# PRAISE FOR CHINESE MEDICAL PSYCHIAT

Bob Flaws and James Lake have produced a masterpiece. While maintaining integrity to the paradigm of TCM, the authors provide an abundance of clinically relevant Western medical information on the diagnosis and treatment of mental-emotional disease. Of even greater importance is their presentation of pattern discriminations, treatment principles, and treatment protocols for Western psychiatric disorders. This text represents a landmark contribution to the professional literature of TCM.

—**Steve Erickson**, Lic. Ac., Dipl. Ac.
Assistant Professor, Northwestern Health Sciences University

Chinese Medical Psychiatry is an excellent addition to the textbook sources on the treatment of diseases with traditional Chinese medicine. This book advances the high standards that Blue Poppy Press has established over the last decade for publication of top quality clinically oriented books on TCM. The book's authors, Bob Flaws and James Lake, have made a significant contribution in writing this fine work on an area of Chinese medicine that, heretofore, has received too little attention. Chinese Medical Psychiatry establishes a new high standard for clinical texts on the often challenging and vitally important speciality of psychiatry from the perspective of Chinese medicine. I welcome the publication of this book and look forward to utilizing it in my clinical practice.

—**Charles May**, M.D., D.O.M., Dipl. Ac. & C.H.
Diplomate, American Boards of Family Practice & Emergency Medicine
Instructor & former Board Member, American Academy of Medical Acupuncture

Psychiatric diseases are among the most commonly encountered illnesses in the American practice of Chinese medicine. Finally, there is a book that comprehensively details the Chinese medical treatment of psychiatric illnesses. Thoroughly researched in the Chinese medical literature, based on Bob Flaws's many years of clinical experience, augmented by research references and case histories, and enhanced by psychiatrist James Lake's succinct and practical Western medical information, this book sets new standards in the understanding and treatment of psychiatric diseases with Chinese medicine.

—**Simon Becker**, Dipl. Ac. & C.H.
Author of A Handbook of Chinese Hematology

It is refreshing to see authors courageous enough to take on this subject. The treatment of mental illness by TCM is a topic long overdue for discussion. It is also a topic historically much avoided by TCM schools and practitioners. This is a gem of a book! It is all here – from frequent joy and lily disease to schizophrenia and bipolar disorder. The chapter on depression and the abundance of abstracts and case histories accompanying each disorder are reasons enough to have this book in your library.

—**Lynn Kuchinski**, M.I.M., Lic. Ac., Dipl. Ac. & C.H.
Author of Controlling Diabetes Naturally with Chinese Medicine

Finally! This invaluable comprehensive resource on the TCM treatment of mental-emotional conditions has been needed in our libraries for too long. This book is sure to help bridge the gap between Western psychiatry and Chinese medicine and become an essential contribution to the treatment of these difficult conditions. A must for any practitioner of Chinese medicine interested in understanding the TCM treatment of psychiatric disorders as well as for every Western psychiatrist eager to gain insight into Chinese medicine.

—**Rosa Schnyer**, L. Ac.
Research specialist, University of Arizona Department of Psychology
Author of Curing Depression Naturally with Chinese Medicine

Chinese Medical Psychiatry fills a nagging void in the English language literature on both the treatment of mental disorders and the nature of the psyche in TCM. Despite the popularity of these subjects within our field, there has been a dearth of rigorously translated information on this topic. This has led to many uninformed attempts to draw parallels between Western psychoanalytic models and TCM theories which have no basis in actual Chinese texts. Bob Flaws and James Lake cut through to the crux of this issue when they explain the evolution of and confusion surrounding the different historical usages of the same terms by shamans, religious philosophers, and naturalistic physicians. In addition, this book, like all Blue Poppy clinical manuals, exhaustively covers diagnosis, pattern differentiation, selection of treatment principles, and formulas and their modifications. However, unlike most other currently available TCM textbooks, it goes a step further by also including research abstracts and case studies. Finally, we have a foundation upon which scholarly discussion of this subject can proceed. This book will form the basis for an entire generation of books on TCM psychiatry.

> —**Todd Luger**, B.S., M.Ac.O.M.
> Director of the Chinese Herb Academy

This is a book in which Chinese and Western medicine find common ground. It is a major step in that process. Recent Western research in the fields of child development, neurology, and personality are fostering a much clearer understanding of the neuorological and physiological aspects of mental and emotional pathology. With these developments, the level of clarity and specificity of Chinese medicine is slowly being matched by Western theories, thereby making a general theory possible. This fine collaboration is surely one of the books that will pave the way.

> —**Ron Kurtz**
> Founder of the Hakomi School of Body-centered Psychotherapy
> Author of *The Body Reveals* (with Hector Prestera, MD)

Finally, a true textbook explaining the relationships of mind/body medicine in Chinese medical terms that is practical and useful for both the serious practitioner and student.

> —**Stuart Watts**, L.Ac., D.O.M., N.D.
> President of the Academy of Oriental Medicine at Austin (AOMA)
> President of the American Association for Teachers of Oriental Medicine (AATOM)
> Board Member of the American Oriental Bodywork Therapy Association (AOBTA)

The authors of *Chinese Medical Psychiatry* have produced a seminal text for both students and practitioners of Chinese medicine who desire to treat mental-emotional disorders. Finally we have a truly holistic clinical manual that encompasses both Chinese medical pattern differentiation and contemporary Western psychiatric theory and practice. This work definitely advances our understanding of how to address the non-duality of psyche and soma.

> —**Liz Bernstein**, D.C., Lic. Ac.

Chinese Medical Psychiatry is a very practical book. I particularly liked the integration of Chinese and Western medicines and the tone with which these elements were presented. Although the treatment of mental-emotional disordes has received considerable attention from Western practitioners, *Chinese Medical Psychiatry* probably contains well more than the sum of everything else on this matter currently in print.

> —**Bob Felt**
> Coauthor of *Understanding Acupuncture*
> Editor of *Redwing Reviews*

# CHINESE MEDICAL PSYCHIATRY

# Chinese Medical Psychiatry

## A Textbook
## &
## Clinical Manual

Including indications for referral to
Western medical services

by

Bob Flaws & James Lake

Published by:
BLUE POPPY PRESS
A Division of Blue Poppy Enterprises, Inc.
4804 SE 69th Avenue
Portland, OR 97206

First Edition, February 2001
Second Printing, May 2003
Third Printing, July 2004
Fourth Printing, November 2005
Fifth Printing, July 2007
Sixth Printing, January 2010
Seventh Printing, April 2011
Eighth Printing, September 2012
Ninth Printing, February 2015
Tenth Printing, October 2016
Eleventh Printing, February 2017
Twelfth Printing, May 2018
Thirteenth Printing, May 2020
Fourteenth Printing, November 2020

ISBN 1-891845-55-1
ISBN 978-1-891845-55-0

Page design: Eric J. Brearton
Cover design: Frank Crawford

COMP Designation: Original work
20  19  18  17  16  15  14
Printed at Frederic Printing, Aurora, CO

Library of Congress Cataloging-in-Publication Data

Flaws, Bob, 1946-
    Chinese medical psychiatry : a textbook & clinical manual : including indications for
referral to Western medical services / by Bob Flaws & James Lake.
        p. ; cm.
    Includes bibliographal references and index.
    ISBN 1-845891-17-9
    1. Medicine, Chinese-Handbooks, manuals, etc. 2. Psychiatry-China-Handbooks,
manuals, etc. 3. Mental illness-China-Handbooks, manuals, etc. 4. Mental
illness-Treatment-China-Handbooks, manuals, etc. I. Lake, James, 1956- II. Title.
    [DNLM: 1. Mental Disorders-therapy. 2. Diagnosis, Differential. 3. Medicine,
Chinese Traditional. 4. Mental Disorders-diagnosis. WM 400 F591c 2000]
RC451.C6.F535 2000
616.89'00951-dc21

00-050752

# ❖ TABLE OF CONTENTS ❖

# ❖ PREFACE ❖

According to the National Institute of Mental Health, 22-23% of the adult U.S. population has a diagnosable mental disorder during any one year period, while 28-30% have either a mental or addictive disorder. Based on these statistics, mental-emotional disorders form a large segment of disease within modern health care, thus presenting clinicians of all kinds with a huge challenge. This book is a textbook and clinical manual of Chinese medical psychiatry (*zhong yi jing shen bing xue*). It is intended for students and professional practitioners of acupuncture and Chinese medicine. Western psychiatrists may also find this book a valuable reference when treating patients who are also being seen by Chinese medical practitioners. It has been coauthored by a Chinese medical practitioner (Bob Flaws) and a board-certified Western psychiatrist (James Lake). In general, Bob Flaws is responsible for all Chinese medical materials in this book, and James Lake is responsible for all Western medical materials included herein.

This textbook is subdivided into three sections or Books. Book 1 deals with the introductory and theoretical materials which are the necessary prerequisite for understanding and using the treatment protocols contained in Books 2 and 3. Book 2 covers the disease causes and mechanisms, patterns and their treatments of 21 traditional Chinese medical psychiatric diseases. These include such diseases as susceptibility to fear and fright, plum pit qi, running piglet, visceral agitation, and lily disease. Book 3 covers the treatment based on pattern discrimination of 12 modern Western medical psychiatric disorders. Most of these are disease categories currently recognized in both the West and the People's Republic of China, at least provisionally for investigative purposes. However, one of these, psychological disturbances due to erroneous qigong, is a diagnostic label currently used only in China. Acupuncture and Chinese medicinal treatments with their modifications are described under each pattern of each disease in both Books 2 and 3.

The dominant system of medicine in the world today is, for the purposes of this book (and following Chinese precedents), simply referred to as Western medicine (*xi yi*). This is also sometimes called allopathic medicine, conventional Western medicine, modern Western medicine, or biomedicine. The most commonly practiced professional system of non-Western medicine in the world today is Chinese medicine (*zhong yi*). This system is also sometimes referred to as Oriental medicine (*dong yi*) and traditional Chinese medicine (TCM). Within this book, we commonly refer to this system as standard professional Chinese medicine. Both Chinese and Western medicines are the enduring and widely employed systems of medicine they are because they consistently produce desirable clinical benefits for a range of medical and psychiatric disorders. Both systems of medicine are founded on conceptual roots that date to antiquity. Nevertheless, both also continue to evolve over time.

Chinese and Western medicine have developed out of rational and empirical approaches reflecting diverse ways of conceptualizing the body and identifying and measuring effects of various internal and external factors on health and illness. This process has resulted in systematic differences in defining, diagnosing, and treating illness and corresponding differences in ways practitioners trained in these two systems construct subjective complaints or symptoms and objective signs into named diseases or disorders. Therefore, these two disparate healing systems employ different conceptual models and empirical methods to identify, understand, and treat various groups of symptoms or disorders. In this regard, it is important for the Chinese medical practitioner to realize that Western psychiatry assumes a biological basis for most common symptom groupings categorized as psychiatric disorders, including schizophrenia, bipolar disorder, major depressive disorder, and many anxiety disorders. The Western medical model further assumes that these largely biologically determined disorders typically manifest as similar groups of symptoms across diverse cultures. In fact, epidemiological studies demonstrate that this is the case with respect to several common psychiatric disorders. This observation is of central importance to Western practitioners of Chinese medicine because it supports the argument that, when Chinese medical treatments used in the People's Republic of China are effective in the treatment of groups of symptoms associated with psychological distress, it is reasonable to infer that similar treatments will yield successful outcomes in non-Chinese patients living in Western countries who manifest similar symptom patterns.

We believe that the continuing evolution of Chinese and Western medicines has, in general, resulted in the refinement of their diagnostic and treatment approaches toward greater efficacy over a period of not less than two millennia of trial and error, clinical experience, and research. In parallel with this progress, ineffective or harmful treatments have been progressively abandoned or modified into treatments that yield more desirable outcomes. As part of this evolutionary process, each system of medicine has received conceptual input from the other. Such cross-fertilization has occurred several times over many centuries. For instance, the Galenic medicine, theriacum, traveled east during the first millennium at roughly the same time Chinese pulse examination traveled west. During the second millennium, Western anatomy had a great impact on Chinese medicine in the Qing dynasty, while Chinese medical massage (*tui na*) was used as the

basis of Pier Henrik Ling's Swedish massage in the late 18th century. Therefore, there is a long history of these two systems of medicine influencing and enriching each other. Recently, however, the trend toward cross-fertilization has accelerated through improved communication between diverse cultures and divergent systems of medicine. This has led to the current situation in which practitioners and institutions from both Chinese and Western medicine increasingly regard the other system as a valid way of understanding health and illness capable of generating effective alternative or complementary treatments for a range of medical or psychiatric disorders.

This trend is illustrated by the choice of many clinicians, in Asia and increasingly in the West, to undergo formal training in the other system of medicine, and this increasing intellectual and institutional openness between Chinese and Western medicines, now accelerated by the emergence of such dual-trained clinicians, has shifted the relationship between traditional Chinese medicine and modern Western medicine in an important way. Until recently, these two systems of medicine (and the majority of their practitioners) viewed each other with mutual disdain and dismissive skepticism. Now, however, instead of dismissing Chinese medicine out of hand, Western physicians are reading, in reputable Western medical journals, about double-blind studies or controlled clinical observations showing the efficacy and safety of its various techniques for the treatment of chronic pain and numerous other medical and psychiatric disorders. (For example, see Bensoussan, Talley, Hing *et al.*'s "Treatment of Irritable Bowel Syndrome with Chinese Herbal Medicine," *Journal of the American Medical Association*, Nov. 11, 1998, p. 1585-1589.) It is equally significant that, at the same time, 40% of the curriculum at provincial Chinese medical schools in China consists of Western medical theory and diagnosis.

Until now, movement toward the integration of Chinese and Western medicines (called *zhong xi yi jie he*, integrated Chinese-Western medicine, in Chinese or simply *xin yi*, new medicine) has been faster in the East than in the West. However, a pivotal moment in the shift toward increasing Western acceptance of Chinese medicine occurred when the National Institutes of Health (NIH) published consensus guidelines on the appropriate uses of acupuncture in late 1998. Though still very much a working document, the NIH consensus guidelines have provided a strong positive endorsement of Chinese medicine from the highest authority of the Western medical establishment. Such an event could not have taken place less than a decade ago because of the previously staunchly conservative nature of the institutions that define and limit acceptable ideas and practices within Western medicine. We believe that the present period of increasing cross-fertilization between Chinese and Western medicine will eventually lead to a new synthesis of medical theories and techniques throughout the world.

Therefore, like many contemporary Chinese medical textbooks produced in the People's Republic of China, this book includes discussions of Western medicine that will help the clinician better understand important Western medical concepts of diagnosis and treatment for the disorders reviewed. Each chapter in Books 2 and 3 begins with a discussion of the Western psychiatric disease categories that are similar to a particular Chinese disease or Chinese disease categories that are similar to a particular Western disease. Because different systems of medicine assign significance to symptoms in different ways, it is reasonable to expect that parallel reviews of the same disorder from the perspectives of Chinese medicine and Western medicine will result in systematic differences in concepts of nosology, diagnosis, and treatment reflecting those differences. In fact, this has been the case in the present effort to place Western psychiatric disorders within the broad framework of Chinese medical concepts of disease classification and diagnosis.

Thinking about discrete groups of symptoms or disorders from the divergent viewpoints of Chinese and Western medicine requires a method that can demonstrate the presence or absence of correspondences of groups of symptoms between these two systems of medicine. In some instances explored in this book, a particular symptom or group of symptoms described in the Chinese medical literature bears phenomenological resemblance to a symptom or disorder conceptualized in Western medicine. On close examination, certain correspondences may be interpreted as etiologically or causally equivalent symptom patterns identified in the two systems of medicine. Equivalent correspondences are infrequent because of systematic differences in approaches to defining, categorizing, and diagnosing illness, and especially mental illness, in divergent systems of medicine. Therefore, rigorous attempts to understand differences between symptoms or disorders as conceptualized in different systems of medicine often lead to only approximate reasonable correspondences.

For example, Chapter 10 in Book 2 discusses frequent joy. This is regarded as a potentially primary disorder of affect regulation in Chinese medicine. The Chinese description of this symptom is interpreted as inappropriate laughter in contemporary Western psychiatry. In contrast to Chinese medicine, conventional Western psychiatry regards inappropriate laughter as an ambiguous symptom that may reflect one of several possible underlying medical (including neurologic) or psychiatric disorders. Therefore, from a contemporary Western medical perspective, in the absence of a specific pattern of associated symptoms, inappropriate laughter does not correspond to a specific underlying disorder. Numerous representative corresponding Western disorders are discussed in the section on differential diagnosis for frequent joy, but it is important to note that this list is not an exhaustive review of possible correspondences. As exact correspondences seldom occur between groups of symptoms described in Chinese and Western medicine, the Chinese medical practitioner or Western physician attempting to "think between" these two divergent systems of medicine is left with the task of inferring reasonable correspondences leading to accurate and clinically useful diagnostic and treatment formulations. *Chinese Medical Psychiatry* is offered to practitioners of Chinese medicine and Western physicians as a bridge to guide their efforts to rigorously think between Chinese medicine and contemporary Western psychiatry.

Most chapters in Books 2 and 3 include the following sections on various Western medical aspects of disorders discussed in the book:

**NOSOLOGY:** Discusses the Western medical classification of disease

**EPIDEMIOLOGY:** Discusses the prevalence and other trends in the occurrence of a disorder (when such data are available)

**DIFFERENTIAL DIAGNOSIS:** Discusses the Western medical understandings of representative medical or psychiatric disorders possibly related to a Chinese disorder

**ETIOLOGY & PATHOPHYSIOLOGY:** Discusses the Western medical concepts of disease causation of Western medical or psychiatric disorders or of Western medical disorders that appear to be related to a Chinese disorder

**WESTERN MEDICAL TREATMENT:** Summarizes current standards of care for Western disorders or of Western medical or psychiatric disorders that appear to be related to a Chinese disorder

**SHORT & LONG-TERM ADVANTAGES & DISADVANTAGES OF WESTERN MEDICAL TREATMENT:** Summarizes potential adverse effects of current Western medical treatments for Western medical disorders that appear to be related to a Chinese disorder

**PROGNOSIS:** Discusses the Western medical understandings of likely short- and long-term outcomes of Western disorders or of Western disorders that appear to be related to a Chinese disorder

**INDICATIONS FOR REFERRAL TO WESTERN MEDICAL SERVICES:** Reviews the warning signs based on history or clinical presentation that point to a possible acute or life-threatening medical or psychiatric emergency requiring urgent Western medical evaluation and treatment (urgent referral) or suggest that referral to Western medical-psychiatric treatment may be appropriate in cases when a condition has not responded to Chinese medical treatment (nonurgent referral)

These sections on Western medicine are intended as a template or guide for Chinese medical practitioners who may find themselves in the position of evaluating patients complaining of symptoms that may indicate the need for urgent referral to Western medical-psychiatric care. These sections are also intended as background information for Chinese medical practitioners who may benefit from collaboration with a Western-trained physician in approaching certain complicated or treatment nonresponsive patients. The ultimate goal of such collaboration is development of an effective integrative treatment plan combining Chinese and Western therapies in order to yield outcomes superior to results available using either system of medicine alone.

The following sections within each chapter in Books 2 and 3 pertain strictly to Chinese medicine. These sections include:

**DISEASE CAUSES AND MECHANISMS:** Discusses the Chinese medical disease causes and disease mechanisms operative in each disease

**PATTERN DISCRIMINATION:** Discusses the main patterns presenting under each disease category

**TREATMENT PRINCIPLES:** Gives the treatment principles appropriate for remedying each element of the pattern discrimination in order of descending importance

**CHINESE MEDICINAL FORMULAS WITH MODIFICATIONS:** Gives at least one Chinese medicinal formula, its ingredients, their dosages, method of administration, and its modifications

**ACUPUNCTURE-MOXIBUSTION FORMULAS WITH MODIFICATIONS:** Gives a basic acupuncture formula with its modifications and supplementing or draining techniques

**CLINICAL TIPS:** Based primarily on Bob Flaws's personal clinical experience, this section discusses special bits of information or techniques for better therapeutic outcomes.

We have also included abstracts of published clinical research (mostly Chinese) as well as numerous Chinese case histories in order to substantiate the safety and effectiveness of Chinese medical treatments for these disorders. Few of these research reports meet the "gold standard" of prospective, randomized, double-blind, placebo-controlled studies, and we acknowledge that all case histories are, by definition, anecdotal. Nevertheless, we believe that the abundant clinical and research evidence contained in this book supports claims of clinical efficacy and safety for Chinese medical treatments of numerous psychiatric disorders. All research summarized in this book is valid, outcomes-based research, and the case histories provide a clear picture of how this medicine is used in the People's Republic of China. It is our hope that this book will stimulate increased open-minded discussion and interest among Western researchers and physicians in the Chinese medical treatment of psychiatric disorders.

Chinese medical materials in this book are based on six main sources, 1) Philippe Sionneau and Lü Gang's *The Treatment of Disease in TCM, Vol. 1: Diseases of the Head & Face, Including Mental & Emotional Disorders*, 2) Li Qing-fu and Liu Du-zhou's *Zhong Yi Jing Shen Bing Xue (Chinese Medical Psychiatry)*, 3) Huang Yue-dong's *Jing Shen Ji Bing Zhong Yi Lin Chuang Zhi Liao (The Chinese Medical Clinical Treatment of Psychiatric Disease)*, 4) Li Qi-lu's *Jing Shen Bing De Zhong Yi Zhi Liao (The Chinese Medical Treatment of Psychiatric Disease)*, 5) Chen Jia-yang's *Shi Yong Zhong Yi Shen Jing Bing Xue (Practical Chinese Medical Neurology)*, and Zhang Hong-du, Zhang Jin-yi & Ding Yu-ling's *Zhong Yi Zhen Jiu Zhi Liao Shen Jing Bing (The Chinese Medical*

*Acupuncture & Moxibustion Treatment of Psychiatric Disease)*. These primary sources have been supplemented by numerous other Chinese and English language sources listed in the Bibliography. The primary sources for the Western medical sections of the text include Kaplan and Saddock's *Comprehensive Textbook of Psychiatry*, Harrison's *Principles of Medicine*, French's *Guide to Differential Diagnosis*, Dunner's *Current Psychiatric Therapy*, Merritt's *Neurology,* Hales and Yudofsky's *The American Psychiatric Press Textbook of Neuropsychiatry,* and the American Psychiatric Association's *Diagnostic & Statistical Manual*, 4th edition (*DSM-IV*), and *Guide to DDX in DSM-4.* Secondary Western medical sources are also listed in the Bibliography at the back of this book.

The Chinese medical terminology used in this book is based on Nigel Wiseman's *English-Chinese Chinese-English Dictionary of Chinese Medicine* (Hunan Science & Technology Press, Changsha,1995) and Wiseman and Feng Ye's *Practical Dictionary of Chinese Medicine* (Paradigm Publications, Brookline, MA, 1998). Whenever the authors have chosen a different term than that suggested by Wiseman and Feng, they have noted this divergence and their reasons in a footnote the first time such a divergence appears. Acupuncture point identifications are based on the World Health Organization's *Standard Acupuncture Point Nomenclature*, however, with the following divergences:

1.We give the Chinese name first, romanized in Pinyin, with channel abbreviation and standard number following in parentheses

2. LU is Lu, ST is St, SP is Sp, HT is Ht, BL is Bl, KI is Ki, PC is Per, TE is TB, LV is Liv, REN is CV, and DU is GV.

Chinese medicinals within formulas are identified by Latin pharmacological nomenclature with the Chinese name written in Pinyin following in parentheses. Chinese medicinals within Clinical Tips sections or Notes which have already been identified by Latin pharmacological nomenclature within their chapter are referred to by their common English name. Chinese medicinal formulas are identified by Chinese name first written in Pinyin followed by English translation in parentheses. In terms of dosages, "g" stands for gram, while *ji* means a single packet of a prescription, most often intended as a one day dose.

To increase the scope and clinical utility of this book for both Chinese medical practitioners and Western physicians, Blue Poppy Press has created a companion website which can be found at *www.chinesemedicalpsychiatry.com*. This website can also be accessed through *www.bluepoppy.com*. It includes summary exhibits taken from the text, articles, book reviews, and extensive links to other websites on pertinent aspects of Chinese medicine, psychiatry, psychotherapy, and neuroscience. In addition, the reader will find a bulletin board for discussion of issues pertaining to the Western practice of Chinese medical psychiatry and the interface between Chinese medicine and Western psychiatry.

The authors hope this book will facilitate open-minded communication and cooperation between Chinese medical practitioners and Western psychiatrists, other physician specialists, and other mental health care professionals with the ultimate goal of improving standards of patient care while simultaneously improving treatment outcomes for the range of psychiatric disorders.

Bob Flaws, Dipl. Ac. & C.H., FNAAOM
James Lake, MD, Board Certified Psychiatrist

❖ Book 1 ❖

# INTRODUCTORY THEORY & FUNDAMENTALS

# A Brief History
# of Chinese
# Medical Psychiatry

## The early foundations of Chinese medicine & psychiatry

The early history of Chinese medicine is the story of the evolution from an ancestor and demon based religious/spiritist medicine to a secular professional medicine based on natural philosophy. In the Shang dynasty (1523-1027 BCE), medical treatment was administered by so-called *wu* shamans and mainly consisted of propitiating unhappy ancestors. In the Zhou dynasty (1027-480 BCE), these *wu* shamans continued propitiating ancestors but also spent more and more time exorcising and propitiating demons through sympathetic magic. Beginning in the mid-500s BCE, we find mention in the surviving written sources of the notion that diseases may also be caused by environmental factors, such as wind, rain, darkness, and brightness.[1] We also find mention of four classes or types of doctors separate from *wu* shamans: physicians, surgeons, dieticians, and veterinary surgeons.[2] By the Han dynasty (206 BCE-220 CE), this secular medicine based on natural philosophy was firmly founded. Its main theories are what Paul U. Unschuld calls "systematic correspondence"[3] and what Birch and Felt call the "qi paradigm."[4]

Undoubtedly, these two approaches to medicine, religious/spiritist and secular/natural, were at first mixed. However, over time, these two approaches to health and healing in China split apart and went their separate ways.[5] Although, shamanism continues to this day as a medical option in Chinese communities around the world,[6] over the years, spiritist ideas and practices were largely removed from the secular, natural medicine which became the basis for standard professional Chinese medicine today. Although many of the technical terms of Chinese medicine, such as *xie qi*, evil qi, and *gui men*, ghost gates (*i.e.*, skin pores), harken back to Chinese medicine's roots in its shamanistic, spiritist past, these terms no longer refer to religious/spiritist concepts.[7]

Likewise, the early history of the Chinese treatment of psychoemotional diseases parallels this same evolution. However, since this is a textbook on the standard contemporary professional Chinese medical diagnosis and treatment of psychoemotional diseases,[8] we will begin our discussion of the history of Chinese medical psychiatry with the three main Han dynasty classics of the medicine of systematic correspondences and the qi paradigm: the *Huang Di Nei Jing (Yellow Emperor's Inner Classic)*, the *Nan Jing (Classic of Difficulties)*, and Zhang Zhong-jing's *Shang Han Za Bing Lun (Treatise on Damage [Due to] Cold & Miscellaneous Diseases)*.

Although descriptions of various mental-emotional disturbances are found in non-medical Chinese texts from before the Warring States period,[9] the *Nei Jing (Inner Classic)* is the first surviving Chinese medical text which includes discussions of the diagnosis and treatment of recognizable psychiatric disorders. For instance, Chapter 30 of the *Su Wen (Simple Questions)* is devoted to diseases of the yang ming. This chapter begins with Huang Di saying, "A person suffering from disorders of the foot yang ming channel will have aversion to crowds of people and heat..."[10] Further on, Huang Di continues, saying:

> I have observed that in severe cases of yang ming disorder, a person can become delirious to the point of running about naked, talking loudly, and not consuming food for several days. At the same time, these patients are able to climb great heights and perform unusual feats, things they cannot do under normal circumstances. Why is this?
>
> Qi Bo answers: The four extremities contain an abundance of yang qi. When there is a repletion of yang in the channels, great stamina results. Thus, the person is capable of physically over-achieving.
>
> Huang Di asks: Why is it they like to run around naked?
>
> Qi Bo answers: It is not that they like to do so, but rather that they are feverish and very hot. They dislike covering themselves and aggravating the heat.
>
> Huang Di asks: What about the behavior of cursing at people, singing, and talking loudly?
>
> Qi Bo replies: When yang evils are replete, they harass the spirit and muddle the senses. Therefore, these people appear crazy and unreasonable and lose their senses of norm and appetite.

The above passage clearly describes mania. The importance of evil heat as a disease cause of mental-emotional problems is further underscored in Chapter 30 of the *Su Wen (Simple Questions)* where Qi Bo says, "Symptoms of lockjaw, mental and emotional disturbance, anxiety, swelling, and inflammation all pertain to fire," as opposed to demonic possession.

In the late Han dynasty, the author of the *Nan Jing (Classic of Difficulties)* further described and classified the two fundamental divisions of mental diseases in Chinese medicine: withdrawal and mania. The Chinese medical disease category of withdrawal covers everything from depression to the syncope of epilepsy, while mania covers all excited, agitated, and hyperactive states. In "Difficulty 20," the author of the *Nan Jing* says, "Double yang results in mania; double yin results in withdrawal," while in "Difficulty 59," it reads:

> How can mania and withdrawal be distinguished?
>
> Answer: At the beginning emission [or outbreak] of mania, there is little lying down and no hunger. One [speaks of] onself [as if] elevated and worthy [of honor]. One discriminates [or points out] one's [special] intelligence and one behaves in an arrogant and haughty way. One frenetically smiles, sings, and is happy and frenetically moves about without break. During the initial outbreak of withdrawal, the mind is not happy. One lies stiffly, staring straight [ahead]. The pulses of the three positions, yin and yang, are all exuberant.

Also in the late Han, Zhang Zhong-jing described a number of psychoemotional disease categories in his *Shang Han Za Bing Lun (Treatise on Damage [Due to] Cold & Miscellaneous Diseases)*. These include vexation and agitation, running piglet, insomnia, somnolence, withdrawal and mania, apprehensiveness, confusion of the heart, deranged speech, depression, fear and disquiet, fright, fidgetiness whether lying or sitting, taciturnity, plum pit qi, and visceral agitation. For instance, Zhang says:

> Evil crying causing the ethereal and corporeal souls to be disquieted is [due to] scanty qi and blood, and scanty qi and blood pertain to the heart. If the heart qi is vacuous, the person must be fearful. When they close their eyes and desire to sleep, they dream of traveling to a far place where their essence spirit is scattered and their ethereal and corporeal souls move about frenetically. Yin qi debility results in withdrawal, while yang qi debility results in mania.[11]

Hua Tuo (died circa 208 CE), writing in the *Zhong Zang Jing (Classic of the Central Viscera)*, ascribed mania and withdrawal primarily to a disease within yang:

> This illness originates in the six yang orbs and therefore belongs to the yang system. When yang energy erupts, it may course up or down,

inward or outward, or it may become inverted. At the peak of its eruption, [a variety of symptoms are manifested]. There are patients who sign and laugh, or conversely, there are patients who weep sorrowfully. There are those who run about; those who moan and groan; those who belittle themselves; those who cannot sleep; those who cannot or will not talk. These varieties of symptoms all originate in the six yang orbs.[12]

This emphasis on yang qi in the disease mechanisms of mania and, to a lesser extent, withdrawal has continued to this day as a major motif within Chinese medicine.

## POST-HAN DEVELOPMENTS

Based on the foundations in nosology, etiology, and therapeutics laid in the above three seminal books, Chinese doctors in succeeding dynasties continued refining and expanding upon these notions. In the early Jin dynasty (282 CE), Huang-fu Mi, author of the *Huang Di Zhen Jiu Jia Yi Jing (Yellow Emperor's Systematic Classic of Acupuncture & Moxibustion)*, describes running piglet as one of the five accumulations in Book 8, Chapter 2:

For running piglet with [qi] surging up into the heart and, in extreme cases, symptoms of inability to catch one's breath, an empty sensation in the heart with diminished qi, death-like reversal, heart vexation and pain, hunger but inability to ingest food, frequent cold in the center with abdominal distention sending a dragging pain to the rib-side region, sudden dragging pain between the lower abdomen and spine, and occasional pressure in the rectum, *Zhong Ji* [CV 3] is the ruling point.[13]

Huang-fu Mi also describes the relationship between sorrow, apprehension, sighing, melancholy, susceptibility to fright and the heart and gallbladder in Book 9, Chapter 5:

For irritability, no desire for food, and ever growing silence, needle the foot tai yin. For irascibility and loquaciousness, needle the foot shao yang. For qi shortage, heart impediment, sorrow, irascibility, qi counterflow, and apprehension and mania, *Yu Ji* (Lu 10) is the ruling point. For heart pain, sentimentality, counterflow inversion, the sensation of a suspended heart as if hungering, faltering and stirring of

the heart, susceptibility to fright, and apprehensiveness, *Da Ling* (Per 7) and *Jian Shi* (Per 5) are the ruling points. For faltering and stirring of the heart, susceptibility to fright, apprehension, and sorrow of the heart, *Nei Guan* (Per 6) is the ruling point. For susceptibility to fright, sorrow and melancholy, reversal, heat in the lower legs and soles of the feet, heat all over the face, and dry throat and thirst, *Xing Jian* (Liv 2) is the ruling point. For spleen vacuity producing diseases of cold, melancholy, and frequent sighing in patients, *Shang Qiu* (Sp 5) is the ruling point. . .[14]

Gallbladder disease is characterized by frequent sighing, a bitter taste in the mouth, retching of stale water, faltering and stirring of the heart, apprehension as if fearing arrest, throat choked as if by a lump, and frequent spitting.[15]

In the Sui dynasty (589-618 CE), Chao Yuan-fang, author of the *Zhu Bing Yuan Hou Lun (Treatise on the Origins & Symptoms of Diseases)*, introduced the notion of evil winds as disease causes of withdrawal and mania in Chapter 37 of his important book:

If wind evils invade the yin, they cause withdrawal. If wind evils invade the yang, they cause mania.

However, according to Tseng Wen-shing, due to the rise of religious Daoism in the first Jin dynasty (265-420 CE) and the subsequent popularity of Buddhism in the Tang dynasty (618-907 CE), a number of religious/spiritist concepts or theories crept back into professional Chinese medicine during this time. Therefore, besides various kinds of wind evils causing withdrawal and mania, Chao Yuan-fang also included two types of insanity due to ghost possession, "ghost evil insanity" and "ghost-bewitched insanity."[16] Likewise, in the Tang dynasty, Sun Si-miao not only accepted Chao's notion of winds as an etiological factor in mental-emotional disease but posited a role for the guardian gods of the four directions and other demons and spirits in the creation of such disease.[17] Sun Si-miao also created an acupuncture protocol for the treatment of mental-emotional problems called the 13 Ghost Points. The reintroduction of spiritist beliefs and practices into professional Chinese medicine was so strong during this period that there was even a department of charms and incantations in the *Tai Yi Shu* (Imperial Medical Academy), the national administrative infrastructure of Chinese medicine during this dynasty.[18]

## NEOCONFUCIAN MEDICINE

In the Song dynasty (960-1280 CE), influenced as it was by Neoconfucian philosophy, professional Chinese medicine returned to a more naturalist approach. As Vivien Ng succinctly says, "Medical theories based on naturalistic (as opposed to supernatural) concepts once again gained currency."[19] Although Chinese laypeople continued to believe mental-emotional diseases were primarily due to possession by malevolent spirits, retribution for sinful deeds, and separation of the soul from the body,[20] by the reign of Yuan Feng (1078-1085 CE), there was no longer a department of charms and incantations at the Imperial Medical Academy.[21] In this same dynasty, Chen Yan introduced the three classes of disease causes, the so-called *san yin*. Chen's system classified all disease causing agents into external causes, internal causes, and neither external nor internal causes. Internal causes refer to the seven affects or emotions. External causes include the six environmental excesses (and later, the concept of pestilential qi), and the neither internal nor external category of disease-causing agents include diet, poisoning, external traumatic injury, sex, and lifestyle (primarily discussed under the headings "activity" and "stillness" or rest). While some Chinese doctors even into the 20th century have continued to include spiritist influences and ghost possession as species of the neither internal nor external causes of disease, the emphasis within professional Chinese medicine from this point on returned to the naturalism of yin-yang and five phase theories and the qi paradigm. Chen Yan's classification of disease causes included the disease causes of mental-emotional disease which have been thought of ever since primarily in terms of these three naturalist categories of causes.[22]

In the Yuan dynasty (1280-1368 CE), Zhu Dan-xi, one of the four great masters of the Jin-Yuan,[23] further expanded the naturalist Chinese ideas of disease causation of withdrawal and mania. Speaking of seasonal diseases in his *Dan Xi Xin Fa Zhi Yao (The Heart & Essence of Dan-xi's Methods of Treatment)*, Zhu says, "Cold damage with intense heat, a replete pulse, and mania or withdrawal is a pattern of superabundance."[24] Speaking of phlegm, Zhu implies that it too may be a cause of withdrawal and mania when he says, "Succus Bambusae (*Zhu Li*) treats phlegm existing around the diaphragm with mania and withdrawal, impaired memory, or wind phlegm."[25] And speaking of heart disease,

Zhu says that mania and withdrawal may be caused by phlegm and heat:

> In terms of mania and withdrawal disease, withdrawal is ascribed to yin and mania with excessive joy is ascribed to yang. Frequent anger with a replete pulse [results in] death. A vacuous [pulse indicates] the possibility of a cure. Roughly speaking, this is mostly due to phlegm bound somewhere in the heart region of the chest. Treatment normally [consists of] settling the heart spirit and opening bound phlegm... People who think dual yin is the cause of withdrawal and dual yang is the cause of mania are wrong. Generally speaking, they are both due to heat.[26]

Speaking about other psychoemotional diseases associated with the heart, Zhu says: "In people with heart vacuity and dwindling, there may arise fearful throbbing, vexation and restlessness, impaired memory, or confounded and clouded spirit after disappointment."[27]

Liu Wan-su, another of the four great masters of the Jin-Yuan, reiterated the naturalist belief that mania is due to heat evils. In his *Shang Han Tiao Ben Xin Fa Lei Cui (Categorized Assembly of Damage [Due to] Cold Branch & Root Heart Methods)*, Liu says, "In the initial [stage] of fire warmth mania and agitation [with] panting and fullness, [use] *Huang Lian Jie Du Tang* (Coptis Resolve Toxins Decoction)."[28] In his *He Jian Liu Shu (He-jian's Six Books)*, Liu says:

> The word *kuang* means "raging, unpredictable wildness." The word *yue* means "perverting all the rules of propriety and normal behavior."
>
> Fire is wild and chaotic and murky. Water is clear and calm and smooth. Fire and Water are opposites. [In the human body,] the kidneys correspond to the evolutive phase Water; they govern and check emotions and willpower (*zhi*). The heart corresponds to the evolutive phase Fire. It regulates the particular emotion joy. Since Fire and Water are opposites, when the evolutive phase Fire is resplendent, Water is depleted, and, so too, are the kidneys. When such a condition prevails, the patient loses control of his or her emotions and becomes *kuangyue*.[29]

Likewise, at roughly the same time, Zhang Zi-he, yet another of the four great masters, described several cases whose illnesses had been caused by extremes of emotion. One of these was a case of not eating due to great anger, another was a case of intractable insomnia due to damage by excessive thinking and worry, and the third was a case of pediatric insomnia due to fright.[30]

Li Dong-yuan, arguably the greatest of the four great masters of the Jin-Yuan, also posited purely naturalist disease causes and mechanisms of psychoemotional disease when he explained:

> Anger, indignation, sorrow, worry, fear, and fright can all cause detriment to the original qi. If yin fire blazes and becomes exuberant, this causes congelation and stagnation to be engendered in the heart and, therefore, the seven passions are not quiet. The heart vessels are the abode of the spirit. If the heart sovereign is not calm, transformation may give rise to fire, and fire is the foe to the seven spirits [i.e., the ethereal soul, corporeal soul, essence, spirit, reflection, intelligence, and mind]. Therefore, it is said that, when yin fire is greatly exuberant, the channel constructive qi is not able to keep fit and nourish the spirit. This is a disease of the [heart] vessels. The spirit has no place [from which to get] nourishment, and fluids and humors do not move. Hence the blood vessels are no longer able to be nourished. The heart spirit is the true qi by another name. If it obtains blood, it is engendered, and engenderment by blood leads to the vessels becoming effulgent. The vessels are the abode of the spirit. If congelation and stagnation are engendered in the heart, the seven spirits will leave the form [i.e., the body] and there will be nothing but fire left within the vessels.[31]

## MING & QING DEVELOPMENTS & TRENDS

In the Ming dynasty (1368-1644 CE), writers on the two preeminent Chinese psychoemotional diseases, withdrawal and mania, emphasized the role of emotions as disease-causing factors even more. They also described the disease mechanisms associated with these conditions in greater detail. In 1515, Yu Tuan-zhuan published his *Yi Xue Zheng Chuan (Orthodox Transmission of the Study of Medicine)* where he said:

> Generally, the disease of mania is due to

replete phlegm fire, while the disease of withdrawal is due to heart blood vacuity. All such diseases are due to high hopes not realized.[32]

Also in the Ming, Zhang Jing-yue wrote, in Book 34 of his *Jing Yue Quan Shu (Jing-yue's Complete Book)*:

> Mania disease is usually due to fire, unfulfilled desires, accumulated worries without outlet, or anger without outlet leading to liver-gallbladder qi stagnation leading to joining of evil fire with wood. If evil qi invades the heart, it leads to the spirit not maintaining its abode. If evil qi invades the stomach, it leads to excessive, ruthless, uncontrollable behavior and movement.[33]

Wang Ken-tang, another famous Chinese medical writer of the Ming dynasty, also talking about the disease causes and mechanisms of withdrawal and mania, had this to say:

> These two diseases [withdrawal and mania] each have their unique causes. They may be due to profuse anger which stirs liver wind, they may be due to great fear which disturbs heart fire, or they may be due to accumulated phlegm which eventually leads to its rising by virtue of its heating up. It ascends but does not descend and subsequently blocks the heart orifices. As a result, the spirit cannot communicate and loses its control.[34]

Zhang Jing-yue, quoted above, was one of the founders of the School of Warm Supplementation. According to this school of thought, the four great masters of the Jin-Yuan had overemphasized the role of evil heat within medicine in general. This opinion colored Zhang's ideas about the disease causes and mechanisms of psychiatric disease. While still accepting that mania is primarily due to heat evils which must be drained and cleared, Zhang and his followers cautioned that one should not lump mania and withdrawal together as a single, heat-induced disease.

> [Zhang] cautioned physicians not to use reflexively heat purgatives to treat madness. It is absolutely imperative, he insists, that they first determine whether the illness is of a yin or yang nature before prescribing medicine for the patient.[35]

The famous Qing dynasty (1644-1911) gynecologist,

Fu Qing-zhu, accepted the admonitions of Zhang Jing-yue's followers that each case of mania and withdrawal must be diagnosed and treated individually. In his *Fu Qing Zhu Nan Nu Ke (Fu Qing-zhu's Andrology & Gynecology)*, Fu says that mania can be caused by vacuity fire, not just replete heat, as well as blood stasis "attacking" the heart. Fu also further clarified that phlegm blocking the heart orifices may come from a cold, vacuous spleen and stomach:

> This disease generally arises from spleen-stomach vacuity cold. [In that case,] when food and drink enter the stomach, they are not transformed into essence but into phlegm. This phlegm then mists the heart orifices, thus causing withdrawal and mania disease.[36]

However, not all Ming and Qing dynasty Chinese doctors accepted the theories of the School of Warm Supplementation. Many continued to adhere to the Jin-Yuan theories of Zhu Dan-xi, Liu Wan-su, Dai Si-gong, *et al.* Because of these doctors' uncompromising criticisms of warm supplementation, they came to be known as the Anti-warm Supplementation School. One of the prominent members of this school was Chen Shi-duo (circa 1687 CE). In his chapter, "The Treatment of Mania," in the *Shi Shi Bi Lu (Confidential Records of the Stone Chamber)*, Chen states:

> The majority of *kuang* cases are "hot" diseases. The patient climbs up high places and sings; discards his or her clothing and runs about naked; jumps into bodies of water; scolds, curses, and threatens to kill people... A *kuang* patient who only scolds people, who is never thirsty and who always refuses to drink water... is suffering from a fever that is caused by pent up *qi* (energy) as well as anger that has not been vented...
>
> A patient who is chronically *kuang*, who brandishes a sharp weapon and [threatens] to kill people, who insults officials, who does not recognize kinfolk, who does not know his or her children, who delights in water, [or] who becomes furious at the sight of food, is suffering from an illness that is caused by an exhaustion of the energy of the heart. The pathogenic agent, heat, takes advantage of this exhaustion to invade the body, thereby causing the illness.[37]

Because of this attribution of mania to yang repletion and heat evils, there was also the notion that mania is typically accompanied by a voracious sexual appetite. As an example of this, Wu Ju-tong, another famous Qing dynasty physician, recorded a case history of a man who had been suffering from mania for seven years. In addition to being extremely violent, the man had an insatiable sexual appetite, demanding to have sexual intercourse with a woman every day. Because the man voiced these demands in loud screams and much wailing while chained hand and foot in his family's compound, the family felt compelled to force the man's concubines to satisfy these demands. When Wu Ju-tong saw this patient, he concluded the man suffered from yang repletion and administered an extremely bitter, cold decoction to drain and discharge heat evils from the patient's body. According to Wu, this treatment was effective and the man made a full recovery from his long illness, including his excessive sexual appetite.[38]

As the above brief summary shows, secular, naturalist ideas on the etiology and, therefore, treatment of psychoemotional disease coalesced during the Han dynasty and were then refined and expanded throughout the succeeding dynasties. While the technical terms of Chinese medicine may have originally been derived from shamanic and spiritist beliefs and religious practices, standard professional Chinese medicine has long since evolved into a secular, naturalist medicine. As Vivien Ng says when speaking of the main literary tradition of Chinese medicine:

> Regardless of their orientation, Chinese physicians universally understood the many forms of madness to be organic disorders, and the language used to explain the pathology of *dian* and *kuang* was not all that different from that used to explain other illnesses. The notion that madness could be a [purely] *mental* illness was never advanced, not even by those who saw a distinct relationship between emotions and madness. The holistic approach of classical Chinese medicine has made the distinction between "physical" and "mental" alien to the Chinese experience. ...behavioral disorders were certainly recognized... but only as manifestations of physiological dysfunction.[39]

## SOMATIZATION OF MENTAL-EMOTIONAL COMPLAINTS

Another historical movement within Chinese medical psychiatry has been the medicalization of psychiatric treatment. Although doctors in the Ming dynasty more strongly emphasized the role of emotional disturbance in the cause of mental-emotional disease than their predecessors (at least in terms of the surviving written record), there has been a progressive and long-standing tendency to somaticize psychoemotional complaints on the part of both Chinese patients and practitioners. From at least the time of Confucius (circa 500 BCE), Chinese have been enjoined not to air their emotional laundry in public, and psychological disturbances have carried a stigma within Chinese society ever since.[40] In the first chapter of the *Zhong Yong (Doctrine of the Mean)*, titled "Heavenly Destiny," Confucius says:

> When joy, anger, sorrow, and joy are not revealed, that is called the mean [or moderation]. If they are revealed but made known only moderately, this is called harmony. Moderation is the great root of everything under heaven, while harmony is the way [*dao*] of revealing under heaven.[41]

Based on such teachings, 25 centuries later, the Chinese-American psychiatrist Tseng Wen-shing says:

> For the Chinese, it is a virtue not to express anger openly. Breaking such a cultural tradition often results in the complication of feeling subsequent regret. In the conservative Chinese society a person is encouraged to be compliant to the situation rather than actively attempting to solve the problems and satisfy his individual needs. He has no choice but to be apprehensive, worrying and thinking about his problems.[42]

Although psychiatric illness has been stigmatized in Chinese society for many hundreds of years, this stigmatization of psychiatric patients increased during the Qing dynasty. According to Vivien Ng, in 1731, the governor general of Sichuan submitted a memorial to the Yong Zheng emperor in which he argued for the implementation of mandatory confinement of the insane.[43] This order was formally incorporated into the Qing Code in 1740. In 1766, this statute was amended to provide for even more stringent conditions of confinement. Placing the insane under house arrest or in prison, even when they had not committed a crime, turned such persons into "criminal deviants." This transformation of madness from illness to criminal deviance generated the need for other new laws dealing with the crimes committed by the insane, thus com-

pounding this process of legal and social stigmatization which continued throughout the rest of the Qing dynasty and setting the stage for the Communist regime's similar stigmatization of mental illness as criminal deviance.

Therefore, Kleinman and Kleinman write, "Dysphoric emotion traditionally in Chinese culture has been regarded as shameful to self and family; for that reason it was not to be revealed outside the family and was seen to dangerously overlap with highly stigmatized mental illness."[44] While patients may describe psychoemotional discomfort in "rationalized" psychoemotional terms to close friends or family members,[45] Chinese typically couch these discomforts or complaints in purely somatic terms when talking about them to outsiders, including their health care providers.[46]

This tendency towards somatization is reinforced by Chinese medical theory itself. Since Chinese patients know that Chinese medicine believes that excessive emotions are themselves damaging to one's health, Chinese patients tend to emphasize somatic complaints when presenting their cases to Chinese doctors to avoid "loss of face" or negative judgment.[47] Further, since Chinese doctors categorize psychiatric complaints under the rubric "internal medicine (*nei ke*)" and treat such complaints primarily with somatic-based therapies (acupuncture and internally administered Chinese herbal medicine), they tend to reinforce this process of somatization. Therefore, because practitioners sanction the patient's bodily idiom of distress, they contribute to this process of somatization.[48]

While this process of somatization of complaints and medicalization of treatment predates the Communist era, its adoption by practitioners and patients alike has also been reinforced, at least in mainland China, by the political upheavals of the Cultural Revolution. As Kleinman and Kleinman remark, "During the Great Proletarian Cultural Revolution, all mental illness, including most notably depression, [was] called into question by the Maoists as wrong political thinking."[49] Kleinman and Kleinman go on to say that, "[Psychiatric labels] spelled disaster during the Cultural Revolution and even in the pragmatic political atmosphere of present-day, post-Maoist China, [1985, such labels] are not public attributions which patients and families wish to be associated."[50]

As a means of escaping the socially negative and politically dangerous consequences of psychiatric diagnoses,

Chinese practitioners and patients, from the mid-20th century on, retained the out-dated Western medical diagnostic label of neurasthenia after this label had fallen out of use in most of the rest of the world. Neurasthenia is a disease diagnosis which was popular in the United States in the latter half of the 19th century and which also became popular in Europe during the first third of the 20th century. However, this diagnostic category is no longer accepted as a professional standard in most of the Western world. Neurasthenia literally means "weak nerves." As originally described in the 19th century, this condition was a combination of chronic fatigue, anxiety, and depression and various somatic complaints, such as headache and insomnia. While this disease category fell out of use in the West by the mid-20th century, it was kept by the Chinese due to its emphasis on somatic complaints and its suggestion that disease is not due to personal emotional factors (read, failure) but to overwork and genes. Therefore, especially during the Cultural Revolution and for some time after, neurasthenia was an extremely common diagnosis in both Western and Chinese medical clinics in China. For instance, when Bob Flaws was an intern in the acupuncture department of the Long Hua Hospital in Shanghai in 1982, almost one quarter of all the patients he saw were labeled as suffering from neurasthenia with primary complaints of headache, insomnia, low back pain, and sexual dysfunction (typically premature ejaculation or involuntary seminal emission).

One extension of the adoption of a primarily somatic label for the diagnosis of numerous patients suffering from what, at least in the West, would be categorized as psychiatric complaints, is an emphasis on external physical or medical treatments as opposed to cognitive or behavioral therapies. As Tseng Wen-shing says:

> The influence of emotional factors upon the occurrence of physical illness has been recognized in Chinese medicine since the beginning. The improvement of the emotional condition as a way to improve illness has been emphasized, particularly for psychosomatic disorders. However, Chinese medicine itself, as medicine, is characterized by its herb-oriented treatment. Therefore, regardless of whether the psychological aspect of illness [has] been recognized, *the treatment always end[s] with the prescription of herb medicine.*[51] [Italics ours]

Interestingly, this emphasis on a medical cause of psy-

chiatric disease (as opposed to psychosocial factors) and, hence, the medical treatment of psychiatric disease via drug therapy parallels these same tendencies (though for different reasons) within Western psychiatry during the 1960s, 70s, and 80s. According to Richard J. Castillo, "...from the 1960s to the mid-1980s, many researchers believed that mental disorders were caused primarily by 'chemical imbalances' in the brain stemming from genetic abnormalities."[52] Based on this belief, mental disorders within the Western medicine of this time were seen as brain diseases, and, therefore, their treatment consisted of changing the brain chemistry through drug therapy. However, just as leading-edge Western psychiatrists have come to the conclusion that mental-emotional disorders cannot be treated by drug therapy alone and require a more holistic treatment, there are signs that, among Chinese patients at least, there is a growing openness to and interest in cognitive and behavioral therapies.[53] If this interest in psychotherapy continues to grow (inversely proportional to a decline in the social and political stigmatization of mental disease in China), then it would not be surprising to witness a growing interest in the future in psychotherapy within Chinese medicine as well.

Already in the West, due to the influence of Carl Jung and Alan Watts, there is a heightened interest in psychotherapy among American and European practitioners of Chinese medicine. Although Chinese medicine has been practiced in the United States by ethnic Chinese for at least 150 years, many of the current Western practitioners of Chinese medicine came to its study via a larger "journey to the East" that was initiated in the 1960s by the likes of Allen Ginsberg, Timothy Leary, and the Beatles and has since gone on to become the New Age movement. For instance, Bob Flaws became interested in Chinese medicine as part of his embrace of Buddhism. Similarly, there are a disproportionate number of Western acupuncturists and practitioners of Chinese medicine who are also Buddhists, Taoists, Sufis, and practitioners of Yoga and Vedanta than in the population as a whole. In the first line of the first chapter of Alan Watts seminal *Psychotherapy East and West*, Watts says:

> If we look deeply into such ways of life as Buddhism, Taoism, Vedanta and Yoga, we do not find either philosophy or religion as these are understood in the West. We find something more nearly resembling psychotherapy.[54]

This linkage between Asian philosophies and religions with psychotherapy and eventually with psychedelics has had a lasting impact on Western practitioners of Chinese medicine, especially the Baby Boomers who came of age in the late 1960s and 70s and who are today the leading lights in this medicine in the West. In his Preface to *Psychotherapy East and West*, Watts traces this historical trend to Carl G. Jung's long psychological commentary appearing in Richard Wilhlem's translation of Chinese alchemical text, *The Secret of the Golden Flower*, published in 1929, to G.R. Heyer's *Der Organismus deer Seele* (1932), and Geraldine Coster's *Yoga and Western Psychology* (1934). Watts goes on to modestly confess:

> I also made some contribution to [this linkage between Asian religions and psychotherapy] in a rather immature book called *The Legacy of Asia and Western Man* (1937), and a little later in *The Meaning of Happiness* (1940), which bore the subtitle "The Quest for Freedom of the Spirit in Modern Psychology and the Wisdom of the East."[55]

From these early beginnings, there has developed a now almost unquestioned assumption (at least on the part of many Western practitioners of Chinese medicine) of the linkage between Asian religions and, by extension, Asian medicine and psychotherapy, and books and articles on the integration of Western psychology and psychotherapy continue to be perennially popular in the English language literature on Chinese medicine.[56] Therefore, it is reasonable to expect the influences of Western psychotherapy to enter Chinese medicine from this route as well.

## THE ADOPTION OF THE *DSM-IV* & THE INTEGRATION OF CHINESE & WESTERN MEDICINES

While the somatically prejudiced label of neurasthenia dominated the Chinese medical diagnosis of mental-emotional disease during the 1970s and 80s and is a common diagnosis even today, due to greater freedom of information between the People's Republic of China and the rest of the world, there has been a shift recently toward the adoption of Western psychiatric diagnoses and criteria. In numerous contemporary Chinese journal articles on the treatment of psychiatric diseases, it is now common for Chinese authors to cite the American Psychiatric Association's *Diagnostic & Statistical Manual*, 4th edition (*i.e.*, the *DSM-IV*), as their standard for disease classification. This has led to a more up-to-date nosology congruent with the rest of modern medicine.[57] In addition, the adoption of modern Western disease diagnoses has led to the treatment of these disorders by integrated Chinese-Western medicine. On the one hand, Western medicines, which are typically stronger acting then their Chinese counterparts, have helped Chinese medicine treat cases which were recalcitrant to its approach alone. On the other, Chinese medicine has achieved treatment success in cases judged a failure with Western medicine alone. Further, Chinese treatment modalities and methodologies have been used to treat the side effects of modern Western drugs as well as enabling the reduction of dosage or complete cessation of powerful but potentially deleterious Western pharmaceuticals. In addition, at least three new modalities have been added to Chinese medicine which have shown themselves useful in treating mental-emotional diseases: electroacupuncture, scalp acupuncture, and ear acupuncture or auriculotherapy.[58]

One example of the innovative integration of Chinese and Western medicines is the Chinese medicinal treatment of amenorrhea as a side effect of Western neuroleptic medicines. He Guo-zhang describes the treatment of 52 cases of amenorrhea as a result of treatment with neuroleptic medicines.[59] All the women in this study suffered from varying degrees of psychological disease as well as secondary amenorrhea after taking either chlorpromazine, perphenazine, haloperidol, sulpiride, or chlorprothixene. These Western medicines had mostly caused yin vacuity with internal heat. Therefore, these patients were treated with Chinese medicinals based on the treatment principles of enriching yin, engendering fluids, and clearing heat assisted by coursing and smoothing the qi mechanism and quickening the blood and freeing the flow of the menses *at the same time as continuing to take their Western psychotropic medications*. After taking Chinese medicinals for these purposes, 18 of these experienced the resumption of their menstrual cycles within 20-76 days. Of the seven whose menses did not resume, three failed to take their Chinese medicinals regularly, while four suspended Chinese medical treatment altogether.

It is clear from the above clinical audit that the Western neuroleptic medicines described above can plunder yin and damage fluids. This is probably because they should be classified as extremely powerful exterior-resolving/qi-rectifying medicinals. Using Chinese medical logic, it should be possible to work out Chinese medical descriptions of Western pharmaceuticals. If and when this occurs, there is the possibility of a truly integrated practice of Chinese and Western medicines wherein Western pharmaceuticals are prescribed on the basis of Chinese pattern discrimination.

## ENDNOTES:

[1] Birch, Stephen J. & Felt, Robert L., *Understanding Acupuncture*, Churchill Livingstone, Edinburgh, 1999, p. 9

[2] *Ibid.*, p. 9

[3] Unschuld, Paul U., *Medicine in China: A History of Ideas*, Univ. of CA Press, Berkeley, 1985, p. 51-100

[4] Birch & Felt, *op. cit.*, p. 89

[5] While some Chinese doctors (mostly in so-called overseas Chinese communities) continue to accept spirit possession as a legitimate medical diagnosis even today, a purely secular, natural version of Chinese medicine can be identified as early as the Warring States period. In the *Nei Jing Su Wen (Inner Classic: Simple Questions)*, Chapter 13, Qi Bo counsels Huang Di that using spiritist methods of treatment is ineffective in "modern" times and instead recommends treatment based on systematic correspondence and the qi paradigm.

[6] Holbrook, Bruce, "Chinese Psycho-social Medicine: Doctor and Dang-ki, An Inter-cultural Analysis," *Bulletin of the Institute of Ethnology*, Academia Sinica, #37, 1974, p. 85-110

[7] For a discussion of this, see Sivin, Nathan, *Traditional Medicine in Contemporary China*, Center for Chinese Studies, Univ. of Michigan, Ann Arbor, 1987, p. 102-106

[8] For the authors, standard professional Chinese medicine means that style of Chinese medicine which forms the basis of the teaching curricula at the 20 or more provincial Chinese medical colleges in the People's Republic of China and which is considered the standard of care by the Chinese Department or Ministry of Health.

[9] Liu Xie-he, "Psychiatry in Traditional Chinese Medicine," *British Journal of Psychiatry*, #138, 1981, p. 429: "A number of ancient books between 1100 BC and 500 BC recorded psychiatric symptoms, ..."

[10] *The Yellow Emperor's Classic of Medicine*, trans. by Ni Mao-xing, Shambhala, Boston & London, 1995, p. 118

[11] Zhang Zhong -jing, *Jin Gui Yao Lue (Essentials from the Golden Cabinet)*, Oriental Healing Arts Institute, Long Beach, CA, 1983, p. 76. Although this book is accompanied by a translation done by Wang Su-yen and Hong-yes Hsu, the above quote was translated by Bob Flaws.

[12] Hua Tuo, quoted and translated by Vivien Ng, *Madness in Late Imperial China: From Illness to Deviance*, Univ. of OK Press, Norman, OK, 1990, p. 35

[13] Huang-fu Mi, *The Systematic Classic of Acupuncture & Moxibustion*, trans. by Yang Shou-zhong & Charles Chace, Blue Poppy Press, Boulder, CO, 1994, p. 505

[14] *Ibid.*, p. 546-547

[15] *Ibid.*, p. 547

[16] Tseng Wen-shing, "The Development of Psychiatric Concepts in Traditional Chinese Medicine," *Archives of General Psychiatry*, #29, 1973, p. 571

[17] *Ibid.*, p. 571

[18] Ruan Fang-fu, *A History of Medicine*, Chinese Culture Books Co., Oakland, CA, 1992, p. 44

[19] Ng, *op. cit.*, p. 36

[20] Veith, Ilza, "The Supernatural in Far Eastern Concepts of Mental Disease," *Bulletin of the History of Medicine*, #37, p. 139

[21] *Ibid.*, p. 44

[22] Tseng, *op. cit.*, p. 572

[23] The Jin in Jin-Yuan refers to the second Jin or Tatar dynasty which held sway in the north of China and was coterminous with the end of the Song dynasty in the south.

[24] Zhu Dan-xi, *The Heart & Essence of Dan-xi's Methods of Treatment*, trans. by Yang Shou-zhong, Blue Poppy Press, Boulder, CO, 1993, p. 39

[25] *Ibid.*, p. 80

[26] *Ibid.*, p. 266

[27] *Ibid.*, p. 264-265

[28] Liu Wan-su, *Shang Han Tiao Ben Xin Fa Lei Cui (Categorized Assembly of Damage [Due to] Cold Branch & Root Heart Methods)*, *Jin Yuan Si Da Yi Jia Ming Zhu Ji Cheng (An Anthology of Famous Jin-Yuan Four Great Masters of Medicine)*, China National Chinese Medicine & Medicinals Press, Beijing, 1997, p. 167

[29] Liu Wan-su, quoted and translated by Vivien Ng, *op. cit.*, p. 37

[30] Zhang Zi-he, *Shi Xing San Liao (Ten Forms, Three Treatments)*, *Jin Yuan Si Da Yi Jia Ming Zhu Ji Cheng*, *op. cit.*, p. 281

[31] Li Dong-yuan, *Pi Wei Lun (Treatise on the Spleen & Stomach)*, *Jin Yuan Si Da Yi Jia Ming Zhu Ji Cheng*, *op. cit.*, p. 437

[32] Quoted by William Yu in "The Song of the Thirteen Ghost Points," *Pacific Journal of Oriental Medicine*, Australia, #4, 1995, p. 9

[33] Quoted by William Yu, *op cit.*, p. 9

[34] Quoted by William Yu, *op. cit.*, p. 9

[35] Ng, *op. cit*, p. 45

[36] Quoted by William Yu, *op. cit.*, p. 9

[37] Chen Shi-duo, quoted by Vivien Ng, *op. cit.*, p. 47

[38] Ng, *op. cit.*, p. 48

[39] *Ibid.*, p. 50

[40] As Vivien Ng points out in *Madness in Late Imperial China*, this stigmatization of mental illness was only governmental and societal. Mental illness was not stigmatized in the mainstream Chinese medical literature. "Precisely because madness was regarded as an organic disorder, it carried no stigma as far as the medical community was concerned. There is no reference in the medical literature to moral turpitude as a cause of madness." (*op. cit.*, p. 50-51)

[41]Kong Zi (Confucius), *Zhong Yong (Doctrine of the Mean)*, Sinolingua, Beijing, 1996, p. 3

[42]Tseng Wen-shing, *op. cit.*, p. 573

[43]Ng, *op. cit.*, p. 63

[44]Kleinman, Arthur & Kleinman, Joan, "Somatization: The Interconnectedness in Chinese Society Among Culture, Depressive Experiences, and the Meanings of Pain," *Culture & Depression*, Univ. of CA Press, Berkeley, 1985

[45]Rationalized in this context is Kleinman's use of this term. It refers to giving an abstract label, such as anger, grief, and depression, to pyschoemotional discomforts.

[46]Cheung, F. & Lau, B., " Situational Variations in Help-seeking Behavior Among Chinese Patients," *Comprehensive Psychiatry*, #23, 1982, p. 253-262; and Cheung, F., "Preferences in Help-seeking Among Chinese Students," *Culture, Medicine and Psychiatry*, #8, 1984, p. 371-380

[47]Kleinman & Kleinman, *op. cit.*, 478

[48]*Ibid.*, p. 439

[49]*Ibid.*, p. 440

[50]*Ibid.*, p. 440

[51]Tseng, *op. cit.*, p. 575

[52]Castillo, Richard J., *Culture & Mental Illness, A Client-centered Approach*, Brooks-Cole Publishing Co., Pacific Grove, CA, 1997, p. 3

[53]Kleinman & Kleinman, *op. cit.*, p. 447

[54]Alan W. Watts, *Psychotherapy East and West,* A New American Library, NY, 1963, p. 11

[55]*Ibid.*, p. vii

[56]For example of Western styles of "psychologizing" acupuncture and Chinese medicine, see Lonny S. Jarret's *Nourishing Destiny: The Inner Tradition of Chinese Medicine*, Spirit Path Press, Stockbridge, MA, 1998, and Leon Hammer's *Dragon Rises, Red Bird Flies*, Station Hill Press, Tarrytown, NY, 1990.

[57]For a discussion of the sociopolitical forces contributing to the ever-growing adoption of *DSM-IV* diagnoses by Chinese medical practitioners, see Lee, S., "Diagnosis Postponed: *Shen Jing Shuai Ruo* & the Transformation of Psychiatry in Post-Mao China," *Culture, Medicine & Psychiatry*, Sept. 1999, p. 381-399.

[58]Although we have not discussed ear acupuncture separately in this text, it is the single most commonly used Chinese medical modality in the West for the treatment of psychiatric disturbances due to drug addiction and substance abuse. It can be a very effective therapy for a variety of mental-emotional diseases. However, since a number of other books deal with ear acupuncture in depth and neither author is particularly experienced in this modality, we have not included it in this book.

[59]He Guo-zhang, "The Chinese Medical Treatment of Amenorrhea due to Neuroleptic Medications," *Xin Zhong Yi (New Chinese Medicine)*, #9, 1995, p. 51-52.

# ❖ 2 ❖

# INTRODUCTORY THEORY

## THE BODY-MIND CONNECTION IN CHINESE MEDICINE

Chinese medicine is based on a very different world-view than that of Western medicine. Since not later than the time of René Descartes, Westerners have tended to think in terms of a body/mind split. There is the body and there is the mind, and many a Western philosopher and scientist has tried to puzzle out the relationship between these two.[1] In order to understand Chinese medical psychiatry, one must first and foremost understand that *no such dualism between the body and mind exists in Chinese medicine*. The body is the material basis for the mind which is seen as the natural expression of the functions of the body. As Li and Liu, the authors of *Zhong Yi Jing Shen Bing Xue (Chinese Medical Psychiatry)* state, "Essence, blood, fluids, and humors are the material basis of the spirit [or mind]."[2] Because there is fundamentally no division between the body and mind in Chinese medicine, there is no theoretical prejudice or hierarchy in Chinese medicine of psychological over somatic functions or symptoms.[3] Psyche and soma are accorded equal status and treatment in Chinese medicine since there is no ontological difference between the two.

The concept of an inseparable bodymind continuum is one of the main characteristics of Eastern thought. In classical Chinese medi-

cine, therefore, mental activity has always been considered to be inseparable from bodily functions, and mental diseases were generally not treated differently from any other disorder.[4]

Because of this non-duality between psyche and soma, physiological events within the body may result in mental-emotional sensations, experiences, and predispositions, while psychological events may have either a beneficial or deleterious effect on the body's physiology. The causative relationship between psyche and soma in Chinese medicine is completely bidirectional.

$$BODY \longleftrightarrow MIND$$

This kind of non-dual, bi-directional relationship is referred to as *ying* or correspondence in Chinese, and correspondence is one of the most important concepts in all of Chinese medical theory.

Till now, many Western students and practitioners of Chinese medicine have believed that modern Chinese medicine is primarily a somatically based medicine and that it gives scant attention to psychological disease. This erroneous but widely held opinion is, at least in part, a function of the non-duality of psyche and soma in Chinese medicine. Because these two aspects of human reality are not clearly divided in Chinese medicine, many Westerners have failed to see and appreciate exactly how Chinese medicine does, in fact, treat psychological disease.[5] Interestingly, Western social scientists are increasingly coming to see the same non-duality. For instance, Western psychiatrists, as evidenced by the *DSM-IV*, commonly divide psychiatric disease into anxiety, somatoform, or mood disorders (among others). However, now, medical anthropologists, such as Richard J. Castillo, specializing in psychiatric anthropology are saying:

> Cross-cultural studies indicate that somatic symptoms are the most common clinical manifestations of anxiety disorders worldwide (Kirmayer, 1984; Kirmayer & Weiss, 1994). The somatization of anxiety is also very common among North American and British patients in primary care settings (Goldberg & Bridges, 1988; Kirmayer & Robins, 1991). This widespread expression of anxiety in the form of somatic symptoms challenges the classification system in DSM-IV that places syndromes with prominent somatic symptoms in a separate category distinct from the anxiety disorders. There is no etiological basis for this distinction, nor does there seem to be much clinical utility in this grouping. Looking at mental illness from a client-centered perspective, separating mental disorders expressing emotional distress into distinct anxiety, somatoform, and mood groupings is questionable.[6]

## THE MIND & SPIRIT IN CHINESE MEDICINE

There are a number of different terms used in Chinese to signify the psyche or mind. These include heart (*xin*), mentality (*xin li*), reflection (*yi*), memory (*ji yi*), spirit (*shen*), heart spirit (*xin shen*), spirit light or spirit brilliance (*shen ming*), essence spirit (*jing shen*), mind (*zhi*), reflection mind (*yi zhi*), spirit mind (*shen zhi*), intelligence power (*zhi li*), and brain (*tou nao*). Although each of these terms has its own uses and connotations, the most commonly used terms in the Chinese medical literature for the mind are spirit and the compound terms which include the word spirit, especially essence spirit (*jing shen*). For instance, in *English-Chinese Medical Dictionary*, all Western medical terms beginning with the prefix "psycho-" begin with the Chinese *jing shen*, and, if one goes to this dictionary's companion volume, *Chinese-English Medical Dictionary*, and looks up *jing shen*, the primary meanings are "spirit, mind, psyche."[7] Likewise, the *Concise English-Chinese Chinese-English Dictionary* defines *jing shen* as mind or consciousness, *jing shen bing* as mental

illnesses or mental disorders, and refers to psychiatry as *jing shen bing xue* or, literally, the study of essence spirit diseases.[8] Therefore, in order to understand how most contemporary Chinese doctors understand the mind within the context of Chinese medicine, one must first understand the Chinese meanings of the word "spirit."

Within Chinese medicine, spirit can have three basic meanings. First, spirit refers to the outward manifestations of the body's life activities, including the manifestations of both normal physiological and pathophysiological activities. Therefore, the *Su Wen* (*Simple Questions*) says, "Obtaining spirit is prosperity [*i.e.*, life]; losing spirit is death." The signs of having spirit or physiologic vitality include bright eyes, normal bearing, clear speech, coherent responses to questions, a normal facial complexion, and normal excretions. The signs of loss of spirit include apathy, abnormal bearing, torpid expression, dark complexion, dull eyes, weak voice, slow, halting speech, and incoherent response to inquiry. When the word spirit is used in this way within Chinese medicine, it is similar to saying that a high-stepping, head-tossing, ready-to-run race horse is spirited.

Secondly, spirit refers to consciousness and the function of thinking-feeling.[9] In that case, it may also be called the spirit mind and spirit brilliance. It is this aspect of the spirit that the *Su Wen* is referring to when its author says, "The hearts holds the office of monarch from whence the spirit brilliance issues." The *Su Wen* also says, "When spirit accumulates in the heart, there is now intelligence." The spirit and its outward manifestation as one's emotional affect are referred to by the collective term "spirit affect." When the word spirit is used in this way within Chinese medicine, it refers to our sentience, cognitive abilities and functions, and to our experience of emotions.

Third, spirit also refers to that which is responsible for all movement and change in the phenomenal world. It is the creative and motivating force of nature "whose substance cannot be seen, but whose function can be seen." (*Xun Zi* [*Hsun Tzu* or *Master Xun*], "The Great Treatise") This definition of spirit is similar to the Christian concept of the Holy Ghost or the Native American concept of the Great Spirit. Although this meaning of spirit is very grand, it does not play any actual, practical role in either diagnosis or treatment within contemporary standard professional Chinese medicine.[10]

As stated above, the body and mind are not seen as two

separate, independently existing entities in Chinese medicine. Wu Dun-xu unequivocally states this in his *Zhong Yi Bing Yin Bing Ji Xue (A Study of Chinese Medical Disease Causes & Disease Mechanisms)*: "Form spirit [*xing shen*, *i.e.*, bodymind] is a single unified concept according to Chinese medical theory."[11] However, the spirit and form or body are seen as a yin-yang pair. In this case, the formal body is the material basis of the spiritual brilliance, while the spirit is the manifestation of the body's physiological activities. More particularly, it is the qi and blood which are the material basis of the spirit. The *Ling Shu (Spiritual Pivot)* says that, "Spirit is made from the essence qi of water and grains." Elsewhere the authors of the *Ling Shu* say:

> Spirit is the righteous qi. Spirit is the abode of the qi. It is qi which transforms spirit. When qi is exuberant, spirit is effulgent. When qi is debilitated, spirit becomes diseased. When qi is severed, spirit perishes.[12]

In other words, spirit is nothing other than the accumulation of qi in the heart which is constructed and nourished by blood and essence. Li Dong-yuan explains this succinctly by saying:

> Qi is the forefather of spirit, and essence is the child of qi. [Thus] qi is the root of [both] essence and spirit. Great is qi! When qi accumulates, it produces essence. When essence accumulates, it renders spirit wholesome.[13]

That spirit is made out of essence and qi is further reiterated by Zhang Jie-gu in the Ming dynasty: "Spirit is engendered by the essence and qi."

Following this line of reasoning, in contemporary professional Chinese medicine, spirit is nothing other than a certain quantity of heart qi. Thus the concept of spirit in Chinese medicine is not "spiritual" in any conventional religious sense. As we have seen, the term "spirit" within the Chinese language as a whole is multivalent. In philosophical-cosmological contexts, it does refer to the ineffable motivating force of the universe. In addition, this same word means "god" and "spirit" in the sense of nature spirits, ghosts, and other nonmaterial beings. However, these other usages of the word spirit should not be conflated with this same word when used in a Chinese medical context.[14]

Because the mind or psyche is referred to as essence spirit, psychiatric or psychological diseases are referred to as essence spirit diseases (*jing shen bing*) in Chinese medicine. When discussing pathological abnormalities of the spirit, Chinese medicine recognizes the following disease conditions of the spirit: loss of spirit, disquieted spirit (also called restless spirit), spirit failing to keep to its abode, clouded spirit, haziness of the spirit, fatigued spirit, lassitude of the spirit, debilitated spirit, abstraction of the spirit, and spirit floating and jumping up. All of these are due to two basic disease mechanisms. Either the spirit is deprived of sufficient construction and nourishment or some evil qi is harassing the spirit. Of the types of evil qi which may harass the spirit, the two main ones are fire heat and phlegm turbidity. Heat causes the spirit to stir restlessly, while phlegm turbidity may block and confound the spirit, thus obscuring its light or brilliance. Thus, all the psychiatric diseases discussed in this book involve dysfunction of the spirit and its brilliance due to one or a combination of these three basic disease mechanisms: malnourishment, evil heat, and/or something blocking or confounding the spirit.

## THE CAUSES OF PSYCHOLOGICAL DISEASE IN CHINESE MEDICINE

Ever since Chen Wu-ze (a.k.a. Chen Yan) published the *San Yin Ji Yi Bing Zheng Fang Lun (The Three Causes & A Unified Treatise on Diseases, Patterns & Formulas)* in 1174 CE, Chinese doctors have divided disease causes into three categories, and these three categories also apply to psychological diseases. These three categories of disease causes are external, internal, and neither internal nor external causes.

## EXTERNAL CAUSES: THE SIX ENVIRONMENTAL EXCESSES

External disease causes refer to the six environmental excesses and pestilential or epidemic qi. The six environmental excesses are: wind, cold, heat, summerheat, dampness, and dryness. If one or more of these external evils assail and enter the body, they may cause various pathological problems depending upon the nature of the evil qi. However, as Huang Yue-dong, author of *Jing Shen Yi Bing Zhong Yi Lin Chuang Zhi Liao (The Clinical Treatment of Psychiatric Diseases with Chinese Medicine)*, says, "There are not many [modern] discussions of external contraction by the six excesses resulting in psychological disease."[15] This is especially the case in terms of the types of psychiatric diseases discussed herein. While Sun Si-miao wrote in the Tang dynasty that, "Wind entering the yang channels leads to mania, while wind entering the yin channels leads to withdrawal," Chinese medicine over the succeeding 12 cen-

| THE SIX ENVIRONMENTAL EXCESSES |
| :---: |
| WIND |
| COLD |
| HEAT |
| DAMPNESS |
| DRYNESS |
| SUMMERHEAT |

turies has emphasized the internal and neither internal nor external causes of disease as the etiological factors of the diseases we discuss in this book.

## INTERNAL CAUSES: THE SEVEN AFFECTS

The internal causes of disease are the seven affects. When the seven affects cause disease, this is commonly referred to as internal damage by the seven affects. The seven affects are joy, anger, anxiety, thought, sorrow, fear, and fright. Five of these—anger, joy, thought, sorrow, and fear—are also referred to as the five minds. Each of these five minds corresponds to one of the five viscera (the liver, heart, spleen, lungs, or kidneys) which in turn correspond to one of the five phases (wood, fire, earth, metal, water). According to the *Su Wen (Simple Questions)* chapter titled "The Great Treatise on the Correspondences & Signs of Yin & Yang," "Humans have five viscera which transform the five qi which, in turn, engender joy, anger, sorrow, anxiety, and fear." Thus A) the five minds and seven affects are produced by their corresponding viscus in response to external and internal stimuli, and B) they are the subjective experience of the function, *i.e.*, qi, of these five viscera. That the seven affects are the manifestation of the functioning of the viscera is further explained by the following passage from the *Ling Shu (Spiritual Pivot)*:

> The liver treasures the blood, and the blood is the abode of the ethereal soul. When liver qi is vacuous, it leads to fear. When replete, it leads to anger...The heart treasures the vessels, and the vessels are the abode of the spirit. When the heart qi is vacuous, this leads to sorrow. When replete, this leads to incessant laughing.

When the arising of these affects is appropriate to the

stimulus involved and is neither excessive in intensity nor continues too long, they are simply the natural expression of life activities and experiences and are not necessarily disease-producing.

| THE SEVEN AFFECTS |
| :---: |
| JOY |
| THOUGHT |
| ANXIETY |
| SORROW |
| FEAR |
| FRIGHT |
| ANGER |

However, if these emotions become excessive or violent, then they damage their corresponding viscera. Therefore, the author of "The Great Treatise on the Correspondences & Signs of Yin & Yang" says, "Violent anger damages yin; violent joy damages yang;" while the author of "One's Spirit" in the *Ling Shu (Spiritual Pivot)* says, "Joy without limit damages the ethereal soul, and damage of the ethereal soul leads to mania." In "Oral Questioning" also in the *Ling Shu (Spiritual Pivot)*, the author says, "Great fright or final [*i.e.*, extreme, deathly] fear lead to the blood and qi dividing and parting, yin and yang tearing apart and becoming vanquished, the channels and network vessels reversing and expiring, the vessel pathways becoming non-free-flowing, yin and yang mutually counterflowing, the defensive and qi procrastinating and lodging, the channels and vessels becoming vacuous and empty, and blood and qi not in sequence..." In the Qing dynasty, Shen Jin-ao reiterated that it is *excessive* emotion that causes disease: "Due to having *great* fear, *great* joy, *great* anxiety, *great* fright, the result is suffering loss of spirit." (Italics ours)

Thus, anger is the mind of the liver, but extreme or prolonged anger also damages the liver. Joy is the mind of the heart, but too much joy damages the heart. Thinking is the mind of the spleen, but too much thinking damages the spleen, sorrow is the mind of the lungs, but excessive sorrow damages the lungs. And fear is the mind of the kidneys, but excessive or prolonged fear damages the kidneys. In addition, the affect of anxiety damages the spleen and heart, while the affect of fright likewise damages the heart and also the gallbladder.

In the Chinese literature, it says, "Anger causes the qi to rise." However, this is not a perfect translation. It is the structure of the English language which imposes such a linear, mechanistic reading of the Chinese. Within the Chinese sentence, anger and rising qi are joined by a linking word (*ze*) that means that one thing normally leads to another. In the same way, joy leads to slackening (*i.e.*, slowing in its flow) of the qi, thought leads to binding of the qi, sorrow leads to scattering of the qi, fears leads to descending of the qi, and fright leads to chaos of the qi. In actual fact, anger and rising qi are one and the same thing. When we say we feel angry, we are feeling a physical sensation of rising qi. When we say that we feel joy, we are feeling a sensation of relaxation in the flow of qi. When we say that we feel fear, we are feeling a sensation of descending qi. The names of these affects or emotions are just abstract labels for felt, physical sensations of the flow of qi. Every thought and emotion is likewise a collection of various physical sensations to which we have given an abstract label. The reality of this universal human experience is kept alive within the English language by such colloquialisms as "blowing one's top" or "getting red in the face" as indications of anger, "being down in the dumps" or "low spirits" as expressions of sorrow, and "peeing in one's pants" as an expression of fear.

The function of each of the various viscera and bowels is associated with and dependent on a particular flow of qi. For instance, the stomach governs downbearing, while the spleen governs upbearing. This is referred to as the qi mechanism. Extreme or prolonged emotions cause extreme and prolonged changes of the flow of qi within the body, and these changes in the flow of qi can inhibit the qi mechanism. When the qi mechanism becomes inhibited, the various viscera and bowels cannot perform their functions correctly. Which viscera and bowels are affected depends on which emotions are involved and these emotions' correspondences with the viscera.

However, all extreme or prolonged emotions can damage and inhibit the qi mechanism as a whole. Since the qi mechanism of the entire body is closely related to the liver's function of governing coursing and discharge, extremes of any emotion can result in liver depression qi stagnation. Qi is yang and, therefore, inherently warm. If qi becomes stagnant and accumulates, depression may transform heat or fire. Therefore, it is said that the seven affects when extreme all transform fire. Mostly, this transformation of evil heat or fire involves liver depression qi stagnation transforming heat.

When a person's viscera and bowels are relatively exuberant and replete and yin and yang are relatively coordinated and in balance, emotions come and go in response to stimuli, but they do not result in enduring pathological changes. However, if a person's viscera and bowels are already vacuous and weak or if they habitually tend towards yin or yang exuberance, extreme or prolonged emotions may easily further damage those already weakened organs or tip the yin-yang balance even further. In that case, abnormal or excessive emotions can easily cause disease. Conversely, when one's mind is soothed and freely flowing and one's emotions are open and light, the qi mechanism is freely and smoothly flowing, the qi and blood are regulated and harmonious, the viscera and bowel function is regulated, and the body's righteous qi is effulgent and exuberant. If the mind is not smoothly flowing and the emotions are depressed, the qi mechanism will counterflow and be in chaos, yin and yang and the qi and blood will lose their regulation, and the viscera and bowel function will become abnormal. Then the body's righteous qi will become decreased and weak. Thus the relationships between the qi and blood, viscera and bowels, and yin and yang and the emotions are completely bi-directional.

Although excessive joy can scatter the heart spirit so that it is not treasured correctly, an appropriate amount of joy can act as the antidote to all the other six affects. This is because joy is relaxing. According to the *Su Wen*, "Joy leads the qi to become harmonious and the mind to extend; thus the constructive and defensive are free-flowing and uninhibited." As we will see below when we discuss the disease causes and mechanisms of individual diseases, internal damage by the seven affects is the most common cause of psychological disease in Chinese medicine.

## NEITHER INTERNAL NOR EXTERNAL CAUSES

The category of neither internal nor external causes of disease is comprised of an indefinite number of disease causes. The only thing that links these disease causes together into a single category is that they are neither the six environmental excesses nor the seven affects.

The most important of these neither internal nor external causes of disease *vis à vis* psychological diseases are: 1) faulty diet, 2) lack of regulation between activity and stillness, 3) lack of discipline in bedroom affairs, 4) iatrogenesis, 5) drug addiction, and 6) parasites.

## FAULTY DIET

According to Chinese medical dietary theory, each of the five flavors corresponds to one of the five phases and, therefore, enters or gathers in especially one of the five viscera. The sour flavor corresponds to the wood phase and, hence, tends to gather in the liver. The bitter flavor corresponds to fire and gathers in the heart. The sweet flavor corresponds to earth and gathers in the spleen. The acrid flavor corresponds to metal and gathers in the lungs, and the salty flavor corresponds to water and tends to gather in the kidneys. A certain amount of each flavor is necessary to promote the function of its corresponding viscus, but an excess of that flavor may damage that same viscus. In addition, each of the flavors tends to have certain physiological effects. The sweet flavor is relaxing but also engenders fluids. The sour flavor is astringing. The bitter flavor is both drying and clearing. The acrid flavor is windy, scattering, and drying. While the salty flavor is softening and descending. Therefore, sweet-flavored foods may relax tension but also engender dampness. A little sweet is necessary to fortify the spleen, but too much sweet damages the spleen. In Chinese dietary theory and therapy, the Doctrine of the Mean reigns supreme.

As stated above, there are three main Chinese disease mechanisms at work in psychological diseases: malnourishment, harassment by heat, and blockage and obstruction. The heart qi and blood and, thus, the spirit primarily receive their nourishment from the spleen. Therefore, if the spleen is damaged by faulty diet, the heart has nowhere from which to receive its nourishment. As stated above, overeating sugars and sweets may damage the spleen. However, the spleen may also be damaged by overeating any foods which are excessively greasy and fatty. Oils and fats also engender fluids, and excessive fluids easily damage the spleen. It is said in Chinese medicine, "The spleen is averse to dampness." Oily, fatty foods in Chinese medicine include fatty meats, dairy products such as milk, butter, and cheese, and fried foods. The spleen's transformation of water and grains is a type of warm transformation liked to the distillation of alcohol wherein the stomach is the fermentation vat and the spleen is the fire under that vat which drive off the finest essence.

Therefore, since the spleen's role in digestion is likened to cooking and steaming, overeating (and overdrinking) chilled and uncooked foods may also damage the spleen. And finally, simply eating too much and especially eating too much hard to digest food may jam the qi mechanism and damage the spleen. If the spleen is damaged by any of these dietary irregularities, it may fail to engender and transform the qi and blood and thus construct and nourish the heart spirit which then becomes disquieted and cannot rest calmly within its abode.

Another cause of malnourishment of the spirit is blood vacuity. Blood is manufactured from the turbid, thick-flavored part of the food sent up to the heart by the spleen. "*Zhuo qi gui xin* (the turbid qi gathers in the heart)." Every food is composed of varying proportions of a yin-yang pair of components, qi and *wei* or qi and flavor. The qi part of food is relatively light and clear and primarily makes the qi, while the *wei* is thick-flavored and relatively turbid and makes the yin, blood, and essence. Some foods have more yang qi and other foods have more yin *wei*, and blood and essence require a certain amount of yin *wei* in the diet in order to provide the building blocks for their manufacture. Foods which provide a high amount of yin flavor tend to be derived from animals. Such foods are also referred to as "bloody, meaty foods" in Chinese medicine. In clinical practice, it is not uncommon to see heart yin and blood vacuity resulting in malnourishment of the spirit due to eating a diet lacking sufficient yin flavor. This type of heart spirit malnourishment is especially common in female vegetarians whose blood vacuity is compounded by their monthly loss of blood via menstruation. As an extension of this, it is also possible to see cases of heart spirit malnourishment in patients who simply are not eating enough, as in anorexia nervosa and bulimia nervosa.[16]

Besides the five flavors, every food is categorized in Chinese medicine as having one of four (or five) natures. These so-called natures are expressions of the inherent temperatures of each food. The four natures are hot, warm, cool, and cold. Since some foods are neither cool or warm but level or neutral, we sometimes count five natures. Hot and warm foods tend to warm yang and are used to treat cool and cold patterns. Foods which are cool and cold tend to cool and clear and are used to treat warm and heat patterns. Over-eating cold-natured foods may damage the spleen and lead to heart spirit malnourishment, while over-eating hot-natured foods may result in evil heat in the body. This evil heat may then flame upwards and harass the heart spirit, thus disquieting it. Foods which are hot in nature include peppers and chilis, cinnamon, dry ginger, white and black pepper, Sichuan pepper, oils and fats, certain meats, like chicken, turkey, tuna, and lamb, certain vegetables, like mustard greens and coriander, and alcohol. In addition, heat can be added to foods depending on how they are prepared. Frying and barbecuing foods are both believed to increase the heat of a food's nature. In traditional Chinese psychiatry, it is believed that a number of psychiatric diseases may be due either in part or *in toto* to over-eating hot-natured foods.

Phlegm and dampness are the two main culprits for blocking the orifices of the heart and confounding and thus disquieting the spirit. Phlegm is nothing other than congealed fluids, and "The spleen is the root of phlegm engenderment." Therefore, the engenderment of phlegm damp evils internally may be the result of any dietary irregularities which damage the spleen and cause it to lose its control over the movement and transformation of water fluids in the body. However, the likelihood of phlegm engenderment is even greater if the patient over-eats foods which have a lot of flavor (*i.e.*, *wei* in the technical sense described above) and which strongly engender fluids. Once again, this includes fatty meats, oils and fats in general, and dairy products. That being said, phlegm can also be engendered by heat which stews the juices and congeals fluids into phlegm. Hence a combination of hot-natured foods and greasy, fatty foods is even more likely to engender phlegm internally.

## LACK OF REGULATION BETWEEN ACTIVITY & STILLNESS

Movement or activity (*dong*, literally "stirring") and stillness (*jing*) form another yin-yang pair within Chinese medicine. Activity, whether mental, verbal, or physical, consumes qi and blood since it is qi and blood which empower and nourish all activity. Therefore, too much activity or stirring may result in either consumption and exhaustion of the heart qi or consumption and depletion of yin blood. Both qi and blood vacuities due to over-stirring may result in disquietude of the spirit. In addition, if too much stirring damages yin, then yin will be unable to control yang which becomes hyperactive. In that case, the heart spirit both lacks nourishment from yin blood and is harassed by hyperactive yang, vacuity heat, or internally stirring wind. When excessive activity consumes too much yin blood and

results in yin vacuity/vacuity heat harassing the heart spirit, this itself will cause even more stirring, and a vicious cycle is created which is hard to break. Literally, patients feel they cannot control their restless stirring.

Appropriate stirring or movement promotes the movement of the qi and blood and the free flow of the qi mechanism. This means that a healthy amount of physical activity can help move the qi and move the blood. Because it also frees the flow and disinhibits the qi mechanism, it promotes spleen-stomach function and thus the engenderment and transformation of qi and blood. Too little activity, on the other hand, may result in qi stagnation and blood stasis. Since the qi moves water fluids as well as the blood and disperses and transforms food, inactivity may also result in phlegm dampness and/or food accumulation and nonengenderment of qi and blood. Therefore, both too much and too little physical activity can lead to disquietude of the spirit.

## LACK OF DISCIPLINE IN BEDROOM AFFAIRS

Bedroom affairs are the traditional Chinese way of referring to sexual activity. According to Chinese medicine, too much or too little sexual activity may result in psychological disease. Sexual desire is a function of ministerial or life-gate fire. Ministerial fire is rooted in the lower burner and connects to the heart and pericardium in the upper burner. This connection between the heart above and ministerial fire below is described by Li Dong-yuan in the *Pi Wei Lun (Treatise on the Spleen & Stomach)*:

> [Heart fire] is a yin fire. It starts from the lower burner and its ligation links to the heart. The heart does not reign [personally. Rather,] ministerial fire is its deputy. Ministerial fire is the fire of the pericardium developing from the lower burner.[17]

As we have seen above, ministerial fire is healthy only as long as it remains level and calm in its lower source. Because ministerial fire is the root of and is connected to the yang qi of all the viscera and bowels, if ministerial fire stirs upward and becomes inflamed, this may also lead to yang hyperactivity and inflaming of fire heat in any of the other organs in the body. Because heat, being yang, has an innate tendency to rise and the heart is located in the upper burner, heat rising up due to stirring of ministerial fire typically accumulates in and harasses the heart, thus disquieting the spirit.

Sexual desire and activity are main ways of stirring ministerial fire. Because sexual maturation in adolescents has to do with the effulgence of the kidneys, and ministerial fire is itself rooted in kidney yang, teenagers tend to be both sexually preoccupied (if not actually active), tend to have symptoms of up-flaming heat, such as acne, and also tend to have easily disquieted spirits. Although excessive sexual intercourse may stir ministerial fire, many Chinese practitioners feel that masturbation is especially inflaming to life-gate fire. In addition, and especially or at least most obviously in men, sexual activity also typically results in a loss or consumption of yin essence which may cause or aggravate vacuity heat.

While the Chinese medical literature tends to focus entirely on excessive sexual desire and activity, lack of sexual release may also have deleterious effects on the bodymind. Orgasm in Chinese medicine is described as yang reaching its extreme and then transforming into yin. It is, quite obviously, a discharge of qi. Therefore, an appropriate amount of orgasms help to relax and free the flow of qi. One of the main causes of functional non-ejaculation in men and inability to orgasm in women is liver depression qi stagnation. However, lack of orgasm can itself lead to the causation or worsening of liver depression. If there is then constant stoking of the ministerial fire by erotic thoughts or stimuli, such as photos, movies, or phone sex, this may lead to depression transforming heat. As with all other aspects of the body/mind relationship, the relationships between sex and physiology and sex and psychology in Chinese medicine are all completely bi-directional.

## IATROGENESIS

Iatrogenesis means that a disease has been caused by one's doctor. A number of adverse psychological symptoms may be caused by various Western medical treatments and medications. However, Western medicine has no monopoly on iatrogenesis. Inappropriate Chinese medical treatment may also cause unwanted psychological side effects. As an example of potential Western medical iatrogenesis, Dr. James W. Long, author of *The Essential Guide to Prescription Drugs 1990*, says that Prednisone may cause insomnia and even "mental and emotional disturbances of serious magnitude."[18] This is because, according to Chinese medicinal classification, Prednisone is a very powerful exterior-resolving medicinal. Exterior-resolving medicinals are windy natured, drying medicinals which

work by upbearing and out-thrusting yang. Thus they can clear heat via out-thrusting and relieve pain via moving and quickening. However, they also damage and consume yin. Therefore, they easily lead to yin vacuity fire effulgence. It is this fire effulgence which then ascends to harass the heart spirit. Because yin and yang are mutually rooted, yin vacuity may eventually reach and damage kidney yang. In that case, there is yin and yang dual vacuity with upward flaming of vacuity heat. In the same way, overuse or inappropriate prescription of powerful acrid, windy and, therefore, moving and drying Chinese medicinals which resolve the exterior, such as Radix Bupleuri (*Chai Hu*), can also damage and consume yin and lead to vacuity heat harassing the heart and disquieting the spirit.

Although there is not the time or the space in this present work to discuss all the various psychological side effects of all modern Western and traditional Chinese medicinals, many Western medicinals and some Chinese medicinals do have the potential for creating psychological iatrogenesis. When psychiatric conditions are the result of iatrogenesis, either A) the offending treatment should be suspended and replaced by some other, safer, less iatrogenic treatment, or B) some other treatment should be combined which will mitigate the side effects of the first treatment while still allowing it to achieve its intended therapeutic effects. Chinese medicinals prescribed on the basis of an individualized pattern discrimination are often very effective for mitigating the iatrogenic effects of modern Western medicinals and treatments.

## DRUG ADDICTION

Use of addictive drugs always begins as a kind of self-medication. We are drawn to various drugs and psychotropic substances because we like the way they make us feel. However, at some point, the long-term side effects of such drugs outweigh their short-term benefits. We have already touched on the deleterious effects of alcohol above. Alcohol is sometimes referred to as "fire water" in English, and this English colloquialism is a good description of what overdrinking alcohol does according to Chinese medicine. According to Jin Zi-jiu, a Qing dynasty Chinese doctor:

Alcohol's nature is violent. It is also able to consume the spirit and damage the blood. Its qi is hot. It mainly disperses and wastes. First it enters the liver and gallbladder. Gallbladder fire runs rampant and blazes. The qi loses its subduing and downbearing and liver yin is plundered. The blood loses its calmness and stillness. Hence there is easy counterflow and upbearing... [However,] alcohol's nature is damp as well as hot. Its dampness damages the spleen and leads to the engenderment of rheum. Then phlegm rheum easily gathers in the coils [of the internal organs].[19]

Jin Zi-jiu then goes on to talk about the ill-effects of alcohol's heat on the lungs. However, alcohol's heat does not just affect the lungs. It also damages the heart, liver, and stomach. When alcohol's heat assails the heart, liver, and stomach, it harasses the heart and disquiets the spirit. When this heat or fire combines with phlegm, then heat disquiets the spirit, while phlegm confounds it. Eventually, Jin Zi-jiu says, evil heat due to overconsumption of the alcohol reaches the kidneys, damaging and consuming kidney yin. This then gives rise to vacuity heat which damages and consumes qi and the constructive, ultimately resulting in wearing away of the qi and damage of the blood.

Huang Yue-dong, writing in the 20th century, explains the deleterious psychological effects of alcohol in the following way:

> [Alcohol] enters the stomach and its qi counterflows upward to the chest. There, it steams the liver and gallbladder resulting in the liver [yang] floating and gallbladder [qi counterflowing] horizontally. This leads to mania and anger...[20]

We drink alcohol because of its powerfully dispersing nature. Alcohol in moderation disinhibits the qi mechanism and resolves depression. Thus it relaxes tension, and we temporarily feel more joyous and carefree.

While smoking tobacco is usually not the sole immediate cause of serious psychological disease, according to Chinese medicine, it can definitely aggravate psychological disease. Jin Zi-jiu says that tobacco's qi is acrid and drying and that it easily consumes the qi and damages the lungs. If the lung qi is damaged, then the qi loses its clearing and depurating. What this means is that smoking tobacco damages and consumes both lung qi and yin. Because the lungs lose their clearing and depurating, there is both lingering heat and deep-lying phlegm, and we have already seen how both heat and phlegm can harass, confound, and disquiet the spirit.

The reason people enjoy smoking tobacco is because it is an upbearing, out-thrusting, exterior-resolving substance. Therefore, it temporarily gives us a sense of more abundant yang qi at the same time as it temporarily resolves depression and frees the flow of qi.

When it comes to more immediately deleterious, so-called recreational drugs, these are commonly divided in terms of their effect into "uppers" and "downers." Those drugs which are considered uppers, such as amphetamines, cocaine, and marijuana, achieve their psychotropic effect, at least in terms of Chinese medicine, by strongly upbearing and also out-thrusting the yang qi. The downside is that they also tend to damage and consume yin, and, therefore, their over- or prolonged use typically leads to first yin vacuity/vacuity heat and then to yin and yang dual vacuity with vacuity heat. Although it is more difficult to explain the Chinese disease mechanisms of "downers," such as heroin, codeine, morphine, etc., Li and Liu say that the deleterious effects of any drug can be treated based on the fundamental principle, "For yang disease, treat yin, and for yin disease, treat yang."[21] In other words, all one ever needs to do in Chinese medicine is analyze the symptoms produced by such drugs in terms of Chinese medical theory and treat them accordingly. Although Li and Liu says that it is these kinds of drugs' toxins flowing into the viscera and bowels which result in the spirit mind becoming befuddled, they likewise refrain from positing any exact disease mechanisms. The identification of such specific disease mechanisms is something useful to be done for the future.

## PARASITES

Most books on Chinese medical psychiatry do not discuss parasites as a disease cause of psychological disease. However, parasites, or at least the traditional Chinese idea of parasites, may play a part in a number of psychological diseases. In Chinese, parasites are called *chong*. Literally, this means worms. Worms are believed to be engendered in a damp, hot environment. Such damp heat is either the result of spleen vacuity or, at the very least, causes spleen vacuity. Since these "worms," dampness, and heat hinder and obstruct the free flow of the qi, virtually all cases of parasitism in Chinese medicine are accompanied by qi stagnation. If such conditions continue and endure for a long time, they may also be complicated by blood stasis.

In Chinese medicine, the concept of worm disease includes tapeworms, roundworms, and pinworms the same as does parasitism in Western medicine. However, the Chinese concept of worm disease also includes a number of other diseases, such as cirrhosis of the liver, which Western medicine does not always consider parasitic. One very ancient type of parasitic syndrome is gu worm (*gu chong*) or simply gu condition (*gu zheng*). Gu worms are associated with complex conditions which simultaneously involve digestive, neuromuscular, and mental-emotional symptoms. In the Tang dynasty, Sun Si-miao wrote:

> There are thousands of gu toxins, all of which may potentially cause different symptoms. Some of them may cause bloody stools, while others initiate the desire to lay in a dark room. Others may bring about bouts of irregular emotions, such as depression that alternates with periods of sudden happiness. Others again cause the extremities to feel heavy and ache all over. Then there are myriads of other symptoms we do not have the space to list in their entirety.[22]

Some of the mental-emotional symptoms Heiner Fruehauf, professor of Chinese medicine at the Northwest Naturopathic College, lists as being the result of gu worms include depression, irritability, irascibility, emotional lability, restlessness, insomnia, confusion, clouded thinking, chaotic thinking, visual and auditory hallucinations, epileptiform seizures, and feeling of possession.[23]

Nigel Wiseman, in *A Practical Dictionary of Chinese Medicine*, gives the primary definition of gu as: "1. Toxin of poisonous *chong* (insects, reptiles, etc.) damaging the liver and spleen, causing blockage of the network vessels, and manifesting in the form of drum distention (gu distention)."[24] Worms in Chinese medicine may be either visible, such as roundworms, pinworms, and tapeworms, or they may be invisible. Gu worms fall into the invisible category. Traditionally, it is believed that the main route of entry of gu worms into the body is through the mouth with the food. Once they enter the body, they spread out diffusely "like oil seeping into flour" as the Qing dynasty doctor, Ran Xi, said. In modern Chinese medicine, *Candida albicans* is considered a species of worms even though candidiasis is not considered a parasitic disease in Western medicine. Similarly, Heiner Fruehauf believes it is often useful to categorize intestinal dysbiosis, leaky gut syndrome, infection by blastocystis hominis, and giardiasis as types of gu worm conditions in Chinese medicine.

When gu worms are associated with psychological disease, it is not that the "worms" *per se* cause the mental-emotional symptoms. As stated above, in these cases there is, at the very least, a combination of spleen vacuity, damp heat, and liver depression. Spleen vacuity may lead to malnourishment of the heart spirit since the spleen is the latter heaven root of qi and blood engenderment and transformation. The heat of damp heat may ascend to harass the heart spirit. Over time, dampness and heat may also give rise to phlegm and fire. In addition, liver depression immediately results in irritability and a tendency towards depression, and secondarily may transform into heat or fire. If damp heat or depressive heat endure, either may damage and consume yin blood giving rise to vacuity heat harassing the heart. Further, qi stagnation may lead to blood stasis. Static blood may directly block the orifices of the heart and may indirectly cause malnourishment of the spirit. This is because static blood inhibits the production of new or fresh blood. Hence it is easy to see that the disease mechanisms associated with gu worm condition could give rise to a variety of psychological symptoms. We will talk further about these mechanisms below under the heading "yin fire."

### FORMER HEAVEN DISEASE CAUSES

In addition to internal, external, and neither internal nor external causes, disease causes within Chinese medicine can also be divided into former and latter heaven disease causes. Latter heaven disease causes are those which are acquired or engendered after parturition. Former heaven disease causes are those which are either inherited or are acquired or engendered in utero. The *Ling Shu* (*Spiritual Pivot*) says, "The human fetus is first produced from essence." Likewise, the *Su Wen* (*Simple Questions*) says, "Without essence, the body has no root." Li and Liu quote these lines in substantiation of their statement that:

> If the parent's bodies are healthy and their essence and qi are full and sufficient, then the constituents making up the fetus's body are also healthy and without ailment. The righteous qi has a surplus, the resistance is strong, and thus the fetus does not suffer from harassment by evils. Nourishment is fully and sufficiently supplied, and hence, after being born, the child is healthy and their intelligence is quick-witted. If, [on the other hand,] the par-

ent's bodies are habitually vacuous and weak, their qi and blood is debilitated and faint, and their essence and qi are not full, this will produce disease within the fetus's unbalanced body. The nourishment for the growth and development of the material substance will be lacking, and, after being born, disease may manifest in either the body or the mind.[25]

Li and Liu then go on to say that the mother's eating and drinking and hunger and satiety without limit, the mother's improper taxation and leisure, and the mother's disease reaching the fetus may all result in psychological as well as bodily disease. For instance, if, during pregnancy, the mother overtaxes herself and/or does not obtain sufficient nourishment, her qi and blood, fluids and humors must become depleted. Therefore, the fetus's endowment must also become insufficient. After birth, the child's body will be vacuous and weak and their intelligence may be decreased. Likewise, if the mother catches a warm disease or pestilential epidemic, evil qi may follow the channels downward to reach the fetal origin, thus disturbing the fetus's growth and development. After birth, this may result in the child's intelligence not developing fully.

Although these traditional Chinese teachings on former heaven disease causes may appear simplistic to modern Western readers, they do underscore the fact that traditional Chinese doctors did know that psychological diseases can be due to either inherited factors or factors acquired in utero.

## THE SIX DEPRESSIONS

In the Yuan dynasty, Zhu Dan-xi formulated a list of six depressions. Zhu said:

> If the blood and qi are surging and harmonious, the tens of thousands of diseases cannot be engendered. However, if one has depression, then all the diseases can be engendered.

This is especially true of psychological disease. Therefore, it is important to understand Zhu's six depressions. The six depressions are qi, blood, dampness, phlegm, food, and fire. Five of these are intimately connected with disease mechanisms leading to symptoms of psychological disease. Qi depression is more commonly called qi stagnation. It is mainly due to unfulfilled desires. The liver governs coursing and

discharge and its nature likes to spread freely. Every desire is the subjective sensation of a movement of qi towards or away from something. When such desires are unfulfilled, the liver qi cannot spread freely and coursing and discharging become inhibited. It is interesting to note that, according to Castillo, "...the development of disordered emotions is closely related to the cognitive construction of situations as uncontrollable."[26] This means that disordered emotions, at least for some Western social scientists, are primarily due to the perception of the individual that they cannot fulfil their desires *vis à vis* a particular situation. In other words, that situation is beyond their control and their qi cannot move freely either towards or away from something within that situation. This view is congruent with Chinese medical theory. However, although unfulfilled desires are one of the main and most immediate causes of liver depression qi stagnation, we will discuss a number of others below under liver depression qi stagnation.

Blood depression is none other than blood stasis. It may be due to traumatic injury severing the channels and vessels, to blood vacuity not nourishing the vessels, to qi vacuity not stirring (*i.e.*, moving) the blood, or to qi stagnation. The qi is the commander of the blood. If the qi moves, the blood moves. When the qi stops, the blood also stops. Because blood stasis is a substantial or material depression, static blood may also hinder and obstruct the free flow of qi. Therefore, the relationship between qi stagnation and blood stasis is bi-directional.

Damp depression is damp accumulation. Dampness may be either externally invading or internally engendered. Dampness is nothing other than water fluids. It is also moved and transformed by the qi. If the qi becomes stagnant, fluids may collect (the Chinese word *ting* can also be translated as "stop") and accumulate, thus transforming into evil dampness. *Vice versa*, if, for any reason, dampness accumulates, because it is a material substance, it may hinder and impede the free flow of qi. Hence damp accumulation may cause or aggravate qi stagnation. In addition, because blood and fluids move together, if dampness accumulates, over time, this will also commonly result in blood stasis.

Phlegm depression is nowadays more commonly referred to as phlegm obstruction. If damp evils linger and endure or are worked on by either cold or heat, they may congeal into phlegm. As with dampness and static blood, material phlegm may hinder and obstruct the free flow of qi. Therefore, phlegm depression may cause or aggravate qi depression. Conversely, long-standing qi stagnation complicated by evil dampness may eventually give rise to phlegm obstruction. And, just as lingering dampness may become complicated by blood stasis, so may phlegm turbidity.

Yet again, food is a material substance which is moved and transformed by the qi. If we eat too much and jam the spaces within the qi mechanism, food may become stagnant and depressed. This material substance then impedes the free and easy flow of qi. So food stagnation may give rise to qi stagnation just as qi stagnation inhibiting the qi mechanism may give rise to food stagnation. When food becomes stagnant, the clear and turbid are not divided and damp turbidity may be engendered. And, if food stagnation becomes chronic and enduring, it may also become complicated by blood stasis.

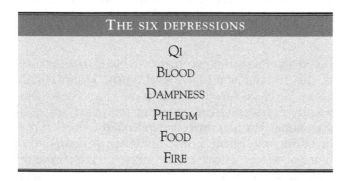

Therefore, immaterial qi and the above four material depressions are all mutually engendering. Any one of these can give rise to any other. In addition, because the body's host or ruling qi is yang and, therefore, warm, if the qi becomes stagnant and accumulates, it may transform into depressive heat. This is what Zhu Dan-xi meant by depressive fire. Because qi stagnation commonly complicates any and all of the above four material depressions, they all may likewise give rise to transformative heat. In other words, blood stasis may become stasis heat, dampness may become damp heat, phlegm may become phlegm heat, and food stagnation may be complicated by stomach heat. Whether or not and how quickly a person transfroms evil heat from depression depends on their constitution, diet, sex, age, and lifestyle. The more yang any of these are, the more likely the person will be to transform depression into heat.

As we have seen above, two of the main causes of psychological disease are evil heat harassing the heart and disquieting the spirit and phlegm turbidity and/or stat-

ic blood blocking the orifices of the heart and confounding the spirit. Because all six of Zhu's depressions can be directly involved in one of these two mechanisms, it is important to understand the disease mechanisms behind and between these six depressions. In addition, because liver depression usually results in spleen vacuity, dampness damages the spleen, and blood stasis and fire heat both damage yin blood, at least four of the six depressions may also play a part in malnourishment of the heart spirit.

## LIVER DEPRESSION QI STAGNATION

As an extension of the above discussion of Zhu Dan-xi's six depressions, in our experience, liver depression qi stagnation is the single most important mechanism in the causation of mental-emotional disorders. Essentially all patients suffering from psychiatric disease exhibit symptoms of this disease mechanism, and this disease mechanism sits squarely in the middle of a number of others. While unfulfilled desires are the main immediate cause of liver depression qi stagnation, loss of the liver's control over coursing and discharge may also be due to the liver's not obtaining sufficient blood to nourish and harmonize it, the liver's not obtaining sufficient yin to enrich and moisten it, and the liver's not obtaining sufficient yang to warm and steam it. In addition, any other stagnation or depression in the body may cause or worsen liver depression qi stagnation. Further, the liver and lungs both participate in the promotion of the free flow of the qi. The liver controls the coursing and discharging of the qi, while the lungs provide the motivating force behind the movement of the qi via their downbearing and depurating. Since the lung qi is rooted in and largely derived from the spleen qi (at least from the latter heaven point of view), spleen qi vacuity leading to a lung qi vacuity may also aggravate liver depression qi stagnation.

Conversely, the liver depression may negatively impact any of the other viscera or bowels which play a main role in the creation or perpetuation of mental-emotional illness. First and foremost, a replete liver will invade the spleen and stomach. Liver assailing the spleen results in spleen qi vacuity and, therefore, blood vacuity as well as dampness, phlegm, and/or food stagnation. Spleen qi vacuity may then lead to kidney yang vacuity, while blood vacuity may lead to yin vacuity. Further, spleen qi vacuity may also lead to lung qi vacuity and/or heart qi and/or blood vacuity. Liver invading the stomach typically gives rise to upward counterflow.

| CAUSES OR AGGRAVATIONS OF LIVER DEPRESSION QI STAGNATION | |
|---|---|
| ❖ Unfulfilled desires inhibiting the qi mechanism | ❖ Yang vacuity not warming & steaming the liver |
| ❖ Anger damaging the liver | ❖ Any of the five other depressions |
| ❖ Blood vacuity not nourishing the liver | ❖ The presence of any evil qi inhibiting the free flow of qi |
| ❖ Yin vacuity not moistening the liver | ❖ Spleen qi vacuity causing lung qi vacuity |

If liver depression transforms into heat, heat may ascend to harass the heart spirit. However, transformative heat may also arise from damp heat, phlegm heat, and stomach heat due to food stagnation. In addition, heat ascending and harassing the heart spirit may also be due to kidney yin vacuity with fire flaring in turn due to enduring depressive heat damaging and consuming yin fluids.

Therefore, it is easy to see the pivotal role liver depression plays in the various disease mechanisms associated with mental-emotional disorders. The main viscera and bowels associated with psychiatric disease in Chinese medicine are the heart, liver, spleen, kidneys, and stomach, and the liver has close reciprocal relationships with all of these. While each of these viscera and bowels has Chinese medical connections to each of the others, in real-life clinical practice, the liver is simply the most commonly diseased of all the Chinese organs, and, therefore, liver-stomach, liver-spleen, heart-liver, and liver-kidney patterns and, by extension, heart-liver-stomach, heart-liver-spleen, and heart-liver-kidney patterns are the most commonly seen patterns. This is why we believe that liver depression plays an important part in the overwhelming majority of patients with psychiatric illness.

## CONSTITUTION & PSYCHOLOGICAL DISEASE

In Chinese medicine, there are four basic body types or constitutions.[27] These are tai yang, shao yang, tai yin, and shao yin. In Chinese, the term for constitution is *chang ti*, "habitual bodily." This means a body that is habitually a certain way. Such a habitual body type may be genetic or it may be due to diet, lifestyle, aging, or disease. In other words, it is not necessarily something we are born with and stays the same throughout our life. It may and usually does change over time and with aging. In terms of the causation of psychiatric illness, different body types predispose one to different diseases mechanisms and, therefore, different patterns of psychiatric disease.

The tai yang is a yang exuberant body type. The person has a well-developed upper body and less well developed lower body. They may be obese in the upper half of their body, but this obesity overlies a well-developed musculature. Tai yang persons typically have a red facial complexion due to yang exuberance, and they easily develop replete heat. If this replete heat harasses the heart, the heart spirit will become disquieted. Because this body type also tends to exhibit phlegm damp signs and symptoms, replete heat is often complicated by dampness and/or phlegm which may further block the orifices of the heart and confound the spirit. In general, patients with this body type should eat less meaty, fried, fatty, oily foods, acrid, hot peppery foods, and not drink too much alcohol. More men tend to be habitually bodily tai yang than women, but women can also exhibit this body type.

The shao yang body type is the body type of the healthy young adult of either sex. From a Western somatotyping point of view, this is the mesomorphic body type. The shao yang body type is an outward sign that yin and yang are in relative balance and the viscera and bowels are functioning relatively normally. Because shao yang body types tend not to be either greatly yin or greatly yang, depending on disease causes and mechanisms as well as their severity and duration, they can become either yin or yang vacuous or replete. However, because this is inherently a yang body type, most often these patients transform heat when ill. If this heat ascends to harass the heart spirit, the spirit will become disquieted.

The tai yin body type is endomorphic. The person is obese, often grossly so, and the tissue is flaccid and without tone. The facial complexion is typically pale, and the lower body is often more obese than the upper body. More women exhibit this body type than men, but either sex can have it. This body type is a result of insufficient yang qi to move and transform phlegm and dampness. In most cases, the spleen is vacuous and weak, and so there is also often qi and blood vacuity.

This means that people with this body type often suffer from phlegm damp conditions and qi and blood vacuity conditions. In terms of psychiatric disease, this further means that people with this body type easily suffer from lack of construction and nourishment of the heart spirit, dampness and phlegm obstructing the heart orifices, and non-free flow of the qi. Tai yin body types need more exercise, should not eat too much, should mostly eat, warm cooked foods, and should not eat chilled, uncooked foods. Because they easily engender phlegm, they also need to be careful about fluid-engendering foods.

The shao yin body type is ectomorphic. The person does not have enough muscle and flesh. Shao yin persons tend towards yin vacuity and, therefore, easily develop vacuity heat. In terms of psychiatric illness, if this vacuity heat and fire flaring ascends to harass the heart, the heart spirit becomes disquieted. In addition, these people often manifest liver depression qi stagnation due to the liver's not obtaining sufficient blood and yin to nourish and moisten it. Shao yin body types need to get adequate rest and to control their impulse to constantly stir. They also need to stay away from stimulating foods and drinks as well as acrid, hot, drying foods and flavors. Instead, they should take care to eat enough "bloody, meaty foods" so as to get enough *wei* to supplement their essence. People with serious cachectic disease, the anorectic, and many of the elderly develop this body type even though they were not born ectomorphic.

---

### THE FOUR YIN-YANG BODY TYPES

❖ **TAI YANG:** Large, beefy, red-faced, overdeveloped upper body, underdeveloped lower body

❖ **SHAO YANG:** Healthy mesomorph, neither fat nor thin, normal muscular tone

❖ **TAI YIN:** Endomorphic, obese, pale-faced, lack of tone, overdeveloped lower body

❖ **SHAO YIN:** Ectomorphic, thin, nervous, restless

---

Just as in Sheldon somatotyping, no one is a pure type, similarly, the above four body types are only rough guidelines for disease tendencies. While most healthy young adults exhibit the shao yang body type, even within that type there may be mixtures. Therefore, one can talk about mixed shao yang-tai yang types, mixed shao-yang-tai yin, and mixed shao yang-shao yin body types. Typically as we age, we move from a more shao yang type to more of one of these other three.

### AGE & SEX

Much of the philosophy of Chinese medicine is based on the theory of universal change found in the *Yi Jing* (*The Classic of Change*). Throughout our life, from conception to death, we are constantly changing. When we are born, our bodies are basically formed and our viscera and bowels are fundamentally present. However, neither our bodies nor our viscera and bowels are yet mature. It takes five or six years for our spleen and stomach to become replete in a healthy sense. Because infants and toddlers are *ipso facto* spleen vacuous and weak, they do not have lots of qi and lots of blood. Therefore, their spirit is easily disquieted and malnourishment of their sinews easily leads to convulsions. In addition, this spleen vacuity leads to easy engenderment of phlegm and dampness.

After five or six, the spleen becomes exuberant and the person begins to make more qi and blood each day than they consume. This surplus is transformed into latter heaven essence. Most of this latter heaven essence is stored in the kidneys where it bolsters and supports the former heaven essence. By the early teens, there is enough essence stored in the kidneys for the kidneys to become exuberant. This leads to exuberance of the life gate fire which, in turn, leads to the awakening of sexual desire. Heat increases in the body; therefore, so does growth, acne (a sign of heat), and a tendency towards emotional lability, irritability, and a lessening of self-control due to heat harassing the heart and disquieting the spirit.

During the late teens, 20s, and early to mid 30s, most shao yang body types have enough qi and blood to nourish their heart spirit but not so much yang qi as to engender evil heat too easily. As long as diet and lifestyle are moderate and normal, yin and yang are in relative balance and so the emotions are also relatively normal. However, as we age, the viscera become weak in the same order that they became mature. In other words, first the spleen becomes vacuous and weak. According to Yan De-xin, one of China's most famous living Chinese medicine geriatric specialists, this spleen vacuity is due to an accumulation of damages due to external invasion, traumatic injury, improper diet, damage by the seven affects, etc. which inhibit the free flow of the qi mechanism and, therefore, liver and spleen function. Because the spleen no longer

## DEVELOPMENTAL STAGES & DISEASE TENDENCIES

❖ **INFANCY:** Viscera & bowel immaturity, qi & blood insufficiency; a tendency to phlegm dampness, food stagnation, and internal stirring of wind

❖ **CHILDHOOD:** At approximately six years of age, the spleen & stomach mature leading to a surplus of qi & blood which is converted into latter heaven essence and stored in the kidneys

❖ **ADOLESCENCE:** Kidneys become effulgent, leading to stirring & hyperactivity of ministerial fire with a tendency to depressive heat. Due to stress of liminality[28], many unfulfilled desires and frustrations. Ergo, a tendency to liver depression qi stagnation.

❖ **ADULTHOOD:** Work & family stress & delayed gratification leading to unfulfilled desires and, therefore, liver depression qi stagnation

❖ **MIDDLE AGE:** Continuance of work & family stress; in addition, decline of spleen due to habitual assault by liver

❖ **LATE MIDDLE AGE/EARLY OLD AGE:** Spleen vacuity reaches the kidneys, leading to qi & yang vacuity; in addition, yin half used up

❖ **OLD AGE:** Decline in qi & blood, disharmony of yin & yang, progressive inhibition of qi flow by blood stasis & phlegm obstruction

engenders and transforms the qi and blood as abundantly as before, there is less of a surplus to be transformed into acquired essence. Over time, this leads first to yin vacuity and then to yin and yang vacuity.

Because of menstruation, gestation, and lactation, all of which consume large amounts of yin blood manufactured by the spleen, women tend to suffer from spleen vacuity more than men. We can see the signs of clinical spleen vacuity crop up or worsen in most Western women around the age of 35. Because the spleen and liver are bi-directionally related, this spleen vacuity tends to be accompanied by a worsening of liver depression. By the time of menopause, the liver is depressed, liver blood and kidney yin as well as spleen qi and kidney yang are all vacuous, and there is vacuity heat. Happily, the cessation of menstruation allows women's spleens and kidneys to recuperate, and, therefore, after menopause, the rate of aging in women as compared to men often tips in their favor. Due to decline in visceral function, most people (Yan De-xin would say all people) develop blood stasis as they age, and many of us develop phlegm.

### THE MENSTRUAL CYCLE & THE EMOTIONS

In Chinese medicine, women's menstrual cycles are divided into four phases, and, depending on what is going on within a woman's body during each of those four phases, she may experience certain psychological disturbances. Phase one is the post-menstrual phase.

blood, and this has left the body relatively yin and blood deficient. Therefore, during phase one, the body attempts to grow yin and replenish blood. Around day 10, yin and blood are once again exuberant. Because yang is transformed out of yin, during phase two, the ovulatory phase, yang grows, the body heats up, and the basal body temperature goes from hypo- to hyperthermal. Phase three lasts from approximately day 16 to the onset of menstruation. During this time, the heart is sending the blood down to the uterus to be stored. This accumulation of blood in the uterus may leave the rest of the woman's body relatively blood vacuous and insufficient if the woman leans in that direction anyway.

## FOUR PHASES OF MENSTRUAL CYCLE

**PHASE 1:** Yin

**PHASE 2:** Yang

**PHASE 3:** Qi

**PHASE 4:** Blood

The liver, like all the rest of the organs and tissues in the body, can only function if it obtains sufficient blood to nourish it. The liver's main function is to govern coursing and discharge or the free flow of qi. Therefore, if the liver is deprived of sufficient blood to nourish it, it will become depressed and its qi will become stagnant. Because of the close reciprocal relationship between the liver and spleen, liver depression causes or exacerbates spleen vacuity. In that case, there will be even less qi and blood engendered and transformed and more phlegm and dampness which may also cause depressive heat.

If conception has not taken place, during phase four, the menstruation itself, the uterus discharges the blood it has been storing and the whole cycle repeats itself. Because yin and blood are relatively empty and vacuous post-menstrually, some women may experience aggravation of vacuity heat harassing the heart spirit during that phase. Because yang becomes exuberant during midcycle, qi depression often transforms into heat at that point in a woman's cycle. And because of blood accumulating in the uterus, liver depression and, therefore, spleen and heart vacuity may also worsen during the premenstruum. This then leads to disquietude of the spirit due to qi stagnation, depressive heat, and/or malnourishment.

## YIN FIRE & PSYCHOLOGICAL DISEASES

Li Gao, a.k.a. (Li) Dong-yuan, one of the four great masters of the Jin-Yuan dynasties, created a theory called yin fire. Yin fire is a pathological fire which arises from the middle and lower burners but disturbs function in the upper burner. The heart is located in the upper burner and is the abode or mansion of the spirit. Therefore, evil heat counterflowing upward from the middle and lower burners easily harasses the heart and disquiets the spirit. We presented Li's seminal discussion of how yin fire harasses the heart spirit in Chapter 1 above.

According to Li, yin fire is the result of five basic disease mechanisms. Each of these five can cause any of the other five. Therefore, when you have one, you tend to have more than one. These five mechanisms are: 1) spleen vacuity, 2) liver depression, 3) damp heat, 4) yin blood vacuity, and 5) stirring of ministerial fire. Although we must present these five disease mecha-

## THE FIVE MECHANISMS OF YIN FIRE:

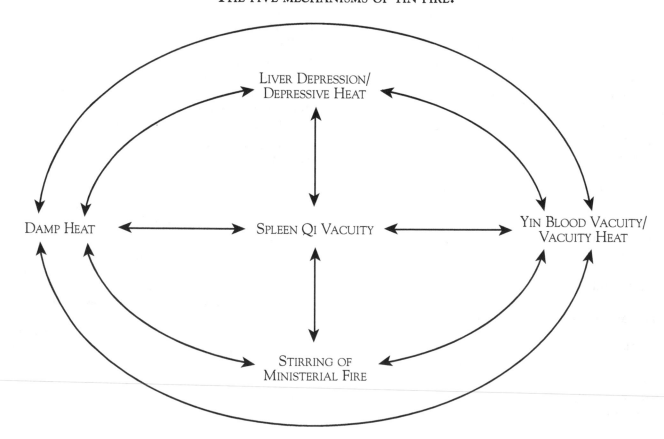

nisms linearly, it is important to understand that they are all mutually engendering.

If, for any reason, the spleen becomes vacuous and weak, dampness may be engendered which percolates down to the lower burner and obstructs the free flow of qi. This may give rise to transformative heat, and thus evil dampness becomes damp heat. The heat component of damp heat floats upward to harass the heart and disquiet the spirit. It may also damage the liver and kidneys. In that case a blood and yin vacuity may give rise to vacuity heat which floats upward to harass the heart and disquiet the spirit.

If the spleen becomes vacuous and weak, it will tend not to engender sufficient qi and blood. Therefore, the heart and the liver will not receive sufficient nourishment. If the heart fails to receive sufficient nourishment, the spirit mind will not be constructed and nourished. If the liver does not receive sufficient nourishment, it will not course and discharge. However, as we have already seen, if, for any other reason, the liver's coursing and discharging is inhibited, liver depression may cause or aggravate spleen vacuity. Further, if the liver becomes depressed and depression transforms heat or fire, heat evils may counterflow upward to harass the heart and disquiet the spirit.

Stirring of ministerial fire may be due to any excessive mental, verbal, or physical activity. However, it is especially due to "sex, drugs, and rock 'n roll." Sex, drugs, and frenetic stirring may all easily cause the ministerial fire to stir upward, leaving its root in its lower source. When ministerial fire stirs upward, it A) damages the spleen qi, B) transforms any other tendency to evil heat in the body, C) damages and consumes yin fluids, and D) leaves the lower burner vacuous and cold.

As stated above, any one of these disease mechanisms may cause any of the others. Therefore, in real-life clinical practice, one rarely sees only one of these patterns. In Westerners especially, with chronic, enduring diseases, one tends to see at least three of these patterns in the overwhelming majority of patients. These are liver depression, spleen vacuity, and some kind of evil heat, whether depressive, vacuity, damp, phlegm, or stasis. Westerners seem particularly prone to complex yin fire scenarios because the modern Western diet and lifestyle so easily damage the liver and spleen and, from there, the heart and kidneys. This is further complicated by over-use of antibiotics damaging the spleen, and antibiotics, corticosteriods, and hormone replacement therapy, including oral birth control pills, tending to create gu worm conditions.

Why we are presenting yin fire theory in this book on psychological diseases is because yin fire, just as gu worm conditions, tends to create a combination of malnourishment of the spirit and evil heat harassing the heart. When there is a complex, multi-mechanism or multi-pattern yin fire scenario producing psychological disease, one cannot rely on simple formulas corresponding to simple, discrete patterns. In that case, one must

---

THAT MEANS THAT, IN COMPLEX YIN FIRE SCENARIOS, ONE WILL HAVE TO KEEP IN MIND FIVE PRINCIPLES:

1. YOU WILL HAVE TO SUPPLEMENT THE SPLEEN AND BOOST THE QI.

2. YOU WILL HAVE TO COURSE THE LIVER AND RECTIFY THE QI.

3. YOU WILL HAVE TO CLEAR SOME KIND OF HEAT SOMEWHERE IN THE BODY.

4. YOU PROBABLY WILL ALSO HAVE TO ADDRESS SOME OTHER SIMULTANEOUS DISEASE MECHANISM, BE THAT BLOOD STASIS, PHLEGM TURBIDITY, FOOD STAGNATION, YIN BLOOD VACUITY, FLUID DRYNESS, OR WHAT HAVE YOU.

5. YOU WILL NEED TO COMBINE THESE THEORIES ACCORDING TO THE PROPORTIONS AND PREDOMINANCES MANIFEST IN THE INDIVIDUAL PATIENT'S PATTERN. IN OTHER WORDS, IN SOME CASES YOU MAY HAVE TO SUPPLEMENT THE SPLEEN, COURSE THE LIVER, AND CLEAR HEAT IN THAT ORDER, WHILE IN OTHER CASES, YOU MAY HAVE TO CLEAR HEAT, COURSE THE LIVER, AND SUPPLEMENT THE SPLEEN. AND YET IN OTHER CASES, YOU MAY HAVE TO PRIMARILY TRANSFORM PHLEGM, CLEAR HEAT, RESOLVE DEPRESSION, AND SUPPLEMENT THE SPLEEN.

treat all the disease mechanisms at the same time. If one does not, the remaining mechanisms will quickly reestablish the single mechanism addressed.

When patients present with a clear-cut, simple repletion, one does not have to worry about yin fire theory. However, the majority of Western patients seeking treatment with acupuncture and Chinese medicine are urban and suburban women working in offices who are between 35-55 years old and suffer from chronic, enduring diseases. In addition, our patients, at least as of this writing, are almost universally outpatients. Therefore, they tend to be what we refer to as the "walking wounded." In terms of psychological illnesses, these patients suffer mostly from depression, bipolar disorder, obsessive-compulsive disorder, somataform, and anxiety disorders, and most of these patients do have mixed vacuity-repletion yin fire patterns.

## TREATMENT BASED ON PATTERN DISCRIMINATION

In contemporary standard professional Chinese medicine, treatment is mainly based on the patient's individual pattern discrimination. That means that, no matter what the patient's disease diagnosis, treatment is chosen based on the patient's actual, personal combination of patterns. This is the single most important thing about Chinese medicine. While the patient's disease diagnosis is taken into account in terms of prognosis and certain empirical acupuncture points or Chinese medicinals, the overall treatment plan is chosen based on the patient's pattern discrimination.

Patterns are constantly shifting due to changes in diet and lifestyle, the seasons, phases of the moon, and weather. Patterns also change and evolve in reaction to treatment. Therefore, in Chinese medicine, patients are typically reevaluated approximately once per week. At each reexamination, the practitioner checks to see if there have been any changes in symptomatology and, therefore, changes in their pattern discrimination. When such changes occur, the practitioner must rediscriminate the pattern(s) and, hence, reformulate the treatment principles and treatment plan. This may involve a few minor modifications of either acupuncture points or Chinese medicinals, or it may require writing and administering a completely different set of points or Chinese medicinal formula.

Chinese medical treatment is largely free of side effects because it is based on individualized pattern discrimi

nation. When a medicine or treatment creates side effects, it is a sign that something about that treatment was not perfectly tailored to that individual. Since health and healing in Chinese medicine are based on balancing all aspects of the bodymind, any treatment which is powerful enough to restore balance must be powerful enough to upset balance if incorrectly prescribed. This is especially so with Chinese medicinals whose ability to create unwanted side effects or iatrogenesis are much greater than acupuncture. Therefore, if a Chinese medicinal causes side effects, it means that, in the process of restoring balance to one part of the body, that medicinal simultaneously pushed another part of the body out of balance. Since all organs, tissues, and qi in the body are interrelated, this is equivalent to "robbing Peter to pay Paul." Hence, whenever a Chinese medical treatment has created side effects, it is because that treatment has not matched all the requirements of bringing that patient's personal pattern back into balance.[29] It is also true that, in China, diarrhea is sometimes caused by strong precipitation in the case of replete heat mania. However, this diarrhea is of only limited duration. Once the patient returns to normal, precipitating medicinals are stopped. In other words, this is a short-term treatment meant to achieve a very specific therapeutic effect. If this diarrhea continues beyond the cessation of the precipitating medicinals, other medicinals are administered to stop this diarrhea.

## TREATING MENTAL-EMOTIONAL DISORDERS WITH CHINESE MEDICINALS

Within Chinese medicine as a whole, the main treatment modality is the internal administration of polypharmacy formulas as water-based decoctions. Although acupuncture is the most well-known modality of Chinese medicine in the West, in China, acupuncture is considered a secondary or adjunctive modality similar to the relationship between Western medicine and physical therapy. This preeminence of internally administered medicinals within Chinese medicine even in terms of the treatment of psychoemotional disorders is reflected in the fact that most Chinese books and articles on this subject only discuss internal medicine, and, if acupuncture and moxibustion are discussed at all, they are clearly accorded secondary status. As Heiner Fruehauf states:

Traditional treatment principles for mental diseases... do not fall outside the realm of standard diagnostic and therapeutic procedures. Even in contemporary China, mental patients usually visit doctors who specialize in "internal medicine," that is the treatment of organ disorders with Chinese herbs, minerals and animal materials.[30]

As the reader will see, we have included ample case histories and abstracts of representative Chinese research supporting that Chinese medicinals alone can be sufficient to treat many patients with mental-emotional disease. However, when using Chinese medicinals for these kinds of disorders, one typically must use large doses of at least some of the medicinals. Within the multi-ingredient formulas found in this book, doses of individual medicinals often range between 30-60g per day, and the total number of grams per day in most formulas for mental-emotional diseases easily exceed 150g per day. As Heiner Fruehauf corroborates when describing a contemporary Chinese treatment protocol for anxiety disorders, "Note again the heavy dosages which are typical for the treatment of mental disorders."[31]

What this means is that Western practitioners should not expect to achieve marked results in the treatment of psychiatric diseases with low potency ready-made pills and powdered extracts. Chinese-made pills tend to be made from either whole ground medicinals or low potency extracts bound with inert filler. Liquid and powdered extracts may achieve similar results as water-based decoctions *when their dosages are equivalent*. However, one should not assume that the recommended daily dosage stated by the manufacturer is sufficient to treat all diseases for which the formula is indicated. In the United States, the Federal Food & Drug Administration (FDA) requires all over-the-counter medications, including Chinese herbal formulas to include a stated daily dose on their packaging. The FDA does not allow this published dose to be a dosage range. Because manufacturers are worried about potential law suits brought by uneducated consumers or even mentally unbalanced consumers, published dosages are routinely low to minimize the likelihood of mishap.

Most of the powdered extracts of Chinese medicinals currently available in the Western marketplace are 5:1 extracts. That means that one gram of extract has been made from five grams of whole Chinese medicinals. If the published daily dosage of most of these powdered extracts is three grams per day, then the total daily dosage equivalent to the

same bulk-dispensed, water-decocted formula is only 15 grams, and 15 grams is typically less than 10% of the standard daily dosage for these kinds of conditions in contemporary professional Chinese medicine. Therefore, if one intends to treat serious mental-emotional disease with internally administered Chinese medicinals, it is important to use a dosage powerful enough to achieve a marked and timely result. Although copious Chinese research proves that Chinese medicinals can treat the kinds of diseases discussed in this book, it is only certain dosages of these medicinals which have been proven effective. Therefore, if one only has access to 5:1 Chinese medicinal powdered extracts, one will typically have to drastically increase the manufacturer's recommended daily dosage in order to see a marked effect. Here in the United States, when one increases the daily dose of such extracts to be equivalent to the dosage levels of bulk-dispensed medicinals used in the People's Republic of China, it is usually less expensive to prescribe water-based decoctions of the whole medicinals.

## TREATING MENTAL-EMOTIONAL DISORDERS WITH ACUPUNCTURE

Although the majority of Chinese literature on the Chinese medical treatment of mental-emotional diseases discusses the internal administration of Chinese medicinals, there have been a number of Chinese studies done showing that acupuncture can be an effective treatment for this group of disorders. Case histories in the chapter on somatoform disorders (Book 3, Chapter 9) even suggest that, at least at some Chinese hospitals, acupuncture is the preferred Chinese medical treatment modality for that condition. As Heiner Fruehauf again states, "[For the treatment of mental-emotional diseases,] the therapeutic focus tends to be on the restoration of uninhibited qi flow, since unbalanced emotions first affect the qi before they influence the physical structure of the body,"[32] and what acupuncture does first and foremost is disinhibit the flow of qi. Therefore, acupuncture can be a very effective treatment for many kinds of mental-emotional disease. In particular, acupuncture is very effective for promoting relaxation in cases of heightened excitation and restlessness. After all, one of the most common responses to acupuncture is for patients to fall asleep on the treatment table.

However, when attempting to treat mental diseases

with acupuncture, it is important that the treatments be scheduled close enough together. Here in the West, it has become a *de facto* standard for many acupuncturists to treatment only once a week. As the case histories and clinical reports included in this book show, in the People's Republic of China, treatments for mental-emotional disorders tend to be scheduled every or not less than every other day. We believe that the Chinese experience shows that the more serious the psychological disease, the more closely treatments should be scheduled. Therefore, many of the failures some Western acupuncturists have experienced in treating these kinds of diseases may have been due to improperly spaced treatment regimes.

## TREATING MENTAL-EMOTIONAL DISORDERS WITH PSYCHOTHERAPY

In Chinese, psychotherapy is called *xin li liao fa*, "psychological treatment method." This corresponds to cognitive-behavioral therapy (CBT) within Western psychiatry. Several different types of Chinese psychotherapy are described in the premodern and contemporary Chinese medical literature. For instance, Liang Guo-yin, in "The 'Using Emotions to Overcome Emotions Method' in the Treatment of Psychiatric Diseases," describes using one emotion to antidote or counteract another emotion.[33] This technique is based on the five phase theory found in the chapter titled, "Great Treatise on the Correspondences & Images of Yin & Yang," in the *Su Wen* (*Simple Questions*) where it says:

> Anger damages the liver. Sorrow overcomes anger. Joy (or excitement) damages the heart. Fear overcomes joy. Thinking damages the spleen. Anger overcomes thinking. Anxiety damages the lungs. Joy overcomes anxiety. Fear damages the kidneys. Thought overcomes fear.

During the Spring and Autumn period (3rd century BCE), roughly the same period in which the *Nei Jing Su Wen* (*Inner Classic: Simple Questions*) was written, there was a famous story of a king of Qi being treated by Dr. Wen Zhi. The king had fallen ill and administration of medicinals had failed to cure him. Wen Zhi made the king angry, and the king promptly recovered.[34] Using this theory, Liang recommends trying to make a person stuck in repetitive thoughts and worries angry in order to jolt them out of this

unproductive "loop," while one should help a person think more clearly about their unreasonable fears. In his article, Liang gives two cases histories of how he used this technique with real-life patients.

Perhaps the most famous Chinese medical proponent of this technique was Zhang Cong-zheng (1156-1228 CE). As Vivien Ng says, Zhang "was famous for his unorthodox methods."[35] The following case history is an example of Zhang's use of this technique.

> Zhang... was once called upon to treat a woman who had suddenly lost all her appetite for food. Moreover, she had frequent screaming fits and was dangerously violent. She was given different medicines but none seemed to work. Feeling desperate, her family overcame their initial reservations about Zhang's methods and turned to him for help.
>
> On the first day of the treatment, Zhang ordered two female assistants to dress up in outlandish fashion and sent them to his patient. When the sick woman saw the weirdly garbed assistants, she burst into laughter for the first time in many months. The next day, Zhang again sent his two assistants to see this patient, this time disguised as animals. Once again, the sick woman laughed heartily. On the third day, he arranged for the patient to witness his two collaborators wolf down an exquisitely prepared meal. With her senses titillated by the sight and smell of the feast, the sick woman recovered her long-lost appetite for food. After several days of similar treatment, she recovered from her long illness.[36]

In this case, we can assume the woman's loss of appetite and anger were due to liver depression transforming into heat which then harassed the heart spirit above plus the liver qi counterflowing horizontally to assail the spleen. Laughter, an expression of joy, relaxes the liver, thus undercutting the two main mechanisms causing the screaming, violence, and loss of appetite.

In the Yuan dynasty, Zhu Dan-xi also believed that certain kinds of mental illness could not be treated successfully with herbal medicine alone. In his *Dan*

| PATHOLOGICAL EMOTION | NEUTRALIZING EMOTION |
| --- | --- |
| ANGER | WORRY AND APPREHENSION |
| JOY | ANGER OR WORRY |
| DESIRE | JOY OR ANGER |
| APPREHENSION | DESIRE OR WORRY |
| FEAR | WORRY AND APPREHENSION |
| GRIEF | APPRENSION OR ANGER |

*Xi Xin Fa (Dan-xi's Heart Methods)*, he identifies the seven affects as the main causes of withdrawal and mania. Because these affects are the cause of these illnesses, Zhu thought it only appropriate to treat them by other, antagonistic emotions. According to Vivien Ng, Zhu proposed the scheme shown above.[37]

While there is a kernel of common sense truth in this methodology and Ng says that Zhu's methodology had many adherents during the Ming and Qing dynasties, the authors of this present work have never seen this method used in clinical practice in China. In fact, Liang's was the only article the authors could find on any kind of psychotherapy in any of the recent Chinese medical journals they researched. Speaking of Zhu Dan-xi's psychotherapy, Liu Xie-he says:

> A systematic psychotherapy called "Huotao" (the living chain) was proposed by Zhu Zhenheng (1281-1358). He attempted to induce different affective reactions in various emotionally disturbed patients for their treatment. But this method is *not used now*.[38] [Italics ours]

It is interesting that the authors could not find Zhu's system of treating emotional illness with emotions in Zhu's *Dan Xi Zhi Fa Xin Yao (The Heart & Essence of Dan-xi's Methods of Treatment)*. This book was published after the *Dan Xi Xin Fa* and is a combination of the *Xin Fa* and Zhu's *Yi Yao (The Essentials of Medicine)*. As the editors of the 1983 edition of the *Xin Yao* state, the version of the *Xin Fa* that currently exists has undergone repeated adulterations and garbling by later generations while the *Dan Xi Zhi Fa Xin Yao* is considered relatively authentic and unadulterated.[39] So either Zhu's method of psychotherapy was a later addition by some unknown editor or Zhu found that it was not that clinically practicable and deleted it from his later work.

Based on Bob Flaws's experience in various Chinese medical hospitals in eastern China from 1982-86, when professional Chinese medical practitioners in China attempt to use verbal therapy for the amelioration of psychiatric disease, they mainly confine themselves to generalized advice on modifying behavior and attitude. As Liu Xie-he says, "Psychotherapy [is] greatly emphasized in traditional Chinese medicine, but it [is] usually practiced in an unstructured manner."[40] Often this advice consists of simply telling the patient to relax. Sometimes it consists of referring the patient to a qigong teacher or class. Qigong is a generic term covering a wide range of mental, movement, and respiratory regimes, covering everything from Zen meditation to yoga to martial arts exercises. In general, qigong can be divided into still qigong (*jing xing qi gong*) and moving or active qigong (*dong xing qi gong*). When qigong is advised to patients with mental-emotional disease, it is mostly the still qigong. This consists of what in the West we would refer to as progressive deep relaxation and is akin to certain kinds of biofeedback therapy. In this type of qigong, the patient uses their volition, imagination, and respiration to relax the entire body and mind.

While many Westerners find Chinese doctors' emphasis on relaxation simplistic for the treatment of long-term psycho-emotional problems, it actually is more profound than many people think. Relaxation results in freeing the flow of the qi mechanism. As we have seen, liver depression qi stagnation sits squarely in the center of most of the disease mechanisms leading to mental-emotional disease. Therefore, any therapy which has a disinhibiting and normalizing effect on the qi flow and, therefore, the qi mechanism will have a salutory effect on the mind and emotions. When one relaxes physically as well as mentally, whatever qi should be upborne is upborne and whatever qi should be downborne is downborne. The psycho-physiological effects of simply letting go are immediate and automatic.[41]

As Western biofeedback therapists know, relaxation is a skill which can be learned but requires practice to perfect. In addition, while almost any negative emotional state can be benefitted by bodymind relaxation, agitated patients may not be able to remain still enough in body and mind to practice relaxation. In such patients, internally administered medicines and/or externally applied physical therapies may help create the space in which to develop the skills and benefits of relaxation.

As we saw above in the case of Zhu Dan-xi, a number of Chinese doctors have recognized that mental-emotional diseases are not always the same as diseases caused by invading pathogens or faulty diet and that the administration of medicines may not achieve a totally satisfactory effect. In the Ming dynasty, Li Zhong-zi, in his *Yi Zong Bi Du* (*A Gathering of Ancestral Medicine Which Must be Studied*) published in 1637, said, "Deep feelings and worry are difficult to doctor [even] with good medicinals." Likewise, Wu Shang-xian, in his *Li Yue Pian Wen* (*Theoretical Rhythmical Prose*) published in 1870, said, "For the feeling of lust, no medicinal is able to cure this; for diseases of the seven affects [*i.e.*, the emotions], they must be treated by the affects [or emotions]." Both these quotes substantiate that internal medical and physical therapies alone, such as acupuncture, may not be sufficient to treat all mental-emotional diseases, and sometimes cognitive and behavioral therapies are necessary as part of an overall treatment plan.

## USING THE CHINESE MEDICAL TREATMENTS IN THIS BOOK

The treatments described in this book are only meant as potential starting places. The formulas and acupuncture points listed under each pattern should not be thought of as recipes in a cookbook. It is assumed that every professional practitioner using this book has completed their professional entry level education in Chinese medicine. That means that one has a firm grasp of basic Chinese medical theory, pattern discrimination, treatment principles and planning, channel and network vessel theory, point theory and usage, Chinese materia medica, formulas and prescriptions, and the modification of acupuncture and/or Chinese medicinal formulas. In addition, it is also expected that practitioners have also completed basic courses in Chinese internal medicine or *nei ke*.

Because every person is unique, real-life patients rarely manifest the simple, discrete patterns presented in textbooks such as this. This kind of textbook is meant for classroom study of each specialty within Chinese medicine. It is not meant to be sufficient unto itself to practice this specialty. Textbooks such as these must be combined with clinical rotations and internships in that specialty so that students see how the information in this kind of textbook is used in real-life practice by well-trained and experienced practitioners. In real life, patients with complex, enduring diseases have complex, multi-pattern presentations. It is the rule rather than the exception that patient's with significant psychiatric disease manifest three *or more* patterns simultaneously. In our experience, it is common in Western practice for patients to manifest seven or eight patterns simultaneously. That means that the treatments suggested in this book under simple, discrete patterns will have to be "mixed and matched" or modified. As Yu Chen wrote in his preface to his famous Qing dynasty collection of case histories, *Gu Qin Yi An An* (*Ancient & Modern Case Histories for Reference*):

> From antiquity to the present, there have been more books on medicine than one can keep track of. For each medical disorder, a special [disease] category has been established, and for each [disease] category, there are numerous [treatment] methods. In the final reckoning, although the number of [treatment] methods may be limited, there is no limit [to the variety of] disorders. Even the variations of a single disease are limitless, and, if several diseases converge on the body of a single patient, the variations are all the more endless... Therefore, it would seem that preoccupation with [individual treatment] methods can take one no further than the carpenter's or wheelwright's square or compass. Medical disorders do not manifest according to square and compass. If the doctor simply tries to treat them according to square and compass, the cases that fit the rule will survive, and those that vary from it will die... What is crucial is the ingenuity of the one using the [treatment] methods.[42]

## ENDNOTES:

[1]Antonio R. Damasio, Ph.D. & M.D., in *Descartes' Error: Emotion, Reason and the Human Brain*, Avon Books, NY, 1994, deconstructs this dualism in terms of contemporary Western medical neuropsychiatry, thus suggesting that contemporary Western and Chinese medical views of the bodymind are

extremely close if not identical philosophically. In 1988, J.A. Hobson, in his Introduction to *Readings from the Encyclopedia of Neuroscience: States of Brain and Mind* (Birkhauser & Co., Boston, MA), introduced the term "mind-brain" to convey this new monistic (*i.e.*, non-dualistic) vision of the relationship between the mind and the brain.

[2]Li Qing-fu & Liu Du-zhou, *Zhong Yi Jing Shen Bing Xue (Chinese Medical Psychiatry)*, Tianjin Science & Technology Publishing Co., Tianjin, 1989, p. 202

[3]This fact is evidenced by Wang Da-yue and Jiang Kun's article, "The Treatment of 41 Cases of Female Sexual Disturbance with Chinese Medicine & Medicinals," appearing in *Shang Hai Zhong Yi Yao Za Zhi (Shanghai Journal of Chinese Medicine & Medicinals)*, #4, 1999, p. 32-33. In this article, somatic and psychological disturbances associated with sex, such as vaginal tract spasm, dyspareunia, bleeding with intercourse, decreased sexual desire, and anorgasmia, are discussed equally and without differentiation alongside such purely somatic signs and symptoms as menstrual dribbling and dripping without cease, continuous leukorrhea, vaginal tract dryness, mouth sores, low back and knee soreness and limpness, and a pale tongue.

[4]Weber, Daniel A. & Hoedeman, Wilhemina, "A Theoretical and Practical Approach to Psychodynamics Using Traditional Chinese Medicine," *Pacific Journal of Oriental Medicine*, #10, p. 27

[5]It is true that, compared to Westerners, Chinese tend to somatize their complaints. Nigel Wiseman, in his "Translator's Preface" to *Fundamentals of Chinese Medicine* (Paradigm Publications, Brookline, MA, 1985, p. xxi-xxii), uses a number of Western anthropological studies to substantiate his statement that: "The clinical gaze of Chinese medicine recognizes the continuum and interaction of the psyche and soma. The methodology has always taken into account the psychosomatic truth that psychological and physiological processes are interactive and have a shared clinical significance... Nevertheless, contemporary Eastern and Western people tend to experience different ends of this continuum in their lives. What may be a single 'energetic' phenomena in Oriental medical theory can be a totally different experience for peoples of different culture." Based on Wiseman's work, Stephen Birch and Robert Felt, the authors of *Understanding Acupuncture* (Churchill Livingstone, Edinburgh, 1999, p. 102) further say: "Illnesses that are recognized as emotional disorders in the West are experienced as physical discomfort in the East. This happens to such an extent that minor psychiatric problems go unrecognized in China because patients report the *secondary* [italics ours], physical complaints and not their anxiety, stress, or depression." However, this does not mean that Chinese medicine does not treat psychological symptoms and complaints effectively. It only means that, for various cultural and sociological reasons, Chinese medicine does not separate psychological diseases from their somatic symptoms and that Chinese patients and their practitioners tend to focus on somatically described complaints as opposed to psychologically rationalized complaints.

[6]Castillo, *op. cit.*, p. 189

[7]*Chinese-English Medical Dictionary*, The Commercial Press & People's Health & Hygiene Press, Hong Kong, 1988, p. 613

[8]*Concise English-Chinese Chinese-English Dictionary*, 2nd edition, Oxford University Press, Hong Kong, 1999, p. 234 (English-Chinese Dictionary) & 351 (Chinese-English Dictionary)

[9]In Chinese medicine, there is no distinction between thoughts and emotions. Both are merely sensations within consciousness. As we will see below, thought is one of the seven "affects."

[10]By standard professional Chinese medicine, we mean that style of Chinese medicine endorsed and standardized by the Department of Health, taught at Chinese medical schools, and practiced in the majority of hospitals and state-run clinics in the People's Republic of China. This is a secular style of Chinese medicine based on a combination of 2,000 years of extant medical literature and the clinical experiences of not less than 100 generations of literate professional practitioners. This style is the continuation of Qing dynasty trends in professional Chinese medicine which have become national standards of care throughout the PRC.

[11]Wu Dun-xu, *Zhong Yi Bing Yin Bing Ji Xue (A Study of Chinese Medical Disease Causes & Disease Mechanisms)*, Shanghai College of Chinese Medicine Press, Shanghai, 1989, p. 93

[12]Quoted by Li & Liu, *op. cit.*, p. 233

[13]Li Dong-yuan, *Pi Wei Lun (Treatise on the Spleen & Stomach)*, trans. by Yang Shou-zhong, Blue Poppy Press, Boulder, CO, 1993, p. 234

[14]Saying that the word spirit within standard professional Chinese medicine does not have spiritual implications in the clinical practice of Chinese medicine is not the same as saying that Chinese medical practitioners do not or should not take into account a patient's religious or spiritual beliefs and practices when attempting to help that patient to heal their illness. While this book is not a text on spiritually based healing practices, it is our belief that, especially in multicultural societies such as in the U.S., practitioners should take into account and even sometimes enlist a patient's spiritual beliefs in the healing transaction.

[15]Huang Yue-dong, *Jing Shen Yi Bing Zhong Yi Lin Chuang Zhi Liao (The Clinical Treatment of Psychiatric Diseases with Chinese Medicine)*, Shanghai Science & Technology Press, Shanghai, 1998, p. 28

[16]In bulimia nervosa, the patient may be eating a large quantity of food, but, because they are vomiting that food back up again, they are not absorbing those nutrients. Anorexia nervosa and bulimia nervosa may be seen as anxiety and obsessive-compulsive disorders, while in Chinese medicine they are covered by the traditional disease categories of fear and fright and anxiety and thinking.

[17]Li Dong-yuan, *Pi Wei Lun (Treatise on the Spleen & Stomach)*, trans. by Yang Shou-zhong, Blue Poppy Press, Boulder, CO, 1993, p. 75-76

[18]Long, James W., *The Essential Guide to Prescription Drugs 1990*, Harper & Row, NY, 1990, p. 805

[19]Jin Zi-jiu, *Jin Zi Jiu Zhuan Ji (A Collection of Jin Zi-jiu's Teachings)*, People's Health & Hygiene Press, Beijing, 1982, p. 85-86

[20]Huang, *op. cit.*, p. 28

[21]Li & Liu, *op. cit.*, p. 257

[22]Sun Si-miao, quoted by Fruehauf, Heiner, "Driving Out Demons and Snakes: Gu Syndrome, a Forgotten Clinical Approach to Chronic Parasitism," *Journal of Chinese Medicine*, #57, May, 1998, p. 12

[23]Fruehauf, *op. cit.*, p. 12

[24]Wiseman, Nigel & Feng Ye, A *Practical Dictionary of Chinese Medicine*, Paradigm Publications, Brookline, MA, 1998, p. 249

[25]Li & Liu, *op. cit.*, p. 261

[26]Castillo, *op. cit.*, p. 173

[27]In actual fact, there are a number of different systems of psychosomatotyping in Chinese medicine. The *Ling Shu (Spiritual Axis)* teaches two completely different systems in two different chapters. In the chapter titled, "Communicating with Heaven," a six-fold division of yin-yang body types is described, while in the chapter titled, "Twenty-five Yin-Yang [Types of] Human," a five phase system is taught. We have chosen to present this four-fold yin-yang division system due to its ease of understanding and its modern clinical utility.

[28]Liminality *vis à vis* adolescence refers to being between two stages, neither wholly adult or wholly child.

[29]Jarisch-Herxheimer reactions are an exception to this rule. Patients with psychological diseases with concomitant intestinal dysbiosis, parasitosis, or candidiasis may experience Herxheimer reactions when initiating Chinese medicinal therapy due to massive die-off of protozoans, yeast, and fungi. These reactions only last 12-24 hours and should be considered a species of "healing crisis."

[30]Fruehauf, Heiner, "Commonly Used Chinese Herb Formulas for the Treatment of Mental Disorders," *The Journal of Chinese Medicine* (UK), #48, 1995, p. 22

[31]*Ibid.*, p. 26

[32]*Ibid.*, p. 22

[33]Liang Guo-yin, "The 'Using Emotions to Overcome Emotions Method' in the Treatment of Psychiatric Disease," *Zhe Jiang Zhong Yi Za Zhi (Zhejiang Journal of Chinese Medicine)*, #9, 1999, p. 399

[34]Liu Xie-he, *op. cit.*, p. 429

[35]Ng, *op. cit.*, p. 38-39

[36]*Ibid.*, p. 38-39

[37]*Ibid.*, p. 41

[38]Liu Xie-he, *op. cit.*, p. 432

[39]Yang Shou-zhong, "Translator's Preface," *The Heart & Essence of Dan-xi's Methods of Treatment*, Blue Poppy Press, Boulder, CO, 1993, p. xv

[40]Liu Xie-he, *op. cit.*, p. 432

[41]David K. Reynolds, author of *The Quiet Therapies: Japanese Pathways to Personal Growth* (Univ. Of Hawaii Press, Honolulu, 1980) describes five systems of Japanese psychotherapy. Three out of five of these can be described, in large part, as the systematic practice of deep relaxation, and all three of these originally derive from Chinese qigong and meditative practices.

[42]Adapted from Sivin, *op. cit.*, p. 92-93

 **3**

# ESSENCE SPIRIT MATERIA MEDICA

Within Chinese medicine, certain medicinals are believed to be especially useful for treating psychiatric diseases. These medicinals are mostly categorized as spirit-quieters, liver-levelers, wind-extinguishers, and orifice-openers. However, they can also come from other categories, such as qi and blood supplements, phlegm-transformers, heat-clearers, etc. Below is a description of some of the most important Chinese medicinals for the treatment of psychological disease. Most Chinese medicinal formulas for the treatment of psychological disease will include one or more of these medicinals.

Included in many of the descriptions below are quotes from the *Shen Nong Ben Cao Jing (The Divine Farmer's Materia Medica Classic)*. This book is the *locus classicus* of Chinese materia medica and was compiled in the early centuries of the first millennium. We have included quotes from this book to show how long a history there is in Chinese medicine of regarding the following medicinals as especially effective for psychological disorders. As in many cultures, psychological disorders in Old China (and even in Hong Kong, Taiwan, and Singapore today) were often ascribed to or associated with demonic possession, ghosts, etc. Modern standard professional Chinese medicine no longer makes use of such spiritist or shamanic concepts even though

medicinals whose use was originally based on such concepts still prove effective in clinical practice.

SPIRIT-QUIETING MEDICINALS

CINNABAR *(Zhu Sha)*

NATURE & FLAVOR: Sweet and cold. Has toxins.

CHANNEL ENTRY: Heart

FUNCTIONS: Settles the heart and quiets the spirit, clears heat and resolves toxins

INDICATIONS: Used for heart fire hyperactivity and exuberance resulting in heart spirit restlessness, vexatious heat within the chest, fright palpitations, racing heart, insomnia, and profuse dreams, Cinnabar is commonly combined with Rhizoma Coptidis Chinensis *(Huang Lian)* and uncooked Radix Rehmanniae *(Sheng Di)* as in *Zhu Sha An Shen Wan* (Cinnabar Quiet the Spirit Pills). For the treatment of blood vacuity heart palpitations and insomnia, Cinnabar should be combined with Radix Angelicae Sinensis *(Dang Gui)*, Semen Zizyphi Spinosae *(Suan Zao Ren)*, and Semen Biotae Orientalis *(Bai Zi Ren)*. For the treatment of fright wind and epilepsy, Cinnabar can be combined with Succinum *(Hu Po)* and Buthus Martensis *(Quan Xie)*.

**DOSAGE:** 0.3-1g

**METHOD OF USE:** Cinnabar is taken in powders and pills. It may also be ground into powder and washed down. It can also be decocted and taken with other medicinals.

**CAUTIONS & CONTRAINDICATIONS:** One should not take too large a dose of this medicinal internally nor should it be taken continuously for a long time. It should be used cautiously in those whose liver and kidney functions are abnormal. In Western clinical practice, it should probably be substituted by Succinum (*Hu Po*), Os Draconis (*Long Gu*), Concha Ostreae (*Mu Li*), Margarita (*Zhen Zhu*), and/or Concha Margaritiferae (*Zhen Zhu Mu*).

**SHEN NONG BEN CAO JING:** "*Dan Sha* is sweet and slightly cold. It treats the hundreds of diseases of the five viscera and body. It nurtures the essence spirit, quiets the ethereal and corporeal souls, boosts the qi, brightens the eyes, and kills spirit demons and evil malign ghosts. Protracted taking may enable one to communicate with the spirit brilliance and prevent senility."

**SUCCINUM (*Hu Po*)**

**NATURE & FLAVOR:** Sweet and level

**CHANNEL ENTRY:** Heart, liver and urinary bladder

**FUNCTIONS:** Settles fright and calms the spirit, disinhibits water and frees the flow of strangury, quickens the blood and transforms stasis

**INDICATIONS:** Used for fright wind, epileptiform conditions, and insomnia, Succinum can be combined with Cinnabar (*Zhu Sha*), Buthus Martensis (*Quan Xie*), and Tuber Ophiopogonis Japonici (*Mai Dong*) in order to settle fright and quiet the spirit. For fright palpitations, disquietude, and insomnia, it can be combined with Caulis Polygoni Multiflori (*Ye Jiao Teng*), Semen Zizyphi Spinosae (*Suan Zao Ren*), Flos Albizziae Julibrissinis (*He Huan Hua*), Cinnabar (*Zhu Sha*), and Sclerotium Poriae Cocos (*Fu Ling*).

**DOSAGE:** 1-1.5g

**METHOD OF USE:** Grind into powder and swallow with the decocted liquid, 0.5g each time. This medicinal is not added to decoctions and boiled.

**MAGNETITUM (*Ci Shi*)**

**NATURE & FLAVOR:** Acrid and cold

**CHANNEL ENTRY:** Liver and kidneys

**FUNCTIONS:** Heavily settles and quiets the spirit, grasps or absorbs the qi and levels panting, boosts the kidneys and subdues yang

**INDICATIONS:** Used for mental-emotional disquietude, heart palpitations, fearful throbbing, insomnia, and fright epilepsy, Magnetite is commonly combined with Cinnabar (*Zhu Sha*). To prevent Magnetite's damaging the stomach, it is commonly combined with Massa Medica Fermentata (*Shen Qu*).

**DOSAGE:** 15-60g

**METHOD OF USE:** Crush and decoct first.

**SHEN NONG BEN CAO JING:** "*Ci Shi* is acrid and cool...It eliminates great fever, vexatious fullness, and deafness."

**OS DRACONIS (*Long Gu*)**

**NATURE & FLAVOR:** Sweet, astringent, and slightly cold

**CHANNEL ENTRY:** Heart and liver

**FUNCTIONS:** Levels the liver and subdues yang, settles, stills, and quiets the spirit, restrains, constrains, secures, and astringes, engenders muscles (*i.e.*, the flesh) and constrains sores

**INDICATIONS:**

1. Used for yin vacuity yang hyperactivity resulting in vexation and agitation, easy anger, and dizziness and vertigo, Os Draconis can be combined with Concha Ostreae (*Mu Li*), Radix Albus Paeoniae Lactiflorae (*Chi Shao*), and Haemititum (*Dai Zhe Shi*) as in *Zhen Gan Xi Feng Tang* (Settle the Liver & Extinguish Wind Decoction).

2. Used for spirit mind restlessness, heart palpitations, and insomnia as well as fright epilepsy and mania and withdrawal. If agitation and stirring are due to yang qi, Os Draconis can be combined with Cinnabar (*Zhu Sha*) and Magnetitum (*Ci Shi*). If due to yin and blood insuf-

ficiency, it may be combined with Semen Zizyphi Spinosae (*Suan Zao Ren*), cooked Radix Rehmanniae (*Shu Di*), and Radix Angelicae Sinensis (*Dang Gui*). If due to heart qi insufficiency, it may be combined with Radix Panacis Ginseng (*Ren Shen*), Sclerotium Poriae Cocos (*Fu Ling*), and Radix Polygalae Tenuifoliae (*Yuan Zhi*).

DOSAGE: 10-30g

METHOD OF USE: Crush and decoct first. For leveling the liver and subduing yang, settling, stilling, and quieting the spirit, use uncooked.

SHEN NONG BEN CAO JING: "*Long Gu* is sweet and level. It mainly treats heart and abdominal demonic influx, spiritual matters, old ghosts, cough and counterflow, diarrhea and dysentery of pus and blood, in females, leaking, concretions and conglomerations, hardness and binding, and, in children, heat qi and fright epilepsy."

DENS DRACONIS (*Long Chi*)

NATURE & FLAVOR: Astringent and cool

CHANNEL ENTRY: Heart and liver

FUNCTIONS: Settles fright and quiets the spirit

INDICATIONS: Fright epilepsy and heart palpitations

DOSAGE: 10-30g

METHOD OF USE: Crush and decoct first.

SHEN NONG BEN CAO JING: "*Long Chi* mainly treats children and adults alike of epilepsy, madness, manic running about, binding qi below the heart, inability to catch one's breath, and various [kinds of] tetany. It kills spiritual matters. Protracted taking makes the body light, enables one to communicate with the spirit brilliance, and lengthens one's life."

CONCHA OSTREAE (*Mu Li*)

NATURE & FLAVOR: Salty, astringent, and slightly cold

CHANNEL ENTRY: Liver and kidneys

FUNCTIONS: Levels the liver and subdues yang, softens the hard and scatters nodulations, restrains, constrains, secures, and astringes

INDICATIONS: Used for yin vacuity yang hyperactivity resulting in vexation and agitation, restlessness, heart palpitations, insomnia, and dizziness and vertigo, Concha Ostreae is commonly combined with Os Draconis (*Long Gu*), Radix Achyranthis Bidentatae (*Niu Xi*), Radix Albus Paeoniae Lactiflorae (*Bai Shao*), and Haemititum (*Dai Zhe Shi*) as in *Zhen Gan Xi Feng Tang* (Settle the Liver & Extinguish Wind Decoction). For heat disease damaging yin resulting in vacuity wind stirring internally and tremors and convulsions of the hands and feet, Concha Ostreae is commonly combined with Plastrum Testudinis (*Gui Ban*), Carapax Amydae Sinensis (*Bie Jia*), uncooked Radix Rehmanniae (*Sheng Di*), and Gelatinum Corii Asini (*E Jiao*) as in *San Jia Fu Mai Tang* (Three Shells Restore the Pulse Decoction).

DOSAGE: 15-30g

METHOD OF USE: Crush and decoct first. For leveling the liver and subduing yang, softening the hard and scattering nodulations, one should use uncooked.

SHEN NONG BEN CAO JING: "*Mu Li* is salty and level. It mainly treats cold damage, [alternating] cold and heat, warm malaria with chills, and fright, indignation, and angry qi."

MARGARITA (*Zhen Zhu*)

NATURE & FLAVOR: Sweet, salty, and cold

CHANNEL ENTRY: Liver and heart

FUNCTIONS: Settles the heart and stabilizes fright, clears the liver and eliminates (eye) screen, clears heat and resolves toxins, restrains and constrains, engenders muscle (*i.e.*, flesh)

INDICATIONS: Used for fright palpitations, epileptiform conditions, and fright wind, Margarita is commonly combined with Os Draconis (*Long Gu*), Concha Ostreae (*Mu Li*), Cinnabar (*Zhu Sha*), Concretio Bambusae Siliceae (*Tian Zhu Huang*), and bile-processed Rhizoma Arisaematis (*Dan Nan Xing*).

DOSAGE: 0.1-0.3g

METHOD OF USE: Powder and swallow with the decocted liquid. This medicinal is not decocted.

## CONCHA MARGARITIFERAE (Zhen Zhu Mu)

NATURE & FLAVOR: Salty, sweet, and cold

CHANNEL ENTRY: Liver and heart

FUNCTIONS: Levels the liver and subdues yang, brightens the eyes and quiets the spirit

INDICATIONS: Used for ascendant liver yang hyperactivity with dizziness, vertigo, tinnitus, eye screen, fright epilepsy, and insomnia

DOSAGE: 15-60g

METHOD OF USE: Crush and decoct first.

## UNCOOKED FRUSTA FERRI (Sheng Tie Luo)

NATURE & FLAVOR: Acrid and cool

CHANNEL ENTRY: Heart and liver

FUNCTIONS: Settles the liver and quiets the spirit

INDICATIONS: Withdrawal and mania, deranged speech after a warm disease, heart palpitations, insomnia, easy fright, easy anger. Used for mania due to phlegm fire harassing the heart, uncooked Frusta Ferri is commonly combined with Cinnabar (Zhu Sha), Bulbus Fritillariae (Bei Mu), Rhizoma Acori Graminei (Shi Chang Pu), and Ramulus Uncariae Cum Uncis (Gou Teng). Used for mania due to intense anger, this medicinal is commonly combined with Radix Glycyrrhizae (Gan Cao).

DOSAGE: 9-30g

METHOD OF USE: Decoct in water and administer. Typically decocted first for 1-1.5 hours.

SHEN NONG BEN CAO JING: "Tie Luo is acrid and level. It mainly treats wind heat, malign wounds, sores, flat abscesses, scabs, and [evil] qi within the skin. Tie mainly fortifies the sinews and cultivates endurance to pain. Tie Jing mainly brightens the eyes and is able to transform copper."

## SEMEN ZIZYPHI SPINOSAE (Suan Zao Ren)

NATURE & FLAVOR: Sweet and level
CHANNEL ENTRY: Heart and liver

FUNCTIONS: Nourishes the heart and quiets the spirit, boosts yin and stops sweating

INDICATIONS: Used for heart-liver blood vacuity leading to the arising of insomnia, profuse dreams, fright palpitations, and racing heart, Semen Zizyphi Spinosae can be combined with Radix Angelicae Sinensis (Dang Gui), Radix Albus Paeoniae Lactiflorae (Bai Shao), Radix Polygoni Multiflori (He Shou Wu), and Arillus Euphoriae Longanae (Long Yan Rou). For the treatment of liver vacuity with heat and vacuity vexation and insomnia, Semen Zizyphi Spinosae is commonly combined with Rhizoma Anemarrhenae Aspeloidis (Zhi Mu) and Sclerotium Poriae Cocos (Fu Ling) as in Suan Zao Ren Tang (Zizyphus Spinosa Decoction). For heart and kidneys not interacting or yin vacuity yang hyperactivity resulting in insomnia, heart palpitations, impaired memory, profuse dreams, and a dry mouth and throat, Semen Zizyphi Spinosae is commonly combined with uncooked Radix Rehmanniae (Sheng Di), Radix Scrophulariae Ningpoensis (Xuan Shen), and Semen Biotae Orientalis (Bia Zi Ren) as in Tian Wang Bu Xin Dan (Heavenly Emperor Supplement the Heart Elixir).

DOSAGE: 10-18g

METHOD OF USE: Decoct in water and administer internally. It may also be ground into powder and swallowed before sleep.

SHEN NONG BEN CAO JING: "Suan Zao is sour and level. It mainly treats heart and abdominal cold and heat and evil binding qi, aching and pain in the limbs, and damp impediment. Protracted taking quiets the five viscera, makes the body light, and prolongs life."

## SEMEN BIOTAE ORIENTALIS (Bai Zi Ren)

NATURE & FLAVOR: Sweet and level

CHANNEL ENTRY: Heart, kidneys, and large intestine

FUNCTIONS: Nourishes the heart and quiets the spirit, moistens the intestines and frees the flow of the stool

INDICATIONS: Used for blood not nourishing the heart leading to the arising of vacuity vexation insomnia, fright palpitations, and racing heart, Semen Biotae Orientalis is commonly combined with Semen Zizyphi

Spinosae (*Suan Zao Ren*), Fructus Schisandrae Chinensis (*Wu Wei Zi*), and Sclerotium Poriae Cocos (*Fu Ling*) as in *Yang Xin Tang* (Nourish the Heart Decoction).

**DOSAGE:** 10-18g

**METHOD OF USE:** Decoct in water and administer internally.

**CAUTIONS & CONTRAINDICATIONS:** Use cautiously in case of loose stools or profuse phlegm.

**SHEN NONG BEN CAO JING:** "*Bai Zi* is sweet and level. It mainly treats fright palpitations, quiets the five viscera, boosts the qi... Protracted taking renders the facial complexion shiny and attractive, sharpens the ears and eyes, and makes one free from hunger, never senile, and the body light while prolonging life."

## RADIX POLYGALAE TENUIFOLIAE (*YUAN ZHI*)

**NATURE & FLAVOR:** Acrid, bitter, and slightly warm

**CHANNEL ENTRY:** Lungs, heart and kidneys

**FUNCTIONS:** Calms the heart and quiets the spirit, dispels phlegm and opens the orifices, rectifies the qi and resolves depression, promotes the interaction between the heart and kidneys

**INDICATIONS:**

1. Used for heart spirit restlessness, fright palpitations, insomnia, and impaired memory. For the treatment of fright palpitations, Radix Polygalae Tenuifoliae can be combined with Cinnabar (*Zhu Sha*) and Dens Draconis (*Long Chi*) as in *Yuan Zhi Wan* (Polygala Pills). For the treatment of insomnia and impaired memory, Radix Polygalae Tenuifoliae can be combined with Radix Panacis Ginseng (*Ren Shen*) and Rhizoma Acori Graminei (*Shi Chang Pu*) as in *Bu Wang San* (No Memory Powder).

2. Used for phlegm obstructing the heart portals resulting in essence spirit confusion and chaos, spirit mind abstraction, and fright epilepsy, Radix Polygalae Tenuifoliae is commonly combined with Rhizoma Acori Graminei (*Shi Chang Pu*), Tuber Curcumae (*Yu Jin*), and Alum (*Bai Fan*).

**DOSAGE:** 3-10g

**METHOD OF USE:** Decoct in water and administer internally.

**CAUTIONS & CONTRAINDICATIONS:** Use cautiously in those with ulcer disease and gastritis.

**SHEN NONG BEN CAO JING:** "*Yuan Zhi* is bitter and warm...It supplements insufficiency, eliminates evil qi, disinhibits the nine orifices, sharpens the wits, brightens the eyes and [improves] the hearing, improves memory, strengthens the will, and doubles one's strength. Protracted taking may make the body light and prevent senility."

## CORTEX ALBIZZIAE JULIBRISSINIS (*He Huan Pi*)

**NATURE & FLAVOR:** Sweet and level

**CHANNEL ENTRY:** Heart and liver

**FUNCTIONS:** Resolves depression and quiets the mind, quickens the blood and disperses swelling

**INDICATIONS:** Used for insomnia, profuse dreams, easy anger, chest oppression, scanty eating, and emotional depression due to liver depression qi stagnation, Cortex Albizziae Julibrissinis can be combined with Radix Salviae Miltiorrhizae (*Dan Shen*) and Caulis Polygoni Multiflori (*Ye Jiao Teng*).

**DOSAGE:** 10-15g

**METHOD OF USE:** Decoct in water and administer internally.

---

**NOTE:** Flos Albizziae Julibrissinis (*He Huan Hua*) quiets the spirit, rectifies the qi, and resolves depression, but does not quicken the blood or disperse swelling.

---

**SHEN NONG BEN CAO JING:** "*He Huan* is sweet and level. It mainly quiets the five viscera, harmonizes the heart will, and makes one happy and worry-free. Protracted taking makes the body light, brightens the eyes, and [makes one feel as if one has] acquired all one's desires."

## CAULIS POLYGONI MULTIFLORI (*Ye Jiao Teng*)

**NATURE & FLAVOR:** Sweet and level

**CHANNEL ENTRY:** Heart and liver

**FUNCTIONS:** Nourishes the blood and quiets the spirit, dispels wind and frees the flow of the network vessels

**INDICATIONS:** Used for heart blood vacuity insomnia, fright palpitations, and profuse dreams, Caulis Polygoni Multiflori is commonly combined with Semen Zizyphi Spinosae (*Suan Zao Ren*) and Semen Biotae Orientalis (*Bai Zi Ren*).

**DOSAGE:** 10-15g

**METHOD OF USE:** Decoct in water and administer internally or use as a wash externally.

## FRUCTUS TRITICI AESTIVI (*Xiao Mai*)

**NATURE & FLAVOR:** Sweet and level

**CHANNEL ENTRY:** Heart

**FUNCTIONS:** Nourishes the heart and quiets the spirit

**INDICATIONS:** For mental-emotional disquietude and insomnia, this medicinal is commonly combined with Radix Glycyrrhizae (*Gan Cao*) and Fructus Zizyphi Jujubae (*Da Zao*) as in *Gan Mai Da Zao Tang* (Licorice, Wheat & Red Dates Decoction).

**DOSAGE:** 15-60g

**METHOD OF USE:** Decoct in water and administer internally.

**NOTE:** There are two forms of Fructus Tritici Aestivi: *Xiao Mai* which is categorized as a spirit-quieter and *Fu Xiao Mai* (Fructus Levis Tritici Aestivi) which is categorized as an astringent. Fructus Levis Tritici Aestivi is mainly for stopping spontaneous perspiration and night sweats by securing the exterior. Unless night sweats or spontaneous perspiration complicate psychological disease, which they sometimes do as in the case of perimenopausal visceral agitation, it is best to use Fructus Tritici Aestivi for the treatment of essence spirit diseases.

## LIVER-LEVELING, YANG-SUBDUING, WIND-EXTINGUISHING MEDICINALS

## CORNU ANTELOPIS SAIGA-TATARICI (*Ling Yang Jiao*)

**NATURE & FLAVOR:** Salty and cold

**CHANNEL ENTRY:** Liver and heart

**FUNCTIONS:** Levels the liver and extinguishes wind, clears the liver and brightens the eyes, clears heat and resolves toxins

**INDICATIONS:**

1. Used for liver wind stirring internally with fright epilepsy and convulsions, especially when extreme heat is stirring the wind, Cornu Antelopis Saiga-tatarici can be combined with Ramulus Uncariae Cum Uncis (*Gou Teng*), Flos Chrysanthemi Morifolii (*Ju Hua*), and uncooked Radix Rehmanniae (*Sheng Di*) as in *Ling Jiao Gou Teng Tang* (Antelope & Uncaria Decoction).

2. Used for ascendant liver yang hyperactivity resulting in dizziness and vertigo, Cornu Antelopis Saiga-tatarici can be combined with Flos Chrysanthemi Morifolii (*Ju Hua*) and Concha Haliotidis (*Shi Jue Ming*).

3. Used for warm heat disease with strong fever and spirit clouding, delirious speech, agitation, and mania or for heat toxin emission of macules, Cornu Antelopis Saiga-tatarici can be combined with Cornu Rhinocerotis (*Xi Jiao*) and Gypsum Fibrosum (*Shi Gao*) as in *Zi Xue San* (Purple Snow Powder).

**DOSAGE:** 3-6g. When taken as a powder, take 0.6-1.5g each time.

**METHOD OF USE:** Decoct alone first, then add to other decocted medicinals and administer. It can also be ground in water to obtain and take as a liquid or taken internally as powder.

**SHEN NONG BEN CAO JING:** "*Ling Yang Jiao* is salty and cold. It mainly brightens the eyes, boosts the qi, lifts yin, removes malign blood and downpour diarrhea, wards off gu toxins, vicious ghosts, and ill matters, quiets the heart qi, and prevents oppressive ghost dreams."

**NOTE:** Because Saiga antelope are an endangered species, one should always substitute Goat Horn, *i.e.*, Cornu Caprae (*Shan Yang Jiao*).

## CALCULUS BOVIS (*Niu Huang*)

**NATURE & FLAVOR:** Bitter and cool

CHANNEL ENTRY: Liver and heart

FUNCTIONS: Extinguishes wind and stops tetany, transforms phlegm and opens the orifices, clears heat and resolves toxins

INDICATIONS:

1. Used for warm heat disease with high fever, spirit clouding, tetany, tremors, and convulsions, and acute pediatric fright wind, Calculus Bovis is commonly combined with Cinnabar (*Zhu Sha*), Buthus Martensis (*Quan Xie*), and Ramulus Uncariae Cum Uncis (*Gou Teng*) as in *Niu Huang San* (Cow Bezoar Powder).
2. Used for the heat of warm heat disease entering the pericardium resulting in spirit clouding, delirious speech and even wind stroke, fright wind, and epilepsy categorized as phlegm heat internal blockage, Calculus Bovis is commonly combined with Secretio Moschi Moschiferi (*She Xiang*), Borneolum (*Bing Pian*), Fructus Gardeniae Jasminoidis (*Zhi Zi*), and Rhizoma Coptidis Chinensis (*Huang Lian*) as in *An Gong Niu Huang Wan* (Quiet the Palace Cow Bezoar Pills).

DOSAGE: 0.2-0.5g

METHOD OF USE: Taken in pills and powders. It is not appropriate to decoct this medicinal.

CAUTIONS & CONTRAINDICATIONS: Use cautiously in pregnant women. It is not appropriate to use this medicinal in those without replete heat patterns.

SHEN NONG BEN CAO JING: "*Niu Huang* is bitter and level. It mainly treats fright epilepsy, [alternating] cold and heat and intense heat, mania, and tetany. It eliminates evils and dispels ghosts."

## RAMULUS UNCARIAE CUM UNCIS (**Gou Teng**)

NATURE & FLAVOR: Sweet and slightly cold

CHANNEL ENTRY: Liver and pericardium

FUNCTIONS: Extinguishes wind and stops tetany, clears heat and levels the liver

INDICATIONS:

1. Used for fright epilepsy, tremors, and convulsions, Ramulus Uncariae Cum Uncis is often combined with Rhizoma Gastrodiae Elatae (*Tian Ma*), Buthus Martensis (*Quan Xie*), and Cornu Antelopis Saiga-tatarici (*Ling Yang Jiao*). If categorized as heat exuberance stirring of wind, Ramulus Uncariae Cum Uncis can be combined with Cornu Antelopis Saiga-tatarici (*Ling Yang Jiao*), Radix Gentianae Scabrae (*Long Dan Cao*), and Flos Chrysanthemi Morifolii (*Ju Hua*).

2. Used for ascendant liver yang hyperactivity dizziness and vertigo, Ramulus Uncariae Cum Uncis is commonly combined with Flos Chrysanthemi Morifolii (*Ju Hua*), Concha Haliotidis (*Shi Jue Ming*), and Radix Albus Paeoniae Lactiflorae (*Bai Shao*).

DOSAGE: 10-15g

METHOD OF USE: Decoct in water and administer internally. When taken in decoction, this medicinal should be added later and cooked for no more than 20 minutes.

## RHIZOMA GASTRODIAE ELATAE (**Tian Ma**)

NATURE & FLAVOR: Sweet and level

CHANNEL ENTRY: Liver

FUNCTIONS: Extinguishes wind and stops tetany, levels the liver and subdues yang, frees the flow of the network vessels and stops pain

INDICATIONS:

1. Used for liver wind stirring internally fright epilepsy, tremors, and convulsions. For the treatment of pediatric high fever fright wind, Rhizoma Gastrodiae Elatae can be combined with Ramulus Uncariae Cum Uncis (*Gou Teng*), Cornu Antelopis Saiga-tatarici (*Ling Yang Jiao*), and Buthus Martensis (*Quan Xie*) as in *Gou Teng Yin* (Uncaria Drink). For the treatment of pediatric spleen vacuity chronic fright, it can be combined with Radix Panacis Ginseng (*Ren Shen*), Rhizoma Atractylodis Macrocephalae (*Bai Zhu*), and Bombyx Batryticatus (*Jiang Can*) as in *Xing Pi San* (Arouse the Spleen Powder). For the treatment of tetanus, Rhizoma Gastrodiae Elatae can be combined with Rhizoma Arisaematis (*Tian Nan Xing*), Radix Ledebouriellae Divaricatae (*Fang Feng*), and Radix Aconiti Coreani Seu Typhonii (*Bai Fu Zi*) as in *Yu Zhen San* (Jade True Powder).

2. Used for headache, dizziness, and vertigo. If due to ascendant liver yang hyperactivity, Rhizoma

Gastrodiae Elatae can be combined with Ramulus Uncariae Cum Uncis (*Gou Teng*), Radix Scutellariae Baicalensis (*Huang Qin*), and Radix Achyranthis Bidentatae (*Niu Xi*) as in *Tian Ma Gou Teng Yin* (Gastrodia & Uncaria Drink). If due to wind phlegm harassing above, Rhizoma Gastrodiae Elatae can be combined with Rhizoma Pinelliae Ternatae (*Ban Xia*), Rhizoma Atractylodis Macrocephalae (*Bai Zhu*), and Sclerotium Poriae Cocos (*Fu Ling*) as in *Ban Xia Bai Zhu Tian Ma Tang* (Pinellia, Atractylodes & Gastrodia Decoction). If categorized as yin and blood insufficiency, Rhizoma Gastrodiae Elatae can be combined with Radix Angelicae Sinensis (*Dang Gui*), Radix Albus Paeoniae Lactiflorae (*Bai Shao*), and cooked Radix Rehmanniae (*Shu Di*).

**DOSAGE:** 3-10g. When ground into powder and swallowed, 1-1.5g each time.

**METHOD OF USE:** Decoct in water and administer internally. It may also be ground into powder and swallowed.

**SHEN NONG BEN CAO JING:** "*Chi Jian* is acrid and warm. It mainly kills demonic and spiritual matters, gu toxins, and malign qi. Protracted taking may boost the qi and strength, help yin grow, make one fat and strong and the body light, and lengthen one's life."

## BUTHUS MARTENSIS (*Quan Xie*)

**NATURE & FLAVOR:** Sweet, acrid, and level. Has toxins.

**CHANNEL ENTRY:** Liver

**FUNCTIONS:** Extinguishes wind and stops tetany, resolves toxins and scatters nodulations, frees the flow of the network vessels and stops pain

**INDICATIONS:** Used for many types of causes resulting in tetany, tremors, and convulsions. For the treatment of acute fright wind, Buthus Martensis can be combined with Rhizoma Gastrodiae Elatae (*Tian Ma*), Ramulus Uncariae Cum Uncis (*Gou Teng*), and Cornu Antelopis Saiga-tatarici (*Ling Yang Jiao*). For the treatment of spleen vacuity chronic fright wind, it can be combined with Radix Codonopsitis Pilosulae (*Dang Shen*), Rhizoma Atractylodis Macrocephalae (*Bai Zhu*), and Rhizoma Gastrodiae Elatae (*Tian Ma*). For the treatment of tetany, it is often combined with Rhizoma Arisaematis (*Tian Nan Xing*) and Scolopendra

Subspinipes (*Wu Gong*) as in *Wu Hu Zhui Feng San* (Five Tigers Expel Wind Powder).

**DOSAGE:** When swallowed after being ground into powder or in pills and powders, 0.5-1g each time. When decocted, one can administer up to 2-5g.

**CAUTIONS & CONTRAINDICATIONS:** This ingredient has toxins. Therefore, the amount used should not be too large nor should this medicinal be administered for too long. Use cautiously in pregnant women and those with blood vacuity engendering wind.

## LUMBRICUS (*Di Long*)

**NATURE & FLAVOR:** Salty and cold

**CHANNEL ENTRY:** Liver, kidneys, lungs, and urinary bladder

**FUNCTIONS:** Clears heat and extinguishes wind, clears the lungs and levels panting, soothes the sinews and frees the flow of the network vessels, disinhibits urination and frees the flow of strangury

**INDICATIONS:** Used for high fever vexation and agitation, fright wind tremors and convulsions, Lumbricus can be used alone or combined with Ramulus Uncariae Cum Uncis (*Gou Teng*), Bombyx Batryticatus (*Jiang Can*), and Cornu Antelopis Saiga-Tatarici (*Ling Yang Jiao*). For the treatment of phlegm fire harassing above mania, agitation, and restlessness, fresh Lumbricus can be used after being washed, dissolved in sugar water, and taken.

**DOSAGE:** 6-15g. When used fresh, one can use up to 10-20g. When ground into powder and swallowed, use 1-3g each time.

**METHOD OF USE:** Decoct in water and administer internally.

**SHEN NONG BEN CAO JING:** "*Bai Jing Qiu Yin* is salty and cold. It mainly treats snake [toxins] and conglomerations. It removes the three [kinds of] worms, hidden corpse, demonic influx, and gu toxins..."

## BOMBYX BATRYTICATUS (*Jiang Can*)

**NATURE & FLAVOR:** Salty, acrid, and level

**CHANNEL ENTRY:** Liver, lungs, and stomach

FUNCTIONS: Dispels wind and stabilizes spasms, transforms phlegm and scatters nodulations

INDICATIONS: Used for various types of spasms and contractures. For those due to phlegm heat, Bombyx Batryticatus can be combined with Calculus Bovis (*Niu Huang*), Rhizoma Coptidis Chinensis (*Huang Lian*), and bile-processed Rhizoma Arisaematis (*Dan Nan Xing*). For enduring convulsions due to spleen vacuity, Bombyx Batryticatus can be combined with Radix Codonopsitis Pilosulae (*Dang Shen*), Rhizoma Atractylodis Macrocephalae (*Bai Zhu*), and Rhizoma Gastrodiae Elatae (*Tian Ma*). For epileptiform conditions, Bombyx Batryticatus can be combined with Buthus Martensis (*Quan Xie*), Sclopendra Suspinipes (*Wu Gong*), and Periostracum Cicadae (*Chan Tui*).

DOSAGE: 3-10g

METHOD OF USE: Decoct in water and administer internally. Use stir-fried for better effect for transforming phlegm. For scattering wind heat, use uncooked.

SHEN NONG BEN CAO JING: "*Bai Jiang Can* is salty. It mainly treats fright epilepsy and night-crying in children..."

## SCOLOPENDRA SUBSPINIPES (*Wu Gong*)

NATURE & FLAVOR: Acrid and warm. Has toxins.

CHANNEL ENTRY: Liver

FUNCTIONS: Extinguishes wind and settles tetany, attacks toxins and scatters nodulations, frees the flow of the network vessels and stops pain

INDICATIONS: Used for children's fright wind, spasms and contractures, tetany, wind stroke hemiplegia, and tetanus, Scolopendra Subspinipes is commonly combined with Buthus Martensis (*Quan Xie*), Bombyx Batryticatus (*Jiang Can*), and Ramulus Uncariae Cum Uncis (*Gou Teng*).

DOSAGE: 2-5g or 1-3 strips. When swallowed as a powder, take 0.6-1g each time. Externally, use a suitable amount.

METHOD OF USE: Commonly taken in powders and pills.

CAUTIONS & CONTRAINDICATIONS: This medicinal is contraindicated in pregnant women or in those with blood vacuity tetany.

SHEN NONG BEN CAO JING: "*Wu Gong* is acrid and warm. It mainly treats demonic influx, gu toxins, and snake, worm, and fish toxins. It kills demonic matters..."

## ORIFICE-OPENING MEDICINALS

## SECRETIO MOSCHI MOSCHIFERI (*She Xiang*)

NATURE & FLAVOR: Acrid and warm

CHANNEL ENTRY: Moves freely through all 12 channels

FUNCTIONS: Opens the orifices and arouses the spirit, quickens the blood and scatters nodulations, stops pain, hastens birth

INDICATIONS: Used for the heat of warm heat disease entering the pericardium spirit clouding, tetany reversal, wind stroke reversal, and fright epilepsy block conditions. If categorized as heat block, Secretio Moschi Moschiferi is commonly combined with Cornu Rhinocerotis (*Xi Jiao*) and Calculus Bovis (*Niu Huang*) as in *Zhi Bao Dan* (Supreme Jewel Elixir). If categorized as cold block, Secretio Moschi Moschiferi is commonly combined with Styrax Liquidus (*Su He Xiang*) and Flos Caryophylli (*Ding Xiang*) as in *Su He Xiang Wan* (Styrax Pills).

DOSAGE: 0.06-0.1g

METHOD OF USE: Only taken in pills and powders, this medicinal should never be decocted.

CAUTIONS & CONTRAINDICATIONS: This medicinal is contraindicated in pregnant women.

SHEN NONG BEN CAO JING: "*She Xiang* is acrid and warm. It mainly keeps off malign qi, kills ghosts and spiritual matters, [cures] warm malaria, gu toxins, epilepsy, and tetanty... Protracted taking eliminates evils to prevent depressive ghost dreams during sleep."

## BORNEOLUM (*Bing Pian*)

NATURE & FLAVOR: Acrid, bitter, and slightly cold

CHANNEL ENTRY: Heart, liver, spleen, and lungs

FUNCTIONS: Opens the orifices and arouses the spirit, clears heat and stops pain

INDICATIONS: Used for wind stroke phlegm reversal, spirit clouding, and fright reversal, Borneolum is often combined with Secretio Moschi Moschiferi (*She Xiang*) as in *An Gong Niu Huang Wan* (Quiet the Palace Cow Bezoar Pills) and *Zhi Bao Dan* (Supreme Jewel Elixir).

DOSAGE: 0.03-0.1g

METHOD OF USE: Only used in pills and powders, this medicinal is never taken in decoction.

## RHIZOMA ACORI GRAMINEI (*Shi Chang Pu*)

NATURE & FLAVOR: Acrid, bitter, and warm

CHANNEL ENTRY: Heart, spleen, and stomach

FUNCTIONS: Opens the orifices and calms the spirit, transforms dampness and harmonizes the stomach

INDICATIONS:

1. Used for damp turbidity confounding the clear orifices resulting in spirit mind clouding and chaos, Rhizoma Acori Graminei is commonly combined with Tuber Curcumae (*Yu Jin*) and Rhizoma Pinelliae Ternatae (*Ban Xia*). Rhizoma Acori Graminei can also be used for withdrawal and torpid intelligence, in which case it is ground into powder, decocted in pig heart soup, and taken.

2. Used for heart qi insufficiency heart palpitations, insomnia, impaired memory, and tinnitus, Rhizoma Acori Graminei is commonly combined with Radix Polygalae Tenuifoliae (*Yuan Zhi*), Sclerotium Poriae Cocos (*Fu Ling*), Radix Panacis Ginseng (*Ren Shen*), and Dens Draconis (*Long Chi*) as in *An Shen Ding Zhi Wan* (Quiet the Spirit & Stabilize the Mind Pills).

3. Used for damp obstructing the spleen with chest oppression and abdominal distention, scanty eating, and torpid intake, Rhizoma Acori Graminei can be combined with Pericarpium Citri Reticulatae (*Chen Pi*), Cortex Magnoliae Officinalis (*Hou Po*), and Rhizoma Pinelliae Ternatae (*Ban Xia*).

DOSAGE: 3-10g

METHOD OF USE: Decoct in water and administer internally.

SHEN NONG BEN CAO JING: "*Chang Pu* is acrid and warm…It opens the orifices of the heart, supplements the five viscera, frees the nine orifices, brightens the eyes and [improves] hearing, and [helps] articulation of the speech. Protracted taking may make the body light, improve memory, prevent confusion, and prolong life."

## STYRAX LIQUIDUS (*Su He Xiang*)

NATURE & FLAVOR: Acrid and warm

CHANNEL ENTRY: Heart and spleen

FUNCTIONS: Opens the orifices and repels filth, scatters cold and stops pain

INDICATIONS: Used for wind stroke phlegm reversal sudden fainting and syncope or epileptiform conditions categorized as cold evils with phlegm turbidity blocking internally, Styrax Liquidus is commonly combined with Secretio Moschi Moschiferi (*She Xiang*), Flos Caryophylli (*Ding Xiang*), and Benzoin (*An Xi Xiang*) as in *Su He Xiang Wan* (Liquid Styrax Pills).

DOSAGE: 0.3-1g

METHOD OF USE: Taken as pills and powders. This medicinal should not be decocted.

CAUTIONS & CONTRAINDICATIONS: This medicinal should not be used for heat block conditions.

## SUPPLEMENTING & BOOSTING MEDICINALS

## RADIX PANACIS GINSENG (*Ren Shen*)

NATURE & FLAVOR: Sweet, slightly bitter, and level

CHANNEL ENTRY: Spleen, lungs, and heart

FUNCTIONS: Greatly supplements the source qi, restores the pulse and secures desertion, supplements the spleen and boosts the lungs, engenders fluids and stops thirst, quiets the spirit and boosts the intelligence

INDICATIONS: Used for heart-spleen vacuity heart spirit restlessness, insomnia, profuse dreams, fright palpitations, impaired memory, bodily fatigue, and lack of strength, Radix Panacis Ginseng is commonly combined with Radix Angelicae Sinensis (*Dang Gui*), Semen Zizyphi Spinosae (*Suan Zao Ren*), and Arillus Euphoriae Longanae (*Long Yan Rou*) as in *Gui Pi Tang* (Return the Spleen Decoction).

DOSAGE: 3-10g. When ground into powder and swallowed, take 1-2g each time. For rescuing from vacuity desertion, one can use doses as large as 15-30g, decocted and taken in divided doses.

METHOD OF USE: When taken in decoction, Radix Panacis Ginseng should be decocted alone over a slow fire and then mixed with the medicinal juice of the other decocted medicinals. It may also be ground into powder and swallowed.

CAUTIONS & CONTRAINDICATIONS: Radix Panacis Ginseng is contraindicated in repletion patterns, heat patterns, and in cases where the righteous qi is not vacuous.

SHEN NONG BEN CAO JING: "Ren Shen is sweet and a little cold. It mainly supplements the five viscera. It quiets the essence spirit, settles the ethereal and corporeal souls, stops fright palpitations, eliminates evil qi, brightens the eyes, opens the heart, and sharpens the wits. Protracted taking makes the body light and prolongs life."

## RADIX GLYCYRRHIZAE (Gan Cao)

NATURE & FLAVOR: Sweet and level

CHANNEL ENTRY: Heart, lungs, spleen, and stomach

FUNCTIONS: Supplements the spleen and boosts the qi, dispels phlegm and stops cough, clears heat and resolves toxins, relaxes tension or cramping and stabilizes pain, regulates and harmonizes other medicinals' natures.

INDICATIONS:

1. For heart qi vacuity and scanty blood, heart palpitations, spontaneous perspiration, and a bound or regulary intermittent pulse, Radix Glycyrrhizae is often combined with uncooked Radix Rehmanniae (Sheng Di), Radix Codonopsitis Pilosulae (Dang Shen), Tuber Ophiopogonis Japonici (Mai Dong), and Ramulus Cinnamomi Cassiae (Gui Zhi) as in Zhi Gan Cao Tang (Mix-fried Licorice Decoction).

2. For spasms and contractions of the four limbs, aching, and pain, Radix Glycyrrhizae is commonly combined with Radix Albus Paeoniae Lactiflorae (Bai Shao). This is then called Shao Yao Gan Cao Tang (Peony & Licorice Decoction).

DOSAGE: 3-6g. As the main medicinal in a formula, it can be used from 10-30g.

METHOD OF USE: Decoct in water and administer internally. This medicinal should be used uncooked when entered with clearing and draining medicinals. It should be used honey mix-fried when entered with supplementing and boosting medicinals.

CAUTIONS & CONTRAINDICATIONS: Radix Glycyrrhizae is contraindicated in case of damp exuberance center fullness and vomiting and spitting. Enduring administration of relatively large doses easily leads to water swelling. When administered at either high doses or for long periods of time, it should be combined with water-seeping medicinals, such as Sclerotium Poriae Cocos (Fu Ling), Rhizoma Alismatis (Ze Xie), and Semen Plantaginis (Che Qian Zi).

## FRUCTUS ZIZYPHI JUJUBAE (Da Zao)

NATURE & FLAVOR: Sweet and slightly warm

CHANNEL ENTRY: Spleen, stomach, heart, and liver

FUNCTIONS: Supplements the center and boosts the qi, nourishes the blood and quiets the spirit, moderates and harmonizes the natures of other medicinals

INDICATIONS: Used for visceral agitation, Fructus Zizyphi Jujubae is commonly combined with Radix Glycyrrhizae (Gan Cao) and Fructus Tritici Aestivi (Xiao Mai) as in Gan Mai Da Zao Tang (Licorice, Wheat & Red Dates Decoction).

DOSAGE: 3-10 fruits. In larger doses, it can be used up to 30-60g.

METHOD OF USE: Decoct in water and administer internally.

CAUTIONS & CONTRAINDICATIONS: This medicinal is able to strengthen dampness. Therefore, it is not appropriate to use in case of damp obstruction abdominal distention, fullness, and oppression.

SHEN NONG BEN CAO JING: "Da Zao is sweet and level. It mainly treats heart and abdominal evil qi, quiets the center, and nourishes the spleen, assists the 12 channels, levels the stomach qi, frees the nine orifices, supplements shortage of qi, shortage of fluids, and insufficiency of the body, [eliminates] great fright and heaviness of the limbs, and harmonizes the hundreds of medicinals. Protracted taking may make the body light and lengthen life."

## ARILLUS EUPHORIAE LONGANAE (*Long Yan Rou*)

NATURE & FLAVOR: Sweet and warm

CHANNEL ENTRY: Heart and spleen

FUNCTIONS: Supplements and boosts the heart and spleen, nourishes the blood and quiets the spirit

INDICATIONS: Used for qi and blood insufficiency heart palpitations, fearful throbbing, impaired memory, insomnia, and a sallow yellow facial complexion, Arillus Euphoriae Longanae is commonly combined with Radix Astragali Membranacei (*Huang Qi*), Radix Codonopsitis Pilosulae (*Dang Shen*), and Radix Angelicae Sinensis (*Dang Gui*) as in *Gui Pi Tang* (Return the Spleen Decoction).

DOSAGE: 10-15g

METHOD OF USE: Decoct in water and administer internally.

SHEN NONG BEN CAO JING: "*Long Yan* is sweet and level. It mainly treats evil qi in the five viscera, quiets the mind, and [relieves] aversion to food. Protracted taking strengthens the ethereal soul, sharpens [the ears and eyes], makes the body light, prevents senility, and enables one to communicate with the spirit brilliance."

## FRUCTUS ALPINIAE OXYPHYLLAE (*Yi Zhi Ren*)

NATURE & FLAVOR: Acrid and warm

CHANNEL ENTRY: Spleen and kidneys

FUNCTIONS: Warms the spleen, opens the stomach, and contains drool, warms the kidneys, secures the essence, and reduces urination, boosts the intelligence

INDICATIONS: Used for spleen-stomach yang vacuity profuse sleeping, Fructus Alpiniae Oxyphyllae can be combined with Radix Codonopsitis Pilosulae (*Dang Shen*), Rhizoma Atractylodis Macrocephalae (*Bai Zhu*), dry Rhizoma Zingiberis (*Gan Jiang*), and Pericarpium Citri Reticulatae (*Chen Pi*).

DOSAGE: 3-6g

METHOD OF USE: Decoct in water and administer internally.

CAUTIONS & CONTRAINDICATIONS: This ingredient is drying and hot and easily damages yin and invigorates fire. Therefore, it is contraindicated in yin vacuity fire effulgence and conditions categorized as damp heat.

## PHLEGM-TRANSFORMING MEDICINALS

## BILE-PROCESSED RHIZOMA ARISAEMATIS (*Dan Nan Xing*)

NATURE & FLAVOR: Bitter and cool

CHANNEL ENTRY: Lungs, liver, and spleen

FUNCTIONS: Clears heat and transforms phlegm, extinguishes wind and stops tetany

INDICATIONS: Used for epileptiform conditions due to phlegm blocking the orifices of the heart and heat harassing the spirit, this medicinal is commonly combined with Rhizoma Acori Graminei (*Shi Chang Pu*), Buthus Martensis (*Quan Xie*), and Succus Bambusae (*Zhu Li*) as in *Ding Xian Wan* (Stabilize Epilepsy Pills). For loss of consciousness due to phlegm heat blocking the heart and confounding the spirit, bile-processed Rhizoma Arisaematis may be combined with Calculus Bovis (*Niu Huang*), Rhizoma Acori Graminei (*Shi Chang Pu*), and Borneolum (*Bing Pian*).

DOSAGE: 3-10g. Do not exceed this dosage.

METHOD OF USE: Decoct in water and administer internally.

CAUTIONS & CONTRAINDICATIONS: Use cautiously in pregnant women.

## CAULIS BAMBUSAE IN TAENIIS (*Zhu Ru*)

NATURE & FLAVOR: Sweet and slightly cold

CHANNEL ENTRY: Lungs, stomach, and gallbladder

FUNCTIONS: Clears heat and transforms phlegm, eliminates vexation and stops vomiting

INDICATIONS: Used for vexation and agitation, insomnia, easy anger, and nausea and vomiting due to hot phlegm, Caulis Bambusae can be combined with Rhizoma Pinelliae Ternatae (*Ban Xia*) and Fructus Immaturus Citri Aurantii (*Zhi Shi*).

**DOSAGE:** 4.5-12g

**METHOD OF USE:** Decoct in water and administer. Typically, for dispelling phlegm, the uncooked is used.

## LAPIS MICAE SEU CHLORITI (*Meng Shi*)

**NATURE & FLAVOR:** Acrid, salty, and cold

**CHANNEL ENTRY:** Lungs and liver

**FUNCTIONS:** Downbears the qi and transforms phlegm, clears the liver, quiets fright, and stops palpitations

**INDICATIONS:** Phlegm accumulations, epilepsy and mania, food stagnation, abdominal concretions. For old or stubborn phlegm causing panting and coughing, fright palpitations, withdrawal and mania, and constipation, Lapis Micae Seu Chloriti is commonly combined with Radix Scutellariae Baicalensis (*Huang Qin*) and Radix Et Rhizoma Rhei (*Da Huang*).

**DOSAGE:** 9-15g when used in decoctions; 1.5-3g when used in pills and powders

**METHOD OF USE:** Decoct in water and administer or grind into powder and use in pills and powders. Typically used calcined. When used in decoction, typically decocted first.

**CAUTIONS & CONTRAINDICATIONS:** Do not use during pregnancy or in those with habitual bodily vacuity and weakness. Use with care in those with spleen-stomach vacuity weakness.

## WATER-DISINHIBITING, DAMPNESS-SEEPING MEDICINALS

## SCLEROTIUM PORIAE COCOS (*Fu Ling*)

**NATURE & FLAVOR:** Sweet, bland, and level

**CHANNEL ENTRY:** Heart, spleen, and kidneys

**FUNCTIONS:** Disinhibits water and percolates dampness, fortifies the spleen and supplements the center, stabilizes the heart and quiets the spirit

**INDICATIONS:**

1. For phlegm rheum collecting internally resulting in dizziness, heart palpitations, and cough, Sclerotium Poriae Cocos is commonly combined with Ramulus Cinnamomi Cassiae (*Gui Zhi*) and Rhizoma Atractylodis Macrocephalae (*Bai Zhu*) as in *Ling Gui Zhu Gan Tang* (Poria, Cinnamon, Atractylodes & Licorice Decoction).

2. Used for heart-spleen insufficiency fright palpitations and insomnia, Sclerotium Poriae Cocos is commonly combined with Radix Codonopsitis Pilosulae (*Dang Shen*), Arillus Euphoriae Longanae (*Long Yan Rou*), and Semen Zizyphi Spinosae (*Suan Zao Ren*) as in *Gui Pi Tang* (Return the Spleen Decoction). When used for phlegm turbidity obstructing internally or heart-kidney not interacting fright palpitations and insomnia, Sclerotium Poriae Cocos is commonly combined with Rhizoma Acori Graminei (*Shi Chang Pu*) and Radix Polygalae Tenuifoliae (*Yuan Zhi*) as in *An Shen Ding Zhi Wan* (Quiet the Spirit & Stabilize the Mind Pills).

**DOSAGE:** 10-30g

**METHOD OF USE:** Decoct in water and administer internally.

**NOTE:** Sclerotium Pararadicis Poriae Cocos (*Fu Shen*) is even more effective for quieting the spirit.

*SHEN NONG BEN CAO JING*: "*Fu Ling* is sweet and level. It mainly treats chest and rib-side counterflow qi, binding pain below the heart due to worry, indignation, fright, and fear, [alternating] cold and heat, vexatious fullness... Protracted taking quiets the ethereal soul, nourishes the spirit, makes one free from hunger, and prolongs life."

## HEAT-CLEARING MEDICINALS

## FRUCTUS GARDENIAE JASMINOIDIS (*Zhi Zi*)

**NATURE & FLAVOR:** Bitter and cold

**CHANNEL ENTRY:** Heart, lungs, stomach, and triple burner

**FUNCTIONS:** Drains fire and eliminates vexation, clears heat and disinhibits dampness, cools the blood and stops bleeding

INDICATIONS: Used for heat disease heart vexation, depression and oppression, agitation and restlessness, this medicinal is commonly combined with Semen Praeparatus Sojae (*Dan Dou Chi*) which is then called *Zhi Zi Chi Tang* (Gardenia & Soya Decoction). For liver depression transforming heat, this medicinal is commonly combined with Cortex Radicis Moutan (*Dan Pi*). If heat toxins have accumulated and are exuberant with symptoms of high fever, vexation and agitation, spirit clouding, and delirious speech, this medicinal is commonly combined with Rhizoma Coptidis Chinensis (*Huang Lian*) and Radix Scutellariae Baicalensis (*Huang Qin*) as in *Qing Wen Bai Du Yin* (Clear the Scourge & Vanquish Toxins Drink).

DOSAGE: 3-10g

METHOD OF USE: Decoct in water and administer internally.

## HERBA LOPHATHERI GRACILIS (*Dan Zhu Ye*)[1]

NATURE & FLAVOR: Sweet, bland, and cold

CHANNEL ENTRY: Heart, stomach, and urinary bladder

FUNCTIONS: Clears heat and eliminates vexation, disinhibits urination

INDICATIONS: Used for heat in the heart channel resulting in vexation, sores in the mouth and on the tongue, and reddish, scanty urination, Herba Lophatheri Gracilis can be combined with Caulis Akebiae (*Mu Tong*) and uncooked Radix Rehmanniae (*Sheng Di*) as in *Dao Chi San* (Abduct the Red Powder).

DOSAGE: 6-12g

METHOD OF USE: Decoct in water and administer internally.

## QI-RECTIFYING MEDICINALS

## LIGNUM AQUILARIAE AGALLOCHAE (*Chen Xiang*)

NATURE & FLAVOR: Acrid, bitter, aromatic, and warm

CHANNEL ENTRY: Kidneys, spleen, and stomach

FUNCTIONS: Moves the qi and stops pain, downbears counterflow and harmonizes the center, promotes the kidneys' grasping or absorbing of the qi

INDICATIONS:

1. Used for chest and abdominal distention, oppression, aching, and pain, stomach cold vomiting and hiccup, including nausea and vomiting in pregnancy, Lignum Aqualariae Agallochae can be combined with Folium Perillae Frutescentis (*Zi Su Ye*).

2. Used for kidney vacuity counterflow panting and rapid breathing, Lignum Aquilariae Agallochae can be combined with Semen Raphani Sativi (*Lai Fu Zi*).

DOSAGE: 1.5-4.5g

METHOD OF USE: Decoct in water and administer internally or taken in powders and pills. When decocted, add later. Some sources say this medicinal should not be decocted.

CAUTIONS & CONTRAINDICATIONS: Use cautiously with those with central qi downward fall and those with yin vacuity with heat symptoms.

NOTE: The *Hai Yao Ben Cao* (Sea of Medicinals Materia Medica) says this medicinal also clears the spirit, while the *Ri Hua Zi Ben Cao* (Ri Hua-zi's Materia Medica) says it supplements the five viscera and boosts the essence. Further, the *Ben Cao Zai Xin* (Materia Medica Once Again Renewed) says it treats liver depression and specifically downbears liver qi. Although modern Chinese materia medica tend not to emphasize this medicinal's psycho-emotional effects, this medicinal is commonly found in formulas designed to treat essence spirit diseases.

## BLOOD-QUICKENING, STASIS-DISPELLING MEDICINALS

## TUBER CURCUMAE (*Yu Jin*)

NATURE & FLAVOR: Acrid, bitter, and cold

CHANNEL ENTRY: Heart, liver, and gallbladder

FUNCTIONS: Quickens the blood and stops pain, moves the qi and resolves depression, cools the blood and clears the heart, disinhibits the gallbladder and recedes jaundice

INDICATIONS:

1. Used for liver qi depression and stagnation and blood

stasis obstructing internally resulting in various types of aching and pain and concretions and conglomerations. For the treatment of chest, rib-side, stomach duct, and abdominal distention and pain, Tuber Curcumae can be combined with Radix Salviae Miltiorrhizae (*Dan Shen*), Radix Bupleuri (*Chai Hu*), Rhizoma Cyperi Rotundi (*Xiang Fu*), and Fructus Citri Aurantii (*Zhi Ke*). For the treatment of hypochondral concretions and lumps, distention, fullness, aching, and pain, Tuber Curcumae can be combined with Radix Salviae Miltiorrhizae (*Dan Shen*), Carapax Amydae Chinensis (*Bie Jia*), Herba Lycopi Lucidi (*Ze Lan*), and Pericarpium Citri Reticulatae Viride (*Qing Pi*).

2. Used for damp warm disease dampness and turbidity misting the clear orifices resulting in chest and stomach duct glomus and oppression, lack of clarity of the spirit mind, and for phlegm internally blocking resulting in vexation and agitation, depression, oppression, epilepsy, and fright mania. For the former, Tuber Curcumae is commonly combined with Rhizoma Acori Graminei (*Shi Chang Pu*), Fructus Gardeniae Jasminoidis (*Zhi Zi*), and Succus Bambusae (*Zhu Li*) as in *Chang Pu Yu Jin Tang* (Acorus & Curcuma Decoction). For the latter, Tuber Curcumae is commonly combined with Alum (*Bai Fan*) as in *Bai Jin Wan* (White & Gold Pills, or Alum & Curcuma Pills).

**DOSAGE:** 6-12g

**METHOD OF USE:** Decoct in water and administer internally.

**CAUTIONS & CONTRAINDICATIONS:** Fears Flos Caryophylli (*Ding Xiang*).

**NOTE:** Although this medicinal is categorized as a blood-quickener, it is often used primarily to move the qi and scatter depression. As the *Ben Cao Bei Yao* (*Materia Medica Full Essentials*) says, it "moves the qi and resolves depression... cools heart heat and scatters liver depression."

EXTERIOR-RESOLVING MEDICINALS

RADIX BUPLEURI (*Chai Hu*)

**NATURE & FLAVOR:** Bitter, acrid, and slightly cold

**CHANNEL ENTRY:** Liver and gallbladder

**FUNCTIONS:** Out-thrusts the exterior and recedes or abates heat, courses the liver and resolves depression, upbears and lifts the yang qi

**INDICATIONS:** Used for liver depression qi stagnation, the symptoms of which are irritability, emotional depression, taciturnity, chest and diaphragmatic fullness and oppression, rib-side and flank distention and pain. In that case, Radix Bupleuri is commonly combined with Rhizoma Cyperi Rotundi (*Xiang Fu*), Radix Ligustici Wallichii (*Chuan Xiong*), and Fructus Citri Aurantii (*Zhi Ke*) as in *Chai Hu Shu Gan San* (Bupleurum Course the Liver Powder). If there is liver depression blood vacuity with menstrual irregularities, one can combine Radix Bupleuri with Radix Angelicae Sinensis (*Dang Gui*) and Radix Albus Paeoniae Lactiflorae (*Bai Shao*) as in *Xiao Yao San* (Rambling Powder).

**DOSAGE:** 3-10g

**METHOD OF USE:** Decoct in water and administer internally.

**CAUTIONS & CONTRAINDICATIONS:** This ingredient's nature and action is upbearing and effusing. Therefore, it is contraindicated in yin vacuity fire effulgence and ascendant hyperactivity of liver yang tinnitus, deafness, dizziness, and headache.

**NOTE:** Although this medicinal is categorized as an exterior-resolving medicinal, when used in pyschological disease, it functions as a qi-rectifying medicinal.

**SHEN NONG BEN CAO JING:** "*Chai Hu* is bitter and level. It mainly treats bound qi in the heart, abdomen, intestines, and stomach, drink and food accumulation and gathering, [alternating] cold and heat, and evil qi."

ASTRINGING & SECURING MEDICINALS

FRUCTUS SCHISANDRAE CHINENSIS (*Wu Wei Zi*)

**NATURE & FLAVOR:** Sour, sweet, and warm

**CHANNEL ENTRY:** Lungs, heart, and kidneys

**FUNCTIONS:** Constrains the lungs and enriches the kidneys, engenders fluids and constrains the sweat, astringes the essence and stops diarrhea, calms the heart and quiets the spirit

**INDICATIONS:** Used for heart blood insufficiency and kidney yin debility and vacuity resulting in vacuity vexation, heart palpitations, insomnia, and profuse dreams, Fructus Schisandrae Chinensis is commonly combined with uncooked Radix Rehmanniae (*Shu Di*), Tuber Ophiopogonis Japonici (*Mai Dong*), Radix Salviae Miltiorrhizae (*Dan Shen*), and Semen Zizyphi Spinosae (*Suan Zao Ren*) as in *Tian Wang Bu Xin Dan* (Heavenly Emperor Supplement the Heart Elixir).

**DOSAGE:** 3-10g. For enriching, supplementing, and boosting yin, use 6-10g.

**METHOD OF USE:** Decoct in water and administer internally.

**CAUTIONS & CONTRAINDICATIONS:** Because this ingredient is sour, astringent, restraining, and constraining, it should not be used in those with exterior evils which have not been resolved, for those with internal replete heat, for the initial stage of cough, nor for the initial emission of measles rash.

**SHEN NONG BEN CAO JING:** "*Wu Wei* is sour and warm. It mainly boosts the qi, [treating] cough and counterflow qi ascent, taxation damage, and languor and emaciation. It supplements insufficiency, fortifies yin, and boosts men's essence."

**ENDNOTES:**

[1] Chinese texts often simply use the term *Zhu Ye*, Folium Bambusae, when identifying this medicinal.

# COMMONLY USED CHINESE FORMULAS IN THE TREATMENT OF PSYCHOEMOTIONAL DISORDERS

The following are some of the most commonly used Chinese medicinal formulas for the treatment of psychoemotional disorders. Readers should note that their proper selection rests primarily on the patient's individual pattern discrimination, not on their disease diagnosis. This is based on the famous Chinese medical saying, "Different diseases, same treatment; same disease, different treatments." In addition, readers should be aware that, in real-life practice, these formulas will have to be modified in terms of the dosages of their ingredients and with various additions and subtractions.

**LIVER QI DEPRESSION & BINDING:** *Chai Hu Shu Gan San* (Bupleurum Course the Liver Powder)

**INGREDIENTS:** Radix Bupleuri (*Chai Hu*), 10-12g, Radix Albus Paeoniae Lactiflorae (*Bai Shao*), 6-10g, Fructus Citri Aurantii (*Zhi Ke*), 6-10g, Radix Ligustici Wallichii (*Chuan Xiong*), 3-6g, Rhizoma Cyperi Rotundi (*Xiang Fu*), 6-10g, Radix Glycyrrhizae (*Gan Cao*), 1-3g

**FUNCTIONS:** Courses the liver and rectifies the qi, harmonizes the blood and resolves depression

**INDICATIONS:** Liver depression qi stagnation with mental-emotional depression, irritability, chest oppression, tendency to sigh, a normal or darkish tongue with thin, white fur, and a bowstring pulse

**LIVER BLOOD VACUITY:** *Si Wu Tang* (Four Materials Decoction)

**INGREDIENTS:** cooked Radix Rehmanniae (*Shu Di*), 10-15g, Radix Angelicae Sinensis (*Dang Gui*), 10-12g, Radix Ligustici Wallichii (*Chuan Xiong*), 6-10g, Radix Albus Paeoniae Lactiflorae (*Bai Shao*), 10-12g

**FUNCTIONS:** Supplements the blood and nourishes the liver

**INDICATIONS:** Insomnia, heart palpitations, a pale white or sallow yellow facial complexion, dry skin and hair, pale lips and tongue, and a fine pulse

**NOTE:** Although this formula is not usually considered a main formula for psychological disturbances, because blood vacuity complicates so many cases of psycho-emotional diseases, especially in women, all or some of its ingredients are often added to other formulas more famous for treating psychological problems.

**LIVER BLOOD VACUITY WITH VACUITY HEAT:** *Suan Zao Ren Tang* (Zizyphus Spinosa Decoction)

**INGREDIENTS:** Semen Zizyphi Spinosae (*Suan Zao Ren*), 15-18g, Sclerotium Poriae Cocos (*Fu Ling*), 6-10g,

Rhizoma Anemarrhenae Aspheloidis (*Zhi Mu*), 6-10g, Radix Ligustici Wallichii (*Chuan Xiong*), 6-10g, Radix Glycyrrhizae (*Gan Cao*), 3-6g

FUNCTIONS: Nourishes the blood and quiets the spirit, clears heat and eliminates vexation

INDICATIONS: Irritability, vexation, insomnia, dizziness, heart palpitations, a dry mouth and throat, a pale tongue with red tip, and a bowstring, fine, rapid pulse

**LIVER BLOOD-KIDNEY YIN VACUITY:** *Liu Wei Di Huang Wan* (Six Flavors Rehmannia Pills)

INGREDIENTS: cooked Radix Rehmanniae (*Shu Di*), 12-25g, Fructus Corni Officinalis (*Shan Zhu Yu*), 10-15g, Radix Dioscoreae Oppositae (*Shan Yao*), 10-15g, Sclerotium Poriae Cocos (*Fu Ling*), 10-12g, Rhizoma Alismatis (*Ze Xie*), 10-12g, Cortex Radicis Moutan (*Dan Pi*), 6-10g

FUNCTIONS: Supplements the kidneys and enriches yin

INDICATIONS: Insomnia, heart palpitations, restlessness and agitation, dizziness, tinnitus, low back and knee soreness and limpness, a dry mouth but no particular desire to drink, a pale tongue with red tip and scanty fur, and a fine, bowstring pulse

**LIVER BLOOD-KIDNEY YIN VACUITY W/ LIVER DEPRESSION:** *Yi Guan Jian* (One Link Decoction)

INGREDIENTS: uncooked Radix Rehmanniae (*Sheng Di*), 10-15g, Radix Glehniae Littoralis (*Sha Shen*), 6-10g, Tuber Ophiopogonis Japonici (*Mai Dong*), 6-10g, Radix Angelicae Sinensis (*Dang Gui*), 6-10g, Fructus Lycii Chinensis (*Gou Qi Zi*), 6-10g, Fructus Meliae Toosendan (*Chuan Lian Zi*), 3-6g

FUNCTIONS: Supplements liver and kidney yin, courses the liver and rectifies the qi

INDICATIONS: Emotional depression, insomnia, heart palpitations, agitation and vexation, chest oppression, breast, rib-side, and abdominal distention and pain, a pale tongue with red tip or a red tongue with scanty fur, and a bowstring, fine pulse

**ASCENDANT LIVER YANG HYPERACTIVITY:** *Tian Ma Gou Teng Yin* (Gastrodia & Uncaria Drink)

INGREDIENTS: Rhizoma Gastrodiae Elatae (*Tian Ma*), 6-10g, Ramulus Uncariae Cum Uncis (*Gou Teng*), 6-10g, Concha Haliotidis (*Shi Jue Ming*), 3-6g, Ramulus Loranthi Seu Visci (*Sang Ji Sheng*), 6-10g, Cortex Eucommiae Ulmoidis (*Du Zhong*), 6-10g, Radix Cyathulae (*Chuan Niu Xi*), 6-10g, Fructus Gardeniae Jasminoidis (*Zhi Zi*), 3-6g, Radix Scutellariae Baicalensis (*Huang Qin*), 6-10g, Herba Leonuri Heterophylli (*Yi Mu Cao*), 6-10g, Caulis Polygoni Multiflori (*Ye Jiao Teng*), 6-10g, Sclerotium Pararadicis Poriae Cocos (*Fu Shen*), 3-6g

FUNCTIONS: Extinguishes wind and subdues yang, settles the liver and quiets the spirit

INDICATIONS: Mania, epilepsy, insomnia, profuse dreams, dizziness, vertigo, tinnitus, a red tongue, and a rapid, bowstring pulse

**LIVER WIND STIRRING INTERNALLY:** *Zhen Gan Xi Feng Tang* (Settle the Liver & Extinguish Wind Decoction)

INGREDIENTS: Radix Achyranthis Bidentatae (*Niu Xi*), 10-15g, Haemititum (*Dai Zhe Shi*), 10-15g, Os Draconis (*Long Gu*), 10-12g, Concha Ostreae (*Mu Li*), 10-12g, Plastrum Testudinis (*Gui Ban*), 10-12g, Radix Scrophulariae Ningpoensis (*Xuan Shen*), 10-12g, Tuber Asparagi Cochinensis (*Tian Men Dong*), 10-12g, Radix Albus Paeoniae Lactiflorae (*Bai Shao*), 10-12g, Herba Artemisiae Capillaris (*Yin Chen Hao*), 3-6g, Fructus Meliae Toosendan (*Chuan Lian Zi*), 3-6g, Fructus Germinatus Hordei Vulgaris (*Mai Ya*), 3-6g, Radix Glycyrrhizae (*Gan Cao*), 3-6g

FUNCTIONS: Settles the liver and extinguishes wind, nourishes yin and leads yang back to its lower source

INDICATIONS: Epilepsy, convulsions, dizziness, vertigo, headache, irritability, mental confusion with moments of clarity, a red, trembling tongue, and a bowstring, surging pulse

**GALLBLADDER-STOMACH DISHARMONY:** *Wen Dan Tang* (Warm the Gallbladder Decoction)

INGREDIENTS: Rhizoma Pinelliae Ternatae (*Ban Xia*), 6-10g, Pericarpium Citri Reticulatae (*Chen Pi*), 6-10g, Sclerotium Poriae Cocos (*Fu Ling*), 10-12g, Fructus Immaturus Citri Aurantii (*Zhi Shi*), 6-10g, Caulis Bambusae In Taeniis (*Zhu Ru*), 6-10g, Radix Glycyrrhizae (*Gan Cao*), 1-3g, Fructus Zizyphi Jujubae (*Da Zao*), 3-5 pieces

FUNCTIONS: Rectifies the qi and transforms phlegm, clears the gallbladder and harmonizes the stomach

INDICATIONS: Emotional depression, insomnia, profuse dreams, nightmares, susceptibility to fright, heart palpitations, profuse phlegm, chest and abdominal oppression and glomus, possible nausea, a dark tongue with slightly yellow, slimy tongue fur, and a slippery, bowstring pulse

**GALLBLADDER-STOMACH DISHARMONY W/ MARKED DEPRESSIVE HEAT:** *Huang Lian Wen Dan Tang* (Coptis Warm the Gallbladder Decoction)

INGREDIENTS: Rhizoma Pinelliae Ternatae (*Ban Xia*), 6-10g, Pericarpium Citri Reticulatae (*Chen Pi*), 6-10g, Sclerotium Poriae Cocos (*Fu Ling*), 10-12g, Fructus Immaturus Citri Aurantii (*Zhi Shi*), 6-10g, Caulis Bambusae In Taeniis (*Zhu Ru*), 6-10g, Rhizoma Coptidis Chinensis (*Huang Lian*), 3-6g, Radix Glycyrrhizae (*Gan Cao*), 1-3g, Fructus Zizyphi Jujubae (*Da Zao*), 3-5 pieces

FUNCTIONS: Clears heat and transforms phlegm, courses the liver and resolves depression

INDICATIONS: Emotional depression, susceptibility to fright, insomnia, profuse dreams, chest and abdominal oppression and distention, profuse phlegm, heart palpitations, dizziness, vertigo, a bitter taste in the mouth, a red tongue with slimy, yellow fur, and a slippery, bowstring, rapid pulse

**LIVER CHANNEL REPLETE FIRE:** *Long Dan Xie Gan Tang* (Gentiana Drain the Liver Decoction)

INGREDIENTS: Radix Gentianae Scabrae (*Long Dan Cao*), 3-6g, Radix Scutellariae Baicalensis (*Huang Qin*), 10-12g, Fructus Gardeniae Jasminoidis (*Zhi Zi*), 6-10g, Rhizoma Alismatis (*Ze Xie*), 6-10g, Semen Plantaginis (*Che Qian Zi*), 6-10g, Caulis Akebiae (*Mu Tong*), 6-10g, uncooked Radix Rehmanniae (*Sheng Di*), 10-12g, Extremitas Radicis Angelicae Sinensis (*Dang Gui Wei*), 6-10g, Radix Bupleuri (*Chai Hu*), 6-10g, Radix Glycyrrhizae (*Gan Cao*)

FUNCTIONS: Drains the liver and gallbladder, clears heat and eliminates dampness

INDICATIONS: Mania, vexation and agitation, irascibility, red eyes, red facial complexion, headache, dizziness, a bitter taste in the mouth, possible dark-colored, burning hot urination, possible thick, yellow vaginal discharge, a red tongue with yellow fur, and a bowstring, rapid, forceful pulse

**HEART-GALLBLADDER QI VACUITY:** *Shi Wei Wen Dan Tang* (Ten Flavors Warm the Gallbladder Decoction)

INGREDIENTS: Rhizoma Pinelliae Ternatae (*Ban Xia*), 6-10g, Fructus Immaturus Citri Aurantii (*Zhi Shi*), 6-10g, Pericarpium Citri Reticulatae (*Chen Pi*), 6-10g, Sclerotium Poriae Cocos (*Fu Ling*), 4.5-10g, Semen Zizyphi Spinosae (*Suan Zao Ren*), 10-12g, Radix Polygalae Tenuifoliae (*Yuan Zhi*), 3-10g, cooked Radix Rehmanniae (*Shu Di*), 10-12g, Radix Panacis Ginseng (*Ren Shen*), 3-6g, Fructus Schisandrae Chinensis (*Wu Wei Zi*), 6-10g, mix-fried Radix Glycyrrhizae (*Gan Cao*), 6-10g, uncooked Rhizoma Zingiberis (*Sheng Jiang*), 5 slices, Fructus Zizyphi Jujubae (*Da Zao*), 3-5 pieces

FUNCTIONS: Transforms phlegm and quiets the heart, supplements and rectifies the qi

INDICATIONS: Anxiety, vexation and agitation, insomnia, heart palpitations, susceptibility to fright, irritability, lassitude of the spirit, lack of strength, chest oppression, a pale but dark tongue with slimy, white fur, and a soggy, bowstring pulse

**LIVER-STOMACH DISHARMONY:** *Xuan Fu Dai Zhe Tang* (Hematite & Inula Decoction)

INGREDIENTS: Flos Inulae Racemosae (*Xuan Fu Hua*), 6-10g, Haemititum (*Dai Zhe Shi*), 10-15g, Radix Panacis Ginseng (*Ren Shen*), 3-6g, Rhizoma Pinelliae Ternatae (*Ban Xia*), 6-10g, uncooked Rhizoma Zingiberis (*Sheng Jiang*), 10-12g, mix-fried Radix Glycyrrhizae (*Gan Cao*), 3-6g, Fructus Zizyphi Jujubae (*Da Zao*), 10-12 pieces

FUNCTIONS: Downbears counterflow and harmonizes the stomach, supplements the spleen and transforms phlegm

INDICATIONS: Ceaseless belching, hiccup, nausea, and vomiting, lassitude of the spirit, fatigue, lack of strength, a swollen tongue with teeth-marks on its edges and slimy, white tongue fur, and a fine, bowstring pulse

**LIVER-STOMACH DEPRESSIVE HEAT & COUNTERFLOW:** *Zuo Jin Wan* (Left Gold Pills)

INGREDIENTS: Rhizoma Coptidis Chinensis (*Huang Lian*), 15-18g, Fructus Evodiae Rutecarpae (*Wu Zhu Yu*), 2-3g

FUNCTIONS: Clears the liver, downbears counterflow, and stops vomiting

INDICATIONS: Vomiting, acid regurgitation, gnawing hunger, hypochondral pain, burping and belching, a bitter taste in the mouth, a red tongue with yellow fur, and a bowstring, rapid pulse

NOTE: This formula is commonly added to other formulas when there is liver assailing the stomach with marked depressive heat and upward counterflow.

LIVER-SPLEEN DISHARMONY: *Xiao Yao San* (Rambling Powder)

INGREDIENTS: Radix Bupleuri (*Chai Hu*), 6-10g, Radix Angelicae Sinensis (*Dang Gui*), 6-10g, Radix Albus Paeoniae Lactiflorae (*Bai Shao*), 6-10g, Rhizoma Atractylodis Macrocephalae (*Bai Zhu*), 6-10g, Sclerotium Poriae Cocos (*Fu Ling*), 6-10g, mix-fried Radix Glycyrrhizae (*Gan Cao*), 3-6g, Herba Menthae Haplocalycis (*Bo He*), 3-6g, uncooked Rhizoma Zingiberis (*Sheng Jiang*), 2-3 slices

FUNCTIONS: Courses the liver and rectifies the qi, fortifies the spleen and eliminates dampness, nourishes and harmonizes the blood

INDICATIONS: Emotional tension and depression, irritability, fatigue, lack of strength, chest oppression, breast, rib-side, and abdominal distention and pain, sighing, a swollen, pale but dark tongue with thin, white fur, and a bowstring, fine pulse

LIVER-SPLEEN DISHARMONY W/ DEPRESSIVE HEAT IN THE BLOOD DIVISION: *Dan Zhi Xiao Yao San* (Moutan & Gardenia Rambling Powder)

INGREDIENTS: Cortex Radicis Moutan (*Dan Pi*), 6-10g, Fructus Gardeniae Jasminoidis (*Zhi Zi*), 6-10g, Radix Bupleuri (*Chai Hu*), 6-10g, Radix Angelicae Sinensis (*Dang Gui*), 6-10g, Radix Albus Paeoniae Lactiflorae (*Bai Shao*), 6-10g, Rhizoma Atractylodis Macrocephalae (*Bai Zhu*), 6-10g, Sclerotium Poriae Cocos (*Fu Ling*), 6-10g, mix-fried Radix Glycyrrhizae (*Gan Cao*), 3-6g, Herba Menthae Haplocalycis (*Bo He*), 3-6g, uncooked Rhizoma Zingiberis (*Sheng Jiang*), 2-3 slices

FUNCTIONS: Courses the liver and rectifies the qi, clears heat and resolves depression, fortifies the spleen and eliminates dampness, nourishes and harmonizes the blood

INDICATIONS: Emotional tension and depression, irritability, fatigue, lack of strength, chest oppression, breast, rib-side, and abdominal distention and pain, sighing, a bitter taste in the mouth, a swollen, dark red tongue with thin, yellow fur, and a rapid, bowstring, fine pulse

LIVER-SPLEEN DISHARMONY W/ DEPRESSIVE HEAT IN THE LUNGS, STOMACH, INTESTINES, LIVER AND/OR GALL-BLADDER: *Xiao Chai Hu Tang* (Minor Bupleurum Decoction)

INGREDIENTS: Radix Bupleuri (*Chai Hu*), 6-10g, Radix Codonopsitis Pilosulae (*Dang Shen*), 10-12g, Rhizoma Pinelliae Ternatae (*Ban Xia*), 6-10g, Radix Scutellariae Baicalensis (*Huang Qin*), 6-10g, mix-fried Radix Glycyrrhizae (*Gan Cao*), 3-6g, uncooked Rhizoma Zingiberis (*Sheng Jiang*), 2-3 slices, Fructus Zizyphi Jujubae (*Da Zao*), 2-3 pieces

FUNCTIONS: Courses the liver and rectifies the qi, fortifies the spleen and boosts the qi, clears heat and transforms phlegm

INDICATIONS: Emotional depression, irritability, profuse dreams, a bitter taste in the mouth, fatigue, profuse phlegm, possible nausea, possible chest and abdominal fullness and distention, a swollen tongue with teeth-marks on its edges and yellow or yellow and white fur, and a slippery, bowstring, rapid pulse

LIVER-SPLEEN DISHARMONY W/ DEPRESSIVE HEAT & SPIRIT DISQUIET: *Chai Hu Jia Long Mu Tang* (Bupleurum Plus Dragon Bone & Oyster Shell Decoction)

INGREDIENTS: Radix Bupleuri (*Chai Hu*), 6-10g, Radix Scutellariae Baicalensis (*Huang Qin*), 6-10g, Rhizoma Pinelliae Ternatae (*Ban Xia*), 6-10g, Radix Codonopsitis Pilosulae (*Dang Shen*), 6-10g, Sclerotium Poriae Cocos (*Fu Ling*), 6-10g, Concha Ostreae (*Mu Li*), 10-12g, Os Draconis (*Long Gu*), 10-12g, Ramulus Cinnamomi Cassiae (*Gui Zhi*), 3-6g, Radix Et Rhizoma Rhei (*Da Huang*), 3-6g, uncooked Rhizoma Zingiberis (*Sheng Jiang*), 2-3 slices, Fructus Zizyphi Jujubae (*Da Zao*), 2-3 pieces

FUNCTIONS: Harmonizes the liver and spleen, clears heat, transforms phlegm, and quiets the spirit

INDICATIONS: Withdrawal and mania, irritability, heart palpitations, insomnia, chest oppression, deranged speech, a red tongue with slimy or dry yellow fur, and a bowstring, rapid pulse

YIN VACUITY-FIRE EFFULGENCE: *Zhi Bai Di Huang Wan* (Anemarrhena & Phellodendron Rehmannia Pills)

INGREDIENTS: Rhizoma Anemarrhenae Aspheloidis (*Zhi*

*Mu*), 6-10g, Cortex Phellodendri (*Huang Bai*), 6-10g, uncooked Radix Rehmanniae (*Sheng Di*), 12-15g, Fructus Corni Officinalis (*Shan Zhu Yu*), 6-10g, Radix Dioscoreae Oppositae (*Shan Yao*), 6-10g, Sclerotium Poriae Cocos (*Fu Ling*), 6-10g, Rhizoma Alismatis (*Ze Xie*), 6-10g, Cortex Radicis Moutan (*Dan Pi*), 3-6g

FUNCTIONS: Clears heat and drains fire, enriches yin and supplements the kidneys

INDICATIONS: Agitation, mania, restlessness, insomnia, profuse dreams, dizziness, low back and knee soreness and limpness, flushed red cheeks, tidal heat, vexatious heat in the hands and feet, night sweats, a red tongue with scanty, yellow fur, and a fine, rapid or surging, rapid pulse

KIDNEY ESSENCE INSUFFICIENCY: *Gui Lu Er Xian Jiao* (Turtle & Deer Two Immortals Glue)

INGREDIENTS: Cornu Cervi (*Lu Jiao*), 12-15g, Plastrum Testudinis (*Gui Ban*), 12-15g, Fructus Lycii Chinensis (*Gou Qi Zi*), 10-15g, Radix Panacis Ginseng (*Ren Shen*), 3-6g

FUNCTIONS: Boosts the essence and fills the marrow

INDICATIONS: Feeble-mindedness, impaired memory, lassitude of the spirit, lack of strength, low back and knee soreness and limpness, and a weak or faint pulse

---

NOTE: When essence insufficiency complicates other patterns, the animal ingredients from this formula can be added to other formulas.

---

**NONINTERACTION BETWEEN THE HEART & KIDNEYS:** With kidney yin vacuity, use *Huang Lian E Jiao Tang* (Coptis & Donkey Skin Glue Decoction)

INGREDIENTS: Rhizoma Coptidis Chinensis (*Huang Lian*), 3-6g, Gelatinum Corii Asini (*E Jiao*), 10-12g, Radix Scutellariae Baicalensis (*Huang Qin*), 10-12g, Radix Albus Paeoniae Lactiflorae (*Bai Shao*), 10-12g, egg yolk (*Ji Zi Huang*), 2 pieces

FUNCTIONS: Drains fire and enriches yin, promotes the interaction of the heart and kidneys

INDICATIONS: Mania, vexation and agitation, insomnia, heart palpitations, a dry mouth and throat, a red tongue with even redder tip and scanty fur, and a fine, rapid, or rapid, surging pulse

With kidney yang vacuity, use *Jiao Tai Wan* (Peaceful Interaction Pills)

INGREDIENTS: Rhizoma Coptidis Chinensis (*Huang Lian*), 18g, Cortex Cinnamomi Cassiae (*Rou Gui*), 3g

FUNCTIONS: Drains and leads fire to move downwards to its lower source, promotes the interaction of the heart and kidneys

INDICATIONS: Mania, vexation and agitation, insomnia, heart palpitations, a dry mouth and throat, cold lower limbs, a red tongue with even redder tip and scanty fur, and a fine, rapid, or rapid, surging pulse

HEART FIRE EFFULGENCE: *San Huang Xie Xin Tang* (Three Yellows Drain the Heart Decoction)

INGREDIENTS: Radix Et Rhizoma Rhei (*Da Huang*), 3-6g, Radix Scutellariae Baicalensis (*Huang Qin*), 6-10g, Rhizoma Coptidis Chinensis (*Huang Lian*), 3-6g

FUNCTIONS: Clears the heart and drains fire

INDICATIONS: Mania, vexation and agitation, heart palpitations, insomnia, constipation, a red tongue tip with possible sores and slimy, yellow fur, and a slippery, rapid pulse

HEART FIRE TRANSMITTED TO THE SMALL INTESTINE: *Dao Chi San* (Abduct the Red Powder)

INGREDIENTS: uncooked Radix Rehmanniae (*Sheng Di*), 10-15g, Caulis Akebiae (*Mu Tong*), 10-12g, Folium Bambusae (*Zhu Ye*), 6-10g, Extremitas Radicis Glycyrrhizae (*Gan Cao Xiao*), 3-6g

FUNCTIONS: Clears the heart and drains fire, seeps dampness and frees the flow of strangury

INDICATIONS: Mania, anxiety, vexation and agitation, restlessness, insomnia, heart palpitations, burning hot, reddish urination, sores on the tip of the tongue, a red tongue tip, and a slippery, rapid pulse

HEART QI VACUITY: *Ding Zhi Wan* (Stabilize the Mind Pills)

INGREDIENTS: Radix Panacis Ginseng (*Ren Shen*), 3-6g,

Sclerotium Poriae Cocos (*Fu Ling*), 10-12g, Rhizoma Acori Graminei (*Shi Chang Pu*), 6-10g, Radix Polygalae Tenuifoliae (*Yuan Zhi*), 6-10g

FUNCTIONS: Supplements and boosts the heart qi, quiets the spirit and stabilizes the mind

INDICATIONS: Apprehensiveness, susceptibility to fear and fright, incessant laughter, a tendency to joy, heart palpitations, anxiety, impaired memory, fatigue, lack of strength, and a weak pulse

HEART SPIRIT DEPRIVED OF NOURISHMENT: *Gan Mai Da Zao Tang* (Licorice, Wheat & Red Dates Decoction)

INGREDIENTS: mix-fried Radix Glycyrrhizae (*Gan Cao*), 10-12g, Fructus Tritici Aestivi (*Huai Xiao Mai*), 30-50g, Fructus Zizyphi Jujubae (*Da Zao*), 10-15 pieces

FUNCTIONS: Nourishes the heart and quiets the spirit, relaxes tension and harmonizes the center

INDICATIONS: Visceral agitation, vexation and agitation, restlessness, insomnia, profuse dreams, alternating bouts of laughing and crying for no reason, frequent yawning, a red or pale red tongue with scanty fur, and a fine, possibly rapid pulse

HEART QI & YIN VACUITY: *Tian Wang Bu Xin Dan* (Heavenly Emperor Supplement the Heart Elixir)

INGREDIENTS: uncooked Radix Rehmanniae (*Sheng Di*), 10-15g, Radix Scrophulariae Ningpoensis (*Xuan Shen*), 10-12g, Tuber Ophiopogonis Japonici (*Mai Dong*), 10-12g, Tuber Asparagi Cochinensis (*Tian Men Dong*), 10-12g, Radix Salviae Miltiorrhizae (*Dan Shen*), 10-12g, Radix Angelicae Sinensis (*Dang Gui*), 6-10g, Sclerotium Pararadicis Poriae Cocos (*Fu Shen*), 10-12g, Semen Biotae Orientalis (*Bai Zi Ren*), 10-12g, Radix Polygalae Tenuifoliae (*Yuan Zhi*), 6-10g, Fructus Schisandrae Chinensis (*Wu Wei Zi*), 10-12g, Semen Zizyphi Spinosae (*Suan Zao Ren*), 10-12g, Radix Platycodi Grandiflori (*Jie Geng*), 6-10g, Radix Panacis Ginseng (*Ren Shen*), 3-6g, Cinnabar (*Zhu Sha*), 1-3g

FUNCTIONS: Nourishes heart and kidney yin, fortifies the spleen and boosts the qi, quiets the spirit and stabilizes the mind

INDICATIONS: Insomnia, profuse dreams, heart palpitations, impaired memory, lassitude of the spirit, lack of strength, a red tongue with scanty fur, and a fine, rapid pulse

HEART-LUNG YIN VACUITY: *Bai He Di Huang Tang* (Lily & Rehmannia Decoction)

INGREDIENTS: Bulbus Lilii (*Bai He*), 30-60g, uncooked Radix Rehmanniae (*Sheng Di*), 15g

FUNCTIONS: Enriches heart and lung yin, clears vacuity heat

INDICATIONS: Lily disease, emotional instability, vexation and agitation, chaotic thinking, restlessness, an unpleasant taste in the mouth, a red tongue with scanty or no fur, and a fine, possibly rapid pulse

HEART-SPLEEN DUAL VACUITY: *Gui Pi Tang* (Restore the Spleen Decoction)

INGREDIENTS: Radix Codonopsitis Pilosulae (*Dang Shen*), 10-12g, Radix Astragali Membranacei (*Huang Qi*), 10-18g, Radix Angelicae Sinensis (*Dang Gui*), 6-10g, Arillus Euphoriae Longanae (*Long Yan Rou*), 10-12g, Rhizoma Atractylodis Macrocephalae (*Bai Zhu*), 6-10g, Sclerotium Poriae Cocos (*Fu Ling*), 10-12g, Radix Polygalae Tenuifoliae (*Yuan Zhi*), 6-10g, Semen Zizyphi Spinosae (*Suan Zao Ren*), 10-12g, mix-fried Radix Glycyrrhizae (*Gan Cao*), 6-10g

FUNCTIONS: Supplements the heart and nourishes the blood, fortifies the spleen and boosts the qi, quiets the spirit and stabilizes the mind

INDICATIONS: Insomnia, profuse dreams, impaired memory, heart palpitations, a pale white or sallow yellow facial complexion, pale lips and nails, dry skin, lassitude of the spirit, lack of strength, a pale, swollen tongue with teethmarks on its edges and thin, white fur, and a fine, forceless pulse

SPLEEN-KIDNEY YANG VACUITY: *Fu Zi Li Zhong Tang* (Aconite Rectify the Center Decoction)

INGREDIENTS: Radix Lateralis Praeparatus Aconiti Carmichaeli (*Fu Zi*), 3-6g, Radix Panacis Ginseng (*Ren Shen*), 10-15g, Rhizoma Atractylodis Macrocephalae (*Bai Zhu*), 6-10g, dry Rhizoma Zingiberis (*Gan Jiang*), 6-10g, mix-fried Radix Glycyrrhizae (*Gan Cao*), 3-6g

FUNCTIONS: Fortifies the spleen and supplements the kidneys, warms yang and scatters cold

INDICATIONS: Withdrawal, lassitude of the spirit, fatigue, somnolence, cold hands and feet, loose stools, possible daybreak diarrhea, a fat tongue with teeth-marks on its edges and white, wet fur, and a deep, slow, faint pulse

**LUNG-SPLEEN QI VACUITY:** *Bu Zhong Yi Qi Tang* (Supplement the Center & Boost the Qi Decoction)

**INGREDIENTS:** Radix Astragali Membranacei (*Huang Qi*), 10-18g, Radix Codonopsitis Pilosulae (*Dang Shen*), 10-12g, Rhizoma Atractylodis Macrocephalae (*Bai Zhu*), 10-12g, mix-fried Radix Glycyrrhizae (*Gan Cao*), 6-10g, Radix Angelicae Sinensis (*Dang Gui*), 6-10g, Radix Bupleuri (*Chai Hu*), 3-10g, Rhizoma Pericarpium Citri Reticulatae (*Chen Pi*), 3-6g, Rhizoma Cimicifugae (*Sheng Ma*), 3-6g

**FUNCTIONS:** Fortifies the spleen and boosts the qi, disinhibits the qi mechanism and upbears yang

**INDICATIONS:** Emotional depression, withdrawal, somnolence, lassitude of the spirit, fatigue, lack of strength, spontaneous perspiration, disinclination to speak and/or a weak voice, dizziness standing up, loose stools or diarrhea, a fat tongue with teeth-marks on its edges and thin, white fur, and a fine, weak, or short pulse

**SPLEEN VACUITY WITH DAMP ENCUMBRANCE:** *Wei Ling San* (Stomach Poria Powder)

**INGREDIENTS:** Rhizoma Alismatis (*Ze Xie*), 10-12g, Sclerotium Poriae Cocos (*Fu Ling*), 10-12g, Sclerotium Polypori Umbellati (*Zhu Ling*), 10-12g, Ramulus Cinnamomi Cassiae (*Gui Zhi*), 3-6g, Rhizoma Atractylodis Macrocephalae (*Bai Zhu*), 6-10g, Cortex Magnoliae Officinalis (*Hou Po*), 6-10g, Pericarpium Citri Reticulatae (*Chen Pi*), 3-6g, Radix Glycyrrhizae (*Gan Cao*), 1-3g, uncooked Rhizoma Zingiberis (*Sheng Jiang*), 1-3 slices, Fructus Zizyphi Jujubae (*Da Zao*), 3-5 pieces

**FUNCTIONS:** Dispels dampness and downbears turbidity, arouses the spleen and disinhibits the qi mechanism

**INDICATIONS:** Confused thinking, impaired memory, heavy-headedness, somnolence, lassitude of the spirit, nausea, chest and abdominal fullness and distention, edema of the face and eyes, watery diarrhea, slimy, white tongue fur, and a soggy, slippery pulse

**YANG MING REPLETE HEAT:** *Da Cheng Qi Tang* (Major Order the Qi Decoction)

**INGREDIENTS:** Radix Et Rhizoma Rhei (*Da Huang*), 10-12g, Mirabilitum (*Mang Xiao*), 6-10g, Cortex Magnoliae Officinalis (*Hou Po*), 10-12g, Fructus Immaturus Citri Aurantii (*Zhi Shi*), 6-10g

**FUNCTIONS:** Drains replete heat from the yang ming and precipitates accumulation

**INDICATIONS:** Withdrawal and mania, epilepsy, vexation and agitation, irascibility, constipation with dry, bound stools, dry, yellow tongue fur, and a deep, forceful pulse

**QI STAGNATION & BLOOD STASIS:** *Xue Fu Zhu Yu Tang* (Blood Mansion Dispel Stasis Decoction)

**INGREDIENTS:** Semen Pruni Persicae (*Tao Ren*), 10-12g, Flos Carthami Tinctorii (*Hong Hua*), 6-10g, Radix Angelicae Sinensis (*Dang Gui*), 6-10g, Radix Ligustici Wallichii (*Chuan Xiong*), 3-6g, Radix Rubrus Paeoniae Lactiflorae (*Chi Shao*), 6-10g, Radix Cyathulae (*Chuan Niu Xi*), 6-10g, Radix Bupleuri (*Chai Hu*), 3-10g, Radix Platycodi Grandiflori (*Jie Geng*), 3-6g, Fructus Citri Aurantii (*Zhi Ke*), 6-10g, uncooked Radix Rehmanniae (*Sheng Di*), 6-12g, Radix Glycyrrhizae (*Gan Cao*), 3-6g

**FUNCTIONS:** Moves the qi and quickens the blood, dispels stasis and stops pain

**INDICATIONS:** Insomnia, profuse dreams, irritability, hysteria, epilepsy, emotional upset which is worse at night, chronic, severe, and/or fixed pain, particularly in the chest or head, varicosities, hemangiomas, liver spots, a sooty black facial complexion, a dark and/or purple tongue or static spots or macules on the tongue, and a bowstring, choppy pulse

**PHLEGM QI DEPRESSION & BINDING:** *Ban Xia Hou Po Tang* (Pinellia & Magnolia Decoction)

**INGREDIENTS:** Rhizoma Pinelliae Ternatae (*Ban Xia*), 6-10g, Cortex Magnoliae Officinalis (*Hou Po*), 6-10g, Folium Perillae Frutescentis (*Zi Su Ye*), 6-10g, Sclerotium Poriae Cocos (*Fu Ling*), 10-12g, uncooked Rhizoma Zingiberis (*Sheng Jiang*), 3-5 slices

**FUNCTIONS:** Rectifies the qi and disperses glomus, downbears counterflow and transforms phlegm

**INDICATIONS:** Plum pit qi, anxiety, depression, chest and abdominal oppression and distention, slimy, white tongue fur, and a bowstring, slippery pulse

**PHLEGM FIRE HARASSING ABOVE:** *Sheng Tie Luo Yin* (Uncooked Iron Filings Drink)

**INGREDIENTS:** uncooked Frusta Ferri (*Tie Luo*), 30-60g, bile-processed Rhizoma Arisaematis (*Dan Nan Xing*), 6-10g, Bulbus Fritillariae Thunbergii (*Zhe Bei Mu*), 6-10g, Radix Scrophulariae Ningpoensis (*Xuan Shen*), 10-15g, Tuber Asparagi Cochinensis (*Tian Men Dong*), 10-12g, Tuber Ophiopogonis Japonici (*Mai Dong*), 10-12g, Fructus Forsythiae Suspensae (*Lian Qiao*), 6-10g, Ramulus Uncariae Cum Uncis (*Gou Teng*), 10-15g, Radix Salviae Miltiorrhizae (*Dan Shen*), 6-10g, Sclerotium Poriae Cocos (*Fu Ling*), 6-10g, Sclerotium Pararadicis Poriae Cocos (*Fu Shen*), 6-10g, Pericarpium Citri Reticulatae (*Chen Pi*), 6-10g, Rhizoma Acori Graminei (*Shi Chang Pu*), 6-10g, Radix Polygalae Tenuifoliae (*Yuan Zhi*), 6-10g, Cinnabar (*Zhu Sha*), 1-3g

**FUNCTIONS:** Drains the heart, eliminates phlegm, and quiets the spirit

**INDICATIONS:** Mania, vexation and agitation, irascibility, insomnia, extreme emotional instability, shouting and yelling at people for no apparent reason, a crimson tongue with slimy, yellow fur, and a bowstring, slippery, rapid pulse

**STASIS & PHLEGM MUTUALLY BINDING:** *Dian Kuang Meng Xing Tang* (Withdrawal & Mania Dream-walking Decoction)

**INGREDIENTS:** Semen Pruni Persicae (*Tao Ren*), 12-24g, Radix Rubrus Paeoniae Lactiflorae (*Chi Shao*), 10-12g, Radix Bupleuri (*Chai Hu*), 6-10g, Pericarpium Arecae Catechu (*Da Fu Pi*), 6-10g, Rhizoma Cyperi Rotundi (*Xiang Fu*), 6-10g, Pericarpium Citri Reticulatae Viride (*Qing Pi*), 6-10g, Fructus Perillae Frutescentis (*Zi Su Zi*), 12-18g, Pericarpium Citri Reticulatae (*Chen Pi*), 10-12g, Rhizoma Pinelliae Ternatae (*Ban Xia*), 6-10g, Caulis Akebiae (*Mu Tong*), 10-12g, Cortex Radicis Mori Albi (*Sang Bai Pi*), 10-12g, Radix Glycyrrhizae (*Gan Cao*), 10-15g

**FUNCTIONS:** Quickens the blood and dispels stasis, moves the qi and abducts phlegm

**INDICATIONS:** Withdrawal & mania, incessant crying, manic laughing, obsessive swearing or singing, a dark, purplish tongue with possible static spots or macules and slimy fur, and a slippery, bowstring, choppy pulse

# 5

# SPIRIT-QUIETING, MIND-STABILIZING ACUPUNCTURE POINTS

The following is a list of psycho-emotional indications for points on the 14 channels as well as several of the most commonly used extra channel points for essence spirit diseases. These indications are based on Andrew Ellis *et al.*'s *Fundamental of Chinese Acupuncture*[1] and Peter Deadman and Mazin Al-Khafaji's article, "The Treatment of Psycho-emotional Disturbance by Acupuncture with Particular Reference to the Du Mai."[2]

**SHANG YANG (LU 1):** Clouding reversal

**TIAN FU (LU 3):** Somnolence, insomnia, sadness, weeping, abstraction of the spirit, impaired memory

**TAI YUAN (LU 9):** Manic raving, agitation

**HE GU (LI 4):** Mania

**YANG XI (LI 5):** Withdrawal & mania, tendency to laughter, susceptibility to fright, seeing ghosts

**TAI YI (ST 23):** Withdrawal & mania, agitation, manic walking

**QI CHONG (ST 30):** Running piglet

**ZU SAN LI (ST 36):** Vexation & agitation, chest oppression, epilepsy, heart palpitations due to vacuity

**FENG LONG (ST 40):** Epilepsy, mania & withdrawal, heart vexation, seeing ghosts, mad laughter

**JIE XI (ST 41):** Deranged speech, fright palpitations, fearful throbbing, mania & withdrawal

**CHONG YANG (ST 42):** Withdrawal & mania

**LI DUI (ST 45):** Withdrawal & mania, profuse dreams, susceptibility to fright, insomnia

**YIN BAI (SP 1):** Withdrawal & mania, profuse dreams, insomnia, vexation and agitation

**GONG SUN (SP 4):** Withdrawal & mania, insomnia, susceptibility to fright, frequent sighing

**SHANG QIU (SP 5):** Withdrawal & mania, anxiety & thinking, nightmares, tendency to laughter

**SAN YIN JIAO (SP 6):** Insomnia, heart palpitations, gallbladder timidity

**SHAO HAI (HT 3):** Impaired memory, mania

**TONG LI (HT 5):** Heart palpitations, fearful throbbing, dizziness, sudden loss of voice, fear of people

**YIN XI (HT 6):** Fright palpitations

**SHEN MEN (HT 7):** Heart vexation, withdrawal & mania, fright palpitations, fearful throbbing, insomnia, epilepsy, a tendency to laughing, impaired memory, visceral agitation, loss of voice, sighing, sadness, talking during sleep

**SHAO FU (HT 8):** Heart palpitations, heart vexation, sorrow, fear, fear of people, sighing, plum pit qi

**SHAO CHONG (HT 9):** Withdrawal & mania, clouding reversal, vexation & agitation, fearful throbbing

**HOU XI (SI 3):** Withdrawal & mania

**YANG GU (SI 5):** Plum pit qi, madness

**ZHI ZHENG (SI 7):** Withdrawal & mania, fright, fear, sorrow, anxiety

**XIAO HAI (SI 8):** Heart vexation, madness

**TING GONG (SI 19):** Madness

**LUO QUE (BL 8):** Withdrawal & mania

**TIAN ZHU (BL 10):** Epilepsy, mania, ceaseless talking, seeing ghosts

**XIN SHU (BL 15):** Epilepsy, fright palpitations, impaired memory, withdrawal & mania

**GE SHU (BL 17):** Withdrawal & mania

**GAN SHU (BL 18):** Withdrawal & mania, epilepsy, profuse anger

**DAN SHU (BL 19):** Irritability, fright palpitations, insomnia

**PI SHU (BL 20):** Lassitude of the spirit

**GAO HUNG SHU (BL 43):** Impaired memory, heart palpitations, insomnia, phlegm fire mania

**PU CAN (BL 61):** Withdrawal & mania, epilepsy

**SHEN MAI (BL 62):** Withdrawal & mania, epilepsy, heart palpitations, insomnia

**JING GU (BL 64):** Withdrawal & mania, epilepsy, heart palpitations

**SHU GU (BL 65):** Withdrawal & mania

**TONG GU (BL 66):** Withdrawal & mania, susceptibility to fright

**YONG QUAN (KI 1):** Clouding reversal, madness, running piglet, heart vexation, irritability, impaired memory, loss of voice, desire to kill people

**TAI XI (KI 3):** Insomnia, profuse dreams, impaired memory

**DA ZHONG (KI 4):** Feeblemindedness, susceptibility to fear and fright, irritability, vexation & oppression, insufficiency of spirit qi, somnolence, agoraphobia

**ZHAO HAI (KI 6):** Epilepsy, running piglet, insomnia, somnolence, nightmares

**FU LIU (KI 7):** Excessive talkativeness, irritability

**ZHU BIN (KI 9):** Withdrawal & mania

**YIN GU (KI 10):** Withdrawal & mania

**QI XUE (KI 13):** Running piglet

**SI MAN (KI 14):** Running piglet

**TONG GU (KI 20):** Heart palpitations, spirit mind abstraction

**TIAN QUAN (PER 2):** Heart palpitations

**QU ZE (PER 3):** Vexation & agitation, heart palpitations, susceptibility to fright

**XI MEN (PER 4):** Heart palpitations, heart vexation, fear & fright, fear of people, insomnia, sadness

**JIAN SHI (PER 5):** Heart palpitations, vexation & agitation, withdrawal & mania, epilepsy, impaired memory, apprehensivness, manic raving, loss of voice

**NEI GUAN (PER 6):** Heart palpitations, withdrawal & mania, epilepsy, impaired memory

**DA LING (PER 7):** Heart palpitations, withdrawal & mania, fright & fear, incessant laughter, heart vexation, sorrow & joy, laughing & crying without constancy

**LAO GONG (PER 8):** Withdrawal & mania, epilepsy, irritability, apprehensiveness, elation, ceaseless laughter, visceral agitation

ZHONG CHONG (PER 9): Fright reversal, clouding reversal, heart vexation, chest oppression

GUAN CHONG (TB 1): Heart vexation

YE MEN (TB 2): Fright palpitations, deranged speech

YANG CHI (TB 4): Heart vexation and chest oppression

SAN YANG LUO (TB 8): Essence spirit listlessness & exhaustion

TIAN JING (TB 10): Plum pit qi, epilepsy

QING LENG YUAN (TB 11): Epilepsy

XIAO LUO (TB 12): Madness

YI FENG (TB 17): Convulsions, mania

CHI MAI (TB 18): Epilepsy, fright & fear

LU XI (TB 19): Insomnia, fright & fear

HE LIAO (TB 22): Convulsions

SI ZHU KONG (TB 23): Epilepsy, mania

TIAN CHONG (GB 9): Madness, wind tetany, susceptibility to fright and fear

WAN GU (GB 12): Insomnia, heart vexation

BEN SHEN (GB 13): Epilepsy

NAO KONG (GB 19): Manic disorders, heart palpitations

FENG CHI (GB 20): Epilepsy, insomnia, madness

ZHE JIN (GB 23): Sighing, tendency to sadness, insomnia

RI YUE (GB 24): Sighing, sorrowfulness

YANG LING QUAN (GB 34): Sighing

YANG JIAO (GB 35): Fright mania

WAI QIU (GB 36): Madness

GUANG MING (GB 37): Grinding teeth

ZU QIAO YIN (GB 44): Nightmares, insomnia, agitation, restlessness

DA DUN (LIV 1): Worried oppression

XING JIAN (LIV 2): Epilepsy, consulsive spasms, insomnia

TAI CONG (LIV 3): Epilepsy, insomnia, fright wind

LI GOU (LIV 5): Plum pit qi, fright palpitations, depression, fear & fright

QU QUAN (LIV 8): Fright mania

ZHANG MEN (LIV 13): Susceptibility to fear, easy anger, insomnia, manic walking, epilepsy, depression

QI MEN (LIV 14): Running piglet

HUI YIN (CV 1): Withdrawal & mania

ZHONG JI (CV 3): Running piglet

GUAN YUAN (CV 4): Running piglet

YIN JIAO (CV 7): Running piglet

ZHONG WAN (CV 12): Urgent or chronic fright wind, withdrawal & mania, running piglet

SHANG WAN (CV 13): Epilepsy, running piglet, heart vexation

JU QUE (CV 14): Withdrawal & mania, epilepsy, heart palpitations, deranged speech, manic rage

JIU WEI (CV 15): Epilepsy, withdrawal & mania, fright palpitations, manic walking, mad singing, dislike of the sound of the human voice

DAN ZHONG (CV 17): Heart palpitations

CHENG JIANG (CV 24): Withdrawal & mania

CHANG QIANG (GV 1): Withdrawal & mania, fright epilepsy

YAO SHU (GV 2): Epilepsy

JI ZHONG (GV 6): Epilepsy

JIN SUO (GV 8): Epilepsy, mania, manic walking, anger damaging the liver

SHEN DAO (GV 11): Impaired memory, fright palpitations, wind epilepsy, distraction, sorrow, worry

SHEN ZHU (GV 12): Epilepsy, manic walking, deranged speech, seeing ghosts, rage with desire to kill people

DA ZHUI (GV 14): Epilepsy

YA MEN (GV 15): Withdrawal & mania, epilepsy

FENG FU (GV 16): Withdrawal & mania, manic walking, ceaseless talking, fright palpitations, suicidal thoughts, sadness

NAO HU (GV 17): Epilepsy

QIANG JIAN (GV 18): Withdrawal & mania, epilepsy

HOU DING (GV 19): Withdrawal & mania, epilepsy

BAI HUI (GV 20): Withdrawal & mania, fright palpitations, impaired memory, epilepsy, heart vexation

QIAN DING (GV 21): Epilepsy

XIN HUI (GV 22): Epilepsy, insomnia, somnolence

SHANG XING (GV 23): Withdrawal & mania

SHEN TING (GV 24): Epilepsy, fright palpitations, insomnia, madness

REN ZHONG (GV 26): Withdrawal & mania, epilepsy, clouding reversal, laughing & crying without constancy, speaking without awareness of a person's high or low status

DUI DUAN (GV 27): Withdrawal & mania

YIN JIAO (GV 28): Withdrawal & mania

SI SHEN CONG (M-HN-1): Withdrawal & mania, epilepsy

YIN TANG (M-HN-3): Insomnia

AN MIAN (N-HN-22): Insomnia, mania, hysteria

## ENDNOTES:

[1]Ellis, Andrew, Wiseman, Nigel & Boss, Ken, *Fundamentals of Chinese Acupuncture*, Paradigm Publications, Brookline, MA, 1988

[2]Deadman, Peter & Al-Khafaji, Mazin, "The Treatment of Psycho-emotional Disturbance by Acupuncture with Particular Reference to the Du Mai," *The Journal of Chinese Medicine*, #47, 1995, p. 30-34

# ❖ 6 ❖

# ACUPUNCTURE FORMULAS FOR COMMONLY SEEN PSYCHIATRIC PATTERNS

Below are the most commonly seen patterns in psycho-emotional diseases. Following each pattern name are several of the main or ruling points for the treatment of that pattern. In real-life practice, depending upon how these patterns combine, other points might be chosen instead. In addition, depending on the patient's main symptoms and complaints, points which are empirically known to be effective for certain signs and symptoms will typically be added to these ruling points.

**LIVER QI DEPRESSION & BINDING:** *Tai Chong* (Liv 3), *He Gu* (LI 4)

**LIVER DEPRESSION TRANSFORMING HEAT:** *Xing Jian* (Liv 2), *Yang Ling Quan* (GB 34)

**LIVER BLOOD-KIDNEY YIN VACUITY:** *Ge Shu* (Bl 17), *Gan Shu* (Bl 18), *Shen Shu* (Bl 23), *Qu Quan* (Liv 8), *Tai Xi* (Ki 3), *San Yin Jiao* (Sp 6)

**LIVER WIND STIRRING INTERNALLY:** Add *Feng Chi* (GB 20) & *Feng Fu* (GV 16) to the above points.

**HEART-GALLBLADDER QI VACUITY:** *Xin Shu* (Bl 15), *Shen Men* (Ht 7), *Tai Chong* (Liv 3), *ZhongWan* (CV 12), *Feng Long* (St 40), *Nei Guan* (Per 6)

**LIVER-SPLEEN DISHARMONY:** *Tai Chong* (Liv 3), *Zu San Li* (St 36), *Zhang Men* (Liv 13), *Pi Shu* (Bl 20)

**KIDNEY ESSENCE INSUFFICIENCY:** *Guan Yuan* (CV 4), *Zhi Shi* (Bl 52), *Shen Shu* (Bl 23)

**NONINTERACTION BETWEEN THE HEART & KIDNEYS:** *Xin Shu* (Bl 15), *Shen Shu* (Bl 23), *Tai Xi* (Ki 3), *Shen Men* (Ht 7), *San Yin Jiao* (Sp 6)

**HEART FIRE EFFULGENCE:** *Shen Men* (Ht 7), *Lao Gong* (Per 8), *Zhong Ji* (CV 3), *Pang Guang Shu* (Bl 28)

**HEART-SPLEEN DUAL VACUITY:** *Xin Shu* (Bl 15), *Ge Shu* (Bl 17), *Pi Shu* (Bl 20), *Shen Men* (Ht 7), *Zu San Li* (St 36)

**SPLEEN-STOMACH VACUITY WEAKNESS:** *Pi Shu* (Bl 20), *Wei Shu* (Bl 21), *Zhong Wan* (CV 12), *Zu San Li* (St 36)

**SPLEEN-KIDNEY YANG VACUITY:** *Pi Shu* (Bl 20), *Wei Shu* (Bl 21), *Shen Shu* (Bl 23), *Ming Men* (GV 4)

**LUNG-SPLEEN QI VACUITY:** *Fei Shu* (Bl 13), *Pi Shu* (Bl 20), *Dan Zhong* (CV 17), *Zu San Li* (St 36)

**SPLEEN VACUITY WITH DAMP ENCUMBRANCE:** *Pi Shu* (Bl 20), *Shang Qi* (Sp 5), *Zu San Li* (St 36), *Zhong Wan* (Cv 12)

**YANG MING REPLETE HEAT:** *Nei Ting* (St 44), *Jie Xi* (St 41), *Tian Shu* (St 25), *Shen Men* (Ht 7), *Lao Gong* (Per 8)

**QI STAGNATION & BLOOD STASIS:** *Tai Zhong* (Liv 3), *He Gu* (LI 4), *Xue Hai* (Sp 10)

PHLEGM QI DEPRESSION & BINDING: *Tai Chong* (Liv 3), *Zhong Wan* (CV 12), *Feng Long* (St 40), *Nei Guan* (Per 6)

PHLEGM DAMPNESS OBSTRUCTING INTERNALLY: *Jiu Wei* (CV 15), *Zhong Wan* (CV 12), *Nei Guan* (Per 6), *Feng Long* (St 40)

PHLEGM FIRE HARASSING ABOVE: *Feng Fu* (GV 16), *Da Zhui* (GV 14), *Shen Zhu* (GV 12), *Lao Gong* (Per 8), *Feng Long* (St 40)

## COMMONLY USED ADJUNCTIVE POINTS IN THE TREATMENT OF PSYCHO-EMOTIONAL DISEASES:

One, some, or all of the following points may be added to the above formulas when the following patterns or symptoms complicate the above patterns.

SPLEEN QI VACUITY: *Pi Shu* (Bl 20), *Zu San Li* (St 36)

SPLEEN DAMPNESS: *Shang Qiu* (Sp 5), *Zu San Li* (St 36), *Zhong Wan* (CV 12)

PHLEGM TURBIDITY: *Feng Long* (St 40), *Zhong Wan* (CV 12)

HEART FIRE: *Da Ling* (Per 7), *Lao Gong* (Per 8)

HEART VACUITY: *Xin Shu* (Bl 15), *Jue Yin Shu* (Bl 14)

STOMACH HEAT: *Nei Ting* (St 44), *Jie Xi* (St 41)

STOMACH DISHARMONY: *Nei Guan* (Per 6), *Zhong Wan* (CV 12), *Zu San Li* (St 36)

LUNG HEAT: *Chi Ze* (Lu 5), *Lie Que* (Lu 7)

LUNG YIN VACUITY: *Lie Que* (Lu 7), *Zhao Hai* (Ki 6)

KIDNEY YIN VACUITY: *Tai Xi* (Ki 3), *San Yin Jiao* (Sp 6)

LIVER-GALLBLADDER HEAT: *Xing Jian* (Liv 2), *Yang Ling Quan* (GB 34)

URINARY BLADDER HEAT: *Zhong Ji* (CV 3), *Pang Guang Shu* (Bl 28)

DISQUIETED SPIRIT: *Shen Men* (Ht 7)

BLOOD HEAT: *Xue Hai* (Sp 10), *Qu Chi* (LI 11)

FOOD STAGNATION: *Nei Ting* (St 44), *Liang Men* (St 21), *Zhong Wan* (CV 12)

HEART PALPITATIONS: *Shen Men* (Ht 7), *Nei Guan* (Per 6), *Jian Shi* (Per 5), *Xin Shu* (Bl 15), *Dan Zhong* (CV 17)

INSOMNIA: *Shen Men* (Ht 7), *Nei Guan* (Per 6), *Yin Tang* (M-HN-3), *Bai Hui* (GV 20), *An Mian* (N-HN-22)

FATIGUE & SOMNOLENCE: *Zu San Li* (St 36), *Bai Hui* (GV 20)

NIGHT SWEATS: *Yin Xi* (Ht 6)

CONSTIPATION: *Nei Ting* (St 44), *Zhi Gou* (TB 6), *Zha Hai* (Ki 6), *Tian Shu* (St 25), *Da Chang Shu* (Bl 25)

PLUM PIT QI: *Tian Tu* (CV 22)

CHEST OPPRESSION: *Dan Zhong* (CV 17)

ABDOMINAL DISTENTION: *Zhang Men* (Liv 13), *Zhong Wan* (CV 12)

HEADACHE & DISTENTION: *Tai Yang* (M-HN-9), *Feng Chi* (GB 20)

DIZZINESS & VERTIGO: *Feng Chi* (GB 20), *Bai Hui* (GV 20)

SYNCOPE: *Ren Zhong* (GV 26), *Shi Xuan* (M-UE-1)

NIGHTMARES: *Hun Men* (Bl 47), *Po Hu* (Bl 42)

MANIA DUE TO HEAT: *Shi Xuan* (M-UE-1)

## LI DONG-YUAN'S YIN FIRE THEORY & ITS ACUPUNCTURE IMPLICATIONS

As we saw in Chapter 1 of this Book, Li Dong-yuan's yin fire theory often plays a part in mental-emotional diseases. If evil heat is engendered internally, whether due to spleen vacuity, liver depression, damp heat, yin blood vacuity, and/or stirring of ministerial fire, this heat will typically ascend to collect in and harass the heart spirit. However, the heart is a yin viscus and fire is a yang evil. Therefore, the yin heart has no intrinsic affinity for yang fire.[1] In addition, because the heart is the ruler of the entire body, if evils attack the heart, it can have drastic implications for the entire bodymind. Therefore, yang evils are commonly shunted to the heart's paired exterior yang channel, the hand small intestine channel. Where being yang, then tend to move upward to the head and neck region. Basing himself on Li Dong-yuan's yin fire theory, Zhu Dan-xi, the fourth of the four great masters of the Jin-Yuan dynasties, says, while explaining upper back and back of the neck pain:

> This [condition] must be due to the heart being damaged by thought and worry. Before the heart contracts disease, the bowel [i.e., the small intestine] becomes diseased. Therefore, the pain started from the scapula on the back.[2]

However, within Li-Zhu thought,[3] there is yet another explanation of how yin fire can move from the heart to the tai yang. The heart treasures the blood, the chong mai is the sea of blood, and the chong mai connects the heart to the lower burner. Therefore, according to Li Dong-yuan, heat in the heart may be transferred to the chong mai. The chong mai is yin and connects with the du mai which is yang. Being yin, the chong mai also has no intrinsic affinity for yang heat evils. Hence heat evils may shift from heart to chong mai to du mai where they counterflow up the governing vessel to flow over into the foot tai yang and thence into the hand tai yang, congesting in and causing symptoms in potentially all three of these yang channels.

> The pattern of center heat disease at the onset arises because the fire of the chong mai attaches itself to that which is inside the two yin[4] and is transmitted to the du mai. What is known as the governing vessel [begins at] *Chang Jiang* under the twenty-first vertebra and is a channel which mutually attaches to the foot tai yang urinary bladder cold qi. The du mai, when exuberant, runs like a great river or a rapidly galloping horse with an uncheckable tremendous momentum. [But] tai yang cold qi is as thin as a thread. When [fire] travels upward against the current of the tai yang cold qi, it surges into the top of the head, turns down the tip of the nose, and enters the hand tai yang in the chest The hand tai yang is *bing* [one of the two heavenly stems corresponding to fire] which is hot qi. The foot urinary bladder is *ren* which is cold qi. *Ren* is able to overwhelm *bing*. But as cold and heat counterflow in the chest, the pulse becomes large and exuberant. Since the hot qi of the hand tai yang small intestine cannot join and enter the urinary bladder channel, the qi of the other 11 channels becomes exuberant and [also] gathers in the chest.[5]

These theories help explain from a classical Chinese medical point of view why chong mai, du mai, small intestine, and urinary bladder points are so important in treating so many Western patients with mental-emotional disturbances. When patients suffer from one of the above scenarios, they typically have psychological complaints, such as insomnia, profuse dreams, irritability, depression, and/or susceptibility to fear and fright, with somatic complaints located along the course of one or more of these channels. Such somatic complaints may include chronic neck and shoulder tension and pain, headaches (both tension and neurovascular), allergic rhinitis, nasosinusitis, TMJ syndrome, and bruxism, to name the most commonly seen in Western clinical practice. In a lesser number of patients, somatic symptoms affecting the foot tai yang and shao yin may extend downward as well, including low back pain and weakness, sciatica, and urinary disturbances. Other symptoms, such as heart palpitations, chest oppression, and plum pit qi, may straddle the body-mind dichotomy. When patients with psycho-emotional problems manifest such a yin fire-chong mai-du mai-tai yang pattern, numerous points will be tender to palpation on these channels and vessels.

Six or seven years ago, Bob Flaws took the above theory and applied it to the acupuncture treatment of fibrocystic breast disease in women displaying a combination of patterns which added up to a yin fire scenario. While these patients' major complaint was premenstrual breast distention and pain and fibrocystic lumps in the breast, Bob Flaws found that all these patients also had one or more psycho-emotional complaints. Most of these women complained of premenstrual tension, irritability, anxiety, and/or depression. In addition, most of these women also suffered from insomnia, profuse dreams, and/or heart palpitations. Although Bob Flaws crafted the following acupuncture protocol as a treatment for yin fire breast disease, when he applied this treatment to these women, they not only reported the disappearance of their premenstrual breast distention and pain and fibrocystic lumps in their breasts but also said they slept much better, had no or fewer heart palpitations, and felt more emotionally stable. This protocol consists of three parts:

1. With the patient lying on their stomach, use a seven star hammer to skin needle the entire upper back from the level of *Ge Shu* (Bl 17) to *Da Zhui* (GV 14) between the medial margins of the scapula.

Seven star hammering should produce erythema of the treated area. Tapping should not be so forceful as to create bleeding. The redder the upper back becomes in response to this tapping, the more likely this protocol will achieve a significant effect. This tapping is to generally free the flow of the tai yang channel qi and disperse exuberant heat evils congesting and counterflowing in these channels.

2. With the patient lying on their back, insert fine gauge filiform needles at the following points: *Tai Chong* (Liv 3), *Tai Xi* (Ki 3), *Shen Mai* (Bl 62), *Hou Xi* (SI 3), *Nei Guan* (Per 6). Use shallow insertion and no or very light manual stimulation. If the patient has any one-sided or predominantly one-sided pathology, such as breast pain, neck or shoulder pain, headache, or TMJ pain, needle *Hou Xi* on the affected side and *Shen Mai* on the opposite side. If bodily discomfort is equally bilateral, then needle these two points bilaterally. In addition, needle all the other points bilaterally.

While these needles are passively retained, press the following points: *Bai Hui* (GV 20) to *Shen Ting* (GV 24), *Tong Tian* (Bl 7) to *Mei Chong* (Bl 3), *Zan Zhu* (Bl 2), *Yin Tang* (M-HN-3), *Tian Chuang* (SI 16) to *Ting Gong* (SI 19), *Zhong Fu* (Lu 1), *Dan Zhong* (CV 17), *Shu Fu* (Ki 27) to *Bu Lang* (Ki 22), and *Qi Tang* (Qi Court). This last point is an extra-channel point located lateral to *Tian Tu* (CV 22) at the anterior attachment of the sternocleidomastoid muscle at the sternoclavicular joint. Needle only those points which are markedly tender to palpation. Use one needle sparrow-pecking technique with shallow insertion and no retention. It will typically take 10-20 minutes using this in-and-out, one needle technique to needle all the tender points. At the end of this needling, remove all the other needles that have been passively retained.

3. With the patient once again lying on their stomach, press the following points: *Feng Chi* (GB 20), *Jian Jing* (GB 21), *Tian Zhu* (Bl 10), *Feng Fu* (GV 16), *Ya Men* (GV 15), *Da Zhui* (GV 14), the tips of the spinous processes from C7-T7, *Da Zhu* (Bl 11) to *Ge Shu* (Bl 17), *Po Hu* (Bl 42) to *Ge Guan* (Bl 46), and *Jian Zhen* (SI 9) to *Jian Zhong Shu* (SI 15). Using one needle sparrow-pecking technique, needle any of these points which are sore to palpation. If the patient has low back pain or dorsal aspect sciatica, continue pressing all the way down the bladder channel, needling all tender points to below the furthest site of discomfort.

If this protocol is truly indicated, the following points will typically be sore to palpation, though they may not be sore bilaterally symmetrically: *Dan Zhong* (CV 17), *Zhong Fu* (Lu 1), *Qi Tang* (Qi Court), *Tian Zong* (SI 11), *Jian Jing* (GB 21), and the tips of the 4th and 5th spinous processes. After needling all the *a shi* points both on the ventral and dorsal sides of the body, these points should be less tender to palpation. In addition, each successive time this treatment is done, less of these points should be tender to palpation. When Bob Flaws uses this protocol to treat benign breast complaints, he normally treats once a week for the first four weeks, once every other week for the next four weeks, and once at the end of the third month of treatment for a total of seven treatments. When mental-emotional disturbances are the major complaint, this treatment may be carried out two or three times per week depending on the severity of the disease.

In terms of the rationale of this protocol, although Dou Han-qing posited *Gong Sun* (Sp 4) and *Nei Guan* (Per 6) as the paired meeting points of the chong mai and yin wei mai, Bob Flaws prefers the combination of *Tai Chong* (Liv 3) and *Nei Guan*. In the *Nei Jing* (*Inner Classic*), *tai chong* is another name for the *chong mai*. Therefore, the ancients who named this point recognized this point's relationship with that vessel. It is Bob Flaws's belief that the combination of *Tai Chong* and *Nei Guan* rectifies and regulates the chong qi as well if not better than Dou's standard coupling. In addition, a liver-spleen disharmony typically sits at the center of most yin fire scenarios, and *Tai Chong* is the earth point on the wood channel. Therefore, it not only courses the liver and rectifies the qi, it harmonizes the liver and spleen. *Nei Guan* rectifies the jue yin qi, loosens the chest, and quiets the spirit. *Tai Xi* (Ki 3) is the source point of the kidneys, and kidney vacuity, whether yin or yang, also often plays a part in yin fire scenarios. If true yin is healthy and replete, it will be able to control upwardly stirring yang. *Hou Xi* (SI 3) and *Shen Mai* (Bl 62) are both main tai yang transport points which regulate the flow of qi in that channel. In addition, these two points are also Dou's paired meeting points for regulating the du mai and yang qiao mai.

As for the one needle sparrow-pecking technique at the *a shi* points, it is a statement of fact within Chinese medicine that, "If there is pain, there is no free flow." In the Tang dynasty, Sun Si-miao introduced the needling of *a shi* points and said that this technique was often the *sine qua non* of success with acupuncture. In Book 29 of Sun's *Qian Jin Yao Fang* (*Essential Formulas [Worth] a Thousand [Pieces of] Gold*), he says, "... regardless of the location of the point, if there is pain, it is called an *a shi* point (and)...it can be needled or moxaed to effect a cure." As Sun explains, *a shi* points are painful points. That means they are the specific places within a channel where the qi is not flowing freely. It is standard procedure in contemporary Chinese acupuncture to A) identify the diseased channel, B) needle ruling points on that channel which are typically distant to the site of pathology but which regulate the flow of qi in that channel, and C) combine these distant ruling points with local points adjacent to the pathology. The use of *a shi* points in the above treatment plan is based on this fundamental acupuncture methodology. In Bob Flaws and Mark Seem's experience, it achieves better results than needling only ruling points or needling local points which are not actually sore to palpation. For more information to this palpatory approach to acupuncture, see Mark Seem's *A New American Acupuncture: Acupuncture Osteopathy, The Myofascial Release of the Bodymind's Holding Patterns* and *Acupuncture Physical Medicine: An Acupuncture Touchpoint Approach to the Treatment of Chronic Fatigue, Pain, and Stress Disorders*, both available from Blue Poppy Press.

## THE THIRTEEN GHOST POINTS

Most Western acupuncturist have heard, at some point in their education, about the 13 ghost points. These are a set of 13 points which, in premodern times, were believed to be preeminently effective for the treatment of psychoemotional disturbances. According to William Yu of Sidney, Australia, such a set of 13 points may date back as far as the Warring States period.[6] However, most sources credit Sun Si-miao with codifying if not creating these in his Tang dynasty *Qian Jin Yao Fang (Essential Formulas [Worth] a Thousand [Pieces of] Gold)*. Since the Tang dynasty, versions of Sun's "Song of the 13 Ghost Points" are found in all major premodern acupuncture and moxibustion compendia, such as Yang Ji-zhou's Ming dynasty *Zhen Jiu Da Cheng (The Great Compendium of Acupuncture & Moxibustion)*. The following translation is based on the text found in Book 9 of Yang's *Great Compendium* where it is titled "Sun True Person's Song of the 13 Ghost Points."[7]

## THE TEXT:

[In terms of] the hundreds of evils causing the disease of withdrawal and mania, when needling, there are 13 points one must know. No matter where one needles the body, first start at *Gui Gong* (Ghost Palace, GV 26).[8] Secondly, needle *Gui Xin* (Ghost Sincerity, Lu 11) and there cannot but be a response.[9] If one starts from the beginning and proceeds step by step, rescue is certain. In men, start on the left, while in women start on the right. The first needle [should be inserted at ] *Ren Zhong-Gui Gong* [till it] stops [*i.e.*, cannot go in any further]. If one started from the left side, remove the needle from the right. The second [needle is inserted] below the nail of the large finger. This is called *Gui Xin* and is needled three *fen* deep. The third needle is below the nail of the large toenail. It is called *Gui Lei* (Ghost Pile, Sp 1 or a point midway

between Liv 1 and Sp 1). The fourth needle [is inserted] above the palm at the point *Da Ling* (Per 7). Continue needling to five *fen* makes this point *Gui Xin* (Ghost Heart). The fifth needle [should be inserted at] *Shen Mai* (Bl 62) which make it *Gui Lu* (Ghost Road). Fire needle this to three *fen* with seven flashes. The sixth needle is located above *Da Zhui* (GV 14). Enter the hair one *cun*. It is called *Gui Zhen* (Ghost Pillow, GV 16). The seventh needle [is located] eight *fen* below the ear. Its name is said *Gui Chuang* (Ghost Bed, St 6). It is essential [to use] warm needle [technique].The eighth needle is at *Cheng Jiang* (GV 24). It is called *Gui Shi* (Ghost Market). One must remember that if one inserts from the left, one must exit from the right. The ninth needle is at *Lao Gong* (Per 8) which makes it *Gui Ku* (Ghost Cave). The tenth needle is at *Shang Xing* (GV 23) and is called *Gui Tang* (Ghost Court).The eleventh needle is below the yin crease [*i.e.*, *Hui Yin*, CV 1], three cones [moxa]. In women, the head of the jade gate [*i.e.*, the clitoris] is called *Gui Zang* (Ghost Treasury). The twelfth [point is at] *Qu Chi* (LI 11) and is called *Gui Tui* (Ghost Leg). Fire needle it until it reaches an essential seven flashes. The thirteenth [point] is at the head of the tongue right in the tongue's center. This point must be called *Gui Feng* (Ghost Seal).The needling is done in opposite fashion on both sides of the hands and feet. If there is only one point, only that has its flow freed [*i.e.*, is needled]. This is the wondrous rhymed formula of our former teacher Sun. [Using it,] mania, raging, and malign ghosts leave without a trace.

## YANG JI-ZHOU'S COMMENTARY:

The first needle is *Gui Gong*, also called *Ren Zhong*; go as far as three *fen*.

The second needle is *Gui Xin*, also called *Shao Chong*; go as far as three *fen*.

The third point is *Gui Lei*, also called *Ji Bai*; go as far as two *fen*.

The fourth is called *Gui Xin*, also called *Da Ling*; go as far as five *fen*.

The fifth is called *Gui Lu*, also called *Shen Mai*; go as far as three *fen*.

The sixth is called *Gui Zhen*, also called *Feng Fu*; go as far as two *fen*.

The seventh is called *Gui Chuang*, also called *Jia Che*; go as far as five *fen*.

The eighth is called *Gui Shi*, also called *Cheng Jiang*; go as far as three *fen*.

The ninth is called *Gui Ku*, also called *Lao Gong*; go as far as two *fen*.

The tenth is called *Gui Tang*, also called *Shang Xing*; go as far as two *fen*.

The eleventh is called *Gui Zang*, also called *Hui Yin* and in women the head of the jade gate; enter three *fen*.

The twelfth is called *Gui Tui*, also called *Qu Chi*; go as far as five *fen*.

The thirteenth is called *Gui Feng* and is located under the central tongue crease. Prick to exit blood. Hold the tongue immovable between two horizontal chopsticks. This method is extremely miraculous. If one adds *Jian Shi* (Per 5) and *Hou Xi* (SI 3), it is even more miraculous.

## AUTHORS' COMMENTARY:

Since the *Zhen Jiu Da Cheng*, other Chinese acupuncturists have created alternative lists of 13 ghost points. One list by Fu Zhui-zhou includes *Ren Zhong* (GV 26), *Shen Ting* (GV 24), *Feng Fu* (GV 16), *Cheng Jiang* (CV 24), *Jia Che* (St 6), *Shao Shang* (Lu 11), *Da Ling* (Per 7), *Jian Shi* (Per 5), *Ru Zhong* (St 17), *Yang Ling Quan* (GB 34), *Yin Bai* (Sp 1), and *Xing Jian* (Liv 2).[10] William Yu also suggests that even Sun did not intend his list of 13 points to be categorically definitive, and that, like so many premodern medical authors, he was merely giving hints upon which he expected his readers to knowingly elaborate.

When the authors look at Sun's 13 ghost points, they are struck by how similar in certain ways they are to Bob Flaws's yin fire acupuncture protocol for chong mai-du mai-tai yang disease. Both protocols appear to use one needle technique. Both protocols use a number of points on the du mai. Both protocols needle *Shen Mai* and pericardium channel points. Both protocols use points at or near the jaw. And both protocols use unilateral or contralateral needling at certain points. As a matter of clini-

cal fact, most women with a yin fire scenario who have one-sided somatic pathologies of the upper body experience their symptoms entirely or primarily on the right side. In any case, the authors of the present work recommend practitioners who choose to use Sun's 13 ghost points to use it flexibly depending on the patient's personal patterns and main clinical signs and symptoms and not use it in a rote, formulaic way.

## ENDNOTES:

[1] Here we are talking solely about yin-yang theory. We are not talking about the heart's five phase correspondence with fire.

[2] Zhu Dan-xi, *The Heart & Essence of Dan-xi's Methods of Treatment*, trans. by Yang Shou-zhong, Blue Poppy Press, Boulder, CO, 1993, p. 189. The scapula is traversed by the hand tai yang small intestine channel.

[3] Li Zhu thought refers to the theories of Li Dong-yuan and Zhu Dan-xi taken as a whole.

[4] *Hui Yin* (CV 1) is that which is located between the front and back yin or genitals and anus respectively.

[5] Li Dong-yuan, *Treatise on the Spleen & Stomach*, trans. by Yang Shou-zhong & Li Jian-yong, Blue Poppy Press, Boulder, CO, 1993, p. 81-82

[6] Yu, Hung-piu (William), "The Song of the Thirteen Ghost Points," *Pacific Journal of Oriental Medicine*, #4, 1995, p. 12

[7] Yang Ji-zhou, *Zhen Jiu Da Cheng (The Great Compendium of Acupuncture & Moxibustion)*, People's Health & Hygiene Publishing Co., Beijing, 1983, p. 362

[8] Readers should keep in mind that withdrawal can refer to syncope and loss of consciousness and *Shui Gou/Ren Zhong* (GV 26) is a main point for arousing the brain and restoring consciousness.

[9] When *Gui Xin/Shao Shang* (Lu 11) is needled, it is most commonly bled or at least drained to clear heat in the upper burner which is harassing the heart spirit, and heat is a major mechanism in mania.

[10] Yu, *op. cit.*, p. 13

# ❖ 7 ❖

# BASIC PRINCIPLES OF LISTENING & COMMUNICATING

The authors wish to emphasize that the following brief review is intended only as an introductory guide to some basic concepts of listening, observing, and communicating that are important for the Chinese medical practitioner to understand in order to achieve a positive therapeutic relationship with a patient who presents with any kind of complaint. As the principal goal of this book is to provide a comprehensive review of Chinese medical approaches to emotional and psychological problems, our goal is to familiarize the practitioner with basic aspects of interactions that often take place in clinics where patients are treated for the range of psychiatric disorders. Unless dually certified, Chinese medical practitioners are not qualified to work with patients in the role of psychotherapists. However, like medical practitioners in all traditions, it is important for them to understand some basic approaches to managing intense emotions and, in unusual cases, how to appropriately refer patients who are in the midst of psychiatric crises. Some patients experience strong feelings of emotional release or distress during the course of Chinese medical treatment for medical disorders. For example, it is not uncommon for patients to experience previously suppressed emotions during acupuncture treatment. As Norman Kraft, a California acupuncturist says in his article, "Flowering of the Heart: Perspectives on Counseling Patients in an Acupuncture Setting," "While many of our patients are relaxed and sedated by an acupuncture treatment, others will connect with emotions long hidden, memories long forgotten, anger long suppressed, fear that was just under the surface."[1] Therefore, the skillful practi-

tioner should be familiar with basic clinical approaches in both kinds of situations.

## WELCOMING THE PATIENT

As Micheal J. Mahoney points out in *Human Change Processes*, the personality of the therapist and the "therapeutic alliances" he or she is capable of engendering with a patient are *eight times* more important to the outcomes of therapy than any specific techniques used during that therapy.

> The bottom line here is that humans can, indeed, help other humans change. It is the *quality* of their (our) relationships with other humans that most powerfully influence the quality of lives and the pace and direction of the developments within them.[2]

In the first minutes of the initial encounter with a new patient, the clinician has a strategic opportunity to establish the expectation of a professional yet cordial relationship with that patient. What is said and felt in these moments significantly determines the future course and outcome of treatment, particularly when psychiatric symptoms are involved. During these moments a patient develops a sense of the practitioner's interest in his or her story by observing the practitioner's greeting, gestures and tone of voice, word choice, and the kinds of questions asked. Communications researchers suggest that 80% of all human communication is nonverbal and is based on physical demeanor or "body language."

Every patient is unique, and every person who comes to a medical practitioner as a patient is worthy of the same respectful open-minded approach as any individual, including patients who "look like" alcoholics or drug addicts. An open, nonjudging heart when meeting a patient for the first time will ensure an open mind, and an open mind will permit more complete and deeper understanding of the patient's distress, more accurate diagnosis, and a more complete and effective approach to treatment. Everyone wins when this approach is taken. In *Grace Unfolding: Psychotherapy in the Spirit of the Tao -te Ching*, Greg Johanson and Ron Kurtz comment on the importance of being welcoming and nonjudgmental when they say:

> The sage or master works without judgement. She is a welcoming presence who can allow for and embrace all being and nonbeing... The sage simply attends to and accommodates what is, especially those things which arise spontaneously in our experience. This attitude of acceptance, inclusion, and trust in what is, is not a technique so much as it is a wordless principle.[3]

A conveyed sense of respectfulness is as central to a successful relationship between any medical practitioner and any patient as are politeness and a cordial or friendly regard. A warm, respectful attitude on the part of the practitioner will ensure that the patient feels comfortable and safe talking about concerns that have brought him or her to treatment. In contemporary Western psychotherapy, this concept is viewed as a fundamental, necessary starting place for adequate communication between patient and therapist and is a central requirement for success in any approach to psychotherapy. Ron Kurtz, body-centered psychotherapist and founder of the Hakomi School, refers to this as "loving presence." According to Kurtz, there are specific techniques which can be learned in order to cultivate this loving presence. One technique is to find something about the patient which the practitioner can admire or respect. This might be their bravery, intelligence, humor, or even the shape of their nose or color of their eyes. For more suggestions on how to cultivate such loving presence, the reader is directed to the Hakomi School home page at *www.ronkurtz.com*. David Kailin, acupuncturist and Ph.D. in Public Health, suggests visualizing each patient in their primordially perfect state as a way of establishing an open, non-judgmental, loving presence.[4]

However, regardless of techniques that are used, the prac-

titioner who helps patients feel comfortable and accepted through clear positive messages of courteous speech and behavior will cultivate a relationship of openness and mutual respect. In achieving this kind of relationship, the practitioner sets the stage for a collaborative approach to identifying problems and arriving at an appropriate or acceptable treatment plan.

## LISTENING

In order to accurately understand the health concerns of any patient, a clinician must be able to listen carefully and to observe accurately. A clinician who is pressured by time constraints or fatigued because of excessive work will probably not listen or observe as skillfully as one who has sufficient time with each patient to not be concerned about time, and who is sufficiently rested and centered on the current patient to permit him or her to accurately observe. When the clinician does not listen attentively to a patient's complaints or does not accurately observe physical or psychological signs, important aspects of history or current symptoms will be missed, the diagnosis will be similarly incomplete or wrong, and the clinician will not be in the best position to develop the most appropriate and most efficacious treatment plan. This, in turn will result in delayed or incomplete response to treatment, prolonged distress for the patient, and frustration in the clinician.

Listening skillfully entails hearing with an open mind or deliberately avoiding or excluding preformed biases about a patient based on previous experience with "similar" patients or information you may have about the patient prior to the initial contact. A useful approach to "listening with an open mind" is to clear the mind for a few minutes before meeting the patient and to read their chart notes, a self-completed patient questionnaire, or other sources of information about the patient only after he or she has had the opportunity to speak for several minutes.

Basic approaches to improving one's capacity to listen skillfully and observe accurately include the following:

1. Try to avoid scheduling patients when you expect to be tired or distracted following a long period of work or illness.

2. Schedule patients in a way that ensures sufficient time with each patient so that both you (the clinician) and the patient do not feel pressed by time.

3. Take frequent brief breaks during the day, especially between patients, in order to refresh and become mental-

ly focused and emotionally centered before seeing each patient.

4. Use the first several minutes of each session to ask open-ended questions or simply listen attentively after inviting the patient to speak. This will give the patient a continuing sense that you are interested, have enough time, and will also provide you with valuable information about important symptoms and other concerns.

5. Make an effort to listen empathically to every patient. A useful approach to achieving empathy is to imagine how you would feel in his or her situation as you listen to the patient's narrative of history and symptoms.

During the initial minutes of each session, it is important to make an effort to observe the patient carefully. This entails noticing outward appearance and behaviors and also being aware of your own subjective, nonrational, or intuitive response to the patient. Such "conscious noticing" will provide valuable information, including an accurate sense of the patient's state of distress and his or her overall physical and emotional well-being. The typical patient will be able to clearly describe certain problems and will likely have limited insight into others. Indeed, it is a well-known fact among psychotherapists that most people who seek counseling arrive with a "chief complaint" that is unrelated to prominent stresses and symptoms that are subsequently identified during the course of treatment. Therefore, even when a patient appears to have insight into apparent central reasons for seeking attention for a psychological or emotional problem, these impressions are often vague, incomplete, or incorrect. The clinician's task is then to skillfully sift through explicit information and his or her subjective responses to the patent during appointments in order to accurately and completely flesh out the patient's actual medical or psychiatric problems.

Skillful, empathic listening and careful observation during each appointment will allow the clinician to accurately assess how well or poorly the patient is doing since the last visit. This information, in turn, will lead to appropriate, useful advise about treatment, resulting in improved physical or psychological health and a more satisfying and meaningful relationship between the clinician and patient.

## CLARIFYING THE PATIENT'S COMPLAINT

A clinician trained in any system of medicine who knows how to listen skillfully and how to observe carefully can use these tools to determine which issues, signs, or symptoms require urgent attention and which do not. It is often helpful to progress gradually from open-ended questions (those that do not lead to a specific yes/no answer) to more specific, directive questions that follow naturally from the patient's responses to initial open-ended questions. For example, "Tell me how you've been" or "How can I help you" are reasonable open-ended questions that can be used during an initial encounter or any subsequent session. It will usually be obvious when the patient begins to speak about concerns that are central reasons for coming for treatment. It will likewise usually be evident when a patient does not describe concerns that are truly central. The latter case may be due to a lack of comfort in disclosing such concerns, especially when there are prominent psychological or emotional problems. However, many patients who have medical or psychological problems are unaware or not completely aware of the nature or magnitude of the problems for which they are seeking medical attention. Other patients are aware of distressing symptoms and have a vague sense of needing to be evaluated or treated but are unable to clearly articulate the sources or symptoms of their distress. The skillful clinician can function as a guide to these patients by helping them to place words around concerns or symptoms. This process often works best when the clinician begins with a few simple open-ended questions and then follows the patient's lead. More directive, close-ended questions can then be asked to verify clinical impressions provided in answers to, "Tell me how you've been," or "How can I help you?" With practice and experience, the clinician will become skilled in using interviewing techniques that result in accurate, complete information while preserving a sense of empathic regard and attentiveness in encounters with all patients.

## REFRAMING

One of the things we as practitioners of Chinese medicine offer our patients is a different view and explanation of their complaints. According to Kraft:

> Many [of our] patients have already been through the wringer of psychiatry and psychology, and are often experts at their own diagnosis. When we approach them with a new viewpoint, they are thrown out of their accustomed viewing of their situation.[5]

Kraft sees this as a good thing, that it gives us an advantage other Western care-givers may lack. The Chinese medical explanation of mental-emotional complaints is based on a unified bodymind, and it uses a number of words and concepts foreign to most Western patients, such as qi, yin and yang, vacuity and repletion. While these Chinese words and ideas may seem exotic and unusual at first, they are, nevertheless, based on a very down-to-earth, human, and humane vision of the world. The Chinese medical description of disease causes and disease mechanisms uses metaphors taken from the every-day natural world. We talk of heat and cold, dampness and dryness, wind and fire, free flow and blockage, normal flow and counterflow. These everyday explanations provide a sense of comprehensibility and manageability which are very empowering to our patients. As Kraft says, "This refocusing gives our patient the ability to see their issues in a new and in a usually much less threatening and engaging way."[6] Therefore, it is important that all practitioners of Chinese medicine be able to explain these concepts in metaphors and images which are easily understandable to our patients. It is also important to explain the fact that the Chinese medical spleen or liver are not the same as the Western biological entities of the same English name. Otherwise, the patient may think they have a disease they do not.

Not only can this reframing process empower our patients in ways biomedical models may not, but the patient is

> ...much more likely to understand the aims and goals of the treatment. Compliance with all parts of the treatment will increase dramatically when the patient is inspired by the methods and excited about the goals.[7]

Therefore, it is extremely important to explain each patient's pattern discrimination, what it does and does not mean, as well as what the patient can do about it. Failure to adequately make such explanations available to the patient is not only potentially legally actionable, but it misses a great opportunity to make use of one of Chinese medicine's most powerful attributes, its ability to provide a holistic, natural, and everyday sense of how the patient is and how they could be. As Kraft eloquently puts it, "In explaining the word Qi, another whole vista of the patient's life is opened."[8]

## PROVIDING A SENSE OF HOPE

As somewhat an extension of the above, many prominent Chinese medical practitioners have commented on the importance of desirable psychological interactions between the clinician and patient in achieving favorable therapeutic outcomes. For example, in 1956 the well-known acupuncturist Cheng Dan-an made a presentation describing the importance of "the concentration of one's mind, faith, and psyche" when treating patients. The following is excerpted from that presentation:

> A great many acupuncturists think that acupuncture treatment, which is a physiotherapy, cures disease through stimulating nerves to adjust the functions of the local parts, internal organs, or tissues... [However, b]ased on 30 years clinical experience, I have come to realize that this idea explains only partly one of the causes of [acupuncture's] curative effect but fails to provide an explanation of its main causes...[The effect of needling,] depends on the concentration of one's mind, faith, and psyche.

> ...In my opinion, the contraction and cause of disease, the relief of that affliction, and the restoration of health may have something to do with the environment, but the main factor underlying these are one's psychological or mental state. According to the teachings of my late father and my own clinical experience, the effect of needling lies mainly in three points: first, the psychological interaction [between patient and practitioner], second, concentration, and third, physical stimulation. It is the combination of these three that works instantaneous wonders.[9]

In going on to explain what he meant by psychological interaction, Cheng says that, "every treatment should be accomplished with concentration." This means that the practitioner should have an "...abundant sense of resoluteness and confidence in order to overcome a disease."[10] According to Cheng, patients who are diseased tend to be full of apprehension and fear and are, therefore, "depressed in spirit." He further stresses that the practitioner should never say anything that might rob the patient of hope. As we will see in the following chapter, providing a sense of manageability of illness, i.e., hope, is one of Antonovsky's three requirements for healing as opposed to curing. Cheng Dan-an stressed the primacy of providing his patients with hope and actively combating hopelessness. What follows can be described as Cheng's rationale for the therapeutic efficacy of hope:

> The reason why I advocate imparting psychological encouragement is to free the spirit of the patient from the talons of disease. To extricate the patient's thought from being immersed all day in worry, anxiety, and depression over the disease, one should, by all means, inspire the

patient with hope and cheer up their spirit. If this is combined with correct treatment, the effect will surely excel that of usual treatment.[11]

Therefore, a basic approach when treating every patient is to instill a sense of hope or belief in the "manageability" of the illness. At the same time, the practitioner should avoid saying or doing anything that suggests feelings of hopelessness or loss of control over the patient's situation. In a similar vein, when describing some of the characteristics of person-centered psychotherapy, Richard J. Castillo writes:

> The cognitive construction of emotions as it relates to mental illness highlights the need for the therapeutic use of hope. Because mental illnesses are so intimately connected to emotions, and therefore to cognition, it is imperative for clinicians to combat hopelessness and helplessness in all clients regardless of their diagnoses. By providing hope to clients, the clinician is creating a therapeutic effect on the client's emotions and, therefore, on their mental disorders.[12]

Recent anthropological research findings have supported the claim that even serious psychiatric disorders, including schizophrenia, may be more amenable to treatment than contemporary Western psychiatry has suggested. For example, two large multinational longitudinal studies sponsored by the World Health Organization have shown that schizophrenic patients in less developed countries have a better course and more favorable long-term outcome than do patients in the most economically developed countries (e.g., Great Britain, the United States, and Denmark).[13] Reported differences in course and outcome do not support contemporary Western theories that argue for a strictly biological etiology of schizophrenia. Therefore, even psychiatric disorders that are presumed to be intractable are not necessarily hopeless in all cases.

## DEALING EFFECTIVELY WITH DIFFICULT PATIENTS

There are seemingly unavoidable moments in every practitioner's career when particularly difficult patients interfere with his or her capacity to establish or maintain a constructive therapeutic relationship. There are also cases in everyone's professional career when patients, for unclear reasons, experience inappropriate negative, sexual, or other feelings toward the practitioner. In many cases, such unexplained, sometimes irrational emotional responses to a practitioner represent underlying psychopathology of which the patient may be unaware. For example, some patients may be extremely argumentative, passive, or help-refusing, while others may come across as overtly hostile. The observant clinician can use this information in order to better understand important aspects of a patient's emotional-psychological makeup. Further, when such feelings are present in the patient and/or the practitioner, they typically interfere with the patient's capacity to respond to treatment and may also interfere with the clinician's willingness to work with the patient. Therefore, practitioner-patient interactions that engender strong negative (and sometimes inappropriate positive) feelings almost always diminish the potential benefit of medical or psychological treatment and can sometimes compromise the patient's care entirely.

Because of these considerations, it is important that practitioners trained in every system of medicine have a basic understanding of how to identify and constructively respond to strong emotions that take place in the context of treatment. The initial and most important concept to keep in mind is to always pay attention to one's intuitive response to a patient. In other words, we should always listen to our gut feelings. It is always significant when the practitioner has a strong emotional response and especially a fearful response. Along these lines, Johanson and Kurtz emphasize the practitioner's ability to remain calm and unattached in the presence of strong emotions:

> The Taoist sage knows that beauty and drama can be invitations to distraction and restlessness as well as being intrinsically edifying. The wise one stays in touch with both her roots and her direction while traveling through glorious vistas. In therapy, rising and falling emotions provide an analogy with the magnificent landscapes Lao Tzu mentions [in chapter 26]. Strong emotion can be the occasion for getting lost in therapy. It can sometimes frighten therapists and overpower them, so that they communicate a verbal or nonverbal message to us to tone it down. Conversely, emotion can seem so rich and full that therapists become fascinated with it for its own sake. They can be involved in trying to promote it subtly even though it is not organically wanting to unfold. Intense, *spontaneous* emotion need only be supported.[14]

## RESPECTING THE POWER OF SUGGESTION

In his article on counseling patients in an acupuncture setting, Norman Kraft points out that we must take great care in particular with what we say and do when patients are experiencing acupuncture. According to Kraft, the acupuncture treatment is a time of great suggestibility. It is an altered state of consciousness akin in many ways to light hypnosis. As Kraft cautions, "While this opens up wonderful possibilities for the healing and helpful use of this state, it is also a time at which the practitioner must be most careful about what they say and do."[15] Although it should be obvious that this is not the time for negative joking or comments, other forms of suggestion may also cause problems. Kraft goes on to tell the following story:

> ...there was a patient I treated at Pacific College who had been seeing another intern for quite a while. When I first spoke with her and inquired whether she found the previous treatments useful, her response was that she enjoyed the treatments and found them useful. Lowering her voice, she then said that the problem was that the previous intern finished each treatment with a short shamanistic ritual. She found this incompatible with her Christianity and, after a time, even began having nightmares populated by South American demons. When she left the care of this intern, the dreams stopped. Our power of suggestion is indeed to be treated with care.[16]

## COGNITIVE DISTORTIONS

Many patients experience distorted ways of thinking or perceiving which limit their capacity for insight during therapy. According to Levy's three stage cognitive model for understanding human emotion,[17] every emotion is preceded by a cognitive assessment. Further, emotional responses are formed only after a person has cognitively assessed a situation. According to this theory, how people cognitively assess situations significantly influences how we emotionally respond to those situations. In other words, if a cognitive assessment is distorted, negative emotions will likely be experienced unnecessarily. In *Feeling Good: The New Mood Therapy*, David Burns identifies 10 cognitive distortions that tend to skew a patient's experiences of mental-emotional distress.[18] It is important to point out that in most cases, cognitive distortions represent unconscious defense mechanisms. Therefore, the patient will typically be unaware that he or she is distorting reality. According to Burns, examples of cognitive distortions include:

1. **ALL-OR-NOTHING THINKING.** This means the patient reports or sees things in an absolute, black and white way. For instance, "There's no way I can ever do that," "That's evil," "The situation is hopeless," "I can't be helped," etc.

2. **OVERGENERALIZING.** The patient experiences his or her situation and the distress it causes as never-ending and always-occurring. For instance, "You always say that," "This always happens to me," "I never get what I need," etc.

3. **NEGATIVE FILTERING.** This means seeing the worst in every situation while simultaneously ignoring the positives. The glass is always half empty as opposed to half full.

4. **DISCOUNTING POSITIVES.** This means refusing to grant value to one's accomplishments or positive qualities.

5. **JUMPING TO CONCLUSIONS.** This refers to a tendency to assume a negative outcome when the outcome has not yet been determined. For instance, "I know this won't work," or "I know you don't like me."

6. **MAGNIFYING & MINIMIZING.** These two cognitive distortions refer to exaggerating negative consequences, or conversely, disregarding or minimizing the actual importance of things in a given context. Magnifying comments might include: "This is a complete disaster!," "It'll be the death of me," or "I can't live without..." A frequently used minimizing comment is "It's OK, it doesn't matter."

7. **EMOTIONAL REASONING.** This refers to a tendency to avoid doing things because of associated unpleasant feelings. Becoming skilled at acting regardless of how one feels about doing a particular thing is a basic principle of Morita Therapy, a school of psychotherapy in Japan. Derived largely from Buddhist teachings, the belief that one needs to do what is necessary regardless of how one feels about the matter is a pervasive idea in Far East Asia. This process does not mean denying one's emotions but acknowledging one's feelings while not allowing them to interfere with necessary actions. "The dogs bark, but the caravan moves on."

8. **TOO MANY "SHOULDS."** Some patients are held captive by shoulds. They tell themselves that they should do this or think that or be a certain kind of person. Such people often feel overwhelmed by a flood of self-imposed unattainable demands or moral judgments on their behavior.

9. **LABELING.** This refers to a tendency to identify oneself with one's shortcomings. For example, instead of saying that an act was foolish, someone might label himself as a fool. Instead of believing that he acted like a jerk, a man internalizes the belief that he *is* a jerk.

10. **BLAMING.** This refers to a tendency to unnecessarily

blame oneself (*i.e.*, when the person is not actually at fault) or, conversely, to blame things on everyone but oneself.

Identifying and assisting patients with cognitive distortions is the domain of cognitive-behavioral therapy. This kind of therapy provides systematic treatments for numerous psychiatric disorders, especially anxiety disorders and less severe forms of depression. Extensive training is necessary to learn the rudiments of any kind of psychotherapy, and the authors are not suggesting that Chinese medical practitioners try to work with their patients as cognitive-behavioral therapists. However, by learning how to recognize specific cognitive distortions, practitioners can help their patients find more skillful ways of expressing their feelings. This will serve the patient-practitioner relationship by bringing accurate information about the patient's emotions and cognitions into the context of treatment. In many cases, this may simply require pointing out to a patient that something he or she just said was a distortion. In addition, recognizing cognitive distortions in their patients can help practitioners avoid the feeling of being "emotionally beat up" by their patients. For example, when the practitioner realizes that a patient's understanding of his or her situation is a distortion of reality, the practitioner can avoid being drawn into that distortion. Finally, it is important to point out that practitioners are sometimes subject to unconscious cognitive distortions of their own. When such distortions take place during treatment, they further complicate clear communication with patients, especially those who have their own cognitive distortions. Therefore, we can try to become aware of our distortions by monitoring our own speech and behavior, with the goal of keeping our interactions with our patients free of our own cognitive distortions. As Johanson and Kurtz remark:

> The work of therapists is not analogous to that of engineers or artists. Therapists do not create something they can stand back from, look at, and claim as their own. Mindful, nonviolent therapy simply helps us discover and affirm the wisdom of our inner experience. When insights emerge, attachments are released, new roads are discovered, and bodies reshape around more realistic, nourishing beliefs, it is not the therapist's doing. It is not their baby.[19]

### KNOWING WHEN & TO WHOM TO REFER FOR ROUTINE OR URGENT FOLLOW-UP

Practitioners trained in any system of medicine should have an understanding of when it is appropriate to refer a patient to a Western physician, psychotherapist, or emergency medical or psychiatric evaluation. It is appropriate to refer patients who are being seen by a Chinese medical practitioner on an ongoing basis to psychotherapists when they continue to experience significant emotional distress. In general, patients who experience persisting symptoms of moderate severity, including depressed mood, anxiety symptoms, disturbed sleep, or other psychological or emotional complaints that have not responded to an appropriate course of Chinese medical treatment and interfere with social or occupational functioning, should be referred to a psychotherapist or psychiatrist for evaluation and, if indicated, ongoing psychotherapy. In cases of severe emotional or psychological symptoms that gravely impair functioning or pose a potential risk to the patient's (or practitioner's) safety, including psychotic symptoms, suicidal or homicidal ideation, or complaints suggestive of a medical emergency, the patient should be referred immediately to emergency medical services. Though uncommon in an out-patient setting, of great concern to any practitioner is the possibility that a patient may be threatening and potentially dangerous. If there is a reasonable concern that the safety of the practitioner or other patients is at risk because of a potentially violent patient, police should be contacted immediately through 911.

In each chapter, a section called, "Indications for referral to Western medical services," describes general and specific reasons for which a patient should be referred to nonurgent or urgent Western medical care respectively. In cases where it is not clear whether persisting emotional or physical symptoms represent an urgent problem warranting referral to an emergency room or less acute concerns that can be adequately managed on a routine outpatient basis, the Chinese medical practitioner should always make the most conservative judgment. That is, when there is reasonable doubt that persisting symptoms represent a potentially life-threatening medical or psychiatric problem, the patient should always be referred to the nearest emergency room.

> The dao of heaven is to benefit [others] and not to harm.
> The dao of the sage is to act but not to compete.[20]

### ENDNOTES:

[1]Kraft, Norman, "Flowering of the Heart," *www.ormed.edu/users/nkraft/ormed.cc.html*, p. 5

[2]Mahoney, Michael J., *Human Change Processes: The Scientific Foundations of Psychotherapy*, Basic Books, NY, 1991, p. 264

[3]Johanson, Greg & Kurtz, Ron, *Grace Unfolding: Psychotherapy in the Spirit of the Tao-te Ching*, Belltower, NY, 1991, p. 9

[4]Kailin, David, "Working Inside the System," workshop notes, Boulder, CO, May 21, 2000

[5]Kraft, *op. cit.*, p. 3

[6]*Ibid.*, p. 7

[7]*Ibid.*, p. 4

[8]*Ibid.*, p. 4

[9]Cheng Dan-an, *Acupuncture and Moxibustion Formulas & Treatments*, trans. by Wu Ming, Blue Poppy Press, Boulder, CO, 1996, p. 1-2

[10]*Ibid.*, p. 2

[11]*Ibid.*, p. 2

[12]Castillo, *op. cit.*, p. 78

[13]*Ibid.*, p. 248-249

[14]Johanson & Kurtz, *op. cit.*, p. 71-72

[15]Kraft, *op. cit.*, p. 5

[16]*Ibid.*, p. 5

[17]Levy, R.I., "Emotion, Knowing, and Culture," *Culture Theory: Essays on Mind, Self & Emotion*, R.A. Shweder & R.A. LeVine, eds., Cambridge University Press, Cambridge, 1984, p. 214-237

[18]Burns, David D., *Feeling Good: The New Mood Therapy*, William Morrow & Co., NY, 1981

[19]Johanson & Kurtz, *op. cit.*, p. 38

[20]Lao-zi, *Da De Jing (The Classic of the Way & Virtue)*, Chapter 81, as found in Gregory C. Richter's *The Gate of All Marvelous Things: A Guide to Reading the Tao Te Ching*, Red Mansions Publishing, SF, 1998, p. 151

# ❖ 8 ❖

# THE INTEGRATION OF CHINESE & WESTERN PSYCHIATRIC TREATMENTS: SOME PRELIMINARY SUGGESTIONS

This book is specifically meant for Western practitioners of acupuncture and Chinese medicine working in a Western milieu. However, it is our hope that Western psychiatrists and other MD specialists may also benefit through improved understanding of Chinese medical approaches to psychiatric disorders. Most Western patients come to acupuncture and Chinese medicine with a preestablished Western medical diagnosis, and many of them are currently taking Western prescription medications or are undergoing other Western medical treatments concurrently. Many patients who are under the care of Chinese medical practitioners do not disclose the specific nature of this on-going treatment to their Western MDs, including their psychiatrists, who may be treating them at the same time for the same or similar complaints. The converse is also probably true. Many patients receiving Western psychiatric treatment may fail to disclose such personal information to their Chinese medical practitioner while being treated for related or quite different complaints. Reasons for such nondisclosure are complex and include patients' reluctance to and possibly also embarrassment at being seen by either physician or Chinese medical practitioner as naïve or misinformed. Many patients may simply regard each kind of medical treatment as an unrelated or independent matter that does not warrant disclosure to other health care providers. The consequences of such nondisclosure for patients include an inherent risk of misdiagnosis or missed diagnosis, subsequent inappropriate treatment, and complications from combining two treatments for which limited information

exists concerning drug-drug or drug-procedure (*e.g.*, acupuncture or moxibustion) interaction risks.

Little reliable information on efficacious and safe combined treatment approaches is presently available to both MDs and Chinese medical practitioners. This factor has substantially limited or curtailed the responsible intentions of open-minded physicians and Chinese medical practitioners who are interested in using integrative treatments that combine Chinese and Western medical approaches in appropriate, safe, and rigorous ways. Ideally, an integrative algorithm will combine approaches that optimize treatment response while simultaneously discouraging or strongly warning against certain combined treatments for which there are identified associated risks or an absence of substantial clinical or research data demonstrating safety and efficacy. To date, only a few specific risks or contraindications have been identified when certain Chinese and Western medical treatments are combined. Examples include the concurrent use of Herba Ephedrae (*Ma Huang*), which contains ephedrine, and numerous anti-hypertensive medications or antidepressants, especially the serotonin-selective re-uptake inhibitors (SSRIs) or monoamine oxidase inhibitors (MAOIs)[1].

Because of these central clinical concerns, important goals of this book are the stimulation of discussion toward the development of a reasonable evidence-based method or algorithm for integrative treatment planning and exploration of important principles of risk that will provide a framework for both Chinese medical practitioners and Western MDs. A principal goal of this work is to facilitate informed, conservative judgments about Chinese and Western therapies that are appropriate and safe to combine based on available information. An equally important goal is to establish reasonable and conservative guidelines that will assist Chinese medical practitioners and Western physicians in their efforts to avoid combining therapies in ways that are inappropriate or unsafe based on available information. These considerations compel the authors to comment on reasonable approaches to the integration of Chinese and Western medicine in Western settings, including a discussion of benefits and risks each system of medicine offers to the other and to Western patients in general.

## THOUGHTS ON THE BENEFITS OF CHINESE MEDICINE TO WESTERN MEDICINE

Based on a combination of more than 20 years of practicing Chinese and Western medicines in the West, we believe that Chinese medicine can benefit Western psychiatric patients in numerous ways. Further, we believe that all these approaches can be safely used in combination with contemporary Western medical treatments of psychiatric disorders.

## PROVIDING A GRADUATED SERIES OF RESPONSES FROM LESS TO MORE RISKY, LESS TO MORE EXPENSIVE

The first of these is providing a graduated series of responses which go from relatively benign with little risk of side effects to more powerful, quick-acting treatments with more risk of side effects. *Primum non nocere* (first do no harm) is a fundamental principle of Western medicine that was established during its early Greco-Roman period of evolution. This maxim is generally interpreted by Western physicians (and often by patients' lawyers) as a caveat against performing procedures or prescribing medications in which the potential risk of harmful consequences may exceed the likely beneficial effects. As scientific advances have permitted synthesis of powerful pharmacological agents, the probability of associated potentially harmful side effects, toxicities, and drug-drug interactions has increased. A consequence of such "progress" is that the principle, "first do no harm," has become the focus of contentious debate in the Western medical community and among patient advocacy groups who are concerned that treatment risks may equal or outweigh potential benefits with respect to certain medical or psychiatric disorders.

A recent report issued by the Institute of Medicine of the National Academy of Sciences highlights this concern. According to this report, approximately 98,000 people die in U.S. hospitals annually as a result of "preventable medical errors." Further, the Institute of Medicine estimates that an additional 100,000 patients die every year because of medical complications due to adverse drug reactions, including drug-drug interactions, side effects, and toxic effects.[2] Because of the above findings and other similar reports, there is a growing concern among Western physicians and patients over high morbidity and mortality associated with synthetic Western medicines or "preventable medical errors." Similar concerns are frequently cited with respect to numerous pharmacological agents currently used in Western medicine to treat psychotic disorders. Many antipsychotics, including older agents like haloperidol (Haldol), chlorpromazine (Thorazine), and more recently introduced drugs like risperidone (Risperdal), quetiapine (Seroquel), and olanzapine (Zyprexa), have a significant associated risk of debilitating, sometimes permanent movement disorders, in addition to numerous other potentially serious side effects, toxicities, and drug-drug interactions (see Short & long-term advantages & disadvantages of Western medical treatment for Schizophrenia, Depression, and Bipolar Affective Disorder, Book 3, for reviews of selected side-effects).

In fact, all Chinese and Western therapies have the potential for producing side effects. If a treatment can bring a person back into balance, when unskillfully or erroneously applied it may also lead to imbalances manifesting as side effects. Clearly, no medical system, modality, or medicine offers a panacea for all disorders or all patients. However, when Chinese medicine is practiced correctly, there is little potential for unwanted or so-called side effects, and there have been negligibly few reports of "preventable medical errors." This is a result of the basic prescriptive methodology of Chinese medicine which aims to apply those specific treatments to individuals which will bring each patient back into his or her personal state of balance. Even when practiced poorly, acupuncture has little potential for side effects, and entry level education in acupuncture is specifically designed to eliminate errors in practice that might cause these side effects (such as hematoma and pneumothorax).[3] In contrast, Chinese medicinals carry a greater risk of side effects. However, due to their being unrefined herbal materials or other naturally occurring products, most Chinese medicinals are not as potent as Western synthetic drugs. Further, Chinese medicinals are prescribed as polypharmacy formulas which are internally designed to mitigate any negative or side effects right from the beginning. In addition, such formulas are individually prescribed on the basis of each person's pattern as opposed to their disease. Because of these factors, professionally prescribed Chinese medicines typically have few if any side effects. In fact, professional practitioners of Chinese medicine are taught to continue rethinking and refining a patient's Chinese medical prescription until it achieves the desired therapeutic effect with zero side effects.

It is accepted that numerous widely used Western antipsychotic medicines (neuroleptics) have serious, potentially intractable side effects. As Richard J. Castillo writes, "In recent years, a growing awareness of the serious side effects of neuroleptics has allowed most clinicians to realize that neuroleptics may be overprescribed and should be used [more] judiciously."[4] Although blocking dopamine receptors with antipsychotic medicines does reduce psychotic symptoms in the majority of symptomatic patients, thus leading to short-term improvement, chronic use of antipsychotic medications may have the effect of up-regulating the dopamine system, exacerbating and prolonging psychotic illnesses.[5] Therefore, based on the principle of first doing no harm, antipsychotic medicines may not be the most appropriate first choice of treatment of certain psychotic disorders but may be more judiciously reserved for the treatment of acute conditions or symptoms that are unresponsive to treatments with fewer associated serious side effects.

Further, Chinese medical treatment is typically cheaper than Western medical treatment (especially so-called Chinese herbal medicine). Assuming that efficacy and safety standards are met, this fact suggests that Chinese medical treatment constitutes a reasonable first choice for patients with non-life-threatening or chronic conditions. Subsequently, nonresponse following appropriate Chinese medical treatment would indicate the need to refer a patient to a Western physician or other appropriate medical practitioner for more potent Western medical treatments that are typically more expensive and carry greater risks of side effects. By extension, a reasonable corollary to this principle is that more expensive Western treatments with higher associated risks of side effects or complications should be avoided in cases where Chinese medical treatments are safe and efficacious. It follows that Western medical approaches can be used separately or in tandem with Chinese medicine in cases where Chinese medical treatments fail to achieve therapeutic outcomes. Concurrent treatment with both Chinese and Western medical treatments should be considered only when there are reasonable grounds (based on documented clinical experience or research findings) to conclude that no or only minor interactions may occur between specific treatments. Thus, with respect to treatments of chronic or non-acute disorders for which Chinese medicine has an established record of efficacy and safety, Chinese medicine can provide a more holistic, safer, and less expensive first treatment option in contrast to the more potent, more specific, and more expensive treatments employed in contemporary Western medicine. Conversely, when Chinese medical treatments have little or no demonstrated efficacy with respect to certain medical or psychiatric disorders, Western treatments may be more appropriate and, in fact, comprise the logical next step toward a graduated series of therapeutic responses.

## TREATING THE SIDE EFFECTS OF WESTERN DRUGS

Secondly, Chinese medicine can be used to effectively manage the side effects of numerous Western drugs and therapies. One of the main complaints of many Western patients is that the side effects of Western medicine are sometimes as bad or worse than the symptoms its medicines seek to treat. Therefore, Western medical practitioners and especially Western psychiatrists often encounter poor patient adherence. Numerous Chinese studies have documented that Chinese medicine, whether acupuncture or Chinese medicinals, can be used to mitigate or eliminate the unwanted side effects of Western medical treatments. Most of these studies describe the results of the Chinese medical treatment of side effects caused by radiation or chemotherapy used to treat various kinds of cancer. However, there is also a relatively large literature describing the Chinese medical treatment of the side effects of corticosteroids (principally prednisone), oral contraceptives, oral and surgical abortifacients, antibiotics, and even antipsychotics.[6]

When Chinese medical practitioners attempt to treat the side effects of Western drugs and therapies, they simply do a pattern discrimination and then apply whatever Chinese medical treatment or medicinals are indicated on the basis of that pattern. In other words, if, after taking a Western medicine, the patient exhibits yin vacuity-vacuity heat signs and symptoms as a side effect, then the Chinese medical treatment principles are to enrich yin and clear vacuity heat. If another patient exhibits the signs and symptoms of spleen vacuity and stomach disharmony after taking Western medicines, then the Chinese medical treatment principles are to fortify the spleen and harmonize the stomach. In other words, use of Chinese medicine to successfully manage the side effects of Western medicine is not predicated on an understanding of the pharmacodynamics or pharmacokinetics of specific

Western medicines. The same Chinese medical prescriptive methodology is applied regardless of the specific Western medicine(s) involved, and this approach is always nothing other than basing treatment on the individual patient's pattern discrimination.

## ACHIEVING BETTER THERAPEUTIC OUTCOMES

Chinese medicine can be used to improve the intended therapeutic effects of Western medicine when prescribed in tandem with Chinese medicines and treatments, with the caveat that potentially unsafe interactions may not have been reported for specific combinations of Chinese medicinals and Western synthetic drugs. Abstracts of numerous Chinese research reports included in Books 2 and 3 show that specific combinations of Chinese and Western medicines are reportedly more effective than Western medicines alone for the treatment of certain diseases in identified populations.

Chinese medicine may also benefit Western patients in another way that is similar to the approach described above. As evidenced by a number of case histories in Books 2 and 3, Chinese medicine is often able to achieve therapeutic effects in diseases or in patients Western medicine is not. Over and over again in the following case histories in this book, we meet patients who have been treated with numerous different Western medications to no avail. However, either Chinese medicine or acupuncture was able to achieve the desired therapeutic effect.[7] In addition, Western medicine simply has no effective specific treatments for certain symptoms or diseases. For instance, Western medicine has little to offer for memory deficits, but Chinese medical practitioners are routinely told by their patients that, after undergoing Chinese medical treatment, their memory has improved.

## PROVIDING COHERENCE IN HEALING

Yet another way Chinese medicine may benefit Western patients is by empowering them. In 1979, Aaron Antonovsky formulated the concept of coherence in healing.[8] According to this theory, coherence means that the patient believes that his or her internal and external environments are predictable and reasonably under control. By gaining coherence, the ill person gains hope and thereby promotes the process of healing. Antonovsky posited three components of coherence within healing. The first is comprehensibility. This refers to a sense of order. It means the ill person can understand the source of illness, the mechanisms of illness, and the effects of those mechanisms on their life. As Castillo points out, "Providing

comprehensibility is one of the key factors in healing mental illness in nonwestern societies."[9] The second component of coherence is manageability. This refers to the belief that the practitioner and patient are competent to meet the demands of the illness. And the third component to coherence in healing is meaningfulness. This refers to providing, or the discovery of, a purpose or lesson behind the disease. We believe that Chinese medicine is an excellent methodology for providing coherence to patients suffering from mental-emotional disorders.

When a Western patient is told that he or she is suffering from an imbalance in their brain chemistry, the patient has little recourse other than to passively rely on pharmacotherapy or other conventional Western medical treatments. Western medical anthropologists refer to this as a "disease-based" or "therapy-centered" approach to treatment. In contrast, Chinese medicine is based on a "patient-centered" approach to care. Chinese medical pattern discriminations explain why a person is experiencing the symptoms they are in very common sense and human terms, at least, that is, once any foreign concepts, such as qi or yin and yang, are introduced. Chinese medical physiology is based on seeing the human body and its activities as a microcosm of the larger phenomenal world. Therefore, the descriptions of Chinese medicine use such easily understandable concepts of hot and cold and dampness and dryness. Because such descriptions can be understood by almost everyone with only a modicum of explanation, Chinese pattern discrimination provides patients with a deep sense of comprehensibility.

For instance, if a patient knows they have too much yang counterflowing upward due to yin vacuity of the kidneys, then they can easily know what foods or activities will tend to aggravate or ameliorate their condition. Any food or activity that wastes or consumes yin will be bad for the patient, but any food or activity which promotes the engenderment, growth, replacement, or augmentation will be good for the patient. Similarly, if a patient is told they have phlegm dampness, any food or activity that engenders phlegm or dampness internally will aggravate their condition, while any food or activity which dries dampness and transforms phlegm will be good for their condition. Recently, a Western psychiatrist with an interest in Chinese medicine told one of the authors how much her psychiatric patients exhibiting yin vacuity-yang hyperactivity signs and symptoms have benefitted from the simple technique of treading in cold water whenever they felt anxious or upset. Cold water (which is yin) applied to the feet (the most yin part of the body) helps to draw or lead yang back to its lower source. This is just one of an almost infinite number of no or low cost, safe, and easy self-remedies based on the common sense, natural world explanations of Chinese medicine. Not only do the human level explanations of Chinese medicine allow for the patient's own dietary and lifestyle modifications, they also give the patient a greater sense of being in control, at least to some degree, of their own destiny with all the therapeutic benefits that entails. Thus the physiological and diagnostic descriptions of Chinese medicine can provide a sense of manageability to Western psychiatric patients, and manageability is the second of Antonovsky's three components of coherence in healing.

In addition, the disease mechanisms of Chinese medicine are all predicated on a loss of balance and harmony between one's inner and outer worlds. One of the most important implications embodied in the movement away from a spiritist/religious theory of disease causation within Chinese medicine to a more secular/naturalist explanation based on systematic correspondences and the qi paradigm is the idea that disease is always an indication that something about the way one is living one's life is out of balance with the natural laws of phenomenal reality. In other words, the experience of disease is not capricious or meaningless and it does have moral value. It is an indication that one needs to change something about the way they are living, bringing their lifestyle back into balance with the natural principles of the phenomenal universe. This moral aspect of Chinese medicine is clearly set forth in the very first chapter of the *Nei Jing Su Wen (Inner Classic: Simple Questions)*:

> Huang Di asked: I've heard that in days of old everyone lived 100 years without showing the usual signs of aging. In our time, however, people age prematurely, living only 50 years. Is this due to a change in environment, or is it because people have lost the correct way of life?

> Qi Bo replied: In the past, people practiced the *dao*. They understood the principles of balance, of yin and yang, as represented by the transformation of the energies of the universe. Thus they formulated practices such as *dao yin* to promote the flow of qi and meditation to help maintain and harmonize themselves with the universe. They ate a balanced diet at regular times, rose and retired at regular hours, avoided overstressing their bodies and minds, and refrained from overindulgence of all kinds. They maintained well-being of body and mind. Thus it is not surprising that they lived to over 100 years.

> These days, people have changed their way of life. They drink wine as though it were water, indulge excessively in destructive activities, drain their essence, and deplete their qi. They do not know the secret of conserving their energy and vitality. Seeking emotional excitement and momentary pleasures, people disregard the natural rhythm and order of the universe. They fail to regulate their lifestyle and diet, and sleep improperly. So it is not surprising that they look old at 50 and die soon after.[10]

Hence, Chinese medicine can also provide psychiatric patients with Antonovsky's third component of coherence in healing, meaningfulness. This can be achieved without imposing a set of religious beliefs or moral precepts that would likely be unacceptable to many patients within our postmodern, multi-cultural society. The concept of health as balance is universal enough and the teachings of Chinese medicine regarding diet and lifestyle are common sense enough that more than two decades of clinical practice in the West suggests that they can typically be accepted by people of all ideological and religious backgrounds.

## PROVIDING HOLISTIC TREATMENT

In contrast to modern Western medicine, Chinese medicine treats the whole person. As we have seen, the signs and symptoms that are pathognomonic of a specific Western disease constitute only a small part of the patient's total signs and symptoms as gathered by the four Chinese medical examinations. The number of signs and symptoms of a Chinese pattern or combination of patterns is always greater than the signs and symptoms associated with their major complaint. Because Chinese medicine treats the patient's pattern, not just their disease, patients undergoing Chinese medical treatment typically experience improvement in all their symptoms across the board. For example, the yin fire acupuncture protocol described in Chapter 6 commonly results in improved sleep and mood, reduced anxiety, decreased neck and shoulder tension, fewer headaches, reduced TMJ discomfort, more regular menstrual cycles, and less frequent urination. In other words, Chinese medicine always treats the whole patient, not just their major complaint. This is because Chinese medicine sees each and every aspect of the patient as part of an integrated whole, and only by bringing the entire organism back into dynamic balance can any one sign or symptom truly be eliminated.

## PROVIDING A NEW PRESCRIPTIVE METHODOLOGY

The authors believe that the Chinese medical prescriptive methodology could also be used to make Western medical treatment safer and more effective. In contrast to Chinese medicine, contemporary Western medicine currently employs a disease-based prescriptive methodology, and, as Richard Castillo writes:

> The disease-centered diagnostic categories that separate psychopathology into mood disorders, psychotic disorders, dissociative disorders, somatoform disorders, anxiety disorders, and so on may be too inflexible to accomodate a client-centered conception of mental illness. The disease-centered classification system may also be based on a false biological determinism. As psychiatry moves into a new era of holistic research, the data that will inform future editions of the DSM-IV may require a different, more client-centered system of classification.[11]

Chinese medicine uses a pattern-based prescriptive methodology. Diseases are like the figure within a ground or a tree within a forest. When Western medicines cause unwanted side effects, it is because that medicine at that dose did not precisely correspond to or match the entirety of the patient's pattern. Regardless of their source, medicines are neither good nor bad in and of themselves. A medicine is good if it achieves a desired therapeutic effect in a specific patient with no unwanted side effects. The authors believe that, if Western physicians could use the Chinese medical prescriptive methodology to more accurately identify the patterns of disease most suited to specific Western medicines or other kinds of medical intervention, patients would experience better therapeutic outcomes with fewer side effects. In other words, we could have all the quick-acting power of Western synthetic drugs while minimizing potential side effects or other undesirable treatment outcomes.

For instance, most of the serotonin selective re-uptake inhibitors (SSRIs), such as fluoxetine (Prozac), proxetine (Paxil), and sertraline (Zoloft), appear to function similar to yang, windy, exterior-resolving, wind dampness treating, and/or qi-rectifying medicinals in Chinese medicine. In some cases, these medicines achieve everyone's (patient's and practitioner's) desired therapeutic effect with no unwanted side effects. In that case, their match with the patient is perfect. However, in other patients, these medicines may cause unwanted oral dryness, anxiety and agitation, and sexual disturbances. According to

Chinese medicine's prescriptive methodology, one must be careful using yang, windy, upbearing, and out-thrusting medicinals with anyone with a tendency to yin vacuity fluid insufficiency since this type of medicinal can damage and cause detriment to righteous yin, thereby causing or aggravating the engenderment of internal heat. Therefore, perhaps these kinds of SSRIs should only be used with care in patients with yin vacuity constitutions and avoided altogether in patients with frank clinical signs and symptoms of yin vacuity-internal heat. In addition, windy, upbearing, and out-thrusting medicinals can also damage qi and ultimately cause detriment to yin and yang. Thus they can deconstruct the spirit, causing a flat or dulled feeling internally and decreased or absent libido or erectile dysfunction.

This approach is similar to either not using or only using a very small dose of Radix Bupleuri (*Chai Hu*) in yin vacuity, yin and yang dual vacuity, or even qi vacuity patients. In addition, knowing the propensity for these kinds of medicinals for damaging yin and qi, they might be combined with other Chinese medicinals that are known to nourish the blood, enrich yin, engender fluids, supplement the qi, and/or clear heat to even further insure that they only create their intended therapeutic effect and not any unwanted side effects. Hence, the greatest benefit Chinese medicine may have to offer to Western medicine is a new, more holistic way of prescribing synthetic drugs.

## THOUGHTS ON THE BENEFITS OF WESTERN MEDICINE TO CHINESE MEDICINE

In terms of what Western medicine has to offer Chinese medicine, there are also several benefits which can be identified. The first of these is Western medicine's empirical approach to diagnosis with its attendant systematic understanding of disease-specific natural history and, therefore, prognosis. For instance, two patients with different Western medical diagnoses may manifest exactly the same Chinese symptom pattern. However, one patient may be suffering from a relatively benign, self-limiting, or transient disorder, such as premenstrual dysphoric disorder, while another may be suffering from a severe, chronic, debilitating disease, such as schizophrenia. Because of its emphasis on history-taking and systematic, empirically based differential diagnosis, Western medicine typically permits greater accuracy in diagnosis in cases of diagnostic ambiguity when the same patient is assessed by a Chinese medical practitioner. Greater diagnostic certainty leads to a more appropriate and comprehensive treatment plan, including combined Chinese and Western medical treatments where appropriate, and also to improved understanding of prognosis.

### PROVIDING BETTER ABILITY TO PROGNOSE

From the Chinese pattern alone, we often cannot fully know and understand the ultimate course of many diseases and, therefore, their prognosis. Although Wu You-ke, a Chinese doctor in the late 18th century said, "Each disease has its own qi," Chinese medicine has never really developed this idea independently, and this, at least in part, is why Western medical disease nosology has largely replaced or at least complements Chinese medical disease nosology in modern Chinese medicine.

### PROVIDING BETTER RECOGNITION OF COMPLICATIONS OR DANGER SIGNS

Secondly, and somewhat as an extension of this first benefit, Western medical disease diagnosis allows for better, more accurate identification of complications or danger signs associated with a particular disorder or its treatment. Knowing a patient has a certain Western psychiatric disease, the well-trained clinician will ask pertinent questions about the patient's behavior and cognitive or mood symptoms between appointments and then place this reported information in the context of his or her observations of the significant symptoms or signs of illness that are apparent or elicited during out-patient visits. For example, a patient who has a history of schizophrenia may disclose subjective experiences of worsening clinical status including increased frequency of auditory hallucinations or new-onset paranoid delusions or depressed mood. This information then provides the clinician with an empirical basis on which to adjust or change medications or refer the patient to another specialist.

### PROVIDING QUICKER, MORE POWERFUL TREATMENTS FOR SERIOUS AND/OR ACUTE CONDITIONS

A prevalent, frequently substantiated belief is that Western medicine often provides more powerful, quicker acting drugs and other treatments than does Chinese medicine. Although it is arguable that Chinese medicine achieves more rounded treatment of the whole person with less potential for side effects, complications, and interactions, it typically does not achieve its effects as rapidly as does Western medicine (acupuncture occasionally excepted). Therefore, especially in cases of severe psychosis, mania, or where there is significant risk of suicide or violent behavior, emergency psychiatric hospitalization and aggressive treatment with Western medicines may rapidly stabilize the patient's condition. Once the patient has been adequately stabilized for hospital discharge, Chinese medical treatments may be employed as maintenance therapies singly or in combination with Western medicine (following reasonable precautions described below).

### PROVIDING BETTER ASSESSMENT & TRACKING OF PROGRESS & OUTCOMES

Western medical tests and examinations may be used to help track and substantiate therapeutic outcomes with Chinese medicine. Changes in signs and symptoms gathered by Chinese medicine's four examinations are often preceded and can be corroborated by changes in such things as blood or urine tests. Many published studies demonstrate that Chinese medical treatments do change the body's biochemistry.[12] While Chinese signs and symptoms only give a rough impression of how such changes are going, laboratory studies often yield precise quantitative data describing clinically useful or important changes in blood chemistry, urine, etc. On the one hand, this data may guide clinicians to alter or adjust their current treatment plan. On the other, it may give the patient increased confidence in their treatment plan and thus catalyze even further any existing placebo effects.

### PROVIDING 24/7 EMERGENCY & IN-PATIENT CARE

Western medical delivery services offer the kind of intensive, 24 hour, seven days a week care that Chinese medicine is as yet unable to provide here in the West. This includes in-patient care which is, as of this writing and as far as we know, unavailable in terms of Chinese medicine outside of a single hospital in southern Germany run by a consortium of Western and Chinese medical doctors. Nevertheless, access to some form of 24 hours per day, seven days per week care and often in-patient care is a medical necessity for many patients suffering from psychiatric disease.

Disorder-specific guidelines for urgent and non-urgent referral to an emergency room or Western medical services are discussed separately in individual chapters in Books 2 and 3. General indications for urgent referral to the nearest emergency room or urgent care facility include:

1. The patient's history or clinical presentation suggest a rapidly progressive, serious, impairing, or untreated medical or psychiatric disorder. For example, sudden-onset change in previous baseline of behavior, cognition, or mood may suggest a rapidly evolving major psychiatric or

medical disorder, including schizophrenia, mania, dementia, neurologic disorders, acute infectious or metabolic processes, etc.

2. The patient's history or clinical presentation points to an on-going pattern of alcohol or substance abuse that is placing the patient's (or other's) safety at risk.

3. The patient is contemplating suicide or violence toward others. In such cases, it is often necessary for the safety of the patient and/or clinician to coordinate urgent care, including transport to an emergency room with local police.

4. In cases where the severity of medical or psychiatric symptoms interferes with the patient's capacity to take care of his or her basic needs of food, clothing, or shelter.

Indications for non-urgent referral to Western medical services include:

1. There are no apparent severe, impairing, or rapidly progressing symptoms suggestive of a rapidly progressive or potentially life-threatening disorder. However, complaints of on-going symptoms have not responded to an appropriate course and duration of Chinese medical treatment.

2. The patient's target symptoms have responded to appropriate Chinese medical treatment, but, during the course of treatment, new, non-acute symptoms have been reported that have not responded to appropriate Chinese medical treatment and may represent an evolving disorder that is unrelated to the disorder being treated.

3. The patient has responded only partially to an appropriate course and duration of Chinese medical treatment and established Western medical treatments suggest that they may benefit from an integrative approach combining appropriate Chinese and Western medical treatments.

4. Reasonable attempts have been made to manage symptoms with appropriate Chinese medical treatments, and the patient has experienced side effects or complications that preclude continuing treatment of this kind. (It should be noted that side effects and complications have been ascribed to Western medical treatments much more frequently than to Chinese medical treatments.)

## ACHIEVING A BETTER THERAPEUTIC OUTCOMES

In the same way that Western physicians and other medically trained specialists may choose to refer to practitioners of Chinese medicine when cases do not respond to Western medical therapy as expected or hoped, Chinese medical practitioners can *and should* refer to Western MDs in cases when Chinese medical treatments fail to achieve expected results. Clearly, no system of medicine is perfect or complete, and all systems of medicine have their relative advantages, deficiencies, and blind spots. For instance, contemporary Western medicine has imaging technology which allows the clinician to see inside the body in a way Chinese medicine is incapable, and many diseases that appear to be due to primary psychological disorders may actually be manifestations of pathological changes in the body or brain which Chinese medicine cannot see until it is often too late. Examples include brain tumors, other kinds of cancer, numerous medical causes of dementia, infectious processes, and metabolic or endocrinological derangement. Specific examples of medical disorders that may manifest as psychiatric symptoms are reviewed in sections on Etiology & Pathophysiology and Differential Diagnosis in respective chapters on the Chinese disorders discussed in this book. Our view is that the interests of Western physicians and other Western medical practitioners, Chinese medical practitioners, and, most of all, patients are best served by intellectual openness to other systems of medicine. We believe that the interests of patients are best served when openness translates into willingness to refer by both Western physicians and Chinese medical practitioners when reasonable treatment efforts by either have not resulted in expected or desirable outcomes.

## MANAGING MEDICAL RELATIONSHIPS

In the course of day-to-day clinical practice in the West, acupuncturists and practitioners of Chinese medicine are often asked to treat patients who are currently taking one or more Western prescription drugs and who do not want to be on those drugs. Therefore, Western practitioners of Chinese medicine frequently have two questions: 1) Should they start administering Chinese medicinals while the patient is concurrently taking Western medications, and 2), if so, how should they adjust or discontinue medications for patients making this request? The first concern has to do with the question of the established safety or inherent risk involved in combining Western pharmaceuticals with Chinese medicinals. Unfortunately, at this time, this is largely *terra incognita*, as all the potential interactions between Western and Chinese medicinals have not been clearly established. Conversely, we know of no published Chinese sources suggesting that certain specific Chinese medicinals should not be taken with certain specific Western medicinals.[13] However, numerous anecdotal reports concerning toxic or lethal interactions suggest that a conservative approach should be followed when Chinese medicinals and Western pharmaceuticals are used concurrently. For example, several deaths have been reported among chronic hepatitis patients in Japan taking *Xiao Chai Hu Tang* (Minor Bupleurum Decoction) along with interferon.[14]

In spite of many newly formed information services or initiatives to monitor and improve quality control of Chinese medicinal herbs, at present there is no definitive database detailing reported or potential medicinal interactions. This situation is made even more complex due to the fact that Chinese doctors prescribe multivalent doses of multi-ingredient formulas. Therefore, our conservative recommendation to Western Chinese medical practitioners is to do what they do in China: proceed cautiously, prescribing only small initial doses for a few days in order to monitor for any unwanted or potentially dangerous drug side effects or interactions. This conservative approach can be extended to the recommendation that doses should be increased only in the absence of unwanted effects. In view of the paucity of published studies documenting the safety of combining specific Chinese and Western medicines, many Western physicians may be reluctant to assume the risk of advising or even permitting their patients to take Chinese medicinals concurrently with Western synthetic medicines. However, it is our hope that the extensive case histories and research abstracts included throughout this book will serve to allay such fears.

The authors are encouraged by the recent acknowledgment by the U.S. National Institutes of Health (NIH), Center for Complementary and Alternative Medicine of inherent problems in the clinical study of compound Chinese herbal formulas. Recently the NIH waived a previous requirement for studies verifying that every possible combination of Chinese medicinal and Western pharmaceutical is safe. Subsequently, the NIH has given permission to the Food and Drug Administration (FDA) to register such formulas as "safe for investigational purposes." We believe this cautious but progressive attitude is an appropriate stance to take when dealing with clinical issues related to lack of knowledge and evolving standards of practice surrounding uses of Chinese medicines in Western countries. Chinese medicine has been used safely in China by millions of people for thousands of years. A recent poll in the People's Republic of China confirmed that a majority of Chinese citizens who use Chinese medicines report few, minor, or no side effects. The results of this survey suggest that the majority of Chinese believe that Chinese medicines can cure diseases, including numerous psychiatric disorders, in cases where Western medicine offers little help.[15] The authors feel strongly that it would be unreasonable not to take advantage of the vast body of accumulated Chinese medical knowledge because contemporary Western scientific approaches to verification of efficacy or mechanism of action have not yet strongly endorsed the many uses of Chinese medicine. Only by employing Chinese medical therapeutics in a Western milieu can clinicians and researchers begin to more completely understand fundamental aspects of Chinese medicine.

Both authors feel strongly that all questions of changing or discontinuing Western medications brought to the attention of a Chinese medical practitioner should be referred to the patient's Western physician. Chinese medical practitioners do not have training in Western medical pharmacology and are, therefore, not in a position to provide competent or safe advice to patients. The only exception to this general rule would apply to Chinese medical clinicians dually licensed to practice Western medicine. It is clearly the case that the Western physician is the legally licensed prescribing physician and, therefore, the clinician with sole authority to recommend dosing changes, alternative Western medications, or discontinuation of Western medications. Further, in most if not all states in the United States, it is illegal for Chinese medical practitioners to offer specific advice concerning dosage or discontinuation of Western medications being used by patients under their care. It follows that in cases when a patient is taking Western medications while undergoing Chinese medical treatment and reported signs or symptoms suggest a need for reevaluation of current medications, the patient should be referred back to his or her prescribing Western physician for consultation. Subsequently, the question of deciding whether, when, or how to discontinue Western medications will be addressed between the patient and his or her Western physician. The authors feel strongly that it is the Chinese medical practitioner's ethical responsibility to contact the patient's Western physician or other medical providers in order to explain the Chinese medical treatments being provided and the rationale for such treatments. However, the authors can think of no instance in which it is or should be the Chinese medical practitioner's responsibility or role to adjust Western medications or advise patients about Western medical care, other than to refer the patient back to their prescribing physician.

ENDNOTES:

[1]Jacobs, Karl. M. & Hirsch, Kenneth A., "Psychiatric Complications of Ma-Huang," *Psychosomatics*, #1, 2000, p. 58-62

[2]Kohn, L.T., Corrigan, J.M., Donaldson, M.S., eds., Institute of Medicine Report, "To Err is Human: Building a Safer Health System," National Academy Press, Washington, DC, Nov. 29, 1999

[3]Yamashita, H. *et al*, "Adverse Events in Acupuncture and Moxibustion Treatment: A Six Year Survey at a National Clinic in Japan," *Journal of Alternative & Complementary Medicine*, #5, 1999, p. 229-236. Of a total of 55,291 acupuncture treatments, only 64 adverse events were reported, *i.e.*, 1.01 events per 1,000 treatments, many of which, such as ecchymosis without pain or transient hypotension, were extremely minor.

[4]Castillo, *op. cit.*, p. 279

[5]*Ibid.*, p. 5

[6]E.g., Jin Pu-fang, "The Treatment of 58 Cases of Post Liver Cancer Chemotherapy Vomiting with *Zhu Ye Shi Gao Tang* (Bamboo Leaf & Gypsum Decoction)," *Zhe Jiang Zhong Yi Za Zhi* (*Zhejiang Journal of Chinese Medicine*), #5, 1995, p. 200

Gong Hao, "The Treatment of 17 Cases of Cancer Chemotherapy Reactions with *Bu Yang Huan Wu Tang* (Supplement Yang & Restore the Five [Viscera] Decoction)," *Zhe Jiang Zhong Yi Za Zhi* (*Zhejiang Journal of Chinese Medicine*), #2, 1996, p. 67

Wei Chang-chun *et al.*, "The Treatment of 20 Cases of Anti-tubercular Medicine's Gastro-intestinal Tract Reactions with Chinese Medicinals," *Ji Lin Zhong Yi Yao* (*Jilin Chinese Medicine & Medicinals*), #4, 1999, p. 17

Zhou Xiong-gen, "A Clinical Audit of the Preventive Treatment of Chemotherapy Gastro-intestinal Tract Reactions with Chinese Medicinals," *Shang Hai Zhong Yi Yao Za Zhi* (*Shanghai Journal of Chinese Medicine & Medicinals*), #6, 1999, p. 24-25

Lin Bei-hong *et al.*, "The Treatment of 30 Cases of Post-chemotherapy Gastro-intestinal Tract Reactions with Acupuncture & Massage," *Si Chuan Zhong Yi* (*Sichuan Chinese Medicine*), #9, 1999, p. 52-53

Li Zong-ju, "The Treatment of 59 Cases of Cancer Chemotherapy Toxic Reactions by the Methods of Regulating & Rectifying the Spleen & Stomach," *Si Chuan Zhong Yi* (*Sichuan Chinese Medicine*), #10, 1999, p. 24-25

He Guo-zhang, "The Chinese Medicine Treatment of 25 Cases of Amenorrhea as a Result of Neuroleptic Medicines," *Xin Zhong Yi* (*New Chinese Medicine*), #9, 1995, p. 51-52

Wu Hong-ying, "The Treatment of [62 Cases of] Post-surgical Abdominal Distention with *Zhu Hou Tang* (Post-surgery Decoction)," *Shan Dong Zhong Yi Za Zhi* (*Shandong Journal of Chinese Medicine*), #1, 1995, p. 34

Zhang Hui-ling, "The Treatment of [40 Cases of] Post-surgical Yin Vacuity Fever with *Sha Shen San Xian Tang* (Glehnia Three Immortals Decoction)," *Zhe Jiang Zhong Yi Za Zhi* (*Zhejiang Journal of Chinese Medicine*), #3, 1995, p. 113

Yang Ji-ping, "The Treatment of [23 Cases of] Post Breast Cancer Surgery Edema of the Upper Arms by the Methods of Boosting the Qi & Quickening the Blood," *Zhe Jiang Zhong Yi Za Zhi* (*Zhejiang Journal of Chinese Medicine*), #5, 1995, p. 222

Mi Yang, "The Treatment of 80 Cases of Post-surgical Abortion Excessive Menstruation with *Gu Jing Wan* (Secure the Menses Pills)," *Hu Bei Zhong Yi Za Zhi* (*Hubei Journal of Chinese Medicine*), #2, 1993, p. 9

Lin Guang-yu *et al.*, "A Clinical Audit of Post Serious Infection Spleen Vacuity Syndrome in Infants," *Zhong Yi Za Zhi* (*Journal of Chinese Medicine*), #1, 1998, p. 38-39

[7]E.g., Liu Ying-feng, "The Chinese Medical Diagnosis & Treatment of [40 Cases of] Antibiotic-resistant Pediatric Respiratory Tract Infections," *Si Chuan Zhong Yi* (*Sichuan Chinese Medicine*), #1, 1996, p. 44-45

[8]Antonovsky, Aaron, *Health, Stress and Coping*, Jossey-Bass & Co., San Francisco, 1979

[9]Castillo, *op. cit.*, p. 79

[10]This is actually a modern paraphrasing of these passages based on Maoshing Ni's *The Yellow Emperor's Classic of Medicine*, Shambhala, Boston, 1995, p. 1. We have chosen to use it rather than a more scholarly accurate, word for word translation since it so clearly elucidates the moral teaching of Chinese medicine *vis à vis* the cause and prevention of disease.

[11]Castillo, *op. cit.*, p. 281

[12]E.g., Wang Xia-ling & Zhou Da-qiao, "An Analysis of Those with Liver Depression & Serum Levels pf [Various] Estrogens," *Hu Bei Zhong Yi Za Zhi* (*Hubei Journal of Chinese Medicine*), #4, 1996, p. 38-39

Li Xiao-ping & Zhang Min-jian, "The Treatment of 86 Cases of Elevated Serum Prolactin in Females with *Xian Mai Tang* (Epimedium & Malted Barley Decoction)," *Fu Jian Zhong Yi Yao* (*Fujian Chinese Medicine & Medicinals*), #5, 1996, p. 27-28

[13]John Chen has made some suggestions along these lines (all using the verb "may"), but these suggestions seem to be based on theory as opposed to real-life case histories or clinical studies. See Chen, John, "Recognition & Prevention of Herb-Drug Interactions," *Clinical Manual of Oriental Medicine*, Lotus Herbs, La Puente, CA, 1998, p. 4/25-4/27

[14]*California Journal of Oriental Medicine*, #1, 1999, p. 48

[15]"Chinese Medicine Preferred," News, News, News, *The Journal of Chinese Medicine*, May, 1999, p. 4

# ❖ Book 2 ❖

# CHINESE ESSENCE SPIRIT DISEASES

## INTRODUCTION

This Book discusses the Chinese disease categories commonly considered essence spirit or psychiatric diseases in traditional Chinese medicine. Most essence spirit diseases resemble syndromes defined in Western psychiatry that have presumed causes and established treatments from the point of view of Western medicine. Others do not correspond to accepted Western medical disease categories and, therefore, have no understood causes or treatments from a Western medical viewpoint. As of this writing, the authors are unaware of any evidence suggesting that Chinese and Western medical treatments for the Chinese diseases described in this Book (or in Book 3) are incompatible, thus resulting in potential harm to the patient. Emerging research data and case reports suggest that judiciously combining or integrating treatments from both systems may result in improved clinical outcomes. Possible approaches to integrative treatments have been discussed above in Book 1, Chapter 8, The Integration of Chinese & Western Psychiatric Treatments.

## THE RELATIONSHIP BETWEEN CHINESE ESSENCE SPIRIT DISEASES & MODERN WESTERN PSYCHIATRIC DISEASES FROM THE CHINESE MEDICAL POINT OF VIEW

One of the confusing things about doing Chinese medicine in the 21st century in the West is the relationship between traditional Chinese disease categories, modern Western disease categories, and Chinese pattern discrimination. While professionally practiced Chinese medicine bases treatment primarily on the patient's individualized pattern discrimination, there is a relationship between patterns and diseases. Over not less than 20 centuries, Chinese doctors have identified the most commonly presenting patterns under each disease. The problem is that we are currently using two different disease nosologies in modern Chinese medicine: 1) traditional Chinese medical disease categories and 2) modern Western medical disease categories. Unfortunately, the commonly seen Chinese patterns have not been worked out for every modern Western medical disease. For instance, in Book 3 on the Chinese medical treatment of Western psychiatric disorders, there are no entries for personality disorders, sexual and gender identity disorders, or eating disorders. Some diagnoses are a fairly recent innovation in the West, and Chinese doctors have yet to adopt them, while other conditions, due to differences in diet and lifestyle, are not as common in China as in the West.

In cases where the patient comes with a modern Western medical diagnosis but the practitioner cannot find anything about that disease in the English language Chinese medical literature, what's a practitioner to do? In that case, the practitioner should simply do a pattern discrimination and treat the patient's pattern. As said above, no matter what the Western medical disease diagnosis, Chinese medical treatment is predicated upon the pattern above all else. However, there is a possible intermediary step which can help guide the practitioner toward the most likely pattern or patterns. This intermediary step consists of doing a traditional Chinese disease diagnosis.

For more than 2,000 years, Chinese doctors have recognized certain disease entities to which they have given specific names. Some of these disease categories are the same as Western medicine, such as headache and insomnia, some are not considered diseases in their own right but are considered symptoms, such as abdominal pain, and some are disease categories unique to Chinese medicine which have no identical equivalent in modern Western medicine, such as the seven mountings. There are literally hundreds of traditional Chinese disease categories. In Chinese, this indeterminate list is often referred to as *za bing* or miscellaneous diseases. These diseases are "miscellaneous" because they are indeterminate in number and also are not part of any particular specialty, such as gynecology or pediatrics, other than general internal medicine or *nei ke*.

Till now, it is our experience that most Western practitioners of acupuncture and Chinese medicine are not very familiar and do not tend to make conscious use of this list of "miscellaneous diseases." Unfortunately, we believe this is a great mistake. This list of miscellaneous diseases can help funnel one to the correct group of patterns whenever a patient presents with a modern Western disease for which no published standard Chinese pattern discrimination yet exists in the English language literature.

For instance, fibromyalgia syndrome (FMS) is not yet a commonly accepted disease diagnosis among Chinese medical practitioners in the People's Republic of China, and, as far as we are aware, there are not yet published, comprehensive Chinese discussions of the pattern discrimination of this condition. Nevertheless, if one knows that the four main symptoms of FMS are muscle-joint aching and pain, insomnia, fatigue, and depression, then one should have no problem in understanding what the patterns are that cover this condition. This is because muscle-joint pain is categorized as the Chinese disease category of impediment, while each of the other three are Chinese disease categories in their own right. Chinese doctors have been writing about all four of these for hundreds of generations, and there is no lack of pre-modern and contemporary literature on each of these in terms of their disease causes and mechanisms, pattern

discrimination, and acupuncture and Chinese medicinal treatment.

The same thing holds true for mental-emotional diseases. For many years, it was a commonly held mistake among Western practitioners that Chinese medicine does not specifically address mental-emotional diseases, that its disease nosology is essentially somatically based. Those who say this are obviously not familiar with the list of Chinese *za bing* or how to use this list in modern Western clinical practice. Within this list, there are a number which, when taken as a whole, do cover the full range of mental-emotional disturbance. However, this list does not look like *The Merck Manual*'s chapter on psychiatric disorders or the *DSM-IV*. Instead of bipolar illness, schizophrenia, senile dementia, and post-traumatic stress syndrome, there are withdrawal and mania, epilepsy, feeblemindedness, insomnia, and impaired memory. By the Ming dynasty, psychological disturbances were divided in the *Yi Xue Ru Men* (*Entering the Gate of the Study of Medicine*) into three main categories and 15 types or subcategories. These three main categories were 1) withdrawal, mania, and epilepsy, 2) vexation and agitation, and 3) fright, palpitations, and fear. The 15 subcategories were: withdrawal, mania, epilepsy, vexation and agitation, deranged speech, picking at one's bedclothes, a tendency to crying for no reason, anger, a tendency to sighing, sorrow, palpitations, fright, fear, forgetfulness, and inability to lie down.[1] While more modern books give slightly different lists, if one understands the major clinical manifestations of any modern Western psychiatric disease, those manifestations are covered by one or more traditional Chinese disease categories.

Therefore, before discussing a number of modern Western psychiatric diseases, we would first like to present a list of traditional Chinese essence spirit disorders. Although *jing shen bing* could be translated as psychiatric diseases, we have chosen a more literal word for word translation in order to help Western practitioners keep this category of disease diagnoses separate from modern Western psychiatric disease diagnoses. Using the disease mechanisms and pattern discrimination described under each of these Chinese disease categories, one should be able to understand and treat *any* modern Western psychiatric disease with Chinese medicine. This is why our first Chinese medical section under each of the modern Western psychiatric diseases discussed in this book has to do with the identification of the Chinese medical diseases that traditionally are used to cover that disorder. We believe that this is an extremely important step in doing contemporary Chinese medicine in the West. If one is unfamiliar or unskilled in using this technique, then one will always be at the mercy of what is currently available on Chinese medicine in English.

## USING THIS TECHNIQUE IN REAL LIFE

As an example of how to use this technique, let us say that a patient suffers from paranoid personality disorder. This is not one of the Western psychiatric disease diagnoses which have yet made it into the Chinese medical literature. However, the fact that no Chinese doctor has worked out a set of pattern discriminations and, therefore, their associated treatment principles and plans is immaterial. According to the *DSM-IV*, persons with this pattern of personality development consistently assume that others will attempt to harm, exploit, or deceive them. In addition, people with this disorder also tend to anger quickly. Knowing these salient clinical manifestations, we can confidently say that people manifesting a paranoid personality disorder have two main Chinese essence spirit diseases: 1) fear and fright and 2) irritability or easy anger. Therefore, the patient's pattern discrimination must include one or more of the patterns which correspond to these two Chinese diseases.

When it comes to irritability, every pattern of this condition is associated with the liver. All are evolutions or complications of liver depression. Therefore, we immediately know that every patient with paranoid personality disorder and irritability has liver depression as part of their overall Chinese pattern discrimination. In terms of fear, there are three Chinese medical disease mechanisms or basic patterns: kidney essence vacuity, qi and blood vacuity, and liver-gallbladder qi vacuity. Because liver-gallbladder qi vacuity is nothing really other than spleen qi vacuity with elements of liver depression and blood vacuity not constructing the heart spirit, this is not really more than a liver-spleen disharmony at root. In a young male with a shao yang body type, of all the patterns listed under fear and fright and irritability, the most likely disease mechanism is liver-spleen disharmony with (heart) qi and

blood vacuity. If fear is more pronounced, then vacuity is probably playing a larger part. If irritability is pronounced, then liver disease is probably more pronounced and evil heat is likely. On the other hand, if the patient had a shao yin body type and was extremely restless and agitated, then the most likely pattern would be kidney yin (or essence) insufficiency, probably with vacuity heat and an element of liver depression due to yin blood not nourishing and emolliating the liver.

Using this same process of triangulation and hypothesis-formation based on age, sex, and body type, one can use various combinations of Chinese essence spirit disease diagnoses to help arrive at pattern discriminations and, hence, their treatments for *any patient of any Western psychiatric disease*. The key to making this process work is teasing out the main *clinical* manifestations of any Western psychiatric disease which are simultaneously traditional Chinese disease categories in their own right. Fear and irritability are examples of traditional Chinese essence spirit diseases. However, since sexual jealousy is not a Chinese essence spirit disease, knowing that patients with paranoid personality disorder tend to be jealous of their spouses or sexual partners does not help advance our Chinese disease diagnosis or ultimate pattern discrimination until or unless one can reframe jealousy into a type of fear, in this case fear of losing or sharing one's partner. Likewise, knowing that persons with this type of personality development are more likely to be seen in hierarchical and egocentric societies also does not immediately lead to a narrowing down of possible patterns with this illness. Therefore, it is important to know what are the main categories of Chinese essence spirit diseases as well as how to analyze more complex symptoms into these relatively basic building blocks of emotion and disease.

## ENDNOTES:

[1] Li Qing-fu & Liu Du-zhou, *Zhong Yi Jing Shen Bing Xue (A Study of Chinese Medical Psychiatric Diseases)*, Tianjin Science & Technology Publishing Co., Tianjin, 1989, p. 7

# ❖ 1 ❖

# WITHDRAWAL & MANIA

Withdrawal and mania, *dian* and *kuang*, are a yin-yang pair of conditions which can either exist separately or alternate back and forth between the two. Withdrawal refers to a torpid, flat, depressed affect with a tendency to taciturnity, uncommunicativeness, and solitariness. It may also include incoherent speech, a lowering of mental faculties, and even syncope and coma. Mania refers to an agitated, excited affect accompanied by inappropriate anger and/or laughing, mental, physical, and emotional restlessness, etc.

The first mention of withdrawal in the Chinese medical literature appears in the *Nei Jing (Inner Classic)*. Both the *Su Wen (Simple Questions)* and *Ling Shu (Spiritual Axis)* refer to "withdrawal disease," "withdrawal and epilepsy," "bone withdrawal disease," and "vessel withdrawal disease." Zhang Zhong-jing's *Jin Gui Yao Lue (Essentials of the Golden Cabinet)* speaks of "withdrawal and dizziness," while Chao Yuan-fang mentions "wind withdrawal" and Sun Si-miao mentions "withdrawal evils." As for the term "mania," it predates the Chinese medical literature, showing up in such early Chinese classics as the *Shang Shu (Book of Shang)* and *Huai Nan Zi (Master Huai Nan)*. The *Su Wen (Simple Questions)* refers to "reversal mania" and "fright mania." Chao Yuan-fang discusses "wind mania." The first use of the compound term "withdrawal and mania" is in the *Ling Shu (Spiritual Axis)*. As mentioned above, by the Ming dynasty, withdrawal, mania, and epilepsy were considered the three major manifestations of essence spirit disease.

In some sense, withdrawal and mania are the grand, over-arching yin-yang dichotomy of all Chinese essence spirit diseases, with numerous other Chinese essence spirit disease categories being subcategories of one or the other of these two. Therefore, many histories of Chinese medical psychiatry simply discuss the evolution of this compound disease category. In fact, it is important to understand that this compound term is *not* a single disease entity. While some patients may alternate between withdrawal and mania, many others will primarily exhibit the symptoms of one or the other. Therefore, the authors have not been able to find any recent Chinese research into this disorder since it is not a single disorder, and this compound term is not used as a diagnostic label in real-life clinical practice.

## NOSOLOGY:

Apparent phenomenological resemblances exist between certain core features of the various Chinese medical patterns of withdrawal and mania and numerous Western psychiatric or medical categories, such as depression, mania, psychotic disorders, anxiety disorders, somatoform disorders, personality disorders, endocrinological disorders, and other medical disorders, including neurologic disorders. However, it is important to again emphasize that nosological categories employed in Chinese medicine do not correspond to established Western medical categories of psychiatric or medical disorders. This is the case even when disorders operationalized in both systems have the same English name. For example, mania is the commonly used English translation of the Chinese term *kuang*. Careful review of the four patterns of mania described below demonstrates that these patterns cover a range of complex psychiatric and possible medical disorders beyond mania per se. Certain patterns of mania resemble core features of mania as it is conceptualized in contemporary Western psychiatric nosology, but other patterns include symptoms which are diagnosed as other disorders in Western psychiatry. In addition, numerous symptoms appearing in the patterns of withdrawal and mania are considered as potentially independent essence spirit diseases, and each of these essence spirit diseases has its own correspondences and similarities to a number of Western psychiatric and medical diagnoses. In view of the order of complexity inherent in these Chinese disease categories, attempts to make inferences about Western medical or psychiatric disorders that correspond to the patterns of withdrawal and mania would be unproductive at best and potentially misguided or confusing at worst. Therefore, the reader is referred to sections on comparative nosology and differential diagnosis in chapters on the respective essence spirit diseases.

## DIFFERENTIAL DIAGNOSIS:

A thorough Western medical-psychiatric differential diagnosis must consider reasonable medical possibilities before assuming a primary psychogenic origin of any of the patterns of withdrawal and mania described below.

## CHINESE DISEASE CAUSES & DISEASE MECHANISMS:

In Chinese medicine, stirring or movement (which include mental stirring, verbal stirring, and physical stirring) is categorized as yang, and stillness is categorized as yin. Therefore, mania, which is characterized as excessive stirring and movement, is categorized as yang, while withdrawal, which is categorized as excessive stillness, is categorized as yin. In the *Su Wen (Simple Questions)*, it says, "All agitation and mania pertain to fire." In "Difficulty 20" in the *Nan Jing (Classic of Difficulties)*, it says, "Double yang leads to mania; double yin leads to withdrawal." Later doctors built upon this early nosological framework in further elaborating the disease causes and mechanisms of withdrawal and mania.

In the Yuan dynasty, Zhu Dan-xi said:

> Withdrawal is categorized as yin, while mania is categorized as yang... Mostly it is caused by phlegm binding within the heart and chest.

In the Qing dynasty, Ye Tian-shi said:

Mania is due to great fright and great fear. The disease is in the liver, gallbladder, and stomach channels. Three yangs combine and ascend and upbear. Therefore, fire blazes leading to phlegm surging. Hence the orifices of the heart become blocked and obstructed. Withdrawal is due to accumulation of worry and accumulation of depression. This disease is in the heart, spleen, and pericardium. These three yin seek shelter and do not diffuse. Hence qi depression leads to phlegm confounding, and the spirit mind becomes obscured.

In general, we can say that withdrawal is either due to the clear qi not being upborne and, therefore, the spirit brilliance not being constructed or some evil causing lack of free flow of the qi and/or blockage of the heart orifices. Heart-spleen dual vacuity and spleen-kidney yang vacuity are the two main mechanisms for nonconstruction of the spirit brilliance. Liver depression due to unfulfilled desires may cause non-free flow of the qi and, therefore, inhibition of the qi mechanism which may also manifest as inhibition of the spirit mind. When it comes to blockage of the heart orifices clouding and confounding the spirit, phlegm and blood stasis are the main culprits. Mania, on the other hand, is primarily due to the heart spirit being harassed by some sort of evil heat or fire. This may be depressive heat, phlegm heat, yang ming replete heat, or vacuity heat. However, some Chinese sources say that blood stasis may also cause mania. In this case, heat has damaged the blood and the blood has become static.

Although some Chinese textbooks list a blood stasis pattern of mania as a discrete pattern without heat, stasis alone does not account for mania. Because static blood inhibits the engenderment of new blood, blood stasis may lead to vacuity heat just as heat damaging the blood (vessels) amy lead to stasis. In any case, all chronic, enduring diseases tend to eventually become complicated with blood stasis. Therefore, in clinical practice, blood stasis typically combines with other disease mechanisms and manifests as simply one element of a more complicated pattern discrimination.

## TREATMENT BASED ON PATTERN DISCRIMINATION:

## 1. WITHDRAWAL

## A. LIVER QI DEPRESSION & BINDING PATTERN

MAIN SYMPTOMS: Emotional depression, a dull affect, taciturnity, illogical speech, irritability and easy anger, if severe, suicidal thoughts, no desire to live, or self-injury, chest and rib-side fullness and oppression, a tendency to sighing, no thought for food or drink, menstrual irregularity in females, a dark tongue with thin, white fur, and a bowstring pulse

**TREATMENT PRINCIPLES:** Course the liver and rectify the qi, resolve depression and arouse the spirit

**FORMULA & MEDICINALS:** *Chai Hu Shu Gan San Jia Wei* (Bupleurum Course the Liver Powder with Added Flavors)

Radix Bupleuri (*Chai Hu*), 12g, Rhizoma Cyperi Rotundi (*Xiang Fu*), 10g, Radix Albus Paeoniae Lactiflorae (*Bai Shao*), 10g, Fructus Citri Aurantii (*Zhi Ke*), 10g, Radix Ligustici Wallichii (*Chuan Xiong*), 6g (added later), Radix Polygalae Tenuifoliae (*Yuan Zhi*), 10g, Caulis Perillae Frutescentis (*Su Geng*), 10g, Lignum Aquilariae Agallochae (*Chen Xiang*), 6g, Radix Glycyrrhizae (*Gan Cao*), 3g

Decoct in water and administer orally in two divided doses, morning and evening, one *ji* per day.

**ADDITIONS & SUBTRACTIONS:** If enduring or extreme depression has transformed heat with a bitter taste in the mouth, more extreme anger, a red tongue, and a bowstring, rapid pulse, one can add Radix Scutellariae Baicalensis (*Huang Qin*) and Rhizoma Coptidis Chinensis (*Huang Lian*). If there is liver depression qi stagnation with spleen vacuity loss of fortification, then use *Xiao Yao San* (Rambling Powder) with additions and subtractions instead. If there is a liver-spleen disharmony with depressive heat, use either *Dan Zhi Xiao Yao San* (Moutan & Gardenia Rambling Powder) or *Xiao Chai Hu Tang* (Minor Bupleurum Decoction) with additions and subtractions.

*Xiao Yao San:* Radix Bupleuri (*Chai Hu*), 3g, Radix Angelicae Sinensis (*Dan Gui*), 10g, Radix Albus Paeoniae Lactiflorae (*Bai Shao*), 10g, Rhizoma Atractylodis Macrocephalae (*Bai Zhu*), 10g, Sclerotium Poriae Cocos (*Fu Ling*), 10g, mix-fried Radix Glycyrrhizae (*Gan Cao*), 6g, Herba Menthae Haplocalycis (*Bo He*), 3-6g (added later), uncooked Rhizoma Zingiberis (*Shen Jiang*), 2 slices (added later)

*Dan Zhi Xiao Yao San:* Cortex Radicis Moutan (*Dan Pi*), 10g, Fructus Gardeniae Jasminoidis (*Zhi Zi*), 10g, Radix Bupleuri (*Chai Hu*), 3-10g, Radix Angelicae Sinensis (*Dan Gui*), 10g, Radix Albus Paeoniae Lactiflorae (*Bai Shao*), 10g, Rhizoma Atractylodis Macrocephalae (*Bai Zhu*), 10g, Sclerotium Poriae Cocos (*Fu Ling*), 10g, mix-fried Radix Glycyrrhizae (*Gan Cao*), 6g

*Xiao Chai Hu Tang:* Radix Bupleuri (*Chai Hu*), 3-10g, Radix Scutellariae Baicalensis (*Huang Qin*), 10-12g, Radix Codonopsitis Pilosulae (*Dang Shen*), 10g, Rhizoma Pinelliae Ternatae (*Ban Xia*), 10g, mix-fried Radix Glycyrrhizae (*Gan Cao*), 6g, Fructus Zizyphi Jujubae (*Da Zao*), 3-5 pieces, uncooked Rhizoma Zingiberis (*Shen Jiang*), 2 slices (added later)

**ACUPUNCTURE:** *Tai Chong* (Liv 3), *Nei Guan* (Per 6), *Shen Men* (Ht 7), *He Gu* (LI 4), *Zu San Li* (St 36), *Dan Zhong* (CV 17). Use draining technique.

**B. PHLEGM QI DEPRESSION & BINDING PATTERN**

**MAIN SYMPTOMS:** Emotional depression, a flat affect, paranoia, lots of worries, nonsensical speech, muttering to oneself, a tendency to sighing, chest and rib-side distention and fullness, no thought for food or drink, possible plum pit qi or the sensation of something stuck in one's throat which cannot be spit up or swallowed down, a tendency to profuse phlegm, fibrocystic breasts in females, slimy tongue fur, and a bowstring, slippery pulse

**TREATMENT PRINCIPLES:** Rectify the qi and resolve depression, transform phlegm and open the orifices

**FORMULA & MEDICINALS:** *Shi Si Wei Wen Dan Tang* (Fourteen Flavors Warm the Gallbladder Decoction)

Magnetitum (*Ci Shi*), 12g, Flouritum (*Zhi Shi Ying*), 12g, Rhizoma Gastrodiae Elatae (*Tian Ma*), 10g, Pericarpium Citri Reticulatae (*Chen Pi*), 10g, Rhizoma Pinelliae Ternatae (*Ban Xia*), 12g, bile-processed Rhizoma Arisaematis (*Dan Nan Xing*), 10g, Radix Polygalae Tenuifoliae (*Yuan Zhi*), 10g, Rhizoma Atractylodis Macrocephalae (*Bai Zhu*), 10g, Sclerotium Poriae Cocos (*Fu Ling*), 12g, Rhizoma Acori Graminei (*Shi Chang Pu*), 15g, Fructus Immaturus Citri Aurantii (*Zhi Shi*), 10g, Caulis Bambusae In Taeniis (*Zhu Ru*), 10g, mix-fried Radix Glycyrrhizae (*Gan Cao*), 5g, Medulla Junci Effusi (*Deng Xin Cao*), 1.5-3g

Decoct in water and administer orally in two divided doses, morning and evening, one *ji* per day.

**ADDITIONS & SUBTRACTIONS:** If complicated by spleen vacuity with fatigue and lassitude of the spirit, add Radix Codonopsitis Pilosulae (*Dang Shen*) and increase the dose of mix-fried Licorice. If there is no evidence of depressive heat disturbing the heart spirit, delete Juncus.

ACUPUNCTURE: *Ren Zhong* (GV 26), *Shen Men* (Ht 7), *Nei Guan* (Per 6), *Zhong Wan* (CV 12), *Zu San Li* (St 36), *Xing Jian* (Liv 2), *Feng Long* (St 40). Use even supplementing-even draining technique.

### C. PHLEGM DAMPNESS OBSTRUCTING INTERNALLY PATTERN

MAIN SYMPTOMS: Difficulty thinking, inattentiveness, a dull, flat affect, slow movements, fatigue, lack of strength, cowering, solitariness, possible visual and auditory hallucinations, torpid food intake, heart vexation, insomnia, a fat swollen tongue with teeth-marks on its edges and slimy, white tongue fur, and a slippery or deep, relaxed (*i.e.*, slightly slow) pulse

TREATMENT PRINCIPLES: Warm yang and fortify the spleen, transform phlegm and open the orifices

FORMULA & MEDICINALS: *Xiang Sha Liu Jun Zi Tang He Li Zhong Tang Jia Wei* (Auklandia & Amomum Six Gentlemen Decoction plus Rectify the Center Decoction with Added Flavors) Radix Codonopsitis Pilosulae (*Dang Shen*), 12g, Rhizoma Atractylodis Macrocephalae (*Bai Zhu*), 10g, Sclerotium Poriae Cocos (*Fu Ling*), 20g, mix-fried Radix Glycyrrhizae (*Gan Cao*), 10g, Radix Auklandiae Lappae (*Mu Xiang*), 6g, Fructus Amomi (*Sha Ren*), 6g (added later), uncooked Rhizoma Zingiberis (*Sheng Jiang*), 10g, dry Rhizoma Zingiberis (*Gan Jiang*), 10g, Pericarpium Citri Reticulatae (*Chen Pi*), 10g, Rhizoma Pinelliae Ternatae (*Ban Xia*), 10g, Rhizoma Atractylodis (*Cang Zhu*), 10g, Radix Polygalae Tenuifoliae (*Yuan Zhi*), 6g, Rhizoma Acori Graminei (*Shi Chang Pu*), 10g, Herba Agastachis Seu Pogostemi (*Huo Xiang*), 10g, Herba Eupatorii Fortunei (*Pei Lan*), 10g

Decoct in water and administer orally in two divided doses, morning and evening, one *ji* per day.

ADDITIONS & SUBTRACTIONS: If there is even more pronounced spleen vacuity with fatigue and lack of strength, one can add Radix Astragali Membranacei (*Huang Qi*) and Rhizoma Cimicifugae (*Sheng Ma*). If spleen vacuity has reached the kidneys and there is low back pain and excessively frequent, possibly turbid urination and/or excessive, white vaginal discharge, one can add Radix Dioscoreae Oppositae (*Shan Yao*) and Semen Dolichoris Lablab (*Bia Bian Dou*).

ACUPUNCTURE: *Dan Zhong* (CV 17), *Zhong Wan* (CV 12), *Nei Guan* (Per 6), *Shen Men* (Ht 7), *Zu San Li* (St 36), *Feng Long* (St 40), *Pi Shu* (Bl 20), *Wei Shu* (Bl 21). Use even supplementing-even draining technique.

### D. HEART-SPLEEN DUAL VACUITY PATTERN

MAIN SYMPTOMS: Excessive thinking, worry, and anxiety, dreaming of ghosts, confusion, heart palpitations, easily frightened, a predilection to sorrow and a desire to cry, impaired memory, difficulty thinking, sluggishness, nonsensical speech, a sallow yellow or pale white facial complexion, reduced intake of food, fatigue, a pale, typically enlarged tongue, and a fine, forceless pulse

TREATMENT PRINCIPLES: Fortify the spleen and nourish the heart, boost the qi and quiet the spirit

FORMULA & MEDICINALS: *Gui Pi Tang Jia Jian* (Restore the Spleen Decoction with Additions & Subtractions)

Mix-fried Radix Astragali Membranacei (*Huang Qi*), 30g, Radix Codonopsitis Pilosulae (*Dang Shen*), 12g, Radix Angelicae Sinensis (*Dang Gui*), 12g, Rhizoma Atractylodis Macrocephalae (*Bai Zhu*), 12g, Sclerotium Pararadicis Poriae Cocos (*Fu Shen*), 30g, Arillus Euphoriae Longanae (*Long Yan Rou*), 12g, Semen Zizyphi Spinosae (*Suan Zao Ren*), 15g, Semen Biotae Oreintalis (*Bai Zi Ren*), 15g, Fructus Schisandrae Chinensis (*Wu Wei Zi*), 10g, Radix Auklandiae Lappae (*Mu Xiang*), 10g, Radix Polygalae Tenuifoliae (*Yuan Zhi*), 6g, mix-fried Radix Glycyrrhizae (*Gan Cao*), 6g, Fructus Zizyphi Jujubae (*Da Zao*), 5 pieces

Decoct in water and administer orally in two divided doses, morning and evening, one *ji* per day.

ACUPUNCTURE: *Xin Shu* (Bl 15), *Pi Shu* (Bl 20), *Nei Guan* (Per 6), *Shen Men* (Ht 7), *Zu San Li* (St 36). Use supplementing technique.

### E. SPLEEN-KIDNEY YANG VACUITY PATTERN

MAIN SYMPTOMS: Advanced age, bodily weakness, or enduring disease which does not heal thus resulting in spleen disease reaching and damaging the kidneys with difficulty thinking, sluggishness, inattention, cowering, scanty speech, no thought for food or drink, bodily vacuity and lack of strength, a lusterless facial complexion, fear of cold, chilled extremities, a pale tongue with thin, white, fur, and a deep, fine, weak pulse

TREATMENT PRINCIPLES: Warm and supplement the spleen and kidneys assisted by transforming phlegm and opening the orifices

FORMULA & MEDICINALS: *Bu Gu Zhi Wan Jia Jian* (Psoraleae Pills with Additions & Subtractions)

Radix Astragali Membranacei (*Huang Qi*), 15g, Radix Codonopsitis Pilosulae (*Dang Shen*), 12g, Fructus Psoraleae Corylifoliae (*Bu Gu Zhi*), 12g, Herba Cistanchis Deserticolae (*Rou Cong Rong*), 12g, Radix Morindae Officinalis (*Ba Ji Tian*), 12g, mix-fried Radix Glycyrrhizae (*Gan Cao*), 6g, Sclerotium Poriae Cocos (*Fu Ling*), 12g, Radix Polygalae Tenuifoliae (*Yuan Zhi*), 10g, Radix Angelicae Sinensis (*Dang Gui*), 10g, Radix Ligustici Wallichii (*Chuan Xiong*), 10g (added later), Semen Biotae Orientalis (*Bai Zi Ren*), 12g, Semen Zizyphi Spinosae (*Suan Zao Ren*), 12g, Fructus Schisandrae Chinensis (*Wu Wei Zi*), 10g, Cortex Cinnamomi Cassiae (*Rou Gui*), 6g (added later)

Decoct in water and administer orally in two divided doses, morning and evening, one *ji* per day.

ADDITIONS & SUBTRACTIONS: If there are concomitant symptoms of blood stasis, one can add Cortex Radicis Moutan (*Dan Pi*) and Tuber Curcumae (*Yu Jin*).

ACUPUNCTURE: Moxa *Shen Shu* (Bl 23), *Ming Men* (GV 4), *Pi Shu* (Bl 20), *Wei Shu* (Bl 21), *Guan Yuan* (CV 4), and *Bai Hui* (GV 20).

## F. BLOOD STASIS OBSTRUCTING INTERNALLY PATTERN

MAIN SYMPTOMS: Emotional lability, irritability, speaking to oneself, torpid spirit, paranoia, delusional thinking, auditory and visual hallucinations, a dark, stagnant facial complexion, piercing, lancinating headache, a dark red tongue with static macules or spots, possible engorged, tortuous sublingual veins, and a bowstring, choppy pulse

TREATMENT PRINCIPLES: Rectify the qi and resolve depression, quicken the blood and transform stasis

FORMULA & MEDICINALS: *Xue Fu Zhu Yu Tang Jia Wei* (Blood Mansion Dispel Stasis Decoction with Added Flavors)

Semen Pruni Persicae (*Tao Ren*), 12g, Flos Carthami Tinctorii (*Hong Hua*), 10g, Radix Angelicae Sinensis (*Dang Gui*), 10g, uncooked Radix Rehmanniae (*Sheng Di*), 10g, Radix Ligustici Wallichii (*Chuan Xiong*), 6g, Radix Rubrus Paeoniae Lactiflorae (*Chi Shao*), 6g, Radix Platycodi Grandiflori (*Jie Geng*), 5g, Radix Cyathulae (*Chuan Niu Xi*), 10g, Radix Bupleuri (*Chai Hu*), 3g, Fructus Citri Aurantii (*Zhi Ke*), 6g, Radix Glycyrrhizae (*Gan Cao*), 6g, Hirudo Seu Whitmania (*Shui Zhi*), 6g

Decoct in water and administer orally in two divided doses, morning and evening, one *ji* per day.

ADDITIONS & SUBTRACTIONS: If there is scanty speech and scanty movement, a lusterless facial complexion, and fatigue and exhaustion, one can add Radix Astragali Membranacei (*Huang Qi*) and Radix Angelicae Sinensis (*Dang Gui*) to boost the qi and supplement the blood.

## 2. MANIA

### A. LIVER DEPRESSION TRANSFORMING FIRE PATTERN

MAIN SYMPTOMS: Emotional tension, agitation, irritability, easy anger, bouts of explosive, possibly violent anger, chest, breast, rib-side, and abdominal distention and pain, menstrual irregularity and PMS in females, a bitter taste in the mouth, possible constipation, headache, a red tongue, red tongue edges, or swollen tongue edges with a thin, yellow, possibly slightly dry fur, and a bowstring, rapid pulse

TREATMENT PRINCIPLES: Course the liver and resolve depression, downbear fire and quiet the spirit

FORMULA & MEDICINALS: *Long Dan Xie Gan Tang Jia Jian* (Gentiana Drain the Gallbladder Decoction with Additions & Subtractions)

Radix Gentianae Scabrae (*Long Dan Cao*), 6-10g, Radix Bupleuri (*Chai Hu*), 6g, Radix Scutellariae Baicalensis (*Huang Qin*), 10g, Rhizoma Coptidis Chinensis (*Huang Lian*), 3-4.5g (added later), Radix Albus Paeoniae Lactiflorae (*Bai Shao*), 10g, Fructus Gardeniae Jasminoidis (*Zhi Zi*), 10g, Cortex Radicis Moutan (*Dan Pi*), 10g, uncooked Radix Rehmanniae (*Sheng Di*), 12g, Radix Angelicae Sinensis (*Dang Gui*), 10g, Rhizoma Alismatis (*Ze Xie*), 10g, Semen Plantaginis (*Che Qian Zi*), 10g, Radix Glycyrrhizae (*Gan Cao*), 3g

Decoct in water and administer orally in two divided doses, morning and evening, one *ji* per day.

ADDITIONS & SUBTRACTIONS: If there is constipation, add Radix Et Rhizoma Rhei (*Da Huang*). If there are heart palpitations and insomnia, add uncooked Os Draconis (*Long Gu*) and Concha Ostreae (*Mu Li*).

ACUPUNCTURE: *Xing Jian* (Liv 2), *Xia Xi* (GB 43), *Lao Gong* (Per 8), *Da Ling* (Per 7), *Da Zhui* (GV 14), *Jian Shi* (Per 5)

### B. PHLEGM FIRE HARASSING ABOVE PATTERN

MAIN SYMPTOMS: Impetuosity, rashness, and impatience, breaking things and injuring other people, cursing and foul speech, an angry look in the eyes, a red facial complexion, red eyes, bound, constipated stools, a red tongue with slimy, yellow fur, and a bowstring, large, slippery, rapid pulse

TREATMENT PRINCIPLES: Settle the heart and flush phlegm, clear the liver and drain fire

FORMULA & MEDICINALS: *Da Huang Huang Lian Xie Xin Tang Jia Wei* (Rhubarb & Coptis Drain the Heart Decoction with Added Flavors)

Radix Et Rhizoma Rhei (*Da Huang*), 15g (added later), Radix Scutellariae Baicalensis (*Huang Qin*), 15g, Rhizoma Coptidis Chinensis (*Huang Lian*), 10g (added later), Rhizoma Anemarrhenae Aspheloidis (*Zhi Mu*), 15g, Fructus Gardeniae Jasminoidis (*Zhi Zi*), 12g, Tuber Curcumae (*Yu Jin*), 12g, Rhizoma Pinelliae Ternatae (*Ban Xia*), 12g, bile-processed Rhizoma Arisaematis (*Dan Nan Xing*), 10g, Concretio Siliceae Bambusae (*Tian Zhu Huang*), 10g, Rhizoma Acori Graminei (*Shi Chang Pu*), 10g

Decoct in water and administer orally in two divided doses, morning and evening, one *ji* per day.

ACUPUNCTURE: *Da Zhui* (GV 14), *Ren Zhong* (GV 26), *Nei Guan* (Per 6), *Lao Gong* (Per 8), *Feng Long* (St 40), *Tai Chong* (Liv 3). Use draining technique.

### C. YANG MING HEAT BINDING PATTERN

MAIN SYMPTOMS: Mania, agitation, deranged speech, a red facial complexion, a tendency to strip off one's clothes, no eating for days, recalcitrant constipation with dry, bound stools, scanty, reddish urine, a red tongue with dry, yellow fur, and a deep, rapid, forceful pulse

TREATMENT PRINCIPLES: Clear and drain the yang ming, calm the spirit and quiet agitation

FORMULA & MEDICINALS: *Da Cheng Qi Tang Jia Wei* (Major Order the Qi Decoction with Added Flavors)

Radix Et Rhizoma Rhei (*Da Huang*), 15g (added later), Mirabilitum (*Mang Xiao*), 10g (dissolved in the hot decoction), Cortex Magnoliae Officinalis (*Hou Po*), 15g, Fructus Immaturus Citri Aurantii (*Zhi Shi*), 12g, Fructus Gardeniae Jasminoidis (*Zhi Zi*), 12g, Fructus Forsythiae Suspensae (*Lian Qiao*), 12g, Radix Scutellariae Baicalensis (*Huang Qin*), 12g, Herba Menthae Haplocalycis (*Bo He*), 6g (added later), Radix Glycyrrhizae (*Gan Cao*), 6g

Decoct in water and administer orally in two divided doses, morning and evening, one *ji* per day.

ADDITIONS & SUBTRACTIONS: If there is thirst with a desire to drink, add Gypsum Fibrosum (*Shi Gao*) and Rhizoma Anemarrhenae Aspheloidis (*Zhi Mu*).

ACUPUNCTURE: *He Gu* (LI 4), *Qu Chi* (LI 11), *Nei Ting* (St 44), *Zhi Gou* (TB 6), *Da Zhui* (GV 14), *Lao Gong* (Per 8). Use draining technique.

### D. YIN VACUITY-FIRE EFFULGENCE PATTERN

MAIN SYMPTOMS: Enduring, long-standing mania which is not too severe, irritability, vexation and agitation, insomnia, excessive speech, susceptibility to fear, heat in the five hearts, afternoon tidal heat, possible malar flushing, possible night sweats, a red tongue with scanty, possibly yellow fur, and a fine, bowstring, rapid pulse

TREATMENT PRINCIPLES: Supplement the kidneys and nourish the liver, downbear fire and quiet the spirit

FORMULA & MEDICINALS: *Er Yin Jian Jia Jian* (Two Yin Decoction with Additions & Subtractions)

Uncooked Radix Rehmanniae (*Sheng Di*), 12-15g, Tuber Ophiopogonis Japonici (*Mai Dong*), 15g, Radix Scrophulariae Ningpoensis (*Xuan Shen*), 15g, stir-fried Semen Zizyphi Spinosae (*Suan Zao Ren*), 12g, Sclerotium Pararadicis Poriae Cocos (*Fu Shen*), 12g, Rhizoma Coptidis Chinensis (*Huang Lian*), 6-10g (added later), Caulis Akebiae (*Mu Tong*), 10g, Medulla Junci Effusi (*Deng Xin Cao*), 10g, Folium Bambusae (*Zhu Ye*), 10g, Radix Codonopsitis Pilosulae (*Dang Shen*), 12g, Rhizoma Acori Graminei (*Shi Chang Pu*), 6g

If yin vacuity-fire effulgence mania is complicated by phlegm heat, use the following *Er Yin Jian* modification:

Semen Trichosanthis Kirlowii (*Gua Lou Ren*), 15g, bile-processed Rhizoma Arisaematis (*Dan Nan Xing*), 10g, Concretio Siliceae Bambusae (*Tian Zhu Huang*), 10g, uncooked Radix Rehmanniae (*Sheng Di*), 15g, Tuber Ophiopogonis Japonici (*Mai Dong*), 15g, Radix Scrophulariae Ningpoensis (*Xuan Shen*), 15g, Radix Cynanchi Atrati (*Bai Wei*), 12g, Cortex Radicis Lycii Chinensis (*Di Gu Pi*), 12g, Rhizoma Coptidis Chinensis (*Huang Lian*), 6g (added later), Caulis Akebiae (*Mu Tong*), 10g, Medulla Junci Effusi (*Deng Xin Cao*), 10g

Decoct in water and administer orally in two divided doses, morning and evening, one *ji* per day.

**ACUPUNCTURE:** *San Yin Jiao* (Sp 6), *Tai Xi* (Ki 3), *Tai Chong* (Liv 3) needled through to *Yong Quan* (Ki 1), *Shen Men* (Ht 7). Use even supplementing-even draining technique.

**ADDITIONS & SUBTRACTIONS:** If there are night sweats, add *Yin Xi* (Ht 6). If there is a chronic dry, sore throat and dry mouth and throat, add *Lie Que* (Lu 7) and *Zhao Hai* (Ki 6) and subtract *Tai Xi*. If there are heart palpitations, add *Nei Guan* (Per 6).

## E. STASIS & HEAT MUTUALLY BINDING PATTERN

**MAIN SYMPTOMS:** Emotional lability, agitation, speaking to oneself, delusional thinking, auditory and visual hallucinations, a dark, stagnant facial complexion, piercing, lancinating headache, a dark red tongue with static macules or spots, possible engorged, tortuous sublingual veins and/or dryish, yellow fur, and a bowstring, rapid, possibly skipping pulse

**TREATMENT PRINCIPLES:** Quicken the blood and transform stasis, clear heat and quiet agitation

**FORMULA & MEDICINALS:** *Qin Lian Si Wu Tang Jia Wei* (Scutellaria & Coptis Four Materials Decoction with Added Flavors)

Semen Pruni Persicae (*Tao Ren*), 12g, Flos Carthami Tinctorii (*Hong Hua*), 10g, Radix Angelicae Sinensis (*Dang Gui*), 10g, uncooked Radix Rehmanniae (*Sheng Di*), 10g, Radix Ligustici Wallichii (*Chuan Xiong*), 6g, Radix Rubrus Paeoniae Lactiflorae (*Chi Shao*), 6g, Radix Platycodi Grandiflori (*Jie Geng*), 5g, Radix Cyathulae (*Chuan Niu Xi*), 10g, Rhizoma Coptidis Chinensis (*Huang Lian*), 3-6g (added later), Radix Scutellariae Baicalensis (*Huang Qin*), 10-12g, Radix Bupleuri (*Chai Hu*), 3g, Fructus Citri Aurantii (*Zhi Ke*), 6g, Radix Glycyrrhizae (*Gan Cao*), 6g, Hirudo Seu Whitmania (*Shui Zhi*), 6g

Decoct in water and administer orally in two divided doses, morning and evening, one *ji* per day.

**ADDITIONS & SUBTRACTIONS:** If there is also constipation, one can add Radix Et Rhizoma Rhei (*Da Huang*) and Mirabilitum (*Mang Xiao*). If there is excitation and restlessness with agitated stirring and lack of calm, one can add Cortex Radicis Moutan (*Dan Pi*) and uncooked Radix Rehmanniae (*Sheng Di*). If sleep at night is restless and there is depression, oppression, and discomfort, one can add Cortex Albizziae Julibrissinisis ((*He Huan Pi*) and Caulis Polygoni Multiflori (*Ye Jiao Teng*).

**ACUPUNCTURE:** *Xue Hai* (Sp 10), *San Yin Jiao* (Sp 6), *He Gu* (LI 4), *Qu Chi* (LI 11), *Tian Shu* (St 25), *Da Zhui* (GV 14). Use draining technique.

### ABSTRACT OF REPRESENTATIVE CHINESE RESEARCH:

*Zhong Guo Zhen Jiu (Chinese National Acupuncture & Moxibustion)*, #5, 1994, p. 8. Wu Ji-hong studied the treatment of 44 out-patient cases of withdrawal and mania with acupuncture. Of these patients, 15 were men and 29 were women. The youngest was 15 years old and the oldest was 48. Their course of disease had lasted from a half month to 20 years. All had been previously diagnosed and treated by Western medicine and either their results had not been marked or side effects were excessive. Therefore, they had stopped their Western medication and come for Chinese medical treatment. The main points used were *Ren Zhong* (GV 26), *Ya Men* (GV 15), and *Da Zhui* (GV 14). The auxiliary points were *Bai Hui* (GV 20), *Si Shen Cong* (M-HN-1), *Nei Guan* (Per 6), *Shen Men* (Ht 7), *Zhong Wan* (CV 12), *Feng Long* (St 40), and *Tai Chong* (Liv 3). Treatment was given once per day until the patient's emotions were stable and then switched to once every other day. Ten treatments equaled one course with a three day rest between successive courses. Of this cohort, 23 cases were cured, 11 cases got a marked effect, eight cases got some effect, and only two cases got no effect. Thus the total amelioration rate was 95.45%.

### REPRESENTATIVE CASE HISTORIES:

#### ❖ CASE 1[1] ❖

The patient was a 48 year old female agricultural worker who was first examined on July 20, 1986. A half year previously, the woman had become taciturn and spoke very little. At times she was tense and agitated and easily angered. Five days before the patient's initial visit, she had had an argument with a neighbor just as night was deepening and she was going to sleep. As a result, she had become emotionally upset and had not been able to sleep for several days. She was arrogant and presumptuous and would curse and swear for no reason. Sometimes she would chant, sometimes she would sing, and laughing gave way to crying without constancy. She moved about forcefully, while her stools were constipated and had not moved for several days. She was diagnosed by a Western medical physician as suffering from manic-depression, and she was administered tranquilizers without effect.

At the time she was seen by the Chinese doctor, she was manic and moving about restlessly. Her face was flushed red, she was alternately laughing and crying, and she spoke unintelligibly. There was profuse, thick phlegm, her tongue was crimson with thick, black, slimy fur, and her pulse was slippery, rapid, and forceful. Therefore, her pattern was discriminated as yang ming heat bind with phlegm heat harassing the heart and she was administered *Gan Sui Gun Tan Tang*: Radix Et Rhizoma Rhei (*Da Huang*), Mirabilitum (*Mang Xiao*), Fructus Citri Aurantii (*Zhi Ke*), Lapis Micae Seu Chloriti (*Meng Shi*), Radix Scutellariae Baicalensis (*Huang Qin*), Lignum Aquilariae Agallochae (*Chen Xiang*), Radix Glycyrrhizae (*Gan Cao*), and Radix Euphorbiae Kansui (*Gan Sui*), 10g each, and Plumula Nelumbinis Nuciferae (*Lian Zi Xin*), 3g.

After administering one *ji* of the above formula, black, sticky, stools were expelled with strands of mucus. Her breath was so foul-smelling it was difficult to bear, but, by evening, all her symptoms were markedly decreased. Thus she was administered another two *ji* of this formula, after which all her symptoms disappeared. On follow-up after half a year, there had been no recurrence.

### ❖ CASE 2[2] ❖

The patient was a 25 year old male worker who was first examined on July 24, 1990. Due to having to leave Zhejiang, his marriage had been called off, and, for the past three months, the man had been depressed. His outward affect was expressionless, he muttered and talked to himself, and, when he spoke, what he said made no sense. In addition, he laughed and cried without constancy. A family member had tried giving him a number of formulas, but none of these had produced any result. When the author of this case saw this patient, the man's eyes looked angry and his face and eyes were both red. His speech was deranged and made no sense, he was shouting curses, and he could neither eat nor sleep. The tongue was red with slimy, yellow fur, and the pulse was bowstring, slippery, and rapid.

Therefore, this patient's pattern was discriminated as fire exuberance and phlegm binding. Because the patient refused to take any more medicine, 120 grams of Mirabilitum (*Mang Xiao*) was made into soup with 300 grams of white radish without the man knowing that this soup contained any medicinals. Soon thereafter, the patient had a number of bowel movements. At first the stools were knotted and black like sheep droppings. Afterwards they became loose and mixed with phlegm drool and had a foul odor. After these bowel movements, his shouting of curses became gradually less and eventually he became calm enough to fall asleep. Therefore, the Mirabilitum was reduced to 60 grams, while the radish remained at the same dose and another *ji* of this soup was administered. After three days, the patient's mind progressively became clear, and he was prescribed medicinals to fortify the spleen and transform phlegm, calm the heart and quiet the spirit. On follow-up five years later, there had been no recurrence.

### ❖ CASE 3[3] ❖

The patient was a 24 year old female cadre who was first examined on Nov. 26, 1990. A half year previously, the patient had begun to laugh and cry without constancy. Her speech was illogical and meaningless, and she was vexed, agitated, and restless. She had been admitted to a hospital where she had been diagnosed as suffering from schizophrenia, for which she was placed on Valium and other Western psychotropic medications. However, these did not achieve a marked effect. Therefore, she was referred for acupuncture and treated with the acupuncture protocol described above under "Abstract of representative Chinese research." After a single treatment, the patient was obviously more calm than before. After one course of treatment, the patient's thinking was clear, and, after one month of treatment, she was judged cured. On follow-up after one year, there had been no recurrence.

### ❖ CASE 4[4] ❖

The patient was a 20 year old unmarried male who was first examined in August 1981. Several years earlier, due to reading books about failing to achieve success, he had become depressed for a long time and had become feeble-minded. His reactions were slow and he muttered and talked to himself. This had recurred four times in the previous four years. Several months before, he had suddenly become manic and had begun raising his hands to hit people. Three to four days later, he had again become feeble-minded. When Wang Ying-yu saw this patient, his facial complexion was somber white and his intelligence was not clear. His four limbs were curled up and spasmotic. His tongue tended towards red, and his pulse was fine and rapid.

Based on the above, the patient's disease was categorized as withdrawal disease and his pattern was categorized as heart blood internally depleted resulting in loss of nourishment of the heart spirit. The patient was pricked to bleed at *Shao Shang* (Lu 11), *Shang Yang* (LI 1), *Zhong Chong* (Per 9), *Guan Chong* (TB 1), *Shao Chong* (Ht 9), *Shao Ze* (SI 1), *Yin Bai* (Sp 1), *Li Dui* (St 45), *Da Dun* (Liv 1), and *Qiao Yin* (GB 44). *Yin Tang* (M-HN-3), *Ren Zhong* (GV 26), *Feng Fu* (GV 16), and *Feng Long* (St 4) were needled with draining method, and *Zu San Li* (St 36) was moxaed. This was done once every day for three days. In addition, the patient was administered three *ji* of *Gan Mai Da Zao Tang Jia Wei* (Licorice, Wheat & Red Date Decoction with Added Flavors): mix-fried Radix Glycyrrhizae (*Gan Cao*), Rhizoma Acori Graminei (*Shi Chang Pu*), and Radix Polygalae Tenuifoliae (*Yuan Zhi*), 6g each, Fructus Tritici Aestivi (*Huai Xiao Mai*), 30g, Fructus Zizyphi Jujubae (*Da Zao*), 10 pieces, Arillus Euphoriae Longanae (*Long Yan Rou*), Semen Zizyphi Spinosae (*Suan Zao Ren*), Rhizoma Cyperi Rotundi (*Xiang Fu*), Radix Albus Paeoniae Lactiflorae (*Bai Shao*), and Radix Salviae Miltiorrhizae (*Dan Shen*), 10g each.

After administering this combined therapy, the patient's mind cleared and became aroused and all his symptoms markedly decreased. Thus the acupuncture was stopped, but the above Chinese medicinal formula was continued for two another weeks. At that point, his mind and emotions returned to normal and he was able to go back to work. On follow-up after 15 years, there had been no recurrence.

❖ CASE 5⁵ ❖

The patient was a 39 year old male who was first examined in August 1959. Several months before, after quarreling with someone, the patient had become psychologically upset. He had begun to frequently break things and injure people. The man was hospitalized where he was treated with no result. Therefore, he was referred to Dr. Wang's clinic. When examined by Dr. Wang, the patient's face and eyes were red and his two eyes had an angry look. He could not sleep at night, he was constipated, and his urine was yellow. His tongue was red with thick, slimy, yellow fur, and his pulse was surging and rapid.

Therefore, the patient's pattern was categorized as heart mind not fulfilled, the five minds transforming fire, and phlegm fire stirring internally, confounding and blocking the clear orifices. The patient's six well points on the

hands were pricked as in the above case, and *Yin Bai* (Sp 1), *Li Dui* (St 45), *Da Dun* (Liv 1), and *Qiao Yin* (GB 44) were strongly needled. This was done one time per day for seven days. In addition, *Shi Jue Ming Tang Jia Wei* (Abalone Shell Decoction with Added Flavors) was administered internally: uncooked Concha Haliotidis (*Shi Jue Ming*), 50g, uncooked Magnetitum (*Ci Shi*), 30g, Lapis Micae Seu Chloriti (*Meng Shi*), 18g, Semen Zizyphi Spinosae (*Suan Zao Ren*), 12g, Rhizoma Acori Graminei (*Shi Chang Pu*) and Radix Polygalae Tenuifoliae (*Yuan Zhi*), 6g each, Radix Et Rhizoma Rhei (*Da Huang*) and Mirabilitum (*Mang Xiao*), 20g each, and Fructus Immaturus Citri Aurantii (*Zhi Shi*), 10g.

After three *ji* of the above formula, the patient's mind had cleared, his gaze became softer, and his stools were freely and easily flowing. Therefore, Rhubarb, Mirabilitum, and Immature Aurantium were deleted from the above formula and another four *ji* were administered. At this point, the patient's disease was cured. He was given regulating and balancing therapy for another one half month, at which time he was considered completely recovered.

❖ CASE 6⁶ ❖

The patient was a 25 year old female who was first examined on Apr. 16, 1974. During the recent year, due to suffering fright, the patient was not able to sleep at night. In addition, her speech was incoherent and she laughed and cried without constancy. She would beat her chest, howling and wailing, nor could she sit calmly in one place. Her Western medical diagnosis was schizophrenia and she had been treated for two months without effect. Therefore, she was referred to the author of this case who found that her pulse was bowstring, fine, and rapid and that her tongue was red with upright prickles on its sides and tip.

Based on the above, the patient's Chinese disease was mania and her pattern was discriminated as liver-gallbladder fire ascending and harassing her heart spirit. Since this had endured for many days, it had also resulted in causing detriment to heart yin. Based on the treatment principles of heavily settling and quieting the spirit accompanied by clearing evil heat from the heart and liver, she was told to stop taking her Western medication and administered *Sheng Tie Lou Yin He Bai He Di Huang Tang Jia Jian* (Iron Filings Drink plus Lily & Rehmannia Decoction with Additions & Subtractions): uncooked Frusta Ferri (*Tie Lou*), 60g, Fructus Tritici Aestivi (*Huai Xiao Mai*), 30g, uncooked Radix Rehmanniae (*Sheng Di*), 12g, Bulbus Lilii (*Bai He*), 12g, Cortex Albizziae Julibrissinis (*He Huan Pi*), 15g, Caulis Polygoni Multiflori (*Ye Jiao Teng*), 30g, Tuber

Ophiopogonis Japonici (*Mai Dong*), 9g, Semen Zizyphi Spinosae (*Suan Zao Ren*), 9g, bile-processed Rhizoma Arisaematis (*Dan Nan Xing*), 9g, Radix Polygalae Tenuifoliae (*Yuan Zhi*), 6g, Radix Glycyrrhizae (*Gan Cao*), 6g, Medulla Junci Effusi (*Deng Xin Cao*), 0.5g. Seven *ji* of this prescription was administered along with nine grams of *Bai Jin Wan* (White Gold Pills) swallowed with the decoction.

At the second visit, the patient reported that she was not able to go to sleep and her mind seemed to have cleared somewhat. The redness of her tongue looked less, and her pulse was simply fine and rapid. Therefore, Juncus was deleted from the original formula and seven more *ji* were administered. At the patient's third visit, her mind was clear and she reported that her chest oppression was relieved. Her pulse was fine and her tongue tip was red. Therefore, the former prescription was replaced with medicinals like Radix Salviae Miltiorrhizae (*Dan Shen*), Rhizoma Coptidis Chinensis (*Huang Lian*), and Radix Pseudostellariae (*Tai Zi Shen*) to continue regulating and balancing this woman's condition. She was followed-up in May of 1978 and there had been no recurrence.

## ❖ CASE 7[7] ❖

The patient was a 16 year old female who was first examined on May 20, 1974. Due to unfulfilled desires, this patient had become depressed and this had turned into withdrawal. Her affect was bland, she was taciturn, and she would not speak. At night, she could not fall asleep and she did not eat. At the time of seeing Dr. Ru, this had been going on for five months. The patient's pulse was bowstring, slippery, and rapid, and her tongue was red with upright prickles and thin, white fur which was thick and slimy at the root.

The patient's disease was diagnosed as withdrawal and her pattern was categorized as liver qi depression and binding transforming fire and engendering phlegm which had ascended and confounded the clear orifices. Based on the treatment principles of settling the heart and quieting the spirit, clearing fire and transforming phlegm, she was told to stop taking her Western medication and was administered seven *ji* of the following medicinals: uncooked Frusta Ferri (*Tie Lou*), 30g, Fructus Tritici Aestivi (*Huai Xiao Mai*), 30g, Bulbus Lilii (*Bai He*), 12g, uncooked Radix Rehmanniae (*Sheng Di*), 12g, Tuber Ophiopogonis Japonici (*Mai Dong*), 9g, Caulis Bambusae In Taeniis (*Zhu Ru*), 9g, processed Rhizoma Pinelliae Ternatae (*Ban Xia*), 9g, Rhizoma Acori Graminei (*Shi Chang Pu*), 9g, and Semen Zizyphi Spinosae (*Suan Zao Ren*), 9g. These were decocted in water and administered internally along with

nine grams of *Zhi Sha An Shen Wan* (Cinnabar Quiet the Spirit Pills) swallowed with the decoction.

At the second visit, the patient reported that her depression had improved. Her affect seemed more open. She was sleeping quietly at night and she was eating a lot. Her tongue was still red with upright prickles, but the white, slimy fur had already transformed and her pulse was merely bowstring and rapid. Therefore, Pinellia was removed from the original formula and Radix Scrophulariae Ningpoensis (*Xuan Shen*), 12g, and processed Rhizoma Arisaematis (*Tian Nan Xing*), 9g, were added and another seven *ji* were prescribed. On the third visit, the patient's affect was even more open and her speech was normal. The above formula was continued for another three months to regulate and balance the patient's condition. On follow-up in May of 1978, there had been no recurrence.

## ❖ CASE 8[8] ❖

The patient was a 38 year old male. Two days before he had been involved in a family argument and, since then, he had become pyschologically abnormal. He was admitted to a hospital where he was diagnosed as being schizophrenic and given fluphenazine and trifluoperazine without effect. Therefore, the patient was referred to Old Doctor Liu for examination and treatment. At the time of examination, the patient's speech was incoherent, his eyes stared angrily at people, and he had bad breath. The patient had not had a bowel movement in several days. His tongue was red with dry, yellow fur, and his pulse was slippery and racing. Therefore, Old Doctor Liu's pattern discrimination was liver depression transforming fire with heart fire internally exuberant. On the basis of this diagnosis, the man was prescribed *Da Huang Huang Lian Xie Xin Tang* (Rhubarb & Coptis Drain the Heart Decoction): Radix Et Rhizoma Rhei (*Da Huang*), 9g, Rhizoma Coptidis Chinensis (*Huang Lian*), 9g, and Radix Scutellariae Baicalensis (*Huang Qin*), 9g. These were decocted in water and administered. At the second examination after having taken three *ji* of this formula, the patient's bowels had moved and he was now able to go to sleep. In addition, his vexation and agitation and all his other symptoms had improved. Therefore, he was given three more *ji* of the same formula, after which his condition was judged cured. On follow-up after nearly seven years, there had been no recurrence.

## ❖ CASE 9[9] ❖

The patient was an 18 year old female who was first seen in August 1970 for withdrawal and mania. The young woman's behavior was eccentric and her speech was agitated and manic. At night, her symptoms got worse. Her six pulses were rapid and racing with the cubit pulses being slippery and forceful. In addition, there was tension, tightness, and hardness from the lower abdomen to the navel. The patient was administered *Di Dang Tang* (Resistance Decoction, *i.e.*, Hirudo Seu Whitmania, *Shui Zhi*, Tabanus, *Meng Chong*, Semen Pruni Persicae, *Tao Ren*, and Radix Et Rhizoma Rhei, *Da Huang*). Because the dispensary lacked Tabanus or Gadfly, only one *ji* was prescribed initially. Later, 20 pieces of Tabanus were added to the formula and another three *ji* were administered. After taking these three *ji*, purple-black static blood mixed with bloody threads and clots descended from the front yin (*i.e.*, vagina). Additionally, when the stools resolved, they were black and gelatinous. The young woman was given some iced sugar water and she fell into a deep sleep. When she woke up, her mind and emotions had returned to normal. She was given a few *ji* of the following medicinals, uncooked Radix Rehmanniae (*Sheng Di*), Radix Cynanchi Atrati (*Bai Wei*), Radix Salviae Miltiorrhizae (*Dan Shen*), Plumula Nelumbinis Nuciferae (*Lian Zi Xin*), Folium Nelumbinis Nuciferae (*He Ye*), and Succinum (*Hu Po*) and she was completely cured.

❖ **CASE 10**[10] ❖

The patient was a 71 year old female who had been mentally ill for more than one year. She had already been treated with fluphenazine, trifluoperazine, and Valium without marked improvement. In the last month, her symptoms had gotten worse. She was emotionally tense and sometimes depressed. She spoke a lot, was paranoid and her speech lacked coherence. In addition, she was susceptible to sorrow and cried a lot. She commonly muttered and talked to herself, and her symptoms were worse at night. These mental-emotional symptoms were accompanied by coughing with profuse phlegm which was clear and watery. Her appetite was poor, her facial complexion was a sallow yellow, her tongue was pale with slimy, white fur, and her pulse was bowstring and moderate or relaxed (*i.e.*, slightly slow).

The patient's Chinese medical pattern was, therefore, categorized as qi mechanism depression and binding with lung-stomach diffusion and downbearing loss of normalcy and phlegm drool congelation and gathering. Another way of saying this would be qi stagnation and phlegm con-

gelation, spleen vacuity unable to transform dampness, and phlegm and dampness joining and obstructing, thus assailing and harassing the heart spirit.

The formula given this woman was *Ban Xia Hou Po Tang Jia Jian* (Pinellia & Magnolia Decoction with Additions & Subtractions): Rhizoma Pinelliae Ternatae (*Ban Xia*), 10g, Cortex Magnoliae Officinalis (*Hou Po*), 10g, Sclerotium Poriae Cocos (*Fu Ling*), 12g, uncooked Rhizoma Zingiberis (*Sheng Jiang*), 6g, Folium Perillae Frutescentis (*Zi Su Ye*), 8g, Pericarpium Citri Erythrocarpae (*Ju Hong*), 9g, and bile-processed Rhizoma Arisaematis (*Dan Nan Xing*), 12g. These were decocted in water and administered internally.

After taking three *ji* of this formula, all the patient's symptoms were greatly diminished. She was able to engage in normal conversation, she no longer drooled, and her cough was less, while her eating was increased. However, at night, she still talked chaotically and slept little. Three more *ji* of the above formula were administered and the woman's mind was clear and crisp. On follow-up after half a year, there had been no recurrence.

**ENDNOTES:**

[1] Lin Tian-zhou, "The Treatment of 10 Cases of Mania with *Gan Sui Gun Tan Tang* (Euphrobia Kansui Roll [Away] Phlegm Decoction)," *Zhe Jiang Zhong Yi Za Zhi (Zhejiang Journal of Chinese Medicine)*, #4, 1993, p. 159

[2] Deng Jing-ming, "The Treatment of Withdrawal & Mania with *Mang Xiao Luo Bu Tang* (Mirabilite & Radish Decoction)," *Zhe Jiang Zhong Yi Za Zhi (Zhejiang Journal of Chinese Medicine)*, #8, 1995, p. 366

[3] Wu Ji-hong, "The Treatment of 44 Cases of Withdrawal & Mania with Acupuncture," *Zhong Guo Zhen Jiu (Chinese National Acupuncture & Moxibustion)*, #5, 1994, p. 8

[4] Cai Sheng-xiang, "Wang Ying-yu's Experiences in the Treatment of Withdrawal & Mania," *Zhe Jiang Zhong Yi Za Zhi (Zhejiang Journal of Chinese Medicine)*, #9, 1996, p. 416

[5] *Ibid.*, p. 416

[6] Ru Shi-mei, *Shang Hai Lao Zhong Yi Jing Yan Xuan Bian (A Selected Collection of Shanghai Old Chinese Doctors' Case Histories)*, *op. cit.*, p. 132-133

[7] *Ibid.*, p. 133

[8] Chen & Zhao, *op. cit.*, p. 172

[9] *Ibid.*, 219

[10] *Ibid.*, p. 398-399

# IRRITABILITY

In Chinese, irritability or *yi nu* is literally "easy anger." This refers to an emotional disposition of easily becoming angry or irritated. In other words, irritability refers to a hot temper which is not under one's volitional control. If easy anger is even more pronounced, it is then referred to as "great anger" or irascibility.[1] However, the disease mechanisms of irascibility are no different than for irritability. It is only a matter of degree. Other Chinese names for this condition include profuse anger, *duo nu*, and a predilection or susceptibility to anger, *shan nu*.

There is no correspondence between the Chinese medicine categories of easy anger or great anger and Western psychiatric disorders or symptoms. However, irritability and anger are frequently observed in the context of a range of behaviors that are categorized as normal or pathological in contemporary Western psychiatry. Psychiatric disorders characterized by easy anger or aggression include intermittent explosive disorder, bipolar affective disorder, antisocial personality disorder, and borderline personality disorder.

## NOSOLOGY:

Individuals with intermittent explosive disorder report an ongoing pattern of loss of control resulting in aggressive or violent behaviors that are disproportionate to circumstances triggering these behaviors. They frequently experience themselves as "losing their tempers," sometimes resulting in violence toward others or destruction of prop-

erty. Individuals with intermittent explosive disorder often have histories of developmental problems or insults to the brain resulting in disinhibition of aggressive impulses. Irritability and aggressive behavior occur often during acute manic episodes in bipolar affective disorder. Individuals with borderline personality disorder frequently experience aggressive or self-injurious impulses in the context of dysfunctional relationships and rapid chaotic changes in mood. In contrast, disregard for the rights of others and indifference to the harmful consequences of aggressive or antisocial behaviors are the hallmarks of antisocial personality disorder. Disinhibited, sometimes aggressive behavior is a frequent consequence of stimulant intoxication, including cocaine and methamphetamine.

## DIFFERENTIAL DIAGNOSIS:

Occasional irritability or anger is considered normal behavior. However, when these symptoms are frequent or continuous and interfere with social or occupational functioning, they may be symptomatic of an underlying psychiatric, medical, or substance abuse problem. Intense anger or aggressive behavior is typical in delirious or demented patients. Hypoglycemia (abnormally low blood sugar) frequently manifests as irritability. Individuals who have experienced traumatic brain injury often experience prolonged emotional dysregulation, including frequent episodes of irritable mood or agitated behavior. Several CNS disorders, including tumors, cerebrovascular accidents (CVA), multiple sclerosis, and others affecting the

---

## DIFFERENTIAL DIAGNOSIS

### 1. MEDICAL DISORDERS

A. DELIRIUM

B. HYPOGLYCEMIA

C. HYPERTHYROIDISM AND OTHER ENDOCRINOLOGIC DISORDERS

D. DEMENTIA

E. HISTORY OF TRAUMATIC BRAIN INJURY

F. CNS DISORDERS, INCLUDING BRAIN TUMORS, MULTIPLE SCLEROSIS (MS), AND CEREBROVASCULAR ACCIDENTS (CVA)

G. CNS DISORDERS OF THE FRONTAL LOBES OR LIMBIC SYSTEM

H. SEIZURE DISORDERS

### 2. EFFECTS OF SUBSTANCES

A. ALCOHOL OR ILLICIT SUBSTANCE INTOXICATION (ESPECIALLY HALLUCINOGENS) OR WITHDRAWAL (ESPECIALLY METHAMPHETAMINES)

B. SIDE EFFECTS OF MEDICATIONS

### 3. PSYCHIATRIC DISORDERS

A. BIPOLAR DISORDER, MANIC PHASE

B. INTERMITTENT EXPLOSIVE DISORDER

C. PERSONALITY DISORDERS, INCLUDING BORDERLINE AND ANTISOCIAL

D. NORMAL RANGE OF BEHAVIOR

---

frontal lobe or limbic system, can result in inappropriate anger or aggressive behavior. In certain kinds of seizure disorders, patients may experience transient intense rage during seizure episodes.

When a patient complains of a persisting pattern or irritable mood or agitated behavior in the absence of identifiable medical etiologies, it is important to rule out ongoing substance abuse. For example, irritability is commonly seen during the withdrawal phase in stimulant abuse, including methamphetamine and cocaine. Prolonged periods of intense irritability associated with racing thoughts, diminished sleep, pressured speech, or psychosis suggest mania, especially when a history of cyclic mood changes has been established.

The differential diagnosis for frequent or severe episodes of aggression is broader than for irritability. In Western psychiatry, occasional aggressive behavior is considered to be within normal range of human behavior. Like irritability, frequent or intense aggression that interferes with functioning is viewed as pathological and suggests underlying medical, psychiatric, or substance abuse problems. Aggressive behavior is commonly seen in bipolar disorder and is sometimes observed during acute stimulant or hallucinogen intoxication. Intermittent explosive disorder is an unusual psychiatric disorder characterized by frequent uncued episodes of intense rage. In addition, several personality disorders, including borderline personality disorder and antisocial personality disorder, are characterized by inappropriate, frequent, and/or intense anger.

### ETIOLOGY & PATHOPHYSIOLOGY:

There is no theoretical or empirical basis for discussing the etiology of irritability. Many psychodynamic and biological theories attempt to explain aggressive behavior. These are too numerous to summarize here. However, animal studies have demonstrated a correlation between decreased brain serotonin and aggressive behavior. A similar relationship holds true for norepinephrine. Medications that increase GABA, the primary inhibitory neurotransmitter, result in decreased aggressive behavior. Lesions in the older regions of the brain are often associated with aggression. Other possible biological correlates of aggression include CNS effects of testosterone and possible genetic influences in cases of antisocial personality disorder and specific chromosomal variants, including XYY karyotype. Some theorists argue that most aggressive behavior can be explained by social learning. In addition, ethology postulates that human aggression is a carry-over from primitive instinctive drives.

### WESTERN MEDICAL TREATMENT:

Many psychotropic medications are used to treat aggressive behavior. These include serotonin-selective re-uptake inhibitors (SSRIs), lithium carbonate, carba-mazepine (Tegretol), the class of beta-blockers, and benzodiazepines. In addition, narcotic antagonists (*e.g.*, naltrexone) are useful in the treatment of aggression. Anti-androgens have been found to reduce aggressive behavior in men who exhibit predatory sexual behavior.

Non-pharmacologic treatments of aggressive behavior include behavior modification techniques and cognitive therapy directed at reshaping self-destructive or destructive patterns of thinking. Physical restraints and seclusion are sometimes required to control extreme aggression when there is a clear threat of suicide or homicide.

## EPIDEMIOLOGY:

The prevalence of inappropriate aggressive behavior is difficult to estimate. There appears to be a relationship between inwardly and outwardly directed aggression. Many studies have demonstrated that suicide and homicide rates are comparable in a given population or culture. In the U.S., for example, the 1990 homicide and suicide rates were 10.2 and 12.3 per 100,000 respectively. There is no clear explanation for the wide variance in homicide and suicide rates between cultures.

## SHORT & LONG-TERM ADVANTAGES & DISADVANTAGES OF WESTERN MEDICAL TREATMENT:

The short term benefit of pharmacotherapy for inappropriate or potentially dangerous aggressive behavior is reduced risk of suicide or homicide. Long-term advantages of conventional Western medical treatments include increased opportunity for normal social and occupational functioning and a diminished probability of suicide, homicide, or destructive behavior.

## PROGNOSIS:

The Western medical prognosis of this condition depends on organicity, chronicity, and symptom severity.

## INDICATIONS FOR REFERRAL TO WESTERN MEDICAL SERVICES:

A patient who displays extreme aggression that disrupts daily functioning is at increased risk for suicidal or homicidal behavior. Violent or suicidal behavior in the context of grossly confused mental state, psychosis, or acute substance intoxication (or withdrawal) is sufficient grounds for emergency medical evaluation to rule out treatable medical or psychiatric causes. Violent patients should be rapidly assessed by clinicians exercising caution. Local police should be contacted to ensure safety for the patient and clinician. Patients who exhibit aggressive behavior that occasionally interferes with daily functioning but does not imminently threaten safety and has failed to respond to appropriate interventions over a reasonable period of time should be referred to a psychiatrist for continuing evaluation or treatment.

## CHINESE DISEASE CAUSES & MECHANISMS:

Anger is the affect or emotion of the liver. Therefore, all disease mechanisms producing easy anger or irritability are associated with the liver viscus. These include liver depression qi stagnation, liver-gallbladder fire heat, whether damp, depressive, or phlegm, and liver blood-kidney yin vacuity. In every case, there is an element of liver depression. This liver depression is nothing other than pent-up qi/unfulfilled desires. When these accumulate to a certain degree, any further stimulus causes this pent-up qi to rush out as a form of over-coursing and over-discharging. This over-coursing and over-discharging itself then damages the liver and inhibits its qi mechanism all the more.

Essentially all chronic, enduring disease is complicated by liver depression, and, therefore, most chronically ill patients are frustrated and irritated. Even if the original cause of the disease was not unfulfilled desires, everyone who is chronically ill has unfulfilled desires. At the very least one wants to be healthy and free from their disease. In addition, in Chinese medicine there is the saying, "In adults, blame the liver." This is because no adults living in a civilized society can immediately fulfill all their desires. To a large extent, to be an adult means to consciously delay gratification of certain desires.

Because liver depression is closely related to blood and yin vacuity, spleen qi vacuity, and kidney yang vacuity and all of these tend to occur or worsen with age, it is no wonder that the elderly are stereotyped as being crotchety and irritable.

## TREATMENT BASED ON PATTERN DISCRIMINATION:

### 1. LIVER DEPRESSION QI STAGNATION PATTERN

MAIN SYMPTOMS: Irritability, chest and rib-side distention and pain, emotional depression, taciturnity, belching, frequent sighing, a dark or normal colored tongue with thin, white fur, and a bowstring pulse

**NOTE:** This pattern rarely presents in its simple form. Rather elements of liver depression tend to complicate the patterns of most chronic, enduring diseases.

**TREATMENT PRINCIPLES:** Course the liver and rectify the qi

**FORMULA & MEDICINALS:** *Chai Hu Shu Gan San Jia Jian* (Bupleurum Course the Liver Powder with Additions & Subtractions)

Radix Bupleuri (*Chai Hu*), 10g, Fructus Citri Aurantii (*Zhi Ke*), 10g, Radix Albus Paeoniae Lactiflorae (*Bai Shao*), 10g, Radix Angelicae Sinensis (*Dang Gui*), 10g, Radix Ligustici Wallichii (*Chuan Xiong*), 6-10g (added later), Rhizoma Cyperi Rotundi (*Xiang Fu*), 10g, Fructus Meliae Toosendan (*Chuan Lian Zi*), 3-6g, Cortex Albizziae Julibrissinisis (*He Huan Pi*), 12g

Decoct in water and administer orally in two divided doses, morning and evening, one *ji* per day.

If there is liver depression complicated with spleen vacuity (as there almost always is in Western patients and especially females), one can use instead either *Xiao Chai Hu Tang* (Minor Bupleurum Decoction) or *Xiao Yao San* (Rambling Powder) as one's guiding formula.

*Xiao Chai Hu Tang* consists of: Radix Bupleuri (*Chai Hu*), 10g, Radix Codonopsitis Pilosulae (*Dang Shen*), 10g, Radix Scutellariae Baicalensis (*Huang Qin*), 10g, Rhizoma Pinelliae Ternatae (*Ban Xia*), 10g, mix-fried Radix Glyycrrhizae (*Gan Cao*), 6g, Fructus Zizyphi Jujubae (*Da Zao*), 3-5 pieces, uncooked Rhizoma Zingiberis (*Sheng Jiang*), 3g (added later). If there is no depressive heat, delete Scutellaria. If there is more severe depressive heat, add Rhizoma Coptidis Chinensis (*Huang Lian*), 3-4.5g (added later).

*Xiao Yao San* consists of: Radix Bupleuri (*Chai Hu*), 10g, Radix Albus Paeoniae Lactiflorae (*Bai Shao*), 10g, Radix Angelicae Sinensis (*Dang Gui*), 10g, Rhizoma Atractylodis Macrocephalae (*Bai Zhu*), 10g, Sclerotium Poriae Cocos (*Fu Ling*), 10g, mix-fried Radix Glycyrrhizae (*Gan Cao*), 6g, Herba Mentha Haplocalysis (*Bo He*), 3-6g (added later), uncooked Rhizoma Zingiberis (*Sheng Jiang*), 3g (added later).

**ACUPUNCTURE:** *Tai Chong* (Liv 3), *Nei Guan* (Per 6), *He Gu* (LI 4), *Shen Men* (Ht 7). Use draining technique.

**ADDITIONS & SUBTRACTIONS:** If liver depression and qi stagnation are severe, add *Qi Men* (Liv 14) and *Gan Shu* (Bl 18). If irascibility is severe, add *Shen Ting* (GV 24). If there is severe cheat oppression, add *Shan Zhong* (CV 17).

## 2. LIVER-GALLBLADDER FIRE EFFULGENCE PATTERN[2]

**MAIN SYMPTOMS:** Irritability, vexation and agitation, a red face and eyes, rib-side pain, a bitter taste in the mouth, a dry mouth, possible headache or vertigo, a red tongue with yellow fur, and a bowstring, rapid pulse

**TREATMENT PRINCIPLES:** Clear the liver and drain gallbladder fire

**FORMULA & MEDICINALS:** *Xie Qing Wan Jia Jian* (Drain the Green Pills with Additions & Subtractions)

Radix Gentianae Scabrae (*Long Dan Cao*), 6g, stir-fried Fructus Gardeniae Jasminoidis (*Zhi Zi*), 10g, Radix Scutellariae Baicalensis (*Huang Qin*), 10g, Radix Et Rhizoma Rhei (*Da Huang*), 3-6g (added later), Radix Angelicae Sinensis (*Dang Gui*), 10g, Radix Ligustici Wallichii (*Chuan Xiong*), 6-10g (added later), Radix Et Rhizoma Notopterygii (*Qiang Huo*), 10g, Radix Ledebouriellae Sesloidis (*Fang Feng*), 10g, Radix Glycyrrhizae (*Gan Cao*), 3g, Herba Menthae Haplocalycis (*Bo He*), 3-6g (added later), Cortex Albizziae Julibrissinis (*He Huan Pi*), 10g

Decoct in water and administer orally in two divided doses, morning and evening, one *ji* per day.

**ADDITIONS & SUBTRACTIONS:** If there is severe vexation and agitation, add Rhizoma Coptidis Chinensis (*Huang Lian*). If there is severe rib-side pain, add Radix Bupleuri (*Chai Hu*), Fructus Meliae Toosendan (*Chuan Lian Zi*), and Rhizoma Corydalis Yanhusuo (*Yan Hu Suo*). If there is severe headache or vertigo, add Spica Prunellae Vulgaris (*Xia Ku Cao*). If there are severe red eyes, add Flos Chrysanthemi Morifolii (*Ju Hua*).

**ACUPUNCTURE:** *Xing Jian* (Liv 2), *Zu Lin Qi* (GB 41), *Nei Ting* (St 44), *Jian Shi* (Per 5). Use draining technique.

## 3. LIVER BLOOD-KIDNEY YIN VACUITY PATTERN

**MAIN SYMPTOMS:** Irritability, dizziness, low back and knee soreness and limpness, a dry throat, dry, rough eyes, heat in the five hearts, possible night sweats, afternoon tidal heat, insomnia, profuse dreams, a red tongue or a pale tongue with red tip, scanty fur, and a fine, rapid or floating, rapid pulse

TREATMENT PRINCIPLES: Supplement the kidneys and enrich yin, nourish the blood and emolliate the liver

FORMULA & MEDICINALS: *Qi Ju Di Huang Wan Jia Wei* (Lycium & Chrysanthemum Rehmannia Pills with Added Flavors) Cooked Radix Rehmanniae (*Shu Di*), 12g, Radix Dioscoreae Oppositae (*Shan Yao*), 10g, Fructus Corni Officinalis (*Shan Zhu Yu*), 10g, Sclerotium Poriae Cocos (*Fu Ling*), 10g, Rhizoma Alismatis (*Ze Xie*), 6g, Cortex Radicis Moutan (*Dan Pi*), 10g, Fructus Lycii Chinensis (*Gou Qi Zi*), 10-12g, Flos Chrysanthemi Morifolii (*Ju Hua*), 10g (steeped afterwards), Cortex Phellodendri (*Huang Bai*), 10g, uncooked Os Draconis (*Long Gu*), 12g (decocted first)

Decoct in water and administer orally in two divided doses, morning and evening, one *ji* per day.

ACUPUNCTURE: *Tai Chong* (Liv 3), *San Yin Jiao* (Sp 6), *Tai Xi* (Ki 3), *Fu Liu* (Ki 7). Use even supplementing-even draining technique.

ENDNOTES

[1]Nigel Wiseman, in *English-Chinese Chinese-English Dictionary of Chinese Medicine*, Hunan Science & Technology Press, Changsha, 1995, only gives a single term, irascibility.

[2]This pattern is being used as a catch-all for all types of liver and gallbladder heat, fire, and yang hyperactivity.

# ❖ 3 ❖

# FREQUENT JOY

For Westerners, it is hard to think that frequent joy could be a disease category. What could be wrong with joy? However, health in Chinese medicine is largely based on the Confucian concept of the Doctrine of the Mean. We are healthy when all our activities, functions, and experiences are in relative, dynamic balance. In Chinese medicine, disease is caused by too much or too little of anything. The Chinese concept of frequent joy refers to frequent, inappropriate or nervous laughter or laughing without reason. It is a type of excited, manic affective state or propensity. In Chinese, frequent joy is *shan xi*.[1]

In Western psychiatry, laughter that is inappropriate or "without reason" is described in different ways depending on its underlying causes. For instance, pathological laughing (or crying) frequently accompanies multiple sclerosis. When there is no underlying organic etiology, inappropriate laughter is usually described as "inappropriate or labile affect."

**NOSOLOGY:**

Since inappropriate laughter (frequent joy) is not a primary disorder in Western psychiatry, there are no identified categories of related disorders that have this symptom in common.

**DIFFERENTIAL DIAGNOSIS:**

Laughter that is inappropriate in a given cultural or social context may be an expression of an underlying neurologic disorder, including multiple sclerosis (MS), encephalomyelitis, or other demyelinating disorders of the central nervous system. When there is a primary identified CNS etiology, it is called "emotional incontinence." The differential diagnosis is made clear by history and a thorough review of current psychological and neurologic symptoms. Inappropriate laughter (or other emotional expression) in a patient with a known diagnosis of MS or

| DIFFERENTIAL DIAGNOSIS | |
|---|---|
| 1. MEDICAL DISORDERS | 2. PSYCHIATRIC DISORDERS |
| NEUROLOGIC DISORDERS, INCLUDING MULTIPLE SCLEROSIS (MS), ENCEPHALOMYELITIS, AND OTHERS | A. BIPOLAR DISORDER<br>B. SCHIZOPHRENIA AND OTHER PSYCHOTIC DISORDERS<br>C. CERTAIN PERSONALITY DISORDERS |

other CNS demyelinating disorder is likely a direct behavioral consequence of the disorder. In MS or other demyelinating disorders, inappropriate laughter is not associated with euphoric mood. In fact, the patient is often confused by his or her behavior.

In the absence of a primary CNS disorder, inappropriate laughter may reflect a range of psychiatric disorders, including bipolar disorder, schizophrenia or other psychotic disorders, and some personality disorders. In conventional Western psychiatry, the diagnostic significance of inappropriate laughter depends on the pattern and history of other associated symptoms. For example, in bipolar disorder, inappropriate laughter (or joy) is associated with an expansive mood, racing thoughts, and diminished need for sleep. Substance abuse, especially amphetamines or hallucinogens, and the effects of certain medications may also sometimes manifest as inappropriate laughter.

## EPIDEMIOLOGY:

The prevalence of inappropriate laughter in Western psychiatric or neurologic disorders is not clearly established, as it has not been examined as a distinct diagnostic entity. One reasonable way to think about it is in terms of the combined prevalence of disorders in which inappropriate laughter occurs. However, such an estimate of combined prevalence of a symptom is not a meaningful or accurate indicator, as this approach does not take into account basic differences in pathogenesis and treatment of the range of occurrences of inappropriate laughter or other emotional expression.

## ETIOLOGY & PATHOPHYSIOLOGY:

Inappropriate laughter in a patient with MS or other demyelinating disorder is a consequence of disturbance in brain functioning caused by direct effects of the disease on brain regions that regulate emotional expression, principally the limbic system and frontal lobes. MS and other demyelinating CNS diseases result from autoimmune damage to the myelin sheaths of nerve fibers. The cause is unknown. When inappropriate laughter is present in the absence of a primary neurologic disorder, it may be interpreted as symptomatic of a primary psychiatric disorder, including bipolar affective disorder (BAD) or schizophrenia. In this case, it is presumably caused by dysregulation in the neurotransmitters that are implicated in the pathogenesis of those disorders (see Book 3, Chapters 6 & 3). The co-occurrence of inappropriate laughter and acute intoxication with a stimulant or hallucinogen is caused by cortical disinhibition.

## WESTERN MEDICAL TREATMENT:

The treatment of inappropriate laughter in Western psychiatry depends on the identified underlying cause(s). Whereas primary psychiatric etiologies are often treatable with pharmacotherapy, most neurologic causes of inappropriate laughter are poorly responsive to treatment. Antidepressants, including tricyclics and serotonin-selective re-uptake inhibitors (SSRIs), are efficacious in some cases when inappropriate laughter is associated with MS or other demyelinating disorders. This behavior typically normalizes with high-dose steroids and other anti-inflammatory agents. In the same way, inappropriate laughter in the context of bipolar disorder, schizophrenia, or other primary psychiatric disorders typically returns to a baseline normal behavior with good response to mood-stabilizing agents like lithium carbonate, carbamazepine (Tegretol), and others. Psychotherapy is not effective treatment of inappropriate laughter per se, though many with MS, BAD, or other, psychiatric disorders benefit from supportive psychotherapy via improved capacity to manage the stress associated with their illness.

## SHORT & LONG-TERM ADVANTAGES & DISADVANTAGES OF WESTERN MEDICAL TREATMENT:

In the context of MS, accepted Western medical treatments of MS include steroids, sedatives, and antispasticity agents. These medications alleviate some of the symptoms of MS but do not arrest demyelination or stop the progressive remitting and relapsing course of this disorder. There is a significant risk of psychiatric side effects with all of these medications. High-dose steroid therapy is frequently accompanied by transient psychosis, mania, or depression which resolve when steroids are discontinued. Concurrent treatment with sedatives used to treat agitation or manic-like symptoms (including inappropriate laughter) in MS patients can cause delirium or disinhibited behavior. Antispasticity agents, including baclofen and others, can cause delirium.

In terms of psychiatric disorders, inappropriate laughter is viewed as a symptom of bipolar affective disorder, schizophrenia, or other underlying psychiatric disorders. Therefore, the advantages and disadvantages of treatment are the same as those described for bipolar disorder and schizophrenia. In general, there are few short-term disadvantages of pharmacologic treatment which results in improved functioning. However, long-term treatment of BAD with lithium carbonate can result in hypothyroidism, kidney disease, or other medical problems. Long-term use of antipsychotic medications in schizophrenia may result in permanent neurologic disorders of abnormal involuntary movement. (See Book 3, Chapter 3, Schizophrenia, for a fuller discussion of these problems)

### INDICATIONS FOR REFERRAL TO WESTERN MEDICAL SERVICES:

When a patient exhibiting inappropriate laughter is confused, agitated, or grossly cognitively impaired, he or she should be referred to the nearest emergency room or urgent care center. These symptoms suggest an underlying delirium or psychosis due to a medical disorder or acute substance intoxication. When a manic or psychotic patient exhibits inappropriate laughter or is threatening suicide or harm to others, the clinician should immediately contact local authorities, requesting that the patient be emergently evaluated for involuntary hospitalization as danger-to-self or danger-to-others. If there is evidence that an individual is functioning at his or her long-standing baseline and symptoms accompanying inappropriate laughter have not responded to appropriate treatment or are progressive, the patient should be referred to a psychiatrist for continued evaluation and treatment.

### CHINESE DISEASE CAUSES & MECHANISMS:

Joy is the affect or emotion associated with the heart viscus and the fire phase. If any type of evil heat harasses the heart spirit, this may manifest as frequent or excessive joy. The main specific types of evil heat or fire causing this condition are heart fire effulgence, non-interaction between the heart and kidneys, phlegm fire harassing the heart, and liver depression effulgent fire, the causes and mechanisms of which we have discussed above.

### TREATMENT BASED ON PATTERN DISCRIMINATION:

### 1. HEART FIRE EFFULGENCE PATTERN

MAIN SYMPTOMS: Frequent laughing without reason, wild or incoherent speech, vexation and agitation, thirst with a desire for chilled drinks, sores of the mouth and on the tip of the tongue, hot, painful, urgent, and/or reddish urine, a red facial complexion, a red tongue, and a rapid pulse

TREATMENT PRINCIPLES: Clear the heart and drain fire

FORMULA & MEDICINALS: *Xie Xin Dao Chi San Jia Jian* (Drain the Heart & Abduct the Red Powder with Additions & Subtractions)

Rhizoma Coptidis Chinensis (*Huang Lian*), 3-6g (added

later), Radix Scutellariae Baicalensis (*Huang Qin*), 10g, Caulis Akebiae (*Mu Tong*), 6-10g, uncooked Radix Rehmanniae (*Sheng Di*), 12g, Folium Lophatheri Gracilis (*Dan Zhu Ye*), 10g, stir-fried Fructus Gardeniae Jasminoidis (*Zhi Zi*), 10g, Medulla Tetrapanacis Papyriferi (*Deng Xin Cao*), 3g, Extremitas Radicis Glycyrrhizae (*Gan Cao Shao*), 10g, Plumula Nelumbinis Nuciferae (*Lian Xin*), 2g

Decoct in water and administer orally in two divided doses, morning and evening, one *ji* per day.

ACUPUNCTURE: *Shen Men* (Ht 7), *Shao Fu* (Ht 8), *Lao Gong* (Per 8), *Da Du* (Sp 2), *Nei Ting* (St 44). Use draining technique.

### 2. NON-INTERACTION BETWEEN THE HEART & KIDNEYS PATTERN

MAIN SYMPTOMS: Frequent laughing without reason, low back and knee soreness and limpness, insomnia, profuse dreams, vexatious heat in the five hearts, afternoon tidal heat, night sweats, seminal emission, tinnitus, a red tongue with scanty fur, and a fine, rapid, floating, rapid, or surging, rapid pulse

TREATMENT PRINCIPLES: Supplement the kidneys and enrich yin, clear the heart and downbear fire

FORMULA & MEDICINALS: *Huang Lian E Jiao Tang Jia Wei* (Coptis & Donkey Skin Glue Decoction with Added Flavors)

Rhizoma Coptidis Chinensis (*Huang Lian*), 6g (added later), Radix Scutellariae Baicalensis (*Huang Qin*), 10g, Gelatinum Corii Asini (*E Jiao*), 10g (dissolved at the end in the decocted liquid), Radix Albus Paeoniae Lactiflorae (*Bai Shao*), 10g, egg yolk (*Ji Zi Huang*), 1 piece (added at the end and stirred into the hot liquid), Rhizoma Acori Graminei (*Shi Chang Pu*), 10g, Radix Polygalae Tenuifoliae (*Yuan Zhi*), 6-10g, cooked Radix Rehmanniae (*Shu Di*), 12-15g

Decoct in water and administer orally in two divided doses, morning and evening, one *ji* per day.

ADDITIONS & SUBTRACTIONS: If there is insomnia with profuse dreams, add uncooked Concha Ostreae (*Mu Li*) and uncooked Os Draconis (*Long Gu*). If there is severe vexation and agitation, add Plumula Nelumbinis Nuciferae (*Lian Xin*), Semen Biotae Orientalis (*Bai Zi Ren*), and stir-fried Semen Zizyphi Spinosae (*Suan Zao*

Ren). If there is seminal emission, add Cortex Phellodendri (*Huang Bai*) and Rhizoma Anemarrhenae Aspheloidis (*Zhi Mu*). If there are night sweats, add calcined Plastrum Testudinis (*Gui Ban*) and Fructus Corni Officinalis (*Shan Zhu Yu*).

**ACUPUNCTURE:** *Xin Shu* (Bl 15), *Ge Shu* (Bl 17), *Tai Xi* (Ki 3), *Fu Liu* (Ki 7), *San Yin Jiao* (Sp 6). Use even supplementing-even draining technique.

### 3. PHLEGM FIRE HARASSING ABOVE PATTERN

**MAIN SYMPTOMS:** Frequent wild laughing without reason, drooling when laughing, profuse phlegm, vexation and agitation, a bitter taste in the mouth, heart palpitations, impaired memory, susceptibility to fright during sleep, slimy, yellow tongue fur, and a slippery, rapid pulse

**TREATMENT PRINCIPLES:** Flush phlegm and downbear fire, clear the heart and quiet the spirit

**FORMULA & MEDICINALS:** *Huang Lian Wen Dan Tang Jia Jian* (Coptis Warm the Gallbladder Decoction with Additions & Subtractions)

Lime-processed Rhizoma Pinelliae Ternatae (*Ban Xia*), 10g, Pericarpium Citri Reticulatae (*Chen Pi*), 10g, Radix Glycyrrhizae (*Gan Cao*), 6g, Fructus Immaturus Citri Aurantii (*Zhi Shi*), 10g, Caulis Bambusae In Taeniis (*Zhu Ru*), 10g, Sclerotium Poriae Cocos (*Fu Ling*), 12g, uncooked Rhizoma Zingiberis (*Sheng Jiang*), 3g (added later), Radix Scutellariae Baicalensis (*Huang Qin*), 10g, Rhizoma Coptidis Chinensis (*Huang Lian*), 3-6g (added later), Rhizoma Acori Graminei (*Shi Chang Pu*), 6g

Decoct in water and administer orally in two divided doses, morning and evening, one *ji* per day.

**ACUPUNCTURE:** *Feng Long* (St 40), *Nei Ting* (St 44), *Da Zhui* (GV 14), *Shen Men* (Ht 7), *Bai Hui* (GV 20). Use draining technique.

### 4. LIVER DEPRESSION-EFFULGENT FIRE PATTERN

**MAIN SYMPTOMS:** Frequent wild laughing without reason, changeable moods, irritability, impatience, frequent nightmares, disturbed sleep, chest and rib-side fullness and distention, red eyes, a red tongue, and a bowstring, rapid pulse

**TREATMENT PRINCIPLES:** Course the liver and rectify the qi, clear heat and discharge fire

**FORMULA & MEDICINALS:** *Xie Gan An Shen Tang* (Drain the Liver & Quiet the Spirit Decoction)

Radix Gentianae Scabrae (*Long Dan Cao*), 6-10g, stir-fried Fructus Gardeniae Jasminoidis (*Zhi Zi*), 10g, Radix Bupleuri (*Chai Hu*), 6-10g, Radix Scutellariae Baicalensis (*Huang Qin*), 10g, Rhizoma Coptidis Chinensis (*Huang Lian*), 3-6g (added later), uncooked Radix Rehmanniae (*Sheng Di*), 12g, Radix Angelicae Sinensis (*Dang Gui*), 10g, Radix Glycyrrhizae (*Gan Cao*), 3g

Decoct in water and administer orally in two divided doses, morning and evening, one *ji* per day.

**ACUPUNCTURE:** *Shen Men* (Ht 7), *Jian Shi* (Per 5), *Xing Jian* (Liv 2), *Zu Lin Qi* (GB 41), *Nei Ting* (St 44). Use draining technique.

### ENDNOTES

[1]Wiseman, *op. cit.*, refers to this as a tendency to joy.

# ANXIETY & THINKING

Anxiety and thinking, *shan you si*, as a Chinese disease category refers to a tendency to worry and continuous or excessive thinking.[1] Worry and anxiety, preoccupation and obsessional thinking are the key symptoms of this disorder. As stated above, Chinese medicine makes no distinction between thoughts and emotions. Both are subjectively experienced sensations.

There is no specific correspondence between anxiety and thinking as a Chinese disease category and any one Western psychiatric symptom or disorder. Symptoms of worry, anxiety, preoccupation, and obsessional thinking occur in numerous psychiatric disorders and are sometimes associated with underlying medical disorders.

## NOSOLOGY:

### 1. PSYCHIATRIC DISORDERS

Occasional worrying or anxiety that do not interfere with social or occupational functioning are not regarded as pathological. Severe or frequent anxiety symptoms imply a primary psychiatric disorder or a medical condition that indirectly causes anxiety or obsessional thinking. When anxiety is pervasive and continuous in the absence of identifiable stressors, it may correspond to the Western psychiatric diagnosis of generalized anxiety disorder. Anxiety with panic attacks may correspond to a Western diagnosis of panic disorder in which anticipation of a panic attack causes generalized anxiety feelings. A long-standing pattern of anxious preoccupation with multiple vague somatic complaints that have no identifiable medical cause may be similar to histrionic personality disorder or a somatoform disorder. Obsessions are also frequent manifestations of depression, phobias, and schizophrenia. Repetitive intrusive thoughts (*i.e.*, obsessions) that seem strange to the patient (and that are sometimes associated with compulsive urges) correspond to a diagnosis of obsessive-compulsive disorder (OCD). In contrast, a long-standing pattern of obsessional thinking in the absence of specific obsessions or compulsions probably corresponds to obsessive-compulsive personality disorder.

### 2. MEDICAL DISORDERS

Anxiety and obsessional thinking are sometimes the result of medical disorders, including encephalitis. Hyperthyroidism is commonly associated with generalized anxiety or panic attacks. Rarely, traumatic brain injury manifests as obsessive-compulsive disorder. Childhood CNS infections with group A beta-hemolytic strep sometimes result in chronic psychiatric symptoms that are equivalent to OCD. By definition, OCD is not caused by an identifiable medical etiology. Brain imaging studies show hyperfunction in the frontal lobes and basal ganglia suggestive of a neurodevelopmental etiology.

## EPIDEMIOLOGY:

The lifetime prevalence of OCD is estimated at 1.5-3%.

## DIFFERENTIAL DIAGNOSIS

### 1. MEDICAL DISORDERS

A. INFECTION OR INJURY OF CNS
B. TOURETTE'S DISORDER
C. OTHER TIC DISORDERS
D. NEUROLOGIC DISORDERS, INCLUDING TOURETTE'S DISORDER, PARKINSON'S DISEASE, AND HUNTINGTON'S DISEASE
E. HISTORY OF TRAUMATIC BRAIN INJURY
F. HISTORY OF CEREBROVASCULAR ACCIDENT (CVA)

### 2. PSYCHIATRIC DISORDERS

A. OBSESSIVE-COMPULSIVE DISORDER (OCD)
B. OBSESSIVE-COMPULSIVE PERSONALITY DISORDER
C. SCHIZOPHRENIA, CATATONIC SUBTYPE, AND OTHER PSYCHOTIC DISORDERS
D. MAJOR DEPRESSIVE EPISODE
E. SPECIFIC PHOBIAS
F  SOCIAL PHOBIAS

The disorder affects women and men equally and typically begins in the second decade of life. For unclear reasons, males tend to be afflicted earlier than females. Obsessive-compulsive disorder typically begins during adolescence. However, onset can be as early as age six, and some individuals develop the disorder in old age. The disorder usually begins gradually, and the individual alternates between relatively asymptomatic periods and transient worsenings in symptom severity that are often stress-related. Many patients experience gradual deterioration throughout the course of their illness, while others slowly improve. Genetic factors clearly play a role in transmission of the disorder, as first degree relatives of individuals diagnosed with OCD are at significantly increased risk of developing OCD compared to more distant relatives or the general population.

### DIFFERENTIAL DIAGNOSIS:

Accurate determination of the cause(s) of anxiety, excessive worry, or obsessions begins with thorough history taking to clarify the general pattern within which these symptoms occur. At this point, a diagnosis of OCD, panic disorder, a primary mood or psychotic disorder or personality disorder will become clear (see Nosology above). A suggestive history may lead to neurologic consultation or laboratory studies may be indicated to identify or rule out treatable medical etiologies. For the purposes of this book, the Western differential diagnosis of anxiety and thinking is regarded as equivalent to that of obsessive-compulsive disorder.

### WESTERN MEDICAL TREATMENT:

Western medical treatments for symptoms of anxiety, worry, or obsessions target the identified primary underlying causes of these symptoms. If possible, underlying medical etiologies are treated. For instance, hypothyroidism may be corrected with hormone replacement therapy.

There are no known treatments in Western medicine for obsessions or anxiety symptoms resulting from traumatic brain injury or CNS infections. Primary psychiatric disorders are treated with medications, psychotherapy, or a combination of the two. A specialized kind of cognitive-behavioral therapy effectively reduces OCD symptom severity. Anxiety disorders associated with obsessions, including OCD, respond to SSRIs and other antidepressant medications. Obsessions or anxiety associated with depression, personality disorders, or schizophrenia respond to several drugs, including SSRIs and benzodiazepines.

### SHORT & LONG-TERM ADVANTAGES & DISADVANTAGES OF WESTERN MEDICAL TREATMENT:

Advantages of pharmacologic treatment include reduced symptom severity and significantly improved social and occupational functioning. Disadvantages of treatment include medication side effects, such as changes in appetite and sexual functioning. Patients who take benzodiazepines for anxiety control may become chemically dependent on these medications, resulting in all the issues, problems, and complications of chemical dependency. Neuroleptics used to manage extreme anxiety or irrational obsessional thinking associated with schizophrenia frequently cause transient abnormal involuntary movements. Prolonged use of typical antipsychotic agents carries a significant risk of tardive dyskinesia, a permanent neurologic disorder of abnormal involuntary movements.

### INDICATIONS FOR REFERRAL TO WESTERN MEDICAL SERVICES:

Extreme anxiety, intense preoccupations, or bizarre obsessions (approaching delusional beliefs) may indicate an acute psychotic process. Urgent medical evaluation is indicated to rule out and treat possible underlying medical causes of these symptoms. Urgent medical referral is also indicated when there is reason to suspect ongoing substance abuse manifesting as chronic anxiety. Many obsessional or extremely anxious patients have co-morbid depression and are at increased risk of suicide. A suicidal patient should be referred to the nearest emergency room for urgent medical-psychiatric assessment. When a patient has not responded to appropriate treatment using approaches prescribed in Chinese medicine and reports ongoing anxiety, preoccupations, or obsessions in the absence of psychosis, substance abuse, or associated medical problems, he or she might benefit from non-urgent referral to a psychiatrist for continuing evaluation.

## CHINESE DISEASE CAUSES & MECHANISMS:

Thinking is the "affect" or mental-emotional sensation or event associated with the spleen. Therefore, on the one hand, over-thinking damages the spleen. According to the *Nei Jing (Inner Classic)*, thinking causes the qi to bind. This binding inhibits the spleen's qi mechanism, hindering and obstructing its upbearing of the clear. On the other hand, over-thinking may be due to a damaged spleen which has lost control over its functions. In addition, worry and anxiety are particularly damaging to the spleen. Because of the five phase relationship of the liver and spleen via the control cycle, in real life, most cases of spleen vacuity are complicated by simultaneous liver depression. As we have seen above, spleen vacuity (with concomitant blood vacuity) may cause liver depression, while liver depression will typically inhibit the spleen's qi mechanism all the more. Thinking binds the qi and liver depression also results in bound qi. Therefore, excessive thinking is commonly seen in those with liver depression and spleen vacuity, what is frequently referred to as a liver-spleen disharmony.

Because the spleen is the latter heaven source of the qi and blood of the heart and lungs, over-thinking, worry, and anxiety are also often seen in patients with heart-spleen and lung-spleen patterns. In the case of lung-spleen vacuity, either lung vacuity may reach the spleen or spleen vacuity may reach the lungs. In the former situation, enduring cough or great sadness may both damage the lungs. If lung vacuity endures and is not cured, it may eventually reach the spleen, thus causing concomitant spleen vacuity. Vice versa, if the spleen is damaged by faulty diet, over-taxation, too little exercise, or over-use of bitter, cold medicinals, spleen vacuity may reach the lungs causing concomitant lung qi vacuity. In either case, over-thinking, worry, and anxiety may occur. The situation is basically the same in terms of heart-spleen dual vacuity. A heart blood vacuity may lead to a spleen qi vacuity, while a spleen qi vacuity may lead to a heart blood vacuity. Likewise, in either case, over-thinking, worry, and anxiety may occur.

## TREATMENT BASED ON PATTERN DISCRIMINATION:

### 1. LIVER-SPLEEN DISHARMONY PATTERN

**MAIN SYMPTOMS:** Persistent anxiety and preoccupation, moodiness, vexation, irritability, chest oppression, breast and/or rib-side distention and pain, poor appetite, loose stools, possible painful diarrhea, possible alternating constipation and diarrhea, menstrual irregularities and PMS in females, a pale, fat tongue which may also be somewhat dark or dull in color, and a bowstring pulse

**TREATMENT PRINCIPLES:** Course the liver and rectify the qi, fortify the spleen and boost the qi

**FORMULA & MEDICINALS:** *Si Ni San Jia Wei* (Four Counterflows Powder with Added Flavors)

Radix Bupleuri (*Chai Hu*), 10g, Radix Albus Paeoniae Lactiflorae (*Bai Shao*), 10g, Herba Menthae Haplocalycis (*Bo He*), 6g (added later), Fructus Citri Aurantii (*Zhi Ke*), 6g, Flos Pruni Mume (*Lu O Mei*), 3g, Flos Rosae Rugosae (*Mei Gui Hua*), 6g, Rhizoma Cyperi Rotundi (*Xiang Fu*), 6-10g, Rhizoma Atractylodis Macrocephalae (*Bai Zhu*), 10g, Radix Codonopsitis Pilosulae (*Dang Shen*), 10g, mix-fried Radix Glycyrrhizae (*Gan Cao*), 6g

Decoct in water and administer orally in two divided doses, morning and evening, one *ji* per day.

**ACUPUNCTURE:** *Qi Men* (Liv 14), *Tai Chong* (Liv 3), *Zhang Men* (Liv 13), *Gong Sun* (Sp 4), *Zu San Li* (St 36). Use even supplementing-even draining technique.

### 2. HEART-SPLEEN DUAL VACUITY PATTERN

**MAIN SYMPTOMS:** Persistent anxiety and preoccupation, obsessional thinking, shortness of breath, disinclination to talk, lassitude of the spirit, heart palpitations, insomnia, torpid intake, loose stools, a sallow yellow or pale white facial complexion, pale lips and nails, a pale, fat tongue with thin fur, and a fine, weak pulse

**TREATMENT PRINCIPLES:** Fortify the spleen and boost the qi, nourish the heart and relieve anxiety

**FORMULA & MEDICINALS:** *Gui Pi Tang Jia Jian* (Restore the Spleen Decoction with Additions & Subtractions)

Rhizoma Atractylodis Macrocephalae (*Bai Zhu*), 10g, Sclerotium Pararadicis Poriae Cocos (*Fu Shen*), 12g, Radix Astragali Membranacei (*Huang Qi*), 10-15g, stir-fried Semen Zizyphi Spinosae (*Suan Zao Ren*), 12g, Radix Polygalae Tenuifoliae (*Yuan Zhi*), 6-10g, Radix Auklandiae Lappae (*Mu Xiang*), 6-10g (added later), Radix Angelicae Sinensis (*Dang Gui*), 10g, Radix Codonopsitis Pilosulae (*Dang Shen*), 10g, Tuber Curcumae (*Yu Jin*), 10g, Arillus Euphoriae Longanae (*Long Yan Rou*), 10g

Decoct in water and administer orally in two divided doses, morning and evening, one *ji* per day.

**ADDITIONS & SUBTRACTIONS:** For insomnia, add Cortex Albizziae Julibrissinis (*He Huan Pi*) and Semen Biotae Orientalis (*Bai Zi Ren*). For severe heart blood vacuity, add Radix Albus Paeoniae Lactiflorae (*Bai Shao*), Gelatinum Corii Asini (*E Jiao*), and Semen Biotae Orientalis (*Bai Zi Ren*). If there is epigastric distention and nausea due to phlegm dampness, add lime-processed Rhizoma Pinelliae Ternatae (*Ban Xia*), Pericarpium Citri Reticulatae (*Chen Pi*), and Fructus Citri Aurantii (*Zhi Ke*).

**ACUPUNCTURE:** *Xin Shu* (Bl 15), *Pi Shu* (Bl 20), *Gong Sun* (Sp 4), *San Yin Jiao* (Sp 6), *Bai Hui* (GV 20). Use supplementing technique.

### 3. LUNG-SPLEEN QI VACUITY PATTERN

**MAIN SYMPTOMS:** Anxiety and preoccupation, moodiness, sorrow, a desire to cry, lassitude of the spirit, fatigue, chest oppression, shortness of breath, a faint voice, sweating on slight exertion, possible persistent, weak cough provoked by talking or exertion, cold hands and feet, loose stools, torpid intake, a pale, fat tongue with thin fur, and a fine, weak pulse

**TREATMENT PRINCIPLES:** Fortify the spleen and boost the qi, supplement the lungs and relieve anxiety

**FORMULA & MEDICINALS:** *Bu Fei Tang* (Supplement the Lungs Decoction)

Radix Codonopsitis Pilosulae (*Dang Shen*), 10g, Radix Astragali Membranacei (*Huang Qi*), 10-15g, cooked Radix Rehmanniae (*Shu Di*), 12g, Fructus Schisandrae Chinensis (*Wu Wei Zi*), 10g, Radix Asteris Tatarici (*Zi Wan*), 10g, Rhizoma Atractylodis Macrocephalae (*Bai Zhu*), 10g, Pericarpium Citri Reticulatae (*Chen Pi*), 3g, mix-fried Radix Glycyrrhizae (*Gan Cao*), 3-6g

Decoct in water and administer orally in two divided doses, morning and evening, one *ji* per day.

**ADDITIONS & SUBTRACTIONS:** If there are loose stools or diarrhea with poor appetite, add Sclerotium Poriae Cocos (*Fu Ling*). For simultaneous food stagnation with loss of appetite, abdominal distention, and loss of taste, add Fructus Germinatus Hordei Vulgaris (*Mai Ya*), Massa Medica Fermentata (*Shen Qu*), and Fructus Crataegi (*Shan Zha*). For spontaneous perspiration, add Fructus Levis Tritici Aestivi (*Fu Xiao Mai*) and Radix Ephedrae (*Ma Huang Gen*).

**ACUPUNCTURE:** *Fei Shu* (Bl 13), *Gao Huang Shu* (Bl 43), *Guan Yuan* (CV 4), *Qi Hai* (CV 6), *Zu San Li* (St 36). Use supplementing technique.

### ENDNOTES

[1]Wiseman, *op. cit.*, refers to this as anxiety and preoccupation.

# ❖ 5 ❖

# FREQUENT SORROW

The Chinese disease category of frequent sorrow or *shan bei* refers to uncontrollable low spirits and a tendency to grieving, melancholy, and crying or a desire to cry.[1] Although there is no clear parallel in Western psychiatry, manifestations of frequent sorrow bear phenomenological resemblance to melancholia and characterologic depression. These terms describe a temperament that is predisposed to depression in the absence of prominent symptoms of psychomotor slowing, change in appetite, reduced energy, and other so-called vegetative symptoms. Depressive or melancholic temperament is typically seen in the context of personality disorders and is accompanied by pervasive feelings of emptiness or loneliness. There is frequently a history of emotional dysregulation, and a chronic pattern of chaotic or abusive relationships. Characterologic depression is not a disorder but a manifestation of several personality disorders. Treatment considerations and indications for referral are identical to those discussed for major depressive disorder.

## CHINESE DISEASE CAUSES & MECHANISMS:

Sorrow is the affect or emotion of the lungs, while tears are the fluid of the liver. Therefore, in Chinese medicine, the causes of sorrow, grief, melancholy, and crying are mostly related to the lungs and liver. When the lungs are healthy and in balance, sorrow is only provoked by appropriate stimuli and is not excessive or inappropriately enduring. In that case, sorrow is an expression of the correct functioning of the lungs. However, if, due to any rea-

son, the lungs become vacuous, they may lose control over their functions, including the production and control of sorrow. Causes which may result in lung qi vacuity include excessive or prolonged grief, over-taxation, and enduring disease. "Sorrow leads the qi to scatter." This means excessive sorrow causes scattering and dispersion of the lung and heart qi. When the lung qi is vacuous, it cannot distribute the finest essence of water and grains transported up to it by the spleen. Therefore, this finest essence accumulates in the lungs. As it is said, "The accumulation of essence in the lungs leads to sorrow." Hence, frequent sorrow may occur. Since lung qi participates with the heart qi in the overall chest or ancestral qi, lung qi vacuity often occurs in combination with heart qi vacuity.

Internally engendered heat flaring upward may also disturb the lungs and cause sorrow and crying. This heat is most commonly depressive heat and may be complicated by lung qi and/or heart blood vacuity due to a concomitant spleen qi vacuity. Just as heat may cause the blood to move frenetically outside its vessels, so heat may force the fluids outside the body. As mentioned above, tears are the fluid of the liver, and the liver and lungs share a mutual five phase relationship via the control cycle. The lungs are supposed to control the liver, but, if the liver becomes depressed and, therefore, replete, the liver may insult the lungs, leading to lung vacuity. In that case, liver depression transforming heat may cause both sorrow and crying. When depressive heat ascends and accumulates in both the lungs and the heart, as it very often does, consuming and damaging yin fluids, there is alternating sorrow and excessive joy. This complex, essentially yin fire pattern may be called a heart vacuity-lung heat pattern.

TREATMENT BASED ON PATTERN DISCRIMINATION:

## 1. HEART-LUNG QI VACUITY PATTERN

MAIN SYMPTOMS: Grief with a tendency to crying, heart palpitations, shortness of breath, fatigue, possibly an enduring, weak cough commonly provoked by exertion or talking, runny nose with clear, watery snivel, a tendency to catch cold, a faint voice, sweating on slight exertion, a pale tongue with thin fur, and a fine, weak pulse

TREATMENT PRINCIPLES: Supplement the heart and lung qi

FORMULA & MEDICINALS: *Bu Fei Tang Jia Jian* (Supplement the Lungs Decoction with Additions & Subtractions)

Radix Panacis Ginseng (*Ren Shen*), 6-10g (decocted first), Radix Astragali Membranacei (*Huang Qi*), 10-15g, cooked Radix Rehmanniae (*Shu Di*), 12g, Fructus Schizandrae Chinensis (*Wu Wei Zi*), 10g, Semen Biotae Orientalis (*Bai Zi Ren*), 12g, stir-fried Semen Zizyphi Spinosae (*Suan Zao Ren*), 12g, Sclerotium Pararadicis Poriae Cocos (*Fu Shen*), 12g, mix-fried Radix Glycyrrhizae (*Gan Cao*), 6-10g

Decoct in water and administer orally in two divided doses, morning and evening, one *ji* per day.

ADDITIONS & SUBTRACTIONS: For profuse sweating, add Fructus Levis Tritici Aestivi (*Fu Xiao Mai*) and Rhizoma Atractylodis Macrocephalae (*Bai Zhu*). If there is borborygmus, torpid intake, and loose stools, add Rhizoma Atractylodis Macrocephalae (*Bai Zhu*) and Pericarpium Citri Reticulatae (*Chen Pi*).

ACUPUNCTURE: *Da Ling* (Per 7), *Jian Shi* (Per 5), *Po Hu* (Bl 42), *Fei Shu* (Bl 13), *Xin Shu* (Bl 15), *Pi Shu* (Bl 20). Use even supplementing-even draining technique. Alternate the use of *Xin Shu* and *Pi Shu* each treatment.

## 2. LIVER FIRE INVADING THE LUNGS PATTERN

MAIN SYMPTOMS: Frequent sorrow and susceptibility to crying alternating with irritability, eructation, chest and rib-side pain and distention, frequent sighing, taciturnity, PMS in females, a bitter taste in the mouth, a dark or reddish tongue with possibly yellow or dryish fur, and a bowstring, rapid pulse

TREATMENT PRINCIPLES: Course the liver and resolve depression, clear the lungs and drain fire

FORMULA & MEDICINALS: *Si Ni San Jia Jian* (Four Counterflows Powder with Additions & Subtractions)

Radix Bupleuri (*Chai Hu*), 10g, Fructus Citri Aurantii (*Zhi Ke*), 10g, Radix Albus Paeoniae Lactiflorae (*Bai Shao*), 10g, Pericarpium Citri Reticulatae Viride (*Qing Pi*), 6g, stir-fried Fructus Gardeniae Jasminoidis (*Zhi Zi*), 6-10g, Radix Scutellariae Baicalensis (*Huang Qin*), 10g, Herba Menthae Haplocalycis (*Bo He*), 6g (added later), Radix Platycodi Grandiflori (*Jie Geng*), 10g, Semen Pruni Armeniacae (*Xing Ren*), 6-10g, Cortex Albizziae Julibrissinisis (*He Huan Pi*), 10g, Radix Glycyrrhizae (*Gan Cao*), 10g

If there is concomitant spleen vacuity, one can use *Xiao Chai Hu Tang Jia Wei* (Minor Bupleurum Decoction with Added Flavors) instead: Radix Bupleuri (*Chai Hu*), 10g, Radix Codonopsitis Pilosulae (*Dang Shen*), 10g, Radix Scutellariae Baicalensis (*Huang Qin*), 10g, Radix Polygalae Tenuifoliae (*Yuan Zhi*), 6-10g, Fructus Schisandrae Chinensis (*Wu Wei Zi*), 6-10g, mix-fried Radix Glycyrrhizae (*Gan Cao*), 6g, Rhizoma Pinelliae Ternatae (*Ban Xia*), 10g, Fructus Zizyphi Jujubae (*Da Zao*), 3-5 pieces, uncooked Rhizoma Zingiberis (*Sheng Jiang*), 3g (added after).

Decoct in water and administer orally in two divided doses, morning and evening, one *ji* per day.

ACUPUNCTURE: *Xing Jian* (Liv 2), *Gan Shu* (Bl 18), *Fei Shu* (Bl 13), *Lie Que* (Lu 7), *Po Hu* (Bl 42), *Hun Men* (Bl 47). Use draining technique.

## 3. HEART VACUITY-LUNG HEAT PATTERN

MAIN SYMPTOMS: Grief and crying for no reason, melancholy, mental abstraction, heart vexation, insomnia, a flushed red facial complexion, heat and sweating in the palms of the hands and soles of the feet, a red tongue with scanty fur, and a bowstring, fine, rapid pulse

TREATMENT PRINCIPLES: Nourish yin and downbear fire, supplement the heart and quiet the spirit

FORMULA & MEDICINALS: *Gan Mai Da Zao Tang Jia Wei* (Licorice, Wheat & Red Date Decoction with Added Flavors)

Uncooked Radix Glycyrrhizae (*Gan Cao*), 10-15g, Fructus Levis Tritici Aestivi (*Xiao Mai*), 20-45g, Fructus Zizyphi Jujubae (*Da Zao*), 6 pieces, Tuber Asparagi Cochinensis (*Tian Dong*), 12g, Tuber Ophiopogonis Japonici (*Mai Dong*), 12g, Radix Albus Paeoniae Lactiflorae (*Bai Shao*), 10g, Radix Angelicae Sinensis (*Dang Gui*), 10g, Bulbus Lilii (*Bai He*), 10g, Sclerotium Pararadicis Poriae Cocos (*Fu Shen*), 12g, Radix Scutellariae Baicalensis (*Huang Qin*), 10g, Flos Albizziae Julibrissinisis (*He Huan Hua*), 10-15g, stir-fried Semen Zizyphi Spinosae (*Suan Zao Ren*), 12g

Decoct in water and administer orally in two divided doses, morning and evening, one *ji* per day.

**ACUPUNCTURE:** *Tai Xi* (Ki 3), *Yin Xi* (Ht 6), *Nei Guan* (Per 6), *San Yin Jiao* (Sp 6), *Xin Shu* (Bl 15), *Shen Shu* (Bl 23), *Gao Huang Shu* (Bl 43). Use even supplementing-even draining technique.

**ENDNOTES**

[1]Wiseman, *op. cit.*, refers to this as a tendency to sorrow.

# ❖ 6 ❖

# SUSCEPTIBILITY TO FEAR & FRIGHT

The Chinese disease category of susceptibility to fear refers to an emotional state characterized by anticipation of the feeling of pain or danger which is often unreasonable or groundless. In other words, it refers to fear of something which is not currently present but which causes fear about the future. Paranoia is a form of this disorder. In Chinese, susceptibility to fear is *shan kong*. Susceptibility to fright describes the emotional state of being easily frightened by minor stimuli or even frightened by nothing. People with the Chinese concept of susceptibility to fright startle more easily than most other people. In Chinese, a susceptibility to fright is *shan jing*. Although these two conditions can be seen as two separate disease diagnoses, many Chinese medical texts simply talk about fear and fright as a single yin-yang dichotomy.

Similar to Chinese medical nosology, Western psychiatry distinguishes between symptoms of generalized fear or anxiety and symptoms of fright or panic. According to the Chinese description above, susceptibility to fear is similar to anticipatory anxiety of pain or danger that is viewed by the patient as unreasonable. This is a subjective state of anxiety. In contrast, susceptibility to fright corresponds to a more intense experience of anxiety typically caused by an observable trigger and accompanied by objective signs of increased startle response, increased heart rate, sweating, trembling, dizziness, and other signs and symptoms of autonomic arousal.

## NOSOLOGY:

Many Western psychiatric symptoms and disorders are phenomenologically similar to the above Chinese categories. Considerable overlap exists between the Western symptoms that resemble or contain elements of these distinct Chinese disorders.

---

### WESTERN PSYCHIATRIC CONDITIONS ASSOCIATED WITH FEAR AND FRIGHT

| SUSCEPTIBILITY TO FEAR | SUSCEPTIBILITY TO FRIGHT |
|---|---|
| GENERALIZED ANXIETY | PANIC ATTACKS, TRIGGERED |
| AGORAPHOBIA | PANIC DISORDER, TRIGGERED |
| PSYCHOSES WITH ANXIETY | POST-TRAUMATIC STRESS DISORDER |
| ADJUSTMENT DISORDER WITH ANXIETY | PHOBIAS WITH PANIC SYMPTOMS |
| OBSESSIVE-CUMPULSIVE DISORDER WITH ANXIETY | |
| SPECIFIC PHOBIAS SOCIAL | |

## 1. GENERALIZED ANXIETY

Susceptibility to fear (generalized anxiety) and susceptibility to fright (panic attacks) or elevated startle response are frequently grouped together in Western psychiatric classification. Like other symptoms reviewed in this section, these may reflect a primary psychiatric disorder or result from a medical disorder or the effects of a substance.

Generalized anxiety disorder exists when symptoms or worry and anxiety persist at least six months in the absence of another psychiatric disorder, and possible contributing medical etiologies or substance abuse have been ruled out. Persisting anxiety in an otherwise healthy individual is a sufficient basis for the diagnosis. Many other categories in Western psychiatric nosology include anxiety as a necessary symptom for diagnosis but require other specific psychiatric symptoms to fulfill diagnostic criteria. For example, in social phobia, an individual experiences anxiety when anticipating embarrassing social situations leading to social avoidance, feelings of dread, and sometimes panic attacks when in certain potentially embarrassing social contexts. Specific phobias pertain to circumscribed fears of specific objects or situations (phobic stimulus). For example, a fear of spiders or a fear of heights might result in avoidance behavior and intense anxiety or panic. Hypochondriasis is a state of generalized anxiety associated with ungrounded beliefs of illness. When such unsubstantiated beliefs and fears are bizarre (with respect to the patient's cultural context), the patient may be delusional. In this case, an underlying psychotic disorder may exist or the patient may be experiencing delusions caused by a medical condition or the effects of a substance or medication. Anxiety associated with bizarre beliefs is often observed in delirium, dementia, and substance intoxication. When anxiety is associated with recurrent intrusive worries, obsessive-compulsive disorder (OCD) may be present (see Chapter 4, this Book, Anxiety & Thinking, and Book 3, Chapter 8, Obsessive-compulsive Disorder). Persisting anxiety symptoms that begin soon after an identifiable traumatic event and are associated with disturbed sleep, increased startle response, or vivid experiences of reliving the trauma (i.e., flashbacks) point to a diagnosis of post-traumatic stress disorder (PTSD).

## 2. PANIC ATTACKS

Panic attacks may occur in many Western psychiatric disorders but only panic disorder requires this symptom to meet diagnostic criteria. After medical disorders or the effects of a substance (including medications) have been ruled out as possible causes, a thorough history will clarify whether panic attacks take place in isolation or during encounters with a feared situation or object. By definition, panic disorder entails uncued panic attacks and anticipatory anxiety of future panic episodes, or situations or objects that may cause them. In contrast, panic episodes in the context of a social situation or during encounters with a feared object suggest social phobia and specific phobia respectively. In contemporary Western psychiatric nosology, uncued panic attacks are described as taking place with or without agoraphobia. Agoraphobia is defined as anticipatory anxiety about being in a place or situation from which escape will be impossible in the event of a panic attack. Agoraphobia can occur in the absence of panic attacks just as panic disorder does not necessarily require the presence of agoraphobia.

### EPIDEMIOLOGY:

The following table summarizes estimated prevalence rates of these disorders.

| WESTERN PSYCHIATRIC ANXIETY DISORDERS & LIFETIME PREVALENCE RATES | |
|---|---|
| DISORDER | LIFETIME PREVALENCE RATE |
| GENERALIZED ANXIETY DISORDER (GAD) | 2.5-8% |
| HYPOCHONDRIASIS | 4-6% |
| POST-TRAUMATIC STRESS DISORDER (PTSD) | 3-10% |
| AGORAPHOBIA | 2.5-6.5% |
| OBSESSIVE-COMPULSIVE DISORDER (OCD) | 2-3% |
| SPECIFIC PHOBIAS | 0.8-2.5% |
| SOCIAL PHOBIA | 2-3% |
| PANIC DISORDER | 1.5-2% |

## DIFFERENTIAL DIAGNOSIS

### 1. MEDICAL DISORDERS

A. NEUROLOGIC DISORDERS
B. ENDOCRINOLOGIC DISORDERS
C. TOXIC EXPOSURE
D. MISCELLANEOUS OTHER MEDICAL DISORDERS

### 2. EFFECTS OF SUBSTANCES

A. ALCOHOL OR ILLICIT SUBSTANCE INTOXICATION OR WITHDRAWAL
B. SIDE EFFECTS OR DISCONTINUATION EFFECTS OF MEDICATIONS

### 3. PSYCHIATRIC DISORDERS

A. PANIC DISORDER WITH OR WITHOUT AGORAPHOBIA
B. SOCIAL PHOBIA
C. SPECIFIC PHOBIAS
D. POST-TRAUMATIC STRESS DISORDER (PTSD)
E. GENERALIZED ANXIETY DISORDER (GAD)
F. SCHIZOPHRENIA AND OTHER PSYCHOTIC DISORDERS
G. PERSONALITY DISORDERS

### DIFFERENTIAL DIAGNOSIS:

As noted above, isolated anxiety or panic attacks are not viewed as disorders in Western psychiatry. Therefore, accurate diagnosis of a disorder that encompasses these symptoms must take into account the broader context or pattern of history, associated medical or psychiatric symptoms, and social or occupational dysfunction within which they are observed. When there is evidence of an underlying related medical disorder or substance abuse, these are investigated and treated if identified as causes of anxiety or panic. A thorough history will clarify the medical differential diagnosis by revealing the degree of association between anxiety or panic symptoms and the course of an identified illness. An extensive list of medical etiologies can result in these symptoms, including neurologic, endocrinologic, toxic, and other diseases. Anxiety or panic can occur prominently during both acute substance intoxication and withdrawal, especially with alcohol and the stimulant drugs of abuse (cocaine and methamphetamine). Chronic use of certain medications, including short-acting sedative-hypnotic agents, can precipiate symptoms that are identical to panic attacks.

When the clinician has ruled out underlying medical etiologies or the effects of a substance, primary psychiatric disorders can be considered. Again, this process is facilitated by good history taking which places anxiety or panic symptoms in the context of co-occurring psychiatric symptoms, current functioning, and pertinent personal and family history. When medical causes have been ruled out, a persisting pattern of panic attacks in the absence of identified precipitants usually points to panic disorder. When panic attacks are accompanied by extreme social avoidance and seemingly irrational fear of being in places from which "escape" is difficult in the event of a panic

attack, the diagnosis is panic disorder with agoraphobia. Panic attacks may also occur in the context of other psychiatric disorders, including post-traumatic stress disorder (PTSD), social or specific phobias, generalized anxiety disorder (GAD), and, less frequently, schizophrenia and other psychotic disorders. Susceptibility to fright includes core symptoms that resemble all of these Western psychiatric disorders, as all include panic attacks. In contrast, susceptibility to fear more closely resembles generalized anxiety disorder (i.e., when there are no co-occurring panic attacks), other anxiety disorders, and certain personality disorders in which anxiety is a prominent symptom.

### ETIOLOGY & PATHOPHYSIOLOGY:

As noted above, medical disorders can manifest as anxiety symptoms including generalized feelings of anxiety and panic attacks. Dysregulation of CNS receptors for GABA (gamma-amino butyric acid), the chief inhibitory neurotransmitter, is believed to underlie generalized anxiety disorder (GAD) and panic disorder. A subset of individuals who have panic disorder are more susceptible to induction of panic by infusion of sodium lactate. The significance of this finding is unclear, but it suggests autonomic dysregulation in the brainstem and limbic system resulting in symptoms that have been classified as panic attacks in Western psychiatric nosology. Panic attacks can result from medical disorders affecting the heart (including cardiac arrhythmias and heart valve pathology), thyroid gland, and adrenals (a rare adrenal tumor called a pheochromocytoma hypersecretes cortisol causing panic-like symptoms). Hypoglycemia, which is sometimes present in diabetic patients or patients with liver disease, can also manifest as panic attacks. In addition, seizure disorder can sometimes manifest as a panic attack.

Brain-imaging studies have implicated abnormal functioning in the prefrontal cortex and limbic system in the pathogenesis of generalized anxiety and other anxiety symptoms. Functional brain imaging studies have demonstrated a general reduction in frontal cerebral blood flow in patients with GAD, panic disorder, or other anxiety disorders. The significance of this finding is not clear. Significant genetic factors contribute to the likelihood of developing panic disorder. Patients who have first-degree relatives with panic disorder are at least four times more likely to develop panic disorder compared to a control population. Twin studies have shown that panic disorder occurred more frequently in identical (monozygotic) twins than fraternal (dizygotic) twins. In addition to the above biological theories of anxiety and panic, many psychoanalytic models have been adduced, starting with Freud's belief that "anxiety disorders" result from "undischarged excitation generated in connection with an unacceptable sexual idea." Psychological causes of anxiety and panic have subsequently been interpreted from many other psychoanalytic theories. These are too numerous to review here.

## WESTERN MEDICAL TREATMENT:

The most efficacious treatment of anxiety depends on the identified underlying cause(s). When anxiety or panic is secondary to a medical disorder, successful treatment of that disorder typically results in resolution of these symptoms. For example, panic attacks typically stop following surgical or pharmacological correction of hyperthyroidism. When panic attacks or generalized feelings of anxiety are tied to underlying psychiatric disorders, treatment response typically includes significant reduction in severity or intensity of anxiety symptoms. Many pharmacologic approaches are used to treat anxiety and panic. There are no best treatment strategies for different kinds of anxiety symptoms. Benzodiazepines, which function as GABA agonists (see pathophysiology section above) are moderately effective in the treatment of generalized anxiety and panic attacks. No specific medication is superior to another. Antidepressant medications, including SSRIs, tricyclics, and MAOIs, are also used with relatively equal efficacy. Cognitive-behavioral therapy and supportive psychotherapy effectively reduce symptom severity and improve overall level of social functioning in patients with generalized anxiety disorder, panic disorder, or other primary psychiatric disorders that include anxiety symptoms. Patients with OCD tend to be more difficult to treat and typically respond to medication doses that are significantly higher than doses required for GAD, phobias, and panic disorders. Anxiety symptoms in the context of an underlying psychotic disorder typically abate with therapeutic response to antipsychotic medications.

## SHORT & LONG-TERM ADVANTAGES & DISADVANTAGES OF WESTERN MEDICAL TREATMENT:

Short-term advantages of pharmacologic treatment of generalized anxiety or panic include significant symptomatic improvement and rapid improvement in social and occupational functioning. However, many patients who suffer from primary anxiety disorders become dependent on benzodiazepines and other anxiolytic medications following prolonged use. Because of the development of physiologic tolerance, these patients frequently require steadily increased doses of a given benzodiazepine to achieve an acceptable level of anxiety relief. Although these patients may experience on-going relief from anxiety, functioning may be impaired over the long-term due to chronic use of high doses of benzodiazepines. The majority of patients taking medications for generalized anxiety or panic attacks experience significant symptomatic improvement and do not become dependent on medications used to treat these symptoms. For these patients, long-term benefits clearly outweigh short- and long-term risks of chemical dependency and associated impairments in social or occupational functioning.

## PROGNOSIS:

The long-term course and prognosis of anxiety symptoms is closely related to the underlying medical or psychiatric etiology. Effective treatment of a medical condition typically results in rapid improvement. However, anxiety symptoms sometimes persist for weeks or months afterwards. Anxiety or panic attacks are sometimes associated with primary psychiatric disorders that are chronic or treatment refractory, including psychotic disorders, OCD, or severe PTSD. In these cases, the long-term course of anxiety symptoms is prognostically poor.

## INDICATIONS FOR REFERRAL TO WESTERN MEDICAL SERVICES:

It is appropriate to refer a patient complaining of generalized anxiety or panic attacks to emergency medical evaluation if there is evidence of an acute underlying medical disorder, substance abuse, or a severe psychiatric disorder that places the patient at risk. An example of the latter case is psychosis accompanied by anxiety and delusional beliefs that might lead to violent or suicidal behavior. Patients who complain of anxiety symptoms that are not associated with severe or acute medical or psychiatric disorders may be non-urgently referred to a psychiatrist if symptomatic improvement does not take place following a reasonable course of appropriate treatment using prescribed Chinese medical approaches.

## CHINESE DISEASE CAUSES & MECHANISMS:

In Chinese medicine, fear is the affect associated with the kidneys. Therefore, kidney vacuity may manifest as susceptibility to fear. Former heaven natural endowment insufficiency, immaturity or aging, enduring disease, over-taxation, unrestrained sexual activity, and over-use of certain medicines and drugs may consume the essence and cause kidney essence insufficiency, thus resulting in susceptibility to fear.

Courage, on the other hand, is seen as the result of two things in Chinese medicine: 1) exuberant heart spirit, and 2) replete gallbladder qi. Therefore, either heart blood-spleen qi vacuity or gallbladder qi vacuity and timidity may result in a lack of courage and, consequently, a susceptibility to fear. Heart blood-spleen qi vacuity is nothing other than a species of qi and blood vacuity. This may be due to immaturity, overtaxation, chronic or great loss of blood, enduring disease, etc. Gallbladder qi vacuity and timidity is actually a combination of qi and blood vacuity, liver depression, and an element of phlegm. Therefore, it is also called heart-gallbladder qi vacuity and may be due to anything which damages the spleen and depresses the liver plus sudden great fright which specifically damages the gallbladder.

In the case of susceptibility to fright, there is an exaggerated startle reflex. Such startling is considered a species of stirring, and stirring always involves a movement of qi in Chinese medicine. The first two mechanisms of susceptibility to fright are very similar to those of susceptibility to fear: heart-gallbladder qi vacuity and liver depression and blood vacuity. In both cases, there is insufficient qi and/or blood to construct and nourish the heart spirit along with an element of liver depression making the flow of the qi mechanism uneasy and, consequently, chaotic. Pent-up stagnant qi is suddenly stimulated to overcourse and overdischarge and this results in chaotic qi flow. When this happens, its outward manifestation is startling.

The second three mechanisms of susceptibility to fright all involve some sort of evil heat. Either yin vacuity/vacuity heat, heart fire effulgence, or phlegm fire harass the heart and disquiet the spirit. Another way of putting this in Chinese is to say the spirit fails to keep to its abode. Failure to keep to one's abode means that one has moved from that abode. If one remembers that spirit is nothing other than an accumulation of qi in the heart, the heart is the ruler of the entire body, and it is qi which propels movement, then it is easy to understand that sudden, chaotic stirring of the spirit may easily result in sudden, chaotic movement of the body.

Yin vacuity is typically due to former heaven natural endowment insufficiency, enduring disease, great or chronic loss of blood, unrestrained sexual activity, aging, and certain medicines and drugs. Phlegm fire is due to a constitutional tendency toward yang exuberance and/or fire heat and accumulated phlegm due to faulty diet and liver depression transforming heat. Heart fire effulgence is usually due to emotional disturbance and/or addiction to acrid, hot, peppery foods or drinking alcohol.

## TREATMENT BASED ON PATTERN DISCRIMINATION:

### 1. KIDNEY ESSENCE INSUFFICIENCY PATTERN

MAIN SYMPTOMS: Susceptibility to fear, heart palpitations, low back and knee soreness and limpness, lassitude of the spirit, dizziness, tinnitus, heart vexation, reduced sleep, seminal emission, night sweats, a red tongue with scanty fur, and a fine, weak pulse

TREATMENT PRINCIPLES: Supplement the kidneys, fill the essence, and fortify the mind

FORMULA & MEDICINALS: *Liu Wei Di Huang Wan Jia Wei* (Six Flavors Rehmannia Pills with Added Flavors)

Cooked Radix Rehmanniae (*Shu Di*), 15g, Fructus Corni Officinalis (*Shan Zhu Yu*), 12g, Radix Dioscoreae Oppositae (*Shan Yao*), 12g, Sclerotium Poriae Cocos (*Fu Ling*), 10g, Rhizoma Alismatis (*Ze Xie*), 6g, Cortex Radicis Moutan (*Dan Pi*), 10g, Radix Polygalae Tenuifoliae (*Yuan Zhi*), 10g, Fructus Lycii Chinensis (*Gou Qi Zi*), 10g, Tuber Ophiopogonis Japonici (*Mai Dong*), 10g, Fructus Schizandrae Chinensis (*Wu Wei Zi*), 10g

Decoct in water and administer orally in two divided doses, morning and evening, one *ji* per day.

ADDITIONS & SUBTRACTIONS: If there are severe night sweats, insomnia, and profuse dreams, add stir-fried Semen Zizyphi Spinosae (*Suan Zao Ren*) and Semen Biotae Orientalis (*Bai Zi Ren*). If there is kidney yang vacuity with impotence, seminal emission, and chilled limbs, add Cornu Cervi (*Lu Jiao*) and Cortex Cinnamomi Cassiae (*Rou Gui*).

ACUPUNCTURE: *Xin Shu* (Bl 15), *Shen Shu* (Bl 23), *Zhi Shi* (Bl 52), *Tai Xi* (Ki 3), *San Yin Jiao* (Sp 6). Use draining technique.

## 2. QI & BLOOD DUAL VACUITY PATTERN

MAIN SYMPTOMS: Intermittent susceptibility to fear, heart palpitations, shortness of breath, a pale white facial complexion, pale lips and nails, fatigue, lack of strength, aversion to wind, spontaneous perspiration, a pale tongue with thin fur, and a fine, weak pulse

TREATMENT PRINCIPLES: Supplement the qi, nourish the blood, and quiet the spirit

FORMULA & MEDICINALS: *Ba Zhen Tang Jia Wei* (Eight Pearls Decoction with Added Flavors)

Radix Codonopsitis Pilosulae (*Dang Shen*), 10g, Rhizoma Atractylodis Macrocephalae (*Bai Zhu*), 10g, Sclerotium Poriae Cocos (*Fu Ling*), 10g, mix-fried Radix Glycyrrhizae (*Gan Cao*), 6g, cooked Radix Rehmanniae (*Shu Di*), 12g, Radix Albus Paeoniae Lactiflorae (*Bai Shao*), 10g, Angelicae Sinensis (*Dang Gui*), 10g, Radix Ligustici Wallichii (*Chuan Xiong*), 6-10g (added later), Rhizoma Acori Graminei (*Shi Chang Pu*), 6g, Radix Polygalae Tenuifoliae (*Yuan Zhi*), 6g

Decoct in water and administer orally in two divided doses, morning and evening, one *ji* per day.

ADDITIONS & SUBTRACTIONS: If there is insomnia, add Sclerotium Pararadicis Poriae Cocos (*Fu Shen*) and stir-fried Semen Zizyphi Spinosae (*Suan Zao Ren*). If there is spontaneous perspiration, add Radix Astragali Membranacei (*Huang Qi*) and Fructus Levis Tritici Aestivi (*Fu Xiao Mai*).

ACUPUNCTURE: *Shen Men* (Ht 7), *Xin Shu* (Bl 15), *San Yin Jiao* (Sp 6), *Zu San Li* (St 36), *Ge Shu* (Bl 17). Use supplementing technique.

## 3. HEART-GALLBLADDER QI VACUITY PATTERN

MAIN SYMPTOMS: Timidity, paranoia, susceptibility to fear and fright, indecisiveness when decision-making is needed, inability to control oneself, rib-side discomfort, heart palpitations, possible heart vexation and/or insomnia, profuse dreams, possible profuse phlegm and/or plum pit qi, a pale tongue with thin fur, and a slightly bowstring, weak, possibly slippery pulse

TREATMENT PRINCIPLES: Supplement the qi, nourish the heart, and quiet the gallbladder

FORMULA & MEDICINALS: *Shi Wei Wen Dan Tang* (Ten Flavors Warm the Gallbladder Decoction)

Radix Codonopsitis Pilosulae (*Dang Shen*), 10g, Sclerotium Poriae Cocos (*Fu Ling*), 10g, mix-fried Radix Glycyrrhizae (*Zhi Gan Cao*), 3-10g, Pericarpium Citri Reticulatae (*Chen Pi*), 6g, lime-processed Rhizoma Pinelliae Ternatae (*Ban Xia*), 10g, Radix Polygalae Tenuifoliae (*Yuan Zhi*), 10g, stir-fried Semen Zizyphi Spinosae (*Suan Zao Ren*), 12g, Fructus Immaturus Citri Aurantii (*Zhi Shi*), 6g, cooked Radix Rehmanniae (*Shu Di*), 12g, Fructus Schisandrae Chinensis (*Wu Wei Zi*), 10g

Decoct in water and administer orally in two divided doses, morning and evening, one *ji* per day.

ACUPUNCTURE: *Shen Ting* (GV 24), *Yang Jiao* (GB 35), *Qi Men* (Liv 14), *Zhang Men* (Liv 13), *Guan Yuan* (CV 4). Use even supplementing-even draining method.

## 4. LIVER DEPRESSION-BLOOD VACUITY PATTERN

MAIN SYMPTOMS: Susceptibility to fright, irritability, vexation and agitation, breast, chest, abdominal, and rib-side distention and fullness especially during the premenstruum, dizziness, headache, moodiness, a pale white facial complexion and pale nails, scanty, delayed, or blocked menstruation in females, a pale tongue with thin fur, and a fine, bowstring pulse

---

NOTE: The main difference between this and the preceding pattern is that there are no specifically heart signs or symptoms listed here.

---

TREATMENT PRINCIPLES: Course the liver and rectify the qi, nourish the blood and quiet the spirit

FORMULA & MEDICINALS: *Xiao Yao San* (Rambling Powder)

Radix Bupleuri (*Chai Hu*), 10g, Radix Angelicae Sinensis (*Dang Gui*), 10g, Radix Albus Paeoniae Lactiflorae (*Bai Shao*), 10g, Rhizoma Atractylodis Macrocephalae (*Bai Zhu*), 10g, Sclerotium Poriae Cocos (*Fu Ling*), 10g, mix-fried Radix Glycyrrhizae (*Gan Cao*), 6g, Herba Menthae Haplocalycis (*Bo He*), 3-6g (added later), uncooked Rhizoma Zingiberis (*Sheng Jiang*), 3g (added later), Fructus Zizyphi Jujubae (*Da Zao*), 3 pieces, uncooked Os Draconis (*Long Gu*), 12g (decocted first), uncooked Concha Ostreae (*Mu Li*), 12g (decocted first)

Decoct in water and administer orally in two divided doses, morning and evening, one *ji* per day.

**ADDITIONS & SUBTRACTIONS:** If blood vacuity is severe, add cooked Radix Rehmanniae (*Shu Di*). If liver depression has transformed into fire with dryness and a bitter taste in the mouth, red eyes, and severe susceptibility to fright, add stir-fried Fructus Gardeniae Jasminoidis (*Zhi Zi*) and Cortex Radicis Moutan (*Dan Pi*) and delete the uncooked Ginger and Mentha. For severe breast or rib-side distention and pain, add Fructus Meliae Toosendan (*Chuan Lian Zi*) and Rhizoma Corydalis Yanhusuo (*Yan Hu Suo*).

**ACUPUNCTURE:** *Da Ling* (Per 7), *Nei Guan* (Per 6), *Tai Chong* (Liv 3), *Qi Men* (Liv 14), *Zu San Li* (St 36). Use even supplementing-even draining technique.

### 5. LIVER BLOOD-KIDNEY YIN VACUITY PATTERN

**MAIN SYMPTOMS:** Susceptibility to fright, vexation, reduced sleep, a pale, white facial complexion, dizziness, low back pain, afternoon tidal heat, night sweats, heat in the palms of the hands and soles of the feet, a red tongue or pale tongue with a red tip, and a fine, bowstring, possibly rapid pulse

**TREATMENT PRINCIPLES:** Nourish the blood and enrich yin, quiet the spirit and relieve fright

**FORMULA & MEDICINALS:** *Gui Shao Di Huang Tang Jia Jian* (Dang Gui & Peony Rehmannia Decoction with Additions & Subtractions)

Radix Angelicae Sinensis (*Dang Gui*), 10g, Radix Albus Paeoniae Lactiflorae (*Bai Shao*), 10g, cooked Radix Rehmanniae (*Shu Di*), 12g, Radix Dioscoreae Oppositae (*Shan Yao*), 10g, Sclerotium Pararadicis Poriae Cocos (*Fu Shen*), 10g, Fructus Corni Officinalis (*Shan Zhu Yu*), 10g, Rhizoma Alismatis (*Ze Xie*), 6g, Cortex Radicis Moutan (*Dan Pi*), 6-10g, stir-fried Semen Zizyphi Spinosae (*Suan Zao Ren*), 12g, Semen Biotae Orientalis (*Bai Zi Ren*), 12g

Decoct in water and administer orally in two divided doses, morning and evening, one *ji* per day.

**ADDITIONS & SUBTRACTIONS:** If there are marked signs and symptoms of vacuity heat, add Rhizoma Anemarrhenae Aspheloidis (*Zhi Mu*) and Cortex Phellodendri (*Huang Bai*).

**ACUPUNCTURE:** *Yin Xi* (Ht 6), *Xin Shu* (Bl 15), *Ge Shu* (Bl 17), *Gan Shu* (Bl 18), *San Yin Jiao* (Sp 6), *Tai Xi* (Ki 3). Use even supplementing-even draining technique.

### 6. PHLEGM FIRE HARASSING ABOVE PATTERN

**MAIN SYMPTOMS:** Susceptibility to fright, heart palpitations, vertigo or dizziness, vexation, insomnia, headache, dryness and bitterness in the mouth, profuse, commonly yellow-colored phlegm, a red tongue with slimy, yellow fur, and a slippery, rapid pulse

**TREATMENT PRINCIPLES:** Clear heat and transform phlegm, quiet the heart and calm the spirit

**FORMULA & MEDICINALS:** *Huang Lian Wen Dan Tang* (Coptis Warm the Gallbladder Decoction)

Lime-processed Rhizoma Pinelliae Ternatae (*Ban Xia*), 10g, Caulis Bambusae In Taeniis (*Zhu Ru*), 10g, Fructus Immaturus Citri Aurantii (*Zhi Shi*), 6g, Pericarpium Citri Reticulatae (*Chen Pi*), 6-10g, Sclerotium Poriae Cocos (*Fu Ling*), 10g, Rhizoma Coptidis Chinensis (*Huang Lian*), 3-6g (added later), Radix Glycyrrhizae (*Gan Cao*), 3g

Decoct in water and administer orally in two divided doses, morning and evening, one *ji* per day.

**ADDITIONS & SUBTRACTIONS:** If there is concomitant liver depression, add Radix Bupleuri (*Chai Hu*) and Fructus Meliae Toosendan (*Chuan Lian Zi*). If there is vomiting, add Folium Eriobotryae Japonicae (*Pi Pa Ye*) and increase the dose of Caulis Bambusae. If there is severe fright, add uncooked Concha Ostreae (*Mu Li*) and uncooked Os Draconis (*Long Gu*).

**ACUPUNCTURE:** *Da Ling* (Per 7), *Zu Lin Qi* (GB 41), *Zhong Wan* (CV 12), *Feng Long* (St 40). Use draining technique.

### 7. HEART FIRE EFFULGENCE PATTERN

**MAIN SYMPTOMS:** Susceptibility to fright, heart vexation, a flushed red facial complexion, red eyes, sores in the mouth and on the tip of the tongue, a preference for chilled drinks, disturbed sleep, difficult, burning, dark-colored urination, a red tongue with thin, yellow fur, and a rapid pulse

**TREATMENT PRINCIPLES:** Clear the heart, discharge fire, and relieve fright

**FORMULA & MEDICINALS:** *Xie Xin Dao Chi San Jia Jian*

(Drain the Heart & Abduct the Red Powder with Additions & Subtractions)

Caulis Akebiae (*Mu Tong*), 5g, uncooked Radix Rehmanniae (*Sheng Di*), 12g, Rhizoma Coptidis Chinensis (*Huang Lian*), 6g (added later), Folium Bambusae (*Zhu Ye*), 10g, Medulla Tetrapanacis Papyriferi (*Deng Xin Cao*), 3g, Plumula Nelumbinis Nuciferae (*Lian Xin*), 3g, calcined Dens Draconis (*Long Chi*), 12g (decocted first), Concha Margaritiferae (*Zhen Zhu Mu*), 12g (decocted first), mix-fried Radix Glycyrrhizae (*Gan Cao*), 6g

Decoct in water and administer orally in two divided doses, morning and evening, one *ji* per day.

**ACUPUNCTURE:** *Lao Gong* (Per 8), *Zhi Zheng* (SI 7), *Shen Men* (Ht 7), *Da Zhong* (Ki 4). Use draining technique.

**CLINICAL TIPS:** Susceptibility to fright due to heart-gall-bladder timidity typically responds well to internally administered Chinese medicinals.

## REPRESENTATIVE CASE HISTORIES:

### ❖ CASE 1[1] ❖

The patient was a 31 year old German female who was first examined in Nanjing in April 1996. Six months before, the patient's house had been burglarized in the middle of the night causing her great fear. Since then, she felt depressed and restless. She said that her heart was disquieted as if someone were chasing her. Whenever she heard any unexpected noise, she had heart palpitations. In addition, the woman suffered from migraine headaches, insomnia, profuse dreams, nightmares, and a suffocating feeling in her throat at night. Her menses were normal, her tongue was pale and purple with thin fur, and her pulse was bowstring and fine. In addition, there was bilateral neck and shoulder tension along the entire trapezius muscle.

The treatment principles in this case were to quiet the gallbladder, calm the heart, and relax tension. The points selected were *Yang Ling Quan* (GB 34), *Jian Jing* (GB 21), and *Shen Men* (Ht 7). Needles were inserted bilaterally at these points and retained for 20 minutes during which time they were manipulated twice. After fast twisting and turning for one minute, the patient reported that her migraine headache and muscle tension were significantly reduced. Because the patient said she still felt tension in the area of *Jian Jing*, the needles in those points were stimulated even more forcefully before being withdrawn. After

withdrawal, cups were applied to *Jian Jing* bilaterally to let some blood.

After this treatment, the patient's mental state was improved. Therefore, this treatment was repeated once a week for five weeks. At the end of that time, all the woman's symptoms had disappeared and the treatment effect was judged stable. Only her sleep was still not entirely normal.

### ❖ CASE 2[2] ❖

The patient was a 36 year old man. Due to suffering a great fright, the main became fearful, filled with dread, and restless each night. He could not bear to be alone at night and needed to be in the company of other people. In addition, he had difficulty sleeping calmly and would wake in fright. When examined, the patient's signs and symptoms included a cold body and chilled limbs and sweating in the centers of his hands and feet. After an episode of fright, he would flatulate and urinate profusely. His eating and drinking were decreased, his tongue was pale with white fur, and his pulse was bowstring.

For these symptoms, the man was prescribed the following Chinese medicinals: Ramulus Cinnamomi Cassiae (*Gui Zhi*), 12g, mix-fried Radix Glycyrrhizae (*Gan Cao*), 24g, uncooked Os Draconis (*Long Gu*), 50g, uncooked Concha Ostreae (*Mu Li*), 50g, uncooked Rhizoma Zingiberis (*Sheng Jiang*), 9g, Fructus Zizyphi Jujubae (*Da Zao*), 6 pieces, Radix Polygalae Tenuifoliae (*Yuan Zhi*), 9g, Arillus Euphoriae Longanae (*Long Yan Rou*), 100g, and Fructus Levis Tritici Aestivi (*Fu Xiao Mai*), 100g. After taking three *ji* of these medicinals, the man's sleep had gradually become quiet and his fear and fright were markedly decreased. The number of episodes of fright had greatly decreased and he no longer had to be constantly with other people. However, sometimes he would still spontaneously perspire and the man was averse to wind. Therefore, 15 grams of uncooked Radix Astragali Membranacei (*Huang Qi*) and nine grams of Radix Albus Paeoniae Lactiflorae (*Bai Shao*) were added to the above formula, and, after taking a number of more *ji*, all the man's symptoms were cured.

### ❖ CASE 3[3] ❖

The patient was a 40 year old male who was initially examined on Dec. 22, 1980. In October of that year, the man had been walking alone late at night when, in the middle of the silence, he heard strange voices coming from nowhere in the middle of a field., sometimes far away and sometimes close. Then suddenly these voices died away. From that time onward, the man's fear and fright took ten thousand forms. His mind was flustered, he couldn't eat or sleep, and he began talking to himself. One month later, his expression and appearance gradually became more abnormal day by day. The man was diagnosed at a local hospital with schizophrenia and treated with sedatives for two months without any apparent effect. When examined by Dr. Huang, the man was paranoid, his mind was flustered and confused, and he had heart palpitations and heart vexation. His abdomen was distended and his upper back was painful. The patient's tongue was slightly pale with thin fur. However, its tip was red. Both inch position pulses were soggy and choppy. The right bar was slightly surging, and the cubit pulses were floating and large. With heavy pressure, they had no force. No neurological pathologies were found.

Based on the above signs and symptoms, the patient's pattern was categorized as heart-kidney dual vacuity with the spirit not keeping to its abode. Therefore, the treatment principles were to supplement and boost the heart and kidneys, quiet the spirit and stabilize the mind. The formula administered for these purposes consisted of: Rhizoma Acori Graminei (*Shi Chang Pu*), 15g, Dens Draconis (*Long Chi*), 30g, Magnetitum (*Ci Shi*), 30g, Radix Polygalae Tenuifoliae (*Yuan Zhi*), 9g, lime-processed Rhizoma Pinelliae Ternatae (*Ban Xia*), 15g, cooked Radix Rehmanniae (*Shu Di*), 18g, Semen Zizyphi Spinosae (*Suan Zao Ren*), 15g, Radix Codonopsitis Pilosulae (*Dang Shen*), 15g, and mix-fried Radix

Glycyrrhizae (*Gan Cao*), 6g. Four *ji* were decocted in water and administered (one *ji* per day).

The second examination occurred on Dec. 26. After taking the above medicinals, the man's psyche gradually had improved. His fear and fright, anxiety and thinking were greatly reduced. His appetite had somewhat increased and his sleep had improved. Therefore, he was prescribed another four *ji* of: Radix Codonopsitis Pilosulae (*Dang Shen*), 15g, cooked Radix Rehmanniae (*Shu Di*), 18g, Semen Zizyphi Spinosae (*Suan Zao Ren*), 15g, Caulis Polygoni Multiflori (*Ye Jiao Teng*), 18g, lime-processed Rhizoma Pinelliae Ternatae (*Ban Xia*), 15g, Magnetitum (*Ci Shi*), 30g, Dens Draconis (*Long Chi*), 30g, Semen Cuscutae Chinensis (*Tu Si Zi*), 15g, Rhizoma Acori Graminei (*Shi Chang Pu*), 15g, and Concha Margaritiferae (*Zhen Zhu Mu*), 30g. When the man was examined again on Dec. 30, all his symptoms were decreased and his mind had returned to normal. Therefore, another five *ji* of the original formula were prescribed and the man was judged cured. On follow-up after one year, he was still fine.

## ENDNOTES:

[1] Qiao Wen-lei, "The Treatment of Stress Syndrome by Acupuncture," trans. by Fu Zhi-wen, *Journal of Chinese Medicine*, #61, 1999, p. 17

[2] Chen & Zhao, *op. cit.*, p. 32-33

[3] Huang Yong-yuan, *Qi Nan Za Zheng Jing Xuan (A Carefully Chosen [Collection of] Strange & Difficult Conditions)*, Guangdong Science & Technology Press, Guangzhou, 1996, p. 107-108

# ❖ 7 ❖

# VEXATION & AGITATION

In Chinese medicine, vexation means annoyance due to a hot, oppressive sensation in the chest. Agitation refers to a restless state of the limbs. The former is a subjective symptom, while the latter is an objective sign. Although they are different, they are usually considered one term since, in most cases, they occur in combination and share the same disease mechanisms. Therefore, it is said:

> If vexation is severe, there must be agitation. If one sees agitation, there must be vexation.

The term vexation and agitation shows up as early as the *Su Wen* (*Simple Questions*) in the Chinese medical literature. Various early Chinese texts have glossed the meaning of agitation as stirring, *dong*, no quiet stillness, *bu an jing*, and anxiety, *you*.

There is no clear parallel between the Chinese medical disease category of vexation and agitation and complementary diagnostic categories in Western psychiatry. Western psychiatry does use descriptive terms like "psychomotor agitation" that probably connote similar but not identical subjective emotion-body or psychosomatic states. In contemporary psychiatry, the concept of somatization refers to the expression of emotional or psychological distress through physical symptom formation. Somatic symptoms typically occur in the absence of conscious awareness of distress. This concept probably captures some aspects of vexation and agitation as described in the Chinese medical literature. Generalized anxiety with somatic symptoms is another way of seeing symptoms included under the disease category of vexation in Chinese medicine. Individuals who experience feelings of restlessness but not frank anxiety often experience unusual body sensations which tend to be the focus of their complaints.

**DIFFERENTIAL DIAGNOSIS:**

Many medical (including neurological) disorders are accompanied by feelings of restlessness. Parkinson's disease, stroke, and brain tumor are included in this category. A common endocrinological cause of restlessness or agitation is hyperthyroidism. A subjective feeling of restlessness in the absence of agitation that results from antipsychotic medications is called akathisia. Side effects of many other medications as well as abuse of alcohol and illicit substances often include feelings of restlessness.

When persisting feelings of restlessness without abnormal movements are accompanied by somatic sensations, anxiety, or fear, the experience may be similar to symptoms that are described as generalized anxiety disorder in contemporary Western psychiatry. If there is no conscious awareness of anxiety or agitation, and the patient is preoccupied by somatic symptoms that have no known medical basis, he or she may fulfill criteria for a conversion disorder. This is a common disorder in which psychological

| DIFFERENTIAL DIAGNOSIS | | |
| --- | --- | --- |
| **1. MEDICAL DISORDERS** | **2. EFFECTS OF SUBSTANCES** | **3. PSYCHIATRIC DISORDERS** |
| A. PARKINSON'S DISEASE<br>B. HISTORY OF CEREBROVASCULAR ACCIDENT (CVA)<br>C. BRAIN TUMORS<br>D. HYPERTHYROIDISM | A. ALCOHOL OR ILLICIT SUBSTANCE INTOXICATION OR WITHDRAWAL<br>B. AKATHISIA AS A SIDE EFFECT OF ANTIPSYCHOTIC MEDICATIONS<br>C. SIDE EFFECTS OF OTHER MEDICATIONS | A. GENERALIZED ANXIETY DISORDER (GAD)<br>B. CONVERSION DISORDER<br>C. DEPRESSION AND OTHER MOOD DISORDERS<br>D. BIPOLAR DISORDER, MANIC PHASE<br>E. SCHIZOPHRENIA, ACUTE EXACERBATION, AND OTHER PSYCHOTIC DISORDERS<br>F. POST-TRAUMATIC STRESS DISORDER (PTSD)<br>G. SOCIAL PHOBIA AND SPECIFIC PHOBIAS<br>H. PERSONALITY DISORDERS |

stress is converted into a somatic symptom that is believed to symbolize an unconscious conflict. Agitation may more closely correspond to conversion disorder than vexation, since agitation entails little or no observable emotional disturbance, a typical finding in conversion disorder. In Western psychiatric theory, extreme emotions are typically expected to be accompanied by a commensurate degree of bodily agitation or feelings of restlessness. For example, an individual who is experiencing rage, grief, terror, euphoria, or other extreme emotions may concurrently experience subjective symptoms of agitation or objective signs of restlessness that match the intensity of his or her emotions. Agitation is frequently observed in the context of severe depression and mania as well as in schizophrenia and other psychotic disorders. Individuals with post-traumatic stress disorder (PTSD) sometimes experience extreme agitation during flashbacks. Social phobia and specific phobias are also sometimes accompanied by subjective symptoms of vexation or physical signs of agitation. Finally, individuals who have borderline, antisocial, or histrionic personality disorder may experience transient episodes of intense agitation.

## ETIOLOGY & PATHOPHYSIOLOGY:

Many theories have been put forward in efforts to explain the neurobiological basis of anxiety. These include dysregulation in GABA (gamma-amino-butyric acid), the primary inhibitory neurotransmitter, resulting in the brain's diminished capacity to adaptively respond to stressful situations. Individuals who are chronically anxious and restless have been observed to become acutely anxious or agitated in response to levels of carbon dioxide in the blood that do not affect the normal population. This has raised the possibility of a genetic predisposition to anxiety in certain populations. Anxiety symptoms, including sudden-onset feelings of agitation and restlessness, occur significantly more often in individuals who have cardiac arrhythmias. For example, mitral valve prolapse, a relatively benign condition, is commonly associated with a higher than average incidence of generalized anxiety and panic. Hyperthyroidism sometimes causes arrhythmias and associated feelings of anxiety and restlessness. This condition can also directly affect normal brain functioning resulting in subjective feelings of anxiety and agitation. The state of restlessness that often accompanies antipsychotic medication use (akathisia) has been attributed to central blockade of dopaminergic neurons that regulate voluntary movement. Subjective feelings of restlessness or agitation that arise during the use of medications may be due to dysregulation of several different neurotransmitters including serotonin, norepinephrine, GABA, dopamine, and others. Chronic alcohol abuse leads to a primary dysregulation in GABA-ergic neurons, resulting in a characteristic syndrome of restlessness and agitation during periods of reduced intake or sudden cessation in drinking. In a similar way, abuse of many illicit substances typically results in dysregulation of one or several neurotransmitters and a concomitant syndrome of restlessness or agitation during intoxication or withdrawal.

## WESTERN MEDICAL TREATMENT:

The most appropriate treatment of restlessness or agitation and associated strong emotions depends on the identified underlying cause(s). Correction of an underlying medical disorder usually leads to significant reduction in restlessness and agitation. For example, successful treatment of hyperthyroidism typically results in rapid return to the patient's pre-morbid non-agitated baseline. When subjective restlessness has been attributed to akathisia secondary to an antipsychotic medication, anticholinergic medications or beta-blockers (a class of antihypertensives) are the recommended treatments in contemporary Western psychiatry. Restlessness that accompanies anxiety usually responds to antianxiety medications, including benzodiazepines and certain antidepressants that affect neurotransmitters implicated in anxiety. Benzodiazepines are used on a routine basis for treatment of baseline anxiety and on an as-needed basis for management of transient episodes of intense restlessness. Antianxiety medications are often effective for somatic symptoms (*i.e.*, when the patient is not conscious of anxiety) in the absence of medical disease, including unusual sensations in the chest or limbs. Hypnosis and cognitive-behavioral therapy are sometimes effective treatments of long-standing symptoms of agitation or restlessness when medical causes have been ruled out. These approaches can significantly add to the effectiveness of pharmacotherapy by providing the patient with skills for improved anxiety management.

## SHORT & LONG-TERM ADVANTAGES & DISADVANTAGES OF WESTERN MEDICAL TREATMENT:

The advantages of effective treatment include improved social and occupational functioning with diminished symptoms of restlessness and agitation. The patient's capacity to tolerate side effects of benzodiazepines must be considered in any treatment plan addressing restlessness or agitation. These frequently include daytime sedation, slowing of reflexes, and cognitive impairment which is especially problematic among the elderly. Long-term use of benzodiazepines can result in physiological dependence with all of its associated medical and psychological complications, including the need for increasing doses to achieve a desired anxiolytic effect (*i.e.*, tolerance), and episodes of withdrawal during periods of interrupted use. Benzodiazepine withdrawal is an unpleasant syndrome of increased autonomic activity characterized by increased heart rate and blood pressure, perspiration, confusion, and frequent feelings of agitation or restlessness.

Side effects of non-benzodiazepine treatments of restlessness and agitation can be unpleasant, resulting in poor compliance or discontinuation. For example, SSRIs (serotonon-selective re-uptake inhibitors) including fluoxetine (Prozac), sertraline (Zoloft), and paroxetine (Paxil), which comprise a principle pharmacological approach for these symptoms in contemporary Western psychiatry, often cause sexual side effects, disturbed sleep, or other side effects that may interfere with social or occupational functioning as much as target symptoms of restlessness or anxiety for which they are intended.

Antipsychotic medications are also sometimes used to treat acute agitation or restlessness. Short-term use of older low-potency typical antipsychotics, including perphenazine (Trilafon), trifluperazine (Mellaril), and others, can result in worsening in subjective feelings of restlessness and abnormal movements that resolve with medication discontinuation. In contrast, chronic use of antipsychotic medications can result in a permanent disorder of abnormal involuntary movement called tardive dyskinesia. Recently introduced atypical antipsychotic agents, including risperidone (Risperdal), olanzapine (Zyprexa), and quetiapine (Seroquel), are associated with a significantly lower incidence of short-term side-effects, including akathisia or abnormal movements. Long-term complications of atypical antipsychotic medication use have not been clearly established. However, several cases of tardive dyskinesia have been reported.

## INDICATIONS FOR REFERRAL TO WESTERN MEDICAL SERVICES:

When severe agitation or restlessness is associated with serious psychiatric symptoms or there is evidence of sudden onset or an underlying acute medical condition, the patient should be referred to the nearest emergency room to rule out delirium, acute psychosis, cardiac arrhythmias, substance intoxication or withdrawal, medication side effects, and other treatable medical etiologies. An agitated patient who voices suicidal or homicidal thoughts should also be emergently evaluated following secure escort to the nearest acute care facility by paramedics or local law enforcement to ensure his or her safety. In cases where agitation or feelings of restlessness are chronic and unchanging, there are no apparent underlying or acute medical issues, and the patient has not responded to an appropriate course of Chinese medical treatment, non-urgent medical or psychiatric referral is indicated to evaluate the patient for possible unidentified medical conditions.

## CHINESE DISEASE CAUSES & MECHANISMS:

There are a number of disease causes and mechanisms described in Chinese medicine that can result in vexation and agitation. However, all these causes and mechanisms involve some kind of evil heat, whether that be true or false heat. For instance, external invasion by wind cold may depress yang within the exterior. When yang is depressed, it transforms into internal heat. Vexation and agitation may then occur if this heat harasses the heart spirit. The Qing dynasty *Lei Zheng Zhi Jian* (*The Treatment of Categorized Conditions*) says:

> Internal heat makes vexation, while external heat makes agitation. Vexation exits from the lungs, and agitation exits from the kidneys. If heat is transmitted from the lungs to kidneys [or *vice versa*], there are both vexation and agitation.

In externally contracted warm diseases, if the evils are not eliminated and remain in the body, they may enter the yang ming channels and struggle there. "The yang ming channel has plenty of qi and plenty of blood." When this invading yang evil combines with the profuse yang qi already in the yang ming, it may make the evil heat even worse. In addition, heat evils can easily bind with the stool, causing blockage of the bowel qi and, therefore, also add another source of depressive heat. If this heat ascends to harass the heart spirit, vexation and agitation may occur.

If an evil qi has not been eliminated but the righteous qi has become vacuous, evils and the righteous qi will fight in between the exterior and interior and thus produce heat which will bind in the shao yang channel. If this heat harasses the heart spirit, it may cause vexation and agitation.

During a warm disease, if heat evils in the qi division remain unresolved, they may fall inward to the heart constructive division and harass the heart spirit. Therefore, there is vexation and agitation.

It is recorded in the *Shang Han Lun* (*Treatise on Damage [Due to] Cold*) that erroneous treatment of an exterior pattern may lead to diaphragm heat. Generally speaking, a tai yang exterior pattern should be cured by using the resolving method. When treated with precipitation, evils may take the chance to invade into the interior where they typically transform into heat. If these heat evils enter the chest above the diaphragm, this may harass the heart spirit. Therefore, vexation and agitation may occur.

If phlegm accumulation endures for a long time due to any of various causes, it will lead to the engenderment of transformative heat. It is also common that depressed qi due to emotional disturbance may transform into fire. If this fire burns the fluids into phlegm and then binds with this phlegm, it may disturb the mind, resulting in vexation and agitation.

If unfulfilled desires or any other reason leads to inhibition of the liver's coursing and discharge, the qi will become stagnant. If this endures or is exacerbated, it may transform into depressive heat. If this heat counterflows upward to accumulate in the chest and harass the heart spirit, it may result in agitation and vexation.

Heart fire effulgence is commonly due to a combination of liver depression transforming fire or excesses of the seven affects transforming fire which ascends to harass the heart spirit complicated and inflamed by faulty diet, *i.e.*, overeating greasy, oily, fatty foods, acrid, hot, peppery foods, and drinking too much alcohol. This fire stirs the spirit, thus causing vexation and agitation.

Yin vacuity may be the result of enduring disease that damages yin, emotional disturbance that transforms heat and consumes the yin, unrestrained sexual activity, or aging with exhaustion of yin. In that case, yin will typically fail to control yang which becomes hyperactive. If this vacuity fire flames upward and harasses the heart spirit, vexation and agitation may occur.

When heat evils cannot be cleared and enter the blood network vessels, they burn the blood and inhibit the movement of the blood. Such blood stasis may then obstruct the orifices of the heart, depriving the heart spirit of proper nourishment. The heart spirit thus becomes disquieted due to a combination of malnourishment and harassment by heat evils. Thus vexation and agitation may occur.

It is also possible that yin evils may be so exuberant and effulgent internally that yang qi is repelled to the exterior. In this case, there are symptoms of false heat but true cold. Because the body's yang qi is forced upward as well as outward, this yang qi disturbs the heart spirit. Thus vexation and agitation may occur.

## TREATMENT BASED ON PATTERN DISCRIMINATION:

### 1. EXTERIOR COLD-DEPRESSED HEAT PATTERN

**MAIN SYMPTOMS:** Vexation and agitation, generalized body pain, fever (literally, emission of heat in Chinese), aversion to cold, no sweating, headache, slight thirst, thin, yellowish white tongue fur, and a floating, tight, rapid pulse

TREATMENT PRINCIPLES: Resolve the exterior and scatter cold, clear heat and eliminate vexation

FORMULA & MEDICINALS: Da Qing Long Tang Jia Jian (Major Blue Dragon Decoction with Additions & Subtractions) Herba Ephedrae (Ma Huang), 10g, Ramulus Cinnamomi Cassiae (Gui Zhi), 6g, mix-fried Radix Glycyrrhizae (Gan Cao), 6g, Semen Pruni Armeniacae (Xing Ren), 10g, uncooked Gypsum Fibrosum (Shi Gao), 25g (decocted first), uncooked Rhizoma Zingiberis (Sheng Jiang), 3g (added later), Fructus Zizyphi Jujubae (Da Zao), 3 pieces, Semen Praeparatus Sojae (Dan Dou Chi), 10g

Decoct in water and administer orally in two divided doses, morning and evening, one ji per day.

ACUPUNCTURE: Shao Fu (Ht 8), Zhi Zheng (SI 7), Feng Men (Bl 12), He Gu (LI 4), Qu Chi (LI 11). Use draining technique.

## 2. YANG MING REPLETE HEAT PATTERN

MAIN SYMPTOMS: Vexation and agitation, high fever, sweating, coarse breathing, thirst, constipation with dry, bound stools, abdominal fullness, pain in the abdomen exacerbated by pressure, in severe cases, delirium, dry, yellow or dry, black tongue fur, and a surging, large, or deep, replete pulse

TREATMENT PRINCIPLES: Clear heat, engender fluids, and greatly precipitate heat binding

FORMULA & MEDICINALS: For heat in the yang ming channel, use Bai Hu Tang Jia Wei (White Tiger Decoction with Added Flavors)

Uncooked Gypsum Fibrosum (Shi Gao), 25g (decocted first), Rhizoma Anemarrhenae Aspheloidis (Zhi Mu), 10g, Radix Glycyrrhizae (Gan Cao), 6g, Semen Oryzae Sativae (Geng Mi), 10g, Semen Praeparatus Sojae (Dan Dou Chi), 10g, stir-fried Fructus Gardeniae Jasminoidis (Zhi Zi), 10g

For heat in the yang ming bowel, use: Da Cheng Qi Tang (Major Order the Qi Decoction)

Radix Et Rhizoma Rhei (Da Huang), 10g (added later), Mirabilitum (Mang Xiao), 6g (dissolved in the decocted liquid), Cortex Magnoliae Officinalis (Hou Po), 10g, Fructus Immaturus Citri Aurantii (Zhi Shi), 6g

Decoct in water and administer orally in two divided doses, morning and evening, one ji per day.

ACUPUNCTURE: He Gu (LI 4), Nei Ting (St 44), Zhi Gou (TB 6), Shang Ju Xu (St 37), Wei Shu (Bl 21), Ran Gu (Ki 2). Use draining technique.

## 3. SHAO YANG GALLBLADDER CHANNEL DEPRESSED FIRE PATTERN

MAIN SYMPTOMS: Vexation and agitation, alternating cold and heat (i.e., fever and chills), chest and rib-side fullness and oppression, a bitter taste in the mouth, inhibited urination, a normal colored or red tongue with half yellow and half white fur, and a bowstring, rapid pulse

TREATMENT PRINCIPLES: Harmonize the shao yang, clear heat, and eliminate vexation

FORMULA & MEDICINALS: Xiao Chai Hu Tang Jia Jian (Minor Bupleurum Decoction with Additions & Subtractions)

Radix Bupleuri (Chai Hu), 12g, Radix Scutellariae Baicalensis (Huang Qin), 10g, Radix Codonopsitis Pilosulae (Dang Shen), 10g, ginger-processed Rhizoma Pinelliae Ternatae (Ban Xia), 10g, mix-fried Radix Glycyrrhizae (Zhi Gan Cao), 6g, Herba Artemisiae Apiaceae (Qing Hao), 10g, stir-fried Fructus Gardeniae Jasminoidis (Zhi Zi), 10g, Os Draconis (Long Gu), 12g (decocted first), Concha Ostreae (Mu Li), 12g (decocted first), uncooked Rhizoma Zingiberis (Sheng Jiang), 5g (added later)

Decoct in water and administer orally in two divided doses, morning and evening, one ji per day.

ACUPUNCTURE: Qi Men (Liv 14), Da Zhui (GV 14), Jian Shi (Per 5), Zu Lin Qi (GB 41). Use draining technique.

## 4. HEAT ENTERING THE CONSTRUCTIVE & BLOOD PATTERN

MAIN SYMPTOMS: Vexation and agitation, insomnia, fever which is worse at night, in severe cases, mania, macules or eruptions on the skin, blood ejection (i.e., hematemesis, epistaxis, hematuria, hemafecia, etc.), a crimson tongue, and a fine, rapid pulse

TREATMENT PRINCIPLES: Clear heat, cool the blood, and eliminate vexation

FORMULA & MEDICINALS: Qing Ying Tang Jia Jian (Clear

the Constructive Decoction with Additions & Subtractions)

Cornu Bubali (*Shui Niu Jiao*), 25g (powdered and swallowed with the decocted liquid), uncooked Radix Rehmanniae (*Sheng Di*), 12g, Radix Scrophulariae Ningpoensis (*Xuan Shen*), 10-15g, Folium Bambusae (*Zhu Ye*), 10g, Tuber Ophiopogonis Japonicae (*Mai Dong*), 12g, Cortex Radicis Moutan (*Dan Pi*), 10g, Radix Salviae Miltiorrhizae (*Dan Shen*), 10g, Rhizoma Coptidis Chinensis (*Huang Lian*), 6g (added later), Flos Lonicerae Japonicae (*Jin Yin Hua*), 10-12g, Fructus Forsythiae Suspensae (*Lian Qiao*), 10-12g

Decoct in water and administer orally in two divided doses, morning and evening, one *ji* per day.

ADDITIONS & SUBTRACTIONS: If there are severe skin eruptions or blood ejection, subtract the Lonicera and Forsythia and add blackened Fructus Gardeniae Jasminoidis (*Zhi Zi*) and Radix Rubrus Paeoniae Lactiflorae (*Chi Shao*) and increase the dosage of uncooked Rehmannia up to 20g.

ACUPUNCTURE: *Shao Fu* (Ht 8), *Lao Gong* (Per 8), *Wei Zhong* (Bl 40), *Qu Chi* (LI 11), *Yong Quan* (Ki 1). Use draining technique on all points except *Wei Zhong* which should be bled with a three-edged needle.

ADDITIONS & SUBTRACTIONS: If there is no bleeding already, prick *Qu Chi* (LI 11), *Shang Yang* (LI 1), *Zhong Chong* (Per 9), *Guan Chong* (TB 1), *Shao Chong* (Ht 9), and *Shao Ze* (SI 1) to bleed.

## 5. DIAPHRAGM HEAT PATTERN

MAIN SYMPTOMS: Vacuity vexation, insomnia, a burning sensation in the region of the heart, chest and diaphragm glomus and oppression with a desire to vomit, thin, yellow tongue fur, and a rapid pulse

TREATMENT PRINCIPLES: Clear the diaphragm and eliminate vexation

FORMULA & MEDICINALS: *Zhi Zi Dou Chi Tang Jia Wei* (Gardenia & Prepared Soybean Decoction with Added Flavors)

Stir-fried Fructus Gardeniae Jasminoidis (*Zhi Zi*), 10g, Semen Praeparatus Sojae (*Dan Dou Chi*), 10g, Herba Menthae Haplocalycis (*Bo He*), 6g, Radix Glycyrrhizae (*Gan Cao*), 3g

Decoct in water and administer orally in two divided doses, morning and evening, one *ji* per day.

ADDITIONS & SUBTRACTIONS: If there is severe internal heat, add uncooked Gypsum Fibrosum (*Shi Gao*).

ACUPUNCTURE: *Yang Xi* (LI 5), *Nei Ting* (St 44), *Ge Shu* (Bl 17), *Shao Fu* (Ht 8), *Qu Ze* (Per 3). Use draining technique.

## 6. PHLEGM FIRE HARASSING ABOVE PATTERN

MAIN SYMPTOMS: Vexatious heat in the heart and agitation, the sound of phlegm in the throat, spitting sticky, thick phlegm, dyspnea, heavy-headedness, vertigo, chest oppression, abdominal distention, nausea, vomiting, slimy, yellow tongue fur, and a slippery, rapid pulse

TREATMENT PRINCIPLES: Clear heat, transform phlegm, and eliminate vexation

FORMULA & MEDICINALS: *Huang Lian Wen Dan Tang Jia Jian* (Coptis Warm the Gallbladder Decoction with Additions & Subtractions)

Lime-processed Rhizoma Pinelliae Ternatae (*Ban Xia*), 10g, Caulis Bambusae In Taeniis (*Zhu Ru*), 10g, Fructus Immaturus Citri Aurantii (*Zhi Shi*), 6g, Pericarpium Citri Reticulatae (*Chen Pi*), 10g, Radix Glycyrrhizae (*Gan Cao*), 3g, Sclerotium Poriae Cocos (*Fu Ling*), 10g, uncooked Rhizoma Zingiberis (*Sheng Jiang*), 3g (added later), Fructus Zizyphi Jujubae (*Da Zao*), 3 pieces, Rhizoma Coptidis Chinensis (*Huang Lian*), 6g (added later), Radix Scutellariae Baicalensis (*Huang Qin*), 10g

Decoct in water and administer orally in two divided doses, morning and evening, one *ji* per day.

ACUPUNCTURE: *Lao Gong* (Per 8), *Nei Ting* (St 44), *Qu Chi* (LI 11), *Da Zhui* (GV 14), *Feng Long* (St 40). Use draining technique.

## 7. LIVER DEPRESSION TRANSFORMING HEAT PATTERN

MAIN SYMPTOMS: Irritability, a bitter taste in the mouth, rib-side distention and pain, breast distention and pain, menstrual irregularity in females, a red tongue with yellow fur, and a bowstring, rapid pulse

TREATMENT PRINCIPLES: Course the liver and rectify the qi, clear heat and resolve depression

FORMULA & MEDICINALS: *Dan Zhi Xiao Yao San* (Moutan & Gardenia Rambling Powder)

Radix Bupleuri (*Chai Hu*), 10g, Radix Albus Paeoniae Lactiflorae (*Bai Shao*), 10g, Radix Angelicae Sinensis (*Dang Gui*), 10g, Rhizoma Atractylodis Macrocephalae (*Bai Zhu*), 10g, Sclerotium Poriae Cocos (*Fu Ling*), 10g, Cortex Radicis Moutan (*Dan Pi*), 10g, Fructus Gardeniae Jasminoidis (*Zhi Zi*), 10g, mix-fried Radix Glycyrrhizae (*Gan Cao*), 6g

Decoct in water and administer orally in two divided doses, morning and evening, one *ji* per day.

ACUPUNCTURE: *Xing Jian* (Liv 2), *Tai Chong* (Liv 3), *Qu Chi* (LI 4), *He Gu* (LI 4), *Zu San Li* (St 36). Use draining technique.

## 8. HEART FIRE EFFULGENCE PATTERN

MAIN SYMPTOMS: Vexation and agitation, heart palpitations, insomnia, urgent, choppy, painful, red urination, sores in the mouth and on the tip of the tongue, a red or red-tipped tongue, and a bowstring, rapid pulse

TREATMENT PRINCIPLES: Clear the heart and downbear fire, disinhibit urination and quiet the spirit

FORMULA & MEDICINALS: *Dao Chi San Jia Wei* (Abduct the Red Powder with Added Flavors)

Uncooked Radix Rehmanniae (*Sheng Di*), 12g, Caulis Akebiae (*Mu Tong*), 10g, Medulla Junci Effusi (*Deng Xin Cao*), 10g, Rhizoma Coptidis Chinensis (*Huang Lian*), 6g (added later), Folium Bambusae (*Zhu Ye*), 6g, Radix Glycyrrhizae (*Gan Cao*), 6g, Succinum (*Hu Po*), 1g (powdered and swallowed with the decocted liquid)

Decoct in water and administer orally in two divided doses, morning and evening, one *ji* per day.

ADDITIONS & SUBTRACTIONS: If there is hematuria, add Herba Ecliptae Prostratae (*Han Lian Cao*) and Herba Cephalanoploris Segeti (*Xiao Ji*). If there is simultaneous yin vacuity, add Herba Dendrobii (*Shi Hu*) and Rhizoma Anemarrhenae Aspheloidis (*Zhi Mu*).

ACUPUNCTURE: *Lao Gong* (Per 8), *Shao Fu* (Ht 8), *Guan Yuan* (CV 4), *Xia Ju Xu* (St 39), *Qian Gu* (SI 2). Use draining technique.

## 9. YIN VACUITY-FIRE EFFULGENCE PATTERN

MAIN SYMPTOMS: Vacuity vexation and agitation, insomnia, heart palpitations, profuse dreams, low back and knee soreness and limpness, heat in the palms of the hands and soles of the feet, afternoon tidal heat, malar flushing, dry throat and mouth, a red tongue with scanty fur, and a fine, rapid, floating, rapid, or surging, rapid pulse

TREATMENT PRINCIPLES: Nourish yin, downbear fire, and eliminate vexation

FORMULA & MEDICINALS: For predominant effulgent fire, use *Huang Lian E Jiao Tang* (Coptis & Donkey Skin Glue Decoction)

Rhizoma Coptidis Chinensis (*Huang Lian*), 6g (added later), Radix Scutellariae Baicalensis (*Huang Qin*), 10g, Radix Albus Paeoniae Lactiflorae (*Bai Shao*), 10g, Gelatinum Corii Asini (*E Jiao*), 10g (dissolved at the end in the decocted liquid), egg yolk (*Ji Zi Huang*), 1 piece (added to the decocted liquid and stirred while the decoction is hot) For predominant kidney yin vacuity, use *Zhi Bai Di Huang Wan* (Anemarrhena & Phellodendron Rehmannia Pills)

Rhizoma Anemarrhenae Aspheloidis (*Zhi Mu*), 10g, Cortex Phellodendri (*Huang Bai*), 10g, cooked Radix Rehmanniae (*Shu Di*), 12g, Fructus Corni Officinalis (*Shan Zhu Yu*), 10g, Rhizoma Alismatis (*Ze Xie*), 6g, Sclerotium Poriae Cocos (*Fu Ling*), 12g, Cortex Radicis Moutan (*Dan Pi*), 10g, Radix Dioscoreae Oppositae (*Shan Yao*), 12g

ACUPUNCTURE: *Yin Xi* (Ht 6), *Fu Liu* (Ki 7), *Ran Gu* (Ki 2), *Tai Xi* (Ki 3), *Jie Xi* (St 41). Use even supplementing-even draining method.

## 10. HEAT & STASIS MUTUALLY BINDING PATTERN

MAIN SYMPTOMS: Vexation and agitation, reddish purple lips and facial complexion, chest, breast, or abdominal pain which is severe, fixed in location, worse at night, and associated with feelings of burning heat, spider nevi, hemagiomas, and varicosities, abnormal vaginal bleeding in females with clots mixed in with bright red blood, a reddish purple tongue with static spots or macules, possible yellow tongue fur, and a bowstring, rapid, possibly choppy pulse[1]

TREATMENT PRINCIPLES: Quicken the blood and transform stasis, clear heat and eliminate vexation

FORMULA & MEDICINALS: *Qin Lian Si Wu Tang Jia Wei* (Scutellaria & Coptis Decoction with Added Flavors)

Radix Scutellariae Baicalensis (*Huang Qin*), 10g, Rhizoma Coptidis Chinensis (*Huang Lian*), 3-4.5g (added later), Semen Pruni Persicae (*Tao Ren*), 10g, Flos Carthami Tinctorii (*Hong Hua*), 10g (steeped afterward), Radix Angelicae Sinensis (*Dang Gui*), 10g, uncooked Radix Rehmanniae (*Sheng Di*), 12g, Radix Ligustici Wallichii (*Chuan Xiong*), 6-10g (added later), Radix Rubrus Paeoniae Lactiflorae (*Chi Shao*), 10g, Radix Cyathulae (*Chuan Niu Xi*), 10g, Radix Salviae Miltiorrhizae (*Dan Shen*), 10g, Radix Bupleuri (*Chai Hu*), 6-10g, Fructus Citri Aurantii (*Zhi Ke*), 6g, Radix Glycyrrhizae (*Gan Cao*), 3g

Decoct in water and administer orally in two divided doses, morning and evening, one *ji* per day.

ACUPUNCTURE: *Xue Hai* (Sp 10), *San Yin Jiao* (Sp 6), *Ge Shu* (Bl 17), *Shen Men* (Ht 7), *Nei Guan* (Per 6). Use draining technique.

## 11. YIN EXUBERANCE-REPELLED YANG PATTERN

MAIN SYMPTOMS: A red facial complexion as if rouged, no aversion to cold, chilly breath, faint respiration, symptoms similar to mania, vexation and agitation, restlessness, a desire to sit in water or in a yin, cool place, reversal chilling of the four limbs, long, clear urination, loose stools with undigested food, oral thirst but no desire to drink or a possible liking for hot drinks, a dark, pale tongue with moist, glossy fur, and a deep, fine pulse

TREATMENT PRINCIPLES: Break yin and rescue yang, stem counterflow and scatter cold

FORMULA & MEDICINALS: *Tong Mai Si Ni Tang* (Free the Flow of the Vessels Four Counterflows Decoction)

Radix Lateralis Praeparatus Aconiti Carmichaeli (*Fu Zi*), 10g, dry Rhizoma Zingiberis (*Gan Jiang*), 4.5g, mix-fried Radix Glycyrrhizae (*Gan Cao*), 6g

Decoct in water and administer orally in two divided doses, morning and evening, one *ji* per day.

ACUPUNCTURE: *Zu San Li* (St 36), *Shen Que* (CV 8), *Guan Yuan* (CV 4). Moxa.

CLINICAL TIPS: Western patients typically need to be explained that vexation refers not just to irritability but to an irritating sensation of heat in their chest before they volunteer this symptom as a complaint.

## REPRESENTATIVE CASE HISTORIES:

### ❖ CASE 1[2] ❖

The patient was a 46 year old, married female who first entered the hospital on Aug. 11, 1987. Two months before, the patient had gotten very worried and angry. Afterwards, she became vexed and agitated and had difficulty sleeping. Other complaints included dizziness and vertigo and a clouded spirit which was sometimes clear and sometimes not. After a period of spirit clouding, the woman's spirit was torpid. The patient had been hospitalized with a diagnosis of functional neurosis and been given Valium and Chinese medicinals to nourish her blood and quiet her spirit. However, none of these had gotten any effect. Therefore, she was referred to the authors of this case who found that, in addition, the patient had generalized heat, a red facial complexion, irritability, poor appetite, normal defecation, yellow-colored urine, slimy, yellow tongue fur, and a soggy, slippery, rapid pulse.

Based on the above signs and symptoms, the patient's pattern was categorized as phlegm fire internally harassing. Therefore, the treatment principles were to clear heat and sweep away phlegm, open the orifices and calm the spirit and the woman was prescribed *Chang Pu Yu Jin Tang Jia Jian* (Acorus & Curcuma Decoction with Additions & Subtractions): Rhizoma Acori Graminei (*Shi Chang Pu*), 9g, Tuber Curcumae (*Yu Jin*), 5g, stir-fried Fructus Gardeniae Jasminoidis (*Zhi Zi*), 9g, Fructus Forsythiae Suspensae (*Lian Qiao*), 9g, Flos Chrysanthemi Morifolii (*Ju Hua*), 9g, Talcum (*Hua Shi*), 9g, Folium Bambusae (*Zhu Ye*), 15g, Cortex Radicis Moutan (*Dan Pi*), 6g, Fructus Arctii Lappae (*Niu Bang Zi*), 3g, Succus Bambusae (*Zhu Li*), a small amount, *Yu Shu Dan* (Jade Pivot Elixir, a Chinese ready-made medicine), 1.5g, and Fructus Tribuli Terrestris (*Bai Ji Li*), 9g.

After taking seven *ji* of the above formula, the patient's spirit mind became clear and awake and her vexation, agitation, and easy anger were all eliminated. However, she still had dizziness and insomnia from time to time. Her tongue fur was slimy and white and her pulse was soggy and slippery. This suggested that the fire had been dispelled but dampness and turbidity were not yet transformed. Therefore, she was given: Rhizoma Acori Graminei (*Shi Chang Pu*), 10g, Fructus Tribuli Terrestris (*Bai Ji Li*), 12g, Flos Chrysanthemi Morifolii (*Ju Hua*), 6g, Talcum (*Hua Shi*), 12g, Caulis Bambusae In Taeniis (*Zhu Ru*), 10g, Rhizoma Pinelliae Ternatae (*Ban Xia*), 10g, Sclerotium Poriae Cocos (*Fu Ling*), 10g, Radix Bupleuri (*Chai Hu*), 6g, Cortex Albizziae Julibrissinis (*He Huan Pi*), 10g, and stir-fried Semen Zizyphi Spinosae (*Suan Zao*

*Ren*), 10g. After taking 20 *ji* of these medicinals, all her symptoms were eliminated. On follow-up after two years, there had been no recurrence.

### ❖ CASE 2³ ❖

The patient was an 18 year old female student who first entered the hospital on Jun. 24, 1979. Normally, this young woman's menses were regular. However, three months before, due to contracting warm heat evils, she had become vexed, agitated, and restless. The patient's spirit mind was abstracted and her sleep was restless. In addition, her menses had not come for three months. Her body was emaciated and her lower abdomen was slightly distended. Therefore, her condition was initially diagnosed as "dry blood taxation," and the patient had been given *Da Huang Zhe Chong Wan* (Rhubarb & Eupolyphaga Pills) without effect. Therefore, she was referred to the authors of this case who found that her facial complexion was sallow yellow, her bones stuck out like firewood, and her lower abdomen was distended, hard, and extremely painful to palpation. The tongue was withered and the pulse was deep, fine, and choppy.

Based on the above signs and symptoms, the patient's pattern was categorized as amassed blood vexation and agitation. Therefore, the treatment principles were to cool the blood and quicken it, settle, still, and quiet the spirit and the patient was prescribed *Tao Ren Cheng Qi Tang Jia Jian* (Persica Order the Qi Decoction with Additions & Subtractions): Radix Et Rhizoma Rhei (*Da Huang*), 15g, Semen Pruni Persicae (*Tao Ren*), 10g, uncooked Radix Rehmanniae (*Sheng Di*), 10g, Cortex Radicis Moutan (*Dan Pi*), 10g, Herba Lycopi Lucidi (*Ze Lan*), 10g, Sedimentum Urinae Hominis (*Ren Zhong Bai*), 4g, and Hirudo (*Shui Zhi*), 3g.

After taking two *ji* of the above formula, the patient passed a lot of black, static blood, her abdominal distention decreased, and the pain stopped. Therefore, at this juncture, it was appropriate to quicken the blood, boost the qi, and abduct stasis and accumulation. This was accomplished by administering four *ji* of the following medicinals: uncooked Radix Rehmanniae (*Sheng Di*), 12g, Radix Astragali Membranacei (*Huang Qi*), 10g, Radix Angelicae Sinensis (*Dang Gui*), 5g, Radix Codonopsitis Pilosulae (*Dang Shen*), 10g, Radix Ligustici Wallichii (*Chuan Xiong*), 10g, Radix Albus Paeoniae Lactiflorae (*Bai Shao*), 10g, Pericarpium Citri Reticulatae (*Chen Pi*), 3g, and Semen Leonuri Heterophylli (*Chong Wei Zi*), 10g. After four *ji* of this prescription, all the patient's symptoms were eliminated and the patient was discharged from the hospital. At that time, she was instructed to take one pill each evening of *Huo Xue An Shen Wan* (Quicken the Blood & Quiet the Spirit Pills, created by the authors) for 60 evenings in order to secure the treatment effect. On follow-up after her next menstruation, it had been regular and normal and there had been no recurrence of her vexation and agitation.

### ❖ CASE 3⁴ ❖

The patient was a 36 year old, married male cadre who entered the hospital on May 6, 1985. The patient was engaged in very taxing mental work. He was so busy at work that he was not able to catch a breath. Gradually, this resulted in his becoming vexed, agitated, and restless. He also developed heart palpitations and insomnia, dizziness, tinnitus, tidal heat, and night sweats. At his local hospital, he had been diagnosed with functional neurosis and was given Western tranquilizers. These medications had not been able to control the patient's pain and suffering and so he came to the authors for examination. At that point, the man had spirit mind abstractions, chaotic thoughts, heart vexation, inability to control himself, a flushed red facial complexion, scanty sleep, profuse dreams, tidal heat, night sweats, dizziness, tinnitus, a dry tongue with scanty fluids, and a fine, rapid pulse.

Based on the above signs and symptoms, the authors of this case categorized this patient's pattern as yin vacuity with fire effulgence. The treatment principles were to enrich the kidneys and nourish the liver, clear heat and calm the spirit. Therefore, they prescribed the man *Liu Wei Di Huang Tang He Suan Zao Ren Tang Jia Jian* (Six Flavors Rehmannia Decoction plus Zizyphus Spinosa Decoction with Additions & Subtractions): cooked Radix Rehmanniae (*Shu Di*), 30g, Fructus Corni Officinalis (*Shan Zhu Yu*), 20g, Sclerotium Pararadicis Poriae Cocos (*Fu Shen*), 20g, Radix Dioscoreae Oppositae (*Shan Yao*), 20g, Radix Polygoni Multiflori (*He Shou Wu*), 20g, Plastrum Testudinis (*Gui Ban*), 20g, Caulis Polygoni Multiflori (*Ye Jiao Teng*), 20g, Semen Zizyphi Spinosae (*Suan Zao Ren*), 20g, mix-fried Radix Glycyrrhizae (*Gan Cao*), 20g, Radix Scrophulariae Ningpoensis (*Xuan Shen*), 20g, Cortex Radicis Moutan (*Dan Pi*), 10g, Radix Ligustici Wallichii (*Chuan Xiong*), 10g, Rhizoma Anemarrhenae Aspheloidis (*Zhi Mu*), 10g, and Fructus Schisandrae Chinensis (*Wu Wei Zi*), 10g.

After taking 30 *ji* of the above formula, the patient's vexation and agitation were eliminated and his sleep was calm. He was given 60 pills of *Suan Zao Ren Wan* (Zizyphus Spinosa Pills) and told to take one every morning and night. The patient was then discharged from the hospital, and, on follow-up, he was fine.

❖ CASE 4[5] ❖

The patient was a 42 year old female who had suffered from heart palpitations for a number of years. After having gotten angry, these had gotten worse in recent days. In addition, the woman complained of chest oppression, worry, restlessness sitting and lying down, vexation and agitation, easy fright, and inability to sleep at night. Her tongue fur was thin and white, while her pulse was fine, rapid, and forceless. Electrocardiogram was normal and her heart rate was 92 beats per minute. Her Western medical diagnosis was vegetative neurological disorder. Her Chinese pattern was categorized as heart yin suffering detriment with blockage of heart yang and consequent floating and jumping of her heart spirit.

Therefore, the woman was prescribed a modification of *Gui Zhi Gan Cao Long Gu Mu Li Tang He Suan Zao Ren Tang* (Cinnamon Twig, Licorice, Dragon Bone & Oyster Shell Decoction plus Zizyphus Spinosa Decoction): Ramulus Cinnamomi Cassiae (*Gui Zhi*), 9g, Radix Glycyrrhizae (*Gan Cao*), 15g, uncooked Os Draconis (*Long Gu*), 30g, uncooked Concha Ostreae (*Mu Li*), 30g, stir-fried Semen Zizyphi Spinosae (*Suan Zao Ren*), 15g,

Radix Ligustici Wallichii (*Chuan Xiong*), 6g, Rhizoma Anemarrhenae Aspheloidis (*Zhi Mu*), 10g, Sclerotium Poriae Cocos (*Fu Ling*), 15g, Cortex Albizziae Julibrissinis (*He Huan Pi*), 15g, Caulis Polygoni Multiflori (*Ye Jiao Teng*), 15g, Radix Pseudostellariae (*Tai Zi Shen*), 15g, and Semen Biotae Orientalis (*Bai Zi Ren*), 9g. After taking three *ji* of these medicinals, the woman's heart palpitations had improved and she was able to sleep approximately five hours per night. Therefore, Fructus Levis Tritici Aestivi (*Fu Xiao Mai*) and Fructus Zizyphi Jujubae (*Da Zao*) were added to the previous formula, thus also incorporating *Gan Mai Da Zao Tang* (Licorice, Wheat & Red Dates Decoction), and the patient was cured.

ENDNOTES

[1] To some extent, the signs and symptoms of this pattern depend on whether blood stasis is mixed with depressive, damp, or phlegm heat.

[2] Li & Liu, *op. cit.*, p. 559-560

[3] *Ibid.*, p. 564-565

[4] *Ibid.*, p. 565-566

[5] Chen & Zhao, *op. cit.*, p. 32

# DERANGED SPEECH

In Chinese medicine, deranged speech refers to incoherent, illogical, nonsensical speech. In Chinese, this term may appear as *yan yu cuo luan, yu yan cuo luan,* or *cu yan wang yu.* The Chinese medicine category of deranged speech does not clearly correspond to any specific Western psychiatric neurologic or medical disorder. Incoherent, illogical, or nonsensical speech is viewed as abnormal or pathological when the severity of this symptom impairs social or occupational functioning. Not all instances of illogical speech reflect underlying medical or psychiatric pathology. Furthermore, there is great disparity in what is considered appropriate or acceptable speech behavior in diverse cultural contexts.

## NOSOLOGY:

Derangement of speech or expressive language that is long-standing implies a pervasive developmental disorder (PDD), such as autism or mental retardation. When onset of incoherent speech coincides with onset or progression of a psychiatric disorder, such as a manic or psychotic episode, this symptom reflects associated cognitive impairment. Cerebrovascular accident affecting the anterior temporal lobe of the dominant (usually left) hemisphere often manifests as loss of expressive language (aphasia) or illogical speech. Deranged speech is commonly observed in delirium and dementia, as well as in patients who are intoxicated with alcohol or are under the influence of illicit substances.

## DIFFERENTIAL DIAGNOSIS:

### 1. MEDICAL DISORDERS

The medical and neurologic differential diagnosis of incoherent, illogical, or nonsensical speech rests on accurate history taking followed by indicated laboratory evaluation to rule out possible underlying organic etiologies. When an acutely ill patient experiences sudden onset disturbance in level of consciousness, delirium is the probable diagnosis. It is important to note that, in delirium, a specific underlying medical disorder or physiologic dysregulation is not always identified. Nonsensical or illogical speech in the context of insidious global cognitive decline in the absence of acute medical illness points to dementia. In contrast, sudden onset of illogical speech or loss of capacity for expressive speech in the absence of other cognitive symptoms suggests cerebrovascular accident (CVA) as the most probable underlying cause. In this case, a complete history frequently points to risk factors for stroke, including hypertension, diabetes, or other medical disorders that increase the risk for cerebrovascular accident. Deranged or illogical speech is sometimes seen in the context of tic disorders which are characterized by sudden, erratic, purposeless movements and associated repetitive, often nonsensical verbalizations (see Chapter 16, this Book, Convulsions). Incoherent speech sometimes manifests as a result of traumatic brain injury (TBI), certain seizure disorders, and CNS tumors. Toxic CNS effects of

| DIFFERENTIAL DIAGNOSIS | | |
|---|---|---|
| 1. MEDICAL DISORDERS | 2. EFFECTS OF SUBSTANCES | 3. PSYCHIATRIC DISORDERS |
| A. DELIRIUM<br>B. DEMENTIA<br>C. CEREBROVASCULAR ACCIDENT (CVA)<br>D. TIC DISORDERS<br>E. TRAUMATIC BRAIN INJURY<br>F. SEIZURE DISORDERS<br>G. CNS TUMORS | A. ALCOHOL OR ILLICIT SUBSTANCES INTOXICATION, CHRONIC ABUSE, OR WITHDRAWAL<br>B. SIDE EFFECTS OF MEDICATIONS | A. SCHIZOPHRENIA AND OTHER PSYCHOTIC DISORDERS<br>B. ACUTE MANIA IN BIPOLAR DISORDER OR SCHIZO-AFFECTIVE DISORDER<br>C. PERVASIVE DEVELOPMENTAL DISORDERS |

substances of abuse during acute intoxication or withdrawal frequently manifest as transiently illogical or incoherent speech. Speech gradually normalizes when the substance is removed or CNS effects of the substance wear off. Medication side effects, including, for instance, those from steroids, can sometimes result in transient confusional states including incoherent speech.

## 2. PSYCHIATRIC DISORDERS

The psychiatric differential diagnosis of deranged speech is also very broad. It includes schizophrenia and other psychotic disorders, acute manic episodes in bipolar or schizoaffective disorder, and pervasive developmental disorders, including autism, Asperger's syndrome, and mental retardation. Disorganized speech in a patient with schizophrenia or other psychotic disorder typically normalizes with response to pharmacologic treatment. Failure to normalize suggests another psychiatric or primary medical cause of incoherent speech. As in psychotic disorders, the illogical speech of the acutely manic patient usually normalizes when manic symptoms are brought under control with appropriate medications.

### ETIOLOGY & PATHOPHYSIOLOGY:

Brain dysfunction of several kinds and degrees of severity manifests as incoherent or illogical speech. A global insult to brain functioning, such as anoxic or traumatic brain injury, results in disorganized speech in the context of gross impairment in sensorium and cognitive functioning. Injury to the left frontal lobe often results in disturbance or loss of expressive language (Broca's aphasia). Other common organic causes of deranged speech include CNS infections such as Herpes encephalitis and HIV encephalopathy. In these cases, the infectious agent directly causes an insult to speech centers in the brain. When disorganized speech is associated with dementia, including Alzheimer's disease, the presumed cause is disruption of brain circuits during the progression of the disease process underlying the specific dementing disorder. In the case of Alzheimer's disease, this entails formation of amyloid plaques and neurofibrillary tangles disrupting circuits in the left fronto-temporal regions that permit normal expressive language. When deranged speech occurs in the context of substance intoxication or withdrawal, it is presumed to be related to global brain dysfunction caused by the direct effects of intoxication or withdrawal on the brain. The current Western psychiatric model of these processes entails generalized dysregulation in functioning of neurotransmitters required for normal functioning of language areas of the brain. In a similar manner, disorganized speech that is a symptom of a major psychiatric disorder reflects dysregulation in brain circuits or neurotransmitter systems that underlie and permit normal expressive language and presumably also normal cognitive and emotional functioning in general.

### WESTERN MEDICAL TREATMENT:

The identified cause(s) of deranged speech will determine the most appropriate or efficacious treatment. If an underlying medical disorder is identified as the cause, successful treatment usually results in normalization of speech. Examples include infectious brain diseases, seizure disorders, and reversible dementias (see Chapter 9, this Book, Feeblemindedness). Incoherent or deranged speech that is due to the intoxication or withdrawal effects of a substance returns to normal with detoxification or maintained sobriety. Deranged speech that is symptomatic of a psychiatric disorder is not different than pharmacologic treatment recommended for the associated disorder. For example, illogical or incoherent speech associated with an acute manic episode typically improves in response to lithium carbonate or other mood-stabilizing agents targeting the abnormal brain state underlying mania. Psychotherapy is not an appropriate or effective treatment of deranged speech.

## SHORT & LONG-TERM ADVANTAGES & DISADVANTAGES OF WESTERN MEDICAL TREATMENT:

Obvious advantages of Western psychiatric treatment of deranged speech include restoration of capacity for normal expressive language and attendant improvements in social and occupational functioning. Because deranged speech is usually regarded as a symptom in Western psychiatry and not an independent disorder, the single most significant advantage of treatment is improvement in an associated primary medical or psychiatric disorder or substance abuse. However, when deranged speech is treated pharmacologically as a symptom of schizophrenia or bipolar disorder, the same potential long-term risks must be considered, including lithium-induced hypothyroidism or renal disease, and permanent movement disorders associated with long-term use of antipsychotic medications.

## PROGNOSIS:

The prognosis of different causes of deranged speech is equivalent to the varying prognoses of associated primary medical or psychiatric disorders. When the cause is an easily treatable medical disorder (*e.g.*, delirium with deranged speech), the prognosis is quite favorable. Transiently deranged speech related to substance intoxication or withdrawal can be expected to resolve without future complications if sobriety is maintained following detoxification. In contrast, incoherent or deranged speech seen in dementia will not respond to known treatments and will continue to worsen. When deranged speech is associated with a major psychiatric disorder, the prognosis depends on the severity or chronicity of that disorder. At their chronic baseline, schizophrenic patients may experience only partial improvement in deranged speech with pharmacologic treatment. In bipolar disorder, on the other hand, incoherent speech is a significant clinical issue only during acute depressive or manic episodes.

## INDICATIONS FOR REFERRAL TO WESTERN MEDICAL SERVICES:

Urgent referral is indicated when there is evidence that deranged speech started abruptly, is associated with a major medical (including neurologic) disorder, substance intoxication or withdrawal, or acute or severe psychiatric symptoms. In these circumstances, Western medical evaluation is necessary to rule out or treat potentially life-threatening underlying causes of incoherent speech. When deranged speech is chronic and there are no known associated acute or severe medical, psychiatric, or substance abuse causes, non-urgent referral to a psychiatrist may help clarify the differential diagnosis and treatment plan if the patient has failed to respond to an appropriate course and duration of Chinese medical treatment.

## CHINESE DISEASE CAUSES & MECHANISMS:

In Chinese medicine, speech is a function of the heart. When heart qi and blood are replete and exuberant, and the heart spirit is quiet, the speech is orderly and coherent. However, when the heart qi and blood are insufficient to construct and nourish the spirit and its functions, then the spirit may become disquieted, the functions of the heart may lose their duty, and the speech may become deranged. Hence, deranged speech is primarily associated with either lack of construction and nourishment of the heart spirit or harassment and blockage of the heart spirit by the three evil qi of phlegm, heat, and static blood. Vacuity mechanisms associated with deranged speech include heart blood-spleen qi vacuity and blood and yin vacuities with vacuity heat. Repletion mechanisms associated with deranged speech include liver depression, blood stasis, phlegm dampness, and phlegm fire.

The Chinese medical explanation for liver depression causing deranged speech is that liver depression may cause disquietude of the ethereal soul. In that case, the ethereal soul cannot follow the orders of the spirit and thus the speech becomes incoherent. While this is not a wrong explanation, in real-life patients, most cases of liver depression deranged speech will be complicated by either blood vacuity, heart-spleen vacuity, kidney yin vacuity, phlegm, dampness, depressive heat, and/or blood stasis.

## TREATMENT BASED ON PATTERN DISCRIMINATION:

### 1. HEART-SPLEEN DUAL VACUITY PATTERN

**MAIN SYMPTOMS:** Deranged speech, disinclination to speak[1], insomnia, heart palpitations, fatigue, lassitude of the spirit, cold hands and feet, a tendency to loose stools, poor appetite, a sallow yellow or pale white facial complexion, pale lips and nails, lack of strength, a pale, fat tongue with teeth-marks on its edges, and a fine, weak, possibly relaxed (*i.e.*, slightly slow) pulse

**TREATMENT PRINCIPLES:** Supplement the heart and nourish the blood, fortify the spleen and boost the qi

**FORMULA & MEDICINALS:** *Gui Pi Tang Jia Wei* (Restore the Spleen Decoction with Added Flavors)

Radix Astragali Membranacei (*Huang Qi*), 10-15g, Radix Codonopsitis Pilosulae (*Dang Shen*), 10g, Rhizoma

Atractylodis Macrocephalae (*Bai Zhu*), 10g, Sclerotium Pararadicis Poriae Cocos (*Fu Shen*), 12g, mix-fried Radix Glycyrrhizae (*Gan Cao*), 6-12g, Radix Angelicae Sinensis (*Dang Gui*), 6-10g, Arillus Euphoriae Longanae (*Long Yan Rou*), 10g, Radix Polygalae Tenuifoliae (*Yuan Zhi*), 6-10g, Radix Auklandiae Lappae (*Mu Xiang*), 6g (added later), Rhizoma Acori Graminei (*Shi Chang Pu*), 6g, uncooked Rhizoma Zingiberis (*Sheng Jiang*), 3g (added later), Fructus Zizyphi Jujubae (*Da Zao*), 3-5 pieces

Decoct in water and administer orally in two divided doses, morning and evening, one *ji* per day.

**ACUPUNCTURE:** *Lian Quan* (CV 23), *Tong Li* (Ht 5), *San Yin Jiao* (Sp 6), *Zu San Li* (St 36), *Xin Shu* (Bl 15), *Pi Shu* (Bl 20). Use even supplementing-even draining technique.

## 2. YIN VACUITY-BLOOD DRYNESS PATTERN

**MAIN SYMPTOMS:** Deranged speech, emotional lability, alternating joy and crying without apparent reason, insomnia, heart palpitations, fatigue, a dry throat, possible night sweats, agitation, a red tongue with scanty, dryish fur, and a fine, possibly rapid, probably bowstring pulse

**TREATMENT PRINCIPLES:** Enrich yin and nourish the blood, clear heat and quiet the spirit

**FORMULA & MEDICINALS:** *Gan Mai Da Zao Tang Jia Jian* (Licorice, Wheat & Red Date Decoction with Additions & Subtractions)

Mix-fried Radix Glycyrrhizae (*Gan Cao*), 10-15g, Fructus Triciti Aestivi (*Huai Xiao Mai*), 15-30g, Bulbus Lilii (*Bai He*), 30g, Semen Zizyphi Spinosae (*Suan Zao Ren*), 12g, Rhizoma Anemarrhenae Aspheloidis (*Zhi Mu*), 10g, Radix Albus Paeoniae Lactiflorae (*Bai Shao*), 10g, Fructus Zizyphi Jujubae (*Da Zao*), 10 pieces

Decoct in water and administer orally in two divided doses, morning and evening, one *ji* per day.

**ACUPUNCTURE:** *San Yin Jiao* (Sp 6), *Tai Xi* (Ki 3), *Shen Men* (Ht 7), *Tong Li* (Ht 5), *Lian Quan* (CV 23), *Xin Shu* (Bl 15), *Ge Shu* (Bl 17). Use even supplementing-even draining technique.

## 3. LIVER DEPRESSION QI STAGNATION PATTERN

**MAIN SYMPTOMS:** Deranged speech, irritability, emotional depression, taciturnity, chest oppression, rib-side dis-

tention, a normal or slightly darkish tongue with thin, white fur, and a fine, bowstring pulse

**TREATMENT PRINCIPLES:** Course the liver and resolve depression

**FORMULA & MEDICINALS:** *Si Ni San Jia Wei* (Four Counterflows Powder with Added Flavors)

Radix Bupleuri (*Chai Hu*), 6g, Fructus Citri Aurantii (*Zhi Ke*), 10g, Radix Albus Paeoniae Lactiflorae (*Bai Shao*), 10g, mix-fried Radix Glycyrrhizae (*Gan Cao*), 6g, Fructus Citri Sacrodactylis (*Fo Shou*), 10g, Fructus Citri Medicae (*Xiang Yuan*), 10g, Flos Rosae Rugosae (*Mei Gui Hua*), 10g, Flos Albizziae Julibrissinis (*He Huan Hua*), 12g, Rhizoma Acori Graminei (*Shi Chang Pu*), 6-10g

Decoct in water and administer orally in two divided doses, morning and evening, one *ji* per day.

**ADDITIONS & SUBTRACTIONS:** If there is insomnia, add Radix Polygalae Tenuifoliae (*Yuan Zhi*) and Semen Zizyphi Spinosae (*Suan Zao Ren*).

**ACUPUNCTURE:** *Tai Chong* (Liv 3), *He Gu* (LI 4), *Qi Men* (Liv 14), *Lian Quan* (CV 23), *Tong Li* (Ht 5). Use draining technique.

## 4. PHLEGM DAMPNESS CONFOUNDING THE ORIFICES PATTERN

**MAIN SYMPTOMS:** Deranged speech, muttering to oneself, slow reactions, mental-emotional confusion or abstraction, dizziness and vertigo, nausea and vomiting, chest and abdominal oppression and fullness, profuse phlegm, a swollen, fat tongue with white, slimy fur, and a slippery, bowstring pulse

**TREATMENT PRINCIPLES:** Transform phlegm and dry dampness, open the orifices and quiet the spirit

**FORMULA & MEDICINALS:** *Dao Tan Tang* (Abduct Phlegm Decoction)

Rhizoma Pinelliae Ternatae (*Ban Xia*), 10g, Rhizoma Arisaematis (*Tian Nan Xing*), 10g, Fructus Immaturus Citri Aurantii (*Zhi Shi*), 6g, Rhizoma Atractylodis Macrocephalae (*Bai Zhu*), 10g, Sclerotium Poriae Cocos (*Fu Ling*), 10g, Pericarpium Citri Reticulatae (*Chen Pi*), 6g, Radix Polygalae Tenuifoliae (*Yuan Zhi*), 6-10g, Rhizoma Acori Graminei (*Shi Chang Pu*), 6g, mix-fried Radix Glycyrrhizae (*Gan Cao*), 3-6g, uncooked Rhizoma Zingiberis (*Sheng Jiang*), 3g (added later)

Decoct in water and administer orally in two divided doses, morning and evening, one *ji* per day.

**ADDITIONS & SUBTRACTIONS:** If there is accompanying spleen qi vacuity, add Radix Codonopsitis Pilosulae (*Dang Shen*) and Radix Astragali Membranacei (*Huang Qi*). If there is simultaneous heart vacuity with insomnia and heart palpitations, add Semen Zizyphi Spinosae (*Suan Zao Ren*), Fructus Schisandrae Chinensis (*Wu Wei Zi*), Semen Biotae Orientalis (*Bai Zi Ren*), and Radix Codonopsitis Pilosulae (*Dang Shen*).

**ACUPUNCTURE:** *Feng Long* (St 40), *Zhong Wan* (CV 12), *Zu San Li* (St 36), *Yin Ling Quan* (Sp 9), *Lian Quan* (CV 23), *Tong Li* (Ht 5). Use even supplementing-even draining technique.

## 5. PHLEGM FIRE HARASSING ABOVE PATTERN

**MAIN SYMPTOMS:** The above signs and symptoms plus profuse yellow phlegm, irritability or even irascibility, a red tongue with yellow, slimy fur, and a slippery, bowstring, rapid pulse

**TREATMENT PRINCIPLES:** Transform phlegm and clear heat, open the orifices and quiet the spirit

**FORMULA & MEDICINALS:** *Huang Lian Wen Dan Tang Jia Wei* (Coptis Warm the Gallbladder Decoction with Added Flavors)

Rhizoma Coptidis Chinensis (*Huang Lian*), 3-6g (added later), Radix Scutellariae Baicalensis (*Huang Qin*), 10g, Rhizoma Acori Graminei (*Shi Chang Pu*), 6g, bile-processed Rhizoma Arisaematis (*Dan Nan Xing*), 3-6g, Rhizoma Pinelliae Ternatae (*Ban Xia*), 10g, Pericarpium Citri Reticulatae (*Chen Pi*), 6-10g, Sclerotium Pararadicis Poriae Cocos (*Fu Shen*), 12g, Fructus Immaturus Citri Aurantii (*Zhi Shi*), 6g, Caulis Bambusae In Taeniis (*Zhu Ru*), 6-10g, Radix Glycyrrhizae (*Gan Cao*), 3-6g, Fructus Zizyphi Jujubae (*Da Zao*), 3-5 pieces

Decoct in water and administer orally in two divided doses, morning and evening, one *ji* per day.

**ACUPUNCTURE:** *Feng Long* (St 40), *Jie Xi* (St 41), *Xing Jian* (Liv 2), *Dan Zhong* (CV 17), *Zhong Wan* (CV 12), *Lian Quan* (CV 23), *Tong Li* (Ht 5). Use draining technique.

## 6. BLOOD STASIS OBSTRUCTING INTERNALLY PATTERN

**MAIN SYMPTOMS:** Deranged speech, especially premenstrually or postpartum in females with either dysmenorrhea or abdominal pain and scanty lochia, possible menstrual irregularity, a dark, dusky facial complexion, spider nevi, hemangiomas, or varicosities, a purplish tongue or possible static spots or macules, engorged, tortuous sublingual veins, and a bowstring, choppy, or bound pulse

**TREATMENT PRINCIPLES:** Quicken the blood and transform stasis, open the orifices and quiet the spirit

**FORMULA & MEDICINALS:** *Tao Hong Si Wu Tang Jia Wei* (Perica & Carthamus Four Materials Decoction with Added Flavors)

Semen Pruni Persicae (*Tao Ren*), 10g, Flos Carthami Tinctorii (*Hong Hua*), 10g (steeped), cooked Radix Rehmanniae (*Shu Di*), 12g, Radix Angelicae Sinensis (*Dang Gui*), 10g, Radix Rubrus Paeoniae Lactiflorae (*Chi Shao*), 10g, Radix Ligustici Wallichii (*Chuan Xiong*), 10-15g (added later), Radix Polygalae Tenuifoliae (*Yuan Zhi*), 6-10g, Rhizoma Acori Graminei (*Shi Chang Pu*), 6g

Decoct in water and administer orally in two divided doses, morning and evening, one *ji* per day.

**ADDITIONS & SUBTRACTIONS:** For simultaneous qi vacuity, add Radix Astragali Membranacei (*Huang Qi*) and Radix Codonopsitis Pilosulae (*Dang Shen*).

**ACUPUNCTURE:** *Xue Hai* (Sp 10), *San Yin Jiao* (Sp 6), *He Gu* (LI 4), *Lian Quan* (CV 23), *Tong Li* (Ht 5). Use draining technique.

**ENDNOTES:**

[1]In Chinese medicine, disinclination to speak refers to a faint voice and reluctance to speak because the patient does not have the energy to speak and speaking is additionally fatiguing.

# ❖ 9 ❖

# FEEBLEMINDEDNESS

Feeblemindedness refers to a chronic or persistent disturbance of the intelligence which is characterized by mental sluggishness, lack of intelligence, foolishness, and/or
clumsiness. In Chinese, this disease is referred to as *chi dai*,
*dai bing*, feeble-minded disease, and *bai chi*, white idiocy.
In minor cases, it manifests as spirit mind abstraction,
diminished speech, mental torpor, or impaired memory. In
severe cases, there may be absence of speech or muttering
to oneself, deranged speech, crying or laughing for no reason, or no desire for food. In such severe cases, this term
is more properly translated as dementia. Hua Tuo was the
first to use the term *chi dai* or feeblemindedness in his Han
dynasty *Shen Yi Mi Chuan (Divine Doctor's Secret
Transmission)*. This literally means idiocy and feeblemindedness. A little later, Huang-fu Mi, in the *Zhen Jiu Jia Yi
Jing (Systematic Classic of Acupuncture & Moxibustion)*
reversed these two words to form *dai chi*. In other premodern books, this disease is referred to as *shen dai*, spirit feeblemindedness.

The Chinese medical disease category of feeblemind-
ness appears to correspond to a spectrum of Western psychiatric disorders of cognitive impairment ranging from
progressive age-related mental slowing to global decline
in cognitive functioning.

## NOSOLOGY:

Contemporary Western psychiatry categorizes all disorders of cognition as organic. That is, there is a presumed

or verified medical etiology for all disorders that affect
cognitive functioning. Alzheimer's disease, vascular
dementia, and alcohol-related dementia comprise three
basic diagnostic categories of dementia in Western psychiatry. Diagnostic criteria for the major categories of
dementia include:

1. Persisting pattern of memory impairment
2. One or more areas of significant cognitive impairment
   (including language and executive functioning)
3. Significant impairment in occupational or social
   functioning
4. Exclusion of delirium or other acute medical disorders
   as the cause of cognitive dysfunction

In addition, each major nosologic category includes specific features. For example, a diagnosis of vascular
dementia requires the presence of identifiable neurological deficits or a documented course of step-wise progression in cognitive decline. In contrast, Alzheimer's disease is diagnosed when specific identifiable causes have
been ruled out. There is a presumption that Alzheimer's
disease is idiopathic (*i.e.*, without a specific identifiable
underlying cause). However, this disorder has been consistently correlated with a specific pattern of neuropathological changes on autopsy (such as amyloid
plaques and neurofibrillary tangles). Feeblemindedness
is a frequent concomitant of several neurological disorders, including Parkinson's disease and Huntington's
disease.

## EPIDEMIOLOGY:

The probability of developing dementia increases with age such that 5% of the population older than 65 is demented at any given time. Dementia becomes more common with increasing old age. In Western cultures approximately 20% of individuals aged 85 or older are demented. It is unclear whether vascular dementia or Alzheimer's disease is the most common cause of dementia, however Alzheimer's disease predominates in the over-75 age group.

## DIFFERENTIAL DIAGNOSIS:

By definition, dementia is a severe, persisting loss of mental capacity. Some dementias are reversible if the underlying cause is accurately diagnosed and treatable. For example, normal pressure hydrocephalus, seizure disorders, chronic vitamin deficiencies ($B_6$ and $B_{12}$), certain endocrinological disorders (including hypothyroidism), and some vascular diseases are potentially treatable and, therefore, reversible causes of dementia. It is essential to distinguish a transient delirium that is caused by an acute and treatable medical problem from the typically insidious pattern of cognitive decline of dementia. Delirium is always associated with disorientation and change in the level of arousal. The delirious patient is frequently agitated and often exhibits psychotic symptoms. In contrast, demented patients are typically alert but occasionally exhibit psychotic or agitated behavior. Cognitive changes accompanying delirium improve as the underlying medical cause responds to treatment. Excluding treatable kinds of dementia, most demented patients continue to decline in baseline mental functioning, and their acute medical causes are seldom identified.

Chronic heavy abuse of alcohol sometimes results in global cognitive impairment. This condition is called alcoholic dementia. In cases where chronic alcohol abuse results in memory loss but cognition and executive functioning are otherwise intact, the probable Western psychiatric diagnosis is alcoholic amnestic disorder. Chronic heavy abuse of marijuana, heroin, and other narcotics sometimes manifests as a dementia-like syndrome which typically resolves with sustained abstinence.

In cases where feeblemindedness persists in the absence of identified underlying medical causes and there is no evidence of associated substance abuse or chronic medication side effects (for example, chronic use of typical antipsychotic agents), the clinician's attention turns to psychiatric disorders as possible explanations for apparent dementia. For unclear reasons, schizophrenics are at increased risk for developing Alzheimer's disease. Individuals who suffer from severe depressed mood that is resistant to treatment sometimes appear to be demented because of symptoms of cognitive slowing or frank cognitive impairment, including memory loss, that may accompany severe depression. This condition has been called "pseudodementia." It is significant that such individuals appear to be at increased risk of developing Alzheimer's disease over the long term, and it has been suggested that symptoms of pseudodementia might actually represent incipient dementia. Finally, many individuals with learn-

| DIFFERENTIAL DIAGNOSIS | | |
|---|---|---|
| 1. MEDICAL DISORDERS | 2. EFFECTS OF SUBSTANCES | 3. PSYCHIATRIC DISORDERS |
| A. NORMAL PRESSURE HYDROCEPHALAS AND OTHER CNS MASS LESIONS<br>B. LONG-TERM COGNITIVE EFFECTS OF POORLY CONTROLLED SEIZURE DISORDERS<br>C. CHRONIC VITAMIN DEFICIENCIES, ESPECIALLY B-VITAMINS<br>D. ENDOCRINOLOGICAL DISORDERS (INCLUDING HYPOTHYROIDISM)<br>E. VASCULAR DISEASES OF THE CNS<br>F. DELIRIUM<br>G. HISTORY OF TRAUMATIC BRAIN INJURY | A. CHRONIC HEAVY ALCOHOL ABUSE<br>B. CHRONIC ABUSE OF MARIJUANA, HEROIN AND OTHER ILLICIT SUBSTANCES<br>C. LONG-TERM COGNITIVE SIDE EFFECTS OF CERTAIN TYPICAL ANTIPSYCHOTIC MEDICATIONS | A. COGNITIVE IMPAIRMENT CONCOMITANT WITH CHRONIC SEVERE SCHIZOPHRENIA<br>B. PSEUDODEMENTIA OF SEVERE RECURRING MAJOR DEPRESSIVE DISORDER<br>C. LEARNING DISORDERS |

ing disorders have selective deficits in one or more areas of executive functioning. Although individuals with learning disorders are able to function well in most situations, in certain social, academic, or occupational contexts, their symptoms may be misrepresented as "feeblemindedness."

## ETIOLOGY & PATHOPHYSIOLOGY:

Western medicine classifies dementias by major etiologic category since dementia results from pathological changes in the brain that manifest as a persisting pattern of global cognitive decline. The specific symptom pattern and severity of cognitive dysfunction depend on location, size and pathophysiology of a brain lesion, or other abnormal aspects of brain functioning underlying dementia. Principle medical causes of dementia include:

1. Trauma (following severe head injury)
2. Infection (*e.g.*, AIDS or neurosyphilis)
3. Cardiac or vascular disease (*e.g.*, stroke)
4. Metabolic disorders (chronic vitamin deficiencies or chronic endocrinological disorders)
5. Degenerative brain disorders (*e.g.*, Alzheimer's disease, Parkinson's disease, Pick's disease)
6. Drugs or toxins (*e.g.*, chronic alcohol abuse, heavy metal toxicity)
7. Other causes (multiple sclerosis, tumor, congenital causes, epilepsy, hydrocephalus)

In addition to the above irreversible dementing disorders, psychiatric disorders are sometimes accompanied by cognitive changes that simulate dementia. The word "pseudodementia" is used to describe persisting severe cognitive dysfunction that is presumed to be secondary to a major psychiatric disorder in the absence of identified medical causes. Western psychiatry regards impaired cognitive functioning that often accompanies severe depression as pseudodementia. However, recent studies of demented populations have demonstrated that individuals who experienced significant cognitive impairment when depressed were more likely to be diagnosed with dementia in later decades. Pseudodementia of severe depression may, therefore, be a risk factor for subsequent development of permanent cognitive impairment. Further research is needed to clarify this issue.

## WESTERN MEDICAL TREATMENT:

Western medicine offers only palliative treatments for early stages of mild to moderate dementia. Two medications, Tacrine and Aricept, are currently available in Western Europe and the U.S. Both inhibit the brain enzyme that breaks down acetylcholine, effectively boosting the availability of this neurotransmitter, thus resulting in mild transient improvement in memory, learning, and general cognitive functioning. The agitation and confusion that frequently accompany dementia are treated symptomatically with small doses of benzodiazepines or low-potency antipsychotics. Considerable research efforts are currently ongoing to develop more effective treatments for Alzheimer's disease and other dementias. To date, no significant breakthroughs in treatment concepts have emerged from conventional Western medicine. Recent double-blind, placebo-controlled studies provide strong evidence for the efficacy of *Ginkgo biloba* preparations in the treatment of Alzheimer's disease that is similar to that of available synthetic drugs. Because of the severe level of cognitive impairment, demented individuals do not have the capacity to benefit from psychotherapy. However, support groups are often beneficial for careproviders, who are at high risk for burnout.

## PROGNOSIS:

The course and prognosis of dementia are highly variable and depend on the nature and severity of underlying causes. For example, early identification and treatment of dementia due to normal pressure hydrocephalus can result in a dramatic and rapid return to the patient's previous baseline cognitive functioning. Correction of metabolic or endocrinological causes of dementia may result in partial or complete recovery of functioning depending on age at onset, duration and severity of symptoms before treatment, previous baseline, and the presence of co-morbid medical or psychiatric disorders. All hereditary or degenerative dementias, including Huntington's disease, Parkinson's disease, and Pick's disease, carry a very poor prognosis. In these disorders, decline is typically insidious, resulting in permanent, severe cognitive dysfunction. Western medicine currently offers no effective treatments for these disorders.

## INDICATIONS FOR REFERRAL TO WESTERN MEDICAL SERVICES:

Evidence of acute onset cognitive dysfunction, change in level of consciousness, confusion or agitation, or the presence of an underlying medical disorder is sufficient basis for urgent evaluation to the nearest emergency room to rule out potentially fatal causes of delirium or reversible causes of dementia. Indications for non-urgent medical-psychiatric referral include a long-standing pattern of cognitive decline without impairment in the level of consciousness that has not responded to an appropriate course of Chinese medical treatment.

## CHINESE DISEASE CAUSES & MECHANISMS:

The clarity and function of the spirit brilliance depends upon effulgent spirit. Spirit is nothing other than an accumulation of qi in the heart. However, qi is engendered from a transformation of blood, yin, and essence, and, once engendered, is also nourished by those yin substances. Feeblemindedness is an inability of the spirit brilliance to function correctly. This in turn may be due to either malnourishment of the heart by blood, yin, and/or essence or some evil qi confounding the spirit, such as phlegm dampness or blood stasis blocking the clear orifices. The types of vacuity leading to malnourishment are blood vacuity mixed with qi depression, liver blood-kidney yin vacuity, and sea of marrow emptiness and vacuity.

## TREATMENT BASED ON PATTERN DISCRIMINATION:

### 1. PHLEGM DAMPNESS CLOUDING THE CLEAR ORIFICES PATTERN

MAIN SYMPTOMS: Spirit mind abstraction, a flat, wooden affect, lack of speech or speaking to oneself, disinclination to talk or to meet visitors, profuse phlegm, heavy-headedness, chest and abdominal fullness and oppression, slimy, white tongue fur, and a bowstring, slippery pulse

TREATMENT PRINCIPLES: Transform dampness and flush away phlegm, open the orifices and boost the intelligence

FORMULA & MEDICINALS: Zhi Mi Tang Jia Jian (Pointing Out Confusion Decoction with Additions & Subtractions)

Lime-processed Rhizoma Pinelliae Ternatae (Ban Xia), 10g, Pericarpium Citri Reticulatae (Chen Pi), 10g, Rhizoma Atractylodis Macrocephalae (Bai Zhu), 10g, Massa Medica Fermentata (Shen Qu), 6g, Rhizoma Acori Graminei (Shi Chang Pu), 10g, Sclerotium Pararadicis Poriae Cocos (Fu Shen), 12g, Radix Polygalae Tenuifoliae (Yuan Zhi), 6g, Radix Panacis Ginseng (Ren Shen), 3g (decocted first), bile-processed Rhizoma Arisaematis (Dan Nan Xing), 5g, Radix Lateralis Praeparatus Aconiti Carmichaeli (Fu Zi), 3g[1], mix-fried Radix Glycyrrhizae (Gan Cao), 6g

Decoct in water and administer orally in two divided doses, morning and night, one ji per day.

ACUPUNCTURE: Xin Hui (GV 22), Yin Ling Quan (Sp 9),

Feng Long (St 40), Zhong Wan (CV 12), Zu San Li (St 36). Use draining technique.

### 2. QI DEPRESSION-BLOOD VACUITY PATTERN

MAIN SYMPTOMS: Feeblemindedness, emotional depression, possible insomnia with impetuosity and impatience, frequent sighing, grief with a tendency to cry, chest and rib-side oppression distention, pale nails, lips, and tongue, and a bowstring, fine pulse

TREATMENT PRINCIPLES: Course the liver and rectify the qi, nourish the blood and boost intelligence

FORMULA & MEDICINALS: If there is a liver-spleen disharmony with blood vacuity, use Xiao Yao San He Gan Mai Da Zao Tang (Rambling Powder plus Licorice, Wheat & Red Date Decoction)

Radix Bupleuri (Chai Hu), 10g, Radix Albus Paeoniae Lactiflorae (Bai Shao), 10g, Rhizoma Atractylodis Macrocephalae (Bai Zhu), 10g, Radix Angelicae Sinensis (Dang Gui), 10g, Sclerotium Poriae Cocos (Fu Ling), 10g, Herba Menthae Haplocalycis (Bo He), 3g (added later), uncooked Rhizoma Zingiberis (Sheng Jiang), 3g (added later), Fructus Ziziphi Jujubae (Da Zao), 6 pieces, Fructus Levis Tritici Aestivi (Fu Xiao Mai), 15g, mix-fried Radix Glycyrrhizae (Gan Cao), 10-15g

If there is a liver depression transforming fire and spleen disharmony with phlegm obstruction, use the following unnamed formula:

Radix Salviae Miltiorrhizae (Dan Shen), 12g, Radix Codonopsitis Pilosulae (Dang Shen), 12g, Rhizoma Pinelliae Ternatae (Ban Xia), 12g, Sclerotium Pararadicis Poriae Cocos (Fu Shen), 12g, Tuber Ophiopogonis Japonici (Mai Dong), 12g, Semen Ziziphi Spinosae (Suan Zao Ren), 12g, Radix Angelicae Sinensis (Dang Gui), 10g, Radix Albus Paeoniae Lactiflorae (Bai Shao), 10g, Radix Trichosanthis Kirlowii (Tian Hua Fen), 10g, Massa Medica Fermentata (Shen Qu), 6g, Radix Glycyrrhizae (Gan Cao), 6g, Pericarpium Citri Reticulatae (Chen Pi), 6g

Decoct in water and administer orally in two divided doses, morning and evening, one ji per day.

ADDITIONS & SUBTRACTIONS: If liver depression is severe, add Tuber Curcumae (Yu Jin) and Cortex Albizziae Julibrissinisis (He Huan Pi). If depressive heat is marked, add stir-fried Fructus Gardeniae Jasminoidis (Zhi Zi) and Cortex Radicis Moutan (Dan Pi) and delete Ginger and

Mentha. If there is insomnia, add Flos Albizziae Julibrissinis (*He Huan Hua*) and stir-fried Semen Zizyphi Spinosae (*Suan Zao Ren*).

ACUPUNCTURE: *Yin Tang* (M-HN-3), *Shen Men* (Ht 7), *Tai Chong* (Liv 3), *Qi Men* (Liv 14), *Zu San Li* (St 36). Use even supplementing-even draining technique.

### 3. LIVER BLOOD-KIDNEY YIN VACUITY PATTERN

MAIN SYMPTOMS: Feeblemindedness, lack of spirit in the eyes, motor ataxia, paraphasia, dizziness, tinnitus, low back and knee soreness and limpness, numbness of the limbs with inhibited flexion and extension, possible heat in the soles of the feet and palms of the hands or night sweats, possible malar flushing and/or emaciation, a red tongue or a pale tongue with red tip, scanty fur, and a fine, commonly bowstring, possibly rapid pulse

TREATMENT PRINCIPLES: Supplement the liver and nourish the blood, enrich the kidneys and boost the intelligence

FORMULA & MEDICINALS: *Da Bu Yuan Jian* (Great Supplement the Origin Decoction)

Cooked Radix Rehmanniae (*Shu Di*), 12g, Fructus Lycii Chinensis (*Gou Qi Zi*), 10g, Fructus Corni Officinalis (*Shan Zhu Yu*), 10g, Cortex Eucommiae Ulmoidis (*Du Zhong*), 10g, Radix Panacis Ginseng (*Ren Shen*), 3-6g (decocted first), Radix Dioscoreae Oppositae (*Shan Yao*), 10g, Radix Polygalae Tenuifoliae (*Yuan Zhi*), 10g, Radix Polygoni Multiflori (*He Shou Wu*), 12g, mix-fried Radix Glycyrrhizae (*Gan Cao*), 3g

Decoct in water and administer orally in two divided doses, morning and evening, one *ji* per day.

Acupuncture: *Si Shen Cong* (M-HN-1), *Feng Chi* (GB 20), *San Yin Jiao* (Sp 6), *Tai Xi* (Ki 3), *Da Zhong* (Ki 4). Use supplementing technique.

### 4. SEA OF MARROW EMPTINESS & VACUITY[2]

Main symptoms: Feeblemindedness, developmental retardation, late closure of the fontanelle in infants, fragile bones, low back and lower limb soreness and weakness, inability to stand for a long period of time, unsteady walking, inability to hold up the head, a pale tongue with scanty fur, and a fine, weak pulse

TREATMENT PRINCIPLES: Supplement the kidneys and foster the essence, fill the marrow and boost the intelligence

Formula & medicinals: *He Che Da Zao Wan Jia Jian* (Placenta Great Construction Pills with Additions & Subtractions)

Placenta Hominis (*Zi He Che*), 3g (powdered and swallowed with the decocted liquid), cooked Radix Rehmanniae (*Shu Di*), 12g, Plastrum Testudinis (*Gui Ban*), 12g (decocted first), Radix Achyranthis Bidentatae (*Niu Xi*), 10g, Cortex Eucommiae Ulmoidis (*Du Zhong*), 10g, Tuber Ophiopogonis Japonicae (*Mai Dong*), 12g, Tuber Asparagi Cochinensis (*Tian Dong*), 12g, Fructus Lycii Chinensis (*Gou Qi Zi*), 10g, Rhizoma Polygonati (*Huang Jing*), 10g, Gelatinum Cornu Cervi (*Lu Jiao Jiao*), 3g (dissolved in the decocted liquid while still hot)

Decoct in water and administer orally in two divided doses, morning and evening, one *ji* per day.

ACUPUNCTURE: *Bai Hui* (GV 20), *Shen Shu* (Bl 23), *Ming Men* (GV 4), *Pi Shu* (Bl 20), *Zu San Li* (St 36). Use supplementing technique.

### 5. QI STAGNATION & BLOOD STASIS PATTERN

MAIN SYMPTOMS: Most cases with this pattern have a history of traumatic injury or birth trauma. Their symptoms include feeblemindedness, apathy, retarded reactions, sluggishness, purple macules on the tongue, and a deep, fine, bowstring pulse.

NOTE: This pattern may be seen alone in its discrete form. However, it also often complicates other of the above patterns.

TREATMENT PRINCIPLES: Quicken the blood, transform stasis, and boost the intelligence

FORMULA & MEDICINALS: *Tong Qiao Huo Xue Tang Jia Jian* (Open the Orifices & Quicken the Blood Decoction with Additions & Subtractions)

Radix Rubrus Paeoniae Lactiflorae (*Chi Shao*), 10g, Radix Ligustici Wallichii (*Chuan Xiong*), 10-15g (added later), Semen Pruni Persicae (*Tao Ren*), 10g, Flos Carthami Tinctorii (*Hong Hua*), 10g, Lumbricus (*Di Long*), 3g, Rhizoma Acori Graminei (*Shi Chang Pu*), 6g, Retinervus Fascicularis Citri Reticulatae (*Ju Luo*), 10g, Fructus Zizyphi Jujubae (*Da Zao*), 3 pieces

ADDITIONS & SUBTRACTIONS: If there is concomitant qi

and blood vacuity, add Radix Angelicae Sinensis (*Dang Gui*) and Radix Astragali Membranacei (*Huang Qi*).

ACUPUNCTURE: *Bai Hui* (GV 20), *Ya Men* (GV 15), *Shen Ting* (GV 24), *Yin Tang* (M-HN-3), *Xue Hai* (Sp 10), *He Gu* (LI 4), *Tai Chong* (Liv 3)

## ABSTRACT OF REPRESENTATIVE CHINESE RESEARCH:

*Shan Xi Zhong Yi (Shanxi Chinese Medicine)*, #1, 2000, p. 12-13: Du Qing-chuan and Ma Rui-lian treated 53 patients with multi-infarct dementia (MID) with *Yi Zhi Huo Xue Tang* (Boost the Intelligence & Quicken the Blood Decoction) based on the principles of enriching and supplementing the liver and kidneys, boosting the qi and quickening the blood. These were compared to 47 cases treated only with *Nao Fu Kang* (piracetam). In the treatment group, there were 31 men and 22 women between the ages of 61-77, with a median age of 66.32 ± 4.38 years. Of the 47 patients in the comparison group, 30 were men and 17 were women. These patients were all 60-79 years old, with a median age of 65.54 ± 4.31 years. All the patients in both groups had experienced the onset of dementia due to cerebrovascular disease within the previous three months and had been diagnosed with MID according to the *DSM-IV* and *ICD-10*. Disturbance in intellect was measured via a dementia-rating scale referred to as the NDS. The median NDS score in the treatment group was 17.24 ± 5.13, while the median score in the comparison group was 18.14 ± 3.67. Therefore, there was no significant statistical difference between these two groups (P>0.05). Serum endothelin levels in both these groups prior to treatment were higher than in a healthy control group of 30 patients.

*Yi Zhi Huo Xue Tang* consisted of: Radix Astragali Membranacei (*Huang Qi*), 60g, Radix Angelicae Sinensis (*Dang Gui*), 10g, Radix Ligustici Wallichii (*Chuan Xiong*), 15g, Hirudo (*Shui Zhi*), 6g, Lumbricus (*Di Long*), 15g, Radix Polygoni Multiflori (*He Shou Wu*), 12g, Fructus Lycii Chinensis (*Gou Qi Zi*), 12g, Rhizoma Acori Graminei (*Shi Chang Pu*), 12g, Fructus Corni Officinalis (*Shan Zhu Yu*), 12g, Rhizoma Anemarrhenae Aspheloidis (*Zhi Mu*), 10g, Rhizoma Atractylodis Macrocephalae (*Bai Zhu*), 15g, and Radix Glycyrrhizae (*Gan Cao*), 6g. Each day, one *ji* of these medicinals was soaked in 700ml of cold water for 1.5 hours. Then they were boiled three times till 400ml of liquid remained. This was administered in three divided doses, morning, noon, and night. After administering five *ji*, two days were skipped before resuming

administration. The patients in the comparison group received 0.8g of piracetam each time, three times per day, administered orally. Both groups were treated for two months, during which time any other treatments for MID were suspended. Serum levels of endothelin (ET) were tested before and after treatment in both groups.

In terms of outcomes, 18 cases experienced marked effect in the treatment group, with another 29 experiencing some effect and six patients no effect. Therefore, the total amelioration rate in the treatment group was 88.68%. In the comparison group, eight cases got a marked effect, 15 got some effect, and 24 cases got no effect, for a total amelioration rate of 48.94%. Hence there was a significant difference in outcomes between these two groups in terms of effectiveness of their respective protocols (P<0.01). In addition, the drop in ET levels in the treatment group from before to after treatment was significant (P<0.01), while decreases in ET levels in the comparison group were not significant (P>0.05).

## REPRESENTATIVE CASE HISTORY:[3]

The patient was a 49 year old male. Due to becoming depressed and angry, the man had developed episodes of feeblemindedness over the last two years. Each episode would begin with a feeling of qi spontaneously surging up under his heart to his throat. When this happened, the man was not able to speak and his body was not able to move. However, his mind was clear. Each of these episodes would last 10 minutes and anywhere from 1-2 to 5-20 of such episodes might occur per day. After an episode had stopped, the man would vomit a large amount of phlegmy fluid and his essence spirit would gradually return to normal. These episodes could also be followed by a headache which could last half a day. The man had been previously treated for epilepsy with both Chinese and Western medicines but with no result. He commonly felt his body was chilled, had cool hands and feet, and a slight degree of stomach and abdominal distention and fullness. Other signs and symptoms included heart vexation, a dry mouth and ability to drink, normal defecation and urination, a red tongue with thick, yellow fur, and a deep, bowstring, forceful pulse.

Therefore, the patient was prescribed the following modified version of Si Ni San (Four Counterflows Powder): Radix Bupleuri (*Chai Hu*), 9g, Radix Albus Paeoniae Lactiflorae (*Bai Shao*), 9g, Fructus Immaturus Citri Aurantii (*Zhi Shi*), 9g, Semen Cassiae Torae (*Cao Jue Ming*), 12g, uncooked Haemititum (*Dai Zhe Shi*), 18g, Rhizoma Pinelliae Ternatae (*Ban Xia*), 9g, and Radix

Glycyrrhizae (*Gan Cao*), 3g. After taking nine *ji* of these medicinals, due to damp heat already being eliminated and his qi mechanism already being smoothly flowing, the patient was given *Er Chen Tang* (Two Aged [Ingredients] Decoction) with additions and subtractions in order to secure the treatment effect. On follow-up after an unspecified period of time, there had been no recurrence.

## ENDNOTES

[1] A small amount of Aconite is added to this formula in order to more effectively melt or transform phlegm. The Chinese word "transform," also means to melt.

[2] This pattern can also be referred to as a kidney essence insufficiency pattern.

[3] Chen & Zhao, *op. cit.*, p. 123-124

# ✦ 10 ✦

# IMPAIRED MEMORY

Impaired memory refers to either partial or total loss of memory about things which have happened either in the recent or distant past. More commonly in English, this is called forgetfulness or amnesia if severe. In the *Nei Jing (Inner Classic)*, this is referred to as *shan wang*, poor memory. Chao Yuan-fang, in the Sui dynasty *Zhu Bing Yuan Hou Lun (Treatise on the Origins & Symptoms of Diseases)*, referred to this *duo wang, excessive forgetfulness*, while Sun Si-miao, in the Tang dynasty *Qian Jin Yao Fang (Essential Formulas [Worth] a Thousand [Pieces of] Gold)*, referred to it as *hao wang*, good at forgetting. The *Sheng Ji Zong Lu (Assembled Records of Imperial Aid)*, published between 1111-1117 CE, introduced the term, *jian wang*, forgetfulness or impaired memory by which it is primarily known today.

Impaired memory is characteristic of many Western medical and psychiatric disorders. Western psychiatry distinguishes between amnestic disorders, characterized by inability to learn or remember, and dementia, in which forgetfulness occurs in the context of global cognitive decline. Delirium is an acute medical condition that is potentially life-threatening. It is characterized by gross disturbance in the level of consciousness that often includes impaired memory. Many psychiatric disorders including PTSD and dissociative disorders are characterized by impairment in the ability to recall selected facts or learn new information. This chapter includes information on the Western medical and psychiatric disease cat-

egories associated with impaired memory excluding dementia, which is discussed in Chapter 9, this Book, Feeblemindedness.

## Nosology:

An individual who is unable to recall learned information or form new memories but who is oriented and has no other cognitive deficits meets diagnostic criteria for amnestic disorder. In contrast, a diagnosis of delirium requires a disturbance in the level of consciousness caused by an identifiable medical or physiological derangement. Gross cognitive impairment is typically associated with delirium. Impaired memory is often found in the context of dissociative disorders in which a traumatic experience is often blocked from conscious recall. In many cases of post-traumatic stress disorder (PTSD) there is amnesia of the traumatic event that precipitated the disorder. Several medical etiologies of impaired memory in the absence of other cognitive symptoms are reviewed below.

## Differential diagnosis:

Chronic alcohol abuse often results in profound memory impairment, including both retrograde (inability to recall recently learned information) and anterograde (inability to form new memories) amnesia. This disorder was previously called Korsakoff's syndrome. Chronic abuse of other substances, including cocaine, methamphetamine, mari-

## DIFFERENTIAL DIAGNOSIS

| 1. MEDICAL DISORDERS | 2. EFFECTS OF SUBSTANCES | 3. PSYCHIATRIC DISORDERS |
|---|---|---|
| A. HISTORY OF TRAUMATIC BRAIN INJURY (TBI)<br>B. SEIZURE DISORDERS<br>C. HISTORY OF CEREBROVASCULAR ACCIDENT (CVA)<br>D. CHRONIC VITAMIN B DEFICIENCY | A. CHRONIC ALCOHOL ABUSE LEADING TO KORSAKOFF'S SYNDROME<br>B. CHRONIC ABUSE OF COCAINE, METHAMPHETAMINE, MARIJUANA OR HEROIN | A. POST-TRAUMATIC STRESS DISORDER (PTSD)<br>B. DISSOCIATIVE IDENTITY DISORDER (IDD) AND OTHER DISSOCIATIVE DISORDERS |

juana, and heroin, can also result in persisting memory impairment in the absence of other cognitive deficits (*i.e.,* following periods of acute intoxication). Head trauma frequently leads to amnesia which may resolve completely or persist indefinitely depending on severity of trauma and the affected brain region. Other common medical disorders that are often associated with amnesia include seizures, cerebrovascular accidents (stroke), and chronic vitamin B deficiency (especially $B_{12}$ and $B_6$). In the acute phase of illness, most of these medical disorders are associated with gross impairment in level of consciousness. However, memory impairment often persists long after delirium has resolved. Medical etiologies are differentiated from psychiatric causes through demonstration of identifiable medical factors that can be clearly linked to onset and severity of memory impairment.

When memory impairment affects functioning in the absence of identifiable associated medical factors or substance abuse, a primary psychiatric disorder is the likely cause. A diagnosis of PTSD can be made only when there is a history of severe trauma during which the individual believed there was a real possibility of being killed or seriously injured, after which symptoms of flashbacks, nightmares, psychic numbing, and increased startle response persisted for at least one month. Dissociative identity disorder (previously known as multiple personality disorder), does not require a documented history of trauma related to a specific problem of memory loss. In this disorder impaired memory is secondary to frequent episodes of dissociation during which the individual experiences him or herself as a distinct ego. Memories formed during dissociative episodes are unavailable to conscious recall when the patient is functioning normally.

### WESTERN MEDICAL TREATMENT:

Unfortunately, Western medicine has no effective treatments for most medical causes of memory loss as most

known medical causes represent severe, often irreversible insults to the brain. Some stroke patients may gradually regain the capacity to form new memories depending on the severity and location of the affected brain region. Alcohol-induced amnestic disorder sometimes improves after long-term treatment with thiamine. Contemporary Western psychiatry offers few effective treatments for PTSD and dissociative disorders. There are no pharmacological agents that directly target dissociative symptoms, but antipsychotics are sometimes helpful during acute dissociative episodes. Benzodiazepines are also sometimes employed to treat severe anxiety symptoms that are frequently seen in PTSD and dissociative identity disorder. Psychogenic amnesia is a mild form of dissociation that is transient and typically resolves without treatment. Supportive psychotherapy and judicious use of hypnotherapy may accelerate recovery to normal pre-morbid psychological functioning in some cases of PTSD and dissociative identity disorder. However, the clinician must carefully assess the severity of dissociative symptoms prior to attempting hypnotherapy in order to minimize risk of inducing an acute dissociative episode, often with psychotic symptoms, during hypnosis.

### SHORT & LONG-TERM ADVANTAGES & DISADVANTAGES OF WESTERN MEDICAL TREATMENT:

The advantages of successful medical treatment of delirium or other potentially life-threatening causes of impaired memory are clear. The use of certain antipsychotic medications to treat dissociative symptoms in dissociative identity disorder or PTSD entails the risk of transient acute neurological side effects (acute dystonic episodes) in the short-term and permanent disorders of involuntary movement (tardive dyskinesia) in the long-term. However, recently introduced antipsychotic medications carry considerably reduced risk for development of tardive dyskinesia.

## PROGNOSIS:

Amnestic syndromes caused by severe head trauma, stroke, or chronic alcohol abuse typically have poor outcomes. Amnesia that is related to CNS infection or mild head trauma is prognostically more favorable. Disorders of forgetting that are psychogenic in origin have favorable outcomes in most cases, but there is a wide range of long-term outcomes depending on the presence of co-morbid psychiatric disorders and treatment response history.

## INDICATIONS FOR REFERRAL TO WESTERN MEDICAL SERVICES:

When there is evidence from the patient's history that memory loss has occurred suddenly and onset was associated with physical trauma, the patient should immediately be referred to the nearest hospital emergency room. This history suggests acute intracranial bleeding which can be lethal if not promptly controlled. Similarly, when there is a history of sudden onset memory loss, associated disorientation and gross confusion, or signs or symptoms of acute medical illness, the patient should be urgently sent to the closest emergency room for evaluation and treatment of delirium. In cases of long-standing memory impairment with associated neurological symptoms, including disturbances in vision, balance, or coordination, the patient should be referred to a neurologist for non-urgent evaluation. Persisting memory loss in the absence of identifiable medical causes that appears to be psychogenic in origin and has not responded to an appropriate course of Chinese medical treatment is an indication for non-urgent referral to a psychiatrist for concurrent evaluation and treatment. In cases where there is persisting memory impairment in the absence of other cognitive deficits and no identified associated medical problems, comprehensive neuropsychological testing may help to clarify the neurological and psychiatric differential diagnosis leading to the most appropriate treatment plan.

## CHINESE DISEASE CAUSES & MECHANISMS:

The Chinese disease causes and mechanisms are similar to profuse dreams discussed above. Either there is insufficient construction and nourishment or the heart spirit or some evil qi is harassing or confounding the heart spirit. As Zhu Dan-xi says, "Impaired memory is mostly due to essence spirit shortage and scantiness, [though] it may also have [i.e., be due to] phlegm." Liu Yi-ren, author of the Qing dynasty Yi Xue Chuan Xin Lu (The Heart Transmission of Medicine), implies that anxiety and thought may cause such essence spirit shortage and scantiness when he says:

The disease of impaired memory is due to excessive anxiety and thought damaging the pericardium. Since the abode of the spirit is not clear, the person is liable to forget in a blink.[1]

However, one disease mechanism we have not discussed above is kidney essence insufficiency. Former heaven natural endowment or habitual bodily vacuity weakness, overtaxation, enduring disease, immaturity or aging, overuse of certain medicinals and drugs, or unrestrained sexual activity may all contribute to kidney essence insufficiency. Being vacuous, kidney essence may then fail to fill the sea of marrow and nourish the brain sufficiently. Therefore, the memory becomes impaired. This is what Lin Xi-tong was referring to when he said, "The heart's spirit resides in the heart, but the heart's essence depends on the kidneys." Wang Ji-an also said:

To treat impaired memory, one must interconnect the heart and kidneys, thus promoting the downward free flow of the heart's spirit brilliance to the kidneys and the upbearing and ascending of the kidneys' essence luster to the brain. The essence is able to engender the qi, while the qi is able to engender the spirit. Hence the spirit is stable and the qi is clear...

## TREATMENT BASED ON PATTERN DISCRIMINATION:

### 1. HEART-SPLEEN DUAL VACUITY PATTERN

Main symptoms: Impaired memory, a sallow yellow facial complexion, lassitude of the spirit, heart palpitations, reduced sleep, profuse dreams, shortness of breath, fatigue, poor appetite, loose stools, menstrual irregularities in females, a pale, commonly enlarged tongue with white fur, and a fine, weak pulse

TREATMENT PRINCIPLES: Fortify the spleen and boost the qi, supplement the heart and nourish the blood

FORMULA & MEDICINALS: Gui Pi Tang Jia Jian (Restore the Spleen Decoction with Additions & Subtractions)

Rhizoma Atractylodis Macrocephalae (Bai Zhu), 10g, Sclerotium Pararadicis Poriae Cocos (Fu Shen), 12g, Radix Astragali Membranacei (Huang Qi), 15g, Radix Codonopsitis Pilosulae (Dang Shen), 10g, mix-fried Radix Glycyrrhizae (Gan Cao), 6g, Radix Angelicae Sinensis (Dang Gui), 10g, Arillus Longanae Euphoriae (Long Yan Rou), 12g, stir-fried Semen Zizyphi Spinosae

(*Suan Zao Ren*), 15g, Radix Polygalae Tenuifoliae (*Yuan Zhi*), 10g, Fructus Alpiniae Oxyphyllae (*Yi Zhi Ren*), 15g, Radix Auklandiae Lappae (*Mu Xiang*), 6-10g (added later)

Decoct in water and administer orally in two divided doses, morning and evening, one *ji* per day.

**ADDITIONS & SUBTRACTIONS:** If either heart blood or heart yin vacuity predominate, subtract Astragalus and add Semen Biotae Orientalis (*Bai Zi Ren*) and Caulis Polygoni Multiflori (*Ye Jiao Teng*). If spleen qi vacuity predominates, replace Spirit of Poria with Sclerotium Poriae Cocos (*Fu Ling*) and add Rhizoma Polygonati (*Huang Jing*) and Pericarpium Citri Reticulatae (*Chen Pi*).

**ACUPUNCTURE:** *Bai Hui* (GV 20), *Shen Men* (Ht 7), *Xin Shu* (Bl 15), *Pi Shu* (Bl 20), *Zu San Li* (St 36). Use supplementing technique.

## 2. KIDNEY ESSENCE INSUFFICIENCY PATTERN

**MAIN SYMPTOMS:** Impaired memory, absentmindedness, lassitude of the spirit, a tendency to let the head fall forward, possible loose teeth, loss and/or early greying of the hair, low back and knee soreness and limpness, weak bones, a pale tongue with white fur, and a vacuous or choppy pulse

**TREATMENT PRINCIPLES:** Supplement the kidneys and boost the essence

**CHINESE MEDICINAL FORMULA:** *He Che Da Zao Wan Jia Jian* (Placenta Great Construction Pills with Additions & Subtractions)

Placenta Hominis (*Zi He Che*), 1g (powdered and swallowed with the decocted liquid), cooked Radix Rehmanniae (*Shu Di*), 12g, Radix Achyranthis Bidentatae (*Niu Xi*), 12g, Cortex Eucommiae Ulmoidis (*Du Zhong*), 10g, calcined Plastrum Testudinis (*Gui Ban*), 20g (decocted first), Fructus Lycii Chinensis (*Gou Qi Zi*), 10g, Rhizoma Polygonati (*Huang Jing*), 10g, Radix Panacis Ginseng (*Ren Shen*), 6-10g (decocted first), Radix Dioscoreae Oppositae (*Shan Yao*), 10g, Fructus Corni Officinalis (*Shan Zhu Yu*), 10g, Radix Polygalae Tenuifoliae (*Yuan Zhi*), 6-10g, Fructus Alpiniae Oxyphyllae (*Yi Zhi Ren*), 15g

Decoct in water and administer orally in two divided doses, morning and evening, one *ji* per day.

**ACUPUNCTURE:** *Si Shen Cong* (M-HN-1), *Jing Gong* (Bl 52), *Shen Shu* (Bl 23), *San Yin Jiao* (Sp 6), *Tai Xi* (Ki 3). Use supplementing technique.

## 3. NON-INTERACTION BETWEEN THE HEART & KIDNEYS PATTERN

**MAIN SYMPTOMS:** Impaired memory, dizziness, tinnitus, heart palpitations, absent-mindedness, low back and knee soreness and limpness, heat in the palms of the hands and soles of the feet, afternoon tidal heat, night sweats, vexation, insomnia, a red tongue with scanty fur, and a fine, rapid pulse

**TREATMENT PRINCIPLES:** Enrich the kidneys, nourish the heart, and promote the interaction between the heart and kidneys

**FORMULA & MEDICINALS:** If kidney yin vacuity is predominant, use *Liu Wei Di Huang Wan Jia Wei* (Six Flavors Rehmannia Pills with Added Flavors)

Cooked Radix Rehmanniae (*Shu Di*), 12g, Radix Dioscoreae Oppositae (*Shan Yao*), 10g, Fructus Corni Officinalis (*Shan Zhu Yu*), 10g, Sclerotium Poriae Cocos (*Fu Ling*), 10g, Rhizoma Alismatis (*Ze Xie*), 6-10g, Cortex Radicis Moutan (*Dan Pi*), 10g, Radix Panacis Ginseng (*Ren Shen*), 6-10g (decocted first), Radix Polygalae Tenuifoliae (*Yuan Zhi*), 6-10g, Fructus Alpiniae Oxyphyllae (*Yi Zhi Ren*), 15g, Plastrum Testudinis (*Gui Ban*), 15g (decocted first)

If heart yang effulgence is predominant, use *Zhen Zhong Dan Jia Jian* (Pillow Elixir with Additions & Subtractions)

Calcined Plastrum Testudinis (*Gui Ban*), 15g (decocted first), uncooked Concha Ostreae (*Mu Li*), 15g (decocted first), Radix Polygalae Tenuifoliae (*Yuan Zhi*), 10g, Rhizoma Acori Graminei (*Shi Chang Pu*), 10g, uncooked Radix Rehmanniae (*Sheng Di*), 12g, Sclerotium Pararadicis Poriae Cocos (*Fu Shen*), 12g, Folium Bambusae (*Zhu Ye*), 10g

Decoct in water and administer orally in two divided doses, morning and evening, one *ji* per day.

**ACUPUNCTURE:** *Si Shen Cong* (M-HN-1), *Yin Xi* (Ht 6), *Xin Shu* (Bl 15), *Shen Shu* (Bl 23), *Zhao Hai* (Ki 6), *San Yin Jiao* (Sp 6). Use even supplementing-even draining technique.

## 4. PHLEGM QI DEPRESSION & BINDING PATTERN

**MAIN SYMPTOMS:** Impaired memory, somnolence, dizziness or vertigo, chest oppression, nausea, reduced food intake, profuse phlegm, the sound of phlegm in the throat, spitting or hacking of phlegm, plum pit qi, slimy, white tongue fur, and a bowstring, slippery pulse

TREATMENT PRINCIPLES: Transform phlegm and quiet the spirit, rectify the qi and resolve depression

FORMULA & MEDICINALS: Wen Dan Tang Jia Jian (Warm the Gallbladder Decoction with Additions & Subtractions)

Lime-processed Rhizoma Pinelliae Ternatae (Ban Xia), 10g, Caulis Bambusae In Taeniis (Zhu Ru), 10g, Fructus Immatrurus Citri Aurantii (Zhi Shi), 6-10g, Pericarpium Citri Reticulatae (Chen Pi), 6-10g, Rhizoma Atractylodis Macrocephalae (Bai Zhu), 10g, Sclerotium Poriae Cocos (Fu Ling), 10g, bile-processed Rhizoma Arisaematis (Dan Nan Xing), 6g, Rhizoma Acori Graminei (Shi Chang Pu), 6g, mix-fried Radix Glycyrrhizae (Gan Cao), 3-6g

ADDITIONS & SUBTRACTIONS: If phlegm depression has transformed into heat with a dry mouth and throat, yellow phlegm, a red facial complexion, a red tongue with slimy, yellow fur, and a slippery, rapid pulse, add Rhizoma Coptidis Chinensis (Huang Lian) and Radix Scutellariae Baicalensis (Huang Qin).

ACUPUNCTURE: Shen Men (Ht 7), Feng Long (St 40), Zu San Li (St 36), He Gu (LI 4). Use draining technique.

## 5. BLOOD STASIS INTERNALLY OBSTRUCTING PATTERN

MAIN SYMPTOMS: Sudden onset of impaired memory which then endures, a dry mouth with a desire for fluids but no desire to swallow, chest oppression, abdominal fullness and pain which is exacerbated by pressure, black stools, a dark, purplish tongue with possible static spots or macules, possible tortuous and engorged sublingual veins, and a bowstring, choppy pulse

TREATMENT PRINCIPLES: Quicken the blood and transform stasis, open the portals and fortify the memory

FORMULA & MEDICINALS: Xue Fu Zhu Yu Tang Jia Jian (Blood Mansion Dispel Stasis Decoction with Additions & Subtractions)

Semen Pruni Persicae (Tao Ren), 10g, Flos Carthami Tinctorii (Hong Hua), 10g (steeped afterwards), Radix Angelicae Sinensis (Dang Gui), 10g, uncooked Radix

Rehmanniae (Sheng Di), 12g, Radix Ligustici Wallichii (Chuan Xiong), 6g (added later), Radix Rubrus Paeoniae Lactiflorae (Chi Shao), 10g, Fructus Citri Aurantii (Zhi Ke), 6-10g, Tuber Curcumae (Yu Jin), 6g, Radix Polygalae Tenuifoliae (Yuan Zhi), 6-10g, Rhizoma Acori Graminei (Shi Chang Pu), 6g

Decoct in water and administer orally in two divided doses, morning and evening, one ji per day.

ACUPUNCTURE: Shao Hai (Ht 3), Si Shen Cong (M-HN-1), Xue Hai (Sp 10), He Gu (LI 4), San Yin Jiao (Sp 6). Use draining technique.

CLINICAL TIPS: When this complaint is due to heart-spleen dual vacuity, it typically responds well to Chinese medicinal treatment. This is the most frequently seen pattern in Western females who complain of impaired memory associated with either the premenstruum, postpartum, or perimenopause.

REPRESENTATIVE CASE HISTORIES:

## ❖ CASE 1[2] ❖

The patient was a 38 year old female peasant farmer who first entered the hospital on Apr. 9, 1981. Two years before, the patient had been bedridden at home due to disease. Then she had suffered worry and had overworked. In the last half year, she felt bodily exhausted and lacked strength. In addition, her memory power had markedly decreased, and sometimes she had insomnia. She went to her local hospital several times for treatment, but her condition only got worse. When seen by the authors of this case, the woman's facial complexion was lusterless, she had heart palpitations, scanty sleep, profuse dreams, lassitude of the spirit, exhaustion, torpid intake, shortness of breath, abdominal distention, loose stools, a pale tongue with thin, white fur, and a fine, weak, forceless pulse.

Based on the above signs and symptoms, the patient's pattern was categorized as heart-spleen dual vacuity, and the treatment principles were to supplement and boost the heart and spleen. The formula prescribed was Gui Pi Tang (Restore the Spleen Decoction): Radix Codonopsitis Pilosulae (Dang Shen), 15g, Radix Astragali Membranacei (Huang Qi), 15g, Rhizoma Atractylodis Macrocephalae (Bai Zhu), 10g, Radix Angelicae Sinensis (Dang Gui), 10g, Sclerotium Poriae Cocos (Fu Ling), 10g, stir-fried Semen Zizyphi Spinosae (Suan Zao Ren), 20g, Arillus Euphoriae Longanae (Long Yan Rou), 15g, mix-fried Radix Glycyrrhizae (Gan Cao), 5g, Radix Polygalae Tenuifoliae

(*Yuan Zhi*), 10g, and Fructus Zizyphi Jujubae (*Da Zao*), 4 pieces.

After taking 20 *ji* of the above formula, the woman's appetite increased, her mental-emotional state improved, and her memory power returned somewhat. Therefore, 18 grams of Os Draconis (*Long Gu*) and 10 grams of Rhizoma Acori Graminei (*Shi Chang Pu*) were added to the original formula in order to quiet the spirit and boost the intelligence. After taking 30 more *ji*, the woman's memory power returned to normal as well as her essence spirit. She was judged cured and discharged from the hospital. At that time, she was recommended to take one pill of *Gui Pi Wan* (Restore the Spleen Pills) each morning and night in order to secure the treatment effect. On follow-up after two years, there had been no recurrence.

### ❖ CASE 2[3] ❖

The patient was a 28 year old female who first entered the hospital on Nov. 8, 1976. This woman's nature was introverted and she did not tend to speak appropriately. Her personality was explosive and agitated. Two years after marrying she had not yet given birth to a child, and her husband and mother-in-law's refusal to adopt a child cut her to her heart. She became entangled in disputes with her mother-in-law and husband and this resulted in her heart becoming vacuous and devitalized. She had little thought for food or drink and could not sleep peacefully at night. She was so distraught that her hair began to fall and her speech became slow and retarded. At the same time, the power of her memory markedly decreased. She went to a hospital where she was diagnosed as suffering from neurasthenia, for which she was given multivitamins and Valium for half a year without much result. When she came to see the authors of this case, her facial complexion was dark and stagnant, her affect was flat, her tongue was purple and dark with static spots and slimy, white fur, and her pulse was bowstring and slippery.

Based on the above signs and symptoms, the patient's pattern was categorized as phlegm and stasis blocking and obstructing the orifices and network vessels.[4] Therefore, the treatment principles were to wash away phlegm and transform stasis, for which *Shou Xing Wan Jia Jian* (Long-life Star Pills with Additions & Subtractions) was prescribed: Radix Polygalae Tenuifoliae (*Yuan Zhi*), 7g, Radix Rubrus Panacis Ginseng (*Hong Shen*), 6g, Radix Astragali Membranacei (*Huang Qi*), 15g, Rhizoma Atractylodis Macrocephalae (*Bai Zhu*), 12g, Radix Glycyrrhizae (*Gan Cao*), 6g, Radix Angelicae Sinensis (*Dang Gui*), 12g, uncooked Radix Rehmanniae (*Sheng Di*), 10g, Radix Albus Paeoniae Lactiflorae (*Bai Shao*), 12g, Sclerotium Poriae Cocos (*Fu Ling*), 15g, Pericarpium Citri Reticulatae (*Chen Pi*), 10g, Cortex Cinnamomi Cassiae (*Rou Gui*), 3g, bile-processed Rhizoma Arisaematis (*Dan Nan Xing*), 10g, Succinum (*Hu Po*), 6g, Cinnabar (*Zhu Sha*), 3g, uncooked Rhizoma Zingiberis (*Sheng Jiang*), 5g, Fructus Schisandrae Chinensis (*Wu Wei Zi*), 10g, and a certain amount of pig's heart blood.

After taking 10 *ji* of the above formula, the woman's eating and drinking increased. Her red tongue with static spots had disappeared, the fur was now slimy and white, and the pulse was simply slippery. Because phlegm and stasis were gradually being eliminated, the following formula was prescribed: Radix Polygalae Tenuifoliae (*Yuan Zhi*), 7g, Rhizoma Arisaematis (*Nan Xing*), 10g, Sclerotium Poriae Cocos (*Fu Ling*), 12g, Rhizoma Atractylodis Macrocephalae (*Bai Zhu*), 12g, Pericarpium Citri Reticulatae (*Chen Pi*), 10g, Radix Rubrus Panacis Ginseng (*Hong Shen*), 6g, Radix Astragali Membranacei (*Huang Qi*), 15g, Radix Angelicae Sinensis (*Dang Gui*), 12g, Radix Albus Paeoniae Lactiflorae (*Bai Shao*), 12g, Cortex Cinnamomi Cassiae (*Rou Gui*), 3g, uncooked Rhizoma Zingiberis (*Sheng Jiang*), 5g, Cinnabar (*Zhu Sha*), 3g, Os Draconis (*Long Gu*), 18g, and calcined Concha Ostreae (*Mu Li*), 18g.

After taking these medicinals, the patient's appetite increased yet again as did the power of her memory. She was able to go to sleep at night and had few dreams. The phlegm was eliminated and the stasis was dispersed. However, because the spleen is the source of phlegm engenderment, she was prescribed the following medicinals to fortify the spleen and eliminate phlegm, rectify the qi and resolve depression: Radix Rubrus Panacis Ginseng (*Hong Shen*), 6g, Rhizoma Atractylodis Macrocephalae (*Bai Zhu*), 15g, Sclerotium Poriae Cocos (*Fu Ling*), 12g, mix-fried Radix Glycyrrhizae (*Gan Cao*), 6g, Pericarpium Citri Reticulatae (*Chen Pi*), 12g, Rhizoma Pinelliae Ternatae (*Ban Xia*), 9g, Fructus Citri Sacrodactylis (*Fo Shou*), 10g, and Tuber Curcumae (*Yu Jin*), 10g. After taking 20 *ji* of these medicinals, her susceptibility to forgetfulness disappeared, the patient was considered cured, and she was discharged from the hospital.

### ❖ CASE 3[5] ❖

The patient was a 41 year old male worker who first entered the hospital on Mar. 5, 1982. His major complaints were impaired memory, feeble-mindedness, slippery essence, and impotence for the previous eight years. He had been treated by a number of other doctors with only very slight results. His affect was dull and he tended to be melancholy. His facial complexion was blackish, he was exhausted, he had seminal emission both with and without dreams. His low back was sore and his lower legs were limp. The patient's tongue was pale and tender and had only scanty fur. His pulse was deep, fine, and forceless.

Based on these signs and symptoms and the fact that the man had had seminal emission for such a long time, his pattern was categorized as kidney essence debility and vacuity. Therefore, the treatment principles were to boost the essence and fill the marrow and the man was prescribed *He Che Da Zao Wan Jia Jian* (Placenta Great Construction Pills with Additions & Subtractions): Placenta Hominis (*Zi He Che*), 12g, cooked Radix Rehmanniae (*Shu Di*), 12g, Radix Dioscoreae Oppositae (*Shan Yao*), 12g, Fructus Corni Officinalis (*Shan Zhu Yu*), 10g, Cortex Eucommiae Ulmoidis (*Du Zhong*), 10g, Fructus Lycii Chinensis (*Gou Qi Zi*), 10g, Cortex Phellodendri (*Huang Bai*), 10g, Tuber Asparagi Cochinensis (*Tian Men Dong*), 10g, Semen Astragali Complanati (*Sha Ji Li*), 10g, calcined Os Draconis (*Long Gu*), 12g, calcined Concha Ostreae (*Mu Li*), 12g, Fructus Schisandrae Chinensis (*Wu Wei Zi*), 5g, Semen Euryalis Ferocis (*Qian Shi*), 12g, Radix Polygalae Tenuifoliae (*Yuan Zhi*), 9g, and Rhizoma Acori Graminei (*Shi Chang Pu*), 9g.

After taking 40 *ji* of the above formula, all the patient's symptoms were markedly decreased. However, his seminal emission had not completely stopped. The authors of this case reasoned that, because his essence pathway was already disinhibited, it would be difficult to secure the essence using decocted medicinals. Therefore, he was given some pills made from Sclerotium Poriae Cocos (*Fu Ling*) and yellow wax (*Huang La*) told to take one each evening to restrain his yin. After taking these pills for one month, his seminal emission stopped. At that point, the original formula was made into pills and he was treated for one more month in order to secure the treatment effect.

## ENDNOTES:

[1] Liu Yi-ren, *The Heart Transmission of Medicine*, trans. by Yang Shou-zhong, Blue Poppy Press, Boulder, CO, 1997, p. 138

[2] Li & Liu, *op. cit.*, p. 612-613

[3] *Ibid.*, p. 616-617

[4] Although the authors of this case do not say so, there was also qi and blood vacuity based on the ingredients in the formula prescribed.

[5] Li & Liu, *op. cit.*, p. 618-619

# PROFUSE DREAMS

Within Chinese medicine, profuse dreams means excessive dreaming which prevents the sleep from being restful. In many cases, there are not just too many dreams, but the dreams themselves are violent, scary, or upsetting. However, violent, scary dreams are also dealt with specifically under the next disease category, oppressive ghost dreams. The lack of restful sleep this condition creates at night results in tiredness and fatigue during the day. The Chinese term for this condition is *duo meng*.

In contemporary Western psychiatry, a persisting pattern of disturbing dreams resulting in arousal from restful sleep is regarded as a sleep disorder. As conceptualized by Western psychiatry, sleep terrors bear phenomenological resemblance to the Chinese medicine category of profuse dreams. Night terrors and nightmares are two kinds of dream experiences that are viewed as pathological because of frequently associated fatigue and disruption in psychological or occupational functioning.

## NOSOLOGY:

Symptoms of disrupted sleep due to awakening caused by frightening dreams are broadly categorized into two primary sleep disorders: sleep terrors and nightmares. These conditions are distinguished by stage of sleep at onset and associated EEG changes. Night terrors typically occur during the 3rd and 4th stages of sleep (*i.e.*, non rapid eye movement sleep), and nightmares occur during rapid eye movement (REM) sleep. Sleep terrors occur during the first half of an individual's normal sleep cycle, are associated with unconscious automatic movements, heavy perspiration, and elevated heart and respiration rates. They are more common in children, and typically there is no memory of the event the following morning. Sleep terrors are associated with an increased probability of psychiatric illness, especially anxiety disorders.

## EPIDEMIOLOGY:

Little is known about the prevalence of sleep terrors or nightmares.

## DIFFERENTIAL DIAGNOSIS:

Anxious or psychotic patients commonly report disturbing dreams causing arousal or partial awakening. However the intensity and frequency of such dreams is usually related to severity of waking psycho-pathology. Therefore, in contrast to night terrors, a persisting pattern of disturbing dreams and disrupted sleep is viewed as an indicator of underlying psychiatric illness. The differential diagnosis of persisting disturbing dreams in the first half of one's sleep cycle includes narcolepsy and epilepsy. The vivid sleep-onset visual hallucinations of narcolepsy may be mistakenly diagnosed as sleep terrors. Certain seizure disorders are also associated with visual disturbances that are likely to occur during the early stages of

| DIFFERENTIAL DIAGNOSIS | |
| --- | --- |
| 1. MEDICAL DISORDERS | 2. PSYCHIATRIC DISORDERS |
| A. NARCOLEPSY<br>B. EPILEPSY<br>C. SEIZURE DISORDERS | A. ANXIETY DISORDERS<br>B. SCHIZOPHRENIA AND OTHER PSYCHOTIC DISORDERS<br>C. POST-TRAUMATIC STRESS DISORDER (PTSD) |

sleep. Patients who suffer from post-traumatic stress disorder (PTSD) often experience recurring nightmares.

## WESTERN MEDICAL TREATMENT:

There is no clearly defined treatment for sleep terrors or nightmares, but tranquilizers, including benzodiazepines, are sometimes effective in suppressing them. Psychotherapy addressing themes of recurring nightmares sometimes results in reduced frequency of disturbing dreams. Improved sleep hygiene may not significantly improve this condition.

## INDICATIONS FOR REFERRAL TO WESTERN MEDICAL SERVICES:

If there is evidence of an underlying seizure disorder or severe psychiatric disorder, including schizophrenia, urgent medical referral is indicated to rule out and treat these etiologies. Patients who experience unresolving night terrors following an appropriate course of Chinese medical treatment or who have other significant daytime symptoms that might reflect an associated psychiatric or neurological disorder should be referred to a psychiatrist or neurologist for continued evaluation including EEG and sleep polysomnography to rule out epilepsy, narcolepsy, and other primary neurologic disorders.

## CHINESE DISEASE CAUSES & MECHANISMS:

In Chinese medicine, healthy sleep should be sound and restful and not disturbed by either too many or too frightening dreams. Normal dreaming which does not disturb sleep shows that the spirit is relatively quiet and calm. In general, the spirit is calm when it is A) nourished by sufficient qi and blood, and B) it is free from harassment by some evil qi.

Qi and blood vacuity may lead to the heart being deprived of proper nourishment. In that case, the spirit may become disquieted and thus unable to remain still and calm during sleep at night. The *Jin Gui Yao Lue* (*Essentials from the Golden Cabinet*) says:

> All types of scanty qi and blood are ascribed [or home] to the heart. If the heart becomes vacuous, people have lots of fears. When they close their eyes and desire to sleep, dreams move and scatter the essence spirit. Thus the ethereal and corporeal souls move frenetically.

The main viscera involved in the construction and nourishment of the spirit are the heart and the spleen. In this case, we speak of heart qi and blood and spleen qi. However, the heart qi and blood are themselves rooted in the spleen, since the spleen is the latter heaven source of qi and blood engenderment and transformation. It is the spleen which upbears the clear of the clear to become the heart qi and the clear of the turbid to become the heart blood. Therefore, anything which causes the spleen to be damaged may result in a qi and blood vacuity. The main causes of spleen qi vacuity are faulty diet, immaturity and aging, overtaxation, overthinking, worry and anxiety as specific types of thought, living in either a cold damp or damp hot environment, erroneous or overuse of cool and cold medicinals, including antibiotics, excessive blood loss, and too little physical exercise and activity. The main direct causes of heart qi and blood consumption and scattering are fear and fright.

The main evil qi which can harass the heart and make the spirit disquieted or restless are fire heat, phlegm, and blood stasis. Fire heat can either be vacuity heat due to yin vacuity, depressive heat, or yin fire. Yin may be or become vacuous and insufficient due to immaturity or aging, enduring disease, over-use of acrid, exterior-resolving, drying, or attacking and draining medicinals and drugs, prolonged over-taxation, enduring evil heat, and excessive sexual activity, including and especially masturbation. If yin becomes so vacuous as to lose control of yang, yang becomes hyperactive and counterflows upward, thus harassing the heart spirit.

Depressive heat is transformed primarily from liver depression qi stagnation. Unfulfilled desires may inhibit the liver's coursing and discharging. Hence the qi does not flow freely but becomes stagnant instead. If this stagnation endures or becomes aggravated, it may transform into heat or fire which likewise ascends to harass the heart spirit above. Anger, when it is expressed is overcoursing and overdischarging. It may damage the liver. If the liver is damaged, it will not do its duties. Its main duty is coursing and discharging. Therefore, the sequela of anger damaging the liver is liver depression, and this depression may easily transform into fire or evil heat. Liver depression may also be due to insufficient blood nourishing the liver. The liver, like all other organs and tissues in the body, can only do its duty when moistened and nourished by sufficient yin blood. In women, the blood collects in the uterus from midcycle to the onset of menstruation. If a woman's blood is not effulgent and replete, this gathering of blood in the uterus may leave the liver temporarily without sufficient nourishment, and hence may also cause or aggravate liver depression. Likewise, yin vacuity due to aging may also cause liver depression due to insufficient moistening and nourishing. Further, liver depression may be due to kidney yang vacuity failing to warm and steam the liver. Kidney yang vacuity is primarily due to either immaturity, aging, or excessive sex, but may be due to overuse of certain medicinals and drugs, such as corticosteroids, methamphetamines, and cocaine. And finally, liver depression may be caused or aggravated by any of the four material or substantial depressions. These are dampness, phlegm, food, and blood. If any of these four are engendered in the body, they may hinder and obstruct the free flow of qi. In that case, the qi becomes stagnant and may transform into depressive heat or fire.

Yin fire is a more complex scenario involving a combination of several factors. These include spleen vacuity, liver depression, blood and yin vacuity, damp heat, and upward stirring of ministerial fire. Upward stirring of ministerial fire may be due to any of the first four factors in the preceding sentence. However, it may also be due to excessive sex, overuse of the same types of medicinals and drugs mentioned above, and excessive psychoemotional stimulation. When ministerial fire stirs upward, it causes heat above while often leaving its lower source vacuous and cold below. This heat counterflows upward and harasses the heart spirit above. Yin fire as a disease mechanism involves several different viscera (the heart, spleen, and liver at the least) and a combination of three or more simple disease mechanisms.

Phlegm may be due to evil heat stewing the juices to congeal into phlegm. In most cases, when heat congeals phlegm, that evil heat is depressive heat or fire. However, phlegm may also be due to spleen vacuity failing to transport and transform water fluids. In that case, water fluids may transform into dampness. If dampness lingers and endures, it may further congeal into phlegm. Since it is the qi which moves fluids, qi stagnation may also cause or aggravate phlegm congelation. Foods which promote the engenderment of phlegm include sweet, fatty, and thick-flavored foods. Thick-flavored foods tend to be animal derivatives, such as dairy products, meats, and eggs as well as greasy, fatty vegetable foods, such as nuts. No matter how phlegm is produced within the body, it may block either the orifices of the heart or the upper clear orifices of the body, i.e., the sensory organs. When phlegm binds with either depressive qi or heat, it is all the more likely to ascend to block the orifices and confound and harass the spirit.

Blood stasis may be due to enduring qi stagnation. This is because the qi is the commander of the blood. If the qi moves, the blood moves. If the qi stops, the blood stops. However, blood stasis may be caused by any of the other three material depressions (dampness, food, and/or phlegm), since any of these may hinder and obstruct the free flow of qi and blood. Blood stasis may also be due to traumatic injury severing the channels and vessels. It is the channels and vessels which promote and canalize the flow of the blood. If the vessels are severed, the blood cannot flow. Such injury to the channels and vessels may include surgery. In addition, blood stasis may be due to either blood vacuity not nourishing the vessels or yang qi vacuity not stirring and pushing the blood. If the blood becomes static internally, this may impede the flow of blood to the heart. Thus the spirit becomes deprived of sufficient construction and nourishment, resulting in heart spirit disquietude. It is also possible for static blood to block the orifices of the heart, thus confounding the heart spirit. To make matters worse, static blood impedes the engenderment of new or fresh blood and leads to blood vacuity. Hence there are several ways that blood stasis internally may result in disquietude of the spirit.

Below are the common patterns associated with profuse dreams. As in all Chinese medical clinical manuals and textbooks, they are presented as simple, discrete patterns. In real-life, the situation is not so easy, and most Western patients with chronic, enduring conditions have a mixed vacuity-repletion pattern made up of several simpler patterns. Nevertheless, the patterns below are the building blocks of such real-life, complicated patterns. When presented with such complicated patterns, one identifies the main patterns and then modifies the treatment under that pattern with additions and subtractions taken from the other, complicating patterns and disease mechanisms.

TREATMENT BASED ON PATTERN DISCRIMINATION:

1. HEART-SPLEEN DUAL VACUITY PATTERN

MAIN SYMPTOMS: Profuse dreams, insomnia, impaired memory[1], reduced food intake, a somber white facial complexion, abdominal distention, loose stools, shortness of breath, disinclination to talk, fatigue, lack of strength, a pale tongue, and a soggy, fine pulse

TREATMENT PRINCIPLES: Fortify the spleen and boost the qi, nourish the heart and supplement the blood

FORMULA & MEDICINALS: Gui Pi Tang Jia Jian (Restore the Spleen Decoction with Additions & Subtractions)

Radix Astragali Membranacei (Huang Qi), 15g, Radix Codonopsitis Pilosulae (Dang Shen), 10g, Rhizoma Atractylodis Macrocephalae (Bai Zhu), 10g, Sclerotium Pararadicis Poriae Cocos (Fu Shen), 12g, Arillus Euphoriac Longanae (Long Yan Rou), 15g, stir-fried Semen Zizyphi Spinosae (Suan Zao Ren), 12g, Radix Auklandiae Lappae (Mu Xiang), 6g (added later), Radix Angelicae Sinensis (Dang Gui), 10g, Radix Polygalae Tenuifoliae (Yuan Zhi), 10g, Rhizoma Acori Graminei (Shi Chang Pu), 6g, Succinum (Hu Po), 1g (powdered and swallowed with the decocted liquid), calcined Dens Draconis (Long Chi), 12g (decocted first), mix-fried Radix Glycyrrhizae (Gan Cao), 6g

If heart blood and spleen qi vacuity are complicated by phlegm heat, use Yi Qi An Shen Tang (Boost the Qi & Quiet the Spirit Decoction) instead:

Radix Angelicae Sinensis (Dang Gui), 10g, Sclerotium Pararadicis Poriae Cocos (Fu Shen), 12g, uncooked Radix Rehmanniae (Sheng Di), 12g, Tuber Ophiopogonis Japonici (Mai Dong), 12g, Semen Zizyphi Spinosae (Suan Zao Ren), 12-15g, Radix Polygalae Tenuifoliae (Yuan Zhi), 6-10g, Radix Panacis Ginseng (Ren Shen), 3-6g (decocted first), Radix Astragali Membranacei (Huang Qi), 15-18g, bile-processed Rhizoma Arisaematis (Dan Nan Xing), 3-6g, Folium Bambusae (Zhu Ye), 10g, Rhizoma Coptidis Chinensis (Huang Lian), 3-6g (added later), Radix Glycyrrhizae (Gan Cao), 3-6g

Decoct in water and administer orally in two divided doses, morning and evening, one ji per day.

ACUPUNCTURE: Shen Men (Ht 7), Xin Shu (Bl 15), Zu San Li (St 36), San Yin Jiao (Sp 6), Yin Bai (Sp 1). Use supplementing technique.

## 2. NONINTERACTION BETWEEN THE HEART & KIDNEYS PATTERN[2]

MAIN SYMPTOMS: Profuse dreams, insomnia, heart vexation, heart palpitations, low back and knee soreness and limpness, afternoon tidal heat, night sweats, seminal emission, a red tongue with scanty or no fur, and a fine, rapid pulse

TREATMENT PRINCIPLES: Nourish yin and downbear fire, promote the interaction between the heart and kidneys

FORMULA & MEDICINALS: Huang Lian E Jiao Tang Jia Jian (Coptis & Donkey Skin Glue Decoction with Additions & Subtractions)

Rhizoma Coptidis Chinensis (Huang Lian), 3-6g (added later), Radix Scutellariae Baicalensis (Huang Qin), 10g, uncooked Radix Albus Paeoniae Lactiflorae (Bai Shao), 10g, Gelatinum Corii Asini (E Jiao), 6g (dissolved at the end), Radix Polygalae Tenuifoliae (Yuan Zhi), 10g, Sclerotium Pararadicis Poriae Cocos (Fu Shen), 12g, Tuber Asparagi Cochinensis (Tian Men Dong), 12g, egg yolk (Ji Zi Huang), 1 piece (added after and stirred or whipped into the final hot decoction)

Decoct in water and administer orally in two divided doses, morning and evening, one ji per day.

ACUPUNCTURE: Yin Xi (Ht 6), Jie Xi (St 41), Tai Xi (Ki 3), Yong Quan (Ki 1). Use even supplementing-even draining technique, and bathe the feet in warm water and then massage Yong Quan strongly just before sleep.

## 3. HEART-GALLBLADDER QI VACUITY PATTERN[3]

MAIN SYMPTOMS: Profuse dreams, nightmares with occasional waking in a fright, impaired memory, timidity, irritability, susceptibility to fright, heart palpitations, possible profuse phlegm, possible plum pit qi, a pale tongue, and a fine, bowstring[4], weak or slippery pulse

TREATMENT PRINCIPLES: Supplement the qi and settle fright, quiet the spirit to stabilize the mind

FORMULA & MEDICINALS: Shi Wei Wen Dan Tang Jia Jian (Ten Flavors Warm the Gallbladder Decoction with Additions & Subtractions)

Lime-processed Rhizoma Pinelliae Ternatae (Ban Xia), 10g, Fructus Immaturus Citri Aurantii (Zhi Shi), 6g, Sclerotium Pararadicis Poriae Cocos (Fu Shen), 12g, stir-fried Semen Zizyphi Spinosae (Suan Zao Ren), 12g, Radix Polygalae Tenuifoliae (Yuan Zhi), 10g, Fructus Schizandrae Chinensis (Wu Wei Zi), 10g, cooked Radix Rehmanniae (Shu Di), 12g, Radix Codonopsitis Pilosulae (Dang Shen), 10g, mix-fried Radix Glycyrrhizae (Gan

*Cao*), 6g, calcined Dens Draconis (*Long Chi*), 12g (decocted first), Magnetitum (*Ci Shi*), 12g (decocted first)

Decoct in water and administer orally in two divided doses, morning and evening, one *ji* per day.

**ADDITIONS & SUBTRACTIONS:** For more obvious liver depression, add Radix Bupleuri (*Chai Hu*) and Fructus Meliae Toosendan (*Chuan Lian Zi*). For more obvious phlegm, add Rhizoma Acori Graminei (*Shi Chang Pu*) and Caulis Bambusae In Taeniis (*Zhu Ru*). If there is depressive heat, add Rhizoma Coptidis Chinensis (*Huang Lian*) and Fructus Gardeniae Jasminoidis (*Zhi Zi*).

**ACUPUNCTURE & MOXIBUSTION:** *Po Hu* (Bl 42), *Shen Men* (Ht 7), *Da Ling* (Per 7), *Shen Que* (CV 8), *San Yin Jiao* (Sp 6). Use even supplementing-even draining technique and moxa *Shen Que*.

### 4. PHLEGM FIRE HARASSING ABOVE PATTERN

**MAIN SYMPTOMS:** Profuse dreams, dizziness, heart palpitations, rashness and impetuosity, irritability or even irascibility, chest oppression, profuse phlegm, a red tongue with slimy, yellow fur, and a slippery, rapid, commonly bowstring pulse

**TREATMENT PRINCIPLES:** Clear heat and transform phlegm

**FORMULA & MEDICINALS:** *Huang Lian Wen Dan Tang Jia Jian* (Coptis Warm the Gallbladder Decoction with Additions & Subtractions)

Rhizoma Coptidis Chinensis (*Huang Lian*), 3-6g (added later), Radix Scutellariae Baicalensis (*Huang Qin*), 6g, lime-processed Rhizoma Pinelliae Ternatae (*Ban Xia*), 10g, Caulis Bambusae In Taeniis (*Zhu Ru*), 6g, Fructus Immaturus Citri Aurantii (*Zhi Shi*), 6g, Pericarpium Citri Reticulatae (*Chen Pi*), 6-10g, Sclerotium Pararadicis Poriae Cocos (*Fu Shen*), 12g, bile-processed Rhizoma Arisaematis (*Dan Nan Xing*), 6-10g, Cortex Albizziae Julibrissinis (*He Huan Pi*), 10g, Radix Polygalae Tenuifoliae (*Yuan Zhi*), 10g, mix-fried Radix Glycyrrhizae (*Gan Cao*), 3-6g

Decoct in water and administer orally in two divided doses, morning and evening, one *ji* per day.

### 5. LIVER FIRE HARASSING INTERNALLY

Main symptoms: Profuse dreams, nightmares, dizziness, irascibility, headache, red eyes, rib-side pain, a bitter taste in the mouth, possible sudden deafness or tinnitus, a red tongue with yellow fur, and a bowstring, rapid pulse

**TREATMENT PRINCIPLES:** Clear the liver and drain fire

**FORMULA & MEDICINALS:** *Long Dan Xie Gan Tang Jia Jian* (Gentiana Drain the Liver Decoction with Additions & Subtractions)

Radix Gentianae Scabrae (*Long Dan Cao*), 10g, Radix Scutellariae Baicalensis (*Huang Qin*), 10g, stir-fried Fructus Gardeniae Jasminoidis (*Zhi Zi*), 10g, Radix Bupleuri (*Chai Hu*), 10g, Radix Albus Paeoniae Lactiflorae (*Bai Shao*), 10g, Extremitas Radicis Angelicae Sinensis (*Dang Gui Wei*), 6-10g, uncooked Radix Rehmanniae (*Sheng Di*), 12g, Radix Ligustici Wallichii (*Chuan Xiong*), 10g (added later), uncooked Radix Glycyrrhizae (*Gan Cao*), 3-6g

Decoct in water and administer orally in two divided doses, morning and evening, one *ji* per day.

**ACUPUNCTURE:** *Xing Jian* (Liv 2), *Feng Chi* (GB 20), *Shen Men* (Ht 7), *Nei Guan* (Per 6), *Zu Qiao Yin* (GB 44). Using draining technique with strong stimulation.

**CLINICAL TIPS:** Most Western patients will not immediately volunteer that they are having profuse dreams. This is something Chinese patients may be used to being asked about but not something Western patients are typically asked. If a Western patient says that they are not sleeping so well, the practitioner must then take care to find out whether the patient cannot go to sleep, cannot stay asleep, or is dreaming so vividly and so much that they do not feel well rested when they get up. If one questions Western patients carefully, one will find that many Western patients experience this symptom. However, it is rarely, if ever, the major complaint. Therefore, the authors have not been able to find any published Chinese research or case histories for this disease category.

### REPRESENTATIVE CASE HISTORIES:

#### ❖ CASE 1[5] ❖

The patient was a 33 year old female who was first examined on Oct. 28, 1984. One year previous, after gradually recovering from a disease, the patient had become constantly sad and was not able to sleep well. She had profuse dreams, her mind was flustered and confused, and her memory power was decreased. A half year later, she commonly dreamed of having sexual intercourse, after which she would awake damp with sweat. In addition, she had heart palpitations, her appetite was habitually poor, and she gradually became emaciated. She had already been treated with both Chinese and Western medicine based on diagnoses of neurasthenia and hysteria. She had been given several different sedatives and sleep medications as well as Chinese medicinals to nourish her heart and quiet her spirit, all to no effect. In the last two months, her dreams had become so abnormal that she was not able to go to sleep at night. During the daytime, she suffered from one-sided headaches. Gradually the patient's condition got worse and worse and she came to see Dr. Huang. At the time of his examination, she had dizziness, heart palpitations, heart fright, generalized loss of strength, torpid intake, low back soreness, and limp feet. Her menses were early and were scanty in amount. Her facial complexion was dark and yellowish green. She was emotionally tense, her tongue was red with thin, yellow fur, and her pulse was bowstring, fine, and rapid.

Based on the above signs and symptoms, the patient's pattern was categorized as liver qi depression and binding, kidney yin depletion and vacuity, and ministerial fire frenetically stirring. The treatment principles were to course the liver and resolve depression, enrich yin and downbear fire. The formula consisted of: Cortex Phellodendri (*Huang Bai*), 30g, uncooked Radix Rehmanniae (*Sheng Di*), 30g, Radix Scrophulariae Ningpoensis (*Xuan Shen*), 24g, Rhizoma Alismatis (*Ze Xie*), 30g, Fructus Amomi (*Sha Ren*), 12g, Os Draconis (*Long Gu*), 30g, Concha Ostreae (*Mu Li*), 30g, Radix Albus Paeoniae Lactiflorae (*Bai Shao*), 12g, Semen Zizyphi Spinosae (*Suan Zao Ren*), 15g, Radix Bupleuri (*Chai Hu*), 12g, and Magnetitum (*Ci Shi*), 30g. These medicinals were decocted in water and administered orally.

On Nov. 1, the patient was re-examined after having taken three *ji* of the above formula. She had still dreamt of intercourse one time, but the night sweats had disappeared and her migraine headaches, her palpitations, and emotional tenseness had remitted. In addition, her eating and drinking had increased. Therefore, the patient was prescribed: Cortex Phellodendri (*Huang Bai*), 30g, cooked Radix Rehmanniae (*Sheng Di*), 24g, Radix Scrophulariae Ningpoensis (*Xuan Shen*), 18g, Rhizoma Alismatis (*Ze Xie*), 30g, Os Draconis (*Long Gu*), 30g, Concha Ostreae (*Mu Li*), 30g, Radix Albus Paeoniae Lactiflorae (*Bai Shao*), 12g, Semen Zizyphi Spinosae (*Suan Zao Ren*), 15g, Radix Bupleuri (*Chai Hu*), 12g, and Magnetitum (*Ci Shi*), 30g. On Nov. 5, after taking four *ji* of these medicinals, the woman's sleep was completely quiet and her dreams of intercourse and heart palpitations had disappeared. However, she was still somewhat emotionally fatigued and she sometimes had

low back soreness. Therefore, seven *ji* of the original formula were prescribed and all her symptoms were cured. On follow-up after one year, there had been no recurrence.

## ❖ CASE 2[6] ❖

The patient was a 25 year old female who was first examined on Aug. 8, 1985. The patient had gotten married one year ago but did not have any wifely feelings for or friendly relationship with her husband. In March of 1985 she had an abortion, after which her sleep progressively became worse and worse. When she went to sleep, she had profuse dreams. The patient also had heart palpitations, easy fright, and occasional headaches. During menstruation, the woman had abdominal pain and breast distention and pain. For the last two weeks, after going to sleep, she would have dreams of sexual intercourse. These would awake her, after which she would have heart palpitations and great perspiration. She had already been examined at her local hospital and been diagnosed with neurasthenia and premenstrual tension (PMT). The patient had been prescribed diazepam and a multivitamin but with no effect. Instead, her condition got worse day by day. At the time she saw Dr. Huang, she had headache, heart palpitations, low back soreness, fatigue, and dreams of intercourse 2-3 times per week. Her affect was devitalized and her emotions were not soothed. Her body was weak, and her facial complexion was sallow yellow and greenish. Her tongue was red with slightly yellow fur, while her pulse was fine, rapid, and slightly bowstring.

Based on the above signs and symptoms, the patient's pattern was categorized as liver qi depression and binding, kidney yin depletion and detriment, and ministerial fire frenetically stirring. The treatment principles were to course the liver and resolve depression, enrich yin and downbear fire. The formula consisted of: Cortex Phellodendri (*Huang Bai*), 18g, uncooked Radix Rehmanniae (*Sheng Di*), 24g, Radix Scrophulariae Ningpoensis (*Xuan Shen*), 24g, Rhizoma Alismatis (*Ze Xie*), 30g, Fructus Amomi (*Sha Ren*), 10g, Os Draconis (*Long Gu*), 30g, Concha Ostreae (*Mu Li*), 30g, Radix Albus Paeoniae Lactiflorae (*Bai Shao*), 12g, Semen Zizyphi Spinosae (*Suan Zao Ren*), 15g, Radix Bupleuri (*Chai Hu*), 10g, and Magnetitum (*Ci Shi*), 30g. These medicinals were decocted in water and administered orally.

The patient was re-examined on Aug. 11. After taking three *ji* of the above medicinals, the dreams of intercourse and the night sweats had disappeared, her affect had markedly improved, and her heart palpitations, low back soreness, and fatigue had all decreased. Therefore, the amount of Phellodendron in the above formula was removed and Radix Dioscoreae Oppositae (*Shan Yao*) and Sclerotium Poriae Cocos (*Fu Ling*) were added. After taking another five *ji*, all the patient's symptoms gradually disappeared and her body returned to health. On follow-up after half a year, there had been no recurrence.

## ENDNOTES:

[1]Wiseman's current suggested term for *jian wang* is forgetfulness. However, we prefer his previous translation as "impaired memory." We do not believe that forgetfulness implies the range of memory impairments that this term covers within Chinese medicine. Nor does the English word forgetfulness imply a potentially treatable medical condition.

[2]This is a pattern of kidney yin (or, more rarely, kidney yang) vacuity below failing to restrain heart fire which is flaring upward.

[3]Although neither the name of this pattern nor the majority of its listed signs and symptoms reflect this fact, liver depression and phlegm complicate this pattern.

[4]Wiseman's current term choice for *xian mai* is a stringlike pulse. However, we prefer bowstring, since stringlike does not necessarily convey the tautness that the Chinese term does.

[5]Huang Yong-yuan, *op. cit.*, p. 114-115

[6]*Ibid.*, p. 115-116

# ❖ 12 ❖

# OPPRESSIVE GHOST DREAMS

Oppressive ghost dreams is Nigel Wiseman's translation of the Chinese *meng yan*. A more succinct and everyday English translation would be nightmares. These are sometimes referred to in Chinese as "malign dreams" and as "upsetting dreams."

In terms of Western psychiatry, the Chinese medical category of oppressive ghost dreams bears phenomenological resemblance to nightmares. However the correspondence is not exact. Nightmares occur in REM (rapid eye movement) sleep and, in contrast to night terrors, the patient recalls disturbing dream content. Although nightmares typically cause awakening, in contrast to night terrors, they are seldom associated with increased heart rate or rapid breathing and are generally experienced as less disturbing than sleep terrors. In Western medicine, sedative-hypnotics are used to suppress dreaming, thus permitting undisrupted sleep. Relaxation exercises before sleep are also often recommended. When there is a related primary psychiatric disorder, appropriate psychotherapy and medications may reduce the intensity or frequency of nightmares. A persisting pattern of arousal from sleep that is unresponsive to appropriate treatment using Chinese medicines or acupuncture warrants referral to a psychiatrist or neurologist to rule out possible underlying neurological disorders including epilepsy and narcolepsy. The reader is referred to Chapter 11, this Book, Profuse Dreams, for a more extensive review of the nosology, differential diagnosis, and treatment for nightmares and night terrors in contemporary Western psychiatry.

CHINESE DISEASE CAUSES & MECHANISMS:

The Chinese disease causes and mechanisms of nightmares are very similar to those of profuse dreams. Either the heart spirit is disquieted because of insufficient construction and nourishment or is harassed by evil qi, namely heat and/or phlegm. Insufficient nourishment of the heart may be due to visceral vacuity not engendering and transforming the qi and blood . The various visceral vacuities associated with nightmares include heart-liver blood vacuity and heart-gallbladder qi vacuity. Blood stasis may also result in blood vacuity since static blood hinders or impedes the engenderment of new or fresh blood.

TREATMENT BASED ON PATTERN DISCRIMINATION:

1. LIVER-GALLBLADDER DEPRESSIVE HEAT PATTERN

MAIN SYMPTOMS: Nightmares, irritability, a bitter taste in the mouth on arising, chest, breast, rib-side, and/or abdominal distention and pain, menstrual irregularity, PMS, or dysmenorrhea in females, possible headaches, red eyes, a dry mouth and throat, a red tongue with dry and/or yellow fur, and a bowstring, rapid pulse

TREATMENT PRINCIPLES: Course the liver and rectify the qi, clear heat and quiet the spirit

FORMULA & MEDICINALS: If there is simple liver-gallbladder repletion, use: *Long Dan Xie Gan Tang Jia Jian* (Gentiana Drain the Liver Decoction with Additions & Subtractions)

Radix Gentianae Scabrae (*Long Dan Cao*), 6g, Radix Scutellariae Baicalensis (*Huang Qin*), 10g, stir-fried Fructus Gardeniae Jasminoidis (*Zhi Zi*), 6-10g, Radix Bupleuri (*Chai Hu*), 6-10g, Radix Albus Paeoniae Lactiflorae (*Bai Shao*), 10-12g, Radix Angelicae Sinensis (*Dang Gui*), 10g, Concha Margaritiferae (*Zhen Zhu Mu*), 12g (decocted first), Succinum (*Hu Po*), 1g (powdered and swallowed with the decocted liquid), Radix Glycyrrhizae (*Gan Cao*), 3-6g

For liver depression transforming heat accompanied by spleen vacuity, use: *Dan Zhi Xiao Yao San Jia Jian* (Moutan & Gardenia Rambling Powder with Additions & Subtractions)

Radix Bupleuri (*Chai Hu*), 6-10g, Radix Angelicae Sinensis (*Dang Gui*), 10g, Radix Albus Paeoniae Lactiflorae (*Bai Shao*), 10-12g, Rhizoma Atractylodis Macrocephalae (*Bai Zhu*), 10g, Sclerotium Pararadicis Poriae Cocos (*Fu Shen*), 12g, stir-fried Fructus Gardeniae Jasminoidis (*Zhi Zi*), 6-10g, Cortex Radicis Moutan (*Dan Pi*), 10g, mix-fried Radix Glycyrrhizae (*Gan Cao*), 6g, Fructus Zizyphi Jujubae (*Da Zao*), 3-5 pieces, uncooked Concha Ostreae (*Mu Li*), 12g (decocted first), Succinum (*Hu Po*), 1g (powdered and swallowed with the decocted liquid)

Decoct in water and administer orally in two divided doses, morning and evening, one *ji* per day.

ACUPUNCTURE: *Xing Jian* (Liv 2), *Feng Chi* (GB 20), *Shen Men* (Ht 7), *Nei Guan* (Per 6), *Zu Qiao Yin* (GB 44). Use draining technique.

## 2. ASCENDANT LIVER YANG HYPERACTIVITY PATTERN

MAIN SYMPTOMS: Nightmares, insomnia, dizziness and vertigo, tinnitus, headache, red eyes, a distended, heavy head with a simultaneous feeling of weakness or lack of grounding in the lower limbs, irritability, irascibility, a red tongue with possibly dry or yellow fur, and a fine, bowstring, rapid pulse[1]

TREATMENT PRINCIPLES: Drain the liver, subdue yang, and quiet the spirit

FORMULA & MEDICINALS: *Tian Ma Gou Teng Yin He Suan Zao Ren Tang Jia Jian* (Gastrodia & Uncaria Drink plus Zizyphus Spinosa Decoction with Additions & Subtractions)

Rhizoma Gastrodiae Elatae (*Tian Ma*), 10g, Ramulus Uncariae Cum Uncis (*Gou Teng*), 10g (added later), Concha Haliotidis (*Shi Jue Ming*), 15g (decocted first), stir-fried Fructus Gardeniae Jasminoidis (*Zhi Zi*), 6-10g, Radix Scutellariae Baicalensis (*Huang Qin*), 6-10g, Radix Achyranthis Bidentatae (*Niu Xi*), 10g, Cortex Eucommiae Ulmoidis (*Du Zhong*), 10g, Ramulus Loranthi Seu Visci (*Sang Ji Sheng*), 12g, Caulis Polygoni Multiflori (*Ye Jiao Teng*), 12-15g, Sclerotium Pararadicis Poriae Cocos (*Fu Shen*), 12g, stir-fried Semen Zizyphi Spinosae (*Suan Zao Ren*), 12g, Radix Ligustici Wallichii (*Chuan Xiong*), 6-15g (added later)

## 3. PHLEGM FIRE HARASSING ABOVE PATTERN

MAIN SYMPTOMS: Nightmares, insomnia, irritability, vexation and agitation, heart palpitations, profuse phlegm, chest and abdominal oppression and fullness, possible nausea and vomiting, a red tongue with thick, slimy, yellow fur, and a slippery, bowstring, rapid pulse

TREATMENT PRINCIPLES: Clear heat and transform phlegm, open the orifices and quiet the spirit

FORMULA & MEDICINALS: If there is constipation, use: *Meng Shi Gun Tan Wan* (Mica Roll Phlegm Pills)

Radix Et Rhizoma Rhei (*Da Huang*), 3-6g (added later), Radix Scutellariae Baicalensis (*Huang Qin*), 10g, Rhizoma Coptidis Chinensis (*Huang Lian*), 3-6g (added later), calcined Lapis Micae Seu Chloriti (*Meng Shi*), 3g (decocted first), Lignum Aquilariae Agallochae (*Chen Xiang*), 1g (powdered and swallowed with the decocted liquid), lime-processed Rhizoma Pinelliae Ternatae (*Ban Xia*), 10g, Rhizoma Acori Graminei (*Shi Chang Pu*), 6g

If there is no constipation, use: *Huang Lian Wen Dan Tang Jia Wei* (Coptis Warm the Gallbladder Decoction with Added Flavors)

Rhizoma Coptidis Chinensis (*Huang Lian*), 3-6g (added later), Radix Scutellariae Baicalensis (*Huang Qin*), 10g, Rhizoma Acori Graminei (*Shi Chang Pu*), 6g, bile-processed Rhizoma Arisaematis (*Dan Nan Xing*), 3-6g, Rhizoma Pinelliae Ternatae (*Ban Xia*), 10g, Pericarpium Citri Reticulatae (*Chen Pi*), 6-10g, Sclerotium Pararadicis Poriae Cocos (*Fu Shen*), 12g, Fructus Immaturus Citri Aurantii (*Zhi Shi*), 6g, Caulis Bambusae In Taeniis (*Zhu Ru*), 6-10g, Radix Glycyrrhizae (*Gan Cao*), 3-6g, Fructus Zizyphi Jujubae (*Da Zao*), 3-5 pieces

Decoct in water and administer orally in two divided doses, morning and evening, one *ji* per day.

**ADDITIONS & SUBTRACTIONS:** Many Chinese practitioners use *Gun Tan Wan* for cases of phlegm fire harassing upward complicated by constipation and *Huang Lian Wen Dan Tang* for cases not complicated by constipation.

**ACUPUNCTURE:** *Feng Long* (St 40), *Nei Ting* (St 44), *Da Ling* (Per 7), *Dan Zhong* (CV 17), *Zhong Wan* (CV 12), *Li Dui* (St 45). Use draining technique.

## 4. HEART-LIVER BLOOD VACUITY PATTERN

**MAIN SYMPTOMS:** Frequent nightmares which occur soon after falling asleep, heart palpitations, tinnitus, impaired memory, a pale, white facial complexion, pale lips and nails, blurred vision, nightblindness, brittle nails, possible numbness of the extremities, scanty menstruation, delayed menstruation, or blocked menstruation, *i.e.*, amenorrhea, in females, a pale tongue with white, possibly dry fur, and a fine, weak, typically also bowstring pulse

**TREATMENT PRINCIPLES:** Supplement the heart and nourish the liver, supplement the blood and quiet the spirit

**FORMULA & MEDICINALS:** *Zhen Zhu Mu Wan Jia Jian* (Mother of Pearl Pills with Additions & Subtractions)

Concha Margaritiferae (*Zhen Zhu Mu*), 15g (decocted first), Radix Angelicae Sinensis (*Dang Gui*), 10g, stir-fried Semen Zizyphi Spinosae (*Suan Zao Ren*), 12-15g, Semen Biotae Orientalis (*Bai Zi Ren*), 12-15g, cooked Radix Rehmanniae (*Shu Di*), 12g, Sclerotium Pararadicis Poriae Cocos (*Fu Shen*), 12g, Caulis Polygoni Multiflori (*Ye Jiao Teng*), 12-15g, Lignum Aquilariae Agallochae (*Chen Xiang*), 1g (powdered and swallowed with the decocted liquid), Succinum (*Hu Po*), 1g (powdered and swallowed with the decocted liquid), calcined Dens Draconis (*Long Chi*), 15g (decocted first)

Decoct in water and administer orally in two divided doses, morning and evening, one *ji* per day.

**ACUPUNCTURE:** *Shen Men* (Ht 7), *Shang Qiu* (Sp 5), *Xin Shu* (Bl 15), *Ge Shu* (Bl 17), *Gan Shu* (Bl 18). Use supplementing technique.

## 5. HEART-GALLBLADDER QI VACUITY PATTERN

**MAIN SYMPTOMS:** Nightmares, waking from sleep in a fright, profuse dreams, insomnia, susceptibility to fright, timidity, paranoia, heart palpitations, chest oppression, possible profuse phlegm or plum pit qi, a pale and/or slightly dark colored tongue with white, possibly slimy fur, and a fine, bowstring, possibly slippery pulse

**TREATMENT PRINCIPLES:** Supplement the heart and gallbladder, boost the qi and quiet the spirit

**FORMULA & MEDICINALS:** *Da Ding Xin Tang Jia Jian* (Major Calm the Heart Decoction with Additions & Subtractions)

Radix Panacis Ginseng (*Ren Shen*), 5g (decocted first), Sclerotium Poriae Cocos (*Fu Ling*), 10g, Sclerotium Pararadicis Poriae Cocos (*Fu Shen*), 10-12g, Radix Polygalae Tenuifoliae (*Yuan Zhi*), 610g, uncooked Os Draconis (*Long Gu*), 15g (decocted first), Cortex Cinnamomi Cassiae (*Rou Gui*), 3g (added later), dry Rhizoma Zingiberis (*Gan Jiang*), 3g, Radix Angelicae Sinensis (*Dang Gui*), 10g, Rhizoma Atractylodis Macrocephalae (*Bai Zhu*), 10g, Radix Albus Paeoniae Lactiflorae (*Bai Shao*), 10-12g, Succinum (*Hu Po*), 1g (powdered and swallowed with the decocted liquid), stir-fried Semen Zizyphi Spinosae (*Suan Zao Ren*), 12-15g, Caulis Polygoni Multiflori (*Ye Jiao Teng*), 15g

Decoct in water and administer orally in two divided doses, morning and evening, one *ji* per day.

**ACUPUNCTURE:** *Shen Men* (Ht 7), *Zu Qiao Yin* (GB 44), *Shang Qiu* (Sp 5), *Xin Shu* (Bl 15), *Gan Shu* (Bl 18). Use even supplementing-even draining technique.

## 6. BLOOD STASIS OBSTRUCTING INTERNALLY PATTERN

**MAIN SYMPTOMS:** Frequent nightmares, piercing, lancinating headache which is fixed in location, purplish green lips and nails, a dark, dusky facial complexion, heart palpitations, chest and/or abdominal pain, worsening of all symptoms in the evening, possible menstrual pain in females, a dark, purplish tongue and/or static spots or macules, and a fine, bowstring, possibly choppy pulse

**TREATMENT PRINCIPLES:** Quicken the blood and transform stasis, open the orifices and quiet the spirit

**FORMULA & MEDICINALS:** *Tong Qiao Huo Xue Tang* (Open the Orifices & Quicken the Blood Decoction)

Radix Rubrus Paeoniae Lactiflorae (*Chi Shao*), 10g, Radix Ligustici Wallichii (*Chuan Xiong*), 10-15g (added later), Semen Pruni Persicae (*Tao Ren*), 10g, Flos Carthami Tinctorii (*Hong Hua*), 10g (steeped), Lumbricus (*Di*

*Long*), 6g, Rhizoma Acori Graminei (*Shi Chang Pu*), 6g, Tuber Curcumae (*Yu Jin*), 10g, Radix Angelicae Sinensis (*Dang Gui*), 10g

**ACUPUNCTURE:** *Da Zhui* (GV 14), *Bai Hui* (GV 20), *Shen Ting* (GV 24), *Xue Hai* (Sp 10), *He Gu* (LI 4), *San Yin Jiao* (Sp 6), *Yin Bai* (Sp 1). Use draining technique on all points except the last one which should be bled.

## REPRESENTATIVE CASE HISTORIES:

### ❖ CASE 1[2] ❖

The patient was a 35 year old female who was first examined on Aug. 25, 1989 as an out-patient. Every night, not long after the patient had fallen asleep, she would awake screaming with fright and fear. Her eyes stared straight ahead, her breathing was rapid, and her heart was thudding. This lasted for 10 minutes, after which she became calm again. She would then lie back down and fall asleep. However, not long after, she would once again wake in a terror. This happened as many as 10 times per night, and eventually the patient became very fatigued during the day. The patient was tested with both EKG and EEG, but these showed no abnormalities. She had been treated with a number of medications, including Valium and antianxiety drugs, but none of these were able to control her disease. Her Western diagnosis was anxiety disorder.

In terms of Chinese medicine, the patient had a bitter taste in her mouth, her pulse was bowstring and fine, and her tongue was pale red with thin, slimy fur. Therefore, she was prescribed *Xue Fu Zhu Yu Tang Jia Jian* (Blood Mansion Dispel Stasis Decoction with Additions & Subtractions): Radix Angelicae Sinensis (*Dang Gui*), Semen Pruni Persicae (*Tao Ren*), Flos Carthami Tinctorii (*Hong Hua*), Radix Platycodi Grandiflori (*Jie Geng*), Radix Rubrus Paeoniae Lactiflorae (*Chi Shao*), Radix Bupleuri (*Chai Hu*), Fructus Immaturus Citri Aurantii (*Zhi Shi*), Radix Ligustici Wallichii (*Chuan Xiong*), Radix Achyranthis Bidentatae (*Niu Xi*), clear Rhizoma Pinelliae Ternatae (*Ban Xia*), and Caulis Bambusae In Taeniis (*Zhu Ru*), 10g each, Concha Haliotidis (*Shi Jue Ming*) and Concha Margaritiferae (*Zhen Zhu Mu*), 30g each, and Pericarpium Citri Reticulatae (*Chen Pi*), 5g. These were decocted in water and administered internally.

After taking seven *ji* of the above formula, the number of episodes was markedly decreased. She still woke up some times, but she was no longer frightened or fearful. Her thinking was clear and she was no longer obviously anxious. However, there was slight pain in the temporal region, chest oppression, vexation heat in the five hearts,

and poor sleep. Her pulse was still bowstring and fine, but her tongue was red with thin fur. Therefore, Dang Gui, Platycodon, Caulis Bambusae, and Orange Peel were removed from the above formula and 10 grams each of uncooked Radix Rehmanniae (*Sheng Di*), Rhizoma Anemarrhenae Aspheloidis (*Zhi Mu*), and Semen Biotae Orientalis (*Bai Zi Ren*) and three grams of Cortex Phellodendri (*Huang Bai*) were added. Another seven *ji* were administered, after which her episodes of fright and fear completely stopped. In April 1992, she had one recurrence, but, after re-administering the above formula, the nightmares ceased. In the following year, the patient was calm and had no further problems sleeping.

### ❖ CASE 2[3] ❖

The patient was a 35 year old female who was first examined on July 25, 1989. She reported that she would not be asleep for very long before she would suddenly scream and sit up awake with both eyes open wide. This was accompanied by rough respiration and palpitations and tachycardia. The condition would last 10 minutes and then begin to calm down. She would then go back to sleep and these episodes would recur as often as 10 times per night. When she did return to sleep, she rested uneasily as if she were walking on thin ice. Cardiac and neurological examinations revealed nothing abnormal. She had received many therapies previously, including antidepressant medications. However, nothing could control her condition.

When the patient came to see the author of this case, she was restless and had a bitter taste in her mouth. Her pulse was fine and bowstring, while her tongue was pale red with thin, slimy fur. The patient was given *Xue Fu Zhu Yu Tang Jia Wei* (Blood Mansion Dispel Stasis Decoction with Added Flavors): Radix Angelicae Sinensis (*Dang Gui*), Semen Pruni Persicae (*Tao Ren*), Flos Carthami Tinctorii (*Hong Hua*), Radix Platycodi Grandiflori (*Jie Geng*), Radix Rubrus Paeoniae Lactiflorae (*Chi Shao*), Radix Bupleuri (*Chai Hu*), Fructus Immaturus Citri Aurantii (*Zhi Shi*), Radix Ligustici Wallichi (*Chuan Xiong*), Radix Achyranthis Bidentatae (*Niu Xi*), Rhizoma Pinelliae Ternatae (*Ban Xia*), and Caulis Bambusae In Taeniis (*Dan Zhu Ru*), 10g each, uncooked Concha Haliotidis (*Sheng Jue Ming*), 30g, Concha Margaritiferae (*Zhen Zhu Mu*), 30g, and Pericarpium Citri Reticulatae (*Chen Pi*), 5g. This was decocted in water and seven *ji* were administered.

The frequency of the episodes markedly diminished even though she would still wake up suddenly. Nevertheless, she no longer had a frightened expression, her mind became clearer, and she was less obviously anxious. She had some slight soreness and pain in the temporal region, chest oppression, vexatious heat in the five hearts, and poor sleep. Her pulse was fine and bowstring, and her tongue was red with thin fur. Therefore, Dang Gui, Platycodon, Caulis Bambusae, and Orange Peel were deleted from the original prescription and uncooked Radix Rehmanniae (*Sheng Di*), 10g, Rhizoma Anemarrhenae Aspheloidis (*Zhi Mu*), 10g, Semen Biotae Orientalis (*Bai Zi Ren*), 10g, and Cortex Phellodendri (*Chuan Bai*), 3g, were added. Seven more *ji* were administered. At this time, the fright ceased altogether. However, the symptoms returned again in April 1992. A single dose of the same prescription was administered and this arrested the illness and, on follow-up after four years, it had not recurred.

## ❖ CASE 3[4] ❖

The patient was a 54 year old cadre who was initially examined on Apr. 10, 1985. The patient had suffered from excessive psychological stress for 10 years during the Cultural Revolution and now commonly had ghost oppressive dreams. When he awoke from these terrible nightmares in which he could not move, he screamed without sound, and felt like he was suffocating, his four limbs would be numb and his breathing was uneasy. In addition, one half of his body dribbled and dripped sweat. This would last for approximately 20 minutes. Other signs and symptoms included heart palpitations, essence spirit listlessness[5], generalized lack of strength, and emaciated body, a greyish facial complexion, and a pale red tongue with white fur. In terms of pulses, his left bar was stirring and did not reach either the inch above or the cubit below. His right pulses were deep and bowstring. His pattern discrimination was undischarged anger resulting in the liver's loss of orderly reaching and the ethereal soul's not keeping quietly in its abode.

Based on the treatment principles of soothing the liver and resolving depression in order to quiet the spirit mind, the man was prescribed the following medicinals: Concha Margaritiferae (*Zhen Zhu Mu*), 30g, Radix Salviae Miltiorrhizae (*Dan Shen*), 10g, Radix Scrophulariae Ningpoensis (*Xuan Shen*), 10g, Radix Angelicae Sinensis (*Dang Gui*), 10g, Radix Albus Paeoniae Lactiflorae (*Bai Shao*), 10g, Sclerotium Pararadicis Poriae Cocos (*Fu Shen*), 10g, Radix Polygalae Tenuifoliae (*Yuan Zhi*), 10g, Rhizoma Acori Graminei (*Shi Chang Pu*), 8g, Radix Bupleuri (*Chai Hu*), 8g, uncooked Radix Glycyrrhizae (*Gan Cao*), 3g, Cortex Radicis Moutan (*Dan Pi*), 10g, stir-fried Fructus Gardeniae Jasminoidis (*Zhi Zi*), 10g, and Cortex Albizziae Julibrissinis (*He Huan Pi*), 10g. After taking 15 *ji* of this prescription with additions and subtractions, there were no obvious symptoms of his condi-

tion and the medicinals were stopped. On follow-up after one year, there had been no recurrence.

## ❖ CASE 4[6] ❖

The patient was a 28 year old female worker who was first examined on Mar. 21, 1959. In April of the preceding year, this woman had given birth to a daughter who suffered from night-crying. The patient's mother was a superstitious peasant who brought in a shaman to treat the baby's night-crying. This shaman said that night-crying was due to spirit possession and proceeded to try to exorcize these spirits. This resulted in terrifying the patient and causing her nightmares. Each night when she went to sleep her whole body was as rigid as if she were paralyzed and her breathing became uneasy. When she woke in a fright, both eyes would stare straight ahead and she would cry for 10 minutes or more. Various previous treatments had failed to cure the woman. The patient had a fat body which was healthy and strong. Her tongue was pale red with thin, white fur. Her pulse was slippery and moderate or relaxed (*i.e.*, slightly slow).

Based on the above signs and symptoms, the patient's pattern was categorized as postpartum emptiness and vacuity of the hundreds of vessels. Therefore, the treatment principles were to nourish the heart and quiet the spirit. Besides receiving psychotherapy, the woman was prescribed the following Chinese medicinals: Radix Pseudostellariae (*Tai Zi Shen*), 20g, Radix Salviae Miltiorrhizae (*Dan Shen*), 10g, Radix Scrophulariae Ningpoensis (*Xuan Shen*), 10g, Radix Angelicae Sinensis (*Dang Gui*), 10g, Radix Albus Paeoniae Lactiflorae (*Bai Shao*), 10g, Radix Polygalae Tenuifoliae (*Yuan Zhi*), 10g, Rhizoma Acori Graminei (*Shi Chang Pu*), 8g, Sclerotium Pararadicis Poriae Cocos (*Fu Shen*), 10g, Tuber Ophiopogonis Japonici (*Mai Dong*), 10g, Fructus Schisandrae Chinensis (*Wu Wei Zi*), 6g, and stir-fried Semen Zizyphi Spinosae (*Suan Zao Ren*), 15g. After taking 15 *ji* of these medicinals, the patient's sleep was quiet and she was able to do her household chores. One month later, the woman was able to return to work.

### ENDNOTES:

[1] The fine pulse suggests an element of yin blood vacuity. In most cases, liver yang becomes hyperactive and ascends due to yin vacuity failing to control.

[2] Hu Ji-ming, "Experiential Knowledge of the Treatment of Sleep Anxiety with *Xue Fu Zhu Yu Tang* (Blood Chamber Dispel Stasis Decoction)," *Zhe Jiang Zhong Yi Za Zhi* (*Zhejiang Journal of Chinese Medicine*), #5, 1993, p. 198

[3] *Ibid.*, p. 198

[4]Chen Jia-yang, *Shi Yong Zhong Yi Shen Jing Xue (A Study of Practical Chinese Medical Neurology)*, Gansu Science & Technology Press, Lanzhou, 1989, p. 431

[5]*I.e.*, mental-emotional torpor and a dull affect

[6]*Ibid.*, p. 432

# ❖ 13 ❖

# INSOMNIA

Insomnia, *bu mian* in Chinese, means either the partial or complete loss of sleep. To be considered pathologic, this condition must have lasted for some time. It does not refer to a single night's lost sleep. In the *Nei Jing (Inner Classic)*, this is also referred to as "inability to close one's eyes," "inability to lie down," and "inability to obtain sleep." In the *Nan Jing (Classic of Difficulties)*, we find the term *bu mian*. Other terms used both historically and now include "scanty sleep" and "loss of sleep."

In conventional Western medicine, insomnia refers to the subjective experience of non-refreshing sleep and may or may not correspond to objectively identifiable disturbances in sleep. Two basic patterns of disturbed sleep are recognized in psychiatry. Dyssomnias include problems initiating and maintaining sleep. Parasomnias are behavioral abnormalities that occur during sleep. Numerous medical or psychiatric disorders are accompanied by insomnia, but there is no clear correspondence between a specific disorder and a discrete pattern of disturbed sleep.

## NOSOLOGY:

Dyssomnias are primary (*i.e.*, not caused by an identified disorder) disturbances in the quality or duration of sleep that are typically associated with daytime fatigue. Excessive sleep and sleep that is delayed or interrupted by frequent awakenings often lead to significant impairments in social and occupational functioning. Shift work or travel across several time zones can result in disturbance of the normal wake-sleep cycle that has been called circadian rhythm sleep disorder. Parasomnias comprise another group of primary sleep disorders associated with pathological patterns of behavior or physiology that occur during sleep, including sleep-walking, sleep-talking, and other "sleep automatisms" as well as impaired sleep caused by irregular breathing (sleep apnea). Secondary sleep disorders are patterns of disturbed sleep-waking that are caused by primary underlying medical and/or psychiatric disorders. Representative medical and psychiatric disorders that are typically accompanied by a pattern of disturbed sleep are discussed below.

## DIFFERENTIAL DIAGNOSIS:

Prior to assuming that a primary psychiatric disturbance is the underlying cause of disturbed sleep, the chief clinical task is to identify or rule out associated medical disorders. A pattern of disrupted sleep with frequent awakenings frequently accompanies neurological disorders, including Parkinson's disease, Huntington's disease, Alzheimer's disease, epilepsy, and cerebrovascular disease. Complicating this matter, contemporary Western pharmacological treatments for these disorders often directly affect sleep. Substance abuse is a common cause of frequent awakening or increased arousal during sleep. Chronic use of alcohol or most short-acting sedative-hypnotic medications is associated with withdrawal during the hours of sleep resulting in disrupted sleep, frequent awakenings, and non-refreshing sleep with residual daytime fatigue.

## DIFFERENTIAL DIAGNOSIS

### 1. MEDICAL DISORDERS

A. DEGENERATIVE NEUROLOGIC DISEASES INCLUDING PARKINSON'S DISEASE, HUNTINGTON'S DISEASE
B. ALZHEIMER'S DISEASE AND OTHER DEMENTIAS
C. SEIZURE DISORDERS
D. HISTORY OF CEREBROVASCULAR ACCIDENT (CVA)
E. SLEEP APNEA (CENTRAL OR OBSTRUCTIVE)
F. RESTLESS LEG SYNDROME

### 2. EFFECTS OF SUBSTANCES

A. ALCOHOL OR ILLICIT SUBSTANCE INTOXICATION OR WITHDRAWAL
B. SIDE EFFECTS OF MEDICATIONS

### 3. PSYCHIATRIC DISORDERS

A. PANIC DISORDER
B. POST-TRAUMATIC STRESS DISORDER (PTSD)
C. GENERALIZED ANXIETY DISORDER (GAD)
D. MOOD DISORDERS
E. SCHIZOPHRENIA AND OTHER PSYCHOTIC DISORDERS

Common and under-diagnosed causes of frequent awakening are sleep apnea and restless leg syndrome. Obese individuals who complain of chronic fatigue may experience repeated brief awakenings throughout the night when the upper airway is transiently obstructed during normal sleep. In contrast, many individuals who are not overweight but experience repeated episodes of transient cessation in the normal rhythm of breathing may have central sleep apnea.

Primary psychiatric causes of disrupted sleep include panic disorder, generalized anxiety, mood disorders, psychotic disorders, and post-traumatic stress disorder (PTSD).

### ETIOLOGY & PATHOPHYSIOLOGY:

Pathological changes in brain regions implicated in many neurological disorders affect sleep directly by disrupting normal functioning of brain circuits that regulate sleep. For instance, many kinds of epilepsy are associated with an increased likelihood of seizure episodes (and awakening) during sleep. The side effects of stimulant-like medication effects often cause disturbed or impaired sleep. Theophylline and many other medications used to treat chronic obstructive pulmonary disease (COPD) are in this category. Obstructive sleep apnea is a disorder in which normal breathing is repeatedly interrupted throughout the night when the upper airway is transiently obstructed by excessive surrounding tissue during normal periods of shallow breathing in an obese individual. This results in multiple episodes of transient hypoxia that stimulate awakening and a "struggle" to breathe in order to bring an adequate supply of oxygen to the brain. Although central sleep apnea is phenomenologically identical to obstructive sleep apnea, the theorized cause is

dysregulation in the brain's sleep regulating center. Disturbed sleep in the context of chronic alcohol or sedative-hypnotic abuse is caused by "rebound" activation of the "arousal" center of the brain as the effects of these substances wear off. In predisposed individuals, panic attacks leading to awakening are sometimes triggered at a certain phase of sleep. Patients who suffer from PTSD often experience recurring nightmares that disrupt restful sleep. Major depression is associated with a pattern of excessive or disrupted sleep for unclear reasons. In contrast, neurochemical changes that underlie mania almost always lead to severely impaired sleep.

### WESTERN MEDICAL TREATMENT:

Correction of treatable medical causes of disturbed sleep will often alleviate the problem. However, disrupted sleep is a concomitant of many neurological disorders for which there is no cure in contemporary Western medicine. For these disorders, including Parkinson's disease, Alzheimer's disease, and others, symptomatic management with sedative-hypnotics sometimes improves the overall quality of sleep. When alcohol or substance abuse is the cause, sedatives should be avoided because of the high relapse risk their use poses to the recovering patient. Sleep usually normalizes within weeks following detoxification. In this population, nonaddictive medications, including antihistamines are a safe alternative to sedative-hypnotics. A pattern of disrupted sleep that is secondary to an underlying psychiatric disorder will gradually resolve in response to effective pharmacologic management of the associated disorder. In all instances where benzodiazepines or other sedative-hypnotic agents are used to treat sleep disorders, it is usually advisable to discontinue them after several weeks in order to reduce the risk of dependence and tolerance (*i.e.*, the requirement for a gradually increasing dose for an equivalent sedating effect). Cognitive and behavioral therapy are often used adjunctively to pharmacological treatment to improve sleep hygiene in patients for whom chronic anxiety has led to impaired sleep.

## SHORT & LONG-TERM ADVANTAGES & DISADVANTAGES OF WESTERN MEDICAL TREATMENT:

All medications used to treat sleep disorders carry the possibility of side effects, including residual daytime sedation and mild cognitive symptoms. Elderly patients are at increased risk for more serious side effects of sedative-hypnotic agents, including orthostatic hypotension (which poses a significant fall risk) and confusional states concomitant with long-term use of benzodiazepines because of their anticholinergic side effects. The most problematic adverse consequence of long-term sedative-hypnotic use is chemical dependence, which is characterized by tolerance, and withdrawal during periods of non-use. Benzodiazepine withdrawal is uncomfortable for healthy young adults and potentially dangerous for elderly medically compromised patients because of associated autonomic activation including increased heart rate, elevated blood pressure, tremulousness, perspiration, and frequent symptoms of anxiety or confusion. Non-benzodiazepine agents used in the treatment of disturbed sleep may also cause unpleasant morning side effects. For example, diphenhydramine (Benadryl) causes dry mouth, urinary retention, blurred vision, and residual morning sedation which can interfere with occupational functioning.

## INDICATIONS FOR REFERRAL TO WESTERN MEDICAL SERVICES:

Urgent referral to a neurologist is indicated when a pattern of disturbed sleep is associated with symptoms that point to an underlying seizure disorder, Parkinson's disease, or another serious neurological disorder. A persisting sleep disturbance that is related to ongoing abuse of alcohol or an illicit substance is a basis for referral to an appropriate rehabilitation program. When there is no evidence of an associated medical disorder or substance abuse and impaired sleep has been unresponsive to appropriate Chinese medical interventions, non-urgent referral to a psychiatrist may help to clarify possible psychogenic causes. A suitable integrative treatment plan can then be devised.

## CHINESE DISEASE CAUSES & MECHANISMS:

In Chinese medicine, sleep is seen as the sinking of the clear yang qi of the heart spirit back down and into the interior of the body to be covered and enfolded by yin. If the heart spirit becomes disquieted either due to malnourishment or harassment by evil qi, it may not sink back down calmly and quietly as it should. In that case, either the person cannot fall asleep or, if they do fall asleep, cannot stay asleep a normal length of time. As Zhang Jing-yue said:

> Sleep is yin and is ruled by the spirit. If the spirit is quiet, this leads to sleep. If the spirit is not quiet, there is no sleep.

The most common types of evil qi harassing the heart spirit and causing insomnia are evil heat or fire and phlegm. Evil heat may include depressive heat, vacuity, phlegm fire, and heart fire effulgence.

The qi of the outside world is the ruling qi when compared to the guest qi of the bodymind. In Chinese medicine, it is a basic principle that the guest qi tends to transform similar to the host or ruling qi. If there is insufficient yin to hold and enfold the yang qi of the spirit, when the yang qi of the tai yang or the sun begins its ascent after midnight, the yang qi of the body may also move upward and outward, thus producing wakefulness when one should still be asleep. This kind of matitudinal or early morning insomnia is mostly due to yin blood vacuity and insufficiency.

Food stagnation due to dietary irregularity may also cause insomnia. The *Nei Jing (Inner Classic)* says, "If there is stomach qi disharmony, there will not be quiet when one lies down." The reason for this is that the defensive yang, retreating from the exterior with the coming of night, is hindered from entering internally by the food retained in the yang ming. Thus the yang qi of the spirit cannot become enfolded by yin. This type of insomnia manifests as inability to fall asleep as opposed to inability to stay asleep.

## TREATMENT BASED ON PATTERN DISCRIMINATION:

### 1. HEART-SPLEEN DUAL VACUITY PATTERN

**MAIN SYMPTOMS:** Difficulty falling asleep, profuse dreams, easily being awakened as one is falling asleep, heart palpitations, impaired memory, a pale white or sallow yellow facial complexion, dizziness, lassitude of the spirit, shortness of breath, disinclination to talk, poor appetite, reduced food intake, loose stools, a pale tongue with thin fur, and a fine, weak pulse

**TREATMENT PRINCIPLES:** Fortify the spleen and boost the qi, nourish the heart and supplement the blood

**FORMULA & MEDICINALS:** *Gui Pi Tang Jia Jian* (Restore the Spleen Decoction with Additions & Subtractions)

Rhizoma Atractylodis Macrocephalae (*Bai Zhu*), 10g, Sclerotium Pararadicis Poriae Cocos (*Fu Shen*), 12g, Radix Astragali Membranacei (*Huang Qi*), 15g, Arillus Euphoriae Longanae (*Long Yan Rou*), 10g, stir-fried Semen Zizyphi Spinosae (*Suan Zao Ren*), 12g, Radix Codonopsitis Pilosulae (*Dang Shen*), 10g, Radix Auklandiae Lappae (*Mu Xiang*), 6-10g (added later), Radix Angelicae Sinensis (*Dang Gui*), 10g, Radix Polygalae Tenuifoliae (*Yuan Zhi*), 10g, mix-fried Radix Glycyrrhizae (*Gan Cao*), 6-15g

Decoct in water and administer orally in two divided doses, noon and before bed at night, one *ji* per day.

**ADDITIONS & SUBTRACTIONS:** If insomnia is severe, add Caulis Polygoni Multiflori (*Ye Jiao Teng*) and Semen Biotae Orientalis (*Bai Zi Ren*). If the memory is impaired, add Rhizoma Acori Graminei (*Shi Chang Pu*) and replace Codonopsis with Radix Panacis Ginseng (*Ren Shen*). If there are profuse dreams, add Succinum (*Hu Po*).

**ACUPUNCTURE:** *Pi Shu* (Bl 20), *San Yin Jiao* (Sp 6), *Shen Men* (Ht 7), *Xin Shu* (Bl 15). Use supplementing technique.

**ADDITIONS & SUBTRACTIONS:** If there are profuse dreams, add *Po Hu* (Bl 42). If there is impaired memory, add *Zhi Shi* (Bl 52) and *Bai Hui* (GV 20). If there are heart palpitations, add *Nei Guan* (Per 6).

## 2. LIVER BLOOD VACUITY TRANSFORMING VACUITY HEAT PATTERN

**MAIN SYMPTOMS:** Insomnia, vexation and agitation, disquieted emotions, irritability, heart palpitations, night sweats, dizziness and vertigo, dry mouth and throat, a pale tongue with red tip, and a fine, bowstring, rapid pulse

**TREATMENT PRINCIPLES:** Nourish yin and clear heat, quiet the spirit and eliminate vexation

**FORMULA & MEDICINALS:** *Suan Zao Ren Tang Jia Jian* (Zizyphus Spinosa Decoction with Additions & Subtractions)

Semen Zizyphi Spinosae (*Suan Zao Ren*), 12g, Rhizoma Anemarrhenae Aspheloidis (*Zhi Mu*), 10g, Sclerotium Poriae Cocos (*Fu Ling*), 10g, Radix Glycyrrhizae (*Gan Cao*), 3-10g, Fructus Tritici Aestivi (*Huai Xiao Mai*), 15-30g

Decoct in water and administer orally in two divided doses, noon and before bed at night, one *ji* per day.

**ADDITIONS & SUBTRACTIONS:** For night sweats, add Concha Ostreae (*Mu Li*) and Fructus Schisandrae Chinensis (*Wu Wei*). For more severe vacuity heat, add Herba Ecliptae Prostratae (*Han Lian Cao*), Fructus Ligustri Lucidi (*Nu Zhen Zi*), and Radix Albus Paeoniae Lactiflorae (*Bai Shao*).

**ACUPUNCTURE:** *Qu Quan* (Liv 8), *Tai Xi* (Ki 3), *San Yin Jiao* (Sp 6), *Po Hu* (Bl 42), *Hun Men* (Bl 47). Use even supplementing-even draining technique.

## 3. NON-INTERACTION BETWEEN THE HEART & KIDNEYS PATTERN

**SYMPTOMS:** Difficulty falling asleep or even insomnia the whole night, dizziness, tinnitus, tidal heat, night sweats, vexatious heat in the five hearts, impaired memory, low back and knee soreness and limpness, seminal emission, a red tongue with scant fur, and a fine, rapid pulse

**TREATMENT PRINCIPLES:** Nourish yin and downbear fire, quiet the heart spirit and promote the interaction between the heart and kidneys

**CHINESE MEDICINAL FORMULA:** *Huang Lian E Jiao Tang Jia Jian* (Coptis & Donkey Skin Glue Decoction with Additions & Subtractions)

Rhizoma Coptidis Chinensis (*Huang Lian*), 6g (added later), Gelatinum Corii Asini (*E Jiao*), 6g (dissolved at the end of decocting), Radix Scutellariae Baicalensis (*Huang Qin*), 10g, Radix Albus Paeoniae Lactiflorae (*Bai Shao*), 10g, egg yolk (*Ji Zi Huang*), 2 pieces (added at end and stirred into the hot decoction), Sclerotium Pararadicis Poriae Cocos (*Fu Shen*), 12g, stir-fried Semen Zizyphi Spinosae (*Suan Zao Ren*), 12g, Cortex Cinnamomi Cassiae (*Rou Gui*), 3g, Radix Polygalae Tenuifoliae (*Yuan Zhi*), 10g

Decoct in water and administer orally in two divided doses, noon and before bed at night, one *ji* per day.

**ADDITIONS & SUBTRACTIONS:** If there is severe insomnia, add Cinnabar (*Zhu Sha*) and Succinum (*Hu Po*). If there is severe vacuity heat, add Radix Scrophulariae Ningpoensis (*Xuan Shen*) and uncooked Radix Rehmanniae (*Sheng Di*). If there is dizziness, add uncooked Concha Margaritiferae (*Zhen Zhu Mu*) and uncooked Os Draconis (*Long Gu*). For tinnitus, add calcined Magnetitum (*Ci Shi*). For seminal emission, add

Cortex Phellodendri (*Huang Bai*) and Rhizoma Anemarrhenae Aspheloidis (*Zhi Mu*).

**ACUPUNCTURE:** *Da Ling* (Per 7), *Tai Xi* (Ki 3), *Shen Men* (Ht 7), *Yong Quan* (Ki 1). Use even supplementing-even draining technique. Bathe the feet in warm water and then massage *Yong Quan* strongly just before sleep.

**ADDITIONS & SUBTRACTIONS:** If heat is severe, add *Nei Ting* (St 44). If there is dizziness, add *Feng Chi* (GB 20). If there is tinnitus, add *Ting Gong* (SI 19). If there is seminal emission, add *Zhi Shi* (Bl 52). If there is severe insomnia, add *An Mian* (M-HN-22).

## 4. HEART YIN VACUITY PATTERN

**MAIN SYMPTOMS:** Difficulty falling asleep, heart palpitations, vacuity vexation, impaired memory, dream emission, profuse dreams, afternoon tidal heat, night sweats, heat in the five hearts, sores in the mouth and on the tip of the tongue, a dry mouth and throat, dry stools, a red tongue with scanty fur, and a fine, rapid pulse

**TREATMENT PRINCIPLES:** Supplement the heart and enrich yin, nourish the blood and quiet the spirit

**FORMULA & MEDICINALS:** *Tian Wang Bu Xin Dan Jia Jian* (Heavenly Emperor Supplement the Heart Elixir with Additions & Subtractions)

Uncooked Radix Rehmanniae (*Sheng Di*), 12g, Radix Codonopsitis Pilosulae (*Dang Shen*), 10g, Radix Salviae Miltiorrhizae (*Dan Shen*), 10g, Radix Scrophulariae Ningpoensis (*Xuan Shen*), 10-15g, Sclerotium Pararadicis Poriae Cocos (*Fu Shen*), 12g, Fructus Schizandrae Chinensis (*Wu Wei Zi*), 10g, Radix Polygalae Tenuifoliae (*Yuan Zhi*), 10g, Radix Angelicae Sinensis (*Dang Gui*), 10g, Tuber Asparagi Cochinensis (*Tian Dong*), 12g, Tuber Ophiopogonis Japonicae (*Mai Dong*), 12g, Semen Biotae Orientalis (*Bai Zi Ren*), 12g, stir-fried Semen Zizyphi Spinosae (*Suan Zao Ren*), 12g

Decoct in water and administer orally in two divided doses, noon and before bed at night, one *ji* per day.

**ADDITIONS & SUBTRACTIONS:** If heart palpitations are severe, add calcined Dens Draconis (*Long Chi*). For night sweats, add calcined Os Draconis (*Long Gu*) and uncooked Radix Albus Paeoniae Lactiflorae (*Bai Shao*). For sores in the mouth and on the tip of the tongue, add Folium Lophatheri Gracilis (*Dan Zhu Ye*) and Rhizoma Coptidis Chinensis (*Huang Lian*).

**ACUPUNCTURE & MOXIBUSTION:** *Yin Xi* (Ht 6), *Xin Shu* (Bl 15), *San Yin Jiao* (Sp 6), *Zhao Hai* (Ki 6). Use even supplementing-even draining technique.

**ADDITIONS & SUBTRACTIONS:** If heart palpitations are severe, add *Nei Guan* (Per 6). For impaired memory, add *Zhi Shi* (Bl 52) with moxibustion. For severe night sweats or afternoon tidal heat, add *Gao Huang Shu* (Bl 43). For sores in the mouth and on the tip of the tongue, add *Lao Gong* (Per 8) and *Liang Quan* (CV 23).

## 5. HEART-GALLBLADDER QI VACUITY PATTERN

**MAIN SYMPTOMS:** Insomnia, fear of sleeping alone, timidity, paranoia, susceptibility to fright, heart palpitations, frequent sighing, dizziness, waking in a fright, possible profuse phlegm and/or plum pit qi, a pale tongue, and a fine, weak, bowstring, possibly slippery pulse

**TREATMENT PRINCIPLES:** Supplement the gallbladder qi, settle fright, and quiet the spirit

**FORMULA & MEDICINALS:** *Ding Zhi Wan Jia Jian* (Stabilize the Mind Pills with Additions & Subtractions)

Radix Panacis Ginseng (*Ren Shen*), 6-10g (decocted first), Sclerotium Poriae Cocos (*Fu Ling*), 10g, Sclerotium Pararadicis Poriae Cocos (*Fu Shen*), 12g, Rhizoma Acori Graminei (*Shi Chang Pu*), 10g, Radix Polygalae Tenuifoliae (*Yuan Zhi*), 10g, stir-fried Semen Zizyphi Spinosae (*Suan Zao Ren*), 12g, calcined Dens Draconis (*Long Chi*), 12g (decocted first), Succinum (*Hu Po*), 1g (powdered and swallowed with the decocted liquid)

Decoct in water and administer orally in two divided doses, noon and before bed at night, one *ji* per day.

**ACUPUNCTURE:** *Da Ling* (Per 7), *Po Hu* (Bl 42), *Shen Ting* (GV 24), *San Yin Jiao* (Sp 6), *Xin Shu* (Bl 15), *Dan Shu* (Bl 19). Alternate the last two points from treatment to treatment and use even supplementing-even draining technique.

## 6. PHLEGM FIRE HARASSING ABOVE PATTERN

**MAIN SYMPTOMS:** Difficulty falling asleep due to severe vexation, chest oppression, epigastric fullness, nausea, vomiting, heavy-headedness, dizziness, a bitter taste in the mouth, a red tongue tip with slimy, yellow fur, and a slippery, rapid pulse

**TREATMENT PRINCIPLES:** Clear heat, transform phlegm, and quiet the spirit

**FORMULA & MEDICINALS:** *Huang Lian Wen Dan Tang Jia Jian* (Coptis Warm the Gallbladder Decoction with Additions & Subtractions)

Rhizoma Coptidis Chinensis (*Huang Lian*), 3-6g (added later), Rhizoma Pinelliae Ternatae (*Ban Xia*), 12g, Sclerotium Paradicis Poriae Cocos (*Fu Shen*), 12g, Caulis Bambusae In Taeniis (*Zhu Ru*), 12g, Fructus Immaturus Citri Aurantii (*Zhi Shi*), 6g, Pericarpium Citri Reticulatae (*Chen Pi*), 6-10g, Rhizoma Acori Graminei (*Shi Chang Pu*), 10g, Radix Polygalae Tenuifoliae (*Yuan Zhi*), 10g, Semen Zizyphi Spinosae (*Suan Zao Ren*), 15g, Os Draconis (*Long Gu*), 15-20g (decocted first), Concha Ostreae (*Mu Li*), 15-20g (decocted first)

Decoct in water and administer orally in two divided doses, noon and before bed at night, one *ji* per day.

**ADDITIONS & SUBTRACTIONS:** If there is constipation, add Semen Trichosanthis Kirlowii (*Gua Lou Ren*) and Radix Et Rhizoma Rhei (*Da Huang*). If there is food stagnation with stomach disharmony, add Semen Panici Miliaciae (*Shu Mi*) and replace lime-processed Pinellia with Pinellia Massa Medica Fermentata (*Ban Xia Qu*). If there is vertigo, add bile-processed Rhizoma Arisaematis (*Dan Nan Xing*) and Rhizoma Gastrodiae Elatae (*Tian Ma*). If there is phlegm rheum mixed with heat with symptoms of a dry throat, surging counterflow heart palpitations, sudden startling, and numb extremities, use *Shi Wei Wen Dan Tang He Shu Mi Tang Jia Jian* (Ten Flavors Warm the Gallbladder Decoction plus Millet Decoction with Additions & Subtractions): Radix Panacis Ginseng (*Ren Shen*), 6g (decocted first), Sclerotium Poriae Cocos (*Fu Ling*), 12g, Semen Zizyphi Spinosae (*Suan Zao Ren*), 12g, Rhizoma Anemarrhenae Aspheloidis (*Zhi Mu*), 6-10g, Caulis Bambusae In Taeniis (*Zhu Ru*), 6-10g, Rhizoma Pinelliae Ternatae (*Ban Xia*), 10g, Semen Panici Miliacei (*Shu Mi*), 15g. In this case, there is more dampness and less heat mixed with qi vacuity and depression.

**ACUPUNCTURE:** *Feng Long* (St 40), *Nei Ting* (St 44), *Zhong Wan* (CV 12), *Shen Men* (Ht 7), *Bai Hui* (GV 20). Use draining technique.

**ADDITIONS & SUBTRACTIONS:** If there is nausea or vomiting, add *Nei Guan* (Per 6). If there is dizziness or vertigo, add *Yin Tang* (M-HN-3).

## 7. LIVER FIRE HARASSING INTERNALLY PATTERN

**MAIN SYMPTOMS:** Difficulty falling asleep due to dizziness and headache, vexation, impatience, irascibility, chest and rib-side distention and fullness, frequent sighing, thirst, a bitter taste in the mouth, red eyes, dark urination, constipation, a red tongue with yellow fur, and a bowstring, rapid pulse

**TREATMENT PRINCIPLES:** Clear the liver, drain fire, and quiet the spirit

**FORMULA & MEDICINALS:** *Xie Qing Wan Jia Jian* (Drain the Green Pills with Additions & Subtractions)

Radix Gentianae Scabrae (*Long Dan Cao*), 6-10g, Radix Scutellariae Baicalensis (*Huang Qin*), 10g, stir-fried Fructus Gardeniae Jasminoidis (*Zhi Zi*), 10g, Radix Et Rhizoma Rhei (*Da Huang*), 3-6g (added later), Radix Bupleuri (*Chai Hu*), 3-10g, Radix Angelicae Sinensis (*Dang Gui*), 10g, Radix Ligustici Wallichii (*Chuan Xiong*), 6-10g (added later), Concha Margaritiferac (*Zhen Zhu Mu*), 15g (decocted first), calcined Dens Draconis (*Long Chi*), 15g (decocted first)

Decoct in water and administer orally in two divided doses, noon and before bed at night, one *ji* per day.

**ADDITIONS & SUBTRACTIONS:** If there is tinnitus or red eyes, add Spica Prunellae Vulgaris (*Xia Ku Cao*). If there is damp heat in the lower burner, add Caulis Akebiae (*Mu Tong*) and Rhizoma Alismatis (*Ze Xie*). If depressive heat is not so severe, use Ye Tian-shi's *Dan Pi Sang Ye Fang* (Moutan & Folium Mori Formula) instead: Cortex Radicis Moutan (*Dan Pi*), 10g, Rhizoma Pinelliae Ternatae (*Ban Xia*), 10g, Ramulus Uncariae Cum Uncis (*Gou Teng*), 12-15g (added later), Folium Mori Albi (*Sang Ye*), 10g, Sclerotium Poriae Cocos (*Fu Ling*), 12g, Pericarpium Citri Erythrocarpae (*Ju Hong*), 6g.

**ACUPUNCTURE:** *Xing Jian* (Liv 2), *Zu Qiao Yin* (GB 44), *Feng Chi* (GB 20), *Shen Men* (Ht 7). Use draining technique.

**ADDITIONS & SUBTRACTIONS:** If dizziness is severe, add *Bai Hui* (GV 20). If headache is severe, add *Tai Yang* (M-HN-9). If there is tinnitus, add *Yi Feng* (TB 17) and *Zhong Zhu* (TB 3). For red eyes, add *Yang Xi* (LI 5) and *Tai Yang* (M-HN-9).

## 8. HEART FIRE EFFULGENCE PATTERN

**MAIN SYMPTOMS:** Insomnia, vexatious heat in the chest and heart, thirst with a desire for chilled drinks, a red facial complexion, sores in the mouth or on the tip of the tongue, painful, short, dark-colored urination, a red tongue tip, and a rapid, forceful pulse

**TREATMENT PRINCIPLES:** Clear the heart, drain fire, and quiet the spirit

**FORMULA & MEDICINALS:** *Dao Chi San Jia Jian* (Abduct the Red Powder with Additions & Subtractions)

Uncooked Radix Rehmanniae (*Sheng Di*), 12g, Caulis Akebiae (*Mu Tong*), 6-10g, Folium Lophatheri Gracilis (*Dan Zhu Ye*), 10g, Extremitas Radicis Glycyrrhizae (*Gan Cao Shao*), 6g, Medulla Tetrapanacis Papyriferi (*Deng Xin Cao*), 3g

Decoct in water and administer orally in two divided doses, noon and before bed at night, one *ji* per day.

**ADDITIONS & SUBTRACTIONS:** For severe insomnia, add Succinum (*Hu Po*) and wine-processed Rhizoma Coptidis Chinensis (*Huang Lian*). For painful urination, add Cortex Phellodendri (*Huang Bai*) and Fructus Gardeniae Jasminoidis (*Zhi Zi*). For multiple sores in the mouth and on the tip of the tongue, add Fructus Forsythiae Suspensae (*Lian Qiao*) and Rhizoma Coptidis Chinensis (*Huang Lian*).

**ACUPUNCTURE:** *Shen Men* (Ht 7), *Lao Gong* (Per 8), *Shao Fu* (Ht 8), *Jie Xi* (St 41). Use draining technique.

## 9. RETAINED HEAT PATTERN

**MAIN SYMPTOMS:** Vacuity vexation, insomnia, fever, profuse sweating, chest and diaphragmatic oppression, thirst with a desire to drink, clamoring stomach, a desire to vomit, a red tongue with scanty fur, and a fine, rapid pulse

**TREATMENT PRINCIPLES:** Engender fluids and supplement the qi, clear heat and eliminate vexation

**FORMULA & MEDICINALS:** *Zhu Ye Shi Gao Tang Jia Jian* (Bamboo Leaf & Gypsum Decoction with Additions & Subtractions)

Folium Bambusae (*Zhu Ye*), 12g, Gypsum Fibrosum (*Shi Gao*), 20g, lime-processed Rhizoma Pinelliae Ternatae (*Ban Xia*), 10g, Tuber Ophiopogonis Japonici (*Mai Dong*), 12g, Radix Pseudostellariae (*Tai Zi Shen*), 10g, Radix Glycyrrhizae (*Gan Cao*), 3-6g, Semen Oryzae Sativae (*Geng Mi*), 10g

Decoct in water and administer orally in two divided doses, noon and before bed at night, one *ji* per day.

**ADDITIONS & SUBTRACTIONS:** If there is severe vexation, add stir-fried Fructus Gardeniae Jasminoidis (*Zhi Zi*) and Semen Praeparatus Sojae (*Dan Dou Chi*).

**ACUPUNCTURE:** *Qu Chi* (LI 11), *He Gu* (LI 4), *Nei Ting* (St 44), *Zhong Wan* (CV 12), *Shen Men* (Ht 7). Use even supplementing-even draining technique.

## 10. FOOD STAGNATION PATTERN

**MAIN SYMPTOMS:** Insomnia, pain, distention, and fullness in the stomach and abdomen, aversion to food, counterflow retching, nausea, thick, slimy tongue fur, and a slippery pulse

**TREATMENT PRINCIPLES:** Disperse food, harmonize the stomach, and quiet the spirit

**FORMULA & MEDICINALS:** *Bao He Wan Jia Jian* (Protect Harmony Decoction with Additions & Subtractions)

Massa Medica Fermentata (*Shen Qu*), 10g, Sclerotium Poriae Cocos (*Fu Ling*), 10g, scorched Fructus Crataegi (*Shan Zha*), 10g, Fructus Forsythiae Suspensae (*Lian Qiao*), 10g, Pericarpium Citri Reticulatae (*Chen Pi*), 10g, Cortex Magnoliae Officinalis (*Hou Po*), 10g, Fructus Immaturus Citri Aurantii (*Zhi Shi*), 10g, Rhizoma Pinelliae Ternatae (*Ban Xia*), 10g, Radix Et Rhizoma Rhei (*Da Huang*), 3g (added later)

Decoct in water and administer orally in two divided doses, noon and before bed at night, one *ji* per day.

**ACUPUNCTURE:** *Nei Guan* (Per 6), *Zhong Wan* (CV 12), *Zhang Men* (Liv 13), *Nei Ting* (St 44). Use draining technique.

**ADDITIONS & SUBTRACTIONS:** If there is grain food stagnation, add *Liang Men* (St 21). If there is meat food stagnation, add *Hua Rou Men* (St 24).

## CLINICAL TIPS:

1. Treatment of insomnia is best given during the second half of the day. Ideally, acupuncture should be administered in the evening one half hour before bed. Likewise, if Chinese medicinals are administered twice per day, the first dose should be administered at noon and the second dose one half hour before bed at night.

2. Insomnia patients need to be advised not to eat too late at night and not to engage in any mental or physical activity soon before going to bed. When insomnia is due to yin and blood vacuity, a glass of warm milk before bed can be helpful.

3. It is important that insomnia patients not sleep later

than usual in the morning in order to try and make up the sleep they lost at night. This only further deregulates one's sleep-wake cycle. Likewise, one should avoid napping during the day for anything more than a half hour.

## ABSTRACTS OF REPRESENTATIVE CHINESE RESEARCH:

*Hei Long Jiang Zhong Yi Yao (Heilongjiang Chinese Medicine & Medicinals)*, #6, 1996, p. 31. Geng Li-wen treated 15 cases of insomnia with *an mo* massage. Of these 15 cases, six were male and nine were female. They ranged in age from 23-50 years old. Their course of disease ranged from 1-12 years. Three of these cases could not sleep at all at night, nine sometimes slept and sometimes were awakened, and three cases had insomnia accompanying bouts of hysteria. Treatment consisted of using one finger pushing as well as point-pressing primarily at *Shen Shu* (Bl 23), *Pang Guang Shu* (Bl 28), *Pi Shu* (Bl 20), *Wei Shu* (Bl 21), *Yao Yang Guan* (GV 3), and *Ming Men* (GV 4). This was followed by various massage techniques on points on the head and face. This was done once every other day, and 10 times equaled one course of treatment. Using this protocol, eight patients were cured, four experienced a marked effect, two got some effect, and one got no result for a total amelioration rate of 93.33%.

*Hei Long Jiang Zhong Yi Yao (Heilongjiang Chinese Medicine & Medicinals)*, #3, 1996, p. 47. Zhuang Dan-hong treated 12 cases of recalcitrant insomnia. Eight of these patients were male and four were female. All were adolescents. Ten were engaged in mental work and two were workers. The treatment method consisted of using a dermal needle one time per day to tap all up and down the governing vessels until the skin was erythematous or there was a very slight degree of bleeding. Using this protocol, Zhuang says that the results were "fully satisfactory," although he fails to give statistical outcomes.

*Hei Long Jiang Zhong Yi Yao (Heilongjiang Chinese Medicine & Medicinals)*, #1, 1995, p. 11-12. Wang Guo-cai *et al.* treated 113 cases of recalcitrant insomnia using a combination of Chinese and Western medicines. In this group, there were 42 men and 71 women who ranged in age from 21-65 years old, with a median age of 41.4 years. Their course of disease had lasted from four months to 17 years, with most cases averaging one year's duration. In all these cases, insomnia was their major complaint. Seventy-three said they had difficulty falling asleep and 29 said they woke early. Fifty-two said their sleep was not deep and they were easily aroused. In addition, 69 had decreased memory power, 62 had accompanying heart palpitations, and 65 had accompanying anxiety, vexation, and agitation. Seventy cases were categorized as yin vacuity, while the remaining 43 cases were categorized as yang vacuity. Depending on these two basic pattern discriminations, the yang vacuity group received *Bu Zhong Yi Qi Tang Jia Jian* (Supplement the Center & Boost the Qi Decoction with Additions & Subtractions) and 25g of amitriptyline two times per day. The yin vacuity group received *Suan Zao Ren Tang Jia Jian* (Zizyphus Spinosa Decoction with Additions & Subtractions) plus 0.5-1mg of lorazepam (Atavin) three times per day. Of these 113 cases, 89 experienced a marked effect, 15 experienced some improvement, and nine cases got no result for a total amelioration rate of 92%. The smallest number of Chinese medicinal *ji* taken was seven and the largest was 23. The shortest number of days of treatment was 10 and the longest was 32.

*Gan Su Zhong Yi Xue Yuan Xue Bao (Gansu College of Chinese Medicine Journal)*, #3, 1996, p. 22-24. Bai Jing-hua *et al.* treated 80 cases of insomnia with Chinese medicinals. Thirty cases were considered the treatment group. They received 30ml of *Tong Zi Yu Ye* (Young Boy Jade Fluid) orally each evening. The other 50 cases were considered the comparison group, and they received 30mg of *Wu Wei Zi Chong Ji* (Schisandra Soluble Granules) orally each evening, with 10 days equaling one course of treatment for both groups. Statistically, in terms of sex, age, and disease duration, these two groups were similar. Six patterns were discriminated in terms of outcomes. These were 1) heart-spleen dual vacuity pattern, 2) heart vacuity-gallbladder timidity pattern, 3) yin vacuity with fire effulgence pattern, 4) phlegm heat internally harassing pattern, 5) liver depression transforming fire pattern, and 6) stasis harassing the heart spirit pattern. Seven patients in the treatment group were cured, 18 got a marked effect, four got some effect, and one case registered no effect for a total amelioration rate of 93.7%. In the comparison group, two cases were cured, 13 cases got a marked effect, 29 cases got some effect, and six cases got no effect for a total amelioration rate of 88%. However, *Wu Wei Zi Chong Ji* achieved a total amelioration rate of 96.7% in patients with heart-spleen dual vacuity. In all other patterns, *Tong Zi Yu Ye* got a better effect, typically by 25% or more.

❖

*Fu Jian Zhong Yi Yao (Fujian Chinese Medicine & Medicinals)*, #6, 1996, p. 16-17. Fan Zhen-hua *et al.* treated 31 cases of insomnia with *Gui Pi Tang Jia Jian* (Restore the Spleen Decoction with Additions & Subtractions). Of these 31 cases, four had simple insomnia, 18 had neurasthenia, six had anxiety disorder, and three where depressed. There were 11 males and 20 females who ranged in age from 22-62 with a median age of 35.80 ± 6.27 years. Their disease course had lasted from two months to five years, with a median duration of 2.12 ± 1.95 years. Twenty-six had difficult falling asleep, 18 had trouble staying asleep, and 16 woke too early. Twenty-three cases had taken Western sleep medications for one month or more with no marked effect. The patients were divided into three patterns: 1) heart-spleen dual vacuity pattern, 2) yin vacuity with fire effulgence pattern, and 3) spleen vacuity with phlegm heat internally harassing pattern. *Gui Pi Tang* was appropriately modified for each of these patterns. One *ji* was decocted in water per day and administered orally in two doses, afternoon and before bedtime. Twelve cases in the heart-spleen dual vacuity group got a marked effect, four got some effect, and five got no effect. Five cases in the yin vacuity with fire effulgence group got a marked effect and two got some effect, and two cases in the spleen vacuity with phlegm fire harassing internally got a marked effect and one got no effect. The total number who got a marked effect was 19 and some effect, six, for a total amelioration rate of 80.6%.

❖

*Jiang Xi Zhong Yi Yao (Jiangxi Chinese Medicine & Medicinals)*, #1, 2000, p. 9: Hong Yan reported on the treatment of 60 cases of insomnia with a combination of *Bai He Zhi Mu Tang* (Lily & Anemarrhena Decoction) and *Gan Mai Da Zao Tang* (Licorice, Wheat & Red Dates Decoction) with additions and subtractions. Of the 60 cases, 15 were male and 45 were female. They ranged in age from 25-67, with a median age of 50 years. Their course of disease had lasted from three months to 10 years. All only slept less than two hours per day. The formula administered consisted of: Bulbus Lilii (*Bai He*), 20g, Rhizoma Anemarrhenae Aspheloidis (*Zhi Mu*), 10g, mix-fried Radix Glycyrrhizae (*Gan Cao*), 10g, Fructus Tritici Aestivi (*Huai Xiao Mai*), 30g, Fructus Zizyphi Jujubae (*Da Zao*), 6 pieces. If there was emotional depression, vexation and agitation, and easy anger, 10 grams each of Radix Bupleuri (*Chai Hu*), Fructus Citri Aurantii (*Zhi Ke*), and Cortex Albizziae Julibrissinis (*He*

*Huan Pi*) and 15 grams of Radix Albus Paeoniae Lactiflorae (*Bai Shao*) were added. If the tongue fur was thick, yellow, and slimy, 6 grams of Rhizoma Coptidis Chinensis (*Huang Lian*) and 10 grams each of Pericarpium Citri Reticulatae (*Chen Pi*), lime-processed Rhizoma Pinelliae Ternatae (*Ban Xia*), Sclerotium Poriae Cocos (*Fu Ling*), and Caulis Bambusae In Taeniis (*Zhu Ru*) were added. If the tongue was dark and purple, 10 grams each of Semen Pruni Persicae (*Tao Ren*), Flos Carthami Tinctorii (*Hong Hua*), cooked Radix Rehmanniae (*Shu Di*), Radix Angelicae Sinensis (*Dang Gui*), and Radix Ligustici Wallichii (*Chuan Xiong*) were added. If there were heart palpitations, 18 grams of Magnetitum (*Ci Shi*) and 10 grams of Tuber Ophiopogonis Japonici (*Mai Dong*) were added. If there was dizziness and vertigo, 15 grams of Rhizoma Acori Graminei (*Shi Chang Pu*) were added. If there was vexatious heat in the five hearts, 20 grams of Semen Zizyphi Spinosae (*Suan Zao Ren*) and 10 grams each of Sclerotium Poriae Cocos (*Fu Ling*) and Radix Ligustici Wallichii (*Chuan Xiong*) were added. One *ji* was administered per day continuously for three weeks. At the end of that time, 30 cases were cured, meaning that their symptoms had disappeared and they were sleeping at least six hours per day. Another 15 cases were judged to have gotten a marked effect, meaning that their symptoms had improved and they were sleeping 4-5 hours per day. Yet another nine cases got some effect, meaning that their symptoms were less and they were sleeping 2-3 hours per day, and six cases got no effect. Thus the total amelioration rate was 90%.

## REPRESENTATIVE CASE HISTORIES:

### ❖ CASE 1[3] ❖

The patient was a 28 year old female who had difficulty falling asleep each night for the past two years. Her mouth and throat were dry, her spirit was listless, and her menstruation was irregular. Her tongue was pale red, and her pulse was bowstring and fine. Therefore, she was prescribed seven *ji* of *Jia Yi Gui Zang Tang* (Jia & Yi Returning & Treasuring Decoction). This consisted of: Concha Margaritiferae (*Zhen Zhu Mu*), 24g, Dens Draconis (*Long Chi*), uncooked Radix Rehmanniae (*Sheng Di*), Radix Salviae Miltiorrhizae (*Dan Shen*), Radix Angelicae Sinensis (*Dang Gui*), Semen Biotae Orientalis (*Bai Zi Ren*), and Flos Albizziae Julibrissinis (*He Huan Hua*), 9g each, Radix Bupleuri (*Chai Hu*) and Herba Menthae Haplocalycis (*Bo He*), 6g each, Radix Albus Paeoniae Lactiflorae (*Bai Shao*), 4.5g, Caulis Polygoni Multiflori (*Ye Jiao Teng*), 12g, Lignum Aquilariae Agallochae (*Chen*

Xiang), 1.5g, and Fructus Zizyphi Jujubae (*Da Zao*), 7 pieces. After taking this prescription, the patient's sleep returned to normal. Two and four years later, the patient once again developed insomnia. Each time, she was represcribed another seven *ji* of this formula which continued to achieve a good effect.

### ❖ CASE 2⁴ ❖

The patient was a 25 year old female who had miscarried one month before. In addition, she had suddenly suffered fright and intimidation. This, plus irritation and anger, had resulted in her being unable to sleep at night in the last few days. The patient's cheeks were flushed red and she complained of spontaneous perspiration as if being drenched. She had fright palpitations, was mentally disturbed, and did not know what to do. Her pulse was fine and rapid and her tongue was red with scanty fur.

This was yin not restraining yang with heart-kidney not interacting. Therefore, the treatment principles were to enrich water and downbear fire, settle timidity and calm the heart. The formula consisted of: Radix Panacis Quinquefolii (*Xi Yang Shen*), 5g, Sclerotium Poriae Cocos (*Fu Ling*), 10g, Dens Draconis (*Long Chi*), 15g, uncooked Concha Haliotidis (*Shi Jue Ming*), 30g, pig blood-processed Radix Salviae Miltiorrhizae (*Dan Shen*), 10g, Cinnabar-processed Medulla Junco Effusi (*Deng Xin Cao*), 3 stalks, Rhizoma Coptidis Chinensis (*Huang Lian*), 1.5g, Folium Bambusae (*Zhu Ye*), 6g, and Fructus Levis Tritici Aestivi (*Fu Xiao Mai*), 30g. Two *ji* of these medicinals were decocted in water and administered internally plus powdered Margarita (*Zhen Zhu*), 0.5g, Succinum (*Hu Po*), 1.5g, and Cinnabar (*Zhu Sha*), 0.5g, swallowed down with the decocted liquid.

On the second visit, the patient reported that she had been able to sleep the night before. However, the sleep was short and she was easily frightened and awakened. Dr. Zhang thought that, according to the *Nei Jing (Inner Classic)*, "Fright had caused the qi to become chaotic, and anger had caused the qi to ascend." Therefore, she was given the following formula: pig blood-processed Radix Salviae Miltiorrhizae (*Dan Shen*), 12g, Dens Draconis (*Long Chi*), 15g, Semen Biotae Orientalis (*Bai Zi Ren*), 8g, Sclerotium Pararadicis Poriae Cocos (*Fu Shen*), 12g, Rhizoma Coptidis Chinensis (*Huang Lian*), 1.5g, uncooked Radix Rehmanniae (*Sheng Di*), 10g, Semen Zizyphi Spinosae (*Suan Zao Ren*), 10g, processed Rhizoma Cyperi Rotundi (*Xiang Fu*), 8g, and *Bu Xin Dan* (Supplement the Heart Elixir), 10g. Five *ji* were decocted in water and administered internally.

After taking these five *ji*, all the patient's symptoms were calmed and her sleeping and eating were normal.

### ❖ CASE 3⁵ ❖

The patient was a 44 year old male who had suffered from insomnia for the past year. Recently, due to a high fever, he had excessively profuse sweating which continued for days and would not stop as well as worry and anxiety, the man had become emotionally upset and could not sleep at all at night. In addition, he experienced dizziness, lack of strength, vexation and agitation, tinnitus, and spontaneous perspiration as well as occasional nausea. His appetite was not good, his pulse was bowstring, and his tongue fur was thin and slimy.

Thus, Dr. Zhang chose to level the liver and harmonize the stomach, calm the heart and quiet the spirit by administering five *ji* of the following formula: Radix Codonopsitis Pilosulae (*Dang Shen*), 10g, mix-fried Radix Astragali Membranacei (*Huang Qi*), 10g, Rhizoma Atractylodis Macrocephalae (*Bai Zhu*), 8g, Sclerotium Pararadicis Poriae Cocos (*Fu Shen*), 10g, processed Rhizoma Pinelliae Ternatae (*Ban Xia*), 8g, Caulis Polygoni Multiflori (*Ye Jiao Teng*), 15g, stir-fried Fructus Immaturus Citri Aurantii (*Zhi Shi*), 6g, ginger-processed Caulis Bambusae In Taeniis (*Zhu Ru*), 6g, powdered Semen Zizyphi Spinosae (*Suan Zao Ren*), 3g, and Fructus Zizyphi Jujubae (*Da Zao*), 5 pieces. In addition, three grams of powdered Semen Zizyphi Spinosae (*Suan Zao Ren*), one gram of Succinum, and 10 grams of *Bai Zi Wan* (Biota Pills) were swallowed with the decoction. After taking these medicinals, the patient was able to sleep throughout the night.

### ❖ CASE 4⁶ ❖

The patient was a 30 year old female cadre whose body was habitually healthy and who previously had been without disease. Ninety days before, due to a violent traffic accident, the child she was carrying was killed. Since then, the patient had been over-working and was anxious and worried. Her essence spirit was listless. Dressing, she knew no warmth, and eating, she knew no flavor. Often she was not able to close her eyes the whole night. She had already been treated with Western medicines, however these had not had any effect. Recently, her insomnia had gotten even more severe, and she lay in bed the whole night tossing and turning.

When seen by Dr. Chen, the patient's facial complexion was somber white. However, both eyes were slightly bloodshot. Her spirit was exhausted, her tongue was dark and purplish, and her pulse was bowstring. Based on her tongue and pulse as well as her history, the patient's pattern was categorized as blood stasis, and, therefore, she was administered *Xue Fu Zhu Yu Tang* (Blood Mansion Dispel Stasis Decoction): Flos Carthami Tinctorii (*Hong Hua*), 9g, Semen Pruni Persicae (*Tao Ren*), 15g, Radix Angelicae Sinensis (*Dang Gui*), 9g, Radix Ligustici Wallichii (*Chuan Xiong*), 9g, Radix Achyranthis Bidentatae (*Niu Xi*), 9g, uncooked Radix Rehmanniae (*Sheng Di*), 12g, Radix Bupleuri (*Chai Hu*), 6g, Radix Rubrus Paeoniae Lactiflorae (*Chi Shao*), 9g, Fructus Citri Aurantii (*Zhi Ke*), 9g, mix-fried Radix Glycyrrhizae (*Gan Cao*), 6g, and Radix Pseudoginseng (*Tian Qi*), 6g. Three *ji* were decocted in water and administered internally, and, after taking these medicinals, the patient was able to sleep at night normally. She was thus given 10 more *ji* of this same formula, and no further recurrence of this problem was seen.

### ❖ CASE 5[7] ❖

The patient was a 27 year old female teacher who had a difficult delivery and had lost a lot of blood. Postpartum, she was not able to sleep at night. She had taken Valium but with no effect. Fifteen days after delivery, she came to the authors of this case for examination. In addition to insomnia, she had lassitude of the spirit, fatigued limbs, dizziness, heart palpitations, a lusterless facial complexion, and occasional lower abdominal pain which was fixed in location. Her lochia was scanty in amount and blackish in color. Her tongue was pale red with thin, white fur. Her pulse was fine and choppy. Based on the large blood loss during delivery, the patient's pattern was categorized as heart-spleen dual vacuity and she was given seven *ji* of *Gui Pi Tang* (Restore the Spleen Decoction) with additional spirit-quieting medicinals. However, there was no marked improvement in her insomnia.

The patient was re-examined, and, although there were signs and symptoms of qi and blood dual vacuity, based on the fixed location lower abdominal pain, scanty lochia which was black in color, and choppy pulse, it was realized that she also presented with the pattern of static blood stopped or gathered internally. Because static blood impedes the engenderment of new or fresh blood, even though there was definite qi and blood vacuity, the authors concluded that transforming stasis should be the ruling principle. Therefore, the woman was administered three *ji* of *Shao Fu Zhu Yu Tang Jia Jian* (Lower Abdomen Dispel Stasis Decoction with Additions & Subtractions): Fructus Foeniculi Vulgaris (*Xiao Hui Xiang*), 8g, dry

Rhizoma Zingiberis (*Gan Jiang*), 10g, Semen Pruni Persicae (*Tao Ren*), 12g, Flos Carthami Tinctorii (*Hong Hua*), 8g, Radix Angelicae Sinensis (*Dang Gui*), 15g, Radix Ligustici Wallichii (*Chuan Xiong*), 10g, Feces Trogopterori Seu Pteromi (*Wu Ling Zhi*), 8g, Radix Astragali Membranacei (*Huang Qi*), 20g, Radix Codonopsitis Pilosulae (*Dang Shen*), 20g, cooked Radix Rehmanniae (*Shu Di*), 20g, Semen Biotae Orientalis (*Bai Zi Ren*), 15g, and Semen Zizyphi Spinosae (*Suan Zao Ren*), 15g.

After taking these three *ji*, the amount of the lochia increased and the abdominal pain decreased. In addition, the patient's sleep at night improved. Hence she was prescribed another seven *ji* of the above formula, after which her sleep markedly improved, her lochia basically ceased, and her abdominal pain was resolved. Therefore, Fennel and dry Ginger were removed from the formula and the amounts of Astragalus and Codonopsis were doubled. Due to this, the patient was able to sleep at night and all her symptoms markedly diminished. The patient was considered cured and advised to eat supplementing foods.

### ❖ CASE 6[8] ❖

The patient was a 35 year old female peasant farmer who first entered the hospital on Dec. 3, 1984. This woman's body was weak and she had many diseases. Her constructive and blood were habitually vacuous. Three years before, she had been the butt of a neighbor's gossip. After that, she developed rib-side distention and fullness with occasional aching and pain and a tendency to sighing. She was also occasionally tense, agitated, and easily angered and she had a hard time falling asleep at night. However, when she did, she had nightmares and tossed and turned all night. In the previous two years, her emotional disease had gotten worse. She had headaches, blurred vision, poor appetite, frequent hiccups, and her menses became irregular and accompanied by menstrual pain. She had been diagnosed as suffering from neurasthenia at her local hospital and treated with Valium and perphenaine without result. Therefore she was referred to the authors of this case for examination. In addition to the above, they determined she had acid regurgitation, a pale tongue with white fur, and a bowstring, fine pulse.

Based on the above signs and symptoms, the authors categorized this woman's pattern as liver depression-blood vacuity. Therefore, the treatment principles were to soothe the liver and rectify the qi, regulate the blood and quiet the spirit. The formula prescribed was *Dan Zhi Xiao Yao San Jia Wei* (Moutan & Gardenia Rambling Powder with Added Flavors): Radix Bupleuri (*Chai Hu*), 10g, Radix Angelicae Sinensis (*Dang Gui*), 18g, Radix Albus Paeoniae Lactiflorae (*Bai Shao*), 12g, Rhizoma Atractylodis Macrocephalae (*Bai Zhu*), 10g, Sclerotium Poriae Cocos (*Fu Ling*), 15g, Radix Glycyrrhizae (*Gan Cao*), 6g, Cortex Radicis Moutan (*Dan Pi*), 7g, Fructus Gardeniae Jasminoidis (*Zhi Zi*), 10g, Fructus Chaenomelis Lagenariae (*Mu Gua*), 10g, Caulis Milletiae Seu Spatholobi (*Ji Xue Teng*), 12g, and vinegar stir-fried Fructus Evodiae Rutecarpae (*Wu Zhu Yu*), 10g.

After taking 16 *ji* of the above formula, the patient's eating and drinking had increased and her chest and rib-side distention and fullness had disappeared. However, her sleep had only somewhat improved. Therefore, 15 grams each of Caulis Polygoni Multiflori (*Ye Jiao Teng*) and Semen Biotae Orientalis (*Bai Zi Ren*) were added in order to subdue yang and quiet the ethereal soul. After taking 15 *ji* of this formula, the patient was cured and discharged from the hospital. On follow-up after two years, there had been no recurrence.

❖ **CASE 7**[9] ❖

The patient was a 33 year old male cadre who was initially examined on Apr. 2, 1961. At the time of this examination, he had already been diagnosed with stomach ulcers and neurasthenia. The patient's major complaints in seeking treatment was heart vexation and insomnia which had gotten worse in the last week. The patient had stomach duct distention, fullness, and burning pain, acid regurgitation, dizziness and heavy-headedness, heart palpitations, and scanty sleep. In the last seven days, he had not been able to sleep at all at night and he was both fearful and frightful. Although his mouth was dry, he had no desire to drink. His tongue was red with white, sticky fur, and his pulse was deep, moderate or relaxed (*i.e.*, slightly slow), and slippery.

Based on the above signs and symptoms, this patient's pattern was categorized as heart-gallbladder qi vacuity with damp heat obstructing the middle burner. Therefore, the treatment principles were to boost the qi and settle fright, quiet the spirit and stabilize the mind, assisted by clearing heat. In order to accomplish these goals, he was prescribed *An Wo Ru Shen Tang Jia Jian* (Quiet Lying Like a Spirit Decoction with Additions & Subtractions): Sclerotium Poriae Cocos (*Fu Ling*), 6g, Sclerotium Pararadicis Poriae Cocos (*Fu Shen*), 6g, uncooked Rhizoma Atractylodis Macrocephalae (*Bai Zhu*), 9g, stir-fried Radix Dioscoreae Oppositae (*Shan Yao*), 9g, Calcitum (*Han Shui Shi*), 4.5g, Radix Pseudostellariae (*Tai Zi Shen*), 9g, stir-fried Semen

Zizyphi Spinosae (*Suan Zao Ren*), 12g, processed Radix Polygalae Tenuifoliae (*Yuan Zhi*), 4.5g, and mix-fried Radix Glycyrrhizae (*Gan Cao*), 3g.

After taking three *ji* of the above formula, the man's sleep had improved and his fear and fright were less. The stomach duct heat was eliminated, but there was still stomach distention and acid regurgitation. His appetite was small and his digestion was slow. His tongue fur was still white and sticky and his pulse was deep and relaxed. Therefore, 1.5 grams of Rhizoma Coptidis Chinensis (*Huang Lian*) and 4.5 grams of Fructus Citri Aurantii (*Zhi Ke*) were added to the above formula. After taking three more *ji*, the man's sleep had increased to the point where he was sleeping four hours per night. The heart palpitations were less, but there was still stomach duct distention and belching, plus his limbs felt heavy, sore, and without strength. His tongue was now red with white fur, and his left pulse was deep and bowstring, while his right pulse was deep and relaxed. Hence, Polygala was removed from the second prescription and Pericarpium Citri Reticulatae (*Chen Pi*), 4.5g, and stir-fried Fructus Germinatus Hordei Vulgaris (*Mai Ya*), 6g, were added. After taking yet three more *ji*, the patient was able to go to sleep at night even though he had profuse dreams. His stomach duct was still not soothed and he had low back soreness and heaviness of the knees. There was generalized fatigue and lack of strength. The pulse and tongue were the same as before. Therefore, the patient was prescribed further decoctions to continue soothing his liver and harmonizing his stomach, but his insomnia was cured.

❖ **CASE 8**[10] ❖

The patient was a 32 year old female. Ever since giving birth two years before, she had been suffering from insomnia. She had been treated previously with *Tian Wang Bu Xin Dan* (Heavenly Emperor Supplement the Heart Elixir), *Zhu Sha An Shen Wan* (Cinnabar Quiet the Spirit Pills), and other such medicines without result. In the last month, the woman's insomnia had gradually gotten worse. It was now not uncommon for her to lie awake the entire night. If she was able to close her eyes, she had nightmares. When examined, it was determined that the woman's signs and symptoms included heart vexation, tension, and agitation, essence spirit abstraction, restlessness, a bitter taste in her mouth, dry throat, vexatious heat in the heart of her hands, short, reddish urination, a red tongue with thin, yellow fur, and a weak, forceless pulse. She was prescribed six *ji* of *Suan Zao Ren Tang* (Zizyphus Spinosa Decoction) without effect. Then she was prescribed several *ji* of *Huang Lian E Jiao Tang*

(Coptis & Donkey Skin Glue Decoction) also without effect.

After thinking a long time about the patient's case, the author of this case consulted with his teacher, Wang Zi-wen, who suggested that this was a case of lily disease. Therefore, the patient was administered *Bai He Di Huang Tang Jia Wei* (Lily & Rehmannia Decoction with Added Flavors): Bulbus Lilii (*Bai He*), 20g, uncooked Radix Rehmanniae (*Sheng Di*), 12g, and Talcum (*Hua Shi*), 10g. After taking six *ji* of this formula, the woman's heart vexation had disappeared and her sleep had increased. Now she was able to sleep 3-4 hours per night at a time. In addition, her affect appeared more stable. Another 12 *ji* of this same formula were prescribed and all this patient's symptoms disappeared.

## ENDNOTES:

[1] This pattern can also be called shao yang gallbladder channel depressive fire.

[2] Retained heat means retained heat evils at the end of a warm heat disease. In this case, heat evils have damaged and consumed yin fluids as well as righteous qi and have not yet been completely eliminated. This combination of vacuity heat and lingering heat evils ascend to harass the heart spirit.

[3] Ding Ying, "The Treatment of Insomnia & Anxiety with *Jia Yi Gui Zang Tang* (Jia & Yi Returning & Treasuring Decoction)," *Zhe Jiang Zhong Yi Za Zhi* (Zhejiang Journal of Chinese Medicine), #10, 1995, p. 446

[4] Zhang Cun-quan, *Shang Hai Lao Zhong Yi Jing Yan Xuan Bian* (Selected Case Histories of Shanghai Old Chinese Doctors), Shanghai Municipal Health Department, Shanghai Science & Technology Press, Shanghai, 1984, p. 139

[5] *Ibid.*, p. 139-140

[6] Chen Gui-fu, "Experiential Knowledge of the Treatment of Insomnia with *Xue Fu Zhu Yu Tang* (Blood Mansion Dispel Stasis Decoction)," *Hei Long Jiang Zhong Yi Yao* (Heilongjiang Chinese Medicine & Medicinals), #5, 1996, p. 35

[7] Xu Bi-hua & Xie Qing-lin, "The Treatment of Three Cases of Insomnia Based on Stasis," *Fu Jian Zhong Yi Yao* (Fujian Chinese Medicine & Medicinals), #3, 1995, p. 61

[8] Li & Liu, *op. cit.*, p. 576-577

[9] *Ibid.*, p. 577-578

[10] Chen Bao-ming & Zhao Jin-xi, *Gu Fang Miao Yong* (Ancient Formulas, Wondrous Uses), Science & Technology Dissemination Press, Beijing, 1994, p. 411-412

# ❖ 14 ❖

# Easily Being Awakened

Easily being awakened, or *yi xing* in Chinese, means that the patient can easily fall asleep but does not sleep soundly. Rather, they are easily wakened. The duration of sleep is short, and it is difficult for the person to get back to sleep after they are awakened. The Chinese disease causes and mechanisms for this condition are the same as for profuse dreams discussed above.

Easily being awakened does not correspond to a primary Western psychiatric disorder. However, sleep that is disrupted by episodes of awakening and difficulty returning to sleep is a symptom that is commonly found in many medical or psychiatric disorders. In conventional Western medicine, insomnia is a nonspecific term that refers to the subjective experience of non-refreshing sleep that may or may not correspond to identifiable disturbances in the normal pattern or quality of sleep. As discussed in Chapter 13, this Book, Insomnia, Western psychiatry recognizes two basic patterns of disturbed sleep: dyssomnias and parasomnias. Dyssomnias are disorders in which the central clinical focus is on problems initiating or maintaining sleep. Easily being awakened would likely be described as middle awakening in contemporary Western psychiatry and is considered a kind of dyssomnia. In contrast to dyssomnias, parasomnias are disorders of sleep in which the focus of clinical attention is a behavioral abnormality that occurs during sleep. Parasomnias include sleep automatisms like sleeptalking or sleepwalking. Although sleep disorders, including easily being awakened, frequently accompany numerous medical or psychiatric disorders, there are no consistent relationships between specific disorders and discrete patterns of disturbed sleep.

### Nosology:

Western approaches to classification of disturbed sleep are reviewed in Chapters 11 and 13, this Book. Because of the wide range of sleep patterns accepted as "normal," disorders of sleep can be understood only after reviewing history and associated clinical symptoms on a case by case basis. By definition, a dyssomnia is characterized by at least one month of disrupted sleep that is typically associated with daytime fatigue and is not caused by an underlying medical or psychiatric disorder. Primary dyssomnias are disturbances in the quality or duration of sleep for which there is no identified medical or psychiatric etiology. Excessive sleep and sleep that is delayed or interrupted by frequent awakenings often lead to significant impairments in social and occupational functioning. A disruptive pattern of insomnia must persist at least one month and cause significant social or occupational impairment. In Western psychiatric nosology, difficulty maintaining sleep (*i.e.,* easily being awakened) is often associated with difficulty initiating sleep. Circadian rhythm sleep disorders are disruptive patterns of frequent awakening that are temporally linked to recent travel across time zones or changes in the sleep-wake cycle related to changes in shifts at work.

In contrast to primary dyssomnias, parasomnias, the other category of primary sleep disorders, are characterized by behaviors that take place during sleep, typically disrupting sleep or causing awakening. As noted, these disorders are associated with physiological abnormalities or pathological patterns of behavior that occur during sleep, including nightmares, sleep terrors, sleep walking, sleep-talking, and other "sleep automatisms" as well as impaired sleep caused by irregular breathing (sleep apnea). Such behaviors interfere with the regular pattern of sleep and are associated with daytime fatigue because they frequently lead to a state of easily being awakened during the course of normal sleep.

In contrast to primary disorders of sleep, secondary sleep disorders are patterns of disturbed sleep-waking that are caused by an identifiable underlying medical or psychiatric disorder. Representative medical and psychiatric disorders that are typically accompanied by a pattern of easily being awakened are discussed below.

### EPIDEMIOLOGY:

Primary insomnia is a common disorder among Western populations surveyed. It is estimated that roughly one-third of all surveyed healthy adults complained of transient insomnia unrelated to medical or psychiatric causes. The prevalence of sleep apnea (obstructive and central combined) is estimated to be as high as 10% and appears to occur in a familial pattern. Two-thirds of surveyed shift workers complained of a sleep disturbance, but the prevalence of sleep disorders among individuals who frequently travel across several time zones has not been clearly established. The prevalence of nightmare disorder has not been clearly established. Sleep terrors are rare in adults but may affect as many as 5% of children in Western populations surveyed. Sleep terrors appear to follow a familial pattern

and are often associated with other sleep automatisms, including sleepwalking. Easily being awakened is a complaint that frequently accompanies many psychiatric disorders. As many as 30-50% of outpatients report middle insomnia at some point during the course of treatment for a major psychiatric disorder. Medically ill patients, alcoholics, and drug addicts report similarly high rates of disrupted sleep.

### DIFFERENTIAL DIAGNOSIS:

The initial task in accurately identifying the cause of easily being awakened is to rule out possible medical etiologies or substance abuse. Many medical or neurological disorders are associated with disrupted sleep. Many neurological disorders, including Parkinson's disease, Huntington's disease, Alzheimer's disease, epilepsy, and cerebrovascular disease, are commonly associated with disorders of initiating and maintaining sleep. Commonly occurring but frequently undiagnosed causes of easily being awakened include sleep apnea and restless leg syndrome. Many obese individuals who complain of chronic fatigue experience repeated brief awakenings throughout the night when the upper airway is transiently obstructed during normal sleep. In contrast, individuals who suffer from central sleep apnea are typically not overweight and experience repeated episodes of transient cessation in the normal rhythm of breathing related to dysregulation in the brain's respiratory drive center.

Many pharmacological treatments for these disorders also often disrupt sleep. A pattern of easily being awakened is also a frequent concomitant of substance abuse, including alcohol and illicit drugs, such as cocaine and methamphetamine. Chronic use of many short-acting sedative-hypnotic medications, including alprazolam (Xanax) and others, is associated with withdrawal during sleep that

| DIFFERENTIAL DIAGNOSIS | | |
|---|---|---|
| **1. MEDICAL DISORDERS** | **2. EFFECTS OF SUBSTANCES** | **3. PSYCHIATRIC DISORDERS** |
| A. PARKINSON'S DISEASE <br> B. HUNTINGTON'S DISEASE <br> C. ALZHEIMER'S DISEASE <br> D. SEIZURE DISORDERS <br> E. CEREBROVASCULAR ACCIDENT (CVA) <br> F. SLEEP APNEA (CENTRAL OR OBSTRUCTIVE) <br> G. RESTLESS LEG SYNDROME | A. ALCOHOL AND ILLICIT SUBSTANCE (INCLUDING COCAINE AND METHAMPHETAMINE) INTOXICATION OR WITHDRAWAL <br> B. SIDE EFFECTS OF MEDICATIONS, INCLUDING SHORT-ACTING SEDATIVE-HYPNOTICS AND CERTAIN ANTIDEPRESSANTS | A. PANIC DISORDER <br> B. GENERALIZED ANXIETY DISORDER (GAD) <br> C. MAJOR DEPRESSION AND OTHER MOOD DISORDERS <br> D. SCHIZOPHRENIA AND OTHER PSYCHOTIC DISORDERS <br> E. POST-TRAUMATIC STRESS DISORDER (PTSD) |

results in a pattern of disrupted sleep including frequent awakenings and non-refreshing sleep with residual daytime fatigue. Certain antidepressants, including for example venlafaxine (Effexor) and fluoxetine (Prozac), are associated with easily being awakened or middle insomnia.

Common underlying psychiatric causes of easily being awakened include panic disorder, generalized anxiety, mood disorders, psychotic disorders, and post-traumatic stress disorder (PTSD).

## ETIOLOGY & PATHOPHYSIOLOGY:

Easily being awakened can point to physiological dysregulation affecting many parts of the body. Pathological changes in brain regions implicated in many neurological disorders affect sleep directly by disrupting normal functioning of brain circuits that regulate sleep. Certain kinds of epilepsy are associated with an increased likelihood of seizure episodes (leading to easily being awakened) during sleep. Medications that have stimulant-like side effects, including theophylline, often cause disturbed or impaired sleep. In obstructive sleep apnea, obese individuals experience transient obstruction of the upper airway by excessive surrounding tissue in the larynx during normal periods of shallow breathing. The resulting pattern of repetitive interruption in normal respiration results in repeated episodes of transient cerebral hypoxia that stimulate awakening and a "struggle" to breathe in order to restore an adequate cerebral oxygen supply. The putative cause of central sleep apnea is dysregulation in the brain's sleep regulating center. Rebound activation of the brain as transient sedating effects wear off is the cause of disrupted sleep and easily being awakened in alcoholics and substance abusers. Individuals who are predisposed to panic attacks may experience panic attacks more frequently during a certain phase of sleep. The specific etiology of this pattern of sleep-related panic attacks has not been clearly established. In PTSD, recurring nightmares disrupt restful sleep, leading to easily being awakened. For unclear reasons, depression is often accompanied by excessive sleep or disrupted sleep. In contrast, by definition, mania is associated with severely impaired sleep.

## WESTERN MEDICAL TREATMENT:

When easily being awakened has been diagnosed in relation to an underlying medical disorder, correction of that disorder often alleviates the problem. However, middle awakening is associated with many neurological disorders, including Alzheimer's disease, Huntington's disease, and Parkinson's disease, for which contemporary Western medicine offers only symptomatic relief with currently available therapies. Sedative-hypnotics sometimes improve the overall quality of sleep for these patients. Sedatives should be avoided when treating sleep disturbances (including easily being awakened) in alcoholics or substance abusers because of the high risk of relapse associated with their use in these populations. Nonaddictive medications, including antihistamines, and some of the more recently introduced sedative-hypnotics, including zolpidem (Ambien) and zaleplon (Sonata), are safe alternatives to traditional benzodiazepines. When disrupted sleep is related to an underlying psychiatric disorder, it will typically resolve with effective pharmacologic treatment of that disorder. It is prudent to discontinue benzodiazepines or other sedative-hypnotic agents after several weeks in order to reduce the risk of dependence and tolerance (i.e., the requirement for a gradually increasing dose for an equivalent sedating effect). In addition to pharmacological management, cognitive and behavioral therapy are sometimes helpful in controlling anxiety symptoms, thus resulting in diminished episodes of awakening and, therefore, indirectly improving the quality of sleep.

## SHORT & LONG-TERM ADVANTAGES & DISADVANTAGES OF WESTERN MEDICAL TREATMENT:

Sedative-hypnotics and all other medications used to treat sleep disorders have associated side effects, including daytime sedation and mild to moderate cognitive impairment. Several more serious possible side effects of sedative-hypnotic agents are more common in the elderly. These include orthostatic hypotension (which poses a significant fall risk in physically impaired patients) and confusion. Chemical dependence is the most serious adverse consequence of long-term sedative-hypnotic use. In dependence, physiological tolerance to large doses of benzodiazepines develops with continued use, and the patient may experience withdrawal symptoms during periods of nonuse. Withdrawal from benzodiazepines or other sedative-hypnotics is uncomfortable for young adults and potentially dangerous for elderly or medically compromised patients because of associated autonomic activation including increased heart-rate, elevated blood pressure, tremulousness, perspiration, and frequent symptoms of anxiety or confusion. Other pharmacological agents used to treat symptoms of easily being awakened sometimes cause unpleasant side effects, including dry mouth, urinary retention, blurred vision, and sedation.

## INDICATIONS FOR REFERRAL TO WESTERN MEDICAL SERVICES:

A pattern of easily being awakened that is associated with other symptoms suggesting an underlying seizure disorder,

Parkinson's disease, or other serious neurological or medical disorder is sufficient basis for urgent referral to the nearest emergency room. A persisting pattern of disturbed sleep in the context of chronic abuse of alcohol or an illicit substance warrants urgent referral to a program for detoxification or rehabilitation. Non-urgent referral to a psychiatrist is appropriate when reasonable efforts have excluded possible medical causes of easily being awakened and there is no evidence of on-going substance abuse. In such cases, when symptoms have been unresponsive to an appropriate course of Chinese medical treatment, consultation with a psychiatrist or neurologist may lead to an integrative treatment strategy.

TREATMENT BASED ON PATTERN DISCRIMINATION:

1. HEART-GALLBLADDER QI VACUITY PATTERN

MAIN SYMPTOMS: Vacuity vexation, heart palpitations, paranoia, timidity, susceptibility to fright, frequent sighing, profuse dreams, easily being awakened, waking in a fright, possible profuse phlegm, a pale tongue, and a bowstring, fine pulse

TREATMENT PRINCIPLES: Nourish the heart and boost the qi, settle fright and quiet the spirit

FORMULA & MEDICINALS: *Suan Zao Ren Tang Jia Wei* (Zizyphus Spinosa Decoction with Added Flavors)

Sclerotium Poriae Cocos (*Fu Ling*), 10g, Radix Panacis Ginseng (*Ren Shen*), 6-10g (decocted first), Radix Polygalae Tenuifoliae (*Yuan Zhi*), 6-10g, Concha Ostreae (*Mu Li*), 15g (decocted first), Semen Zizyphi Spinosae (*Suan Zao Ren*), 12-15g, Radix Albus Paeoniae Lactiflorae (*Bai Shao*), 10g, Rhizoma Anemarrhenae Aspheloidis (*Zhi Mu*), 10g, Radix Ligustici Wallichii (*Chuan Xiong*), 10g (added later), Radix Glycyrrhizae (*Gan Cao*), 3-10g

Decoct in water and administer orally in two divided doses, noon and before bed at night, one *ji* per day.

ACUPUNCTURE: *Da Ling* (Per 7), *Xin Shu* (Bl 15), *Shen Men* (Ht 7). Use even supplementing-even draining technique.

2. HEART-SPLEEN DUAL VACUITY PATTERN

MAIN SYMPTOMS: Profuse dreams, easily being awakened, impaired memory, excessive thinking, lassitude of the spirit, lack of strength, a white facial complexion, loose stools, a pale tongue with thin, white fur, and a fine, weak pulse

TREATMENT PRINCIPLES: Fortify the spleen and boost the qi, nourish the heart and quiet the spirit

FORMULA & MEDICINALS: *Gui Pi Tang Jia Jian* (Restore the Spleen Decoction with Additions & Subtractions)

Sclerotium Pararadicis Poriae Cocos (*Fu Shen*), 12g, stir-fried Semen Zizyphi Spinosae (*Suan Zao Ren*), 12g, Rhizoma Atractylodis Macrocephalae (*Bai Zhu*), 10g, Radix Astragali Membranacei (*Huang Qi*), 15g, Arillus Euphoriae Longanae (*Long Yan Rou*), 12g, Radix Panacis Ginseng (*Ren Shen*), 5g (decocted first), Semen Biotae Orientalis (*Bai Zi Ren*), 12g, Caulis Polygoni Multiflori (*Ye Jiao Teng*), 12g, Fructus Zizyphi Jujubae (*Da Zao*), 3 pieces, mix-fried Radix Glycyrrhizae (*Gan Cao*), 6g

Decoct in water and administer orally in two divided doses, noon and before bed at night, one *ji* per day.

ACUPUNCTURE: *Shen Men* (Ht 7), *Xin Shu* (Bl 15), *Pi Shu* (Bl 20), *San Yin Jiao* (Sp 6). Use supplementing technique.

3. NON-INTERACTION BETWEEN THE HEART & KIDNEYS PATTERN

MAIN SYMPTOMS: Easy and frequent waking up, profuse dreams, difficulty falling asleep again, reduced sleep, vexation and agitation, heart palpitations, low back and knee soreness and limpness, seminal emission, possible afternoon tidal heat, night sweats, a red tongue with white fur, and a fine, rapid pulse

TREATMENT PRINCIPLES: Enrich yin and downbear fire, promote the interaction between the heart and kidneys

FORMULA & MEDICINALS: *Huang Lian E Jiao Tang Jia Jian* (Coptis & Donkey Skin Glue Decoction with Additions & Subtractions)

Rhizoma Coptidis Chinensis (*Huang Lian*), 6g (added later), Radix Scutellariae Baicalensis (*Huang Qin*), 10g, Radix Albus Paeoniae Lactiflorae (*Bai Shao*), 10g, Gelatinum Corii Asini (*E Jiao*), 6g (dissolved at the end in the hot decoction), egg yolk (*Ji Zi Huang*), 1 piece (added at the end and stirred or whipped into the hot decoction), Radix Polygalae Tenuifoliae (*Yuan Zhi*), 6-10g, Sclerotium Pararadicis Poriae Cocos (*Fu Shen*), 12g, Tuber Asparagi Cochinensis (*Tian Dong*), 12g, stir-fried Semen Zizyphi Spinosae (*Suan Zao Ren*), 12g, Semen Biotae Orientalis (*Bai Zi Ren*), 12g

Decoct in water and administer orally in two divided doses, noon and before bed at night, one *ji* per day.

**ACUPUNCTURE:** *Yin Xi* (Ht 6), *Jie Xi* (St 41), *Tai Xi* (Ki 3), *Yong Quan* (Ki 1), *Yin Tang* (M-HN-3). Use even supplementing-even draining technique. Bathe the feet in warm water and then massage *Yong Quan* strongly just before bed or if one wakes up.

### 4. LIVER FIRE HARASSING INTERNALLY PATTERN

**MAIN SYMPTOMS:** Easily being awakened, profuse dreams or nightmares that disturb the sleep, irritability, heart vexation, headache, red eyes, a red facial complexion, rib-side pain, a bitter taste in the mouth, tinnitus, a red tongue with yellow fur, and a bowstring, rapid pulse

**TREATMENT PRINCIPLES:** Clear the liver and gallbladder, drain fire and quiet the spirit

**FORMULA & MEDICINALS:** *Long Dan Xie Gan Tang Jia Jian* (Gentiana Drain the Liver Decoction with Additions & Subtractions)

Radix Gentianae Scabrae (*Long Dan Cao*), 6-10g, Radix Scutellariae Baicalensis (*Huang Qin*), 10g, stir-fried Fructus Gardeniae Jasminoidis (*Zhi Zi*), 10g, Radix Bupleuri (*Chai Hu*), 10g, Radix Albus Paeoniae Lactiflorae (*Bai Shao*), 10g, Radix Angelicae Sinensis (*Dang Gui*), 10g, uncooked Radix Rehmanniae (*Sheng Di*), 12g, Radix Ligustici Wallichii (*Chuan Xiong*), 6-10g (added later), Rhizoma Anemarrhenae Aspheloidis (*Zhi Mu*), 10g, uncooked Radix Glycyrrhizae (*Gan Cao*), 3-6g, Rhizoma Coptidis Chinensis (*Huang Lian*), 3-6g (added later)

Decoct in water and administer orally in two divided doses, noon and before bed at night, one *ji* per day.

**ACUPUNCTURE:** *Xing Jian* (Liv 2), *Zu Qiao Yin* (GB 44), *Shen Men* (Ht 7), *Nei Guan* (Per 6). Use draining technique.

**CLINICAL TIPS:**

1. This is rarely a patient's major complaint. Typically, Western patients do not distinguish this complaint from insomnia in general.

2. As with insomnia, when administering Chinese medicinals in two daily doses, the first dose should be given at noon and the second dose should be administered a half hour before bed at night.

# ❖ 15 ❖

# SOMNOLENCE

Somnolence, *shi mian*, literally means addiction to sleep in Chinese. It refers to sleepiness while awake and a virtually permanent desire to sleep. Generally speaking, the duration of sleep is long, and, after waking, the patient soon falls asleep again. Other Chinese synonyms are *shi wo*, addiction to lying down, and *hao mian*, good at or easy to sleep. The term somnolence first shows up in the *Su Wen (Simple Questions)* where it is also referred to by the synonym "good at or easy lying down." In the *Ling Shu (Spiritual Axis)*, the same disorder is referred to as "profuse lying down" and "quiet lying down." Zhang Zhong-jing, in his Han dynasty *Shang Han Za Bing Lun (Treatise on Damage [Due to] Cold & Miscellaneous Diseases)*, refers to it as "desiring to sleep," "profuse sleeping," and "desiring to lie down."

In Western medicine, excessive daytime sleepiness or a continuous desire to sleep can significantly impair social and occupational functioning. Somnolence is a persisting change in level of arousal that accompanies numerous medical or psychiatric disorders. Contemporary Western psychiatry discerns three categories of abnormal somnolence: primary hypersomnia, narcolepsy, and patterns of excessive sleep or somnolence that are secondary to underlying medical or psychiatric disorders.

## NOSOLOGY:

According to the *DSM-IV*, primary hypersomnia is a disorder of the sleep-wake cycle characterized by excessive sleepiness that persists at least one month in the absence of identifiable underlying medical or psychiatric causes. A clinical determination of "excessive" sleepiness requires that the patient's complaint of sleepiness is a significant departure from his/her usual well-adjusted sleep pattern, is associated with significant occupational or social impairment and is outside of "normal" culturally expected behavior. Narcolepsy is characterized by irresistible urges to sleep accompanied by sudden loss of voluntary muscle tone (cataplexy). Sleep attacks take place without warning in the absence of fatigue, and the patient often experiences vivid hypnagogic hallucinations preceding sleep or hypnopompic hallucinations immediately before awakening. Several medical and psychiatric disorders are frequently accompanied by excessive daytime somnolence that interferes with social or occupational functioning. These are briefly reviewed in the following sections.

## DIFFERENTIAL DIAGNOSIS:

Hypothyroidism is commonly associated with hypersomnia and excessive daytime somnolence. Individuals who suffer from this endocrinological disorder are typically overweight and chronically fatigued and may be depressed. A pattern of disrupted sleep and excessive daytime somnolence is characteristic of sleep apnea. Lesions in the brain stem or hypothalamus (where the circadian pacemaker is located) can result in excessive nighttime sleeping or daytime somnolence. Seizure disorders sometimes masquerade as primary sleep disorders including

| DIFFERENTIAL DIAGNOSIS | | |
|---|---|---|
| **1. MEDICAL DISORDERS**<br><br>A. HYPOTHYROIDISM<br>B. LESIONS IN HYPOTHALAMUS<br>C. SEIZURE DISORDERS<br>D. DIFFUSE BRAIN INJURY CAUSED BY HEAD TRAUMA | **2. EFFECTS OF SUBSTANCES**<br><br>A. ALCOHOL OR ILLICIT SUBSTANCE INTOXICATION OR WITHDRAWAL<br>B. SIDE EFFECTS OF MEDICATIONS | **3. PSYCHIATRIC DISORDERS**<br><br>A. DEPRESSION<br>B. BIPOLAR DISORDER, DEPRESSED PHASE |

hypersomnia. Diffuse brain injury caused by trauma sometimes manifests as increased somnolence. In such cases a documented history of head trauma and the presence of focal neurological symptoms help to clarify the diagnosis. Many illicit substances as well as prescription and over-the-counter medications can result in prolonged sleep or increased daytime sleepiness.

Depression is the psychiatric disorder that is most commonly associated with increased sleep or excessive daytime somnolence. However, depressed patients frequently experience periods of severe insomnia. The sleep behavior of bipolar patients typically alternates between normal or prolonged sleep and severely diminished sleep as the patient cycles between depressive and manic episodes.

### ETIOLOGY & PATHOPHYSIOLOGY:

Excessive somnolence in the context of unresolving medical or psychiatric symptoms can reasonably be ascribed to the diagnosed disorder until proven otherwise. Hypersomnia accompanying hypothyroidism is due to a general lowering of basal metabolic rate that manifests as chronic fatigue and increased nighttime sleep. Somnolence in the context of underlying sleep apnea is caused by chronically non-refreshing sleep. Central nervous system lesions affecting the hypothalamus or brainstem disrupt normal functioning of brain circuits that permit normal sleep. Hypersomnia associated with diffuse brain injury has a similar etiology. Chronic abuse of marijuana, heroin and other illicit substances that function as CNS depressants typically leads to hypersomnia and excessive daytime somnolence. Many psychopharmacological agents, including many antidepressants and some over-the-counter medications (*e.g.*, dephenhydramine), have significant sedating side effects. When depression is the cause of hypersomnia, the underlying cause is believed to be dysregulation in serotonin, norepinephrine, or other neurotransmitters that are implicated in the pathogenesis of depression.

### WESTERN MEDICAL TREATMENT:

Symptomatic management of the underlying (primary) medical or psychiatric disorder often results in normalization in sleep behavior and diminished daytime somnolence. Obstructive sleep apnea is easily managed through a special night-time breathing apparatus (Continuous Positive Airway Pressure) or surgery. In contrast, there is no clearly effective treatment for central sleep apnea. Narcolepsy frequently responds to stimulants, including methylphenidate. Excess daytime somnolence or hypersomnia associated with depressed mood typically normalize as the patient responds to pharmacological therapy. Prolonged sleep or somnolence caused by chronic substance abuse or inappropriate use of medications is best managed in a chemical dependency program.

### SHORT & LONG-TERM ADVANTAGES & DISADVANTAGES OF WESTERN MEDICAL TREATMENT:

Principle advantages of successful pharmacological treatment of hypersomnia and excessive daytime somnolence include improved social and occupational functioning. There are no serious short-term disadvantages of contemporary pharmacological treatments of hypersomnia. Many patients who use methylphenidate (Ritalin) or other stimulants experience unpleasant side effects, including headaches, decreased appetite, anxiety, and sometimes disrupted sleep. Long-term disadvantages of conventional Western medical treatments are identical to problems associated with short-term treatment.

### PROGNOSIS:

Identification of a treatable medical cause of increased somnolence is prognostically favorable. In contrast, the absence of a clear cause or the presence of a primary disorder that is refractory to treatment is prognostically unfavorable. Although conventional Western medicine offers no cures for narcolepsy, the judicious use of stimulants permits most patients afflicted with narcolepsy to lead relatively normal lives.

## INDICATIONS FOR REFERRAL TO WESTERN MEDICAL SERVICES:

Excessive daytime somnolence or hypersomnia that is associated with a recent history (days to one week) of head trauma warrants emergency medical evaluation to rule out intracranial bleeding or other potentially life-threatening causes of change in the level of arousal. However, in the absence of new-onset underlying medical or psychiatric symptoms, persisting somnolence warrants routine medical or psychiatric consultation when the patient has not responded to appropriate Chinese medical interventions.

## CHINESE DISEASE CAUSES & MECHANISMS:

Somnolence can be due to various causes. However, basically, it is either due to insufficient yang qi to upbear and engender the heart spirit or some evil blocking and confounding the heart spirit. The vacuity mechanisms for somnolence include spleen qi vacuity, kidney yang vacuity, heart-spleen dual vacuity, kidney essence insufficiency. We have discussed all the causes and disease mechanisms of these above. The primary evil qi responsible for causing somnolence are phlegm and dampness. Damp depression hinders and obstructs the clear yang from being upborne. Such damp encumbrance is usually associated with spleen vacuity, in which case, a vacuous, weak spleen fails to transport and transform water fluids which then gather and collect and transform into evil dampness. It is also possible for the phlegm of phlegm heat to confound and cloud the heart spirit, thus causing somnolence even though heat typically causes wakefulness and agitation. In this case, phlegm is more pronounced than heat and is commonly accompanied by an element of spleen vacuity.

## TREATMENT BASED ON PATTERN DISCRIMINATION:

### 1. SPLEEN QI VACUITY WEAKNESS PATTERN

MAIN SYMPTOMS: Somnolence, lassitude of the spirit, a pale white facial complexion, shortness of breath, disinclination to talk, poor appetite, diarrhea or loose stools, possible undigested grains in the stools, a tender, pale tongue with slimy fur, and a fine, weak pulse

TREATMENT PRINCIPLES: Fortify the spleen and boost the qi, upbear the clear and vitalize the spirit

FORMULA & MEDICINALS: Bu Zhong Yi Qi Tang (Supplement the Center & Boost the Qi Decoction)

Radix Astragali Membranacei (Huang Qi), 15g, Radix Codonopsitis Pilosulae (Dang Shen), 10g, Rhizoma Atractylodis Macrocephalae (Bai Zhu), 10g, mix-fried Radix Glycyrrhizae (Zhi Gan Cao), 6g, Pericarpium Citri Reticulatae (Chen Pi), 6g, Radix Angelicae Sinensis (Dang Gui), 6g, Radix Bupleuri (Chai Hu), 3g, Rhizoma Cimicifugae (Sheng Ma), 3-4.5g

If spleen vacuity is complicated by food stagnation with fatigue and somnolence especially after eating, use: Er Chen Tang Jia Wei (Two Aged [Ingredients] Decoction with Added Flavors)

Rhizoma Pinelliae Ternatae (Ban Xia), 12g, Sclerotium Poriae Cocos (Fu Ling), 10g, Pericarpium Citri Reticulatae (Chen Pi), 10g, Rhizoma Atractylodis Macrocephalae (Bai Zhu), 15g, Radix Codonopsitis Pilosulae (Dang Shen), 15g, Fructus Germinatus Hordei Vulgaris (Mai Ya), 10g, Massa Medica Fermentata (Shen Qu), 6g, Fructus Crataegi (Shan Zha), 6g, Radix Glycyrrhizae (Gan Cao), 3-6g

Decoct in water and administer orally in two divided doses, morning and evening, one ji per day.

ADDITIONS & SUBTRACTIONS: If complicated by phlegm confounding the spirit, add Rhizoma Pinelliae Ternatae (Ban Xia), Sclerotium Poriae Cocos (Fu Ling), Radix Polygalae Tenuifoliae (Yuan Zhi), and bile-processed Rhizoma Arisaematis (Dan Nan Xing).

ACUPUNCTURE: Bai Hui (GV 20), Feng Chi (GB 20), Zu San Li (St 36), San Yin Jiao (Sp 6). Use supplementing technique.

### 2. SPLEEN-KIDNEY YANG VACUITY

MAIN SYMPTOMS: Somnolence, lassitude of the spirit, disinclination to talk, fear of cold, cold hands and feet, spontaneous perspiration on exertion or movement, sleeping with the limbs huddled, dizziness, low back and knee soreness and limpness, nocturia, long, clear urination, possible clear, watery vaginal discharge, decreased libido, a pale tongue with white fur, and a fine, weak pulse

TREATMENT PRINCIPLES: Fortify the spleen and boost the qi, warm yang and supplement the kidneys

FORMULA & MEDICINALS: Fu Zi Li Zhong Wan He Shen Qi

*Wan Jia Wei* (Aconite Rectify the Center Pills plus Kidney Qi Pills with Added Flavors)

Radix Codonopsitis Pilosulae (*Dang Shen*), 10g, Radix Lateralis Praeparatus Aconiti Carmichaeli (*Fu Zi*), 6g, dry Rhizoma Zingiberis (*Gan Jiang*), 6g, Rhizoma Atractylodis Macrocephalae (*Bai Zhu*), 10g, mix-fried Radix Glycyrrhizae (*Zhi Gan Cao*), 6g, cooked Radix Rehmanniae (*Shu Di*), 12g, Fructus Corni Officinalis (*Shan Zhu Yu*), 10g, Radix Dioscoreae Oppositae (*Shan Yao*), 10g, Sclerotium Poriae Cocos (*Fu Ling*), 10g, Rhizoma Alismatis (*Ze Xie*), 6g, Cortex Radicis Moutan (*Dan Pi*), 6-10g, Semen Alpiniae Oxyphyllae (*Yi Zhi Ren*)

Decoct in water and administer orally in two divided doses, morning and evening, one *ji* per day.

**ADDITIONS & SUBTRACTIONS:** If complicated by phlegm confounding the spirit, add Rhizoma Pinelliae Ternatae (*Ban Xia*), Sclerotium Poriae Cocos (*Fu Ling*), Radix Polygalae Tenuifoliae (*Yuan Zhi*), and bile-processed Rhizoma Arisaematis (*Dan Nan Xing*).

**ACUPUNCTURE:** *Tai Yang* (M-HN-9), *Shen Mai* (Bl 62), *Shen Que* (CV 8), *Qi Hai* (CV 6), *Guan Yuan* (CV 4). Use supplementing technique on the first two points and moxibustion on the last three.

## 3. HEART-SPLEEN DUAL VACUITY PATTERN

**MAIN SYMPTOMS:** Somnolence, fatigue, heart palpitations, reduced food intake, lack of strength, a sallow yellow or pale white facial complexion, dizziness, impaired memory, abdominal distention, loose stools, a pale, typically enlarged tongue with thin, white fur, and a fine, weak pulse

**TREATMENT PRINCIPLES:** Fortify the spleen and boost the qi, nourish the heart and supplement the blood

**FORMULA & MEDICINALS:** *Gui Pi Tang Jia Jian* (Restore the Spleen Decoction with Additions & Subtractions)

Rhizoma Atractylodis Macrocephalae (*Bai Zhu*), 12g, Radix Astragali Membranacei (*Huang Qi*), 15g, Arillus Euphoriae Longanae (*Long Yan Rou*), 10g, stir-fried Semen Zizyphi Spinosae (*Suan Zao Ren*), 12g, Radix Polygalae Tenuifoliae (*Yuan Zhi*), 6-10g, Radix Angelicae Sinensis (*Dang Gui*), 10g, Radix Codonopsitis Pilosulae (*Dang Shen*), 10g, Radix Auklandiae Lappae (*Mu Xiang*), 6g (added later), Rhizoma Acori Graminei (*Shi Chang Pu*), 6g

Decoct in water and administer orally in two divided doses, morning and evening, one *ji* per day.

**ACUPUNCTURE:** *Xin Shu* (Bl 15), *Pi Shu* (Bl 20), *Zu San Li* (St 36), *San Yin Jiao* (Sp 6), *Shen Mai* (Bl 62). Use supplementing technique.

## 4. KIDNEY ESSENCE INSUFFICIENCY PATTERN

**MAIN SYMPTOMS:** Somnolence, fatigue, tinnitus, deafness, impaired memory, difficulty thinking, dull affect, a tendency to lower the head, low back and knee soreness and limpness, a pale tongue, and a fine, weak pulse

**TREATMENT PRINCIPLES:** Enrich the kidneys and foster the essence, supplement the marrow and strengthen the brain

**FORMULA & MEDICINALS:** *He Che Da Zao Wan Jian Jian* (Placenta Great Construction Pills with Additions & Subtractions)

Placenta Hominis (*Zi He Che*), 1g (powdered and swallowed with the decocted liquid), Tuber Ophiopogonis Japonicae (*Mai Dong*), 12g, cooked Radix Rehmanniae (*Shu Di*), 12g, Radix Achyranthis Bidentatae (*Niu Xi*), 12g, Cortex Eucommiae Ulmoidis (*Du Zhong*), 10g, Fructus Lycii Chinensis (*Gou Qi Zi*), 10g, Gelatinum Plastri Testudinis (*Gui Ban Jiao*), 10g (dissolved in the decocted liquid), Gelatinum Cornu Cervi (*Lu Jiao Jiao*), 9g (dissolved in the decocted liquid), Sclerotium Poriae Cocos (*Fu Ling*), 10g, Fructus Amomi (*Sha Ren*), 3g (added later)

Decoct in water and administer orally in two divided doses, morning and evening, one *ji* per day.

**ACUPUNCTURE:** *Bai Hui* (GV 20), *Zu San Li* (St 36), *San Yin Jiao* (Sp 6), *Tai Xi* (Ki 3), *Zhao Hai* (Ki 6), *Shen Mai* (Bl 62). Use supplementing technique.

## 5. DAMPNESS ENCUMBERING THE SPLEEN PATTERN

**MAIN SYMPTOMS:** Somnolence, lassitude of the spirit, a sensation as if one had a bag over, or a band wrapped tightly around, one's head, heavy, encumbered limbs, chest oppression and abdominal distention, poor appetite, loose stools, slimy, white tongue fur, and a soggy, slippery pulse

**TREATMENT PRINCIPLES:** Eliminate dampness and arouse the spleen

**FORMULA & MEDICINALS:** *Ping Wei San Jia Jian* (Level the Stomach Powder with Additions & Subtractions)

Rhizoma Atractylodis (*Cang Zhu*), 12g, Cortex Magnoliae Officinalis (*Hou Po*), 10g, Pericarpium Citri Reticulatae (*Chen Pi*), 10g, Herba Agastachis Seu Pogostemi (*Huo Xiang*), 10g, lime-processed Rhizoma Pinelliae Ternatae (*Ban Xia*), 10g, Sclerotium Poriae Cocos (*Fu Ling*), 10g, Rhizoma Acori Graminei (*Shi Chang Pu*), 6g, Herba Eupatorii Fortunei (*Pei Lan*), 10g

Decoct in water and administer orally in two divided doses, morning and evening, one *ji* per day.

**ACUPUNCTURE:** *Yin Ling Quan* (Sp 9), *San Yin Jiao* (Sp 6), *Zu San Li* (St 36), *Yin Tang* (M-HN-3), *Er Jian* (LI 2), *San Jian* (LI 3). Alternate the last two points between treatments and use even supplementing-even draining technique.

### 6. PHLEGM HEAT CLOUDING & SINKING PATTERN

**MAIN SYMPTOMS:** Somnolence, difficulty thinking, heavy-headedness, profuse yellow phlegm, plum pit qi, irritability, heart vexation, chest and abdominal fullness and oppression, possible nausea and vomiting, a red facial complexion and red eyes, taciturnity[1] alternating with talkativeness, possible deranged speech, possible heart palpitations, a red tongue with slimy, yellow fur, and a slippery, bowstring, rapid pulse

**TREATMENT PRINCIPLES:** Clear heat and transform phlegm, open the orifices and arouse the spirit

**FORMULA & MEDICINALS:** *Huang Lian Wen Dan Tang Jia Jian* (Coptis Warm the Gallbladder Decoction with Additions & Subtractions)

Rhizoma Pinelliae Ternatae (*Ban Xia*), 12g, Caulis Bambusae In Taeniis (*Zhu Ru*), 12g, Rhizoma Acori Graminei (*Shi Chang Pu*), 12g, Sclerotium Poriae Cocos (*Fu Ling*), 10g, Pericarpium Citri Reticulatae (*Chen Pi*), 10g, Fructus Immaturus Citri Aurantii (*Zhi Shi*), 10g, Rhizoma Coptidis Chinensis (*Huang Lian*), 6g (added later), Radix Glycyrrhizae (*Gan Cao*), 3g

Decoct in water and administer in two divided doses, morning and evening, one *ji* per day.

**ADDITIONS & SUBTRACTIONS:** If accompanied by spleen vacuity as most cases of phlegm heat somnolence are, one can add Radix Codonopsitis Pilosulae (*Dang Shen*) and Rhizoma Atractylodis (*Cang Zhu*).

**ACUPUNCTURE:** *Feng Long* (St 40), *Zu San Li* (St 36), *Jie Xi* (St 41), *Jian Shi* (Per 5), *Dan Zhong* (CV 17), *Zhong Wan* (CV 12). Use even supplementing-even draining technique.

**ADDITIONS & SUBTRACTIONS:** If there is plum pit qi, add *Tong Li* (Ht 5) and *Lian Quan* (CV 23). If there is pronounced spleen vacuity, add *Pi Shu* (Bl 20) and *Wei Shu* (Bl 21).

**CLINICAL TIPS:** Spleen qi vacuity somnolence typically responds very well to relatively large doses of Radix Astragali Membranacei (*Huang Qi*) and Radix Codonopsitis Pilosulae (*Dang Shen*).

### ABSTRACTS OF REPRESENTATIVE CHINESE RESEARCH:

*Hei Long Jiang Zhong Yi Yao* (*Heilongjiang Chinese Medicine & Medicinals*), #3, 1995, p. 16-17: Wang Gui-rong and Dan Shu-fang treated 20 cases of frequently occurring somnolence with Chinese medicinals. Of these 20 patients, 14 were female and six were male. Six cases were between 20-30 years old, 10 cases were 31-40, and four cases were over 40 years of age. Five cases had thin, weak bodies, 10 cases were fat, and five cases were neither fat nor thin. The longest course of disease was five years and the shortest was 90 days. Chinese medicinals were prescribed on the basis of individualized pattern discrimination, with four patterns being used: 1) dampness obstructing the spleen and stomach, 2) spleen vacuity with damp exuberance, 3) damp heat obstructing the center, and 4) yang vacuity. Using this protocol, 12 cases were cured, six improved, and two got no result for a total amelioration rate of 90%. The most number of *ji* administered was 60 and the least was 10.

*Zhong Yi Za Zhi* (*Journal of Chinese Medicine*), #8, 1996, p. 486: Huo Xiao-le and Gao Yun-wang report on the treatment of 32 cases of recurrent somnolence with *Xing Nao Jie Mian Tang* (Arouse the Brain & Relieve Sleep Decoction). Of the 32 patients in this study, 26 were male and six were female. They ranged in age from 7-32, with the majority being 7-12 years old. Their course of disease had lasted from one month to 15 years. The formula used in this study consisted of: Fructus Alpiniae Oxyphyllae (*Yi Zhi Ren*), 12g, Radix Puerariae (*Ge Gen*), 10g, Radix

Ligustici Wallichii (*Chuan Xiong*), 10g, Radix Polygalae Tenuifoliae (*Yuan Zhi*), 10g, Rhizoma Acori Graminei (*Shi Chang Pu*), 10g, Sclerotium Poriae Cocos (*Fu Ling*), 15g, Flos Carthami Tinctorii (*Hong Hua*), 5g, Herba Menthae Haplocalycis (*Bo He*), 6g, Rhizoma Cimcifugae (*Sheng Ma*), 6g, and Borneolum (*Bing Pian*), 0.3g (swallowed with the decoction). One *ji* was administered per day in the morning on an empty stomach. Using this protocol, 26 patients (81.25%) were cured, four (12.5%) experienced a marked effect, and two (6.25%) got no effect. Thus the total amelioration rate was 93.7%.

## REPRESENTATIVE CASE HISTORIES:

### ❖ CASE 1 [2] ❖

The patient was a 42 year old female who was first examined on Jul. 7, 1990. The patient's major complaint was somnolence. She frequently desired to sleep and yawned. Even at work she would have to have short naps. Although she was easily aroused, after waking, she immediately was fatigued and wanted to lie down again. This typically happened several times per day. In addition, she had loss of strength in her arms and legs and there was a sticky, slimy sensation in her mouth. Her tongue was red with thick, yellow, turbid, slimy fur, and her pulse was soggy and moderate or relaxed (*i.e.*, slightly slow). EEG, brain angiogram, and brain CT scan were all normal. She had been taking an unspecified Western medication which had failed to get any result. Thus she was referred to the authors of this case.

Based on the above signs and symptoms, the patient's pattern was categorized as dampness and turbidity encumbering the spleen. Therefore, she was prescribed the following medicinals: Herba Agastachis Seu Pogostemi (*Huo Xiang*), 15g, Herba Eupatorii Fortunei (*Pei Lan*), 15g, Cortex Magnoliae Officinalis (*Hou Po*), 15g, Fructus Amomi (*Sha Ren*), 5g, Radix Angelicae Dahuricae (*Bai Zhi*), 15g, Radix Et Rhizoma Ligustici Chinensis (*Gao Ben*), 15g, Radix Ligustici Wallichii (*Chuan Xiong*), 15g, Rhizoma Atractylodis (*Cang Zhu*), 15g, Rhizoma Acori Graminei (*Shi Chang Pu*), 15g, Tuber Curcumae (*Yu Jin*), 15g, Rhizoma Pinelliae Ternatae (*Ban Xia*), 10g, and Rhizoma Cyperi Rotundi (*Xiang Fu*), 15g.

After taking 10 *ji* of the above formula with additions and subtractions, the patient only reported fatigue and a continued desire to lie down. The sticky, slimy sensation in her mouth was less. Therefore, Rhizoma Atractylodis was replaced with Rhizoma Atractylodis Macrocephalae (*Bai Zhu*), Angelica Dahurica, Ligusticum Chinensis,

Ligusticum Wallichium, and Curcuma were deleted, and Sclerotium Poriae Cocos (*Fu Ling*) and Radix Codonopsitis Pilosulae (*Dang Shen*) were added to fortify the spleen, supplement the qi, and secure the root. After 30 *ji* all the patient's symptoms had disappeared. On follow-up some time later, there had been no recurrence.

### ❖ CASE 2 [3] ❖

The patient was a 65 year old female who was first examined on Jun. 5, 1992. The patient was obese. Her major complaint was that after eating she always felt like going to sleep. This had been going on for 10 years. She had previously tried both Chinese and Western medicine for this problem but without result. In the month before coming to see the authors of this case, her somnolence had gotten worse. Her tongue was pale and fat with teeth-marks on its edges and thin, slimy fur. Her pulse was soggy. EEG and brain angiogram showed evidence of early stage arteriosclerosis. Liver function and liver and spleen ultrasonography showed no abnormalities.

Based on the above signs and symptoms, the authors categorized this woman's pattern as spleen vacuity with damp exuberance. The medicinals she was prescribed consisted of: Rhizoma Atractylodis Macrocephalae (*Bai Zhu*), 30g, Sclerotium Poriae Cocos (*Fu Ling*), 30g, Radix Codonopsitis Pilosulae (*Dang Shen*), 30g, Pericarpium Citri Reticulatae (*Chen Pi*), 15g, Rhizoma Cyperi Rotundi (*Xiang Fu*), 15g, Fructus Amomi (*Sha Ren*), 15g, Rhizoma Acori Graminei (*Shi Chang Pu*), 15g, Rhizoma Pinelliae Ternatae (*Ban Xia*), 10g, Fructus Perillae Frutescentis (*Zi Su Zi*), 15g, Radix Glycyrrhizae (*Gan Cao*), 10g, Massa Medica Fermentata (*Shen Qu*), Fructus Crataegi (*Shan Zha*), Fructus Germinatus Hordei Vulgaris (*Mai Ya*), and Semen Raphani Sativi (*Lai Fu Zi*), 15g each.

After taking 10 *ji* of the above medicinals, the woman's somnolence had markedly decreased. Each day, she only had three episodes or less. Therefore, Perilla and Pinellia were removed and the patient was prescribed another 30 *ji*, after which she was considered cured. One year later, she again had a recurrence of this problem, but its duration was short and, after taking another 20 *ji*, she was again cured. On follow-up after that, there had been no recurrence.

### ❖ CASE 3 [4] ❖

The patient was a 48 year old woman who was first examined on Aug. 16, 1990. This woman had suffered from somnolence for the past year and frequently desired to sleep. At the same time, her head was heavy, and this feeling did not decrease after being roused from sleep. In addition, there was heart vexation, oppression, anxiety, and agitation, a bitter taste and sticky, slimy feeling in the mouth, and oral thirst but no desire to drink. Her menses were sometimes early and sometimes late. The patient's tongue was red with slimy, yellow fur, and her pulse was soggy and rapid. EEG and brain angiogram showed no abnormalities.

Based on the above signs and symptoms, the authors of this case categorized this patient's pattern as damp heat obstructing the center and prescribed the following medicinals: Rhizoma Coptidis Chinensis (*Huang Lian*), 10g, Radix Scutellariae Baicalensis (*Huang Qin*), 15g, Fructus Gardeniae Jasminoidis (*Zhi Zi*), 15g, Rhizoma Pinelliae Ternatae (*Ban Xia*), 10g, Cortex Magnoliae Officinalis (*Hou Po*), 15g, Pericarpium Citri Reticulatae (*Chen Pi*), 15g, Rhizoma Acori Graminei (*Shi Chang Pu*), 15g, and Rhizoma Phragmitis Communis (*Lu Gen*), 15g. One *ji* of these medicinals were decocted in water and administered in two divided doses along with 0.03 grams of Borneolum (*Bing Pian*) swallowed with the decoction.

After taking 10 *ji* of the above formula, the somnolence, headache, and vexation and oppression had all decreased. Therefore, the Borneol was eliminated and 10 more *ji* were prescribed, after which all the patient's symptoms disappeared. However, because there was a faint amount of lassitude of the spirit a couple of times per day, Coptis and Scutellaria were removed and Fructus Citri Sacrodactylis (*Fo Shou*), Rhizoma Corydalis Yanhusuo (*Yuan Hu*), Cortex Albizziae Julibrissinis (*He Huan Pi*), and Radix Polygalae Tenuifoliae (*Yuan Zhi*) were added. After taking yet another 20 *ji*, the patient's spirit was clear, her qi was crisp, and her emotions were calm and harmonious. On follow-up, there had been no recurrence.

❖ CASE 4[5] ❖

A 35 year old female was first examined on May 6, 1990. Two months previous, she had developed a generalized fever and body ache after being soaked in a drenching rain. This was treated successfully. However, she became somnolent. When examined, she reported that she was experiencing fatigue and somnolence, heaviness in her head and body, diminished appetite, a bland taste in her mouth and lack of thirst, soft, pasty stools, clear, long urination, and a clear, thin vaginal discharge. Her tongue was pale and had thin, white fur, while her pulse was soggy

and moderate or relaxed (*i.e.*, slightly slow). The patient's pattern was categorized as spleen-stomach vacuity and dampness assaulting spleen yang.

Treatment to supplement the middle and fortify the spleen, transform dampness and free the flow of yang was, therefore, indicated. She was administered *Wan Dai Tang* with modifications. This consisted of: stir-fried Rhizoma Atractylodis Macrocephelae (*Bai Zhu*), 30g, stir-fried Radix Dioscoreae Oppositae (*Shan Yao*), 30g, Radix Codonopsitis Pilosulae (*Dang Shen*), 15g, Rhizoma Atractylodes (*Cang Zhu*), 12g, stir-fried Semen Plantaginis (*Che Qian Zi*), 12g, Pericarpium Citri Reticulatae (*Chen Pi*), 6g, Radix Bupleuri (*Chai Hu*), 6g, Ramulus Cinnamomi Cassiae (*Gui Zhi*), 8g, Radix Ledebouriellae Divaricatae (*Fang Feng*), 6g, Sclerotium Poriae Cocos (*Fu Ling*), 6g, and Rhizoma Acori Graminei (*Shi Chang Pu*), 6g. Three *ji* of this prescription was administered in decoction and all of her symptoms diminished. With administration of three more *ji*, all of her symptoms disappeared completely and did not return.

❖ CASE 5[6] ❖

The patient was a 36 year old male cadre who had been somnolent for more than a half year. In recent days, this had gotten worse. His essence spirit was devitalized and his head felt heavy, oppressed, and distended. Sometimes he was able to work, but other times he had to find a place to hide in order to sleep. The patient's pulses were deep and faint. In particular, the cubit positions were weak and forceless, while the man's tongue was pale with thin, white fur. In the *Shang Han Lun* (*Treatise on Damage [Due to] Cold*), it says, "Shao yin disease: a faint, fine pulse and only a desire to sleep." Therefore, the man was prescribed *Ma Huang Fu Zi Xi Xin Tang* (Ephedra, Aconite & Asarum Decoction): Herba Ephedrae (*Ma Huang*), 6g, Radix Lateralis Praeparatus Aconiti Carmichaeli (*Fu Zi*), 10g, and Herba Asari Cum Radice (*Xi Xin*), 3g. After taking three *ji* of this formula, the man's head and brain felt clear and aroused and his whole body felt lighter. Because his tongue and pulse were as before, the cadre was given nine more *ji* of these medicinals, after which his disease was completely cured.

❖ CASE 6[7] ❖

The patient was a 51 year old male who had first experienced unusual sleepiness three months before. No matter how much he slept, after waking, he still felt tired, even when he had slept for 24 hours. This somnolence had progressively worsened so that he would sometimes fall asleep while working and even while eating. He was diagnosed as suffering from narcolepsy and prescribed various stimulants, such as caffeine. However, the results were not long-lasting. Therefore, he was referred for acupuncture. When the acupuncture doctor examined this patient, it was found that the man was obese, his appetite was poor, and he complained of abdominal distention and loose stools. His tongue was pale with slimy, white fur, and his pulse was deep and moderate (or relaxed, *i.e.*, slightly slow).

Based on the above signs and symptoms, the patient's pattern was categorized as spleen vacuity with damp encumbrance. Therefore, the treatment principles were, in general, to supplement yang while draining yin. The acupuncture points selected consisted of: *Zu San Li* (St 36), *San Yin Jiao* (Sp 6), *Shen Mai* (Bl 62), *Zhao Hai* (Ki 6), and *Bai Hui* (GV 20). Treatment was given once every day for two days, after which the patient felt that his mind was clearer. After five treatments, the man could stay awake with conscious effort during the day. After 10 treatments, all of his symptoms were markedly improved and acupuncture treatment was, therefore,

ceased. On follow-up after three months, there had been no recurrence of narcolepsy and the patient had returned to work.

## ENDNOTES:

[1] Taciturnity refers to an emotional predisposition not to speak to others. The patient has the qi to speak but does not want to speak.

[2] Wang Gui-rong & Dan Shu-fang, "The Chinese Medicinal Treatment of 20 Cases of Frequently Occurring Somnolence," *Hei Long Jiang Zhong Yi Yao Za Zhi (Heilongjiang Chinese Medicine & Medicinals)*, #3, 1995, p. 16

[3] *Ibid.*, p. 17

[4] *Ibid.*, p. 17

[5] Qian Sheng, "New Uses for *Wan Dui Tang* (Arresting Vaginal Discharge Decoction)," *Zhong Yi Za Zhi (Journal of Chinese Medicine)*, #9, 1993, p. 550

[6] Chen & Zhao, *op. cit.*, p. 54

[7] *Acupuncture Case Histories from China*, ed. by Chen Ji-rui & Nissi Wang, Eastland Press, Seattle, 1988, p. 123-125

# ❖ 16 ❖

# Convulsions

Nigel Wiseman currently translates the Chinese *chou chu* as "convulsions." Wiseman previously translated this term as convulsive spasm.[1] The English word "convulsions" may cause some readers to think this diagnostic category is less inclusive than it is. In English (at least in American English), convulsions imply "a violent, involuntary contraction or spasm of the muscles."[2] However, in Chinese medicine, convulsions include various tics, spasms, and sudden, uncontrollable, commonly jerky movements, including tremors. In Chinese, these are also referred to as *chou dong*, jerking or spasmodic contracture, *chou feng*, tugging wind or clonic spasm, *qi zong*, tugging and slackening, *zhuan jin*, cramp, *zhen chan*, tremor, and *jing bing*, tetany disease depending on their severity and location. Therefore, the Chinese term translated by Wiseman as convulsions covers a much wider range of conditions than this English word normally covers. To help distinguish seizures from tics, Chinese doctors also use the terms *shen shun dong*, twitching of the body, and simply *shun* for spasmodic blinking of the eye(s).[3]

The Chinese diagnostic category of convulsions refers to numerous abnormal movements, including tics, spasms and sudden jerky movements. These symptoms resemble features of several neurologic disorders described in Western medicine, including tic disorders, Parkinson's disease, Parkinsonism, and other less common degenerative neurologic disorders. Abnormal involuntary movements, behaviors, and vocalizations of tic disorders also sometimes resemble symptoms observed in certain

seizure disorders. However, these categories are etiologically disparate (see Chapter 17, this Book, Epilepsy, for a discussion of seizure disorders). Both Western and Chinese medicine describe tics using similar descriptive language, therefore the phenomenology of tics is probably equivalent in these two systems of medicine. However other apparent neurologic symptoms, including sudden jerky movements, are more difficult to characterize but probably correspond to Parkinson's disease, Parkinsonism, or numerous less common degenerative neurologic disorders.

## Nosology:

The first three patterns under convulsions describe tics that are related to stress, irritability, or anger. Similar symptoms would not lead to the diagnosis of a formal tic disorder in Western medicine. This is because, in Western medicine, abnormal movements which are transient, stress-induced, do not occur in the context of other symptoms that imply a serious psychiatric or neurologic disorder (such as Parkinson's disease), and apparently cease when the causative stressful situation is resolved, are not categorized as tic disorders. In contrast to these first three patterns, the fourth pattern, extreme heat stirring wind, describes repeated numerous, strong tics and spasms and associated heart vexation, tension, and agitation, possible spirit clouding and deranged speech. Abnormal movement symptoms included in this pattern resemble features of many neurologic disorders, including tic disorders,

Parkinson's disease, Parkinsonism, and possibly multiple sclerosis (MS) or other degenerative neurologic disorders. Further, in contrast to the first three patterns listed under convulsions, the last pattern includes symptoms that resemble prominent psychiatric symptoms, such as easy anger, heart vexation, spirit clouding, and deranged speech. The presence of concomitant psychiatric symptoms suggests certain neurologic disorders that are often associated with changes in mood or cognition, as well as somatoform disorders that can sometimes manifest as apparent neurologic symptoms.

Western medicine defines tics as sudden, involuntary, nonrhythmic movements. Western medicine differentiates motor tics from vocal tics and simple tics involving one movement from complicated patterns of abnormal involuntary movements or vocal behaviors. Several tic disorders are described in current Western psychiatric nosology, including Tourette's disorder which is characterized by a pattern of multiple motor tics exhibited at the same or different times as vocal tics. The disorder begins before age 18, tics occur several times daily for at least one year, and there is considerable associated social or occupational impairment. Western psychiatry contrasts Tourette's disorder to chronic motor or vocal tic disorder in which either motor or vocal tics (but not both) are present. All other aspects of these disorders are identical to Tourette's. Transient tic disorder is diagnosed when tics are present for at least four weeks but not longer than one year. With the exception of a limited course, all other aspects of this disorder are identical to Tourette's disorder.

Repetitive abnormal involuntary movements are also characteristic of Parkinson's disease and Parkinsonism. However, in contrast to tic disorders, involuntary movements are rhythmic. Parkinson's disease and Parkinsonism share many common neurological symptoms but have different causes. Parkinsonism has numerous possible etiologies in contrast to Parkinson's disease in which there is no identified underlying cause. Parkinson's disease is a degenerative neurologic disorder characterized by slowing of voluntary movements, pill-rolling tremor at rest, and gait disturbance. The disorder usually progresses slowly, and early stages are sometimes characterized by psychiatric symptoms, including depressed mood, diminished capacity to express emotions (*i.e.*, masked face), etc. In early or mild Parkinson's disease or Parkinsonism, the individual often appears apathetic or restless. These changes are actually neuropsychiatric symptoms caused by the same CNS pathology that leads to grossly abnormal movements in more advanced stages of illness.

It is important to note that common features of early or mild forms of Parkinson's disease or Parkinsonism resemble central aspects of the Chinese category of lily disease (see Chapter 21, this Book). In an analogous manner, early or mild forms of multiple sclerosis are often accompanied by psychiatric complaints in the absence of abnormal movements. Progression of the disorder typically leads to a complex pattern of abnormal movements, weakness, and gait disturbance in the context of psychiatric symptoms, including erratic irritable or labile mood changes, impaired memory, etc. As these degenerative disorders evolve from chiefly psychiatric symptoms in early or mild forms to complex psychosomatic symptoms in later stages or more severe forms, the Chinese medical interpretation of associated symptom patterns might be expected to shift from lily disease to convulsions or tetany disease. It follows that, when a patient is evaluated during early or mild stages of Parkinson's disease, Parkinsonism, multiple sclerosis, or other degenerative neurological disorders, the most likely Chinese medical diagnosis will be lily disease. Conversely, according to Chinese medical diagnostic criteria, more advanced or severe forms of these disorders would likely be diagnosed as convulsions.

## EPIDEMIOLOGY:

Tic disorders are generally first diagnosed during childhood. A persisting pattern of abnormal involuntary movements or vocalizations, in the absence of a degenerative neurologic disorder, may occur in 10-15% of children and adolescents, with peak prevalence rates between 7-11 years of age. In Tourette's disorder, motor tics tend to develop initially, followed in time by vocal tics. In a similar manner, most afflicted individuals experience simple tics which often evolve into complex tics. All tic disorders are more common among boys than girls. Race, ethnicity, and socioeconomic status are not correlated with increased risk of tic disorders.

In contrast to tic disorders, Parkinson's disease or the various forms of Parkinsonism are typically diagnosed in late adulthood or old age. In most cases, symptoms begin before age 55. However individuals afflicted with rare inherited forms of these disorders may become symptomatic as early as 20 years of age. Most individuals who are initially diagnosed with Parkinsonism are subsequently diagnosed with Parkinson's disease, since a specific cause is never established. Parkinson's disease is more common among males in Western populations and occurs at a rate of approximately 160 in 100,000. There are few epidemiological data on the various forms of Parkinsonism. In contrast to Parkinson's disease, individuals afflicted with

MS typically first become symptomatic sometime during the third or fourth decade. In rare cases, the disorder is first diagnosed in childhood or old age. Multiple sclerosis usually follows a remitting-relapsing course, and afflicted individuals may have prolonged disease-free intervals that last decades.

## DIFFERENTIAL DIAGNOSIS:

### 1. MEDICAL DISORDERS

The initial goal of differential diagnosis in a patient who presents with abnormal involuntary movements or vocalizations is to rule out possible medical etiologies. Specific kinds of abnormal movements are characteristic of various neurologic disorders, including tic disorders, Parkinson's disease, Parkinsonism, Huntington's disease, and several more obscure disorders. By definition, abnormal movements are always involuntary in tic disorders and all degenerative neurologic disorders. However, the abnormal movements of tic disorders and Huntington's disease are nonrhythmic in contrast to the rhythmic movements of Parkinson's disease and Parkinsonism. Early stages or mild forms of these disorders are often missed or misdiagnosed by Western physicians. During the course of both Parkinson's disease and Parkinsonism, afflicted individuals often experience psychiatric symptoms, including depressed mood, diminished expressiveness, reduced attention span, and anxious or dependent personality changes. Many or all of these symptoms may emerge prior to grossly abnormal movements. The emergence of unambiguous neurologic symptoms combined with positive laboratory results or diagnostic imaging studies eventually confirms a diagnosis of Parkinson's disease or Parkinsonism.

A persisting pattern of abnormal involuntary movements or vocal tics can also result from traumatic brain injury and stroke. Acute or chronic neurologic side effects of certain medications, substance intoxication, or poisoning are sometimes indistinguishable from the abnormal movements of tic disorders or Parkinson's disease. Subjective feelings of restlessness (akithisia) and self-limiting abnormal movements (dystonias) are frequent side effects of most antipsychotic medications. Chronic use of antipsychotic medications, especially the older or typical agents, is associated with significant risk of developing a Parkinsonian movement disorder called tardive dyskinesia which typically continues after the antipsychotic in question has been discontinued. Further, Parkinsonism has been attributed to CNS exposure to MPTP, an illicit substance found in some street drugs. Vocal tics rarely result

from medication side effects. A thorough history will generally suggest the likelihood of underlying medical or neurologic disease. Tourette's disorder is commonly observed in mental retardation and autism and is believed to be part of a heritable chromosomal abnormality.

Multiple sclerosis and other CNS demyelinating disorders are sometimes associated with erratic involuntary, typically nonrhythmic movements that are sometimes described as tics or spasms. Further, many individuals afflicted with MS report erratic changes in mood, depression, mania, irritability, and sometimes psychotic symptoms that resemble features of the fourth pattern including easy anger, heart vexation, and agitation. Deranged speech can be a manifestation of psychosis or a direct consequence of demyelination affecting the speech center of the brain. Early or mild forms of MS are often associated with psychiatric symptoms before abnormal movements become evident. Magnetic resonance imaging (MRI) of the brain is the definitive study that confirms the presence of lesions of demyelination. Special studies of the cerebrospinal fluid are also done to clarify the diagnosis, but positive findings are not specific to multiple sclerosis.

### 2. PSYCHIATRIC DISORDERS

When Parkinson's disease, Parkinsonism, multiple sclerosis, and other neurologic disorders have been ruled out by history, normal neurologic examination, or normal laboratory studies, the practitioner must consider various psychiatric disorders as possible explanations for the observed symptom pattern. Like lily disease, some aspects of convulsions resemble features of the broad category of somatoform disorders (see Book 3, Chapter 9, Somatoform Disorders) as defined in contemporary Western psychiatry. In Western medical differential diagnosis, a somatoform disorder is the presumed diagnosis when possible medical causes of somatic symptoms have been ruled out or have not been verified by laboratory studies or physical examination. All somatoform disorders are characterized by persisting somatic complaints, including, in some cases, apparent abnormal motor functioning in the context of a normal neurologic examination. Somatic symptoms, including unusual movements that resemble tremors or tics, are often associated with identifiable psychological stresses. Conversion disorder is a kind of somatoform disorder that is associated with apparent abnormal sensory or motor functioning in the context of a normal neurologic examination. Patients afflicted with conversion disorder are often described as "hysterical" and tend to exaggerate or distort perceptions of normal bodily sensations. In many cases, conversion disorder is associated with depression or other major psychiatric histories. Some individuals complain of constant vague somatic symptoms that are never found to have a medical basis but do not complain of changes in sensory or motor functioning. In a Western medical setting, such patients would typically receive a diagnosis of hypochondriasis or histrionic personality disorder.

Unusual somatic symptoms often occur in the context of depressed mood. When a depressed patient complains of somatic symptoms that are consistently worse during periods of severe depression, major depressive episode with somatization is the probable diagnosis. Somatic symptoms also occur in the course of schizophrenia and other psychotic disorders, suggesting somatic delusions. Schizophrenia is the likely diagnosis in patients who experience paranoia, delusions, auditory hallucinations, or other psychotic symptoms and complain of disturbing somatic symptoms in the absence of medical explanations.

Somatic complaints occur commonly in anxiety disorders, including panic disorder and generalized anxiety disorder (GAD). Individuals afflicted with obsessive-compulsive disorder (OCD) sometimes give the appearance of tics or other abnormal stereotyped movements because of repetitive rituals that are compulsively repeated. Patients with OCD generally report ongoing obsessions that are related to observed rituals and have normal neurologic exam findings. Some individuals who complain of unusual sensations or movement symptoms are actually feigning symptoms (malingering) or deliberately creating them (factitious disorder) by introducing a foreign substance into his or her body. A current psychodynamic interpretation of factitious disorder is that the individual creates symptoms in order to identify with a sick role. Conversely, a common motivation for feigning symptoms is hope of financial gain from a legal settlement related to alleged

circumstances of illness onset. Because of the above considerations, somatoform disorder can only be diagnosed when malingering and factitiousness have been ruled out.

ETIOLOGY & PATHOPHYSIOLOGY:

## 1. TIC DISORDERS

There is no clearly established explanation of tic disorders in Western medicine. However, emerging evidence points to developmental abnormalities in certain brain regions that control movement, especially the basal ganglia. Magnetic resonance imaging and functional brain imaging studies have shown consistent abnormalities in these brain regions. Other research suggests an underlying derangement in dopamine. Abnormal EEG patterns are present in up to two-thirds of patients with Tourette's or other tic disorders. Other theories view tic disorders as a result of endocrinologic or immunologic dysregulation during critical developmental periods. Women who experience complications during pregnancy are significantly more likely to have offspring who develop Tourette's disorder. Reasons for this remain unclear.

## 2. PARKINSON'S DISEASE & PARKINSONISM

Parkinson's disease has no identified cause (i.e., it is idiopathic) in contrast to Parkinsonism in which there are numerous identified neurologic, infectious, metabolic, vascular, genetic, or drug-induced causes of abnormal involuntary movements. A finding of degeneration of dopamine-containing neurons in the substantia nigra, a small region located at the base of the brain, is always associated with Parkinson's disease, but the primary cause of degenerative changes in this specific brain region is never established. In contrast, Parkinsonism is diagnosed when one of numerous possible infectious, metabolic,

## DIFFERENTIAL DIAGNOSIS

### 1. MEDICAL DISORDERS

A. TIC DISORDERS
B. PARKINSON'S DISEASE
C. PARKINSONISM
D. HUNTINGTON'S DISEASE
E. MULTIPLE SCLEROSIS
F. OTHER DEGENERATIVE DISORDERS OF THE CNS

### 2. EFFECTS OF SUBSTANCES

A. SOMATOFORM DISORDERS (INCLUDING CONVERSION DISORDER)
B. HYPOCHONDRIASIS
C. MAJOR DEPRESSIVE EPISODE WITH SOMATIZATION
D. SCHIZOPHRENIA WITH SOMATIC DELUSIONS
E. GENERALIZED ANXIETY DISORDER (GAD)
F. PANIC ATTACK
G. OBSESSIVE-COMPULSIVE DISORDER
H. MALINGERING
I. FACTITIOUS DISORDERS

toxic, traumatic, vascular, or genetic disorders has been established as the cause of observed neurologic symptoms. The various underlying causes of Parkinsonism can affect different parts of the brain, including the basal ganglia, substantia nigra, cerebellum, or multiple brain circuits.

### 3. MULTIPLE SCLEROSIS & OTHER DEGENERATIVE DISORDERS OF THE CNS

Other neurologic disorders that sometimes manifest as persisting abnormal involuntary movements include diffuse lewy body disease and MS. Lewy body disease is a degenerative disorder affecting subcortical brain regions and resulting in abnormal movement symptoms that typically follow rapid cognitive decline and dementia. Multiple sclerosis is an autoimmune disorder of the central nervous system resulting in focal areas of demyelination and inflammation in the white matter of the brain and spinal cord. Western medicine has not confirmed the cause or causes of MS, but this disorder is probably related to the body's misdirected immune response to an otherwise benign viral illness, resulting in wide-spread autoimmune destruction of myelin surrounding CNS nerve fibers.

### 4. SOMATOFORM DISORDERS & OTHER PSYCHIATRIC DISORDERS

Many neurobiological and psychodynamic theories have been advanced in efforts to explain somatoform disorders. Western medical and psychiatric theories about the etiology of conversion disorder are reviewed in Book 3, Chapter 9, Somatoform Disorders. Recently, neurobiological models have come into greater acceptance as explanations of certain somatoform disorders, including conversion disorder and hypochondriasis. For example, cortical dysfunction may result in impaired attention causing distorted perceptions of normal bodily sensations. Non-biological models of somatoform disorders derive from psychoanalytic theories and social learning theory. Contemporary Western medical views of the causes of major depression, obsessive-compulsive disorder, and schizophrenia are reviewed in Chapters 4, 8, and 3, Book 3. Hypochondriasis and histrionic personality disorder are discussed in Chapter 9, Book 3, Somatoform Disorders.

### WESTERN MEDICAL TREATMENT:

### 1. TIC DISORDERS

Antipsychotic medications work by antagonizing CNS dopamine receptors and sometimes alleviate tic symp-

toms. For unclear reasons, many patients do not respond to these medications. Education and social support are often helpful in cases where tic symptoms are associated with significant social impairment. Cognitive and behavioral therapy sometimes benefits patients who suffer from tic disorders by providing skills or insights that permit improved coping with social or occupational consequences of abnormal movements or vocalizations.

### 2. PARKINSON'S DISEASE, PARKINSONISM, & MS

In contemporary Western medicine, medications, physical therapy, surgery, and electroconvulsive therapy are used as treatments for Parkinson's disease and Parkinsonism. Pharmacological agents that increase CNS dopamine, including L-dopa, are current Western treatments of these disorders. Surgery and ECT are sometimes used in cases that are refractory to pharmacological treatment. There are presently no cures for Parkinson's disease. Numerous pharmacological treatments are used for MS, including intravenous steroids for controlling acute attacks and beta-interferon for controlling the course of the illness by reducing the number of relapses. Numerous immunosuppressant drugs, including emerging experimental treatments, are also used.

### 3. SOMATOFORM DISORDERS & OTHER PSYCHIATRIC DISORDERS

There are no specific pharmacological treatments for somatoform disorders. Numerous psychotropic medications have been employed to treat these disorders. Current treatments for conversion disorder are reviewed in Book 3, Chapter 9, Somatoform Disorders. In contemporary Western psychiatry, serotonin-selective re-uptake inhibitors (SSRIs) are commonly used in the management of somatoform disorders. Sedative-hypnotics are used as adjunctive treatments of transient anxiety symptoms that are frequently reported by individuals who have long-standing somatic complaints. Many somatoform disorders, including somatization disorder, pain disorder, and body dysmorphic disorder, sometimes improve with supportive psychotherapy and cognitive-behavioral therapy. Western medical treatments for major depressive disorder and obsessive-compulsive disorder are reviewed in Book 3, Chapters 4 and 8 respectively. Treatments for hypochondriasis and histrionic personality disorder are discussed in Book 3, Chapter 9, Somatoform Disorders. Current Western treatments of other anxiety disorders included in the differential diagnosis of convulsions are described in Book 3, Chapter 7, Anxiety Disorders.

## SHORT & LONG-TERM ADVANTAGES & DISADVANTAGES OF WESTERN MEDICAL TREATMENT:

### 1. TIC DISORDERS

When antipsychotic medications are effective, benefits include improved social and occupational functioning. Short-term disadvantages of antipsychotic medications include the risk of reversible abnormal involuntary movements which would further exacerbate target symptoms of the tic disorder being treated. Recent advances in psychopharmacology have led to new atypical antipsychotic medications, including risperidone, that are equally efficacious as older typical antipsychotics, but have minimal risks. The risk of developing medication induced side effects is also mitigated by the fact that many tic disorders are transient, requiring pharmacologic treatment of limited duration.

### 2. PARKINSON'S DISEASE, PARKINSONISM & MS

Anti-Parkinsonian agents usually result in significantly improved quality of life. However, many complications of long-term treatment with dopamine agonists complicate the course of Parkinson's disease and Parkinsonism. These include unpleasant medication side effects, on-and-off effects, and movement disorders that usually normalize when the medication causing these symptoms is discontinued. Adverse behavioral effects of L-dopa and dopamine agonists include auditory or visual hallucinations, vivid dreams, drowsiness, confusion, agitation, delusions, depression, and mania. Chronic steroid therapy for MS can result in numerous medical complications secondary to immunosuppression as well as agitated or manic states and, sometimes, frank psychosis. Chemotherapeutic agents often precipitate depressed mood.

### 3. SOMATOFORM DISORDERS & OTHER PSYCHIATRIC DISORDERS

Individuals who respond to pharmacological treatments of somatoform disorders typically report significant reduction in severity of baseline somatic symptoms, in addition to diminished anxiety and markedly improved social and occupational functioning. However, these benefits must be viewed with respect to risks of drug side effects. Common side effects of SSRIs include upset stomach and other gastrointestinal complaints, fatigue or "activation," and sometimes insomnia, diminished libido, and an uncomfortable subjective sense of diminished capacity for emotional expression. Chronic use of benzodiazepines and other sedative-hypnotics carries the risk of chemical dependency with all of its complications. Advantages and disadvantages associated with Western medical treatments of major depressive disorder, obsessive-compulsive disorder, schizophrenia, and the various anxiety disorders are reviewed in other chapters.

## PROGNOSIS:

### 1. TIC DISORDERS

The course and prognosis of tic disorders is highly variable and depends on age at onset, chronicity, symptom severity, and frequency. Most tic disorders are transient and resolve without the need for pharmacologic treatment. In contrast, Tourette's disorder is a life-long condition but, in most cases, symptom severity and frequency diminish starting in adolescence. Patients with Tourette's disorder sometimes have complete remissions lasting several years. When Tourette's or another tic disorder occurs together with another medical or neurologic disorder, there is typically more severe impairment in functioning than in simple tic disorders. In cases of co-morbid attenton deficit disorder (ADD), the degree of social or occupational impairment is significantly greater.

### 2. PARKINSON'S DISEASE, PARKINSONISM & MS

Parkinson's disease follows a progressive insidious course. Since the introduction and widespread use of L-dopa, the five year mortality rate of Parkinson's disease has dropped significantly and average life expectancy has increased by several years. Nevertheless, there is no cure for Parkinson's disease. The various forms of Parkinsonism have more benign long-term outcomes which are further improved with medications. Successful treatment of the identified underlying cause(s) of Parkinsonism sometimes improves or completely eliminates abnormal movements and other Parkinsonian symptoms. However, in many cases, neurological damage caused by CNS infections, medications, toxic, traumatic, or vascular insults is irreversible, and Parkinsonian symptoms persist indefinitely. The prognosis of MS is highly variable depending on age at onset, frequency, and severity of relapses. Milder forms are associated with fewer relapses and less severe physical or cognitive impairment.

### 3. SOMATOFORM DISORDERS & OTHER PSYCHIATRIC DISORDERS

Like all psychiatric disorders, prognosis and long-term course are related to chronicity, symptom severity, and treatment responsiveness. Most kinds of somatoform disorder have relatively favorable prognosis if there are no co-occurring psychiatric or neurological disorders. Other important predictors of long-term outcome include the level of pre-morbid social-psychological functioning, and the nature of symptom onset. Rapid onset is usually associated with a more favorable long-term course. When conversion disorder is diagnosed in hospitalized patients, most cases resolve quickly without pharmacological or other kinds of treatment. Patients who complain of chronic or severe symptoms or suffer from other psychiatric syndromes will likely respond less rapidly or completely to treatment and will therefore continue to experience significant impairment for an indefinite period. Difficult social or legal circumstances typically predict poor outcomes. In contrast to conversion disorder, hypochondriasis usually has a chronic life-long course interrupted by transient periods of symptomatic worsening or improvement. Typical long-term courses of major depressive disorder, schizophrenia, obsessive-compulsive disorder, and the various anxiety disorders described above are reviewed in other chapters.

## INDICATIONS FOR REFERRAL TO WESTERN MEDICAL SERVICES:

Emergency medical referral is indicated whenever there is evidence of an acute or rapidly evolving medical (including neurologic) or psychiatric disorder that might be life-threatening. These include, for example, cerebrovascular accident, traumatic brain injury, psychosis, and severe depression with suicidal thoughts. In general, urgent referral to the nearest emergency room is appropriate when there is evidence that an acute medical disorder, for example, cerebrovascular accident (*i.e.*, stroke), trauma, infection, or metabolic derangement, coexists with new onset neurologic symptoms. Intoxication with alcohol or an illicit substance also warrants urgent medical referral. Patients suffering from transient or chronic tic disorders in the absence of underlying medical disease may benefit from non-urgent referral to a neurologist. Such referral is indicated when an appropriate course of Chinese medical treatment has not resulted in clinical improvement. Evidence of progressive degenerative neurologic disease, including Parkinson's disease, MS, or acute-onset Parkinsonism always warrants referral to a neurologist.

Routine referral to a Western-trained psychiatrist or neurologist will help to clarify the differential diagnosis in cases where chronic symptoms that are not life-threatening have failed to improve during an appropriate course of Chinese medical treatment. In such cases, development of an integrative treatment plan combining Chinese and Western medical therapies might prove more beneficial to the patient than either approach alone.

## CHINESE DISEASE CAUSES & MECHANISMS:

The two main mechanisms of convulsions in Chinese medicine are malnourishment of the sinews and stirring of wind. The sinews only maintain their proper extension and remain relaxed when they receive proper moistening and nourishment. If, for any reason, the sinews lack proper moistening and nourishment, they dry out and contract. When they contract, they may cause convulsions or tugging and slackening. The sinews may be deprived of proper nourishment if an evil qi congests in and obstructs the channels and network vessels or if yin blood is insufficient. The common evils which may congest and obstruct the channels and network vessels are wind, cold, and dampness. For instance, if wind cold external evils invade the network vessels of the shao yang and yang ming, cold may causes contraction and constriction, while wind may cause erratic movement. In addition, qi stagnation, blood stasis, and phlegm may all also hinder and obstruct the free flow of the channels and network vessels, thus depriving the sinews of proper moistening and nourishment.

Wind is nothing other than stirring or extremely mobile qi. The qi may be stirred and transformed into wind internally by either extreme heat or by yin and blood vacuity failing to control yang. Extreme heat or fire may directly result in transformation of wind. In addition, heat or fire may damage and consume yin fluids and thus give rise to wind due to a combination of both heat and insufficient yin to control yang. Because the *Nei Jing* (*Inner Classic*) says that, "All wind shaking and vertigo pertain to the liver," yin blood vacuity resulting in internal stirring of wind is ascribed to the liver. Because static blood inhibits the engenderment of new or fresh blood, blood stasis may not only obstruct the channels and network vessels, it may also result in a yin and blood vacuity. However, Chinese internal medicine textbooks do not typically list a separate blood stasis pattern of tugging and slackening. Most cases of tics and spasms in real-life Western practice are due to a combination of two or more of the above factors. External contraction of wind cold evils is not a cause of psychiatric tics and spasms but rather of conditions such as Bell's palsy. Therefore, we will not discuss that pattern of tics and spasms below.

## TREATMENT BASED ON PATTERN DISCRIMINATION:

### 1. LIVER DEPRESSION TRANSFORMING HEAT WITH BLOOD VACUITY PATTERN

MAIN SYMPTOMS: Facial tics which typically occur during

episodes of stress or anger, irritability, easy anger, chest, breast, rib-side, and/or abdominal distention and fullness, possible PMS or early or excessive menstruation in females, a dark red tongue or a pale tongue with red and/or inflated tongue edges with white or yellow fur, and a fine, bowstring, possibly rapid pulse

**TREATMENT PRINCIPLES:** Course the liver and rectify the qi, clear heat and resolve depression, nourish the blood and extinguish wind

**FORMULA & MEDICINALS:** *Dan Zhi Xiao Yao San Jia Wei* (Moutan & Gardenia Rambling Powder with Added Flavors)

Cortex Radicis Moutan (*Dan Pi*), 10g, Fructus Gardeniae Jasminoidis (*Zhi Zi*), 10g, Radix Bupleuri (*Chai Hu*), 3-10g, Radix Angelicae Sinensis (*Dang Gui*), 10g, Radix Albus Paeoniae Lactiflorae (*Bai Shao*), 10-18g, Rhizoma Atractylodis Macrocephalae (*Bai Zhu*), 10g, Sclerotium Poriae Cocos (*Fu Ling*), 10g, mix-fried Radix Glycyrrhizae (*Gan Cao*), 6g, Ramulus Uncariae Cum Uncis (*Gou Teng*), 10-15g (added later), Periostracum Cicadae (*Chan Tui*), 10g

Decoct in water and administer orally in two divided doses, morning and evening, one *ji* per day.

**ADDITIONS & SUBTRACTIONS:** If there is no obvious depressive heat, delete the Moutan and Gardenia. If there is more marked blood vacuity, add Caulis Milletiae Seu Spatholobi (*Ji Xue Teng*) and Radix Polygoni Multiflori (*He Shou Wu*). If there are red, itchy eyes, add Flos Chrysanthemi Morifolii (*Ju Hua*) and Herba Equiseti Hiemalis (*Mu Zei Cao*).

**ACUPUNCTURE:** *Tai Chong* (Liv 3), *He Gu* (LI 4), *Feng Chi* (GB 20), *Ge Shu* (Bl 17), *Gan Shu* (Bl 18). Use even supplementing-even draining technique.

**ADDITIONS & SUBTRACTIONS:** For more obvious liver heat, add *Xing Jian* (Liv 2). For tics of the eyes, add *Tai Yang* (M-HN-9), *Zan Zhu* (Bl 2), and *Tong Zi Liao* (GB 1). For tics of the lips, add *Di Cang* (St 4) and *Ren Zhong* (GV 26) for tics of the upper lip, or *Cheng Jiang* (CV 24) for tics of the lower lip. For tics of the jaws, add *Ju Liao* (St 3), *Jia Che* (St 6), and *Quan Liao* (SI 18). For tics of the shoulder, add *Jian Yu* (LI 15), *Jian Zhen* (SI 9), and *Jian Liao* (TB 14). For tics of the arms, add *Wai Guan* (TB 5) and *Qu Chi* (LI 11). And for tics of the neck, add *Da Zhui* (GV 14) and *Tian Zhu* (Bl 10).

## 2. LIVER BLOOD VACUITY PATTERN

**MAIN SYMPTOMS:** Slight tics often associated with the menses in females, a pale white facial complexion, pale lips and nails, dizziness, possible blurred vision or night-blindness, scanty menstruation, dry, brittle nails, dry hair and skin, a pale tongue with thin, possibly dry white fur, and a fine, bowstring pulse

**TREATMENT PRINCIPLES:** Supplement the liver and nourish the blood, relax the sinews and extinguish wind

**FORMULA & MEDICINALS:** *Si Wu Tang He Da Ding Feng Zhu Jia Jian* (Four Materials Decoction plus Major Stabilize Wind Pearls with Additions & Subtractions)

Cooked Radix Rehmanniae (*Shu Di*), 12g, Radix Angelicae Sinensis (*Dang Gui*), 10g, Radix Albus Paeoniae Lactiflorae (*Bai Shao*), 10g, Radix Ligustici Wallichii (*Chuan Xiong*), 10g (added later), Gelatinum Corii Asini (*E Jiao*), 10g (dissolved at the end in the hot decoction), Fructus Schisandrae Chinensis (*Wu Wei Zi*), 10g, Tuber Ophiopogonis Japonici (*Mai Dong*), 12g, Plastrum Testudinis (*Gui Ban*), 12g (decocted first), Carapax Amydae Sinensis (*Bie Jia*), 12g (decocted first), Concha Ostreae (*Mu Li*), 12g (decocted first)

Decoct in water and administer orally in two divided doses, morning and evening, one *ji* per day.

**ADDITIONS & SUBTRACTIONS:** If there is constipation, add Semen Cannabis Sativae (*Huo Ma Ren*). If there is static blood obstructing the network vessels, add Buthus Martensis (*Quan Xie*) and Scolopendra Subspinipes (*Wu Gong*). If there is accompanying qi vacuity with fatigue and lack of strength, add Radix Astragali Membranacei (*Huang Qi*) and Radix Codonopsitis Pilosulae (*Dang Shen*). If there are loose stools due to spleen vacuity, add Radix Dioscoreae Oppositae (*Shan Yao*) and Rhizoma Atractylodis Macrocephalae (*Bai Zhu*). If there is dizziness, vacuity vexation, and insomnia, one can add Fructus Gardeniae Jasminoidis (*Zhi Zi*), Herba Lophatheri Gracilis (*Dan Zhu Ye*), Flos Chrysanthemi Morifolii (*Ju Hua*), and Caulis Polygoni Multiflori (*Ye Jiao Teng*). If there is torpid intake and abdominal fullness, one can add Fructus Amomi (*Sha Ren*), Endothelium Corneum Gigeriae Galli (*Ji Nei Jin*), and Pericarpium Citri Reticulatae (*Chen Pi*).

**ACUPUNCTURE:** *Ge Shu* (Bl 17), *Gan Shu* (Bl 18), *Shen Shu* (Bl 23), *Qu Quan* (Liv 8), *San Yin Jiao* (Sp 6), *He Gu* (LI 4), *Feng Chi* (GB 20). Use even supplementing-even draining technique.

ADDITIONS & SUBTRACTIONS: Depending on the localization of the tics, use the same added points as above.

### 3. LIVER WIND INTERNAL STIRRING PATTERN

MAIN SYMPTOMS: Tics occasioned or aggravated by bouts of stress and/or anger, headache and distention, dizziness, tinnitus, heaviness or a feeling of unsteadiness in the lower limbs, a dark red tongue with yellow, possibly dry fur, and a fine, bowstring, forceful, possibly rapid pulse

NOTE: Although this pattern is somewhat similar to the one above, it includes heat and/or ascendant liver yang hyperactivity.

TREATMENT PRINCIPLES: Level or calm the liver and extinguish wind

FORMULA & MEDICINALS: *Tian Ma Gou Teng Yin Jia Jian* (Gastrodia & Uncaria Drink with Additions & Subtractions)

Rhizoma Gastrodiae Elatae (*Tian Ma*), 12g, Ramulus Uncariae Cum Uncis (*Gou Teng*), 12-15g (added later), Concha Haliotidis (*Shi Jue Ming*), 15g (decocted first), Fructus Gardeniae Jasminoidis (*Zhi Zi*), 10g, Radix Scutellariae Baicalensis (*Huang Qin*), 10g, Radix Achyranthis Bidentatae (*Niu Xi*), 12g, Cortex Eucommiae Ulmoidis (*Du Zhong*), 10g, Buthus Martensis (*Quan Xie*), 6g, Radix Ligustici Wallichii (*Chuan Xiong*), 6g (added later)

Decoct in water and administer orally in two divided doses, morning and evening, one *ji* per day.

ADDITIONS & SUBTRACTIONS: If yin and blood vacuity are pronounced, add Radix Angelicae Sinensis (*Dang Gui*), Radix Albus Paeoniae Lactiflorae (*Bai Shao*), cooked Radix Rehmanniae (*Shu Di*), and Fructus Lycii Chinensis (*Gou Qi Zi*).

ACUPUNCTURE: *Tai Chong* (Liv 3), *He Gu* (LI 4), *Feng Chi* (GB 20), *Bai Hui* (GV 20). Use draining technique or even supplementing-even draining technique.

ADDITIONS & SUBTRACTIONS: If yin vacuity is marked, add *Tai Xi* (Ki 3) and *San Yin Jiao* (Sp 6). Depending on the localization of the tics, use the same added points as above under pattern #1.

### 4. EXTREME HEAT STIRRING WIND PATTERN

MAIN SYMPTOMS: Repeated, numerous, strong tics and spasms, a red facial complexion, red eyes, easy anger, abdominal distention, constipation, dry throat, oral thirst, heart vexation, tension, and agitation, if severe, possible spirit clouding and deranged speech, a red tongue with yellow, slimy, possibly dry fur, and a bowstring, rapid pulse

TREATMENT PRINCIPLES: Discharge fire and assist fluids, nourish yin and increase humors, extinguish wind and resolve tetany

FORMULA & MEDICINALS: For replete heat in the yang ming, use *Zeng Ye Cheng Qi Tang Jia Wei* (Increase Fluids & Order the Qi Decoction with Added Flavors)

Radix Scrophulariae Ningpoensis (*Xuan Shen*), 15-30g, Tuber Ophiopogonis Japonici (*Mai Dong*), 12-24g, uncooked Radix Rehmanniae (*Sheng Di*), 12-24g, Radix Et Rhizoma Rhei (*Da Huang*), 6-10g (added later), Mirabilitum (*Mang Xiao*), 4.5g (dissolved in the decocted liquid), Lumbricus (*Di Long*), 6g, Buthus Martensis (*Quan Xie*), 6g, Flos Chrysanthemi Morifolii (*Ju Hua*), 10g (steeped), Ramulus Uncariae Cum Uncis (*Gou Teng*), 10-15g (added later)

If extreme heat has damaged qi and fluids, use *Bai Hu Jia Ren Shen Tang Jia Jian* (White Tiger Plus Ginseng Decoction with Additions & Subtractions)

Gypsum Fibrosum (*Shi Gao*), 30g (decocted first), Rhizoma Anemarrhenae Aspheloidis (*Zhi Mu*), 10g, mix-fried Radix Glycyrrhizae (*Gan Cao*), 3-6g, Radix Panacis Ginseng (*Ren Shen*), 6g (decocted first), Lumbricus (*Di Long*), 6g, Buthus Martensis (*Quan Xie*), 6g, Flos Chrysanthemi Morifolii (*Ju Hua*), 10g (steeped), Ramulus Uncariae Cum Uncis (*Gou Teng*), 10-15g (added later)

Decoct in water and administer orally in two divided doses, morning and evening, one *ji* per day.

ADDITIONS & SUBTRACTIONS: If vexation and agitation are severe, add Herba Lophatheri Gracilis (*Dan Zhu Ye*) and Fructus Gardeniae Jasminoidis (*Zhi Zi*).

ACUPUNCTURE: *Nei Ting* (St 44), *Qu Chi* (LI 11), *Yang Ling Quan* (GB 34), *Da Zhui* (GV 14), *Feng Chi* (GB 20). Use draining technique.

ADDITIONS & SUBTRACTIONS: Depending on the localization of the tics, use the same added points as above under pattern #1. If phlegm is blocking the orifices, add *Feng Long* (St 40). If there is concomitant blood stasis, add *Xue Hai* (Sp 10).

## ABSTRACTS OF REPRESENTATIVE CHINESE RESEARCH:

*Zhong Yi Za Zhi (Journal of Chinese Medicine)*, #11, 1993, p. 678-679: Xu Zhu-qian reported on the treatment of 52 cases of pediatric Tourette's disorder between February 1991 and February 1992. Of the 52 cases, 41 were boys and 11 were girls. Their ages ranged from 4-15 years, with the median age being nine. The course of disease had lasted from three months to 12 years, with a median duration of two years eight months. The treatment consisted of administering the following Chinese medicinals internally as a water-based decoction: Flos Magnoliae Lileflorae (*Xin Yi Hua*), 10g, Fructus Xanthii Sibirici (*Cang Er Zi*), 10g, Radix Scrophulariae Ningpoensis (*Xuan Shen*), 10g, Radix Isatidis Seu Baphicacanthi (*Ban Lan Gen*), 10g, Radix Sophorae Subprostratae (*Shan Dou Gen*), 5g, Rhizoma Pinelliae Ternatae (*Ban Xia*), 3g, and Ramulus Uncariae Cum Uncis (*Gou Teng*), 10g, plus individual additions and subtractions based on each case's presenting signs and symptoms. The medicinals were boiled down to 100ml of liquid which was administered orally in four divided doses per day. Twenty-eight days equaled one course of treatment. After one course of treatment, 28 cases (53.8%) were judged cured, 17 cases (32.7%) were judged markedly improved, five cases (9.6%) experienced some improvement, and two cases (3.8%) got no result. Thus the total amelioration rate was 96.1%.

*Zhong Yi Za Zhi (Journal of Chinese Medicine)*, #7, 1993, p. 423-424: Yi Lian-chong *et al.* reported on the treatment of 156 cases of pediatric Tourette's disorder. One hundred two cases were boys and 54 were girls. One hundred fourteen cases were between 6-10 years old, and 42 were 11-15. The course of disease ranged from six days to one year. Seventy-eight cases had already been treated by Western medicine, and 36 cases had received Chinese medicinals and acupuncture. Eighty-four cases showed some abnormality on EEG examination, six cases showed x-ray abnormalities, and another six showed CT scan abnormalities. Treatment consisted of needling *Nei Ting* (St 44), *Qu Chi* (LI 11), *Pian Li* (LI 6), and *Si Bai* (St 2) in the 66 cases whose Chinese pattern was categorized as yang ming heat accumulation, while treatment consisted of needling *Shen Men* (Ht 7), *Fu Liu* (Ki 7), *Ya Men* (GV

15), and *Lian Quan* (CV 23) in the 90 cases whose pattern was categorized as sea of marrow insufficiency. One treatment was given per day, with two weeks equaling one course of treatment and a maximum of three courses being given. Of the 156 cases treated in this manner, 114 cases (73.1%) were cured, 30 cases (19.25%) were brought under control, and 12 cases (7.7%) experienced no result. Thus the total amelioration rate was 92.3%. Eight-one percent of the patients in the yang ming heat accumulation group were cured as opposed to only 66.7% of those manifesting sea of marrow insufficiency being cured.

*Zhong Yi Za Zhi (Journal of Chinese Medicine)*, #9, 1999, p. 569: Zhang Hong reported on the treatment of 36 cases of Tourette's disorder with ear acupuncture point pressure using magnetized pellets. Twenty-two of these patients were boys and 14 were girls. Their ages ranged from 4-13 years, with a median age of nine. Their course of disease had lasted from 1-4 years, with a median duration of 1.5 years. One case had CT scan abnormalities, and three cases had EEG abnormalities. Nineteen cases had previously been treated with Chinese or Western medicines. All were diagnosed with Tourette's disorder based on the criteria in the *DSM-III*. The main ear points consisted of Liver, Kidneys, Spirit Gate, and Brain. The auxiliary points consisted of Subcortex, Heart, Spleen, and Stomach points depending which of these were abnormally reactive. Depending on the severity of the disease 5-7 of these points were selected and magnetized pellets afixed over each with adhesive. Patients were instructed to press each pellet for 2-3 minutes each time, three times per day. Every other day, the points were switched from one ear to the other, with 10 treatments equaling one course. After from 1-3 such courses, 14 cases (38.9%) were cured, 19 cases (52.8%) were improved, and three cases (8.3%) got no result, for a total amelioration rate of 91.7%.

*Shang Hai Zhong Yi Yao Za Zhi (Shanghai Journal of Chinese Medicine & Medicinals)*, #4, 1999, p. 30-31: Chen Wei-bin, Chen Yan-ping, and Xu Gang reported on the treatment of 12 cases of infantile convulsions treated based on the liver. All 12 cases were seen as out-patients and all were diagnosed according to the criteria in the *DSM-IV*. These children's ages ranged from 8-13 years old, with a median age of 9.1. Their disease had lasted from eight months to three years. Of these 12 cases, one had transient convulsions, six had chronic active convulsions, and five cases were diagnosed with Tourette's disorder. Epilepsy was excluded in all cases and EEG was normal in all cases. The patients were divided into two groups according to pattern discrimination: 1) liver depression transforming fire and stirring wind pattern and 2) liver-kidney yin vacuity stirring wind pattern. The patients in the liver depression transforming fire group received the following Chinese medicinals administered in decoction: Cortex Radicis Moutan (*Dan Pi*), stir-fried Fructus Gardeniae Jasminoidis (*Zhi Zi*), Spica Prunellae Vulgaris (*Xia Ku Cao*), and Sclerotium Poriae Cocos (*Fu Ling*), 10g each, Radix Bupleuri (*Chai Hu*), Flos Chrysanthemi Morifolii (*Ju Hua*), and Rhizoma Coptidis Chinensis (*Huang Lian*), 5g each, Ramulus Uncariae Cum Uncis (*Gou Teng*), 15g, and Concha Haliotidis (*Shi Jue Ming*), 20g. The patients in the liver-kidney yin vacuity group received: uncooked Radix Rehmanniae (*Sheng Di*), cooked Radix Rehmanniae (*Shu Di*), Radix Dioscoreae Oppositae (*Shan Yao*), Cortex Radicis Moutan (*Dan Pi*), Radix Glehniae Littoralis (*Sha Shen*), Tuber Ophiopogonis Japonici (*Mai Dong*), Tuber Curcumae (*Yu Jin*), and Fructus Ligustri Lucidi (*Nu Zhen Zi*), 10g each, and Plastrum Testudinis (*Gui Ban*), 12g. In addition, all patients received acupuncture every other day at: *Bai Hui* (GV 20), *Da Zhui* (GV 14), *Shen Men* (Ht 7), *Gan Shu* (Bl 18), and *Dan Shu* (Bl 19) with 15 minutes needle retention per time and stimulation one time every five minutes with draining technique. Ten such treatments equaled one course of treatment. After three months of treatment, nine cases (75%) were cured, two cases (16.7%) improved, and one case (8.3%) got no result. Among those who were cured were the one case of transient convulsions, four cases of chronic active convulsions, and four cases of Tourette's disorder. Both cases who improved had chronic active convulsions, and the patient who did not respond to this protocol had Tourette's disorder.

❖

*He Nan Zhong Yi (Henan Chinese Medicine)*, #1, 2000, p. 53: Chen Bang-guo reported on the treatment of 31 cases of facial muscle spasm with acupuncture. There were 14 males and 17 females in this study. Fourteen were between 35-45 and 17 were over 45 years of age. The longest disease course was five years and the shortest was three months. Three cases had bilateral convulsions. All the rest experienced one-sided muscle jerking or tics. Twelve were left-sided and 16 were right-sided. Treatment consisted of needling *He Gu* (LI 4) with twisting draining technique, stimulating the needle every 10 minutes, with a 30 minute needle retention time. In addition, the local facial nerve trunk was stimulated with acupuncture. One

treatment was given per day, and 10 such treatments equaled one course, after which there was a 2-3 day rest before starting the next course. All the patients in this study received two such courses of treatment. Using this technique, 17 cases were considered clinically cured, seven were deemed to have gotten a marked effect, six got some effect, and only one got no effect, for a total amelioration rate of 97%.

REPRESENTATIVE CASE HISTORIES:

❖ CASE 1[4] ❖

The patient was a nine year old girl who experienced uncontrollable twitching of the eyelids, corners of the mouth, neck, abdomen, and four limbs. There was a repetitive odd sound in her throat, her nose was blocked, and her appetite was a little reduced. Her defecation and urination were normal. Her facial complexion was somber white and lusterless. Her tongue was slightly red with slimy, slightly yellow fur, and her pulse was slippery and forceful. EEG and CT scans were without apparent abnormality. The patient was diagnosed as suffering from Tourette's disorder and her pattern was categorized as wind phlegm attached to the lungs. Therefore, she was treated with the same Chinese medicinal formula described in the first Chinese abstract above plus Buthus Martensis (*Quan Xie*), 3g, and Scolopendra Subspinipes (*Wu Gong*), 1 piece.

After taking 10 *ji* of this formula, the strange sound in the patient's throat, the squeezing of her eyebrows, and the blinking of her eyes were brought under control and the twitching movement of her limbs was markedly reduced. Therefore, the above formula was continued with additions and subtractions for another 13 *ji*. At that point, the girl's body no longer twitched. However, because her appetite was still not normal and she had a sallow yellow facial complexion, she was prescribed *Liu Jun Zi Tang Jia Wei* (Six Gentlemen Decoction with Added Flavors). After seven or more *ji* of this formula to improve her spleen and stomach function, the patient was judged cured and there was no recurrence of the twitching.

❖ CASE 2[5] ❖

The patient was an 11 year old girl who was first examined on Nov. 8, 1990. For the past three years, she had been nodding her head, blinking her eyelids, and shrugging her shoulders uncontrollably. In the last half year, her condition had gotten worse. Now she uttered odd sounds from her throat. Fatigue and emotional stress made her symptoms worse. On examination it was found that she also had heavy-headedness and distention, was easily angered, rash, and impetuous, was nauseous, and had a torpid intake. Her sleep was not calm at night, her stools were constipated, her tongue was red with yellow fur, and her pulse was bowstring and rapid. Serologic examination was normal. EEG showed a moderate degree abnormality. The patient's pattern was categorized as phlegm heat brewing internally with yang hyperactivity stirring wind. Therefore, the treatment principles were to settle the liver and extinguish wind, clear heat and transform phlegm, nourish yin and soothe the sinews, for which she was given modified Zhen Gan Xi Feng Tang (Settle the Liver & Extinguish Wind Decoction): Spica Prunellae Vulgaris (Xia Ku Cao), Flos Chrysanthemi Morifolii (Ju Hua), and Ramulus Uncariae Cum Uncis (Gou Teng), 20g each, uncooked Os Draconis (Long Gu), uncooked Concha Ostreae (Mu Li), and Radix Albus Paeoniae Lactiflorae (Bai Shao), 25g each, Tuber Asparagi Cochinensis (Tian Men Dong), Radix Scrophulariae Ningpoensis (Xuan Shen), Tuber Curcumae (Yu Jin), and Sclerotium Poriae Cocos (Fu Ling), 15g each, Rhizoma Coptidis Chinensis (Huang Lian), Fructus Citri Sacrodactylis (Fo Shou), and Haemititum (Dai Zhe Shi), 10g each. In addition, the child was forbidden acrid, spicy food.

After taking 10 ji of this formula, the symptoms were slightly less. The defecation was easier and the food intake had increased. In addition, the girl's sleep at night was calm. After another 10 ji, the patient's facial and shoulder twitching had decreased by 2/3-3/4. However, her head still felt dizzy and distended. Therefore, 30 grams of Radix Puerariae (Ge Gen) were added to her formula and another five ji were prescribed. Now all her symptoms were greatly reduced, her head only felt slightly dizzy and distended, and her tongue and pulse had returned to normal. For another three months, the girl was administered Herba Dendrobii (Shi Hu), Fructus Lycii Chinensis (Gou Qi Zi), Radix Salviae Miltiorrhizae (Dan Shen), Fructus Perillae Frutescentis (Zi Su Zi), Cortex Radicis Moutan (Dan Pi), Cortex Albizziae Julibrissinis (He Huan Pi), and bile-processed Rhizoma Arisaematis (Dan Nan Xing) to nourish yin and supplement the kidneys, quicken the blood and clear the heart, resolve depression and quiet the spirit. At the end of those three months, all the patient's symptoms had been completely eliminated. On follow-up after two years, there had been no recurrence and her EEG had returned to normal.

### ❖ CASE 3[6] ❖

The patient was an 11 year old boy who had had "un-self-controllable" convulsions for five years. These had started when the boy was seven years old after he failed to be

selected for a swim team. Three years ago, he had been treated with orally administered haloperidol, but this had made him somnolent and he had stopped taking this medication. The child was habitually angry and easily became excited. His stools were constipated, his sleep was not calm, his mouth was dry with a bitter taste, his tongue was red with thin, white fur, and his pulse was bowstring. Therefore, his pattern was discriminated as liver qi depression and binding transforming fire which then harassed and stirred the spirit brilliance, plus lack of nourishment of the sinews and vessels. The treatment principles were to clear the liver and drain fire, quiet the spirit, stabilize the mind, and extinguish wind.

Thus the boy was given: Cortex Radicis Moutan (Dan Pi), stir-fried Fructus Gardeniae Jasminoidis (Zhi Zi), Radix Rubrus Paeoniae Lactiflorae (Chi Shao), Radix Albus Paeoniae Lactiflorae (Bai Shao), Spica Prunellae Vulgaris (Xia Ku Cao), and Ramulus Uncariae Cum Uncis (Gou Teng), 10g each, Concha Margaritiferae (Zhen Zhu Mu) and Concha Haliotidis (Shi Jue Ming), 20g each, Flos Chrysanthemi Morifolii (Ju Hua) and Pericarpium Citri Reticulatae (Chen Pi), 5g each, and uncooked Radix Glycyrrhizae (Gan Cao), 3g. In addition, he was acupunctured at Bai Hui (GV 20), Shen Men (Ht 7), Gan Shu (Bl 18), and Dan Shu (Bl 19) one time every other day. After two months of Chinese medicinals and acupuncture, his convulsions had disappeared and there had been no recurrence on follow-up after one year.

### ❖ CASE 4[7] ❖

The patient was a 45 year old male. One year prior, this man had begun to experience twitching of his left eyelid. This twitching gradually spread to involve his entire left cheek. It was more pronounced whenever the man was under stress or excited, and no other cause for this condition could be found. In addition, the patient had a bowstring pulse and thin, white tongue fur. Based on these signs and symptoms, the man's pattern was categorized as external contraction of wind evils lodging in and obstructing the tai yang and yang ming channels. Acupuncture was thus performed once per day at Hou Xi (SI 3) and Shen Mai (Bl 62) on the right side, at He Gu (LI 4) and Feng Chi (GB 20) on the left side, and at Zu San Li (St 36) bilaterally. After four such treatments, the facial spasm had improved but the twitching eyelid continued. Therefore, another 14 treatments were administered, after which the twitching was basically brought under control. When the patient became excited, he still would sometimes experience mild twitching of the same eyelid. Hence another 10 treatments were given, after which it is assumed that all the symptoms were eliminated because, on follow-up after six months, there had been no recurrence.

### ❖ CASE 5[8] ❖

A 42 year old male was seen for the main complaint of tremor in all his limbs for more than two years. Two and a half years before, the patient had developed dizziness, a stiff neck, insomnia, and an unsteady gait which a local doctor had diagnosed as neurasthenia. Therefore, the man was treated with sedatives and glutamic acid but without any result. A half year later, a mild tremor appeared in his left leg accompanied by slowed movement of that leg and reduced step length. Some time after, the tremor also affected both of the patient's hands. At this point, he was diagnosed as suffering from Parkinson's disease and was prescribed Artane, 1mg each time three times per day. However, due to intolerable side effects, such as dizziness, blurred vision, and vomiting, and its lack of clinical effect, this drug was suspended and replaced by Levodopa. This medicine was administered for half a year, during which time the patient's symptoms improved slightly initially only to be followed by sudden complete inability to use his arms and legs. The patient's mind was clear but his affect was slightly dull. He had difficulty turning his head and saliva drooled from the corner of his mouth. His muscular tonus was increased and there was cogwheel rigidity.

The patient was treated with scalp acupuncture at the chorea and tremor-controlling area on both sides of his head. After the first treatment, the patient felt that his neck was more flexible and his mind was much clearer. He could straighten his back, walk with bigger strides, and change directions more easily. However, these improvements only lasted for three hours. The patient received 30 scalp acupuncture treatments with the same results after each treatment. Therefore, in order to lengthen the interval of relief, the needle-embedding method was used with the same results. In other words, as long as the needles were embedded, the man experienced relief, but, when the needles were withdrawn, his symptoms returned within a few hours.

### ❖ CASE 6[9] ❖

The patient was an 18 year old male whose main complaint was involuntary torsion of the whole body for half a day. Two months previously, the young man had developed insomnia and headache. He had been diagnosed as suffering from "neurosis" and was prescribed haloperidol for this. After taking this medication for the third time, he developed a painful feeling in his upper back which later developed into torsional spasm of his head and body to the left. Upon examination, it was found that the young man's mental state was clear but his facial expression was abnormal due to the forced spasm. His head was passively turned to the left 100E. His right arm and torso also twisted intermittently to the left for 30 seconds to two minutes at a time every several minutes. When such an attack occurred, the patient's head sweated. Scalp acupuncture was performed at the upper half of the chorea and tremor-controlling area on both sides of the head. After the first treatment, the severity of the torsion spasm was markedly relieved and the interval between attacks lengthened to 10 minutes. The following morning, the patient was almost normal except for increased muscular tonus and cogwheel rigidity. Therefore, a second treatment was given and the patient fully recovered.

### ❖ CASE 7[10] ❖

The patient was a 43 year old female cadre who had experienced right-sided facial muscle jerking for one year. This was in reaction to work stress and taxation fatigue. The patient had previously tried Chinese and Western medicines without satisfactory result. Therefore, she had come for acupuncture treatment. Sometimes the woman's condition was better and sometimes it was worse. Her upper and lower right eyelids and the corners of her mouth jerked noticeably for 40 minutes per episode. Therefore, acupuncture was performed at the facial nerve trunk and at He Gu (LI 4) one time per day. After three treatments, the woman's right-sided facial muscle convulsions had decreased, but she still experienced several minutes of twitching of the corner of her mouth each day. After 10 treatments, her facial muscle jerking completely disappeared. She was treated three more times in order to secure the treatment effect, at which time the woman was judged clinically cured. On follow-up after half a year, there had been no recurrence.

### ENDNOTES:

[1]Wiseman, Nigel, Glossary of Chinese Medical Terms and Acupuncture Points, Paradigm Publications, Brookline, MA, 1990, p. 33

[2]Webster's New World Dictionary of the American Language, ed. by David B. Guralnik & Jospeh H. Friend, The World Publishing Co., Cleveland, 1964, p. 324

[3]Shaui Xue-zhong, Chinese-English Terminology of Traditional Chinese Medicine, Hunan Science & Technology Press, Changsha, 1983, p. 513-514

[4]Xu Zhu-qian, "The Treatment of 52 Cases of Pediatric Tourette's Syndrome Based on the Lungs," Zhong Yi Za Zhi (Journal of Chinese Medicine), #11, 1993, p. 679

[5]Zhang Wu-sheng, "The Treatment of Tourette's Syndrome with Pueraria," *Zhong Yi Za Zhi (Journal of Chinese Medicine)*, #6, 1999, p. 326

[6]Chen Wei-bin *et al.*, "The Treatment of 12 Cases of Pediatric Convulsions Based on the Liver," *Shang Hai Zhong Yi Yao Za Zhi (Shanghai Journal of Chinese Medicine & Medicinals)*, #4, 1999, p. 31

[7]*Acupuncture Case Histories, op. cit.*, p. 129-130

[8]Jiao Shun-fa, *Scalp Acupuncture and Clinical Cases*, Foreign Languages Press, Beijing, 1997, p. 71-72

[9]*Ibid.*, p. 73-74

[10]Chen Dang-guo, "The Treatment of 31 Cases of Facial Muscle Spasm by Needling the Facial Nerve Trunk & *He Gu* (LI 4)," *He Nan Zhong Yi (Henan Chinese Medicine)*, #1, 2000, p. 53

# ❖ 17 ❖

# EPILEPSY

Wiseman translates the Chinese *dian xian* simply as "epilepsy." While this Chinese disease category does cover the Western medical disease of epilepsy, it also covers conditions which in Western medicine are not considered epilepsy *per se*. *Dian* is the same character meaning "withdrawal" we saw in *dian kuang*, withdrawal and mania. *The Pinyin Chinese-English Dictionary* edited by Wu Jing-rong simply gives epilepsy for the word *xian*.[1] However, this character is made from the homologous word *xian* meaning a not busy, idle, and unoccupied surmounted by the disease radical, suggesting pathological idleness or loss of consciousness and volition. Since this condition covers epilepsy and other conditions not considered epilepsy by Western medicine, we prefer to call this condition "epileptiform disease." It is characterized by essence spirit abstraction. If it is severe, there is sudden falling and loss of consciousness. Foaming drool may be spit from the mouth, the eyes may stare straight upward, and there may be convulsions of the four limbs.

The term epilepsy is first found in the *Su Wen (Simple Questions)* where its authors refer to "epilepsy reversal." The *Zhu Bing Yuan Hou Lun (Treatise on the Origins & Symptoms of Diseases)* refers to "fright epilepsy," "wind epilepsy," and "food epilepsy." The *Qian Jin Yao Fang (Essential Formulas [Worth] a Thousand [Pieces of] Gold)* talks about "the five viscera epilepsies," *i.e.*, liver epilepsy, spleen epilepsy, lung epilepsy, kidney epilepsy, and heart epilepsy. Sun Si-miao also discusses horse, cow, sheep, pig, dog and chicken epilepsies based on various noises the

patient may utter during an epileptic episode. And the *Tai Ping Sheng Hui Fang (Tai Ping [Era] Imperial Grace Formulary)* of the Song dynasty speaks of "heat epilepsy." As stated above, the most common Chinese term in use today for this condition is *dian xian*.

With the exception of the first pattern, which appears to correspond to a generalized tonic-clonic seizure, the five patterns of *dian xian* described below do not correspond to discrete diagnostic categories within Western medicine or psychiatry. However, features included in patterns described in the Chinese medical literature resemble symptoms of several Western diseases. The following section compares and contrasts various symptom patterns described in the Chinese literature with Western medical or psychiatric syndromes. It is interesting that Western medicine identifies numerous psychiatric symptoms that are associated with seizure disorders but are not required to diagnose various subtypes of these disorders. In contrast to this approach, in Chinese medical diagnosis, psychiatric symptoms appear to be as central as neurologic symptoms.

## NOSOLOGY:

Western medicine identifies two basic patterns of epilepsy: generalized and partial seizures. Generalized seizures have no focal starting point in the brain. Most kinds of generalized seizures are characterized by abrupt loss of consciousness (*grand mal*) or change in level of consciousness (*petit mal*). Generalized seizures are typically associated with rhythmic contraction and relaxation of voluntary muscles. In contrast to such tonic-clonic seizures, partial seizures more commonly occur in the absence of associated abnormal involuntary movements. Partial seizures begin in a specific focus in the brain and subsequently spread or generalize to other brain regions. The specific pattern of generalization corresponds to a predictable constellation of associated neurological or psychiatric symptoms. Partial seizures are classified as complex or simple depending on the presence or absence of altered level of consciousness or unusual psychiatric sequellae.

## EPIDEMIOLOGY:

Seizure disorders typically begin during childhood or early adulthood. Onset can take place at any age as a result of traumatic brain injury or other serious insult to the brain. Of the roughly 20-40 million people worldwide who are diagnosed with seizure disorders, three-fourths had their first seizure before age 18, and as many as 20% may have inherited a familial predisposition to develop a seizure disorder.

## DIFFERENTIAL DIAGNOSIS:

In clarifying the differential diagnosis of seizure disorders, the initial task is to rule out possible underlying or confounding medical disorders manifesting as symptoms that resemble a seizure. These include common medical causes of sudden-onset loss of consciousness or change in level of consciousness. Cardiac arrhythmias, myocardial infarction, and cerebrovascular accidents (stroke) are commonly associated with loss of consciousness. Further, temporary occlusion of one of the major arteries supplying the brain can result in a transient ischemic attack (TIA). This is regarded as a warning sign of impending stroke and can manifest as acute onset change in the level of consciousness with associated confusion, disorientation, or complete loss of consciousness. However, these medical emergencies are rarely associated with abnormal rhythmic movements and are distinguishable from epilepsy because of other associated symptoms. Although electroencephalography (EEG) never conclusively rules out the presence of an underlying seizure disorder, normal EEG results following loss of consciousness point to other etiologies. Intoxication with alcohol or illicit substances can result in altered level of consciousness or frank loss of consciousness. Inappropriate high doses of numerous medications, including sedative-hypnotics, opiates, and others, can also result in change in level of consciousness or loss of consciousness. A thorough history, laboratory studies, including urine toxicology and blood alcohol level, and

the absence of other typical seizure-like symptoms will generally clarify the diagnosis. It is important to note, however, that seizures frequently occur in the context of abuse or withdrawal from alcohol or illicit substances, in which case urine and serology studies frequently do not reveal their presence.

As noted earlier, consistent patterns of correspondences between certain kinds of seizure disorders and certain psychiatric symptoms have been observed. Some of these patterns resemble patterns of epilepsy described in the Chinese medical literature. Western medicine distinguishes abnormal behaviors or psychiatric symptoms associated with seizure disorders on the basis of timing of occurrence of these symptoms with respect to seizure activity. Seizure-associated symptoms can occur immediately before (pre-ictal); during (ictal); or between (inter-ictal) seizure activity. It is often difficult to distinguish epilepsy with associated psychiatric manifestations from a primary co-existing psychiatric disorder. Among others, conversion disorders, anxiety disorders, and many disorders of impulse control are often associated with seizure disorders. The second Chinese medical pattern of liver fire and phlegm heat includes "clouding of consciousness, convulsions," and "at normal times (*i.e.*, between seizures), the emotions are tense and agitated and there is heart vexation, and insomnia." A pattern of persisting emotional disturbance included as a central feature of this pattern of epilepsy resembles frequently observed inter-ictal disturbances in personality discussed in the Western psychiatric literature. Borderline personality disorder is more frequently diagnosed in patients with seizure disorders than the normal population. This disorder is characterized by persisting dysregulation in the individual's capacity for emotional self-regulation in which anger, agitation, and other psychological symptoms that resemble vexation interfere with social and occupational functioning. The borderline patient often behaves in an impulsive, immature, or self-destructive way, and subsequently there is often an associated history of chaotic interpersonal relationships. Schizophrenia-like syndromes, in which psychotic symptoms are prominent between seizures, have been observed at higher-than-chance rates in epileptic populations. As discussed in Chapter 7, this Book, the Chinese disease category of vexation and agitation is sometimes present "at normal times (*i.e.*, between seizures) and likely corresponds to certain psychotic symptoms observed during inter-ictal periods that have been described in the Western medical literature. In Western psychiatry, however, the temporal relationship between seizure activity and psychosis is highly variable, and prominent psychotic symptoms including auditory or visual hallucinations, agitation, and paranoia may occur

## DIFFERENTIAL DIAGNOSIS

### 1. MEDICAL DISORDERS

A. SEIZURE DISORDERS
B. MYOCARDIAL INFARCTION
C. CEREBROVASCULAR ACCIDENT (CVA)
D. TRANSIENT ISCHEMIC ATTACK (TIA)

### 2. EFFECTS OF SUBSTANCES

A. ALCOHOL OR ILLICIT SUBSTANCE INTOXICATION OR WITHDRAWAL
B. SIDE EFFECTS OF MEDICATIONS

### 3. PSYCHIATRIC DISORDERS

A. CONVERSION DISORDER
B. ANXIETY DISORDERS
C. DISORDERS OF IMPULSE CONTROL
D. BORDERLINE PERSONALITY DISORDER (BPD)
E. HISTRIONIC PERSONALITY DISORDER (HPD)
F. SCHIZOPHRENIA AND OTHER PSYCHOTIC DISORDERS
G. MAJOR DEPRESSIVE EPISODE
H. PSEUDOSEIZURES

before, during, or after resolution of a seizure. Many patients who suffer from a schizophrenia-like syndrome between seizures also experience prominent mood symptoms which are included in several Chinese medical patterns of epilepsy.

Spleen-stomach vacuity weakness is the fourth Chinese pattern described as a variant of epilepsy in Chinese medicine. In this pattern, lassitude of the spirit and lack of strength imply depressed mood. Further, the Chinese medical description of "dizziness, torpid intake, lusterless facial complexion and soggy or weak pulse" resembles psychosomatic symptoms that are often associated with depressed mood in Western psychiatry. In fact, depression is the psychiatric disorder that is most commonly observed in patients with seizure disorders. When seizure activity does not conform to a described pattern or is observed in a patient with normal EEG findings, pseudo-seizures must be considered in the differential diagnosis. In contemporary Western psychiatry, pseudoseizures are viewed as non-epileptic seizures and are conceptualized as psychosomatic symptoms caused by an underlying psychiatric disorder. Psychiatric disorders that are frequently associated with pseudoseizures include conversion disorders and certain personality disorders, including borderline personality disorder and histrionic personality disorder.

### ETIOLOGY & PATHOPHYSIOLOGY:

Many epileptic individuals are eventually found to have temporal and, less commonly, frontal lobe lesions. However, in the majority of cases, a specific cause is never identified. Epileptogenic brain lesions can result from head trauma, brain tumors, or congenital anomalies in brain development. Psychiatric disturbances that commonly accompany temporal lobe seizures are often directly caused by seizure activity or indirectly by chronic CNS changes resulting from repeated seizure activity. Chronic seizures may result in dysregulation of specific neurotransmitters, including increased dopamine or GABA, and a higher than chance probability of psychiatric syndromes that are associated with these changes, for example, schizophrenia-like symptom patterns or depression. Behavioral or psychological changes are frequent responses to feelings of loss of control in patients with seizure disorders. These can include depression, either social withdrawal or increased dependent behavior, and generalized anxiety.

### WESTERN MEDICAL TREATMENT:

Administration of anti-seizure medications is the established standard of care for seizure disorders in Western medicine. These include principally carbamazepine (Tegretol), valproic acid (Depakote), phenytoin (Dilantin), and more recently introduced drugs like GABA-pentin (Neurontin) and lamotrigine (Lamictal). Carbamazepine, valproic acid, GABA-pentin, and lamotrigine are appropriate choices for treatment of seizure-related mood disorders including depressive or manic episodes. Antipsychotic medications are used to treat schizophrenia-like syndromes. However, many antipsychotics lower the seizure threshold or interact with anti-seizure medications, thus increasing the risk of breakthrough seizure activity. Psychosurgery is sometimes indicated for individuals who fail to respond to anti-seizure medications and who experience frequent seizures or associated psychiatric syndromes that cause significant impairment in functioning.

SHORT & LONG-TERM ADVANTAGES & DISADVAN-
TAGES OF WESTERN MEDICAL TREATMENT:

Successful treatment of a seizure disorder and any associated psychiatric syndromes results in improved cognitive,
social, and occupational functioning. When medications
effectively prevent seizure episodes, less cumulative
seizure-induced brain damage occurs over the long-term.
Disadvantages of conventional Western medical treatments include all potential risks of side effects, toxicities,
and drug interactions of anti-seizure medications. These
are too numerous to describe in this brief review. Many
antipsychotic medications used to treat seizure-related
psychotic syndromes directly lower the seizure threshold
and also interact with antiseizure medications, lowering
their bio-availability, hence further increasing the risk of
seizures. If there is uncertainty regarding a complaint that
may be a medication side effect or interaction, the patient
should be referred to his or her treating physician.

Complications of psychosurgery include failure to control
seizures and failure to resolve associated psychiatric syndromes. In unusual cases, following surgery, the patient
may experience temporary apathy, mutism, and loss of
capacity for certain complex learned behaviors.

PROGNOSIS:

Because most seizure disorders respond to medication, the
majority of afflicted individuals have favorable prognoses.
In most cases, good seizure control with medications corresponds to alleviation of associated psychiatric symptoms. However, some individuals complain of psychiatric
syndromes that persist long after seizure activity has been
adequately controlled.

INDICATIONS FOR REFERRAL TO
WESTERN MEDICAL SERVICES:

A history or clinical presentation that suggests the possibility of an underlying seizure disorder is always a sufficient basis for urgent medical referral in order to rule out
acute or life-threatening causes, including head trauma,
stroke, brain tumors, or the effects of alcohol or an illicit
substance. In cases where chronic seizure activity or associated psychiatric syndromes in the absence of acute or
severe symptoms have failed to respond to a sufficient
course of Chinese medical treatment, the patient may
benefit from non-urgent referral to a psychiatrist or neurologist for continuing evaluation and development of an
optimized treatment plan combining appropriate elements of Chinese and Western medical therapies.

CHINESE DISEASE CAUSES & DISEASE MECHANISMS:

The causes of epileptiform condition in Chinese medicine
are divided into former heaven or prenatal and latter
heaven or postnatal. If the mother experiences great fright
during pregnancy, this may damage the fetus causing
essence damage and kidney depletion. In that case, after
birth kidney yin may fail to control liver yang which
becomes hyperactive and may engender wind. When this
wind stirs internally, it may give rise to epileptiform conditions.

In terms of latter heaven causes and mechanisms, if the
seven affects are unregulated, and especially if there is
great fright and fear, the qi mechanism may counterflow and become chaotic. "Fright leads to qi chaos,"
while "Fear leads to qi descent." If the qi mechanism
becomes chaotic and counterflows, the viscera and
bowels will not be harmonious and thus easily suffer
detriment. If the liver and kidneys suffer detriment,
then yin may not restrain yang. Hyperactive yang may
then go on to engender heat and/or wind. If the spleen
and stomach suffer detriment, this easily leads to the
creation of phlegm turbidity gathering internally. If this
situation endures, external evils, emotional stimuli, or
faulty diet may provoke phlegm turbidity to follow qi
counterflow, fire flaring, and/or wind stirring to confound and block the clear orifices. If this is severe, it
may cause epileptiform condition. In addition, stagnant
qi and phlegm turbidity may give rise to blood stasis or
blood stasis may be caused directly due to traumatic
injury. In that case, static blood may obstruct the blood
vessels preventing yin, blood, essence, and qi from
ascending to fill the sea of marrow. If severe, this may
also result in epileptiform condition. As Liu Yi-ren
says, "Generally speaking, epilepsy is ascribed to
phlegm, fire, and fright."

TREATMENT BASED ON PATTERN DISCRIMINATION:

1. LIVER WIND & PHLEGM TURBIDITY PATTERN

MAIN SYMPTOMS: There may either be prodromal dizziness, chest oppression, and lack of strength or there may
be no marked prodromal signs and symptoms. During the
episode itself, there is sudden falling, consciousness is not
clear, there are convulsions, and there may be spitting of
drool. Sounds like the bleating of sheep or the grunting of
pigs may be heard. There may also be incontinence of
both urination and defecation.

TREATMENT PRINCIPLES: Flush phlegm and extinguish
wind, open the orifices and stabilize epilepsy

FORMULA & MEDICINALS: *Ding Xian Wan Jia Jian* (Stabilize Epilepsy Pills with Additions & Subtractions)

Succus Bambusae (*Zhu Li*), 10-15ml (swallowed with the decocted liquid), Rhizoma Acori Graminei (*Shi Chang Pu*), 12g, bile-processed Rhizoma Arisaematis (*Dan Nan Xing*), 10-12g, processed Rhizoma Pinelliae Ternatae (*Ban Xia*), 10g, Rhizoma Gastrodiae Elatae (*Tian Ma*), 10g, Buthus Martensis (*Quan Xie*), 1.5-3g (powdered and swallowed with the decocted liquid), Bombyx Batryticatus (*Jiang Can*), 6-10g, Sclerotium Pararadicis Poriae Cocos (*Fu Shen*), 10g, Radix Polygalae Tenuifoliae (*Yuan Zhi*), 10g
Decoct in water and administer orally in two divided doses, morning and evening, one *ji* per day.

ACUPUNCTURE: *Tai Chong* (Liv 3), *Feng Long* (St 40), *Nei Guan* (Per 6), *Yao Qi* (M-BW-29, an empirical point for epilepsy located two *cun* above the tip of the coccyx). Use draining technique.

## 2. LIVER FIRE & PHLEGM HEAT PATTERN

MAIN SYMPTOMS: During the episode there is clouding of consciousness, convulsions, and spitting of drool. At normal times, the emotions are tense and agitated and there is heart vexation, insomnia, spitting of hard-to-expectorate phlegm, a dry mouth with a bitter taste, constipation, a red tongue with slimy, yellow fur, and a bowstring, slippery, rapid pulse.

TREATMENT PRINCIPLES: Clear the liver and drain fire, transform phlegm and open the orifices

FORMULA & MEDICINALS: *Long Dan Xie Gan Tang He Di Tan Tang Jia Jian* (Gentiana Drain the Liver Decoction plus Flush Phlegm Decoction with Additions & Subtractions)

Radix Gentianae Scabrae (*Long Dan Cao*), 15-20g, Radix Scutellariae Baicalensis (*Huang Qin*), 10-12g, Fructus Gardeniae Jasminoidis (*Zhi Zi*), 10g, processed Rhizoma Pinelliae Ternatae (*Ban Xia*), 10g, Pericarpium Citri Erythrocarpae (*Ju Hong*), 6-10g, bile-processed Rhizoma Arisaematis (*Dan Nan Xing*), 10-12g, Rhizoma Acori Graminei (*Shi Chang Pu*), 12g

Decoct in water and administer orally in two divided doses, morning and evening, one *ji* per day.

ADDITIONS & SUBTRACTIONS: If there is headache with profuse phlegm, add Concha Haliotidis (*Shi Jue Ming*),

Ramulus Uncariae Cum Uncis (*Gou Teng*), Succus Bambusae (*Zhu Li*), and Lumbricus (*Di Long*).

ACUPUNCTURE: *Xing Jian* (Liv 2), *Shen Men* (Ht 7), *Nei Guan* (Per 6), *Feng Long* (St 40), *Yao Qi* (M-BW-29). Use draining technique.

ADDITIONS & SUBTRACTIONS: If there is phlegm fire congestion and repletion and constipation, add *Zu San Li* (St 36) and *Tian Shu* (St 25).

## 3. YIN VACUITY-YANG HYPERACTIVITY PATTERN

MAIN SYMPTOMS: Epileptiform attacks enduring for days, impaired memory, low back pain, dizziness, dry stools, a red tongue with scanty fur, and a fine, rapid pulse

TREATMENT PRINCIPLES: Enrich and supplement the liver and kidneys, subdue yang and quiet the spirit

FORMULA & MEDICINALS: *Zuo Gui Wan Jia Jian* (Restore the Left [Kidney] Pills with Additions & Subtractions)

Cooked Radix Rehmanniae (*Shu Di*), 12-15g, Radix Dioscoreae Oppositae (*Shan Yao*), 12g, Fructus Corni Officinalis (*Shan Zhu Yu*), 10g, Fructus Lycii Chinensis (*Gou Qi Zi*), 10g, Gelatinum Plastri Testudinis (*Gui Ban Jiao*), 12-15g (dissolved at the end in the hot decoction)

Decoct in water and administer orally in two divided doses, morning and evening, one *ji* per day.

ADDITIONS & SUBTRACTIONS: If yin vacuity and yang hyperactivity are heavy, add uncooked Concha Ostreae (*Mu Li*) and Carapax Amydae Chinensis (*Bie Jia*). If there is heart spirit restlessness, add Semen Biotae Orientalis (*Bai Zi Ren*) and Magnetitum (*Ci Shi*). If phlegm fire is severe, add Bulbus Fritillariae (*Bei Mu*), Concretio Bambusae Siliceae (*Tian Zhu Huang*), and Caulis Bambusae In Taeniis (*Zhu Ru*). If there is vexatious heat within the heart, add scorched Fructus Gardeniae Jasminoidis (*Zhi Zi*) and Plumula Nelumbinis Nuciferae (*Lian Zi Xin*). If the stools are dry, add Radix Scrophulariae Ningpoensis (*Xuan Shen*) and Semen Cannabis Sativae (*Huo Ma Ren*). If there is lassitude of the spirit, a somber facial complexion, and the condition endures and does not recover, also administer *He Che Da Zao Wan* (Placenta Great Construction Pills, a Chinese ready-made medicine).

*He Che Da Zao Wan* consist of: Placenta Hominis (*Zi He Che*), Plastrum Testudinis (*Gui Ban*), Cortex Phellodendri

(*Huang Bai*), Cortex Eucommiae Ulmoidis (*Du Zhong*), Radix Achyranthis Bidentatae (*Niu Xi*), Tuber Asparagi Cochinensis (*Tian Men Dong*), Tuber Ophiopogonis Japonici (*Mia Dong*), cooked Radix Rehmanniae (*Shu Di*)

ACUPUNCTURE: *Tai Chong* (Liv 3), *San Yin Jiao* (Sp 6), *Gan Shu* (Bl 18), *Shen Shu* (Bl 23), *Shen Men* (Ht 7). Mostly use supplementing technique but drain *Tai Chong*.

ADDITIONS & SUBTRACTIONS: If there is vexatious heat in the heart, add *Jian Shi* (Per 5). If there is dry stool constipation, add *Da Chang Shu* (Bl 25) and *Tian Shu* (St 25). If there is lassitude of the spirit and a lusterless facial complexion, add *Pi Shu* (Bl 20) and *Zu San Li* (St 36).

## 4. SPLEEN-STOMACH VACUITY WEAKNESS PATTERN

MAIN SYMPTOMS: Epileptiform condition which endures without cure, lassitude of the spirit, lack of strength, occasional dizziness, torpid intake, cold hands and feet, a lusterless facial complexion, loose stools, possible nausea and/or vomiting, a pale tongue, and a soggy or weak pulse

TREATMENT PRINCIPLES: Fortify the spleen and boost the qi, harmonize the stomach and transform turbidity

FORMULA & MEDICINALS: *Liu Jun Zi Tang* (Six Gentlemen Decoction)

Radix Codonopsitis Pilosulae (*Dang Shen*), 10-12g, Sclerotium Poriae Cocos (*Fu Ling*), 10-12g, stir-fried Rhizoma Atractylodis Macrocephalae (*Bai Zhu*), 10g, mix-fried Radix Glycyrrhizae (*Gan Cao*), 3g, processed Rhizoma Pinelliae Ternatae (*Ban Xia*), 10-12g, Pericarpium Citri Reticulatae (*Chen Pi*), 6-10g

Decoct in water and administer orally in two divided doses, morning and evening, one *ji* per day.

ADDITIONS & SUBTRACTIONS: If vomiting is severe, add Caulis Bambusae In Taeniis (*Zhu Ru*) and Fructus Citri Aurantii (*Zhi Ke*). If there is phlegm harassing the heart spirit with restlessness, add Rhizoma Acori Graminei (*Shi Chang Pu*), Radix Polygalae Tenuifoliae (*Yuan Zhi*), Rhizoma Arisaematis (*Tian Nan Xing*), and Bombyx Batryticatus (*Jiang Can*).

ACUPUNCTURE: *Pi Shu* (Bl 20), *Wei Shu* (Bl 21), *Zhong Wan* (CV 12), *Feng Long* (St 40), *Zu San Li* (St 36), *Zhang Men* (Liv 13). Use even supplementing-even draining technique.

ADDITIONS & SUBTRACTIONS: If there is nausea and vomiting, add *Nei Guan* (Per 6).

## 5. BLOOD VESSEL STASIS & OBSTRUCTION PATTERN

MAIN SYMPTOMS: Habitual headache which is fixed in location, either pounding or piercing in nature, worse at night, static macules on the edges of the tongue, a choppy or small, bowstring pulse, and a possible history of traumatic injury to the head

TREATMENT PRINCIPLES: Quicken the blood and dispel stasis, open the orifices and extinguish wind

FORMULA & MEDICINALS: *Tong Qiao Huo Xue Tang He Zhi Jing San Jia Jian* (Free the Flow of the Orifices & Quicken the Blood Decoction plus Stop Tetany Powder with Additions & Subtractions)

Semen Pruni Persicae (*Tao Ren*), 10g, Flos Carthami Tinctorii (*Hong Hua*), 3-10g (steeped), Radix Rubrus Paeoniae Lactiflorae (*Chi Shao*), 10-15g, Radix Ligustici Wallichii (*Chuan Xiong*), 6-12g (added later), Cortex Radicis Moutan (*Dan Pi*), 10-12g, Tuber Curcumae (*Yu Jin*), 10g, Buthus Martensis (*Quan Xie*), 1-1.5g, Scolopendra Subspinipes (*Wu Gong*), 1-1.5g

Decoct in water and administer orally in two divided doses, morning and evening, one *ji* per day.

ADDITIONS & SUBTRACTIONS: If headache is severe, add Feces Trogopterori Seu Pteromi (*Wu Ling Zhi*) and Pollen Typhae (*Pu Huang*). If there is simultaneous qi vacuity, add Radix Astragali Membranacei (*Huang Qi*) and Radix Codonopsitis Pilosulae (*Dang Shen*). If there is simultaneous blood vacuity, add Radix Angelicae Sinensis (*Dang Gui*) and uncooked Radix Rehmanniae (*Sheng Di*).

ACUPUNCTURE: *Xue Hai* (Sp 10), *Tai Chong* (Liv 3), *He Gu* (LI 4), *Feng Chi* (GB 20), *Bai Hui* (GV 20), *Yin Tang* (M-HN-3). Use draining technique.

## ABSTRACTS OF REPRESENTATIVE CHINESE RESEARCH:

*Zhe Jiang Zhong Yi Za Zhi* (*Zhejiang Journal of Chinese Medicine*), #10, 1995, p. 454. Zhang Fu-cun and Wei Bao-yong, treated 14 cases of epilepsy by embedding catgut at governing vessel points. Of the 14 patients described in this study, 10 were male and four were female. The youngest was six and the oldest was 42 years old. Their course of disease had lasted from three months to 14 years.

The disease was primary onset in nine cases and secondary onset in five cases. Thirteen of the patients had taken dilantin and other such anti-epileptic drugs for a long time. Attacks occurred from 1-4 times per day to 1-2 times per year. Typically, convulsions lasted 10 minutes. Catgut was embedded at *Jin Suo* (GV 8) and left in place for seven days.[2] This was done once a year for three years which constituted one course of treatment. During this treatment, drinking any alcohol was prohibited. Using this protocol, five case were cured and had no recurrences within five years. Seven cases got some response in that the number of occurrences decreased and their duration shortened. Two cases experienced no result. Thus the total amelioration rate was 85.7%.

❖

*Jiang Su Zhong Yi* (*Jiangsu Chinese Medicine*), #11, 1999, p. 37. Gan De-shou *et al.* studied the comparative effects of a specific acupuncture protocol against the use of Dilantin in 60 cases of epilepsy. Among the 30 patients in the acupuncture group, 18 were male and 12 were female. The youngest was six and the oldest was 43 years of age. The shortest course of disease was three months and the longest was 10 years. EEG and CT scan showed that none of these patients had focal pathological changes in their brains, and the comparison group receiving dilantin was statistically similar to the acupuncture treatment group. Based on the treatment principles of enriching fluids and extinguishing wind, the points used consisted of *Cheng Jiang* (CV 24), *Dan Zhong* (CV 17), *Jiu Wei* (CV 14), *Zhong Wan* (CV 12), *Guan Yuan* (CV 4), *Lie Que* (Lu 7), and *Zhao Hai* (Ki 6). The needles were stimulated once every five minutes and retained for 30 minutes per treatment. Ten treatments equaled one course, and there was a 3-5 day intermission between courses. Treatment typically lasted 2-3 courses. During this treatment, other anti-seizure medications were gradually reduced or stopped. Patient's in the comparison group received 0.1g of Dilantin three times per day plus a multi-vitamin. Using this regime, in the acupuncture treatment group, 22 patients were almost cured, seven improved, and one got no result for a total amelioration rate of 96.7%. In the comparison group, 14 cases were almost cured, 14 cases improved, and two cases got no result for a total amelioration rate of 93.3%. Thus there was a marked statistical difference in nearly cured rates between these two groups (P<0.05) even though there was no marked statistical difference in over-all amelioration rates (P>0.05).

❖

*Si Chuan Zhong Yi* (*Sichuan Chinese Medicine*), #11, 1999, p. 32: Zhang Yong-xia reported on the treatment of 44 cases of epilepsy using a formula called *Zhi Xian Ling* (Stop Epilepsy Magic [Medicine]). Twenty-six patients were male and 18 were female. Twenty-five cases were 1-18 years old and 19 cases were 19-26 years old. All the patients had had occurrences of seizures. The shortest disease course was one week and the longest was three years. Nine cases had a history of encephalitis, six had histories of external injury to the brain, one had had brain surgery, and 28 cases were of unknown etiology. Thirty-nine patients had epileptic EEG brain waves, while the brain waves in five cases were normal. CT scans were abnormal in 13 cases and normal in 31. All these patients were diagnosed according to the criteria in the 1991 *Xian Dai Zhong Yi Nei Ke Xue* (*A Study of Modern Chinese Medicine Internal Medicine*) and the 1994 *Zhong Yi Bing Zheng Zhen Duan Liao Xiao Biao Zhun* (*Criteria for Chinese Medical Disease & Pattern Diagnosis, Treatment & Outcomes*).

❖

The formula consisted of: artificial Calculus Bovis (*Ren Gong Niu Huang*), Rhizoma Gastrodiae Elatae (*Tian Ma*), Fructus Crataegi (*Shan Zha*), Ramulus Uncariae Cum Uncis (*Gou Teng*), Radix Polygalae Tenuifoliae (*Yuan Zhi*), and Succinum (*Hu Po*), 30g each, Bombyx Batryticatus (*Jiang Can*), Scolopendra Subspinipes (*Wu Gong*), Buthus Martensis (*Quan Xie*), Fructus Liquidambaris Taiwaniae (*Lu Lu Tong*), and Rhizoma Acori Graminei (*Shi Chang Pu*), 20g each, Concha Ostreae (*Mu Li*), Os Draconis (*Long Gu*), and Concha Margaritiferae (*Zhen Zhu Mu*), 50g each, Radix Salviae Miltiorrhizae (*Dan Shen*), 16g, bile-processed Rhizoma Arisaematis (*Dan Nan Xing*), 10g, and Concretio Silicea Bambusae (*Tian Zhu Huang*), 15g. All these medicinals were ground into powder and 3-5g were administered each time either in hot water or mixed with honey 2-3 times per day. Three months equaled one course of treatment, and treatment lasted 1-2 courses. Using this protocol, 28 cases (65%) got a marked effect, 11 cases (28%) experienced fair improvement, and five cases (7%) got no result. Thus the total amelioration rate was 93%.

REPRESENTATIVE CASE HISTORIES:

❖ CASE 1[3] ❖

The patient was a 40 year old female who was first examined on Jan. 11, 1975. In April of the preceding year, after having malaria, the patient began having episodes of cramps which were accompanied by clouding of her spirit mind. After half a day, she would wake up. In addition, even during normal times she was dizzy. Her right pulse was bowstring, slippery, and rapid, while her left pulse was fine, rapid, and slippery. Therefore, her pattern was categorized as malarial evils causing phlegm and stasis mutual binding which had then ascended to harass the clear orifices and resulted in the onset of epilepsy. For this, the patient was prescribed: uncooked Radix Albus Paeoniae Lactiflorae (*Bai Shao*), 12g, uncooked Semen Coicis Lachryma-jobi (*Yi Yi Ren*), 12g, processed Radix Polygoni Multiflori (*He Shou Wu*), 12g, Radix Angelicae Sinensis (*Dang Gui*), 9g, Radix Codonopsitis Pilosulae (*Dang Shen*), 9g, Pericarpium Citri Reticulatae (*Chen Pi*), 9g, Massa Medica Fermentata (*Shen Qu*), 9g, stir-fried Fructus Citri Aurantii (*Zhi Ke*), 9g, Sclerotium Poriae Cocos (*Fu Ling*), 9g, uncooked Radix Glycyrrhizae (*Gan Cao*), 4.5g, and Fructus Zizyphi Jujubae (*Da Zao*), 5 pieces. Seven *ji* of these medicinals were decocted in water and administered internally along with 15 grams of *Bai Jin Wan* (White Gold Pills) swallowed with the decoction.

At her second visit, the patient reported that, since taking these medicinals, she had not had an episode of cramping. However, she could not sleep at night. Her right pulse was slippery and rapid, and her left was fine, rapid, and slippery. Her tongue fur was clean. Therefore, she was prescribed seven *ji* of *Shi Wei Wen Dan Tang* (Ten Flavors Warm the Gallbladder Decoction): uncooked Rhizoma Atractylodis Macrocephalae (*Bai Zhu*), 9g, Sclerotium Poriae Cocos (*Fu Ling*), 9g, Radix Codonopsitis Pilosulae (*Dang Shen*), 9g, stir-fried Semen Zizyphi Spinosae (*Suan Zao Ren*), 9g, Radix Angelicae Sinensis (*Dang Gui*), 9g, Pericarpium Citri Reticulatae (*Chen Pi*), 4.5g, stir-fried Fructus Citri Aurantii (*Zhi Ke*), 4.5g, Radix Polygalae Tenuifoliae (*Yuan Zhi*), 3g, and mix-fried Radix Glycyrrhizae (*Gan Cao*), 3g.

On Jan. 17, the patient returned for her third visit. Her cramps had not recurred. Sometimes she was dizzy, but at night, her sleep was quiet. Her pulse was deep and fine and her tongue was red. The patient reported that her menstruation had continued for a half month without stopping. Therefore, her pattern was re-discriminated as depressive heat causing the blood to move frenetically and the patient was prescribed seven *ji* of the following medicinals: uncooked Concha Ostreae (*Mu Li*), 15g, Fructus Ligustri Lucidi (*Nu Zhen Zi*), 9g, Herba Ecliptae Prostratae (*Han Lian Cao*), 9g, processed Radix Polygoni Multiflori (*He Shou Wu*), 9g, Radix Angelicae Sinensis (*Dang Gui*), 9g, Sclerotium Poriae Cocos (*Fu Ling*), 9g, Fructus Tritici Aestivi (*Huai Xiao Mai*), 9g, Cortex

Radicis Moutan (*Dan Pi*), 4.5g, Radix Albus Paeoniae Lactiflorae (*Bai Shao*), 4.5g, Radix Rubrus Paeoniae Lactiflorae (*Chi Shao*), 4.5g, uncooked Radix Glycyrrhizae (*Gan Cao*), 3g. On follow-up in Oct. 1977, the epilepsy had not occurred again.

## ❖ CASE 2[4] ❖

The patient was a 45 year old, unmarried worker who was first hospitalized on Aug. 4, 1983. The patient was habitually arrogant and short-tempered. He was easily irritated and easily angered. Five years before he had caught a cold and developed a high fever which would not abate. After treatment, the power of the fever greatly diminished. However, it still continued and the patient developed rigid falling and staring straight. There were convulsions of his four limbs and he vomiting foamy drool from his mouth. His facial complexion was reddish purple, and he uttered a noise like sheep bleating. At the same time, his urine became incontinent and he bit the tip of his tongue. After he awakened, his body was fatigued and lacked strength. Similar seizures recurred once every 2-3 months, and the man was diagnosed as suffering grand mal epilepsy. The man was prescribed anti-seizure medication and, as long as he took them, they controlled his seizures. However, if he stopped taking them, the seizures returned. In the last year, due to getting divorced and problems at work, he had become even more irritable, and this had provoked a worsening of his disease so that he had 5-6 attacks every day. After these attacks passed, his heart was vexed and the man was agitated and anxious. He rushed about manically, did not evade dangerous situations, and was unable to sleep at night. This would go on for 3-4 days and then his movement would relax only to be followed by another set of seizures. Numerous prior formulas by a number of different doctors had all proved ineffective. When the authors of this case examined this man, his eyes had an angry look, he was manically cursing and shouting, he was agitated and restless, his stools were dry and bound, his urine was reddish yellow, his tongue was red with slimy, yellow fur, and his pulse was bowstring, slippery, and rapid.

Based on the above signs and symptoms, the patient's pattern was categorized as phlegm and fire mutually binding with liver wind stirring internally. Therefore, the treatment principles were to clear heat and wash away phlegm, level the liver and extinguish wind, quiet the spirit and settle fright. The formula prescribed was *Ding Xian Zhi Kuang Tang* (Stabilize Epilepsy & Stop Mania Decoction): Rhizoma Gastrodiae Elatae (*Tian Ma*), 10g, Bulbus Fritillariae Cirrhosae (*Chuan Bei Mu*), 10g, Rhizoma Pinelliae Ternatae (*Ban Xia*), 7g, Cinnabar-processed

Sclerotium Pararadicis Poriae Cocos (*Fu Shen*), 12g, Bombyx Batryticatus (*Jiang Can*), 9g, bile-processed Rhizoma Arisaematis (*Dan Nan Xing*), 10g, Buthus Martensis (*Quan Xie*), 9g, Rhizoma Acori Graminei (*Shi Chang Pu*), 12g, Succinum (*Hu Po*), 2g, Pericarpium Citri Reticulatae (*Chen Pi*), 10g, Radix Polygalae Tenuifoliae (*Yuan Zhi*), 7g, Radix Salviae Miltiorrhizae (*Dan Shen*), 15g, Tuber Ophiopogonis Japonici (*Mai Dong*), 12g, Radix Glycyrrhizae (*Gan Cao*), 6g, Cinnabar (*Zhu Sha*), 2g, Succus Bambusae (*Zhu Li*), 10g.

After taking 40 *ji* of the above formula, the patient only had one episode of convulsions and these were less stong than before. When he awakened, his spirit was clear and his manic symptoms all disappeared. He was thirsty and desired to drink, his stools were still dry and bound, and his urine was slightly yellow. His tongue was red with slimy, yellow fur, and his pulse was bowstring and slippery. Thus heat had already decreased. Now the treatment principles were to level the liver and extinguish wind, sweep away phlegm and open the orifices. The formula prescribed for these purposes consisted of: powdered Cornu Antelopis Saiga-tatarici (*Ling Yang Jiao*), 5g, Ramulus Uncariae Cum Uncis (*Gou Teng*), 12g, artificial Calculus Bovis (*Niu Huang*), 7g, Buthus Martensis (*Quan Xie*), 10g, calcined Lapis Chloriti Seu Micae (*Meng Shi*), 30g, Radix Et Rhizoma Rhei (*Da Huang*), 6g, Lignum Aquilariae Agallochae (*Chen Xiang*), 9g, bile-processed Rhizoma Arisaematis (*Dan Nan Xing*), 10g, and Succus Bambusae (*Zhu Li*), 12g.

At the patient's third examination after taking 20 *ji* of the above medicinals, his epilepsy had not recurred a single time. Therefore, he was discharged from the hospital and prescribed one pill per day of *Kang Xian Ling* (Anti-epilepsy Efficacious [Medicine]). This is a formula created by the authors.

### ❖ CASE 3⁵ ❖

The patient was a 36 year old male worker with a habitually debilitated and weak physique who entered the hospital on Mar. 13, 1981. Eight years before, the man had been working down a well and had received a violent electric shock. Since then, he was always frightened and afraid. This ultimately developed into a history of episodes of spirit mind abstraction. At the same time, his hands and feet spasmed and his body became rigid. Two years previously, he had developed tugging wind condition. When the disease occurred, the patient would suddenly fall down on the ground. There were convulsions of his four limbs and the sound of phlegm rattling in his throat, the man became unconscious, and white foam was vomit-

ed from his mouth. After these attacks, his head was heavy and the patient was exhausted and desired to lie down to sleep. Initially, these attacks occurred 1-3 times per year. However, at the time this man was examined by this case's authors, they were occurring increasingly frequently, and hence the man had been hospitalized. At the time of the author's examination, the man complained of headache and heavy-headedness, restless sleep, occasional vexation and tenseness, chest and abdominal fullness and oppression, scanty eating and torpid intake, deviation of the mouth and eyes, and discomfort in his limbs. His tongue fur was slimy and yellow, and his pulse was slippery and slightly rapid. Electroencephalogram showed a mild degree of abnormality.

Based on the above signs and symptoms, the authors of this case categorized this man's pattern as phlegm heat stirring wind. The treatment principles were to sweep away phlegm and open the orifices, clear heat, extinguish wind, and stop tetany. Their initial formula consisted of: calcined Lapis Chloriti Seu Micae (*Meng Shi*), 30g, bile-processed Rhizoma Arisaematis (*Dan Nan Xing*), 10g, Buthus Martensis (*Quan Xie*), 9g, Lignum Aquilariae Agallochae (*Chen Xiang*), 7g, uncooked Radix Rehmanniae (*Sheng Di*), 9g, cooked Radix Rehmanniae (*Shu Di*), 9g, ginger-processed Rhizoma Pinelliae Ternatae (*Ban Xia*), 6g, Radix Et Rhizoma Rhei (*Da Huang*), 9g, Pumice (*Fu Hai Shi*), 15g, Ramulus Uncariae Cum Uncis (*Gou Teng*), 10g, and Rhizoma Gastrodiae Elatae (*Tian Ma*), 9g.

After taking the above medicinals for three months, the number of seizures had decreased to two times per month. The patient's mental-emotional state was quite good and he reported no uncomfortable sensations. Therefore he was discharged from the hospital. The formula he had taken was made up into a powder and the patient was instructed to take a specified amount of this powder once every morning. On follow-up after six months, there had been no seizures and his EEG had returned to normal.

### ❖ CASE 4⁶ ❖

The patient was a 16 year old male who had had encephalitis when he was eight years old. Since then he had suffered from epileptic seizures which had increasingly become more severe. Various types of previous treatment had failed to cure the young man's condition. The patient's signs and symptoms included abdominal muscular tension and spasm, liver enlargement with pressure pain, and a bowstring pulse. The young man was prescribed *Chai Hu Qing Gan San* (Bupleurum Clear the Liver Powder) without effect. Then he was given *Chai Hu*

*Jia Long Gu Mu Li Tang* (Bupleurum Plus Dragon Bone & Oyster Shell Decoction) also without result. In fact, when he had been given the *Chai Hu Qing Gan San*, his seizures had gotten worse, remaining unconscious for three hours with episodes three nights in a row. Therefore, based on the urgency of these episodes and the nature of his mental-emotional symptoms, the patient was prescribed *Gan Mai Da Zao Tang* (Licorice, Wheat & Red Dates Decoction). After taking this formula, it was as if the young man had awoken from a dream, and there were no further occurrences of seizures. On follow-up after two months, the patient had only had two slight episodes.

### ❖ CASE 5[7] ❖

The patient was a seven year old female who had been previously healthy. The girl had seizures at school and was admitted to a local hospital's intensive care unit. She experienced an average of four status epileptic episodes per day lasting a few minutes per episode. She was administered pentobarbital infusion, phenytoin sodium (Dilantin), carbamazepine (Tegretol), and phenobarbital for seizure control. Despite appropriate therapeutic levels of these medications, the patient continued to have complex partial seizures with rhythmic spike and wave activity in both right and left temporal lobes seen on EEG. Several attempts at tapering off pentobarbital failed, and the patient underwent craniotomy for brain biopsy, but no abnormality was noted. Due to a grim prognosis, acupuncture treatment was requested by both the ICU care team and the parents in an attempt to control the seizures.

The girl was treated with acupuncture at *Feng Chi* (GB 20), *Nei Guan* (Per 6), and *San Yin Jiao* (Sp 6). Needles were retained for 10 minutes per treatment with electroacupuncture at *San Yin Jiao*. Three such treatments were administered the first week with two treatments per week for the next four weeks. After the second treatment, EEG showed moderate generalized cortical dysfunction with no electrographic seizures and no overt seizure activity noted. The patient was then weaned off the pentobarbital drip and was transferred to a regular ward. Following decannulation of her tracheotomy tube (which had been inserted due to peripheral cyanosis and significant desaturation), the child was transferred to a rehabilitation facility. There were no complications to the acupuncture treatment.

### ENDNOTES:

[1] *The Pinyin Chinese-English Dictionary*, ed. by Wu Jing-rong, Beijing Foreign Languages Institute, The Commercial Press, Beijing, 1991, p. 748

[2] For an explanation of this technique, please see Shanghai College of Traditional Chinese Medicine, *Acupuncture: A Comprehensive Text*, trans. by John O'Connor & Dan Bensky, Eastland Press, Seattle, 1981, p. 463-467

[3] Jin Shou-shan, *Shang Hai Lao Zhong Yi Jing Yan Xuan Bian (A Selected Collection of Shanghai Old Chinese Doctors' Case Histories)*, op. cit., p. 123

[4] Li & Liu, op. cit., p. 500-501

[5] *Ibid.*, p. 504-505

[6] Chen & Zhao, op. cit., p. 440

[7] Lin Yuan-chi & Hong, Gene G., "Acupuncture Treatment of Pediatric Status Epilepticus," *Medical Acupuncture*, Fall/Winter 1999/2000, p. 43-44

# ❖ 18 ❖

# PLUM PIT QI

Plum pit qi, *mei he qi*, refers to a subjective feeling of something stuck in the throat which can neither be swallowed down nor spit up. In the Chinese literature the something stuck in the throat is described as feeling similar to a piece of meat. This relatively commonly seen condition corresponds to both physiological and psychological conditions in terms of Western medical nosology. For instance, it can cover post-sinus drip as well as neurotic esophageal stenosis or what is also sometimes referred to as globus hystericus. In Chinese medicine, this pattern is seen primarily in women, and, although Chinese medicine has no hard and fast division between body and mind, it is considered one of the more psychological maladies. The *Ling Shu* (*Spiritual Axis*) referred to this condition as "[something] situated within the throat." Zhang Zhong-jing, in his chapter on miscellaneous disease of women in the *Jin Gui Yao Lue* (*Essentials from the Golden Cabinet*) called it "a small slice of cooked meat." In the Tang dynasty, Sun Si-miao also likened it to "cooked meat."

In Western psychiatry, a feeling that something is stuck in the throat in the absence of evidence of a medical explanation is classified as conversion disorder. By definition, a conversion disorder is a disturbance of sensory, motor, or combined sensory-motor functioning that is not consistent with known medical or neurological disease patterns and is, therefore, construed as psychogenic in origin. Globus hystericus is a conversion disorder in which the primary symptom is motor dysfunction in swallowing associated with the subjective feeling of a lump in the throat.

## NOSOLOGY:

Western psychiatry classifies four primary categories of conversion disorders:

1. Those presenting motor symptoms or deficits
2. Those presenting sensory symptoms or deficits
3. Those presenting seizures or convulsions
4. Those with a mixed presentation (*i.e.*, presenting with two or more different kinds of conversion symptoms)

The principle criterion required to formally diagnosis conversion disorder is the presence of one or more symptoms interfering with motor or sensory function in the absence of a demonstrable medical or neurological cause. By definition, conversion symptoms cannot be feigned or deliberately created by the patient, are associated with significant social or occupational impairment, and coincide in timing of onset or exacerbation with identifiable psychological stressors. Globus hystericus is a specific pattern of motor dysfunction affecting swallowing that fulfills these criteria.

## EPIDEMIOLOGY:

Conversion disorders may be relatively common. Epidemiologic studies estimate incidence rates from 10-300 cases per 100,000 in the general (*i.e.*, non-psychiatrically ill) populations. This means that, at any given moment, conversion symptoms may be present in 0.3% of

---

### DIFFERENTIAL DIAGNOSIS

| 1. MEDICAL DISORDERS | 2. EFFECTS OF SUBSTANCES | 3. PSYCHIATRIC DISORDERS |
|---|---|---|
| A. DEGENERATIVE NEUROLOGIC DISORDERS, INCLUDING MULTIPLE SCLEROSIS (MS) AND MYASTHENIA GRAVIS<br>B. SEIZURE DISORDERS<br>C. CEREBROVASCULAR ACCIDENT (CVA)<br>D. MYOCARDIAL INFARCTION | A. ALCOHOL OR ILLICIT SUBSTANCE ABUSE OR WITHDRAWAL<br>B. SIDE EFFECTS OF NONPRESCRIPTION OR PRESCRIPTION MEDICATIONS<br>3. PSYCHIATRIC DISORDERS | A. CONVERSION DISORDER<br>B. SOMATOFORM DISORDER<br>C. SOMATIC DELUSION IN SCHIZOPHRENIA<br>D. HYPOCHONDRIASIS<br>E. DISSOCIATIVE DISORDERS<br>F. MALINGERING<br>G. FACTITIOUS DISORDERS |

---

the population. In contrast, the lifetime prevalence of conversion disorders may be as high as 33% of the general population. Onset of conversion disorders (including globus hystericus) ranges from early childhood to old age. All types of conversion disorders are 2-5 times more common in women than men. An interesting trend is over-representation of rural and undereducated populations. Some studies have suggested familial patterns. However, the question of increased familial risk, including possibly genetic predisposition, remains unclear.

### DIFFERENTIAL DIAGNOSIS:

The primary consideration in making a diagnosis of conversion disorder is exclusion of medical or neurologic causes. Early manifestations of degenerative neurologic disorders, including multiple sclerosis and myasthenia gravis, are frequently misdiagnosed as conversion symptoms and only retrospectively, when these disorders have progressed to the point where brain imaging, serologic studies, or other diagnostic procedures can yield unambiguous positive findings, are they recognized as medical conditions. Unusual presentations of seizure disorders, cerebrovascular accidents (strokes), and myocardial infarction sometimes manifest as transient motor or sensory deficits, thus requiring that these disorders be definitively ruled out. Chronic effects of a substance or medication side effects must also be ruled out as probable causes of the identified motor or sensory symptom.

When possible organic etiologies have been excluded, the psychiatric differential diagnosis must be further clarified. This is accomplished by careful history-taking to determine a clinical course suggestive of an underlying pattern of a major psychiatric disorder in which the specific conversion symptom is present as part of a larger pattern of psychopathology. For example, when a conversion symptom is associated with several other somatic complaints

(all also in the absence of verified medical causes), including pain symptoms, gastrointestinal symptoms, sexual dysfunction, and neurologic symptoms, the Western psychiatric diagnosis is somatoform disorder. In an analogous way, persisting physical complaints experienced by a schizophrenic patient are regarded as somatic delusions in the context of underlying psychosis and are not diagnosed as an independent conversion disorder. Individuals who are morbidly preoccupied with beliefs that a somatic symptom represents serious underlying neurological or medical disease fulfill criteria for hypochondriasis. In contrast, individuals with conversion disorders typically exhibit an inappropriate absence of concern for or indifference ("la belle indifference") to a belief that a serious underlying medical disorder exists. Symptoms of apparent motor or sensory dysfunction sometimes occur in dissociative disorders, in which case conversion disorder and dissociative disorder may be diagnosed together. Finally, it is necessary to distinguish conversion symptoms in which symptoms are not intentionally feigned from factitious disorder or malingering in which there are primary unconscious or deliberate conscious motives respectively to "create" a symptom giving the appearance of a functional deficit.

### ETIOLOGY & PATHOPHYSIOLOGY:

Many neurobiological and psychodynamic theories have been put forward in attempts to explain the etiologic basis of conversion symptoms. Results of functional brain imaging studies and neuropsychological examination of patients diagnosed with conversion disorders often point to abnormalities in interhemispheric communication or hypofunction of the dominant cerebral hemisphere leading to sensorimotor processing defects that are manifested as conversion symptoms.

Classical psychoanalytic theory understands conversion

disorders as resulting from unconscious intrapsychic conflicts in which symptom formation (or its functional consequences) represents a symbolic resolution of the conflict. According to this view, anxiety associated with the underlying unconscious conflict is typically diminished with conversion symptom formation. Social theorists have suggested that conversion symptom formation permits the conflicted individual to express a role or wish that is forbidden within his or her cultural context or broader framework of social expectations.

Until now there is no single accepted explanation of conversion phenomena. It is likely that many discrete pathophysiological and sociocultural mechanisms result in conversion symptom formation.

### Western medical treatment:

If neurologic or medical disease is identified as the underlying cause of difficulty swallowing or another complaint of lost sensory or motor functioning, appropriate medical evaluation and treatment must be pursued. When known organic causes have been ruled out, Western medicine regards the symptom as psychogenic in origin. If careful history taking determines that the symptom fulfills criteria for a conversion disorder, several psychological therapies may be useful. These include hypnotherapy (sometimes assisted by intravenous amytal or lorazepam) to increase suggestibility that the symptom will resolve following hypnosis. Anxiolytic medications, including benzodiazepines, may permit the patient to have sufficient control over anxiety during psychotherapy to gain insight into the need to maintain a conversion symptom when exploring symbolic or psychodynamic meanings of the symptom. Insight sometimes results in dramatic improvements in functioning. Cognitive-behavioral treatment approaches to conversion disorders include active discouragement of maintaining or depending on a symptom and modifying the patient's environment to motivate him or her to use the affected body part. There are no psychopharmacological treatments that effectively treat conversion symptoms or its hypothesized underlying neurobiological or psychodynamic causes.

### Short & long-term advantages & disadvantages to Western medical treatment:

Advantages of successful treatment of globus hystericus or other conversion disorders include restoration of normal sensory or motor functioning and removal of occupational or social impairments caused by those symptoms. There are no obvious disadvantages of treatment since there are no risks associated with hypnotherapy and cognitive-behavioral therapy.

### Prognosis:

Many studies examining the long-term courses of patients diagnosed with conversion disorders show that a significant percentage (ranging from 20-50%) had subsequently been diagnosed with a medical or neurologic disorder that retrospectively accounted for the supposed conversion symptom. These "organic" disorders frequently included degenerative diseases of the spinal cord, peripheral nerves, and muscles. Other studies have concluded that as many as one-third of diagnosed cases of conversion disorder were later diagnosed with a major psychiatric disorder, frequently schizophrenia. In view of the high degree of diagnostic inaccuracy, the clinical course and prognosis of actual conversion disorders is difficult to ascertain. However, it is established that, when conversion symptoms remit during the course of medical hospitalization addressing the conversion symptom, only a small percentage of patients experience relapses on one-year and five-year follow-up. As many as 90% of psychiatric in-patients no longer manifest conversion symptoms by the time of discharge. Prognostically favorable factors include rapid onset; a high level of pre-morbid functioning; the absence of co-morbid psychiatric, medical, or neurologic disorders; and no pending litigation.

### Indications for referral to Western medical services:

Urgent referral to a nearby emergency room or urgent care center is warranted in cases when the presenting symptom may represent a potentially dangerous or acute medical or neurologic problem, including stroke, seizure disorder or myocardial infarction. In cases where underlying organic pathology has been excluded and the conversion symptom has failed to respond to appropriate Chinese medical interventions, routine referral to a Western physician is indicated to rule out possible underlying medical or neurologic causes of any symptom pattern that is inconsistent with a described disorder. In such cases, psychiatric evaluation and treatment with hypnotherapy or cognitive-behavioral therapy will likely prove beneficial.

### Chinese disease causes & disease mechanisms:

In Chinese medicine, the feeling of constriction or something stuck in the throat is believed to be due to phlegm blocking the orifice of the throat. This phlegm may be engendered by spleen vacuity or it may be brewed and transformed by some sort of evil heat. However, no matter where and how it is formed, it is drafted up to lodge in the throat by either upwardly counterflowing qi due to liver depression or some species of evil heat. Therefore, in most case of plum pit qi, no matter what else is going on, there is a core disease mechanism of phlegm and qi depression and binding. If liver depression transforms heat, then there may be a combination of phlegm and heat mutually binding. If this heat damages and consumes yin fluids, it may give rise to yin vacuity fire effulgence, however still complicated by phlegm nodulation. If qi stagnation and phlegm nodulation last for a long time, this will inevitably transform into blood stasis, qi stagnation, and phlegm obstruction.

## TREATMENT BASED ON PATTERN DISCRIMINATION:

### 1. PHLEGM QI DEPRESSION & BINDING

**MAIN SYMPTOMS:** A feeling of something caught in the back of the throat which can neither be spit up or swallowed down, chest and abdominal fullness and oppression, profuse phlegm, irritability, possible PMS, menstrual irregularity, or fibrocystic lumps in the breast in females, slimy, white tongue fur, and a slippery, bowstring pulse

**TREATMENT PRINCIPLES:** Move the qi and downbear counterflow, transform phlegm and disinhibit the throat

**FORMULA & MEDICINALS:** *Ban Xiao Hou Po Tang Jia Wei* (Pinellia & Magnolia Decoction with Added Flavors)

Rhizoma Pinelliae Ternatae (*Ban Xia*), 10-12g, Cortex Magnoliae Officinalis (*Hou Po*), 10g, Sclerotium Poriae Cocos (*Fu Ling*), 12g, Pericarpium Citri Reticulatae (*Chen Pi*), 6g, uncooked Rhizoma Zingiberis (*Sheng Jiang*), 6g (added later), Caulis Perillae Frutescentis (*Su Geng*), 10g, Spica Prunellae Vulgaris (*Xia Ku Cao*), 15g, Bulbus Fritillaria (*Bei Mu*), 6g, Rhizoma Acori Graminei (*Shi Chang Pu*), 6g, Radix Bupleuri (*Chai Hu*), 3-6g

Decoct in water and administer orally in two divided doses, morning and evening, one *ji* per day.

**ADDITIONS & SUBTRACTIONS:** For more severe qi stagnation, add Tuber Curcumae (*Yu Jin*) and Pericarpium Citri Reticulatae Viride (*Qing Pi*). For simultaneous abdominal distention, add Fructus Amomi (*Sha Ren*) and Radix Auklandiae Lappae (*Mu Xiang*). For more serious inhibition of the throat, add Radix Playtcodi Grandiflori (*Jie Geng*) and Radix Scrophulariae Ningpoensis (*Xuan Shen*).

**ACUPUNCTURE:** *Tai Chong* (Liv 3), *Nei Guan* (Per 6), *Feng Long* (St 40), *Zu San Li* (St 36), *Dan Zhong* (CV 17), *Zhong Wan* (CV 12), *Tian Tu* (CV 22). Use draining technique.

### 2. PHLEGM HEAT HARASSING ABOVE PATTERN

**MAIN SYMPTOMS:** The same sort of symptoms as above plus a red tongue with slimy, yellow fur, and a slippery, bowstring, rapid pulse

**TREATMENT PRINCIPLES:** Clear heat and transform phlegm, resolve depression and disinhibit the throat

**FORMULA & MEDICINALS:** *Huang Lian Wen Dan Tang Jia Wei* (Coptis Warm the Gallbladder Decoction with Added Flavors)

Rhizoma Coptidis Chinensis (*Huang Lian*), 3-6g (added later), Radix Scutellariae Baicalensis (*Huang Qin*), 10g, Rhizoma Acori Graminei (*Shi Chang Pu*), 6g, Spica Prunellae Vulgaris (*Xia Ku Cao*), 15g, Radix Scrophulariae Ningpoensis (*Xuan Shen*), 15g, Bulbus Fritillariae (*Bei Mu*), 10g, Rhizoma Pinelliae Ternatae (*Ban Xia*), 10g, Pericarpium Citri Reticulatae (*Chen Pi*), 6-10g, Sclerotium Pararadicis Poriae Cocos (*Fu Shen*), 12g, Fructus Immaturus Citri Aurantii (*Zhi Shi*), 6g, Caulis Bambusae In Taeniis (*Zhu Ru*), 6-10g, Radix Glycyrrhizae (*Gan Cao*), 3-6g, Fructus Zizyphi Jujubae (*Da Zao*), 3-5 pieces

Decoct in water and administer orally in two divided doses, morning and evening, one *ji* per day.

**ACUPUNCTURE:** *Xing Jian* (Liv 2), *Jie Xi* (St 41), *Feng Long* (St 40), *Tian Tu* (CV 22), *Dan Zhong* (CV 17), *Zhong Wan* (CV 12). Use draining technique.

### 3. YIN VACUITY-LIVER DEPRESSION PATTERN

**MAIN SYMPTOMS:** A sensation of something obstructing and stopping the throat which can neither be coughed up nor swallowed down, a dry mouth and throat, heat in the hearts of the hands and feet, lingering rib-side pain, possible menstrual pain and/or PMS, possible scanty, delayed, or blocked menstruation, a red tongue with scanty fur, and a bowstring, fine, rapid pulse

**TREATMENT PRINCIPLES:** Enrich yin and downbear fire, emolliate the liver and scatter nodulation

**FORMULA & MEDICINALS:** *Yi Guan Jian Jia Jian* (One Link Decoction with Additions & Subtractions)

Fructus Meliae Toosendan (*Chuan Lian Zi*), 10g, Radix Glehniae Littoralis (*Sha Shen*), 12g, Tuber Ophiopogonis Japonici (*Mai Dong*), 12g, uncooked Radix Rehmanniae (*Sheng Di*), 12g, Fructus Lycii Chinensis (*Gou Qi Zi*), 10g, Radix Angelicae Sinensis (*Dang Gui*), 10g, Radix Scrophulariae Ningpoensis (*Xuan Shen*), 15g, Tuber Curcumae (*Yu Jin*), 10g, Radix Platycodi Grandiflori (*Jie Geng*), 10g, Radix Albus Paeoniae Lactiflorae (*Bai Shao*), 10g

Decoct in water and administer orally in two divided doses, morning and evening, one *ji* per day.

**ACUPUNCTURE:** *Lie Que* (Lu 7), *Zhao Hai* (Ki 6), *San Yin Jiao* (Sp 6), *Tai Chong* (Liv 3), *Qi Men* (Liv 14), *Tian Tu* (CV 22), *Feng Long* (St 40). Use supplementing technique on the first three points and even supplementing-even draining method on the last four points.

## 4. LUNG-KIDNEY YIN VACUITY, PHLEGM FIRE FLAMING UPWARD PATTERN

**MAIN SYMPTOMS:** A feeling of something caught in the back of the throat which can neither be spit up or swallowed down, a dry mouth and throat, thirst but no great desire to drink, heat in the hearts of the hands and feet, afternoon tidal heat, possible night sweats, possible palpitations, vexation and agitation, insomnia, tinnitus, dizziness, a red tongue with dry and/or scanty, possibly yellow fur, and a bowstring, fine, rapid pulse

**NOTE:** The difference between this pattern and the preceding one is that there is more liver depression in the preceding pattern and more vacuity heat in this pattern.

**TREATMENT PRINCIPLES:** Nourish the lungs and enrich the kidneys, clear heat and disinhibit the throat

**FORMULA & MEDICINALS:** *Yi Guan Jian Jia Wei* (One Link Decoction with Added Flavors)

Tuber Ophiopogonis Japonicae (*Mai Dong*), 12g, Radix Glehnia Littoralis (*Sha Shen*), 12g, uncooked Radix Rehmanniae (*Sheng Di*), 12g, Fructus Lycii Chinensis (*Gou Qi Zi*), 12g, Radix Angelicae Sinensis (*Dang Gui*), 10g, Radix Albus Paeoniae Lactiflorae (*Bai Shao*), 10g, Radix Scrophulariae Ningpoensis (*Xuan Shen*), 10g, Bulbus Fritlariae (*Bei Mu*), 10g, Spica Prunellae Vulgaris (*Xia Ku Cao*), 15g, Concha Ostreae (*Mu Li*), 12g (decocted first), Rhizoma Anemarrhenae Aspheloidis (*Zhi Mu*), 10g, Radix Scutellariae Baicalensis (*Huang Qin*), 10-12g,

Fructus Meliae Toosendan (*Chuan Lian Zi*), 6-10g

Decoct in water and administer orally in two divided doses, morning and evening, one *ji* per day.

**ADDITIONS & SUBTRACTIONS:** If there is insomnia and more pronounced disquietude of the heart spirit, add Semen Zizyphi Spinosae (*Suan Zao Ren*) and Semen Biotae Orientalis (*Bai Zi Ren*).

**ACUPUNCTURE:** *Lie Que* (Lu 7), *Zhao Hai* (Ki 6), *San Yin Jiao* (Sp 6), *Feng Long* (St 40), *Nei Ting* (St 44), *Tian Tu* (CV 22). Use even supplementing-even draining technique.

## 5. BLOOD STASIS OBSTRUCTING THE NETWORK VESSELS PATTERN

**MAIN SYMPTOMS:** A feeling of something caught in the back of the throat which can neither be spit up or swallowed down, chest, rib-side, or abdominal fixed or piercing pain, possible menstrual irregularity and/or dysmenorrhea in females, enduring disease whose symptoms get worse in the afternoon or evening, spider nevi, hemangiomas, or varicosities, a dark, dusky facial complexion, a dark, purplish tongue or possible static spots and macules, and a bowstring, choppy, possibly bound pulse

**TREATMENT PRINCIPLES:** Quicken the blood and transform stasis, free the flow of the network vessels and disinhibit the throat

**FORMULA & MEDICINALS:** *Xue Fu Zhu Yu Tang Jia Jian* (Blood Mansion Dispel Stasis Decoction with Additions & Subtractions)

Semen Pruni Persicae (*Tao Ren*), 10g, Flos Carthami Tinctorii (*Hong Hua*), 10g (steeped), Radix Angelicae Sinensis (*Dang Gui*), 10g, Radix Ligustici Wallichii (*Chuan Xiong*), 10g (added later), Radix Rubrus Paeoniae Lactiflorae (*Chi Shao*), 10g, Radix Bupleuri (*Chai Hu*), 10g, Fructus Immaturus Citri Aurantii (*Zhi Shi*), 6g, Radix Platycodi Grandiflori (*Jie Geng*), 6g, Radix Cyathulae (*Chuan Niu Xi*), 10g, Tuber Curcumae (*Yu Jin*), 10g, Spica Prunellae Vulgaris (*Xia Ku Cao*), 15g, Radix Salviae Miltiorrhizae (*Dan Shen*), 10g

Decoct in water and administer orally in two divided doses, morning and evening, one *ji* per day.

**ADDITIONS & SUBTRACTIONS:** If the throat is dry and painful, add Radix Scrophulariae Ningpoensis (*Xuan*

Shen) and Radix Trichosanthis Kirlowii (*Tian Hua Fen*).

**ACUPUNCTURE:** *Xue Hai* (Sp 10), *He Gu* (LI 4), *Tai Chong* (Liv 3), *San Yin Jiao* (Sp 6), *Tian Tu* (CV 22), *Lian Quan* (CV 23). Use even supplementing-even draining technique.

**CLINICAL TIP:** Plum pit qi typically responds well to both acupuncture and/or Chinese medicinals. Some Chinese doctors regard Spica Prunellae Vulgaris (*Xia Ku Cao*) as an empirical specific for this condition.

## ABSTRACTS OF REPRESENTATIVE CHINESE RESEARCH:

*Zhe Jiang Zhong Yi Za Zhi* (*Zhejiang Journal of Chinese Medicine*), #5, 1993, p. 210. Yang Ding-you treated 23 cases of plum pit qi using *Gua Di Dan Fan San* (Melon Pedicle & Chalcanthitum Powder). Of these 23 patients, 19 were female and four were male. Their ages ranged from 19-57 years old. All suffered from a feeling of something stuck in their throat that could neither be spit up or swallowed down. The duration of disease had lasted from five months to four years. Equal amounts of Pediculus Melonis (*Gua Di*) and Chalcanthitum (*Dan Fan*) were ground into powder and mixed. Each day, 0.5-1.0g of this mixture were administered in a white sugar soup. Depending on whether the patient was strong or weak, this was administered one time per day or every other day. Typically, vomiting occurred one hour after administration. In most cases, 2-4 administrations resulted in cure. In terms of actual outcomes, 19 patients were cured, meaning the sensation in their throat disappeared, two patients registered good improvement, meaning the sensation in their throat decreased, and two patients got no effect, meaning there was no change from before to after treatment in this sensation.

*Zhong Yi Za Zhi* (*Journal of Chinese Medicine*), #10, 1994, p. 613. Li Ya-le *et al.* treated a total of 220 cases of plum pit qi disease with two different Chinese medicinal protocols. All the patients met the criteria set forth for plum pit qi disease developed at the 1991 Chinese National Ear, Nose & Throat Symposium. These criteria include varying degrees of emotional depression as well as the sensation of something stuck in the throat. Within the total study, there were 98 men and 122 women. Their ages ranged from 7-68 years old. Seventy-one point eight-two percent were between 25-55. Their course of disease had lasted from as short as one day to as long as five years. However, in 67.27% of cases, it had lasted from three months to one year. These 220 patients were divided into

two groups whose age and disease course were statistically similar. One hundred eighty patients were given *Mei He Qi Chong Ji* (Plum Pi Qi Soluble Granules), 20g each time, 2-3 times per day. The other 40 patients were given *Xiao Yao Wan* (Rambling Pills), one pill each morning and evening.[1] In both cases, one course of treatment equaled 10 days. Forty-eight of the *Mei He Qi Chong Ji* group were cured, 56 registered a marked effect, 73 got some effect, and only three got no effect. Thus the total amelioration rate in this group was 98.3%. In the *Xiao Yao Wan* group, five patients were cured, seven got a marked effect, 16 got some effect, and twelve got no effect for a total amelioration rate of 69.7%. Hence there was a marked statistical difference between these two groups (P<0.05).

*Shang Hai Zhong Yi Yao Za Zhi* (*Shanghai Journal of Chinese Medicine & Medicinals*), #5, 1998, p. 24. Zhou Gui-juan treated a total of 23 patients with plum pit qi with *Ban Xia Hou Po Tang* (Pinellia & Magnolia Decoction). Nineteen of these patients were female and four were male. The youngest was 21 and the oldest was 58. Their course of disease had lasted from several years to 1-2 weeks. Depending on accompanying signs and symptoms, a number of other medicinals were added to this standard prescription. Thus each patient received a modification of this basic formula. At the end of this study, 22 out of 23 patients experienced either complete disappearance of the foreign sensation in their throat or great reduction in this sensation. The shortest course of treatment to cure was five *ji* and the longest was 20 *ji*. In a small number cases, their plum pit qi returned due to emotional stimulus. However, readministration of this formula remitted the symptoms once again.

❖

*Ji Lin Zhong Yi Yao* (*Jilin Chinese Medicine & Medicinals*), #4, 1993, p. 19. Jin Ming-mo treated 40 cases of plum pit qi using *Shun Qi Xiao Shi Hua Tan Tang* (Normalize the Qi, Disperse Food & Transform Phlegm Decoction). Among these 40 cases, 12 were men and 28 were women. Ten cases ranged in age from 18-30 years old, 21 cases were 31-40 years old, five cases were 41-50 years old, and the rest were over 50. The course of disease had lasted from as long as three years to as short as seven days. Further, 23 cases were from emotional causes, seven were due to undisciplined diet, and the rest were due to upper respiratory tract infection. The formula consisted of Pericarpium Citri Reticulatae (*Chen Pi*), 10g, Pericarpium Citri Reticulatae Viride (*Qing Pi*), 10g, bile-processed Rhizoma Arisaematis (*Dan Nan Xing*), 10g,

Rhizoma Pinelliae Ternatae (*Ban Xia*), 10g, Fructus Perillae Frutescentis (*Zi Su Zi*), 10g, Semen Raphani Sativi (*Lai Fu Zi*), 10g, Radix Bupleuri (*Chai Hu*), 10g, Rhizoma Cimicifugae (*Sheng Ma*), 10g, Radix Platycodi Grandiflori (*Jie Geng*), 10g, and Rhizoma Cyperi Rotundi (*Xiang Fu*), 10g. If there was emotional upset, Semen Biotae Orientalis (*Bai Zi Ren*), stir-fried Semen Zizyphi Spinosae (*Suan Zao Ren*), and Cortex Cinnamomi Cassiae (*Rou Gui*) were added. If there was food stagnation, Massa Medica Fermentata (*Shen Qu*), Endothelium Corneum Gigeriae Galli (*Ji Nei Jin*), and stir-fried Fructus Germinatus Hordei Vulgaris (*Mai Ya*) were added. And, if there was upper respiratory tract infection, Flos Lonicerae Japonicae (*Jin Yin Hua*), Radix Isatidis Seu Baphicacanthi (*Ban Lan Gen*), and Herba Taraxaci Mongolici Cum Radice (*Pu Gong Ying*) were added. One *ji* was decocted in water and administered per day in two divided doses. Twenty-eight cases were cured, eight cases improved, and four cases got no result. Thus the total amelioration rate was 90%. Cure included no recurrence within six months.

*Bei Jing Zhong Yi (Beijing Chinese Medicine)*, #6, 1993, p. 48. Li Xin-cun treated 64 cases of chronic laryngitis, which he equated with plum pit qi, with *Xue Fu Zhu Yu Tang* (Blood Mansion Dispel Stasis Decoction). Among these patients, 23 were men and 41 were women. The youngest was 18 and the oldest was 54 years old. The shortest disease course was eight days and the longest was four years. *Xue Fu Zhu Yu Tang* consisted of: Radix Angelicae Sinensis (*Dang Gui*), 15g, Flos Carthami Tinctorii (*Hong Hua*), 10g, Semen Pruni Persicae (*Tao Ren*), 10g, Fructus Citri Aurantii (*Zhi Ke*), 10g, Radix Bupleuri (*Chai Hu*), 10g, Radix Rubrus Paeoniae Lactiflorae (*Chi Shao*), 15g, Radix Ligustici Wallichii (*Chuan Xiong*), 10g, Radix Platycodi Grandiflori (*Jie Geng*), 10g, Radix Cyathulae (*Chuan Niu Xi*), 15g, uncooked Radix Rehmanniae (*Sheng Di*), 15g, and Radix Glycyrrhizae (*Gan Cao*), 10g, one *ji* per day. If there was a dry, sore throat, Radix Scrophulariae Ningpoensis (*Xuan Shen*), Radix Trichosanthis Kirlowii (*Tian Hua Fen*), and mix-fried Foliu Eriobotryac Japonicae (*Pi Pa Ye*) were added. If there was an itchy throat, Rhizoma Belancandae (*She Gan*) and Herba Menthae Haplocalycis (*Bo He*) were added. If there was the feeling as if something were stuck in the throat, Caulis Perillae Frutescentis (*Su Geng*) and Rhizoma Pinelliae Ternatae (*Ban Xia*) were added. Ten *ji* equaled one course of treatment. In terms of outcomes, 52 cases were cured, 11 experienced marked improvement, and only one got no

result. Thus the total amelioration rate was 98.4%. The smallest number of *ji* was eight and the largest was 20, with an average of 14.

*Shang Hai Zhong Yi Yao Za Zhi (Shanghai Journal of Chinese Medicine & Medicinals)*, #1, 1992, p. 20-21. Zhang Jian-hua treated 54 cases of plum pit qi with *Bai Mei Li Yan Tang* (Peony & Mume Disinhibit the Throat Decoction). This consisted of: Radix Albus Paeoniae Lactiflorae (*Bai Shao*), 9g, Flos Pruni Mume (*Lu E Mei*), 4.5g, Radix Adenophorae Strictae (*Nan Sha Shen*), 4.5g, Bulbus Lilii (*Bai He*), 9g, Radix Platycodi Grandiflori (*Jie Geng*), 4.5g, Rhizoma Belamcandae (*She Gan*), 4.5g, and Radix Glycyrrhizae (*Gan Cao*), 3g, one *ji* per day. A number of other ingredients were added to this base formula depending on signs and symptoms. Two weeks equaled one course of treatment. Using this protocol, 21 cases experienced marked improvement, 28 cases experienced some improvement, and five cases got no result. Thus the total amelioration rate was 90.7%.

*Si Chuan Zhong Yi (Sichuan Chinese Medicine)*, #11, 1993, p. 33-34. Yuan Chang-hua treated 49 cases of plum pit qi. Of these, 13 were men and 36 were women. Their ages ranged from 18-76 years old. Their disease course had lasted from two weeks to three years. Treatment was given on the basis of pattern discrimination, with four patterns being used: 1) liver depression qi stagnation pattern, 2) phlegm depressed in the chest and diaphragm pattern, 3) yin vacuity with liver depression pattern, and 4) blood stasis obstructing the network vessels pattern. Chinese medicinal decoctions were administered on this basis. Thirty-nine patients were cured, seven cases improved, and three cases got no result for a total amelioration rate of 93.8% Among those cured, there were no relapses within one year.

*Zhe Jiang Zhong Yi Za Zhi (Zhejiang Journal of Chinese Medicine)*, #1, 2000, p. 17: Liu Chang-ming treated 60 cases of plum pit qi between Mar. 1994 and Oct. 1997 with family-transmitted *Wu Hua Yin* (Five Flowers Drink). Of these 60 patients, 24 were male and 36 were female. The youngest was 18 and the oldest was 63, with 71.10% being 35-55 years old. The shortest course of disease was two months and the longest was four years and nine months, with 68% of cases suffering from this condition four months to one year. The diagnostic criteria for inclusion in this study were based on those promulgated at the 1991 National Chinese Medicine Ear, Nose & Throat Symposium. These included a history of emotional stress or emotional trauma, an abnormal sensation of something in the throat, and either no observed abnormality of the throat or accompanying inflammation. Those suffering from malignant diseases were excluded. In 20 cases, the throat was normal; in 13 cases there was accompanying chronic laryngitis; in 17 cases there was accompanying chronic gastritis; in seven cases there was accompanying chronic pharyngitis or tonsillitis; and in three cases there was accompanying chronic rhinitis.

Treatment consisted of all patients being administered *Wu Hua Yin*: Flos Pruni Mume (*Lu E Mei*), 8g, Flos Magnoliae Offiicinalis (*Hou Po Hua*), Flos Citri Sacrodactylis (*Fo Shou Hua*), and mix-fried Radix Glycyrrhizae (*Gan Cao*), 6g each, Flos Inulae Racemosae (*Xuan Fu Hua*), Flos Albizziae Julibrissinis (*He Huan Hua*), bamboo juice-processed Rhizoma Pinelliae Ternatae (*Ban Xia*), and Caulis Perillae Frutescentis (*Su Geng*), 10g each. Additions and subtractions were made depending on each patient's symptoms. One *ji* was administered orally per day after being boiled two times. A half month equaled one course of treatment and four such courses were given. Based on criteria promulgated at the same 1991 symposium described above, 11 cases were cured. This meant that their symptoms decreased within one half month, had disappeared after two months, and there was no recurrence after 12 months. Eighteen cases were judged to have gotten a marked effect. This meant that their symptoms had decreased after half a month and had disappeared after two months, but had recurred within 12 months. Twenty-four cases got some effects. This meant that their symptoms had decreased in half a month and had partially disappeared after two months. Seven patients experienced no effect, meaning there was no marked change from before to after treatment. Thus the total amelioration rate was 88.33%, and there were no obvious adverse reactions. This formula is safe and able to be taken by those who are weak, pregnant, or breast-feeding

## REPRESENTATIVE CASE HISTORIES:

### ❖ CASE 1[2] ❖

The patient was a 38 year old female who was first examined on July 15, 1991. For the previous year she had been emotionally depressed. This had resulted in chest and rib-side distention and fullness, chest oppression, a tendency to sighing, and vomiting after meals. She had previously been hospitalized for the treatment of neurogenic vomit-ing where she had been treated with vitamin B6, a multi-vitamin, Valium, and *Xiao Yao Wan* (Rambling Pills). After taking these medicines, her vomiting stopped and her symptoms lessened. However, she still sometimes felt something obstructing her throat which she could neither spit up nor swallow down. Whenever the patient felt emotionally upset, this sensation in her throat got worse. She had already had several barium meal x-rays of the esopha-gus, and no abnormalities had been found. She had also gone to a Chinese medical hospital where she had been diagnosed with plum pit qi and given more than 20 *ji* of *Ban Xia Hou Po Tang* (Pinellia & Magnolia Decoction). Initially this had achieved some improvement, but, with continued administration, this improvement got less and her emotional stress got more. Because the woman was worried about esophageal cancer, she went to many doc-tors, but none of the treatment she received achieved any marked effect.

When the patient came to see the author of this case, her throat was pale red, moist, and glossy. Her respiration was nor-mal, and her swallowing was easy and unobstructed. There was no aching and pain in her throat, but yet she felt like she had something stuck in her throat. Her tongue fur was white and slimy, and her pulse was bowstring and slippery. Therefore, her pattern was discriminated as phlegm rheum following qi coun-terflow and moving upward where it was binding in the throat. Based on the saying in the *Nei Jing* (*Inner Classic*), "For disease in the upper, abduct and skip," one *ji* of *Gua Di Dan Fan San* (Melon Pedicle & Chalcanthitum Powder) was given once per day. This consisted of 0.5g of Pediculus Melonis (*Gua Di*) and Chalcanthitum (*Dan Fan*) administered in a white sugar soup.

After two days, the patient was re-examined where the patient said that, after taking this "soup," she had vomit-ed 150-200ml of sticky, thick fluids. The next day her chest area felt soothed and easy and the feeling in her throat had disappeared. Therefore, in order to secure the treatment effect, she was administered *Shao Ting Pian* (lit-erally, "Slightly Stopping Tablets," an unidentified medi-cine) to extend her vomiting. She once again vomited some mucousy fluids which were half the amount of the previous time. After taking this medicine, the patient felt some slight aching in her stomach region and her stools were loose. Two days after stopping this medicine, this dis-appeared. On follow-up after a half year, none of her pre-vious symptoms had returned.

### ❖ CASE 2[3] ❖

The patient was a 46 year old female. Nine months previ-ous, the patient had experienced emotional upset. At that time, she felt something in her throat which she could neither spit up nor swallow down. When eating, her throat was normal, and there was no obvious aching or pain. She also experienced abdominal distention and oppression extending to both rib-side regions. She had tried numerous formulas but without result. Examination revealed that her lips were slightly dry, her urine was yellow, and her stools were dry. Her tongue fur was slightly yellow, and her pulse was bowstring and slippery.

Therefore, the patient's pattern was discriminated as liver depression qi stagnation with loss of harmony of the spleen and stomach and phlegm and qi counterflowing up. The treatment principles were to course the liver and resolve depression, rectify the qi and transform phlegm. The medicinals used consisted of Shun Qi Xiao Shi Hua Tan Tang as described above under the research abstracts plus Cortex Cinnamomi Cassiae (Rou Gui), 10g, and Fructus Gardeniae Jasminoidis (Zhi Zi), 10g.

After three ji, the patient's symptoms had disappeared. After another five ji, her disease was completely cured. On follow-up after one year, there had been no recurrence.

❖ CASE 3[4] ❖

The patient was a 42 year old female who complained of phlegm in her throat accompanied by feeling out of sorts for the previous three months. She could neither cough this phlegm up nor swallow it down. In addition, she had chest oppression, inability to relax, dizziness, a bitter taste and sticky feeling in her mouth, thirst but no desire to drink, insomnia, profuse dreams, a red tongue with slimy, yellow fur, and a bowstring, slippery, pulse.

The disease diagnosis was plum pit qi, and her Chinese pattern was categorized as phlegm depression of the chest and diaphragm with phlegm and qi binding and transforming into heat. Therefore, the treatment principles were to transform phlegm and clear heat, disinhibit the qi and scatter nodulation. The formula used was Wen Dan Tang Jia Wei (Warm the Gallbladder Decoction with Added Flavors): Rhizoma Pinelliae Ternatae (Ban Xia) and Sclerotium Poriae Cocos (Fu Ling), 5g each, Pericarpium Citri Reticulatae (Chen Pi), Fructus Immaturus Citri Aurantii (Zhi Shi), Radix Scutellariae Baicalensis (Huang Qin), Caulis Bambusae In Taeniis (Zhu Ru), and Tuber Curcumae (Yu Jin), 10g each, Fructus Trichosanthis Kirlowii (Gua Lou) and Spica Prunellae Vulgaris (Xia Ku Cao), 30g each, Bulbus Fritillariae Thunbergii (Zhe Bei Mu), 12g, and Radix Platycodi Grandiflori (Jie Geng), 6g. One ji was decocted in water per day and administered internally.

After taking three ji, the patient was re-examined. The chest oppression was decreased and her sleep was improved. The other symptoms were the same as before. Therefore, 15 grams of Rhizoma Belamcandae (She Gan) were added to the above medicinals to strengthen their ability to clear heat and disinhibit the throat, transform phlegm and scatter nodulation. After taking another three ji, the patient was extremely happy. Her throat condition was quite obviously improved and her tongue fur had turned from yellow and glossy to thin and slimy. Therefore, no further change was made in her formula. Three more ji were administered, and the patient was completely cured. On follow-up after one year, there had been no recurrence.

❖ CASE 4[5] ❖

The patient was a 45 year old female who had been depressed, withdrawn, and taciturn for two years. The patient reported that she felt discomfort in her throat as if there was something blocking it. The woman was diagnosed as suffering from functional neurosis and given sedatives. However, this had not resolved her symptoms. At the time of examination by the authors of this case history, the woman's pulse was bowstring and slippery and her tongue was fat with slimy, white fur. Therefore, due to a combination of depressed qi and phlegm counterflowing upward, she was prescribed Xuan Fu Hua Dai Zhe Shi Tang Jian Jian (Inula & Hematite Decoction with Additions & Subtractions): Flos Inulae Racemosae (Xuan Fu Hua), Haemititum (Dai Zhe Shi), Rhizoma Pinelliae Ternatae (Ban Xia), mix-fried Radix Glycyrrhizae (Gan Cao), uncooked Rhizoma Zingiberis (Sheng Jiang), Cortex Magnoliae Officinalis (Hou Po), Caulis Perillae Frutescentis (Su Gen), and Pumice (Hai Fu Shi), dosages unspecified. After taking seven ji of this formula, all the woman's symptoms remitted.

❖ CASE 5[6] ❖

The patient was a 43 year old female. A half year previously, she had been involved in a domestic argument and had been gossiped about. Afterwards, the woman experienced chest and rib-side fullness and pain. She had no thought for eating or drinking. She also had dizziness and tinnitus. On her own initiative, she took Shu Gan He Wei Wan (Soothe the Liver & Harmonize the Stomach Pills) which slightly decreased the chest and rib-side fullness and pain and the dizziness. However, she gradually developed a feeling in her throat as if something were stuck and which she could neither spit up nor swallow down. She also had phlegm which was white in color and which she could not easily expectorate.

Emotionally, the woman suffered from fear and fright. She went to the ENT department at the author of the case's hospital but was told there was no abnormality seen. Therefore, she was diagnosed as suffering from neurotic esophageal stenosis and referred to a Chinese medical practitioner who found her tongue pale with slimy, white fur, and her pulse deep and bowstring. Accordingly, the woman's Chinese medical pattern was categorized as qi mechanism depression and obstruction with phlegm qi congealing and binding. Hence the woman was prescribed *Ban Xia Hou Po Tang* (Pinellia & Magnolia Decoction): Rhizoma Pinelliae Ternatae (*Ban Xia*), 12g, Cortex Magnoliae Officinalis (*Hou Po*), 12g, Sclerotium Poriae Cocos (*Fu Ling*), 12g, Folium Perillae Frutescentis (*Zi Su Ye*), 10g, and uncooked Rhizoma Zingiberis (*Sheng Jiang*), 3 slices.

After taking four *ji* of these medicinals, the woman's phlegm had decreased. However, she still had a feeling of something blocking her throat. Her tongue and pulse were as before. Therefore, 20 grams of Semen Trichosanthis Kirlowii (*Gua Lou Ren*), 6 grams of Bulbus Fritillariae Cirrhosae (*Chuan Bei Mu*), and 10 grams of Pericarpium Citri Reticulatae (*Chen Pi*) were added to the above formula. The patient took another four *ji* and reported that the sensation of blockage in her throat was markedly diminished. Each day, her eating and drinking increased. Her tongue was pale red with thin, white fur, and her pulse was only slightly bowstring. After taking yet another four *ji* of this formula, all her symptoms had been eliminated and the disease was considered cured.

## ENDNOTES

[1]The difference between these two approaches to treatment is that *Xiao Yao Wan* course the liver and rectify the qi, fortify the spleen and eliminate dampness, while *Mei He Qi Chong Ji* loosen the chest and rectify the qi, transform phlegm and scatter nodulation, harmonize the stomach and downbear counterflow, and eliminate vexation and disinhibit the throat. Whereas the first protocol is a general one for treating liver depression with spleen dampness, the second protocol is specific for treating upwardly counterflowing qi binding with phlegm in the throat.

[2]Yang Ding-you, "The Treatment of 23 Cases of Plum Pit Qi with *Gua Di Dan Fan San* (Melon Pedicle & Chalcanthitum Powder)," *Zhe Jiang Zhong Yi Za Zhi (Zhejiang Journal of Chinese Medicine)*, #5, 1993, p. 210

[3]Jin Ming-mo, "The Treatment of 40 Cases of Plum Pit Qi with *Shun Qi Xiao Shi Hua Tan Tang* (Normalize the Qi, Disperse Food & Transform Phlegm Decoction)," *Ji Lin Zhong Yi Yao (Jilin Chinese Medicine & Medicinals)*, #4, 1993, p. 19

[4]Yuan Chang-hua, "An Explanation of the Pattern Discrimination Treatment of 49 Cases of Plum Pit Qi," *Si Chuan Zhong Yi (Sichuan Chinese Medicine)*, #11, 1993, p. 33-34

[5]Chen & Zhao, *op. cit.*, p. 182

[6]*Ibid.*, p. 397-398

# ❖ 19 ❖

# VISCERAL AGITATION

Visceral agitation is a paroxysmal mental disease most prevalent in women. The viscus implied by the name is the heart, and the agitation refers to agitation of the blood due to damaged yin and to the rashness, impetuousity, and impatience that characterize this condition. The Chinese literature usually further says this condition is most common in adolescent females. However, it may also be used to describe severe premenstrual tension, and it is often seen in perimenopausal women. Visceral agitation often begins as melancholy, depression, and emotional lability but then progresses to alternating laughing and crying for no reason, sighing for no apparent reason, and vexation and agitation. In severe cases, such as postpartum when there has been a great loss of blood and body fluids, there may be convulsions with a white facial complexion and possible complete loss of consciousness. The first mention of visceral agitation within the Chinese medical literature is in Zhang Zhang-jing's *Jin Gui Yao Lue (Essentials of the Golden Cabinet)* where it is specifically ascribed to women.

The Chinese medical disorder "visceral agitation" incorporates many symptoms that do not correspond to a distinct Western medical or psychiatric diagnosis. However, several nosologic categories in Western psychiatry bear resemblance to aspects of this disorder. These include premenstrual dysphoric disorder (formerly known as premenstrual syndrome or PMS), mood disorders associated with the perimenopause, and postpartum mood disorders. Histrionic personality disorder and hysteroid dysphoria also have many symptoms in common with visceral agitation.

## NOSOLOGY:

Paroxysmal outbursts of impetuosity, impatience, and rashness that are associated with emotional lability and are more commonly observed in women (especially during adolescence) have the flavor of histrionic personality disorder in Western psychiatric nosology. In this disorder, a pervasive dysregulation of emotional experience and behavior is associated with inappropriate, often dramatic displays that change rapidly from moment to moment in the absence of apparent external causes. The histrionic individual often behaves in a seductive or provocative manner and insists on being the center of attention, is easily influenced by others, and considers relationships to be more intimate or meaningful than they actually are. Individuals with histrionic personality disorder or other personality disorders are frequently dysphoric or anxious and sometimes become extremely agitated without apparent cause. Occasions of unusually great stress may lead to transient worsening in baseline psychopathology, including extremely theatrical displays of inappropriate emotionality or impetuosity which subside in intensity when the stressor is removed.

Hysteroid dysphoria is a descriptive category that is no longer in current use in Western psychiatric nosology but which alludes to a symptom pattern observed in visceral agitation, including emotional lability, melancholic depression, and rash or inappropriate behavior reflected in unstable relationships. Individuals who were formerly given this diagnostic label are now typically diagnosed with bipolar affective disorder or histrionic personality disorder according to the *DSM-IV*. However, a pattern of almost continuous dysregulation in mood and interpersonal functioning are not central to either of these diagnostic categories. Contemporary Western psychiatry regards these symptom patterns as mood disorders in women related to endocrinologic factors around the time of menarche, in the immediate four week postpartum period, during the days before onset of menses, or during the perimenopause. A significant number (up to 15%) of women experience depressed mood in the immediate postpartum period, and some women become frankly psychotic. Premenstrual syndrome (PMS), which has been renamed premenstrual dysphoric disorder in the *DSM-IV*, is characterized by severe periodic irritable, labile, or depressed mood with onset before the start of menses and resolution with the beginning of a menstrual cycle. These symptoms result in significant impairments in social or occupational functioning. In contrast, perimenopausal mood changes more often include anxiety and fatigue than depressed mood. These symptoms occur during the brief period of months or years before menopause as ovarian sensitivity to estrogen steadily declines. Although mood lability is often accompanied by impatience, rashness, and impetuosity, these aspects of visceral agitation are not considered core symptoms of female mood disorders related to endocrinologic factors.

## EPIDEMIOLOGY:

Prevalence estimates of histrionic personality disorder range from 2% in the general population to 15% in outpatient mental health clinic populations. As many as 5% of women may fulfill criteria for premenstrual dysphoric disorder, but as many as 50% of women experience some changes in mood premenstrually. It has been estimated that 10-15% of women experience significantly depressed or labile mood in the initial postpartum period. Although the prevalence of postpartum psychosis is only 0.1%, the risk of recurring psychosis may be as great as 50% in women who have had an initial postpartum psychotic episode. The frequency of occurrence of perimenopausal mood changes remains unclear. However, a significant subset of perimenopausal women who are genetically vulnerable to bipolar disorder may experience an acute exacerbation or first manic episode during the perimenopause.

## DIFFERENTIAL DIAGNOSIS:

The clinician must first rule out possible medical etiologies or chronic effects of a substance that manifest as impatience, impetuosity, rashness, lability, or other personality changes. Chronic use of (or withdrawal from) heroin or other opiates or stimulants (including cocaine and methamphetamine) can result in a pervasive pattern of labile or irritable mood. A long-standing pattern of pervasive social dysfunction in the absence of major medical disorders, including neurologic disease (*e.g.*, CNS mass, lesion, or seizure disorder), head trauma, or substance abuse implies a primary psychiatric disorder. The diagnostic challenge in this case is to distinguish between histrionic personality disorder, other personality disorders, and major mood disorders, including bipolar disorder. The clinician's task is complicated by the possibility of several independent disorders occurring in one patient. Histrionic personality disorder is characterized by a pervasive pattern of dysfunction in behavior and emotional experience with onset in adolescence or early adulthood. More specifically, the histrionic individual is inappropriately seductive or dramatic, awkward or uncomfortable

---

## DIFFERENTIAL DIAGNOSIS

| 1. MEDICAL DISORDERS | 2. EFFECTS OF SUBSTANCES | 3. PSYCHIATRIC DISORDERS |
|---|---|---|
| A. CNS DISORDERS, INCLUDING MASS LESIONS, SEIZURE DISORDERS, ETC.<br>B. HISTORY OF HEAD TRAUMA | A. ALCOHOL OR ILLICIT SUBSTANCE INTOXICATION OR WITHDRAWAL<br>B. SIDE EFFECTS OF MEDICATIONS | A. HISTRIONIC PERSONALITY DISORDER (HPD)<br>B. OTHER PERSONALITY DISORDERS<br>C. MAJOR DEPRESSIVE DISORDER<br>D. BIPOLAR AFFECTIVE DISORDER (BAD)<br>E. PREMENSTRUAL DYSPHORIC DISORDER (PMDD) |

when not the center of attention. He or she is also easily suggestible and influenced by others and tends to regard relationships as more meaningful or intimate than they are. In contrast, hysteroid dysphoria is an atypical presentation of depressed mood in the context of emotional lability and an unstable relationship pattern. When there is evidence of cyclic mood changes that are not associated with menstrual periods, a primary diagnosis of bipolar disorder is likely. Mood changes associated with the luteal phase of the menstrual cycle point to premenstrual dysphoric disorder. However, some women with histrionic personalities experience transient worsening in baseline lability and mood symptoms just prior to onset of menses.

## ETIOLOGY & PATHOPHYSIOLOGY:

Personality changes, including rashness, impetuosity, and impatience, accompanying medical or neurologic disorders are the direct result of derangements in brain functioning caused by the disorder. A similar presentation that is transient and recurrent, corresponding to menstrual cycles or other endocrinologic changes in women is presumably related to effects of endocrinologic dysregulation on brain function. However, no consistent correspondence has been established between endocrinologic markers and cognitive or mood symptoms observed in women diagnosed with premenstrual dysphoric disorder, postpartum depression, or perimenopausal mood disorders. Therefore, while a biological diathesis or cause is presumed by contemporary Western psychiatry, it has not yet been clearly demonstrated. A recently introduced hypothesis is based on the model that some women who have a preexisting genetic or other biological vulnerability may manifest symptoms when exposed to certain endocrinologic or other stressors at certain critical periods of the reproductive cycle. This hypothesis has also not been substantiated by epidemiologic or other data. Several psychodynamic or psychoanalytic explanations of histrionic personality disorder have also been advanced. These are too numerous and subtle to review for purposes of this discussion.

## WESTERN MEDICAL TREATMENT:

The Western medical appropriate treatment of a pattern of lability associated with impetuosity, rashness, and impatience, depends on the biological or psychiatric causes of these symptoms. When an associated medical or neurological disorder has been identified (see Differential diagnosis above), treatment of this primary disorder can result in dramatic relief and sometimes removal of the dysfunctional symptom pattern described as visceral agitation in Chinese medicine. For example, if the cause is an atypical seizure disorder, appropriate pharmacotherapy will control the disorder resulting in normalization of associated aberrant behaviors or emotional displays. If the identified medical cause is an operable intracranial mass, surgical removal will often result in return to pre-morbid functioning. In an analogous manner, abstinence from a substance of abuse will typically result in dramatic improvement in baseline functioning which will be maintained so long as abstinence continues. Lability associated with impetuosity, rashness, or impatience seen in female mood disorders sometimes responds to hormonal replacement therapy (HRT), including estrogens and progesterone. However, efficacy of treatments using gonadal steroids is still poorly defined since the same hormones may precipitate manic, depressive, or psychotic episodes. Other treatments include serotonin-selective re-uptake inhibitors, such as fluoxetine (Prozac), sertraline (Zoloft), or paroxetine (Paxil). When a cyclic mood pattern confirms a diagnosis of bipolar affective disorder, the patient is typically started on a mood-stabilizing agent. These include lithium carbonate, carbamazepine (Tegretol), valproic acid (Depakote), and the more recently introduced drugs, lamotragine (Lamictal) and gabapentin (Neurontin). Recent evidence suggests that cognitive-behavioral therapy or individual dynamic psychotherapy results in reduction of symptom severity and improved social or interpersonal functioning in histrionic personality disorder. Antidepressants or anxiolytics are sometimes used to treat target symptoms that result in significant psychological or social morbidity in histrionic personality disorder or other personality disorders.

## SHORT & LONG-TERM ADVANTAGES & DISADVANTAGES TO WESTERN MEDICAL TREATMENT:

Advantages and disadvantages of medical or surgical treatments of etiologies underlying mood lability are numerous and depend on the nature of the intervention. There are no significant short-term disadvantages of pharmacologic treatments for psychiatric disorders manifesting as lability or "rashness, impetuosity, or impatience." Long-term side effects of lithium carbonate therapy include drug-induced hypothyroidism and renal dysfunction. Possible long-term negative consequences of hormonal therapy for treatment of premenstrual dysphoric disorder or perimenopausal mood disorder include an increased incidence of breast cancer, many other medical complications, and the possible induction of a psychotic or manic episode.

PROGNOSIS:

The long-term outcome of medical or neurologic disorders associated with lability is highly variable and depends on the nature and severity of the underlying disorder. Certain seizure disorders associated with lability or mood symptoms respond well to medications. Others are refractory to medication management and eventually require stereotaxic brain surgery for adequate control of seizures. Individuals who exhibit mood lability, rashness, or impetuosity associated with substance abuse may remain abstinent for years or experience frequent relapses of drug use depending on their social circumstances and their affiliation with an appropriate drug rehabilitation program.

Personality disorders typically carry unfavorable prognoses in view of the pervasive and chronic nature of symptoms that comprise these disorders. However, a broad range of severity exists in core personality disorder symptoms. Social circumstances and the presence of co-morbid psychiatric disorders or substance abuse also significantly influence long-term outcome in histrionic personality disorder or others. When lability, impetuosity, or rashness are associated with bipolar disorder, they can reasonably be expected to improve during periods of appropriate pharmacotherapeutic treatment. However, in more refractory cases of rapid cycling bipolar disorder or mixed manic and depressive states, symptoms of lability will also likely be relatively less responsive to mood-stabilizing medications. Mood disorders related to women's reproductive cycles may be mild, moderate, or severe. Symptoms sometimes remit or worsen in the absence of apparent external causes.

INDICATIONS FOR REFERRAL TO
WESTERN MEDICAL SERVICES:

Urgent medical referral is indicated if there is evidence of an acute or potentially life-threatening medical or psychiatric disorder. For example, a patient who complains of extreme mood lability and a history of symptoms suggestive of epilepsy should be referred to the nearest emergency room for a thorough medical evaluation including an EEG and CT of the head. Urgent medical referral is also indicated when there is evidence of on-going substance abuse that is causing significant impairment in social or occupational functioning. Lability in the context of an acute manic episode also warrants urgent medical referral to rule out possible medical-neurological etiologies of mania and assist the patient with an appropriate referral to psychiatric treatment.

Impetuosity, rashness, or impatience associated with mood disorders in the premenstrual, post-partum, or peri-menopausal period require urgent medical evaluation only in cases when the patient is severely impaired or at risk of suicide because of these symptoms. For example, a profoundly depressed woman who has given birth two weeks ago may attempt suicide or possibly experience a psychotic episode, which places both the woman and infant at considerable risk.

If chronic symptoms of lability, impetuosity, rashness, or impatience occur independently from other potentially serious or acute medical or psychiatric symptoms and the individual has failed to respond to an adequate trial of prescribed Chinese medicines or acupuncture, non-urgent psychiatric referral may be useful to clarify the differential diagnosis and establish an optimized combined treatment program.

CHINESE DISEASE CAUSES & DISEASE MECHANISMS:

Visceral agitation is primarily due to lack of construction and nourishment of the heart spirit and harassment of the spirit by some sort of evil heat. Lack of construction and nourishment of the heart is, in turn, mainly due to heart-spleen dual vacuity. Evil heat may be depressive heat, phlegm heat, or vacuity heat. In real-life clinical practice, liver depression is always operative in cases of visceral agitation. It is typically liver depression-spleen vacuity which are the root mechanisms for heart-spleen dual vacuity and for the engenderment of both depressive and phlegm heat. Likewise, it is typically enduring or severe depressive heat which damages and consumes yin blood which then gives rise to yin vacuity effulgent fire or yin vacuity yang hyperactivity. Because most cases of visceral agitation present with at least four simultaneous disease mechanisms (liver depression, depressive heat, spleen vacuity, and heart blood vacuity), the heat involved in visceral agitation is perhaps best described as a species of yin fire.

TREATMENT BASED ON PATTERN DISCRIMINATION:

1. HEART SPIRIT LACK OF NOURISHMENT PATTERN

MAIN SYMPTOMS: Devitalized essence spirit, abstraction, sorrowfulness without apparent cause and abnormal laughing and crying, heart vexation, insomnia, profuse dreams, susceptibility to fright, heart palpitations, lassitude of the spirit, a tender, red tongue, and a fine, bowstring pulse

TREATMENT PRINCIPLES: Enrich the heart and supplement the spleen, nourish the blood and quiet the spirit

**FORMULA & MEDICINALS:** If symptoms of yin and blood vacuity are more pronounced, use: *Gan Mai Da Zao Tang Jia Wei* (Licorice, Wheat & Red Date Decoction with Added Flavors)

Stir-fried Semen Zizyphi Spinosae (*Suan Zao Ren*), 12g, uncooked Radix Rehmanniae (*Sheng Di*), 12g, Bulbus Lilii (*Bai He*), 12g, mix-fried Radix Glycyrrhizae (*Gan Cao*), 10-15g, Fructus Tritici Aestivi (*Huai Xiao Mai*), 15-30g, Fructus Zizyphi Jujubae (*Da Zao*), 5-15 pieces

If symptoms of liver depression are more pronounced, use: *Xiao Yao San He Gan Mai Da Zao Tang Jia Wei* (Rambling Powder plus Licorice, Wheat & Red Date Decoction with Added Flavors)

Radix Bupleuri (*Chai Hu*), 6g, Herba Menthae Haplocalycis (*Bo He*), 3-6g (added later), Radix Albus Paeoniae Lactiflorae (*Bai Shao*), 10g, Radix Angelicae Sinensis (*Dang Gui*), 10g, Rhizoma Atractylodis Macrocephalae (*Bai Zhu*), 10g, Sclerotium Pararadicis Poriae Cocos (*Fu Shen*), 12g, mix-fried Radix Glycyrrhizae (*Gan Cao*), 10g, Fructus Tritici Aestivi (*Huai Xiao Mai*), 15-30g, Semen Zizyphi Spinosae (*Suan Zao Ren*), 12-15g, Caulis Polygoni Multiflori (*Ye Jiao Teng*), 10-15g, Fructus Zizyphi Jujubae (*Da Zao*), 5 pieces

If complicated by phlegm heat, use: *Wen Dan Tang He Gan Mai Da Zao Tang Jia Jian* (Warm the Gallbladder Decoction plus Licorice, Wheat & Red Date Decoction with Additions & Subtractions)

Lime-processed Rhizoma Pinelliae Ternatae (*Ban Xia*), 10g, Sclerotium Poriae Cocos (*Fu Ling*), 10g, Pericarpium Citri Reticulatae (*Chen Pi*), 6g, Fructus Citri Aurantii (*Zhi Ke*), 6g, Caulis Bambusae In Taeniis (*Zhu Ru*), 6-10g, Radix Glycyrrhizae (*Gan Cao*), 6g, Radix Bupleuri (*Chai Hu*), 6-10g, Radix Albus Paeoniae Lactiflorae (*Bai Shao*), 10g, Rhizoma Cyperi Rotundi (*Xiang Fu*), 10g, Cortex Radicis Moutan (*Dan Pi*), 10g, Fructus Gardeniae Jasminoidis (*Zhi Zi*), 6g, Fructus Tritici Aestivi (*Huai Xiao Mai*), 15-30g, Fructus Zizyphi Jujubae (*Da Zao*), 5 pieces

If heart-spleen dual vacuity is more pronounced, use: *Gui Pi Tang He Gan Mai Da Zao Tang Jia Wei* (Restore the Spleen Decoction plus Licorice, Wheat & Red Date Decoction with Added Flavors)

Radix Astragali Membranacei (*Huang Qi*), 10-15g, Radix Codonopsitis Pilosulae (*Dang Shen*), 10g, Rhizoma Atractylodis Macrocephalae (*Bai Zhu*), 10g, Sclerotium Pararadicis Poriae Cocos (*Fu Shen*), 12g, Radix Angelicae Sinensis (*Dang Gui*), 6-10g, Arillus Euphoriae Longanae (*Long Yan Rou*), 10g, Radix Auklandiae Lappae (*Mu Xiang*), 6g (added later), Radix Polygalae Tenuifoliae (*Yuan Zhi*), 6-10g, Semen Zizyphi Spinosae (*Suan Zao Ren*), 12g, Fructus Tritici Aestivi (*Huai Xiao Mai*), 15-30g, Fructus Zizyphi Jujubae (*Da Zao*), 5 pieces, Rhizoma Acori Graminei (*Shi Chang Pu*), 6g, mix-fried Radix Glycyrrhizae (*Gan Cao*), 10-12g

Decoct in water and administer orally in two divided doses, morning and evening, one *ji* per day.

**ADDITIONS & SUBTRACTIONS:** If there is plum pit qi, add Rhizoma Pinelliae Ternatae (*Ban Xia*) and Cortex Magnoliae Officinalis (*Hou Po*). If there is even more pronounced qi stagnation, add Fructus Citri Sacrodactylis (*Fo Shou*) and Cortex Albizziae Julibrissinisis (*He Huan Pi*). If liver depression has transformed heat, add Cortex Radicis Moutan (*Dan Pi*), Fructus Gardeniae Jasminoidis (*Zhi Zi*), and Radix Scutellariae Baicalensis (*Huang Qin*).

**ACUPUNCTURE:** *Ren Zhong* (GV 26), *Bai Hui* (GV 20), *Nei Guan* (Per 6), *Shen Men* (Ht 7). Use even supplementing and draining technique.

**ADDITIONS & SUBTRACTIONS:** During a hysterical crisis, use *Ren Zhong* (GV 26), *Lao Gong* (Per 8), and *Yong Quan* (Ki 1). For pronounced chest oppression, add *Dan Zhong* (CV 17). For plum pit qi, add *Feng Long* (St 40), *Lian Quan* (CV 23) and *Tong Li* (Ht 5). For heart spirit lack of nourishment, add *Xin Shu* (Bl 15), *Ge Shu* (Bl 17), and *San Yin Jiao* (Sp 6). For abnormal laughing and weeping, add *Hou Xi* (SI 3). For essence spirit abstraction, add *Xin Shu* (Bl 15) and *Hun Men* (Bl 47)

## 2. HEART-LIVER FIRE EFFULGENCE PATTERN

**MAIN SYMPTOMS:** Heart vexation, easy anger, lack of tranquility when sitting or lying down, crying and laughing without constancy, profuse dreams, susceptibility to fright, a red tongue with thin, yellow fur, and a bowstring, fine, rapid pulse

**TREATMENT PRINCIPLES:** Clear the liver and resolve depression, tranquilize the heart and quiet the spirit

**FORMULA & MEDICINALS:** *Dan Zhi Xiao Yao San Jia Wei* (Moutan & Gardenia Rambling Powder with Added Flavors)

Flouritum (*Zhi Shi Ying*), 15g, Os Draconis (*Long Gu*), 12g, Concha Ostreae (*Mu Li*), 12g, Cortex Albizziae Julibrissinis (*He Huan Pi*), 12g, Radix Bupleuri (*Chai Hu*), 9g, Rhizoma Atractylodis Macrocephalae (*Bai Zhu*), 9g, Sclerotium Poriae Cocos (*Fu Ling*), 12g, Radix Angelicae Sinensis (*Dang Gui*), 9g, Radix Albus Paeoniae Lactiflorae (*Bai Shao*), 9g, Cortex Radicis Moutan (*Dan Pi*), 9g, Fructus Gardeniae Jasminoidis (*Shan Zhi*), 9g, mix-fried Radix Glycyrrhizae (*Gan Cao*), 6g

Decoct in water and administer orally in two divided doses, morning and evening, one *ji* per day.

**ADDITIONS & SUBTRACTIONS:** If heart vexation and insomnia are severe, add Magnetitum (*Ci Shi*), Tuber Ophiopogonis Japonici (*Mai Dong*), and Fructus Schisandrae Chinensis (*Wu Wei Zi*). If there is chest and rib-side distention and oppression with a dry mouth and bitter taste, add Radix Scutellariae Baicalensis (*Huang Qin*), uncooked Radix Rehmanniae (*Sheng Di*), and Pericarpium Citri Reticulatae Viride (*Qing Pi*). If there is headache and dizziness, add Concha Haliotidis (*Shi Jue Ming*), Flos Chrysanthemi Morifolii (*Ju Hua*), and Folium Mori Albi (*Sang Ye*).

**ACUPUNCTURE:** *Tai Chong* (Liv 3), *San Yin Jiao* (Sp 6), *Feng Fu* (GV 16), *Shao Fu* (Ht 8). Use draining method.

### 3. LIVER-KIDNEY INSUFFICIENCY PATTERN

**MAIN SYMPTOMS:** Heart vexation, irritability, insomnia, heart palpitations, susceptibility to fright, dry mouth, dry stools, heat in the five hearts, dizziness, tinnitus, low back and knee soreness and limpness, a red tongue with scanty, possibly dry, possibly yellow fur, and a fine, bowstring, rapid or surging, rapid pulse

**TREATMENT PRINCIPLES:** Enrich the kidneys and clear the liver, nourish the heart and quiet the spirit

**FORMULA & MEDICINALS:** For yin vacuity/vacuity heat, use *Bai He Di Tang Wan He Zi Shui Qing Gan Yin* (Lily & Rehmannia Pills plus Enrich Water & Clear the Liver Drink)

Bulbus Lilii (*Bai He*), 10g, uncooked Radix Rehmanniae (*Sheng Di*), 12g, cooked Radix Rehmanniae (*Shu Di*), 12g, Radix Dioscoreae Oppositae (*Shan Yao*), 10g, Fructus Corni Officinalis (*Shan Zhu Yu*), 10g, Cortex Radicis Moutan (*Dan Pi*), 6-10g, Sclerotium Poriae Cocos (*Fu Ling*), 10g, Rhizoma Alismatis (*Ze Xie*), 6-10g, Radix Bupleuri (*Chai Hu*), 3-6g, Radix Albus Paeoniae Lactiflorae (*Bai Shao*), 10g, Fructus Gardeniae Jasminoidis

(*Zhi Zi*), 6-10g, Semen Zizyphi Spinosae (*Suan Zao Ren*), 12-15g, Radix Angelicae Sinensis (*Dang Gui*), 10g

For yin vacuity and yang hyperactivity, use *Tian Ma Gou Teng Yin He Gan Mai Da Zao Tang Jia Wei* (Gastrodia & Uncaria Drink plus Licorice, Wheat & Red Date Decoction with Added Flavors)

Rhizoma Gastrodiae Elatae (*Tian Ma*), 10g, Ramulus Uncariae Cum Uncis (*Gou Teng*), 10g (added later), Cortex Eucommiae Ulmoidis (*Du Zhong*), 10g, Radix Achyranthis Bidentatae (*Niu Xi*), 10g, Concha Haliotidis (*Shi Jue Ming*), 12g (decocted first), uncooked Radix Rehmanniae (*Sheng Di*), 12g, Fructus Gardeniae Jasminoidis (*Zhi Zi*), 6-10g, Radix Scutellariae Baicalensis (*Huang Qin*), 10g, Radix Bupleuri (*Chai Hu*), 3-6g, Sclerotium Pararadicis Poriae Cocos (*Fu Shen*), 12g, Caulis Polygoni Multiflori (*Ye Jiao Teng*), 10-15g, Fructus Tritici Aestivi (*Huai Xiao Mai*), 10-15g, Radix Glycyrrhizae (*Gan Cao*), 6-10g, Fructus Zizyphi Jujubae (*Da Zao*), 5 pieces

For yin vacuity with phlegm fire pattern, use *Wen Dan Tang Jia Wei* (Warm the Gallbladder Decoction with Added Flavors)

Rhizoma Pinelliae Ternatae (*Ban Xia*), 12g, Pericarpium Citri Reticulatae (*Chen Pi*), 9g, Sclerotium Poriae Cocos (*Fu Ling*), 9g, Fructus Immaturus Citri Aurantii (*Zhi Shi*), 6g, Caulis Bambusae In Taeniis (*Zhu Ru*), 9g, bile-processed Rhizoma Arisaematis (*Dan Nan Xing*), 9g, Semen Lepidii Seu Descuraniae (*Ting Li Zi*), 9g, Rhizoma Anemarrheae Aspheloidis (*Zhi Mu*), 9g, Tuber Ophiopogonis Japonici (*Mai Dong*), 12g, Caulis Polygoni Multiflori (*Ye Jiao Teng*), 12g, Radix Glycyrrhizae (*Gan Cao*), 6g, Fructus Zizyphi Jujubae (*Da Zao*), 5 pieces

Decoct in water and administer in two divided doses, morning and evening, one *ji* per day.

**ACUPUNCTURE:** *Ren Zhong* (GV 26), *Bai Hui* (GV 20), *Shen Men* (Ht 7), *Nei Guan* (Per 6), *Tai Xi* (Ki 3), *San Yin Jiao* (Sp 6), *Guan Yuan* (CV 4). Use even supplementing-even draining technique.

**ADDITIONS & SUBTRACTIONS:** If agitation is severe, add *Yong Quan* (Ki 1). If there is pronounced liver depression, add *Tai Chong* (Liv 3) and *Zhi Gou* (TB 6). If liver depression is transforming fire, add *Xing Jian* (Liv 2) and *Xia Xi* (GB 43). If there is chest oppression, add *Dan Zhong* (CV 17). If there is plum pit qi, add *Feng Long* (St 40). If there is accompanying blood stasis, add *Xue Hai* (Sp 10). If there is accompanying phlegm, add *Zhong Wan* (CV 12) and *Feng Long* (St 40).

ABSTRACT OF REPRESENTATIVE
CHINESE RESEARCH:

*Fu Jian Zhong Yi Yao (Fujian Chinese Medicine &
Medicinals)*, #1, 2000, p. 59-60: Lin Fa-kai treated 58
women for visceral agitation with *Bai He Run Fei Tang Jia
Wei* (Lily Moisten the Lungs Decoction with Added
Flavors) between 1988-1996. Twenty of the patients in
this study were 25-35 years old, 15 were 36-46 years old,
and 33 were 47 years old or older. Twelve were unmarried
and 46 were married. In 30 cases, the disease course had
lasted 3-10 months, in 26 cases it had lasted 1-3 years, and
in two cases it had lasted more than three years. Eleven
cases had been previously treated with Chinese medicine,
27 cases had been already treated with Western medicine,
and 20 cases had been treated with both Chinese and
Western medicine.

*Bai He Run Fei Tang Jia Wei* consisted of: Bulbus Lilii
(*Bai He*), 50-100g, stir-fried Rhizoma Atractylodis
Macrocephalae (*Bai Zhu*), Tuber Curcumae (*Yu Jin*),
Fructus Zizyphi Jujubae (*Da Zao*), and Fructus Citri
Sacrodactylis (*Fo Shou*), 12-15g each, Radix Dioscoreae
Oppositae (*Shan Yao*) and Fructus Levis Tritici Aestivi
(*Fu Xiao Mai*), 30g each, Rhizoma Acori Graminei (*Shi
Chang Pu*), Tuber Ophiopogonis Japonici (*Mai Men
Dong*), Radix Polygalae Tenuifoliae (*Yuan Zhi*), stir-fried
Semen Zizyphi Spinosae (*Suan Zao Ren*), and Radix
Glehniae Littoralis (*Sha Shen*), 15g each. If liver qi
depression and binding was relatively severe, Radix
Bupleuri (*Chai Hu*), Radix Albus Paeoniae Lactiflorae
(*Bai Shao*), and Rhizoma Cyperi Rotundi (*Xiang Fu*)
were added. If there was heat phlegm depression and
binding, Bulbus Fritillariae Thunbergii (*Zhe Bei Mu*),
Caulis Bambusae In Taeniis (*Zhu Ru*), and Sclerotium
Pararadicis Poriae Cocos (*Fu Shen*) were added. If there
was constipation, Radix Et Rhizoma Rhei (*Da Huang*),
Semen Pruni (*Yu Li Ren*), and Semen Cannabis Sativae
(*Huo Ma Ren*) were added. If there was yin vacuity with
yang hyperactivity, uncooked Radix Rehmanniae (*Sheng
Di*), Concha Margaritiferae (*Zhen Zhu Mu*), and Tuber
Asparagi Cochinensis (*Tian Men Dong*) were added. If
there was blood stasis obstruction and stagnation, Radix
Salviae Miltiorrhizae (*Dan Shen*), Caulis Milletiae Seu
Spatholobi (*Ji Xue Teng*), and Herba Lycopi Lucidi (*Ze
Lan*) were added. One *ji* was decocted in water and
administered per day, and two weeks equaled one course
of treatment. During the time these medicinals were
administered, patients were forbidden to eat acrid, peppery foods or to drink alcohol.

After administering 2-5 courses of the above medicinals,
41 cases were judged cured. This meant that their psyches
had returned to normal, their symptoms had disappeared,
and there was no recurrence when followed up in 1999.
Fourteen cases got some effect. This meant that their psyches had returned to normal, their symptoms had disappeared, but there was one or more recurrences after one
year of stopping treatment. Three cases experienced no
effect. This meant that their psychological symptoms
were the same as before starting treatment or that any
improvements were only transitory. Thus, the total amelioration rate was 91.66%. In closing, the author mentioned that it was his opinion that most cases of female
visceral agitation are due to liver qi depression and binding but that the heart and lungs are also intimately
involved.

REPRESENTATIVE CASE HISTORIES:

### ❖ CASE 1[1] ❖

The patient was a 17 year old female who was first examined on Jul. 31, 1967. In the last month, due to her emotions not being fulfilled, the patient complained of
insomnia, chest oppression, outbreaks of crying, and lack
of constancy of joy and anger. At times when this was
severe, there were spasms and contractions, stiffness of
the four limbs, and essence spirit rigidity. Typically, it
was excessive thinking, anxiety, and worry that afterwards easily caused an outbreak of this disease. The
amount of food eaten was less than normal, but her two
excretions and her menses were mostly normal. Her
tongue fur was thin and white, and her pulse was deep
and fine.

The patient's pattern was discriminated as liver depression
not soothed causing the onset of visceral agitation. Based
on the treatment principles of soothing the liver and
resolving depression, loosening the chest and rectifying
the qi, she was treated with two formulas. The first formula consisted of: *Dan Zhong* (CV 17), *Zhong Wan* (CV
12), *Qi Hai* (CV 6), *Nei Guan* (Per 6), *He Gu* (LI 4), *Zu
San Li* (St 36), *Tai Chong* (Liv 3). The second formula was
Five Viscera Transports Plus *Ge Shu* Formula, *i.e.*, *Fei Shu*
(Bl 13), *Xin Shu* (Bl 15), *Ge Shu* (Bl 17), *Gan Shu* (Bl 18),
*Pi Shu* (Bl 20), and *Shen Shu* (Bl 23). These two formulas
were used alternately, one time every other day with
draining technique.

After needling five times according to the above methods,
the chest oppression and suffocating feeling were somewhat decreased. Spasms and contractions had not
occurred in the last two weeks. Therefore, the above treatment methods were continued three more times. At that
time, her chest oppression was eliminated and her sleep

was quiet and good. Her affect had taken a turn for the better, and she talked and laughed freely. She was then prescribed *Ping Gan Shu Luo Wan* (Level the Liver & Soothe the Network Vessels Pills), one pill each time, two times per day. After 20 pills, her clinical condition was judged cured.

### ❖ CASE 2[2] ❖

This patient was a 29 year old female who was first examined on May 21, 1968. In the last month, the patient had been crying and laughing without constancy. There was also dizziness, insomnia, vexation and agitation, chest region suffocation and oppression, excessive thinking, excessive worry, excessive paranoia, susceptibility to sighing, essence spirit abstraction, easy fright and fear, no desire to eat or drink, dry stools, and yellow urine. Her expression was apathetic. Her tongue fur was thin and white, while her pulse was deep, fine, and bowstring. Based on these signs and symptoms, her pattern discrimination was liver depression qi stagnation causing the onset of visceral agitation. The treatment principles were to soothe the liver and resolve depression. Based on these principles, she was treated with the following formula: *Bai Hui* (GV 20), *Dan Zhong* (CV 17), *Nei Guan* (Per 6), *He Gu* (LI 4), *Tai Chong* (Liv 3) with draining technique.

After needling two times with the above formula, her chest region suffocation and oppression were greatly reduced, but there was still essence spirit abstraction. Sometimes the patient walked aimlessly about the room and did not like to make contact with others. Therefore, the same formula was administered four more times, by which time the chest oppression had already been eliminated and her vexation and agitation were greatly reduced. Her abnormal crying and laughing no longer occurred. Therefore, acupuncture was stopped while observing her condition. On follow-up, there had been no recurrence and she was able to work again.

### ❖ CASE 3[3] ❖

The patient was a 30 year old female who was first examined on Aug. 12, 1967. Due to her emotions not being fulfilled, the patient had essence spirit abstraction, chest oppression and suffocation, tension, agitation, and disquietude, laughing and crying without constancy, excessive paranoia, fright, and fear, and auditory hallucinations for the past two years. There was also disquieted sleep at night, easily being aroused, profuse dreaming, head distention and pain, lack of strength in the four limbs, poor appetite, and delayed, scanty, purplish colored menstruation. Her facial complexion was yellowish white and lus-

terless. Her tongue fur was thin, white, and slightly slimy. Her pulse was deep and fine. The pattern discrimination in this case was liver depression not soothed and heart-spleen both damaged causing the onset of visceral agitation. The treatment principles used were to supplement and boost the heart and spleen, soothe the liver and resolve depression. Two formulas were used. The first formula was Five Viscera Transports Plus *Ge Shu* Formula plus *Bai Hui* (GV 20). The second formula consisted of: *Zhong Wan* (CV 12), *Qi Hai* (CV 6), *Nei Guan* (Per 6), *San Yin Jiao* (Sp 6), *Shen Men* (Ht 7), *Zu San Li* (St 36), and *Tai Chong* (Liv 3). These two formulas were used alternately and needled twice each week with supplementing technique.

After two months of acupuncture, the auditory hallucinations had disappeared, her emotions were comparatively quiet and still, and her outbreaks of sadness and crying were reduced. Her sleep took a turn for the better, and her nighttime dreaming was less. Acupuncture treatment was continued for two whole months. After this, the outbreaks of excessive paranoia were markedly diminished, and her sleep was markedly improved, while her mood was happy. Again the original formulas were used to treat another two months, and all the remaining symptoms disappeared. Clinically, her disease condition was judged cured. Ttreatment was, therefore, ceased to observe her condition. The patient recovered and went back to work, and the condition did not recur.

### ❖ CASE 4[4] ❖

The patient was a 38 year old, married female peasant farmer who was hospitalized on Jun. 13, 1978. Five years previously, the patient's sister-in-law had hit her in a fight. At that time, the patient had fainted, her four limbs had become rigid, and her hands and feet had spasmed. After she awakened, she cried and laughed without constancy and weeped and wailed. She developed insomnia and was vexed, anxious, and restless. Then suddenly she was like a normal person again. In the past year she had again had frequent bouts of anxiety, each day having several such episodes. After these bouts receded, she felt as if her head were clouded and her brain distended. In addition, there was chest and rib-side discomfort and fullness, easy anger, and occasional hiccups. She had been diagnosed at a hospital in Xian with hysteria and treated but without success. At the time of the authors' examination, the patient's facial complexion was greenish blue, her tongue was red with white fur, and her pulse was bowstring.

Based on the above signs and symptoms, this woman's Chinese disease was diagnosed as visceral agitation and her pattern was categorized as liver qi not soothed resulting in heart spirit disturbance. The treatment principles were to soothe the liver and regulate the qi, downbear counterflow and course depression. Therefore, the patient was prescribed *Chen Xiang Jiang Qi Tang Jia Wei* (Aquilaria Downbear Counterflow Decoction with Added Flavors): Lignum Aquilariae Agallochae (*Chen Xiang*), 9g, Fructus Meliae Toosendan (*Chuan Lian Zi*), 10g, Rhizoma Cyperi Rotundi (*Xiang Fu*), 10g, Fructus Amomi (*Sha Ren*), 5g, mix-fried Radix Glycyrrhizae (*Gan Cao*), 6g, Fructus Tritici Aestivi (*Huai Xiao Mai*), 30g, stir-fried Semen Zizyphi Spinosae (*Suan Zao Ren*), 18g, Radix Polygalae Tenuifoliae (*Yuan Zhi*), 6g, Fructus Zizyphi Jujubae (*Da Zao*), 5 pieces, and Cinnabar (*Zhu Sha*), 2g.

After taking nine *ji* of the above formula, the woman's emotions became more stable. She was able to sleep for 5-6 hours each night. However, she still had occasional hiccups and her four limbs emitted coolness. Thus 10 grams of Flos Inulae Racemosae (*Xuan Fu Hua*) and 7 grams of vinegar stir-fried Fructus Evodiae Rutecarpae (*Wu Zhu Yu*) were added to her formula to downbear counterflow and stop vomiting, warm the center and scatter cold. After taking 25 *ji* of this formula, all the woman's symptoms had disappeared and she was discharged from the hospital with 60 *Xiao Yao Wan* (Rambling Pills). The patient was instructed to take one pill each morning and evening on an empty stomach. On follow-up after two years, there had been no recurrence.

### ❖ CASE 5⁵ ❖

The patient was a 28 year old, married woman who was hospitalized on May 5, 1979. Three years before, the patient had gotten in an argument and been hit. Since then, her indignation and anger had not been resolved. Initially once every two months and now once every 2-3 days she would collapse to the ground and pound the earth, incessantly yelling and crying. Sometimes she would hit people or curse at them. She acted as if she were possessed, and several shaman had tried treating her for spirit possession but without success. Eventually the woman's condition got so bad she was brought to the hospital where she was diagnosed as suffering from hysteria. However, Western medication was also not markedly helpful. The patient's facial complexion was greenish yellow. Her intake was scanty and her stools were loose. There was counterflowing chilling of her four limbs, her tongue was red with thin, white fur, and her pulse was bowstring and moderate or relaxed (*i.e.*, slightly slow).

Based on the above signs and symptoms, the authors of

this case diagnosed her traditional Chinese disease as visceral agitation and her pattern was categorized as liver-spleen disharmony. The treatment principles were to soothe the liver and rectify the qi, regulate and harmonize the liver and spleen. Therefore, the prescription consisted of *Xiao Yao San Jia Jian* (Rambling Powder with Additions & Subtractions): Radix Angelicae Sinensis (*Dang Gui*), 30g, stir-fried Radix Albus Paeoniae Lactiflorae (*Bai Shao*), 18g, Radix Bupleuri (*Chai Hu*), 10g, Sclerotium Poriae Cocos (*Fu Ling*), 15g, Rhizoma Atractylodis Macrocephalae (*Bai Zhu*), 10g, Radix Glycyrrhizae (*Gan Cao*), 6g, uncooked Rhizoma Zingiberis (*Sheng Jiang*), 3g, Fructus Zizyphi Jujubae (*Da Zao*), 3 pieces, Radix Auklandiae Lappae (*Mu Xiang*), 6g, Rhizoma Cyperi Rotundi (*Xiang Fu*), 10g, and Radix Et Rhizoma Nardostachydis (*Gan Song*), 9g.

After taking 20 *ji* of the above formula, the woman's symptoms were reduced by half. Therefore, she was given 60 *Xiao Yao Wan* (Rambling Pills) and instructed to take one pill each morning. She was also given 60 *Xiang Sha Yang Wei Wan* (Auklandia & Amomum Nourish the Stomach Pills) and instructed to take one pill of these every night in order to continue regulating and rectifying her condition. On follow-up after two years, there had been no recurrence.

### ❖ CASE 6⁶ ❖

The patient was a 23 year old, married female homemaker who was admitted to the hospital on Oct. 14, 1980. One month before she had gotten into an argument. Since then she tended to be sorrowful, cried a lot, was paranoid, and had insomnia and profuse dreams. The patient was easily agitated, had torpid intake, a bitter taste in her mouth, and short, reddish urine. The patient had already been treated with hydrotherapy and with Chinese medicinals for quieting the spirit and stabilizing the mind as well as coursing the liver and rectifying the qi, picking out phlegm and clearing heat. However, none of these treatments had been successful. Therefore the patient was referred to the authors of this case. When seen by the authors, the patient had lassitude of the spirit, lack of strength, a red tongue with redder tip and faintly yellow fur, and a deep, fine, rapid pulse. She said she desired to eat but could not eat and desired to sleep but could not sleep.

Based on the above signs and symptoms, the patient's Chinese disease was diagnosed as visceral agitation and her pattern was categorized as yin vacuity with yang hyperactivity. The treatment principles were to enrich yin and clear heat, nourish the heart and quiet the spirit.

Therefore, she was prescribed *Bai He Di Huang Tang He Gan Mai Da Zao Tang Jia Jian* (Lily & Rehmannia Decoction plus Licorice, Wheat & Red Date Decoction with Additions & Subtractions): Bulbus Lilii (*Bai He*), 60g, uncooked Radix Rehmanniae (*Sheng Di*), 15g, uncooked Radix Glycyrrhizae (*Gan Cao*), 10g, Fructus Tritici Aestivi (*Huai Xiao Mai*), 20g, Sclerotium Poriae Cocos (*Fu Ling*), 15g, and stir-fried Semen Zizyphi Spinosae (*Suan Zao Ren*), 20g.

After taking three *ji* of the above formula, all the patient's symptoms were decreased greatly by half, while her sorrow and crying were already eliminated. Her urination was free-flowing, and her mouth and center were both harmonious. Although she was able to eat, the amount was still scanty however. In addition, she was able to go to sleep. Therefore, 24 grams of uncooked Concha Ostreae (*Mu Li*) were added to her prescription in order to assist yin and subdue yang. After taking six *ji* of this formula, all the patient's symptoms had disappeared and her mental-emotional state returned to normal. Her eating and drinking increased and her sleep was appropriately calm. Because her affect was still slightly apprehensive, she was told to take one pill of *Bai He Wan* (Lily Pills) each morning and one pill of *Zhi Bai Di Huang Wan* (Anemarrhena & Phellodendron Rehmannia Pills) each night. Then she was discharged from the hospital.

### ❖ CASE 7[7] ❖

The patient was a 38 year old woman who became abnormally sorrowful after the sudden death of her son. This continued for a long time without her returning to normal. Each afternoon and evening she would talk to herself and laugh and cry without constancy. She was able to go to sleep at night, but she would wake several times each night in a fright. In addition, she complained of heart palpitations, restlessness, vexation and agitation, and essence spirit abstraction. However, from early morning to noon she was like a normal person. This had been going on for the past two months. She had received previous treatment. Due to this, sometimes she was better, sometimes she was worse, and definitely this treatment had not been able to secure her condition. At her examination, it was found that the woman had hypochondral distention and discomfort, dry mouth but no desire to drink, a tendency to great sighing, and easy excitement. Her pulse was rapid and large but forceless, while her tongue fur was slimy and white. Therefore, her pattern was categorized as heart-liver blood vacuity with blood dryness and liver tension and simultaneous phlegm and heat. For this, the patient was prescribed three *ji* of *Gan Cao Xie Xin Tang* (Licorice Drain the

Heart Decoction): mix-fried Radix Glycyrrhizae (*Gan Cao*), 30g, Rhizoma Pinelliae Ternatae (*Ban Xia*), 10g, Radix Codonopsitis Pilosulae (*Dang Shen*), 15g, dry Rhizoma Zingiberis (*Gan Jiang*), 6g, Rhizoma Coptidis Chinensis (*Huang Lian*), 5g, and Radix Scutellariae Baicalensis (*Huang Qin*), 10g. After this, the patient's symptoms were markedly improved. Hence another 10 *ji* of this formula were prescribed and the patient was completely cured.

### ❖ CASE 8[8] ❖

The patient was a 32 year old, married cadre who was first examined in June 1995. Due to constant arguing, the patient had become emotionally depressed. Gradually she developed bouts of sorrow and crying. She had already been treated with both Chinese and Western medicine for one year. However, when her condition did not heal, she came to see the author of the article from which this case is taken. At the time the patient was examined, she laughed and cried without constancy, was unable to control herself, had a tendency to sighing, and experienced heart vexation and lability. Both rib-sides were distended and painful, her menstruation was irregular, and her stools were not crisp. In addition, her urine was reddish yellow, her tongue was pale red with yellow fur, and her pulse was bowstring, fine, and rapid.

Based on the above, the patient's pattern was categorized as liver qi depression and binding transforming fire. This fire had "killed" the stomach, scorched the lungs, and accumulated in the heart. The treatment principles were to course the liver and boost the stomach, moisten the lungs and clear the heart. *Bai He Run Fei Tang Jia Wei* (Lily Moisten the Lungs Decoction with Added Flavors) was used for these purposes. It consisted of: Bulbus Lilii (*Bai He*), 100g, Fructus Levis Tritici Aestivi (*Fu Xiao Mai*), 30g, Radix Dioscoreae Oppositae (*Shan Yao*), 30g, stir-fried Semen Zizyphi Spinosae (*Suan Zao Ren*), 15g, Tuber Curcumae (*Yu Jin*), 10g, stir-fried Rhizoma Atractylodis Macrocephalae (*Bai Zhu*), 15g, mix-fried Radix Glycyrrhizae (*Gan Cao*), 6g, Radix Albus Paeoniae Lactiflorae (*Bai Shao*), 12g, Fructus Meliae Toosendan (*Chuan Lian Zi*), 9g, Fructus Citri Sacrodactylis (*Fo Shou*), Rhizoma Acori Graminei (*Shi Chang Pu*), and vinegar-processed Radix Bupleuri (*Chai Hu*), 12g each, and Fructus Zizyphi Jujubae (*Da Zao*), 7 pieces.

After one course of treatment, the patient's crying and laughing no longer occurred and her psyche returned to normal. Therefore, the original formula was continued for another two courses, after which she was judged cured. On follow-up at the end of 1999, there had been no recurrence.

## ENDNOTES

[1] Yu Hui-chan & Han Fu-ru, *Golden Needle Wang Le-ting: A 20th Century Master's Approach to Acupuncture*, trans. by Shuai Xuezhong, Blue Poppy Press, Boulder, CO, 1997, p. 171-172

[2] *Ibid.*, p. 172-173

[3] *Ibid.*, p. 173-174

[4] Li & Liu, *op. cit.*, p. 526-527

[5] *Ibid.*, p. 528-529

[6] *Ibid.*, p. 533-534

[7] Chen & Zhao, *op. cit.*, p. 166

[8] Lin Fa-kai, "The Treatment of 56 Cases of Female Visceral Agitation with *Bai He Run Fei Tang Jia Wei* (Lily Moisten the Lungs Decoction with Added Flavors)," *Fu Jian Zhong Yi Yao (Fujian Chinese Medicine & Medicinals)*, #1, 2000, p. 59-60

# ❖ 20 ❖

# RUNNING PIGLET

Running piglet, *ben tun*, refers to a subjective sensation of upsurge from the lower abdomen to the chest and possibly even the throat. This is typically accompanied by gripping abdominal pain, chest oppression, rapid breathing, dizziness, heart palpitations, and heart vexation. The term is first found in the *Ling Shu (Spiritual Axis)* where it is considered a minor form of bone withdrawal or bone epileptiform disease.[1]

> If kidney vessel cramping is severe, this is bone withdrawal disease. If there is faint cramping, this is deep reversal running piglet.

In the *Nan Jing (Classic of Difficulties)*, running piglet is one of the *wu ji* or five accumulations.

> Kidney accumulation is called running piglet. It emits from the lower abdomen and ascends to reach below the heart. It is pig-like in form.

Because the *Su Wen (Simple Questions)* refers to kidney accumulation as "thoroughfare mounting," running piglet and thoroughfare mounting have mostly become synonymous.

This Chinese disease category includes symptom patterns that contain somatic complaints but few or no accompanying emotional or psychological symptoms. Palpitations that begin at the level of the umbilicus and ascend, irregular or intermittent pulse, or a "subjective sensation of upsurge" from the lower abdomen to the chest and throat, dizziness and sensations of coldness at the extremities appear to be core characteristics of the variant symptom patterns described. Although these symptom patterns do not match discrete syndromes in contemporary Western medicine or psychiatry, many apparent similarities exist between symptom descriptions in these two disparate paradigms. Core features of panic attacks (see Chapter 6, Fear & Fright, this Book) are remarkably close to the Chinese medical patterns of running piglet. An apparent distinction is the pronounced absence of associated fear or anxiety symptoms which are central to a diagnosis of panic disorder.

Other patterns included under running piglet also resemble features of certain somatoform disorders in contemporary Western psychiatry, including conversion disorder and pain disorder. In addition to primary psychiatric disorders, consideration must be given to acute or chronic medical disorders that sometimes manifest as irregular heartbeat, dizziness, distressing sensations in the abdomen or precordial area, and coldness in the extremities. Among other possible medical etiologies, myocardial infarction, cardiac arrhythmias, hyperthyroidism, metabolic derangements, esophageal reflux, and disorders of autonomic regulation (dysautonomias) often manifest as symptom patterns that are similar to those described under running piglet.

## NOSOLOGY:

A panic attack is characterized by sudden-onset of feelings of intense fear or dread accompanied by signs of autonomic arousal, such as increased heart rate, shortness of breath, perspiration and dizziness. An enduring pattern or panic attacks that are not cued by identifiable stresses may point to a diagnosis of panic disorder if medical etiologies and substance abuse have been eliminated as possible causes and prominent symptoms of anticipatory anxiety occur between panic attacks. Somatoform disorders are reviewed in detail in Book 3, Chapter 9. In overview, conversion disorder, pain disorder, and others included in this broad nosologic category are characterized by persisting somatic complaints in the absence of substantiating medical findings. The individual experiences significant social or occupational impairment and symptoms are not intentionally created or feigned (*i.e.*, unlike factitious disorder or malingering). As conceptualized in Western psychiatry, panic attacks and numerous somatic complaints frequently occur in the context of other major psychiatric disorders, including schizophrenia and other psychotic disorders, major depressive disorder, and the spectrum of anxiety disorders.

## DIFFERENTIAL DIAGNOSIS:

Before assuming that a symptom pattern is psychogenic in origin, reasonable attempts must be made to rule out potentially serious medical causes, including cardiac arrhythmias, disorders of the stomach (or other organs including the esophagus), and disorders of the autonomic nervous system. A thorough history and routine electrocardiogram (EKG) will frequently verify or rule out underlying medical disease. Specialized laboratory tests may be required to rule out other disorders, including hyperthyroidism, other endocrinological disorders, and metabolic derangements. Medication side effects as well as alcohol or illicit substance abuse must also be ruled out as causes of anxiety or somatic symptoms.

When probable medical etiologies have been excluded, the psychiatric differential diagnosis is further clarified by a detailed psychiatric history in order to determine whether panic attacks or other somatic complaints represent the core problem or are associated with another primary psychiatric disorder. The presence of two or more psychiatric disorders further complicates this task. The clinician must then determine whether and how specific somatic complaints are related to one or both disorders. For example, when panic attacks do not occur in the context of a pervasive pattern of other anxiety symptoms, depression or psychosis, the most likely diagnosis is panic disorder. Conversely, post-traumatic stress disorder (PTSD) is characterized by panic attacks that are evoked by vivid memories of a life-threatening event (flashbacks) or a location or situation that reminds the individual of a previous trauma. In a simi-

| DIFFERENTIAL DIAGNOSIS | | |
|---|---|---|
| **1. MEDICAL DISORDERS** | **2. EFFECTS OF SUBSTANCES** | **3. PSYCHIATRIC DISORDERS** |
| A. DISORDERS OF THE HEART, INCLUDING ARRHYTHMIAS | A. ALCOHOL OR ILLICIT SUBSTANCE INTOXICATION OR WITHDRAWAL | A. PANIC DISORDER |
| B. DISORDERS OF THE STOMACH AND UPPER GASTROINTESTINAL TRACT | B. SIDE EFFECTS OF MEDICATIONS | B. POST-TRAUMATIC STRESS DISORDER (PTSD) |
| C. DISORDERS OF THE AUTONOMIC NERVOUS SYSTEM | | C. SOMATOFORM DISORDER |
| D. HYPERTHYROIDISM | | D. MAJOR DEPRESSIVE EPISODE WITH SOMATIZATION |
| E. OTHER ENDOCRINOLOGICAL DISORDERS | | E. SCHIZOPHRENIA OR OTHER PSYCHOTIC DISORDERS |
| F. METABOLIC DERANGEMENTS | | F. GENERALIZED ANXIETY DISORDER (GAD) |
| G. NEUROLOGIC DISORDERS, INCLUDING MULTIPLE SCLEROSIS (MS) | | G. MALINGERING |
| H. CHRONIC PAIN SYNDROMES | | H. FACTITIOUS DISORDER |
| I. DISORDERS CAUSING SEXUAL DYSFUNCTION | | |
| J. SYSTEMIC LUPUS ERYTHEMATOSUS (SLE) | | |
| K. ACUTE INTERMITTENT PORPHYRIA | | |

lar manner, persisting somatic complaints that have no identified medical basis and occur in isolation from other psychiatric symptoms point to a somatoform disorder as the most likely diagnosis. The particular somatoform disorder will be determined by the specific symptom pattern observed. Book 3, Chapter 9 reviews diagnostic criteria for several representative somatoform disorders. When somatic symptoms occur primarily or exclusively in the context of a broader pattern of symptoms that is characteristic of another primary psychiatric disorder, contemporary Western psychiatry views those somatic complaints as secondary to that disorder. In Western psychiatric nosology, a somatoform disorder and another major psychiatric disorder may be diagnosed concurrently (with some exceptions) when symptom patterns fulfilling diagnostic criteria for two disorders are simultaneously present.

## ETIOLOGY & PATHOPHYSIOLOGY:

Subjective sensations associated with cardiac arrhythmias, myocardial infarction, and disorders of the upper gastrointestinal system commonly lead to feelings of distress and anxiety and can evoke full-blown panic attacks in susceptible individuals. Dysregulation of the autonomic nervous system can be caused by a tumor, infection, metabolic or endocrinological disorders, medication side-effects, and substance abuse or withdrawal. Distressing somatic symptoms and anxiety are frequent concomitants of autonomic dysregulation.

## WESTERN MEDICAL TREATMENT:

When sensations of running piglet are due to medical as opposed to psychiatric causes, Western medical treatment consists of treating the underlying medical etiology. For information on the Western medical treatment, prognosis, short and long-term advantages and disadvantages, and indications for referral to Western medical services for the psychiatric causes of this disorder, see Book 2, Chapter 6, Fear & Fright, and Book 3, Chapter 7, Anxiety Disorders.

## CHINESE DISEASE CAUSES & DISEASE MECHANISMS:

There are three major mechanisms of this condition, all of which involve upward counterflow. The first is upward counterflow due to heart yang insufficiency with external assailing of cold evils resulting in the thoroughfare qi counterflowing upward. In the *Shang Han Lun* (*Treatise on Damage [Due to] Cold*), heart yang vacuity is seen as mainly due to iatrogenesis. Profuse sweating, either due to moxibustion or medicinal therapy, results in loss of not only sweat but heart qi and yang, since "sweat is the fluid of the heart."

> When the heart yang is sufficient, it settles and contains the kidney water, preventing it from flooding. If the heart yang is damaged, it is unable to control the kidney water which begins to move. Movement of the kidney water is felt as palpitations below the umbilicus and it may be followed by running piglet.[2]

However, heart yang vacuity may also be due to overtaxation, enduring disease, and debility due to aging. In that case, running piglet disease may be provoked by sudden or intense fear or fright.

The second mechanism associated with running piglet is due to spleen yang insufficiency with water qi ascending and intimidating. Spleen yang vacuity may be due to aging, enduring disease, unregulated eating and drinking, and iatrogenesis. And the third mechanism of running piglet is due to liver qi surging and counterflowing. Liver qi surging and counterflowing may be due to unfulfilled desires, anger, and frustration causing qi stagnation. Because the qi is yang, when it becomes stagnant and accumulates, it may counterflow upward. It may also be due to liver yin insufficiency failing to control yang which then counterflows upward. Liver yin vacuity may be due to aging, excessive blood and/or fluid loss, enduring heat damaging yin fluids, long-term "recreational" drug use, and iatrogenesis.

In real life, because the close interrelationships between the spleen and heart and spleen and liver, it is not so easy to discriminate such clear-cut, simple patterns. Spleen vacuity may lead to heart vacuity, and liver depression typically complicates spleen vacuity. However, it is extreme emotional stress and especially fear or fright which set the stage for this traditional Chinese disease.

## TREATMENT BASED ON PATTERN DISCRIMINATION:

### 1. HEART YANG VACUITY WITH UPSURGING OF YIN COLD QI OF THE KIDNEYS PATTERN

MAIN SYMPTOMS: Palpitations below the umbilicus ascending to below the heart, shortness of breath, chilled limbs, possible cyanosis of the nails and chest pain, a dark, possibly purplish tongue, and a possibly regularly intermittent pulse

TREATMENT PRINCIPLES: Warm and free the flow of heart yang, level upsurge and downbear counterflow

FORMULA & MEDICINALS: *Gui Zhi Jia Gui Tang* (Cinnamon Twig Plus Cinnamon Decoction)

Ramulus Cinnamomi Cassiae (*Gui Zhi*), 15g, Radix Albus Paeoniae Lactiflorae (*Bai Shao*), 10g, mix-fried Radix Glycyrrhizae (*Gan Cao*), 10g, Fructus Zizyphi Jujubae (*Da Zao*), 12 pieces, uncooked Rhizoma Zingiberis (*Sheng Jiang*), 3 slices

Decoct in water and administer orally in two divided doses, morning and evening, one *ji* per day.

ADDITIONS & SUBTRACTIONS: If leveling kidney evils, use Cortex Cinnamomi Cassiae (*Rou Gui*). If resolving tai yang evils, use Cinnamon Twigs.

ACUPUNCTURE: *Xin Shu* (Bl 15), *Shen Shu* (Bl 23), *Guan Yuan* (CV 4). Moxa all three points in this order.

## 2. SPLEEN YANG INSUFFICIENCY WITH WATER QI ASCENDING & INTIMIDATING PATTERN

MAIN SYMPTOMS: Palpitations below the abdomen which may stretch to below the heart, fatigue, lack of strength, counterflow chilling of the four limbs, loose stools, edema, the sound of water sloshing about under the heart, a swollen, pale tongue with teeth-marks on its edges and thin, white, slimy fur, and a weak, faint, moderate (*i.e.*, slightly slow), or even a slow pulse

TREATMENT PRINCIPLES: Warm and supplement spleen yang, seep water, level upsurging, and downbear counterflow

FORMULA & MEDICINALS: *Ling Gui Cao Zao Tang* (Poria, Cinnamon, Licorice & Red Dates Decoction)

Sclerotium Poriae Cocos (*Fu Ling*), 25g, Ramulus Cinnamomi Cassiae (*Gui Zhi*), 12g, mix-fried Radix Glycyrrhizae (*Gan Cao*), 6g, Fructus Zizyphi Jujubae (*Da Zao*), 15 pieces

Decoct in water and administer orally in two divided doses, morning and evening, one *ji* per day.

ACUPUNCTURE: *Xin Shu* (Bl 15), *Pi Shu* (Bl 20), *Wei Shu* (Bl 21), *Shui Fen* (CV 9), *Da Ling* (Per 7). Moxa the first four points in this order and needle the last point with draining method.

## 3. LIVER QI COUNTERFLOWING UPWARD PATTERN

MAIN SYMPTOMS: Periumbilical palpitations followed by an upsurging of qi from the abdomen to the sternum when the patient becomes upset, chilled limbs and body when nervous but restoration of the heat in the limbs when relaxed and at ease, heart palpitations, white, slimy tongue fur, and a bowstring pulse which tends to be hooked, *i.e.*, floating in the inch and deep in the cubit

TREATMENT PRINCIPLES: Level the liver and downbear upward counterflow

FORMULA & MEDICINALS: *Ben Tun Tang Jia Jian* (Running Piglet Decoction with Additions & Subtractions)

Radix Albus Paeoniae Lactiflorae (*Bai Shao*), 18g, Rhizoma Pinelliae Ternatae (*Ban Xia*), 12g, Radix Albus Paeoniae Lactiflorae (*Bai Shao*), 10g, Radix Angelicae Sinensis (*Dang Gui*), 10g, Radix Puerariae (*Ge Gen*), 10g, Lignum Aquilariae Agallochae (*Chen Xiang*), 10g, Radix Ligustici Wallichii (*Chuan Xiong*), 10g, Radix Glycyrrhizae (*Gan Cao*), 10g, uncooked Rhizoma Zingiberis (*Sheng Jiang*), 7 pieces

Decoct in water and administer orally in two divided doses, morning and evening, one *ji* per day.

ADDITIONS & SUBTRACTIONS: If liver depression qi stagnation has transformed into depressive heat, add Radix Scutellariae Baicalensis (*Huang Qin*).

ACUPUNCTURE: *Tai Chong* (Liv 3), *Dan Zhong* (CV 17), *Nei Guan* (Per 6), *Gong Sun* (Sp 4)

## 4. LIVER YIN INSUFFICIENCY WITH LIVER QI SURGING & COUNTERFLOWING PATTERN

MAIN SYMPTOMS: A feeling of qi flowing upward from the lower abdomen, chest oppression, throat tightness, dizziness, vertigo, thin or emaciated body, dry, rough eyes, thin tongue with scanty fluids and scanty or even peeled fur, and a bowstring, fine, rapid pulse

TREATMENT PRINCIPLES: Enrich yin and nourish the blood, level surging and downbear counterflow

FORMULA & MEDICINALS: *Yi Guan Jian Jia Wei* (One Link Decoction with Added Flavors)

Radix Glehniae Littoralis (*Sha Shen*), 15-20g, uncooked Radix Rehmanniae (*Sheng Di*), 15-20g, Fructus Lycii

Chinensis (*Gou Qi Zi*), 12-15g, Tuber Ophiopogonis Japonici (*Mai Dong*), 10-12g, Radix Angelicae Sinensis (*Dang Gui*), 10-12g, Fructus Meliae Toosendan (*Chuan Lian Zi*), 10g, Haemititum (*Dai Zhe Shi*), 10g

Decoct in water and administer orally in two divided doses, morning and evening, one *ji* per day.

**ADDITIONS & SUBTRACTIONS:** For a dry mouth with a bitter taste, add Rhizoma Coptidis Chinensis (*Huang Lian*). For constipation, add Semen Biotae Orientalis (*Bai Zi Ren*) and Fructus Citri Aurantii (*Zhi Ke*).

**ACUPUNCTURE:** *Tai Xi* (Ki 3), *San Yin Jiao* (Sp 6), *Tai Chong* (Liv 3), *Guan Yuan* (CV 4), *Qi Hai* (CV 6), *Dan Zhong* (CV 17), *Da Ling* (Per 7). Use even supplementing-even draining technique on the first five points and draining method on the last two.

**CLINICAL TIPS:** This condition is not unfrequently experienced by Western patients who lack a medical label for it. Therefore, it is the authors' experience that it commonly goes unreported. However, when reported, it does typically respond well to acupuncture. It is rarely, if ever, Western patients' major complaint, and it is typically only discovered by careful questioning and reframing. For instance, a Western patient may simply gloss over this symptom by saying that they have been gassy lately.

**ABSTRACT OF CHINESE RESEARCH:**

*He Nan Zhong Yi (Henan Chinese Medicine)*, #3, 2000, p. 62-63: Du Qiu-yao and Wang Lin treated 26 patients with running piglet qi with acupuncture-moxibustion. Sixteen of these patients were males and 10 were female. The youngest was 13 and the oldest was 66 years of age. In 18 case, their pattern was liver-kidney qi counterflow, while in the other eight cases, their pattern was cold water counterflowing upward. Treatment consisted of needling *Qi Hai* (CV 6) and *Guan Yuan* (CV 4). If there was liver-kidney qi counterflow, *Zhang Men* (Liv 13), *Tai Chong* (Liv 3), *Gong Sun* (Sp 4), and *Nei Guan* (Per 6) were added. If there was cold water counterflowing upward, *Dan Zhong* (CV 17), *San Yin Jiao* (Sp 6), and *Qi Chong* (St 30) were added. *Qi Hai* and *Tai Chong* were moxaed with sparrow-pecking method. *Nei Guan* was needled with even supplementing-even draining technique. *Zhang Men* and *Gong Sun* were needled with draining method. *Guan Yuan* was indirectly moxaed over ginger. *Qi Chong* was moxaed with sparrow-pecking technique, and *Dan Zhong* was needled with draining method.

Using the above protocol, 20 patients were cured. This meant that, after one course of treatment, all their symptoms disappeared and there was no recurrence on follow-up after one year. Improvement meant that, after two courses of treatment, the symptoms basically disappeared, but there was a recurrence within one year. However, all the symptoms were markedly less. Based on these criteria, the remaining six cases were judged improved. Thus the total amelioration rate was 100%.

**REPRESENTATIVE CASE HISTORIES:**

### ❖ CASE 1[3] ❖

The patient was a 64 year old female homemaker. During the summer months of 1996, while sitting on a small stool outside her apartment to take advantage of the cool evening, suddenly, a neighbor's small dog came up behind her, jumped up on her back, and knocked her to the ground. The next day she began to have abdominal distention and vomiting. This continued and became a sensation of qi surging from her lower abdomen to her throat. Every day, this would occur 10 or more times. These episodes were accompanied by fear and anxiety and a kind of suffering she could not explain in words and which she could not control. In addition, there was a difficult to bear aching and painful sensation in her lower abdomen.

The patient went to her local hospital where she was examined. A CT scan showed no abnormalities and all her blood work was normal. She was treated with metronidazole for three days with no result. Therefore, the patient was referred to the authors for examination and treatment at which time, her tongue was pale with glossy, white fur and her pulse was deep and bowstring. Based on these findings plus her other signs and symptoms, her Chinese medical pattern was discriminated as fear and fright damaging the liver and kidney qi resulting in upward counterflow and surging and thus running piglet. Therefore, the treatment principles were to level the liver and downbear counterflow, rectify the qi and harmonize the constructive. The formula used was *Ben Tun Tang Jian Jian* (Running Piglet Decoction with Additions & Subtractions): Radix Ligustici Wallichii (*Chuan Xiong*), 10g, Radix Angelicae Sinensis (*Dang Gui*), 15g, Radix Albus Paeoniae Lactiflorae (*Bai Shao*), 20g, Radix Glycyrrhizae (*Gan Cao*), 10g, Radix Puerariae (*Ge Gen*), 10g, Rhizoma Pinelliae Ternatae (*Ban Xia*), 10g, Radix Scutellariae Baicalensis (*Huang Qin*), 10g, uncooked Rhizoma Zingiberis (*Sheng Jiang*), 7 slices, Lignum Aquilariae Aggalochae (*Chen Xiang*), 10g, and Sclerotium Poriae Cocos (*Fu Ling*), 10g.

After three *ji* of this formula, the vomiting had disappeared and the number of times the qi counterflowed and surged were reduced to 5-6 times per day. Her feeling of anxiety was also lessened as was her abdominal discomfort. Therefore, the patient was given four more *ji* of the above formula, after which she was completely cured. On follow-up after one year, there had not been any recurrence.

## ❖ CASE 2[4] ❖

The patient was a 43 year old female who was first examined on Sept. 6, 1994. The patient reported that, for the last three months, she had experienced episodes of qi surging upward from her lower abdomen to her chest and rib-side. If severe, it could extend to her throat. Additionally, her chest felt oppressed and her throat felt tight, and there was accompanying dizziness so that she could not move. Before coming to the author of this case, the patient had been diagnosed as suffering from running piglet at an outpatient clinic. Based on that diagnosis, she had been treated with modified *Gui Zhi Jia Gui Tang* (Cinnamon Twig Plus Cinnamon Decoction) and *Ling Gui Cao Zao Tang* (Poria, Cinnamon, Licorice & Red Dates Decoction) with no effect. On re-examination, the doctor at that clinic found her throat and mouth were dry and her stools were constipated. Therefore, thinking this a case of liver qi depression and binding, he treated the patient with *Chai Hu Shu Gan San Jian Jian* (Bupleurum Course the Liver Powder with Additions & Subtractions). However, after administering this, there were no marked signs of improvement and the patient was referred to the author of this case.

The author found that the woman's body was emaciated and her facial complexion was pale. Both eyes were dry and rough. Her tongue body was thin and small with scanty fluids and both edges were bright and peeled with no fur. In addition, her pulse was bowstring, fine, and rapid. Therefore, her pattern was discriminated as liver yin insufficiency with inability to moisten and nourish the large intestine. This had resulted in the intestinal qi not being able to transmit and conduct, and thus the qi had surged and counterflowed upward. The treatment principles were to enrich yin and nourish the blood, free the flow of the bowels and downbear turbidity. The medicinals used were: Radix Glehniae Littoralis (*Sha Shen*) and uncooked Radix Rehmanniae (*Sheng Di*), 20g each, Fructus Lycii Chinensis (*Gou Qi Zi*), Radix Angelicae Sinensis (*Dang Gui*), and Tuber Ophiopogonis Japonici (*Mai Dong*), 15g each, and Fructus Germinatus Horedi Vulgaris (*Mai Ya*), Fructus Meliae Toosendan (*Chuan Lian Zi*), Fructus Citri Aurantii (*Zhi Ke*), and Semen Biotae Orientalis (*Bai Zi Ren*), 10g each.

After taking five *ji* of this prescription, the surging qi had leveled and the bowel qi was freely flowing. However, the patient was still sometimes dizzy. Thus, Aurantium was deducted from the above formula and 15g of Flos Chrysanthemi Morifolii (*Ju Hua*) was added. After taking five *ji* of this formula, all her symptoms were eliminated.

## ❖ CASE 3[5] ❖

This patient was one of 30 in a clinical audit on the treatment of running piglet with *Xuan Fu Dai Zhe Tang* (Inula & Hematite Decoction). She was 39 years old, had an introverted disposition, and was first examined on May 10, 1990. Four months earlier, qi had begun to surge upward episodically from her lower abdomen to her chest and epigastric region during an argument with a customer. Thereafter, this feeling recurred, initially one time every 4-5 days but gradually increasing to once every day. The patient had sought previous treatments but none had been successful. The patient reported that, each day around 4 o'clock in the afternoon, she felt something moving in her lower right abdomen. This continued for 10 minutes and then the feeling moved upward. If this feeling were severe, when it reached her chest and epigastric region, it could make her vomit phlegm drool. This would be followed by fainting and falling to the ground. When she revived, she was like a normal person.

The patient's tongue was coated with thin, white fur, and her pulse was bowstring. Based on these signs and symptoms, her pattern was discriminated as depression and anger damaging the liver with liver qi counterflowing upward resulting in running piglet. Therefore, the treatment principles were to settle the liver and downbear counterflow. The formula consisted of a combination of *Xuan Fu Dai Zhe Tang* and *Gui Zhi Jia Gui Tang* (Cinnamon Twig Plus Cinnamon Decoction): Flos Inulae Racemosae (*Xuan Fu Hua*), 10g, Haemititum (*Dai Zhe Shi*), 30g, ginger-processed Rhizoma Pinelliae Ternatae (*Ban Xia*), 10g, Radix Codonopsitis Pilosulae (*Dang Shen*), 10g, Ramulus Cinnamomi Cassiae (*Gui Zhi*), 15g, Radix Albus Paeoniae Lactiflorae (*Bai Shao*), 10g, Radix Glycyrrhizae (*Gan Cao*), 7g, uncooked Rhizoma Zingiberis (*Sheng Jiang*), 3 slices, and Fructus Zizyphi Jujubae (*Da Zao*), 4 pieces. These were decocted in water and one *ji* was administered per day.

After taking three *ji* of the above formula, the running piglet qi sensation was decreased, yet there was still a feeling as if there was an animal moving about inside in the lower right abdomen. This movement lasted for 10 minutes, surged upward, then stopped. Therefore, the patient was given five more *ji* of the original formula and was cured. On follow-up after three months, there had been no recurrence.

### ❖ CASE 4⁶ ❖

The patient was a 48 year old, ill-tempered male who commonly argued with others. Consequently, the man's pattern was categorized as liver depression qi stagnation. The previous month, he had a quarrel with his children during which he began to feel an upward surging feeling in the area below his umbilicus. This was followed by the feeling of something surging upward into his chest and throat which eventually arrived at his head. After some time, this feeling subsided again to the periumbilical region. After repeated attacks of this sort, the patient became restless and frightened. He developed insomnia, was even more irritable, and even considered committing suicide.

One evening, the patient was severely frightened by a dream and sought out treatment by knocking at the author's door around midnight. His tongue fur was thin and white, and his pulse was slippery and surging. Both his eyelids and hands were trembling. Therefore, his pattern was discriminated as spleen yang vacuity with water qi surging upward harassing the heart spirit above and he was prescribed *Ling Gui Cao Zao Tang Jia Wei* (Poria, Cinnamon, Licorice & Red Dates Decoction with Added Flavors): Sclerotium Poriae Cocos (*Fu Ling*), 20g, Ramulus Cinnamomi Cassiae (*Gui Zhi*), 10g, Radix Glycyrrhizae (*Gan Cao*), 6g, Rhizoma Atractylodis Macrocephalae (*Bai Zhu*), 10g, Cortex Albizziae Julibrissinis (*He Huan Pi*), 30g, Caulis Polygoni Multiflori (*Ye Jiao Teng*), 30g, Rhizoma Anemarrhenae Aspheloidis (*Zhi Mu*), 12g, Radix Ligustici Wallichii (*Chuan Xiong*), 6g. These were decocted in water and one *ji* was administered internally per day.

After taking five *ji* of this formula, the patient's sleep had improved and all his other symptoms had gradually disappeared. On follow-up after one year, there had been no recurrence.

### ❖ CASE 5⁷ ❖

The patient was a 49 year old female who was first examined on Oct. 15, 1964 after having had an appendectomy. At the time of being discharged from the hospital, she was diagnosed with limited ileitis. Soon thereafter, the patient had felt a sensation of qi ascending from her lower abdomen and surging to her throat which felt as if it were being burnt. This was so severe, she wished to die. At the time of her initial visit, there was epigastric pain

and discomfort, poor appetite, pain within the throat, generalized bodily burning heat, dizziness, and a red tongue. The left pulse was deep and fine. Therefore, Dr. Zhang's treatment principles were to settle counterflow, descend the qi, and abduct (ministerial) fire to return it to its residence or source in the lower burner. His prescription consisted of: calcined Concha Ostreae (*Mu Li*), 30g, Flouritum (*Zhi Shi Ying*), 15g, calcined Os Draconis (*Long Gu*), 12g, uncooked Radix Albus Paeoniae Lactiflorae (*Bai Shao*), 12g, calcined Haemititum (*Dai Zhe Shi*), 12g, Flos Inulae Racemosae (*Xuan Fu Hua*), 9g, mix-fried Radix Glycyrrhizae (*Gan Cao*), 9g, Lignum Dalbergiae Odoriferae (*Jiang Xiang*), 1.5g, and Cortex Cinnamomi Cassiae (*Rou Gui*), 1.2g. Two *ji* of these medicinals were decocted in water and administered internally.

On the second visit, the patient reported that the feeling of running piglet was soothed after taking the above medicinals. She frequently passed flatus, her appetite was still poor, there was still epigastric pain and oppression, and a hot sensation in her chest and abdomen. Her tongue was red and her pulse was deep and fine. Therefore, the patient was prescribed three *ji* of the following medicinals: calcined Concha Ostreae (*Mu Li*), 30g, calcined Concha Arcae Inflatae (*Wa Leng Zi*), 30g, Flouritum (*Zhi Shi Ying*), 15g, calcined Os Draconis (*Long Gu*), 12g, calcined Haemititum (*Dai Zhe Shi*), 12g, Flos Inulae Racemosae (*Xuan Fu Hua*), 9g, processed Rhizoma Cyperi Rotundi (*Xiang Fu*), 9g, stir fried Fructus Citri Aurantii (*Zhi Ke*), 9g, Flos Pruni Mume (*Lu O Mei*), 4.5g, Fructus Citri Sacrodactylis (*Fo Shou*), 3g, and Lignum Aquilariae Agallochae (*Chen Xiang*), 1.5g.

At the third visit, the patient reported that the running piglet qi had stopped, that she had an appetite, and that the epigastric pain and the hot feeling in her abdomen, chest, and all around her body were less. However, she was belching frequently and had profuse dreams during sleep at night which led to fright and fear. Her tongue was still red and her pulse was fine and slightly deep. Dr. Zhang decided that the patient's kidney vacuity had still not recuperated. Therefore he prescribed four *ji* of the following medicinals: calcined Concha Ostreae (*Mu Li*), 30g, calcined Concha Arcae Inflatae (*Wa Leng Zi*), 30g, Fructus Lycii Chinensis (*Gou Qi Zi*), 9g, Fructus Tribuli Terrestris (*Bai Ji Li*), 9g, processed Rhizoma Cyperi Rotundi (*Xiang Fu*), 9g, stir-fried Fructus Citri Aurantii (*Zhi Ke*), 9g, Fructus Citri Sacrodactylis (*Fo Shou*), 4.5g, and Lignum Aquilariae Agallochae (*Chen Xiang*), 1.5g. After taking a total of nine *ji*, the patient's condition was basically cured.

ENDNOTES:

[1] Bone here refers to the kidneys.

[2] Zhang Zhong-jing, *Shang Han Lun*, trans. by Craig Mitchell, Feng Ye & Nigel Wiseman, Paradigm Publications, Brookline, MA, 1999, p. 171

[3] Zhang Xiao-hui & Cao Jing-long, "A Short Discussion of Experiences Treating Running Piglet," *Ji Lin Zhong Yi Yao (Jilin Chinese Medicine & Medicinals)*, #1, 1999, p. 42

[4] Qiu Zhi-qiang, "The Treatment of Running Piglet with *Yi Guan Jian* (One Link Decoction)," *Zhe Jiang Zhong Yi Za Zhi (Zhejiang Journal of Chinese Medicine)*, #10, 1999, p. 431

[5] Qian Tian-lei, "The Treatment of Running Piglet Qi Diseases with *Xuan Fu Dai Zhe Tang* (Inula & Hematite Decoction)," *Bei Jing Zhong Yi (Beijing Chinese Medicine)*, #1, 1996, p. 30-31

[6] Wang Zhan-xi, *Shang Han Lun Lin Chuang Yan Jiu (Clinical Studies [Based on] the Treatise on Damage [Due to] Cold)*, People's Health & Hygiene Press, Beijing, 1983, p. 95

[7] Zhang Zhen-xia, *Shang Hai Lao Zhong Yi Jing Yan Xuan Bian (A Selected Collection of Shanghai Old Chinese Doctors' Case Histories)*, *op. cit.*, p. 156-157

# ❖ 21 ❖

# LILY DISEASE

Lily disease, *bai he bing*, is first described as a disease category in Zhang Zhong-jing's late Han dynasty *Jin Gui Yao Lue* (*Essentials of the Golden Cabinet*). The Chinese name of this disease is based on the fact that Bulbus Lilii (*Bai He*) is the main ingredient in every formula Zhang recommends for its treatment. In this disease, the patient feels like eating but is unable to eat. They feel like lying down, *i.e.*, sleeping but cannot lie down. They feel like moving but cannot move. Their affect is restless, but they also tend to be taciturn and speak little. They may feel cold without there being cold (*i.e.*, chills), or they may feel hot without there being heat (*i.e.*, fever). In addition, there may be a bitter taste in the mouth, reddish urine, and a faint, rapid pulse. As Zhang Zhong-jing says, it is as if the person were possessed even though their body is harmonious or normal. Zhang also says that not all medicinals are able to treat this condition since many medicinals may provoke diarrhea and/or vomiting.[1]

The seven Chinese patterns included under lily disease share several core characteristics, namely:

1. The desire to move without being able to move
2. The desire to lie down (*i.e.*, sleep) without being able to lie down
3. The patient feels like eating but is unable to eat
4. The patient may feel cold or hot in the absence of coldness or heat in the environment

In addition to these basic features, numerous somatic, behavioral, or psychological complaints are described

under lily disease. None of these corresponds to discrete diagnostic categories in Western medicine. However, many symptoms included within the various patterns of lily disease resemble certain psychiatric disorders, including conversion disorder and hypochondriasis (see Book 3, Chapter 9, Somatoform Disorders). Furthermore, many of these patterns are phenomenologically similar to early or mild forms of certain neurologic disorders described in contemporary Western medicine, including Parkinson's disease, Parkinsonism, multiple sclerosis (MS), and possibly other degenerative neurological disorders. Early or mild forms of these disorders are sometimes accompanied by psychiatric symptoms when physical symptoms like tremor or abnormal gait are not yet present. Therefore, early or mild forms of Parkinson's disease, Parkinsonism, MS, and other degenerative neurological disorders are sometimes difficult to distinguish from psychiatric disorders, including depression, incipient schizophrenia, certain somatoform disorders, and histrionic personality disorder. These possibilities are discussed in the sections that follow.

The Chinese medical literature on lily disease stipulates that individuals afflicted with this disorder typically have no physical signs or symptoms pointing to neurological or other kinds of medical disorders. Therefore, it is important to distinguish between early or mild forms of certain neurologic disorders, which may arguably correspond to core features of lily disease and later, more severe forms which are clearly unlike lily disease. More severe or advanced forms of Parkinson's disease, Parkinsonian syndromes, or other neurologic disorders in which abnormal movements are obviously present and result in significant impairment are included under the broad Chinese disease category of Convulsions (see Chapter 16, this Book).

## NOSOLOGY:

Neuropsychiatric symptoms that often occur in the early stages or mild forms of Parkinson's disease or Parkinsonism resemble some features of lily disease, including restless affect at the same time as taciturnity and speaking little, withdrawn affect, faint voice, difficulty sleeping, brooding and unhappiness, and a tendency to sorrow. Later in the course of the illness but sometime before grossly abnormal movements are apparent, an individual may begin to experience difficulty initiating purposeful behaviours. For example, he or she may desire to move without being able to move or desire to lie down without being able to lie down, etc. The insidious progression of symptoms like these might be construed as gradual changes in personality, and the afflicted individual might be viewed as passive, unmotivated, or apathetic. This group of symptoms commonly associated with Parkinson's disease could easily be misinterpreted as depression or possibly even early dementia. In contrast, early or mild forms of MS (or other demyelinating disorders of the central nervous system) sometimes manifest as other patterns included under lily disease, for example, laughing and crying without constancy, emotional rashness and impetuosity, paranoia, numbness and tingling, and garrulousness. As in Parkinson's disease, gross abnormalities are seldom identified on neurologic exam in early or mild forms of MS or other degenerative neurologic diseases.

Parkinson's disease and Parkinsonism share common neurological symptoms but are etiologically distinct. By definition, in contrast to Parkinson's disease in which there is no identified underlying cause, Parkinsonism has numerous identifiable underlying medical causes. Parkinson's disease is a degenerative neurologic disorder that is typically characterized by insidious onset. When the pre-morbid histories of individuals who have subsequently been diagnosed with Parkinson's disease are closely examined, there is a significantly greater than chance incidence of psychiatric symptoms that can be retrospectively interpreted as early symptoms of this disorder.

As the patient's illness progresses from exclusively or predominantly psychiatric symptoms to a combined physical-psychiatric symptom pattern, the Chinese medical interpretation of this evolving disorder in the same patient typically shifts from the broad diagnostic category of lily disease to the broad category of convulsions. Therefore, if a patient is evaluated during early or mild stages of a disorder that Western medicine classifies as Parkinson's disease, Parkinsonism, MS, or other less common degenerative neurological disorders, he or she might be diagnosed with lily disease. In contrast, patients at more advanced stages of illness, with more severe forms of these disorders (*i.e.*, in which abnormal movement symptoms are prominent), or, in some cases, even patients who had previously been diagnosed with lily disease would likely receive a diagnosis of convulsions.[2]

## EPIDEMIOLOGY:

Eighty percent of individuals who are initially diagnosed with Parkinsonism are eventually diagnosed with Parkinson's disease. In other words, a specific cause is never established. Symptoms begin before age 55 in the majority of cases. However, some unusual heritable forms of Parkinsonism may begin as early as 20 years of age. In surveyed Western populations, Parkinson's disease occurs more commonly among males and has a prevalence rate of approximately 160 in 100,000. The various Parkinsonian syndromes affect many individuals, but limited epidemiological data exist for these disorders. In multiple sclerosis, symptoms typically begin during the third or fourth decade, but the disorder may (rarely) start in childhood or old age. In most cases, MS follows a remitting-relapsing course, and disease-free intervals may last from weeks to decades.

## DIFFERENTIAL DIAGNOSIS:

### 1. MEDICAL DISORDERS

Many patterns of lily disease refer to other Chinese essence spirit diseases, including deranged speech, profuse dreams, easy fright, easily being awakened, and excessive thinking and worrying. These disorders are examined separately in other chapters. As these Chinese medical disorders describe somatic and psychiatric symptoms that commonly occur in early stages or mild forms of Parkinson's disease, Parkinsonism, multiple sclerosis, or other degenerative diseases of the central nervous system, all of these disorders must be ruled out before a psychogenic cause can be presumed. Careful history-taking usually clarifies the differential diagnosis, pointing to one or more probable medical etiologies. However, many uncommon degenerative neurological disorders sometimes manifest as psychiatric syndromes, especially in the early stages of disease. Because these disorders are uncommon and often subtle, it is often problematic to detect or confirm them. Therefore, in many cases, neurologic disease cannot be ruled out definitively even in cases where there is an absence of confirmatory data. Continuing progression of neurodegenerative disorders, including development of specific neurologic symptoms, and confirmation by laboratory or diagnostic imaging studies will typically clarify the diagnosis.

Before developing the striking abnormal movements that are hallmarks of Parkinson's disease, many individuals experience mood changes, typically depression. Others notice feelings of restlessness that are not explained by identified medical problems. Many report a diminished capacity to concentrate or impaired attention. Still others experience subtle changes in personality, including a diminished range of emotional reactivity (flattening of affect) or decreased talkativeness. Many patients experience insidious cognitive slowing (sometimes called bradyphrenia) and overall cognitive decline that typically progress to dementia in advanced stages of illness. As both Parkinson's disease and Parkinsonism progress, voluntary movements become slow and deliberate (bradykinesia), and the patient experiences progressive difficulty initiating movements. In the absence of abnormal movements, many symptoms of early or mild Parkinson's disease or Parkinsonism bear striking resemblance to features of lily disease.

Psychiatric symptoms often begin during (and are presumed to be caused by) incipient degeneration of the basal ganglia, eventually resulting in florid abnormal movements that are the hallmark of Parkinson's disease. As the disorder progresses, psychiatric symptoms typically become more pronounced and are ultimately accompanied by prominent physical signs, including unilateral pill-rolling tremor at rest, slowed voluntary movements, hypotension, loss of balance, and festinating gait (i.e., short, rapid steps). The diminished emotional reactivity of early Parkinson's disease typically progresses to a complete loss of the individual's capacity to express emotions through facial expressions (mask-like face). Like Parkinson's disease, many forms of Parkinsonism are accompanied by numerous psychological changes, including depressed mood, diminished expressiveness, reduced attention span, and anxious or dependent personality changes. A diversity of possible causes of Parkinsonism (see Etiology) results in the broad variation of associated psychiatric and physical symptom patterns depending on specific psychiatric effects of underlying drug-related, infectious, vascular, traumatic, genetic, or other cause(s). In both Parkinson's disease and Parkinsonism, prominent symptoms of autonomic dysregulation may result in sensations of coolness or heat or erratic changes in heart rate or blood pressure. "The individual may feel coldness or heat in the absence of coldness or heat in the environment." Further, akithisia can occur in both disorders. This neurologic symptom is characterized by subjective feelings of restlessness and, in later stages, difficulty or frank inability to remain still. Therefore, as Parkinson's disease or Parkinsonism progresses, the patient may experience subjective feelings of restlessness in the context of increasing difficulties initiating purposeful behaviors. For example, he or she may experience a desire to move without being able to move, a desire to lie down without being able to lie down, or a desire to eat without being able to eat.

As noted above, many individuals in the early stages of MS report erratic changes in mood, including depression, mania, and irritability as well as impaired concentration and, during symptomatic periods, laughing and crying with no constancy. Unusual sensations, like numbness and tingling, are also common in MS, and patients often complain of fatigue and disrupted sleep. Magnetic resonance imaging (MRI) of the brain is the definitive diagnostic study that confirms the presence of lesions of demyelination in almost all cases. Special studies of the cerebrospinal fluid are also done to clarify the diagnosis, but positive findings are not specific to multiple sclerosis.

## 2. PSYCHIATRIC DISORDERS

The work of differential diagnosis turns to a consideration of psychiatric disorders that are reasonable explanations of the observed symptom pattern when Parkinson's disease, Parkinsonism, MS, and other neurologic disorders have been ruled out by history, normal neurologic examination, or normal findings on diagnostic imaging studies (e.g., normal MRI when MS is suspected). Many aspects of lily disease resemble features of the broad category of somatoform disorders (see Book 3, Chapter 9) as defined in contemporary Western psychiatry. Western medical differential diagnosis assumes that a somatoform disorder is the likely explanation when reasonable attempts to identify medical causes of somatic symptoms have yielded no or equivocal findings. Somatoform disorders are characterized by persisting somatic complaints, including apparent abnormal or diminished sensory or motor functioning in the absence of evidence for underlying medical causes and with normal neurologic examination results. Onset of many somatoform disorders and episodes of exacerbation are often associated with identifiable psychological stresses, and a co-morbid major psychiatric disorder is frequently identified.

Accurate diagnosis of a specific somatoform disorder

depends on the specific symptom pattern, course, and severity. A thorough history usually clarifies the psychiatric differential diagnosis, indicating whether somatic symptoms are primary (*i.e.*, the diagnosis is a somatoform disorder) or secondary to another psychiatric disorder. When depression is the patient's chief complaint and somatic symptoms are consistently worse during periods of severe depression, major depressive episode with somatization is the most likely diagnosis. Reports of unusual somatic symptoms in the context of a previously diagnosed psychotic disorder, including schizophrenia and other psychotic disorders, suggest the possibility of somatic delusions. When a previously undiagnosed patient complains of prominent somatic symptoms without apparent medical basis and also experiences paranoia, delusions, auditory hallucinations, or other psychotic symptoms, schizophrenia is the most likely diagnosis. Some patterns of lily disease include nonspecific features that resemble a psychotic prodrome, *i.e.*, the early stages of an evolving psychotic disorder, including schizophrenia. These include, for example, clouded head, seeming as if possessed, a desire to speak but inability to speak, paranoia, and confused disorderly dreams.

Many patients who have anxiety disorders, including panic disorder and generalized anxiety disorder (GAD), complain of somatic symptoms. However, the focus of clinical attention in these disorders is not somatic symptoms but debilitating panic attacks or generalized anxiety symptoms. In cases of persisting somatic complaints in the absence of significant psychiatric symptoms, the correct diagnosis depends on whether symptoms are intentionally caused or feigned. A factitious disorder is diagnosed when a patient manufactures somatic symptoms by introducing an agent into his or her body with the intention of creating these symptoms. The current psychodynamic view is that such patients create symptoms in order to identify with a sick role. Conversely, an individual who reports somatic symptoms but does not actually experience them is malingering. Contemporary Western psychiatry attributes deliberate feigning of symptoms to undisclosed hopes of financial reward that may result from legal settlements related to alleged circumstances of illness onset. A somatoform disorder can only be diagnosed when malingering and factitiousness have been ruled out. The specific types of somatoform disorders are described in Book 3, Chapter 9.

## ETIOLOGY & PATHOPHYSIOLOGY:

### 1. PARKINSON'S DISEASE, PARKINSONISM & MS

By definition, Parkinson's disease has an identified primary cause. In contrast, numerous forms of Parkinsonism are highly variable in presentation, and are secondary consequences of other neurologic, infectious, metabolic, vascular, genetic, or drug-induced disorders. Parkinson's disease is caused by the degeneration of dopamine-containing neurons in the substantia nigra, a small region located at the base of the brain. Parkinson's disease is diagnosed when primary causes of degenerative changes in the substantia nigra have not been identified. In contrast, Parkinsonism is caused by numerous infectious, metabolic, toxic, traumatic, vascular, and genetic disorders that affect various parts of the brain, including the basal ganglia, substantia nigra, cerebellum, or multiple brain circuits. Diffuse Lewy body disease is a progressive dementing disorder that affects many subcortical brain regions, often resulting in abnormal movement symptoms significantly after the patient has become demented. Multiple sclerosis is an autoimmune disorder of the central nervous system resulting in focal areas of demyelination and inflammation in the white matter of the brain and spinal cord. Numerous possible causes have been advanced, but until now none has been confirmed. The most widely accepted theory suggests that this demyelinating disorder of the

| DIFFERENTIAL DIAGNOSIS | |
|---|---|
| **1. MEDICAL DISORDERS** | **2. PSYCHIATRIC DISORDERS** |
| A. EARLY OR MILD FORMS OF PARKINSON'S DISEASE | A. SOMATOFORM DISORDERS |
| B. EARLY OR MILD FORMS OF PARKINSONISM | B. HYPOCHONDRIASIS |
| C. EARLY OR MILD FORMS OF MULTIPLE SCLEROSIS | C. HISTRIONIC PERSONALITY DISORDER |
| D. EARLY OR MILD FORMS OF OTHER DEGENERATIVE NEUROLOGIC DISORDERS | D. MAJOR DEPRESSIVE EPISODE WITH SOMATIZATION |
| | E. PSYCHOTIC DIORDERS, INCLUDING SCHIZOPHRENIA |
| | F. GENERALIZED ANXIETY DISORDER (GAD) |
| | G. FACTITIOUS DISORDER |
| | H. MALINGERING |

central nervous system is triggered to the body's misdirected immune response to an otherwise benign viral illness, thus resulting in wide-spread autoimmune destruction of the myelin surrounding nerve fibers.

## 2. SOMATOFORM DISORDERS

The pathogenesis of somatoform disorders has not been clearly established. Several neurobiological and psychodynamic theories have been advanced in attempts to explain symptom patterns that are included under the broad grouping of somatoform disorders. Contemporary Western models of conversion disorder are reviewed in Book 3, Chapter 9, Somatoform Disorders. Recent studies support a neurobiological models of certain somatoform disorders, including conversion disorder and hypochondriasis. For example, cortical dysfunction may result in impaired attention causing distorted perceptions of normal bodily sensations. Hypochondriasis and pain disorder may have similar neurobiological etiologies. Non-biological models of somatoform disorders derive from psychoanalytic theories and social learning theory.

## WESTERN MEDICAL TREATMENT:

### 1. PARKINSON'S DISEASE, PARKINSONISM & MS

In contemporary Western medicine, medications, physical therapy, surgery, and electroconvulsive therapy are used as treatments of Parkinson's disease and Parkinsonian syndromes. Medications that are effective against many neurological symptoms of these disorders are ones that release dopamine in the brain or stimulate CNS dopamine receptors. Clozapine, an atypical antipsychotic agent, is sometimes provided together with L-dopa to prophylax against psychotic symptoms that are frequent side-effects of L-dopa and other dopamine agonists. Surgical interventions are sometimes necessary when symptoms are unresponsive to medications. Electroconvulsive therapy (ECT) is sometimes effective in alleviating or slowing progression of Parkinson's disease or Parkinsonian syndromes. There are presently no cures for Parkinson's disease. Successful treatment of the identified underlying cause(s) of Parkinsonism sometimes improves or completely eliminates abnormal movements and other Parkinsonian symptoms. However, in many cases, neurological damage caused by CNS infections, medications, toxic, traumatic, or vascular insults is irreversible, and Parkinsonian symptoms persist indefinitely. Numerous pharmacological treatments are used for MS. Intravenous steroids are used to control acute attacks, and regular use of Beta-interferon is used to control the course of the illness by reducing the number of relapses. Numerous

immunosuppressant drugs, including emerging experimental treatments, are also used.

## 2. SOMATOFORM DISORDERS

There are no specific pharmacological treatments for somatoform disorders. Numerous psychotropic medications have been employed to treat these disorders. Current treatments for conversion disorder are reviewed in Book 3, Chapter 9, Somatoform Disorders. In contemporary Western psychiatry, serotonin-selective re-uptake inhibitors (SSRIs) are commonly used in the management of most somatoform disorders. Sedative-hypnotics are used adjunctively to SSRIs for management of transient anxiety symptoms that are frequently reported by individuals who have long-standing somatic complaints. Somatization disorder, pain disorder, and body dysmorphic disorder sometimes respond to supportive psychotherapy and cognitive-behavioral therapy.

## SHORT & LONG-TERM ADVANTAGES & DISADVANTAGES OF WESTERN MEDICAL TREATMENT:

### 1. PARKINSON'S DISEASE, PARKINSONISM & MS

Anti-Parkinsonian agents usually result in significantly improved quality of life. However, many complications of long-term treatment with dopamine agonists complicate the course of Parkinson's disease and Parkinsonian syndromes. These include unpleasant medication side-effects, on-and-off effects, and movement disorders that usually normalize when the causative medication is discontinued. Adverse behavioral effects of L-dopa and dopamine agonists include auditory or visual hallucinations, vivid dreams, drowsiness, confusion, agitation, delusions, depression, and mania. Chronic steroid therapy for MS can result in numerous medical complications secondary to immunosuppression as well as agitated or manic states and sometimes frank psychosis. Chemotherapeutic agents often precipitate depressed mood.

### 2. SOMATOFORM DISORDERS

Individuals who respond to pharmacological treatment for somatoform disorders typically report significant reduction in severity of baseline somatic symptoms in addition to diminished anxiety and markedly improved social and occupational functioning. However, these benefits must be viewed with respect to risks of drug side effects. Common side effects of SSRIs include upset stomach and other gastrointestinal complaints, fatigue or "activation," and sometimes insomnia, diminished libido, and an uncomfortable subjective sense of diminished capacity for emotional expression. Chronic use of benzodiazepines and other sedative-hypnotics carries the risk of chemical dependency with all of its complications.

## PROGNOSIS:

### 1. PARKINSON'S DISEASE, PARKINSONISM & MS

Parkinson's disease follows a progressive, insidious course. Since the introduction and widespread use of L-dopa, the five year mortality rate of Parkinson's disease has dropped significantly and average life expectancy has increased by several years. Nevertheless, there is no cure for Parkinson's disease. Parkinsonian syndromes have more benign long-term outcomes which are further improved with medications. The prognosis of MS is highly variable depending on age at onset and frequency and severity of relapses. Milder forms are associated with fewer relapses and less severe physical or cognitive impairment.

### 2. SOMATOFORM DISORDERS

Like all psychiatric disorders, prognosis and long-term course are related to chronicity, symptom severity, and treatment responsiveness. Most somatoform disorders have relatively favorable prognosis if there are no co-occurring psychiatric or neurological disorders. Other important predictors of long-term outcome include the level of pre-morbid social-psychological functioning and the nature of symptom onset. Rapid onset is usually associated with a more favorable long-term course. When conversion disorder is diagnosed in hospitalized patients, most cases resolve quickly without pharmacological or other kinds of treatment. Patients who complain of chronic or severe symptoms or suffer from other psychiatric syndromes will likely respond less rapidly or completely to treatment and will, therefore, continue to experience significant impairment for an indefinite period. Difficult social or legal circumstances typically predict poor outcomes. In contrast to conversion disorder, hypochondriasis usually has a chronic life-long course interrupted by transient periods of symptomatic worsening or improvement.

### INDICATIONS FOR REFERRAL TO WESTERN MEDICAL SERVICES:

Parkinson's disease and Parkinsonian syndromes are progressive neurologic disorders. Western medicine offers many treatments for these disorders that are moderately effective. Thorough history-taking and accurate diagnosis are essential to ensure that appropriate treatment is initiated in a timely manner. Therefore, evidence of progressive degenerative neurologic disease, including Parkinson's disease, multiple sclerosis, or acute-onset Parkinsonian syndromes, *always* warrants referral to a neurologist. Urgent referral to an emergency room is indicated when there is evidence of an acute medical condition, for example, trauma, infection, or metabolic derangements that cause or co-exists with observed neurologic symptoms characteristic of Parkinson's disease (see above). Urgent referral to an appropriate hospital-based or residential treatment program is also warranted in cases of alcohol or illicit substance abuse that may underlie reported somatic, mood, or anxiety symptoms.

Non-urgent referral to a psychiatrist or neurologist will help to clarify the medical and psychiatric differential diagnoses in cases where moderate symptoms (in the absence of identified acute medical or psychiatric disorders) have failed to respond to an appropriate course of Chinese medical treatment. In such cases, the Chinese medicine practitioner and Western-trained physician may be able to develop an integrative treatment plan that is more beneficial to the patient than either approach alone.

## CHINESE DISEASE CAUSES & MECHANISMS:

Due to depression and binding of the seven affects or after great illness, there is lack of nourishment of the heart spirit which thus becomes disquieted. Such malnourishment of the heart spirit may be due to various types of yin vacuity and may be aggravated by liver depression, phlegm, and/or heat, the latter two of which may ascend and also harass the spirit, hence disquieting it all the more.

## TREATMENT BASED ON PATTERN DISCRIMINATION:

### 1. HEART-LUNG YIN VACUITY WITH INTERNAL HEAT PATTERN

**MAIN SYMPTOMS:** A desire but inability to eat, a desire to lie down but inability to lie down, a desire to move but inability to move, a restless affect at the same time as taciturnity and speaking little, a possible cold feeling without there being cold (*i.e.*, chills) or a possible hot feeling without there being heat (*i.e.*, fever). In addition, there may be a bitter taste in the mouth, reddish urine, and a faint, rapid pulse.

**TREATMENT PRINCIPLES:** Enrich yin and clear heat, quiet the spirit and stabilize the mind

**FORMULA & MEDICINALS:** *Bai He Da Zao Tang Jia Wei* (Lily & Red Date Decoction with Added Flavors)

Bulbus Lilii (*Bai He*), 15-60g, Rhizoma Anemarrhenae Aspheloidis (*Zhi Mu*), 10g, uncooked Radix Rehmanniae (*Sheng Di*), 15g, Radix Glycyrrhizae (*Gan Cao*), 6g, Fructus Tritici Aestivi (*Huai Xiao Mai*), 15-30g, Fructus Zizyphi Jujubae (*Da Zao*), 5 pieces

Decoct in water and administer orally in two divided doses, morning and evening, one *ji* per day.

**ADDITIONS & SUBTRACTIONS:** If there is marked oral dryness, add Radix Trichosanthis Kirlowii (*Tian Hua Fen*) and Radix Glehniae Littoralis (*Sha Shen*). If heat signs are marked, add Talcum (*Hua Shi*), uncooked Concha Ostreae (*Mu Li*), and Os Draconis (*Long Gu*).

**ACUPUNCTURE:** *Fei Shu* (Bl 13), *Xin Shu* (Bl 15), *Shen Men* (Ht 7), *Nei Guan* (Per 6), *Tai Xi* (Ki 3), *San Yin Jiao* (Sp 6). Use even supplementing-even draining method for the first four points and supplementing method for the last two.

## 2. PHLEGM HEAT HARASSING ABOVE PATTERN

**MAIN SYMPTOMS:** Essence spirit abstraction and restlessness, deranged speech, laughing and crying without constancy, a desire to eat but inability to eat, a desire to move but inability to move, headache and distention, emotional rashness and impetuosity, chest and rib-side fullness and oppression, vexation and agitation, restless sleep, scanty sleep and easily being awakened, profuse dreams, easy fright, a red facial complexion, a red tongue tip with thin, yellow, slightly slimy fur, and a slippery, rapid pulse

**TREATMENT PRINCIPLES:** Clear heat and eliminate phlegm, nourish yin and quiet the spirit

**FORMULA & MEDICINALS:** *Bai He Hua Tan Tang* (Lily Transform Phlegm Decoction)

Bulbus Lilii (*Bai He*), 15-60g, Rhizoma Anemarrhenae Aspheloidis (*Zhi Mu*), 10g, uncooked Radix Rehmanniae (*Sheng Di*), 15g, Fructus Trichosanthis Kirlowii (*Gua Lou*), 10g, Semen Pruni Armeniacae (*Xing Ren*), 10g, Fructus Immaturus Citri Aurantii (*Zhi Shi*), 6g, Pericarpium Citri Reticulatae (*Chen Pi*), 10g, Rhizoma Pinelliae Ternatae (*Ban Xia*), 10g, Sclerotium Poriae Cocos (*Fu Ling*), 12g, bile-processed Rhizoma Arisaematis (*Dan Nan Xing*), 10g, Radix Scutellariae Baicalensis (*Huang Qin*), 10g, Radix Glycyrrhizae (*Gan Cao*), 6g

Decoct in water and administer orally in two divided doses, morning and evening, one *ji* per day.

**ACUPUNCTURE:** *Xin Shu* (Bl 15), *Shen Men* (Ht 7), *Da Ling* (Per 7), *Dan Zhong* (CV 17), *Zhong Wan* (CV 12), *Feng Long* (St 40), *San Yin Jiao* (Sp 6). Use even supplementing-even draining method on all these points except for *San Yin Jiao*, *Da Ling*, and *Feng Long*. Supplement *San Yin Jiao* and drain *Da Ling* and *Feng Long*.

## 3. LIVER DEPRESSION-YIN VACUITY PATTERN

**MAIN SYMPTOMS:** A slightly red facial complexion, quick, bright eyes, a desire to move but inability to move, great sighing, irritation and vexation, chest and rib-side distention and fullness, sighing, possible acid regurgitation, insomnia, profuse dreams, a red tongue with slightly yellow fur, reddish urination, and a slightly bowstring, fine, rapid pulse

**TREATMENT PRINCIPLES:** Enrich yin and resolve depression, soothe the liver and harmonize the stomach

**FORMULA & MEDICINALS:** *Bai He Li Yu Tang* (Lily Rectify Depression Decoction)

Bulbus Lilii (*Bai He*), 15-60g, uncooked Radix Rehmanniae (*Sheng Di*), 12g, Rhizoma Anemarrhenae Aspheloidis (*Zhi Mu*), 10g, Pericarpium Citri Reticulatae Viride (*Qing Pi*), 6g, Pericarpium Citri Reticulatae (*Chen Pi*), 6g, Fructus Immaturus Citri Aurantii (*Zhi Shi*), 6g, calcined Concha Arcae Inflatae (*Wa Leng Zi*), 15g, Radix Auklandiae Lappae (*Mu Xiang*), 9g

Decoct in water and administer orally in two divided doses, morning and evening, one *ji* per day.

**ACUPUNCTURE:** *Xin Shu* (Bl 15), *Shen Men* (Ht 7), *Tai Xi* (Ki 3), *San Yin Jiao* (Sp 6), *Bai Hui* (GV 20), *Yin Tang* (M-HN-3), *Qi Men* (Liv 14), *Zhong Wan* (CV 12). Use supplementing technique on the first four points and draining technique on the last four.

## 4. SPLEEN DEPRESSION-LUNG DAMAGE PATTERN

**MAIN SYMPTOMS:** A flushed red facial complexion, excessive thinking and worrying, fatigued limbs, aversion to stir, a faint voice, a quiet, withdrawn affect, possible melancholy, a desire to eat but inability to eat, emission of coolness from the four limbs, numbness and tingling, paranoia, clouded head, torpid spirit, difficulty falling asleep at night, a bitter taste in the mouth, reddish urination, a red tongue, and a deep, fine pulse

TREATMENT PRINCIPLES: Enrich yin and supplement the lungs, fortify the spleen and resolve depression

FORMULA & MEDICINALS: *Bai He Li Pi Tang* (Lily Rectify the Spleen Decoction)

Bulbus Lilii (*Bai He*), 15-60g, Rhizoma Anemarrhenae Aspheloidis (*Zhi Mu*), 10g, uncooked Radix Rehmanniae (*Sheng Di*), 12g, Ramulus Cinnamomi Cassiae (*Gui Zhi*), 6g, Rhizoma Atractylodis (*Cang Zhu*), 10g, Fructus Meliae Toosendan (*Chuan Lian Zi*), 10g, Fructus Amomi (*Sha Ren*), 4.5g, Haemititum (*Dai Zhe Shi*), 12g

Decoct in water and administer orally in two divided doses, morning and evening, one *ji* per day.

ACUPUNCTURE: *Xin Shu* (Bl 15), *Fei Shu* (Bl 13), *Shen Men* (Ht 7), *Zu San Li* (St 36), *San Yin Jiao* (Sp 6), *Tai Chong* (Liv 3), *Bai Hui* (GV 20), *Yin Tang* (M-HN-3). Supplement the first five points and drain the last three.

## 5. LOSS OF REGULATION BETWEEN YIN & YANG PATTERN

MAIN SYMPTOMS: A sometimes red, sometimes white facial complexion, difficulty sleeping, profuse dreams, a desire to speak but inability to speak, a desire to stop speaking but inability to stop speaking, a desire to lie down but inability to lie down, a desire to sleep but inability to sleep, brooding and unhappiness, taciturnity, occasional heart vexation, occasional stretching and yawning, alternating sorrow and joy, seeming as if possessed, a red tongue, and a fine, rapid, forceless pulse

TREATMENT PRINCIPLES: Regulate and put in good order yin and yang

FORMULA & MEDICINALS: *Bai He Gui Fu Long Mu Tang* (Lily, Cinnamon, Aconite, Dragon Bone & Oyster Shell Decoction)

Bulbus Lilii (*Bai He*), 15-60g, Rhizoma Anemarrhenae Aspheloidis (*Zhi Mu*), 10g, uncooked Radix Rehmanniae (*Sheng Di*), 12g, Cortex Cinnamomi Cassiae (*Rou Gui*), 10g, Radix Lateralis Praeparatus Aconiti Carmichaeli (*Fu Zi*), 10g, uncooked Os Draconis (*Long Gu*), 12g, uncooked Concha Ostreae (*Mu Li*), 12g

Decoct in water and administer orally in two divided doses, morning and evening, one *ji* per day.

ACUPUNCTURE: *Xin Shu* (Bl 15), *Shen Shu* (Bl 23), *Ming Men* (GV 4), *Guan Yuan* (CV 4), *San Yin Jiao* (Sp 6), *Shen Men* (Ht 7), *Bai Hui* (GV 20), *Yin Tang* (M-HN-3). Supplement the first six points, adding moxa to *Shen Shu* and *Ming Men*. Drain the last two points.

## 6. LUNG-KIDNEY YIN VACUITY PATTERN

MAIN SYMPTOMS: Both cheeks slightly red, fatigue, lack of strength, a tendency to sorrow and a desire to cry, occasionally appearing to shrink in fear, paranoia, vexatious heat in the five hearts, steaming bones, tidal heat, easy fright, possible seminal emission and/or urinary incontinence, impotence, premature ejaculation, reddish urine, a slightly red tongue, and a fine, rapid pulse

TREATMENT PRINCIPLES: Enrich and supplement the lungs and kidneys, quiet the corporeal soul and stabilize the mind

FORMULA & MEDICINALS: *Bai He Ding Zhi Tang* (Lily Stabilize the Mind Decoction)

Bulbus Lilii (*Bai He*), 15-60g, Rhizoma Anemarrhenae Aspheloidis (*Zhi Mu*), 10g, uncooked Radix Rehmanniae (*Sheng Di*), 15g, Cortex Radicis Lycii Chinensis (*Di Gu Pi*), 10g, Radix Polygoni Multiflori (*He Shou Wu*), 10g, mix-fried Carapax Amydae Sinensis (*Bie Jia*), 15g

Decoct in water and administer orally in two divided doses, morning and evening, one *ji* per day.

ACUPUNCTURE: *Fei Shu* (Bl 13), *Xin Shu* (Bl 15), *Shen Shu* (Bl 23), *Tai Xi* (Ki 3), *San Yin Jiao* (Sp 6), *Da Zhui* (GV 14), *Bai Hui* (GV 20), *Yin Tang* (M-HN-3). Supplement the first five points, bleed *Da Zhui*, and drain the last two points.

## 7. NON-INTERACTION BETWEEN THE HEART & KIDNEYS PATTERN

MAIN SYMPTOMS: A flushed red facial complexion, vexation and agitation, a desire to sleep but inability to sleep, tossing and turning in bed restlessly, laughing and crying with no constancy, a tendency to stretch, lots of yawning, difficulty falling asleep, nightmares, confused, disorderly dreams, counterflow chilling of the lower extremities, garrulousness, reddish urination, a red tongue, and a fine, rapid pulse

TREATMENT PRINCIPLES: Nourish the heart and enrich the kidneys, join and free the flow between the heart and kidneys

**Formula & medicinals:** *Bai He Zi Shen Tang* (Lily Enrich the Kidneys Decoction)

Bulbus Lilii (*Bai He*), 15-60g, Rhizoma Anemarrhenae Aspheloidis (*Zhi Mu*), 10g, uncooked Radix Rehmanniae (*Sheng Di*), 15g, Rhizoma Coptidis Chinensis (*Huang Lian*), 3-6g, Cortex Cinnamomi Cassiae (*Rou Gui*), 10g, uncooked Os Draconis (*Long Gu*), 12g, uncooked Concha Ostreae (*Mu Li*), 12g, Gelatinum Corii Asini (*E Jiao*), 10g

Decoct in water and administer orally in two divided doses, morning and evening, one *ji* per day.

**Acupuncture:** *Xin Shu* (Bl 15), *Shen Shu* (Bl 23), *Ming Men* (GV 4), *Guan Yuan* (CV 4), *San Yin Jiao* (Sp 6), *Shen Men* (Ht 7), *Bai Hui* (GV 20), *Yin Tang* (M-HN-3). Supplement the first six points, adding moxa to *Shen Shu* and *Ming Men*. Drain the last two points.

**Clinical tips:** Lily disease is not a common diagnosis since its key symptoms are either shared with a number of other essence spirit diseases or are relatively amorphous and ill-defined. The fact that this diagnosis is rarely used in present-day China is evidenced by the fact that the authors could only find a single clinical audit discussing its treatment.

**Abstract from representative Chinese research:**

*Bei Jing Zhong Yi (Beijing Chinese Medicine)*, #3, 1999, p. 3: Yang Wei-hua *et al.* treated 56 patients with lily disease. Of these, 25 were men and 31 were women. All had been sick for 1-5 years. Eight cases were 60 years old or older, and all had been treated with such Western medicines as vitamin C, a multi-vitamin, and tranquilizers but without success. In terms of Western disease diagnosis, all had been labeled as suffering from anxiety disorder. Treatment consisted of internal administration of *Bai He Da Zao Tang* (Lily & Red Date Decoction) as described above under "Treatment based on pattern discrimination." Using this protocol, 20 patients were cured, 28 got a marked effect, and eight got no effect for a total amelioration rate of 85%. Cure meant that all symptoms disappeared and there was no recurrence within one year.

**Representative case histories:**

**❖ Case 1³ ❖**

The patient was a 56 year old female. For the past two years, she had suffered from anxiety, spontaneous perspiration, a dry mouth with a bitter taste, and inhibited urination. She had already been treated in the internal medicine and psychiatric departments with various types of orally administered Chinese and Western medicines but without marked effect. Therefore, she was referred to the authors of this case for examination. At that time, it was determined that, two years prior, the patient had suffered from a high fever which had not abated for one month even though she had been treated with large amounts of Western antibiotics and cold and cooling Chinese medicinals. Afterwards, the woman gradually developed headache, insomnia, impaired memory, spontaneous perspiration, a dry mouth with bitter taste, oral thirst, inability to sit or lie down calmly and occasional chills and occasional emission of heat even though her body temperature was normal. At times the woman was emotionally flustered and anxious. Her urine was short, reddish, rough, and painful. After defecation, she sometimes felt dizzy, and her stools were typically dry. Her tongue was red with scanty fur, and her pulse was fine and rapid.

Therefore, the patient's Chinese disease diagnosis was labeled as lily disease and her pattern was categorized as heart-lung yin vacuity with internal heat. The treatment principles were to enrich yin and clear heat, quiet the spirit and stabilize the mind. The formula consisted of *Bai He Da Zao Tang Jia Wei* (Lily & Red Date Decoction with Added Flavors): Bulbus Lilii (*Bai He*), 12g, uncooked Radix Rehmanniae (*Sheng Di*), 15g, Radix Glycyrrhizae (*Gan Cao*), 6g, Fructus Tritici Aestivi (*Huai Xiao Mai*), 15g, Fructus Zizyphi Jujubae (*Da Zao*), 5 pieces, uncooked Os Draconis (*Long Gu*) and Concha Ostreae (*Mu Li*), 20g each, Talcum (*Hua Shi*), 10g, Radix Trichosanthis Kirlowii (*Tian Hua Fen*), 15g, Semen Zizyphi Spinosae (*Suan Zao Ren*), 10g, Medulla Junci Effusi (*Deng Xin Cao*), 10g, and Medulla Tetrapanacis Papyriferi (*Tong Cao*), 10g. These medicinals were decocted in water and administered internally.

After taking 10 *ji* of the above formula, the dry mouth and emotional anxiety were 80% better. Therefore, the same ingredients were made into honey pills, each pill weighing 10g. Each day, the patient took one pill three times. She continued this regime for one month when her disease was judged cured. On follow-up after one year, there had been no recurrence.

**❖ Case 2⁴ ❖**

The patient was a 42 year old male worker who was first hospitalized in November 1972. The patient's main complaints were timidity and shrinking in fright, anxiety disturbance, a tendency to sorrow, a desire to cry, dream emission, and impotence, all of which had gotten worse during the last four months. Two years previously, the patient had suffered from pulmonary tuberculosis with a dry cough, oral thirst, lack of strength, and tidal heat. He had been treated with antitubercular drugs, and his disease had remitted. However, he still had low back encumbrance, lack of strength, emission of heat from his hands, feet, and heart, poor sleep, dream emission, and slippery essence. He was treated with both Chinese and Western medicine and this had gotten some improvement but had not eliminated the root of his condition. Some time later, the patient had become anxious, worried, and depressed. In addition, in the last four months, he had developed insomnia and night sweats. On examination, the patient's facial complexion was a somber white with flushed red cheeks, his urine was reddish, his tongue was red with no fluids or fur, and his pulse was fine and rapid.

Based on the above signs and symptoms, this patient's pattern was categorized as lung-kidney yin vacuity, for which he was prescribed *Bai He Ding Zhi Tang Jia Wei* (Lily Stabilize the Mind Decoction with Added Flavors): Bulbus Lilii (*Bai He*), 30g, Rhizoma Anemarrhenae Aspheloidis (*Zhi Mu*), 12g, uncooked Radix Rehmanniae (*Sheng Di*), 15g, Cortex Radicis Lycii Chinensis (*Di Gu Pi*), 15g, Radix Polygoni Multiflori (*He Shou Wu*), 18g, mix-fried Carapax Amydae Sinensis (*Bie Jia*), 10g, Bulbus Fritillariae Thunbergii (*Zhe Bei Mu*), 10g, and Herba Houttuyniae Cordatae Cum Radice (*Yu Xing Cao*), 15g.

After taking 10 *ji* of the above formula, the patient's disease remitted. There was now only slight melancholy, low back encumbrance, lack of strength, and dream emission. His pulse and tongue were the same as above. Therefore, the formula was changed slightly: Bulbus Lilii (*Bai He*), 30g, Rhizoma Anemarrhenae Aspheloidis (*Zhi Mu*), 12g, uncooked Radix Rehmanniae (*Sheng Di*), 15g, Cortex Radicis Lycii Chinensis (*Di Gu Pi*), 12g, Radix Polygoni Multiflori (*He Shou Wu*), 10g, Carapax Amydae Sinensis (*Bie Jia*), 10g, Bulbus Fritillariae Thunbergii (*Zhe Bei Mu*), 10g, Herba Houttuyniae Cordatae Cum Radice (*Yu Xing Cao*), 12g, Os Draconis (*Long Gu*), 18g, Rhizoma Cibotii Barometsis (*Gou Ji*), 10g, and Herba Epimedii (*Yin Yang Huo*), 10g.

After taking 20 *ji* of this formula, the clinical condition had completely disappeared. When the man was discharged from the hospital, he was advised to take one pill of *Bai He Wan* (Lily Pills) each morning, one pill of *Long Mu Wan* (Dragon Bone & Oyster Shell Pills) each noon, and one pill of *Di Huang Wan* (Rehmannia Pills) each evening and to continue this regime for 60 days. On fol-

low-up after two years, there had been no recurrence.

### ❖ CASE 3[5] ❖

The patient was a 20 year old female student who was first admitted to the hospital on May 17, 1978. During the previous three years, the patient had difficulties with a boy at her school who had hit her. Since then, she had become vexed and agitated at night and unable to sleep. Her grades had markedly gone down, she did not like to see people, and her spirit mind was abstracted. She had been treated at various hospitals before with sedatives and tranquilizers as well as Chinese medicinals to rectify her qi and quiet her spirit. However, the results had not been good and, therefore, she was referred to the authors of this case. At the time of examination, the patient's signs and symptoms included emotional depression, restlessness, chest and rib-side distention and fullness, burping and belching, acid regurgitation, scanty eating, a bitter taste in her mouth, reddish urine, a red tongue with slightly yellow fur, and a bowstring, fine, slightly rapid pulse.

Based on these signs and symptoms, the authors of this case categorized the young woman's pattern as liver depression transforming fire with fire consuming and damaging liver yin. The treatment principles were to enrich yin and resolve depression, harmonize the stomach and clear heat. The formula prescribed was *Bai He Li Yu Tang Jia Jian* (Lily Rectify Depression Decoction with Additions & Subtractions): Bulbus Lilii (*Bai He*), 60g, uncooked Radix Rehmanniae (*Sheng Di*), 30g, Rhizoma Anemarrhenae Aspheloidis (*Zhi Mu*), 15g, Pericarpium Citri Reticulatae (*Qing Pi*), 6g, Pericarpium Citri Reticulatae (*Chen Pi*), 6g, Fructus Citri Sacrodactylis (*Fo Shou*), 6g, Rhizoma Coptidis Chinensis (*Huang Lian*), 7g, Fructus Evodiae Rutecarpae (*Wu Zhu Yu*), 3g, and calcined Concha Arcae Inflatae (*Wa Leng Zi*), 15g.

After taking six *ji* of the above formula, the patient's eating and drinking increased slightly. Therefore, the dose of Buddha Hand Citron was increased in the original formula in order to strengthen the coursing of depression. At her third examination, the patient reported that the belching and acid regurgitation had disappeared, her eating and drinking had increased yet again, and her chest and rib-side distention and fullness had decreased. Therefore, Concha Arca was removed and 20 grams of stir-fried Semen Zizyphi Spinosae (*Suan Zao Ren*) was added. At her fourth examination, the patient's eating and drinking were normal and her chest and rib-side distention and fullness had disappeared. Her sleep had increased, her spirit mind abstraction had decreased, as had her heart palpitations and restlessness. Based on the principles of enriching yin and resolving depression, settling, stilling, and quieting the spirit, the patient was prescribed: Bulbus Lilii (*Bai He*), 30g, uncooked Radix Rehmanniae (*Sheng Di*), 30g, Rhizoma Anemarrhenae Aspheloidis (*Zhi Mu*), 15g, uncooked Concha Ostreae (*Mu Li*), 24g, Talcum (*Hua Shi*), 10g, Radix Glehniae Littoralis (*Sha Shen*), 15g, Tuber Ophiopogonis Japonici (*Mai Dong*), 15g, Fructus Meliae Toosendan (*Chuan Lian Zi*), 6g, stir-fried Semen Zizyphi Spinosae (*Suan Zao Ren*), 25g, and uncooked Dens Draconis (*Long Chi*), 24g.

After taking 10 *ji* of this formula, all her symptoms basically disappeared. In order to secure the treatment effect, she was prescribed *Bai He Li Yu Tang* with Fructus Schisandrae Chinensis (*Wu Wei Zi*), 10g, and Sclerotium Pararadicis Poriae Cocos (*Fu Shen*), 10g. At the same time as taking 10 *ji* of these medicinals, the patient was treated with psychotherapy, at which point she was judged cured. When she was discharged from the hospital, she was given 30 pills each of *Xiao Yao Wan* (Rambling Pills) and *Bai He Wan* (Lily Pills) and instructed to take one pill of the former every morning and one pill of the latter every night. On follow-up after one year, there had been no recurrence.

### ❖ CASE 4[6] ❖

The patient was a 52 year old female cadre who was first hospitalized on Jun. 20, 1975. When the patient was young, she was a good student who strived to make progress. She graduated from university and joined a work brigade were she became embroiled in the upheavals of the Cultural Revolution and was politically persecuted. In August 1969, the patient's eating and drinking became poor and she had difficulty sleeping. When she tried to pay attention, she found she could not concentrate. This downward trend continued until, in May 1972, the patient gradually seldom spoke and avoided other people. She isolated herself and was very melancholy. To others, it seemed as if she were possessed by a spirit. She was diagnosed and treated for a "functional psychological condition" for three months and her symptoms improved but were not completely eliminated. In September 1974, the patient's symptoms got worse. Her four limbs were fatigued and emitted coolness and she was sorrowful and cried frequently. At the time the authors of this case examined the woman, her facial complexion was flushed red, her head was lowered, she did not speak, sometimes she cried, she dreaded cold, her reactions were slow, her eating and drinking had become abnormal, and she had a bitter taste in her mouth. Her tongue was red and her pulse was deep and weak.

Based on these signs and symptoms, the authors categorized the patient's pattern as spleen depression damaging the lungs. Therefore, the treatment principles were to enrich yin and supplement the lungs, arouse the spleen and resolve depression, and the formula prescribed was *Bai He Li Pi Tang Jia Wei* (Lily Rectify the Spleen Decoction with Added Flavors): Bulbus Lilii (*Bai He*), 50g, Rhizoma Anemarrhenae Aspheloidis (*Zhi Mu*), 12g, uncooked Radix Rehmanniae (*Sheng Di*), 15g, Ramulus Cinnamomi Cassiae (*Gui Zhi*), 6g, Rhizoma Atractylodis (*Cang Zhu*), 15g, Fructus Amomi (*Sha Ren*), 9g, and Fructus Zanthoxyli Bungeani (*Chuan Jiao*), 9g.

After taking 20 *ji* of the above medicinals, the patient's melancholy and crying had disappeared and she was able to control her behavior and emotions. Her sleep increased, but her eating and drinking remained poor and she occasionally had hypochondral distention and fullness. Her tongue was not red and her pulse was now bowstring. Therefore, she was given: Radix Auklandiae Lappae (*Mu Xiang*), 6g, Fructus Amomi (*Sha Ren*), 9g, Radix Codonopsitis Pilosulae (*Dang Shen*), 15g, Rhizoma Atractylodis Macrocephalae (*Bai Zhu*), 12g, Sclerotium Poriae Cocos (*Fu Ling*), 12g, Radix Glycyrrhizae (*Gan Cao*), 6g, Pericarpium Citri Reticulatae (*Chen Pi*), 9g, Rhizoma Pinelliae Ternatae (*Ban Xia*), 9g, Bulbus Lilii (*Bai He*), 15g, and Tuber Curcumae (*Yu Jin*), 10g. After taking 20 *ji* of this prescription, all the patient's symptoms disappeared and she was discharged from the hospital. At that time, she was given 30 pills each of *Bai He Wan* (Lily Pills) and *Xiang Sha Yang Wei Wan* (Auklandia & Amomum Nourish the Stomach Pills) and told to take one pill of the former each morning and one pill of the latter each night.

### ❖ CASE 5[7] ❖

The patient was a 13 year old female who had suffered extreme fright in April 1960 after watching a postmortem dissection of a human body. Since then, she had such uncontrollable diarrhea, she had to stay indoors. She was taken to a hospital where she was told she was not diseased. After being sent home, she was not able to lift her neck and her head rolled from side to side. She was not able to speak and she lacked intelligence (*i.e.*, was not respondent). She was given sedatives for two days, but with no results. Therefore, she was referred to a Chinese doctor for examination and treatment. This Chinese doctor found that the girl's pulse was floating and rapid and that her tongue was red and lacked fur. There were no other particular signs or symptoms. Therefore, she was treated for lily disease by administering *Bai He Zhi Mu*

*Tang* (Lily & Anemarrhena Decoction): Bulbus Lilii (*Bai He*), 7 pieces, and Rhizoma Anemarrhenae Aspheloidis (*Zhi Mu*), 4.5g. After taking one *ji* of this prescription, the patient was able to lift her neck 7/10 and the rolling of her head from side to side was reduced. However, she could still not speak. After another *ji*, the patient was able to lift her neck completely and her head no longer rolled from side to side. Because she reported that her mouth was dry and she was very thirsty, she was given one *ji* of *Gua Lou Mu Li San* (Trichosanthes & Oyster Shell Powder): Fructus Trichosanthis Kirlowii (*Gua Lou*) and Concha Ostreae (*Mu Li*), 9g each. At this point the patient's disease was judged cured.

## ENDNOTES

[1] Interestingly, Bulbus Lilii (*Bai He*) is a main spirit-quieting anti-gu medicinal according to the Qing dynasty school of anti-gu medicine, and, in terms of modern Western disease categories, gu diseases correspond to intestinal dysbiosis, parasitosis, amebiasis, and candidiasis. In such cases, many bitter, cold heat-clearing, dampness-eliminating Chinese medicinals may provoke Jarish-Herxheimer reactions.

[2] In the case of MS, the usual Chinese disease diagnosis is wilting condition (*wei zheng*). However, if there was spasticity, convulsions might be a secondary disease diagnosis.

[3] Yang Wei-hua *et al.*, "A Clinical Audit of the Treatment of 56 Cases of Lily Disease with *Bai He Da Zao Tang* (Lily & Red Date Decoction)," *Bei Jing Zhong Yi (Beijing Chinese Medicine)*, #3, 1999, p. 35

[4] Li & Liu, *op. cit.*, p. 546-547

[5] Li & Liu, *op. cit.*, p. 541-542

[6] Li & Liu, *op. cit.*, p. 543-544

[7] Chen & Zhao, *op. cit.*, p. 412-413

# ❖ Book 3 ❖

# THE TREATMENT OF WESTERN PSYCHIATRIC DISEASES WITH CHINESE MEDICINE

The chapters within this Book deal with putatively Western psychiatric disorders. Either these are A) current diagnostic categories found in the *DSM-IV*, such as schizophrenia, major depressive disorder, and bipolar affective disorder, B) provisional Western medical diagnostic labels under investigation, such as premenstrual dysphoric disorder and perimenopausal syndrome, or C) Western medical diagnoses which were once considered standard but are no longer so according to the *DSM-IV*, such as hysteria. The chapters in this have been arranged in order similar to the *DSM-IV*, beginning with idisorders usually first diagnosed in infancy, childhood, or adolescence," progressing to mood, anxiety, and somatoform disorders, and ending with provisional diagnostic labels under investigation.

There are a number of philosophical issues surrounding the use of culturally determined, essentially Anglo-American diagnostic labels within Chinese medicine. In addition, some Western clinicians are questioning the utility of some of these labels which artificially create boundaries where none actually exist in real-life patients. For instance, it is now assumed by many that depression always includes elements of anxiety and that there is no hard and fast demarcation between mood disorders, cognitive disorders, and somatoform disorders.[1]

Be that as it may, there are several reasons for introducing these Western psychiatric disease categories in this work. The first and foremost of these is that, due to the world-wide hegemony of Western medicine, contemporary Chinese practitioners themselves, rightly or wrongly, are increasingly adopting these labels. Discussions of mental-emotional disease are, more and more, being framed in terms of these Western diagnostic labels within the Chinese medical literature. Therefore, literary research into the Chinese medical treatment of mental-emotional complaints increasingly requires searching the literature via these keywords.

Secondly, Western patients often come to the clinics of Western practitioners of Chinese medicine with these diagnoses pre-established by an MD. In that case, patients typically deem it important that their Chinese medical practitioners treat them for what they, the patient, take to be their diagnosis, i.e., their Western medical diagnosis. While the Chinese medical practitioner may reframe the Western medical diagnosis into one or more traditional Chinese disease diagnoses for their own pattern discrimination purposes, Western patients usually want assurance that they are being treated specifically for their Western medical diagnosis even when they go to a practitioner of Chinese medicine. As Richard Castillo points out, "Curing is... likely to have a poor outcome if the disease diagnosed is not simultaneously the illness that has brought the client in for treatment."[2]

Further, as Chinese medicine becomes more and more integrated into the dominant Western health care delivery system, Western practitioners of Chinese medicine need to be able to work within the framework of that system. Third party payers, such as insurance companies, Medicaid and Medicare, Workman's Compensation, HMOs, and PPOs, reimburse based on the treatment of Western disease diagnoses (identified by CPT and ICD-10 codes). In addition, as more and more Western patients receive integrated Chinese-Western medical treatment, Chinese medical practitioners will need to work and, therefore, communicate all the more with Western MDs. Since MDs tend to be more powerful within Western society (even within Chinese society) than Chinese medical practitioners, Chinese medical practitioners are, by and large, required to speak the language of the dominant paradigm.

## ENDNOTES

[1]Castillo, *op. cit.*, p. 172

[2]*Ibid.*, p. 33

# ATTENTION DEFICIT HYPERACTIVITY DISORDER (ADHD)

Attention deficit hyperactivity disorder (ADHD) is a problem that is usually diagnosed in children but can last throughout adolescence and into adulthood. As its name implies, it is characterized by poor attention span and easy distractibility and by hyperactivity and impulsivity.

## NOSOLOGY:

As presently conceived in the *DSM-IV*, three principal symptom patterns are included as sub-types of ADHD. In all patterns, symptoms must have their onset before the age of seven, persist at least six months, cause significant impairment, and not be better explained by a psychiatric or medical disorder or the effects of a medication or substance abuse. The predominantly inattentive subtype is characterized by a persisting pattern of at least five symp-

toms demonstrating consistent inability to maintain attention. The predominantly hyperactive-impulsiveness subtype is characterized by at least five symptoms demonstrating a pattern of excessive nondirected movement or impulsiveness. In the combined inattentive-hyperactive type, the patient must experience at least six inattentive symptoms and at least six hyperactivity symptoms. The following table lists representative symptoms included under inattentive and hyperactive subtypes of ADHD as defined in Western psychiatry.

An explicit and central aspect of the Western psychiatric diagnosis is symptom onset before age seven. This requirement has led to considerable vagueness and ambiguity in efforts to correctly diagnose adults who present with ADHD-like symptomatology but for whom an accurate

| SYMPTOM PATTERNS OF ADHD IN WESTERN PSYCHIATRY | |
|---|---|
| INATTENTIVE SUBTYPE | HYPERACTIVE SUBTYPE |
| 1. DIFFICULTY SUSTAINING ATTENTION<br>2. DOES NOT FOLLOW THROUGH WITH INSTRUCTIONS<br>3. DIFFICULTY ORGANIZING TASKS<br>4. EASILY DISTRACTED<br>5. AVOIDS TASKS THAT REQUIRE SUSTAINED MENTAL EFFORT | 1. OFTEN RESTLESS OR FIDGETS WITH HANDS WHEN SITTING<br>2. RUNS OR CLIMBS EXCESSIVELY OR WHEN INAPPROPRIATE TO DO SO<br>3. OFTEN BLURTS OUT ANSWERS INAPPROPRIATELY<br>4. HAS DIFFICULTY WAITING TURN<br>5. OFTEN INTERRUPTS OR INTRUDES ON OTHERS |

developmental history cannot be clearly established. For these reasons, the recently established residual adult sub-type of ADHD is viewed as a controversial diagnosis by many Western-trained psychiatrists.

Interestingly, some patterns included under ADHD as defined below describe easy anger, pronounced irritability, and vexation and agitation. Although these symptom patterns are not viewed as core features of ADHD as conceptualized in contemporary Western psychiatry, they resemble aspects of two other disorders that are frequently co-morbid with ADHD in surveyed Western populations: oppositional defiant disorder and conduct disorder. Inclusion of angry, irritable mood or agitated, aggressive behavior in the Chinese but not the Western psychiatric concept of ADHD likely points to a systematic difference between the nosologies of Chinese and Western medicine and not to actual differences in phenomenology or occurrence of similar symptom patterns in Chinese and Western culture.

EPIDEMIOLOGY:

Many factors confound efforts to estimate prevalence rates for symptom patterns that are included as subtypes of ADHD as defined in Western psychiatry. Rigorous comparisons between studies done at different times or in different countries is difficult because of substantial changes in diagnostic criteria for ADHD over the years. Because of this, significant differences in understanding of ADHD continue to exist between many Western countries, and there are no uniform epidemiologic data. Conservative prevalence estimates of ADHD among school-age children in Western cultures range from 2-8% depending on study methodology and diagnostic criteria used. Most surveys show a higher prevalence in boys than in girls. Further, boys tend to exhibit hyperactive or mixed type symptoms, whereas girls tend to exhibit the inattentive symptom pattern more frequently. Some studies suggest that most school-age children diagnosed with ADHD in Western cultures have the combined type symptom pattern as conceptualized in *DSM* and *ICD* classification systems.[1] Other studies suggest a high co-morbidity of ADHD and conduct disorder. The prevalence of ADHD in adult populations is difficult to estimate because of problems inherent in confirming the required symptom pattern during childhood and the often ambiguous presentation of predominantly inattentive-type symptoms in adulthood.

DIFFERENTIAL DIAGNOSIS:

In clarifying the differential diagnosis, the initial task is to determine whether the behavioral or cognitive presentation of a child brought to clinical attention is consistent with the abnormal or dysfunctional symptom patterns described as sub-types of ADHD. Cultural norms and the influence of social context (*i.e.*, family or other social factors) on behavior must be weighed in order to determine whether a persisting maladaptive behavioral pattern is present. In cases where a pattern of abnormal behavior has been established, acute medical causes must be ruled out. Certain seizure disorders, diseases of the central nervous system, toxic exposure, or metabolic diseases can manifest as symptom patterns that resemble hyperactivity or impaired attention and concentration. The effects of certain prescription medications (including, for example, bronchodilators) or illicit substances can manifest as hyperactivity, inattentiveness, or heightened impulsiveness. A careful history usually suggests or excludes possible medical etiologies.

---

## DIFFERENTIAL DIAGNOSIS

| 1. MEDICAL DISORDERS | 2. EFFECTS OF SUBSTANCES | 3. PSYCHIATRIC DISORDERS |
|---|---|---|
| A. SEIZURE DISORDERS | A. SIDE EFFECTS OF MEDICATIONS (*E.G.*, BRONCHODILATORS) | A. ATTENTION DEFICIT HYPER-ACTIVITY DISORDER (ADHD) |
| B. DISEASES OF THE CNS | B. ALCOHOL OR ILLICIT SUBSTANCE INTOXICATION OR WITHDRAWAL | B. GENERALIZED ANXIETY DISORDER (GAD) |
| C. TOXIC EXPOSURE | | C. SEPARATION ANXIETY |
| D. METABOLIC DISEASES | | D. OPPOSITIONAL-DEFIANT DISORDER |
| | | E. CONDUCT DISORDER |
| | | F. LEARNING DISORDERS |
| | | G. PERCEPTUAL OR COGNITIVE PROCESSING DEFICITS |

In most cases, underlying medical problems are not identified, and a primary diagnosis of ADHD is assumed. However a symptom pattern that looks like ADHD in the absence of evidence for associated medical problems does not necessarily imply a primary diagnosis of ADHD. Many disorders, including generalized anxiety disorder (GAD) and separation anxiety disorder, are phenomenologically similar to ADHD in many respects. As noted above (see Nosology), significant overlap exists between features of oppositional defiant disorder (ODD) or conduct disorder and features of ADHD. Whereas ODD and conduct disorder are characterized by a marked and persisting pattern of oppositional or antisocial behavior, these are not typical features of ADHD. A thorough behavioral history usually permits the clinician to determine whether one, both, or neither disorder is present.

Several neuropsychological tests give validated measures of abnormalities in attention and provide clues to the nature and severity of specific neuropsychological deficits manifesting as ADHD sub-types. Findings of learning disabilities or specific perceptual or cognitive processing deficits complicate the diagnostic picture, as these symptom patterns may represent primary neuropsychological abnormalities or may be secondary to the same brain dysfunction syndrome that underlies and manifests as ADHD.

## ETIOLOGY & PATHOPHYSIOLOGY:

Contemporary Western psychiatry views ADHD as multi-factorial in origin. Several competing theories have been proposed as models of brain dysfunction manifesting as symptom patterns that are presently categorized as sub-types of ADHD. Definitive evidence has not been established for any of these. The following table (page 280) summarizes important aspects of several representative theoretical models of pathogenesis.

## WESTERN MEDICAL TREATMENT:

Symptoms generally resolve rapidly when medical etiologies, medication side-effects, or substance abuse is identified and successfully treated. When primary medical causes and other psychiatric disorders have been eliminated, contemporary Western treatments typically include behavioral modification therapy and stimulant medications. Stimulants, including methylphenidate (Ritalin), dextroamphetamine, and pemoline (Cylert), are accepted standard treatments in contemporary Western psychiatry. All stimulants work as central dopamine agonists. Antidepressant medications, including tricyclic antidepressants, serotonin-selective re-uptake inhibitors

(SSRIs), and monoamine oxidase inhibitors (MAOIs), and atypical antidepressants (e.g., buproprion [Wellbutrin] and venlavaxine [Effexor]), have also been used with moderate success. Although there is no clearly established standard of treatment, psychiatrists increasingly favor SSRIs or atypical agents because of reduced risk of side effects, drug-drug interactions, or toxicities. Clonidine, anticonvulsants, and certain antipsychotic medications have also been used to a limited extent (because of significant side effect problems) with varying degrees of success.

Studies have demonstrated efficacy for both behavioral therapy and pharmacotherapy, and there is evidence for relatively greater treatment response when these modalities are combined. However, the efficacy of both approaches is related to numerous factors that are difficult to quantify, including co-morbidity, symptom severity, supportive family environment, and availability of specially adapted school programs.

Limited evidence from controlled studies suggests that strictly controlling diet to eliminate refined sugar and certain food additives favorably affects a small percentage of children with ADHD. In a similar vein, there is also limited evidence for the efficacy of megadose vitamin therapy or supplementation with essential fatty acids.

EEG biofeedback is a promising emerging treatment of ADHD that has yielded clinical improvements through selective suppression of lower (theta) EEG frequencies or selective stimulation of higher frequencies (alpha or beta).

## SHORT & LONG-TERM ADVANTAGES & DISADVANTAGES OF WESTERN MEDICAL TREATMENT:

When behavioral therapy alone is effective, medications and their potential side effects do not become treatment issues. However, in Western countries, medications are prescribed to treat most cases of childhood ADHD. Stimulants used to treat ADHD are typically accompanied by numerous behavioral side effects (or withdrawal effects) which sometimes interfere with the therapeutic effects of these medications. These include irritable mood, insomnia, appetite suppression with weight loss, subjective feelings of restlessness, and restricted expression of emotions. More serious but infrequent side effects of stimulants include visual hallucinations and abnormal movements (tics). Further, all stimulants may suppress growth hormone, resulting in transient delayed growth if used during childhood. Although the stimulant medications used to treat ADHD are not addictive in the same way

## ADHD: Western Models of Pathogenesis

| MODEL | ARGUMENTS AND EVIDENCE |
|---|---|
| GENETIC | • Four times higher incidence in first degree relatives of patients with ADHD<br>• 50% of Tourette's patients have ADHD<br>• higher rates of antisocial personality disorder among fathers in adoptive studies<br>• Higher rates of depression and anxiety in first degree relatives |
| CEREBRAL DYSFUNCTION | • Decreased frontal lobe metabolism on functional brain imaging<br>• Frontal cortical atrophy in adults diagnosed with ADHD as children |
| THTROID DYSFUNCTION | • Significant positive correlation between abnormal thyroid functions and some cases of ADHD<br>• Some symptoms improved with thyroid hormone replacement |
| AMINE HYPOTHESIS | • Low cerebrospinal fluid and serum levels of dopamine and serotonin and their metabolites<br>• Dopamine agonists effectively reduce symptom severity in many ADHD patients |
| ENVIRONMENTAL MODELS | • Many children diagnosed with ADHD have documented history of minor brain insults including fetal exposure to infections, birth trauma, nutritional deficiency and neonatal exposure to toxins<br>• Some children with ADHD may be hypersensitive to food additives or dyes (inconclusive evidence)<br>• Some children diagnosed with ADHD may be hypersensitive to refined sugar (also inconclusive)<br>• Some ADHD patients have a much higher requirement for vitamins than the normal population (limited evidence)  Psychosocial models |
| PSYCHOLOGICAL MODELS | • Children who experienced neglect or loss in early childhood exhibited higher rates of ADHD |

that illicit narcotics (*e.g.*, methamphetamine and cocaine) are addictive, abruptly stopping or reducing them can result in a mild rebound syndrome associated with irritability, mood changes, and disturbed sleep.

Non-stimulant medications used to treat ADHD have other kinds of side effects that differ depending on drug class. Serotonin-selective re-uptake inhibitors may cause sedation or agitation, changes in appetite, or anxiety. The older antidepressant agents (tricyclics) are seldom used in contemporary Western psychiatric treatment of ADHD because of significant side effects associated with these drugs, including changes in heart rate and blood pressure, visual blurring, dizziness, constipation, sedation, and dry mouth. Chronic use of clonidine can result in hypotension, and its sudden discontinuation can cause rebound hypertension. Because of potentially serious permanent side effects, antipsychotics are seldom used with the exception of severe symptoms that have not responded to adequate trials on all other available pharmacological agents. Deleterious consequences of EEG biofeedback have not been reported to date.

## PROGNOSIS:

The course and prognosis of ADHD depend on symptom severity and the presence of co-morbid medical or psychiatric disorders. Most children who respond to treatment with stimulants or other medications are generally able to adapt to public school environments, but many require special resource programs and more individualized supervision than their peers. Although many children diagnosed with ADHD experience gradual reduction in baseline symptom severity (including disruptive or impulsive behavior) with long-term treatment, some continue to pose behavioral problems through high school. Some studies have suggested that children diagnosed with ADHD are at higher risk of drug use or delinquency than their non-ADHD peers. It is estimated that approximately one half of all children diagnosed with ADHD are subsequently diagnosed with other psychiatric disorders in adolescence or early adulthood. These include bipolar disorder, conduct disorder, antisocial personality disorder, alcohol or substance abuse, and various anxiety disorders. Reasons for this association are not clearly established.

## INDICATIONS FOR REFERRAL TO WESTERN MEDICAL SERVICES:

Urgent referral to the nearest emergency room or urgent care center is indicated in cases of persisting hyperactivity, distractibility, or impulsive behavior where history and clinical presentation suggest an underlying medical etiology or substance abuse. These include seizure disorders, diseases of the central nervous system, exposure to toxins, and substance abuse. The conventional Western approach to discerning possible underlying medical causes of ADHD-like symptom patterns is described in the section on differential diagnosis.

When symptoms have not responded to an appropriate duration and course of Chinese medical treatment, non-urgent referral to a Western trained psychiatrist may clarify the differential diagnosis, thus leading to an optimized integrative treatment plan.

## CHINESE DISEASE CATEGORIZATION:

The main symptoms of attention deficit hyperactivity disorder as described in the Chinese medical literature correspond to the Chinese disease categories of irritability (*yi nu, duo nu*), insomnia (*bu mian*), profuse dreams (*duo meng*), oppressive ghost dreams (*meng yan*), vexation and agitation (*fan zao*), and impaired memory (*jian wang*).

## CHINESE DISEASE CAUSES & MECHANISMS:

In Chinese medicine, hyperactivity has mainly to do with the Chinese spirit residing in the heart. If the spirit is healthy, then it is, *ipso facto*, calm. If the spirit is calm, the mind is not agitated nor the body restless. Therefore, according to Chinese medicine, there are three basic mechanisms which may result in pediatric hyperactivity. Either the spirit is not nourished sufficiently, some sort of evil qi, such as heat or wind, harasses the heart spirit, or some sort of evil qi, such as phlegm turbidity or blood stasis, block the orifices of the heart.

The Chinese disease causes and mechanisms of attention deficit disorder (ADD) are very similar to those of hyperactivity, either there is insufficient qi and blood to construct the spirit mind, there is some evil qi harassing the heart spirit making it disquieted, or some evil qi is blocking the heart orifices, thus misting and confounding the heart spirit.

## TREATMENT BASED ON PATTERN DISCRIMINATION:

### 1. SPLEEN VACUITY-LIVER HYPERACTIVITY PATTERN

MAIN SYMPTOMS: Uncontrollable fidgeting, emotional tension, easy anger, poor sleep, fatigue, diminished appetite, easily developing diarrhea due to emotional stress, thin, white tongue fur, and a bowstring pulse

SYMPTOM ANALYSIS: Emotional tension, easy anger, and the bowstring pulse are all liver depression symptoms. Fatigue and diminished appetite are spleen vacuity symptoms. In this context, poor sleep and uncontrollable fidgeting are due to malnourishment of the spirit which is, consequently, disquieted. Diarrhea due to stress or emotional upset is due to liver assailing the spleen. The thin, white tongue fur says that there is neither evil heat nor phlegm turbidity.

TREATMENT PRINCIPLES: Fortify the spleen and harmonize the liver

FORMULA & MEDICINALS: *Yi Gan San* (Repress the Liver Powder)

Radix Bupleuri (*Chai Hu*), 3-10g, Ramulus Uncariae Cum Uncis (*Gou Teng*), 6-12g, Radix Angelicae Sinensis (*Dang Gui*), 4.5-10g, Radix Ligustici Wallichii (*Chuan Xiong*), 6-12g, Rhizoma Atractylodis Macrocephalae (*Bai Zhu*), 6-10g, Sclerotium Poriae Cocos (*Fu Ling*), 6-12g, mix-fried Radix Glycyrrhizae (*Gan Cao*), 3-10g

Decoct in water and administer orally in two divided doses, morning and evening, one *ji* per day.

FORMULA ANALYSIS: Within this formula, Bupleurum courses the liver and rectifies the qi. Uncaria settles and extinguishes liver wind and quiets the spirit. Dang Gui nourishes the blood to harmonize the liver and treats the blood to treat wind. Ligusticum moves the qi within the blood as well as guides the effects of the other medicinals upward to the head. Atractylodes, Poria, and mix-fried Licorice all fortify the spleen and, therefore, help construct the heart spirit.

ADDITIONS & SUBTRACTIONS: If spirit disquiet is pronounced, add Cortex Albizziae Julibrissinis (*He Huan Pi*) and Caulis Polygoni Multiflori (*Ye Jiao Teng*) or Os Draconis (*Long Gu*) and Concha Ostreae (*Mu Li*). If there is depressive heat, add Radix Scutellariae Baicalensis (*Huang Qin*) and/or Rhizoma Coptidis Chinensis (*Huang Lian*). If fatigue due to spleen vacuity is more pronounced, add Radix Codonopsitis Pilosulae (*Dang Shen*). If there is accompanying phlegm turbidity, add Rhizoma Pinelliae Ternatae (*Ban Xia*), Rhizoma Acori Graminei (*Shi Chang Pu*), and Pericarpium Citri Reticulatae (*Chen Pi*).

ACUPUNCTURE: *Tai Chong* (Liv 3), *He Gu* (LI 4), *Zu San Li* (St 36), *Shen Men* (Ht 7). Use even supplementing-even draining technique.

ADDITIONS & SUBTRACTIONS: If concentration is scattered, add *Bai Hui* (GV 20), *Si Shen Cong* (M-HN-1), and *Da Ling* (Per 7). If there is hyperactive stirring, add *Ding Shen* (N-HN-32), *An Mian* (N-HN-22), and *Xin Shu* (Bl 15). If the emotions are labile and there is vexation and agitation, add *Shen Ting* (GV 24), *Dan Zhong* (CV 17), and *Zhao Hai* (Ki 6).

## 2. HEART-SPLEEN DUAL VACUITY PATTERN

MAIN SYMPTOMS: A sallow yellow or somber white facial complexion, pale nails, pale lips, fatigue, insomnia, profuse dreams, heart palpitations, shortness of breath, poor appetite, a tendency to loose stools, impaired memory, a fat, pale tongue with teeth-marks on its edges and thin, white fur, and a fine, weak pulse

SYMPTOM ANALYSIS: The sallow yellow or somber white facial complexion, pale lips and nails, pale tongue, and fine pulse all are due to blood vacuity. The fatigue, shortness of breath, poor appetite, tendency to loose stools, fat tongue with teeth-marks on its edges, and weak pulse all are due to spleen qi vacuity. The insomnia, profuse dreams, impaired memory, and heart palpitations are due to qi and blood not constructing and nourishing the heart spirit.

TREATMENT PRINCIPLES: Fortify the spleen and supplement the heart, boost the qi and nourish the blood

FORMULA & MEDICINALS: *Gui Pi Tang He Gan Mai Da Zao Tang Jia Jian* (Restore the Spleen Decoction plus Licorice, Wheat & Red Dates Decoction with Additions & Subtractions)

Radix Pseudostellariae (*Tai Zi Shen*), 6-10g, Sclerotium Paradicis Poriae Cocos (*Fu Shen*), 6-12g, Rhizoma Atractylodis Macrocephalae (*Bai Zhu*), 6-10g, Radix Angelicae Sinensis (*Dang Gui*), 4.5-10g, Radix Astragali Membranacei (*Huang Qi*), 6-12g, Radix Polygalae Tenuifoliae (*Yuan Zhi*), 4.5-10g, Semen Zizyphi Spinosae (*Suan Zao Ren*), 6-12g, Rhizoma Acori Graminei (*Shi Chang Pu*), 3-10g, Fructus Schisandrae Chinensis (*Wu Wei Zi*), 6-10g, Fructus Zizyphi Jujubae (*Da Zao*), 2-5 pieces, Fructus Tritici Aestivi (*Huai Xiao Mai*), 12-25g, mix-fried Radix Glycyrrhizae (*Gan Cao*), 3-10g

Decoct in water and administer orally in two divided doses, morning and evening, one *ji* per day.

FORMULA ANALYSIS: Wheat, Astragalus, Pseudostellaria, Poria, Atractylodes, Schisandra, and mix-fried Licorice all supplement the spleen and, therefore, heart and lung qi. Dang Gui, Zizyphus Spinosa, and Red Dates nourish heart blood. Polygala and Acorus both transform phlegm and open the orifices. In addition, Polygala rectifies the qi and resolves depression. Spirit of Poria, Polygala, Zizyphus Spinosa, Acorus, and Wheat all also quiet the spirit.

ACUPUNCTURE: *Xin Shu* (Bl 15), *Ge Shu* (Bl 17), *Gao Huang Shu* (Bl 47), and *Pi Shu* (Bl 20). Use supplementing technique. Additions and subtractions same as for pattern #1 above.

### 3. YIN VACUITY-YANG HYPERACTIVITY PATTERN

MAIN SYMPTOMS: Besides tending to be thin, children with this pattern also have a red tongue with diminished fur or a pale tongue with a red tip. Their pulses are fine and rapid, and they tend to suffer from poor concentration, insomnia, heart palpitations, easy agitation, easy anger, excessive movement and speech, dizziness, tinnitus, possible low back pain, possible enuresis, flushed cheeks, dry mouth and throat, and possible night sweats.

ANALYSIS OF SYMPTOMS: A thin body suggests former heaven natural endowment yin insufficiency. A dry mouth and throat, red tongue with scanty fur and a fine rapid pulse tend to confirm this. The poor concentration, insomnia, heart palpitations, easy agitation, easy anger, excessive movement and speech, dizziness, flushed cheeks, and night sweats are all evidence of upwardly counterflowing yang not being controlled by yin. The enuresis and low back pain specifically indicate kidney yin vacuity as the root of this condition.

TREATMENT PRINCIPLES: Enrich and nourish kidney yin, level the liver and subdue yang, calm the heart and boost the intelligence

FORMULA & MEDICINALS: *Zuo Gui Yin Jia Wei* (Restore the Left [Kidney] Drink with Added Flavors)

Cooked Radix Rehmanniae (*Shu Di*), 6-12g, Fructus Corni Officinalis (*Shan Zhu Yu*), 6-10g, Fructus Lycii Chinensis (*Gou Qi Zi*), 6-10g, Sclerotium Poriae Cocos (*Fu Ling*), 6-10g, Radix Dioscoreae Oppositae (*Shan Yao*), 6-10g, mix-fried Radix Glycyrrhizae (*Gan Cao*), 3-6g, Rhizoma Anemarrhenae Aspheloidis (*Zhi Mu*), 6-10g, Cortex Phellodendri (*Huang Bai*), 6-10g, Plastrum Testudinis (*Gui Ban*), 10-15g, Fructus Ligustri Lucidi (*Nu Zhen Zi*), 6-10g, uncooked Os Draconis (*Long Gu*), 10-15g, uncooked Concha Ostreae (*Mu Li*), 10-15g, Rhizoma Acori Graminei (*Shi Chang Pu*), 6-10g

Decoct in water and administer orally in two divided doses, morning and evening, one *ji* per day.

ANALYSIS OF FORMULA: Within this formula, cooked Rehmannia, Lycium, Plastrum Testudinis, and Ligustrum all supplement the kidneys and enrich yin. These are aided by Cornus which supplements kidney yin and yang in a balanced way, by Dioscorea which supplements the

spleen and kidney qi, and by Poria and mix-fried Licorice which supplement spleen and stomach yin in order to bolster and support the kidneys. Anemarrhena and Phellodendron clear vacuity heat above, while Dragon Bone, Oyster Shell, and Plastrum Testudinis all heavily settle and subdue yang. In addition, Plastrum Testudinis also enriches yin. In this formula, Acorus quiets the spirit and boosts the intelligence. Other spirit-quieting medicinals include Dragon Bone, Oyster Shell, and Poria.

ADDITIONS & SUBTRACTIONS: If the concentration is scattered and the memory is poor, add Fructus Alpiniae Oxyphyllae (*Yi Zhi Ren*) and Radix Linderae Strychnifoliae (*Wu Yao*). If night-time sleep is not quiet and there are spasms and contractions of the hands and feet, add Semen Zizyphi Spinosae (*Suan Zao Ren*), Caulis Polygoni Multiflori (*Ye Jiao Teng*), Ramulus Uncariae Cum Uncis (*Gou Teng*), and Radix Albus Paeoniae Lactiflorae (*Bai Shao*).

ACUPUNCTURE: *Tai Xi* (Ki 3), *San Yin Jiao* (Sp 6), *Nei Guan* (Per 6), *Da Zhui* (GV 14), *Qu Chi* (LI 11). Use supplementing technique on the first two points and draining technique on the last three points. Additions and subtractions same as pattern #1 above.

### 4. PHLEGM HEAT HARASSING INTERNALLY PATTERN

MAIN SYMPTOMS: Excessive movement and speech, difficulty controlling oneself, lack of concentration, easy anger, pronounced irritability, vexation and agitation, possible nausea, profuse phlegm, chest and abdominal fullness and oppression, torpid intake, possible bad breath, a bitter taste in the mouth, yellow-red urination, red tongue edges and slimy, yellow tongue fur, and a slippery, rapid, bowstring pulse

ANALYSIS OF SYMPTOMS: Excessive movement and speech, difficulty controlling oneself, lack of concentration, easy anger, pronounced irritability, vexation and agitation, are all due to heat harassing the heart spirit above. This heat is corroborated by the bad breath, yellow-red urine, red tongue, yellow tongue fur, and rapid pulse. The signs and symptoms of phlegm include the profuse phlegm, chest and abdominal fullness and oppression, torpid intake, slimy tongue fur, and slippery pulse. The bowstring pulse and red tongue edges along with the anger and irritability show that the heat is depressive heat arising from the liver-gallbladder.

TREATMENT PRINCIPLES: Clear heat and disinhibit dampness, transform phlegm and calm the heart

**FORMULA & MEDICINALS:** *Huang Lian Wen Dan Tang Jia Jian* (Coptis Warm the Gallbladder Decoction with Additions & Subtractions)

Rhizoma Pinelliae Ternatae (*Ban Xia*), 6-12g, Pericarpium Citri Reticulatae (*Chen Pi*), 6-10g, Sclerotium Poriae Cocos (*Fu Ling*), 6-10g, Cortex Magnoliae Officinalis (*Hou Po*), 6-10g, Tuber Curcumae (*Yu Jin*), 6-10g, Rhizoma Acori Graminei (*Shi Chang Pu*), 6-10g, Talcum (*Hua Shi*), 6-10g, Fructus Citri Aurantii (*Zhi Ke*), 6-10g, Fructus Forsythiae Suspensae (*Lian Qiao*), 6-10g, Rhizoma Coptidis Chinensis (*Huang Lian*), 1.5-6g, Radix Glycyrrhizae (*Gan Cao*), 1.5-3g

Decoct in water and administer orally in two divided doses, morning and evening, one *ji* per day.

**FORMULA ANALYSIS:** Pinellia and Orange Peel transform phlegm and eliminate dampness. They also harmonize the stomach and rectify the qi. Other medicinals in this formula which rectify the qi are Aurantium, Magnolia, and Curcuma. Another medicinal which transforms phlegm is Acorus, while another medicinal which eliminates turbid dampness is Magnolia. Poria and Talcum both seep dampness and, therefore, not only aid in eliminating phlegm and dampness but also lead heart fire down and out of the body via urination. Coptis and Forsythia simply clear heat in the heart and stomach, and Licorice harmonizes all the other medicinals in this formula. Spirit-quieting medicinals in this formula include Poria and Acorus. In addition, Curcuma is an empiric specific for loosening the chest and eliminating oppression.

**ADDITIONS & SUBTRACTIONS:** If there is concomitant yin vacuity, add cooked Radix Rehmanniae (*Shu Di*), Bulbus Lilii (*Bai He*), and Herba Dendrobii (*Shi Hu*). If there is accompanying constipation due to more exuberant heat evils, add Radix Et Rhizoma Rhei (*Da Huang*), Radix Scutellariae Baicalensis (*Huang Qin*), and Fructus Gardeniae Jasminoidis (*Zhi Zi*). If there is more profuse phlegm and marked chest oppression, add Lapis Micae Seu Chloriti (*Meng Shi*) and Lignum Aquilariae Agallochae (*Chen Xiang*).

If there is phlegm confounding the orifices but no or very minor heat, use *Chang Zhi Long Mu Tang* (Acorus, Polygala, Dragon Bone & Oyster Shell Decoction): Rhizoma Acori Graminei (*Shi Chang Pu*), 6-10g, mix-fried Radix Polygalae Tenuifoliae (*Yuan Zhi*), 6-10g, uncooked Os Draconis (*Long Gu*), 6-12g, uncooked Concha Ostreae (*Mu Li*), 6-12g, and Succinum (*Hu Po*), 0.5-2g. If there is then concomitant yang qi vacuity, add Radix Astragali

Membranacei (*Huang Qi*), Cornu Cervi (*Lu Jiao*), and Radix Lateralis Praeparatus Aconiti Carmichaeli (*Fu Zi*).

**ACUPUNCTURE:** *Feng Long* (St 40), *Zhong Wan* (CV 12), *Nei Guan* (Per 6), *Da Zhui* (GV 14), *Qu Chi* (LI 11). Use draining technique. Additions and subtractions same as pattern #1 above.

## 5. STATIC BLOOD OBSTRUCTING INTERNALLY PATTERN

**MAIN SYMPTOMS:** Poor concentration, difficulty studying, easy anger over nothing, excessive movement and restlessness, dry, withered hair and scaly skin, prominent blue green sinews (*i.e.*, veins), possible history of birth trauma with intracranial hemorrhage, a blue-green or dull, dark facial complexion, a dark and/or purple tongue or static spots or macules, engorged, tortuous sublingual veins, and a deep, choppy, fine, choppy, or bound, regularly intermittent pulse

**ANALYSIS OF SYMPTOMS:** Most of the signs and symptoms in the above list indicate blood stasis. The poor concentration, difficulty studying, and excessive movement are due to a disquieted spirit due to a combination of blockage of the portals of the heart and heart blood and essence vacuity not constructing and nourishing the spirit. The latter is based on the idea that static blood inhibits the engenderment of new or fresh blood. The easy anger shows that there is qi stagnation, not just blood stasis.

**TREATMENT PRINCIPLES:** Quicken the blood and transform stasis, nourish the blood and engender essence, calm the spirit and boost the intelligence

**FORMULA & MEDICINALS:** *Huo Xue An Shen Tang* (Quicken the Blood & Quiet the Spirit Decoction)

Semen Pruni Persicae (*Tao Ren*), 6-10g, Flos Carthami Tinctorii (*Hong Hua*), 6-10g, Radix Ligustici Wallichii (*Chuan Xiong*), 3-6g, Radix Rubrus Paeoniae Lactiflorae (*Chi Shao*), 3-6g, Rhizoma Acori Graminei (*Shi Chang Pu*), 6-10g, Fructus Alpiniae Oxyphyllae (*Yi Zhi Ren*), 6-10g, Fructus Corni Officinalis (*Shan Zhu Yu*), 6-10g, cooked Radix Rehmanniae (*Shu Di*), 6-12g, Rhizoma Polygonati (*Huang Jing*), 6-10g

Decoct in water and administer orally in two divided doses, morning and evening, one *ji* per day.

**ANALYSIS OF FORMULA:** Persica, Carthamus, Red Peony, and Ligusticum all quicken the blood and transform stasis.

Alpinia, Cornus, cooked Rehmannia, and Polygonatum supplement yin and yang, thus boosting and filling the essence. Acorus opens the heart orifices, quiets the spirit, and boosts the intelligence as does Alpinia.

**ADDITIONS & SUBTRACTIONS:** If there is excessive movement and restless fidgeting, add Os Draconis (*Long Gu*) and Concha Ostreae (*Mu Li*). If there is essence spirit lassitude, fatigue, shortness of breath, and heart palpitations, add Radix Astragali Membranacei (*Huang Qi*) and Radix Angelicae Sinensis (*Dang Gui*). If there is torpid intake, a sallow yellow facial complexion, and lack of strength of the four limbs, add Radix Codonopsitis Pilosulae (*Dang Shen*), Rhizoma Atractylodis Macrocephalae (*Bai Zhu*), Sclerotium Poriae Cocos (*Fu Ling*), and Radix Dioscoreae Oppositae (*Shan Yao*). If there is simultaneous vexatious heat in the five hearts, insomnia, profuse dreams, bodily emaciation, and a red tongue with scanty fur, add Plastrum Testudinis (*Gui Ban*), uncooked Radix Rehmanniae (*Sheng Di*), Rhizoma Anemarrhenae Aspheloidis (*Zhi Mu*), and Cortex Phellodendri (*Huang Bai*).

**ACUPUNCTURE:** *Xue Hai* (Sp 10), *He Gu* (LI 4), *Xin Shu* (Bl 15), *Ge Shu* (Bl 17), *Shen Shu* (Bl 23). Use draining technique on the first three points and supplementing technique on the last two. Additions and subtractions same as pattern #1 above.

## 6. YANG QI INSUFFICIENCY PATTERN

**MAIN SYMPTOMS:** Poor concentration, excessive movement but not over-excitation, lassitude of the spirit, a somber white facial complexion, torpid intake, loose stools, low back and knee soreness and limpness, a cold body and chilled limbs, a pale tongue with moist fur, and a deep, weak pulse

**SYMPTOM ANALYSIS:** The poor concentration, excessive movement but not overexcitation, and lassitude of the spirit are due to nonconstruction of the heart spirit by the yang qi of the spleen and kidneys. The torpid intake and loose stools indicate spleen qi vacuity weakness, while the low back and knee soreness and weakness indicate a kidney vacuity. The somber white facial complexion, cold body and chilled limbs, pale tongue, and deep, weak pulse all suggest vacuity cold due to yang qi insufficiency. The moist tongue fur shows that yang qi is too vacuous and weak to transport and transform fluids properly.

**TREATMENT PRINCIPLES:** Supplement the kidneys and boost the qi, strengthen the will (or mind) and quiet the spirit

**FORMULA & MEDICINALS:** *Shen Qi Wan Jia Wei* (Kidney Qi Pills with Added Flavors)

Cooked Radix Rehmanniae (*Shu Di*), 6-12g, Fructus Corni Officinalis (*Shan Zhu Yu*), 6-10g, Radix Dioscoreae Oppositae (*Shan Yao*), 6-10g, Sclerotium Poriae Cocos (*Fu Ling*), 6-10g, Rhizoma Alismatis (*Ze Xie*), 6-10g, Cortex Radicis Moutan (*Dan Pi*), 3-6g, Radix Lateralis Praeparatus Aconiti Carmichaeli (*Fu Zi*), 3-6g, Cortex Cinnamomi Cassiae (*Rou Gui*), 3-6g, Fructus Alpiniae Oxyphyllae (*Yi Zhi Ren*), 6-10g, Rhizoma Acori Graminei (*Shi Chang Pu*), 6-10g

Decoct in water and administer orally in two divided doses, morning and evening, one *ji* per day.

**FORMULA ANALYSIS:** Cooked Rehmannia nourishes the blood and supplements the kidneys. Although this pattern is one of yang qi vacuity, yin is the mother of yang from which yang is transformed and grows. Cornus and Dioscorea both supplement the kidney qi. Dioscorea also supplements the spleen qi and helps eliminate dampness. Poria likewise fortifies the spleen, seeps dampness, and also quiets the spirit. Alisma seeps dampness and also prevents supplementation of yang resulting in flaming fire. It is aided in this latter job by Moutan which also quickens the blood and transforms stasis. Aconite and Cinnamon both strongly warm yang and invigorate the kidneys, while Alpinia and Acorus both boost the intelligence.

**ACUPUNCTURE & MOXIBUSTION:** *Shen Shu* (Bl 23), *Ming Men* (GV 4), *Zhi Shi* (Bl 51), *Guan Yuan* (CV 4), *Zu San Li* (St 36). Moxa all points.

**CLINICAL TIPS:** In Chinese medicine, activity is yang. Therefore, in real-life hyperactive patients, there is typically either depressive, phlegm, or vacuity heat and pure vacuity patterns are rarely seen.

## REPRESENTATIVE ABSTRACTS OF CHINESE RESEARCH:

*Zhong Guo Zhong Xi Yi Jie He Za Zhi* (*Chinese Journal of Integrated Chinese-Western Medicine*), #7, 1999, p. 410-411: Li Xue-rong and Chen Zhi-jian conducted a prospective, double-blind study of 70 children diagnosed as suffering from hyperactivity. All these children were 6-14 years old and all met the diagnostic criteria for pediatric hyperactivity in *DSM-IV*. In addition, all these children were assessed by the Conners hyperactivity index before and after treatment. The 70 children were divided into treatment and comparison groups which were, in terms of sex, age, disease duration, and severity of symptoms statistically similar (P , 0.05). The 37 children in the treatment group were administered *Duo Dong Ning* (Hyperactivity Calmer) orally. This consisted of: Fructus Lycii Chinensis (*Gou Qi Zi*), cooked Radix Rehmanniae (*Shu Di*), Fructus Schisandrae Chinensis (*Wu Wei Zi*), Radix Panacis Ginseng (*Ren Shen*), Sclerotium Poriae Cocos (*Fu Ling*), and Radix Glycyrrhizae (*Gan Cao*). Children under eight years of age were given three grams of this formula per day in pill form. Children eight and over were given six grams per day. The 33 children in the comparison group were given 10mg per day of Ritalin, and four weeks equaled one course of treatment. In terms of outcomes, there was no statistically marked difference in therapeutic effectiveness between the Chinese medicinals and Ritalin (P>0.05). However, the children in the Ritalin group experienced more severe side effects, such as loss of appetite, than those treated with Chinese medicinals (P<0.05).

*Si Chuan Zhong Yi* (*Sichuan Chinese Medicine*), #12, 1999, p. 46: Zhang Guang-shuan *et al.* reported on the treatment of 42 cases of pediatric hyperactivity with integrated Chinese-Western medicine. As part of the disease definition, the authors included decreased ability to concentrate and emotional lability as well as excessive physical activity. All the patients were seen as out-patients and all were diagnosed based on Chinese national criteria for pediatric hyperactivity. Among the 42 cases, 30 were boys and 12 were girls. All were between 5-12 years of age, and their disease course had lasted from as short as four months to as long as 4.5 years. The Chinese medicinal treatment consisted of: Radix Bupleuri (*Chai Hu*), 6-12g, Radix Scutellariae Baicalensis (*Huang Qin*), 5-10g, Fructus Tribuli Terrestris (*Bai Ji Li*), 6-10g, Radix Astragali Membranacei (*Huang Qi*), 20-40g, Radix Codonopsitis Pilosulae (*Dang Shen*), 10-15g, Folium Bambusae (*Zhu Ye*), 6-10g, Fructus Ligustri Lucidi (*Nu Zhen Zi*), 6-12g, and Concha Margaritiferae (*Zhen Zhu Mu*), 10-20g. If there was heart-liver fire depression, 15 grams of Ramulus Uncariae Cum Uncis (*Gou Teng*), 30 grams of Folium Mori Albi (*Sang Ye*), and 12 grams of Radix Albus Paeoniae Lactiflorae (*Bai Shao*) were added. If there was spleen qi vacuity weakness, eight grams of Rhizoma Atractylodis Macrocephalae (*Bai Zhu*), 20 grams of Sclerotium Poriae Cocos (*Fu Ling*), and 10 grams of Fructus Alpiniae Oxyphyllae (*Yi Zhi Ren*) were added. If there was yin vacuity with yang hyperactivity, eight grams of cooked Radix Rehmanniae (*Shu Di*), 20 grams of Plastrum Testudinis (*Gui Ban*), and 10 grams of Fructus Corni Officinalis (*Shan Zhu Yu*) were added. In addition, the children were give one gram of Ritalin per day. One

month equaled one course of treatment. During this treatment a clear bland diet was administered, and greatly acrid, greatly hot, greatly bitter, and greatly cold foods were prohibited. Typically, treatment lasted from 1-3 courses. In 22 cases (52.4%) all the symptoms disappeared. In 15 cases (35.7%) symptoms partially remitted, and in five cases (11.9%) there was no improvement in symptoms. Thus the total amelioration rate was 88.1%.

*Hu Bei Zhong Yi Za Zhi* (*Hubei Journal of Chinese Medicine*), #3, 1994, p. 33: Zhao Qi-ran and Peng Hong-xing reported on the treatment of 30 cases of pediatric hyperactivity using *Gui Zhi Tang* (Cinnamon Twig Decoction). In this study, there were 21 boys and nine girls ranging in age from 2-13 years old. The course of their disease had lasted from as short as five days to as long as four years. *Gui Zhi Tang* consisted of: Ramulus Cinnamomi Cassiae (*Gui Zhi*), 6g, Radix Albus Paeoniae Lactoflorae (*Bai Shao*), 15g, mix-fried Radix Glycyrrhizae (*Gan Cao*), 4g, uncooked Rhizoma Zingiberis (*Sheng Jiang*), 4 slices, and Fructus Zizyphi Jujubae (*Da Zao*), 4 pieces. One *ji* was decocted per day and administered, with seven days equaling one course of treatment. Using this protocol, eight cases were judged cured, 17 markedly improved, three improved, and two experienced no effect. Thus the total amelioration rate was 93.3%.

❖

*Zhe Jiang Zhong Yi Za Zhi* (*Zhejiang Journal of Chinese Medicine*), #10, 1994, p. 469: Sun Hao reported on the treatment of 53 cases of pediatric hyperactivity using a standard formula. Among these 53 children, there were 48 boys and five girls. Twenty-nine were between the ages of 6-7 years old, 13 were between 8-9, and eight cases were 10 years old or above. All had been previously examined by Western physicians and neurological conditions had been ruled out. The formula administered consisted of: cooked Radix Rehmanniae (*Shu Di*), Radix Albus Paeoniae Lactiflorae (*Bai Shao*), Fructus Corni Officinalis (*Shan Zhu Yu*), and Sclerotium Pararadicis Poriae Cocos (*Fu Shen*), 10-15g each, Fructus Schisandrae Chinensis (*Wu Wei Zi*), 3-5g, Fructus Lycii Chinensis (*Gou Qi Zi*), 10g, mix-fried Radix Polygalae Tenuifoliae (*Yuan Zhi*), 5-10g, uncooked Os Draconis (*Long Gu*) and uncooked Concha Ostreae (*Mu Li*), 20-30g each, mix-fried Radix Glycyrrhizae (*Gan Cao*), 5g, Fructus Zizyphi Jujubae (*Da Zao*), 3-5 pieces, and Fructus Tritici Aestivi (*Huai Xiao Mai*), 50-100g. One *ji* of this formula was administered per day for 10 days, after which the doses were multiplied by a factor of eight and powdered. For the next three months, patients received 10 grams of this powder two times per day mixed with sugar and hot water. Using this protocol, 39 children were cured, 10 children improved, and four children got no effect. Thus the total amelioration rate was 92.4%.

❖

*Zhong Yi Za Zhi (Journal of Chinese Medicine)*, #11, 1994, p. 696: Sun Hao again reported on the treatment of five boys and one girl for hyperactivity. Four of these cases were between 7-9 years, one was six, and the other was 10 years old. The formula used in this study was *Gan Mai Da Zao Tang* (Licorice, Wheat & Red Dates Decoction) composed of: Radix Glycyrrhizae (*Gan Cao*), 10g, Fructus Tritici Aestivi (*Huai Xiao Mai*), 50g, and Fructus Zizyphi Jujubae (*Da Zao*), 10 pieces. After one month of treatment, the hyperactivity was markedly decreased in two cases, after two months, all four other patients' hyperactivity was basically under control. After three months of treatment, all six children were able to sit still in class and their academic achievement markedly rose.

REPRESENTATIVE CASE HISTORIES:

❖ CASE 1[2] ❖

The patient was a 12 year old boy who was first examined on Mar. 6, 1988. According to the boy's mother, the child's spirit was not calm and he was prone to fear. For the last year he had been hyperactive. He also suffered from insomnia and profuse dreams. His throat was dry and his mouth was parched. His studies were not good and his emotions were not stable. Sometimes he broke things and acted violently. He had not responded to his teacher's admonishments. The boy's essence spirit was listless and he reported being fatigued. In addition, his tongue was red with scanty fur and his pulse was fine and rapid. EEG was normal. He was diagnosed as being hyperactive, and his pattern was categorized as kidney water insufficiency with heart fire flaming upward. Therefore, he was prescribed the following form of *Huang Lian E Jiao Tang Jia Jian* (Coptis & Donkey Skin Glue Decoction with Additions & Subtractions): Rhizoma Coptidis Chinensis (*Huang Lian*), 4g, Gelatinum Corii Asini (*E Jiao*) and Radix Albus Paeoniae Lactiflorae (*Bai Shao*), 9g each, Radix Scutellariae Baicalensis (*Huang Qin*), cooked Radix Rehmanniae (*Shu Di*), Radix Dioscoreae Oppositae (*Shan Yao*), Semen Zizyphi Spinosae (*Suan Zao Ren*), uncooked Concha Ostreae (*Mu Li*), and Plastrum Testudinis (*Gui Ban*), 10g each, Radix Bupleuri (*Chai Hu*) and Cortex Radicis Moutan (*Dan Pi*), 8g each. Five *ji* of this formula were ground into powder, and 9-15

grams of this powder were decocted in water and administered two times per day.

After taking these five *ji*'s worth of medicinals, the boy's mind seemed to be clear and awake and his emotions had become stable. His sleep had improved, but he still was hyperactive. Therefore, 10 grams of Radix Polygalae Tenuifoliae (*Yuan Zhi*) and six grams of Rhizoma Acori Graminei (*Shi Chang Pu*) were added to the original formula and seven more *ji* were prescribed. After this, the boy's movement was markedly more restrained and his eating and drinking had increased. Another seven *ji* were administered, after which the boy was judged cured. There had been no recurrence on follow-up after two years.

❖ CASE 2[3] ❖

The patient was a 13 year old girl who was first examined on Oct. 5, 1989. The girl's emotions were unstable her memory was poor, she was emotionally tense, and she moved hyperactively. Her emotions had been tense and upset for the last year, but had gotten worse in the last month when she had been frightened by ghost stories by country relatives. Her facial complexion was sallow yellow. Externally she appeared to be tense and anxious. Her tongue was pale with white fur, and her pulse was fine and rapid. When pressed heavily, the pulse became forceless. Electroencephalogram was normal. Her pattern was categorized as kidney water insufficiency with ascendant liver yang hyperactivity. Therefore, she was prescribed *Er Xian Tang Jia Wei* (Two Immortals Decoction with Added Flavors): Herba Epimedii (*Xian Ling Pi*), Radix Morindae Officinalis (*Ba Ji Tian*), Rhizoma Curculignis Orchioidis (*Xian Mao*), Radix Angelicae Sinensis (*Dang Gui*), Herba Cistanchis Deserticolae (*Rou Cong Rong*), Fructus Ligustri Lucidi (*Nu Zhen Zi*), and Cortex Albizziae Julibrissinis (*He Huan Pi*), 8g each, stir-fried Semen Zizyphi Spinosae (*Suan Zao Ren*), 12g, Radix Albus Paeoniae Lactiflorae (*Bai Shao*), 10g, Rhizoma Anemarrhenae Aspheloidis (*Zhi Mu*) and Cortex Phellodendri (*Huang Bai*), 6g each.

After taking five *ji* of the above medicinals, the girl's spirit was calm and her emotions were stable. Her responses to others were comprehensible, but her pulse and tongue were as before. Therefore, 15 grams of processed Radix Polygoni Multiflori (*He Shou Wu*) and six grams of Ramulus Uncariae Cum Uncis (*Gou Teng*) were added to the formula and another 23 *ji* were administered. After this, the patient's essence spirit was strong and good, her emotions were positive, and her grades had gone up. On follow-up after one year, there had been no recurrence.

### ❖ CASE 3[4] ❖

The patient was a nine year old boy who was first examined on Jul. 7, 1988. According to his mother, the boy's mind was listless yet he moved about restlessly. He had cut class for the last three months. For the last year, he was easily frightened and easily aroused from sleep. After waking, he would cry. In addition, the boy was fatigued, his body lacked strength, his reactions were slow, and his memory was not good. In recent days, he had become vexed, agitated, and restless with no thought for food or drink. The child's body was thin and his head hung down. His tongue was pale with white fur, and his pulse was deep, fine, and weak, especially so in the cubit positions. Electroencephalogram was normal. His pattern was categorized as kidney essence vacuity detriment with brain marrow not full.

Thus the boy was prescribed modified *Er Xian Tang Jia Jian* (Two Immortals Decoction with Additions & Subtractions): Rhizoma Curculiginis Orchioidis (*Xian Mao*), Herba Epimedii (*Xian Ling Pi*), Radix Morindae Officinalis (*Ba Ji Tian*), Herba Cistanchis Deserticolae (*Rou Cong Rong*), Radix Angelicae Sinensis (*Dang Gui*), cooked Radix Rehmanniae (*Shu Di*), Fructus Ligustri Lucidi (*Nu Zhen Zi*), Fructus Corni Officinalis (*Shan Zhu Yu*), Gelatinum Corni Cervi (*Lu Jiao Jiao*), Plastrum Testudinis (*Gui Ban*), stir-fried Semen Zizyphi Spinosae (*Suan Zao Ren*), and Fructus Alpiniae Oxyphyllae (*Yi Zhi Ren*), 9g each, and mix-fried Radix Glycyrrhizae (*Gan Cao*), 3g.

After taking five *ji* of the above medicinals, the boy's emotions and hyperactivity were all markedly improved. In addition, his eating and drinking had increased. Mix-fried Licorice and Zizyphus Spinosa were removed from the formula, but one pill per day of *Ren Shen Jian Pi Wan* (Ginseng Fortify the Spleen Pills) was added, a half pill taken each morning and night. Another 26 *ji* were administered, after which time the boy was judged cured. On fol-low-up after one year, there had been no recurrence, his body was stronger and healthier than before, and his studies had improved.

### ❖ CASE 4[5] ❖

The patient was an eight year old, male student who was first examined on May 10, 1996. The student's grades had been unusually low and he had been easily excited to movement for the last half year. He was seen to make small movements throughout his classes, his concentration was unstable, he habitually glanced right and left, and he was easily moved to either tears or anger. His teachers had tried numerous times to alter this behavior but without improvement. In addition, the child had insomnia, night sweats, and bruxism. The tip of his tongue was slightly red, and his pulse was bowstring and fine. Therefore, he was categorized as displaying a heart-liver fire depression pattern. He was treated with the integrated Chinese-Western medical protocol described by Zhang Guang-shuan *et al.* in the second Chinese research report above. This treatment lasted for two months, after which all his symptoms disappeared, and his grades gradually improved.

### ENDNOTES

[1] 2I.e., *International Classification of Disease*, 10th edition (*ICD 10*), World Health Organization

[2] Wang Shi-biao & Duan Ji-hong, "The Treatment of Pediatric Hyperactivity Based on the Kidneys," *Shang Hai Zhong Yi Yao Za Zhi (Shanghai Journal of Chinese Medicine & Medicinals)*, #3, 1993, p. 22

[3] *Ibid.*, p. 22-23

[4] *Ibid.*, p. 23

[5] Zhang Guang-shuan *et al.*, "The Treatment of 42 Cases of Pediatric Hyperactivity with Integrated Chinese-Western Medicine," *Si Chuan Zhong Yi (Sichuan Chinese Medicine)*, #12, 1999, p. 46

# 2

# SENILE DEMENTIA

Senile dementia refers to dementia in the elderly. While this is a common diagnostic label in modern Chinese medicine, this is not a current diagnostic label in modern Western psychiatry. Some Western clinician's divide dementia in the elderly into Alzheimer's and non-Alzheimer's types. No such distinction is made in modern Chinese medicine. The following Chinese medical description of this modern Chinese disease category comes from Yan De-xin's *Aging & Blood Stasis*:

> Senile dementia ... refers to mental disease which occurs before or after 65 years of age. Its pathological change is extensive cerebral atrophy which is marked in the frontal lobe. The weight of the brain is at least 100g lighter than that of a normal elderly person. The neurons are atrophic, and the number and quality of nerve cells are reduced. Because the average length of human life has been prolonged, the incidence of senile dementia is gradually rising...

> Senile dementia is characterized by numerous disease causes and variability in the conditions associated with this disease. The majority of elderly persons around 65 years of age have numerous types of diseases in their bodies. In addition, their bodies and psychological activities, including their brains, have slowly degenerated. Because immunity in the aged declines, their resistance to

disease is already weakened. In addition, owing to various diseases, they regularly take different kinds of drugs, but their ability to break down and excrete these drugs' toxins is also weakened. Thus, chronic drug toxicity is one of the disease causes of this disease. Loneliness and solitude caused by unpleasant emotional experiences in life, such as separation from sons and daughters, bereavement of spouses, and decrease in social activities are internal psychological factors of this disease. It also sometimes happens that, during acute attacks of infectious disease, disturbances of consciousness appear and that, when the acute attack is over, senile dementia manifests itself!

## NOSOLOGY:

Contemporary Western psychiatry categorizes all disorders of cognition as organic. That is, there is a presumed or verified medical etiology for all disorders that affect cognitive functioning. Alzheimer's disease, vascular dementia, and alcohol-related dementia comprise three basic diagnostic categories of dementia in Western psychiatry. Diagnostic criteria for the major categories of dementia include:

❖ Persisting pattern of memory impairment
❖ One or more areas of significant cognitive impairment (including language and executive functioning)

❖    Significant impairment in occupational or social functioning

❖    Exclusion of delirium or other acute medical disorders as the cause of cognitive dysfunction

In addition, each major nosologic category includes specific features. For example, a diagnosis of vascular dementia requires the presence of identifiable neurological deficits or a documented course of step-wise progression in cognitive decline. In contrast, Alzheimer's disease is diagnosed when specific identifiable causes have been ruled out. There is a presumption that Alzheimer's disease is idiopathic (*i.e.*, without a specific identifiable underlying cause). However, this disorder has been consistently correlated with a specific pattern of neuropathological changes on autopsy (such as amyloid plaques and neurofibrillary tangles). Dementia is also a frequent concomitant of several neurological disorders, including Parkinson's disease and Huntington's disease.

### EPIDEMIOLOGY:

The probability of developing dementia increases with age such that 5% of the population older than 65 is demented at any given time. Dementia becomes more common with increasing old age. In Western cultures approximately 20% of individuals aged 85 or older are demented. It is unclear whether vascular dementia or Alzheimer's disease is the most common cause of dementia, however Alzheimer's disease predominates in the over-75 age group.

### DIFFERENTIAL DIAGNOSIS:

By definition, dementia is a severe, persisting loss of mental capacity. Some dementias are reversible if the underlying cause is accurately diagnosed and treatable. For example, normal pressure hydrocephalus, seizure disorders, vitamin deficiencies, and certain endocrinological disorders, and some vascular dementias are potentially reversible causes of dementia. It is essential to distinguish a transient delirium that is caused by an acute and treatable medical problem from the typically insidious pattern of cognitive decline of dementia. Delirium is always associated with disorientation and change in the level of arousal. The delirious patient is frequently agitated and often exhibits psychotic symptoms. In contrast, demented patients are typically alert but occasionally exhibit psychotic or agitated behavior. Cognitive changes accompanying delirium improve as the underlying medical cause responds to treatment.

Excluding treatable kinds of dementia, most demented patients continue to decline in baseline mental functioning, and their acute medical causes are seldom identified.

### ETIOLOGY & PATHOPHYSIOLOGY:

Western medicine classifies dementias by major etiologic category since dementia results from pathological changes in the brain that manifest as a persisting pattern of global cognitive decline. The specific symptom pattern and severity of cognitive dysfunction depend on location, size and pathophysiology of a brain lesion, or other abnormal aspects of brain functioning underlying dementia. Principle medical causes of dementia include:

1. Trauma (following severe head injury)
2. Infection (*e.g.*, AIDS or neurosyphilis)
3. Cardiac or vascular disease (*e.g.*, stroke)
4. Metabolic disorders (chronic vitamin deficiencies or chronic endocrinological disorders)
5. Degenerative brain disorders (*e.g.*, Alzheimer's disease, Parkinson's disease, Pick's disease)
6. Drugs or toxins (*e.g.*, chronic alcohol abuse, heavy metal toxicity)
7. Other causes (multiple sclerosis, tumor, congenital causes, epilepsy, hydrocephalus)

In addition to the above irreversible dementing disorders, psychiatric disorders are sometimes accompanied by cognitive changes that simulate dementia. The word "pseudodementia" is used to describe persisting severe cognitive dysfunction that is presumed to be secondary to a major psychiatric disorder in the absence of identified medical causes. Western psychiatry regards impaired cognitive functioning that often accompanies severe depression as pseudodementia. However, recent studies of demented populations have demonstrated that individuals who experienced significant cognitive impairment when depressed were more likely to be diagnosed with dementia in later decades. Pseudodementia of severe depression may, therefore, be a risk factor for subsequent development of permanent cognitive impairment. Further research is needed to clarify this issue.

### WESTERN MEDICAL TREATMENT:

Western medicine offers only palliative treatments for early stages of mild to moderate dementia. Two medications, Tacrine and Aricept, are currently available in Western Europe and the U.S. Both inhibit the brain enzyme that breaks down acetylcholine, effectively boost-

## DIFFERENTIAL DIAGNOSIS

| 1. MEDICAL DISORDERS | 2. EFFECTS OF SUBSTANCES | 3. PSYCHIATRIC DISORDERS |
|---|---|---|
| A. METABOLIC DISORDERS | A. CHRONIC ALCOHOL ABUSE | A. PSEUDODEMENTIA |
| I. VITAMIN DEFICIENCIES, INCLUDING $B_{12}$ AND FOLIC ACID | B. DRUG INTOXICATION | |
| II. HYPERCALCEMIA ASSOCIATED WITH HYPERPARATHYROIDISM | | |
| III. HYPOGLYCEMIA | | |
| IV. HYPOTHYROIDISM | | |
| V. ORGAN SYSTEM FAILURE, E.G., HEPATIC, RESPIRATORY, OR RENAL ENCEPHALOPATHY | | |
| VI. PELLAGRA | | |
| | | |
| B. STRUCTURAL DISORDERS | | |
| I. ALZHEIMER'S DISEASE | | |
| II. AMYOTHROPHIC LATERAL SCLEROSIS (ALS) | | |
| III. BRAIN TRAUMA, INCLUDING SURGERY AND RADIATION | | |
| IV. BRAIN TUMOR | | |
| V. CEREBRELLAR DEGENERATION | | |
| VI. COMMUNICATING HYDROCEPHALUS | | |
| VII. HUNTINGTON'S DISEASE | | |
| VIII. MULTIPLE SCLEROSIS (MS) | | |
| IX. NORMAL-PRESSURE HYDROCEPHALUS | | |
| X. PARKINSON'S DISEASE | | |
| XI. PICK'S DISEASE | | |
| XII. VASCULAR DISEASE | | |
| XIII. WILSON'S DISEASE | | |
| | | |
| C. INFECTIOUS DISORDERS | | |
| I. BACTERIAL ENDOCARDITIS | | |
| II. CREUTZFELD-JAKOB DISEASE | | |
| III. HIV DEMENTIA | | |
| IV. NEUROSYPHILIS | | |
| V. TUBERCULAR & FUNGAL MENINGITIS | | |
| VI. VIRAL ENCEPHALITIS | | |

ing the availability of this neurotransmitter, thus resulting in mild transient improvement in memory, learning, and general cognitive functioning. The agitation and confusion that frequently accompany dementia are treated symptomatically with small doses of benzodiazepines or low-potency antipsychotics. Considerable research efforts are currently ongoing to develop more effective treatments for Alzheimer's disease and other dementias. To date, no significant breakthroughs in treatment concepts have emerged from conventional Western medicine. Recent double-blind, placebo-controlled studies provide strong evidence for the efficacy of *Ginkgo biloba* preparations in the treatment of Alzheimer's disease that is similar to that of available synthetic drugs. Because of the severe level of cognitive impairment, demented individuals do not have the capacity to benefit from psychotherapy. However, support groups are often beneficial for care-providers, who are at high risk for burnout.

## PROGNOSIS:

The course and prognosis of dementia are highly variable and depend on the nature and severity of underlying causes. For example, early identification and treatment of dementia due to normal pressure hydrocephalus can result in a dramatic and rapid return to the patient's previous baseline cognitive functioning. Correction of metabolic or endocrinological causes of dementia my result in partial or complete recovery of functioning depending on age at onset, duration and severity of symptoms before treatment, previous baseline, and the presence of co-morbid medical or psychiatric disorders. All hereditary or degenerative dementias, including Huntington's disease, Parkinson's disease, and Pick's disease, carry a very poor prognosis. In these disorders, decline is typically insidious, resulting in permanent, severe cognitive dysfunction. Western medicine currently offers no effective treatments for these disorders.

## INDICATIONS FOR REFERRAL TO WESTERN MEDICAL SERVICES:

Evidence of acute onset cognitive dysfunction, change in level of consciousness, confusion or agitation, or the presence of an underlying medical disorder is sufficient basis for urgent evaluation in the nearest emergency room to rule out potentially fatal causes of delirium or reversible causes of dementia. Indications for non-urgent medical-psychiatric referral include a long-standing pattern of cognitive decline without impairment in the level of consciousness that has not responded to an appropriate course of Chinese medical treatment.

## CHINESE DISEASE CATEGORIZATION:

What is referred to as senile dementia in the modern Chinese medical literature mainly corresponds to the traditional Chinese disease categories of feeble-mindedness (*chi dai*), impaired memory (*jian wang*), deranged speech (*yan yu cuo luan*), and withdrawal and mania (*dian kuang*).

## CHINESE DISEASE CAUSES & MECHANISMS:

Due to decline in visceral function and especially that of the kidneys and spleen, during old age, qi and blood become progressively vacuous and debilitated, and hence the constructive and defensive are not well-regulated. Therefore, clear yang is not upborne, and turbid yin is not downborne, and the spirit brilliance suffers progressive

damage and detriment day by day. In addition, due to a variety of disease causes and mechanisms, there appear qi stagnation, blood stasis, and phlegm congelation which mist and confound the orifices of the heart. For instance, qi, blood, yin, and yang vacuities may all engender or aggravate liver depression qi stagnation, while any enduring depression of any disease evil in the body will eventually give rise to blood stasis. Further, because the spleen and kidneys are two of the three viscera which control water fluids in the body, decline in the function of either or both of these typically gives rise to dampness which then may congeal into phlegm. Because lack of movement and activity are usually a by-product of the qi and yang vacuity that characterize aging, a tendency to qi stagnation, blood stasis, and phlegm congelation is even more common in the elderly due to their more sedentary lifestyle. Other disease causes resulting in the disease mechanisms associated with this condition include the side effects of the many medications many elderly take on a regular basis and their interactions. Thus qi and blood are not able to fill and nourish the mansion of the original spirit, *i.e.*, the brain. Rather, there is bewilderment and chaos in the mechanism responsible for the spirit brilliance which develop into the symptoms of this disease.

## TREATMENT BASED ON PATTERN DISCRIMINATION:

### 1. KIDNEY ESSENCE INSUFFICIENCY PATTERN

**MAIN SYMPTOMS:** Feeble-mindedness in the elderly, difficulty thinking, mental confusion, impaired memory, essence spirit abstraction, deafness, tinnitus, susceptibility to fear, easy fright, low back and knee soreness and weakness, atrophy of the lower limbs, lack of strength, a pale tongue with thin, white fur, and a deep, weak pulse, especially in the cubit positions

**ANALYSIS OF SYMPTOMS:** Many of these symptoms are kidney vacuity symptoms, such as low back and knee soreness and weakness, deafness, tinnitus, and susceptibility to fear. Most of the rest of the symptoms indicate that kidney essence and blood are insufficient to fill the sea of marrow, *i.e.*, the brain.

**TREATMENT PRINCIPLES:** Supplement the kidneys and fill the essence, boost the marrow and fortify the brain

**FORMULA & MEDICINALS:** *Da Zao Wan Jia Jian* (Great Construction Pills with Additions & Subtractions)

Placenta Hominis (*Zi He Che*), 3g (swallowed with the

decoction), Cortex Eucommiae Ulmoidis (*Du Zhong*), 9g, Radix Achyranthis Bidentatae (*Niu Xi*), 12g, Tuber Ophiopogonis Japonici (*Mai Dong*), 12g, Tuber Asparagi Cochinensis (*Tian Men Dong*), 12g, cooked Radix Rehmanniae (*Shu Di*), 12g, Radix Panacis Ginseng (*Ren Shen*), 6g, Fructus Alpiniae Oxyphyllae (*Yi Zhi Ren*), 15g, Gelatinum Plastri Testudinis (*Gui Ban Jiao*), 12g, Gelatinum Cornu Cervi (*Lu Jiao Jiao*), 12g

Decoct in water and administer orally in two divided doses, morning and evening, one *ji* per day.

**ANALYSIS OF FORMULA:** Within this formula, Placenta, Turtle Shell Glue, and Deer Antler Glue are all meaty, bloody medicinals which nourish the blood and supplement the essence. They are aided in this by cooked Rehmannia which nourishes the blood and enriches yin. Ophiopogon and Asparagus help supplement the essence by engendering fluids and enriching yin. Achyranthes supplements liver and kidney yin and strengthens the low back, while Eucommia supplements the liver and kidney yang and strengthens the low back. Ginseng greatly supplements the source qi in order to transform essence, and Alpinia Oxyphylla supplements the kidneys and boosts the intelligence.

**ACUPUNCTURE:** *Shen Shu* (Bl 23), *Zhi Shi* (Bl 52), *Guan Yuan* (CV 4), *Da Zhong* (Ki 4), *San Yin Jiao* (Sp 6). Use supplementing technique.

## 2. YIN VACUITY-INTERNAL HEAT PATTERN

**MAIN SYMPTOMS:** Dizziness, vertigo, impaired memory, scanty sleep, deafness, tinnitus, low back and leg soreness and weakness, a parched throat and dry tongue, a thin, emaciated body, vexatious heat in the five hearts, red cheeks, tidal heat, night sweats, worsening of symptoms as evening approaches, a red tongue with dry, scanty fur, and a fine, rapid pulse

**ANALYSIS OF SYMPTOMS:** Dizziness, vertigo, impaired memory, scanty sleep, deafness, tinnitus, low back and leg soreness and weakness, a worsening of symptoms as evening approaches, dry, scanty tongue fur, and a fine pulse all suggest kidney yin vacuity. A parched throat and dry tongue, vexatious heat in the five hearts, red cheeks, tidal heat, night sweats, a red tongue, and a rapid pulse all indicate internal heat.

**TREATMENT PRINCIPLES:** Nourish yin and clear heat assisted by supplementing the kidneys

**FORMULA & MEDICINALS:** *Zhi Bai Di Huang Wan Jia Wei* (Anemarrhena & Phellodendron Rehmannia Pills with Added Flavors)

Rhizoma Anemarrhenae Aspheloidis (*Zhi Mu*), 9g, Cortex Phellodendri (*Huang Bai*), 9g, cooked Radix Rehmanniae (*Shu Di*), 12-15g, Fructus Corni Officinalis (*Shan Zhu Yu*), 9g, Radix Dioscoreae Oppositae (*Shan Yao*), 9g, Sclerotium Poriae Cocos (*Fu Ling*), 9g, Cortex Radicis Moutan (*Dan Pi*), 6-9g, Rhizoma Alismatis (*Ze Xie*), 6-9g, Radix Polygalae Tenuifoliae (*Yuan Zhi*), 6-9g

Decoct in water and administer orally in two divided doses, morning and evening, one *ji* per day.

**ANALYSIS OF FORMULA:** Anemarrhena and Phellodendron both clear vacuity, while Anemarrhena also enriches yin. Cooked Rehmannia nourishes the blood and enriches yin. Cornus supplements the kidney qi. Dioscorea supplements both the spleen and kidney qi. Poria fortifies the spleen, seeps dampness, and quiets the spirit. It helps lead ministerial fire back down to its lower source by guiding yang into the yin tract. Alisma, which also seeps dampness, helps Poria in both these tasks, while Moutan clears vacuity heat at the same time as it quickens the blood. Polygala transforms phlegm, quiets the spirit, and helps promote the interaction between the heart and kidneys.

**ADDITIONS & SUBTRACTIONS:** If heat is severe, add Rhizoma Coptidis Chinensis (*Huang Lian*). If insomnia is marked, add Semen Zizyphi Spinosae (*Suan Zao Ren*) and Semen Biotae Orientalis (*Bai Zi Ren*). If agitation and restlessness are pronounced, add Os Draconis (*Long Gu*), Concha Ostreae (*Mu Li*), and Magnetitum (*Ci Shi*). For concomitant liver depression qi stagnation, add Fructus Meliae Toosendan (*Chuan Lian Zi*), Tuber Curcumae (*Yu Jin*), and/or a little Radix Bupleuri (*Chai Hu*). If there are night sweats and heart palpitations, add Fructus Levis Tritici Aestivi (*Fu Xiao Mai*) and Fructus Schisandrae Chinensis (*Wu Wei Zi*). If yin vacuity and heat engender internally stirring of wind, add Lumbricus (*Di Long*), Rhizoma Gastrodiae Elatae (*Tian Ma*), and Ramulus Uncariae Cum Uncis (*Gou Teng*). If there is concomitant blood stasis, add Radix Salviae Miltiorrhizae (*Dan Shen*) and Herba Leonuri Heterophylli (*Yi Mu Cao*).

**ACUPUNCTURE:** *Tai Xi* (Ki 3), *San Yin Jiao* (Sp 6), *Shen Shu* (Bl 23), *Guan Yuan* (CV 4), *Yin Xi* (Ht 6), *Da Ling* (Per 7), *Shen Men* (Ht 7). Supplement the first four points and drain the last three.

### 3. SPLEEN-KIDNEY YANG VACUITY PATTERN

MAIN SYMPTOMS: Feeble-mindedness, slow movement, scanty speech or, if severe, no speech, difficulty thinking, confused thoughts, decreased memory power, loss of intelligence, fatigue, lack of strength, dizziness, deafness, tinnitus, low back and knee soreness and weakness, cold hands and feet, poor appetite, a tendency to loose stools, if severe, cockcrow diarrhea, nocturia, clear, long urination, a pale, enlarged tongue with slimy, white fur, and a deep, weak, possible moderate (*i.e.*, slightly slow), or slow pulse

ANALYSIS OF SYMPTOMS: Poor appetite, loose stools, fatigue, lack of strength, an enlarged tongue, and a weak pulse all indicate spleen qi vacuity. Dizziness, deafness, tinnitus, low back and knee soreness and weakness, nocturia, clear, long urination, and a deep, slow pulse indicate kidney yang vacuity. Cold hands and feet indicate a general yang qi vacuity. The slimy tongue fur shows that yang qi is not moving and transforming body fluids correctly, while the mental-emotional symptoms have to due with failure of clear yang to be upborne and thus construct the spirit brilliance.

TREATMENT PRINCIPLES: Warm and supplement the spleen and kidneys, upbear the clear and boost the intelligence

FORMULA & MEDICINALS: *Jia Wei Shen Qi Wan* (Added Flavors Kidney Qi Pills)

Fructus Alpiniae Oxyphyllae (*Yi Zhi Ren*), 15g, Radix Astragali Membranacei (*Huang Qi*), 12-18g, Radix Codonopsitis Pilosulae (*Dang Shen*), 8-15g, Rhizoma Atractylodes (*Bai Zhu*), 9g, Sclerotium Poriae Cocos (*Fu Ling*), 9-12g, cooked Radix Rehmanniae (*Shu Di*), 12-15g, Radix Dioscoreae Oppositae (*Shan Yao*), 9g, Fructus Corni Officinalis (*Shan Zhu Yu*), 9-18g, Rhizoma Alismatis (*Ze Xie*), 9g, Cortex Radicis Moutan (*Dan Pi*), 6-9g, Radix Lateralis Praeparatus Aconiti Carmichaeli (*Fu Zi*), 6-9g, Cortex Cinnamomi Cassiae (*Rou Gui*), 6-9g, Rhizoma Acori Graminei (*Shi Chang Pu*), 6-9g, Radix Polygalae Tenuifoliae (*Yuan Zhi*), 6-9g

Decoct in water and administer orally in two divided doses, morning and evening, one *ji* per day.

ANALYSIS OF FORMULA: Astragalus, Codonopsis, Atractylodes, and Poria all fortify the spleen and supplement the qi. Cornus supplements the kidney qi, while Dioscorea supplements both the spleen and kidney qi. Alpinia Oxyphylla supplements the kidney qi, invigorates

yang, and boosts the intelligence. Alisma seeps dampness and prevents flaming of ministerial fire due to yang-supplementation, and Moutan quickens the blood and transforms stasis. Aconite and Cortex Cinnamomi strongly warm the interior and supplement yang. Polygala transforms phlegm, quiets the spirit, and promotes the interaction between the heart and kidneys, while Acorus transforms phlegm, open the orifices, and quiets the spirit.

ACUPUNCTURE: *San Yin Jiao* (Sp 6), *Fu Liu* (Ki 7), *Shen Shu* (Bl 23), *Ming Men* (GV 4), *Pi Shu* (Bl 20), *Wei Shu* (Bl 21), *Shen Que* (CV 8), *Guan Yuan* (CV 4). Supplement the first two points and moxa all the rest.

### 4. QI & BLOOD DUAL VACUITY PATTERN

MAIN SYMPTOMS: Heart palpitations, impaired memory, insomnia, profuse dreams, a sallow yellow facial complexion, a bland affect, scanty speech, spontaneous perspiration on slight exertion, decreased eating and drinking, abdominal distention, loose stools, fatigue, a desire to lie down, a pale tongue, and a fine, forceless pulse

NOTE: This pattern can also be called heart-spleen dual vacuity pattern.

ANALYSIS OF SYMPTOMS: Fatigue, a desire to lie down, scanty speech, spontaneous perspiration on slight exertion, and a forceless pulse all indicate qi vacuity. A sallow yellow facial complexion, a pale tongue, and a fine pulse indicate blood vacuity. In this case, the bland affect, heart palpitations, impaired memory, insomnia, and profuse dreams are all due to qi and blood vacuity not nourishing and constructing the heart spirit. Hence the spirit is not quiet or calm. In addition, decreased eating and drinking, abdominal distention, and loose stools are spleen vacuity symptoms. They occur in this pattern because the spleen is the latter heaven root of qi and blood engenderment and transformation.

TREATMENT PRINCIPLES: Supplement the qi and nourish the blood, calm the heart and quiet the spirit

FORMULA & MEDICINALS: *Gui Pi Tang* (Restore the Spleen Decoction)

Fructus Alpiniae Oxyphyllae (*Yi Zhi Ren*), 15g, Radix Astragali Membranacei (*Huang Qi*), 9-45g, Radix Codonopsitis Pilosulae (*Dang Shen*), 9-18g, Rhizoma Atractylodis Macrocephalae (*Bai Zhu*), 9-12g, Sclerotium

Poriae Cocos (*Fu Ling*), 9-12g, mix-fried Radix Glycyrrhizae (*Gan Cao*), 6-15g, Radix Angelicae Sinensis (*Dang Gui*), 6-9g, Semen Zizyphi Jujubae (*Suan Zao Ren*), 12-15g, Arillus Euphoriae Longanae (*Long Yan Rou*), 9g, Radix Auklandiae Lappae (*Mu Xiang*), 6-9g, Radix Polygalae Tenuifoliae (*Yuan Zhi*), 6-9g, uncooked Rhizoma Zingiberis (*Sheng Jiang*), 2 slices, Fructus Zizyphi Jujubae (*Da Zao*), 2-10 pieces

Decoct in water and administer orally in two divided doses, morning and evening, one *ji* per day.

**ANALYSIS OF FORMULA:** Alpinia Oxyphylla supplements the kidneys, invigorates yang, and boosts the intelligence. Astragalus, Codonopsis, Atractylodes, Poria, and mix-fried Licorice all fortify the spleen and boost the qi. Longans, Dang Gui, and Zizyphus Spinosa nourish the blood and quiet the spirit. Polygala supplements the heart, rectifies the qi, transforms phlegm, and quiets the spirit. Auklandia rectifies the qi and harmonizes the liver and spleen, while Red Dates and uncooked Ginger not only harmonize all the other medicinals in this formula but also help supplement the qi and nourish the blood.

**ACUPUNCTURE:** *Xin Shu* (Bl 15), *Ge Shu* (Bl 17), *Pi Shu* (Bl 20), *Shen Men* (Ht 7), *Zu San Li* (St 36), *San Yin Jiao* (Sp 6). Use supplementing technique.

## 5. PHLEGM MISTING THE CLEAR ORIFICES PATTERN

**MAIN SYMPTOMS:** Feeble-mindedness, scanty speech, deranged speech, a depressed affect, difficulty thinking, confused thoughts, slow movement, profuse phlegm, chest and abdominal oppression and fullness, somnolence, inability to control one's own activities, possible nausea and vomiting of phlegm drool, a feeling as if something were stuck in the throat which can neither be spit up or swallowed down, a fat, enlarged tongue which is pale and dark at the same time and has slimy, white fur, and a slippery or bowstring, slippery pulse

**ANALYSIS OF SYMPTOMS:** Profuse phlegm, nausea and vomiting of phlegm drool, plum pit qi, slimy tongue fur, and a slippery pulse all indicate phlegm. Chest and abdominal oppression and fullness, a dark tongue, and a bowstring pulse indicate that phlegm is complicated by qi stagnation. The feeble-mindedness, scanty speech, deranged speech, depressed affect, difficulty thinking, confused thoughts, and inability to control or take care of oneself are all due to phlegm misting the clear orifices and harassing the heart spirit. The pale, enlarged tongue suggests that

spleen vacuity is responsible for the phlegm turbidity or has subsequently been damaged by phlegm dampness.

**TREATMENT PRINCIPLES:** Transform phlegm and open the orifices, settle the heart and quiet the spirit

**FORMULA & MEDICINALS:** *Wen Dan Tang Jia Wei* (Warm the Gallbladder Decoction with Added Flavors)

Rhizoma Pinelliae Ternatae (*Ban Xia*), 9-12g, Sclerotium Poriae Cocos (*Fu Ling*), 9-12g, Pericarpium Citri Reticulatae (*Chen Pi*), 6-9g, Caulis Bambusae In Taeniis (*Zhu Ru*), 6-9g, Fructus Immaturus Citri Aurantii (*Zhi Shi*), 6-9g, Radix Glycyrrhizae (*Gan Cao*), 3-9g, Rhizoma Acori Graminei (*Shi Chang Pu*), 9g, uncooked Rhizoma Zingiberis (*Sheng Jiang*), 2-3 slices

Decoct in water and administer orally in two divided doses, morning and evening, one *ji* per day.

**ANALYSIS OF FORMULA:** Pinellia, Orange Peel, Immature Aurantium, and uncooked Ginger all transform phlegm and rectify the qi. Acorus transforms phlegm, opens the orifices, and quiets the spirit. Poria fortifies the spleen and helps eliminate dampness via seeping it. It also quiets the spirit. Caulis Bambusae downbears counterflow and eliminates vexation, and Licorice harmonizes all the other medicinals in this formula.

**ADDITIONS & SUBTRACTIONS:** If there is phlegm heat, add Rhizoma Coptidis Chinensis (*Huang Lian*), bile-processed Rhizoma Arisaematis (*Dan Nan Xing*), Concha Cyclinae Meretricis (*Hai Ge Ke*), and Lapis Micae Seu Chloriti (*Meng Shi*). If spleen vacuity is marked, add Radix Codonopsitis Pilosulae (*Dang Shen*) and Rhizoma Atractylodis Macrocephalae (*Bai Zhu*) and change uncooked to mix-fried Licorice.

**ACUPUNCTURE:** *Feng Long* (St 40), *Zhong Wan* (CV 12), *Dan Zhong* (CV 17), *Tai Chong* (Liv 3), *Nei Guan* (Per 6). Drain all points.

## 6. STASIS STAGNATING IN THE BRAIN NETWORK VESSELS PATTERN

**MAIN SYMPTOMS:** A history of external injury to the head region, a bland affect, difficulty thinking, confused thoughts, slow reactions, impaired memory, abstraction, scanty speech, dizziness and vertigo, vertex pain, fixed, localized pain, possible lancinating pain, an enduring condition which does not heal, age spots, varicosities, cherry hemangiomas, greenish blue lips, a sooty facial complexion, dry, scaly skin, a dark, purplish tongue or possible static macules or spots and thin, white fur, and a fine, bowstring, and/or choppy pulse

ANALYSIS OF SYMPTOMS: The majority of the above signs and symptoms indicate blood stasis. Then, because of this stasis and stagnation, the spirit brilliance is impaired.

TREATMENT PRINCIPLES: Quicken the blood and transform stasis, nourish the blood and fortify the brain

FORMULA & MEDICINALS: *Tong Qiao Huo Xue Tang Jia Jian* (Free the Flow of the Orifices & Quicken the Blood Decoction with Additions & Subtractions)

Radix Rubrus Paconiae Lactiflorae (*Chi Shao*), 9g, Semen Pruni Persicae (*Tao Ren*), 9g, Flos Carthami Tinctorii (*Hong Hua*), 9g, Radix Ligustici Wallichii (*Chuan Xiong*), 9-15g, Bulbus Allii Fistulosi (*Cong Bai*), 9g, Rhizoma Acori Graminei (*Shi Chang Pu*), 9g, Radix Polygalae Tenuifoliae (*Yuan Zhi*), 9g, Radix Salviae Miltiorrhizae (*Dan Shen*), 9g, Fructus Zizyphi Jujubae (*Da Zao*), 2-3 pieces, uncooked Rhizoma Zingiberis (*Sheng Jiang*), 2 slices

Decoct in water and administer orally in two divided doses, morning and evening, one *ji* per day.

ANALYSIS OF FORMULA: Within this formula, Red Peony, Persica, Carthamus, Ligusticum, and Salvia all quicken the blood and transform stasis. Scallions move the qi and free the flow of yang. Polygala rectifies the qi, transforms phlegm, and quiets the spirit, while Acorus transforms phlegm, opens the orifices, and quiets the spirit. Red Dates and uncooked Ginger harmonize the other medicinals in the formula.

ACUPUNCTURE: *Tai Chong* (Liv 3), *He Gu* (LI 4), *Xue Hai* (Sp 10), *San Yin Jiao* (Sp 6), *Feng Chi* (GB 20), *Yin Tang* (M-HN-3). Use draining technique.

### 7. TOXINS DAMAGING THE BRAIN NETWORK VESSELS PATTERN

MAIN SYMPTOMS: Symptoms associated with either a heat disease or poisoning, difficulty thinking, confused thoughts, unclear speech, emotional lability, heart vexation, insomnia, lassitude of the spirit, decreased intake, if extreme, lower limb paralysis, non-freely flowing urination and/or defecation, loss of memory power, a red tongue with scanty fur, and a fine, rapid pulse

ANALYSIS OF SYMPTOMS: In this case, the symptoms

either indicate heat, such as the red tongue and rapid pulse, or harassment of the heart spirit by heat evils.

TREATMENT PRINCIPLES: Clear heat and resolve toxins, open the orifices and quiet the spirit

FORMULA & MEDICINALS: *Huang Lian Jie Du Tang* (Coptis Resolve Toxins Decoction)

Rhizoma Coptidis Chinensis (*Huang Lian*), 3-9g, Radix Scutellariae Baicalensis (*Huang Qin*), 9g, Cortex Phellodendri (*Huang Bai*), 9g, Fructus Gardeniae Jasminoidis (*Zhi Zi*), 6-12g

Decoct in water and administer orally in two divided doses, morning and evening, one *ji* per day.

ANALYSIS OF FORMULA: All four of these medicinals are bitter and cold and clear heat and eliminate dampness. When combined together in this way, they also clear heat and resolve toxins.

ACUPUNCTURE: *Shi Xuan* (M-UE-1), *Ren Zhong* (GV 26). Bleed both points.

### 8. LIVER DEPRESSION QI STAGNATION PATTERN

MAIN SYMPTOMS: Emotional depression, vexation and agitation, easy anger, chest and abdominal oppression and discomfort which is relieved by belching and/or flatulence, no gusto in eating, lassitude of the spirit, lack of strength, insomnia, profuse dreams, thin, white tongue fur, and a bowstring pulse

ANALYSIS OF SYMPTOMS: All these symptoms are due to either qi stagnation or inhibition of the qi mechanism.

TREATMENT PRINCIPLES: Course the liver and rectify the qi, boost the intelligence and quiet the spirit

FORMULA & MEDICINALS: *Xiao Yao San Jia Wei* (Rambling Powder with Added Flavors)

Radix Bupleuri (*Chai Hu*), 3-9g, Tuber Curcumae (*Yu Jin*), 9g, Radix Angelicae Sinensis (*Dang Gui*), 9g, Radix Albus Paeoniae Lactiflorae (*Bai Shao*), 9-18g, Radix Polygalae Tenuifoliae (*Yuan Zhi*), 9g, Rhizoma Atractylodis Macrocephalae (*Bai Zhu*), 9-12g, Sclerotium Poriae Cocos (*Fu Ling*), 9-12g, mix-fried Radix Glycyrrhizae (*Gan Cao*), 6-9g, Herba Menthae Haplocalycis (*Bo He*), 3-6g, uncooked Rhizoma Zingiberis (*Sheng Jiang*), 2 slices

Decoct in water and administer orally in two divided doses, morning and evening, one *ji* per day.

**ANALYSIS OF FORMULA:** Bupleurum, Curcuma, and Mentha course the liver and rectify the qi. Polygala also rectifies the qi along with transforming phlegm and quieting the spirit. Dang Gui and Peony nourish the blood and harmonize the liver, while Atractylodes, Poria, and mix-fried Licorice fortify the spleen and supplement the qi. Poria and Licorice also quiet the spirit, and uncooked Ginger helps Poria eliminate dampness at the same time as it helps Bupleurum move the qi. In addition, it and Licorice harmonize all the other medicinals in this formula.

**ACUPUNCTURE:** *Tai Chong* (Liv 3), *He Gu* (LI 4), *Dan Zhong* (CV 17), *Nei Guan* (Per 6), *Zu San Li* (St 36). Use draining technique.

**CLINICAL TIPS:** Although Chinese medicine has traditionally emphasized the role of kidney essence vacuity in geriatric diseases, Yan De-xin suggests that kidney vacuity in the elderly is typically complicated by blood stasis. In addition, if there is feeblemindedness and clouded spirit, one must also factor in phlegm misting the clear orifices.

**ABSTRACTS OF REPRESENTATIVE CHINESE RESEARCH:**

*Zhong Guo Zhong Xi Yi Jie He Za Zhi (Chinese Journal of Integrated Chinese-Western Medicine)*, #7, 1999, p. 405-106: In this study, Wang Can-hui *et al.* studied the treatment methods of enriching the kidneys and quickening the blood on 26 cases of vascular dementia by administering seven grams per day of modified *San Jia San* (Three Scales Powder) made into the form of pills. There were 19 males and seven females in this study who ranged in age from 50-78, with a median age of 64.5 ± 14.5 years. These patients' disease course had lasted from 0.5-5.0 years, with a median duration of 2.2 ± 1.4 years. Fourteen cases suffered from cerebral infarction, 10 cases from cerebral hemorrhage, and two cases from hypertension. In 10 cases, CT scan showed atrophic changes in the brain. The formula consisted of: Plastrum Testudinis (*Gui Ban*), Carapax Amydae Chinensis (*Bie Jia*), Concha Ostreae (*Mu Li*), Eupolyphaga Seu Ophisthoplatia (*Di Bie Chong*), Lumbricus (*Di Long*), Bombyx Batryticatus (*Jang Can*), Radix Angelicae Sinensis (*Dang Gui*), Radix Rubrus Paeoniae Lactiflorae (*Chi Shao*), Radix Polygoni Multiflori (*He Shou Wu*), Rhizoma Acori Graminei (*Shi Chang Pu*), and Radix Eleuthrococci Senticosi (*Ci Wi Jia*). Patients were evaluated by the Hagayakawa dementia scale (HDS), the mini mental state examination (MMSE), and single entry scoring of MMSE. A marked improvement was scored in these patients' HDS and MMSE from before to after treatment (P<0.01). Therefore, this study suggests that these Chinese medicinals are able to reverse the process of vascular dementia and improve intelligence in vascular dementia patients.

*Si Chuan Zhong Yi (Sichuan Chinese Medicine)*, #5, 1999, p. 30: In this study, Zhu Jun-cheng reported on the treatment of 54 cases of senile dementia with the methods of boosting the qi and quickening the blood plus *Nao Fu Kang* (Restore Brain Health) and vitamin C in comparison to a group of 48 patients who were treated with *Nao Fu Kang* and vitamin C alone. Of these 54 patients, 22 were males and 32 were females. They ranged in age from 58-85, with a median age of 70.5 years, and their course of disease had lasted from 0.5-6 years. Thirty cases had coincidental senile dementia, while the remaining 24 cases had multiple sclerosis dementia. There was no marked statistical difference between this and the comparison group in terms of sex, age, disease duration, etc. (P + 0.05). The Chinese medicinals consisted of: Radix Angelicae Sinensis (*Dang Gui*) and Radix Codonopsitis Pilosulae (*Dang Shen*), 15g each, Radix Astragali Membranacei (*Huang Qi*), 20g, Radix Rubrus Paeoniae Lactiflorae (*Chi Shao*), Radix Ligustici Wallichii (*Chuan Xiong*), Radix Puerariae (*Ge Gen*), Rhizoma Acori Graminei (*Shi Chang Pu*), and Fructus Alpiniae Oxyphyllae (*Yi Zhi Ren*), 10g each. If there was yang hyperactivity, 15 grams of Ramulus Uncariae Cum Unics (*Gou Teng*) and 10 grams each of Radix Scutellariae Baicalensis (*Huang Qin*) and Rhizoma Gastrodiae Elatae (*Tian Ma*) were added. If there was yin vacuity, 10 grams each of cooked Radix Rehmanniae (*Shu Di*), Fructus Corni Officinalis (*Shan Zhu Yu*), and Cortex Radicis Moutan (*Dan Pi*) were added. If there was spleen vacuity, 15 grams of Rhizoma Atractylodis Macrocephalae (*Bai Zhu*) and 10 grams of Semen Dolichoris Lablab (*Bai Bian Dou*) were added. And if there was wind and phlegm exuberance, 10 grams each of Bombyx Batryticatus (*Jiang Can*) and Radix Typhonii Seu Aconiti Coreani (*Bai Fu Zi*) were added. One *ji* was administered per day, and six weeks equaled one course of therapy. All patients in both groups received *Nao Fu Kang*, 0.4g, and vitamin C, 0.1g, orally three times per day. In the Chinese medical group, 18 patients (33.33%) were cured, 30 (55.56%) got some effect, and six (11.11%) got no effect for a total amelioration rate of 88.89%. In the comparison group, six patients (12.5%) were cured, 24 (50%) got some effect, and 18 (37.5%) got no effect for a total amelioration rate of 62.5% Thus there were marked statistical differences between the treatment and comparison groups both in terms of cure rate (P< 0.01) and total amelioration rate (P<0.01).

*Shang Hai Zhong Yi Yao Za Zhi (Shanghai Journal of Chinese Medicine & Medicinals)*, #5, 1999, p. 13-15: Chen Xin-xin and Fan Hua-chang reported on the comparative treatment of 60 cases of senile dementia due to cerebral infarction with *Xing Nao Jing Zhu She Ye* (Arouse the Brain Injectable Fluid) manufactured by the Wuxi Pharmaceutical Company. All 60 patients in this study were diagnosed with cerebral infarction by CT scan and all had suffered from dementia for less than three months. Various Western medical tests and texts were cited as criteria for the diagnosis of dementia, including *DSM-IV*. They were then divided into two, statistically similar groups. In the treatment group, there were 22 men and eight women who were 46-78 years of age, with a median age of 68 years. In the treatment group, besides standard antihypertension and anti-infection medicine, 40-60ml of *Xing Nao Jing* were given per day intravenously for 14 days. The comparison group received the same antihypertensive and anti-infection medicine plus 20ml intravenously per day of *Sheng Mai Zhen Zhu She Ye* (Engender the Pulse Injectable Fluid) for 14 days. Using this protocol, the treatment group scored a total amelioration rate of 70%, while the comparison group only scored a total amelioration rate of 20%. Results showed that *Xing Nao Xing* enhanced the speed of blood flow in the common carotid artery, decreased peripheral resistance of the blood vessels of the brain, improved nervous function, decreased the symptoms of dementia, and improved lifestyle and activities.

❖

*Zhe Jiang Zhong Yi Za Zhi (Zhejiang Journal of Chinese Medicine)*, #8, 1995, p. 357: Yang Su-cheng reported on the treatment of 26 cases of senile dementia with water needle (*i.e.*, point injection acupuncture). Nineteen of these cases were male and seven were female. The youngest was 55 and the oldest was 88 years old. All suffered from marked decreases in memory power, comprehension, decision-making, computation, direction, and thinking. The main point needled was *Shen Shu* (Bl 23). Auxiliary points were *Zu San Li* (St 36) and *San Yin Jiao* (Sp 6). Each point was injected with 2ml of *Ren Shen Zhu She Ye* (Ginseng Injectable Fluid) and 4ml of *Fu Fang Dang Gui Zhu She Ye* (Compound Dang Gui Injectable Fluid) every other day, with 10 days equaling one course of treatment. A four day rest period was given between each successive course. Of the 26 patients treated with this protocol, 24 experienced results in 1-3 courses of treatment. Only two cases got no

results. Treatment effects were based on criteria established at the May 1990 All China Chinese Medicine Symposium on Geriatrics held in Beijing.

*Xin Zhong Yi (New Chinese Medicine)*, #12, 1996, p. 31: Yang Zheng-zhi reported on the treatment of 18 cases of senile dementia using cupping at upper back transport points. There were 10 men and eight women in this study who ranged in age from 65-81, with a median age of 69.4 years. Their disease course had lasted from seven months to five years. All had been diagnosed as suffering from dementia according to the criteria in *Shi Yong Shen Jing Bing Xue (A Practical Study of Neurological Diseases)*. In all cases, CT scans showed either brain atrophy or multiple cerebral infarction. Cupping was done at *Da Zhui* (GV 14) and at *Shen Shu* (Bl 23) for 30 minutes each time, one time per day, with 15 days equaling one course of treatment. After 9-12 such courses of therapy, six cases got a marked effect, 10 got some effect, and two got no effect

❖

*The Journal of Chinese Medicine*, #6, 2000, p. 54: Geng Jian described the treatment of 50 cases of senile dementia by acupuncture combined with inhalation of herbal medicinals and oxygen. Seventy males and 30 females aged 56-81 years were divided into treatment and control groups of 50 patients each. Among these 100 patients as a whole, there were 68 cases of multiple infarctional dementia and 42 cases of primary degenerative dementia. The control group was intravenously administered 30ml of brain tissue extract in 250ml of 5% glucose per day. The treatment group received acupuncture while simultaneously inhaling an infusion of Chinese medicinals via an oxygen nebulizer. The medicinals in this infusion consisted of: Secretio Moschi Moschiferi (*She Xiang*), Fructus Gleditschiae Chinensis (*Zao Jiao*), Borneolum (*Bing Pian*), and Radix Ligustici Wallichii (*Chuan Xiong*). Two groups of acupuncture points were needled on alternate days: 1) *Si Shen Cong* (M-HN-1), *Bai Hui* (GV 20), *Shen Men* (Ht 7), *Feng Long* (St 40), and *Nei Guan* (Per 6), and 2) *Gan Shu* (Bl 18), *Shen Shu* (Bl 23), and *Zu San Li* (St 36). The first group of points were needled with draining method, while the second group were needled with supplementing method. In the treatment group, 12 patients were judged cured, 36 improved, and two cases got no effect. Thus the total amelioration rate in the treatment group was 96%. In the control group, eight were cured, 30 improved, and 12 got no effect. Hence the total amelioration rate in the control group was only 76%.

REPRESENTATIVE CASE HISTORIES:

### ❖ CASE 1[2] ❖

The patient was a 63 year old male who was first hospitalized on Jul. 12, 1992. Both of the man's legs had lacked strength for one month. His disease condition had gradually become more pronounced. His reactions were slow and his sleep was restless with profuse dreams. In addition, he had tinnitus. His appetite was OK and his two excretions were normal. His tongue was pale with scanty fur, and his pulse was deep and fine. CT scan showed cerebral cortex atrophy. Other exams and tests were used to confirm a diagnosis of senile dementia. After being admitted to the hospital, the man was needled at *Nei Guan* (Per 6), *Shang Xing* (GV 23), *Yin Tang* (M-HN-3), *Si Shen Cong* (M-HN-1), *Feng Chi* (GB 20), *Tian Zhu* (Bl 10), *San Yin Jiao* (Sp 6), *Wan Gu* (GB 12), and head motor area (*i.e.*, scalp acupuncture line) for 20 minutes each time, two times per day for three months, at the end of which time, all the patient's symptoms were markedly improved. EEG was improved from before treatment, both legs had more strength, his reactions were more sensitive, and the man was improved enough to be discharged from the hospital.

### ❖ CASE 2[3] ❖

The patient was a 67 year old female who was first examined on Mar. 8, 1990. For the past year, the patient had been experiencing dizziness, tinnitus, fatigue, and lack of strength. Over that time, essence spirit feeble-mindedness had increased. She was also fearful, had impaired memory, and spoke little. In addition, she tended to be angry and her behavior had become eccentric. At the time of seeing the author of this case history, the woman had already been diagnosed with senile dementia and had taken various Chinese and Western medicine with no apparent effect. At the time of being examined, the patient's affect was bland, her emotions were unstable, she cried for no reason, she tended to sit torpidly, her thinking was slow, and her movements were slow and decreased. She had no memory of recent events, but her long-term memory was OK. She also had no ability to compute or tell direction.

Her tongue was pale with white fur, and her pulse was deep and fine. She was given two courses of water needle treatment as described above under "representative Chinese research" and all her symptoms decreased. On follow-up after two years, her reactions were sharp and quick and her emotions were stable.

### ❖ CASE 3[4] ❖

The patient was a 65 year old retired, alcoholic worker. During the last year, the man had become easily moved to anger and yelling at people. His memory had decreased, he was commonly suspicious, he had visual hallucinations, and he tended to sleep during the daytime. In addition, his urination had become incontinent. A local hospital had diagnosed the man with senile dementia and he had taken various Chinese and Western medicine with no apparent effect. In 1990, the man underwent one course of acupuncture and all his symptoms disappeared. At the time of writing this case three years later, the man was still in good health. Acupuncture consisted of inserting 28 gauge needles to connect all four *Si Shen Cong* (M-HN-1) to *Bai Hui* (GV 20). After insertion, warm supplementation hand technique was used to produce a warm, hot feeling around the needles. Then the needles were withdrawn. This was done one time every other day, with 15 times equaling one course of treatment. A five day rest was given between each successive such course of treatment.

### ENDNOTES

[1] Yan De-xin, *Aging & Blood Stasis: A New TCM Approach to Geriatrics*, trans. by Tang Guo-shen & Bob Flaws, Blue Poppy Press, Boulder, CO, 1995, p. 243-244

[2] He Jun & Li Qiu-yang, "Jottings on the Acupuncture Treatment of Senile Dementia," *Tian Jin Zhong Yi (Tianjin Chinese Medicine)*, #3, 1993, p. 43

[3] Yang Shu-cheng, "The Water Needle Treatment of 26 Cases of Senile Dementia," *Zhe Jiang Zhong Yi Za Zhi (Zhejiang Journal of Chinese Medicine)*, #8, 1995, p. 357

[4] Ye Heng, "The Treatment of Senile Dementia by Needling *Si Shen Cong* (M-HN-1)," *Zhe Jiang Zhong Yi Za Zhi (Zhejiang Journal of Chinese Medicine)*, #11, 1993, p. 520

# 3

# SCHIZOPHRENIA

Schizophrenia is a severe disorder of thought characterized by distorted perceptions of reality, impaired reasoning, disorganized speech and behavior, and lost capacity for the spontaneous experience of emotions. Delusional beliefs and auditory or visual hallucinations may also be present, and there is typically diminished motivation and grossly impaired occupational and social functioning. The general definition of schizophrenia includes the requirement of a time course that is greater than six months.

Schizophrenics typically have a higher than chance occurrence of neurologic soft signs, including diminished dexterity and increased blink reflex. There is a higher than chance occurrence of apraxia or inability to carry out tasks which is attributed to dysfunction of the right parietal lobe. Neuro-psychological test data and functional brain-imaging studies reveal dysfunction in the temporal and frontal lobes, principle brain regions in language and executive functioning including abstract reasoning. Schizophrenics tend to score lower on standardized intelligence tests before disease onset, and intelligence continues to deteriorate during the course of chronic psychotic illness.

As many as 25% of individuals experiencing psychosis are also depressed. Marked change in the individual's previous baseline of emotional responsiveness typically occurs during the acute phase, i.e., when symptoms are most pronounced. This may include either extreme emotional withdrawal, intense, inappropriate, or self-destructive emotions, and possibly extreme rage or anxiety.

## NOSOLOGY:

Western psychiatry identifies five sub-types of schizophrenia depending on the symptoms that are most prominent. The following table summarizes core features of the sub-types of schizophrenia as defined in contemporary Western psychiatry.

According to Western psychiatric diagnostic criteria, in all sub-types of schizophrenia, the individual experiences a disturbance in occupational or social functioning and psychotic symptoms that are not caused by a medical problem, the effects of a medication, or illicit substance abuse. Western psychiatry categorizes symptoms into other psychotic disorders based on symptom type, the presence of identifiable medical or other causes, and symptom duration. Symptom patterns that are similar to schizophrenia but continue for shorter periods of time are defined as other kinds of psychotic disorders as summarized in the table on the following page.

## PROMINENT SYMPTOMS OF SCHIZOPHRENIA SUBTYPES

| SCHIZOPHRENIA SUB-TYPES | PROMINENT SYMPTOMS |
| --- | --- |
| PARANOID | • Delusions or hallucinations<br>• Does not exhibit disorganized or catatonic behavior |
| DISORGANIZED | • Disorganized Disorganized speech, behavior, or inappropriate affect<br>• Does not exhibit catatonic behavior |
| CATATONIC | • Motoric immobility (including posturing) or excessive motor activity<br>• Extreme negativism<br>• Repeats words or actions of others |
| UNDIFFERENTIATED | • Meets criteria for schizophrenia in general but there are no other specific distinguishing symptoms |
| RESIDUAL | • Symptoms are present but in an attenuated form |

## PSYCHOTIC DISORDERS RELATED TO SCHIZOPHRENIA

| OTHER PSYCHOTIC DISORDERS | BASIC CRITERIA |
| --- | --- |
| SCHIZOPHRENIFORM DISORDER | • Same symptom pattern as schizophrenia<br>• Symptoms continue for at least one month but less than six months |
| BRIEF PSYCHOTIC DISORDER | • Same symptom pattern as schizophrenia<br>• Symptoms continue for at least one day but less than one month |
| DELUSIONAL DISORDER | • Non-bizarre delusions<br>• Symptoms last at least one month<br>• Never previously diagnosed as schizophrenic |
| SCHIZOAFFECTIVE DISORDER | • Same basic symptom pattern as schizophrenia<br>• In context of manic or depressive symptoms during the period of active psychosis |
| SUBSTANCE-INDUCED PSYCHOTIC DISORDER | • There is evidence that psychotic symptoms are due to the effects of a substance and the patient is not psychotic when not using that substance |

## EPIDEMIOLOGY:

The worldwide prevalence of schizophrenia is 0.2-2% in most Western and Asian countries surveyed. The prevalence of schizophrenia appears to be greater in lower socioeconomic classes in urban areas. However, the apparent increased rate of schizophrenia in these populations may be an artifact of downward social migration that typically occurs during the course of the illness. Schizophrenia is diagnosed in approximately 1 in 10,000 adults annually. The average age at onset is between the late teens and the early 30s, but the disorder may first occur during childhood or old age. Although schizophrenia is generally believed to affect men and women equally, some studies have suggested that men are disproportionately affected by this disorder. Further, women appear to be older at the time of initial symptom onset, experience more mood symptoms than men, and have a more favorable overall long-term course. Biological relatives of schizophrenics have a significantly greater risk (perhaps as much as 10 times greater) of developing schizophrenia than the average population. Impaired capacity to function socially may account for a disproportionate occurrence of schizophrenia in single versus married persons. Despite its relatively low prevalence and incidence, because of the severely impairing cognitive symptoms that characterize schizophrenia and the absence of effective treatment in many cases, patients with schizophrenia occupy 25% of all hospital beds in the U.S. and account for 20% of all Social Security disability days.

## DIFFERENTIAL DIAGNOSIS:

In clinical practice, psychosis often has an underlying medical cause, including neurologic disease. In general, psychotic symptoms are common in the context of medical disorders associated with changes in the level or quality of consciousness, including brain tumors, other CNS lesions, hyperthyroidism, systemic lupus erythematosus (SLE), some advanced cases of multiple sclerosis (MS), delirium, and dementia. Certain prescription medications sometimes cause psychosis. For example, high dose steroids, which are used to treat many immunological disorders, can result in a fulminant psychotic syndrome. Medications that target CNS dopamine receptors, including principally drugs used to treat Parkinson's disease (e.g., L-Dopa and compound drugs containing it), and others, sometimes cause psychosis. Chronic use or acute intoxication of illicit substances is frequently associated with psychosis that is sometimes difficult to distinguish from a primary psychiatric disorder. Well-known examples of illicit substances that result in psychosis during acute intoxication include methamphetamines, cocaine, and

hallucinogens like LSD or PCP. Chronic use of marijuana or heroin sometimes manifests as a psychotic syndrome. Because of numerous possible primary medical or substance-induced causes of psychosis, the initial task in clarifying the differential diagnosis is to rule out reasonable possibilities based on history, clinical presentation, and, where possible, laboratory or diagnostic studies. For example, a history of evolving psychosis in the context of progressive neurologic changes points to a lesion in the CNS. Diagnostic imaging with a CT-scan or MRI will confirm or rule out the presence of a brain lesion. When there is reasonable evidence that psychosis is related to acute intoxication or chronic substance abuse, urine toxicology will typically confirm the diagnosis. Discontinuation of a prescription medication will confirm or rule out a suspected relationship between that medication and a psychotic syndrome. Medical disorders and the effects of substances must be ruled out with tests and a complete history before schizophrenia can be correctly diagnosed and appropriately treated.

When a thorough history and appropriate laboratory or other diagnostic studies have ruled out reasonable underlying medical causes of psychosis, a primary psychiatric disorder is assumed to exist. Accurate diagnosis of schizophrenia or other psychotic disorders requires careful review of history and a thorough mental status examination to determine the course of the disorder, degree of impairment, and the presence or absence of specific symptoms. Schizophreniform disorder is diagnosed when a pattern of psychotic symptoms that is identical to that seen in schizophrenia persists longer than one month but resolves completely within six months of onset. In a similar way, brief psychotic disorder is diagnosed when a schizophrenia-like symptom pattern lasts at least one day but never persists longer than one month.

Before schizophrenia can be conclusively diagnosed, other primary psychiatric disorders that are sometimes associated with psychosis must be ruled out. Individuals afflicted with mood disorders, including major depressive disorder and bipolar disorder (type I only), sometimes experience transient psychotic episodes when acutely depressed or manic respectively. In the absence of a complete history, schizoaffective disorder is difficult to distinguish from schizophrenia. In the absence of medical causes, the diagnosis is confirmed by episodes of concurrent psychosis and acute mania or profoundly depressed mood interspersed with episodes of psychosis unaccompanied by mood symptoms. Delusional disorder is another psychotic disorder that is difficult to distinguish from schizophrenia because of similarities in history and symptomatology. In this disorder, the individual experiences nonbizarre delusions, in

## DIFFERENTIAL DIAGNOSIS

| 1. MEDICAL DISORDERS | 2. EFFECTS OF SUBSTANCES | 3. PSYCHIATRIC DISORDERS |
|---|---|---|
| A. CNS LESIONS INCLUDING BRAIN TUMORS | A. ALCOHOL OR ILLICIT SUBSTANCE INTOXICATION OR CHRONIC USE | A. SCHIZOPHRENIA |
| B. HYPERTHYROIDISM | B. SIDE EFFECTS OF CERTAIN MEDICATIONS INCLUDING STEROIDS, L-DOPA, OTHERS | B. BRIEF PSYCHOTIC DISORDER |
| C. SYSTEMIC LUPUS ERYTHEMATOSUS (SLE) | | C. SCHIZOPHRENIFORM DISORDER |
| D. MULTIPLE SCLEROSIS (MS) | | D. SCHIZOAFFECTIVE DISORDER |
| E. DELIRIUM | | E. BIPOLAR DISORDER (TYPE I ONLY) |
| F. DEMENTIA | | F. DELUSIONAL DISORDER |
| | | G. MAJOR DEPRESSIVE EPISODE WITH PSYCHOTIC FEATURES |
| | | H. DISSOCIATIVE DISORDERS, INCLUDING DISSOCIATIVE IDENTITY DISORDER |
| | | I. POST-TRAUMATIC STRESS DISORDER (PTSD) |
| | | J. SEVERE PERSONALITY DISORDERS, INCLUDING BORDERLINE, SCHIZOID, AND SCHIZOTYPAL |

contrast to typically bizarre delusions of paranoid schizophrenia, and the individual has not previously been diagnosed with schizophrenia. Other Western psychiatric disorders that sometimes manifest with psychotic symptoms include post-traumatic stress disorder (PTSD), dissociative disorders (including, principally, dissociative identity disorder), and certain personality disorders, including borderline, schizoid, and schizotypal personality disorders.

### ETIOLOGY & PATHOPHYSIOLOGY:

Currently, there is no consensus over the etiology of psychotic disorders in Western psychiatry. However, most researchers believe that a number of factors may lead to the pathogenesis of psychosis, including genetic predisposition resulting in increased susceptibility to stress or possibly emergence of psychosis *de novo*. Abnormalities in specific chromosomes have been implicated, including chromosomes 5, 11, and 18. Such genetic predisposition may affect the functioning or CNS levels of specific neurotransmitters (or their CNS receptors) that are consistently abnormal in schizophrenics. These include dopamine, serotonin, GABA, and glutamate. Brain-imaging studies have revealed abnormalities in metabolism, especially affecting the frontal lobes. In addition to biological theories of the pathogenesis of schizophrenia, many social and psychological theories have been advanced. Possible sociopsychological factors include fail-

ure of the ego to achieve constancy during early psychological development, etc.

### WESTERN MEDICAL TREATMENT:

Individuals who are unable to function because of the severity of psychotic symptoms are typically hospitalized for pharmacological treatment for presumed neurochemical causes. Psychotic patients frequently experience delusions or auditory hallucinations resulting in homicidal or suicidal thoughts. Patients who express homicidal or suicidal thoughts should be hospitalized immediately. If the patient is unable or unwilling to cooperate with psychiatric hospitalization, the clinician is obligated to contact the emergency medical system so that paramedics or local law enforcement can perform an emergency assessment and place the patient on a hold (5150) if indicated. Principle goals of hospitalization are accurate diagnosis (including appropriate medical evaluation to rule out underlying medical causes), psychiatric stabilization, and safety. When symptomatology is less severe and the patient is able to function independently, an appropriate medical workup and medication management may take place on an out-patient basis.

Antipsychotic medications are used singly or in combination depending on the nature and severity of symptoms and treatment response history on a case by case basis. All medications currently used in contemporary Western psychiatry function as dopamine receptor antagonists, consistent with the hypothesis that a CNS hyper-dopaminergic state causes or is clinically correlated with the emergence of psychosis and that correction of this neurochemical derangement will, therefore, eliminate psychotic symptoms. More recently introduced antipsychotic medications antagonize both dopamine and serotonin receptors and appear to treat the so-called negative symptoms of schizophrenia, including withdrawal and diminished spontaneous speech, more effectively. These newer antipsychotics have been called atypical agents. Their chronic use is associated with some degree of risk for development of severe neurologic side effects that have been historically associated with chronic use of earlier typical antipsychotic agents, such as Thorazine (chlorpromazine) and Haldol (haloperidol). In addition, medications with other CNS properties are used to treat the nonpsychotic symptoms that often accompany psychosis. These include sedatives for the treatment of agitation that often accompanies acute psychosis and medications that counter the neurologic side effects of antipsychotic agents. Although used infrequently for the treatment of schizophrenia, electroconvulsive therapy (ECT) is sometimes employed in cases of catatonic schizophrenia where symptoms have not responded to appropriate medication trials.

In addition to pharmacological approaches, individual, family, and group psychotherapy are sometimes recommended in the treatment of psychotic disorders. Support groups or family therapy following specific cognitive-behavioral models have been correlated with reduced relapse rates. In schizophrenia, the focus is on support and relapse prevention. Studies have demonstrated greater effectiveness of treatment strategies that combine medication management and supportive individual and group therapy than approaches that rely on medications alone.

## PROGNOSIS:

Long- and short-term prognoses for diagnosed patients with schizophrenia who are receiving conventional Western psychiatric treatments are disappointingly poor. Using accepted outcomes criteria, several prospective and retrospective studies have consistently demonstrated that only 10-20% of schizophrenic patients show improvement or absence of continued decline over a 10 year period following their initial hospitalization and the initiation of treatment. Furthermore, at least 50% of schizophrenic patients have demonstrably poor out-comes despite compliance with recommended conventional Western treatments. The majority of patients receiving available Western medical therapies for psychotic disorders continue to experience frequent exacerbations requiring hospitalization and co-morbid mood disorders and have a high rate of suicide attempts and completed suicides. It is estimated that 40-60% of schizophrenics receiving currently available conventional Western medical treatments continue to be severely impaired throughout their lives.

## SHORT & LONG-TERM ADVANTAGES AND DISADVANTAGES OF WESTERN MEDICAL TREATMENT:

From the Western psychiatric perspective, the advantages of acute hospitalization are obvious, including removal of the patient from the stressors that might have precipitated a psychotic episode and confinement in a controlled, safe setting where consequences of erratic behaviors or severe breakdown in cognitive functioning will not be potentially life-threatening or a danger to others. Studies demonstrate that early aggressive treatment, including hospitalization where appropriate, and the initiation of appropriate pharmacologic therapy typically yields a more rapid return to the patient's previous level of psychological functioning, resulting in reduced individual disruption and, therefore, reduced loss in productivity. Long-term advantages of continuing treatment (so-called maintenance therapy) are believed to be a reduced risk of relapse and overall improved social and occupational functioning. However, it is estimated that these treatments for schizophrenia and other psychotic disorders only effectively diminish or relieve symptoms in 50% of cases, while placebos typically achieve effectiveness rates of 30% or higher.

In other words, more than half of schizophrenics who comply with recommended Western treatment approaches have poor out-comes. This means frequent relapses and continuing insidious decline in cognitive functioning, including occupational and social functioning, and a continued pattern of acute exacerbations requiring hospitalization. In view of the inherent long-term risks in the chronic maintenance use of most antipsychotic medications, high relapse rates to acute psychotic states among even compliant patient populations, and sometimes unimpressive differences between placebo and antipsychotic medications, psychiatrists must frequently weigh the short-term benefits against the long-term risk of permanent neurologic side effects associated with available conventional treatments. This dilemma has led an increasing number of psychiatrists to investigate nonconventional and non-Western paradigms and treatments for schizophrenia and other psychiatric disorders which tend to respond poorly to available contemporary Western psychiatric therapies.

## INDICATIONS FOR REFERRAL TO WESTERN MEDICAL SERVICES:

It is generally advisable to refer individuals experiencing psychotic symptoms for medical-psychiatric evaluation. Mild to moderate symptoms that do not markedly interfere with functioning or pose safety risks to the patient or others may be adequately managed on an out-patient basis. When symptoms are so severe that functioning is grossly impaired or the patient poses a real threat to themself or others, emergency medical evaluation is appropriate and necessary for reasons described above. When there is clinical uncertainty about a patient's safety or capacity to meet such basic needs as food, clothing, or shelter, it is always advisable to immediately arrange for an emergency medical evaluation. In those instances where psychotic individuals are grossly impaired, agitated, or paranoid and unable to cooperate with a referral to the closest hospital emergency room, it is necessary for the patient's safety to initiate the local emergency response network through 911.

In nonemergency cases where psychotic symptoms have persisted or only partially responded to treatment, professional practitioners of Chinese medicine should consult with the patient's psychiatrist in an effort to clarify the diagnosis and develop an integrated Chinese-Western medical treatment plan. It is the authors' opinion that Western acupuncturists and practitioners of Chinese medicine not holding dual licensure as both Chinese doctor and Western MD are not adequately trained to cope with all the ramifications of schizophrenia and other such psychoses.

## CHINESE DISEASE CATEGORIZATION:

Persons exhibiting the signs and symptoms of schizophrenia in Western medicine are traditionally categorized as suffering from the Chinese disease categories of *dian kuang*, withdrawal and mania, *kuang zheng*, manic condition, or *chi dai*, feeblemindedness.

## CHINESE DISEASE CAUSES & DISEASE MECHANISMS:

According to Chinese medical theory, the causes of schizophrenia are closely related to damage due to excesses of the five minds and seven affects. For instance, excessive anger, fear, and fright or unfilled thoughts and preoccupations may cause disturbances in the function of the viscera and bowels and loss of regulation in the balance of yin and yang. This may then produce qi depression, phlegm congelation, fire evils, blood stasis, and other such pathological changes which may cloud the heart orifices and harass and cause chaos to the spirit brilliance, thus resulting in loss of psychological normalcy. The causes and mechanisms of schizophrenia may also be closely related to former heaven natural endowment and constitutional strength and weakness. If the righteous qi exists internally and yin is level (or calm) while yang is secreted, then psychological stimuli may cause psycho-emotional discomfort but they will not cause disease. However, if the natural endowment is habitually vacuous or if yin or yang are inclined in one direction or another, then such stimuli may lead to the spirit brilliance's easily being harassed with the consequent development of withdrawal and mania.

## TREATMENT BASED ON PATTERN DISCRIMINATION:

### 1. ACUTE EPISODES

### A. YANG DISEASE PATTERN

**MAIN SYMPTOMS:** Excited, agitated stirring, visual hallucinations, delusions, difficulty thinking and disturbed, chaotic thoughts, odd, unusual, eccentric behavior, form exuberant, body replete, a red facial complexion and red eyes, dry stools, a red tongue with yellow fur, and a bowstring or bowstring, rapid, forceful pulse

**ANALYSIS OF SYMPTOMS:** Habitual bodily exuberance combined with excesses of the five minds lead to "double yang" which then leads to mania. In mania, the six spirits lose control and the heart spirit is not calm. Therefore, there is excited, agitated stirring, visual hallucinations, delusions, difficulty thinking and disturbed, chaotic thoughts, odd, erratic behavior, etc., all of which are yang-natured symptoms. Likewise, the red facial complexion, red eyes, dry stools, red tongue with yellow fur, and the rapid pulse are all signs of yang qi exuberant internally.

**TREATMENT PRINCIPLES:** Drain fire, flush phlegm, quicken the blood and dispel stasis, heavily settle and quiet the spirit

**COMMONLY USED FORMULAS:** Choose from *Long Dan Xie Gan Tang* (Gentiana Drain the Liver Decoction), *Di Tan Tang* (Flush Phlegm Decoction), *Dian Kuang Meng Xing Tang* (Withdrawal & Mania Dream Arousal Decoction), and *Sheng Tie Luo Yin* (Uncooked Iron Filings Drink).

**ANALYSIS OF FORMULAS:** The commonly seen disease mechanisms of yang-natured withdrawal and mania are 1)

phlegm fire harassing upward, 2) static blood obstructing and stagnating, and 3) heart spirit smothered and harassed. *Long Dan Xie Gan Tang* is the main formula for draining liver-gallbladder replete fire. It is appropriate to use for liver-gallbladder replete heat with extreme fire heat resulting in psychomotor excitation as the main symptom of schizophrenia. *Di Tan Tang* is very good for flushing phlegm and opening the orifices. Therefore, it is mainly used in schizophrenia accompanied by white or yellow slimy tongue fur, a slippery, bowstring pulse, and other such signs of phlegm confounding the heart orifices and turbid qi clouding the heart. *Dian Kuang Meng Xing Tang* is mainly suitable for quickening the blood and breaking stasis, moving the qi and resolving depression. It is relatively effective in cases of delusional and adolescent schizophrenia whose clinical manifestations are emotional lability, behavioral disturbances, excited, agitated stirring, and delusions. These may also be accompanied by menstrual irregularity, greenish black or purplish red static spots or static macules on the lips and tongue, a choppy pulse, and other such symptoms of blood stasis. *Sheng Tie Luo Yin* has the effects of settling the heart and softening phlegm, quieting the spirit and stabilizing the mind. It mainly treats phlegm fire harassing above resulting in withdrawal and mania. Nowadays, it is mostly used to treat patients with acute episodes of agitated and manic schizophrenia.

## FORMULA INGREDIENTS:

*Long Dan Xie Gan Tang:* Radix Gentianae Scabrae (*Long Dan Cao*), Radix Scutellariae Baicalensis (*Huang Qin*), Fructus Gardeniae Jasminoidis (*Zhi Zi*), Radix Bupleuri (*Chai Hu*), Extremitas Radicis Angelicae Sinensis (*Dang Gui Wei*), uncooked Radix Rehmanniae (*Sheng Di*), Rhizoma Alismatis (*Ze Xie*), Semen Plantaginis (*Che Qian Zi*), Caulis Akebiae (*Mu Tong*), Radix Glycyrrhizae (*Gan Cao*)

*Di Dan Tang:* Rhizoma Pinelliae Ternatae (*Ban Xia*), Pericarpium Citri Erythrocarpae (*Ju Hong*), Sclerotium Poriae Cocos (*Fu Ling*), Fructus Immaturus Citri Aurantii (*Zhi Shi*), Caulis Bambusae In Taeniis (*Zhu Ru*), bile-processed Rhizoma Arisaematis (*Dan Nan Xing*), Rhizoma Acori Graminei (*Shi Chang Pu*), Radix Panacis Ginseng (*Ren Shen*), Radix Glycyrrhizae (*Gan Cao*)

*Dian Kuang Meng Xing Tang:* Semen Pruni Persicae (*Tao Ren*), Radix Bupleuri (*Chai Hu*), Rhizoma Cyperi Rotundi (*Xiang Fu*), Caulis Akebiae (*Mu Tong*), Radix Rubrus Paeoniae Lactiflorae (*Chi Shao*), Rhizoma Pinelliae Ternatae (*Ban Xia*), Pericarpium Arecae Catechu (*Da Fu Pi*), Pericarpium Citri Reticulatae Viride (*Qing Pi*), Pericarpium Citri Reticulatae (*Chen Pi*), Cortex Radicis Mori Albi (*Sang Pi*), Fructus Perillae Frutescentis (*Su Zi*), Radix Glycyrrhizae (*Gan Cao*)

*Sheng Tie Luo Yin:* Frusta Ferri (*Tie Luo*), bile-processed Rhizoma Arisaematis (*Dan Nan Xing*), Bulbus Fritillariae (*Bei Mu*), Radix Scrophulariae Ningpoensis (*Xuan Shen*), Tuber Asparagi Cochinensis (*Tian Dong*), Tuber Ophiopogonis Japonici (*Mai Dong*), Fructus Forsythiae Suspensae (*Lian Qiao*), Ramulus Uncariae Cum Uncis (*Gou Teng*), Radix Salviae Miltiorrhizae (*Dan Shen*), Sclerotium Poriae Cocos (*Fu Ling*), Sclerotium Pararadicis Poriae Cocos (*Fu Shen*), Pericarpium Citri Reticulatae (*Chen Pi*), Rhizoma Acori Graminei (*Shi Chang Pu*), Radix Polygalae Tenuifoliae (*Yuan Zhi*), Cinnabar (*Zhu Sha*)[1]

## ACUPUNCTURE:

A. *Zhong Wan* (CV 12), *Shen Men* (Ht 7), *San Yin Jiao* (Sp 6)

B. *Xin Shu* (Bl 15), *Gan Shu* (Bl 18), *Pi Shu* (Bl 20), *Feng Long* (St 40)

Alternate the use of these two groups of points using draining technique and strong stimulation. If yang-natured symptoms are pronounced, one can simply needle *Huan Tiao* (GB 30) bilaterally with a relatively thick, four *cun* needle and strong stimulation. This can create a spirit-quieting effect.

## B. YIN DISEASE PATTERN

**MAIN SYMPTOMS:** A flat affect, abnormally slow reactions, lack of will, difficulty thinking, fatigued, form vacuous, body weak, qi timidity, lassitude of the spirit, a somber white facial complexion, a pale tongue, and a deep, fine pulse

**ANALYSIS OF SYMPTOMS:** Natural endowment insufficiency combined with depression and binding of the seven affects result in "double yin" and lead to withdrawal. If withdrawal and mania have endured for a long time, both qi and blood may have become vacuous and yang qi devitalized. Thus the essence spirit has nothing to arouse it and, therefore, the affect is flat, reactions are slow, there is lack of will or determination, thinking is difficult, and the patient is fatigued. These are all yin type symptoms. A vacuous form and weak body, qi timidity, lassitude of the spirit, a somber, white facial complexion, a pale tongue, and a deep, fine pulse are all signs of yang qi insufficiency with yin qi exuberant internally.

**TREATMENT PRINCIPLES:** Nourish the blood and supplement the heart, warm yang and excite

**COMMONLY USED FORMULAS:** *Yang Xin Tang* (Nourish the Heart Decoction), *Di Huang Yin Zi* (Rehmannia Drink), *Wen Yang Xing Fen Tang* (Warm Yang & Excite Decoction)

**ANALYSIS OF FORMULAS:** In yin-natured withdrawal and mania, qi and blood depletion and vacuity and kidney yang insufficiency are commonly seen. The heart governs the blood and the treasuring of the spirit. If the blood filling the heart channel is insufficient, is no way to nourish the spirit. Hence the spirit becomes disquieted or restless. *Yang Xin Tang* boosts the qi and supplements the blood, nourishes the heart and quiets the spirit. It can be used in chronic psychological diseases, geriatric psychological diseases, and postpartum psychological disease where there are essence spirit listlessness, fright palpitations, restlessness, insomnia, impaired memory, a bright facial complexion with scanty luster, a pale tongue, a fine, forceless pulse, and other such symptoms of qi and blood dual vacuity. *Di Huang Yin Zi* and *Wen Yang Xing Fen Tang* both have the effect of warming yang and supplementing the kidneys, vitalizing and exciting the yang qi. They are mainly used in the treatment of chronic, simple, or catatonic types of schizophrenia where the affect is indifferent, dull, cowering, withdrawn, etc. accompanied by a bright, white facial complexion, reversal chilling of the four limbs, a pale tongue, and a deep, fine pulse.

**FORMULA INGREDIENTS:**

*Yang Xin Tang:* Radix Astragali Membranacei (*Huang Qi*), Sclerotium Poriae Cocos (*Fu Ling*), Sclerotium Pararadicis Poriae Cocos (*Fu Shen*), Radix Angelicae Sinensis (*Dang Gui*), Radix Ligustici Wallichii (*Chuan Xiong*), mix-fried Radix Glycyrrhizae (*Gan Cao*), Pinellia Massa Medica Fermentata (*Ban Xia Qu*), Semen Biotae Orientalis (*Bai Zi Ren*), Semen Zizyphi Spinosae (*Suan Zao Ren*), Radix Polygalae Tenuifoliae (*Yuan Zhi*), Fructus Schisandrae Chinensis (*Wu Wei Zi*), Radix Panacis Ginseng (*Ren Shen*), Cortex Cinnamomi Cassiae (*Rou Gui*)

*Di Huang Yin Zi:* Dry Radix Rehmanniae (*Di Huang*), Radix Morindae Officinalis (*Ba Ji Tian*), Fructus Corni Officinalis (*Shan Zhu Yu*), Herba Dendrobii (*Shi Hu*), Herba Cistanchis Deserticolae (*Rou Cong Rong*), Radix Lateralis Praeparatus Aconiti Carmichaeli (*Fu Zi*),

Fructus Schisandrae Chinensis (*Wu Wei Zi*), Cortex Cinnamomi Cassiae (*Rou Gui*), Sclerotium Poriae Cocos (*Fu Ling*), Tuber Ophiopogonis Japonici (*Mai Dong*), Rhizoma Acori Graminei (*Shi Chang Pu*), Radix Polygalae Tenuifoliae (*Yuan Zhi*)

*Wen Yang Xing Fen Tang:* Radix Codonopsitis Pilosulae (*Dang Shen*), cooked Radix Rehmanniae (*Shu Di*), Herba Epimedii (*Yin Yang Huo*), Herba Cistanchis Deserticolae (*Rou Cong Rong*), Plastrum Testudinis (*Gui Ban*), Radix Lateralis Praeparatus Aconiti Carmichaeli (*Fu Zi*), Radix Astragali Membranacei (*Huang Qi*), mix-fried Radix Glycyrrhizae (*Gan Cao*), Cortex Cinnamomi Cassiae (*Rou Gui*), dry Rhizoma Zingiberis (*Gan Jiang*)

**ACUPUNCTURE:**

A. *Ren Zhong* (GV 26), *Shao Shang* (Lu 11), *Yin Bai* (Sp 1), *Da Ling* (Per 7), *Feng Long* (St 40)

B. *Feng Fu* (GV 16), *Da Zhui* (GV 14), *Shen Zhu* (GV 12)

C. *Jiu Wei* (CV 15), *Shang Wan* (CV 13), *Zhong Wan* (CV 12), *Feng Long* (St 40)

D. *Ren Zhong* (GV 26), *Feng Fu* (GV 16), *Lao Gong* (Per 8), *Da Ling* (Per 7)

Choose one set of points each time, alternating the use of all four sets with even supplementing-even draining technique.

**2. REMITTENT STAGE**

**A. LIVER QI DEPRESSION & BINDING PATTERN**

**MAIN SYMPTOMS:** Emotional depression, a dull affect, taciturnity, illogical speech, a tendency to uncommon anger, if severe, suicidal thoughts and no desire to live, self-injury, chest and rib-side fullness and oppression, a tendency to sighing, no thought for food or drink, menstrual irregularity in females, a dark tongue with thin, white fur, and a bowstring pulse

**ANALYSIS OF SYMPTOMS:** Unfulfilled desires and frustration may inhibit the qi mechanism or excessive anger may damage the liver. Hence the liver loses its control over coursing and discharging and the qi becomes stagnant and accumulates. The liver may also lose control over coursing and discharging in females prior to menstruation if the blood accumulating in the uterus leaves liver blood insufficient. In any case, lack of coursing and discharge results in emotional depression, a dull affect, taciturnity, no desire to live, no desire to eat or drink, and menstrual irregularity in women. Qi stagnation leads to chest and rib-side fullness and oppression and sighing. When the qi becomes stagnant and accumulates, it eventually has to counterflow. This leads to easy anger and physical violence against both oneself and others. A dark tongue and a bowstring pulse are both signs of inhibited qi and, therefore, blood flow.

**TREATMENT PRINCIPLES:** Course the liver and resolve depression

**FORMULA & MEDICINALS:** *Chai Hu Shu Gan San Jia Wei* (Bupleurum Course the Liver Decoction with Added Flavors)

Radix Bupleuri (*Chai Hu*), 12g, Rhizoma Cyperi Rotundi (*Xiang Fu*), 10g, Radix Albus Paeoniae Lactiflorae (*Bai Shao*), 10g, Fructus Citri Aurantii (*Zhi Ke*), 10g, Radix Ligustici Wallichii (*Chuan Xiong*), 6g (added later), Radix Polygalae Tenuifoliae (*Yuan Zhi*), 10g, Caulis Perillae Frutescentis (*Su Geng*), 10g, Lignum Aquilariae Agallochae (*Chen Xiang*), 6g, Radix Glycyrrhizae (*Gan Cao*), 3g

Decoct in water and administer orally two times per day in divided doses, morning and evening, one *ji* per day.

**ANALYSIS OF FORMULA:** Bupleurum, Cyperus, Aurantium, Caulis Perillae, and Aquilaria all course the liver and rectify the qi. Polygala rectifies the qi and resolves depression at the same time as it quiets the spirit. Peony nourishes the blood and, therefore, emolliates and harmonizes the liver, while Ligusticum moves the qi within the blood. Licorice harmonizes all the other medicinals in the formula.

**ADDITIONS & SUBTRACTIONS:** If enduring or extreme depression has transformed heat with a bitter taste in the mouth, more extreme anger, a red tongue, and a bowstring, rapid pulse, one can add Radix Scutellariae Baicalensis (*Huang Qin*) and Rhizoma Coptidis Chinensis (*Huang Lian*). If there is liver depression qi stagnation with spleen vacuity loss of fortification, then use *Xiao Yao San* (Rambling Powder) with additions and subtractions instead. If there is a liver-spleen disharmony with depressive heat, use either *Dan Zhi Xiao Yao San* (Moutan & Gardenia Rambling Powder) or *Xiao Chai Hu Tang* (Minor Bupleurum Decoction) with additions and subtractions.

*Xiao Yao San:* Radix Bupleuri (*Chai Hu*), Radix Angelicae Sinensis (*Dan Gui*), Radix Albus Paeoniae Lactiflorae (*Bai Zhu*), Rhizoma Atractylodis Macrocephalae (*Bai Zhu*), Sclerotium Poriae Cocos (*Fu Ling*), mix-fried Radix

Glycyrrhizae (*Gan Cao*), Herba Menthae Haplocalycis ((*Bo He*), uncooked Rhizoma Zingiberis (*Shen Jiang*)

*Dan Zhi Xiao Yao San:* Cortex Radicis Moutan (*Dan Pi*), Fructus Gardeniae Jasminoidis (*Zhi Zi*), Radix Bupleuri (*Chai Hu*), Radix Angelicae Sinensis (*Dan Gui*), Radix Albus Paeoniae Lactiflorae (*Bai Shao*), Rhizoma Atractylodis Macrocephalae (*Bai Zhu*), Sclerotium Poriae Cocos (*Fu Ling*), mix-fried Radix Glycyrrhizae (*Gan Cao*)

*Xiao Chai Hu Tang:* Radix Bupleuri (*Chai Hu*), Radix Scutellariae Baicalensis (*Huang Qin*), Radix Codonopsitis Pilosulae (*Dang Shen*), Rhizoma Pinelliae Ternatae (*Ban Xia*), mix-fried Radix Glycyrrhizae (*Gan Cao*), Fructus Zizyphi Jujubae (*Da Zao*), uncooked Rhizoma Zingiberis (*Shen Jiang*)[2]

**ACUPUNCTURE:** *Tai Chong* (Liv 3), *Nei Guan* (Per 6), *Shan Men* (Ht 7), *He Gu* (LI 4), *Zu San Li* (St 36), *Dan Zhong* (CV 17). Use draining technique.

## B. PHLEGM QI DEPRESSION & BINDING PATTERN

**MAIN SYMPTOMS:** Emotional depression, a flat affect, paranoia, lots of worries, illogical speech, murmuring to oneself, laughing and crying without constancy, a tendency to sighing, chest and rib-side distention and fullness, no thought for food or drink, possible plum pit qi or the sensation of something stuck in one's throat which cannot be spit up or swallowed down, a tendency to profuse phlegm, slimy tongue fur, and a bowstring, slippery pulse

**ANALYSIS OF SYMPTOMS:** Excessive thinking and worrying may lead to liver qi binding and depression and the spleen's loss of fortification and movement. This may then give rise to phlegm turbidity. If qi depression binds with phlegm, this may obstruct and confound the spirit brilliance. Therefore, there are a flat, dull affect, emotional depression, paranoia, lots of worries, illogical speech, laughing and crying without constancy, and various other such psychological abnormalities. If the liver qi becomes depressed, the liver channel will not be smoothly or easily flowing. Thus there are a tendency to sighing and chest and rib-side distention and fullness. Because there is phlegm turbidity obstructing the center and the spleen qi is not transporting, there is no thought of eating or drinking. Plum pit qi is a symptom of phlegm and qi mutually binding, while profuse phlegm obviously indicates phlegm. The slimy tongue fur and the bowstring, slippery pulse are both signs of phlegm and qi depression and binding.

**TREATMENT PRINCIPLES:** Rectify the qi and resolve depression, transform phlegm and open the orifices

**FORMULA & MEDICINALS:** *Shun Qi Dao Tan Tang He Kong Xian Dan Jia Jian* (Normalize the Qi & Abduct Phlegm Decoction plus Control Drool Elixir with Additions & Subtractions)

Pericarpium Citri Reticulatae (*Chen Pi*), 10g, Rhizoma Pinelliae Ternatae (*Ban Xia*), 10g, bile-processed Rhizoma Arisaematis (*Dan Nan Xing*), 10g, Sclerotium Poriae Cocos (*Fu Ling*), 15g, Rhizoma Cyperi Rotundi (*Xiang Fu*), 10g, Rhizoma Acori Graminei (*Shi Chang Pu*), 15g, Radix Auklandiae Lappae (*Mu Xiang*), 7g, *Kong Xian Dan* (a Chinese ready-made medicine whose ingredients are Radix Euphorbiae Kansui, *Gan Sui*, Radix Euphorbiae Seu Knoxiae, *Da Ji*, and Semen Sinapis Albae, *Bai Jie Zi*), 2-3 pills swallowed with the other decocted medicinals

Decoct in water and administer orally two times per day in divided doses, morning and evening, one *ji* per day. Take the *Kong Xian Dan* by washing them down with the liquid decoction.

**FORMULA ANALYSIS:** *Shun Qi Dao Tan Tang* downbears the qi and transforms phlegm, resolves depression and opens the orifices. Within this formula, Pinellia, Orange Peel, bile-processed Arisaema, and Poria disinhibit the qi and transform phlegm. Cyperus, Auklandia, and Acorus resolve depression and open the orifices, broaden the center and downbear the qi. These are combined with *Kong Xian Dan* in order to attack and dispel the phlegm drool and thus eliminate phlegm turbidity of the chest and diaphragm. This leads to the liver being able to move and the phlegm turbidity obtaining clearing. Hence the psychological symptoms are remitted.

**ADDITIONS & SUBTRACTIONS:** If there is chest and diaphragmatic fullness and oppression, with profuse phlegm drool in the mouth, a slippery, large pulse, and a strong, replete body, one can use *San Sheng San* (Three Sages Powder) to promote vomiting, seize the phlegm drool by force, and hurry the other medicinals' effect. This is comprised of Pediculus Cucumeris Melonis (*Gua Di*), Radix Et Rhizoma Veratri (*Li Lu*), and Radix Ledebouriellae Divaricatae (*Fang Feng*). If there is spirit clouding with a dull affect, confused, chaotic speech, an absence of eye-blinking, and slimy, white tongue fur evidencing phlegm confounding the heart orifices, it is appropriate to pick away the phlegm and open the orifices, rectify the qi and scatter nodulation by first administering *Su He Xiang Wan* (Liquid Styrax Pills, a ready-made medicine) to penetratingly and aromatically open the orifices. Then use *Si Qi Tang* (Four [to] Seven Decoction) with added bile-processed Rhizoma

Arisaematis (*Dan Nan Xing*), Tuber Curcumae (*Yu Jin*), Rhizoma Acori Graminei (*Shi Chang Pu*), and Radix Polygalae Tenuifoliae (*Yuan Zhi*) in order to transform phlegm and move the qi. If there is insomnia and easy fright, agitation, vexation, and restlessness, a red tongue with yellow fur, and a slippery, rapid pulse due to qi depression transforming heat, phlegm and heat combining and brewing, this phlegm and heat ascending and harassing the heart spirit, one should clear heat and transform phlegm. In that case, one may use *Wen Dan Tang* (Warm the Gallbladder Decoction) plus Rhizoma Coptidis Chinensis (*Huang Lian*) combined with *Bai Jin Wan* (White & Gold Pills). If also accompanied by spirit clouding and chaotic mind, one can also use *Zhi Bao Dan* (Ultimate Treasure Elixir, a ready-made medicine) in order to clear the heart and open the orifices.

*Si Qi Tang* is comprised of: Rhizoma Pinelliae Ternatae (*Ban Xia*), Cortex Magnoliae Officinalis (*Hou Po*), Sclerotium Poriae Cocos (*Fu Ling*), uncooked Rhizoma Zingiberis (*Sheng Jiang*), Folium Perillae Frutescentis (*Zi Su Ye*), and Fructus Zizyphi Jujubae (*Da Zao*).

*Wen Dan Tang* is comprised of: Rhizoma Pinelliae Ternatae (*Ban Xia*), Pericarpium Citri Reticulatae (*Chen Pi*), Sclerotium Poriae Cocos (*Fu Ling*), Fructus Immaturus Citri Aurantii (*Zhi Shi*), Caulis Bambusae In Taeniis (*Zhu Ru*), Radix Glycyrrhizae (*Gan Cao*), and Fructus Zizyphi Jujubae (*Da Zao*).

*Bai Jin Wan* is comprised of Alumen (*Bai Fan*) and Tuber Curcumae (*Yu Jin*) in a 3:7 ratio. The pills are traditionally made using Fructus Gleditschiae Chinensis (*Zao Jiao*) juice, though these days water and flour are also commonly used.

*Zhi Bao Dan* is comprised of: Cornu Rhinocerotis (*Xi Jiao*)[3], Calculus Bovis (*Niu Huang*), Carapax Eretmochelydis Imbricatae (*Dai Mao*), Borneolum (*Bing Pian*), Secretio Moschi Moschiferi (*She Xiang*), Benzoinum (*An Xi Xiang*), Cinnabar (*Zhu Sha*), Succinum (*Hu Po*), Realgar (*Xiong Huang*).

**ACUPUNCTURE:** *Ren Zhong* (GV 26), *Shen Men* (Ht 7), *Nei Guan* (Per 6), *Zhong Wan* (CV 12), *Zu San Li* (St 36), *Xing Jian* (Liv 2), *Feng Long* (St 40). Use even supplementing-even draining technique.

## C. PHLEGM DAMPNESS OBSTRUCTING INTERNALLY PATTERN[4]

**MAIN SYMPTOMS:** Difficulty thinking, inattentiveness, a

dull, flat affect, slow movements, fatigue, lack of strength, cowering, solitariness, possible visual and auditory hallucinations, torpid food intake, heart vexation, insomnia, a fat swollen tongue with teeth-marks on its edges and slimy, white tongue fur, and a slippery or deep, relaxed (*i.e.*, slightly slow) pulse

**ANALYSIS OF SYMPTOMS:** This pattern is mostly due to excessive worrying, thinking, and anxiety or over-taxation and fatigue damaging the spleen which then loses control over its fortification and transportation. This results in water dampness collecting internally. This gathers and accumulates and produces disease. It is also possible for contraction of yin cold water dampness to cause detriment to the central palace. The yang qi becomes debilitated and this results in the qi's not transforming fluids. Phlegm and dampness then obstruct the center and produce disease. In either case, phlegm and dampness encumber the spleen and the spleen and stomach's upbearing and downbearing lose their normalcy. This then leads to torpid intake and, if severe, abdominal distention and loose stools. Damp turbidity obstructing the center results in the clear yang being unable to fill above. Instead, turbid evils counterflow upward confounding and blocking the heart orifices. Hence there is difficulty thinking, inattentiveness, a dull, flat affect, cowering, and solitariness. Because the spleen is damaged, the qi and blood are depleted and vacuous and fail to nourish the heart spirit. Neither do they fill and nourish the whole body. This leads to heart vexation, insomnia, slow movement, fatigue, and lack of strength. The fat tongue body, white, slimy fur, and slippery or deep, relaxed pulse are all symptoms of phlegm dampness internally obstructing.

**TREATMENT PRINCIPLES:** Warm yang and fortify the spleen, transform phlegm and open the orifices

**FORMULA & MEDICINALS:** *Xiang Sha Liu Jun Zi Tang He Li Zhong Tang Jia Wei* (Auklandia & Amomum Six Gentlemen Decoction plus Rectify the Center Decoction with Added Flavors)

Radix Codonopsitis Pilosulae (*Dang Shen*), 12g, Rhizoma Atractylodis Macrocephalae (*Bai Zhu*), 10g, Sclerotium Poriae Cocos (*Fu Ling*), 20g, mix-fried Radix Glycyrrhizae (*Gan Cao*), 10g, Radix Auklandiae Lappae (*Mu Xiang*), 6g, Fructus Amomi (*Sha Ren*), 6g (added later), uncooked Rhizoma Zingiberis (*Sheng Jiang*), 10g, dry Rhizoma Zingiberis (*Gan Jiang*), 10g, Pericarpium Citri Reticulatae (*Chen Pi*), 10g, Rhizoma Pinelliae Ternatae (*Ban Xia*), 10g, Rhizoma Atractylodis (*Cang Zhu*), 10g, Radix Polygalae Tenuifoliae (*Yuan Zhi*), 6g, Rhizoma Acori

Graminei (*Shi Chang Pu*), 10g, Herba Agastachis Seu Pogostemi (*Huo Xiang*), 10g, Herba Eupatorii Fortunei (*Pei Lan*), 10g

Decoct in water and administer orally in two divided doses, morning and evening, one ji per day.

**FORMULA ANALYSIS:** Within this formula, Codonopsis and Licorice fortify the spleen and supplement the spleen. Atractylodes Macrocephala fortifies the spleen and dries dampness, while Atractylodes dries dampness and fortifies the spleen. These are assisted by Poria which fortifies the spleen and percolates dampness, but also supplements the heart and quiets the spirit. Pinellia, Orange Peel, and uncooked Ginger all harmonize the center and transform phlegm. Acorus and Polygala also transform phlegm. However, Acorus also opens the orifices, while Polygala also resolves depression and quiets the spirit. Auklandia and Amomum rectify the qi. Dry Ginger warms the center and thus assists in the supplementation of the spleen. And Agastaches and Eupatorium both aromatically penetrate and transform dampness, thus also aiding the supplementation of the spleen.

**ADDITIONS & SUBTRACTIONS:** If there is even more pronounced spleen vacuity with fatigue and lack of strength, one can add Radix Astragali Membranacei (*Huang Qi*) and Rhizoma Cimicifugae (*Sheng Ma*). If spleen vacuity has reached the kidneys and there is low back pain and excessively frequent, possibly turbid urination and/or excessive, white vaginal discharge, one can add Radix Dioscoreae Oppositae (*Shan Yao*) and Semen Dolichoris Lablab (*Bia Bian Dou*).

**ACUPUNCTURE:** *Dan Zhong* (CV 17), *Zhong Wan* (CV 12), *Nei Guan* (Per 6), *Shen Men* (Ht 7), *Zu San Li* (St 36), *Feng Long* (St 40), *Pi Shu* (Bl 20), *Wei Shu* (Bl 21). Use even supplementing-even draining technique.

### D. PHLEGM FIRE HARASSING ABOVE PATTERN

**MAIN SYMPTOMS:** Emotional tension and agitation, breaking things and injuring other people, foul speech, an angry look in the eyes, a red facial complexion, red eyes, bound, constipated stools, a red tongue with slimy, yellow fur, and a bowstring, large, slippery, rapid pulse

**ANALYSIS OF SYMPTOMS:** Sudden, violent anger damages the liver. Liver fire suddenly and sharply arises, and phlegm and fire congest and become exuberant. These then ascend and harass the spirit brilliance, thus causing emotional tension and agitation, breaking things, injuring people, speaking foul language, and both eyes looking angry. Liver fire suddenly and violently becoming exuberant ascends to harass the clear orifices. Therefore, the face and eyes are red. The bound, constipated stools, the red tongue with yellow, slimy fur, and the bowstring, large, slippery, rapid pulse are all categorized as phlegm fire congestion and exuberance, yang qi solitary[5] and exuberant signs.

**TREATMENT PRINCIPLES:** Settle the heart and flush phlegm, clear the liver and drain fire

**FORMULA & MEDICINALS:** *Sheng Tie Luo Yin Jia Jian* (Uncooked Iron Filings Drink with Additions & Subtractions)

Uncooked Frusta Ferri (*Tie Luo*), 30-60g, bile-processed Rhizoma Arisaematis (*Dan Nan Xing*), 10g, Bulbus Frtillariae (*Bei Mu*), 12g, Pericarpium Citri Erythrocarpae (*Ju Hong*), 12g, Rhizoma Acori Graminei (*Shi Chang Pu*), 12g, Radix Polygalae Tenuifoliae (*Yuan Zhi*), 12g, Sclerotium Pararadicis Poriae Cocos (*Fu Shen*), 12g, Radix Scrophulariae Ningpoensis (*Xuan Shen*), 12g, Tuber Asparagi Cochinensis (*Tian Dong*), 12g, Tuber Ophiopogonis Japonici (*Mai Dong*), 12g, Fructus Forsythiae Suspensae (*Lian Qiao*), 12g, Cinnabar (*Zhu Sha*), 1g (taken in two divided doses washed down with the decoction)

First decoct the Frusta Ferri, remove the dregs, retain the juice, and cook all the other medicinals in that juice. Then divide into two doses and administer orally morning and evening , one *ji* per day.

**FORMULA ANALYSIS:** Within this formula, Frusta Ferri and Cinnabar heavily settle and quiet the spirit, settle the heart and stop mania. Bile-processed Arisaema, Red Citrus, Poria, and Fritillaria clear and flush phlegm turbidity. Acorus and Polygala transform phlegm turbidity and open the heart orifices. Asparagus and Ophiopogon, Scrophularia, and Forsythia nourish yin and clear heat. When all these medicinals are used together, they clear the liver and drain fire, flush phlegm and diffuse the orifices, settle, still, and quiet the spirit. This formula is appropriate for patients who are markedly excited and agitated.

**ADDITIONS & SUBTRACTIONS:** If phlegm and fire are congesting and exuberant and yellow, slimy tongue fur is severe, one can add *Meng Shi Shi Tan Wan* (Mica Roll Phlegm Pills)[6] to drain fire and dispel phlegm. One can also use *An Gong Niu Huang Wan* (Quiet the Palace

Bezoar Pills, a ready-made medicine) to clear the heart and open the orifices. If there is mainly liver-gallbladder fire exuberance with manic speech, constipation, red urine, and a bowstring, replete pulse, one can use *Dang Gui Long Hui Wan* (Dang Gui, Gentiana & Aloe Pills) to drain the liver and clear fire. If there is mainly yang ming heat exuberance with constipation, coarse, yellow tongue fur, and a replete, large pulse, one can use *Da Cheng Qi Tang* (Major Order the Qi Decoction) plus Fructus Gleditschiae Chinensis (*Zao Jiao*) and pig bile to wash away and flush filth and turbidity. If the spirit mind is clear but there are vexation and insomnia due to phlegm fire harassing internally, one can use *Wen Dan Tang* (Warm the Gallbladder Decoction) plus *Zhu Sha An Shen Wan* (Cinnabar Quiet the Spirit Pills, a ready-made medicine) to transform phlegm and quiet the spirit.

*Meng Shi Shi Tan Wan:* Rhizoma Gastrodiae Elatae (*Tian Ma*), Secretio Bambusae Siliceae (*Tian Zhu Huang*), Realgar (*Xiong Huang*), Mica Schist (*Meng Shi*), bile-processed Rhizoma Arisaematis (*Dan Nan Xing*), Pulvis Semenis Crotonis Tiglii (*Ba Dou Shuang*), Radix Aconiti Coreani Seu Typhonii Gigantei (*Bai Fu Zi*), uncooked Radix Glycyrrhizae (*Gan Cao*), Buthus Martensis (*Quan Xie*), Radix Ledebouriellae Divaricatae (*Fang Feng*), Secretio Moschi Moschiferi (*She Xiang*)

*An Gong Niu Huang Wan:* Calculus Bovis (*Niu Huang*), Cornu Rhinocerotis (*Xi Jiao*), Secretio Moschi Moschiferi (*She Xiang*), Rhizoma Coptidis Chinensis (*Huang Lian*), Radix Scutellariae Baicalensis (*Huang Qin*), Fructus Gardeniae Jasminoidis (*Zhi Zi*), Realgar (*Xiong Huang*), Borneolum (*Bing Pian*), Tuber Curcumae (*Yu Jin*), Cinnabar (*Zhu Sha*), Maragarita (*Zhen Zhu*)

*Dang Gui Long Hui Wan:* Radix Angelicae Sinensis (*Dang Gui*), Radix Gentianae Scabrae (*Long Dan Cao*), Fructus Gardeniae Jasminoidis (*Zhi Zi*), Rhizoma Coptidis Chinensis (*Huang Lian*), Cortex Phellodendri (*Huang Bai*), Radix Scutellariae Baicalensis (*Huang Qin*), Herba Aloes (*Lu Hui*), Radix Et Rhizoma Rhei (*Da Huang*), Radix Auklandiae Lappae (*Mu Xiang*), Secretio Moschi Moschiferi (*She Xiang*)

*Da Cheng Qi Tang:* Radix Et Rhizoma Rhei (*Da Huang*), Mirabilitum (*Mang Xiao*), Fructus Immaturus Citri Aurantii (*Zhi Shi*), Cortex Magnoliae Officinalis (*Hou Po*)

*Zhu Sha An Shen Wan:* Cinnabar (*Zhu Sha*), Rhizoma Coptidis Chinensis (*Huang Lian*), Radix Angelicae Sinensis (*Dang Gui*), uncooked Radix Rehmanniae (*Sheng Di*), mix-fried Radix Glycyrrhizae (*Gan Cao*)

ACUPUNCTURE: *Da Zhui* (GV 14), *Ren Zhong* (GV 26), *Nei Guan* (Per 6), *Lao Gong* (Per 8), *Feng Long* (St 40), *Tai Chong* (Liv 3). Use draining technique.

## E. HEART-SPLEEN DUAL VACUITY PATTERN

MAIN SYMPTOMS: Excessive thinking, worry, and anxiety, dreaming of ghosts, confusion, heart palpitations, easily frightened, a predilection to sorrow and a desire to cry, poor memory, difficulty thinking, sluggishness, illogical speech, a somber white facial complexion, reduced intake of food, fatigue, a pale tongue, and a fine, forceless pulse

ANALYSIS OF SYMPTOMS: Due to habitual bodily or natural endowment insufficiency or possible withdrawal disease enduring for a long time, the heart and spleen are both vacuous, heart blood is depleted internally, and the heart spirit lacks nourishment. Therefore, there is excessive thinking, worry, and anxiety, dreaming of ghosts, confusion, heart palpitations, easy fright, a predilection for sorrow and a desire to cry, poor memory, difficulty thinking, and sluggishness. Due to scanty blood and qi debility and the spleen's loss of fortification and transportation, there is reduced intake and fatigue. These and a pale tongue and a fine, forceless pulse are all symptoms of heart-spleen dual vacuity and qi and blood dual debility.

TREATMENT PRINCIPLES: Fortify the spleen and nourish the heart, boost the qi and quiet the spirit

FORMULA & MEDICINALS: *Gui Pi Tang* (Restore the Spleen Decoction)

Mix-fried Radix Astragali Membranacei (*Huang Qi*), 30g, Radix Codonopsitis Pilosulae (*Dang Shen*), 12g, Radix Angelicae Sinensis (*Dang Gui*), 12g, Rhizoma Atractylodis Macrocephalae (*Bai Zhu*), 12g, Sclerotium Pararadicis Poriae Cocos (*Fu Shen*), 30g, Arillus Euphoriae Longanae (*Long Yan Rou*), 30g, Semen Zizyphi Spinosae (*Suan Zao Ren*), 30g, Radix Auklandiae Lappae (*Mu Xiang*), 10g, Radix Polygalae Tenuifoliae (*Yuan Zhi*), 6g, mix-fried Radix Glycyrrhizae (*Gan Cao*), 6g, Fructus Zizyphi Jujubae (*Da Zao*), 6 pieces, uncooked Rhizoma Zingiberis (*Sheng Jiang*), 6g

Decoct in water and administer orally in two divided doses, morning and evening, one *ji* per day.

ANALYSIS OF FORMULA: Within this formula, Codonopsis and Astragalus sweetly and warmly boost the qi and greatly supplement the spleen qi. Atractylodes, bitter and warm, fortifies the spleen and dries dampness. Spirit of

Poria fortifies the spleen and quiets the spirit. Mix-fried Licorice sweetly and warmly regulates the center, boosts the qi, and fortifies the spleen. Longans sweetly and warmly boost the heart spirit and supplement the blood in order to quiet the spirit, boost the intelligence and calm the heart. Dang Gui combined with Astragalus boosts the qi and engenders the blood. Auklandia, acrid and warm, moves the qi and scatters stagnation in order to resolve stagnant qi as well as rectify the qi and arouse the spleen. Polygala quiets the spirit, boosts the intelligence, and resolves depression. Ziyphus Spinosa calms the heart and quiets the spirit. Ginger and Red Dates harmonize the stomach and fortify the spleen, regulate and harmonize the constructive and defensive in order to promote engenderment and transformation. When all these medicinals are used together, they fortify the spleen and boost the qi, supplement the blood and nourish the heart, and thus the heart spirit is automatically quieted.

ADDITIONS & SUBTRACTIONS: If there is excessive thinking, worry, and anxiety, a predilection to sorrow and a desire to cry, fright, fear, and restlessness, and a disquieted heart spirit, one can use *Yang Xin Tang* (Nourish the Heart Decoction) to fortify the spleen and boost the qi, nourish the heart and quiet the spirit.

ACUPUNCTURE: *Xin Shu* (Bl 15), *Pi Shu* (Bl 20), *Nei Guan* (Per 6), *Shen Men* (Ht 7), *Zu San Li* (St 36). Use supplementing technique.

## F. YANG VACUITY DEPLETION & DETRIMENT PATTERN

MAIN SYMPTOMS: Advanced age, bodily weakness, or enduring disease which does not heal thus resulting in spleen disease reaching and damaging the kidneys with difficulty thinking, sluggishness, inattention, cowering, scanty speech, no thought for food or drink, bodily vacuity and lack of strength, a lusterless facial complexion, fear of cold, chilled extremities, a pale tongue with thin, white, fur, and a deep, fine, weak pulse

ANALYSIS OF SYMPTOMS: This pattern is mostly due to violent disease and/or enduring disease, overeating uncooked, chilled foods, and over-use of cool and cold medicinals, any of which may damage spleen yang. If this endures, it will evolve into spleen-kidney yang qi vacuity weakness. When spleen yang is devitalized, there is no thought of eating or drinking, torpid intake, and loose stools. If severe, there are undigested grains in the stools. Because the spleen is the source of qi and blood engenderment and transformation, there is inability to nourish the face and the limbs. Hence, the lusterless facial complexion and chilled extremities. Yin rules stillness and yang governs stirring. If yang is insufficient to push stirring, thinking is difficult and sluggish, there is inattentiveness and cowering, and speech is diminished. If spleen yang does not transform water dampness and these congeal into phlegm, the clear orifices will be confounded and blocked, thus producing various psychological symptoms. If yang qi is unable to warm and cook, there will be fear of cold and chilled limbs. The pale tongue with thin, white fur and the deep, fine, weak pulse are all symptoms of yang vacuity with qi and blood insufficiency.

**TREATMENT PRINCIPLES:** Warm and supplement the spleen and kidneys assisted by transforming phlegm and opening the orifices

**FORMULA & MEDICINALS:** *Wen Yang Xi Fen Tang Jia Jian* (Warm Yang & Excite Decoction with Additions & Subtractions)

Radix Codonopsitis Pilosulae (*Dang Shen*), 20g, cooked Radix Rehmanniae (*Shu Di*), 15g, Radix Lateralis Praeparatus Aconiti Carmichaeli (*Fu Zi*), 10g, Cortex Cinnamomi Cassiae (*Rou Gui*), 10g, Herba Cistanchis Deserticolae (*Rou Cong Rong*), 15g, Herba Epimedii (*Yin Yang Huo*), 15g, dry Rhizoma Zingiberis (*Gan Jiang*), 6g, Plastrum Testudinis (*Gui Ban*), 15g, Pericarpium Citri Reticulatae (*Chen Pi*), 10g, Rhizoma Pinelliae Ternatae (*Ban Xia*), 10g, mix-fried Radix Glycyrrhizae (*Gan Cao*), 6g, Sclerotium Poriae Cocos (*Fu Ling*), 15g

Decoct in water and administer orally in two divided doses, morning and evening, one *ji* per day.

**FORMULA ANALYSIS:** Within this formula, Codonopsis, mix-fried Licorice, and Poria fortify the spleen and supplement the qi. Poria also percolates dampness and quiets the spirit. Dry Ginger warms the spleen and thus aids its supplementation. Cistanches invigorates yang and supplements the kidneys as does Epimedium. Cinnamon and Aconite warm the yang of both the spleen and the kidneys. Pinellia and Orange Peel transform phlegm, while cooked Rehmannia and Tortoise Plastrum enrich yin. Since yin and yang are mutually rooted, when supplementing yang, it is also important to supplement yin.

**ADDITIONS & SUBTRACTIONS:** For more severe phlegm blocking the orifices of the heart, one may add Rhizoma Acori Graminei (*Shi Chang Pu*) and Radix Polygalae Tenuifoliae (*Yuan Zhi*). If there are concomitant symptoms of blood stasis, one can add Cortex Radicis Moutan

(*Dan Pi*) and Tuber Curcumae (*Yu Jin*). If there is more pronounced qi vacuity with fatigue and lack of strength, one can add Radix Astragali Membranacei (*Huang Qi*) and Radix Dioscoreae Oppositae (*Shan Yao*).

**ACUPUNCTURE:** Moxa *Shen Shu* (Bl 23), *Ming Men* (GV 4), *Pi Shu* (Bl 20), *Wei Shu* (Bl 21), *Guan Yuan* (CV 4), and *Bai Hui* (GV 20).

## G. YIN VACUITY-FIRE EFFULGENCE PATTERN

**MAIN SYMPTOMS:** Manic disease enduring for a long time and gradually worsening, fatigue, excessive speech, susceptibility to fright, emotional anxiety and tension, occasional vexation, emaciated form, a red facial complexion, vexatious heat in the five hearts or centers, a dry mouth but no desire to drink, a red tongue with scanty or possibly no fur, and a fine, rapid pulse[7]

**ANALYSIS OF SYMPTOMS:** Enduring, protracted mania consumes the qi and damages yin. Thus the qi becomes insufficient and this leads to manic heat which gradually worsens as well as lassitude and listlessness of the essence spirit. If yin is insufficient, this leads to inability to control heart fire. Thus vacuity fire harasses above and the heart spirit loses its nourishment. This results in excessive speaking, susceptibility to fright, emotional anxiety and tension, occasional vexation, and other such symptoms. An emaciated form, red face, vexatious heat in the five hearts, a dry mouth but no desire to drink, a red tongue with scanty fur, and a fine, rapid pulse are all symptoms of yin vacuity fire effulgence.

**TREATMENT PRINCIPLES:** Enrich yin and downbear fire, quiet the spirit and stabilize the mind

**FORMULA & MEDICINALS:** *Er Yin Jian* (Two Yin Decoction)

Uncooked Radix Rehmanniae (*Sheng Di*), 30g, Tuber Ophiopogonis Japonici (*Mai Dong*), 12g, Radix Scrophulariae Ningpoensis (*Xuan Shen*), 12g, Sclerotium Poriae Cocos (*Fu Ling*), 12g, Semen Zizyphi Spinosae (*Suan Zao Ren*), 20g, Rhizoma Coptidis Chinensis (*Huang Lian*), 10g, Caulis Akebiae (*Mu Tong*), 8g, Folium Bambusae (*Zhu Ye*), 12g, Medulla Junci Effusi (*Deng Xin Cao*), 3g, Radix Glycyrrhizae (*Gan Cao*)

Decoct in water and administer orally in two divided doses, morning and evening, one *ji* per day.

**ANALYSIS OF FORMULA:** Within this formula, uncooked

Rehmannia and Ophiopogon are the ruling medicinals which enrich kidney yin and downbear heart fire. Scrophularia also enriches yin, while Coptis clears heart fire. Zizyphus Spinosa enriches yin, nourishes the heart, and quiets the spirit. These are the adjunctive medicinals. Poria blandly percolates, Akebia clears and disinhibits, and Bamboo Leaves clear the heart. Thus these medicinals help eliminate evil heat in the heart channel via urination. Juncus enters the heart, and Licorice regulates all the other medicinals and harmonizes the center. These are the messengers and assistants. When used together, they eliminate heat evils from the heart channel, supplement kidney yin, join the heart and kidneys, and promote the interaction between water and fire. Hence all the symptoms are automatically eliminated.

**ADDITIONS & SUBTRACTIONS:** If the stools are dry, add Semen Cannabis Sativae (*Huo Ma Ren*), Semen Pruni (*Yu Li Ren*), and Semen Pruni Persicae (*Tao Ren*) to moisten the intestines and free the flow of the stools. If there is a dry mouth, torpid intake, and no thought for food or drink, add scorched *San Xian* (Three Immortals, *i.e.,* Massa Medica Fermentata, *Shen Qu,* Fructus Crataegi, *Shan Zha,* and Fructus Germinatus Hordei Vulgaris, *Mai Ya*) in order to disperse food and abduct stagnation. If there is devitalized essence spirit with sluggish and scanty stirring, it is appropriate to add Radix Pseudostellariae (*Tai Zi Shen*), mix-fried Radix Astragali Membranacei (*Huang Qi*), and Rhizoma Cimicifugae (*Sheng Ma*) to boost the qi and lift the spirit.

**ACUPUNCTURE:** *Shen Men* (Ht 7), *Da Ling* (Per 7), *Tai Chong* (Liv 3) needled through to *Yong Quan* (Ki 1), *San Yin Jiao* (Sp 6). Use even supplementing-even draining technique.

## H. BLOOD STASIS OBSTRUCTING INTERNALLY PATTERN

**MAIN SYMPTOMS:** Emotional lability, sometimes agitated, sometimes still, speaking to oneself, torpid spirit, paranoia, delusional thinking, auditory and visual hallucinations, a dark, stagnant facial complexion, piercing, lancinating headache, a dark red tongue with static macules or spots, possible engorged, tortuous sublingual veins, and a bowstring, choppy pulse

**ANALYSIS OF SYMPTOMS:** Withdrawal disease enduring for a long time which continues insidiously without ceasing may result in qi stagnation and blood stasis. Static blood then obstructs internally and the heart spirit is not calm. Therefore, there is emotional lability, sometimes agita-

tion, sometimes stillness, paranoia, delusional thinking, and visual and auditory hallucinations. The dark, stagnant facial complexion, piercing headache, dark red tongue with static macules or spots, and the bowstring, choppy pulse are all symptoms of blood stasis obstructing internally.

**TREATMENT PRINCIPLES:** Rectify the qi and resolve depression, quicken the blood and transform stasis

**FORMULA & MEDICINALS:** *Xue Fu Zhu Yu Tang Jia Wei* (Blood Mansion Dispel Stasis Decoction with Added Flavors)

Semen Pruni Persicae (*Tao Ren*), 12g, Flos Carthami Tinctorii (*Hong Hua*), 10g, Radix Angelicae Sinensis (*Dang Gui*), 10g, uncooked Radix Rehmanniae (*Sheng Di*), 10g, Radix Ligustici Wallichii (*Chuan Xiong*), 6g, Radix Rubrus Paeoniae Lactiflorae (*Chi Shao*), 6g, Radix Platycodi Grandiflori (*Jie Geng*), 5g, Radix Cyathulae (*Chuan Niu Xi*), 10g, Radix Bupleuri (*Chai Hu*), 3g, Fructus Citri Aurantii (*Zhi Ke*), 6g, Radix Glycyrrhizae (*Gan Cao*), 6g, Hirudo Seu Whitmania (*Shui Zhi*), 6g

Decoct in water and administer orally in two divided doses, morning and evening, one *ji* per day.

**ANALYSIS OF FORMULA:** Within this formula, Dang Gui, Persica, and Carthamus are the main medicinals which quicken the blood and dispel stasis. Ligusticum and Red Peony are the main adjunctive medicinals which assist in quickening the blood and dispelling stasis. Hirudo also assists in quickening the blood by breaking the blood and freeing the flow of the network vessels. Uncooked Rehmannia combined with Dang Gui nourishes and quickens the blood. It promotes the dispelling of stasis without damaging yin blood. Cyathula dispels stasis and frees the flow of the blood vessels. Bupleurum, Platycodon, and Aurantium course the liver, rectify the qi, and broaden the chest in order to resolve and eliminate qi stagnation. When the qi moves, the blood will move. These are the assistant and messenger medicinals. When all these medicinals are used together, they quicken the blood and dispel stasis, move the qi and move the blood. Hence all the symptoms are automatically cured.

**ADDITIONS & SUBTRACTIONS:** If there is the simultaneous appearance of a bitter taste in the mouth and dry throat, short, reddish urination, and a feeling internally of brewing heat, one should add Caulis Akebiae (*Mu Tong*) and Radix Scutellariae Baicalensis (*Huang Qin*) to clear heat and drain fire. If there is also constipation, one can use *Dian Kuang Meng Xing Tang Jia Jian* (Withdrawal & Mania Dream-arousing Decoction with Additions & Subtractions) instead. If there is excitation and restlessness with agitated stirring and lack of calm, one can add Cortex Radicis Moutan (*Dan Pi*) and uncooked Radix Rehmanniae (*Sheng Di*) to clear fire hidden within the blood. If sleep at night is restless and there is depression, oppression, and discomfort, one can add Cortex Albizziae Julibrissinis ((*He Huan Pi*) and Caulis Polygoni Multiflori (*Ye Jiao Teng*) to resolve depression and quiet the spirit. If there is scanty speech and scanty movement, a lusterless facial complexion, and fatigue and exhaustion, one can add Radix Astragali Membranacei (*Huang Qi*) and Radix Angelicae Sinensis (*Dang Gui*) to boost the qi and supplement the blood.

*Dian Kuang Meng Xing Tang Jia Jian:* Pericarpium Citri Reticulatae (*Chen Pi*), 10g, Pericarpium Citri Reticulatae Viride (*Qing Pi*), 10g, Semen Pruni Persicae (*Tao Ren*), 10g, Flos Carthami Tinctorii (*Hong Hua*), 10g, Hirudo Seu Whitmania (*Shu Zhi*), 10g, Radix Salviae Miltiorrhizae (*Dan Shen*), 20g, Radix Bupleuri (*Chai Hu*), 10g, Fructus Perillae Frutescentis (*Zi Su Zi*), 15g, Caulis Akebiae (*Mu Tong*), 6g, Radix Rubrus Paeoniae Lactiflorae (*Chi Shao*), 10g, Radix Glycyrrhizae (*Gan Cao*), 10g, Cortex Radicis Mori Albi (*Sang Bai Pi*), 10g, Rhizoma Pinelliae Ternatae (*Ban Xia*), 10g, Radix Et Rhizoma Rhei (*Da Huang*), 18g, Radix Gentianae Scabrae (*Long Dan Cao*), 12g[8]

**ACUPUNCTURE:** *Shen Men* (Ht 7), *Nei Guan* (Per 6), *Xue Hai* (Sp 10), *He Gu* (LI 4), *Xin Shu* (Bl 15), *Ge Shu* (Bl 17), *Gan Shu* (Bl 18). Use draining technique.

**CLINICAL TIPS:** Phlegm fire (meaning liver depression with depressive heat harassing the spirit and phlegm misting the heart orifices) is extremely common in schizophrenic patients. Pure vacuity patterns are not that commonly seen.

**ABSTRACTS OF REPRESENTATIVE CHINESE RESEARCH:**

*Shan Xi Zhong Yi (Shanxi Chinese Medicine),* #6, 1986, p. 26: Zhang Yong-xiang *et al.* reported on the treatment of 24 cases of schizophrenia. Eighteen of these cases were orally administered *Huang Niu Jiao Jian Ji* (Yellow Cow Horn Decocted Formula). This consisted of a decoction of 20-50g of Cornu Tauri (*Huang Niu Jiao*) per day. Administration of other anti-schizophrenic drugs was suspended four days before administering these Chinese medicinals. This was combined with Chinese medicinal

treatment based on each patient's pattern discrimination. These medicinals were administered for two months. The other six patients were administered 3g of *Huang Niu Jiao Fen* (Yellow Cow Horn Powder) orally, three times per day at the same time as a small dose of anti-schizophrenic medication. Among the 24 cases treated soley with Chinese medicinals, 17 cases or 70.8% were either cured or experienced a marked effect. Another six cases or 25% experienced improvement, while only one case experienced no effect. Thus the total amelioration rate in this group was 95.8%.

*Shan Xi Yi Xue Za Zhi (Shanxi Medical Journal),* #5, 1982, p. 14: Zhang Yi-yin used *Dan Wei Fu Ling Jian* (Single Flavor Poria Decoction) to treat 57 cases of schizophrenia. This consisted of 60g of Sclerotium Poriae Cocos (*Fu Ling*) decocted in water and administered per day. Three of these cases were judged cured, 11 were judged to have experienced a marked effect, 16 improved, and 27 experienced no effect. Thus the total amelioration rate with this protocol was only 57%.

❖

*Zhong Yi Za Zhi (Journal of Chinese Medicine),* #9, 1986, p. 31: Yang Chun-lin *et al.* used *Bei Huang Pian* (Perisca & Rhubarb Tablets) as the main treatment of 186 cases of schizophrenia. All these patients were discriminated as presenting a blood stasis pattern with no bodily vacuity. This medicine was manufactured as follows: Semen Pruni Persicae (*Tao Ren*), 20g, Radix Et Rhizoma Rhei (*Da Huang*), 40g, and Radix Rubrus Paeoniae Lactiflorae (*Chi Shao*), 40g, were made into 50 sugar-coated pills. At first, 10-15 of these pills were administered orally each day. If there was no diarrhea, this dose was increased to 20-30 pills two times per day. At the same time, a small amount of Western medicine was administered. Sixty-eight point seven percent were judged to have experienced a marked effect from this protocol. That meant that susceptibility to anger was not constant and visual and auditory hallucinations, and eccentric behavior were improved.

❖

*Jiang Xi Zhong Yi Yao (Jiangxi Chinese Medicine & Medicinals),* #6, 1984, p. 32: Yang Bei-quan *et al.* treated 30 cases of adolescent female withdrawal and mania with *Tao He Cheng Qi Tang Jia Jian* (Persica Order the Qi Decoction with Additions & Subtractions). This consisted of: Semen Pruni Persicae (*Tao Ren*), Flos Carthami Tinctorii (*Hong Hua*), Ramulus Cinnamomi Cassiae (*Gui Zhi*), Radix Et Rhizoma Rhei (*Da Huang*), Rhizoma Acori

Graminei (*Shi Chang Pu*), Radix Polygalae Tenuifoliae (*Yuan Zhi*), blackened Fructus Gardeniae Jasminoidis (*Zhi Zi*), Radix Salviae Miltiorrhizae (*Dan Shen*), Radix Rubrus Paeoniae Lactiflorae (*Chi Shao*), and Rhizoma Corydalis Yanhusuo (*Yan Hu Suo*). Thirty-five days equaled one course of treatment. During acute episodes, 10mg of haloperidol was administered via intramuscular injection. In terms of treatment outcomes, six cases were judged cured, 17 were deemed to have gotten a marked effect, four got some improvement, and three experienced no effect. Thus the total amelioration rate was 90%.

*Zhong Guo Zhong Xi Yi Jie He Za Zhi* (*Chinese Journal of Integrated Chinese-Western Medicine*), #7, 1993, p. 408-409: Zhu-ge D.Y. & Chen J.K. reported on the treatment of 60 patients with schizophrenia. These 60 patients were divided into two groups. One group was treated with chlorpromazine and electroacupuncture, while the other group was treated with chlorpromazine alone. Treatment outcomes were assessed by the Brief Psychiatric Rating Scale (BPRS). At this study's endpoint, the total amelioration rates between these two groups were similar. However, marked effects appeared earlier in the course of treatment with the combined therapy, less chlorpromazine was needed in patients in the combined therapy group, and patients in this group displayed fewer side effects.

*Zhong Yi Za Zhi* (*Journal of Chinese Medicine*), #1, 1996, p. 34-35: Feng Xiu-jie and Ma Liang reported on the treatment of 122 cases of schizophrenia using Chinese medicinals. Fifty of these patients were female and 72 were male. They ranged in age from the teens to more than 50 years old, with 72.13% being 21-40 years of age. These patients were divided into eight patterns: 1) phlegm fire internally binding and ascending to harass the brain spirit (24 cases), 2) liver fire internally blazing and scorching the brain spirit (16 cases), 3) liver depression and phlegm binding and ascending to the brain spirit (17 cases), 4) liver depression and spleen vacuity with malnourishment of the brain above (13 cases), 5) liver-kidney dual vacuity failing to boost the brain above (17 cases), 6) spleen-kidney dual vacuity failing to boost the brain above (23 cases), 7) heart-spleen dual vacuity with malnourishment of the brain above (6 cases), 8) qi vacuity and blood stasis with loss of regulation of the brain spirit (6 cases). Each of these eight groups of patients received one *ji* of Chinese medicinals per day appropriate to their pattern discrimination, with 30-60 *ji* equaling one course of treatment.

Using this protocol, 66 patients were considered cured, 55 were improved, and only one case got no result. Thus the total amelioration rate was 99.18%.

*Zhe Jiang Zhong Yi Za Zhi* (*Zhejiang Journal of Chinese Medicine*), #6, 1999, p. 264: Ren Wan-wen reported on the comparative treatment of 80 cases of schizophrenia with Western antipsychotic medicinals alone and antipsychotic medicinals plus pressure at ear points. All the patients in this study had been diagnosed with schizophrenia. The treatment group (receiving the combined therapy) consisted of 50 patients between the ages of 18-51 years old. The comparison group which received drug therapy only and consisted of 30 patients was statistically similar in terms of sex, age, and disease duration. The ear points consisted of Heart, Brain, Kidney, Spirit Gate, and Frontal Lobe. Each time, Vaccaria seeds were tapped over 2-3 of these points which the patient was supposed to press 1-2 minutes each time several times per day. After 3-5 days, depending on whether the disease nature had increased or decreased and the patient's history, the points were changed. Along with this, both groups received either chlorpromazine ≤ 350mg per day or similar medications. Treatment lasted 2-3 months. Of the 50 patients who received combined treatment, 20 were cured, 21 were markedly improved, seven improved, and only two got no effect. In the comparison group, eight cases were cured, eight got a marked effect, six improved, and eight got no result. Thus there was a marked difference in total amelioration rates between these two groups (P< 0.01).

*Psychiatry & Clinical Neuroscience*, #12, 1998, p. 329_330: Wang B. divided 80 schizophrenic patients into two groups of 40. One group was treated with traditional Chinese medicine to quicken the blood and dispel stasis and the other group was treated with antipsychotic drugs. Both groups were observed by the rating methods of BPRS, TESS, and CGI scale as well as undergoing hemorheology tests. The results showed that such Chinese medicinals for quickening the blood and dispelling stasis has fewer side effects on schizophrenic patients than did the antipsychotic drugs. In addition, there was objective evidence of changes in these patients' hemorheology. Therefore, the author concluded that Chinese medicine is superior in effect to Western antipsychotic drugs in terms of combating anxiety and depression as well as for psychomotor inhibition. However, it is less effective for controlling psychomotor excitation as compared to antipsychotic drugs.

*The Journal of Chinese Medicine*, UK, #48, 1995, p. 25-26: Heiner Fruehauf reported on Qiao Yu-chuan's treatment of 415 patients with schizophrenia. Each patient was administered a water-based decoction made from: Gypsum Fibrosum (*Shi Gao*), 155g, Radix Et Rhizoma Rhei (*Da Huang*), 62g, uncooked Frusta Ferri (*Sheng Tie Luo*), 31g, Lapis Micae Seu Chloriti (*Meng Shi*), 31g, Caulis Polygoni Multiflori (*Ye Jiao Teng*), 31g, Radix Scutellariae Baicalensis (*Huang Qin*), 24g, and Cortex Phellodendri (*Huang Bai*), 24g. These medicinals were boiled three times to yeild a total of 2,000ml of medicinal liquid. This was divided into six portions and one portion was administered every two hours. One course of treatment equaled two weeks. Accompanying diarrhea was expected and left untreated. After two weeks of this treatment, *Gui Pi Tang* (Restore the Spleen Decoction) or other such harmonizing formula was advised. Using this protocol, 330 patients were reported cured, 42 improved, and three got no result. Forty-one patients discontinued treatment before completion of the trial. Thus the total amelioration rate was 98.6%.

In a consecutive study conducted by the same research team and also reported on by Fruehauf (p. 26), three variations of this formula were used: Schizophrenia Formula #1 for liver depression and fire flaming, Schizophrenia Formula #2 for blood vacuity and phlegm fire, and Schizophrenia Formula #3 for yang ming channel replete heat. Depending on their pattern discrimination, 500 schizophrenic patients were given one of these three formulas. Among these 500 patients, 229 were males and 271 were females. Their course of disease had lasted from several months to 30 years, and the patients were of all ages. Four hundred one of these patients were judged cured, 93 improved, and six got no result.

According to the authors of *Zhong Yi Fang Ji De Yao Li He Yong* (*The Use & Pharmacology of Chinese Medicine Formulas & Prescriptions*) edited by Deng Wen-long, Chongqing, 1990, p. 422, since 1959, there have been at least eight reports in major Chinese medical journals concerning the use of *Gan Mai Da Zao Tang* (Licorice, Wheat & Red Dates Decoction) for the treatment of schizophrenia.

For instance, Heiner Fruehauf, in *The Journal of Chinese*

*Medicine*, UK, #48, 1995, p. 25 reports on the use of *Gan Mai Da Zao Tang* plus Concha Ostreae (*Mu Li*) and Os Draconis (*Long Gu*) for the treatment of 79 cases of schizophrenia who had not responded to any other medications. The patients in this study took this formula from 7-70 days plus a small amount of chlorpromazine (maximum dose was 200mg per day). Of these 79 cases, five were judged cured, 23 markedly improved, and 17 got no result. This study first appeared in Chinese in *Zhe Jiang Zhong Yi Za Zhi* (*Zhejiang Journal of Chinese Medicine*), #6, 1982.

In the same journal (p. 25), Fruehauf also reports on the treatment of 146 schizophrenic patients by Cheng Men-xue using *Gan Mai Da Zao Tang* (Licorice, Wheat & Red Dates Decoction) plus *Bai He Gu Jin Tang* (Lily Secure Metal Decoction). All 146 of these patients also were not responding to Western medications. One hundred seventeen of these patients took 200mg of chlorpromazine per day along with these Chinese medicinals. Treatment lasted from 7-98 days, with an average duration of 16.8 days. After which time, 11 were judged cured, 44 markedly improved, and 64 improved. Thus the total amelioration rate was 81.4%.

### REPRESENTATIVE CASE HISTORIES:

### ❖ CASE 1[9] ❖

The patient was a 20 year old female who had given birth only 20 days before. Due to bickering over trivial affairs with her neighbor, the woman had become annoyed and psychologically disturbed. She swore at people, she threw things and broke them, and sometimes she glared and clenched her fists. Her demeanor was intimidating even when she was not doing anything. She yelled and cried incessantly. She was vexed and agitated and did not sleep. It had already been seven nights since she had slept. Her affect was excited. Hence her Western medical diagnosis was schizophrenia and she had been given various sedatives to no avail. When examined by the Chinese medical practitioner, both the patient's eyes stared straight ahead as if oblivious to human beings. She had not had a bowel movement for a number of days, and there was lower abdominal pain on pressure. At the time of the onset of this disease, her lochia had already ceased. Her pulse was bowstring, slippery, and forceful. Her lips were crimson red, and her tongue fur was yellow and slimy. Therefore, her pattern was discriminated as qi and fire joining and depressed with heat and blood binding and inhibiting the bowel qi. Therefore stasis heat was fuming above.

The treatment principles in this case were to free the flow

of the bowels and drain heat, move stasis and scatter nodulation. The formula chosen was *Kuang Xing Tang* (Mania Arousal Decoction): Radix Bupleuri (*Chai Hu*), 12g, Radix Et Rhizoma Rhei (*Da Huang*), 9g, Fructus Immaturus Citri Aurantii (*Zhi Shi*), 9g, Cortex Radicis Moutan (*Dan Pi*), 12g, Semen Pruni Persicae (*Tao Ren*), 12g, Radix Rubrus Paeoniae Lactiflorae (*Chi Shao*), 9g, Rhizoma Pinelliae Ternatae (*Ban Xia*), 9g, Caulis Bambusae In Taeniis (*Zhu Ru*), 9g, uncooked Rhizoma Zingiberis (*Sheng Jiang*), 12g, Fructus Gardeniae Jasminoidis (*Zhi Zi*), 9g, Tuber Curcumae (*Yu Jin*), 9g, Pericarpium Citri Reticulatae (*Chen Pi*), 9g. These medicinals were decocted in water and administered orally, one *ji* per day. After administering one *ji* of this formula, the patient had a large bowel movement and discharged a lot of fecal matter which included some mucousy matter. That night she was able to go to sleep. When she woke the next morning, her affect was bright and intelligent and her previous abstraction seemed like a dream. Her lochia was expelled and her disease was completely cured.

### ❖ CASE 2 ❖

The patient was a 38 year old female. Due to emotional stimulation, she had become agitated and restless. She could not sit or lie down calmly. She had chest oppression, emotional depression, and no desire to eat. Sometimes she was sorrowful and cried and was not able to control herself. Other times she would dash about and run out into the street. She spoke to herself, yelled loudly, howled, and shouted. Sometimes she felt cold and sometimes she felt warm. Her upper back and neck felt as if they were burning. In addition, the patient had head distention and pain, she expectorated thick, sticky phlegm, and she had a dry mouth and throat. She had already been hospitalized and treated based on a diagnosis of schizophrenia. However, that previous treatment had not been effective. When she was referred to the Chinese medical clinic, her pulse was deep, bowstring, and fine, while her tongue fur was thin and white. The patient's pattern was discriminated as liver depression qi stagnation, depression transforming fire, and fire burning and damaging fluids. Thus fluids and been made into phlegm, and phlegm and heat were harassing above. This resulted in the patient's spirit not being calm.

The treatment principles in this case were to clear heat and transform phlegm, calm the heart and quiet the spirit. Therefore, she was prescribed *Long Mu Bai Wei Ju Ye Tang* (Dragon Bone, Oyster Shell, Cynanchus & Orange Leaf Decoction): uncooked Os Draconis (*Long Gu*), 30g, uncooked Concha Ostreae (*Mu Li*), 30g, Radix Cynanchi Atrati (*Bai Wei*), 12g, Folium Citri Reticulatae (*Ju Ye*),

12g, uncooked Radix Rehmanniae (*Sheng Di*), 12g, uncooked Radix Albus Paeoniae Lactiflorae (*Bai Shao*), 12g, Radix Cyathulae (*Chuan Niu Xi*), 12g, Radix Scrophulariae Ningpoensis (*Xuan Shen*), 9g, Tuber Ophiopogonis Japonici (*Mai Dong*), 9g, Fructus Gardeniae Jasminoidis (*Zhi Zi*), 9g, Caulis Bambusae In Taeniis (*Zhu Ru*), 9g, stir-fried Fructus Citri Aurantii (*Zhi Ke*), 6g, uncooked Radix Glycyrrhizae (*Gan Cao*), 3g. These were decocted in water and administered orally, one *ji* per day.

This was combined with *Zhu Hu San* (Cinnabar & Succinum Powder). This consisted of Cinnabar (*Zhu Sha*), 12g, and Succinum (*Hu Po*), 18g. These were powdered, mixed together, and divided up into 12 bags. Each evening, one bag was administered before sleep, washed down with warm water. After administering this powder for four nights, it was discontinued. Altogether, 30 *ji* of the above prescription were administered, after which all the symptoms disappeared, and the patient was judged cured.

### ❖ CASE 3 ❖

The patient in this case was a 30 year old male farmer. He was first examined on March 10, 1963. One month before, there were some family problems and he had contracted wind cold. For this he had taken too much deer penis (*Lu Bian*). Afterwards, he had suddenly begun breaking things and injuring people, including his relatives. He climbed onto the roof and took off his clothes. The patient's strength was magnified much greater than usual. He did not distinguish between filth and cleanliness, and he did not know hunger or thirst. He was treated based on a diagnosis of schizophrenia, but without result. When he was referred for Chinese medicine, his facial complexion was dark red, his tongue was purplish red, and this tongue fur was slimy and yellow. His pulse was bowstring and large. Therefore, his pattern was discriminated as phlegm fire flaming upward obstructing and blocking the heart orifices.

The treatment principles in this case were to transform phlegm and open the orifices, clear fire and quiet the spirit. The formula prescribed was *Tie Luo Yin* (Iron Filings Drink): Tuber Ophiopogonis Japonici (*Mai Dong*), 12g, Tuber Asparagai Cochinensis (*Tian Men Dong*), 12g, Bulbus Fritillariae Thunbergii (*Zhe Bei Mu*), 12g, Radix Salviae Miltiorrhizae (*Dan Shen*), 12g, Radix Scrophulariae Ningpoensis (*Xuan Shen*), 12g, Sclerotium Poriae Cocos (*Fu Ling*), 12g, Sclerotium Pararadicis Poriae Cocos (*Fu Shen*), 12g, Ramulus Uncariae Cum Uncis (*Gou Teng*), 12g, Fructus Forsythiae Suspensae

(*Lian Qiao*), 12g, Pericarpium Citri Reticulatae (*Chen Pi*), 5g, bile-processed Rhizoma Arisaematis (*Dan Nan Xing*), 5g, Rhizoma Acori Graminei (*Shi Chang Pu*), 5g, Radix Polygalae Tenuifoliae (*Yuan Zhi*), 5g, Cinnabar (*Zhu Sha*), 3g (swallowed with the decocted liquid), uncooked Frusta Ferri (*Tie Luo*), 200g (decocted for one hour first).

These medicinals were decocted in water and administered orally, one *ji* per day, for two days. At that time, all his symptoms were greatly reduced. On Mar. 12, he was re-examined, his speech was normal, and his emotions were once again under his control. Four more *ji* of the above formula was prescribed without the Frusta Ferri. After taking these medicinals, the patient was judged cured. On follow-up 10 years later, there had been no recurrence.

### ❖ CASE 4 ❖

The patient was a 21 year old female who was newly married for half a month. During this time she had gradually become melancholic, sorrowful, and irritable. This eventually turned into mania. The patient could not sleep at night, her speech was incoherent, and sometimes she yelled maniacally. When she was examined, it was seen that her facial complexion was red and her body was replete. Her tongue was also red with yellow fur, and her pulse was slippery, rapid, and forceful. Her Western medical diagnosis was schizophrenia, while her Chinese pattern was discriminated as liver-gallbladder depressive heat mixed with phlegm which was confounding and blocking the heart orifices.

The treatment principles in this case were to clear and drain the liver and gallbladder, flush phlegm and open the orifices. Therefore, she was prescribed *Jia Jian Long Dan Xie Gan Tang* (Modified Gentiana Drain the Liver Decoction): Radix Gentianae Scabrae (*Long Dan Cao*), 9g, Fructus Gardeniae Jasminoidis (*Zhi Zi*), 9g, Radix Scutellariae Baicalensis (*Huang Qin*), 9g, stir-fried Radix Bupleuri (*Chai Hu*), 3g, uncooked Radix Rehmanniae (*Sheng Di*), 12g, bile-processed Rhizoma Arisaematis (*Dan Nan Xing*), 6g, Rhizoma Acori Graminei (*Shi Chang Pu*), 6g, Tuber Curcumae (*Yu Jin*), 9g, uncooked Radix Et Rhizoma Rhei (*Da Huang*), 15g, cooked Radix Et Rhizoma Rhei (*Da Huang*), 15g, Mirabilitum (*Xuan Ming Fen*), 12g, Rhizoma Coptidis Chinensis (*Huang Lian*), 3g, uncooked Frusta Ferri (*Tie Luo*), 30g. One *ji* of the above medicinals was decocted in water and administered orally each day for two days.

On the third day, the patient was re-examined and already

her affect was greatly changed. The patient explained herself that, after taking the medicinals, she had had several bowel movements which were a shiny black color and were gelatinous in consistency. At night she was much quieter, her spirit was clear, and her speech was normal. Therefore, the patient was administered five *ji* of *Jia Jian Dan Zhi Xiao Yao San* (Modified Moutan & Gardenia Rambling Powder) in decoction, after which she was judged fine. This consisted of: Cortex Radicis Moutan (*Dan Pi*), 9g, Fructus Gardeniae Jasminoidis (*Zhi Zi*), 9g, Radix Scutellariae Baicalensis (*Huang Qin*), 9g, Radix Angelicae Sinensis (*Dang Gui*), 10g, Radix Albus Paeoniae Lactiflorae (*Bai Shao*), 9g, Sclerotium Poriae Cocos (*Fu Ling*), 9g, Rhizoma Atractylodis Macrocephalae (*Bai Zhu*), 9g, Radix Glycyrrhizae (*Gan Cao*), 3g, Herba Menthae Haplocalycis (*Bo He*), 3g (added later), Tuber Curcumae (*Yu Jin*), 9g. The patient was followed up four years after taking these medicinals, and no recurrence had been seen.

### ❖ CASE 5[10] ❖

The patient was a 29 year old married female who had already had one child and was first examined on Apr. 10, 1989. In December 1988, the patient had been diagnosed as schizophrenic. Her sleep was restless at night and she moved around manically and frenetically. She occasionally hit people, and she laughed and cried without constancy. At other times, she was feeble-minded. Three months prior, she had been treated at a psychiatric hospital with Artane, chlorpromazine, and other Western drugs, her symptoms had improved, and she had been discharged. However, in the last month, her symptoms had returned, she had not been sleeping well, and she was referred to the case's author for examination and treatment. At that time, the patient complained of dizziness, heart palpitations, restlessness, scanty intake, and loose stools. Her lips were red, her tongue was coated with slimy, white fur, and her pulse was bowstring, slippery, and forceful.

Therefore, Dr. Lin prescribed *Chai Hu Jia Long Gu Mu Li Tang Jia Wei* (Bupleurum Plus Dragon Bone & Oyster Shell Decoction with Added Flavors): Radix Bupleuri (*Chai Hu*), Rhizoma Pinelliae Ternatae (*Ban Xia*), and Radix Scutellariae Baicalensis (*Huang Qin*), 10g each, Radix Pseudostellariae (*Tai Zi Shen*), Sclerotium Poriae Cocos (*Fu Ling*), and Os Draconis (*Long Gu*), 15g each, wine-processed Radix Et Rhizoma Rhei (*Da Huang*), 9g, Ramulus Cinnamomi Cassiae (*Gui Zhi*), 6g, uncooked Concha Ostreae (*Mu Li*), 30g, uncooked Rhizoma Zingiberis (*Sheng Jiang*), 6g, Fructus Zizyphi Jujubae (*Da Zao*), 5 pieces, and uncooked Frusta Ferri (*Tie Luo*), 120g.

After taking 10 *ji* of this formula, the patient's symptoms slightly decreased. Her affect improved when she was not manic at night. Because these medicinals had had some effect, the doseage of her Western medications was decreased. Another 30 *ji* of the original formula was administered, after which the disease's nature was marked improved. At that point, the Western medications were stopped and she was administered a combination of *Wen Dan Tang* (Warm the Gallbladder Decotation) and *Gan Mai Da Zao Tang* (Licorice, Wheat & Red Dates Decotation) for regulating treatment for two months. The patient was considered cured and there had been no recurrence on the follow-up in 1996.

## ENDNOTES

[1] This medicinal is a mercuric compound. Although it has been used in Chinese medicine for over 2,000 years, it is toxic and its use is forbidden by the U.S. Food & Drug Administration. In most instances, it can be substituted with Succinum (*Hu Po*) which is nontoxic. In formulas where there are already both Cinnabar and Succinum, one can delete the Cinnabar and increase the doses of the remaining heavy, yang-subduing, spirit-quieting medicinals.

[2] Liver depression complicates essentially all enduring disease in adults. If liver depression was not the original cause of disease, then it will become the result of disease, since every disease is associated with unfulfilled desires either for or against something. Therefore, some appropriate qi-rectifying medicinals are either found in or should be added to formulas for all other patterns of schizophrenia.

[3] This medicinal is derived from a severely endangered species. It should be substituted by Cornu Bubali (*Shui Niu Jiao*).

[4] The difference between this pattern and the preceding one is that, in pattern B, there is more liver depression qi stagnation, while in pattern C, there is more spleen vacuity.

[5] In other words, yang is so exuberant, it is no longer being controlled by its complement yin.

[6] We assume this is a ready-made medicine available on the Chinese market.

[7] Kidney yang vacuity often complicates yin and qi dual vacuity patterns, especially in perimenopausal women. In that case, one or more yang-invigorating, kidney supplementing medicinals should be added to other formulas appropriate for that pattern. When kidney yang vacuity complicates yin vacuity where there is vacuity heat, the only symptoms of yang vacuity may be low back pain, cold feet, nocturia, and decreased sexual desire.

[8] Whenever withdrawal and mania disease endures for a long time, it will commonly be accompanied by some blood stasis symptoms. In that case, one should add some blood-quickening, stasis-transforming medicinals as appropriate to whatever other formulas have been chosen based on the patient's pattern discrimination.

[9] Li Wen-liang & Qi Qiang, *Qian Jia Miao Fang (Ten Thousand Families' Wonderous Formulas)*, People's Liberation Army Press, Beijing, 1985, p. 481-486. This citation covers cases 1-4.

[10] Lin Tian-hua, "A Survey of the Treatment of Neurological & Psychological Diseases with *Chai Hu Jia Long Gu Mu Li Tang* (Bupleurum Plus Dragon Bone & Oyster Shell Decoction)," *Bei Jing Zhong Yi (Beijing Chinese Medicine)*, #3, 1996, p. 47-48

# DEPRESSION

Contemporary Western psychiatry regards persisting patterns of depressed, manic, or mixed depressed-manic mood that interfere with normal social or occupational functioning as mood disorders. Depressive mood disorders occur with many degrees of severity and in the context of numerous concomitant medical or psychiatric disorders. Major depressive disorder is the most severe disorder of persisting depressed mood. Major depressive disorder was previously referred to as unipolar disorder to distinguish it from bipolar disorder. Other mood disorders described in Western psychiatric literature include cyclothymic disorder, dysthymic disorder, adjustment disorder with depressed mood, and persisting mood changes related to medical disorders, medication side effects, or the chronic effects of alcohol or illicit substance abuse.

## NOSOLOGY:

The two broad pattern discriminations discussed in this chapter contain numerous groups of symptoms that resemble core features of major depression as it is operationalized in contemporary Western psychiatric nosology. Most of the patterns below include prominent somatic complaints, persisting depressed mood, and excessive restlessness or agitation (e.g., vexation and agitation) or diminished energy and listlessness. While particular patterns do not correspond exactly to accepted types of depression as defined in Western psychiatry, some important common characteristics exist between Chinese medical conceptions of depression and contemporary Western psychiatric concepts. For example, many groups of symptoms described as sub-types of the liver qi depression and binding pattern appear to resemble what has been described as agitated depression in the West. This type of depression is characterized by persisting feelings of sadness in the context of irritable, agitated, or angry mood. In contrast, many described groups of symptoms included under the Chinese diagnostic category of vacuity patterns appear to closely resemble what has been described as vegetative depression in Western psychiatry. In this type of depressive mood disorder, the individual experiences feelings of lassitude, fatigue, disinterest, loss of energy, and sometimes diminished libido. Therefore, the distinction in Chinese medicine between the two general categories of liver qi depression and binding pattern and vacuity patterns is at least phenomenologically similar to the dichotomy of agitated versus vegetative depression in contemporary Western descriptive nosology.

According to contemporary Western psychiatry, a major depressive episode is strictly defined with respect to symptom type, severity, and duration. At least five symptoms causing significant distress or social or occupational impairment must persist at least two weeks. Among these, the individual must experience either depressed mood or persisting feelings of loss of pleasure in activities that are typically enjoyable to that person. Included among the other four symptoms necessary to fulfill diagnostic criteria for a major depressive episode, an individual may experience: change in appetite (increase or decrease), persisting feelings of worthlessness or guilt, thoughts of death or suicidal impulses, change in sleep (increased or decreased need for sleep), or persisting fatigue. The formal definition further stipulates that these symptoms must not be better explained by another previously diagnosed major psychiatric disorder and may not be related to a known medical disorder or the effects of a substance (including medications, alcohol, or illicit substances). Persisting depressed mood may point to numerous possible medical or psychiatric disorders depending on history and the particular symptom pattern disclosed during a diagnostic interview. The various diagnostic possibilities are reviewed in the following section.

## EPIDEMIOLOGY:

Major depression is most common between 20-45 years of age, and the average age of occurrence for initial major depressive episodes is 40. Based on many well-controlled studies, it is a significant but poorly understood fact that depression is roughly twice as prevalent in women as in men. Reasons for this are not clear. There have been no significant reported differences in the prevalence of major depression based on ethnicity, socio-economic status, or race. As many as 15% of the general population will experience severe depression during the course of their lives, and the incidence of major depression at any given time in surveyed Western populations may be as high as 3%. The majority of individuals experiencing major depression contemplate suicide, and as many as 20% attempt suicide sometime during the course of their illness. Depressed women attempt suicide twice as often as men, but men who attempt suicide are twice as likely to succeed compared to women. As many as 90% of depressed patients experience co-morbid anxiety, and many depressed patients abuse alcohol or illicit substances, possibly in an attempt to self-medicate their symptoms. It is estimated that nearly 50% of depressed individuals never receive treatment, and many patients receiving treatment are not successfully treated, *i.e.*, their symptoms do not improve. The incidence of depression may be underestimated in children and the elderly due to differences in symptomatology in these age groups resulting in frequent misdiagnosis or missed diagnosis. In school-age children, for example, antisocial behavior, academic problems, or school avoidance may mask underlying depressed mood. Depression in the elderly is frequently misdiagnosed because individuals in this age group tend to focus on somatic complaints which then become the primary concern of the treating Western physician.

## DIFFERENTIAL DIAGNOSIS:

Episodes of major depression and mania can be precipitated or exacerbated by numerous medical disorders, including endocrinological disease (especially thyroid and adrenal dysfunction), cancer, infectious diseases (such as HIV and hepatitis), neurologic disorders (such as epilepsy and brain tumors), cerebrovascular accidents (CVA), and head injuries. Systemic lupus erythematosus (SLE) and multiple sclerosis (MS) are disorders in which depressive (or manic) mood symptoms sometimes track periods of acute illness as these disorders follow their typical remitting-relapsing courses. Contemporary Western psychiatry characterizes persisting depressed mood related to a known underlying medical cause as a mood disorder due to a general medical condition. Chronic use of alcohol or certain illicit drugs, especially marijuana, can also result in persistent, typically depressive, mood changes. Many over-the-counter and prescription drugs are known to have depressive or mood-elevating side effects. Antihypertensives, antibiotics, chemotherapeutic agents, antiarrhythmics, and anti-Parkinsonian medications frequently cause depressive mood changes, while steroid use has been associated with manic states. A persisting pattern of depressed mood that is etiologically related to substance abuse or medication side effects is called a substance induced mood disorder. Accurate diagnosis of underlying organic causes of mood changes is necessary in order to achieve the most effective treatment plan. Therefore, Western psychiatry begins with a medical workup with the goal of identifying, treating, or eliminating underlying biological causes.

A mood disorder that is not found to have a medical etiology following an appropriate workup is regarded as a primary mood disorder. The severity, course, and pattern of symptoms will then determine the most likely Western psychiatric diagnosis. An individual who complains of chronic depressed mood that is sustained and of moderate intensity and has never attempted suicide or experienced suicidal thoughts has dysthymic disorder. According to current diagnostic criteria in Western psychiatry, a major depressive episode can be diagnosed only when an individual experiences severe depressed mood for a period of at least two weeks in the context of impaired social or occupational functioning and at least five other associated symptoms, including persisting feelings of worthlessness or hopelessness, loss of interest in life or activities, social avoidance, changed (increased or decreased) appetite, disturbed sleep, and sometimes, persisting thoughts of suicide. Recurring episodes of major depression lead to a diagnosis of major depressive disorder. Some individuals experience psychotic symptoms, including auditory hallucinations or delusions, during the course of a major depressive episode. However, many schizophrenics experience bouts of depressed mood at times during the course of their illness. Therefore, it is important to distinguish schizophrenia with depressed features from a major depressive episode with psychotic features. A long-standing history of progressive deterioration in functioning in the context of pervasive psychotic symptoms is characteristic of schizophrenia. When prominent psychotic symptoms occur during periods of normal mood and there is a history of major depressive illness at times when the patient is experiencing active psychotic symptoms, the likely diagnosis is schizoaffective disorder.

A history of recurring major depressive episodes interspersed with manic or hypomanic episodes (see Chapter 6, this Book) leads to a diagnosis of bipolar affective disorder. Recurring episodes of moderate depressed mood interspersed with hypomanic (but never full-blown manic) episodes is labeled cyclothymic disorder. When an individual experiences transient depressed mood following severe stress and there is no previous history of depression, the diagnosis is "adjustment disorder, depressed." Individuals who have primary anxiety disorders frequently experience periods of depressed mood, either in response to feelings of helplessness or as a concomitant of CNS neurochemical changes that also predispose them to

anxiety disorders. These include post-traumatic stress disorder (PTSD) and generalized anxiety disorder (GAD) as well as social and specific phobias. Finally, many individuals who have personality disorders, principally borderline personality disorder, experience periods of intense despair, sometimes accompanied by thoughts of dying or suicidal ideation. Aspects of borderline personality disorder that distinguish it from major depression and other mood disorders include a long-standing pattern of disruptive interpersonal relationships, self-destructive behavior, rapidly shifting affect, lack of insight, and (sometimes) intrusive suicidal thoughts.

## ETIOLOGY & PATHOPHYSIOLOGY:

Although biological and psychosocial theories continue to advance multifactorial causal explanations, the etiology of mood disorders is not clearly established within conventional Western medicine. The following are some of the interesting findings or observations that characterize contemporary understandings of mood disorders from a Western medical perspective.

Animal and human studies have demonstrated consistent associations between abnormal levels of specific neurotransmitters and depressed mood. However, there appears to be no simple correlation between a specific neurotrans-

## DIFFERENTIAL DIAGNOSIS

### 1. MEDICAL DISORDERS

A. ENDOCRINOLOGICAL DISORDERS (INCLUDING HYPOTHYROIDISM AND ADRENAL DYSFUNCTION)

B. CANCER

C. SYSTEMIC LUPUS ERYTHEMATOSUS (SLE)

D. MULTIPLE SCLEROSIS (MS) AND OTHER IMMUNOLOGICAL DISORDERS

E. INFECTIOUS DISEASES (INCLUDING HIV AND HEPATITIS)

F NEUROLOGIC DISORDERS (INCLUDING EPILEPSY AND BRAIN TUMORS)

G. CEREBROVASCULAR ACCIDENTS (CVA)

H. TRAUMATIC BRAIN INJURY

### 2. EFFECTS OF SUBSTANCES

A. ALCOHOL OR ILLICIT SUBSTANCE ABUSE (COMMONLY MARIJUANA)

B. EFFECTS OF MEDICATIONS (E.G., CHEMOTHERAPY AGENTS, SOME ANTIHYPERTENSIVES, AND ANTI-PARKINSONIAN DRUGS)

### 3. PSYCHIATRIC DISORDERS

A. DYSTHYMIC DISORDER

B. MAJOR DEPRESSIVE DISORDER

C. SCHIZOPHRENIA WITH DEPRESSED MOOD

D. SCHIZOAFFECTIVE DISORDER

E. BIPOLAR DISORDER (TYPE I AND II)

F. CYCLOTHYMIC DISORDER

G. ADJUSTMENT DISORDER WITH DEPRESSED MOOD

H. ANXIETY DISORDERS, INCLUDING POST-TRAUMATIC STRESS DISORDER (PTSD), GENERALIZED ANXIETY DISORDER (GAD), AND SOCIAL AND SPECIFIC PHOBIAS

I. BORDERLINE PERSONALITY DISORDER

mitter or cerebral spinal fluid (CSF) level and depressed mood. To date, neurotransmitters principally implicated in the pathogenesis of depression are serotonin and nor-epinephrine. However, recent research suggests that dopamine, GABA (the chief inhibitory neurotransmitter), and many others may also be indirectly involved in pathological mood changes. Primary endocrine imbalances may also be tied to depression or mania, including dysfunction in the hypothalamus, pituitary, thyroid, and adrenals. In addition, accumulating evidence from brain-imaging studies suggests that depressive mood changes are related to diminished metabolic activity in the frontal cortex and possibly to lesions in the hypothalamus or other components of the brain's primitive limbic circuits.

Genetic studies have demonstrated strong familial inheritance patterns for both bipolar and unipolar depression. However, the significance (*i.e.*, for aggressive treatment planning) of genetic predispositions to mood disorders is obscured by complex psychosocial factors that are difficult to control in longitudinal studies. Some researchers contend, for example, that life stressors and familial patterns of extreme dysfunction comprise the primary risk factors for development of mood disorders. Other factors that have been proposed as contributing causes of depressed mood include certain personality styles (especially antisocial or paranoid), maladaptive psychodynamic defenses (*e.g.*, inwardly directed rage or failure to achieve mirroring at a critical developmental age), and learned self-defeating cognitive patterns (including pessimism and negative distortions).

## WESTERN MEDICAL TREATMENT:

Hospitalization is required when symptom severity impairs daily functioning or the patient is suicidal. The goals of hospitalization are safety, medical evaluation, and psychiatric stabilization. In cases where there is no previous psychiatric history, a thorough medical workup is performed to rule out or identify possible biological causes. This may include neurologic assessment with brain-imaging if the history is suggestive of a primary CNS process (*e.g.*, history of head trauma, seizure, or brain tumor), serologic studies, including complete blood count, urinalysis, thyroid hormone studies, and urine toxicology screen if there is evidence of drug abuse or inappropriate use of prescription medications. Identified causative biological factors are corrected when possible, and any non-resolving acute psychiatric symptoms are addressed with psychopharmacology and supportive psychotherapy. In the acute hospitalized setting, insight-oriented psychotherapy is inappropriate and potentially confusing or disruptive.

When symptoms of depression or mania are not sufficiently impairing to warrant hospitalization, they are managed on an out-patient basis. Combined medication management and psychotherapy are the recommended treatment for depression, whereas manic symptoms are treated with pharmacotherapy alone. There is evidence that many psychotherapeutic approaches are helpful for depressed patients who are not suicidal. Several studies have shown that cognitive therapy is often as effective as pharmacotherapy in the treatment of depression, but the prevailing view in contemporary Western psychiatry is that cognitive therapy in combination with an appropriate antidepressant is more effective than either treatment alone.

Numerous antidepressant medications belonging to different drug classes are used to treat unipolar depression in contemporary Western psychiatry. Although less popular than more recently introduced medications, the tricyclic antidepressants (TCAs, *e.g.*, imiprimine, desiprimine, nortriptyline, and amitriptyline) are no less effective. However, as a class, the serotonin-selective re-uptake inhibitors (SSRIs) have fewer side effects than TCAs, resulting in improved compliance and possibly improved long-term outcomes. Monoamine oxidase inhibitors (MAOIs) comprise another class of antidepressants. However, these are infrequently used in contemporary Western psychiatry because of potentially dangerous interactions with other medications or certain foods. Many novel antidepressant medications with superior side effect profiles have recently been introduced in the U.S. These include citalopram (Celexa), mirtazepine (Remeron), and reboxetine (Vestra).

In addition to synthetic psychotropic medications, Western-trained psychiatrists are prescribing St. John's Wort preparations and other natural products, including SAMe (S-adenosyl methionine), and *Ginkgo biloba* at increasing rates. Although many depressed individuals use St. John's Wort or other natural products in conjunction with synthetic psychotropics, clinical data have not yet established an acceptable level of risk due to interactions or toxicities using this approach.

## SHORT & LONG-TERM ADVANTAGES & DISADVANTAGES OF WESTERN MEDICAL TREATMENT:

The short-term and on-going efficacy and advantages of conventional Western pharmacologic treatments for major depressive disorder are clearly established for most medications in current use. Numerous controlled, double-blind studies demonstrate that significant clinical gains are derived from these therapies, including maintained euthymic mood and improved social and occupational functioning. Outcomes data also consistently support the value of cognitive therapy for major depressive disorder. However, this optimistic picture is in stark contrast to a long list of potentially serious side effects or toxicities commonly associated with many antidepressants. The following table lists significant toxicities or drug-drug interactions for representative antidepressants in widespread current use in contemporary Western psychiatry.

## PROGNOSIS:

Major depressive disorder is a chronic disorder. One-fourth of depressed patients requiring hospitalization experience recurring severe depression within six months of discharge. The chance of recurring depression continues to increase, approaching 75% five years after the initial depressive episode. The rate of recurrence and symptom severity on recurrence are much lower among patients taking antidepressants prophylactically. The natural history of untreated major depressive disorder appears to result in increasingly frequent depressive episodes of progressively increasing severity. The absence of co-morbid medical, psychiatric, and substance abuse problems is prognostically favorable, whereas social isolation and unstable family functioning often lead to poor long-term outcomes.

## INDICATIONS FOR REFERRAL TO WESTERN MEDICAL SERVICES:

A patient who voices suicidal thoughts requires hospitalization for safety. When a suicidal or psychiatrically impaired patient refuses voluntary hospitalization, the clinician has a professional obligation to activate the emergency medical response system in order to rapidly bring the patient to the attention of local police or paramedics. This will result in an emergency assessment, and, if indicated, the patient will be placed on an involuntary hold and transported to the nearest emergency room for medical and psychiatric evaluation. Non-urgent consultation with a psychiatrist is indicated when a patient does not improve following a reasonable period of treatment or there is evidence of an underlying untreated medical problem or substance abuse.

## CHINESE DISEASE CATEGORIZATION:

In traditional Chinese medicine, emotional depression is categorized as depressive condition (*yu zheng*), withdrawal (*dian*), vacuity taxation (*xu lao*), insomnia (*bu mian*), vexation and agitation (*fan zao*), and visceral agitation (*zang zao*). During the 1970s and 80s, the disease diagnosis of neurasthenia (*shen jing shuai rou*) was popular in the People's Republic of China, but this has largely been replaced by the disease category of depressive condition.

## CHINESE DISEASE CAUSES & DISEASE MECHANISMS:

The Chinese medical causes and mechanisms of depression mostly revolve around the liver viscus. In the eighteenth century *Za Bing Yuan Liu Xi Zhu* (*Wonderous Lantern Peering into the Origin & Development of Miscellaneous Diseases*), it says, "All depression can be classified as a liver disease."[1] Essentially all patients with depression exhibit signs and symptoms of liver depression no matter what other disease mechanisms are also at work. Thus liver depression is, we believe, the *sine qua non* of depression. This opinion is substantiated by the following lines from the Qing dynasty *Zheng Zhi Hui Bu* (*Complete Collection of Patterns & Treatments*) by Li Yong-cui:

> In all the many cases of depression, their cause is qi which is not regulated or coursing. Treatment must first normalize [the flow] of qi.

## DRUG TOXICITY, SIDE EFFECTS & INTERACTIONS

| TRICYCLIC ANTIDEPRESSANTS (TCAs) | SEROTONIN-SELECTIVE RE-UPTAKE INHIBITORS (SSRIs) |
| --- | --- |
| ❖ Serious toxicity (lethality) in overdose<br>❖ Interacts with SSRIs to result in potentially toxic levels when used in combination<br>❖ Affects serum levels of many other medications by affecting liver enzymes | ❖ Common sexual side-effects<br>❖ Common GI side-effects<br>❖ Common sedation or insomnia side-effects<br>❖ Affects serum levels of other drugs through live enzymes |

The method of normalizing the qi is aimed at the liver and is used for the liver's loss of orderly reaching and the qi's loss of coursing and discharge. It is the same as coursing the liver and rectifying the qi and is what is meant by the *Su Wen* (*Simple Questions*) when it says, "For wood depression, out-thrust it.""

Liver depression can be due to a number of causes. One of the most immediate is unfulfilled desires. All desire is the subjective experience of a movement of qi towards something we want or away from something we don't want. When such desires remain unfulfilled, this inhibits the liver's qi mechanism. The liver's qi mechanism is responsible for coursing and discharge. This means the spreading and extension of the qi. If the liver's qi mechanism becomes depressed, then the qi becomes stagnant.

However, other causes of liver depression include blood loss or vacuity, faulty diet, too little exercise, anger, and aging. In order for the liver to perform its functions correctly, it must receive sufficient moistening and nourishing from the blood. Therefore, if the yin blood becomes vacuous and insufficient for any reason, such as loss or non-engenderment, this can cause or aggravate liver depression. Secondly, if faulty diet leads to food stagnation, damp accumulation, or phlegm obstruction, any of these three yin depressions may cause or aggravate qi stagnation. These evil yin accumulations hinder and obstruct the free flow of the qi and this then can inhibit the liver's qi mechanism. Third, exercise promotes the movement of the qi and blood. Therefore, too little physical exercise can lead to or aggravate liver depression qi stagnation. Fourth, anger is the affect or emotion of the liver. When it is expressed, it is a form of over-coursing and over-discharging which damages the liver. Therefore, the sequela of such over-coursing and over-discharging is inhibited coursing and discharging. Again, this results in consumption of yin, depletion of yang, and vacuity of both the spleen and kidneys. According to Chinese five phase theory, healthy spleen and kidneys keep the liver qi smoothly and freely flowing. Yin blood nourishes and emolliates the liver, while kidney yang warms and steams the liver, promoting its function. The spleen is the latter heaven source of qi and blood engenderment and transformation. If the spleen is healthy, there is sufficient blood to nourish the liver and sufficient qi to empower coursing and discharging.

When the liver becomes depressed, almost always, automatically the spleen becomes vacuous and weak. If the spleen becomes vacuous and weak, it not only does not engender and transform qi and blood, but it also fails to transport and transform water fluids. These then may gather and accumulate, transforming into evil dampness. If evil dampness lingers and endures, it may congeal into phlegm. In that case, phlegm fluids may hinder the free flow of the qi, block the orifices of the heart, and confound the upper clear orifices, the sense organs. The tendency for phlegm and dampness to be engendered internally is increased if one overeats sugars and sweets which damage the spleen and engender dampness or fats and hard-to-digest, thick-flavored foods.

Since qi is yang, if the liver becomes depressed and the qi becomes stagnant and accumulates, stagnant qi may transform into depressive heat or fire. Since heat and fire are yang, they inherently have a tendency to flare upward, thus harassing the heart spirit above. Evil fire and heat can also stew the juices and congeal fluids into phlegm. In that case, upwardly flaring fire may draft phlegm along with it so that, not only is the spirit harassed by evil heat, the heart orifices are blocked and confounded. If evil heat endures in the body for a long time or is severe, it may consume yin fluids and lead to a yin blood insufficiency. In that case, yin is insufficient to control yang which becomes hyperactive and tends to ascend all the more to harass the heart spirit.

On the other hand, enduring spleen vacuity may eventually reach the kidneys. Latter heaven spleen qi is rooted in and bolstered by former heaven kidney yang. In many people, and especially in women who tend toward spleen vacuity more than men in any case, the spleen becomes vacuous and weak in the mid to late thirties. This then leads to a spleen qi and kidney yang vacuity in the mid to late forties and early fifties and on into the sixties. If kidney yang fails to warm and steam the liver, liver depression becomes all the worse.

Thus it is easy to see there is a very close relationship between the Chinese viscera of the liver, spleen, kidneys, and heart and depression as well as between liver depression, spleen qi vacuity, blood vacuity, yin vacuity, yang vacuity, phlegm, and fire. Although the pattern discrimination given below presents each of these disease mechanisms as separate patterns, in real-life Western patients, they appear in groups of three or more. For instance, most Western females with depression have liver depression, spleen vacuity, and some kind of evil heat. In addition, depending on their age, constitution, and life-style, they may also have phlegm and/or kidney vacuity. That kidney vacuity may be either yin, yang, or both yin and yang. Hence it is not uncommon to see patients in clinical practice who do not have one or the other of the patterns presented below but combinations of up to eight of them. In such complicated cases (which are the norm and *not* the exception in Western practice), one must create individualized treatment plans which are, nevertheless, made from the building blocks described below.

**TREATMENT BASED ON PATTERN DISCRIMINATION:**

**1. LIVER QI DEPRESSION & BINDING PATTERN**

**MAIN SYMPTOMS:** Irritability, a tendency to sigh, taciturnity, solitariness, premenstrual breast distention and pain, chest oppression and rib-side pain, lower abdominal distention and pain, discomfort in the stomach and epigastrium, diminished appetite, possible delayed menstruation whose amount is either scanty or profuse, darkish, stagnant menstrual blood, the menses unable to come easily, a normal or slightly dark tongue with thin, white fur, and a bowstring pulse

**ANALYSIS OF SYMPTOMS:** If, for any reason, the liver loses its control over coursing and discharge, the qi will become stagnant and will not flow smoothly nor spread freely. This results in irritability, taciturnity, and solitariness. The liver channel traverses the lower abdomen and mixes with the stomach. Then it spreads across the chest and ribsides. Therefore, if there is liver qi depression and stagnation, there is abdominal distention, rib-side pain, and chest oppression which produces a desire to sigh, while, in females there is typically non-movement of menstruation. If the liver qi assails the stomach, the stomach loses its harmony and downbearing. Therefore, there is epigastric oppression and belching and burping, lack of appetite, and, in some cases, even nausea and vomiting. The slightly dark tongue and the bowstring pulse are both signs of liver depression qi stagnation.

**NOTE:** Although essentially all patients with depression manifest liver depression qi stagnation, it rarely presents in such a pure, simple, and discrete form. In real-life, it is always complicated by spleen vacuity, stomach disharmony, depressive heat, blood vacuity, yin vacuity and/or yang vacuity, phlegm, dampness, etc.

**TREATMENT PRINCIPLES:** Course the liver, rectify the qi, and resolve depression

**FORMULA & MEDICINALS:** *Chai Hu Shu Gan San Jia Wei* (Bupleurum Course the Liver Powder)

Radix Bupleuri (*Chai Hu*), 3g, stir-fried Fructus Citri Aurantii (*Zhi Ke*), 10g, Radix Albus Paeoniae Lactiflorae (*Bai Shao*), 12g, mix-fried Radix Glycyrrhizae (*Gan Cao*), 10g, processed Rhizoma Cyperi Rotundi (*Xiang Fu*), 10g, Tuber Curcumae (*Yu Jin*), 10g, Radix Ligustici Wallichii (*Chuan Xiong*), 6g (added later)

Decoct in water and administer orally in two divided doses, morning and evening, one *ji* per day

**ANALYSIS OF FORMULA:** Bupleurum, Aurantium, and Cyperus all course the liver and rectify the qi. White Peony emolliates and harmonizes the liver. Ligusticum moves the qi within the blood as well as leads the other medicinals to move upward to the head and downward to the uterus. It helps prevent blood stasis due to qi stagnation. Mix-fried Licorice supplements the spleen based on the saying, "When the liver is diseased, first treat the spleen." It also harmonizes all the other medicinals and helps prevent the acrid, windy, and, therefore, drying medicinals from damaging yin blood.

**ADDITIONS & SUBTRACTIONS:** If there is concomitant spleen vacuity, add Radix Codonopsitis Pilosulae (*Dang Shen*) and Rhizoma Atractylodis Macrocephalae (*Bai Zhu*). If there is concomitant blood vacuity, add Radix Angelicae Sinensis (*Dang Gui*).

**ACUPUNCTURE:** *Tai Chong* (Liv 3), *He Gu* (LI 4), *Zu San Li* (St 36), *Nei Guan* (Per 6). Use draining technique.

**2. LIVER DEPRESSION TRANSFORMING FIRE PATTERN**

**MAIN SYMPTOMS:** All the above signs and symptoms plus the following differences: First, the patient is not just irritable, they are downright angry. Secondly, there is a bitter taste in their mouth in the mornings when they wake or possible acid regurgitation. And third, there is a red tongue with yellow fur and a bowstring, rapid pulse. Other symptoms may include tinnitus, headache, red eyes, dry mouth, dry, bound, constipated stools, violent outbursts of anger, cursing, shouting, and physically throwing or destroying things.

**ANALYSIS OF SYMPTOMS:** If qi depression transforms into fire, fire's nature is to flare upward. Therefore, it follows the liver vessels and moves upward. This results in headache, red eyes, and tinnitus. If liver fire attacks the stomach, the stomach and intestines will have heat. Therefore, the mouth is dry, there is a bitter taste, and there may be acid regurgitation, while the stools are constipated and bound. The emotional tension, agitation, and easy anger, the red tongue with yellow fur, and the bowstring, rapid pulse are all signs of liver fire.

TREATMENT PRINCIPLES: Course the liver and rectify the qi, clear heat and resolve depression

FORMULA & MEDICINALS: *Dan Zhi Xiao Yao San* (Moutan & Gardenia Rambling Powder)

Cortex Radicis Moutan (*Dan Pi*), 10g, scorched Fructus Gardeniae Jasminoidis (*Zhi Zi*), 10g, Radix Bupleuri (*Chai Hu*), 10g, Rhizoma Atractylodis Macrocephalae (*Bai Zhu*), 10g, Radix Albus Paeoniae Lactiflorae (*Bai Shao*), 12g, Radix Angelicae Sinensis (*Dang Gui*), 10g, Sclerotium Poriae Cocos (*Fu Ling*), 12g, mix-fried Radix Glycyrrhizae (*Gan Cao*), 6g

Decoct in water and administer orally in two divided doses, morning and evening, one *ji* per day.

ANALYSIS OF FORMULA: Within this formula, Moutan and Gardenia clear heat and resolve vexation. Bupleurum courses the liver and resolves depression. Dang Gui and White Peony nourish the blood and emolliate the liver, while Atractylodes, Poria, and mix-fried Licorice fortify the spleen and supplement the qi.

ADDITIONS & SUBTRACTIONS: For more pronounced yin and blood vacuity, add cooked Radix Rehmanniae (*Shu Di*) and Radix Polygoni Multiflori (*He Shou Wu*). For insomnia, add Cortex Albizziae Julibrissinis (*He Huan Pi*) and Caulis Polygoni Multiflori (*Ye Jiao Teng*). For more serious spleen qi vacuity with fatigue and lassitude of the spirit, add Radix Astragali Membranacei (*Huang Qi*) and Radix Codonopsitis Pilosulae (*Dang Shen*). If liver-gallbladder ministerial fire ascends to bind in the upper burner, add Folium Eriobotryae Japonicae (*Pi Pa Ye*), Tuber Curcumae (*Yu Jin*), and Pericarpium Trichosanthis Kirlowii (*Gua Lou Pi*). If depressive heat leads to wind, add Ramulus Uncariae Cum Uncis (*Gou Teng*) and Rhizoma Gastrodiae Elatae (*Tian Ma*).

ACUPUNCTURE: *Xing Jian* (Liv 2), *He Gu* (LI 4), *Qu Chi* (LI 11), *Feng Chi* (GB 20), *Nei Guan* (Per 6), *Nei Ting* (St 44). Use draining technique.

## 3. BLOOD MOVEMENT DEPRESSION & STAGNATION PATTERN[2]

MAIN SYMPTOMS: Emotional depression, vexation and agitation, thoughts of suicide, a dark, dusky facial com- plexion, rib-side and flank distention and pain, possible amenorrhea or painful menstruation in females, a dark, purplish tongue, possibly having static spots or macules, white fur, and a deep, bowstring, and/or choppy pulse

ANALYSIS OF SYMPTOMS: If liver depression endures or is severe, the qi may fail to move the blood. The blood, therefore, becomes static due to the qi's being stagnant. Thus, there is a combination of liver depression qi stagna- tion signs and symptoms, such as the rib-side distention and bowstring pulse along with blood stasis symptoms, such as lower abdominal or menstrual pain, a purple tongue, or a choppy pulse.

TREATMENT PRINCIPLES: Course the liver and move the qi, quicken the blood and transform stasis

FORMULA & MEDICINALS: For predominant qi stagnation, use *Jin Ling Zi San Jia Wei* (Melia Powder with Added Flavors)

Fructus Meliae Toosendan (*Chuan Lian Zi*), 15g, Rhizoma Corydalis Yanhusuo (*Yan Hu Suo*), 10g (added later), Semen Pruni Persicae (*Tao Ren*), 10-12g, Extremitas Radicis Angelicae Sinensis (*Dang Gui Wei*), 10g, Tuber Curcumae (*Yu Jin*), 6-10g, Lignum Dalbergiae Odoriferae (*Jiang Xiang*), 6-10g

Decoct in water and administer orally in two divided doses, morning and evening, one *ji* per day.

ANALYSIS OF FORMULA: Melia moves and rectifies the qi. Persica and Dang Gui Tails quicken the blood and dispel stasis. Curcuma and Dalbergia quicken the blood and move the qi. Curcuma treats liver depression qi stagna- tion, while Dalbergia treats spleen-stomach qi stagnation.

For predominant blood stasis, use *Xue Fu Zhu Yu Tang* (Blood Mansion Dispel Stasis Decoction)

Semen Pruni Persicae (*Tao Ren*), 10-12g, Flos Carthami Tinctorii (*Hong Hua*), 10g (steeped afterwards), Radix Angelicae Sinensis (*Dang Gui*), 10g, Radix Ligustici Wallichii (*Chuan Xiong*), 10-15g (added later), Radix Rubrus Paeoniae Lactiflorae (*Chi Shao*), 10g, Radix Cyathulae (*Chuan Niu Xi*), 10g, Radix Bupleuri (*Chai Hu*), 3-6g, Radix Platycodi Grandiflori (*Jie Geng*), 6g, Fructus Citri Aurantii (*Zhi Ke*), 10g, uncooked Radix Rehmanniae (*Sheng Di*), 12g, Radix Glycyrrhizae (*Gan Cao*), 3g

Decoct in water and administer orally in two divided doses, morning and evening, one *ji* per day.

ANALYSIS OF FORMULA: Within this formula, Persica, Carthamus, Ligusticum, Red Peony, and Cyathula all quicken the blood and dispel stasis, while Bupleurum, Aurantium, and Platycodon all rectify and move the qi. In addition, Bupleurum and Platycodon both upbear the clear yang. Dang Gui and uncooked Rehmannia both nourish and move the blood. They help prevent the attacking and moving medicinals from damaging yin blood. Licorice harmonizes all the medicinals in this formula. Hence the blood is quickened and the qi is moved, all without damaging the blood and fluids.

ACUPUNCTURE: *Xue Hai* (Sp 10), *Xin Shu* (Bl 15), *Ge Shu* (Bl 17), *Dan Shu* (Bl 18), *He Gu* (LI 4). Use draining technique. Also use a three-edged needle to puncture and bleed any small, visible varicosities.

## 4. PHLEGM QI DEPRESSION & BINDING PATTERN

MAIN SYMPTOMS: Plum pit qi, *i.e.*, discomfort within the throat as if there were something obstructing and blocking the throat which can neither be swallowed down nor spit out, oppression within the chest, possible simultaneous rib-side pain, slimy, white tongue fur, and a bowstring, slippery pulse

ANALYSIS OF SYMPTOMS: If liver depression assails the spleen and the spleen loses its movement and fortification, then dampness will be engendered. If this lingers and endures, it may congeal into phlegm. Phlegm and qi thus become depressed and bound in the chest and above the diaphragm. Therefore, one sees discomfort within the throat as if there were something blocking and obstructing it which can neither be swallowed down nor spit out. This is called plum pit qi because the Chinese liken this sensation to having a plum pit stuck in one's throat. If qi loses its soothing, then there is oppression within the chest. The rib-sides are the place where the liver channel spreads. If the channels and network vessels of the liver become depressed and stagnant, then there is rib-side pain. The slimy, white tongue fur and the bowstring, slippery pulse are symptoms of liver depression mixed with phlegm dampness.

TREATMENT PRINCIPLES: Transform phlegm, disinhibit the qi, and resolve depression

FORMULA & MEDICINALS: *Si Qi Tang* (Four [to] Seven Decoction)

Caulis Perillae Frutescentis (*Su Geng*), 10g, Flos Magnoliae Officinalis (*Chuan Bu Hua*), 5g, Rhizoma Pinelliae Ternatae (*Ban Xia*), 10g, Sclerotium Poriae Cocos (*Fu Ling*), 12g, uncooked Rhizoma Zingiberis (*Sheng Jiang*), 2 slices (added later), Fructus Zizyphi Jujubae (*Da Zao*), 5g

Decoct in water and administer orally in two divided doses, morning and evening, one *ji* per day.

ANALYSIS OF FORMULA: Within this formula, Caulis Perillae rectifies the qi, broadens the chest, and downbears counterflow. Flos Magnoliae likewise rectifies the qi at the same time as it eliminates phlegm and dampness, whereas Pinellia transforms phlegm and dampness while downbearing counterflow. Both are assisted by uncooked Ginger which also transforms phlegm and dampness, moves the qi and downbears counterflow. Poria and Red Dates fortify the spleen and supplement the qi. They are included since the spleen is the source of phlegm engenderment. Poria and Red Dates both also have an ability to quiet the heart.

ADDITIONS & SUBTRACTIONS: For severe qi stagnation, add Radix Bupleuri (*Chai Hu*), Tuber Curcumae (*Yu Jin*), Rhizoma Cyperi Rotundi (*Xiang Fu*), and Pericarpium Citri Reticulatae Viride (*Qing Pi*). For more severe chest oppression, add Tuber Curcumae (*Yu Jin*) and Fructus Citri Aurantii (*Zhi Ke*). For abdominal distention, add Radix Auklandiae Lappae (*Mu Xiang*) and Fructus Amomi (*Sha Ren*).

ACUPUNCTURE: *Tai Chong* (Liv 3), *Feng Long* (St 40), *Zhong Wan* (CV 12), *Nei Guan* (Per 6), *Dan Zhong* (CV 17), *Zu San Li* (St 36). Use even supplementing-even draining technique.

## 5. PHLEGM FIRE OBSTRUCTING THE QI PATTERN

MAIN SYMPTOMS: Insomnia, a heavy, full, stuffy, or tight feeling in the head, profuse phlegm, chest oppression, aversion to food, burping and belching, acid regurgitation, possible nausea, heart vexation, a bitter taste in the mouth, vertigo and dizziness, slimy, yellow tongue fur, and a slippery, rapid, bowstring pulse. In cases of depression, the person will feel both profoundly apathetic and tired yet restless and anxious or may alternate between one and the other.

ANALYSIS OF SYMPTOMS: Basically, this pattern is the same as the one above it except for the addition of heat or fire. The manifestations of this heat are the heart vexation, agitation, and insomnia, the bitter taste in the mouth, the yellow tongue fur, and the rapid pulse.

TREATMENT PRINCIPLES: Transform phlegm and clear heat, harmonize the stomach and quiet the spirit

**FORMULA & MEDICINALS:** *Huang Lian Wen Dan Tang Jia Wei* (Coptis Warm the Gallbladder Decoction with Added Flavors)

Caulis Bambusae In Taeniis (*Zhu Ru*), 6g, Fructus Immaturus Citri Aurantii (*Zhi Shi*), 6g, Rhizoma Pinelliae Ternatae (*Ban Xia*), 10g, Pericarpium Citri Reticulatae (*Chen Pi*), 6-10g, Sclerotium Poriae Cocos (*Fu Ling*), 12g, Tuber Curcumae (*Yu Jin*), 10g, Rhizoma Acori Graminei (*Shi Chang Pu*), 6-10g, Radix Polygalae Tenuifoliae (*Yuan Zhi*), 6-10g, Radix Glycyrrhizae (*Gan Cao*), 3g, uncooked Rhizoma Zingiberis (*Sheng Jiang*), 3-6g (added later), Rhizoma Coptidis Chinensis (*Huang Lian*), 3-6g (added later)

Decoct in water and administer orally in two divided doses, morning and evening, one *ji* per day.

**ANALYSIS OF FORMULA:** Within this formula, Pinellia, Caulis Bambusae, Aurantium, Orange Peel, and uncooked Ginger all transform phlegm and rectify the qi. Caulis Bambusae also clears heat and eliminates vexation, while Coptis clears the heart and drains fire. Curcuma broadens the chest, and Acorus and Polygala open the orifices and quiet the spirit. Licorice harmonizes all the other medicinals in this formula.

**ACUPUNCTURE:** *Feng Long* (St 40), *Dan Zhong* (CV 17), *Zhong Wan* (CV 12), *Jie Xi* (St 41), *Jian Shi* (Per 5). Use draining technique.

## VACUITY PATTERNS

### 1. DEPRESSION CAUSING DETRIMENT TO THE HEART QI PATTERN

**MAIN SYMPTOMS:** Mental-emotional abstraction, restlessness, sorrow and anxiety, a tendency to crying, frequent yawning, a pale tongue with thin, white fur, and a bowstring, fine pulse

**ANALYSIS OF SYMPTOMS:** If anxiety and depression are not resolved, the heart qi is consumed and damaged and the qi and blood become depleted and unable to nourish the heart spirit. Therefore, one sees mental-emotional abstraction, restlessness, and other such symptoms. The pale tongue with thin, white fur and the bowstring, fine pulse are signs of qi depression and blood vacuity.

**TREATMENT PRINCIPLES:** Nourish the heart and supplement the qi, resolve depression and quiet the spirit

**FORMULA & MEDICINALS:** *Ren Shen Gan Mai Fang Jia Wei* (Ginseng, Licorice & Wheat Formula with Added Flavors)

Fructus Tritici Aestivi (*Huai Xiao Mai*), 30g, mix-fried Radix Glycyrrhizae (*Gan Cao*), 10-12g, Sclerotium Poriae Cocos (*Fu Ling*), 12g, Semen Alpiniae Oxypohyllae (*Yi Zhi Ren*), 10g, Rhizoma Acori Graminei (*Shi Chang Pu*), 6-10g, Cortex Albizziae Julibrissinis (*He Huan Hua*), 15g, Caulis Polygoni Multiflori (*Ye Jiao Teng*), 15g

Decoct in water and administer orally in two divided doses, morning and evening, one *ji* per day.

**ANALYSIS OF FORMULA:** Within this formula, Ginseng, Wheat, Poria, Caulis Polygoni, and mix-fried Licorice all nourish the heart and quiet the spirit. Flos Albizziae resolves depression and quiets the spirit, while Acorus opens the orifices of the heart and quiets the spirit. Alpinia Oxyphylla supplements the spleen and kidneys and boosts the intelligence. Fortification of the spleen promotes the lungs' diffusing and downbearing of the qi. Supplementing the kidneys and invigorating yang, promotes the liver's coursing and discharging via ministerial fire's warming and steaming.

**ACUPUNCTURE:** *Shen Men* (Ht 7), *Nei Guan* (Per 6), *Tai Chong* (Liv 3), *Xin Shu* (Bl 15), *Dan Zhong* (CV 17), *Bai Hui* (GV 20). Use even supplementing-even draining technique.

### 2. HEART-SPLEEN DUAL VACUITY PATTERN

**MAIN SYMPTOMS:** Excessive thinking with a tendency to worry, heart palpitations, gallbladder timidity, scanty sleep, impaired memory, a lusterless facial complexion, dizziness, lassitude of the spirit, devitalized eating and drinking, a pale tongue, and a fine, weak pulse. In depressed patients exhibiting this pattern, there is pronounced confusion, lack of concentration, lack of strength in the arms and legs, and severe fatigue.

**ANALYSIS OF SYMPTOMS:** If the heart is taxed by thinking and worry, the heart and spleen may both become vacuous. The heart thus loses its nourishment and, therefore one sees heart palpitations, timidity, scanty sleep, and poor memory. The spleen and stomach are the source of the engenderment and transformation of the qi and blood. If the spleen does not fortify and move, then eating and drinking are diminished and scanty and the source of qi and blood is insufficient. Therefore, one sees a lusterless facial complexion, dizziness, lassitude of the spirit, fatigue, lack of strength, a pale tongue, and a fine, weak pulse.

**TREATMENT PRINCIPLES:** Fortify the spleen and nourish the heart, boost the qi and supplement the blood

**FORMULA & MEDICINALS:** *Gui Pi Tang Jia Jian* (Restore the Spleen Decoction with Additions & Subtractions)

Radix Codonopsitis Pilosulae (*Dang Shen*), 10g, Radix Astragali Membranacei (*Huang Qi*), 10-15g, Rhizoma Atractylodis Macrocephalae (*Bai Zhu*), 10g, Radix Angelicae Sinensis (*Dang Gui*), 10g, Sclerotium Poriae Cocos (*Fu Ling*), 10g, Radix Polygalae Tenuifoliae (*Yuan Zhi*), 4.5g, stir-fried Semen Zizyphi Spinosae (*Suan Zao Ren*), 12g, Radix Auklandiae Lappae (*Mu Xiang*), 6g (added later), Arillus Euphoriae Longanae (*Long Yan Rou*), 10g, mix-fried Radix Glycyrrhizae (*Gan Cao*), 6g

Decoct in water and administer orally in two divided doses, morning and evening, one *ji* per day.

**ANALYSIS OF FORMULA:** Within this formula, Astragalus and Codonopsis greatly supplement the spleen and heart qi. They are assisted in this by Atractylodes, Poria, and mix-fried Licorice. Dang Gui, Longans, and Zizyphus Spinosa all supplement and nourish the blood. Longans supplement the heart and nourish the blood, while Zizyphus Spinosa nourishes the liver and quiets the spirit. Auklandia and Polygala both rectify the qi. In addition, Auklandia harmonizes the liver and spleen, while Polygala also resolves depression, quiets the spirit, and transforms phlegm.

**ADDITIONS & SUBTRACTIONS:** If depression is transforming heat, add Cortex Radicis Moutan (*Dan Pi*) and Fructus Gardeniae Jasminoidis (*Zhi Zi*).

**ACUPUNCTURE:** *Xin Shu* (Bl 15), *Ge Shu* (Bl 17), *Pi Shu* (Bl 20), *Shen Men* (Ht 7), *San Yin Jiao* (Sp 6), *Zu San Li* (St 36). Use supplementing technique.

### 3. SPLEEN-KIDNEY YANG VACUITY PATTERN

**MAIN SYMPTOMS:** Emotional listlessness and depression, a predilection to lie down, little stirring or movement, heart vexation, fright and fear, heart palpitations and loss of sleep, a somber white facial complexion, impotence in men or involuntary seminal emission, clear, watery vaginal discharge in females, decreased or absent libido in both men and women, low back soreness, cold feet, a fat,

pale tongue with possible teeth-marks on its edges and white fur, and a deep, fine pulse

**NOTE:** This pattern does not present in its pure form when associated with depression. However it commonly complicates liver depression and even yin vacuity patterns.

**ANALYSIS OF SYMPTOMS:** If spleen qi vacuity endures or worsens and reaches the kidneys, kidney yang may also become vacuous and insufficient. Therefore, the signs and symptoms of qi vacuity are even more pronounced, such as a predilection to lie down and not move, plus there are symptoms of specifically kidney yang vacuity, such as lack of libido, low back soreness, and cold feet. Many women exhibit this pattern as they enter their perimenopausal years.

**TREATMENT PRINCIPLES:** Warm the kidneys and fortify the spleen, invigorate yang and boost the qi

**FORMULA & MEDICINALS:** *Ji Sheng Shen Qi Wan Jia Wei* (Aid The Living Kidney Qi Pills with Added Flavors)

Radix Astragali Membranacei (*Huang Qi*), 10-15g, Radix Codonopsitis Pilosulae (*Dang Shen*), 10g, Rhizoma Atractylodis Macrocephalae (*Bai Zhu*), 10g, Sclerotium Poriae Cocos (*Fu Ling*), 12g, cooked Radix Rehmanniae (*Shu Di*), 12-15g, Radix Dioscoreae Oppositae (*Shan Yao*), 10g, Fructus Corni Officinalis (*Shan Zhu Yu*), 10g, Rhizoma Alismatis (*Ze Xie*), 6g, Cortex Radicis Moutan (*Dan Pi*), 6-10g, Cortex Cinnamomi Cassiae (*Rou Gui*), 6g, Radix Lateralis Praeparatus Aconiti Carmichaeli (*Fu Zi*), 3-6g

Decoct in water and administer orally in two divided doses, morning and evening, one *ji* per day.

**ANALYSIS OF FORMULA:** Within this formula, Astragalus, Codonopsis, Atractylodes, Dioscorea, and Poria all fortify the spleen and boost the qi. In addition, Dioscorea also supplements the kidneys. Cornus and Rehmannia both supplement the kidneys. Rehmannia enriches kidney yin, while Cornus supplements kidney qi. Since yin and yang are mutually rooted, when supplementing yang it is also appropriate to supplement yin and vice versa. This is referred to as seeking yang within yin. Alisma combined with Poria seeps dampness and prevents upward flaring of fire effulgence, while Moutan quickens the blood and transforms stasis. Most chronic, enduring diseases are complicated by an element of blood stasis. Cinnamon and Aconite warm yang and invigorate the kidneys.

ADDITIONS & SUBTRACTIONS: If there is marked qi depression, add Fructus Meliae Toosendan (*Chuan Lian Zi*) and Radix Auklandiae Lappae (*Mu Xiang*). If there effulgent fire flaring above, add Rhizoma Anemarrhenae Aspheloidis (*Zhi Mu*) and Cortex Phellodendri (*Huang Bai*).

ACUPUNCTURE: Moxa *Pi Shu* (Bl 20), *Ming Men* (GV 4), *Shen Shu* (Bl 23), *Shen Que* (CV 8), *Guan Yuan* (CV 4), and/or *Zu San Li* (St 36).

## 4. YIN VACUITY-FIRE EFFULGENCE PATTERN

MAIN SYMPTOMS: Vertigo and dizziness, heart palpitations, insomnia, profuse dreams, heart vexation, heat in the five hearts, easy anger, possible involuntary seminal emission in men, low back soreness, menstrual irregularities in women, aversion to people, possible suicidal thoughts, a dry mouth and throat, a red tongue, and a bowstring, fine, and rapid pulse. In patients with depression, there is lots of anxiety, vexation and agitation, and restlessness.

ANALYSIS OF SYMPTOMS: If kidney yin is insufficient and the blood and body fluids are consumed by heat, depleted yin may not be able to control yang and hence yang floats upward. Therefore, one may see vertigo, dizziness, and easy anger. If there is yin and blood depletion and consumption, then the heart spirit loses its nourishment. In addition, yin vacuity gives rise to heat, and vacuity heat harasses the spirit. Therefore, there are heart palpitations, scanty sleep, and vexation and agitation. If kidney yin is insufficient, then the low back mansion loses its nourishment and thus there is low back soreness. Because there is yin vacuity with fire effulgence, effulgent fire harasses and stirs the essence chamber. Hence the essence is not secured and there is seminal emission. If the liver and kidneys lose their nourishment, the *chong* and *ren* will be unregulated. Therefore, there are menstrual irregularities. The red tongue and bowstring, fine, rapid pulse are both signs of yin vacuity.

TREATMENT PRINCIPLES: Enrich yin and clear heat, settle the heart and quiet the spirit

FORMULA & MEDICINALS: *Zi Shui Qing Gan Yin* (Enrich Water & Clear the Liver Drink)

Uncooked Radix Rehmanniae (*Sheng Di*), 12g, Fructus Corni Officinalis (*Shan Zhu Yu*), 10g, Sclerotium Poriae Cocos (*Fu Ling*), 12g, Radix Angelicae Sinensis (*Dang Gui*), 10g, Radix Dioscoreae Oppositae (*Shan Yao*), 10g, Cortex Radicis Moutan (*Dan Pi*), 6-10g, Rhizoma Alismatis (*Ze Xie*), 6-10g, Radix Albus Paeoniae Lactiflorae (*Bai Shao*), 10g, Radix Bupleuri (*Chai Hu*), 1.5-3g, stir-fried Fructus Gardeniae Jasminoidis (*Zhi Zi*), 10g, Fructus Zizyphi Jujubae (*Da Zao*), 5g

Decoct in water and administer orally in two divided doses, morning and evening, one *ji* per day.

ANALYSIS OF FORMULA: Cooked Rehmannia, Dang Gui, and White Peony all nourish liver blood, while Rehmannia also supplements and enriches the kidneys. Cornus supplements the kidney qi, and Dioscorea supplements both the spleen and kidneys. Poria aids in the fortification of the spleen at the same time as it also works with Alisma to percolate dampness. Moutan both quickens and cools the blood, preventing upward flaring of effulgent fire. A small amount of Bupleurum is used to course the liver and rectify the qi, remembering that, in depression, it is enduring depressive heat that commonly consumes yin blood and causes fire effulgence. This is also why Gardenia is in this formula. It clears heat and resolves depression. Red Dates harmonize all the other medicinals in this formula as well as quiet the spirit.

ACUPUNCTURE: *Tai Xi* (Ki 3), *Zhao Hai* (Ki 6), *San Yin Jiao* (Sp 6), *Shen Men* (Ht 7), *Nei Guan* (Per 6), *Bai Hui* (GV 20), *Feng Chi* (GB 20), *Yin Tang* (M-HN-3). Use even supplementing-even draining technique.

CLINICAL TIPS: The most common pattern of unipolar depression among Western patients is liver depression and spleen vacuity with depressive heat. This may then be complicated by more serious qi or blood and, therefore, even yin or yang vacuity or by phlegm turbidity or phlegm heat.

## ABSTRACTS OF REPRESENTATIVE WESTERN RESEARCH:

*Journal of Psychological Science*, #5, 1998, p. 397-401: Allen, B. and Schnyer, R.N. studied the effects of acupuncture on 38 women, aged 18-45, suffering from depression. Those women who met the criteria for the study received a SCID interview (Structural Clinical Interview) conducted by qualified psychologists. A traditional Chinese medical diagnosis was then conducted by an acupuncturist to determine their Chinese pattern discrimination, treatment principles, and acupuncture treatment plan. These treatments were designed by the assessing acupuncturist but were administered by four other acupuncturists. Neither the assessing acupuncturist nor the treating acupuncturists knew which treatment group the patient was in.

Participants were assigned to one of three groups: specific, non-specific, and wait-list. Patients assigned to the specific group each received acupuncture treatment specifically to treat depression. Patients assigned to the nonspecific group received treatment for their Chinese pattern of disharmony but which did not address depression directly. Patients assigned to the wait-list group waited before receiving specific treatment. All treatments were tailored to the individual and were based on Chinese medical pattern discrimination.

The specific group received eight weeks of specific treatment. The nonspecific group received eight weeks of nonspecific treatment and then eight weeks of specific treatment. While the wait-list group waited eight weeks and then received eight weeks of specific treatment. Each eight week segment consisted of 12 sessions: two sessions per week for four weeks; then one session per week for four more weeks. By the end of this study, all participants had received specific treatment to address their pattern of disharmony as it related to their depression.

In addition to the SCID interview at the beginning of the study, participants were also administered the Hamilton Rating Scale for Depression (HRSD) before treatment began and again after four and eight weeks in the specific treatment group and, in addition, after 12 and 16 weeks in the nonspecific and wait-list treatment groups. Patients also filled out self-report forms. Alliance to the therapist and resistance to treatment were also measured.

After completion of the specific treatment, using the DSM-IV remission criteria, 64% of the women experienced full remission, 18% of the women experienced partial remission, and 18% experienced no remission. Using the Hamilton Rating Scale as the criterion for remission, 70% of all women experienced remission, while 30% did not. These results compare favorably to both psychotherapy and pharmacotherapy whose effectiveness falls between 65-70%. Specific acupuncture treatment produced a significant reduction of symptoms over time and it demonstrated greater reduction in symptoms over eight weeks than the nonspecific group. However, it did not demonstrate a significantly greater reduction than the wait-list group. These preliminary findings suggest that acupuncture is as effective as pharmacotherapy or psychotherapy as a treatment for depression.

❖

*American Journal of Chinese Medicine*, #3, 1976, p. 289-292: Kurland, H. D. conducted a three year study comparing electroconvulsive therapy (ECT) with acupuncture treatment in functional psychoses. Acupuncture effects were augmented by the simultaneous, non-painful electrical stimulation of eight acupuncture needles. The resulting treatment is called Acupuncture Electric Stimulation Therapy (Acu-EST). Each patient was utilized as her own control, treating exacerbations of depression alternately with ECT and Acu-EST. Acu-EST was not found to be a panacea and did not enable the discontinuation of antidepressant and neuroleptic medication. Individual Acu-EST treatments were often less effective than individual ECT treatments. However, series of Acu-EST did assist in producing significant remissions in depressive symptomatology. Because it did not produce the temporary disabling memory defects which occurred with ECT, Acu-EST was more easily adaptable to outpatient treatment.

*Zh. Nevropatologie & Psikhiatrie Im S. S. Korsakova (Journal of Neuropathology & Psychiatry...)*, #12, 1983, p. 1853-1855: Kochetkov, V.D., Mikhailova, A.A., and Dallakian, I.G. treated 41 neurotic patients with pronounced depressive-hypochondriac symptomatology with acupuncture. A decrease in the psycho-emotional and algetic symptoms (sleep restoration, increased working capacity) following acupuncture was attended by certain changes in the nocturnal and diurnal EEG with the prevailing activation of the synchronizing mechanisms of nonspecific brain systems which suggests that the structures of the thalamocortical and nonspecific cerebral level are involved in the realization of the acupuncture therapeutic effect and that it is advisable to activate the synchronizing cerebral mechanisms.

*Zh. Nevropatologie & Psikhiatrie Im S. S. Korsakova (Journal of Neuropathology & Psychiatry...)*, #4, 1987, p. 604_608: Poliakov, S.E. treated 167 patients with depression associated with manic-depressive psychosis and schizophrenia with acupuncture. This study established that, as judged by the characteristics of psychotropic activity and potency of acupuncture's anti-depressive action, this mode of treatment most resembles the administration of balanced antidepressants of the pyrasidol type. Acupuncture was found to be effective in some patients showing resistance to antidepressants. The paper presents the results of psychological, biochemical, and electrophysiologic examinations of patients in the process of the treatment.

❖

*Nervenarzt (Neurology)*, #11, 1998, p. 961-967: Roschke, J., Wolf, C., Kogel, P., Wagner, P., and Bech, S. studied the comparative treatment of depression in 70 patients with acupuncture and mianserin drug therapy. These 70 inpatients were divided into three different treatment groups. All patients were pharmacologically treated with the tetracyclic antidepressant mianserin. The verum group (n = 22) received acupuncture at specific points considered to be effective in the treatment of depression. The placebo group (n = 24) was treated with acupuncture at nonspecific locations, and the control group (n = 24) received only pharmacological treatment. Acupuncture was applied three times a week over a period of four weeks. Psychopathology was rated by judges blind to verum/placebo conditions twice a week over eight weeks with the CGI, GAS, BRMS, and BfS rating scales. Additionally applied acupuncture improved the course of depression more than pharmacological treatment with mianserin did by itself.

### ABSTRACTS OF REPRESENTATIVE CHINESE RESEARCH:

*Journal of Traditional Chinese Medicine*, #5, 1985, p. 3-8: Luo H., Jia Y., and Zhan L. treated 47 patients diagnosed with clinical depression with a mean duration of 5-6 months. Patients were randomly assigned to treatment groups receiving either acupuncture or Western medication. Acupuncture patients received electrical stimulation for one hour per day (except Sundays) for five weeks via needles inserted at two points, one on the scalp and one on the forehead. Patients in the Western medication group all took the same dosage of amitriptyline three times a day for five weeks. Each patient was tested weekly using standard psychiatric rating scales. The severity of depression at onset was statistically similar for both groups. In addition, patients were interviewed by two psychiatrists at the onset and at completion of treatment to independently assess treatment outcomes. After five weeks of treatment, 70% of the acupuncture treatment group were judged either cured or markedly improved, while only 65% of the medication group were judged cured or markedly improved. In addition, the Clinical Global Impression (CGI) index found significantly fewer side effects in the acupuncture group.

*Journal of Traditional Chinese Medicine*, #14, 1994, p. 14-18: Yang X., Liu H., Luo H., and Jia Y. compared the effects of acupuncture and electroacupuncture to antidepressant medication for the treatment of clinical depression. There were 41 patients in this study who had all been diagnosed with either unipolar depression or bipolar affective disorder with disease courses lasting from four months to five years. These patients were randomly assigned to receive either acupuncture or amitriptyline. Patients in the acupuncture group received a common set of eight points based on pattern discrimination. Electrical stimulation was applied to four of these common points per treatment. Treatment was given six times per week for six weeks. The medication group began their doses of amitriptyline at 25mg per day and reached a maximum of 300mg by the end of the six weeks. Dose regimens were individualized based on efficacy and side effects. Measured by the Hamilton Rating Scale, factors of anxiety somatization, cognitive disturbance, retardation, sleep disturbance, and feelings of despair in both the acupuncture and control groups showed obvious decrease in mean values, and the change in anxiety somatization was markedly significant in the acupuncture group as compared to that in the control group (P < 0.01). After six weeks of acupuncture, the power of slow wave delta significantly decreased, while that of the fast wave alpha significantly increased as compared to before and during treatment (P < 0.05).

*Psychiatry & Clinical Neuroscience*, #12, 1998, p. 338-340: Luo H., Meng F., Jia Y., and Zhao X. found that electroacupuncture treatment is as effective as amitriptyline for patients with depression. In this study, two consecutive clinical studies on the treatment of depression with electroacupuncture were conducted. The first study was double-blind, placebo-controlled in which 29 depressed inpatients were recruited. Patients were randomly divided into three groups: electroacupuncture plus placebo; amitriptyline; and electroacupuncture plus amitriptyline. All patients received electroacupuncture and/or amitriptyline treatment for six weeks. The Hamilton Rating Scale for Depression, Clinical Global Impression (CGI) index, and ASBERG scales for the side effects of antidepressants were used to evaluate the therapeutic efficacy and side effects. Based on the results and research protocol of the first study, a multi_centered collaborative study was conducted in which 241 inpatients with depression were recruited. Patients were randomly divided into two treatment groups: the electroacupuncture plus placebo and the amitriptyline groups. The results from both studies showed that the therapeutic efficacy of electroacupuncture was equal to that of amitriptyline for depressive disorders (P > 0.05). In addition, electroacupuncture got a better therapeutic effect for anxiety somatization and for cognitive process disturbance of depressed patients than did amitriptyline (P < 0.05). Moreover, the side effects of electroacupuncture were much less than that of amitriptyline (P < 0.001).

*Shang Hai Zhong Yi Yao Za Zhi (Shanghai Journal of Chinese Medicine & Medicinals), #2, 1994, 14-16:* Han Zhong-bo discusses the treatment of depression using internally administered Chinese medicinals based on pattern discrimination. Of the 58 patients in this study, 25 were male and 33 were female. They ranged in age from 20-65 years old, with a median age of 40. All had been diagnosed with clinical depression based on the criteria in *Zhong Guo Jing Shen Yi Bing Fen Lei Yu Zhen Duan Biao Zhun (Chinese National Criteria for the Division of Types & Diagnosis of Psychiatric Diseases, i.e., CCMD-II).* Four patterns were used to divide this cohort: 1) liver-kidney insufficiency pattern (17 cases), 2) spleen vacuity with liver depression pattern (22 cases), 3) yin vacuity with internal dryness pattern (10 cases), and 4) qi stagnation-blood stasis pattern (9 cases). In addition, if there was recalcitrant insomnia small amounts of either of three Western sedatives were given via intramuscular injection. If blood pressure was high, antihypertensive medications were administered. Patients were assessed at two, four, and eight week intervals. Using this protocol, 21 patients were either judged cured or markedly improved, 28 patients got some result, and nine patients experienced no effect. Thus the total amelioration rate was 84%. Of the four patterns, those in the qi stagnation-blood stasis group got the highest rate of cure or marked improvement (56%). The liver-kidney insufficiency group registered a 35% cure or marked improvement rate, the spleen vacuity-liver depression group registered a 27% cure or marked improvement rate, and the yin vacuity with internal dryness group registered a 40% cure or marked improvement rate.

*Shang Hai Zhong Yi Yao Za Zhi (Shanghai Journal of Chinese Medicine & Medicinals), #5, 1999, p. 20-22:* Jiang You-qian treated 26 cases of clinical depression using Chinese medicinals administered on the basis of pattern discrimination. Of these 26 patients, 17 were male and nine were female. The oldest was 73 years old and the youngest was 16. Their disease course had lasted from 4-9 months. Diagnostic criteria were based on *CCMD-2.* The SDS rating of depression for these patients was $41.88 \pm 10.5$. The four patterns used in this study were: 1) liver depression qi stagnation pattern (8 cases), 2) liver depression with phlegm heat pattern (4 cases), 3) heart-spleen dual vacuity pattern (9 cases), and 4) heart-kidneys not interacting pattern (5 cases). Chinese medicinal treatment was combined with psychotherapy but not with Western antidepressant drugs. Four weeks equaled one course of treatment, and two courses of treatment were given. During this time, patients were evaluated once every two weeks. Using this protocol, 13 patients were judged to have gotten a marked effect, nine patients got some effect, and four patients got no effect. Of the four patterns, those with liver depression qi stagnation got the highest rate of effectiveness, while those with heart-kidneys not interacting got the highest rate of ineffectiveness.

*Shang Hai Zhong Yi Yao Za Zhi (Shanghai Journal of Chinese Medicine & Medicinals), #11, 1999, p. 23:* Ni Ai-ti and Wu Li-ying treated 100 women with postmastectomy depression using internally administered Chinese medicinals on the basis of pattern discrimination. These women were selected out of a larger group of 370 women who had undergone mastectomies for the treatment of breast cancer between 1994-1998. The three patterns used were: 1) liver depression qi stagnation pattern (40 cases), 2) liver depression transforming fire pattern (30 cases), and 3) chong and ren loss of regulation pattern (30 cases). Pattern discrimination and diagnostic criteria were based on the Shanghai Municipal Department of Health's *Zhong Yi Bing Zheng Zhen Liao Chang Gui (Standards of Chinese Medical Disease & Pattern Diagnosis & Treatment).* Using this protocol, five women were cured, 32 improved, and three got no result in the liver depression qi stagnation group (92.5% total effectiveness). Five women were cured, 21 improved, and four got no result in the liver depression transforming fire group (86.7% total effectiveness), and 14 women were cured, 13 improved, and three got no result in the chong and ren loss of regulation group (90.0% total effectiveness). On follow-up after four years, five of these women had died, two had suffered metastasis, and the other 93 women's physical condition and quality of life were considered quite good.

❖

*Zhe Jiang Zhong Yi Za Zhi (Zhejiang Journal of Chinese Medicine), #3, 1996, p. 131:* Yang Dan-hong and Feng Li-ping treated 34 cases of menopausal depression with a combination of scalp and body acupuncture. All these women had previously been treated with Chinese and/or Western medicines without effect. These women ranged in age from 41-54 years old, and the course of their disease had lasted from as short as one month to as long as five years. Scalp acupuncture locations included the middle crown line, the middle forehead line, and side of the forehead lines 1, 2, and 3. Body acupuncture was based on three different patterns: 1) ascendant liver yang hyperactivity pattern (16 cases), 2) heart-kidneys not interacting pattern (11 cases), and 3) phlegm qi depression and binding pattern (7 cases). The first pattern group was needled bilaterally at *Gan Shu* (Bl 18), *Jian Shi* (Per 5), *Xing Jian* (Liv 2), and *Zhi Gou* (TB 6). The second pattern group was needled at *Xin Shu* (Bl 15), *Shen Shu* (Bl 23), *Shen Men* (Ht 7), and *Tai Xi* (Ki 3), and the third pattern group was needled at *Zhong Wan* (CV 12) and *Dan Zhong* (CV 17) on the midline and at *Feng Long* (St 40) and *Zu San Li* (St 36) bilaterally. Patients were needled once every other day, with 10 treatments equaling one course of treatment. Using this protocol, 17 patients were cured, nine experienced a marked effect, four improved, and four got no result. Thus the total amelioration rate was 88.2%.

❖

*Tian Jin Zhong Yi (Tianjin Chinese Medicine)*, #3, 1996, p. 11: Lin Hong treated a total of 90 patients for postpartum depression using either regular or electroacupuncture. The oldest woman in this study was 34 years old and the youngest was 20. The shortest course of disease was two days and the longest was two months. All the women were diagnosed as being clinically depressed according to the criteria set forth in *ICD-10*. Thirty-eight cases experienced the onset of this condition within one week postpartum, and the other 77 experienced its onset within four weeks postpartum. Fifty-three of these women received electroacupuncture, while the other 37 received regular or "fine needle" acupuncture. Both the regular acupuncture and the electroacupuncture groups received the same set of points: *Shen Men* (Ht 7), *Ben Shen* (GB 13), *Xin Shu* (Bl 15), *Shen Dao* (GV 11), and *Hou Xi* (SI 3). Treatment was given every day, with five treatments equaling one course of treatment. In the electroacupuncture group, 22 cases got a marked effect, 16 got a moderate effect, nine got some effect, and six got no effect for a total amelioration rate of 88.68%. In the regular acupuncture group, nine got a marked effect, seven got a moderate effect, eight got some effect, and 13 got no effect for a total amelioration rate of 64.87%. Thus there was a statistically significant difference in effectiveness between these two groups (P<0.05).

❖

*Si Chuan Zhong Yi (Sichuan Chinese Medicine)*, #2, 1999, p. 25: Xu Chao-gang reported on the Chinese medicinal treatment of 40 cases of post-stroke depression. Twenty-two of these patients were male and 18 were female. These patients ranged in age from 40-72 years old, with a median age of 57 years. Twenty-seven cases had cerebral infarction and 13 had cerebral hemorrhage. Thirty-two suffered from complete paralysis, while eight were only partially paralyzed. The Chinese medicinal formula administered to these patients consisted of: uncooked Radix Rehmanniae (*Sheng Di*), Radix Angelicae Sinensis (*Dang Gui*), Tuber Ophiopogonis Japonici (*Mai Dong*), and Radix Bupleuri (*Chai Hu*), 12g each, Radix Dioscoreae Oppositae (*Shan Yao*), stir-fried Semen Zizyphi Spinosae (*Suan Zao Ren*), Cortex Eucommiae Ulmoidis (*Du Zhong*), and Radix Achyranthis Bidentatae (*Niu Xi*), 15g each, calcined Os Draconis (*Long Gu*), 30g, Radix Polygalae Tenuifoliae (*Yuan Zhi*), Rhizoma Acori Graminei (*Shi Chang Pu*), Radix Albus Paeoniae Lactiflorae (*Bai Shao*), and Herba Leonuri Heterophylli (*Yi Mu Cao*), 10g each, and Radix Salviae Miltiorrhizae (*Dan Shen*), 20g. If the stools were dry, 20 grams of Herba Cistanchis Deserticolae (*Rou Cong Rong*) were added. If there was indigestion and torpid intake, 10 grams of Fructus Crataegi (*Shan Zha*) and nine grams of Fructus Citri Aurantii (*Zhi Ke*) were added. If there was insomnia and night-time fright, 20 grams of Caulis Polygoni Multiflori (*Ye Jiao Teng*) were added. One *ji* was administered per day along with psychological counseling. Using this protocol for 7-20 days and based on the 1995 *Zhong Yi Bing Zheng Zhen Duan Liao Xiao Biao Zhun (Chinese Medical Disease & Pattern Diagnosis & Treatment Effectiveness Criteria)*, 33 cases were judged cured, four were improved, and three got no result. Thus the total amelioration rate was 93%.

❖

*The Journal of Chinese Medicine*, #6, 2000, p. 56-57: Wu Jin-rong *et al.* reported on the treatment of 40 cases of depression with modified *Wen Dan Tang* (Warm the Gallbladder Decoction). Of these 40 cases, there were 13 cases of liver depression qi stagnation, 18 cases of phlegm qi depression and binding, six of heart-spleen dual vacuity, and three of yin vacuity fire effulgence. The formula administered consisted of: Pericarpium Citri Reticulatae (*Chen Pi*), 15g, Rhizoma Pinelliae Ternatae (*Ban Xia*), 10g, Sclerotium Poriae Cocos (*Fu Ling*), 15g, Caulis Bambusae In Taeniis (*Zhu Ru*), 15g, Fructus Immaturus Citri Aurantii (*Zhi Shi*), 10g, and Tuber Curcumae (*Yu Jin*), 12g. If there was severe qi vacuity, Radix Astragali Membranacei (*Huang Qi*), 20g, and Radix Codonopsitis Pilosulae (*Dang Shen*), 15g, were added. If there was severe blood stasis, Radix Salviae Miltiorrhizae (*Dan Shen*), 20g, and Radix Ligustici Wallichii (*Chuan Xiong*), 15g, were added. If there was severe insomnia, Semen Biotae Orientalis (*Bai Zi Ren*), 15g, Cortex Albizziae Julibrissinis (*He Huan Pi*), 10g, and Radix Polygalae Tenuifoliae (*Yuan Zhi*), 6g, were added. For more marked qi stagnation, Radix Bupleuri (*Chai Hu*), 15g, and Rhizoma Cyperi Rotundi (*Xiang Fu*), 10g, were added. For torpid intake, scorched Fructus Crataegi (*Shan Zha*), Fructus Germinatus Hordei Vulgaris (*Mai Ya*), and Massa Medica Fermentata (*Shen Qu*), 10g each, and Fructus Amomi (*Sha Ren*), 6g, were added. For constipation, Herba Cistanchis Deserticolae (*Rou Cong Rong*), 20g, and Radix Et Rhizoma Rhei (*Da Huang*), 6g, were added. One *ji* of these medicinals was administered per day, with 15 days equaling one course of treatment and 2-3 such courses given. After this treatment, 19 cases were cured, 16 improved, and five got no effect, for a total amelioration rate of 87.5%.

Heiner Fruehauf, in *The Journal of Chinese Medicine*, UK, #48, 1995, p. 24, reported on the treatment of 35 cases of depression with *Chai Hu Jia Long Gu Mu Li Tang* (Bupleurum Plus Dragon Bone & Oyster Shell Decoction). Of these 35 cases, 15 were reported cured, 10 were markedly improved, nine improved, and one showed no result. Thus the total amelioration rate using this protocol was 97.1%. This study first appeared in Chinese in *Shan Dong Zhong Yi Za Zhi (Shandong Journal of Chinese Medicine)*, #3, 1984.

In another study reported on by Fruehauf (p. 24), 54 cases of depression were also treated with *Chai Hu Jia Long Gu Mu Li Tang*. In that study, 32 patients were judged cured, 19 improved, and three got no result. Thus the total amelioration rate was 94.4%. This study first appeared in Chinese in *Liao Ning Zhong Yi Za Zhi (Liaoning Journal of Chinese Medicine)*, #12, 1984.

## REPRESENTATIVE CASE HISTORIES:

### ❖ CASE 1[3] ❖

The patient was a 43 year old female who was first examined on Mar. 25, 1974. The patient complained that she thought too much and worried too much and was exceedingly depressed. In the last half year, her emotions had been bitter and oppressed. Her speech had suddenly become inhibited, and she pronounced her words unclearly. She felt as if the root of her tongue was stiff and the tongue tip had shortened and withdrawn toward the root. There was chest area suffocation and oppression, no taste for food or drink, and epigastric and abdominal distention and fullness after eating. She had not been able to work for the past half year. Her essence spirit was listless and devitalized, and her sleep was poor with profuse dreams. Her two excretions and her menses were normal. She had been examined at an unnamed hospital and diagnosed as

neurotic. Previous Western medical treatment had been ineffective. Her facial complexion was yellow and her body was emaciated. Her tongue fur was thin, white, and slightly dry. Her pulse was deep, fine, and bowstring. Therefore, her pattern was discriminated as liver depression qi stagnation with spleen-stomach disharmony. The treatment principles were to soothe the liver and resolve depression, fortify the spleen and harmonize the stomach. The formula used was Old Ten Needles Formula, *i.e.*, *Zhong Wan* (CV 12), *Qi Hai* (CV 6), *Tian Shu* (St 25), *Nei Guan* (Per 6), *Zhang Men* (Liv 13), *Zu San Li* (St 36), plus *Lian Quan* (CV 23), with draining technique.

After six treatments with the above formula, the patient's speech was somewhat more flowing and uninhibited than before. Her abdominal distention, suffocation, and oppression had gradually lessened, and her sleep was somewhat better. However, lying down to sleep at night, she still had profuse dreams, and sometimes there were nightmares and fright arousal (*i.e.*, waking in a startle). Therefore, Dr. Wang changed to Five Viscera Transports Plus *Ge Shu* Formula, *i.e.*, *Fei Shu*, Bl 13, *Xin Shu*, Bl 15, *Ge Shu*, Bl 17, *Gan Shu*, Bl 18, *Pi Shu*, Bl 20, and *Shen Shu*, Bl 23. These were needled three times each week for two weeks. After these treatments. The patient's essence spirit was improved, and her speech was even more flowing and uninhibited. Her tongue body still felt hard, but most of the symptoms basically disappeared. Thus points were chosen as before, and the two formulas were used alternately three times each week.

At her May 25 examination, the patient reported that each night she was able to sleep for eight hours. Her chest oppression had already greatly decreased. She was hungry and felt like eating. After eating, her abdominal distention was also reduced. Therefore, treatment was continued with the original formula. At her Jun. 21 examination, the patient reported that all her symptoms had basically disappeared. Hence treatment was stopped. On follow-up a half year later, there had been no recurrence.

### ❖ CASE 2[4] ❖

The patient was a 40 year old female who was first examined on Apr. 4, 1979. The patient had had chest and ribside distention and oppression for half a year. This was due to her comrades speaking out of the corners of their mouths (*i.e.*, gossiping). This resulted in habitual suffocation and oppression within her chest. She had been administered *Shu Gan Wan* (Soothe the Liver Pills) without seeing any change for the better. In fact, her situation worsened day by day. Her stomach and epigastrium reaching over to both lateral costal regions were distended. Her upper back felt sore and heavy. She had no desire to eat and could not go to sleep easily. She was not able to lie down, and prolonged sitting led to heart vexation and chaotic thoughts. Her whole body lacked strength. She was dizzy and her stools were dry, but her urination was normal. There was a slight degree of lower leg edema, her body was fat, and her tongue fur was white and slimy. In the center, it was slightly yellow. The tongue proper was crimson. The pulse was deep and slippery. Therefore, the pattern discrimination was liver loss of orderly reaching, wood depression, and earth congestion, and the treatment principles were to soothe the liver and fortify the spleen, loosen the chest and rectify the qi. The formula consisted of *Shang Wan* (CV 13), *Zhong Wan* (CV 12), *Xia Wan* (CV 10), *Qi Hai* (CV 6), *Tian Shu* (St 25), *Nei Guan* (Per 6), and *Zu San Li* (St 36). These points were needled one time every other day with draining technique.

After three treatments, the chest region suffocation and oppression were decreased. The lateral costal region was still distended, and the sleep was still not good. Therefore, the treatment plan was changed to include two formulas: Five Viscera Transports Plus *Ge Shu* and Old Ten Needles Formula (*i.e.*, the Three Wan, *Tian Shu*, *Nei Guan*, and *Zu San Li*). These two groups of formulas were used alternately. Each formula was needled continuously two times. After needling for one month, the patient's chest and abdominal suffocation and oppression had already been eliminated, and her rib-side distention had disappeared. Eating and sleeping were both good. However, when she became taxed, there was dizziness and heart vexation. Therefore, the previous formulas plus *Bai Hui* (GV 20), *Dan Zhong* (CV 17), and *Feng Chi* (GB 20) were continued for six more times. By then, all the symptoms were eliminated.

### ❖ CASE 3[5] ❖

This patient was a 50 year old female who was first examined on Sept. 14, 1963. The patient had suffered from heart palpitations and insomnia for half a year. In March of 1962, the patient had been worried and anxious plus she had overtaxed herself to an excessive degree. This resulted in heart palpitations, shortness of breath, insomnia, and impaired memory. Chinese medicinals had been administered without marked effect. Recently, she had felt dizziness and distention of the head. In addition, there was reduced eating and drinking, dry stools, normal urination, a blackish, lusterless facial complexion, and an emaciated body. Her tongue proper was pale with a red tip. Her speech was without force, and her pulse was deep and

relaxed (*i.e.*, slightly slow). Her pattern was discriminated as excessive thought and worry damaging both the heart and spleen, and the treatment principles were to supplement and boost the qi and blood, nourish the heart and quiet the spirit. Two formulas were used to accomplish these ends: 1) *Shen Men* (Ht 7), *Nei Guan* (Per 6), *Zhong Wan* (CV 12), *Qi Hai* (CV 6), *Zhang Men* (Liv 13), *Zu San Li* (St 36), *San Yin Jiao* (Sp 6), and 2) Five Viscera Transports Plus *Ge Shu* Formula. These two formulas were used alternately, three times each week with supplementing technique.

After 12 treatments, the patient's sleep, heart palpitations, and shortness of breath were all greatly improved. Therefore, the above treatment methods were continued for one month, after which her symptoms were all eliminated.

### ❖ CASE 4[6] ❖

The patient was an 11 year old male who was first examined on Nov. 9, 1991. During the last half year, each day when the boy returned from school he spent great amounts of energy studying and concentrating until he eventually became obsessed with his schoolwork and never went out to play. Over time, the boy became psychologically tense and unable to endure vexation. This continued to the point where he became melancholic and sorrowful, giving out great sighs. Eventually this turned into incessant crying. Occasionally, the boy muttered and spoke to himself. In addition, there was headache and dread of chill. The boy's mind was clear with appropriate responses. His tongue was pale red with thin, white fur, and his pulse was bowstring and forceful.

Dr. Zeng diagnosed the boy as suffering from depression and categorized his pattern as unsoothed depression and anger resulting in heart spirit loss of normalcy. Therefore, the treatment principles were to course the liver and resolve depression, nourish the heart and quiet the spirit. Accordingly, Dr. Zeng performed acupuncture bilaterally at *Xing Jian* (Liv 2) and *Shen Men* (Ht 7), using draining method at *Xing Jian* and even supplementing-even draining method at *Shen Men*. After obtaining the qi, the boy began to cry. The needles were retained for 20 minutes, after which the crying ceased. After another 10 minutes, all the patient's symptoms disappeared as if he were a normal person. On follow-up three years later, there had been no recurrence.

### ❖ CASE 5[7] ❖

The patient was a 27 year old, married female worker who

entered the hospital on Jan. 7, 1984 complaining of heart vexation, insomnia, depression, and melancholy which had gotten bad in the last three months. The patient's personality was introverted and she tended to speak inappropriately. She was taciturn and answered questions scantily. In the fall of 1982, she had begun to experience chest and rib-side fullness and oppression, emotional lability, insomnia, and profuse dreams. Eventually she had become depressed and did not desire to see people. She cried frequently and sighed a lot. Previous treatment had been ineffective. The patient's facial complexion was faintly red. There was a bitter taste in her mouth and dry throat. In addition, she experienced headaches, dizziness, and tinnitus. Her stools were constipated, and her urine was reddish yellow. Her tongue was red with yellow fur, and her pulse was bowstring and rapid.

Based on the above signs and symptoms, the authors categorized this patient's pattern as enduring liver depression transforming into heat. The treatment principles were to course the liver and resolve depression, drain fire and quiet the spirit. Therefore, they prescribed *Chai Hu Qing Gan Tang* (Bupleurum Clear the Liver Decoction): Radix Bupleuri (*Chai Hu*), 10g, uncooked Radix Rehmanniae (*Sheng Di*), 12g, Radix Angelicae Sinensis (*Dang Gui*), 12g, Radix Rubrus Paeoniae Lactiflorae (*Chi Shao*), 9g, Radix Ligustici Wallichii (*Chuan Xiong*), 9g, Fructus Forsythiae Suspensae (*Lian Qiao*), 10g, Fructus Arctii Lappae (*Niu Bang Zi*), 10g, Radix Scutellariae Baicalensis (*Huang Qin*), 10g, Fructus Gardeniae Jasminoidis (*Zhi Zi*), 12g, Radix Trichosanthis Kirlowii (*Tian Hua Fen*), 10g, Radix Stephaniae Tetrandrae (*Fang Ji*), 9g, and Radix Glycyrrhizae (*Gan Cao*), 6g.

After taking 10 *ji* of the above formula, there was no obvious effect. The patient had not defecated for four days and she had no thought for food or drink. Therefore, 10 grams each of Radix Et Rhizoma Rhei (*Da Huang*) and Mirabilitum (*Mang Xiao*) were added to the above formula in order to free the flow of her stools and drain fire. After eight *ji* of this formula, she had 2-3 bowel movements per day and her eating and drinking increased, and all her other symptoms had decreased by half. Therefore, the doses of Rhubarb and Mirabilite were also halved. At her fourth examination, all her symptoms had disappeared. She was discharged from the hospital and told to take one *Xiao Yao Wan* (Rambling Pill) in the morning and three *Xie Gan Wan* (Drain the Liver Pills) at night for 30 days in order to continue regulating and rectifying her condition. On follow-up after two years, there had been no recurrence.

❖ CASE 6[8] ❖

The patient was a 29 year old female homemaker who entered the hospital on Mar. 15, 1978. Her facial complexion was flushed red and her eye whites were injected. She complained of insomnia and profuse dreams, rashness, and easy anger. She had headache and distention, and sometimes over the last half year her limbs felt numb and tingling. The patient's personality was slightly introverted and she spoke little. She appeared anxious and unstable. In addition, the patient reported tinnitus, dizziness, dry, itchy eyes, blurred vision, rib-side discomfort, and occasional low back soreness. For the last half year her condition had been worse and she laughed and cried without constancy. Further, she took little interest in human affairs. After being hospitalized, she had been treated with Western medicine for one month but without apparent improvement. And finally, the patient's tongue was red with scanty fluids and her pulse was fine and rapid.

Based on the above signs and symptoms, the patient's pattern was categorized as enduring depression transforming heat which had consumed and damaged yin essence. Therefore, the treatment principles were to enrich and nourish yin and essence, clear heat and eliminate vexation. The formula prescribed was *Qi Ju Di Huang Tang Jia Wei* (Lycium & Chrysanthemum Rehmannia Decoction with Added Flavors): uncooked Radix Rehmanniae (*Sheng Di*), 15g, cooked Radix Rehmanniae (*Shu Di*), 12g, Fructus Corni Officinalis (*Shan Zhu Yu*), 10g, Rhizoma Alismatis (*Ze Xie*), 12g, Cortex Radicis Moutan (*Dan Pi*), 10g, Radix Dioscoreae Oppositae (*Shan Yao*), 15g, Sclerotium Poriae Cocos (*Fu Ling*), 15g, Fructus Lycii Chinensis (*Gou Qi Zi*), 15g, Flos Chrysanthemi Morifolii (*Ju Hua*), 15g, Fructus Citri Sacrodactylis (*Fo Shou*), 10g, and Tuber Curcumae (*Yu Jin*), 9g.

After taking 20 *ji* of the above formula, the dizziness and the red eyes had disappeared and the chest and abdominal discomfort were eliminated. However, there was still laughing and crying without constancy. Therefore, uncooked Rehmannia, Buddha Hand Citron, and Curcuma were removed and Fructus Levis Tritici Aestivi (*Fu Xiao Mai*), 20g, Radix Glycyrrhizae (*Gan Cao*), 10g, Bulbus Lilii (*Bai He*), 20g, and Semen Zizyphi Spinosae (*Suan Zao Ren*), 15g, were added. After taking 14 *ji* of this formula, the emotional lability disappeared, the sleep had improved, and eating and drinking increased. However, there was still numbness of the limbs and low back soreness. Radix Angelicae Sinensis (*Dang Gui*), 15g, Fructus Chaenomelis Lagenariae (*Mu Gua*), 10g, and Caulis Milletiae Seu Spatholobi (*Ji Xue Teng*), 18g, were added to the above formula and, after taking another 30 *ji*, the patient was cured and discharged from the hospital. On follow-up after two years, there had been no recurrence.

### ❖ CASE 7[9] ❖

The patient was a 45 year old, married peasant farmer who was admitted to the hospital on Jul. 15, 1983. The patient complained of being fearful and having difficulty sleeping for the last year. He had no thought for food or drink, his whole body lacked strength, and his head was dizzy and felt clouded. In the same last year, the patient had also developed heart palpitations and heart vexation and had no desire to go outdoors. He had been hospitalized when he had talked of killing himself. His facial complexion was lusterless and he was averse to movement and liked stillness. The man was taciturn and talked little. His abdomen was distended, his stools were loose, and he was easily frightened. The patient's tongue was pale and tender with thin, slimy fur, and his pulse was fine and weak.

Thus it was judged that unresolved worry and anxiety had damaged the patient's heart and spleen and his qi and blood had become vacuous and insufficient. The treatment principles were to fortify the spleen and boost the qi, supplement the heart and quiet the spirit. Therefore, he was prescribed *Gui Pi Tang* (Restore the Spleen Decoction): Rhizoma Atractylodis Macrocephalae (*Bai Zhu*), 10g, Sclerotium Pararadicis Poriae Cocos (*Fu Shen*), 12g, Radix Astragali Membranacei (*Huang Qi*), 12g, Radix Panacis Ginseng (*Ren Shen*), 6g, Radix Auklandiae Lappae (*Mu Xiang*), 6g, Radix Glycyrrhizae (*Gan Cao*), 6g, Radix Angelicae Sinensis (*Dang Gui*), 15g, Radix Polygalae Tenuifoliae (*Yuan Zhi*), 9g, Arillus Euphoriae Longanae (*Long Yan Rou*), 10g, and Semen Zizyphi Spinosae (*Suan Zao Ren*), 18g.

After taking 30 *ji* of the above formula, all the patient's symptoms had decreased. However, his emotions were not yet soothed and he still had heat and chest depression and oppression accompanied by long sighs. Therefore, Tuber Curcumae (*Yu Jin*), 10g, and Fructus Citri Sacrodactylis (*Fo Shou*), 9g, were added to the above formula in order to rectify the qi and open depression. After taking 15 *ji* of this formula, all the man's symptoms were greatly decreased, but his dizziness had gotten worse. For this, 10 grams of Radix Ligustici Wallichii (*Chuan Xiong*) and nine grams of Radix Angelicae Dahuricae (*Bai Zhi*) were added to his formula to quicken the blood, dispel wind, and stop pain. After taking yet another 12 *ji*, all the symptoms were eliminated and the man was discharged from the hospital with 30 pills of *Shi Quan Da Bu Wan* (Ten [Ingredients] Completely & Greatly Supplementing Pills)

and 30 pills of *Xiang Sha Liu Jun Zi Wan* (Auklandia & Amomum Six Gentlemen Pills). The patient was instructed to take one pill of the former each morning and one pill of the latter each evening in order to continue regulating and rectifying his condition.

### ❖ CASE 8[10] ❖

The patient was a 50 year old male cadre who was first examined on May 5, 1997. One month previously, the man had suffered a cerebral infarction as diagnosed by CT scan. After treatment for this, his symptoms had improved. However, as days wore on, the man's emotional state deteriorated. For the last seven days, he had been easily angered and complained of heart vexation due to loss of strength of his limbs on his left side and inability to walk. The man's speech was reduced, he was sorrowful, his appetite was poor, and he had insomnia. His tongue was red with scanty fur, and his pulse was bowstring and fine. His Chinese pattern discrimination was that, due to eating fried foods and being addicted to alcohol, his yin had been damaged. Thus his liver-kidney yin were vacuous and liver yang hyperactivity was harassing, depressing, and damaging his spirit. The man was administered the basic formula described above by Xu Chao-gang under "Abstracts of representative Chinese research," plus10 grams of Fructus Crataegi (*Shan Zha*) and psychotherapy. After six days, the man's emotional state was markedly improved, and after nine days, his outlook was positive.

### ❖ CASE 9[11] ❖

The patient was a 48 year old male driver. Two years before, the man had fallen from his bicycle and broken his right arm. Although the bone healed, the man complained of weakness in that arm and worried that this weakness would prevent him from driving. This worrying had eventually led to the man becoming depressed. In the last year he had developed insomnia, nightmares, chest oppression, poor appetite, and impaired memory. In addition, he often laughed or wept for no apparent reason. His tongue was pale with slimy, white fur, while his pulse was bowstring and fine. Neurological and EEG examinations were normal.

Based on the above signs and symptoms, the man's pattern was categorized as heart-spleen dual vacuity with liver depression qi stagnation. Therefore, the treatment principles were to course the liver and fortify the spleen, calm the heart and quiet the mind. He was treated with acupuncture at the following points: *Nei Guan* (Per 6), *Shen Men* (Ht 7), *Dan Zhong* (CV 17), *Zu San Li* (St 36), *San Yin Jiao* (Sp 6), and *Tai Chong* (Liv 3). *Shen Men* and

*Zu San Li* were supplemented, while the other points were needled with even supplementing-even draining technique. Treatment was administered one time per day, with six treatments equaling one course. A one day rest was allowed between courses.

After two such courses, the man's appetite was markedly improved and he was able to fall asleep more easily. His crying was less, but the patient still laughed uncontrollably. In addition, his nightmares continued unabated. It was determined that phlegm due to spleen vacuity not properly controlling the movement and transformation of water fluids also was playing a part in his disease mechanisms. Therefore, *Tong Li* (Ht 5) and *Feng Long* (St 40) were added to the above points to regulate and drain the heart as well as transform phlegm, and *Nei Guan* was discontinued. After three treatments with these points, the man's uncontrollable laughter ceased and his nightmares decreased. Hence *Tong Li* was discontinued. Three more treatments were given, after which his symptoms all gradually subsided, his weight increased, and his complexion improved. At this point, the patient's tongue was pink with thin, white fur, and his pulse was only slightly bow-string. On follow-up after six months, there had been no recurrence of his previous depression.

## ENDNOTES

[1] Quoted by Heiner Fruehauf, "Commonly Used Chinese Herb Formulas for the Treatment of Mental Disorders," *Journal of Chinese Medicine*, UK, #48, 1995, p. 22

[2] This is just another name for blood stasis.

[3] Yu & Han, *op. cit.*, p. 162-64

[4] *Ibid.*, p. 164-165

[5] *Ibid.*, p. 165-166

[6] Zeng Jian-ya, *Zhong Guo Zhen Jiu (Chinese Acupuncture & Moxibustion)*, #4, 1994, p. 31

[7] Li & Liu, *op. cit.*, p. 517

[8] *Ibid.*, p. 525-526

[9] *Ibid.*, p. 523-524

[10] Xu Chao-gang, "The Treatment of 40 Cases of Post-stroke Depression Mainly by Enriching Yin & Quieting the Spirit," *Si Chuan Zhong Yi (Sichuan Chinese Medicine)*, #2, 1999, p. 25

[11] *Acupuncture Case Histories from China*, ed. by Chen Ji-rui & Nissi Wang, Eastland Press, Seattle, 1988, p. 114-116

# ❖ 5 ❖

# POSTPARTUM DEPRESSION

Postpartum depression, also called "baby blues" refers to depression experienced in the postpartum period. Such depression may appear within 24 hours of delivery. It is usually limited in duration (36-48 hours) and is very common. This type of depression may require treatment if it lasts for more than 72 hours or is associated with lack of interest in the infant, suicidal or homicidal thoughts, hallucinations, or psychotic behavior. Contemporary Western psychiatry recognizes many syndromes that occur in the immediate postpartum time frame. However, in the current nosology (see below), these symptom patterns are described as "specifiers" of broader categories of mood disorders or psychotic disorders. According to *DSM-IV* criteria, postpartum onset means that symptoms begin sometime during the first four weeks after childbirth. Other Western mental health organizations define the postpartum period as lasting up to one year following childbirth. Definitional differences in the time-frame required for symptom onset will significantly influence the number of cases diagnosed as postpartum disorders.

## NOSOLOGY:

The *DSM-IV* mentions postpartum onset as a specifier in seven separate psychiatric disorders (see table below). Depressed mood with or without psychotic symptoms is the focus of clinical attention in four of these. Manic or mixed depressive-manic symptoms with or without psychotic symptoms are specified in the remaining three symptom patterns.

## DISORDERS WITH POSTPARTUM ONSET ACCORDING TO THE *DSM-IV*

- ❖ Major depressive disorder—single episode
- ❖ Major depressive disorder—recurrent
- ❖ Bipolar disorder I—single manic episode
- ❖ Bipolar disorder I—most recent episode manic
- ❖ Bipolar disorder I—most recent episode mixed
- ❖ Bipolar disorder I—most recent episode depressed
- ❖ Bipolar disorder II—depressed

The same general criteria required to diagnose an episode of major depression, mania, or mixed manic-depressive symptoms (see preceeding chapter) are also required to diagnose postpartum depression. In Western psychiatric nosology, psychotic symptoms sometimes occur together with a manic or depressive episode but are not necessary to diagnose either. This appears to be analogous to the second symptom pattern under the broad heading of postpartum depression in which "the patient appears on the verge of mania; if extreme there may be visual and auditory hallucinations." It is interesting that all four patterns included in postpartum depression contain references to heart palpitations, dizziness, spontaneous perspiration, or similar somatic complaints that resemble descriptions of panic attacks as conceptualized in Western psychiatry. Although panic attacks can occur in the context of depressive, manic, or mixed manic-depressive episodes, they are not regarded as core or required symptoms of mood disorders. Here again we observe that differences between symptom patterns of postpartum depression in Chinese and Western psychiatry are analogous to differences between symptom patterns of ADHD, seizure disorders, and other broad diagnostic categories as viewed from these two paradigms. That is, certain symptoms that are regarded as incidental to a Western psychiatric diagnosis are viewed as core features of a Chinese diagnostic category that resembles the Western diagnosis. Such differences are probably expressions of systematic differences between logical assumptions underlying disease classification in Chinese and Western medicine.

## EPIDEMIOLOGY:

Epidemiologic surveys of Western populations indicate that prevalence rates of postpartum psychiatric disorders vary depending on number of pregnancies. Postpartum psychosis occurs in first-time pregnancies at a rate of one in 500 (0.005%), and almost one-third of women who have had a postpartum psychotic episode experience similar symptoms in subsequent pregnancies.

## DIFFERENTIAL DIAGNOSIS:

Symptom patterns of several medical disorders that begin or worsen during or soon after pregnancy resemble postpartum psychiatric disorders. Ruling out delirium is the most important medical consideration in the differential diagnosis of postpartum depression or psychosis. Delirium in the postpartum period can be caused by medication side effects, infection, or blood loss. By definition, delirium is characterized by a change in level of consciousness, confusion, and disorientation. The delirious patient typically alternates between alert wakefulness and confused stupor. Specific medical disorders that may undergo exacerbation

during or after pregnancy include multiple sclerosis (MS), systemic lupus erythematosus (SLE), hyperthyroidism, hypothyroidism, and other endocrinological disorders. It is difficult to distinguish postpartum mood or psychotic symptoms from neuropsychiatric sequelae of these or other medical disorders on the basis of clinical findings alone. Laboratory studies and brain-imaging usually clarify the differential diagnosis, verifying or excluding possible underlying medical causes.

Chronic abuse of alcohol or illicit substances during pregnancy or following delivery can result in persisting depressed mood. Use of certain prescription medications, including antihypertensives and steroids, can also result in depressive mood changes.

When primary medical disorders have been excluded, a thorough history clarifies the psychiatric differential diagnosis. The goal is to establish a pattern of mood or psychotic symptoms that occur predominantly in the weeks following childbirth. When this pattern cannot be established, other primary psychiatric disorders must be considered. For unclear reasons, transient worsening in schizophrenia, obsessive-compulsive disorder (OCD), and many anxiety disorders sometimes takes place in the postpartum time frame. According to the *DSM-IV* approach, the correct diagnosis depends on the long-term course and specific symptom pattern.

## ETIOLOGY & PATHOPHYSIOLOGY:

Many biological, psychological, and social theories have been advanced as putative explanations of postpartum psychiatric syndromes. Most of these derive from observations of effects of specific neuroendocrinological changes on mood and behavior. This approach to understanding the pathogenesis of psychiatric disorders with postpartum

| DIFFERENTIAL DIAGNOSIS | | |
|---|---|---|
| 1. MEDICAL DISORDERS | 2. EFFECTS OF SUBSTANCES | 3. PSYCHIATRIC DISORDERS |
| A. DELIRIUM <br> B. MULTIPLE SCLEROSIS (MS) <br> C. SYSTEMIC LUPUS ERYTHEMATOSUS (SLE) <br> D. HYPERTHYROIDISM OR HYPOTHYROIDISM <br> E. OTHER ENDOCRINOLOGICAL DISEASES | A. CHRONIC ABUSE OF ALCOHOL OR ILLICIT SUBSTANCES <br> B. SIDE EFFECTS OF MEDICATIONS | A. SCHIZOPHRENIA AND OTHER PSYCHOTIC DISORDERS <br> B. OBSESSIVE-COMPULSIVE DISORDER (OCD) <br> C. ANXIETY DISORDERS |

onset can be traced to the discovery that anterior pituitary damage caused by a sudden transient drop in blood pressure during delivery manifests as symptom patterns that closely match diagnostic criteria for postpartum psychosis or depression. This disorder, called Sheehan's syndrome, is characterized by depression, agitation, confusion, and auditory or visual hallucinations. Further, hormonal replacement therapy with cortisone and thyroxine (two master hormones whose production declines in Sheehan's syndrome) typically results in normalization of postpartum psychiatric syndromes. Other evidence suggests that severe agitation or psychotic symptoms tend to occur in the first days following childbirth in contrast to depressed mood, which gradually evolves over a period of weeks. A neuroendocrinological basis for this pattern has not been clearly established. Independently from pituitary dysregulation in Sheehan's syndrome, maternal thyroid hormone serum levels typically change from high to low between the final trimester and the first postpartum days. The majority of women who experience this change in serum thyroid hormone levels report psychiatric symptoms that resemble postpartum depression. Treatment with thyroid hormone effectively reverses depressed mood and other psychiatric symptoms in approximately 50% of cases. In addition to pituitary-mediated hormonal influences, dysregulation in several neurotransmitters has been implicated as a possible cause of postpartum psychiatric syndromes. Studies investigating the role of serotonin, dopamine and norepinephrine have been inconclusive to date.

Although many studies have explored the potential contribution of psychological and social factors to the pathogenesis of postpartum psychiatric disorders, no causal relationships have been established. Numerous psychoanalytic or psychodynamic models have been proposed over the decades since Freud's early work more than a century ago. However, none has improved our understanding of postpartum disorders.

## WESTERN MEDICAL TREATMENT:

Prompt treatment of identified medical etiologies (including hypothyroidism) usually leads to rapid clinical improvement in symptoms of agitation, psychosis, or depression. Aggressive treatment of postpartum psychotic states with high potency antipsychotics in the first days after symptom onset is usually more effective than starting treatment several weeks into the illness. Delaying the start of treatment can be a consequence of unreported or unrecognized psychotic symptoms. For unclear reasons, delayed treatment sometimes results in refractory psychot-

ic states. The standard of care in contemporary Western psychiatry is to continue antipsychotic medications at least six weeks after a therapeutic response has been achieved and as long as one year after onset of postpartum psychotic symptoms. Antipsychotics may be safely continued during breast-feeding. Because of the very high risk of recurring psychosis following subsequent pregnancies, it is reasonable to start antipsychotics at childbirth in women with a history of postpartum psychosis.

In contrast to postpartum psychosis, which typically starts in the first days after childbirth, postpartum depressive or manic states tend to evolve gradually over several months. Most classes of antidepressants, including SSRIs, tricyclic agents, and atypical agents, have been used with some success. Several studies of nursing mothers have demonstrated that most antidepressants are secreted into the breast milk at concentrations that affect infants, resulting in significant behavioral side effects or discontinuation syndromes. As the long-term consequences of neonatal exposure to antidepressants have not been established, the recommended conservative approach is to avoid breast-feeding if severe postpartum psychiatric symptoms interfere with functioning, placing the mother's or infant's welfare at risk.

Progesterone therapy has been used to treat postpartum depression but with mixed results. When depressive symptoms are severe or refractory to trials of appropriate medications, electroconvulsive therapy (ECT) is considered to be the most reasonable alternative treatment available in contemporary Western medicine. Women who experience postpartum depression or mania are several times more likely to have clinically significant mood changes during or after future pregnancies. Because of the high probability of recurrence, prophylactic treatment is often started after subsequent births. Supportive psychotherapy often benefits mothers who are coping with the fatigue, anxiety, and stresses of caring for an infant while depressed. Perhaps the optimum treatment approach is combined medications and psychotherapy.

## SHORT & LONG-TERM ADVANTAGES & DISADVANTAGES OF WESTERN MEDICAL TREATMENT:

Successful treatment of postpartum psychotic states or mood disorders significantly improves the mother's capacity to care for her self and to competently manage her newborn infant. Disadvantages of treatment with conventional medications include the potential for side effects in the mother and infant (if the mother is nursing) and unknown long-term effects on the infant. Electroconvulsive therapy has no identified or serious long-term risks but frequently causes temporary amnesia, headaches, confusion, or dizziness.

## PROGNOSIS:

When recognized and treated early and aggressively, both postpartum psychosis and postpartum mood disorders usually improve rapidly. However, in cases where the start of treatment is delayed, these disorders may progress and become refractory to subsequent treatment. Untreated postpartum psychotic or mood disorders may persist for months or years.

## INDICATIONS FOR REFERRAL TO WESTERN MEDICAL SERVICES:

Urgent referral to the nearest emergency room is indicated when there is evidence of an acute medical problem, such as delirium, multiple sclerosis, hyperthyroidism, or hypothyroidism, or the patient is psychotic or suicidal. In cases where underlying medical causes have been ruled out and the patient has not responded to an adequate trial of appropriate Chinese medical treatment, non-urgent referral to a psychiatrist may be beneficial to clarify the differential diagnosis and coordinate an integrative treatment plan.

## CHINESE DISEASE CATEGORIZATION:

*Chan hou jing ji* refers to postpartum fright and anxiety with heart palpitations. *Chan hou huang hu* literally means that one is abstracted from their surroundings as if in a trance postpartum. As a disease category, it includes impaired memory, restlessness and agitation, and confused, chaotic speech. *Chan hou xu fan* means postpartum vacuity vexation, agitation, lack of tranquility, restless fidgeting, and insomnia.

## CHINESE DISEASE CAUSES & MECHANISMS:

Most postpartum mental-emotional disorders are rooted in vacuity. Due to excessive blood and fluid loss during delivery and consumption of blood and fluids due to breast-feeding, heart qi and blood may become vacuous and weak. The heart treasures the spirit, and heart blood nourishes and secures the spirit. Therefore, if heart qi and blood become vacuous and weak, the spirit may become unsettled and nervous. This then may give rise to fright palpitations, impaired memory, and deranged speech. Since heart qi and blood are rooted in the spleen, heart vacuity is typically complicated by spleen vacuity, and

spleen vacuity may give rise to fatigue, somnolence, lethargy, and lack of strength. Because the spleen qi and kidney yang are mutually rooted, spleen qi vacuity may also involve kidney yang vacuity.

However, a righteous postpartum vacuity is often complicated by various types of evil qi. For instance, postpartum blood vacuity may fail to nourish and moisten the liver sufficiently which then fails to control coursing and discharge. Hence the liver becomes depressed and the qi becomes stagnant, leading to irritability and easy anger. If liver depression transforms heat, this heat may ascend to harass the heart spirit. If it endures, it will also further consume yin and blood. If the liver invades the spleen, the spleen may become even more vacuous and weak. If the spleen fails to do its duty in controlling the movement and transformation of body fluids, dampness may be engendered which may further give rise to phlegm and turbidity misting and obstructing the clear orifices. Likewise, yin vacuity may engender internal heat. When this ascends and collects in the heart, it harasses the spirit, causing vexation and agitation, impaired memory, dizziness, insomnia, and heart palpitations. It is also possible for a righteous vacuity to allow for easy contraction of external wind evils which then cause heart palpitations, fearful throbbing, heart vexation, restlessness, insomnia, profuse dreams, and/or mental-emotional chaos and confusion.

In addition, it is possible to have completely replete postpartum disease mechanisms of essence spirit disorders. If spoilt blood (*i.e.*, static blood) is retained after delivery and penetrates upward, it may disturb the heart spirit causing heart palpitations, oppression, agitation, and insomnia. If severe, such spoilt or static blood may even result in mania, visual and auditory hallucinations, and deranged speech.

## TREATMENT BASED ON PATTERN DISCRIMINATION:

### 1. HEART QI VACUITY WEAKNESS PATTERN

**MAIN SYMPTOMS:** There are postpartum heart palpitations, nervous anxiety, vertigo, dizziness, impaired memory, deranged speech, spontaneous perspiration, vexation and agitation, insomnia, and a pale white or sallow yellow facial complexion. The tongue is pale and dry, and the pulse is bowstring and fine.

**ANALYSIS OF SYMPTOMS:** All the signs and symptoms in this pattern indicate qi and blood vacuity not nourishing and constructing the heart spirit.

**TREATMENT PRINCIPLES:** Boost the qi and nourish the blood, quiet the spirit and tranquilize palpitations

**FORMULA & MEDICINALS:** *Gui Pi Tang Jia Wei* (Restore the Spleen Decoction with Added Flavors)

Radix Panacis Ginseng (*Ren Shen*), 6g, Rhizoma Atractylodis Macrocephalae (*Bai Zhu*), 9g, Arillus Euphoriae Longanae (*Long Yan Rou*), 9g, Radix Polygalae Tenuifoliae (*Yuan Zhi*), 6g, Sclerotium Pararadicis Poriae Cocoris (*Fu Shen*), 12g, Radix Auklandiae Lappae (*Mu Xiang*), 6-9g, Radix Astragali Membranacei (*Huang Qi*), 9-18g, Radix Angelicae Sinensis (*Dang Gui*), 9g, mix-fried Radix Glycyrrhizae (*Gan Cao*), 6-9g, Semen Zizyphi Spinosae (*Zao Ren*), 12g, Tuber Ophiopogonis Japonici (*Mai Dong*), 12g, Fructus Schisandrae Chinensis (*Wu Wei Zi*), 9g, Concha Ostreae (*Mu Li*), 12g, Dens Draconis (*Long Chi*), 12g

Decoct one *ji* in water per day and administer orally in two divided doses, morning and evening.

**ANALYSIS OF FORMULA:** Within this formula, Ginseng, Atractylodes, Poria, Astragalus, and mix-fried Licorice all fortify the spleen and boost the qi. In addition, Ginseng and Spirit of Poria both quiet the spirit. Longans supplement the heart and spleen, meaning that they supplement heart blood and spleen qi. Dang Gui and Zizyphus Spinosa also nourish the blood. In addition, Zizyphus Spinosa quiets the spirit. Ophiopogon and Schisandra both engender fluids. Ophiopogon also clears the heart and transforms phlegm, while Schisandra supplements the chest qi. Polygala and Auklandia both rectify the qi. Polygala also supplements the heart and transforms phlegm, while Auklandia harmonizes the liver and spleen. Dragon's Teeth and Oyster Shell both heavily subdue yang and quiet the spirit.

**ACUPUNCTURE:** *Xin Shu* (Bl 15), *Ge Shu* (Bl 17), *Pi Shu* (Bl 20), *Shen Men* (Ht 7), *Zu San Li* (St 36), *Bai Hui* (GV 20), *Yin Tang* (M-HN-3). Use supplementing technique on the first five points and draining technique on the last two.

### 2. BLOOD STASIS PENETRATING THE HEART PATTERN

**MAIN SYMPTOMS:** There are postpartum heart palpitations, sitting and sleeping are not calm, and the lochia does not descend. Sometimes the patient appears on the verge of mania. If extreme, there may be visual and auditory hallucinations, deranged speech, and acting as if possessed. In addition, there is loss of sleep, lower abdominal distention and pain, the facial complexion is purple and dark, and the lips are a deep red. The tongue has static spots or macules, and the pulse is bowstring, choppy, and forceful.

**ANALYSIS OF SYMPTOMS:** Non-descension of the lochia, lower abdominal distention and pain, a purple and/or dark facial complexion, dark lips, static macules or spots on the tongue, and a bowstring, choppy pulse all indicate qi stagnation and blood stasis. That stasis is causing spirit disquietude is indicated by the accompanying heart palpitations and other mental-emotional complaints.

**TREATMENT PRINCIPLES:** Free the flow of the channels and quicken the network vessels

**FORMULA & MEDICINALS:** *Jia Wei Chuan Xiong San* (Added Flavors Ligusticum Powder)

Radix Ligustici Wallichii (*Chuan Xiong*), 15g, uncooked Radix Rehmanniae (*Sheng Di*), 12g, Radix Albus Paeoniae Lactiflorae (*Bai Shao*), 9g, Radix Achyranthis Bidentatae (*Niu Xi*), 9g, Pollen Typhae (*Pu Huang*), 9g, Feces Trogopterori Seu Pteromi (*Wu Ling Zhi*), 9g

Decoct one *ji* in water per day and administer orally in two divided doses, morning and evening.

**ANALYSIS OF FORMULA:** Pollen Typhae, Flying Squirrel Feces, Ligusticum, and uncooked Rehmannia all quicken the blood and dispel stasis. Achyranthes supplements the liver and kidneys and also leads the blood to move downward. Peony nourishes the blood and thus harmonizes the liver. In addition, uncooked Rehmannia also clears any heat in the blood.

**ACUPUNCTURE:** *Xue Hai* (Sp 10), *San Yin Jiao* (Sp 6), *Tai Chong* (Liv 3), *He Gu* (LI 4), *Qi Hai* (CV 6), *Guan Yuan* (CV 4). Use draining technique.

### 3. YIN VACUITY-FIRE EFFULGENCE PATTERN

**MAIN SYMPTOMS:** Postpartum heart vexation, restlessness, dizziness, tinnitus, impaired memory, insomnia, heart palpitations, night sweats, vexatious heat in the hands and feet, tidal heat, flushed red cheeks, a dry mouth but no particular thirst, low back and knee soreness and weakness, a red tongue with scanty, dry fur, and a bowstring, fine, rapid pulse

**ANALYSIS OF SYMPTOMS:** Dizziness, tinnitus, a dry mouth,

night sweats, low back and knee soreness and weakness, scanty, dry tongue fur, and a fine pulse all indicate yin vacuity. That yin vacuity has given rise to internal heat is evidenced by night sweats, vexatious heat in the hands and feet, tidal heat, flushed red cheeks, a red tongue, and a rapid pulse. The bowstring pulse is due to yin blood not nourishing and moistening the liver properly. The heart vexation, restlessness, impaired memory, insomnia, and heart palpitations all show that heat is harassing and disquieting the heart spirit.

**TREATMENT PRINCIPLES:** Nourish yin and clear heat, quiet the spirit and tranquilize palpitations

**FORMULA & MEDICINALS:** *Ren Shen Dang Gui Tang Jia Wei* (Ginseng & Dang Gui Decoction with Added Flavors)

Radix Panacis Ginseng (*Ren Shen*), 6g, Radix Angelicae Sinensis (*Dang Gui*), 9g, cooked Radix Rehmanniae (*Shu Di*), 12g, Tuber Asparagi Cochinensis (*Tian Dong*), 12g, Cortex Cinnamomi Cassiae (*Rou Gui*), 3g, Radix Albus Paeoniae Lactiflorae (*Bai Shao*), 9g, Tuber Ophiopogonis Japonici (*Mai Dong*), 12g, Caulis Bambusae In Taeniis (*Zhu Ru*), 9g, Rhizoma Anemarrhenae Aspheloidis (*Zhi Mu*), 9g

Decoct one *ji* in water per day and administer orally in two divided doses, morning and evening.

**ANALYSIS OF FORMULA:** Within this formula, Ginseng supplements the heart qi, engenders fluids, and quiets the spirit. Dang Gui, Peony, and cooked Rehmannia nourish the blood and, therefore, enrich yin. Ophiopogon clears the heart at the same time as it engenders fluids and transforms phlegm. Asparagus supplements the kidneys and enriches yin. Caulis Bambusae clears depressive heat and downbears counterflow, and Anemarrhena drains fire at the same time as it supplements the kidneys and enriches yin.

**ADDITIONS & SUBTRACTIONS:** If yin vacuity causes internal engenderment of the heat which damages stomach and intestinal fluids with constipation and marked thirst, then use *Zeng Ye Cheng Qi Tang Jia Wei* (Increase Fluids Order the Qi Decoction with Added Flavors): Radix Scrophulariae Ningpoensis (*Xuan Shen*), 15g, Os Draconis (*Long Gu*), 15g, Concha Ostreae (*Mu Li*), 15g, Tuber Ophiopogonis Japonici (*Mai Dong*), 12g, uncooked Radix Rehmanniae (*Sheng Di*), 12-24g, Radix Et Rhizoma Rhei (*Da Huang*), 9g, Mirabilitum (*Mang Xiao*), 4.5g

Decoct one *ji* in water per day and administer orally in two divided doses, morning and evening.

**ACUPUNCTURE:** *Xin Shu* (Bl 15), *Shen Shu* (Bl 23), *Shen Men* (Ht 7), *Yin Xi* (Ht 6), *Da Ling* (Per 7), *Tai Xi* (Ki 3), *San Yin Jiao* (Sp 6), *Bai Hui* (GV 20), *Yin Tang* (M-HN-3). Use even supplementing-even draining technique.

### 4. RIGHTEOUS VACUITY WITH CONTRACTION OF EVILS PATTERN

**MAIN SYMPTOMS:** Dizziness, headache, agitation and restlessness, heart palpitations, fearful throbbing, heart vexation, insomnia, profuse dreams, if severe, chaotic and confused thinking, possible tics and spasms or convulsions, alternating fever and chills, a pale, possibly enlarged tongue with white fur, and a faint, forceless pulse

**ANALYSIS OF SYMPTOMS:** Dizziness, headache, tics and spasms, and alternating fever and chills all evidence external contraction by wind evils. However, the alternating fever and chills also show that the righteous is vacuous and weak internally. The pale, enlarged tongue and faint, forceless pulse further corroborate a righteous vacuity. That wind is harassing the heart spirit internally is indicated by the agitation and restlessness, heart palpitations, fearful throbbing, heart vexation, profuse dreams, etc.

**TREATMENT PRINCIPLES:** Course wind and dispel evils, harmonize the qi and blood and quiet the spirit

**FORMULA & MEDICINALS:** *Xiao Chai Hu Tang He Si Wu Tang Jia Wei* (Minor Bupleurum Decoction plus Four Materials Decoction with Added Flavors)

Os Draconis (*Long Gu*), 12-15g, Concha Ostreae (*Mu Li*), 12-15g, Radix Bupleuri (*Chai Hu*), 9g, Radix Codonopsitis Pilosulae (*Dang Shen*), 9-18g, Radix Scutellariae Baicalensis (*Huang Qin*), 9g, Rhizoma Pinelliae Ternatae (*Ban Xia*), 9g, Radix Angelicae Sinensis (*Dang Gui*), 9g, Radix Albus Paeoniae Lactiflorae (*Bai Shao*), 9-18g, cooked Radix Rehmanniae (*Shu Di*), 9-12g, Radix Ligustici Wallichii (*Chuan Xiong*), 6-9g, mix-fried Radix Glycyrrhizae (*Gan Cao*), 6g, uncooked Rhizoma Zingiberis (*Sheng Jiang*), 2 slices, Fructus Zizyphi Jujubae (*Da Zao*), 3 pieces

Decoct one *ji* in water per day and administer orally in two divided doses, morning and evening.

**ANALYSIS OF FORMULA:** Bupleurum and uncooked Ginger resolve the exterior and out-thrust evils. The ingredients of *Si Wu Tang* (Four Materials Decoction), *i.e.*, Dang Gui, Peony, Ligusticum, and cooked Rehmannia nourish the blood. Codonopsis and mix-fried Licorice fortify the spleen and supplement the qi. Red Dates supplement the heart and help harmonize the constructive and defensive. Scutellaria clears heat from the liver, gallbladder, lungs, stomach, and intestines, while Dragon Bone and Oyster Shell heavily subdue yang and quiet the spirit.

ACUPUNCTURE: *Feng Chi* (GB 20), *Feng Fu* (GV 16), *Feng Men* (Bl 12), *Bai Hui* (GV 20), *Yin Tang* (M-HN-3), *Wai Guan* (TB 5), *He Gu* (LI 4). Drain all points.

CLINICAL TIPS: In most women with postpartum depression, postpartum vacuity of qi, blood, and/or yin plays a large part. However, this postpartum vacuity is always complicated in real-life by liver depression qi stagnation, and this qi stagnation may be further complicated by blood stasis. Although the Chinese literature does not say anything about phlegm turbidity, if the patient overeats fatty, greasy, so-called nutritious food postpartum and their spleen is vacuous and weak, there may also be complications from phlegm misting the orifices. Righteous vacuity with external contraction of evils mostly describes postpartum deranged speech, clouded spirit, and convulsions due to high fever associated with acute postpartum endometritis. This is not so commonly seen in developed countries.

REPRESENTATIVE CASE HISTORY:

Neither the patient's age, marital status, occupation, or date of first examination are given in this case history. The patient had given birth twice before without problem. However, after her third delivery, she developed a number of psychological complaints, including insomnia, anxiety, and vexation and agitation. These were accompanied by heart fluster (*i.e.*, fright palpitations), shortness of breath, sweating, disinclination to speak, headache, lack of strength, and generalized soreness and pain. Her heart rate was 100 BPM, her respiratory rate was 24 times per minute, her temperature was 36.6EC, and her blood pressure was 13.3/8.0kPa. Her abdomen was level and soft, neither her liver or spleen were enlarged, and her uterus had shrunk to 3.0 *cun* below her navel. There was a slight degree of pressure pain over the uterus, her lochia was slightly profuse in amount, fresh red in color, and had a fishy odor. Her two excretions were normal. The patient's tongue was pale with thin, white fur, and her pulse was fine, rapid, and forceless. Her throat was slightly hyperemic, but neither tonsils or her submaxillary glands were enlarged.

Based on the above signs and symptoms, the patient was diagnosed as suffering from postpartum insomnia and her pattern was categorized as great postpartum damage to the true source or origin. Therefore, her qi and blood were both debilitated and unable to enrich and nourish the heart spirit. Therefore, the treatment principles were to supplement the qi, nourish the blood, and quiet the spirit. The medicinals she was given consisted of: Radix Panacis Ginseng (*Ren Shen*), 15g, Radix Astragali Membranacei (*Huang Qi*), 25g, Rhizoma Atractylodis Macrocephalae (*Bai Zhu*), 15g, Radix Angelicae Sinensis (*Dang Gui*), 15g, Sclerotium Pararadicis Poriae Cocos (*Fu Shen*), 30g, Radix Polygalae Tenuifoliae (*Yuan Zhi*), 25g, Semen Zizyphi Spinosae (*Suan Zao Ren*), 25g, Cortex Albizziae Julibrissinis (*He Huan Pi*), 15g, Radix Auklandiae Lappae (*Mu Xiang*), 15g, Arillus Euphoriae Longanae (*Long Yan Rou*), 25g, Fructus Schisandrae Chinensis (*Wu Wei Zi*), 15g, cooked Radix Rehmanniae (*Shu Di*), 30g, mix-fried Radix Glycyrrhizae (*Gan Cao*), 5g, Fructus Zizyphi Jujubae (*Da Zao*), 5 pieces, uncooked Rhizoma Zingiberis (*Sheng Jiang*), 3 slices, and Gelatinum Corii Asini (*E Jiao*), 20g. One *ji* was administered per day, decocted in water, and given in two divided doses, morning and evening.

A half hour after taking the first dose of the above medicinals, the patient was able to go to sleep. This was the first time she had slept in three days. She continued taking Chinese medicinals for regulating and rectifying treatment, and all her symptoms were cured.

ENDNOTES

[1] Zhou Yan-yu & Gan Shu-juan, "The Treatment of Postpartum Insomnia with *Gui Pi Tang Jia Wei* (Restore the Spleen Decoction with Added Flavors)," *Ji Lin Zhong Yi Yao* (*Jilin Chinese Medicine & Medicinals*), #6, 1999, p. 23

# ❖ 6 ❖

# BIPOLAR AFFECTIVE DISORDER (BAD)

Bipolar affective disorder is the current standard Western medical name for what was previously and still is commonly referred to as manic-depressive disorder or manic depression. It is one of the three major affective disorders (along with unipolar depression and schizoaffective disorder). This disorder is characterized by repeated (*i.e.*, at least two) episodes in which the patient's mood and activity levels are significantly disturbed. On some occasions, this disturbance consists of an elevation of mood and increased energy and activity (mania or hypomania) and, on other occasions, of a lowering of mood and decreased energy and activity (depression). Characteristically, recovery is usually complete between episodes. Manic episodes tend to begin abruptly and last from two weeks to five months (median duration four months). Depression tends to last longer (median duration six months). Episodes of both kinds often follow stressful life events or other mental trauma, but the presence of such stress is not essential for this diagnosis. Age of first onset may come at any time from childhood to old age. The frequency of episodes and the pattern of remissions and relapses are both very variable, though remissions tend to get shorter as time goes on, and depression tends to become commoner and last longer after middle age.

## NOSOLOGY:

Contemporary Western psychiatry distinguishes two major sub-types of bipolar disorder, type I and type II. Type I is characterized by cyclic mood changes in which episodes of severe depression alternate with acute mania. Some patients experience more frequent manic episodes, while others are more often depressed. Similar to patients with unipolar depression, during depressive episodes those with bipolar affective disease tend to withdraw socially and report absence of pleasure in activities that previously held their interest. They also report diminished energy, loss of libido, and absence of motivation at work. They frequently experience impaired concentration or short-term memory. There may be increased or decreased appetite accompanied by weight gain or loss. The normal sleep pattern is frequently disrupted. They may awaken early and have difficulty returning to sleep or may sleep excessively but still not feel refreshed.

During manic episodes, the individual experiences grandiose or irritable mood and diminished need for sleep. They may talk rapidly, develop hypersexual feelings toward others, and spend money irrationally. Psychosis is sometimes seen, including delusional beliefs, paranoia, or auditory hallucinations. However, when a mood disorder is primary, psychiatric symptoms typically arise after a sustained change in mood. By definition, an individual with type I bipolar disorder is severely impaired during a manic episode.

In bipolar type II, depressive episodes alternate with hypomanic episodes. These are relatively mild, nonpsychotic periods of time usually lasting one week or less. Although euphoric and requiring less sleep than normal, symptoms are not severe enough to impair social or occupational functioning.

Patients are considered rapid cyclers if they have four or more depressive or manic episodes in one year. Some individuals experience a seasonal pattern, typically including depressive mood swings during the fall and manic symptoms during spring (*i.e.*, during periods of increasing daylength). This pattern is called seasonal affective disorder (SAD).

Patients with major depressive episodes and a family history of bipolar affective disorder are unofficially called bipolar type III. These patients typically exhibit subtle hypomanic tendencies, and their temperament is called hyperthymic. This means that they tend to be driven, ambitious, and goal-oriented.

As many as 90% of all depressed patients, including those with bipolar affective disorder, experience co-morbid anxiety, and many type I bipolar patients abuse alcohol or illicit substances, possibly in an attempt to self-medicate their symptoms.

## EPIDEMIOLOGY:

It is estimated that bipolar disorder afflicts approximately 1-3% of adult populations worldwide. For unclear reasons, this disorder is more common in surveyed Western populations in higher socioeconomic classes and among single or divorced individuals. Most cases of bipolar disorder are eventually referred to mental health care. Bipolar disorder is equally prevalent among men and women across cultures. In contrast to major depressive disorder (which typically begins at age 40 or later), the initial episode of bipolar disorder occurs earlier, usually in the third or fourth decade of life. Reasons for the observed difference in age at onset are not clearly established but probably reflect a complex interplay of biological (including genetic, endocrinological, and CNS), psychosocial, and economic factors.

## DIFFERENTIAL DIAGNOSIS:

Mood changes, including both depression and mania, can be precipitated by several medical disorders, including endocrinologic disease (especially thyroid and adrenal dysfunction), cancer, infectious diseases (including HIV, hepatitis, and others), neurologic disorders (including epilepsy and brain tumors), or head injuries. Many over-the-counter and prescription drugs are known to have depressive or mood-elevating side effects. Antihypertensives,

antibiotics, chemotherapeutic agents, anti-arrhythmics and anti-Parkinsonian medications frequently cause depressive mood changes. Steroid use has been associated with manic states as well as depression and psychosis. Chronic use of alcohol and illicit drugs can also result in a persisting pattern of mood changes typically corresponding to degrees of intoxication and withdrawal. Chronic use of steroids for pulmonary, rheumatologic, or other kinds of medical disorders is frequently associated with mania. Many antidepressant medications carry a significant risk of inducing a manic episode when used by patients who have bipolar disorder, but also sometimes when used by a patient with major depressive disorder. Tricyclic antidepressants are associated with the greatest risk for inducing mania, followed by serotonin-selective re-uptake inhibitors (SSRIs), while atypical antidepressants, including buproprion (Wellbutrin) and MAOIs, appear to have the lowest associated risk of inducing manic episodes in bipolar patients. Accurate diagnosis of underlying organic causes of mood changes is necessary for elaboration of the most effective treatment plan. Therefore, Western psychiatric diagnosis always starts with a medical workup with the goals of identifying, treating, or eliminating underlying biological causes.

A persisting pattern of cyclic mood changes that does not have an identified underlying medical etiology following a thorough workup is regarded as a primary mood disorder. Bipolar affective disorder is diagnosed when the history or current presentation includes prominent symptoms of mania or hypomania. The differentiation between bipolar I and bipolar II is contained in the distinction between mania and hypomania. This distinction is one of degree and duration of symptoms. A manic episode is more severe and, according to the current Western medical definition, manic-like symptoms, including pressured speech, racing thoughts, euphoric mood, grandiosity, and diminished need for sleep, must last at least five days. In general, an acute manic episode results in grossly impaired functioning and may be accompanied by psychotic symptoms, including auditory hallucinations, disorganized thinking, or (typically grandiose) delusions. In contrast, a hypomanic episode is shorter in duration, does not result in impaired social or occupational functioning, and is never accompanied by psychotic symptoms. In order to establish a diagnosis of bipolar disorder, there must be a history of at least one manic (bipolar type I) or hypomanic episode (bipolar type II). Both types of bipolar disorder are characterized by recurring episodes of major depression which may have onset before or after an initial episode of mania or hypomania. In cases where mild manic symptoms (hypomania) fluctuate with depressive mood changes that are not severe or impairing, the likely Western diagnosis is cyclothymic disorder, essentially a mild form of cyclic mood disorder.

An important goal of psychiatric differential diagnosis is distinguishing between mood disorders such as bipolar disorder or cyclothymic disorder and psychotic disorders which may be accompanied by mood symptoms, such as schizoaffective disorder or schizophrenia. In mood disorders, the most concerning clinical problem is a persisting pattern of mood changes. This is in contrast to psychotic disorders in which changes in mood often occur but are not the primary focus of clinical attention. Schizoaffective disorder is an interesting disorder in that it is characterized by prominent mood symptoms and psychosis with the caveat that mood changes are present for a substantial period of time during periods of psychosis. This symptom pattern stands in contrast to schizophrenia or other psychotic disorders in which mood symptoms may be present but are typically not prominent and, by definition, do not occur during phases of active psychosis. Prominent mood symptoms, including depression, euphoria, and irritability, are also characteristic of certain personality disorders, most notably borderline personality disorder. Personality disorders often occur together with mood disorders, and there is on-going debate in academic psychiatry as to whether borderline personality disorder represents a particular form of rapid-cycling bipolar disorder. In general, borderline personality disorder is characterized by an enduring pattern of disturbance in emotional regulation resulting in rapid mood swings or lability, a history of failed, contentious relationships, impulsive, self-destructive behaviors, including self-cutting or suicidal gestures, and a disturbed sense of identity that interferes with normal social functioning. In contrast

to bipolar disorder, patients with borderline personality disorder typically experience very rapid (*i.e.*, typically several hours and always less than one day) changes in mood in the context of a long-standing pattern of dysfunction in interpersonal relationships and self-destructive behaviors.

## ETIOLOGY & PATHOPHYSIOLOGY:

Numerous biological, psychological, and social theories have been proposed as explanations of bipolar disorder. The emphasis on neurobiological theories in contemporary Western psychiatry has favored hypotheses of dysregulation in the limbic system as explaining the pathogenesis of manic and depressive mood episodes. The limbic system is a complex network of evolutionarily primitive brain circuits implicated in the expression and regulation of mood states. Accumulating research evidence suggests that hereditary factors play a significant role in the pathogenesis of bipolar I disorder and probably less of a role in bipolar II disorder. Family studies, including adoptive twin studies, have demonstrated that biological offspring of bipolar parents have a significantly greater chance of developing bipolar disorder than offspring of non-bipolar parents. The widely accepted view in contemporary Western psychiatry is that individuals who are more likely to develop bipolar disorder because of a genetic or neurobiological predisposition tend to experience acute manic (or depressive) states in the context of severe psychosocial stresses which somehow "trigger" manic episodes. In addition to prevailing neurobiological models, various psychoanalytic explanations of mania have argued that acute manic states result when unconscious sexual urges overwhelm normal ego defense mechanisms, resulting in the expression of hypersexual urges and

| DIFFERENTIAL DIAGNOSIS | | |
|---|---|---|
| 1. MEDICAL DISORDERS | 2. EFFECTS OF SUBSTANCES | 3. PSYCHIATRIC DISORDERS |
| A. ENDOCRINOLOGIC DISEASES INCLUDING THYROID AND ADRENAL DYSFUNCTION<br>B. CANCER<br>C. INFECTIOUS DISEASES INCLUDING HIV, HEPATITIS AND OTHERS<br>D. NEUROLOGIC DISEASES INCLUDING EPILEPSY AND BRAIN TUMORS | A. ALCOHOL ABUSE OR ILLICIT SUBSTANCES<br>B. MEDICATION SIDE EFFECTS | A. BIPOLAR DISORDER (TYPE I OR II)<br>B. MAJOR DEPRESSIVE DISORDER<br>C. CYCLOTHYMIC DISORDER<br>D. SCHIZOAFFECTIVE DISORDER<br>E. SCHIZOPHRENIA AND OTHER PSYCHOTIC DISORDERS<br>F. BORDERLINE PERSONALITY DISORDER (AND OTHER PERSONALITY DISORDERS) |

behavior and other cognitive and behavioral symptoms of mania.

## WESTERN MEDICAL TREATMENT:

Principal treatments of bipolar disorder in contemporary Western psychiatry are lithium carbonate, valproic acid (Depakote), and carbamazepine (Tegretol). All of these medications are used as treatments of acute manic episodes and as maintenance therapies for prevention of recurring depressive or manic episodes in bipolar patients. In recent years, other drugs have been employed as maintenance therapies in the treatment of bipolar disorder. These include calcium channel blockers (traditionally used to treat high blood pressure) and novel antiseizure medications, such as gabapentin (Neurotonin), lamotrigine (Lamictal), and others. The more recently introduced agents are typically used as adjunctive agents in combination with more established drugs in the treatment of severe or refractory forms of bipolar disorder. Another common approach is the combined use of mood stabilizers and antidepressants as maintenance therapies. For example, a commonly used approach in the U.S. and Western Europe is to combine lithium carbonate with a serotonin-selective re-uptake inhibitor, such as paroxetine (Paxil), fluoxetine (Prozac), or sertraline (Zoloft). When symptoms of bipolar disorder are severely impairing and refractory to trials on several different medications or combined medication regimens, electroconvulsive therapy (ECT) is sometimes recommended. Numerous studies show that ECT often alleviates severe symptoms that are nonresponsive to available pharmacological treatments. In this treatment, a weak electrical current is passed through the brain after the patient is placed under general anesthesia. A typical course of ECT lasts several weeks and entails 6-12 separate treatments. One ECT procedure generally lasts a few hours and may be done on an out-patient basis if the patient does not require psychiatric hospitalization for safety.

## SHORT & LONG-TERM ADVANTAGES & DISADVANTAGES OF WESTERN MEDICAL TREATMENT:

The short-term benefits and long-term efficacy of conventional Western pharmacologic treatments for bipolar disorder are clearly established for lithium carbonate. Numerous controlled, double-blind studies and years of clinical experience have substantiated that most patients benefit from these through stabilization of mood swings and improved social and occupational functioning. In contrast, fewer data support the use of more recently introduced mood stabilizers, including gaba-pentin and lamotrigine. However, this optimistic picture is in stark contrast to a long list of potentially serious side effects or toxicities commonly associated with most currently used mood-stabilizers. The following table lists significant toxicities or drug-drug interactions for representative mood-stabilizers in widespread current use in contemporary Western psychiatry. The side effects and contraindications of antidepressants have been discussed in Chapter 4, this Book, Depression.

Side effects of ECT include transient amnesia, muscle soreness, headache, and dizziness. When these complications occur following ECT, they are generally mild and typically subside in hours to days. There are no absolute contraindications to ECT. However, elderly and medically impaired patients are at substantially greater risk of experiencing complications.

## PROGNOSIS:

Bipolar disorder is a chronic, recurring disorder that typ-

| DRUG TOXICITY, SIDE EFFECTS & INTERACTIONS | | |
|---|---|---|
| LITHIUM CARBONATE | TEGRETOL (CARBAMAZEPINE) | DEPAKOTE (VALPROIC ACID) |
| TREMOR | BLURRED VISION | TREMOR |
| WEIGHT GAIN | NAUSEA | HAIR LOSS |
| DIARRHEA | SEDATION | WEIGHT GAIN |
| THIRST, POLYURIA | HYPONATREMIA (LOW SERUM SODIUM) | BLOOD DISORDERS |
| HYPOTHYROIDISM | BLOOD DISORDERS | INTERACTS WITH MANY OTHER DRUGS BY AFFECTING LIVER ENZYMES (REQUIRES ROUTINE MONITORING) |
| IMPAIRED RENAL FUNCTION (UNCOMMON) | LIVER DAMAGE (REQUIRES ROUTINE MONITORING) | |
| REQUIRES ROUTINE MONITORING | | |

ically begins with a depressive episode. Untreated manic or depressive episodes can last up to three months resulting in significant social and occupational impairment. As in unipolar depression, the frequency of manic episodes typically increases over time. Onset at an early age (*e.g.*, in the teens) is prognostically unfavorable since bipolar disorder is often misdiagnosed when it first appears in childhood. Overall, bipolar patients have a less favorable prognosis than unipolar depressed patients. This is because only one half of patients on maintenance pharmacotherapy have adequate symptom control at any time during the course of their illness. Prognostically favorable aspects of history include short duration of manic episodes, late age at onset, and the absence of co-morbid medical or psychiatric disorders and substance abuse. Factors that are prognostically poor include long-standing impairment in pre-morbid functioning, poor response to medication, and male gender. Approximately one-third of all bipolar patients experience severe chronic symptoms resulting in social or occupational impairment. Another 30% continue to experience recurrences but function adequately, while one-third are in partial remission at any given time in the course of their illness.

## INDICATIONS FOR REFERRAL TO WESTERN MEDICAL SERVICES:

A patient who voices suicidal thoughts requires hospitalization for safety. Similarly, patients who are grossly impaired because of manic or psychotic symptoms also warrant hospitalization. When a suicidal or psychiatrically impaired patient refuses voluntary hospitalization, the clinician has a professional obligation to activate the emergency medical response system in order to rapidly bring the patient to the attention of local police or paramedics. This will result in an emergency assessment, and, if indicated, the patient will be placed on an involuntary hold and transported to the nearest emergency room for medical and psychiatric evaluation. Non-urgent consultation with a psychiatrist is indicated when a patient does not improve following a reasonable period of treatment or there is evidence of an underlying untreated medical problem or substance abuse.

## CHINESE DISEASE CATEGORIZATION:

In Chinese medicine, bipolar disorder, or what is more commonly called manic depression, is mostly categorized as withdrawal (*dian*), mania (*kuang*), and/or epilepsy (*xian*) depending on its clinical signs and symptoms, including mania, vexation and agitation, depression, etc.

According to the *Ling Shu* (*Spiritual Axis*):

> Mania preceded by spontaneous sorrow, frenetic joy, bitterness, anger, and susceptibility to fear is obtained by worry and hunger... Mania may [also] be preceded by sleepless and lack of appetite and may be characterized by the delusion that one is a lofty sage, eloquent speaker, or respectable noble. One may be capable of all sorts of abusive words and be restless both day and night.

These are certainly the clinical symptoms of at least the manic part of bipolar disorder.

## CHINESE DISEASE CAUSES & MECHANISMS:

In Chinese medicine, the disease evils associated with this condition are mostly internal engenderment of (depressed) qi, fire, phlegm, and stasis. The site of this disease is located in the heart, liver, spleen, and kidneys. The disease can be divided into yin and yang, vacuity and repletion. Mania is mainly due to evil repletion. Its disease nature is categorized as yang. In the case of withdrawal, typically there is simultaneous vacuity and repletion, with vacuity being more prominent and repletion less. Therefore, its disease nature is categorized as yin. If mania endures for a long time, replete evils damage and cause detriment to the righteous qi and the disease nature can turn from yang to yin or mania can produce withdrawal. On the other hand, if withdrawal does not heal, righteous vacuity may lead to evil exuberance and the disease nature may turn from yin to yang, thus producing mania. Therefore, yin and yang, vacuity and repletion are closely interrelated in this condition.

Most cases of this condition are believed in Chinese medicine to be due to great fright and great fear, excessive stimulation by the seven affects, and the five minds transforming fire. This leads to fire exuberance and phlegm congestion with qi and blood counterflow and chaos harassing and causing chaos to the spirit brilliance. This then results in mania. In terms of the depression pole of bipolar disorder, worrying and thinking may become depressed and bound and not be able to extend themselves or frustrated anger may not be discharged. In either case, the qi may become depressed and the blood static, and hence the heart spirit may become clouded and concealed. The modern Chinese medical diagnosis and treatment of this condition depends on whether the patient is in a manic or depressive state combined with their personal pattern discrimination.

TREATMENT BASED ON PATTERN DISCRIMINATION:

## 1. MANIC STATE

### A. LIVER DEPRESSION-BLOOD HEAT PATTERN

MAIN SYMPTOMS: High spirits, tension, agitation, easy anger, difficulty thinking, rushing about, meddlesomeness, intrusiveness, bilateral rib-side distention and pain, insomnia, profuse dreams, a bitter taste in the mouth, dry mouth, a crimson tongue with scanty fur, and a bowstring, rapid pulse

SYMPTOM ANALYSIS: Due to habitual bodily yang exuberance and emotional tension and agitation, the liver qi becomes depressed and stagnant. If the yang qi becomes fiercely exaggerated, blood heat may harass internally and the spirit brilliance may lose its control. Hence, there are the symptoms of an upsurge of spirits, tension, agitation, easy anger, difficulty thinking, rushing about, meddlesomeness, intrusiveness, and other such symptoms of psycho-emotional excitation. Due to liver channel depression and stagnation and qi depression not diffusing, there is bilateral rib-side distention and pain. Due to blood heat internally harassing and disquietude of the heart spirit, there is insomnia, profuse dreams, etc., while the dry mouth, the bitter taste in the mouth, the crimson tongue with scanty fur, and the bowstring, rapid pulse are all symptoms of liver depression-blood heat.

TREATMENT PRINCIPLES: Course the liver and drain heat, resolve depression and quiet the spirit

FORMULA & MEDICINALS: *Chai Hu Qing Gan Yin* (Bupleurum Clear the Liver Drink)

Radix Bupleuri (*Chai Hu*), 10g, Fructus Gardeniae Jasminoidis (*Zhi Zi*), 10g, Cortex Radicis Moutan (*Dan Pi*), 15g, Pericarpium Citri Reticulatae Viride (*Qing Pi*), 5g, Caulis Perillae Frutescentis (*Su Geng*), 10g, Radix Albus Paeoniae Lactiflorae (*Bai Shao*), 10g, Ramulus Uncariae Cum Uncis (*Gou Teng*), 15g (added later)

Decoct in water and administer orally in two divided doses, morning and evening, one *ji* per day.

FORMULA ANALYSIS: Within this formula, Bupleurum courses the liver and resolves depression. Gardenia, bitter and cold, clears heat from the three burners. Moutan cools the blood and clears fire hidden within the blood. Together, these are the ruling medicinals in this formula. Green Orange Peel and Caulis Perillae

rectify the qi and harmonize the center. White Peony nourishes yin and emolliates the liver, thus relaxing liver urgency, cramping, or tension. Uncaria enters the liver channel where it levels the liver and quiets the spirit. When all these medicinals are used together, they clear the liver and drain fire, resolve depression and quiet the spirit.

ADDITIONS & SUBTRACTIONS: If the formal body is strong and replete and there is agitation, worry, and restlessness with a bowstring, forceful pulse, one can add uncooked Frusta Ferri (*Tie Luo*), Mica Schist (*Meng Shi*), and Magnetitum (*Ci Shi*) to heavily settle and quiet the spirit, repress and control mania. If there is a bitter taste in the mouth, a dry mouth, heart vexation, restlessness, constipation, and a desire to drink due to fire hyperactivity and exuberance, one can add Rhizoma Coptidis Chinensis (*Huang Lian*), Radix Scutellariae Baicalensis (*Huang Qin*), Radix Et Rhizoma Rhei (*Da Huang*), and Plumula Nelumbinis Nuciferae (*Lian Zi Xin*).

ACUPUNCTURE: *Xing Jian* (Liv 2), *He Gu* (LI 4), *Qu Chi* (LI 11), *Xue Hai* (Sp 10), *Shen Men* (Ht 7), *Feng Chi* (GB 20), *Bai Hui* (GV 20). Use draining technique.

### B. LIVER DEPRESSION-PHLEGM FIRE PATTERN

MAIN SYMPTOMS: Emotional tension and agitation, excited, impetuous behavior, a bitter taste in the mouth, raving, bilateral rib-side distention and pain, insomnia, profuse dreams, dizziness, headache, spitting yellow phlegm from the mouth, a red tongue with slimy, yellow fur, and a bowstring, slippery, rapid pulse

ANALYSIS OF SYMPTOMS: Systemic phlegm fire exuberance and emotional tension and agitation lead to the yang qi inclined towards hyperactivity. If this is coupled with unfulfilled desires and liver qi depression and stagnation, then fierce exaggeration of the yang qi may lead to the two evils of phlegm and fire mutually stirring and harassing the spirit brilliance. Hence there is excited, rash, impetuous behavior, raving, and a bitter taste in the mouth. Liver channel depression and stagnation with phlegm fire ascending to harass the clear orifices results in bilateral rib-side distention and pain, insomnia, profuse dreams, dizziness, and headache, while spitting yellow phlegm from the mouth, a red tongue with slimy, yellow fur, and a bowstring, slippery, rapid pulse are all symptoms of phlegm fire internally brewing with liver qi depression and binding.

TREATMENT PRINCIPLES: Course the liver and resolve depression, transform phlegm and drain fire

**FORMULA & MEDICINALS:** *Qing Qi Hua Tan Tang He Gun Tan Wan* (Clear the Qi & Transform Phlegm Decoction plus Roll Phlegm Pills)

Pericarpium Citri Reticulatae (*Chen Pi*), 10g, Semen Pruni Armeniacae (*Xing Ren*), 10g, Fructus Immaturus Citri Aurantii (*Zhi Shi*), 10g, Radix Scutellariae Baicalensis (*Huang Qin*), 15g, Fructus Trichosanthis Kirlowii (*Gua Lou*), 15g, Sclerotium Poriae Cocos (*Fu Ling*), 15g, bile-processed Rhizoma Arisaematis (*Dan Nan Xing*), 15g, processed Rhizoma Pinelliae Ternatae (*Ban Xia*), 12g, *Gun Tan Wan* (Roll Phlegm Pills), 9g

*Gun Tan Wan* consist of: Calcined Mica Schist (*Meng Shi*), Radix Et Rhizoma Rhei (*Da Huang*), Radix Scutellariae Baicalensis (*Huang Qin*), Lignum Aquilariae Agallochae (*Chen Xiang*)

Decoct in water and administer orally in two divided doses, morning and evening, one *ji* per day.

**ANALYSIS OF FORMULA:** Within this formula, bile-processed Arisaema is the main medicinal which clears heat and transforms phlegm. It is assisted by Scutellaria and Fructus Trichosanthis which, together, clear heat and transform phlegm. Orange Peel and Immature Aurantium course the liver and resolve depression, rectify the qi and transform phlegm. These are likewise adjunctive medicinals. The spleen is the source of phlegm engenderment and the lungs are the place where phlegm is stored. Therefore, Poria is used to fortify the spleen and percolate dampness. Armeniacae moistens the intestines and stops cough. Pinellia dries dampness and transforms phlegm. These are the assisting and messenger medicinals. Because the essence spirit has lost control due to phlegm fire being exuberant internally, *Gun Tan Wan* are added to increase the power of downbearing fire and dispelling phlegm.

**ADDITIONS & SUBTRACTIONS:** If one is rash and impetuous and there is uncontrollable manic behavior, one can add uncooked Frusta Ferri (*Tie Luo*), Magnetitum (*Ci Shi*), and Haemititum (*Dai Zhe Shi*) to heavily settle and quiet the spirit. If there is constipation with yellowish red urine, add Radix Et Rhizoma Rhei (*Da Huang*) and Mirabilitum (*Mang Xiao*) to free the flow of the bowels and drain fire. If there is headache and dizziness, add Flos Chrysanthemi Morifolii (*Ju Hua*), Ramulus Uncariae Cum Uncis (*Gou Teng*), and Fructus Tribuli Terrestris (*Bai Ji Li*) to level the liver and stop tetany.

**ACUPUNCTURE:** *Xiang Jian* (Liv 2), *Feng Long* (St 40), *Zhong Wan* (CV 12), *Dan Zhong* (CV 17), *Shen Men* (Ht 7), *Lao Gong* (Per 8), *Feng Chi* (GB 20), *Bai Hui* (GV 20). Use draining technique with strong stimulation.

## C. QI STAGNATION & BLOOD STASIS PATTERN

**MAIN SYMPTOMS:** Emotional lability, changes in disease nature, sometimes agitated and impulsive, sometimes torpid and wooden, manic speech exiting from the mouth, a predilection to unstable anger, chest region fullness and oppression, headache with piercing, lancinating pain, red, bloodshot eyes, a dark, purplish tongue, possible static macules, or engorged, tortuous sublingual veins, and a bowstring, choppy pulse

**ANALYSIS OF SYMPTOMS:** If mania endures for a long time, this will lead to qi stagnation and blood stasis. Hence there is emotional lability, sometimes impetuousity and sometimes taciturnity and passivity, raving speech, a predilection to unstable anger, etc. In addition, static blood obstructing and stagnating prevents the clear yang from spreading. Thus the vessels and network vessels are not freely flowing. This results in chest region fullness and oppression and piercing head pain, while the red, bloodshot eyes, the dark, purplish tongue, static macules, engorged sublingual veins, and bowstring, choppy pulse are all signs of blood stasis obstructing internally.

**TREATMENT PRINCIPLES:** Quicken the blood and transform stasis, rectify the qi and resolve depression

**FORMULA & MEDICINALS:** *Dian Kuang Meng Xing Tang* (Withdrawal & Mania Dream-arousing Decoction)

Semen Pruni Persicae (*Tao Ren*), 24g, Radix Bupleuri (*Chai Hu*), 10g, Radix Rubrus Paeoniae Lactiflorae (*Chi Shao*), 20g, Caulis Akebiae (*Mu Tong*), 10g, Pericarpium Arecae Catechu (*Da Fu Pi*), 10g, Pericarpium Citri Reticulatae (*Chen Pi*), 10g, Cortex Radicis Mori Albi (*Sang Bai Pi*), 10g, Rhizoma Cyperi Rotundi (*Xiang Fu*), 6g, Rhizoma Pinelliae Ternatae (*Ban Xia*), 6g, Pericarpium Citri Reticulatae Viride (*Qing Pi*), 6g, Fructus Perillae Frutescentis (*Zi Su Zi*), 12g, Radix Glycyrrhizae (*Gan Cao*), 15g

Decoct in water and administer orally in two divided doses, morning and evening, one *ji* per day.

**ANALYSIS OF FORMULA:** This formula was created by the Qing dynasty doctor, Wang Qing-ren, to treat qi and blood congealing and stagnating in the brain resulting in withdrawal and mania. Within this formula, a heavy dose of Perica is combined with Red Peony as the main medicinals. Together, these cool the blood and transform stasis in order to free the flow of congealed and stagnant qi and blood within the brain orifices. Bupleurum and Cyperus rectify the qi and resolve depression. Green Orange Peel, Orange Peel, Pericarpium Arecae, and Fructus Perillae move and rectify the qi. Akebia frees and disinhibits the blood vessels, leading the blood to move downward. Pinellia harmonizes the stomach and transforms phlegm, and Licorice harmonizes all the other medicinals.

**ADDITIONS & SUBTRACTIONS:** If there is excitation and restlessness, add Cortex Radicis Moutan (*Dan Pi*), uncooked Radix Rehmanniae (*Sheng Di*), and Lumbricus (*Di Long*). If there is insomnia and disquieted sleep, add Radix Sophorae Flavescentis (*Ku Shen*) and Caulis Polygoni Multiflori (*Ye Jiao Teng*). If there is raving speech, hasty breathing, a red facial complexion, bad breath, and constipation, add Radix Et Rhizoma Rhei (*Da Huang*) and Rhizoma Coptidis Chinensis (*Huang Lian*). If phlegm is profuse and there is chest oppression, add bile-processed Rhizoma Arisaematis (*Dan Nan Xing*), Tuber Curcumae (*Yu Jin*), and fresh Succus Bamusae (*Zhu Li*). If there is rash, impetuous behavior and inability to control oneself, one can add calcined Mica Schist (*Meng Shi*) and Lignum Aquilariae Agallochae (*Chen Xiang*). If there is severe psycho-emotional excitation, one can add uncooked Frusta Ferri (*Tie Luo*), clear Mica Schist (*Meng Shi*), and Rhizoma Anemarrhenae Aspheloidis (*Zhi Mu*).

**ACUPUNCTURE:** *Tai Chong* (Liv 3), *He Gu* (LI 4), *Xue Hai* (Sp 10), *Xin Shu* (Bl 15), *Ge Shu* (Bl 17), *Gan Shu* (Bl 18), *Feng Chi* (GB 20), *Bai Hui* (GV 20). Use draining technique.

## D. FIRE EXUBERANCE DAMAGING YIN PATTERN

**MAIN SYMPTOMS:** Enduring withdrawal and mania, essence spirit listlessness, sometimes stillness, sometimes agitation, illogical speech, heart vexation, insomnia, excessive speaking, susceptibility to fright, vexatious heat in the five hearts, a dry throat with scanty fluids, a red tongue with scanty fur, and a fine, rapid pulse

**ANALYSIS OF SYMPTOMS:** If mania endures for a long time, it may consume and exhaust the righteous qi. Yin essence becomes depleted and vacuous, and vacuity fire harasses internally. Hence there is essence spirit lassitude, sometimes stillness and sometimes agitation, and illogical speech. If heart yin becomes insufficient and the heart spirit loses its nourishment, then there is heart vexation, insomnia, excessive speaking, and susceptibility to fright. Vexatious heat in the five hearts, a dry throat with scanty fluids, a red tongue with scanty fur, and a fine, rapid pulse are all symptoms of yin vacuity fire effulgence.

**TREATMENT PRINCIPLES:** Supplement the kidneys and enrich yin, clear fire and quiet the spirit

**FORMULA & MEDICINALS:** *Er Yin Jian* (Two Yin Decoction)

Uncooked Radix Rehmanniae (*Sheng Di*), 30g, Tuber Ophiopogonis Japonici (*Mai Dong*), 15g, Radix Scrophulariae Ningpoensis (*Xuan Shen*), 15g, Rhizoma Coptidis Chinensis (*Huang Lian*), 10g (added later), Caulis Akebiae (*Mu Tong*), 10g, Folium Bambusae (*Zhu Ye*), 10g, Medulla Junci Effusi (*Deng Xin Cao*), 5g, Sclerotium Pararadicis Poriae Cocos (*Fu Shen*), 15g, Semen Zizyphi Spinosae (*Suan Zao Ren*), 15g, Radix Glycyrrhizae (*Gan Cao*), 6g

Decoct in water and administer orally in two divided doses, morning and evening, one *ji* per day.

**ANALYSIS OF FORMULA:** Within this formula, uncooked Rehmannia, Ophiopogon, and Scrophularia nourish yin and clear heat. Coptis, Akebia, Folium Bambusae, and Juncus discharge heat and clear the heart. Spirit of Poria, Zizyphus Spinosa, and Licorice nourish the heart and quiet the spirit. Together, these medicinals have the effect of enriching yin in order to clear vacuity fire, nourishing the heart and quieting the spirit. They are appropriate for enduring mania damaging yin with vacuity fire internally harassing.

**ADDITIONS & SUBTRACTIONS:** If there are heart palpitations and restlessness with excessive speaking, susceptibility to fright, worry and anxiety, one can add *Qian Jin Ding Zhi Wan* (*Thousand [Pieces of] Gold* Stabilize the Mind Pills) in order to quiet the spirit and stabilize the mind. If there is heart vexation, chest oppression, sometimes agitation and sometimes depression, and susceptibility to joy and sighing, one can add Radix Bupleuri (*Chai Hu*), Radix Albus Paeoniae Lactiflorae (*Bai Shao*), and Flos Inulae (*Xuan Fu Hua*) to course the liver and resolve depression. If there is heart vexation, insomnia, excessive fear, and susceptibility to fright which endures for a long time without ceasing, one can add Radix Salviae Miltiorrhizae (*Dan Shen*) and Succinum (*Hu Po*) to quicken the blood and quiet the spirit.

*Qian Jin Ding Zhi Wan* consist of: Radix Panacis Ginseng (*Ren Shen*), Sclerotium Poriae Cocos (*Fu Ling*), Rhizoma Acori Graminei (*Shi Chang Pu*), and Radix Polygalae Tenuifoliae (*Yuan Zhi*).

**ACUPUNCTURE:** *San Yin Jiao* (Sp 6), *Tai Xi* (Ki 3), *Tai Chong* (Liv 3) needled through to *Yong Quan* (Ki 1), *Shen*

*Men* (Ht 7), *Nei Guan* (Per 6), *Feng Chi* (GB 20), *Bai Hui* (GV 20). Mostly use even supplementing-even draining technique with light stimulation. However, many Western patients with this pattern do not like acupuncture. They are too nervous and high-strung. Therefore, acupuncture can be counterproductive in these patients.

## 2. DEPRESSIVE STATE

### A. LIVER QI DEPRESSION & BINDING PATTERN

**MAIN SYMPTOMS:** Low spirits, many worries, susceptibility to anxiety, sorrow, hopelessness, decreased movement, slowed reactions, rib-side distention and pain, abdominal distention, scanty eating, loose stools which are not crisp, a pale tongue, and a bowstring, relaxed (*i.e.*, slightly slow) pulse

**ANALYSIS OF SYMPTOMS:** The liver rules coursing and discharge, and its nature likes to spread and extend itself freely. If the liver qi becomes depressed, the qi will bind and fail to spread and coursing and discharge will lose their normalcy. Hence there are low spirits or a depressed affect, many worries, susceptibility to anxiety, sorrow, hopelessness, slow reactions, etc. If there is liver depression qi stagnation, the channel and vessel qi mechanism will not be smoothly and easily flowing, thus there is rib-side distention and pain due to the liver qi counterflowing horizontally. Such horizontal counterflow may also attack the spleen and assail the stomach resulting in abdominal distention, loose, uncrisp stools, and scanty eating, while the pale tongue and bowstring, relaxed pulse are all signs of liver-stomach disharmony.

**TREATMENT PRINCIPLES:** Course the liver and resolve depression, rectify the qi and harmonize the center

**FORMULA & MEDICINALS:** *Chai Hu Shu Gan Tang* (Bupleurum Course the Liver Decoction)

Radix Bupleuri (*Chai Hu*), 10g, Rhizoma Cyperi Rotundi (*Xiang Fu*), 10g, Fructus Citri Aurantii (*Zhi Ke*), 10g, Pericarpium Citri Reticulatae (*Chen Pi*), 7g, Radix Ligustici Wallichii (*Chuan Xiong*), 5g (added later), Radix Albus Paeoniae Lactiflorae (*Bai Shao*), 10g, mix-fried Radix Glycyrrhizae (*Gan Cao*), 6g

Decoct in water and administer orally in two divided doses, morning and evening, one *ji* per day.

**ANALYSIS OF FORMULA:** This formula is made from *Si Ni San* (Four Counterflows Powder) plus Ligusticum, Cyperus, and Orange Peel. Within it, Bupleurum,

Cyperus, Aurantium, and Orange Peel course the liver and resolve depression, rectify the qi and harmonize the center. Ligusticum, White Peony, and Licorice quicken the blood and stabilize pain, emolliate the liver and relax urgency, tension, or cramping.

**ADDITIONS & SUBTRACTIONS:** If qi depression is relatively severe, one can add Tuber Curcumae (*Yu Jin*) and Pericarpium Citri Reticulatae Viride (*Qing Pi*) to assist the function of resolving depression. If the five depressions (*i.e.*, food, dampness, phlegm, blood, or fire) are complicating this condition, one can add *Yue Ju Wan* (Escape Restraint Pills) to move the qi and resolve depression.[1] If there is sorrow, a desire to commit suicide, and muddled, confused intelligence, one can combine *Su He Xiang Wan* (Liquid Styrax Pills) to warm, free the flow of, and open the orifices, transform turbidity and arouse the brain. If spleen and blood vacuity are more pronounced, with fatigue, possible water swelling, a fat, pale tongue, and a fine, bowstring pulse, one may use *Xiao Yao San* (Rambling Powder) instead. If spleen vacuity and/or stomach disharmony are pronounced with depressive heat in the lungs and/or stomach and phlegm dampness, one may use *Xiao Chai Hu Tang* (Minor Bupleurum Decoction) instead.

*Yue Ju Wan* is composed of: Rhizoma Cyperi Rotundi (*Xiang Fu*), Rhizoma Atractylodes (*Cang Zhu*), Radix Ligustici Wallichii (*Chuan Xiong*), Massa Medica Fermentata (*Shen Qu*), Fructus Gardeniae Jasminoidis (*Zhi Zi*).

**ACUPUNCTURE:** *Tai Chong* (Liv 3), *He Gu* (LI 4), *Zu San Li* (St 36), *Dan Zhong* (CV 17), *Zhong Wan* (CV 12), *Qi Hai* (CV 6). Mostly use draining technique.

### B. LIVER BLOOD STASIS & STAGNATION PATTERN

**MAIN SYMPTOMS:** Emotional depression, suicidal thoughts or behavior, vexation and agitation, difficulty thinking, slowness making connections in the mind, slow movement, a dark, dusky facial complexion, bilateral rib-side pain, blocked menstruation in females, a dark, purplish tongue or possible static spots, and a bowstring, choppy pulse[2]

**ANALYSIS OF SYMPTOMS:** Due to unfulfilled desires and worry and thought, the qi binds. If the qi remains depressed for some time, blood movement will also become unsmooth or uneasy. This then results in qi stagnation and blood stasis. Liver qi becomes depressed and bound and static blood obstructs and stagnates, the essence spirit will be devitalized and thus there is emotional depression, suicidal thoughts or behavior, vexation and agitation, difficulty thinking, slowness making connections within the mind, and slowed movements. The dark, dusky facial complexion, bilateral rib-side pain, blocked menstruation in females, dark, purplish tongue or static spots, and the bowstring, choppy pulse are all symptoms of qi stagnation and blood stasis.

**TREATMENT PRINCIPLES:** Quicken the blood and transform stasis, rectify the qi and resolve depression

**FORMULA & MEDICINALS:** *Xue Fu Zhu Yu Tang* (Blood Mansion Dispel Stasis Decoction)

Semen Pruni Persicae (*Tao Ren*), 12g, Flos Carthami Tinctorii (*Hong Hua*), 10g, Radix Angelicae Sinensis (*Dang Gui*), 10g, uncooked Radix Rehmanniae (*Sheng Di*), 10g, Radix Ligustici Wallichii (*Chuan Xiong*), 6g (added later), Radix Rubrus Paeoniae Lactiflorae (*Chi Shao*), 6g, Radix Platycodi Grandiflori (*Jie Geng*), 5g, Radix Cyathulae (*Chuan Niu Xi*), 10g, Radix Bupleuri (*Chai Hu*), 3g, Fructus Citri Aurantii (*Zhi Ke*), 6g, Radix Glycyrrhizae (*Gan Cao*), 3g

Decoct in water and administer orally in two divided doses, morning and evening, one *ji* per day.

**ANALYSIS OF FORMULA:** This formula is made from *Tao Hong Si Wu Tang* (Persica & Carthamus Four Materials Decoction) and *Si Ni San* (Four Counterflows Powder) plus Platycodon and Cyathula. Within this formula, Dang Gui, Persica, and Carthamus are the main medicinals which quicken the blood and dispel stasis. Ligusticum and Red Peony assist these main medicinals in quickening the blood and dispelling stasis and are the adjunctive medicinals. Uncooked Rehmannia combined with Dang Gui both nourishes and quickens the blood. It helps insure that dispelling stasis does not result in damaging yin blood. Cyathula dispels stasis and frees the flow of the blood vessels. Bupleurum, Playtcodon, and Aurantium course the liver, rectify the qi, and broaden the chest in order to resolve and eliminate any bitterness due to qi stagnation. In addition, if the qi moves, the blood moves. Licorice regulates and harmonizes all the other medicinals in this formula. When these medicinals are combined together, the blood is quickened and the qi is moved. Thus all the symptoms are automatically cured.

**ADDITIONS & SUBTRACTIONS:** If qi depression is heavy with suicidal thoughts and behavior, add Flos Pruni Persicae (*Tao Hua*), Tuber Curcumae (*Yu Jin*), and Rhizoma Acori Graminei (*Shi Chang Pu*) to dispel stasis, open the orifices, and arouse the brain. If blood stasis is

severe, add Lignum Dalbergiae Odoriferae (*Jiang Xiang*), blast-fried Squama Manitis Pentadactylis (*Chuan Shan Jia*), and Lignum Sappan (*Su Mu*).

**ACUPUNCTURE:** *Tai Chong* (Liv 3), *He Gu* (LI 4), *Xue Hai* (Sp 10), *San Yin Jiao* (Sp 6), *Shen Men* (Ht 7), *Nei Guan* (Per 6), *Dan Zhong* (CV 17), *Qi Hai* (CV 6). Mostly use draining technique.

## C. HEART-SPLEEN DUAL VACUITY PATTERN

**MAIN SYMPTOMS:** Emotional depression, lack of interest, self-blame, self-reproach, decreased activity, excessive thinking, excessive worry, heart vacuity qi timidity, *i.e.*, timidity and fearfulness, insomnia, impaired memory, fatigue and exhaustion, a pale white or sallow yellow, lusterless facial complexion, scanty eating, loose stools, a pale, enlarged tongue with white fur, and a fine, weak pulse[3]

**ANALYSIS OF SYMPTOMS:** Due to over-taxation of the heart by thinking and worrying, the heart spirit suffers detriment damage and the spleen becomes vacuous and weak. This leads to loss of normalcy of transportation and transformation and the qi and blood engenderment and transformation become insufficient. Hence the heart loses the place from which it receives nourishment and the heart spirit is not engendered. This results in emotional depression, lack of interest, self-blame and self-reproach, too much thinking and worrying, timidity, etc. If the spleen loses its fortification and movement, the qi and blood will not be full. Thus there are fatigue and exhaustion, a lusterless facial complexion, scanty eating, loose stools, etc., while a pale tongue with white fur and a fine, weak pulse are all signs of qi and blood insufficiency.

**TREATMENT PRINCIPLES:** Fortify the spleen and nourish the heart, boost the qi and supplement the blood

**FORMULA & MEDICINALS:** *Gui Pi Tang* (Restore the Spleen Decoction)

Radix Codonopsitis Pilosulae (*Dang Shen*), 15g, mix-fried Radix Astragali Membranacei (*Huang Qi*), 15g, Radix Angelicae Sinensis (*Dang Gui*), 5g, stir-fried Rhizoma Atractylodis Macrocephalae (*Bai Zhu*), 10g, Sclerotium Poriae Cocos (*Fu Ling*), 10g, mix-fried Radix Glycyrrhizae (*Gan Cao*), 6g, Arillus Euphoriae Longanae (*Long Yan Rou*), 15g, stir-fried Semen Zizyphi Spinosae (*Suan Zao Ren*), 15g, Radix Polygalae Tenuifoliae (*Yuan Zhi*), 10g, Radix Auklandiae Lappae (*Mu Xiang*), 5g, uncooked Rhizoma Zingiberis (*Sheng Jiang*), 6g, Fructus Zizyphi Jujubae (*Da Zao*), 3 pieces

Decoct in water and administer orally in two divided doses, morning and evening, one *ji* per day.

ANALYSIS OF FORMULA: Within this formula, Codonopsis and Astragalus sweetly and warmly boost the qi, greatly supplementing the spleen qi. Atractylodes, bitter and warm, fortifies the spleen and dries dampness. Poria blandly percolates and fortifies the spleen. Mix-fried Licorice, sweet and warm, regulates the center, boosts the qi, and fortifies the spleen. When the spleen and stomach obtain nourishment, then engenderment and transformation are effulgent and exuberant, heart blood is full and sufficient, and the spirit is autmatically quieted. Longans sweetly and warmly boost the heart and spleen and supplement the qi and blood in order to quiet the spirit, boost the intelligence, and calm the heart. When Dang Gui is combined with Astragalus, it boosts the qi and engenders the blood. Auklandia is acrid and warm. It moves the qi and scatters stagnation in order to resolve stagnant qi as well as rectify the qi and arouse the spleen. Polygala quiets the spirit, boosts the intelligence, and resolves depression. Zizyphus Spinosa calms the heart and quiets the spirit, while Zizyphus Jujuba and mix-fried Licorice harmonize the stomach and fortify the spleen, regulate and harmonize the constructive and defensive in order to promote engenderment and transformation. When the qi is effulgent, the blood is automatically engendered, and, when heart blood is full, the heart spirit is automatically quieted.

ADDITIONS & SUBTRACTIONS: If depression is severe with poor sleep at night, one can add Tuber Curcumae (*Yu Jin*), Fructus Citri Aurantii (*Zhi Ke*), and Flos Albizziae Julibrissinis (*He Huan Hua*) to open depression and quiet the spirit. If eating is scanty and there is disinclination to speak, one can add Fructus Amomi (*Sha Ren*) and Pericarpium Citri Reticulatae (*Chen Pi*) in order to rectify the qi and disperse food.

ACUPUNCTURE: *Shen Men* (Ht 7), *Tai Bai* (Sp 3), *Zu San Li* (St 36), *Xin Shu* (Bl 15), *Ge Shu* (Bl 17), *Pi Shu* (Bl 20). Use supplementing technique.

### D. SPLEEN-KIDNEY YANG VACUITY PATTERN

MAIN SYMPTOMS: Essence spirit listlessness, low spirits, addiction to lying down, scanty movement, diminished willpower, sorrow, ennui, decreased sexual desire, impotence and seminal emission in males, clear, watery vaginal discharge and/or early menstruation in females, a somber white facial complexion, lack of warmth in the four extremities, a fat, pale tongue with teeth-marks on its edges and white fur, and a deep, fine pulse[4]

ANALYSIS OF SYMPTOMS: If enduring depression is not resolved, detriment may reach the spleen and kidneys, in which case both the spleen and kidneys are vacuous and yang qi is devitalized. This results in essence spirit listlessness, low spirits, a constant desire to lay down, scanty movement, diminished willpower, sorrow, ennui, and decreased libido. The somber white facial complexion, lack of warmth in the four limbs, fat, pale tongue with white fur, and the deep, fine pulse are all symptoms of spleen-kidney yang vacuity.

TREATMENT PRINCIPLES: Fortify the spleen and boost the qi, warm yang and supplement the kidneys

FORMULA & MEDICINALS: *Wen Yang Xing Fen Tang* (Warm Yang & Excite Decoction)

Radix Codonopsitis Pilosulae (*Dang Shen*), 15g, cooked Radix Rehmanniae (*Shu Di*), 15g, Herba Epimedii (*Xian Ling Pi*), 5g, Herba Cistanchis Deserticolae (*Rou Cong Rong*), 15g, Plastrum Testudinis (*Gui Ban*), 15g, Radix Lateralis Praeparatus Aconiti Carmichaeli (*Fu Zi*), 10g, Radix Astragali Membranacei (*Huang Qi*), 10g, mix-fried Radix Glycyrrhizae (*Gan Cao*), 10g, Cortex Cinnamomi Cassiae (*Rou Gui*), 6g, dry Rhizoma Zingiberis (*Gan Jiang*), 6g

Decoct in water and administer orally in two divided doses, morning and evening, one *ji* per day.

ANALYSIS OF FORMULA: Within this formula, Codonopsis, Astragalus, and mix-fried Licorice fortify the spleen and boost the qi in order to promote the source of engenderment and transformation. Epimedium and Cistanches supplement the kidneys and invigorate yang. Plastrum Testudinis and cooked Rehmannia enrich the kidneys and foster the essence, thus seeking yang within yin. Aconite, dry Ginger, and Cortex Cinnamomi warm yang and excite, vitalizing the yang qi. When all these medicinals are used together, their effect is to fortify the spleen and boost the qi, vitalize and excite yang qi.

ADDITIONS & SUBTRACTIONS: If the essence spirit is devitalized with addiction to lying down, scanty movement, shortness of breath, disinclination to speak, scanty eating, and loose stools, one can add stir-fried Rhizoma Atractylodis Macrocephalae ((*Bai Zhu*), Rhizoma Cimicifugae (*Sheng Ma*), Pericarpium Citri Reticulatae (*Chen Pi*), and stir-fried Fructus Germinatus Hordei Vulgaris (*Mai Ya*) to fortify the spleen and boost the qi. If depression is not resolved and the willpower is decreased, one can add Radix Bupleuri (*Chai Hu*), Radix Polygalae Tenuifoliae (*Yuan Zhi*), Tuber Curcumae (*Yu Jin*), and

Fructus Citri Aurantii (*Zhi Ke*) to course the liver and resolve depression. If thinking is slow and difficult, behavior is slow and relaxed, and there is terminal dribbling of urination, one can add Semen Cuscutae Chinensis (*Tu Si Zi*), Semen Alpiniae Oxyphyllae (*Yi Zhi Ren*), Radix Linderae Strychnifoliae (*Wu Yao*), and Rhizoma Acori Graminei (*Shi Chang Pu*) to supplement the kidneys and open the orifices.

**ACUPUNCTURE:** Moxa *Zu San Li* (St 36), *Guan Yuan* (CV 4), *Qi Hai* (CV 6), *Shen Shu* (Bl 23), *Ming Men* (GV 4), *Pi Shu* (Bl 20), and *Bai Hui* (GV 20). If this pattern only complicates some other pattern and results in a mixed vacuity-repletion pattern overall, then only moxa *Guan Yuan* (CV 4).

**CLINICAL TIPS:** During depressive episodes, look for liver depression with spleen vacuity as the core disease mechanisms. This may then be complicated by blood, yin, and/or yang vacuities as well as phlegm turbidity. During manic episodes, there will always be some kind of evil heat. This is either depressive heat, phlegm heat, or vacuity heat.

**ABSTRACTS OF REPRESENTATIVE CHINESE RESEARCH:**

*Jiang Xi Zhong Yi Za Zhi (Jiangxi Journal of Chinese Medicine)*, #5, 1989, p. 197: Wang Cun-xi used self-composed *Meng Xia Cheng Qi Tang* (Mica & Pinellia Order the Qi Decoction) in the treatment of 310 cases of manic condition. This was comprised of Mica Schist (*Meng Shi*) and Radix Scutellariae Baicalensis (*Huang Qin*), 20g each, Rhizoma Pinelliae Ternatae (*Ban Xia*), Fructus Forsythiae Suspensae (*Lian Qiao*), Fructus Immaturus Citri Aurantii (*Zhi Shi*), and Rhizoma Acori Graminei (*Shi Chang Pu*), 10g each, Tuber Curcumae (*Yu Jin*), 15g, Cortex Magnoliae Officinalis (*Hou Po*), 12g, and Radix Et Rhizoma Rhei (*Da Huang*) and Mirabilitum (*Mang Xiao*), 10-30g each, with additional modifications depending on each patient's pattern discrimination. One *ji* of these medicinals were administered orally per day. During the acute stage, a small dose of Western medicine, such as 5-10mg

of haloperidol, were injected intramuscularly. Each evening, 50-200mg of cholrpromazine hydrochloride was administered orally. If, after administration of the above formula for 2-3 *ji*, there was no diarrhea, the dose of Mirabilitum and Rhubarb was increased. One hundred sixty-five patients were judged cured, 129 were judged improved, and 16 cases were deemed to have gotten no effect. Thus the total amelioration rate was 94%. The shortest course of disease was 15 days and the longest was 120 days, with a median duration of 76 days.

*Zhong Xi Yi Jie He Za Zhi (Journal of Integrated Chinese-Western Medicine)*, #8, 1984, p. 465: Zhang Liang-dong *et al.* used *Jia Wei Xiao Yao San* (Added Flavors Rambling Powder) as the main treatment of 26 cases of affective psychoses. Of these 26 patients, 13 were manic depressive, 10 were anxious and depressed, and three were simply manic. Because most of these patients suffered from insomnia, they were given 5-10mg of Valium before bed each night. After eight weeks of treatment, 16 cases were judged to have markedly improved, seven cases improved, and three cases got no effect. Thus the total amelioration rate was 88.5%.

**ENDNOTES**

[1] Although the text refers to the five depressions, *Yue Ju Wan* only treats four of these. It does not treat phlegm depression unless phlegm-transforming ingredients are added to it.

[2] This pattern is a combination of liver depression qi stagnation signs and symptoms with blood stasis signs and symptoms. Therefore, it could also be called qi stagnation and blood stasis pattern.

[3] This pattern often complicates liver depression and depressive heat in women. In real-life practice, it does not typically manifest as a simple, discrete pattern.

[4] This pattern is very common in perimenopausal women where it complicates liver depression and/or yin vacuity with either depressive or vacuity heat. In that case, the main symptoms of spleen qi vacuity are fatigue, cold hands and nose, orthostatic hypotension, easy bruising, loose stools, and a fat tongue, while the main symptoms of kidney yang vacuity will be low back pain, cold feet, nocturia, and decreased sexual desire.

# 7

# ANXIETY DISORDERS

Anxiety is an unpleasant emotional state. Anxiety disorders are a class of psychiatric disorders characterized by persisting or recurrent fear that may or may not be associated with a specific object or situation. Anxiety is often accompanied by physiologic changes and behavior similar to those caused by fear. Anxiety disorders are the most common class of psychiatric disorders. However, they are often not recognized and, therefore, commonly go untreated.

### NOSOLOGY:

Contemporary Western psychiatry distinguishes between panic attacks, panic disorder, and numerous primary psychiatric disorders that may include but do not require the presence of panic attacks to fulfill diagnostic criteria. The later category of disorders includes social and specific phobias, post-traumatic stress disorder (PTSD), generalized anxiety disorder (GAD), psychotic disorders, and numerous medical disorders that can manifest with panic-like symptoms. Representative medical disorders include hyperthyroidism (less commonly hypothyroidism), cardiac arrhythmias, and seizure disorders (see Differential Diagnosis below).

Western psychiatric nosology defines a panic attack as a transient experience of intense fear associated with arousal of the autonomic nervous system which may be accompanied by increased heart rate, perspiration, shortness of breath, or subjective feelings of dread. A panic attack may

occur spontaneously or may be cued by an identifiable stressor. Panic disorder is diagnosed when a pattern of recurring spontaneous panic attacks is associated with anticipatory anxiety of future attacks. Further, it must be established that these symptoms are not caused by a medical disorder or the effects of a substance and are not better explained by another co-existing psychiatric disorder. Panic attacks and associated anticipatory anxiety typically cause significant social and occupational impairment. In contemporary Western psychiatry, a clinical history of panic attacks that does not meet the above criteria cannot be formally diagnosed as panic disorder. For example, although patients with generalized anxiety disorder (GAD) frequently experience panic symptoms, the focus of clinical attention is personal and social distress caused by long-standing symptoms of anxiety or worry. In contrast to panic disorder and GAD, histrionic personality disorder is characterized by an enduring pattern of emotional dysregulation and attention-seeking behavior that may sometimes include panic attacks or other anxiety symptoms. Panic attacks sometimes occur during the course of major depressive disorder but are viewed as incidental features in this disorder. A diagnosis of depression requires that minimum criteria for duration and severity be met for a least five cardinal symptoms, including depressed mood, appetite change, "interest," sleep behavior, and others. Vegetative symptoms often associated with depression include feelings of lassitude or fatigue, reduced appetite, or loss of energy or initiative. Agitated symptoms can include easy anger, vexation, insomnia, and feelings of restlessness. Like histrionic personality disorder and generalized anxiety disorder, post-traumatic stress disorder may include panic attacks, but these are not required diagnostic criteria. The same holds for social and specific phobias in which the individual experiences recurring feelings of intense anxiety in social contexts or when exposed to a specific object or circumstance respectively.

## EPIDEMIOLOGY:

Panic disorder affects 1-2% of North American and European populations. A significantly higher percentage of individuals who report panic attacks experience some but not all symptoms required for a diagnosis of panic disorder. In surveyed Western populations, more women than men have panic disorder. In other surveys of Western populations, generalized anxiety disorder and social phobia are regarded as two of the most commonly occurring anxiety disorders. Both disorders have been observed more frequently in women than men. Prevalence estimates for GAD and social phobia are 8% and 3% respectively. Because of methodological difficulties inherent in designing studies on PTSD, prevalence estimates range from 1-19% of Western populations surveyed. Panic symptoms and anxiety states are frequent concomitants of numerous medical disorders. However, few epidemiologic studies have been done in this area.

## DIFFERENTIAL DIAGNOSIS:

Several common and unusual medical disorders can manifest as panic attacks, generalized anxiety states, agitation, and depression. Prior to assuming that any or all symptoms associated with the four patterns described under anxiety disorders are primary psychological complaints, probable medical etiologies must be ruled out. Panic-like symptoms and generalized anxiety are frequent concomitants of hyperthyroidism, However, hypothyroid states are also, though less frequently, associated with panic attacks. Other endocrinologic causes (including hyperparathyroidism and adrenal tumor) as well as cardiac arrhythmias, seizure disorders, hypoglycemia (and all its possible causes), medication side-effects, and CNS effects of illicit substances can manifest as panic attacks, agitation, or sustained generalized anxiety. Depression sometimes masks several underlying (often undiagnosed) medical disorders, including hypothyroidism and disorders of the central nervous system, but can also result from chronic substance abuse or medication side-effects. The medical differential diagnosis of major depressive disorder is reviewed in more detail in Chapter 4 of this Book, Depression.

When plausible medical etiologies have been ruled out, continuing symptoms are presumed to be psychogenic in origin until proven otherwise. One or several primary psychiatric disorders may be present. When the principal complaint is untriggered (i.e., not associated with an external stimulus) panic attacks in the absence of other anxiety symptoms, the Western diagnosis is panic disorder. Contemporary Western psychiatry distinguishes two major categories or symptom patterns of panic disorder. One pattern is characterized by panic attacks alone. In the other pattern, panic attacks are associated with agoraphobia, a condition in which intense fear is experienced in places from which escape or avoidance might be difficult or impossible in the event of a panic attack. In contrast to panic disorder, many other anxiety disorders may include panic attacks in the context of other more pervasive psychiatric symptoms that are the focus of clinical attention. For example, panic attacks may occur during the course of generalized anxiety disorder in which symptoms of excessive worry or anxiety that are not due to underlying medical conditions cause long-term distress or impairment in social or occupational functioning. In PTSD, panic attacks sometimes accompany flashbacks or recurring nightmares in which a life-threatening trauma is re-experienced. Although panic attacks can occur during the course of PTSD or obsessive-compulsive disorder, they are not necessary to fulfill diagnostic criteria for these disorders. Similarly, panic attacks may take place during the course of social phobia or specific phobias but are not necessary to diagnose these disorders. Specific phobias frequently manifest as panic attacks when the phobic object or situation is encountered (e.g., spiders in arachnophobia or heights in acrophobia), but again, their presence is not required to diagnose any specific phobia. Schizophrenics and individuals with other psychotic disorders sometimes experience agitation, heightened anxiety, or panic during the course of their illness. However, in Western psychiatry these symptoms are not core diagnostic criteria for the psychotic disorders.

## ETIOLOGY & PATHOPHYSIOLOGY:

Dozens of medical disorders can sometimes manifest as anxiety, agitation, or panic attacks. These are too numerous to review in detail for purposes of this discussion but can be broadly categorized as endocrinological, neurological, inflammatory; toxic, systemic, and idiopathic disorders. All of these types of disorders directly or indirectly affect normal CNS functioning resulting in the range of observed symptomatology. Research evidence suggests that medical etiologies of anxiety symptoms are mediated through different metabolic, endocrinologic, or neurophysiological path-

## DIFFERENTIAL DIAGNOSIS

| 1. MEDICAL DISORDERS | 2. EFFECTS OF SUBSTANCES | 3. PSYCHIATRIC DISORDERS |
|---|---|---|
| A. HYPERTHYROIDISM OR HYPOTHYROIDISM<br>B. OTHER ENDOCRINOLOGICAL DISORDERS INCLUDING HYPERPARATHYROIDISM, ADRENAL TUMORS, OTHERS<br>C. CARDIAC ARRHYTHMIAS<br>D. SEIZURE DISORDERS<br>E. HYPOGLYCEMIA | A. ALCOHOL OR ILLICIT SUBSTANCE INTOXICATION OR WITHDRAWAL<br>B. SIDE EFFECTS OF MEDICATIONS | A. PANIC DISORDER WITH OR WITHOUT AGORAPHOBIA<br>B. GENERALIZED ANXIETY DISORDER (GAD)<br>C. POST-TRAUMATIC STRESS DISORDER (PTSD)<br>D. OBSESSIVE-COMPULSIVE DISORDER (OCD)<br>E. SOCIAL PHOBIA AND SPECIFIC PHOBIAS<br>F. SCHIZOPHRENIA AND OTHER PSYCHOTIC DISORDERS |

ways. The pathophysiology of panic disorder has been extensively studied. Dysregulation in many neurotransmitter systems, hormones, and the autonomic nervous system have been postulated as primary underlying causes of panic attacks or increased susceptibility to them. Implicated neurotransmitters include GABA, norepinephrine, serotonin, and cholecystokinin. Dysregulation of the hypothalamic-pituitary-adrenal axis resulting in abnormal elevation of blood cortisol may predispose certain individuals to generalized anxiety states or panic attacks. Diseases affecting the thyroid commonly manifest as panic attacks. Cardiac arrhythmias and seizure disorders are sometimes initially misdiagnosed as panic disorder only to be confirmed by laboratory findings or the patient's subsequent clinical course. Hypoglycemia, which accompanies numerous medical disorders including diabetes, many disorders of the liver, and pancreatic cancer can manifest as a pattern of recurring panic attacks or increased arousal. Genetic factors likely also play a significant role in several symptoms or disorders, including panic disorder, obsessive-compulsive disorder (OCD), and social phobia.

Psychogenic causes should be considered only after plausible medical etiologies have been ruled out. Numerous psychoanalytic, behavioral, and cognitive models of panic disorder, generalized anxiety states, and other anxiety syndromes have been advanced. However, to date, there is little consensus surrounding psychological models that best explain clinically observed symptom patterns.

### WESTERN MEDICAL TREATMENT:

Medical treatments of identified biological causes of anxiety states or panic attacks directly or indirectly target presumed metabolic, endocrinologic, or neurophysiological mechanisms whose dysregulation results in those symptom patterns. Anxiety symptoms improve significantly in most cases soon after effective treatment has been initiated. Anxiety states or panic attacks that do not resolve following correction of a presumed medical cause may be multifactorial and/or psychogenic in origin. Contemporary Western psychiatry describes many pharmacological treatments for unresolving patterns of anxiety symptoms. Sedative-hypnotic medications, including principally benzodiazepines, comprise the mainstay of traditional Western treatment for anxiety. Among others, these include clonazepam (Klonopin), lorazepam (Ativan), diazepam (Valium), and alprazolam (Xanax). Benzodiazepines reduce or alleviate anxiety and panic symptoms by increasing CNS activity of GABA, the brain's major inhibitory neurotransmitter. Serotonin-selective re-uptake inhibitors (SSRIs), tricyclic antidepressants (TCAs), and monoamine oxidase inhibitors (MAOIs) are also commonly used to treat the range of anxiety disorders, including panic disorder and generalized anxiety disorder. In contemporary Western psychiatry, there is little consensus regarding *best* treatments of specific anxiety disorders. Virtually all classes of psychopharmacological drugs have been explored in clinical trials. Variable outcomes suggest considerable subjective differences between individuals who report similar anxiety symptoms.

Cognitive-behavioral therapies (CBT) have demonstrated efficacy against most anxiety disorders, including panic disorder, GAD, social and specific phobias, OCD, and some cases of PTSD. Among other techniques, CBT includes progressive muscle relaxation, exposure and response prevention, deep breathing exercises, visualization (including guided imagery), and others. Many patients benefit more from combined psychopharmacological treatment and cognitive-behavioral therapy than from either treatment modality alone.

## SHORT & LONG-TERM ADVANTAGES & DISADVANTAGES OF WESTERN MEDICAL TREATMENT:

Advantages of effective Western medical treatment generally include improved social and occupational functioning as an indirect consequence of diminished symptom severity. The less anxious individual is able to think more clearly at work and function more smoothly in social contexts. Sustained reduction in the severity or frequency of anxiety symptoms is associated with reduced risk of co-morbid depression, other anxiety disorders, and substantially reduced risk of alcohol or substance abuse. Short-term disadvantages of conventional pharmacological treatment with benzodiazepines include sedation and interference with normal cognitive functioning which can become problematic in elderly or demented patients who have diminished cognitive reserve. Other psychopharmacologic agents commonly used to treat anxiety disorders have numerous associated side effects which vary from drug to drug. These include sexual dysfunction, gastrointestinal distress, dry mouth, hypotension, and others.

Chronic benzodiazepine use results in dependence and all related medical and psychological complications including tolerance (the need for increasing doses to achieve a given anxiety reducing effect) and withdrawal following rapid cessation. As benzodiazepines are potentiated by alcohol and certain prescription medications and illicit substances, individuals who abuse alcohol or drugs or who are being treated for certain medical disorders are at risk of potentially dangerous, sometimes lethal interactions.

## PROGNOSIS:

The long-term outcomes of anxiety states associated with underlying medical disorders depend on chronicity, severity, and responsiveness of these disorders to conventional medical treatments. When there is an identified medical etiology, anxiety symptoms typically resolve following successful treatment. In certain cases, however, anxiety symptoms may persist following resolution of an underlying medical disorder. This is often the case, for example, following successful treatment of viral or bacterial encephalitis. Panic disorder follows a fluctuating, chronic course, but its overall prognosis is usually quite good. In contrast, social phobia and obsessive-compulsive disorder (OCD) are typically less responsive to available Western psychiatric treatments and, therefore, often result in long-term impairment in social and occupational functioning. Generalized anxiety disorder (GAD) is often diagnosed together with another more impairing psychiatric disorder (typically depression) which may be the primary focus of clinical attention. Little information is available on long-term outcomes in cases of GAD. The expected course of post-traumatic stress disorder (PTSD) is highly variable and depends on pre-morbid (i.e., pretraumatic) social adjustment, the presence of other psychiatric or medical disorders, and symptom severity. It is estimated that one-third of PTSD patients gradually improve but continue to experience symptoms throughout life. Approximately 10% remain unchanged or develop more severe symptoms, and the remaining 60% recover to varying degrees but may experience relapses throughout the course of their lives.

## INDICATIONS FOR REFERRAL TO WESTERN MEDICAL SERVICES:

The patient should be referred to the nearest emergency room or urgent care center when history or clinical presentation suggests associated acute or progressive medical illness, including heart disease, seizure disorder, or other neurologic illness, cardiovascular disease, or an infectious process. Abuse of alcohol or an illicit substance that has resulted in impaired functioning or places the patient at risk is also sufficient basis for urgent medical referral.

In cases where acute, severe, or progressive medical problems have been excluded as possible causes of the four symptom patterns under anxiety disorders, routine referral to a psychiatrist may clarify the differential diagnosis and lead to a more efficacious integrative treatment plan if symptoms have failed to respond to an appropriate course and duration of Chinese medical treatment.

## CHINESE DISEASE CATEGORIZATION:

In Chinese medicine, the symptoms which Western medicine categorizes as anxiety disorders are mostly categorized as fright and fear (jing kong), fright palpitations (jing ji), and fearful throbbing (zheng chong).

## CHINESE MEDICAL DISEASE CAUSES & DISEASE MECHANISMS:

In Chinese medicine, this disease is believed to be caused primarily by habitual bodily righteous vacuity and recurrent stimulation of the seven affects. These internally damage the three viscera of the heart, liver, and spleen. This then results in irregularity of the function of the viscera and bowels, disturbance in the flow of qi and blood, and thus substantial depletion and detriment. Unfulfilled desires or damage due to anger may result in liver depression qi stagnation. Because of the close reciprocal relationship between the liver and spleen, liver qi repletion typically results in spleen qi vacuity. If liver depression endures and transforms into fire, this evil heat may consume and damage yin fluids. When this evil heat flares upward, it may harass the heart and disquiet the spirit. On the other hand, over-thinking and too much worry and anxiety may directly damage the heart and spleen, causing a heart blood-spleen qi vacuity. In that case, the spirit will be deprived of nourishment and will typically also become disquieted. If spleen vacuity leads to phlegm engenderment and liver depression leads to transformative heat, then a combination of phlegm heat may harass the heart spirit. It is also possible for enduring qi stagnation to result in blood stasis. If this static blood obstructs internally, it may deprive the heart spirit of nourishment and block the heart orifices. Often such blood stasis combines with depressive heat, thus forming heat stasis. In that case, heat harasses the spirit, while stasis blocks the orifices.

By now, the reader should be aware that there are close reciprocal relationships between the liver and spleen, spleen and heart, liver and kidneys, qi and phlegm, qi and blood, and qi and heat. Therefore, in real-life practice, these various disease mechanisms often tend to complicate each other.

### TREATMENT BASED ON PATTERN DISCRIMINATION:

### 1. HEART QI VACUITY & BLOOD STASIS PATTERN

**MAIN SYMPTOMS:** Sudden onset of tension, fear, and dread, tension stretching from *Da Zhui* (GV 14) to the head, a feeling of doom and approaching death causing incessant moaning, restless sitting, crying and sighing, rapid, distressed breathing, heart jumping rapidly, chest oppression, a suffocating feeling in the chest, heart palpitations, shortness of breath, listlessness of the essence spirit, insomnia, profuse dreams, a dark, pale tongue with white fur, and a fine, weak, possibly bound or regularly intermittent pulse

**NOTE:** This pattern is a combination of heart-spleen dual vacuity and qi stagnation and blood stasis.

**ANALYSIS OF SYMPTOMS:** If the seven affects damage internally, the heart qi may become insufficient. Thus the heart's stirring of the vessels (*i.e.*, promotion of blood flow) may lack strength. This results in the heart palpitations, shortness of breath, and listlessness of the essence spirit. If the heart qi is vacuous and insufficient, then breathing may become rapid and hasty. Likewise, there may be crying and sighing. If the heart qi and heart blood are vacuous and insufficient, then the heart spirit will lack nourishment. Hence sitting is restless and there is tension, fear, and dread. If the heart qi is insufficient, then chest yang will also be devitalized and the heart vessels will be blocked and obstructed. Thus one may see chest oppression or a suffocating feeling in the chest. The dark tongue with white fur and the fine, weak or bound, regularly intermittent pulses are all signs of heart qi vacuity mixed with static blood blocking and obstructing.

**TREATMENT PRINCIPLES:** Boost the qi and nourish the heart, quicken the blood and free the flow of the vessels

**FORMULA & MEDICINALS:** *Tian Wang Bu Xin Dan* (Heavenly Emperor Supplement the Heart Elixir)

Uncooked Radix Rehmanniae (*Sheng Di*), 30g, Fructus Schisandrae Chinensis (*Wu Wei Zi*), 10g, Radix Angelicae Sinensis (*Dang Gui*), 15g, Tuber Asparagi Cochinensis (*Tian Men Dong*), 15g, Tuber Ophiopogonis Japonici (*Mai Dong*), 15g, Semen Biotae Orientalis (*Bai Zi Ren*), 15g, Semen Zizyphi Spinosae (*Suan Zao Ren*), 15g, Radix Panacis Ginseng (*Ren Shen*), 10g (decocted first), Radix Scrophulariae Ningpoensis (*Xuan Shen*), 10g, Sclerotium Poriae Cocos (*Fu Ling*), 10g, Radix Salviae Miltiorrhizae (*Dan Shen*), 10g, Radix Platycodi Grandiflori (*Jie Geng*), 10g

Decoct in water and administer orally in two divided doses, morning and evening, one *ji* per day.

**ANALYSIS OF FORMULA:** Within this formula, uncooked Rehmannia, Scrophularia, Asparagus, and Ophiopogon enrich yin and nourish the blood, nourish the heart and quiet the spirit. Ginseng and Poria boost the heart qi and quiet the heart spirit. Biota and Polygala calm the heart and quiet the spirit. Salvia and Dang Gui supplement the blood and nourish the heart at the same time as they quicken the blood and free the flow of the vessels. The sourness of Schisandra and Zizyphus Spinosa restrains the heart qi from floating and stirring, being worn away and stirring. They also are able to quiet the spirit. Platycodon guides the other medicinals to the upper part of the body and the site of the disease. When all these medicinals are used together, they boost the qi and nourish the blood, nourish the heart and quiet the spirit, quicken the blood and free the flow of the vessels.

ADDITIONS & SUBTRACTIONS: If there is a suffocating, oppressive feeling in the chest or possible piercing pain due to devitalized chest yang and static blood obstructing and stagnating, one can add Tuber Curcumae (*Yu Jin*), Ramulus Cinnamomi Cassiae (*Gui Zhi*), and Radix Rubiae Cordifoliae (*Qian Cao*). If there is tension, disquietude, and heart qi floating upward, one can add Os Draconis (*Long Gu*), Concha Margaritiferae (*Zhen Zhu Mu*), and uncooked Concha Ostreae (*Mu Li*). If there is emotional lability, tension, agitation, easy anger, headache, and dizziness due to liver depression transforming fire, then one can add Radix Bupleuri (*Chai Hu*), Fructus Gardeniae Jasminoidis (*Zhi Zi*), and Radix Scutellariae Baicalensis (*Huang Qin*) or administer in addition *Dan Zhi Xiao Yao Wan* (Moutan & Gardenia Rambling Pills, a Chinese ready-made medicine).

*Dan Zhi Xiao Yao Wan* consist of: Cortex Radicis Moutan (*Dan Pi*), Fructus Gardeniae Jasminoidis (*Zhi Zi*), Radix Bupleuri (*Chai Hu*), Radix Angelicae Sinensis (*Dang Gui*), Radix Albus Paeoniae Lactiflorae (*Bai Shao*), Rhizoma Atractylodis Macrocephalae (*Bai Zhu*), Sclerotium Poriae Cocos (*Fu Ling*), mix-fried Radix Glycyrrhizae (*Gan Cao*).

If there is liver depression with spleen qi and blood vacuity but no particular blood stasis, use *Xiao Yao San Jia Wei* (Rambling Powder with Added Flavors) instead: Radix Bupleuri (*Chai Hu*), 3-10g, Radix Angelicae Sinensis (*Dang Gui*), 10-18g, Radix Albus Paeoniae Lactiflorae (*Bai Shao*), 10g, Rhizoma Atractylodis Macrocephalae (*Bai Zhu*), 10g, Sclerotium Poriae Cocos (*Fu Ling*), 10g, mix-fried Radix Glycyrrhizae (*Gan Cao*), 6-10g, Caulis Polygoni Multiflori (*Ye Jiao Teng*), 12g, Cortex Albizziae Julibrissinis (*He Huan Pi*), 12g, uncooked Rhizoma Zingiberis (*Sheng Jiang*), 2-3 slices (added later), Herba Menthae Haplocalycis (*Bo He*), 3g (added later).

ACUPUNCTURE: *Tai Chong* (Liv 3), *Xue Hai* (Sp 10), *He Gu* (LI 4), *Shen Men* (Ht 7), *Nei Guan* (Per 6), *Zu San Li* (St 36), *Xin Shu* (Bl 15), *Ge Shu* (Bl 17). Use even supplementing-even draining technique.

## 2. LIVER DEPRESSION-PHLEGM FIRE PATTERN

MAIN SYMPTOMS: Emotional depression, anxiety, worry, sorrow, tension, vexation and agitation, easy anger, a tendency to sighing, insomnia, profuse dreams, chest and diaphragmatic fullness and oppression, bilateral rib-side distention and pain, profuse, thick phlegm, a red tongue with slimy, yellow fur, and a bowstring or bowstring, slippery, rapid pulse

ANALYSIS OF SYMPTOMS: If there is emotional depression, then the liver qi is depressed and bound and the qi mechanism has lost its regulation/regularity. Hence the affect is depressed and there is anxiety, worry, sorrow, and tension, rib-side pain, and a tendency to sigh. If the qi has remained depressed for some time, qi stagnation may engender phlegm. If both endure, they may engender fire. In that case, phlegm fire harassing internally may produce symptoms of vexation and agitation, easy anger, chest and diaphragmatic fullness and oppression, profuse, thick, possibly yellow-colored phlegm, insomnia, and profuse dreams. The red tongue with slimy, yellow fur and the bowstring, slippery, rapid pulse are signs of liver qi depression and binding and phlegm fire brewing internally.

TREATMENT PRINCIPLES: Course the liver and resolve depression, clear heat and transform phlegm

FORMULA & MEDICINALS: *Chai Hu Shu Gan San He Xiao Xian Xiong Tang* (Bupleurum Course the Liver Powder plus Minor Sinking Chest Decoction)

Radix Bupleuri (*Chai Hu*), 10g, Pericarpium Citri Reticulatae (*Chen Pi*), 10g, Radix Albus Paeoniae Lactiflorae (*Bai Shao*), 15g, Fructus Citri Aurantii (*Zhi Ke*), 10g, mix-fried Radix Glycyrrhizae (*Gan Cao*), 6g, Radix Ligustici Wallichii (*Chuan Xiong*), 6g (added later), Rhizoma Cyperi Rotundi (*Xiang Fu*), 6g, Rhizoma Coptidis Chinensis (*Huang Lian*), 6g (added later), Rhizoma Pinelliae Ternatae (*Ban Xia*), 10g, Fructus Trichosanthis Kirlowii (*Gua Lou*), 30g

Decoct in water and administer orally in two divided doses, morning and evening, one *ji* per day.

ANALYSIS OF FORMULA: This formula uses Bupleurum and White Peony to mainly course the liver, resolve depression, and clear heat. These are then combined with Aurantium, Orange Peel, Ligusticum, and Cyperus to course the liver and move the qi, quicken the blood and free the flow of the network vessels. Coptis, Pinellia, and Trichosanthes are used from *Xiao Xian Xiong Tang* to clear heat and transform phlegm. Thus they eliminate the phlegm fire harassing within the chest. Mix-fried Licorice regulates and harmonizes all the other medicinals. When all these medicinals are used together, they course the liver and resolve depression, clear heat and transform phlegm.

ADDITIONS & SUBTRACTIONS: If there is heart vexation and disquietude, short, reddish urination, and constipation, one can add wine-fried Radix Et Rhizoma

Rhei (*Da Huang*), Fructus Gardeniae Jasminoidis (*Zhi Zi*), and Radix Scutellariae Baicalensis (*Huang Qin*) to clear and discharge fire from all three burners. If there is headache, dizziness, a red facial complexion, red eyes, vexation and agitation, and irritability, one can add Radix Gentianae Scabrae (*Long Dan Cao*), Rhizoma Alismatis (*Ze Xie*), Flos Chrysanthemi Morifolii (*Ju Hua*), and Bombyx Batryticatus (*Jiang Can*) to clear the liver and drain fire, brighten the eyes and stop tetany. If phlegm turbidity is relatively severe, add Bulbus Fritillariae Cirrhosae (*Chuan Bei Mu*), Rhizoma Pinelliae Ternatae (*Ban Xia*), and Rhizoma Atractylodis Macrocephalae (*Bai Zhu*) to transform phlegm and dispel dampness. If there is a splitting headache with a red facial complexion, and stiff neck, add Radix Achyranthis Bidentatae (*Niu Xi*), Concha Haliotidis (*Shi Jue Ming*), and Spica Prunellae Vulgaris (*Xia Ku Cao*) to level the liver and subdue yang.

**ACUPUNCTURE:** *Xing Jian* (Liv 2), *Jian Shi* (Per 5), *He Gu* (LI 4), *Feng Long* (St 40), *Dan Zhong* (CV 17), *Zhong Wan* (CV 12). Mostly use draining technique.

## 3. HEART QI STAGNATION & BLOOD STASIS PATTERN

**MAIN SYMPTOMS:** Episodes of anxiety and worry which endure for a long time and do not heal, tension, wanness and sallowness, fearful throbbing, impaired memory, fear and dread, shaking, trembling, a torpid, stagnant affect, chest area oppression and pain, venter and abdominal burping and belching or hiccup, a dark, stagnant facial complexion, dark, greenish circles around the eyes, a dark red tongue or static spots and macules, and a deep, bowstring, or fine, choppy pulse

**ANALYSIS OF SYMPTOMS:** If the seven affects are repressed or there is excessive fear and fright, the qi mechanism may become depressed and stagnant and hence the blood movement may not be smooth or easily flowing. If this endures, it will lead to the blood's movement also becoming stagnant. Static blood will then obstruct the heart vessels. It is also possible for enduring disease to enter the network vessels causing static blood to obstruct internally. In any case, the symptoms of such static blood internally obstructing are episodic anxiety and worry which endures for a long time and does not heal accompanied by other static blood signs and symptoms. If the heart qi becomes depressed and stagnant and the movement of the blood loses its smoothness or easiness, then the heart spirit may become disquieted. This then produces the tension, wanness and sallowness, fearful throbbing, impaired memory, fear and fright, restlessness, and the torpid, stagnant affect, etc.

**TREATMENT PRINCIPLES:** Quicken the blood and move stagnation, settle the heart and quiet the spirit

**FORMULA & MEDICINALS:** *Xue Fu Zhu Yu Tang Jia Jian* (Blood Mansion Dispel Stasis Decoction with Additions & Subtractions)

Radix Salviae Miltiorrhizae (*Dan Shen*), 15g, Radix Angelicae Sinensis (*Dang Gui*), 15g, Radix Ligustici Wallichii (*Chuan Xiong*), 10g (added later), Radix Albus Paeoniae Lactiflorae (*Chi Shao*), 12g, Semen Pruni Persicae (*Tao Ren*), 12g, Flos Carthami Tinctorii (*Hong Hua*), 10g (steeped), Radix Bupleuri (*Chai Hu*), 15g, Fructus Citri Aurantii (*Zhi Ke*), 12g, Rhizoma Cyperi Rotundi (*Xiang Fu*), 15g, Tuber Curcumae (*Yu Jin*), 15g, Dens Draconis (*Long Chi*), 15g (decocted first), Radix Polygalae Tenuifoliae (*Yuan Zhi*), 10g, Succinum (*Hu Po*), 6g (swallowed with the decocted liquid), mix-fried Radix Glycyrrhizae (*Gan Cao*), 6g

Decoct in water and administer orally in two divided doses, morning and evening, one *ji* per day.

**ANALYSIS OF FORMULA:** Within this formula, Salvia, Dang Gui, Ligusticum, Red Peony, Persica, and Carthamus all quicken the blood and transform stasis, nourish the blood and quiet the spirit. Bupleurum, Aurantium, Cyperus, and Curcuma move the qi and resolve depression, rectify the qi and quiet the spirit. Dragon's Teeth, Polygala, and Succinum quiet the spirit and stabilize the mind, settle the heart and quiet the spirit. When all these medicinals are used together, they quicken the blood and move stagnation, settle the heart and quiet the spirit, clear heat and nourish the blood.

**ADDITIONS & SUBTRACTIONS:** If there is heart spirit vexation and chaos, chaotic qi and heat within the chest, tension, anxiety and worry, insomnia, profuse dreams, and a red tongue due to heart fire flaming upward burning and damaging yin blood, then also administer *Zhu Sha An Shen Wan* (Cinnabar Quiet the Spirit Pills, a Chinese ready-made medicine) in order to settle the heart and quiet the spirit, clear heat and nourish the blood.

*Zhu Sha An Shen Wan* consist of: Cinnabar (*Zhu Sha*), Rhizoma Coptidis Chinensis (*Huang Lian*), Radix Angelicae Sinensis (*Dang Gui*), uncooked Radix Rehmanniae (*Sheng Di*), and Radix Glycyrrhizae (*Gan Cao*).

**ACUPUNCTURE:** *Tai Chong* (Liv 3), *He Gu* (LI 4), *Xue Hai* (Sp 10), *Shen Men* (Ht 7), *Nei Guan* (Per 6), *Yin Tang* (M-HN-3), *Dan Zhong* (CV 17), *Xin Shu* (Bl 15). Mostly use draining technique.

## 4. HEART-SPLEEN DUAL VACUITY PATTERN

**MAIN SYMPTOMS:** Fear and dread, worry and anxiety, fright palpitations, insomnia, profuse dreams, impaired memory, fatigue, lassitude of the spirit, lack of strength in the four limbs, scanty eating, loose stools, cold hands and feet, a pale white, somber white, or swallow yellow facial complexion, pale lips and nails, a pale, fat, swollen tongue with teeth-marks on its edges and thin, white fur, and a fine, weak pulse

**ANALYSIS OF SYMPTOMS:** If heart qi and blood are insufficient to construct and nourish the spirit, there will be fear and dread, worry and anxiety, fright palpitations, insomnia, profuse dreams, and impaired memory. Spleen qi vacuity is responsible for the fatigue, lassitude of the spirit, lack of strength, scanty eating, loose stools, cold hands and feet, fat, swollen tongue, and weak pulse. Blood vacuity is responsible for the pale, white, somber white, or sallow yellow facial complexion, pale lips and nails, and pale tongue, and fine pulse.

**TREATMENT PRINCIPLES:** Fortify the spleen and supplement the heart, nourish the blood and quiet the spirit

**FORMULA & MEDICINALS:** *Gui Pi Tang* (Restore the Spleen Decoction)

Radix Panacis Ginseng (*Ren Shen*), 3-6g (decocted first), Radix Astragali Membranacei (*Huang Qi*), 12-15g, Radix Angelicae Sinensis (*Dang Gui*), 10g, Arillus Euphoriae Longanae (*Long Yan Rou*), 10g, Rhizoma Atractylodis Macrocephalae (*Bai Zhu*), 10g, Sclerotium Poriae Cocos (*Fu Ling*), 10g, Semen Zizyphi Spinosae (*Suan Zao Ren*), 12g, mix-fried Radix Glycyrrhizae (*Gan Cao*), 6-10g, Radix Auklandiae Lappae (*Mu Xiang*), 6g (added later), Radix Polygalae Tenuifoliae (*Yuan Zhi*), 6-10g, Fructus Zizyphi Jujubae (*Da Zao*), 3-5 pieces, uncooked Rhizoma Zingiberis (*Sheng Jiang*), 1-3 slices (added later)

Decoct in water and administer orally in two divided doses, morning and evening, one *ji* per day.

**ANALYSIS OF FORMULA:** Ginseng, Astragalus, Atractylodes, Poria, and mix-fried Licorice supplement the spleen and boost the qi. Dang Gui, Zizyphus Spinosa, Longans, and Red Dates supplement the heart and nourish the blood. Together, these two groups of medicinals construct and nourish the heart spirit, thus quieting and calming it. Auklandia, Polygala, and uncooked Ginger all rectify the qi and resolve depression.

**ADDITIONS & SUBTRACTIONS:** To supplement the blood more, add cooked Radix Rehmanniae (*Shu Di*) and Radix Albus Paeoniae Lactiflorae (*Bai Shao*). To course the liver and rectify the qi, add a little Radix Bupleuri (*Chai Hu*). To settle, still, and quiet the spirit even more, add Os Draconis (*Long Gu*) and Concha Ostreae (*Mu Li*). To nourish the heart and quiet the spirit more, add Semen Biotae Orientalis (*Bai Zi Ren*).

**ACUPUNCTURE:** *Zu San Li* (St 36), *Shen Men* (Ht 7), *Nei Guan* (Per 6), *San Yin Jiao* (Sp 6), *Xin Shu* (Bl 15), *Ge Shu* (Bl 17), *Pi Shu* (Bl 20). Use supplementing technique.

## 5. YIN VACUITY-FIRE EFFULGENCE PATTERN

**MAIN SYMPTOMS:** Fear and dread, susceptibility to fright, vexation and agitation, dizziness, tinnitus, insomnia, heart palpitations, afternoon tidal heat, possible night sweats, malar flushing, vexatious heat in the five hearts, insomnia, a dry mouth and throat, low back and knee soreness and weakness, excessive night-time urination which is scanty in amount and yellow in color, a red tongue with scanty fur, and a fine, rapid or surging, rapid, rootless pulse

**ANALYSIS OF SYMPTOMS:** If, for any reason, yin becomes so vacuous as to be insufficient to control yang, yang will become hyperactive and flame upward. Thus vacuity fire harasses the heart and disquiets the spirit. This accounts for the fear and dread, susceptibility to fright, vexation and agitation, dizziness, tinnitus, heart palpitations, insomnia, tidal heat, night sweats, vexatious heat, the red tongue, and the rapid pulse. Yin vacuity is responsible for the low back and knee soreness and weakness, the numerous but scanty night-time urination, dry mouth and throat, the scanty fur, and the fine or surging, rootless pulse.

**TREATMENT PRINCIPLES:** Clear the heart and nourish yin, settle fright and quiet the spirit

**FORMULA & MEDICINALS:** *Huang Lian E Jiao Tang* (Coptis & Donkey Skin Glue Decoction)

Rhizoma Coptidis Chinensis (*Huang Lian*), 3-6g (added later), Gelatinum Corii Asini (*E Jiao*), 10-12g (dissolved in the decocted liquid while still hot), Radix Scutellariae Baicalensis (*Huang Qin*), 10-12g, Radix Albus Paeoniae Lactiflorae (*Bai Shao*), 10-12g, egg yolks (*Ji Zi Huang*), 2 pieces (stirred into the hot decoction after it has been strained)

Decoct in water and administer orally in two divided doses, morning and evening, one *ji* per day.

**ANALYSIS OF FORMULA:** Coptis and Scutellaria clear the heart and drain fire. Donkey Skin Glue greatly supplements yin blood as do the egg yolks. White Peony also supplements the blood and restrains yin.

**ADDITIONS & SUBTRACTIONS:** For dry throat, add Radix Scrophulariae Ningpoensis (*Xuan Shen*) and Tuber Ophiopogonis Japonici (*Mai Dong*). For heart vexation, add Fructus Gardeniae Jasminoidis (*Zhi Zi*) and Folium Bambusae (*Zhu Ye*). For pronounced susceptibility to fright, add Concha Margaritiferae (*Zhen Zhu Mu*) and Concha Ostreae (*Mu Li*). For scanty, dark-colored urine, add Medulla Junci Effusi (*Deng Xin Cao*) and Medulla Tetrapanacis Papyriferi (*Tong Cao*).

**ACUPUNCTURE:** *Tai Xi* (Ki 3), *Fu Liu* (Ki 7), *San Yin Jiao* (Sp 6), *Yin Xi* (Ht 6), *Jian Shi* (Per 5), *Bai Hui* (GV 20), *Yin Tang* (M-HN-3). Use even supplementing-even draining technique.

**CLINICAL TIPS:** As in most psychiatric diseases, mixed repletion and vacuity patterns are the most common in Western patients.

**ABSTRACTS OF REPRESENTATIVE CHINESE RESEARCH:**

*Tian Jin Zhong Yi (Tianjin Chinese Medicine)*, #6, 1996, p. 7: Liu Zheng-xue and Tai Xiu-ping treated 71 cases of anxiety disorder with *Jiao Hu Ning Chong Ji* (Anxiety-calming Soluble Granules). According to the Hamilton scale of anxiety, all these patients scored greater than 20 points. Within this group, there were 24 males and 47 females who ranged in age from 16-81 years old, with 55% being middle-aged or elderly. Their disease course had lasted from 3-11 months. *Jiao Hu Ning Chong Ji* is designed to course the liver and rectify the qi, quicken the blood and transform stasis, nourish the blood and quiet the spirit. It is comprised of: Radix Bupleuri (*Chai Hu*), Tuber Curcumae (*Yu Jin*), Radix Auklandiae Lappae (*Mu Xiang*), Radix Salviae Miltiorrhizae (*Dan Shen*), uncooked Radix Rehmanniae (*Sheng Di*), Radix Ligustici Wallichii (*Chuan Xiong*), and Concha Margaritiferae (*Zhen Zhu Mu*). Each packet weighed 8g, and two packets were administered three times per day, with some patients receiving a maximum of three packets three times per day. The course of treatment was six weeks. Thirty-nine of these patients also received 0.5-1.0mg of lorazepam each evening and 0.25mg two times during the day. Using this protocol, 21 patients were cured, 25 patients were markedly improved, 16 patients improved, and nine patients got no result. Improvement in Hamilton anxiety scores was a part of outcome criteria. The statistical significance in the reduction of these scores was P<0.001. Most of the patients in this study presented either liver depression qi stagnation or liver depression and blood stasis patterns, and the treatment outcomes of these patients was better than those patients exhibiting a liver-kidney yin vacuity pattern.

*Shang Hai Zhong Yi Yao Za Zhi (Shanghai Journal of Chinese Medicine & Medicinals)*, #11, 1998, p. 26: Huang Yi-dong treated 60 cases of anxiety disorder using integrated Chinese-Western medicine. Of the 60 patients in this study, 16 were male and 44 were female. Twenty-eight cases were 45 years of age or older, and 32 cases were under 45. The youngest patient was 15 and the oldest was 71. Forty-four were married, 12 were unmarried, two were widowed, and two were divorced. Sixteen were workers, 20 were cadres, 16 were retired, and eight were students. Among these patients' complaints were anxiety, depression, tension, insomnia, muscular, sensory, circulatory, respiratory, digestive, and neurological disturbances. The longest course of disease was 30 years, the shortest was one half month, and the median duration was five years. The Chinese medical treatment consisted of the internal administration of water-decocted medicinals prescribed on the basis of five different patterns: 1) heart spirit not calm with qi and yin dual vacuity (34 cases), 2) ascendant liver yang hyperactivity (8 cases), 3) liver depression qi stagnation (4 cases), 4) yin vacuity with fire effulgence (6 cases), and 5) kidney yang vacuity detriment (8 cases). One *ji* of Chinese medicinals was administered per day. The Western medical treatment in 44 cases consisted of hydroxyzine, 50mg per day. Another four cases received 37mg of amitryptiline per day, and the remaining 12 cases received 50mg of meperidine per day. At night, all these patients also received a suitable amount of sedative, such as diazepam (Valium), lorazepam, trazadone, etc. Patients were assessed at two, four, six, eight, and 12 week intervals. Patients' symptoms were numerically evaluated before, during, and after this treatment, and there was a statistically marked decrease in these numbers (P<0.001).

*Zhe Jiang Zhong Yi Za Zhi (Zhejiang Journal of Chinese Medicine)*, #1, 1990 as reported by Heiner Fruehauf, *The Journal of Chinese Medicine*, UK, #48, 1995, p. 26: Ding Fou-ting treated 266 patients for anxiety disorder with a standard formula modified according to pattern discrimination plus acupuncture given on the basis of pattern discrimination. The standard formula was called *Ning Shen Jie Lu Tang* (Calm the Spirit & Resolve Anxiety Decoction). It consisted of: Dens Draconis (*Long Chi*), 30g, Magnetitum (*Ci Shi*), 30g, Semen Zizyphi Spinosae (*Suan Zao Ren*), 15g, Radix Polygalae Tenuifoliae (*Yuan Zhi*), 15g, Rhizoma Acori Graminei (*Shi Chang Pu*), 15g, Tuber Curcumae (*Yu Jin*), 24g, Rhizoma Nardostachydis (*Gan Song*), 12g, Cortex Albizziae Julibrissinis (*He Huan Pi*), 9g, Radix Glycyrrhizae (*Gan Cao*), 9g, Succinum (*Hu Po*), 3g, and Cinnabar (*Zhu Sha*), 3g. The base acupuncture formula consisted of: *Feng Fu* (GV 16), *Bai Hui* (GV 20), *Tong Li* (Ht 5), *Shen Men* (Ht 7), and *Nei Guan* (Per 6).

If there was liver depression qi stagnation, Radix Albus Paeoniae Lactiflorae (*Bai Shao*), 24g, Rhizoma Cyperi Rotundi (*Xiang Fu*), 24g, Radix Bupleuri (*Chai Hu*), 18g, Pericarpium Citri Reticulatae Viride (*Qing Pi*), 12g, and Radix Glycyrrhizae (*Gan Cao*), 9g, were added to the above medicinal formula, and *Gan Shu* (Bl 18) and *Xing Jian* (Liv 2) were added to the acupuncture protocol. If there was simultaneous phlegm obstruction, Fructus Immaturus Citri Aurantii (*Zhi Shi*), 12g, uncooked Rhizoma Zingiberis (*Sheng Jiang*), 12g, Rhizoma Cyperi Rotundi (*Xiang Fu*), 12g, bile-processed Rhizoma Arisamatis (*Dan Nan Xing*), 9g, Sclerotium Poriae Cocos (*Fu Ling*), 15g, Rhizoma Pinelliae Ternatae (*Ban Xia*), 15g, Pumice (*Fu Hai Shi*), 30g, Lapis Micae Seu Chloriti (*Meng Shi*), 30g, and Folium Perillae Frutescentis (*Zi Su Ye*), 5g, were added to the medicinals, and *Fei Shu* (Bl 13), *He Gu* (LI 4), *Lie Que* (Lu 7), *Tian Tu* (CV 22), and *Feng Long* (St 40) were added to the acupuncture. If there was concomitant heart blood vacuity, Polygala, Acorus, and Curcuma were reduced to nine grams each, Zizyphus Spinosa was increased to 30g, and Radix Codonopsitis Pilosulae (*Dang Shen*), 30g, Radix Angelicae Sinensis (*Dang Gui*), 30g, Fructus Schisandrae Chinensis (*Wu Wei Zi*), 30g, Arillus Euphoriae Longanae (*Long Yan Rou*), 30g, Sclerotium Pararadicis Poriae Cocos (*Fu Shen*), 15g, Tuber Ophiopogonis Japonici (*Mai Dong*), 15g, and Fructus Zizyphi Jujubae (*Da Zao*), 15g, were added to the medicinals, while *Xin Shu* (Bl 15) and *Pi Shu* (Bl 20) were added to the acupuncture. If there was blood stasis, Radix Salviae Miltiorrhizae (*Dan Shen*), 30g, Semen Pruni Persicae (*Tao Ren*), 15g, Flos Carthami Tinctorii (*Hong Hua*), 15g, Radix Rubrus Paeoniae Lactiflorae (*Chi Shao*), 15g, and Hirudo Seu Whitmania (*Shui Zhi*), 15g, were added to the medicinals, while *Xue Hai* (Sp 10) and *Ge Shu* (Bl 17) were added to the acupuncture.

Of the 266 cases participating in this study, all were judged cured. On follow-up after one year, 211 remained without recurrence. Thirty-one cases reported reoccur-

rences, but these were cured by repeating the above treatments. Twenty-four cases died of unrelated diseases.

*Shanghai Journal of Acupuncture & Moxibustion*, 1998, p. 68-70: Liu, Zhang, and Liu studied 240 patients diagnosed as suffering from anxiety disorder. They divided these 240 patients into three groups of 80 patients apiece. One group was treated with acupuncture at *Nei Guan* (Per 6), *Zu San Li* (St 36), *Tai Chong* (Liv 3), *Shen Shu* (Bl 23), *Ming Men* (GV 4), and *Qu Chi* (LI 11). A second group was treated with psychological relaxation and biofeedback therapy, while the third group was treated with the above acupuncture points plus psychological relaxation and biofeedback therapy. One course of treatment equaled 10 days, and 1-4 courses of treatment were given. At the end of treatment, 21 acupuncture, 16 desensitization, and 42 combined therapy patients were symptom-free, while 34 acupuncture patients, 36 desensitization patients, and 23 combined therapy patients got a marked effect. On one year follow-up, 48% of the combined group continued to be normal. Less than half that percentage had remained normal in the other two groups.

## REPRESENTATIVE CASE HISTORIES:

## ❖ CASE 1[1] ❖

The patient was a 27 year old female who habitually had periods of excessive heart beating. In addition, there were purple macules on her lower limbs. Her menses were relatively profuse in amount, and premenstrually she experienced abdominal pain, dizziness on movement, and decreased visual acuity. Her tongue had a red tip with thin fur, and her pulse was bowstring and rapid. Dr. Liu diagnosed this patient's disease as fearful throbbing and discriminated her pattern as heart-spleen dual vacuity not able to contain the blood. Therefore, the treatment principle was to restore the spleen, for which he prescribed the following medicinals: Fructus Tritici Aestivi (*Huai Xiao Mai*), 30g, Radix Pseudostellariae (*Tai Zi Shen*), 9g, mix-fried Radix Astragali Membranancei (*Huang Qi*), 9g, Gelatinum Piscis (*Yu Biao Jiao*), 9g, calcined Concha Ostreae (*Mu Li*) and Os Draconis (*Long Gu*), 15g each, uncooked Pollen Typhae (*Pu Huang*), 9g, carbonized Cortex Radicis Moutan (*Dan Pi*), 9g, Radix Angelicae Sinensis (*Dang Gui*), 6g, mix-fried Radix Polygalae Tenuifoliae (*Yuan Zhi*), 6g, mix-fried Radix Glycyrrhizae (*Gan Cao*), 3g, and Fructus Zizyphi Jujubae (*Da Zao*), 5 pieces.

After taking 21 *ji* of the above formula, the patient's menstruation was normal, there was no abdominal pain, the purple macules disappeared, her sleeping and eating became good again, and there were no further episodes of fearful throbbing.

### ❖ CASE 2[2] ❖

The patient was a 14 year old male who was first examined on Jul. 24, 1975. During his younger years, he had been an active person. However, in May of 1975, his activity had become excessive after an outburst of anger while saddling a horse. This was accompanied by his feeling heart palpitations, chest oppression, shortness of breath, and distressed rapid breathing. At such times, his heart could beat more than 200 BPM. He was taken to a hospital for emergency diagnosis and treatment, after which his symptoms remitted. However, whenever he was active these symptoms would recur. At the time Dr. Xu examined this patient, he had chest oppression, shortness of breath, distressed rapid breathing, and taxation fatigue, all of which were worsened after worry or anger. His pulse was fine and bowstring, and his tongue was pale.

Based on the above, Dr. Xu's assessment of this case was that anger had damaged the young man's liver and taxation fatigue had damaged his spleen. Because his liver and spleen were both insufficient, his qi and blood were vacuous and scanty. Thus his heart had no place from which to receive nourishment and hence the patient experienced heart palpitations, fearful throbbing, fearfulness, and restlessness. Dr. Xu's treatment principles were to supplement and boost the heart qi and enrich and nourish heart blood, assisted by settling the heart and calming the spirit. Based on these principles, he prescribed: Os Draconis (*Long Gu*), 30g, Haemititum (*Dai Zhe Shi*), 30g, Bulbus Lilii (*Bai He*), 30g, Concha Cypreae Maculae (*Zi Bei Chi*), 24g, uncooked Radix Rehmanniae (*Sheng Di*), 15g, Tuber Ophiopogonis Japonici (*Mai Dong*), 15g, Radix Salviae Miltiorrhizae (*Dan Shen*), 15g, Radix Codonopsitis Pilosulae (*Dang Shen*), 12g, Fructus Schisandrae Chinensis (*Wu Wei Zi*), 9g, mix-fried Radix Glycyrrhizae (*Gan Cao*), 9g, and Rhizoma Acori Graminei (*Shi Chang Pu*), 6g.

After taking seven *ji* of the above formula, the patient's chest oppression and shortness of breath improved. Therefore, he was re-prescribed another 20 *ji*, after which all the symptoms disappeared and did not return.

### ENDNOTES

[1] Liu Shu-yi, *Shang Hai Lao Zhong Yi Jing Yan Xuan Bian (A Selected Collection of Shanghai Old Chinese Doctors' Case Histories)*, *op. cit.*, p. 63

[2] Xu Song-nian, *Ibid.*, p. 210-211

# 8

# OBSESSIVE-COMPULSIVE DISORDER

Obsessive-compulsive disorder is a type of anxiety disorder which is characterized by recurrent, unwanted, intrusive ideas, images, or impulses that seem silly, weird, nasty, or horrible (obsessions) and by urges to do something that will lessen the discomfort due to those obsessions (compulsions).

## NOSOLOGY:

Diagnosis of obsessive-compulsive disorder (OCD) requires the presence of obsessions, compulsions, or both. In Western psychiatry, an obsession is defined as a recurring intrusive thought that is experienced as irrational. Fear of contamination when anticipating coming into contact with ordinary objects is a frequently cited obsession in OCD. Strong anxiety feelings often accompany obsessions. A compulsion is an urge to act or think that is difficult to resist and which often results in reduction in anxiety associated with the corresponding obsession (when one is present). Compulsive hand-washing, for example, often occurs in response to obsessional fears of contamination. The diagnosis of OCD requires that obsessions and/or compulsions occupy a significant part of the day, interfere with social or occupational functioning, and, in contrast to delusions, are acknowledged by the patient as unreasonable or irrational thoughts.

Symptoms of tension, worry and anxiety, fear and dread, restlessness, and susceptibility to excessive suspicion or paranoia may be present in the context of OCD but are not required core diagnostic criteria. Most symptoms included under the Chinese diagnosis "obsessive-compulsive disorder" appear to correspond to anxiety symptoms or somatic complaints as these are conceptualized in Western psychiatric nosology. There is no clear correlation between the Chinese disease category and discreet Western psychiatric disorders. Criteria used to discern various symptom patterns are described below under the section on differential diagnosis.

## EPIDEMIOLOGY:

OCD usually begins in childhood or early adulthood. The life-time prevalence of OCD has been estimated at 2-5% in surveyed (largely Western) populations. There is a higher-than-chance occurrence of OCD in first-degree relatives of individuals diagnosed with OCD. There is also a non-random familial association between OCD and Tourette's disorder (see Book 2, Chapter 16, Convulsions, for a discussion of tic disorders).

## DIFFERENTIAL DIAGNOSIS:

Before diagnosing OCD, possible underlying medical causes must be ruled out. While uncommon, brain injury or infection can manifest as obsessions or compulsions. A careful medical history will suggest the possibility of insults to the central nervous system as precipitants of a disturbance that is eventually diagnosed as OCD.

Numerous psychiatric disorders share core OCD symptoms. The presence of obsessive or compulsive personality traits in contrast to frank symptoms of obsessions or compulsions points to obsessive-compulsive personality disorder. The principle distinguishing feature is the presence of an obsessive or compulsive style that is a long-standing aspect of personality but does not cause marked distress or interfere with social or occupational functioning. In addition, obsessive-compulsive personality disorder is not characterized by the presence of specific obsessions or compulsions as described above. Some individuals who have obsessive personality traits also suffer from OCD and, therefore, experience frank obsessions. Hence it is sometimes difficult to clearly differentiate these two disorders. Obsessions or compulsions often occur during the course of schizophrenia and sometimes meet full diagnostic criteria for OCD. This is then diagnosed as OCD occurring together with schizophrenia. Conversely, severe OCD symptoms sometimes approach the intensity of delusions characteristic of schizophrenia and other psychotic disorders. However, in most cases of severe OCD, the patient is aware that his or her obsessions are irrational. That is, in contrast to the delusional patient, the obsessional patient is typically able to distinguish irrational obsessions from reality (*i.e.*, their reality testing is intact). Ruminations of depressed individuals are sometimes misdiagnosed as obsessions. In most cases, ruminations occur only or principally during a major depressive episode and typically have themes of guilt, worthlessness, or low self-esteem that are viewed as congruent with the patient's underlying depressed mood. In contrast, obsessions are typically experienced as irrational and intrusive and have themes that do not necessarily reflect depressed (or other) mood states. Obsessional thinking or frank obsessions frequently occur in the context of anxiety disorders, including specific phobias and social phobia. In such cases, phobic avoidance of an object or situation is associated with fears that have an intrusive, obsessional quality. In contrast to OCD, core symptoms in phobias are specific fears and avoidance behaviors with respect to certain objects or contexts, in the absence of compulsive rituals. Finally, OCD is often difficult to distinguish from Tourette's disorder or other tic disorders (see Book 2, Chapter 16 for a discussion of this family of Western psychiatric disorders that approximate the Chinese disease category of "convulsions"). Complex rhythmic involuntary movements seen in tic disorders are sometimes difficult to distinguish from rituals of OCD.

## ETIOLOGY & PATHOPHYSIOLOGY:

Several neurobiological and psychodynamic theories have been advanced in efforts to explain the origins of obsessions and compulsions. However, no single theory has adequately explained the observed course or phenomenology of obsessive-compulsive disorder. A popular current neurobiological theory views OCD symptoms as concomitants of developmental abnormalities or injury affecting specific brain regions implicated in the regulation of movement, including the basal ganglia and parts of the frontal lobes. Functional brain imaging studies (including MRI and PET) have demonstrated consistent abnormalities in these brain regions implying dysregulation of a complex circuit that manifests as obsessions or compulsions. Significantly, successful response to pharmacological or other treatments typically results in normalization of brain functioning as demonstrated by functional brain imaging data. In rare cases where OCD is precipitated by brain trauma or infection, there is evidence that the same brain regions are affected.

At the level of neuro-pharmacology, OCD symptoms uniformly respond to drugs that increase available brain serotonin more so than drugs that affect other neurotransmitters. Complicating this picture is the absence of consistent findings of dysregulation in brain serotonin among patients diagnosed with OCD. It is, therefore, likely that dysregulation of neurotransmitters other than serotonin is central to the pathogenesis of OCD.

## DIFFERENTIAL DIAGNOSIS

### 1. MEDICAL DISORDERS

A. INFECTION OR INJURY OF CNS
B. NEUROLOGIC DISORDERS, INCLUDING TOURETTE'S DISORDER, PARKINSON'S DISEASE, AND HUNTINGTON'S DISEASE
C. OTHER TIC DISORDERS
D. HISTORY OF CEREBROVASCULAR ACCIDENT (CVA)

### 3. PSYCHIATRIC DISORDERS

A. OBSESSIVE-COMPULSIVE DISORDER (OCD)
B. OBSESSIVE-COMPULSIVE PERSONALITY DISORDER
C. SCHIZOPHRENIA AND OTHER PSYCHOTIC DISORDERS
D. MAJOR DEPRESSIVE EPISODE
E. SPECIFIC PHOBIAS
F. SOCIAL PHOBIAS

Psycho-dynamic theories of OCD incorporate unconscious defense mechanisms that manifest as obsessions or compulsions to protect the ego from anxiety. Isolation, undoing, and reaction formation are defense mechanisms postulated in psychodynamic models of OCD.

## WESTERN MEDICAL TREATMENT:

Most medical etiologies of OCD cause irreversible pathological changes in the brain. These include traumatic brain injury and certain kinds of bacterial infections (notably Group A beta-hemolytic streptococcus) that permanently alter normal functioning of those brain regions implicated in OCD. In these cases, pharmaco-therapy sometimes results in diminished symptom severity.

Contemporary Western psychiatric treatments of OCD include pharmacotherapy and a specific type of cognitive-behavioral therapy. Several medications have been used to treat obsessions and compulsions, but there is no cure, and most treatments yield only moderate improvements with frequent relapses. Most available psychopharmacological agents have been tried singly or in combination. Currently there is no considered best treatment, and most drugs have yielded roughly equivalent results. Drugs commonly used to treat OCD in the U.S. and Europe are clomipramine (Anafranil) and the serotonin-selective re-uptake inhibitors (SSRIs), including fluoxetine (Prozac), paroxetine (Paxil), sertraline (Zoloft), and fluvoxamine (Luvox). These medications, which are used in contemporary Western psychiatry to treat depression, are typically effective against OCD at higher doses. Citalopram (Celexa) is a SSRI that has only recently been introduced to the U.S. but has well-documented efficacy against OCD at high doses based on extensive clinical experience with this drug in Europe. Benzodiazepines are sometimes used adjunctively with SSRIs to treat anxiety associated with OCD. Combining two or more medications is a commonly used approach to treatment of OCD symptoms that have not responded to a single agent. However, there is little evidence to substantiate improved efficacy when two drugs are used in combination, and treatment response is often confounded by medication side effects further complicating the clinical picture. Antipsychotic medications are sometimes helpful in combination with SSRIs when OCD symptoms are severe or refractory or there is evidence of a co-morbid psychotic disorder. When severe OCD has been refractory to all available pharmacological treatment approaches, electroconvulsive therapy (ECT) is sometimes used. To date, there are few studies on the effectiveness of ECT in the treatment of OCD, and most have equivocal findings. Psycho-surgery has been tried in

a few extreme cases of OCD in which impaired functioning threatens the patient's safety or capacity to care for his or her basic needs. At least four different neurosurgical approaches have been tried. All have been found to be only moderately successful, and all have an associated risk of postoperative seizure disorder.

In addition to pharmacological treatments, electroconvulsive therapy, and neurosurgery, cognitive-behavioral therapy often yields improvements in the severity or frequency of OCD symptoms. Thought-stopping and both imaginary and *in vivo* exposure therapy are specific techniques that address obsessions or compulsions. Many treatment protocols for OCD combine pharmacotherapy with cognitive-behavioral therapy interventions that are optimized to address the patient's specific pattern of OCD symptoms.

## SHORT & LONG-TERM ADVANTAGES & DISADVANTAGES OF WESTERN MEDICAL TREATMENT:

Contemporary Western treatments of OCD provide relief in some cases and result in little or no improvement in others. Most available pharmacological approaches are generally effective for obsessive and compulsive symptoms of moderate severity. Existing treatments are less effective for OCD symptoms that are severe or chronic or that occur in combination with another major psychiatric disorder. Many studies have demonstrated that combining medications and behavioral therapy yields more rapid improvement than either approach alone. Successful treatment of OCD results in improved occupational and social functioning. Medications used to treat OCD have associated side effects which can cause subjective distress and sometimes become the focus of future obsessions. Short-term and long-term benefits and disadvantages of contemporary Western treatments are roughly equivalent. An exception is the possibility of chemical dependence when benzodiazepines are used over long periods.

## PROGNOSIS:

The typical course and outcome of OCD are difficult to predict in most cases. Although many factors affect outcome, there is no consistent correlation between specific factors and prognosis. In contemporary Western psychiatry, OCD has a fluctuating course in which periods of diminished symptomatology alternate with transient periods of symptomatic worsening. Patients who have moderate symptoms and no co-morbid psychiatric disorders generally have better long-term courses. Conversely, the presence of other psychiatric or medical disorders or severe or chronic symptoms is often associated with poor outcomes.

## INDICATIONS FOR REFERRAL TO WESTERN MEDICAL SERVICES:

Urgent referral to the nearest emergency room is justified when there is evidence of an acute underlying medical problem, including traumatic brain injury or infection. Urgent referral is also warranted when there is an ongoing pattern of substance abuse manifesting as obsessions which place the patient's safety at risk. Out-patient psychiatric referral should be expedited when severe OCD symptoms impair occupational or social functioning. In cases where moderate OCD symptoms have failed to respond to appropriate Chinese medical treatment, the patient may benefit from non-urgent referral to a psychiatrist for continuing clarification of the medical and psychiatric differential diagnosis and development of an optimized treatment plan combining appropriate Chinese and Western approaches.

## CHINESE MEDICAL CATEGORIZATION:

In Chinese medicine, the symptoms associated with obsessive-compulsive disorder are traditionally categorized under the diseases vexation and agitation (*fan zao*), depression condition (*yu zheng*), impaired memory (*jian wang*), and abject demeanor (*bie die*). The English translation of the name of this last Chinese disease category is problematic since the second word, *die*, does not appear in any of our Chinese-English dictionaries. The *Jian Ming Zhong Yi Ci Dian* (*A Plain & Clear Dictionary of Chinese Medicine*) says that this disease category first appears in the Chinese medical literature in Tai Yuan-li's Ming dynasty *Zheng Zhi Yao Lue* (*Essentials of Patterns & Treatments*). The *Za Bing Yuan Liu Xi Zhu* (*Rhinoceros [i.e., Sharp, Incisive] Candle [i.e., Light] on the Source & Course of the Miscellaneous Diseases*) says:

> *Bie die* is a type of heart blood insufficiency and fearful throbbing disease. In this condition, there is glomus and blockage in the heart center [*i.e.,* epigastric region], inability to eat or drink, the intelligence is as if drunk, the heart [or mind] is commonly apologetic, and the person tends to stay indoors in the dark or remain behind doors. [This condition] is seen in people who are frightened, reclusive, and have no place [*i.e.,* are ashamed to show their face].[1]

## CHINESE MEDICAL DISEASE CAUSES & DISEASE MECHANISMS:

The Chinese descriptions of this condition center on the heart and gallbladder's relationship to courage and, conversely, timidity and also to the gallbladder's relationship to decision-making. If the heart is over-taxed over a long period of time, phlegm turbidity will accumulate and assail the gallbladder. This then results in heart vacuity and gallbladder timidity. In this case, the heart becomes vacuous and one can no longer control oneself, remembering that the heart is the emperor or sovereign of the bodymind. If the gallbladder becomes timid, then decision-making becomes abnormal. What the Chinese texts typically do not explain is that over-taxation of the heart and engenderment of phlegm turbidity also involve the liver and spleen. If the spleen becomes vacuous due to over-taxation, then it will fail to fortify and move. Failure of fortification means that it will no longer engender the qi and blood correctly. This then is the cause of heart vacuity. Failure to move means that it will no longer transport and move water fluids. These may gather and collect, engendering evil dampness which, over time, may congeal into phlegm. In addition, phlegm turbidity will inhibit the qi mechanism and cause or at least aggravate liver depression qi stagnation. Therefore, this disease mechanism is somewhat more complex than terse Chinese descriptions may at first seem.

The second mechanism of this condition does explicitly involve the liver. If the emotions are repressed and depressed, disease will reach or affect the liver. The liver becomes depressed and the qi becomes stagnant. If this endures and is not resolved, then qi stagnation will lead to blood stasis involving the gallbladder. Hence decision-making is abnormal.

## TREATMENT BASED ON PATTERN DISCRIMINATION:

### 1. HEART-GALLBLADDER QI VACUITY PATTERN

**MAIN SYMPTOMS:** Compulsive thoughts and actions, tension, worry and anxiety, inability to control oneself, heart vacuity gallbladder timidity, easily frightened by touching things, fear and dread, restlessness, susceptibility to excessive suspicion or paranoia, vacuity vexation, insomnia, dizziness or vertigo, possible profuse phlegm and/or plum pit qi, a pale tongue with white fur, and a fine or bowstring, fine pulse

**ANALYSIS OF SYMPTOMS:** If over-taxation affects the heart and over-thinking damages the spleen, then the spleen will lose its fortification and movement. Fluids will accumulate and produce phlegm. Phlegm turbidity will then assail the gallbladder and the gallbladder will lose its ability to make decisions. Thus there is uncontrollable worry and anxiety and compulsive behavior as a reaction to those worries and anxieties. If the heart qi is depleted and vacuous and the gallbladder qi is not calm, then one sees tension, worry and anxiety, easy fright due to touching things, fear and dread, restlessness, heart palpitations, and insomnia. If phlegm turbidity obstructs the center and the clear yang is not upborne, then there will be dizziness and chest oppression. The pale tongue with white fur and the fine or bowstring, fine pulse are signs of heart vacuity with phlegm obstruction.

**TREATMENT PRINCIPLES:** Nourish the heart and quiet the spirit, dry dampness and transform phlegm

**FORMULA & MEDICINALS:** *Wen Dan Tang Jia Wei* (Warm the Gallbladder Decoction with Added Flavors)

Rhizoma Pinelliae Ternatae (*Ban Xia*), 15g, Caulis Bambusae In Taeniis (*Zhu Ru*), 15g, Fructus Immaturus Citri Aurantii (*Zhi Shi*), 10g, Pericarpium Citri Reticulatae (*Chen Pi*), 10g, uncooked Rhizoma Zingiberis (*Sheng Jiang*), 10g (added later), mix-fried Radix Glycyrrhizae (*Gan Cao*), 6g, Sclerotium Pararadicis Poriae Cocos (*Fu Shen*), 30g, Tuber Ophiopogonis Japonici (*Mai Dong*), 15g, Radix Polygalae Tenuifoliae (*Yuan Zhi*), 10g, Dens Draconis (*Long Chi*), 21g (decocted first), Rhizoma Acori Graminei (*Shi Chang Pu*), 15g, Succinum (*Hu Po*), 6g (powdered and swallowed with the decocted liquid)

Decoct in water and administer orally in two divided doses, morning and evening, one *ji* per day.

**ANALYSIS OF FORMULA:** Within this formula, the ingredients of *Wen Dan Tang* dry dampness and transform phlegm, clear heat and eliminate vexation (Caulis Bambusae), thus quieting "the mansion of center stillness." This promotes the gallbladder's obtaining of quiet and calm. Poria, Ophiopogon, Polygala, and Acorus are added to nourish the heart and quiet the spirit, free the flow of the orifices and downbear turbidity. Dragon's Teeth and Succinum heavily settle and quiet the spirit. When all these medicinals are used together, heart vacuity obtains nourishment, gallbladder qi obtains calm, and the heart spirit obtains quiet and stillness.

**ADDITIONS & SUBTRACTIONS:** If there is chest oppression and profuse phlegm, add Fructus Trichosanthis Kirlowii (*Gua Lou*) and Bulbus Fritillariae Thunbergii (*Zhe Bei Mu*) to clear heat and transform phlegm. If there is emotional tension and agitation, heart vexation, and easy anger, add Radix Bupleuri (*Chai Hu*), Fructus Gardeniae Jasminoidis (*Zhi Zi*), and Radix Gentianae Scabrae (*Long Dan Cao*) to course the liver and drain fire.

If there is stomach venter distention and oppression with torpid intake and scanty eating, add Fructus Amomi (*Sha Ren*), Radix Auklandiae Lappae (*Mu Xiang*), and stir-fried Endothelium Corneum Gigeriae Galli (*Ji Nei Jin*) to disperse, abduct, and harmonize the center. If there is insomnia and profuse dreams, add Semen Zizyphi Spinosae (*Suan Zao Ren*), Cortex Albizziae Julibrissinis (*He Huan Pi*), and Caulis Polygoni Multiflori (*Ye Jiao Teng*) to settle, still, and quiet the spirit. If there is compulsive reactive behavior and inability to control oneself, add Magnetitum (*Ci Shi*), Concha Ostreae (*Mu Li*), and Tuber Asparagi Cochinensis (*Tian Men Dong*) to heavily settle and quiet the spirit.

**ACUPUNCTURE:** *Shen Men* (Ht 7), *Nei Guan* (Per 6), *Feng Long* (St 40), *Zu San Li* (St 36), *Dan Zhong* (CV 17), *Zhong Wan* (CV 12), *Zu Qiao Yin* (GB 44). Use even supplementing-even draining technique.

## 2. QI & BLOOD STASIS & STAGNATION PATTERN

**MAIN SYMPTOMS:** Compulsive behavior and inability to control one's thoughts, emotional lability, tension and agitation, stirring and fear, a dark, dusky facial complexion, bilateral rib-side distention and pain or generalized body pain, piercing headache, insomnia, profuse dreams, a purplish, dark tongue or static spots and macules, and a bowstring, choppy pulse

**ANALYSIS OF SYMPTOMS:** If the emotions are repressed and depressed, disease may reach the liver resulting in liver depression qi stagnation. If this endures and is not resolved, there will be both qi stagnation and blood stasis. This may then affect both the liver and gallbladder. In that case, the gallbladder qi may become disquieted and decision-making may become abnormal. Therefore, there is compulsive behavior and difficulty controlling one's thoughts, the emotions are labile, and there is tension and agitation, stirring and fear, insomnia and profuse dreams. If static blood obstructs the liver channel and qi and blood coursing and movement become unregulated, then one may see bilateral rib-side pain or generalized body pain. If there is static blood obstructing and stagnating, then the clear yang may not be upborne. In that case, one may see a piercing headache. The purplish, dark tongue and the bowstring, choppy pulse are signs of static blood obstructing internally.

**TREATMENT PRINCIPLES:** Course the liver and rectify the qi, quicken the blood and transform stasis

**FORMULA & MEDICINALS:** *Xue Fu Zhu Yu Tang* (Blood Mansion Dispel Stasis Decoction)

Semen Pruni Persicae (*Tao Ren*), 12g, Flos Carthami Tinctorii (*Hong Hua*), 10g (steeped), Radix Angelicae Sinensis (*Dang Gui*), 10g, uncooked Radix Rehmanniae (*Sheng Di*), 10g, Radix Ligustici Wallichii (*Chuan Xiong*), 6g (added later), Radix Rubrus Paeoniae Lactiflorae (*Chi Shao*), 10g, Radix Achyranthis Bidentatae (*Niu Xi*), 10g, Radix Platycodi Grandiflori (*Jie Geng*), 6g, Radix Bupleuri (*Chai Hu*), 3g, Fructus Citri Aurantii (*Zhi Ke*), 6g, Radix Glycyrrhizae (*Gan Cao*), 3g

Decoct in water and administer orally in two divided doses, morning and evening, one *ji* per day.

**ANALYSIS OF FORMULA:** Within this formula, Dang Gui, Ligusticum, Red Peony, Persica, and Carthamus all quicken the blood and dispel stasis. Achyranthes dispels static blood and frees the flow of the blood vessels at the same time as it leads the blood to move downward. Bupleurum courses the liver and resolves depression, upbears and outthrusts the clear yang. Platycodon and Aurantium open fullness and move the qi. When the qi moves, the blood moves. Uncooked Rehmannia cools the blood and clears heat. When combined with Dang Gui, it is also able to nourish and moisten the blood. This promotes the expulsion of stasis without damaging yin blood. Licorice regulates and harmonizes all the other medicinals. This formula not only moves blood division stasis and stagnation but is also able to resolve depression and binding of the qi division.

**ADDITIONS & SUBTRACTIONS:** For compulsive reactive behavior, such as compulsive hand-washing, and inability to control oneself, add Radix Trichosanthis Kirlowii (*Gua Lou Gen*), Ramulus Cinnamomi Cassiae (*Gui Zhi*), Radix Albus Paeoniae Lactiflorae (*Bai Shao*), and Bombyx Batryticatus (*Jiang Can*) to free the flow of the network vessels, stop tetany, and control stirring. If there are obsessional thoughts and uncontrollable worries and anxieties, one can add Rhizoma Acori Graminei (*Shi Chang Pu*), Concretio Bambusae Siliceae (*Tian Zhu Huang*), and Secretio Moschi Moschiferi (*She Xiang*) to free the flow of the orifices, arouse the spirit, and control worry.

**ACUPUNCTURE:** *Tai Chong* (Liv 3), *He Gu* (LI 4), *Xue Hai* (Sp 10), *Shen Men* (Ht 7), *Nei Guan* (Per 6), *Xin Shu* (Bl 15), *Ge Shu* (Bl 17), *Bai Hui* (GV 20), *Yin Tang* (M-HN-3). Use draining technique.

**CLINICAL TIPS:** Both patterns of this psychiatric disease involve liver depression. Often there is both repletion, in the form of qi stagnation, depressive heat, phlegm, and/or blood stasis, combined with spleen and, therefore, heart vacuity. Simple qi stagnation and blood stasis are not so commonly seen in real-life practice.

**ENDNOTES**

[1]Research Institute, Guangzhou College of Chinese Medicine, *Jian Ming Zhong Yi Ci Dian (A Plain & Clear Dictionary of Chinese Medicine)*, People's Health & Hygiene Press, Beijing, 1986, p. 540. Based on this definition, it appears this disease category might also cover agoraphobia.

# 9

# SOMATOFORM DISORDERS

Somatoform disorders are another class of psychiatric disorders. In China, these are still referred to by the outmoded name "hysteria." As used in China, hysteria is equivalent to what are now called somatoform disorders in *DSM-IV*. As a group, somatoform disorders are characterized by physical symptoms that suggest but are not fully explained by a physical disorder and that cause significant distress or interfere with social, occupational, or other functioning. Most cases of hysteria in China correspond to conversion disorders, a subset of somatoform disorders. Conversion disorders are characterized by physical symptoms caused by psychologic conflict which is unconsciously converted to resemble those of a neurologic disorder. Such symptoms typically consist of impaired coordination or balance, weakness, or paralysis of an arm or leg or loss of sensation in part of the body. Other symptoms include simulated convulsions; loss of one of the special senses, such as vision (blindness, double vision) or hearing (deafness); aphonia; difficulty swallowing; sensation of a lump in the throat; and urinary retention. Generally, onset of symptoms is linked to a socially or psychologically stressful event.

## NOSOLOGY:

Somatoform disorders are diagnosed in contemporary Western psychiatry when persisting complaints of unusual bodily sensations or apparent loss of normal sensory or motor functioning suggest underlying medical etiologies

in the absence of demonstrated pathology. In current Western psychiatric nosology, six specific somatoform disorders are included under the broad category of somatoform disorders. Diagnostic criteria that are common to all somatoform disorders include the following: symptoms must cause significant occupational or social impairment; medical etiologies must be ruled out; the symptom or symptoms must not be deliberately produced or feigned; and the symptoms are not better explained by another major psychiatric disorder. The following table lists these disorders and their principle specific diagnostic criteria.

Several Chinese disorders included as subtypes of hysteria include lily disease, plum pit qi, and running piglet. These have been discussed in Book 2. A patient complaining to a Western-trained psychiatrist of symptoms included under each of these Chinese diagnostic groupings would likely be diagnosed with one or more somatoform disorders. However, as noted above, no clear correspondence exists between symptom patterns described in the Chinese and Western psychiatric disease categories. Lily disease is an interesting Chinese disease category in that it includes prominent depression, sleep disturbance, and unusual somatic complaints (*i.e.*, subjective sensations of heat or cold and a bitter taste in the mouth). An individual presenting to a Western-trained clinician might be diagnosed with depression with somatization, a somatoform disorder, or both disorders depending on the established history of symptom severity and duration that

## MAIN CRITERIA OF SOMATOFORM DISORDERS ACCORDING TO THE *DSM-IV*

| DISORDER | PRINCIPLE DIAGNOSTIC CRITERIA |
|---|---|
| SOMATIZATION DISORDER | • Onset before age 30<br>• At least 4 pain symptoms, 2 gastrointestinal symptoms, one pseudo-neurological symptom, and one sexual symptom |
| CONVERSION DISORDER | • Impaired motor or sensory functioning that cannot be explained<br>• An apparent link exists between the symptom and psychological factors |
| UNDIFFERENTIATED SOMATIZATION DISORDER | • At least one somatic complaint lasts longer than six months<br>• The patient experiences distress that is disproportionate to symptom severity |
| PAIN DISORDER | • One or more pain symptoms cause significant social or occupational impairment<br>• An apparent link exists between the pain symptom or symptoms and psychological factors |
| HYPOCHRONDRIASIS | • Bodily sensations that last longer than six months and are interpreted as signs of serious illness in the absence of documented evidence of pathology<br>• The patient continues to believe he/she has a serious illness despite evidence to the contrary |
| BODY DYSMORPHIC DISORDER | • The patient is preoccupied by an imagined deficit or distorted perception of a physical defect |

determine the ongoing focus of clinical attention. Several other discreet patterns under hysteria include depressed or labile mood and multiple somatic symptoms or physiological irregularities (*e.g.*, menstrual irregularity), aberrant behaviors (*e.g.*, frequent sighing, torpid sitting), or sleep disturbances. Paranoia and agitation are described features of certain patterns. As Western psychiatric nosology is presently conceived, these Chinese medical patterns do not correspond to established ways of classifying psychiatric disorders in Western cultures. An individual presenting with such complaints would therefore not fit existing Western diagnoses. Hypochondriasis might be viewed as the most probable diagnosis but would fail to explain mood changes, paranoia, disturbed sleep, or other core features of the Chinese medical pattern. In contrast, running piglet is characterized by somatic symptoms but no apparent psychological symptoms. The principle complaints in running piglet are a sensation (of qi) surging upward from the lower abdomen to the chest and epigastrium or throat and associated pain and sensations of heat or cold. In cases where possible medical explanations have been ruled out, this kind of persisting symptom pattern would probably lead to a diagnosis of hypochondriasis or somatoform disorder not otherwise specified, a non-specific catch-all category for psychosomatic symptom patterns that do not fit presently established diagnostic categories for the somatoform disorders. As mentioned above and discussed in Book 2, Chapter 18, the symptom pattern classified as plum pit qi is phenomenologically close to the Western psychiatric category globus hystericus which is viewed as an unusual kind of conversion disorder.

## EPIDEMIOLOGY:

Prevalence rates of somatoform disorders are difficult to estimate because of subtle and poorly defined differences between these disorders and unusual medical disorders or other more common psychiatric disorders for which they may be mistaken. Based on limited surveys of Western populations, somatization disorder may affect as many as one out of 50 in the general adult population. For unclear reasons, somatization disorder is more frequently reported among women and is significantly more common in female relatives of women who carry the same diagnosis. Estimated prevalence rates of conversion disorder vary widely depending on the population surveyed. Studies of out-patients at mental health clinics suggest that one to two percent of psychiatric outpatients meet criteria for conversion disorder. In contrast, surveys of medical or psychiatric inpatients suggest that conversion symptoms are much more common in those acute-care settings. As defined in the *DSM-IV*, pain disorder may affect 10-15% of Western populations surveyed.

## DIFFERENTIAL DIAGNOSIS:

The medical and psychiatric differential diagnoses of the somatoform disorders are extremely broad. Symptoms required to diagnose somatization disorder (see the table above) can mimic or mask the spectrum of medical disorders that manifest as chronic pain, gastrointestinal distress, neurological disease, or sexual dysfunction. Despite these complex considerations, somatoform disorders are often easily distinguished from primary medical disorders because of the absence of positive findings on repeated examinations or laboratory studies. Conversely, several unusual chronic medical disorders are difficult to diagnose with certainty and tend to have a remitting and relapsing course and equivocal associated laboratory findings even in confirmed cases of illness. Examples include multiple

sclerosis (MS), systemic lupus erythematosus (SLE), and acute intermittent porphyria (AIP). A further complication is the fact that many patients who are initially diagnosed with a somatoform disorder are subsequently found to have an unusual medical disorder that is consistent with early manifestation of the illness. These individuals are typically re-diagnosed and started on appropriate treatments for their actual medical problems only after several years and considerable suffering.

Western medical differential diagnosis assumes that a psychosomatic disorder is the likely explanation when reasonable attempts to identify medical causes of somatic symptoms have yielded no or equivocal findings. The most accurate diagnosis then depends on the specific symptom pattern, including course, symptom severity, and duration. A thorough history usually clarifies the psychiatric differential diagnosis, indicating whether somatic symptoms are primary (*i.e.*, a somatoform disorder exists) or secondary (*i.e.*, symptoms are caused by or associated with another psychiatric disorder). For example, in cases where the most prominent symptom is depression and somatic complaints are experienced as more severe or associated with increased social or occupational impairment during periods of severe depression, the most likely diagnosis is generally considered to be major depressive episode with somatization symptoms. In contrast, schizophrenia or another psychotic disorder is the most probable underlying psychiatric diagnosis when complaints of unusual somatic symptoms occur in the context of a broader pattern of psychosis, possibly including paranoia, delusions, auditory hallucinations, or other psychotic symptoms. Somatic complaints frequently accompany anxiety disorders, including panic disorder and generalized anxiety disorder (GAD). However, in these disorders, debilitating panic attacks or pervasive feelings of anxiety and not somatic symptoms constitute the primary clinical focus. When a pattern of somatic symptoms that has no

| DIFFERENTIAL DIAGNOSIS | |
|---|---|
| **1. MEDICAL DISORDERS** | **2. PSYCHIATRIC DISORDERS** |
| A. NEUROLOGIC DISORDERS, INCLUDING MULTIPLE SCLEROSIS (MS) | A. SOMATOFORM DISORDER |
| B. GASTROINTESTINAL DISORDERS | B. MAJOR DEPRESSIVE EPISODE WITH SOMATIZATION |
| C. CHRONIC PAIN SYNDROMES | C. SCHIZOPHRENIA OR OTHER PSYCHOTIC DISORDERS |
| D. DISORDERS CAUSING SEXUAL DYSFUNCTION | D. PANIC DISORDER |
| E. SYSTEMIC LUPUS ERYTHEMATOSUS (SLE) | E. GENERALIZED ANXIETY DISORDER (GAD) |
| F. ACUTE INTERMITTENT PORPHYRIA | F. MALINGERING |
| | G. FACTITIOUS DISORDER |

established medical basis persists in the absence of significant mood, anxiety, or psychotic symptoms, the diagnosis depends on whether these symptoms are deliberately caused or feigned. A patient who pretends to experience somatic symptoms but actually has no symptoms is malingering. The accepted understanding in Western psychiatry is that feigning symptoms is generally motivated by hopes of financial reward. A patient who deliberately creates symptoms and, on examination, is found to have signs of a disorder that cannot be explained is diagnosed with a factitious disorder. In Western psychiatric theory, the accepted understanding is that such patients create symptoms in order to identify with a sick role (see Etiology & Pathophysiology below). A somatoform disorder can only be diagnosed when malingering and factitiousness have been ruled out. The specific symptom pattern, kind and severity of impairment will generally lead to the correct diagnosis (see table above).

## ETIOLOGY & PATHOPHYSIOLOGY:

Many neurophysiological and psychodynamic theories have been advanced in attempts to explain the pathogenesis of somatoform disorders. Evidence is emerging for a neurobiological basis of somatization disorder. Recent studies have demonstrated cortical dysfunction that may result in impairments in attention manifesting as distorted or exaggerated perceptions of normal bodily sensations. A similar neurobiological etiology has been proposed for hypochondriasis and pain disorder. Numerous theories derived from psychoanalytic models or social learning theory have also been advanced in efforts to explain various somatoform disorders. Body dysmorphic disorder is interesting in that it frequently occurs together with major depressive disorder, and there is some evidence of familial and cultural patterns of transmission.

## WESTERN MEDICAL TREATMENT:

Effective pharmacological treatments have not been established for most somatoform disorders. Serotonin-selective re-uptake inhibitors (SSRIs) and monoamine oxidase inhibitors (MAOIs) have yielded positive results in the management of somatoform disorders, although their mechanism of action has not been clearly established. Benzodiazepines and other sedative-hypnotics are sometimes used for management of panic symptoms or transient increases in anxiety commonly associated with somatic complaints. Highly structured supportive therapy and cognitive-behavioral interventions are sometimes useful in cases of somatization disorder, pain disorder, and body dysmorphic disorder.

## SHORT & LONG-TERM ADVANTAGES & DISADVANTAGES OF WESTERN MEDICAL TREATMENT:

Advantages of successful treatment include significant reduction in baseline somatic and anxiety complaints as well as improved social and occupational functioning. Disadvantages of contemporary Western treatments of somatoform disorders include risks of drug side effects or (in the case of benzodiazepines and other sedative-hypnotic medications) chemical dependency. There are no known disadvantages associated with long-term psychotherapy or cognitive-behavioral therapy.

## PROGNOSIS:

Cases of conversion disorder have a variable prognosis depending on the presence of co-morbid psychiatric or neurologic disorders, the nature of symptom onset (i.e., sudden or insidious), and level of social-psychological adaptation. Most hospitalized cases of conversion disorder resolve relatively quickly without treatment. Chronic duration and the presence of other psychiatric disorders are prognostically unfavorable. On-going litigation or other stressful social or legal circumstances are also predictive of a poor outcome. Hypochondriasis typically follows a chronic life-long course, including periods of transient symptomatic worsening or improvement. Individuals who complain of chronic pain and have been diagnosed with pain disorders often continue to experience considerable debility throughout life. The long-term outcome of body dysmorphic disorder is generally poor as most cases fail to respond to available Western medical treatments.

## INDICATIONS FOR REFERRAL TO WESTERN MEDICAL SERVICES:

Urgent referral to the nearest emergency room is indicated when there is evidence that an acute or progressive medical disorder or the effects of a substance may underlie reported somatic, mood, or anxiety symptoms. Non-urgent referral to a psychiatrist may be useful to clarify the medical-psychiatric differential diagnosis or to establish an optimized integrative treatment plan in cases where acute medical etiologies have been excluded and symptoms persist after completion of a prescribed course of Chinese medical treatment.

## CHINESE DISEASE CATEGORIZATION:

Traditionally in Chinese medicine, somatoform disorders

fall under the categories of visceral agitation (*zang zao*), lily disease (*bai he bing*), depression condition (*yu zheng*), reversal pattern (*jue zheng*), plum pit qi (*mei he qi*), and running piglet qi (*ben tun qi*). Lily disease is a form of mental depression characterized by emotional lability, taciturnity, a desire to sleep without being able to sleep, a desire to move without being able to move, a desire to eat without being able to eat, subjective sensations of heat when there is no heat and cold when there is no cold, a bitter taste in the mouth, yellow urine, etc. It is due to depression and binding of the seven affects or the sequela of a great heat disease when heart-lung yin vacuity engenders internal heat. Reversal pattern refers to fainting and loss of consciousness of human affairs. Running piglet qi, or simply running piglet, is an ancient disease category. In the *Nan Jing (Classic of Difficulties)*, it is listed as one of the five accumulations and specifically the accumulation pertaining to the kidneys. Its symptoms are a sensation of qi surging upward from the lower abdomen to the chest and epigastrium or even the throat. At the time of onset, the pain and bitterness (*i.e.*, suffering) are severe. There may be abdominal pain mixed with cold and heat, and the condition may endure for days and days. Running piglet is mostly due to kidney yin cold qi counterflowing upward or liver channel qi and fire surging and counterflowing.

## CHINESE DISEASE CAUSES & DISEASE MECHANISMS:

According to Chinese medicine, hysteria is mainly caused by habitual bodily heart, liver, and spleen weakness as well as stimuli by the seven affects and reactions to those stimuli. In those who tend toward repletion, the disease is located mainly in the heart, liver, and spleen. This condition is mostly caused by loss of regulation of the seven affects, worry, thinking, vexation, and annoyance, or extreme emotional tension. The qi mechanism is disturbed and this causes phlegm rheum to accumulate. This results in liver qi stagnation and counterflow with phlegm and qi blocking and obstructing. If liver wind stirs internally, wind and phlegm may ascend and harass the heart spirit above. If phlegm and qi become depressed and bind, the channels and vessels will become inhibited. If phlegm and fire harass the heart, the heart spirit will not be calm. Qi depression and phlegm obstruction may both also produce blood stasis which then stagnates in and obstructs the channels and vessels. Hence the sinews and the bones lose their construction and nourishment. Other complications due to qi stagnation include food accumulation and depressive heat. In those who tend to vacuity, there is heart spirit delusion due to heart-spleen dual vacuity, spleen-stomach vacuity weakness, heart-kidney yang vacuity, or liver-kidney depletion and detriment.

Typically, either in the initial phase of the disease or during acute episodes, repletion is more important and vacuity is less. Initially, we can also say that the damage is to the qi division. If this disease endures for some time without cure or during remittent stages, then habitual bodily visceral weakness is more important, and pathological changes are more moderate in degree and tend to be due to vacuity. For instance, liver fire may damage yin, or the liver may check spleen earth and the spleen may lose its fortification, etc. In addition, vacuity and repletion may exist simultaneously. In that case, the viscera and bowels lose their regulation, the qi and blood counterflow and become chaotic, and vacuity and repletion become mixed. Because there are so many ways hysteria can manifest, there are relatively a lot of different Chinese patterns corresponding to these manifestations.

## TREATMENT BASED ON PATTERN DISCRIMINATION:

### 1. LIVER QI DEPRESSION & BINDING, HEART SPIRIT DELUSION PATTERN

**MAIN SYMPTOMS:** Emotional depression, emotional anxiety, heart spirit restlessness, paranoia, easy fright, a tendency to sorrow and crying, abnormal susceptibility to anger, frequent sighing, chest and rib-side distention and pain, venter (*i.e.*, epigastric) oppression, torpid intake, irregular defecation, menstrual irregularity and/or PMS in females, a pale or slightly dark tongue with thin, white fur, and a bowstring, fine pulse

**ANALYSIS OF SYMPTOMS:** The liver rules coursing and discharge and its nature likes to spread and extend. The liver's channel traverses the rib-side and penetrates the diaphragm. If the liver qi becomes depressed and bound, coursing and discharge lose their normalcy and the qi mechanism is inhibited. This then manifests as emotional depression, abnormal anger, frequent sighing, chest and rib-side distention and pain, etc. If the liver qi is depressed and bound, then the liver will attack the spleen and assail the stomach. This results in venter oppression, torpid intake, and irregular defecation. The heart spirit delusion is due to malnourishment of the heart. Its symptoms include the anxiety, restlessness, paranoia, easy fright, a tendency to sorrow and crying, the pale tongue, and the fine pulse. The darkish tongue with thin, white fur and the bowstring pulse are signs of liver depression qi stagnation.

**TREATMENT PRINCIPLES:** Course the liver and resolve depression, rectify the qi and smooth the flow of the center

**FORMULA & MEDICINALS:** *Chai Hu Shu Gan Tang He Gan Mai Da Zao Tang* (Bupleurum Course the Liver Decoction plus Licorice, Wheat & Red Date Decoction)

Radix Bupleuri (*Chai Hu*), 12g, Fructus Citri Aurantii (*Zhi Ke*), 10g, Radix Albus Paeoniae Lactiflorae (*Bai Shao*), 12g, Fructus Citri Aurantii (*Zhi Ke*), 10g, Rhizoma Cyperi Rotundi (*Xiang Fu*), 10g, Radix Ligustici Wallichii (*Chuan Xiong*), 6g (added later), mix-fried Radix Glycyrrhizae (*Gan Cao*), 10g, Fructus Tritici Aestivi (*Huai Xiao Mai*), 15-30g, Fructus Zizyphi Jujubae (*Da Zao*), 5-10 pieces

Decoct in water and administer orally in two divided doses, morning and evening, one *ji* per day.

**ANALYSIS OF FORMULA:** Within this formula, Bupleurum, Aurantium, Cyperus, and Orange Peel course the liver and resolve depression, rectify the qi and smooth the flow of the center. Ligusticum and White Peony quicken the blood and free the flow of the network vessels, emolliate the liver and relax tension. Mix-fried Licorice, Red Dates, and Wheat all supplement and nourish the heart and quiet the spirit.

**ADDITIONS & SUBTRACTIONS:** If liver depression is severe, one can choose from and add Flos Inulae Racemosae (*Xuan Fu Hua*), Tuber Curcumae (*Yu Jin*), Pericarpium Citri Reticulatae Viride ((*Qing Pi*), Fructus Citri Sacrodactylis (*Fo Shou*), Flos Pruni Mume (*Lu O Mei*), etc. in order to assist the effect of coursing the liver and resolving depression. If there is burping and chest and venter discomfort, one can add Flos Inulae Racemosae (*Xuan Fu Hua*), Haemititum (*Dai Zhe Shi*), and Rhizoma Pinelliae Ternatae (*Ban Xia*) to level the liver, harmonize the stomach, and downbear counterflow. If there is simultaneous food stagnation with abdominal distention, one can add Massa Medica Fermentata (*Shen Qu*), Fructus Germinatus Hordei Vulgaris (*Mai Ya*), Fructus Crataegi (*Shan Zha*), and Endothelium Corneum Gigeriae Galli (*Ji Nei Jin*) to disperse food and transform stagnation. If liver depression has endured for days and qi depression has transformed into fire with emotional tension, agitation, and easy anger, a dry mouth with a bitter taste, and red tongue with yellow fur, then one may add Fructus Gardeniae Jasminoidis (*Zhi Zi*), Rhizoma Coptidis Chinensis (*Huang Lian*), and Cortex Radicis Moutan (*Dan Pi*) to cool the liver and drain fire. If heart qi vacuity is severe and the blood is not nourishing the heart, add Semen Zizyphi Spinosae (*Suan Zao Ren*), Arillus Euphoriae Longanae (*Long Yan Rou*), Radix Angelicae Sinensis (*Dang Gui*), Semen Biotae Orientalis (*Bai Zi Ren*), Sclerotium Pararadicis Poriae Cocos (*Fu Shen*), etc. If, due to prolonged administration of relatively high doses of Licorice, edema develops, add Sclerotium Poriae Cocos (*Fu Ling*) and Cortex Albizziae Julibrissins (*He Huan Pi*).

If liver-spleen disharmony is more pronounced, use *Jie Yu Tang* (Resolve Depression Decoction): Rhzoma Atractylodis Macrocephalae (*Bai Zhu*), 10g, Sclerotium Poriae Cocos (*Fu Ling*), 10g, Radix Albus Paeoniae Lactiflorae (*Bai Shao*), 10g, Radix Angelicae Sinensis (*Dang Gui*), 10g, Radix Bupleuri (*Chai Hu*), 10g, Radix Glycyrrhizae (*Gan Cao*), 10g, Radix Polygalae Tenuifoliae (*Yuan Zhi*), 10g, Rhizoma Acori Graminei (*Shi Chang Pu*), 10g, Concha Ostreae (*Mu Li*), 15g (decocted first), Os Draconis (*Long Gu*), 15g (decocted first), Magnetitum (*Ci Shi*), 24g (decocted first), Fructus Zizyphi Jujubae (*Da Zao*), 10g, Succinum (*Hu Po*), 3g (swallowed in two divided doses with the decocted liquid)

**ACUPUNCTURE:** For liver depression & binding: *Nei Guan* (Per 6), *He Gu* (LI 4), *San Yin Jiao* (Sp 6), *Zu San Li* (St 36), *Tai Chong* (Liv 3), *Feng Chi* (GB 20), *Dan Zhong* (CV 17). Use draining technique. For heart spirit delusion: *Shen Men* (Ht 7), *Hou Xi* (SI 3), *San Yin Jiao* (Sp 6), *Nei Guan* (Per 6), etc. Use mostly supplementing technique.

## 2. LIVER DEPRESSION TRANSFORMING FIRE WITH QI COUNTERFLOWING UPWARD PATTERN

**MAIN SYMPTOMS:** Due to emotional stimulation, there is a subjective sensation of qi surging upward from the lower abdomen to the throat accompanied by a desire to die, fright palpitations, restlessness, aversion to the sound of human voices, possible abdominal pain or vomiting, vexatious thirst, panting counterflow, first cold, then heat, the qi returning incessantly, whitish yellow tongue fur, and a bowstring, rapid pulse

**ANALYSIS OF SYMPTOMS:** In this case, there is a combination of heat and cold. The subjective sensation of qi surging upward is liver depression. The qi becomes stagnant and accumulates. Eventually it has to vent itself somewhere. Because qi is yang, it most commonly counterflows upward. This also causes the fright palpitations, restlessness, abdominal pain or vomiting, and the asthmatic panting. Alternating cold and hot sensations and the whitish yellow tongue fur show that there is both heat and cold. The heat is depressive cold, while the cold is not true cold. It is reversal chilling or counterflow chilling due to heat being depressed internally. The bowstring pulse is due to liver depression, while the rapid pulse is due to heat. The aversion to the sound of human voices is also due to liver depression.

**TREATMENT PRINCIPLES:** Level the liver, downbear counterflow, and normalize the flow of qi

**FORMULA & MEDICINALS:** *Ben Tun Tang* (Running Piglet Decoction)

Radix Glycyrrhizae (*Gan Cao*), 10g, Radix Ligustici Wallichii (*Chuan Xiong*), 10g, Radix Angelicae Sinensis (*Dang Gui*), 10g, Rhizoma Pinelliae Ternatae (*Ban Xia*), 12-15g, Radix Scutellariae Baicalensis (*Huang Qin*), 12g, Radix Puerariae (*Ge Gen*), 18g, Radix Albus Paeoniae Lactiflorae (*Bai Shao*), 18g, uncooked Rhizoma Zingiberis (*Sheng Jiang*), 3 slices, Cortex Radicis Pruni Triflora (*Gan Li Gen Bai Pi*), 6g

Decoct in water and administer orally in two divided doses, morning and evening, one *ji* per day.

**ANALYSIS OF FORMULA:** Within this formula, Licorice, White Peony, and Pueraria all relax tension and release the muscles. Ligusticum and Pueraria both tend to be upbearing and ascending. Although there is upward counterflow, that upward counterflow is due to extreme liver depression. Therefore, paradoxically, upbearing the clear yang, which disinhibits the qi mechanism, restores proper downbearing of counterflow. Pinellia and Ginger also downbear and descend counterflow. They specifically work on the stomach qi. However, because the stomach channel is so full of qi and blood, harmonizing the stomach qi can affect the qi of the entire body and especially the liver qi due to the close reciprocal relationship between these two organs. In addition, since Ginger's warm acridity promotes the circulation of qi and blood to the extremities, it also eliminates the counterflow chilling sensations. Scutellaria, on the other hand, clears depressive heat. Cortex Pruni is also cooling and thirst relieving.

**ACUPUNCTURE:** *Zhong Wan* (CV 12), *Nei Guan* (Per 6), *Zu San Li* (St 36), *Gong Sun* (Sp 4), *Shang Wan* (CV 13), *Guan Yuan* (CV 4), *He Gu* (LI 4). Use draining technique or even supplementing-even draining technique.

### 3. LIVER DEPRESSION-PHLEGM OBSTRUCTION PATTERN

**MAIN SYMPTOMS:** Emotional depression, low spirits, chest and abdominal fullness and oppression, torpid sitting, taciturnity, the sound of phlegm in the throat, profuse phlegm, plum pit qi, torpid intake, a pale tongue with slimy, white fur, and a bowstring, slippery pulse

**ANALYSIS OF SYMPTOMS:** If the seven affects damage internally, the liver qi may become depressed. In that case, the qi will stagnate and dampness will obstruct. If dampness gathers, it may engender phlegm. If phlegm and qi harass internally, they may confound and block the spirit brilliance. Thus one sees emotional depression, low spirits, torpid sitting, and taciturnity. When phlegm and qi counterflow upward to the chest and diaphragm, then one hears the sound of phlegm in the throat and the patient may feel the sensation of something stuck in the throat. Profuse phlegm, chest oppression, torpid intake, slimy, white tongue fur, and a bowstring, slippery pulse are all signs of liver depression mixed with phlegm.

**TREATMENT PRINCIPLES:** Course the liver and rectify the qi, transform phlegm and resolve depression

**FORMULA & MEDICINALS:** *Ban Xia Hou Po Tang* (Pinellia & Magnolia Decoction)

Rhizoma Pinelliae Ternatae (*Ban Xia*), 10g, Sclerotium Poriae Cocos (*Fu Ling*), 12g, Folium Perillae Frutescentis (*Zi Su Ye*), 10g, Cortex Magnoliae Officinalis (*Hou Po*), 6g, uncooked Rhizoma Zingiberis (*Sheng Jiang*), 10g (added later)

Decoct in water and administer in two divided doses, morning and evening, one *ji* per day.

**ANALYSIS OF FORMULA:** This formula uses acrid and warm Pinellia to transform phlegm and open binding, harmonize the stomach and downbear counterflow. Magnolia is acrid, bitter, and warm. It is said that Magnolia's "bitterness is able to descend the qi and discharge repletion and fullness, while its warmth is able to boost the qi and scatter dampness and fullness." When these two medicinals are combined Magnolia's qi-moving assists Pinellia's transforming of phlegm, while Pinellia's downbearing of counterflow assists Magnolia's moving of the qi. These are then combined with uncooked Ginger whose acridity scatters binding and bitterness downbears counterflow, hence descending the qi and scattering fullness, resolving depression and broadening the chest. Perilla Leaves enter the lung. Their nature is slightly acrid and warm. They aromatically penetrate, course and scatter. Thus they assist Pinellia's downbearing of counterflow and harmonization of the stomach.

**ADDITIONS & SUBTRACTIONS:** If qi depression predominates, add Radix Bupleuri (*Chai Hu*), Rhizoma Cyperi Rotundi (*Xiang Fu*), Fructus Citri Sacrodactylis (*Fo Shou*), and Fructus Citri Aurantii (*Zhi Ke*) to increase the power of rectifying the qi and opening depression. If phlegm depression is severe, then one can add Concha Cyclinae Meretricis (*Hai Ge Ke*), Radix Asteris Tatarici (*Zi Wan*), Bulbus Fritillariae (*Bei Mu*), Pericarpium Citri Reticulatae (*Chen Pi*), and Fructus Trichosanthis Kirlowii (*Gua Lou*) to increase the strength of transforming phlegm and moving the qi.

**ACUPUNCTURE:** *Zu San Li* (St 36), *San Yin Jiao* (Sp 6), *Zhong Wan* (CV 12), *Feng Long* (St 40), *Gan Shu* (Bl 18), *Dan Zhong* (CV 17). Use draining technique.

## 4. PHLEGM HEAT HARASSING ABOVE PATTERN

**MAIN SYMPTOMS:** Vexation, agitation, disquietude or restlessness, abnormal susceptibility to anger, vexation and oppression within the chest, insomnia, profuse dreams, a bitter taste in the mouth, oral thirst, possible spitting of yellow phlegm, yellow urine, constipation, a red tongue with slimy, yellow or glossy, yellow fur, and a slippery, bowstring, rapid pulse

**ANALYSIS OF SYMPTOMS:** The vexation, agitation, restlessness, abnormal susceptibility to anger, vexation, profuse dreams, bitter taste, oral thirst, yellow urine, and constipation are due to evil heat harassing the heart and damaging fluids. The chest oppression and profuse phlegm are due to phlegm obstruction. The red tongue with slimy, yellow or glossy, yellow fur and slippery, bowstring, rapid pulse are all signs of phlegm heat.

**TREATMENT PRINCIPLES:** Transform phlegm and clear heat, resolve depression and quiet the spirit

**FORMULA & MEDICINALS:** *Huang Lian Wen Dan Tang* (Coptis Warm the Gallbladder Decoction)

Rhizoma Coptidis Chinensis (*Huang Lian*), 3-6g (added later), Rhizoma Pinelliae Ternatae (*Ban Xia*), 10g, Caulis Bambusae In Taeniis (*Zhu Ru*), 10g, Pericarpium Citri Reticulatae (*Chen Pi*), 10g, Sclerotium Poriae Cocos (*Fu Ling*), 12g, Fructus Immaturus Citri Aurantii (*Zhi Shi*), 10g, Radix Glycyrrhizae (*Gan Cao*), 3-6g, Fructus Zizyphi Jujubae (*Da Zao*), 3-5 pieces

Decoct in water and administer orally in two divided doses, morning and evening, one *ji* per day.

**ANALYSIS OF FORMULA:** Pinellia, Poria, Orange Peel, and Caulis Bambusae all transform phlegm. Caulis Bambusae, Coptis, and uncooked Licorice all clear heat. Poria,

Licorice, and Red Dates all fortify the spleen, supplement the heart, and quiet the spirit. While Pinellia, Caulis Bambusae, Orange Peel, and Immature Aurantium all rectify the qi and resolve depression. In addition, Licorice and Red Dates harmonize all the other medicinals in this formula and protect the stomach from damage.

**ADDITIONS & SUBTRACTIONS:** If there is more serious vexation and agitation, insomnia, and profuse dreams, add Os Draconis (*Long Gu*), Concha Ostreae (*Mu Li*), and Concha Margaritiferae (*Zhen Zhu Mu*). If there is heart fire effulgence, then add Cinnabar (*Zhu Sha*) and uncooked Frusta Ferri (*Tie Lou*). If there is constipation, add Radix Et Rhizoma Rhei (*Da Huang*), Mirabilitum (*Mang Xiao*), and Cortex Magnoliae Officinalis (*Hou Po*).

**ACUPUNCTURE:** *Shen Men* (Ht 7), *Feng Long* (St 40), *Jian Shi* (Per 5), *Zu San Li* (St 36), *Tian Shu* (Bl 10), *Gan Shu* (Bl 18). Use draining technique.

## 5. QI STAGNATION & BLOOD STASIS PATTERN

**MAIN SYMPTOMS:** Emotional lability, emotional depression and melancholy, sorrow and crying, emotional torpor and stagnation, chest and rib-side fullness and oppression, dark circles under the eyes, headache, insomnia, profuse dreams, easy fright, if severe, lack of use of the limbs, sleep-walking, a dark, purplish tongue or possible static spots and macules, and a bowstring, choppy pulse

**NOTE:** This pattern tends to complicate other patterns that either have endured for some time or are severe. It does not usually appear as a simple, discreet pattern.

**ANALYSIS OF SYMPTOMS:** The main cause of hysteria neurosis is damage by the seven affects. This results in qi stagnation which, in turn, may result in blood stasis. As it is said, "If the qi moves, the blood moves; if the qi stops, the blood stops." When emotional depression causes inhibition of the qi mechanism, then the mechanism of engenderment is blocked and severed. Hence the essence spirit has no place from which to receive qi and blood and thus also suffers damage. If this continues for a long time and is not resolved, then this must damage the construction and blood. Thus the viscera and bowels lose their moistening, the heart spirit loses it blood nourishment, the heart spirit becomes disquieted, and the symptoms of hysteria result.

**TREATMENT PRINCIPLES:** Quicken the blood and transform stasis, nourish the blood and moisten the viscera

FORMULA & MEDICINALS: *Tao Hong Si Wu Tang Jia Wei* (Persica & Carthamus Four Materials Decoction with Added Flavors)

Semen Pruni Persicae (*Tao Ren*), 10g, Flos Carthami Tinctorii (*Hong Hua*), 10g (steeped), Radix Angelicae Sinensis (*Dang Gui*), 10g, Radix Rubrus Paeoniae Lactiflorae (*Chi Shao*), 30g, Radix Ligustici Wallichii (*Chuan Xiong*), 10g (added later), uncooked Radix Rehmanniae (*Sheng Di*), 12g, Radix Bupleuri (*Chai Hu*), 10g, Rhizoma Cyperi Rotundi (*Xiang Fu*), 12g, Os Draconis (*Long Gu*), 30g (decocted first), mix-fried Radix Glycyrrhizae (*Gan Cao*), 6g, Succinum (*Hu Po*), 6g (powdered and swallowed with the decocted liquid)

Decoct in water and administer in two divided doses, morning and evening, one *ji* per day.

ANALYSIS OF FORMULA: Persica and Carthamus combined with the Four Materials (*i.e.*, Dang Gui, Rehmannia, Ligusticum, and Peony) strongly supplement and strongly quicken the blood. Hence this is a good formula for treating blood vacuity and blood stasis. The combination of Bupleurum and Cyperus courses the liver and rectifies the qi, resolves depression and moves the qi. When the blood obtains qi, it moves; when the qi obtains blood, it is smoothly flowing. When the viscera and bowels obtain qi and blood, they are moistened and nourished. Thus depression and stagnation obtain coursing and resolution. In addition, Dragon Bone, Succinum, and mix-fried Licorice are added to calm the heart and stabilize the mind, emolliate and harmonize the blood vessels. Hence this combination of medicinals promotes the spreading and extension of the qi mechanism, the filling and exuberance of the blood vessels, the transformation of static blood, the free flow of the vessels and network vessels, the moistening of the five viscera, and the stabilization of the heart spirit.

ADDITIONS & SUBTRACTIONS: If there is chest oppression, tension and agitation, a bitter taste in the mouth, and yellow tongue fur, one can add Rhizoma Coptidis Chinensis (*Huang Lian*) and Fructus Gardeniae Jasminoidis (*Zhi Zi*) to clear heat and eliminate vexation. If there is chest glomus with sighing, then add Fructus Citri Sacrodactylis (*Fo Shou*) and Tuber Curcumae (*Yu Jin*) to rectify the qi and resolve depression. If there are heart palpitations and insomnia, add Sclerotium Pararadicis Poriae Cocos (*Fu Shen*) and stir-fried Semen Zizyphi Spinosae (*Suan Zao Ren*) to calm the heart and quiet the spirit.

ACUPUNCTURE: *Xue Hai* (Sp 10), *Tai Chong* (Liv 3), *He Gu* (LI 4), *San Yin Jiao* (Sp 6). Use draining technique.

## 6. HEART SPIRIT DEPRIVED OF NOURISHMENT PATTERN

MAIN SYMPTOMS: Disquietude or restlessness of the heart spirit, an anxious, worried affect, sorrow and desire to cry, mental instability, lots of stretching and yawning, heart vexation, inability to lie down, restlessness when sitting or lying down, heart palpitations, a pale tongue with thin, white fur, and a fine, weak pulse

NOTE: The difference between this pattern and pattern #1 is that, in pattern #1, liver depression is primary and heart vacuity is secondary. Here, heart vacuity is primary and liver depression is secondary in importance.

ANALYSIS OF SYMPTOMS: If the seven affects are unregulated and there is worry, thinking, vexation and annoyance or excessive emotional tension, the liver qi may become depressed and bound and the heart qi may be consumed and damaged. Thus construction and blood are insufficient and this may result in malnourishment of the heart spirit. In that case, one will see heart spirit restlessness, a worried, anxious affect, sorrow and a desire to cry, mental instability, lots of stretching and yawning, heart vexation, inability to lie down, restlessness when sitting or lying down, etc. The heart palpitations, pale tongue with thin, white fur, and the fine, weak pulse are all symptoms of heart blood insufficiency.

TREATMENT PRINCIPLES: Sweetly moisten and relax tension, nourish the heart and quiet the spirit

FORMULA & MEDICINALS: *Gan Mai Da Zao Tang Jia Wei* (Licorice, Wheat & Red Date Decoction with Added Flavors)

Radix Glycyrrhizae (*Gan Cao*), 10g, Fructus Tritici Aestivi (*Huai Xiao Mai*), 30g, Fructus Zizyphi Jujubae (*Da Zao*), 15 pieces, Semen Biotae Orientalis (*Bai Zi Ren*), 10g, stir-fried Semen Zizyphi Spinosae (*Suan Zao Ren*), 15g, Sclerotium Pararadicis Poriae Cocos (*Fu Shen*), 12g, Dens Draconis (*Long Chi*), 30g (decocted first), Concha Ostreae (*Mu Li*), 30g (decocted first)

Decoct in water and administer orally in two divided doses, morning and evening, one *ji* per day.

ANALYSIS OF FORMULA: *Gan Mai Da Zao Tang* is effective for nourishing the heart and quieting the spirit, sweetly moistening and relaxing tension or urgency. This formula is suggested in Zhang Zhong-jing's *Jin Gui Yao*

*Lue* (*Essentials from the Golden Cabinet*) for visceral agitation. Its rationale is based on the idea that, "When the liver suffers urgency or tension, relax that tension with sweet foods." The ingredients in this formula supplement the center and boost the qi as well as moisten visceral agitation. When Biota, Zizyphus Spinosa, and Spirit of Poria are added to this base, they can strengthen its effect of nourishing the heart and quieting the spirit. Dragon's Teeth and Oyster Shell settle, still, and quiet the spirit. Therefore, when all these medicinals are used together, their effect is to nourish the heart and quiet the spirit.

**ADDITIONS & SUBTRACTIONS:** For a lusterless facial complexion, lassitude of the spirit, fatigue, heart palpitations, and insomnia, add Radix Angelicae Sinensis (*Dang Gui*), Radix Albus Paeoniae Lactiflorae (*Bai Shao*), Radix Astragali Membranacei (*Huang Qi*), etc. to supplement the qi and nourish the blood. If there is a heart qi insufficiency with restless heart spirit, an anxious, worried affect, restlessness when sitting and lying down, one can also administer *Ren Shen Hu Po Wan* (Ginseng & Succinum Pills, a Chinese ready-made medicine) in order to nourish the blood and nourish the spirit, quiet the spirit and stabilize the mind. If there is heart qi insufficiency with worrying and depression damaging the spirit with mental-emotional restlessness, heart palpitations, and insomnia, then one can also give *An Shen Ding Zhi Wan* (Quiet the Spirit & Stabilize the Mind Pills, a Chinese ready-made medicine).

*Ren Shen Hu Po Wan* consist of: Radix Panacis Ginseng (*Ren Shen*), Succinum (*Hu Po*), Sclerotium Pararadicis Poriae Cocos (*Fu Shen*), Sclerotium Poriae Cocos (*Fu Ling*), Rhizoma Acori Graminei (*Shi Chang Pu*), Radix Polygalae Tenuifoliae (*Yuan Zhi*), Cinnabar (*Zhu Sha*), Resina Olibani (*Ru Xiang*), Semen Zizyphi Spinosae (*Suan Zao Ren*).

*An Shen Ding Zhi Wan* consist of: Radix Panacis Ginseng (*Ren Shen*), Rhizoma Atractylodis Macrocephalae (*Bai Zhu*), Sclerotium Pararadicis Poriae Cocos (*Fu Shen*), Sclerotium Poriae Cocos (*Fu Ling*), Rhizoma Acori Graminei (*Shi Chang Pu*), Radix Polygalae Tenuifoliae (*Yuan Zhi*), Cinnabar (*Zhu Sha*), Tuber Ophiopogonis Japonici (*Mai Dong*), Semen Zizyphi Spinosae (*Suan Zao Ren*), Calculus Bovis (*Niu Huang*), Arillus Euphoriae Longanae (*Long Yan Rou*).

**ACUPUNCTURE:** Shen Men (Ht 7), Nei Guan (Per 6), Dan Zhong (CV 17), Yin Tang (M-HN-3). Use supplementing technique.

## 7. HEART-LIVER QI COUNTERFLOW WITH MALNOURISHMENT OF THE NETWORK VESSELS PATTERN

**MAIN SYMPTOMS:** One-sided or lower limb paralysis or wilting, weakness, and lack of strength after either sudden anger or sorrow, inability to stand or walk, heart palpitations, restlessness, chest oppression, rib-side pain, dizziness, vertigo, a pale red or dark red tongue with thin, white fur, and a bowstring, fine pulse. The difference between this pattern, the one above it, and pattern #1 is that this pattern specifically describes hysterical paralysis.

**ANALYSIS OF SYMPTOMS:** The paralysis, wilting, weakness, lack of strength, inability to walk or stand, dizziness and vertigo, pale tongue, and fine pulse are due to lack of nourishment of the vessels and network vessels. The chest and rib-side oppression and pain, dark tongue, and bowstring pulse are all indications of liver depression. The heart palpitations and restlessness are due to heart vacuity.

**TREATMENT PRINCIPLES:** Course the liver, nourish the heart, and calm the network vessels

**FORMULA & MEDICINALS:** *Gan Mai Da Zao Tang He Xiao Yao San Jia Jian* (Licorice, Wheat & Red Date Decoction plus Rambling Powder with Additions & Subtractions)

Radix Bupleuri (*Chai Hu*), 3-10g, Radix Angelicae Sinensis (*Dang Gui*), 10g, Radix Albus Paeoniae Lactiflorae (*Bai Shao*), 15-18g, Rhizoma Atractylodis Macrocephalae (*Bai Zhu*), 10g, Sclerotium Poriae Cocos (*Fu Ling*), 10g, mix-fried Radix Glycyrrhizae (*Gan Cao*), 10-15g, Fructus Tritici Aestivi (*Huai Xiao Mai*), 15-30g, Fructus Zizyphi Jujubae (*Da Zao*), 10-15 pieces, uncooked Rhizoma Zingiberis (*Sheng Jiang*), 2 slices

**ANALYSIS OF FORMULA:** Within this formula, Bupleurum courses the liver and rectifies the qi. Dang Gui nourishes and quickens the blood. White Peony nourishes the blood and emolliates the liver, thus relaxing tension and cramping. Atractylodes, Poria, mix-fried Licorice, Red Dates, and Triticus all supplement and nourish the heart and spleen. All, except Atractylodes, also quiet the spirit. Uncooked Ginger harmonizes all the other medicinals in the formula as well as promotes the movement of the qi and blood to and within the extremities.

**ADDITIONS & SUBTRACTIONS:** If the disease has endured for some time and there is static blood obstructing the network vessels, add Radix Rubrus Paeoniae Lactiflorae (*Chi Shao*), Squama Manitis Pentadactylis (*Chuan Shan Jia*), Radix Achyranthis Bidentatae (*Niu Xi*), and Semen Pruni Persicae (*Tao Ren*).

ACUPUNCTURE: *Shen Men* (Ht 7), *Nei Guan* (Per 6), *Dan Zhong* (CV 17).

ADDITIONS & SUBTRACTIONS: For the upper extremities, add *He Gu* (LI 4), *Hou Xi* (SI 3), *Qu Chi* (LI 11), *Jian Yu* (LI 15). For the lower extremities, add *Yong Quan* (Ki 1), *Tai Chong* (Liv 3), *Yang Ling Quan* (GB 34), *Feng Shi* (GB 31), *Huan Tiao* (GB 30). Use even supplementing-even draining technique.

## 8. HEART-SPLEEN DUAL VACUITY, QI & BLOOD INSUFFICIENCY PATTERN

MAIN SYMPTOMS: Essence spirit abstraction, heart palpitations, gallbladder timidity, excessive thinking, susceptibility to suspicions, insomnia, impaired memory, nighttime sleep not quiet, profuse dreams, easily awakened, dizziness, lassitude of the spirit, devitalized eating and drinking, a pale white or sallow yellow, lusterless facial complexion, a pale tongue, and a fine, weak pulse

ANALYSIS OF SYMPTOMS: Over-taxation of the heart due to too much thinking and worrying over a long period of time may lead to damage of the heart and spleen. The heart and spleen may also both become vacuous if, after a great disease, there is qi and blood insufficiency. In this case, the heart loses its nourishment and the spirit thus becomes disquieted. This is the cause of the heart palpitations, gallbladder timidity, excessive thinking, susceptibility to suspicion, insomnia, impaired memory, etc. The spleen and stomach are the latter heaven root and the source of qi and blood engenderment and transformation. If the spleen does not fortify and move, eating and drinking become devitalized and, therefore, the source of both qi and blood becomes insufficient. This results in the lusterless facial complexion, dizziness, lassitude of the spirit, pale tongue, and fine, weak pulse.

TREATMENT PRINCIPLES: Supplement and boost the heart and spleen, nourish the blood and quiet the spirit

FORMULA & MEDICINALS: *Gui Pi Tang* (Restore the Spleen Decoction)

Radix Codonopsitis Pilosulae (*Dang Shen*), 15g, Radix Astragali Membranacei (*Huang Qi*), 15g, Rhizoma Atactylodis Macrocephalae (*Bai Zhu*), 10g, Radix Polygalae Tenuifoliae (*Yuan Zhi*), 10g, Semen Zizyphi Spinosae (*Suan Zao Ren*), 12g, Sclerotium Pararadicis Poriae Cocos (*Fu Shen*), 12g, Arillus Euphoriae Longanae (*Long Yan Rou*), 10g, Radix Angelicae Sinensis (*Dang Gui*), 10g, Radix Auklandiae Lappae (*Mu Xiang*), 6g

(added later), mix-fried Radix Glycyrrhizae (*Gan Cao*), 6g, uncooked Rhizoma Zingiberis (*Sheng Jiang*), 3 slices, Fructus Zizyphi Jujubae (*Da Zao*), 6 pieces

Decoct in water and administer orally in two divided doses, morning and evening, one *ji* per day.

ANALYSIS OF FORMULA: Within this formula, Codonopsis and Astragalus are sweet and warm and boost the qi. They also greatly supplement the spleen qi. Atractylodes is bitter and warm. It fortifies the spleen and dries dampness. Poria blandly percolates or seeps and fortifies the spleen. Mix-fried Licorice is sweet and warm, and it regulates the center, boosts the qi, and fortifies the spleen. Together, the above medicinals form *Si Jun Zi Tang Jia Huang Qi* (Four Gentlemen Decoction plus Astragalus). This combination boosts the qi and supplements the center, fortifies the spleen and boosts the stomach. If the spleen and stomach obtain nourishment, engenderment and transformation are effulgent and exuberant and heart blood is full and sufficient. Therefore, the spirit is automatically quieted. Longans sweetly and warmly boost the heart spirit and supplement the qi and blood in order to quiet the spirit. They also boost the intelligence and calm the heart. Dang Gui combined with Astragalus boosts the qi and engenders blood. Auklandia is acrid and warm. It moves the qi and scatters stagnation in order to resolve depressed and stagnant qi and blood, rectify the qi and arouse the spleen. Polygala quiets the spirit, boosts the intelligence, and resolves depression, and Zizyphus Spinosa calms the heart and quiets the spirit. When all these medicinals are used together, heart blood is filled and the heart spirit is automatically quieted.

ADDITIONS & SUBTRACTIONS: If there is serious heart blood insufficiency, add cooked Radix Rehmanniae (*Shu Di*) and Radix Albus Paeoniae Lactiflorae (*Bai Shao*) to enrich yin and nourish the blood. If insomnia is relatively severe, add Flos Albizziae Julibrissinis (*He Huan Hua*) and Semen Biotae Orientalis (*Bai Zi Ren*) to nourish the heart and quiet the spirit. If qi depression is not smoothly or easily flowing, add Tuber Curcumae (*Yu Jin*) and Cortex Albizziae Julibrissinis (*He Huan Pi*) to rectify the qi and resolve depression. And if there is yin vacuity fire effulgence, add uncooked Radix Rehmanniae (*Sheng Di*), Tuber Ophiopogonis Japonici (*Mai Dong*), and Rhizoma Coptidis Chinensis (*Huang Lian*) to enrich yin and clear heat.

ACUPUNCTURE: *Gong Sun* (Sp 4), *Nei Guan* (Per 6), *Zu San Li* (St 36), *Xin Shu* (Bl 15), *Zhong Wan* (CV 12), *Shen Men* (Ht 7). Use supplementing or even supplementing-even draining technique.

## 9. LIVER-KIDNEY INSUFFICIENCY WITH MALNOURISHMENT OF THE SINEWS & BONES PATTERN

MAIN SYMPTOMS: A relatively long disease course, former heaven natural endowment insufficiency, or bodily emaciation, knee and lower leg wilting and weakness, inability to stand, if severe, atrophy of the large muscles of the legs, lower and upper back pain, dizziness and vertigo, a thin, small tongue which is red in color and has scanty fur, and a fine, weak or fine, rapid pulse

ANALYSIS OF SYMPTOMS: The relatively long disease course suggests that, "Enduring disease has damaged the kidneys." The bodily emaciation suggests constitutional yin vacuity. The lower and upper back pain, dizziness and vertigo, red tongue with scanty fur, and fine pulse are all signs of yin vacuity. The inability to stand, the knee and lower leg wilting and weakness, and the atrophy of the large muscles in the legs indicate malnourishment by yin blood. The rapid pulse suggests that yin is insufficient to control yang, while the weak pulse suggests a qi and yin vacuity.

TREATMENT PRINCIPLES: Supplement and boost the liver and kidneys, nourish yin and clear heat

FORMULA & MEDICINALS: Hu Qian Wan Jia Jian (Hidden Tiger Pills with Additions & Subtractions)

Cortex Phellodendri (Huang Bai), 10g, Rhizoma Anemarrhenae Aspheloidis (Zhi Mu), 10g, cooked Radix Rehmanniae (Shu Di), 12-15g, Plastrum Testudinis (Gui Ban), 12-15g (decocted first), Radix Albus Paeoniae Lactiflorae (Bao Shao), 10-15g, Radix Angelicae Sinensis (Dang Gui), Radix Achyranthis Bidentatae (Niu Xi), 10g, Herba Cynomorii Songarici (Suo Yang), 6g, Pericarpium Citri Reticulatae (Chen Pi), 6g

Decoct in water and administer orally in two divided doses, morning and evening, one ji per day.

ANALYSIS OF FORMULA: Cooked Rehmannia, Plastrum Testudinis, White Peony, Dang Gui, and Achyranthes all nourish the blood and enrich yin. Cynomorium invigorates yang and strengthens the sinews and bones. It is used both for its empirical action of strengthening the sinews and bones and also based on the principle of "searching for yin within yang." Phellodendron and Anemarrhena clear vacuity heat, while Orange Peel harmonizes all the medicinals in the formula and prevents damage to the spleen by any enriching, slimy, stagnating medicinals.

ADDITIONS & SUBTRACTIONS: If there is concomitant yang vacuity, add Herba Epimedii (Xian Ling Pi), Radix Morindae Officinalis (Ba Ji Tian), Fructus Psoraleae Corylifoliae (Bu Gu Zhi), etc. If there is yin vacuity yang hyperactivity with malnourishment of the heart spirit manifesting as sorrow and tendency to crying, paranoia, easy fright, afternoon tidal heat, vexatious heat in the five hearts, a dry mouth and throat, dizziness and vertigo, scanty, reddish urine, a red tongue with scanty fur, and a fine, rapid pulse but no particular signs or symptoms of malnourishment of the sinews and bones, use Zhi Bai Di Huang Tang Jia Bai He Zao Ren (Anemarrhena & Phellodendron Rehmannia Decoction plus Lily & Zizyphus Spinosa) instead.

Zhi Bai Di Huang Tang Jia Bai He Zao Ren is comprised of: Bulbus Lilii (Bai He), 12g, Semen Zizyphi Spinosae (Suan Zao Ren), 12g, Rhizoma Anemarrhenae Aspheloidis (Zhi Mu), 10g, Cortex Phellodendri (Huang Bai), 10g, cooked Radix Rehmanniae (Shu Di), 12-15g, Radix Dioscoreae Oppositae (Shan Yao), 10g, Fructus Corni Officinalis (Shan Zhu Yu), 10g, Sclerotium Poriae Cocos (Fu Ling), 10g, Cortex Radicis Moutan (Dan Pi), 6-10g, Rhizoma Alismatis (Ze Xie), 6-10g.

ACUPUNCTURE: Gan Shu (Bl 18), Shen Shu (Bl 23), Tai Xi (Ki 3), San Yin Jiao (Sp 6), Bai Hui (GV 20).

ADDITIONS & SUBTRACTIONS: For upper extremity paralysis, add Jian Yu (LI 15) and Qu Chi (LI 11). For lower extremity paralysis, add Huan Tiao (GB 30), Yang Ling Quan (GB 34), Tai Chong (Liv 3), Zu San Li (St 36), Jie Xi (St 41). Use supplementing technique.

## 10. YIN VACUITY-LUNG HEAT PATTERN

MAIN SYMPTOMS: A feeling of something obstructing the throat, a red, dry, sore throat, dry cough, vexatious heat, night sweats, heat in the five hearts, a red tongue with thin, yellow fur, and a fine, rapid pulse

ANALYSIS OF SYMPTOMS: The inhibition of the throat, dry throat, the dry cough, night sweats, thin fur, and fine pulse are all indications of yin vacuity. The red, sore throat, vexatious heat, heat in the five hearts, red tongue with yellow fur, and the rapid pulse all indicate heat.

TREATMENT PRINCIPLES: Nourish yin, moisten the lungs, and clear heat

FORMULA & MEDICINALS: Yang Yin Qing Fei Tang (Nourish Yin & Clear the Lungs Decoction)

Uncooked Radix Rehmanniae (Sheng Di), 15-20g, Radix

Scrophulariae Ningpoensis (*Xuan Shen*), 10-15g, Tuber Ophiopogonis Japonici (*Mai Dong*), 12g, Radix Albus Paeoniae Lactiflorae (*Bai Shao*), 10g, Cortex Radicis Moutan (*Dan Pi*), 10g, Bulbus Fritillariae Cirrhosae (*Chuan Bei Mu*), 6-10g, Herba Menthae Haplocalycis (*Bo He*), 3-6g (added later), Radix Glycyrrhizae (*Gan Cao*), 3g

Decoct in water and administer orally in two divided doses, morning and evening, one *ji* per day.

**ANALYSIS OF FORMULA:** Within this formula, uncooked Rehmannia is the ruling medicinal for enriching yin and clearing vacuity heat. It is assisted in this by Scrophularia and Ophiopogon which both specifically moisten the lungs. Moutan clears heat from the blood division at the same time as it quickens the blood. This condition is an enduring one which is often complicated by an element of blood stasis. Fritillaria Cirrhosa clears heat and transforms phlegm. However, unlike Fritillaria Thunbergium, it also engenders fluids and nourishes yin. Mentha courses the liver, resolves depression, and clears heat, while Licorice harmonizes the other medicinals while also clearing heat and engendering fluids.

**ADDITIONS & SUBTRACTIONS:** For vexatious heat and night sweats, add Rhizoma Anemarrhenae Aspheloidis (*Zhi Mu*) and Cortex Radicis Lycii Chinensis (*Di Gu Pi*). For insomnia, add Semen Zizyphi Spinosae (*Suan Zao Ren*) and Caulis Polygoni Multiflori (*Ye Jiao Teng*).

**ACUPUNCTURE:** *Fei Shu* (Bl 13), *Tai Xi* (Ki 3), *Tai Yuan* (Lu 9), *Yu Ji* (Lu 10). Mostly use supplementing technique.

## 11. COLD WATER COUNTERFLOWING UPWARD, HEART YANG INSUFFICIENCY PATTERN

**MAIN SYMPTOMS:** Due to stimulation by fright and fear there is a sensation of palpitations stirring below the umbilicus. This is followed by qi surging and counterflowing upward with heart fluster and restlessness, insomnia, profuse dreams, a cold body and chilled limbs, a pale tongue with slimy, white fur, and a bowstring, tight pulse which is possibly insufficient in the left *cun* position.

**ANALYSIS OF SYMPTOMS:** Fear is the affect or emotion of the kidneys, while fright causes the qi to become chaotic. The sensation of stirring below the umbilicus and the upward surging of qi are symptoms that the kidney qi has lost its root in its lower source. One of the functions of the kidney qi is to govern the water of the entire body. If

the kidney qi becomes dysfunctional, water fluids may not be transformed. When the kidney qi surges upward, it may carry with it these untransformed water fluids which harass the heart and disquiet the spirit. This produces the symptoms of heart fluster (*i.e.*, palpitations), insomnia, profuse qi, etc. The cold limbs and body and the pale tongue with white, slimy fur are all symptoms that ministerial fire is no longer warming and steaming the body nor transforming water as it should. The bowstring, tight pulse shows that this condition is due to extreme nervous tension and disturbance to the smooth flow of qi. The insufficient left inch position suggests that ministerial fire is no longer promoting the engenderment of heart yang.

**TREATMENT PRINCIPLES:** Warm yang, transform water, and downbear counterflow

**FORMULA & MEDICINALS:** *Gui Zhi Jia Gui Tang* (Cinnamon Twig Plus Cinnamon Decoction)

Ramulus Cinnamomi Cassiae (*Gui Zhi*), 15g, Radix Albus Paeoniae Lactiflorae (*Bai Shao*), 10g, uncooked Rhizoma Zingiberis (*Sheng Jiang*), 6g (added later), Radix Glycyrrhizae (*Gan Cao*), 3-6g, Fructus Zizyphi Jujubae (*Da Zao*), 2 pieces

Decoct in water and administer orally in two divided doses, morning and evening, one *ji* per day.

**ANALYSIS OF FORMULA:** This formula is given in the *Shang Han Lun* (*Treatise on Damage [Due to] Cold*) as a specific for running piglet condition. Cinnamon Twigs resolve the exterior, while White Peony relaxes tension. The combination of these two medicinals harmonizes the constructive and defensive. This results in resolving the muscular tension. Red Dates, Licorice, and uncooked Ginger all also help harmonize the constructive and defensive, while Licorice and Red Dates also nourish the heart and quiet the spirit.

**ACUPUNCTURE:** *Zhong Wan* (CV 12), *Shang Wan* (CV 13), *Guan Yuan* (CV 4). Use supplementing technique and add moxibustion.

## 12. PHLEGM TURBIDITY BLOCKING THE ORIFICES, LIVER WIND INTERNALLY STIRRING PATTERN

**MAIN SYMPTOMS:** Sudden aphasia, sudden syncope, the sound of phlegm in the throat, reversal chilling of the four extremities, possible arched back rigidity, both eyes staring upward, the two excretions normal, thin, white tongue fur, and a slippery, bowstring, rapid pulse

**NOTE:** The difference between this pattern and phlegm qi depression and binding is largely one of degree of severity of the symptoms.

**ANALYSIS OF SYMPTOMS:** The sudden aphasia, loss of consciousness, and reversal chilling of the extremities, when combined with the sound of phlegm in the throat and the slippery pulse, suggest phlegm blocking the orifices. The suddenness of the attack, the arched back rigidity, the eyes staring upward, and the bowstring, rapid pulse suggest liver wind internally stirring. The two excretions and the tongue fur being normal suggest that this is not either a spleen, kidney, or heat pattern.

**TREATMENT PRINCIPLES:** Flush phlegm and open the orifices, settle tetany and extinguish wind

**FORMULA & MEDICINALS:** *Dao Tan Tang Jia Wei* (Abduct Phlegm Decoction with Added Flavors)

Rhizoma Pinelliae Ternatae (*Ban Xia*), 12g, Sclerotium Poriae Cocos (*Fu Ling*), 10g, Pericarpium Citri Reticulatae (*Chen Pi*), 6-10g, Fructus Immaturus Citri Aurantii (*Zhi Shi*), 6g, Rhizoma Arisaematis (*Tian Nan Xing*), 6g, Radix Glycyrrhizae (*Gan Cao*), 3-6g, Bulbus Fritillariae (*Bei Mu*), 10g, Rhizoma Acori Graminei (*Shi Chang Pu*), 6-10g, Buthus Martensis (*Quan Xie*), 6g, Os Draconis (*Long Gu*), 12g (decocted first), Concha Ostreae (*Mu Li*), 12g (decocted first)

Decoct in water and administer orally in two divided doses, morning and evening, one *ji* per day.

**ANALYSIS OF FORMULA:** Pinellia, Poria, Orange Peel, and Licorice fortify the spleen, dry dampness, and transform phlegm. Arisaema and Acorus transform phlegm and open the orifices. Immature Aurantium helps transform phlegm at the same time as it strongly rectifies the qi. Fritillaria also transforms phlegm. Scorpion extinguishes wind and resolves tetany while freeing the flow of the network vessels. Dragon Bone and Oyster Shell heavily settle, still, and quiet the spirit.

**ACUPUNCTURE:** *Ren Zhong* (GV 26), *He Gu* (LI 4), *Tai Chong* (Liv 3), *Feng Long* (St 40), *Zhong Wan* (CV 12), *Zu San Li* (St 36). Use draining technique.

**ABSTRACTS OF REPRESENTATIVE CHINESE RESEARCH:**

*Bei Jing Zhong Yi* (Beijing Chinese Medicine), #6, 1999, p.

40: Wang Jian-guo reported on the treatment of 11 cases of hysterical aphasia by needling *Yong Quan* (Ki 1). The youngest patient in this study was 16 and the oldest was 45 years old. All were females. The longest course of disease was one week and the shortest was two days. Aphasia was the main clinical symptom. This was commonly accompanied by vexation and agitation, dizziness, insomnia, torpid spirit, a red tongue with yellow fur, and a bowstring, fine pulse. *Yong Quan* was needled bilaterally with 28-30 gauge needles and heavy twisting and turning draining hand technique until the patient was not able to bear the pain and then gave out a sound. Once the patient's voice returned to normal, they were also needled at *San Yin Jiao* (Sp 6) to enrich yin and moisten dryness. Using this technique, all 11 cases were deemed cured.

*Hei Long Jiang Zhong Yi Yao* (Heilongjiang Journal of Chinese Medicine & Medicinals), #3, 1995, p. 41: Liu Bing-jiu treated 39 cases of hysteria using acupuncture with sparrow-pecking technique at *Yong Quan* (Ki 1). This was based on the author's identification of this disease's traditional Chinese counterpart being visceral agitation and the statement in the *Ling Shu* (Spiritual Axis) that, "If the disease is in the viscera, choose the well [points]," *Yong Quan* being the well point of the foot shao yin kidney channel. Sparrow-pecking technique with strong stimulation was used bilaterally on this point for 10-40 minutes in order to arouse patients from an acute hysteric episode. Of the 39 patients in this study, 15 were "cured" with 10 minutes of treatment, 17 were "cured" with 20 minutes of treatment, and seven were "cured" with 40 minutes of treatment. Liu says that these episodes appeared after marked psychological shock and were characterized by excitement, convulsions, hyperactivity, and hypersensitivity.

Heiner Fruehauf, in *The Journal of Chinese Medicine*, UK, #48, 1995, p. 24, reports on a number of published Chinese clinical audits treating various types of hysteria with *Xiao Yao San* (Rambling Powder): *Xin Jiang Zhong Yi Yao* (Xinjiang Chinese Medicine & Medicinals), #2, 1986, hysterical aphasia; *Xin Zhong Yi* (New Chinese Medicine), #1, 1983 & *Shang Hai Zhong Yi Yao Za Zhi* (Shanghai Journal of Chinese Medicine & Medicinals), #3, 1983, hysterical blindness; and *Si Chuan Zhong Yi* (Sichuan Chinese Medicine), #9, 1986, hysterical seizures.

REPRESENTATIVE CASE HISTORIES:

#### ❖ CASE 1: Sudden hysterical blindness[3] ❖

The patient was a 26 year old, male worker who was first examined on July, 19, 1963. This young man was habitually headstrong and self-willed. However, his discipline was not strong. Several days before he got into a quarrel at work and had become emotionally upset. Both his eyes stared straight ahead. He wouldn't speak and he wouldn't eat or drink. Likewise, he wouldn't sleep but rushed outside. Since that day, his field of vision was only about the size of a plate. He had no peripheral vision at all. In addition, the patient reported that he experienced chest oppression, a suffocating feeling, and dizziness. He was examined at a Western medical hospital and was diagnosed as suffering from hysterical blindness. At his Chinese medical examination, the patient's tongue was red with slimy, white fur. His pulse was deep and bowstring. Therefore his pattern was discriminated as great anger damaging the liver with the liver vessels becoming depressed and stagnant. Therefore, their connection to the eyes was not free-flowing and thus there occurred sudden blindness.

Based on this pattern discrimination, the treatment principles were to level the liver, resolve depression, and brighten the eyes. The formula prescribed was *Xie Gan Ming Mu Tang* (Drain the Liver & Brighten the Eyes Decoction). This consisted of: uncooked Concha Haliotidis (*Shi Jue Ming*), 24g, Fructus Tribuli Terrestris (*Bai Ji Li*), 10g, Radix Gentianae Scabrae (*Long Dan Cao*), 6g, stir-fried Fructus Gardeniae Jasminoidis (*Zhi Zi*), 6g, uncooked Radix Rehmanniae (*Sheng Di*), 10g, Radix Angelicae Sinensis (*Dang Gui*), 10g, Radix Ligustici Wallichii (*Chuan Xiong*), 6g, Semen Celosiae (*Qing Xiang Zi*), 10g, and Flos Chrysanthemi Morifolii (*Ju Hua*), 10g. After administering these medicinals, the patient was able to think clearly again, his visual acuity returned to normal, and the dizziness, chest oppression, and suffocating feeling all disappeared.

#### ❖ Case 2: Hysterical deafness[4] ❖

The patient was a 37 year old male cadre who was first examined on May 10, 1963. The patient was habitually tense and agitated and easily lost his temper. Three weeks previous, he had a critical assignment with a deadline for completion. A coworker said he was not equal to this task and the patient became emotionally upset. Suddenly, his two ears became deaf and he could not hear the words spoken to him. This made the man even more tense and agitated. His bowel movements were only one time every two

to three days and were dry. He was diagnosed at the ear, nose, and throat department of the hospital as suffering from neurotic hearing disturbance. Previous treatments had not been effective so he came to the Chinese medical hospital for treatment. There it was noted that his tongue was red with thick, slimy, yellow fur. His pulse was bowstring and forceful. Therefore, his pattern was discriminated as sudden anger damaging the liver causing liver-gallbladder fire to counterflow upward to assail the clear orifices and thus block and obstruct the orifices of the ears. Based on this pattern discrimination, the treatment principles were to drain liver-gallbladder fire, diffuse and free the flow of the clear orifices. The formula prescribed was *Long Dan Xie Gan Tang Jia Wei* (Gentiana Drain the Liver Decoction with Added Flavors) and consisted of: Radix Gentianae Scabrae (*Long Dan Cao*), 10g, stir-fried Fructus Gardeniae Jasminoidis (*Zhi Zi*), 8g, Radix Scutellariae Baicalensis (*Huang Qin*), 10g, uncooked Radix Rehmanniae (*Sheng Di*), 10g, Radix Angelicae Sinensis (*Dang Gui*), 10g, Radix Bupleuri (*Chai Hu*), 8g, uncooked Radix Glycyrrhizae (*Gan Cao*), 3g, Caulis Akebiae (*Mu Tong*), 3g, Rhizoma Alismatis (*Ze Xie*), 10g, Semen Plantaginis (*Che Qian Zi*), 10g, Radix Et Rhizoma Rhei (*Da Huang*), 6g, and Flos Chrysanthemi Morifolii (*Ju Hua*), 10g. After administering one *ji* of these medicinals, the patient was able to hear the sound of voices. After three *ji*, his hearing had returned basically to normal. He was able to go about his business by himself, and all his daily activities became normal.

#### ❖ CASE 3: Hysterical aphasia[5] ❖

The patient was a 42 year old, female homemaker who was first examined on Dec. 28, 1965. Several days before, a family member had died. The patient's relationship with the deceased was especially close. Therefore, her heart emotions were damaged by sorrow and, that evening, she had not slept. At the same time, her affect became stiff and dull. The next day, she could not speak. When asked what was the matter, she beat her hands upon her chest. For two days she had not eaten anything. When examined, it was found that her tongue was pale red with thin, yellow fur, while her pulse was deep and bowstring. Therefore, her pattern was discriminated as qi depression with phlegm binding.

The treatment principles employed were to resolve depression and transform phlegm, open the orifices and emit the voice. The formula prescribed was *Wen Dan Tang Jia Jian* (Warm the Gallbladder Decoction with Additions & Subtractions) and consisted of: Pericarpium Citri Erythrocarpae (*Ju Hong*), 6g, lime-processed Rhizoma Pinelliae Ternatae (*Ban Xia*), 6g, Sclerotium Poriae Cocos

(*Fu Ling*), 12g, Caulis Bambusae In Taeniis (*Zhu Ru*), 10g, Fructus Citri Aurantii (*Zhi Ke*), 6 slices, Tuber Curcumae (*Yu Jin*), 6g, Rhizoma Acori Graminei (*Shi Chang Pu*), 10 slices, Radix Polygalae Tenuifoliae (*Yuan Zhi*), 10g, Cortex Albizziae Julibrissinis (*He Huan Pi*), 10g, Semen Oroxyli Indici (*Mu Hu Die*), 10g, and Fructus Trichosanthis Kirlowii (*Gua Lou*), 15g. After administering one *ji* of these medicinals, the patient could sleep. When she woke up the next morning, she was able to speak again.

### ❖ CASE 4: Hysterical syncope & convulsions[6] ❖

The patient was a 29 year old female who was first examined on March 20, 1975. The patient had a history of recurrent fainting, and she had had an episode on the day she was first examined. These fainting spells had begun in 1971. When they occurred, they lasted from a few minutes to 20 minutes or more, during which time she was unconscious of human affairs and her hands and feet tugged and stirred. After she awakened, the patient was fatigued and felt weak. Both her eyes showed little spirit, and she reported that her vision was blurred. Emotionally, she was sorrowful and experienced heart vexation and easy agitation. She kept up a torrential flow of words that never stopped and she burped repeatedly. The patient slept little and had nightmares when she did. Her stools were dry and bound and she only defecated two times per week. Her menses were excessively heavy, and she had a thick, foul-smelling, white vaginal discharge. Her pulse was fine, and she had a pale tongue with thin fur. Her pattern was discriminated as liver depression fire effulgence harassing and smothering her clear palaces.

The treatment principles in this case were to course the liver and resolve depression, clear fire and calm the spirit. The formula prescribed consisted of: Radix Scutellariae Baicalensis (*Huang Qin*), 9g, Rhizoma Anemarrhenae Aspheloidis (*Zhi Mu*), 9g, Cortex Phellodendri (*Huang Bai*), 9g, Ramulus Uncariae Cum Uncis (*Gou Teng*), 9g (added later), Herba Artemisiae Apiaceae (*Qing Hao*), 4.5g, Fructus Tribuli Terrestris (*Bai Ji Li*), 9g, Caulis Bambusae In Taeniis (*Zhu Ru*), 4.5g, Flos Citri Sacrodactylis (*Fo Shou Hua*), 2.4g, Flos Citri Aurantii (*Dai Dai Hua*), 2.4g, Fructus Akebiae Trifoliatae (*Ba Yue Zha*), 9g, Tuber Curcumae (*Yu Jin*), 9g, uncooked Rhizoma Zingiberis (*Sheng Jiang*), 9g, Pericarpium Trichosanthis Kirlowii (*Gua Lou Pi*), 9g, Cortex Ailanthi Altissimi (*Chun Gun Pi*), 9g, Concha Margaritiferae (*Zhen Zhu Mu*), 30g, *Ding Zhi Dan* (Stabilize the Mind Elixir, a Chinese ready-made medicine), 12g (wrapped during decoction).

The second examination occurred on March 28 after the patient had taken four *ji* of the above medicinals. Her eyes now had spirit, her emotions were soothed and easy, and all her symptoms were eliminated. However, her throat was dry and there was a thick, profuse secretion from her right nostril. When she spit some phlegm, it contained threads of blood. Her pulse was fine, and her tongue was pale with thin fur. Therefore, her current pattern was discriminated as qi stagnation somewhat eased but depressive fire not cleared. Therefore, the treatment principles were to rectify the qi and resolve depression, clear fire and calm the spirit. The patient was prescribed: Radix Scutellariae Baicalensis (*Huang Qin*), 9g, Rhizoma Anemarrhenae Aspheloidis (*Zhi Mu*), 9g, Cortex Phellodendri (*Huang Bai*), 9g, Fructus Forsythiae Suspensae (*Lian Qiao*), 9g, Radix Bupleuri (*Chai Hu*), 9g, Ramulus Uncariae Cum Uncis (*Gou Teng*), 9g (added later), Fructus Tribuli Terrestris (*Bai Ji Li*), 9g, Fructus Akebiae Trifoliatae (*Ba Yue Zha*), 9g, Tuber Curcumae (*Yu Jin*), 9g, uncooked Rhizoma Zingiberis (*Sheng Jiang*), 9g, Rhizoma Pinelliae Ternatae (*Ban Xia*), 4.5g, Pericarpium Trichosanthis Kirlowii (*Gua Lou Pi*), 18g, Cortex Ailanthi Altissimi (*Chun Gen Pi*), 9g, Caulis Bambusae In Taeniis (*Zhu Ru*), 6g, Concha Margaritiferae (*Zhen Zhu Mu*), 30g, *Ding Zhi Dan* (Stabilize the Mind Elixir), 12g (wrapped).

The case history ends here with the assumption that these medicinals successfully treated the symptoms seen at the second examination. The psychiatric symptoms were eliminated after the first prescription. In the author's end discussion of this case, he says that the diagnosis was yin vacuity fire effulgence. In other words, there was both yin vacuity *and* liver depression with fire effulgence. The first formula cleared vacuity heat more, and more moderately rectified the qi, while the second formula cleared depressive heat more, and more strongly rectified the qi.

### ❖ CASE 5: Hysterical dysphagia[7] ❖

The patient was a 47 year old female cadre. During the previous half month, she had been suffering from chest oppression, and, during the last three days, she had progressively more and more difficulty swallowing when eating. Prior treatments with both Western and Chinese medicines were ineffective. Examination in the internal medicine department of the hospital in which this case took place had ruled out organic pathology of the esophagus. The patient was, therefore, diagnosed as suffering from hysterical dysphagia and referred to the acupuncture department.

According to Dr. Huang, the patient's Chinese disease diagnosis was plum pit qi and her pattern was categorized as liver depression qi stagnation due to excessive anxiety and thinking with depression engendering phlegm. Therefore, the treatment principles were to rectify the qi and transform phlegm, resolve depression and disinhibit the throat. For these purposes, acupuncture was performed at *Nei Guan* (Per 6), *Dan Zhong* (CV 17), *Tian Tu* (CV 22), *Zu San Li* (St 36), and *Hou Xi* (SI 3). *Hou Xi* was needled on the right side only. The needles were retained for 30 minutes, during which time *Nei Guan* was stimulated with lifting and thrusting and twisting manipulations every five minutes. After this treatment, the patient felt that her chest oppression had loosened and she was able to swallow water with no difficulty. The same treatment was carried out every day for the next five days, after which time the patient was completely cured.

### ❖ CASE 6: Hysterical hiccups[8] ❖

The patient was a 50 year old female peasant who explained that, due to problems within her home, she felt unhappy and oppressed. Besides feeling persistent chest oppression, she had gradually developed worse and worse episodes of hiccups which had now continued for three years. Previous treatments with Western and Chinese medicines had been ineffective. The internal medicine department of the hospital had ruled out organic pathology and diagnosed the woman as suffering from hysterical hiccups. Therefore, the patient was referred to the acupuncture department.

Dr. Huang categorized this woman's Chinese disease as running piglet and her pattern as a liver-spleen disharmony causing chaotic counterflow and upward surging of the spleen and stomach qi. Therefore, the treatment principles were to calm the spirit and quiet the heart, soothe and resolve depression and binding of the spleen and stomach qi, and free the flow of and disinhibit the qi mechanism. Based on these principles, Dr. Huang needled *Ren Zhong* (GV 26), *Nei Guan* (Per 6), *Zu San Li* (St 36), and *Hou Xi* (SI 3). *Hou Xi* was needled on the right side only. Lifting and thrusting and twisting manipulations were carried out at *Nei Guan* every five minutes, and the needles were retained for 30 minutes. After this treatment, the patient felt that her chest oppression had been soothed and her hiccups ceased. The next day, the patient reported that her chest still felt loose but that she still had occasional bouts of light hiccups. The patient was treated once per day for five days, after which the hiccups disappeared and the patient was cured.

### ❖ CASE 7: Hysterical aphonia[9] ❖

The patient was a 27 year old male peasant. According to his companion, the patient was having an argument during which he was "accidentally" struck in the front of the chest. The patient suddenly felt unendurable pressure in his chest and had difficulty speaking. This then gradually developed into aphonia which had lasted for one half year. Treatment at his local hospital had been ineffective, so he was referred to the hospital where the author of this case worked. Examinations by various specialists ruled out both organic pathology and pathological neural responses. Therefore, the Western medical diagnosis was hysterical aphonia.

Dr. Huang diagnosed this patient's Chinese disease as visceral agitation and categorized his pattern as loss of regulation of the qi mechanism due to external injury of the network vessels resulting in blockage of the heart qi. Therefore, the treatment principles were to open the heart orifices and regulate and rectify the qi mechanism. *Ren Zhong* (GV 26), *Tian Tu* (CV 22), *Nei Guan* (Per 6), *Dan Zhong* (CV 17), *Zu San Li* (St 36), and *Hou Xi* (SI 3) were needled, with *Hou Xi* only being needled on the left. During stimulation of the needles, the patient was instructed to try to speak when he felt the needle sensation reach the chest. Lifting and thrusting and twisting manipulations were repeated every five minutes and the needles were retained for 30 minutes. After the needles were removed, the patient could make strong sounds as well as multisyllable speech. After being treated again the next day, the man's voice was clear and his speech was lucid. Therefore he was judged cured.

### ❖ CASE 8: Hysterical lower limb paralysis[10] ❖

The patient was a 19 year old female student who was initially examined on May 20, 1970. Two months before, after getting angry at school, the patient had suddenly developed paralysis of her right lower leg so that she was unable to stand. In addition, the patient felt like there was something blocking her throat, she had a suffocating feeling in her chest, and she sometimes had epigastric pain. When she entered the hospital, there were no abnormalities in her four limbs or spinal column and her cerebrospinal fluid and blood were all normal. Other than being emotionally labile, there were no other psychological abnormalities. The patient's tongue was red with slightly slimy, white fur, while her pulse was deep, fine, and bowstring.

Based on the above signs and symptoms, the patient's pattern was categorized as liver depression and blood vacuity with the blood not nourishing the sinews and the network vessels losing their harmony. Therefore, the treatment principles were to soothe the liver and resolve depression, nourish the blood, nourish the sinews, and free the flow of the network vessels. The medicinals prescribed consisted of: Radix Pulsatillae Chinensis (*Bai Tou Weng*), 10g, Cortex Fraxini (*Qin Pi*), 10g, Rhizoma Coptidis Chinensis (*Huang Lian*), 3g, Cortex Phellodendri (*Huang Bai*), 6g, Radix Angelicae Sinensis (*Dang Gui*), 10g, Radix Albus Paeoniae Lactiflorae (*Bai Shao*), 12g, uncooked Rhizoma Atractylodis Macrocephalae (*Bai Zhu*), 6g, Sclerotium Poriae Cocos (*Fu Ling*), 12g, Radix Glycyrrhizae (*Gan Cao*), 3g, Radix Bupleuri (*Chai Hu*), 6g, Ramulus Mori Albi (*Sang Zhi*), 15g, Fructus Chaenomelis Lagenariae (*Mu Gua*), 10g, and Fasciculus Vascularis Luffae Cylindricae (*Si Gua Luo*), 6g.

After taking an undisclosed number of *ji* of this formula, the patient's lower limbs gradually became able to flex and extend and her emotional state improved. Another six *ji* of this formula with additions and subtractions was pre-scribed, after which she was able to stand and, slowly, slowly, was able to walk again.[11]

## ENDNOTES

[1]Chen Jia-yang, *Shi Yong Zhong Yi Shen Jing Bing Xue (A Study of Practical Chinese Medical Neurology)*, Gansu Science & Technology Press, Lanzhou, 1989, p. 472-473

[2]*Ibid.*, p. 495

[3]*Ibid.*, p. 404-405

[4]*Shang Hai Lao Zhong Yi Jing Yan Xuan Bian (A Selected Collection of Shanghai Old Chinese Doctors' Experiences)*, *op. cit.*, p. 295

[5]Huang Xing-yi, "Experiences in the Treatment of Hysterical Disease with Acupuncture," *Zhong Guo Zhen Jiu (Chinese Acupuncture & Moxibustion)*, #2, 1995, p. 44

[6]*Ibid.*, p. 44

[7]*Ibid.*, p. 44

[8]Chen Jia-yang, *op. cit.*, p. 340-341

[9]In the author's commentary on this case, she says that the ingre-dients of *Bai Tou Weng Tang* (Pulsatilla Decoction) were used to cool the blood in order to treat the tight sinews, a somewhat unusual use of this formula.

# ❖ 10 ❖

# PREMENSTRUAL DYSPHORIC DISORDER

Premenstrual dysphoric disorder (PMDD) or severe PMS is a biologically based medical condition that causes impaired social and occupational functioning and affects interpersonal relationships. As defined in the *DSM-IV*, it is characterized by somatic complaints (including fatigue, headaches, pain, and others) and emotional symptoms (including lability, irritability, and marked depressed or anxious mood) during the days before onset of menses (*i.e.*, during the luteal phase) and symptom resolution soon after onset of menses (*i.e.*, during the follicular phase). Risk factors include a family history of mood disorders and a personal history of depression or postpartum depression.

Because of on-going debate over the most appropriate name for this symptom pattern and the absence of unambiguous evidence for the existence (or neuroendocrinological correlates) of core features, premenstrual dysphoric disorder continues to be listed under "criteria proposed for further study" in the *DSM-IV*. However, the *International Categorization of Disease*, 10th edition (*ICD-10*), includes the disorder as an established disorder under the name premenstrual tension syndrome, and this latter name is also sometimes found in the contemporary Chinese medical literature.

## NOSOLOGY:

The research criteria for PMDD list 11 symptoms:

1. Marked depressed mood

2. Persistent anger or irritability

3. Marked anxiety or tension

4. Sudden sadness or depression

5. Difficulty concentrating

6. Lack of interest in activities once enjoyed

7. Noticeable lack of energy

8. Marked change in appetite

9. Insomnia or hypersomnia

10. Feeling overwhelmed or out of control

11. Other physical symptoms, such as joint pain or breast tenderness and/or distention

According to the current definition, at least five of these must be present for a significant period of time during the luteal phase for at least one year. Further, to meet diagnostic criteria, these symptoms must significantly impair social or occupational functioning and cannot be better explained by another medical or psychiatric disorder.

## EPIDEMIOLOGY:

Prevalence estimates of PMDD are difficult to establish because of inherent problems identifying specific symptoms and rating symptom severity in survey studies that typically rely on histories that are self-reported in the context of social and cultural variables that likely influence the objectivity of reported symptoms. PMDD-like symptoms may affect one in six women in Western populations surveyed, and some data suggest that three-fourths of all women may experience a mild form of this disorder. Most women are able to continue working during the most symptomatic period, but as many as one in four may experience significant impairment in social functioning because of premenstrual symptoms. Apparently, only a small percentage of women who report symptoms of PMDD become severely impaired.

## DIFFERENTIAL DIAGNOSIS:

Most women experience transient somatic symptoms or changes in mood shortly before or during menstruation. A determination of PMDD is based on assessment of the severity of a recurring pattern of symptoms that substantially interfere with normal social or occupational functioning. Expectations of normal functioning and learned coping strategies vary greatly between cultures, resulting in differences in self-reported levels of distress associated with similar somatic or psychological symptoms. Because of issues and other factors (above) that limit the validity of epidemiologic data, Western psychiatry continues to view PMDD as a provisional diagnosis only.

The initial task of differential diagnosis is to rule out possible underlying medical causes of recurring dysphoric mood coinciding with onset of menses. Exacerbation of numerous medical disorders can accompany menstruation. Among others, these include diseases of the thyroid and other endocrinological disorders; endometriosis; systemic lupus erythematosus (SLE), certain seizure disorders, and metabolic disorders. Medication side effects and behavioral or mood changes caused by alcohol or illicit substance use must also be considered. Thorough history-

taking and laboratory studies generally clarify the medical differential diagnosis, confirming or excluding more common possibilities. When medical etiologies have been excluded, the psychiatric differential diagnosis is further clarified by careful history-taking. The most important question is whether somatic or mood symptoms that occur before menstruation are associated with an exacerbation of another primary psychiatric disorder. For unclear reasons (see Etiology below), individuals with mood disorders sometimes experience transient worsening around the time of menses. The same is true for certain somatoform disorders and eating disorders.

## ETIOLOGY & PATHOPHYSIOLOGY:

Contemporary Western medicine has not advanced a satisfactory explanation for PMDD. Many neuroendocrinological theories have proposed a central role for dysregulation in estrogen, progesterone, endorphins, cortisol, thyroid hormones, as well as certain CNS neurotransmitters – especially serotonin. Despite ongoing research, most studies continue to yield equivocal data. Another kind of biological model for PMDD is based on emerging evidence for a central relationship between chronobiological (including circadian) rhythms and cyclic mood changes. An analogous model has been proposed as an explanation for seasonally recurring mood changes that are characteristic of seasonal affective disorder. Though limited data have been obtained to date, preliminary findings are promising, and it has been reported that some women diagnosed with PMDD have responded to the same light exposure and sleep deprivation therapies that are effective against seasonal affective disorder. In addition to the above neuroendocrinological models, epidemiologic studies suggest possible genetic or familial factors, since the majority of women diagnosed with PMDD were found to

## DIFFERENTIAL DIAGNOSIS

| 1. MEDICAL DISORDERS | 2. EFFECTS OF SUBSTANCES | 3. PSYCHIATRIC DISORDERS |
|---|---|---|
| A. THYROID DISEASE | A. ALCOHOL AND ILLICIT SUBSTANCE | A. MAJOR DEPRESSIVE EPISODE |
| B. OTHER ENDOCRINOLOGICAL | INTOXICATION OR WITHDRAWAL | B. BIPOLAR AFFECTIVE DISORDER |
| DISORDERS | B. SIDE EFFECTS OF MEDICATIONS | (BAD) |
| C. ENDOMETRIOSIS | | C. SOMATOFORM DISORDERS, |
| D. SYSTEMIC LUPUS ERYTHEMATOSUS | | INCLUDING CONVERSION |
| E. (SLE) | | DISORDER AND OTHERS |
| SEIZURE DISORDERS | | D. EATING DISORDERS |

have mothers who met criteria for major depressive disorder or PMDD. In the past, psychoanalytic theories were proposed as explanations of mood changes and somatic symptoms associated with menstruation. None of these formulations has withstood the test of time and clinical evidence.

## WESTERN MEDICAL TREATMENT:

Numerous treatments of PMDD have been tried in the context of contemporary Western medicine. These range from dietary modifications, exercise, and psychotherapy to various pharmacological agents, including antidepressants, mood-stabilizers, and sedative-hypnotics, to hormonal replacement therapies (HRT). To date, more than 50 treatments have been tried, all with limited success. It has been suggested that this poor record of treatment response may be due in large part to a grossly inadequate or simplistic understanding of the underlying cause(s) of PMDD.

## SHORT & LONG-TERM ADVANTAGES & DISADVANTAGES OF WESTERN MEDICAL TREATMENT:

Antidepressants and mood-stabilizers have an associated risk of unpleasant side effects, some of which can be mistaken for symptoms of PMDD. These include insomnia or sedation, weight gain, nervousness or irritability, and decreased libido. Sedative-hypnotic use always poses a short-term risk of sedation and a long-term risk of chemical dependence. Hormonal replacement therapy poses several potential risks, including an increased risk of breast cancer in a genetically susceptible population of women, infertility, dermatologic problems, and many other medical complications that may be mistakenly identified as PMDD symptoms.

## PROGNOSIS:

Limited epidemiological data support the view that untreated PMDD symptoms tend to progress and worsen. It has been suggested that some cases evolve into major depressive disorder. Anecdotal reports support the view that PMDD symptom severity increases in relationship to total number of pregnancies. The reasons for this are unclear. In most cases, symptom severity diminishes by the mid 40s, but unusual cases continue well into the menopause.

## INDICATIONS FOR REFERRAL TO WESTERN MEDICAL SERVICES:

Urgent referral to the nearest emergency room or urgent care center is indicated when history or clinical presentation suggest an underlying acute medical problem including a seizure disorder, systemic lupus erythematosus (SLE), hyperthyroidism or other endocrinological disorders, endometriosis, possible toxic exposure, or active abuse of alcohol or illicit substances. In cases where medical etiologies have been ruled out and the patient has not responded to an appropriate course of Chinese medical treatment, nonurgent referral to a psychiatrist may prove useful in clarifying the differential diagnosis or developing an optimized integrative treatment plan combining Chinese and contemporary Western therapies.

## CHINESE DISEASE CATEGORIZATION:

Premenstrual dysphoric disorder corresponds to an indefinite number of menstrual movement (*jing xing*) diseases. *Jing xing* means menstrual movement. Disease names prefaced by these two words refer to conditions cyclically associated with the approach or onset of menstruation. Most of the traditional Chinese disease categories discussed in Book 2 could have the words "menstrual movement" prefacing them. For instance, some of the common premenstrual essence spirit complaints recognized by Chinese medicine include menstrual movement insomnia (*jing xing bu mian*), menstrual movement fatigue (*jing xing juan dai*), menstrual movement irritability (*jing xing duo nu*), menstrual movement tension (*jing xing jin zhang*), menstrual movement impaired memory (*jing xing jian wang*), menstrual movement fright and fear (*jing xing jing kong*), menstrual movement anxiety and depression (*jing xing you yu*), menstrual movement feeble-mindedness (*jing xing chi dai*), menstrual movement raving (*jing xing wang yan*), menstrual movement hallucinations (*jing xing wang jian*), menstrual movement convulsions (*jing xing chou chu*), menstrual movement epilepsy (*jing xing dian xian*), and menstrual movement withdrawal and mania (*jing xing dian kuang*).

## CHINESE DISEASE CAUSES & MECHANISMS:

During the second half of a woman's cycle, the blood is sent down from the heart to the uterus. If a woman's blood tends to be scanty, this may leave the heart malnourished above. Thus the spirit becomes disquieted. In addition, there may also be insufficient blood to nourish the liver. In that case, the liver may fail to do its duty of controlling coursing and discharge. Therefore, the liver becomes depressed and the qi becomes stagnant. Because of the interrelationships between the heart and spleen, heart and liver, and liver and kidneys, heart blood vacuity may lead to spleen qi vacuity, liver depression transforming into heat may give rise to heart fire effulgence, and liver blood vacuity may evolve into kidney yin vacuity with ascendant yang hyperactivity. Because of the relationship of qi to blood and static blood to the engenderment of new blood, blood stasis may be engendered or worsened premenstrually. In addition, blood stasis may be caused or aggravated by enduring dampness and/or phlegm or by vacuity cold due to spleen-kidney yang vacuity. Because of the spleen's role in the movement and transformation of water fluids, spleen vacuity may give rise to dampness, phlegm, and/or turbidity. Because of the spleen qi's relationship with kidney yang, spleen vacuity may give rise to spleen-kidney yang vacuity. Further, either due to yin and blood vacuity or fire effulgence, wind may be engendered internally. Thus there are good Chinese medical reasons why any and all of the main disease mechanisms of essence spirit disease may be initiated or aggravated during the premenstruum.

**TREATMENT BASED ON PATTERN DISCRIMINATION:**

**1. HEART BLOOD VACUITY PATTERN**

**MAIN SYMPTOMS:** Several days before the menses, there is sadness and desire to cry, sudden essence spirit abstraction, inability to control oneself, restless sleep at night, heart palpitations, fearful throbbing, taciturnity, scanty speech, and excessive worry and anxiety. The tongue is pale with thin fur, and the pulse is fine, moderate or relaxed (*i.e.*, slightly slow), and forceless.

**ANALYSIS OF SYMPTOMS:** All the signs and symptoms of this pattern are due to heart blood not nourishing and constructing the heart spirit which thus becomes restless or disquieted.

**TREATMENT PRINCIPLES:** Nourish the heart and quiet the spirit

**FORMULA & MEDICINALS:** *Gan Mai Da Zao Tang Jia Bai He Di Huang Tang* (Licorice, Triticus & Red Dates Decoction Plus Lily & Rehmannia Decoction)

Fructus Tritici Aestivi (*Huai Xiao Mai*), 25-60g, mix-fried Radix Glycyrrhizae (*Gan Cao*), 10-15g, Fructus Zizyphi Jujubae (*Da Zao*), 5-10 pieces, Bulbus Lilii (*Bai He*), 15-60g, uncooked Radix Rehmanniae (*Sheng Di*), 15g, Semen Zizyphi Spinosae (*Zao Ren*), 12g, Radix Polygalae Tenuifoliae (*Yuan Zhi*), 10g

Decoct one *ji* in water per day and administer orally in two divided doses, morning and evening.

**ANALYSIS OF FORMULA:** All the medicinals in this formula supplement and nourish either heart qi or heart blood. In addition, all except cooked Rehmannia quiet the spirit. In addition, Polygala transforms phlegm, rectifies the qi, and promotes the interaction between the heart and kidneys.

**ADDITIONS & SUBTRACTIONS:** If qi vacuity is more severe, use *Gui Pi Tang Jia Wei* (Restore the Spleen Decoction with Added Flavors)

Radix Astragali Membranacei (*Huang Qi*), 10-18g, Radix Codonopsitis Pilosulae (*Dang Shen*), 10g, Sclerotium Poriae Pararadicis (*Fu Shen*),12g, Rhizoma Atractylodis Macrocephalae (*Bai Zhu*), 10g, mix-fried Radix Glycyrrhizae (*Gan Cao*), 10g, Radix Polygalae Tenuifoliae (*Yuan Zhi*), 10g, Rhizoma Acori Graminei (*Shi Chang Pu*), 10g, Radix Angelicae Sinensis (*Dang Gui*), 10g, stir-fried Semen Zizyphi Spinosae (*Suan Zao Ren*), 12g, Arillus Euphoriae Longanae (*Long Yan Rou*), 10g, Radix Auklandiae Lappae (*Mu Xiang*), 6-10g

Decoct one *ji* in water per day and administer orally in two divided doses, morning and evening.

**ACUPUNCTURE:** *Xin Shu* (Bl 15), *Shen Men* (Ht 7), *Ge Shu* (Bl 17), *Pi Shu* (Bl 20), *Zu San Li* (St 36), *Bai Hui* (GV 20), *Yin Tang* (M-HN-3). Supplement the first five points and drain the last two.

**2. LIVER-SPLEEN DISHARMONY PATTERN**

**MAIN SYMPTOMS:** Premenstrual irritability, emotional lability, fatigue, lack of strength, constipation, loose stools, or alternating constipation and diarrhea, cold hands, chest oppression and a tendency to sigh, a craving for sweets, a tendency to water swelling, premenstrual breast distention and pain, premenstrual abdominal distention and pain and/or menstrual pain, a pale but dark, swollen or enlarged tongue with thin, white, possibly slightly slimy fur, and a bowstring, fine pulse

**Analysis of symptoms:** The premenstrual irritability and lability, constipation, chest oppression, tendency to sigh, breast and abdominal distention and pain, dark tongue, and bowstring pulse are all directly due to liver depression qi stagnation. The fatigue, lack of strength, loose stools, cold hands, craving for sweets, edema, pale, enlarged tongue, and fine pulse are all due to spleen qi vacuity. The possibly slimy tongue fur shows that spleen vacuity is not controlling water fluids properly.

TREATMENT PRINCIPLES: Course the liver and rectify the qi, fortify the spleen and boost the qi

FORMULA & MEDICINALS: *Xiao Yao San* (Rambling Powder)

Radix Bupleuri (*Chai Hu*), 6-10g, Radix Albus Paeoniae Lactiflorae (*Bai Shao*), 10-12g, Radix Angelicae Sinensis (*Dang Gui*), 6-10g, Rhizoma Atractylodis Macrocephalae (*Bai Zhu*), 10g, Sclerotium Poriae Cocos (*Fu Ling*), 10-12g, mix-fried Radix Glycyrrhizae (*Gan Cao*), 6-12g, Herba Menthae Haplocalycis (*Bo He*), 6g, uncooked Rhizoma Zingiberis (*Sheng Jiang*), 2 pieces

Decoct one *ji* in water per day and administer orally in two divided doses, morning and evening.

ANALYSIS OF FORMULA: Bupleurum courses the liver and rectifies the qi. It is aided in this by Mint and uncooked Ginger. Peony and Dang Gui nourish the blood and thus harmonize the liver. Poria, Atractylodes, and mix-fried Licorice fortify the spleen and supplement the qi. In addition, Poria quiets the spirit and seeps dampness, while uncooked Ginger harmonizes the stomach and transforms dampness.

ADDITIONS & SUBTRACTIONS: If there is marked premenstrual breast distention and pain, add Rhizoma Cyperi Rotundi (*Xiang Fu*), Pericarpium Citri Reticulatae (*Chen Pi*), Folium Citri Reticulatae (*Ju Ye*), Semen Citri Reticulatae (*Ju He*), and/or Pericarpium Citri Reticulatae Viride (*Qing Pi*). If there are loose stools or diarrhea, add Radix Auklandiae Lappae (*Mu Xiang*) and Fructus Amomi (*Sha Ren*). If spleen vacuity is more pronounced with marked fatigue and lack of strength, add Radix Astragali Membranacei (*Huang Qi*) and Radix Codonopsitis Pilosulae (*Dang Shen*). If spleen vacuity is complicated by kidney yang vacuity, add Herba Epimedii (*Xian Ling Pi*) and Rhizoma Curculiginis Orchioidis (*Xian Mao*) or dry Rhizoma Zingiberis (*Gan Jiang*) and Radix Lateralis Praeparatus Aconiti Carmichaeli (*Fu Zi*) depending on the signs and symptoms.

ACUPUNCTURE: *Tai Chong* (Liv 3), *He Gu* (LI 4), *Zu San Li* (St 36), *San Yin Jiao* (Sp 6), *Nei Guan* (Per 6). Use even supplementing-even draining technique on all points.

ADDITIONS & SUBTRACTIONS: If spleen vacuity is pronounced, add *Pi Shu* (Bl 20) and *Wei Shu* (Bl 21). If chest oppression and breast distention are pronounced, add *Dan Zhong* (CV 17), *Ru Gen* (St 18), and *Liang Qiu* (ST 34). If there is either abdominal distention or pain, add *Qi Hai* (CV 6), *Tian Shu* (St 25), and *Gui Lai* (St 29). If there is spleen dampness, add *Shang Qiu* (Sp 5) and *Zhong Wan* (CV 12).

### 3. LIVER DEPRESSION-FIRE EFFULGENCE PATTERN

MAIN SYMPTOMS: Three to seven days or more before the menses, the emotions become agitated. There is heart vexation and easy anger or mania, agitation, and restlessness. The throat is dry, there is a bitter taste in the mouth, and there is chest, breast, and/or rib-side distention and pain. The tongue is red with thick, slimy, yellow fur, and the pulse is bowstring, fine, and rapid.

ANALYSIS OF SYMPTOMS: Easy anger shows the liver is depressed, as does the chest, breast, and/or rib-side distention and pain and the bowstring pulse. The dry throat, heart vexation, bitter taste in the mouth, mania, agitation, restlessness, a red tongue with yellow fur, and rapid pulse all indicate that depression has transformed heat which is ascending to harass the heart spirit.

TREATMENT PRINCIPLES: Clear the liver and resolve depression, drain fire and quiet the spirit

FORMULA & MEDICINALS: For replete liver channel fire, use *Long Dan Xie Gan Tang Jia Jian* (Gentiana Drain the Liver Decoction with Additions & Subtractions)

Radix Gentianae Scabrae (*Long Dan Cao*), 6-10g, Rhizoma Alismatis (*Ze Xie*), 10g, Semen Plantaginis (*Che Qian Zi*), 10g, uncooked Radix Rehmanniae (*Sheng Di*), 12g, Extremitas Radicis Angelicae Sinensis (*Dang Gui*), 10g, Fructus Gardeniae Jasminoidis (*Shan Zhi*), 6-10g, Radix Scutellariae Baicalensis (*Huang Qin*), 10g, uncooked Radix Glycyrrhizae (*Gan Cao*), 3-6g, Cortex Radicis Moutan (*Dan Pi*), 6-10g, Rhizoma Coptidis Chinensis (*Huang Lian*), 3-6g, Ramulus Uncariae Cum Uncis (*Gou Teng*), 10-12g, Os Draconis (*Long Gu*), 12g, Concha Ostreae (*Mu Li*), 12g

Decoct one *ji* in water per day and administer orally in two divided doses, morning and evening.

ANALYSIS OF FORMULA: Gentiana, Scutellaria, Coptis, and Gardenia are all bitter, cold medicinals which clear heat and drain fire. Uncooked Rehmannia, which is sweet and cold clears heat from the blood as does Moutan. Moutan and Dang Gui rootlets also quicken the blood and transform stasis. Alisma and Plantago seep dampness, thus leading evil heat down and out via urination. Uncaria clears and settles the liver. Dragon Bone and

Oyster Shell subdue yang and quiet the spirit, while uncooked Licorice clears heat and harmonizes all the other medicinals in this formula.

**ADDITIONS & SUBTRACTIONS:** For heart-liver fire effulgence, use *Huang Lian Qing Xin Yin Jia Jian* (Coptis Clear the Heart Drink with Additions & Subtractions)

Rhizoma Coptidis Chinensis (*Huang Lian*), 3-12g, Radix Scutellariae Baicalensis (*Huang Qin*), 10-12g, Radix Gentianae Scabrae (*Long Dan Cao*), 6-10g, Plumula Nelumbinis Nuciferae (*Lian Xin*), 3-6g, uncooked Radix Rehmanniae (*Sheng Di*), 12-15g, Radix Angelicae Sinensis (*Dang Gui*), 10g, Semen Zizyphi Spinosae (*Suan Zao Ren*), 12g, Sclerotium Pararadicis Poriae Cocos (*Fu Shen*), 10-12g, Radix Polygalae Tenuifoliae (*Yuan Zhi*), 10g, Radix Glycyrrhizae (*Gan Cao*), 3-10g, Magnetitum (*Ci Shi*), 15-25g

If depressive heat is mixed with spleen vacuity, use *Dan Zhi Xiao Yao San Jia Wei* (Moutan & Gardenia Rambling Powder with Added Flavors)

Cortex Radicis Moutan (*Dan Pi*), 6-10g, Fructus Gardeniae Jasminoidis (*Shan Zhi*), 6-10g, Radix Bupleuri (*Chai Hu*), 10g, Radix Angelicae Sinensis (*Dang Gui*), 10g, Radix Albus Paeoniae Lactiflorae (*Bai Shao*), 10-18g, Rhizoma Atractylodis Macrocephalae (*Bai Zhu*), 10g, Sclerotium Poriae Cocos (*Fu Ling*), 10-12g, mix-fried Radix Glycyrrhizae (*Gan Cao*), 6-10g, Herba Menthae Haplocalycis (*Bo He*), 6g, Caulis Polygoni Multiflori (*Ye Jiao Teng*), 15g, Cortex Albizziae Julibrissinis (*He Huan Pi*), 15g

If there is liver depression/depressive heat with spleen vacuity and phlegm dampness and/or constipation, use *Chai Hu Jia Long Gu Mu Li Tang Jia Wei* (Bupleurum Plus Dragon Bone & Oyster Shell Decoction with Added Flavors)

Radix Bupleuri (*Chai Hu*), 10g, Radix Codonopsitis Pilosulae (*Dang Shen*), 6g, Rhizoma Pinelliae Terantae (*Ban Xia*), 10g, Sclerotium Poriae Cocos (*Fu Ling*), 10-12g, Radix Scutellariae Baicalensis (*Huang Qin*), 10g, Os Draconis (*Long Gu*), 12g, Concha Ostreae (*Mu Li*), 12g, Radix Angelicae Sinensis (*Dang Gui*), 6-10g, Radix Albus Paeoniae Lactiflorae (*Bai Shao*), 10-15g, Ramulus Cinnamomi Cassiae (*Gui Zhi*), 6g, Radix Et Rhizoma Rhei (*Da Huang*), 3-6g, uncooked Rhizoma Zingiberis (*Sheng Jiang*), 2 slices, Fructus Zizyphi Jujubae (*Da Zao*), 3 pieces

If there is depressive heat in the liver, lungs, and stomach with possible complicating phlegm and/or dampness, use

*Xiao Chai Hu Tang Jia Wei* (Minor Bupleurum Decoction with Added Flavors)

Radix Bupleuri (*Chai Hu*), 10g, Radix Codonopsitis Pilosulae (*Dang Shen*), 10-12g, Rhizoma Pinelliae Terantae (*Ban Xia*), 10g, Radix Scutellariae Baicalensis (*Huang Qin*), 10g, Radix Angelicae Sinensis (*Dang Gui*), 6-10g, Radix Albus Paeoniae Lactiflorae (*Bai Shao*), 10g, mix-fried Radix Glycyrrhizae (*Gan Cao*), 6-10g, uncooked Rhizoma Zingiberis (*Sheng Jiang*), 2-3 slices, Fructus Zizyphi Jujubae (*Da Zao*), 3-5 pieces

**ACUPUNCTURE:** *Xiang Jian* (Liv 2), *Yang Ling Quan* (GB 34), *He Gu* (LI 4), *Da Ling* (Per 7), *Shen Men* (Ht 7), *Bai Hui* (GV 20), *Da Zhui* (GV 14). Drain all points. If there is concomitant spleen vacuity, add *Zu San Li* (St 36), *Pi Shu* (Bl 20), and *Wei Shu* (Bl 21). If there is concomitant phlegm, add *Feng Long* (St 40) and *Zhong Wan* (CV 12). If there is simultaneous blood vacuity, add *Ge Shu* (Bl 17) and *Gan Shu* (Bl 18). If there is simultaneous spleen dampness, add *Shang Qiu* (Sp 5).

## 4. PHLEGM QI DEPRESSION & BINDING PATTERN

**MAIN SYMPTOMS:** Premenstrual emotional depression, dizziness as if one's head were covered in a bag, profuse, sticky phlegm, fatigue, somnolence, if severe, spontaneous sadness and spontaneous weeping, crying out as if in pain, or deep silence, an anxious heart laden with cares, thin, white, slimy tongue fur, and a soggy, fine or bowstring, slippery pulse

**ANALYSIS OF SYMPTOMS:** The premenstrual depression, deep silence, and bowstring pulse all indicate qi depression. The dizziness, sticky phlegm, slimy tongue fur, and slippery pulse all indicate phlegm. The fatigue, somnolence, soggy and/or fine pulse indicate that the liver has invaded the spleen with consequent spleen vacuity, while the emotional lability and anxiety show that phlegm is misting the orifices and disquieting the spirit.

**TREATMENT PRINCIPLES:** Rectify the qi and resolve depression, transform phlegm and open the orifices

**FORMULA & MEDICINALS:** *Ban Xia Hou Po Tang Jia Wei* (Pinellia & Magnolia Decoction with Added Flavors)

Rhizoma Pinelliae Ternatae (*Ban Xia*), 10g, Cortex Magnoliae Officinalis (*Hou Po*), 10g, Folium Perillae Frutescentis (*Zi Su Ye*), 10-12g, Sclerotium Poriae Cocos (*Fu Ling*), 10-12g, Radix Angelicae Sinensis (*Dang Gui*), 6-10g, Radix Albus Paeoniae Lactiflorae (*Bai Shao*), 10g, uncooked Rhizoma Zingiberis (*Sheng Jiang*), 3 slices

Decoct one *ji* in water per day and administer orally in two divided doses, morning and evening.

ANALYSIS OF FORMULA: Within this formula, Pinellia, Magnolia, Foilum Perillae, and uncooked Ginger all transform phlegm and rectify the qi. Poria helps eliminate dampness and turbidity by fortifying the spleen and seeping dampness. It also quiets the spirit. Dang Gui and Peony nourish the blood and harmonize the liver, thus allowing it to course and discharge.

ADDITIONS & SUBTRACTIONS: If there is phlegm turbidity clouding the heart orifices, use *Ban Xia Bai Zhu Tian Ma Tang Jia Wei* (Pinellia, Atractylodes & Gastrodia Decoction with Added Flavors)

Rhizoma Pinelliae Ternatae (*Ban Xia*), 10g, Rhizoma Gastrodiae Elatae (*Tian Ma*), 10g, Rhizoma Atractylodis Macrocephalae (*Bai Zhu*), 10g, Sclerotium Poriae Cocos (*Fu Ling*), 10-12g, Pericarpium Citri Reticulatae (*Chen Pi*), 6-10g, Radix Angelicae Sinensis (*Dang Gui*), 6-10g, Radix Albus Paeoniae Lactiflorae (*Bai Shao*), 10-12g, Radix Glycyrrhizae (*Gan Cao*), 3-10g, uncooked Rhizoma Zingiberis (*Sheng Jiang*), 2-4 slices, Fructus Zizyphi Jujubae (*Da Zao*), 2-4 pieces

If there is phlegm heat harassing above, use *Sheng Tie Luo Yin Jia Jian* (Uncooked Iron Filings Drink with Additions & Subtractions)

Pericarpium Citri Reticulatae (*Chen Pi*), 10g, Sclerotium Poriae Cocos (*Fu Ling*), 10g, lime-processed Rhizoma Pinelliae Ternatae (*Ban Xia*), 10g, Fructus Citri Aurantii (*Zhi Ke*), 10g, Caulis Bambusae In Taeniis (*Zhu Ru*), 10g, uncooked Frusta Ferri (*Tie Luo*), 15g, Ramulus Uncariae Cum Uncis (*Gou Teng*), 10-12g, Radix Salviae Miltiorrhizae (*Dan Shen*), 10g, Fructus Forsythiae Suspensae (*Lian Qiao*), 10g, Tuber Ophiopogonis Japonici (*Mai Dong*), 12g, Bulbus Fritillariae Thunbergii (*Zhe Bei Mu*), 10g, Radix Scrophulariae Ningpoensis (*Xuan Shen*), 15g, bile-processed Rhizoma Arisaematis (*Dan Nan Xing*), 10g, Radix Polygalae Tenuifoliae (*Yuan Zhi*), 10g, Rhizoma Acori Graminei (*Shi Chang Pu*), 10g

If there is phlegm wind, use *Ding Xian Wan Jia Jian* (Stabilize Epilepsy Pills with Additions & Subtractions)

Rhizoma Gastrodiae Elatae (*Tian Ma*), 10g, Bulbus Fritillariae Cirrhosae (*Chuan Bei Mu*), 10g, ginger-processed Rhizoma Pinelliae Ternatae (*Ban Xia*), 10-12g, Sclerotium Poriae Cocos (*Fu Ling*), 10-12g, Sclerotium Pararadicis Poriae Cocos (*Fu Shen*), 10-12g, bile-processed Rhizoma Arisaematis (*Dan Nan Xing*), 10g,

Rhizoma Acori Graminei (*Shi Chang Pu*), 10g, Buthus Martensis (*Quan Xie*), 3-6g, Bombyx Batryticatus (*Jiang Can*), 10g, Succinum (*Hu Po*), 1-3g, Medulla Junci Effusi (*Deng Xin Cao*), 1-3g, Pericarpium Citri Reticulatae (*Chen Pi*), 6-10g, Radix Polygalae Tenuifoliae (*Yuan Zhi*), 10g, Radix Salviae Miltiorrhizae (*Dan Shen*), 10g, Tuber Ophiopogonis Japonici (*Mai Dong*), 12g

ACUPUNCTURE: *Tai Chong* (Liv 3), *Feng Long* (St 40), *Zhong Wan* (CV 12), *Shen Men* (Ht 7), *Nei Guan* (Per 6). Use draining technique.

ADDITIONS & SUBTRACTIONS: If there is phlegm fire, replace *Tai Chong* with *Xing Jian* (Liv 2) and replace *Nei Guan* with *Lao Gong* (Per 8).

## 5. YIN VACUITY WITH ASCENDANT LIVER YANG HYPERACTIVITY PATTERN

MAIN SYMPTOMS: Premenstrual irascibility, easy anger, dizziness, vertigo, tinnitus, head distention and/or pain, profuse dreams, insomnia, a red face and red eyes, low back pain, a red tongue, and a bowstring, fine, rapid or surging, rapid pulse

ANALYSIS OF SYMPTOMS: Irascibility and easy anger indicate liver depression as does the bowstring pulse. However, the dizziness, vertigo, tinnitus, head distention and/or pain, the red face, eyes, and tongue, and rapid pulse show that depression has transformed heat which has led to ascendant hyperactivity of yang. Likewise, a surging pulse also confirms upward counterflow of yang. The profuse dreams and insomnia are due to heat harassing and disquieting the heart spirit, while the low back pain and possibly fine pulse show that depressive heat has consumed yin or that yin vacuity has engendered heat.

TREATMENT PRINCIPLES: Clear the liver and subdue yang, nourish the blood and enrich the kidneys

FORMULA & MEDICINALS: *Tian Ma Gou Teng Yin* (Gastrodia & Uncaria Drink)

Rhizoma Gastrodiae Elatae (*Tian Ma*), 10g, Ramulus Uncariae Cum Uncis (*Gou Teng*), 12-15g, Concha Haliotidis (*Shi Jue Ming*), 18-24g, Fructus Gardeniae Jasminoidis (*Zhi Zi*), 10g, Radix Scutellariae Baicalensis (*Huang Qin*), 10g, Herba Leonuri Heterophylli (*Yi Mu Cao*), 10-12g, Radix Cyathulae (*Chuan Niu Xi*), 12g, Cortex Eucommiae Ulmoidis (*Du Zhong*), 10-12g, Ramulus Loranthi Seu Visci (*Sang Ji Sheng*), 10-24g, Caulis Polygoni Multiflori (*Ye Jiao Teng*), 10-30g, Sclerotium Pararadicis Poriae Cocos (*Fu Shen*), 10-15g

Decoct one *ji* in water per day and administer orally in two divided doses, morning and evening.

**ANALYSIS OF FORMULA:** Gastrodia and Uncaria both settle the liver and extinguish wind. Uncaria also clears the liver as do Scutellaria and Gardenia. Abalone Shell heavily subdues yang and quiets the spirit. Eucommia and Loranthus supplement the kidneys, while Cyathula both quickens the blood and leads the blood to move downwards. Since blood is the mother of qi, this helps lead yang back down to its lower source. Leonurus also quickens the blood but without damaging yin blood. Caulis Polygoni and Spirit of Poria both quiet the spirit. However, the former also nourishes the liver, while the latter also seeps dampness, thus leading heat down and out through urination.

**ADDITIONS & SUBTRACTIONS:** If there is yin vacuity with fire effulgence, use *Huang Lian E Jiao Ji Zi Huang Tang Jia Wei* (Coptis, Donkey Skin Glue & Chicken Egg Yolk Decoction with Added Flavors)

Rhizoma Coptidis Chinensis (*Huang Lian*), 3-12g, Radix Scutellariae Baicalensis (*Huang Qin*), 10-12g, Radix Albus Paeoniae Lactiflorae (*Bai Shao*), 10-18g, Gelatinum Corii Asini (*E Jiao*), 12g, Bulbus Lilii (*Bai He*), 15-30g, uncooked Radix Rehmanniae (*Sheng Di*), 12-15g, Sclerotium Pararadicis Poriae Cocos (*Fu Shen*), 12-15g, chicken egg yolks (*Ji Zi Huang*), 2-3

**ACUPUNCTURE:** *Bai Hu* (GV 20), *Feng Chi* (GB 20), *Yin Tang* (M-HN-3), *Da Ling* (Per 7), *Tai Chong* (Liv 3), *San Yin Jiao* (Sp 6), *Tai Xi* (Ki 3). Drain the first four points, use even supplementing-even draining technique at *Tai Chong*, and supplement the last three points.

## 6. SPLEEN-KIDNEY YANG VACUITY PATTERN

**MAIN SYMPTOMS:** Premenstrual feeble-mindedness, essence spirit abstraction, no thought for food or drink, cold hands and feet, low back and knee pain and weakness, nocturia, dizziness, loose stools, lassitude of the spirit, lack of strength, a pale, enlarged tongue with teethmarks on its edges and thin, white fur, and a deep, weak pulse

**ANALYSIS OF SYMPTOMS:** The feeble-mindedness, essence spirit abstraction, dizziness, lassitude of the spirit, and lack of strength all indicate lack of clear yang qi to construct and make brilliant the heart spirit. The lack of appetite, loose stools, and enlarged tongue all indicate specifically spleen qi vacuity, while the low back and knee pain and weakness and nocturia indicate specifically kidney vacu-

ity. The pale tongue, cold hands and feet and deep, weak pulse show that there is a yang vacuity.

**TREATMENT PRINCIPLES:** Warm and supplement the spleen and kidneys

**FORMULA & MEDICINALS:** *Jian Gu Tang Jia Jian* (Fortifying & Securing Decoction with Additions & Subtractions)

Radix Codonopsitis Pilosulae (*Dang Shen*), 10g, Rhizoma Atractylodis Macrocephalae (*Bai Zhu*), 10g, Sclerotium Poriae Cocos (*Fu Ling*), 10-12g, Semen Coicis Lachryma-jobi (*Yi Yi Ren*), 21g, Radix Morindae Officialis (*Ba Ji Tian*), 10g, dry Rhizoma Zingiberis (*Gan Jiang*), 6-10g, Radix Auklandiae Lappae (*Mu Xiang*), 6-10g

Decoct one *ji* in water per day and administer orally in two divided doses, morning and evening.

**ANALYSIS OF FORMULA:** Codonopsis, Atractylodes, and Poria fortify and supplement the spleen qi. In addition, Poria quiets the spirit. Coix helps Poria seep dampness. Since the spleen and kidneys both govern water fluids in the body, spleen-kidney dual vacuity is commonly complicated by dampness. Morinda supplements the kidneys and invigorates yang. Dry Ginger warms the interior and promotes the supplementation of the spleen. Auklandia rectifies the qi and eliminates dampness.

**ADDITIONS & SUBTRACTIONS:** If there is diarrhea, add Semen Dolichoris Lablab (*Bai Bian Dou*), roasted Radix Puerariae (*Ge Gen*), and Fructus Psoraleae Corylifoliae (*Bu Gu Zhi*). If bodily cold and chilled limbs are marked, add Radix Lateralis Praeparatus Aconiti Carmichaeli (*Fu Zi*), Cortex Cinnamomi Cassiae (*Rou Gui*), and Radix Dipsaci (*Xu Duan*). If there is shortness of breath and a falling, sagging sensation in the lower abdomen, add Radix Astragali Membranacei (*Huang Qi*) and Rhizoma Cimicifugae (*Sheng Ma*). If there is chest oppression and abdominal distention, add Rhizoma Cyperi Rotundi (*Xiang Fu*) and Fructus Citri Aurantii (*Zhi Ke*).

For spleen-kidney yang vacuity complicated by blood stasis, use *Si Ni Tang Jia Wei* (Four Counterflows Decoction with Added Flavors)

Radix Lateralis Praeparatus Aconiti Carmichaeli (*Fu Zi*), 6-10g, Radix Angelicae Sinensis (*Dang Gui*), 10g, Radix Dioscoreae Oppositae (*Shan Yao*), 10g, Sclerotium Poriae Cocos (*Fu Ling*), 10-12g, cooked Radix Rehmanniae (*Shu Di*), 15g, Herba Epimedii (*Xian Ling Pi*), 10g, Rhizoma

Curcumae Zedoariae (*E Zhu*), 10g, Rhizoma Sparganii (*San Leng*), 10g, Radix Rubrus Paeoniae Lactiflorae (*Chi Shao*), 10g, Radix Ligustici Wallichii (*Chuan Xiong*), 10g, dry Rhizoma Zingiberis (*Gan Jiang*), 6-10g

**ACUPUNCTURE:** *Guan Yuan* (CV 4), *Shen Que* (CV 8), *Zhong Wan* (CV 12), *Pi Shu* (Bl 20), *Wei Shu* (Bl 21), *Shen Shu* (Bl 23), *Ming Men* (GV 4). Moxa all points.

### 7. QI STAGNATION & BLOOD STASIS PATTERN

**MAIN SYMPTOMS:** Severe, fixed menstrual pain with dark, blackish blood and/or blood clots, delayed or scanty menstruation, possible blocked menstruation, premenstrual breast, chest, rib-side, or abdominal distention and pain, irritability, easy anger, a sooty dark facial complexion, purplish, dark lips, age spots, spider nevi, or other visible varicosities, aggravation of symptoms at night, a dark, possibly purple tongue and/or static macules or spots, and a bowstring, fine, choppy pulse

**ANALYSIS OF SYMPTOMS:** Severe, fixed menstrual pain, dark, blackish blood, blood clots, delayed or scanty, possibly blocked menstruation, a sooty, dark facial complexion, purplish, dark lips, age spots, varicosities large and small, a purple tongue or possible static spots or macules, and a choppy pulse all indicate blood stasis as do worsening symptoms at night. Irritability, easy anger, chest, breast, rib-side, and abdominal distention and pain, and a bowstring pulse indicate qi stagnation. The fine pulse indicates that either static blood is hindering the creation of new, fresh blood or that blood vacuity is the cause of liver depression and/or blood stasis.

**TREATMENT PRINCIPLES:** Move the qi and quicken the blood, dispel stasis and stop pain

**FORMULA & MEDICINALS:** *Xue Fu Zhu Yu Tang* (Blood Mansion Dispel Stasis Decoction)

Semen Pruni Persicae (*Tao Ren*), 12g, Flos Carthami Tinctorii (*Hong Hua*), 10g, Radix Angelicae Sinensis (*Dang Gui*), 10g, Radix Ligustici Wallichii (*Chuan Xiong*), 10g, Radix Rubrus Paeoniae Lactiflorae (*Chi Shao*), 10g, Radix Cyathulae (*Chuan Niu Xi*), 10g, Radix Bupleuri (*Chai Hu*), 3-10g, Radix Platycodi Gandiflori (*Jie Geng*), 6-10g, Fructus Citri Aurantii (*Zhi Ke*), 6-10g, uncooked Radix Rehmanniae (*Sheng Di*), 10-15g, Radix Glycyrrhizae (*Gan Cao*), 3-6g

Decoct one *ji* in water per day and administer orally in two divided doses, morning and evening.

**ACUPUNCTURE:** *Tai Chong* (Liv 3), *He Gu* (LI 4), *Xue Hai* (Sp 10), *San Yin Jiao* (Sp 6), *Guan Yuan* (GV 4), *Qi Hai* (CV 6). Use draining technique.

**CLINICAL TIPS:** The most common pattern of premenstrual dysphoria is a liver-spleen disharmony with blood vacuity and possible dampness. In ectomorphic patients and/or women in their 40s, blood vacuity may be complicated by yin vacuity, while spleen qi vacuity may be complicated by kidney yang vacuity. Most Western women with premenstrual dysphoria disorder have at least three patterns concomitantly and often five or six.

### ABSTRACT OF REPRESENTATIVE CHINESE RESEARCH:

*Yun Nan Zhong Yi Zhong Yao Za Zhi* (*Yunnan Journal of Chinese Medicine & Chinese Medicinals*), #5, 1996, p. 9-10: In this clinical audit, Liang Xiang-yun reports on the treatment of 60 cases of premenstrual tension based on pattern discrimination. The patients in this study were 16-45 years old. Six were unmarried. Their duration of illness was between five months and 15 years. Besides various somatic complaints, psycho-emotional complaints included vexation and agitation, irritability, and insomnia. Six patterns were discriminated: 1) liver depression qi stagnation (22 cases), spleen-kidney yang vacuity (6 cases), 3) heart-spleen dual vacuity (5 cases), 4) yin vacuity-fire effulgence (18 cases), 5) blood vacuity engendering wind (2 cases), and 6) static blood obstructing the network vessels (7 cases).

The formula used for pattern #1 was *Chai Hu Shu Gan San Jia Jian* (Bupleurum Course the Liver Powder with Additions & Subtractions). The formula for pattern #2 was *Jian Gu Tang Jia Jian* (Fortifying & Securing Decoction with Additions & Subtractions). The formula for pattern #3 was *Gui Pi Tang Jia Jian* (Restore the Spleen Decoction with Additions & Subtractions). The formula for pattern #4 was *Zhi Bai Di Huang Tang Jia Jian* (Anemarrhena & Phellodendron Rehmannia Decoction with Additions & Subtractions). The formula for pattern #5 was *Yang Xue Chu Feng Tang Jia Jian* (Nourish the Blood & Dispel Wind Decoction with Additions & Subtractions), and the formula for pattern #6 was *Xue Fu Zhu Yu Tang Jia Jian* (Blood Mansion Dispel Stasis Decoction with Additions & Subtractions). These medicinals were administered beginning 7-15 days before the onset of menstruation. The number of *ji* administered each cycle was between three and seven. After menstruation, all patients received 3-9 *ji* of *Ba Zhen Tang Jia Jian* (Eight Pearls Decoction with Additions & Subtractions), these additions and subtractions were made depending on their pattern.

Treatment continued for anywhere from 1-6 cycles. Treatment was assessed after five cycles. Complete disappearance of all premenstrual symptoms, including psychoemotional symptoms, was considered a cure. Thus 37 cases (62%) were deemed cured, 19 cases got a good result, and four cases experienced no result. Therefore, the total amelioration rate was 93%.

## REPRESENTATIVE CASE HISTORIES:

### ❖ CASE 1[1] ❖

The patient was a 30 year old female who was first examined on Jan. 31, 1974. The patient complained of premenstrual dizziness, headache, heart fluster, shortness of breath, nausea, chest oppression and pain, a dry mouth with a preference for chilled drinks, vexation and agitation., easy anger, fatigue, listlessness of the four limbs, and lack of strength. After her menses came, all these symptoms disappeared. Her menstruation was 3-7 days early, its color was dark red, and its volume was moderate. At the time of menstruation, there was also lumbar aching and pain. The patient said that her premenstrual symptoms were so bad, she could not work during each premenstruum.

Based on these signs and symptoms, the woman's pattern was categorized as liver depression transforming fire with yin vacuity and yang hyperactivity. Therefore, the treatment principles were to nourish yin and clear heat, cool the blood and level or calm the liver. The formula prescribed consisted of: Folium Mori Albi (Sang Ye), 9g, Flos Chrysanthemi Morifolii (Ju Hua), 9g, Radix Scutellariae Baicalensis (Huang Qin), 9g, Rhizoma Thalactri Foliosi (Ma Wei Lian), 9g, uncooked Radix Albus Paeoniae Lactiflorae (Bai Shao), 9g, uncooked Radix Rehmanniae (Sheng Di), 12g, Fructus Trichosanthis Kirlowii (Tian Hua Fen), 15g, Cortex Radicis Moutan (Dan Pi), 9g, Fructus Gardeniae Jasminoidis (Zhi Zi), 9g, Radix Achyranthis Bidentatae (Niu Xi), 9g, Fructus Ligustri Lucidi (Nu Zhen Zi), 9g, and Herba Ecliptae Prostratae (Han Lian Cao), 9g.

After taking three ji of the above formula, the dizziness, headache, heart fluster, vexation and agitation, insomnia, and chest oppression were all decreased. Therefore, Trichosanthes was removed from the formula and 15 grams of Gelatinum Corii Asini (E Jiao) were added. On Apr. 13, the patient was re-examined and she was advised to take 3-6 ji of the above formula a few days before each menstruation. The patient followed these instructions, her essence spirit returned to normal and so did her menstrual cycle. After this, the woman was able to work all day during each premenstruum.

### ❖ CASE 2[2] ❖

The patient was an 18 year old female who was first examined on Sept. 3, 1978. The patient's menarche had occurred at 15 years of age and, up until recently, her menstruation had been normal. However, a half year ago the patient had experienced a fright at the onset of her menstruation. Since then for the last half year, the patient had been experiencing menstrual movement emotional abnormality such that she did not know her family members, had no thought for food or drink, and both her eyes had a blank, stagnant look. When these premenstrual symptoms were severe, she would climb on high, sing, and take her clothes off. The patient had been hospitalized and treated but discharged after her symptoms seemed to improve. However, not long after her premenstrual emotional abnormalities had recurred and she was referred to the author of this case's hospital for examination. At that examination, it was found that the patient had profuse, sticky phlegm. Her tongue fur was yellow and slimy, and her pulse was soggy and slippery.

Based on the above signs and symptoms, the patient's pattern was categorized as phlegm turbidity ascending and misting the clear orifices with heart-liver fire effulgence harassing and causing chaos to the spirit brilliance. Therefore, the patient was prescibed Huang Lian Wen Dan Tang Jia Jian (Coptis Warm the Gallbladder Decoction with Additions & Subtractions): Rhizoma Coptidis Chinensis (Huang Lian), 3g, ginger-processed Rhizoma Pinelliae Ternatae (Ban Xia), 9g, Fructus Immaturus Citri Aurantii (Zhi Shi), 9g, Sclerotium Poriae Cocos (Fu Ling), 9g, Pericarpium Citri Reticulatae (Chen Pi), 9g, Rhizoma Acori Graminei (Shi Chang Pu), 9g, Tuber Curcumae (Yu Jin), 9g, ginger-processed Caulis Bambusae In Taeniis (Zhu Ru), 12g, bile-processed Rhizoma Arisaematis (Dan Nan Xing), 9g, uncooked Radix Et Rhizoma Rhei (Da Huang), 9g (added later), and uncooked Frusta Ferri (Tie Luo), 30g (cooked first).

After seven ji, the patient's slimy, yellow tongue fur had already transformed and her essence spirit gradually became vitalized. Therefore she was given Si Wu Tang Jia Jian (Four Materials Decoction with Additions & Subtractions) to nourish the blood and regulate the menses: Radix Angelicae Sinensis (Dang Gui), 9g, Radix Rubrus Paeoniae Lactiflorae (Chi Shao), 9g, Radix

Ligustici Wallichii (*Chuan Xiong*), 6g, uncooked Radix Rehmanniae (*Sheng Di*), 12g, cooked Radix Rehmanniae (*Shu Di*), 12g, Sclerotium Poriae Cocos (*Fu Ling*), 9g, Pericarpium Citri Reticulatae (*Chen Pi*), 9g, Herba Leonuri Heterophylli (*Yi Mu Cao*), 12g, Rhizoma Cyperi Rotundi (*Xiang Fu*), 9g, and Flouritum (*Zhi Shi Ying*), 12g.

After seven *ji* of this second formula, the patient's menses returned to normal and there was no recurrence of her menstrual movement essence spirit abnormality. On follow-up a half year later, her mind was bright and clear, her studies were good, and there had been no recurrence.

### ❖ CASE 3[3] ❖

The patient was a 20 year old female who was first examined on Oct. 29, 1976. Menarche had occurred when the patient was 15 years old, and her menses always came sometimes early, sometimes late, at no fixed schedule. During the last year, the patient had developed premenstrual and menstrual vexation and agitation, easy anger, sadness, a tendency to cry, emotional aloofness, and an inability to control herself. These symptoms were accompanied by heart palpitations, insomnia, profuse dreams, impaired memory, pain at the vertex of her head, slight facial edema, poor appetite, and yellow urine. Her last menstruation had begun on Oct. 22. Her tongue was pale red with static spots and slightly yellow fur. Her pulse was deep and fine.

Based on these signs and symptoms, the patient's pattern was categorized as liver depression qi stagnation with liver qi counterflowing horizontally and assailing the spleen. Therefore, the treatment principles were to course the liver and resolve depression assisted by fortifying the spleen and hence she was administered one *ji* per day of the following medicinals: Tuber Curcumae (*Yu Jin*), 12g, Fructus Citri Sacrodactylis (*Fo Shou*), 12g, Radix Salviae Miltiorrhizae (*Dan Shen*), 15g, Sclerotium Poriae Cocos (*Fu Ling*), 25g, Caulis Polygoni Multiflori (*Ye Jiao Teng*), 30g, Fructus Tribuli Terrestris (*Bai Ji Li*), 12g, and Rhizoma Alismatis (*Ze Xie*), 15g.

On Nov. 19, the patient was examined again when her menses were due. The patient's symptoms were the same as before. Therefore, she was prescribed the following medicinals to course the liver and resolve depression, nourish the blood and free the flow of menstruation: Tuber Curcumae (*Yu Jin*), 12g, Radix Albus Paeoniae Lactiflorae (*Bai Shao*), 15g, Radix Salviae Miltiorrhizae (*Dan Shen*), 15g, Cortex Albizziae Julibrissinis (*He Huan Pi*), 12g, Caulis Polygoni Multiflori (*Ye Jiao Teng*), 30g,

Radix Glycyrrhizae (*Gan Cao*), 6g, Radix Achyranthis Bidentatae (*Niu Xi*), 15g, Sclerotium Poriae Cocos (*Fu Ling*), 25g, and Ramulus Loranthi Seu Visci (*Sang Ji Sheng*), 25g.

On Dec. 10, the young woman was examined for the third time. Her last menses had come on Nov. 26, and her premenstrual symptoms had been slightly less. The prescribing physician decided that her liver depression was slightly resolved but that her spleen damage had yet to recover based on her facial edema and abdominal distention. Therefore, the patient was prescribed: Tuber Curcumae (*Yu Jin*), 12g, Pericarpium Citri Reticulatae Viride (*Qing Pi*), 6g, Radix Salviae Miltiorrhizae (*Dan Shen*), 12g, Rhizoma Atractylodis Macrocephalae (*Bai Zhu*), 12g, Sclerotium Poriae Cocos (*Fu Ling*), 25g, Ramulus Loranthi Seu Visci (*Sang Ji Sheng*), 30g, Caulis Polygoni Multiflori (*Ye Jiao Teng*), 30g, and Rhizoma Alismatis (*Ze Xie*), 12g.

On Dec. 31, the patient was examined for the fourth time. Her premenstrual symptoms preceding her last menses had been markedly decreased. However, her sleep had still not been good. Therefore, the patient was prescribed: Tuber Curcumae (*Yu Jin*), 12g, Bulbus Lilii (*Bai He*), 25g, Rhizoma Cyperi Rotundi (*Xiang Fu*), 10g, Radix Salviae Miltiorrhizae (*Dan Shen*), 12g, Radix Albus Paeoniae Lactiflorae (*Bai Shao*), 15g, Rhizoma Atractylodis Macrocephalae (*Bai Zhu*), 12g, Sclerotium Poriae Cocos (*Fu Ling*), 25g, Radix Glycyrrhizae (*Gan Cao*), 6g, and Caulis Polygoni Multiflori (*Ye Jiao Teng*), 30g.

On Jan. 21, 1977, the patient was seen a fifth and final time. Her last menstruation had come only two days early and she had not experienced any premenstrual symptoms. Her mood was good as was her appetite. Her face was still just slightly puffy. Therefore, she was prescribed: Tuber Curcumae (*Yu Jin*), 12g, Rhizoma Cyperi Rotundi (*Xiang Fu*), 10g, Radix Albus Paeoniae Lactiflorae (*Bai Shao*), 15g, Sclerotium Poriae Cocos (*Fu Ling*), 25g, Radix Salviae Miltiorrhizae (*Dan Shen*), 12g, Radix Achyranthis Bidentatae (*Niu Xi*), 15g, Caulis Polygoni Multiflori (*Ye Jiao Teng*), 30g, and Rhizoma Dioscoreae Hypoglaucae (*Bi Xie*), 20g. On follow-up after two years, the patient's treatment effect was stable.

### ❖ CASE 4[4] ❖

The patient was a 36 year old married woman who was first examined on Jan. 6, 1976. The patient's last menses had come on Nov. 30, 1975. Her menses were typically late. Two to three days before the onset of each menstruation, the woman became emotionally depressed and cried for no reason. In addition, she experienced vexation and agitation and easy anger and was not able to control herself. When extreme, she would yell and scream and even hit her family members. After menstruation, her emotions all returned to normal. Other premenstrual symptoms included edema of the four limbs, lumbosacral soreness, lower abdominal pain, dry, bound stools, and easy fright and profuse dreams at night. These symptoms had been recurring for the past eight years. Her tongue was swollen with teeth-marks on its edges and thin, yellow fur, while her pulse was fine and bowstring.

Based on these signs and symptoms, the patient's pattern was categorized as qi and yin dual vacuity with liver depression qi stagnation. Because of enduring depression, there was also transformative fire resulting in heart-liver fire mixed with phlegm heat. This was misting the clear orifices above resulting in these premenstrual mental-emotional complaints. Therefore, the treatment principles were to course the liver and open depression, use bitter and cold medicinals to discharge heat, upbear the clear and downbear the turbid, flush phlegm and perfuse the orifices using *Da Chai Hu Tang Jia Jian* (Major Bupleurum Decoction with Additions & Subtractions): Radix Bupleuri (*Chai Hu*), 9g, Spica Prunellae Vulgaris (*Xia Ku Cao*), 12g, Rhizoma Coptidis Chinensis (*Huang Lian*), 3g, Radix Scutellariae Baicalensis (*Huang Qin*), 6g, processed Radix Et Rhizoma Rhei (*Da Huang*), 6g, Rhizoma Acori Graminei (*Shi Chang Pu*), 9g, Tuber Curcumae (*Yu Jin*), 6g, Concretio Silicae Bambusae (*Tian Zhu Huang*), 9g, bile-processed Rhizoma Arisaematis (*Dan Nan Xing*), 9g, ginger-processed Rhizoma Pinelliae Ternatae (*Ban Xia*), 6g, Sclerotium Poriae Cocos (*Fu Ling*), 9g, *Bai Jin Wan* (White Gold Pills), 9g (swallowed with the decoction). Fourteen *ji* of these medicinals were prescribed.

On Jan. 20, the patient was examined the second time. Her menses had come on Jan. 17. Because of taking the above formula, much stasis was precipitated and she experienced lower abdominal distention and pain and the expulsion of clots. There had still been premenstrual emotional tension, vexation and agitation, easy anger, profuse dreams, and dry, bound stools. However, all these were less than before. Her pulse was still fine and bowstring, and her tongue was still fat and enlarged. It was judged that heart fire was somewhat less but that liver fire was still blazing. Therefore, she was prescribed the following medicinals to settle the liver and discharge heat: Radix Bupleuri (*Chai Hu*), 9g, Spica Prunellae Vulgaris (*Xia Ku Cao*), 12g, Radix Gentianae Scabrae (*Long Dan Cao*), 6g, Radix Scutellariae Baicalensis (*Huang Qin*), 6g, processed Radix Et Rhizoma Rhei (*Da Huang*), 9g, Tuber Curcumae (*Yu Jin*), 6g, Radix Angelicae Sinensis (*Dang Gui*), 9g,

Semen Aeschuli (*Suo Luo Zi*), 9g, Magnetitum (*Ci Shi*), 12g, Concha Margaritiferae (*Zhen Zhu Mu*), 30g, Ramulus Uncariae Cum Uncis (*Gou Teng*), 12g, and Lapis Micae Seu Chloriti (*Meng Shi*), 12g, one *ji* per day.

On Mar. 30, the patient reported that her last menses had arrived on Mar. 20. Due to the bitter, cold, heat-discharging, phlegm fire clearing medicinals, the patient's premenstrual dysphoria was better. She had not yelled or screamed. However, she had still felt heart vexation and had cried for no reason. Her face had been edematous, her upper abdomen had been distended, and her night-time sleep had still been harassed by dreams. Therefore, she was prescribed: Radix Bupleuri (*Chai Hu*), 9g, Rhizoma Cyperi Rotundi (*Xiang Fu*), 6g, Tuber Curcumae (*Yu Jin*), 9g, Rhizoma Acori Graminei (*Shi Chang Pu*), 9g, bile-processed Rhizoma Arisaematis (*Dan Nan Xing*), 9g, Concretio Silicea Bambusae (*Tian Zhu Huang*), 9g, ginger-processed Rhizoma Pinelliae Ternatae (*Ban Xia*), 6g, Sclerotium Poriae Cocos (*Fu Ling*), 9g, Fructus Immaturus Citri Aurantii (*Zhi Shi*), 9g, processed Radix Et Rhizoma Rhei (*Da Huang*), 6g, Lapis Micae Seu Chloriti (*Meng Shi*), 12g, Magnetitum (*Ci Shi*), 18g, Concha Margaritiferae (*Zhen Zhu Mu*), 30g, one *ji* per day.

On Jun. 8, The patient came for her examination. She had been taking the above medicinals for several months and she no longer had any premenstrual mental-emotional abnormalities. However, she still did have some edematous swelling of her extremities and her whole body lacked strength. Her tongue was fat and enlarged with slimy fur, and her pulse was fine. Therefore, her pattern was categorized as a liver-spleen disharmony with water dampness stagnation and accumulation, and she was prescribed seven *ji* of the following formula: Ramulus Cinnamomi Cassiae (*Gui Zhi*), 6g, Radix Stephaniae Tetrandrae (*Fang Ji*), 9g, uncooked Radix Astragali Membranacei (*Huang Qi*), 12g, Rhizoma Atractylodis Macrocephalae (*Bai Zhu*), 6g, Sclerotium Poriae Cocos (*Fu Ling*), 12g, Sclerotium Polypori Umbellati (*Zhu Ling*), 9g, Rhizoma Alismatis (*Ze Xie*), 6g, Pericarpium Citri Reticulatae (*Chen Pi*), 6g, ginger-processed Rhizoma Pinelliae Ternatae (*Ban Xia*), 6g, Rhizoma Acori Graminei (*Shi Chang Pu*), 9g, Tuber Curcumae (*Yu Jin*), 6g, and Fructus Immaturus Citri Aurantii (*Zhi Shi*), 9g.

After taking these medicinals, all the swelling and edema receded, and the patient was given *Xiao Yao San* (Rambling Powder) and *Si Ling San* (Four [Ingredients] Poria Powder) to course and regulate the liver and spleen, divide and move water dampness, and thus secure the therapeutic effect. On follow-up one year after ceasing taking these medicinals, there had been no recurrence.

### ❖ CASE 5[5] ❖

The patient was a 17 year old unmarried female who was first examined on Oct. 5, 1972. Her last menses had arrived on Sept. 14, and menarche had occurred when she was 15 years old. In the last several months, the patient had developed premenstrual dizziness, headache, a red, sore, swollen throat, a temperature of 39EC, and mental-emotional vexation, agitation, and restlessness. When this was severe, there was even spirit clouding and incoherent speech. The patient was constipated and experienced cramping and pain in her lower abdomen. These symptoms would last for 3-4 days before each menstruation. After menstruation, she would gradually return to normal and all these symptoms would disappear. The young woman's tongue tip and edges were red and prickly, and her pulse was fine, bowstring, and rapid.

Based on these signs and symptoms, the patient's pattern was categorized as yin vacuity with internal heat and heart-liver fire blazing internally. Thus phlegm fire was misting and confounding the clear orifices. Based on this, the patient was prescribed seven *ji* of the following medicinals: uncooked Radix Et Rhizoma Rhei (*Da Huang*), 9g, Radix Gentianae Scabrae (*Long Dan Cao*), 6g, blackened Fructus Gardeniae Jasminoidis (*Zhi Zi*), 6g, Caulis Akebiae (*Mu Tong*), 6g, uncooked Radix Rehmanniae (*Sheng Di*), 24g, Radix Scrophulariae Ningpoensis (*Xuan Shen*), 9g, Tuber Ophiopogonis Japonici (*Mai Dong*), 6g, Cortex Radicis Lycii Chinensis (*Di Gu Pi*), 6g, Radix Scutellariae Baicalensis (*Huang Qin*), 6g, and Folium Bambusae (*Zhu Ye*), 9g.

The patient's second examination occurred on Oct. 12. After taking the above medicinals, the patient's defecation had become freely flowing and easy. Because the patient was moving towards her menses, 14 *ji* of the following preventive formula were prescribed to continue clearing the liver and promote the division of the clear: uncooked Radix Et Rhizoma Rhei (*Da Huang*), 9g, Radix Scutellariae Baicalensis (*Huang Qin*), 6g, Caulis Akebiae (*Mu Tong*), 6g, Cortex Radicis Lycii Chinensis (*Di Gu Pi*),

9g, uncooked Radix Rehmanniae (*Sheng Di*), 15g, Radix Scrophulariae Ningpoensis (*Xuan Shen*), 9g, Tuber Ophiopogonis Japonici (*Mai Dong*), 6g, ginger-processed Rhizoma Pinelliae Ternatae (*Ban Xia*), 6g, bile-processed Rhizoma Arisaematis (*Dan Nan Xing*), 9g, Tuber Curcumae (*Yu Jin*), 6g, Rhizoma Acori Graminei (*Shi Chang Pu*), 9g, and *Meng Shi Di Tan Wan* (Mica Flush Phlegm Pills), 12g (swallowed with the decoction).

On Oct. 28, the patient was examined for the third and final time. Her last menses had come on Oct. 21. During this premenstruum, the patient's emotions were stable, and, during menstruation, she did not have a fever. In fact, she had been like any other normal person. This meant that her liver fire had been leveled. In order to secure the therapeutic effect, the patient was prescribed another seven *ji* of the following formula: processed Radix Et Rhizoma Rhei (*Da Huang*), 6g, Radix Scutellariae Baicalensis (*Huang Qin*), 6g, Caulis Akebiae (*Mu Tong*), 6g, Cortex Radicis Lycii Chinensis (*Di Gu Pi*), 9g, uncooked Radix Rehmanniae (*Sheng Di*), 18g, Radix Scrophulariae Ningpoensis (*Xuan Shen*), 9g, Tuber Ophiopogonis Japonici (*Mai Dong*), 6g, bile-processed Rhizoma Arisaematis (*Dan Nan Xing*), 9g, Tuber Curcumae (*Yu Jin*), 9g, Magnetitum (*Ci Shi*), 18g, Lapis Micae Seu Chloriti (*Meng Shi*), 18g, and Rhizoma Acori Graminei (*Shi Chang Pu*), 9g.

### ENDNOTES

[1]Liu Feng-wu, *The Essence of Liu Feng-wu's Gynecology*, trans. by Shuai Xue-zhong & Bob Flaws, Blue Poppy Press, Boulder, CO, 1998, p. 141-142

[2]Yue Xiu-zhen, *Fu Ke Ming Yi Zheng Zhi Jing Hua (An Efflorescence of Famous Gynecologists Patterns & Treatments)*, Shanghai University of Chinese Medicine Press, Shanghai, 1995, p. 76-77

[3]Yang Yi-ya, *Fu Ke (Gynecology)*, Hubei Science & Technology Press, Shijiazhuang, 1996, p. 184-185

[4]Tang Ji-fu, *Shang Hai Lao Zhong Yi Jing Yan Xuan Bian*, *op. cit.*, p. 471-472

[5]*Ibid.*, p. 473-474

# PERIMENOPAUSAL SYNDROME

Persisting psychosomatic symptom patterns that begin shortly before or after onset of menopause have been recognized and treated in the context of Western medicine for decades. Symptoms of perimenopausal mood disorders include psychological and emotional symptoms, such as irritable, depressed, or labile mood, subjective feelings of agitation, cognitive slowing, and impaired short-term memory. However, the perimenopause is also characterized by many somatic symptoms, such as dizziness, irregular menstrual flow, constipation, insomnia, sweats, hot flashes, and subjective complaints of generalized weakness or soreness. Unlike premenstrual dysphoric disorder, for which provisional diagnostic criteria have been formulated (see the preceeding chapter) in Western psychiatry, there is yet no consensus among psychiatrists regarding the validity of distinct perimenopausal mood disorders. Reasons for this reflect difficulties inherent in systematically defining a mood disorder in contemporary Western psychiatry. The value of epidemiological data is limited by methodological problems obtaining reliable descriptive information describing mood symptoms that are somehow causally linked to biological or social changes of the perimenopause. Further, many studies have suggested that a significant percentage of women who report persisting mood changes during the perimenopause have histories of mood disorders previous to onset of the menopause. Finally, cross-cultural surveys of women entering the menopause suggest that reported experiences of distressing somatic or psychological symptoms during the transition to menopause are highly variable between cultures

and that these differences are probably related to variations in subjective expectations of the menopause that exist between disparate cultures.

## NOSOLOGY:

No formal Western psychiatric diagnosis is characterized by a pattern of psychosomatic symptoms circumscribed to the years before and after onset of the menopause. The absence of a Western diagnostic label points to a lack of consensus over whether psychological and somatic symptom patterns observed during the perimenopause constitute a disorder, *i.e.*, a symptom pattern that is empirically verifiable and stable over time across an identified high-risk group. Despite this unresolving debate, a rapidly growing medical-psychiatric literature has contributed to improved understanding of social and physiological causes and effective treatment of perimenopausal mood changes. Some investigators have used the term perimenopausal syndrome to describe these changes.

## EPIDEMIOLOGY:

In the U.S., approximately 40 million women are postmenopausal. Roughly one-third of these are receiving hormonal replacement therapy (HRT) or other therapies addressing physiological or mood symptoms. Menopause typically starts at age 51. However, some women may be symptomatic as early as the mid 30s. Most women who complain of significant disturbances in mood around the time of menopause have histories of depression or other mood symptoms earlier in life. Because formal diagnostic criteria for perimenopausal syndrome do not yet exist in Western psychiatric nosology, epidemiologic surveys cannot estimate prevalence rates of this disorder.

### DIFFERENTIAL DIAGNOSIS:

The initial task in differential diagnosis is to determine whether reported somatic, mood, or cognitive symptoms are within the normal range of expected behavior. Because of diverse cultural expectations for normal behavior around the time of menopause, this is a judgement that is meaningful only when made with the understanding of a specific cultural and social context in mind. In cases where reported experiences cause significant distress or impairment, they are typically identified as symptoms. Medical or psychiatric explanations are then sought. Perimenopausal changes in mood, cognition, or memory point to numerous possible underlying medical disorders. Dementia must be ruled out when gradual decline in memory is a prominent symptom. Progressive symptoms of emotional lability or irritability in the context of headaches may point to a brain tumor or other pathological CNS process. Tumors in or near the pituitary sometimes manifest as "skipped periods" typical of early menopause and are often associated with emotional lability, mood changes, and visual disturbances. Both excessive activity and inactivity of the parathyroid gland can result in psychiatric symptom patterns that approximate those associated with perimenopausal syndrome. These include cognitive impairment, irritability, or depression and mania. Lability, irritability, and memory impairment are also commonly seen in diabetes and hypothyroidism. Finally, alcohol or substance abuse or withdrawal can sometimes manifest as psychosomatic complaints similar

to those reported during the perimenopause. Neurological evaluation, appropriate laboratory studies, and brain imaging studies generally confirm or exclude these possibilities.

When medical causes have been excluded as reasonable explanations, a thorough history can clarify the psychiatric differential diagnosis. Most women who experience severe mood symptoms during the perimenopause have histories of depression. Therefore, in cases where a clear history of recurring depression or manic-depressive cycles has been established and medical etiologies have not been identified, it is assumed that mood symptoms during the perimenopause point to a recurring episode of a primary pre-existing psychiatric disorder. Women who become symptomatic in the perimenopause often have histories of major depression, dysthymia, cyclothymia, and bipolar disorder. A careful review of history will often clarify the primary psychiatric diagnosis.

### ETIOLOGY & PATHOPHYSIOLOGY:

Menopause is a term used to describe physiological, behavioral, and psychological changes that occur as normal consequences of naturally declining functioning of the ovaries. The menopause generally takes place gradually over a period of years as the number of estrogen-secreting ovarian follicles decreases. Declines in serum estrogen and progesterone cause changes in levels of many other reproductive hormones. Estrogen is known to increase serotonin levels in the brain by inhibiting an enzyme (monoamine oxidase) that normally breaks down serotonin and other neurotransmitters. The decline in circulating estrogen, therefore, leads to a relative decline in serotonin which has been implicated in the pathogenesis of depression. Hormonal and neurotransmitter changes

---

### DIFFERENTIAL DIAGNOSIS

| 1. MEDICAL DISORDERS | 2. EFFECTS OF SUBSTANCES | 3. PSYCHIATRIC DISORDERS |
|---|---|---|
| A. ALZHEIMER'S DISEASE AND OTHER DEMENTIAS<br>B. BRAIN TUMORS, INCLUDING TUMORS OF THE PITUITARY<br>C. OTHER PRIMARY CNS DISEASES<br>D. HYPOPARATHYROIDISM OR HYPERPARATHYROIDISM<br>E. HYPOTHYROIDISM<br>F. CNS EFFECTS OF DIABETES | A. ALCOHOL AND ILLICIT SUBSTANCE INTOXICATION OR WITHDRAWAL<br>B. SIDE EFFECTS OF MEDICATIONS | A. MAJOR DEPRESSIVE EPISODE<br>B. DYSTHYMIA<br>C. CYCLOTHYMIA<br>D. BIPOLAR DISORDER (I OR II) |

are believed to manifest as psychosomatic symptom patterns associated with the perimenopause. In addition to biological models, some have suggested that the Western experience of menopause as a time of considerable distress is a socially conditioned group phenomenon related to anxiety or dysphoria over loss of control of the circumstances of one's reproductive life.

## WESTERN MEDICAL TREATMENT:

Successful treatment of underlying medical causes of lability, depression, and memory loss typically alleviates these complaints. In cases where a major psychiatric disorder is identified as the cause of somatic or psychological symptoms during the perimenopause, conventional Western treatments include antidepressant or mood-stabilizing medications and psychotherapy. Treatment responses are often improved when medications and psychotherapy are combined. When a perimenopausal syndrome does not cause marked impairment, the initial, more conservative approach is to start hormone replacement therapy (HRT). Many natural and synthetic forms of estrogen and progesterone are available. However, standard approaches to their use have not yet been established. Women who are impaired by psychiatric symptoms as part of a perimenopausal syndrome or who do not respond to an initial trial on HRT will likely benefit from antidepressants. It has been suggested that vitamin B6 eases the severity of perimenopausal symptoms. Some clinicians advocate stress management programs and aerobic exercise as approaches to minimize impairment during the perimenopause.

## SHORT & LONG-TERM ADVANTAGES & DISADVANTAGES OF WESTERN MEDICAL TREATMENT:

Early aggressive hormone replacement therapy protects against osteoporosis, a debilitating long-term consequence of estrogen deficiency. Estrogen therapy in the absence of progesterone in menopausal women significantly increases the risk of uterine cancer. It appears likely that estrogen replacement increases the risk of developing breast cancer in women who are genetically susceptible. A woman's level of functioning and general mood are markedly improved when HRT is successful.

In addition to risks and benefits of hormonal replacement therapy, women being treated for perimenopausal mood symptoms should be evaluated with respect to the potential advantages of antidepressant medication therapy in general. The benefits and long-term efficacy of conventional Western pharmacologic treatments for major depressive disorder are clearly established. The results of controlled studies with thousands of depressed patients consistently demonstrate significant clinical improvements in mood when antidepressant medications are used at recommended doses. Some women respond to cognitive therapy or supportive therapy, and many benefit from involvement in support groups for women undergoing menopause. Although the majority of depressed perimenopausal women tolerate antidepressant medications without significant problems, a significant minority must discontinue medications because of side effects or the risk of interactions with other prescription medications. While little is known about possible deleterious consequences of long-term antidepressant use in general, even less is known about potentially harmful effects of chronic antidepressant use in elderly women.

## INDICATIONS FOR REFERRAL TO WESTERN MEDICAL SERVICES:

Urgent referral to the nearest emergency room is indicated if history or clinical presentation suggest dementia or other progressive neurological disorders, brain tumor, endocrinological disorders (including hypothyroidism or hyperthyroidism), or a severe, untreated psychiatric disorder. A patient who voices suicidal thoughts should be carefully assessed and referred immediately to the nearest emergency room. It may be necessary to contact local authorities to ensure her safety during transport. Alcohol or substance abuse merit referrals to appropriate rehabilitation services if abuse is chronic and does not jeopardize the patient's welfare. Referral to emergency medical evaluation is also appropriate when an on-going pattern of substance abuse impairs social or occupational functioning or places the patient or others at risk. Routine referral to a psychiatrist is often helpful when patients who have no underlying medical problems fail to respond to an appropriate course and duration of Chinese medical treatment.

## CHINESE DISEASE CATEGORIZATION:

In contemporary Chinese gynecology, the disease category of perimenopausal syndrome is well-established. One of the most common Chinese translations of this disease category is *jue jing qian hou zhu zheng*. Literally this means "cessation of menstruation before and after various pathoconditions." Depending on the main presenting signs and symptoms, perimenopausal mood disorder may also be categorized as irritability (*yi nu*), vexation and agitation (*fan zao*), impaired memory (*jian wang*), fatigue (*juan dai*), insomnia (*bu mian*), visceral agitation (*zang zao*), etc.

## CHINESE DISEASE CAUSES & MECHANISMS:

It is said in the opening chapters of the *Nei Jing Su Wen* (*Inner Classic: Simple Questions*) that, at seven times seven or 49 years of age, kidney essence is exhausted in females and thus the *tian gui* ceases. In other words, at approximately 50 years of age, the ren mai is vacuous and not freely flowing, while the chong mai is debilitated and its blood is scanty. This is based on the fact that both the chong and ren arise from the uterus and carry or are filled with primarily kidney qi and essence blood. However, this is not the whole story.

Just as the maturation of the spleen-stomach creating a superabundance of acquired or latter heaven essence plays a part in the initial arrival of the *tian gui*[1] or menarche, so does the decline of the spleen-stomach and, therefore, a decline in the production and storage of acquired essence play an important part in the cessation of the *tian gui*. The *Nei Jing* (*Inner Classic*) also says that the yang ming begins to decline at the age of 35 in a woman and that this is why the facial skin develops wrinkles since it is no longer nourished by sufficient blood. As the spleen's ability to engender postnatally abundant blood and acquired essence declines, this places more of a burden on kidney essence if blood is to regularly fill to overflowing the chong mai/bao gong/uterus. If this burden were allowed to continue indefinitely, this would exhaust the kidneys all the more and lead to premature aging and debility.

But this is not the case. Somehow, the body recognizes what a drain that the kidneys' participation in the maintenance of regular menstruation is after the spleen and stomach have begun to decline and slack off in their participation in the engenderment and transformation of blood. Therefore, a change is initiated primarily in the relationship between the kidneys and heart via the uterus and chong mai/bao mai. Rather than sending blood down from the heart, the bao mai reverses the direction of its flow, sending essence up to nourish the spirit residing in the heart. Instead of preparing the uterus for the growth of a physical addition to the community of humankind, the blood focuses on the heart to nourish the woman's spirit.

However, this change is initiated by blood vacuity and insufficiency of yin essence. Therefore, as the bao mai reverses its flow, it is easy for yang to come out of control and to counterflow upward. This may manifest as evil heat ascending and harassing above. This heat may accumulate in the liver, the lungs, or the heart causing symptoms of dysfunction in any of these viscera. Along with symptoms of vacuity heat, fire, and rising, rootless yang, such as migraine headaches, hypertension, tinnitus, dizziness,

heart palpitations, insomnia, restlessness, anxiety, emotional lability, and hot flashes, yin may be insufficient to nourish the structure of the body and, therefore, symptoms of dryness, atrophy, shrinkage, and malnourishment of the various tissues of the body may also manifest. These include dry skin, lumbar soreness, vaginal dryness and atrophy, greying of the hair, and stiffness of the sinews. As yang counterflows upward away from its lower source, it may leave the lower body vacuous and cold with cold feet, polyuria, nocturia, urinary incontinence, and/or decreased sexual desire.

It is interesting to note that those women who seem to have the worst and most prolonged difficulties with perimenopausal complaints are those women with a long history of liver depression qi stagnation. All transformations in the body are managed by the qi mechanism. The change in life in women is just such a transformation. If there is liver depression, the qi mechanism is not freely flowing and uninhibited. If the liver is depressed, A) it may transform heat which further damages and consumes yin blood, B) it may assail the spleen, thus damaging the spleen's engenderment and transformation of the qi and blood, and C) qi stagnation may give rise to blood stasis. In addition, if the spleen becomes vacuous and weak and fails to maintain its control over the movement and transformation of body fluids, this may give rise to evil dampness, and, if this evil dampness endures or is cooked by depressive heat, it may congeal into phlegm.

In other words, the weakening and decline of the kidneys by themselves are not sufficient to create the kinds of symptoms one finds in women with perimenopausal syndrome, and this is especially so when it comes to perimenopausal mood disorders. While some perimenopausal essence spirit disturbances may be due to insufficient nourishment and construction of the heart spirit by essence and blood, most are complicated by one or more species of evil qi. These evil qi include qi stagnation, blood stasis, phlegm turbidity, depressive heat, damp heat, and/or vacuity heat. Evil heat harasses the spirit causing it to be restless, while phlegm turbidity and blood stasis mist the clear orifices and obstruct the network vessels respectively.

## TREATMENT BASED ON PATTERN DISCRIMINATION:

### 1. LIVER-KIDNEY YIN VACUITY PATTERN

**MAIN SYMPTOMS:** Dizziness, blurred vision, heart vexation, easy anger, emotional lability, insomnia, easy waking, menses sometimes profuse, sometimes scanty, possible spotting without cessation, pale red blood, tinnitus, tidal heat, hot flashes and night sweats, heat in the center of the hands, feet, and heart, soreness and weakness in the low back and knees, constipation, insomnia, a dry mouth but no particular desire to drink, a dry, reddish tongue with scanty or no fur, and a bowstring, fine, rapid pulse

**ANALYSIS OF SYMPTOMS:** Dizziness, blurred vision, scanty menstruation, tinnitus, low back and knee soreness and weakness, a dry mouth, constipation, scanty or no tongue fur, and a fine pulse all indicate yin vacuity and fluid insufficiency. Profuse menstruation, tidal heat, hot flashes, night sweats, heat in the five hearts, a red tongue, and rapid pulse all indicate heat. Easy anger and the bowstring pulse are due to liver depression due to lack of nourishing and moistening, while heart vexation, emotional lability, insomnia, and easy waking are all due to heat harassing and disquieting the heart spirit.

**TREATMENT PRINCIPLES:** Enrich yin and nourish the liver

**FORMULA & MEDICINALS:** *Geng Nian An Tang* (Climacteric-quieting Decoction)

Uncooked Radix Rehmanniae (*Sheng Di*), 12-24g, cooked Radix Rehmanniae (*Shu Di*), 12-24g, Radix Polygoni Multiflori (*He Shou Wu*), 12-24g, Rhizoma Alismatis (*Ze Xie*), 10g, Sclerotium Poriae Cocos (*Fu Ling*), 10-15g, Cortex Radicis Moutan (*Dan Pi*), 6-10g, Radix Scrophulariae Ningpoensis (*Xuan Shen*), 10-15g, Tuber Ophiopogonis Japonicae (*Mai Dong*), 10-12g, Fructus Schisandrae Chinensis (*Wu Wei Zi*), 10-12g, Fructus Corni Officinalis (*Shan Zhu Yu*), 10g

Decoct one *ji* in water per day and administer orally in two divided doses, morning and evening.

**ANALYSIS OF FORMULA:** Within this formula, the two Rehmannias nourish the blood, enrich yin, and clear vacuity heat. Vacuity heat is also cleared by Scrophularia, Moutan, and even Ophiopogon. Ophiopogon and Schisandra engender fluids, while Cornus supplements both kidney yin and yang evenly. Polygonum likewise nourishes the blood and enriches yin. Poria fortifies the spleen and seeps dampness. Alisma also seeps dampness. Therefore, these two medicinals help lead upwardly counterflowing yang back to its lower source via urination.

**ADDITIONS & SUBTRACTIONS:** If sweating is profuse, add Fructus Levis Tritici Aestivi (*Fu Xiao Mai*) and aged Semen Setariae Italicae (*Kang Gu Lao*). If there is heart vexation, add Fructus Gardeniae Jasminoidis (*Zhi Zi*) and Semen Praeparatus Sojae (*Dan Dou Chi*). If there are profuse dreams, add Radix Albus Paeoniae Lactiflorae (*Bai Shao*) and Fructus Chaenomelis Lagenariae (*Mu Gua*). If there is insomnia, add Magnetitum (*Ci Shi*), Concha Margaritiferae (*Zhen Zhu Mu*), and Caulis Polygoni Multiflori (*Ye Jiao Teng*). If there is headache, add Fructus Viticis (*Man Jing Zi*), Radix Angelicae Dahuricae (*Bai Zhi*), and Flos Chrysanthemi Morifolii (*Ju Hua*). If there is dizziness, add Herba Dendrobii (*Shi Hu*), Radix Platycodi Grandiflori (*Jie Geng*), and Radix Glycyrrhizae (*Gan Cao*). And if there is low back and leg pain, add Radix Dipsaci (*Chuan Duan*), Ramulus Loranthi Seu Visci (*Ji Sheng*), and Radix Achyranthis Bidentatae (*Niu Xi*).

If yin vacuity is complicated by fire effulgence with more pronounced signs and symptoms of heat, use *Zhi Bai Di Huang Wan Jia Wei* (Anemarrhena & Phellodendron Rehmannia Pills with Added Flavors)

Cooked Radix Rehmanniae (*Shu Di*), 12-24g, Fructus Corni Officinalis (*Shan Zhu Yu*), 10g, Radix Dioscoreae Oppositae (*Shan Yao*), 10g, Sclerotium Poriae Cocos (*Fu Ling*), 10-15g, Rhizoma Alismatis (*Ze Xie*), 10g, Cortex Radicis Moutan (*Dan Pi*), 10g, Cortex Phellodendri (*Huang Bai*), 10-12g, Rhizoma Anemarrhenae Aspheloidis (*Zhi Mu*), 10-12g, Concha Ostreae (*Mu Li*), 12-30g, Os Draconis (*Long Gu*), 12-30g

**ACUPUNCTURE:** *Tai Xi* (Ki 3), *San Yin Jiao* (Sp 6), *Guan Yuan* (CV 4), *Shen Shu* (Bl 23), *Shen Men* (Ht 7), *Nei Guan* (Per 6). Use even supplementing-even draining method at all points.

**ADDITIONS & SUBTRACTIONS:** If there is profuse sweating, add *He Gu* (LI 4) and *Fu Liu* (Ki 7).

## 2. HEART & KIDNEYS NOT INTERACTING PATTERN

**MAIN SYMPTOMS:** Scanty menses which are pale red in color or blocked menstruation, dizziness, tinnitus, vexation and agitation, insomnia, heart palpitations, impaired memory, low back and knee soreness and weakness, tidal heat, night sweats, constipation, short, reddish urination, a flushed red facial complexion, dry throat but no desire to drink, a red tongue tip with possible sores and scanty or no fur, and a fine, rapid or fine, weak, rapid pulse

**NOTE:** The red tongue tip and sores on the tip of the tongue combined with short, reddish, possibly painful urination differentiate this pattern from the above. In a lesser percentage of cases, this same named pattern may describe heart fire effulgence above with kidney yang vacuity below.

ANALYSIS OF SYMPTOMS: The above signs and symptoms are a combination of kidney yin vacuity with heart fire effulgence. Kidney yin vacuity signs and symptoms include scanty and/or blocked menstruation, dizziness, tinnitus, low back and knees soreness and weakness, short urination, thirst, constipation, scanty or no tongue fur, and a fine pulse. Signs and symptoms of heart fire effulgence include vexation and agitation, insomnia, heart palpitations, tidal heat, night sweats, sores on the tongue, reddish urine, a flushed red facial complexion, a red tongue tip, and a rapid pulse.

TREATMENT PRINCIPLES: Enrich yin and tranquilize the heart, quiet the spirit and promote the interaction between the heart and kidneys

FORMULA & MEDICINALS: *Liu Wei Di Huang Tang He Huang Lian E Jiao Tang* (Six Flavors Rehmannia Decoction plus Coptis & Donkey Skin Glue Decoction)

Cooked Radix Rehmanniae (*Shu Di*), 12-24g, Fructus Corni Officinalis (*Shan Zhu Yu*), 9g, Radix Dioscoreae Oppositae (*Shan Yao*), 9g, Sclerotium Poriae Cocos (*Fu Ling*), 9-15g, Cortex Radicis Moutan (*Dan Pi*), 9g, Rhizoma Alismatis (*Ze Xie*), 9g, Rhizoma Coptidis Chinensis (*Huang Lian*), 6-15g, Gelatinum Corii Asini (*E Jiao*), 9g, Radix Scutellariae Baicalensis (*Huang Qin*), 9-12g, Radix Albus Paeoniae Lactiflorae (*Bai Shao*), 9g, egg yolk (*Ji Zi Huang*), 2-3 pieces (stirred later into the strained, hot decoction)

Decoct one *ji* in water per day and administer orally in two divided doses, morning and evening.

ANALYSIS OF FORMULA: Cooked Rehmannia supplements the kidneys and enriches yin as do Donkey Skin Glue and egg yolks. Peony nourishes the blood, and the blood and essence share a common source. Cornus supplements both kidney yin and yang in an even way. Dioscorea supplements both the spleen and kidneys, while Poria supplements the spleen and seeps dampness. Moutan both clears vacuity heat and quickens the blood. Alisma seeps dampness and thus helps Poria lead yang into the yin tract. Coptis and Scutellaria clear heat and drain fire. In particular, Coptis is the main medicinal for clearing heat from the heart.

ACUPUNCTURE: *Shen Men* (Ht 7), *Da Ling* (Per 7), *Xin Shu* (Bl 15), *Tai Xi* (Ki 3), *San Yin Jiao* (Sp 6), *Shen Shu* (Bl 23). Drain the first three points and supplement the last three.

## 3. ASCENDANT LIVER YANG HYPERACTIVITY PATTERN

MAIN SYMPTOMS: Dizziness and vertigo with a sense of the feet not being grounded, head distention and pain, heart vexation, easy anger, hot sensations in the body and face especially in the afternoon, sweating, low back and knee soreness and weakness, profuse menstrual bleeding or lingering menstrual flow, a red tongue with scanty fur, and a fine, bowstring, rapid pulse

NOTE: This pattern is distinguished from the above two patterns by the prominent head distention and pain, dizziness and vertigo with a feeling of being ungrounded.

ANALYSIS OF SYMPTOMS: Dizziness, vertigo, a feeling of ungroundedness, head distention and pain, sweating, and hot sensations in the body and face all indicate yang counterflowing upward. Easy anger points to the liver, since anger is the affect of the liver. This is corroborated by the bowstring pulse. Low back and knee soreness and weakness, scanty tongue fur, and a fine pulse suggest underlying yin vacuity, with yin failing to control yang. The profuse menstrual bleeding, red tongue, and rapid pulse all show the presence of evil heat, heat and yang being one of a kind.

TREATMENT PRINCIPLES: Enrich yin and descend fire, level the liver and subdue yang

FORMULA & MEDICINALS: *Tian Ma Gou Teng Yin* (Gastrodia & Uncaria Drink)

Rhizoma Gastrodiae Elatae (*Tian Ma*), 10g, Ramulus Uncariae Cum Uncis (*Gou Teng*), 10-15g, Concha Haliotidis (*Shi Jue Ming*), 12-24g, Ramulus Loranthi Seu Visci (*Sang Ji Sheng*), 12-15g, Cortex Eucommiae Ulmoidis (*Du Zhong*), 10g, Radix Cyathulae (*Chuan Niu Xi*), 10g, Fructus Gardeniae Jasminoidis (*Zhi Zi*), 10g, Radix Scutellariae Baicalensis (*Huang Qin*), 10-12g, Herba Leonuri Heterophylli (*Yi Mu Cao*), 10g, Sclerotium Pararadicis Poriae Cocos (*Fu Shen*), 10-15g

Decoct one *ji* in water per day and administer orally in two divided doses, morning and evening.

ANALYSIS OF FORMULA: Within this formula, Gastrodia and Uncaria level and clear the liver. Abalone Shell heavily subdues yang, and Scutellaria and Gardenia clear the liver. Cyathula quickens the blood and leads it to move downward. Poria leads yang downward by seeping dampness, thus leading yang into the yin tract. Spirit of Poria also quiets the spirit. Leonurus quickens the blood without damaging yin blood, and Eucommia and Loranthus both supplement the liver and kidneys.

**ACUPUNCTURE:** *Tai Xi* (Ki 3), *San Yin Jiao* (Sp 6), *Guan Yuan* (CV 4), *Shen Shu* (Bl 23), *Feng Chi* (GB 20), *Bai Hui* (GV 20), *Tai Yang* (M-HN-9). Supplement the first four points and drain the rest.

**ADDITIONS & SUBTRACTIONS:** If there is headache, add *Lie Que* (Lu 7). If there is dizziness, add *Yin Tang* (M-HN-3).

## 4. LIVER WIND STIRRING INTERNALLY PATTERN

**MAIN SYMPTOMS:** Dizziness, vertigo, headache, tics and spasms, tremors, easy anger, vexation and agitation, a red tongue with scanty fur, and a fine, bowstring, possibly rapid pulse

**NOTE:** This pattern is differentiated from pattern #3 above primarily by the presence of tics, spasms, and tremors.

**ANALYSIS OF SYMPTOMS:** Dizziness, vertigo, headache, and tics and spasms, tremors, or even convulsions, when taken as a group are all wind signs and symptoms. Easy anger and the bowstring pulse indicate the disease is located in the liver, while the fine pulse and red tongue with scanty fur suggest yin vacuity. The vexation and agitation is due to vacuity heat and wind harassing and disquieting the heart spirit.

**TREATMENT PRINCIPLES:** Level the liver and extinguish wind

**FORMULA & MEDICINALS:** *Ling Yang Gou Teng Tang* (Antelope & Uncaria Decoction)

Cornu Caprae (*Shan Yang Jiao*), 12-15g, Folium Mori Albi (*Sang Ye*), 10g, Bulbus Fritillariae Cirrhosae (*Chuan Bei Mu*), 10g, uncooked Radix Rehmanniae (*Sheng Di*), 12-24g, Ramulus Uncariae Cum Uncis (*Gou Teng*), 10-12g, Sclerotium Poriae Cocos (*Fu Ling*), 10-15g, Flos Chrysanthemi Morifolii (*Ju Hua*), 10-15g, Radix Glycyrrhizae (*Gan Cao*), 6g, Caulis Bambusae In Taeniis (*Zhu Ru*), 10-12g, Radix Albus Paeoniae Lactiflorae (*Bai Shao*), 10-18g

Decoct one *ji* in water per day and administer orally in two divided doses, morning and evening.

**ANALYSIS OF FORMULA:** Goat Horn settles the liver and extinguishes wind. Uncaria settles and clears the liver and extinguishes wind. Folium Mori and Chrysanthemum clear the liver as does Caulis Bambusae. In addition, Caulis Bambusae downbears counterflow. Peony nourishes the blood and harmonizes the liver. Uncooked Rehmannia enriches yin and clears vacuity heat. Poria seeps dampness and leads yang back into the yin tract, while Licorice harmonizes all the medicinals in this formula.

**ADDITIONS & SUBTRACTIONS:** For hypertension, add Radix Achyranthis Bidentatae (*Huai Niu Xi*) and Fructus Tribuli Terrestris (*Bai Ji Li*).

**ACUPUNCTURE:** *Tai Xi* (Ki 3), *San Yin Jiao* (Sp 6), *Guan Yuan* (CV 4), *Shen Shu* (Bl 23), *Feng Chi* (GB 20), *Bai Hui* (GV 20), *Feng Fu* (GV 16), *Yin Tang* (M-HN-3). Supplement the first four points and drain the rest.

## 5. SPLEEN-KIDNEY YANG VACUITY PATTERN

**MAIN SYMPTOMS:** A somber white facial complexion, a withered, listless essence spirit, fatigue, lack of strength, impaired memory, low back and knee soreness and weakness, dizziness, poor appetite, abdominal distention, a bland, tastelessness in the mouth, thin, loose stools, frequent urination which is clear and long or scanty urination with edematous swelling possibly of the face, profuse, pale-colored menses, chilled extremities, especially chilled feet, decreased sexual desire, profuse, white, watery vaginal discharge, a pale, white tongue with thin, white fur, and a deep, small, moderate (*i.e.*, slightly slow); deep, weak; or deep, fine, forceless pulse

**NOTE:** This pattern rarely, if ever, presents perimenopausally in its pure form. However, it commonly complicates other perimenopausal patterns.

**ANALYSIS OF SYMPTOMS:** Fatigue, lack of strength poor appetite, abdominal distention, a bland, tasteless mouth, and thin, loose stools all specifically indicate spleen vacuity. Low back and knee soreness and weakness, clear, long urination, chilled feet, and decreased sexual desire all specifically indicate kidney yang vacuity. The other signs and symptoms all corroborate generalized yang qi vacuity.

**TREATMENT PRINCIPLES:** Warm and supplement the kidneys and spleen

**FORMULA & MEDICINALS:** *You Gui Wan Jia Wei* (Restore the Right [Kidney] Pills with Added Flavors)

Cooked Radix Rehmanniae (*Shu Di*), 12-24g, Radix Lateralis Praeparatus Aconiti Carmichaeli (*Fu Zi*), 6-10g, Cortex Cinnamomi Cassiae (*Rou Gui*), 6-10g, Radix Codonopsitis Pilosulae (*Dang Shen*), 10-18g, Fructus Psoraleae Corylifoliae (*Bu Gu Zhi*), 10g, Rhizoma Curculiginis Orchiodis (*Xian Mao*), 10-15g, Herba Epimedii (*Xian Ling Pi*), 10-15g, Fructus Corni Officinalis (*Shan Zhu Yu*), 10g, Fructus Lycii Chinensis (*Gou Qi Zi*), 10g, Radix Dioscoreae Oppositae (*Shan Yao*), 10g, Cortex Eucommiae Ulmoidis (*Du Zhong*), 10-12g, Radix Angelicae Sinensis (*Dang Gui*), 10g, Semen Cuscutae Chinensis (*Tu Si Zi*), 10g, Gelatinum Cornu Cervi (*Lu Jiao Jiao*), 10g (dissolved at end in the strained decoction)

Decoct one *ji* in water per day and administer orally in two divided doses, morning and evening.

**ANALYSIS OF FORMULA:** Cooked Rehmannia supplements the kidneys and enriches yin. Yin is the root of yang. Aconite and Cortex Cinnamomi strongly warm yang. Codonopsis specifically supplements the spleen qi, while Dioscorea supplements both the spleen and kidney qi and Psoralea supplements both spleen and kidney yang. Cornus supplements both kidney yin and yang. Cuscuta supplements and invigorates kidney yang but also boosts the essence. Deer Antler Glue, Eucommia, Curculigo, and Epimedium only supplement the kidneys and invigorate yang. Dang Gui nourishes and quickens the blood, and blood is the mother of the qi.

**ADDITIONS & SUBTRACTIONS:** If there is diarrhea, abdominal distention, and abdominal pain due to liver-spleen disharmony, delete Dang Gui and Lycium and add Rhizoma Atractylodis Macrocephalae (*Bai Zhu*), Pericarpium Citri Reticulatae (*Chen Pi*), stir-fried Radix Ledebouriellae Divaricatae (*Fang Feng*), and Radix Albus Paeoniae Lactiflorae (*Bai Shao*) to regulate the liver and to harmonize the spleen. If accompanied by profuse menstruation or flooding and leaking, add Cacumen Biotae Orientalis (*Ce Bai Ye*), carbonized Petriolus Trachycarpi (*Zong Lu*), and Radix Pseudoginseng (*San Qi*). For edema of the face and feet, delete cooked Rehmannia and add Cortex Sclerotii Poriae Cocos (*Fu Ling Pi*), uncooked Radix Astragali Membranacei (*Huang Qi*), and Radix Stephaniae Tetrandrae (*Feng Ji*).

**ACUPUNCTURE:** *PI SHU* (BL 20), *WEI SHU* (BL 21), *SHEN SHU* (Bl 23), *Ming Men* (GV 4), *Shen Que* (CV 8), *Zu San Li* (St 36). Moxa all points.

## 6. KIDNEY YIN & YANG DUAL VACUITY PATTERN

**MAIN SYMPTOMS:** Dizziness, vertigo, tinnitus, low back soreness and lack of strength, lack of warmth in the four extremities, alternating hot and cold sensations or hot above and cold below, decreased sexual desire, nocturia, a pale tongue with a red tip or a red tongue with scanty fur, and a deep, fine, bowstring or vacuous, surging, possibly rapid pulse

**NOTE:** This is the single most common pattern of perimenopausal complaints. However, it is usually complicated by other patterns as well, such as liver depression qi stagnation at the least.

**ANALYSIS OF SYMPTOMS:** Dizziness, vertigo, tinnitus, hot sensations above, a red tongue with scanty fur, and a fine, rapid, possibly surging pulse all indicate yin vacuity with heat above. Low back soreness can indicate any kidney vacuity, but cold sensations in the lower body, decreased sexual desire, nocturia, and a deep pulse indicate yang vacuity with cold below. A bowstring pulse indicates liver depression either due to liver blood vacuity or yang vacuity failing to warm and steam the liver.

**TREATMENT PRINCIPLES:** Supplement both kidney yin and yang aided by descending fire

**FORMULA & MEDICINALS:** *Er Xian Tang He Er Zhi Wan Jia Jian* (Two Immortals Decoction plus Two Ultimates Pills with Additions & Subtractions)

Rhizoma Curculiginis Orchioidis (*Xian Mao*), 10-15g, Herba Epimedii (*Xian Ling Pi*), 10-15g, Radix Angelicae Sinensis (*Dang Gui*), 10g, Rhizoma Anemarrhenae Aspheloidis (*Zhi Mu*), 10-12g, Cortex Phellodendri (*Huang Bai*), 10-12g, Fructus Ligustri Lucidi (*Nu Zhen Zi*), 12-15g, Herba Ecliptae Prostratae (*Han Lian Cao*), 12-15g

Decoct one *ji* in water per day and administer orally in two divided doses, morning and evening.

**ANALYSIS OF FORMULA:** Curculigo and Epimedium nourish liver blood at the same time as supplementing the kidneys and invigorating yang. Dang Gui nourishes the liver. Ligustrum and Eclipta enrich yin without being slimy and stagnating. And Anemarrhena and Phellodendron clear vacuity and help lead yang back to its lower source.

ADDITIONS & SUBTRACTIONS: If there are either night sweats, heart palpitations, or vexation and agitation, add *Gan Mai Da Zao Tang* (Licorice, Wheat & Red Dates Decoction): mix-fried Radix Glycyrrhizae (*Zhi Gan Cao*), Fructus Levis Tritici Aestivi (*Fu Xiao Mai*), and Fructus Zizyphi Jujubae (*Da Zao*). To increase this subsequent formula's heart-nourishing and spirit-quieting effects, also add Semen Biotae Orientalis (*Bai Ren*), Semen Zizyphi Spinosae (*Zao Ren*), and Sclerotium Pararadicis Poriae Cocos (*Fu Shen*). If there is concomitant spleen vacuity, add Radix Astragali Membranacei (*Huang Qi*), Radix Codonopsitis Pilosulae (*Dang Shen*), and mix-fried Radix Glycyrrhizae (*Gan Cao*). If there is concomitant liver depression, add Fructus Meliae Toosendan (*Chuan Lian Zi*) and Radix Auklandiae Lappae (*Mu Xiang*).

ACUPUNCTURE: *Tai Xi* (Ki 3), *San Yin Jiao* (Sp 6), *Qu Quan* (Liv 8), *Yin Xi* (Ht 6), *Shen Men* (Ht 7), *Bai Hui* (GV 20), *Shen Shu* (Bl 23), *Ming Men* (GV 4). Supplement the first three points, drain the next three, and moxa the last two.

## 7. HEART-SPLEEN DUAL VACUITY PATTERN

MAIN SYMPTOMS: Heart palpitations, shortness of breath, impaired memory, insomnia, a sallow yellow facial complexion, listless spirit, fatigue, lack of strength, reduced appetite, stomach and abdominal distention, a pale, fat, enlarged tongue with teeth-marks on its edges and thin fur, and a fine, soggy pulse

ANALYSIS OF SYMPTOMS: All these symptoms indicate either blood vacuity or spleen qi vacuity.

TREATMENT PRINCIPLES: Supplement the heart and nourish the blood, fortify the spleen and boost the qi

FORMULA & MEDICINALS: *Gui Pi Tang* (Restore the Spleen Decoction)

Radix Codonopsitis Pilosulae (*Ren Shen*), 10-18g, Radix Astragali Membranacei (*Huang Qi*), 10-60g, Radix Angelicae Sinensis (*Dang Gui*), 10g, Arillus Euphoriae Longanae (*Long Yan Rou*), 10-12g, Rhizoma Atractylodis Macrocephalae (*Bai Zhu*), 10-15g, Radix Auklandiae Lappae (*Mu Xiang*), 6-10g, Sclerotium Poriae Cocos (*Fu Ling*), 10-15g, Radix Polygalae Tenuifoliae (*Yuan Zhi*), 6-10g, Semen Zizyphi Spinosae (*Suan Zao Ren*), 12-25g, mix-fried Radix Glycyrrhizae (*Gan Cao*), 6-18g, uncooked Rhizoma Zingiberis (*Sheng Jiang*), 2-3 slices, Fructus Zizyphi Jujubae (*Da Zao*), 2-12 pieces

Decoct one *ji* in water per day and administer orally in two divided doses, morning and evening.

ANALYSIS OF FORMULA: Codonopsis, Astragalus, Atractylodes, Poria, and mix-fried Licorice all supplement the spleen and boost the qi. Poria also quiets the spirit. Red Dates, Longans, Dang Gui, and Zizyphus Spinosa nourish the blood and quiet the spirit. Polygala and Auklandia both rectify the qi. Polygala also transforms phlegm and quiets the spirit. Uncooked Ginger helps fortify the spleen, rectify the qi, and, when combined with Licorice and Red Dates, harmonizes the entire formula.

ADDITIONS & SUBTRACTIONS: If the kidneys are also vacuous, add cooked Radix Rehmanniae (*Shu Di*). If menstrual bleeding is profuse or there is flooding and leaking, add stir-fried Radix Sanguisorbae (*Di Yu*). If there is loss of sleep, add Os Draconis (*Long Gu*) and Concha Ostreae (*Mu Li*).

ACUPUNCTURE: *Xin Shu* (Bl 15), *Ge Shu* (Bl 17), *Pi Shu* (Bl 20), *Shen Men* (Ht 7), *Zu San Li* (St 36). Supplement all points.

## 8. LIVER DEPRESSION QI STAGNATION PATTERN

MAIN SYMPTOMS: Irritability, chest and epigastric fullness and oppression, rib-side distention and pain, a tendency to sigh frequently, a dark or normal colored tongue with thin, white fur, and a bowstring pulse

NOTE: This pattern essentially complicates all other perimenopausal patterns.

ANALYSIS OF SYMPTOMS: All these symptoms are due to an inhibited qi mechanism and the liver's loss of control over coursing and discharge.

TREATMENT PRINCIPLES: Course the liver and rectify the qi

FORMULA & MEDICINALS: *Xiao Yao San* (Rambling Powder)

Radix Bupleuri (*Chai Hu*), 10g, Radix Angelicae Sinensis (*Dang Gui*), 10g, Radix Albus Paeoniae Lactiflorae (*Bai Shao*), 10-15g, Rhizoma Atyractylodis Macrocephalae (*Bai Zhu*), 10g, Sclerotium Poriae Cocos (*Fu Ling*), 10-15g, mix-fried Radix Glycyrrhizae (*Gan Cao*), 6-10g, uncooked Rhizoma Zingiberis (*Sheng Jiang*), 2 slices, Herba Menthae Haplocalycis (*Bo He*), 3-6g

Decoct one *ji* in water per day and administer orally in two divided doses, morning and evening.

**ANALYSIS OF FORMULA:** Bupleurum courses the liver and rectifies the qi. It is aided in these functions by Mint. Atractylodes, Poria, and mix-fried Licorice all supplement the spleen and boost the qi. Poria and Licorice also quiet the spirit. Dang Gui and Peony nourish the blood and harmonize the liver. Peony also moderates or relaxes tension, and especially so when combined with Licorice. Uncooked Ginger helps Poria eliminate any dampness at the same time as it helps Bupleurum move the qi and disinhibit the qi mechanism.

**ADDITIONS & SUBTRACTIONS:** If liver depression transforms heat, then delete Ginger and Mint and add Cortex Radicis Moutan (*Dan Pi*) and Fructus Gardeniae Jasminoidis (*Zhi Zi*), thus creating *Dan Zhi Xiao Yao San* (Moutan & Gardenia Rambling Powder). If there is more serious blood and yin vacuity, add cooked Radix Rehmanniae (*Shu Di*), thus creating *Hei Xiao Yao San* (Black Rambling Powder).

**ACUPUNCTURE:** *Tai Chong* (Liv 3), *He Gu* (LI 4), *Zu San Li* (Per 6), *Nei Guan* (Per 6). Drain all points except *Zu San Li*, for which use even supplementing-even draining technique.

## 9. PHLEGM & QI MUTUALLY BINDING PATTERN

**MAIN SYMPTOMS:** Obesity, chest oppression, profuse phlegm, possible plum pit qi, abdominal distention, belching, nausea, lack of appetite, edema, loose stools, slimy, white tongue fur, and a slippery or slippery, bowstring pulse

**ANALYSIS OF SYMPTOMS:** Obesity is an indication of exuberant phlegm dampness. Profuse phlegm, plum pit qi, nausea, slimy tongue fur, and a slippery pulse all suggest the presence of phlegm. Chest oppression, abdominal distention, belching, and a bowstring pulse indicate liver depression qi stagnation, while lack of appetite, loose stools, and edema suggest an underlying spleen vacuity not controlling the movement and transformation of body fluids.

**TREATMENT PRINCIPLES:** Rectify the qi, transform phlegm, and fortify the spleen

**FORMULA & MEDICINALS:** *Ban Xia Hou Po Tang* (Pinellia & Magnolia Decoction)

Rhizoma Pinelliae Ternatae (*Ban Xia*), 10-12g, Cortex Magnoliae Officinalis (*Hou Pu*), 10g, Sclerotium Poriae Cocos (*Fu Ling*), 10-12g, uncooked Rhizoma Zingiberis (*Sheng Jiang*), 2-3 slices, Folium Perillae Frutescentis (*Su Ye*), 10g

Decoct one *ji* in water per day and administer orally in two divided doses, morning and evening.

**ANALYSIS OF FORMULA:** Within this formula, Pinellia, Magnolia, uncooked Ginger, and Folium Perillae all transform phlegm and downbear counterflow. In addition, Perilla harmonizes the liver and spleen, while Pinellia, Magnolia, and Ginger harmonize the stomach. Poria aids in the elimination of dampness and turbidity by fortifying the spleen and seeping dampness. It also quiets the spirit.

**ADDITIONS & SUBTRACTIONS:** For more severe qi stagnation, add Radix Bupleuri (*Chai Hu*), Tuber Curcumae (*Yu Jin*), Rhizoma Cyperi Rotundi (*Xiang Fu*), and Pericarpium Citri Reticulatae Viride (*Qing Pi*). For vomiting, add Fructus Amomi (*Sha Ren*) and Fructus Cardamomi (*Bai Dou Kou*). For more severe chest oppression and abdominal fullness, add Tuber Curcumae (*Yu Jin*) and Fructus Citri Aurantii (*Zhi Ke*). For chest pain, add Fructus Trichosanthis Kirlowii (*Gua Lou*) and Bulbus Allii (*Xie Bai*). For abdominal distention, add Fructus Amomi (*Sha Ren*). For rib-side pain, add Fructus Meliae Toosendan (*Chuan Lian Zi*) and Rhizoma Corydalis Yanhusuo (*Yan Hu Suo*). For pain and swelling in the throat, add Radix Scrophulariae Ningpoensis (*Yuan Shen*) and Radix Platycodi Grandiflori (*Jie Geng*).

**ACUPUNCTURE:** *Feng Long* (St 40), *Zhong Wan* (CV 12), *Nei Guan* (Per 6), *Dan Zhong* (CV 17). Drain all points.

**ADDITIONS & SUBTRACTIONS:** If there is plum pit qi, add *Tian Tu* (CV 22). If there is spleen vacuity, add *Zu San Li* (St 36) and *Pi Shu* (Bl 20).

## 10. PHLEGM HEAT HARASSING UPWARD PATTERN

**MAIN SYMPTOMS:** Vexation and agitation, profuse, possibly yellow phlegm, heart palpitations, insomnia, profuse dreams, chest oppression, possible nausea and vomiting, a red tongue with slimy, yellow fur, and a bowstring, slippery, rapid pulse

**ANALYSIS OF SYMPTOMS:** Heat is evidenced by the vexation and agitation, yellow-colored phlegm, red tongue with yellow fur, and rapid pulse. Phlegm is evidenced by the profuse phlegm, nausea and vomiting, slimy tongue fur, and slippery pulse. Concomitant qi stagnation is evidenced by the chest oppression and bowstring pulse. The heart palpitations, insomnia, and profuse dreams are due to a combination of heat and phlegm harassing the heart spirit.

TREATMENT PRINCIPLES: Clear heat and transform phlegm, course the liver and eliminate vexation

FORMULA & MEDICINALS: Wen Dan Tang (Warm the Gallbladder Decoction)

Rhizoma Pinelliae Ternatae (Ban Xia), 10-12g, Pericarpium Citri Reticulatae (Chen Pi), 10g, Sclerotium Poriae Cocos (Fu Ling), 10-12g, Fructus Immaturus Citri Aurantii (Zhi Shi), 6-10g, Caulis Bambusae In Taeniis (Zhu Ru), 10g, Radix Glycyrrhizae (Gan Cao), 3-6g, Fructus Zizyphi Jujubae (Da Zao), 2-3 pieces

Decoct one ji in water per day and administer orally in two divided doses, morning and evening.

ANALYSIS OF FORMULA: Within this formula, Pinellia transforms phlegm, and Caulis Bambusae clears depressive heat at the same time as it downbears counterflow. Orange Peel and Immature Aurantium rectify the qi and also transform phlegm. Poria supplements the spleen and seeps dampness. It also quiets the spirit. Licorice and Red Dates harmonize the other ingredients in the formula, but also supplement the heart and quiet the spirit in their own right.

ADDITIONS & SUBTRACTIONS: For a bitter taste in the mouth, add Rhizoma Coptidis Chinensis (Huang Lian). This then becomes Huang Lian Wen Dan Tang (Coptis Warm the Gallbladder Decoction). For headache, dizziness, vertigo, nausea, and vomiting, add Herba Agastachis Seu Pogostemi (Huo Xiang) and Rhizoma Acori Graminei (Shi Chang Pu). For dampness and heat, add Herba Artemisiae Apiaceae (Qing Hao) and Radix Scutellariae Baicalensis (Huang Qin). If there is abdominal distention, add Percarpium Arecae Catechu (Da Fu Pi) and Semen Raphani Sativi (Lai Fu Zi). If there is indigestion due to food stagnation, add Massa Medica Fermentata (Shen Qu) and Endothelium Corneum Gigeriae Galli (Nei Jin). If there is phlegm misting the portals of the heart, add Rhizoma Arisaematis (Nan Xing) and Rhizoma Acori Graminei (Chang Pu).

ACUPUNCTURE: Zhong Wan (CV 12), Feng Long (St 40), Dan Zhong (CV 17), Da Ling (Per 7), Xing Jian (Liv 2). Drain all points.

## 11. BLOOD STASIS OBSTRUCTING THE NETWORK VESSELS PATTERN

MAIN SYMPTOMS: Heart vexation, irritability, possible painful lumps in the breasts, possible flooding and leaking with dark-colored blood containing clots, possible uterine myomas, rib-side and abdominal distention and pain, heart palpitations, insomnia, hot flashes, symptoms worse at night, a dark, dusky facial complexion, visible broken capillaries or varicosities, chloasma or "liver spots" on the face and skin, black spots or floating threads in the visual field, a purple or dark-colored tongue with possible static spots or macules and thin, dry fur, and a bowstring, fine, choppy, and/or deep pulse

NOTE: This pattern primarily complicates other perimenopausal patterns.

ANALYSIS OF SYMPTOMS: Essentially all these signs and symptoms indicate blood stasis. The irritability is due to concomitant liver depression qi stagnation.

TREATMENT PRINCIPLES: Quicken the blood and dispel stasis

FORMULA & MEDICINALS: Gui Zhi Fu Ling Wan He Xue Fu Zhu Yu Tang (Cinnamon Twig & Poria Pills plus Blood Mansion Dispel Stasis Decoction)

Ramulus Cinnamomi Cassiae (Gui Zhi), 6-10g, Sclerotium Poriae Cocos (Fu Ling), 10-12g, Radix Rubrus Paeoniae Lactiflorae (Chi Shao), 10g, Cortex Radicis Moutan (Dan Pi), 10g, Semen Pruni Persicae (Tao Ren), 10g, Flos Carthami Tinctorii (Hong Hua), 10g, Radix Angelicae Sinensis (Dang Gui), 10g, Radix Ligustici Wallichii (Chuan Xiong), 10g, Radix Cyathulae Officinalis (Chuan Niu Xi), 10-12g, Radix Bupleuri (Chai Hu), 3-10g, Radix Platycodi Grandiflori (Jie Geng), 6g, Fructus Citri Aurantii (Zhi Ke), 6-10g, uncooked Radix Rehmanniae (Sheng Di), 12-15g, Radix Glycyrrhizae (Gan Cao), 3-6g

Decoct one ji in water per day and administer orally in two divided doses, morning and evening.

ANALYSIS OF FORMULA: Red Peony, Moutan, Persica, Carthamus, Ligusticum, Cyathula, and uncooked Rehmannia all quicken the blood and dispel stasis, Red Peony, Moutan, and uncooked Rehmannia also clear heat and cool the blood, while Cyathula leads the blood to move downwards. Dang Gui both nourishes and quickens the blood. Cinnamon Twigs lead the qi to move downward at the same time as freeing the flow of the channels and vessels via warming and moving. Poria induces the qi to move downwards by guiding yang into the yin tract. Bupleurum, Platycodon, and Aurantium all rectify the qi to move the blood. Bupleurum and Platycodon also upbear the clear. Licorice harmonizes all the other medicinals in this formula.

**ACUPUNCTURE:** *San Yin Jiao* (Sp 6), *Xue Hai* (Sp 10), *Tai Chong* (Liv 3), *He Gu* (LI 4). Drain all points.

**ADDITIONS & SUBTRACTIONS:** If there is lower abdominal pain, add *Gui Lai* (St 29), *Tian Shu* (St 25), *Zhong Ji* (CV 3), *Guan Yuan* (CV 4), and/or *Qi Hai* (CV 6). If there is chest pain, add *Dan Zhong* (CV 17) and *Nei Guan* (Per 6). If spirit unrest is marked, add *Shen Men* (Ht 7). If there is agitated stirring, add *Shi Xuan* (M-UE-1) and *Ren Zhong* (GV 26).

**CLINICAL TIPS:** Most Western women with perimenopausal syndrome have a liver-spleen disharmony as well as a liver blood-kidney yin and yang vacuity with some sort of internal heat. Either depressive or phlegm heat may exist coterminously with spleen qi and kidney yang vacuity below. Likewise, phlegm may exist simultaneously with yin vacuity and fluid dryness.

**ABSTRACTS OF REPRESENTATIVE CHINESE RESEARCH:**

*Tian Jin Zhong Yi (Tianjin Chinese Medicine)*, #3, 1994, p. 7-8: Zhang Da-ying describes the combined acupuncture and Chinese medicinal treatment of 557 cases of perimenopausal syndrome based on pattern discrimination. The women in this study were 45-55 years old, with an average age of 48. In 90% of cases, there was insomnia, while in 87.6% of cases there were profuse dreams, tenseness, agitation, easy anger, and restlessness. Patients were discriminated into three basic patterns: 1) yin vacuity-yang hyperactivity (226 cases), 2) qi stagnation and blood stasis (256 cases), and 3) phlegm dampness obstructing internally (35 cases). The yin vacuity-yang hyperactivity patients received *Geng Nian An Tang* (Climacteric-quieting Decoction) with individualized additions and subtractions. They were also needled at *Tai Xi* (Ki 3), *San Yin Jiao* (Sp 6), *Tai Chong* (Liv 3), *Shui Gou* (GV 26), and *Nei Guan* (Per 6) with individualized additional points following their symptoms. The qi stagnation and blood stasis patients received *Xue Fu Zhu Yu Tang* (Blood Mansion Dispel Stasis Decoction) with individualized additions and subtractions. They were needled at *Xue Hai* (Sp 10),

*San Yin Jiao* (Sp 6), *Tian Shu* (St 25), and *Zhang Men* (Liv 13). The phlegm dampness obstructing internally patients received *Wen Dan Tang* (Warm the Gallbladder Decoction) with added flavors depending on individual signs and symptoms, and they were needled at *Feng Long* (St 40), *Di Ji* (Sp 8), *Zu San Li* (St 36), *Li Gou* (Liv 5), and *Shui Gou* (GV 26). Of the 557 patients treated with the above protocol, 18 cases (3.2%) were judged completely cured, 227 cases (40.8%) were markedly improved, 298 cases (53.3%) got some effect, and 14 cases (2.5%) got no effect. Thus the total amelioration rate was 97.3%.

*Guo Yi Lun Tan (Forum on Chinese Medicine)*, #5, 1996, p. 37: Cao Guo-rong describes the treatment of 22 cases of menopausal syndrome with *Bu Xin Tang Jia Wei* (Supplement the Heart Decoction with Added Flavors). *Bu Xin Tang Jia Wei* consisted of: cooked Radix Rehmanniae (*Shu Di*), uncooked Radix Rehmanniae (*Sheng Di*), Radix Scrophulariae Ningpoensis (*Xuan Shen*), Semen Zizyphi Spinosae (*Suan Zao Ren*), Tuber Ophiopogonis Japonici (*Mai Dong*), Tuber Asparagi Cochinensis (*Tian Men Dong*), Radix Salviae Miltiorrhizae (*Dan Shen*), Sclerotium Poriae Cocos (*Fu Ling*), and Radix Angelicae Sinensis (*Dang Gui*), 12g each, Fructus Schisandrae Chinensis (*Wu Wei Zi*), Radix Codonopsitis Pilosulae (*Dang Shen*), Semen Biotae Orientalis (*Bai Zi Ren*), Radix Polygalae Tenuifoliae (*Yuan Zhi*), and Cortex Radicis Lycii Chinensis (*Di Gu Pi*), 10g each, Concha Ostreae (*Mu Li*) and Os Draconis (*Long Gu*), 20g each, Radix Platycodi Gandiflori (*Jie Geng*), 6g, and Cinnabar (*Zhu Sha*), 2g. One ji of these medicinals were administered per day with individual additions and subtractions, and all the patients in this study obtained a full recovery with administration of 8-32 ji.

*Yun Nan Zhong Yi Zhong Yao Za Zhi (Yunnan Journal of Chinese Medicine & Chinese Medicinals)*, #5, 1996, p. 19: Guo Xiao-ming treated 58 cases of menopausal syndrome using the methods of supplementing the kidneys and quieting the heart. The major symptoms of this group of patients were dizziness, tinnitus, heart palpitations, agitation, heart fluster, easy anger, tidal heat, sweating, insomnia, and profuse dreams. The basic formula consisted of: cooked Radix Rehmanniae (*Shu Di*), Fructus Corni Officinalis (*Shan Zhu Yu*), Fructus Lycii Chinensis (*Gou Qi Zi*), calcined Os Draconis (*Long Gu*), calcined Concha Ostreae (*Mu Li*), and Caput Rhizomatis Nelumbinis Nuciferae (*He Ding*). Depending on whether patients manifested predominantly yin vacuity (43 cases) or predominantly yang hyperactivity (15 cases), other medicinals were added as well as yet other additions based on major symptoms or complaints. Within 6-8 *ji* of these medicinals, 48 cases registered marked improvement, and the other 10 cases improved. Thus the total amelioration rate was 100%.

*Bei Jing Zhong Yi (Beijing Chinese Medicine)*, #3, 1988, p. 17: In this clinical audit, Ma Sheng-hua reported on the treatment of 179 cases of menopausal syndrome via the liver. These women's symptoms consisted of hot flashes, red face, sweating, emotional dysphoria, dizziness and vertigo, heart palpitations, and insomnia. The diagnostic criteria for inclusion in this study were based on *Fu Chan Ke Xue (A Study of Gynecology & Obstetrics)*, while the criteria for pattern discrimination were based on *Zhong Yi Bing Zheng Zhen Duan Liao Xiao Biao Zhun (Criteria for Chinese Medical Diseases, Patterns, Diagnosis, Treatment & Effects)*. Patients in this study were discriminated into four patterns: 1) liver depression qi stagnation (56 cases), 2) heart-liver fire effulgence (74 cases), 3) liver-kidney yin vacuity (32 cases), and 4) liver blood-spleen qi vacuity (17 cases). Patients in each of these four groups received one *ji* per day of a Chinese medicinal formula prescribed for that group, and 4-6 weeks equaled one course of treatment.

Among the 56 cases of liver depression qi stagnation, 11 got a marked effect, 36 got some effect, and nine got no effect. Among the 74 cases of heart-liver fire effulgence, 15 got a marked effect, 48 got some effect, and 11 got no effect. Among the 32 cases of liver-kidney yin vacuity, six got a marked effect, 20 got some effect, and six got no effect, and among the 17 cases of liver-spleen dual vacuity, three got a marked effect, 11 got some effect, and three got no effect. Thus the total amelioration rate was 82.4%.

*Si Chuan Zhong Yi (Sichuan Chinese Medicine)*, #4, 1998, p. 38-39: Fu Ji-hong *et al.* reported on the treatment of 48 cases of menopausal syndrome with *Xiong Ju Qin Yao Tang* (Ligusticum, Chrysanthemum, Scutellaria & Peony Decoction). All the women in this study were 43-55 years old. Among them, there were eight cases of kidney yin vacuity, three cases of kidney yang vacuity, 24 cases of liver depression (17 of which had transformed fire and seven of which had transformed ascendant liver yang hyperactivity), six cases of spleen vacuity with exuberant dampness, and seven cases of heart-spleen dual vacuity. *Xiong Ju Qin Shao Tang* consisted of: Radix Ligustici

Wallichii (*Chuan Xiong*), Fructus Crataegi (*Shan Zha*), Radix Scutellariae Baicalensis (*Huang Qin*), Fructus Immaturus Sophorae Japonicae (*Huai Hua Mi*), Ramulus Loranthi Seu Visci (*Sang Ji Sheng*), Spica Prunellae Vulgaris (*Xia Ku Cao*), Flos Chrysanthemi Morifolii (*Ju Hua*), and Radix Albus Paeoniae Lactiflorae (*Bai Shao*), 20g each, Radix Salviae Miltiorrhizae (*Dan Shen*) and Rhizoma Alismatis (*Ze Xie*), 24g each, and uncooked Concha Ostreae (*Mu Li*), 30g. If there was kidney yang vacuity, *You Gui Wan* (Restore the Right [Kidney] Pills) were also prescribed. If there was kidney yin vacuity, *Zuo Gui Wan* (Restore the Left [Kidney] Pills) were also prescribed. If there was spleen vacuity, *Gui Pi Tang* (Restore the Spleen Decoction) with additions and subtractions was concomitantly administered. Using this protocol, 35 cases were cured, 12 cases improved, and only one case experienced no result. Thus the total amelioration rate was 98.2%.

*Si Chuan Zhong Yi (Sichuan Chinese Medicine)*, #6, 1999, p. 38: In this clinical audit, Luo Dai-hua reported on the treatment of 35 cases of menopausal syndrome. The women in this study were 43-57 years old. Their main symptoms included alternating hot and cold, spontaneous perspiration and night sweats, dizziness and vertigo, low back soreness, heart vexation, insomnia, and tenseness, agitation, and easy anger. All these patients received *Geng Nian Yin* (Climacteric Drink) with additions and subtractions based on their main complaints. *Geng Nian Yin* consisted of: uncooked Radix Rehmanniae (*Sheng Di*), Radix Lithospermi Seu Arnebiae (*Zi Cao*), Ramulus Loranthi Seu Visci (*Sang Ji Sheng*), Ramulus Uncariae Cum Uncis (*Gou Teng*), and Fructus Germinatus Hordei Vulgaris (*Mai Ya*), 15g each, Herba Epimedii (*Xian Ling Pi*), Radix Angelicae Sinensis (*Dang Gui*), and Rhizoma Cyperi Rotundi (*Xiang Fu*), 10g each. One *ji* was administered per day. Of these 35 cases, 24 (68.5%) were cured, 10 cases (28.5%) improved, and one case (2%) got no result. Thus the total amelioration rate was 98%. The largest number of *ji* administered was 42, the smallest was five, and the average was 11.

*Si Chuan Zhong Yi (Sichuan Chinese Medicine)*, #8, 1999, p. 49: In this study, Li Shi-qian treated 100 cases of menopausal syndrome with *Du Qi Wan Jia Chai Shao Gui* (Capital Qi Pills plus Bupleurum, Peony & Cinnamon). The women in this study were 40-55 years of age, with a median age of 46, and all experienced varying degrees of tidal heat, heart fluster, easy agitation, impaired memory, and torpid intake. *Du Qi Wan Jia Chai Shao Gui* consisted of: uncooked Radix Rehmanniae (*Sheng Di*), 24g, Radix Dioscoreae Oppositae (*Shan Yao*), Sclerotium Poriae Cocos (*Fu Ling*), and Radix Albus Paeoniae Lactiflorae (*Bai Shao*), 15g each, Semen Zizyphi Spinosae (*Suan Zao Ren*), Rhizoma Alismatis (*Ze Xie*), Cortex Radicis Moutan (*Dan Pi*), Radix Bupleuri (*Chai Hu*), and Ramulus Cinnamomi Cassiae (*Gui Zhi*), 10g each, and Fructus Schisandrae Chinensis (*Wu Wei Zi*), 6g. Additions and subtractions were made on an individual basis depending on major complaints, with one *ji* of medicinals being administered per day. Using this protocol, 68 cases registered a marked effect, 23 cases got some effect, and nine cases got no effect for a total amelioration rate of 91%. The smallest number of *ji* were 10, the largest was 30, and the average was 15.

❖

*Bei Jing Zhong Yi (Beijing Chinese Medicine)*, #2, 1998, p. 28-29: In this clinical audit, Ma Yue-hong reported on the treatment of 40 cases of menopausal syndrome with *Bu Xin Dan Jia Jian* (Supplement the Heart Elixir with Additions & Subtractions). The women in this study were 46-55 years old. Clinically, their main symptoms were heart palpitations, heart fluster, hot flashes, sweating, vacuity vexation, insomnia, dizziness, tinnitus, emotional lability, tension, agitation, and easy anger. *Bu Xin Dan Jia Jian* consisted of: uncooked Radix Rehmanniae (*Sheng Di*), Radix Angelicae Sinensis (*Dang Gui*), Tuber Ophiopogonis Japonici (*Mai Dong*), Semen Biotae Orientalis (*Bai Zi Ren*), Semen Zizyphi Spinosae (*Suan Zao Ren*), Radix Pseudostellariae (*Tai Zi Shen*), Radix Scrophulariae Ningpoensis (*Xuan Shen*), Radix Salviae Miltiorrhizae (*Dan Shen*), Sclerotium Poriae Cocos (*Fu Ling*), Radix Polygalae Tenuifoliae (*Yuan Zhi*), Fructus Schisandrae Chinensis (*Wu Wei Zi*), Bulbus Lilii (*Bai He*), and Concha Margaritiferae (*Zhen Zhu Mu*). Individual additions and subtractions were made to this base formula based on pattern discrimination and major complaints. Ten *ji* equaled one course of treatment. Diagnostic and outcome criteria were based on *Zhong Yi Bing Zheng Zhen Duan Liao Xiao Biao Zhun* (Criteria for Chinese Medical Diseases, Patterns, Diagnosis, Treatment & Effects). Based on these criteria, 22 cases (55%) were cured, 17 cases (42.5%) improved, and one case (2.5%) got no effect. Therefore, the total amelioration rate was 97.5%. The largest number of *ji* administered was 40 and the smallest was 15.

❖

*Zhe Jiang Zhong Yi Za Zhi (Zhejiang Journal of Chinese*

*Medicine)*, #11, 1999, p. 477: Ye Feng and Yang Hai-hua treated 60 cases of menopausal syndrome with *Gui Zhi Tang Jia Wei* (Cinnamon Twig Decoction with Added Flavors). All the women in this study were 42-58 years of age, with a median age of 50.3 years. Main symptoms included facial flushing, easy sweating, menstrual irregularity, headache, dizziness, vexation and agitation, easy anger, nervous tension, heart palpitations, insomnia, and restlessness. The basic formula consisted of: Ramulus Cinnamomi Cassiae (*Gui Zhi*), Radix Albus Paeoniae Lactiflorae (*Bai Shao*), Radix Glycyrrhizae (*Gan Cao*), Tuber Curcumae (*Yu Jin*), and Fructus Citri Sacrodactylis (*Fo Shou*), 9g each, Radix Angelicae Sinensis (*Dang Gui*) and uncooked Radix Rehmanniae (*Sheng Di*), 12g each, Fructus Zizyphi Jujubae (*Da Zao*), 30g, and uncooked Rhizoma Zingiberis (*Sheng Jiang*), 3g. One *ji* was administered per day, with 28 days equaling one course, and modifications were made for the patterns of 1) liver fire tending towards hyperactivity, 2) heart and kidneys not interacting, 3) heart-spleen dual vacuity, and 4) phlegm dampness brewing and binding. Using this protocol, 24 patients were deemed cured and 36 improved. Thus the amelioration rate was 100%.

❖

*Jiang Su Zhong Yi (Jiangsu Chinese Medicine)*, #3, 1999, p. 30: Wang Li-feng treated 40 cases of menopausal syndrome with *Zi Shen Qing Xin Tang* (Enrich the Kidneys & Clear the Heart Decoction). All the women in this study were 42-55 years of age. Major symptoms included menstrual irregularity, tidal heat, sweating, and emotional lability. *Zi Shen Qing Xin Tang* consisted of: uncooked Radix Rehmanniae (*Sheng Di*), Fructus Ligustri Lucidi (*Nu Zhen Zi*), Herba Ecliptae Prostratae (*Han Lian Cao*), Sclerotium Poriae Cocos (*Fu Ling*), and stir-fried Semen Zizyphi Spinosae (*Suan Zao Ren*), 12g each, calcined Concha Cypraeae Maculae (*Zi Bei Chi*), 20g, and Plumula Nelumbinis Nuciferae (*Lian Xin*), Cortex Albizziae Julibrissinis (*He Huan Pi*), and Fructus Levis Tritici Aestivi (*Fu Xiao Mai*), 10g each. One *ji* was administered per day, and modifications were made on the basis of five complicating patterns: 1) liver channel depressive fire, 2) spleen-stomach disharmony, 3) phlegm turbidity, 4) blood stasis, and 5) kidney yang vacuity. Using this protocol, 30 cases experienced a marked effect, eight got some effect, and two got no effect for a total amelioration rate of 95%.

*Shang Hai Zhong Yi Yao Za Zhi (Shanghai Journal of Chinese Medicine & Medicinals)*, #5, 1999, p. 29: Cheng Ke-lan treated 36 cases of menopausal syndrome with *Xiao Yao*

*San Jia Jian* (Rambling Powder with Additions & Subtractions). The women in this study ranged from 40-55 years of age. Psycho-emotional and functional neurological symptoms included vexation and agitation, easy anger, a tendency to sorrow, easy fright, insomnia, profuse dreams, heart palpitations, fearful throbbing, sweating, and tidal heat. The formula consisted of: Radix Albus Paeoniae Lactiflorae (*Bai Shao*), Radix Angelicae Sinensis (*Dang Gui*), and Fructus Lycii Chinensis (*Gou Qi Zi*), 15g each, Semen Zizyphi Spinosae (*Suan Zao Ren*), Sclerotium Poriae Cocos (*Fu Ling*), and Rhizoma Atractylodis Macrocephalae (*Bai Zhu*), 12g each, mix-fried Radix Glycyrrhizae (*Gan Cao*), 9g, Radix Bupleuri (*Chai Hu*), 6g, and dry Rhizoma Zingiberis (*Gan Jiang*), 3 slices. One *ji* was administered per day, modified based on four complicating patterns: 1) yin vacuity-liver depression (16 cases), 2) heart-lung depression and binding (8 cases), 3) heart and kidneys not interacting (6 cases), and 4) spleen-kidney yang vacuity (6 cases). Criteria for pattern discrimination were based on *Shang Hai Shi Zhong Yi Zhen Liao Chang Gui* (*Shanghai Municipal Standards for Chinese Medical Diagnosis & Treatment*). Using this protocol, 23 patients were cured, nine improved, and four got no result. Thus the total amelioration rate was 88.8%.

❖

*Shang Hai Zhong Yi Ya Za Zhi* (*Shanghai Journal of Chinese Medicine & Medicinals*), #8, 1999, p. 30: Wang Wen-wei and Xu Jian-zhong treated 32 cases of menopausal syndrome with *Yi Geng Tang* (Control the Climacteric Decoction). The women in this study were 43-56 years of age, the criteria for menopausal syndrome were Kuppeman's criteria of 1959, and mental-emotional and functional neurological compliants included tidal heat, insomnia, dizziness, heart palpitations, vexation and agitation, insomnia, depression, and sweating. *Yi Geng Tang* consisted of undisclosed amounts of: Herba Epimedii (*Xian Ling Pi*), Radix Morindae Officinalis (*Ba Ji Tian*), uncooked Radix Rehmanniae (*Sheng Di*), Radix Albus Paeoniae Lactiflorae (*Bai Shao*), Fructus Lycii Chinensis (*Gou Qi Zi*), Semen Cuscutae Chinensis (*Tu Si Zi*), Plastrum Testudinis (*Gui Ban*), Herba Cistanchis Deserticolae (*Rou Cong Rong*), Rhizoma Anemarrhenae Aspheloidis (*Zhi Mu*), Cortex Phellodendri (*Huang Bai*), Rhizoma Coptidis Chinensis (*Huang Lian*), and Sclerotium Poriae Cocos (*Fu Ling*). One *ji* was administered per day, three months equaled one course, and modifications were made on the basis of five complicating patterns: 1) yin vacuity, 2) yang vacuity, 3) ascendant liver yang hyperactivity, 4) qi stagnation, and 5) phlegm obstruction. After one course of treatment, 12 cases got a

marked effect, 16 cases got some effect, and four cases got no effect for a total amelioration rate of 87.5%.

REPRESENTATIVE CASE HISTORIES:

### ❖ CASE 1[2] ❖

The patient was a 52 year old female worker who complained of facial flushing, sweating, tenseness, agitation, and easy anger for one month. This patient was first examined on Oct. 12, 1998. For the last half year, this woman's menstrual cycle had been irregular, sometimes coming as short as 20 days and as long as 90 days. The menses were scanty, and they contained clots. In addition, the patient reported heart palpitations, chest oppression, and clamoring stomach. She had been examined at a hospital and prescribed a multi-vitamin and vitamin $B_1$ but without effect. Her tongue edges and tip were red with thin, white fur, while her pulse was fine and bowstring. Therefore, her pattern was categorized as liver-kidney insufficiency with water not moistening wood and yin and yang loss of regularity. She was administered *Gui Zhi Tang Jia Wei* (Cinnamon Twig Decoction with Added Flavors) as described above under "Representative abstracts" plus nine grams each of Cortex Radicis Moutan (*Dan Pi*) and Fructus Gardeniae Jasminoidis (*Zhi Zi*). After taking seven *ji* the facial flushing and sweating were decreased, but all her other symptoms remained. Therefore, Fructus Meliae Toosendan (*Chuan Lian Zi*), 9g, Fructus Cardamomi (*Bai Dou Kou*), 6g, and Fructus Lycii Chinensis (*Gou Qi Zi*), 12g, were added. After taking seven *ji* of this prescription, all her symptoms were greatly reduced, and, after 14 *ji*, all her symptoms were cured.

### ❖ CASE 2[3] ❖

The patient was a 49 year old female who was first examined on Apr. 20, 1997. This woman's menstruation had been ceased for two years. She complained of vexatious heat in the five hearts, insomnia, heart palpitations, vexation and agitation, easy anger, hot flashes, sweating, dizziness, tinnitus, low back soreness, upper back pain, epigastric distention, a dry mouth, nocturnal polyuria, and poor appetite. Her tongue edges and tip were red with thin, white fur, and her pulse was bowstring and fine. Based on these signs and symptoms, her pattern was categorized as kidney vacuity with liver depression and she was prescribed the following formula: uncooked Radix Rehmanniae (*Sheng Di*), 24g, Semen Zizyphi Spinosae (*Suan Zao Ren*), Rhizoma Alismatis (*Ze Xie*), Fructus Mori Albi (*Sang Shen*), Cortex Radicis Moutan (*Dan Pi*), Radix Bupleuri (*Chai Hu*), Ramulus Cinnamomi Cassiae (*Gui Zhi*), and Rhizoma Anemarrhenae Aspheloidis (*Zhi Mu*),

10g each, Sclerotium Pararadicis Poriae Cocos (*Fu Shen*), 30g, Radix Albus Paeoniae Lactiflorae (*Bai Shao*), Radix Dioscoreae Oppositae (*Shan Yao*), Cortex Phellodendri (*Huang Bai*), Fructus Lycii Chinensis (*Gou Qi Zi*), and Flos Chrysanthemi Morifolii (*Ju Hua*), 15g each, and Fructus Schisandrae Chinensis (*Wu Wei Zi*), 6g. One *ji* was decocted in water and administered per day.

After taking five *ji* of the above medicinals, the vexatious heat in the five hearts, insomnia, and heart palpitations improved, while the hot flashes, and sweating disappeared, the emotions improved, and all the other symptoms decreased. Therefore, another 10 *ji* of the same medicinals were administered, after which all her symptoms disappeared and the patient was judged clinically cured. In order to secure the therapeutic effect, the woman was prescribed *Zhi Bai Di Huang Wan* (Anemarrhena & Phellodendron Rehmannia Pills).

❖ CASE 3[4] ❖

The patient was a 48 year old female who was first examined on May 20, 1997. This woman's menses had been irregular for two years. Their amount was scanty, their color was red, and her cycle was long. For the last half year, the woman had experienced marked emotional abnormality. She was vexed and agitated and easily angered. In addition, she complained of chest and rib-side distention and pain, facial flushing and hot flashes, heart palpitations, impaired memory, headache, sweating, low back soreness and lower limb weakness, insomnia, and anxiety. Her tongue was red with thin, yellow fur, and her pulse was bowstring, fine, and slightly rapid. The woman had previously been treated with *Xiao Yao San Jia Jian* (Rambling Powder with Additions & Subtractions) without effect.

Based on these signs and symptoms, the woman was diagnosed as suffering from menopausal syndrome, and her pattern was categorized as kidney yin insufficiency with loss of harmony of the heart and liver. Therefore, she was prescribed *Zuo Gui Yin Jia Jian* (Restore the Left [Kidney] Drink with Additions & Subtractions): Fructus Lycii Chinensis (*Gou Qi Zi*), Radix Albus Paeoniae Lactiflorae (*Bai Shao*), and Fructus Ligustri Lucidi (*Nu Zhen Zi*), 15g each, uncooked Radix Rehmanniae (*Sheng Di*), Concha Margaritiferae (*Zhen Zhu Mu*), and Caulis Polygoni Multiflori (*Ye Jiao Teng*), 20g each, Fructus Corni Officinalis (*Shan Zhu Yu*), Semen Zizyphi Spinosae (*Suan Zao Ren*), Flos Chrysanthemi Morifolii (*Ju Hua*), and Ramulus Uncariae Cum Uncis (*Gou Teng*), 12g each, Radix Bupleuri (*Chai Hu*), 6g, and Radix Glycyrrhizae (*Gan Cao*), 3g.

After taking four *ji* of the above medicinals, the woman's hot flashes and headache went away and all her other symptoms improved. Therefore, Chrysanthemum and Uncaria were removed and 12 grams of Radix Polygoni Multiflori (*He Shou Wu*) and 10 grams of Radix Angelicae Sinensis (*Dang Gui*) were added. After taking eight *ji* of this formula, all the patient's symptoms were completely eliminated. On follow-up after one year, the patient's condition was fine and there had been no recurrence of the previous signs and symptoms.

❖ CASE 4[5] ❖

The patient was a 42 year old female who was first examined on Jun. 26, 1997. The woman was obese, her menses were regular, and she had no history of menstrual pain. For the last two months, this patient experienced upper back coldness, a desire for warmth, dizziness, headache, epigastric oppression, vomiting, heart palpitations, profuse dreams, a slight degree of lower limb edema, low back pain, a tendency to sorrow and crying for no reason, and nocturnal polyuria. The woman had been treated by a number of other doctors with various formulas to no effect. When examined by the author of this case, her facial complexion was greenish yellow. The woman was wearing thick clothes, her tongue was pale with slimy, white fur, and her pulse was soggy and moderate (*i.e.*, slightly slow). The internal medicine department had diagnosed this woman with functional neurological disorder and rheumatic arthritis, while the gynecology department had diagnosed her with menopausal syndrome.

Based on the above signs and symptoms the woman's Chinese medical pattern was discriminated as kidney yang insufficiency with dampness obstructing and not moving. Therefore, she was prescribed *Bu Shen Tang He Er Chen Tang Jia Jian* (Supplement the Kidneys Decoction plus Two Aged [Ingredients] Decoction with Additions & Subtractions): Fructus Corni Officinalis (*Shan Zhu Yu*), Radix Dioscoreae Oppositae (*Shan Yao*), Sclerotium Poriae Cocos (*Fu Ling*), Herba Epimedii (*Xian Ling Pi*), Fructus Rubi Chingii (*Fu Pen Zi*), and cooked Radix Rehmanniae (*Shu Di*), 12g each, Rhizoma Curculiginis Orchioidis (*Xian Mao*), lime-processed Rhizoma Pinelliae Ternatae (*Ban Xia*), Pericarpium Citri Reticulatae (*Chen Pi*), and Fructus Amomi (*Sha Ren*), 10g each, Semen Coicis Lachryma-jobi (*Yi Yi Ren*), 20g, and Radix Glycyrrhizae (*Gan Cao*), 3g.

After taking four *ji* of the above formula, the patient's fear of cold decreased and her nausea and vomiting stopped. At this point, the patient's tongue fur was thin and white and her pulse was deep and moderate. Therefore, Coix and Pinellia were removed from the original formula and 20 grams of Radix Astragali Membranacei (*Huang Qi*), 10g each of Fructus Psoraleae Corylifoliae (*Bu Gu Zhi*), Succinum (*Hu Po*), and Cortex Eucommiae Ulmoidis (*Du Zhong*), and 12 grams of Fructus Rosae Laevigatae (*Jin Ying Zi*) were added. After taking 30 *ji* of this prescription, all the patient's symptoms were eliminated and the patient was judged cured. On follow-up after three months, there had been no recurrence.

### ❖ CASE 5[6] ❖

The patient was a 55 year old female who was first examined on Jun. 22, 1986. In 1982, this woman's menstrual cycle had become irregular and she had started to have hot flashes which had gradually increased in severity. In addition, there was dizziness, heart vexation, a dry mouth, a feeling of internal heat, anger, tenseness, and agitation. The patient's last menses had begun on Apr. 10, 1986 and had lasted for five days. Its amount tended to be profuse. There had been no menstruation the last two months. The patient had three children and had had three artificial abortions. She had a history of hypertension, her tongue fur was thin and slimy, and her pulse was fine and bowstring.

Based on the above signs and symptoms, the patient was treated with the following principles: nourish yin and level the liver, clear the heart and quiet the spirit. The medicinals she was administered consisted of: uncooked Radix Rehmanniae (*Sheng Di*), 30g, uncooked Radix Albus Paeoniae Lactiflorae (*Bai Shao*), 15g, uncooked Radix Cynanchi Atrati (*Bai Wei*), 9g, Concha Haliotidis (*Shi Jue Ming*), 30g, Dens Draconis (*Long Chi*), 15g, Rhizoma Coptidis Chinensis (*Huang Lian*), 3g, Tuber Ophiopogonis Japonici (*Mai Dong*), 9g, Flos Chrysanthemi Morifolii (*Ju Hua*), 9g, and Herba Ecliptae Prostratae (*Han Lian Cao*), 15g.

After taking 14 *ji* of the above formula, the patient's sleep was good and her heart vexation, internal heat, hot flashes, and sweating were all markedly improved. Her oral dryness was also decreased. However, there was abdominal distention, many bowel movements per day, and repeated flatulence. Her pulse was now deep, fine, and bowstring, and her tongue fur was thin. Therefore, Folium Mori Albi (*Sang Ye*), 9g, Sclerotium Polypori Umbellati (*Zhu Ling*), 15g, Sclerotium Poriae Cocos (*Fu Ling*), 15g, Radix Salviae Miltiorrhizae (*Dan Shen*), 9g, and Pericarpium Arecae Catechu (*Da Fu Pi*), 9g, were added and another 14 *ji* were prescribed.

The patient's third examination occurred on Aug. 3. All her symptoms had improved, but there was still some internal heat and sweating. Thus nine grams of Radix Scutellariae Baicalensis (*Huang Qin*) were added to the above formula and another 14 *ji* were prescribed. On Aug. 17, the patient reported that the internal heat and sweating were gone and that the volume of her urine had increased. Her blood pressure was normal (17/11kPa), and her menses had not come in four months. Therefore the patient was given another two weeks of the same formula to consolidate the therapeutic effect.

### ❖ CASE 6[7] ❖

The patient was a 53 year old female who was first examined on Aug. 17, 1997. The woman's menses had stopped two years ago. For the last year, she had experienced recurrent bouts of dizziness, heart palpitations, and insomnia. She had difficulty controlling herself emotionally and easily became angry. When her condition was severe, she could not lie down quietly and was not able to go to sleep at night. This resulted in her not being able to go to work like normal. The patient had been previously administered *Xiao Yao San* (Rambling Powder) and *Huang Lian E Jiao Tang* (Coptis & Donkey Skin Glue Decoction). These had lessened her symptoms, but, when she stopped taking them, her symptoms would return. On examination, the patient's tongue tended towards red with thin fur, and her pulse was fine and somewhat rapid. The respiratory sounds in both the patient's lungs were normal, her ECG was normal, and her blood pressure was 140/90mmHg. Her Western medical diagnosis was climacteric syndrome, and her Chinese pattern was categorized as liver-kidney yin vacuity with loss of regulation of yin and yang. Her Chinese medicinal formula consisted of: Herba Epimedii (*Xian Ling Pi*), 12g, Rhizoma Anemarrhenae Aspheloidis (*Zhi Mu*), 10g, Cortex Phellodendri (*Huang Bai*), 10g, Radix Salviae Miltirorrhizae (*Dan Shen*), 10g, uncooked Concha Ostreae (*Mu Li*), 15g, uncooked Os Draconis (*Long Gu*), 15g, uncooked Radix Rehmanniae (*Sheng Di*), 15g, and Radix Bupleuri (*Chai Hu*), 6g. One *ji* of this formula was administered per day for one half month, after which all her symptoms had basically disappeared. Her blood pressure descended to 118/82mmHg, and the patient was already back at work. On numerous follow-ups, none of this woman's symptoms had returned.

### ENDNOTES

[1] *Tian gui* means heavenly water. Sometimes *tian gui* means the menstruate and sometimes it is seen as something more basic or fundamental. In this instance, readers may equate it with the menses.

[2] Ye Feng & Yang Hai-hua, "The Treatment of 30 Cases of Climacteric Syndrome with *Gui Zhi Tang Jia Wei* (Cinnamon

Twig Decoction with Added Flavors)," *Zhe Jiang Zhong Yi Za Zhi* (*Zhejiang Journal of Chinese Medicine*), #11, 1999, p. 477

[3]Li Shi-qian, "The Treatment of 100 Cases of Climacteric Syndrome with *Du Qi Wan Jia Chai Shao Gui* (Capital Qi Pills plus Bupleurum, Peony & Cinnamon)," *Si Chuan Zhong Yi* (*Sichuan Chinese Medicine*), #8, 1999, p. 49

[4]Liu Zong-bao, "Knowledge Gained by Experience in the Treatment of Climacteric Syndrome," *Si Chuan Zhong Yi* (*Sichuan Chinese Medicine*), #6, 1999, p. 10

[5]*Ibid.*, p. 10-11

[6]Le Tuo-zhen, *op. cit.*, p. 93-94

[7]Hu Wei-yong, "Epimedium in the Treatment of Climacteric Syndrome," *Zhong Yi Za Zhi* (*Journal of Chinese Medicine*), #12, 1999, p. 711

# ❖ 12 ❖

# PSYCHOLOGICAL DISTURBANCES DUE TO ERRONEOUS QIGONG

*Qi gong* literally means "qi work." In contemporary China, this term encompasses everything from meditation to martial arts. In general, there are two broad divisions of qigong, still qigong and active qigong. In still qigong, practitioners assume a static position and work with either or both their breath and their thoughts. There are various breathing patterns used in qigong, such as breathing through the mouth or the nose, accentuating inhalation or exhalation, holding the breath either on the inhalation or exhalation, breathing in by expanding the abdomen, breathing in while contracting the abdomen, etc. In terms of thoughts, one may try to still or decrease the number of their thoughts, they may try to cultivate specific thoughts, such as harmony and peace, or they may engage in various types of simple or complex visualizations. In active qigong, bodily movement may be rapid or slow, patterned or random. These movements are typically coordinated, however, with specific breathing patterns and/or specific thoughts or visualizations. Additionally, different types of qigong are done in order to 1) remedially treat disease, 2) prevent disease and promote good health and longevity, 3) achieve supernormal physical and/or mental powers and abilities, and 4) achieve some sort of spiritual enlightenment. Not all types of qigong achieve all four of these goals, nor are all types of qigong suitable for all constitutions, ages, and sexes or for all times of the day, days of the month, or months of the year.

In the People's Republic of China, tens of millions of people practice qigong on a regular basis. A certain percent-

age of these people also practice qigong incorrectly. Either the style of qigong is not right for them or they are doing something wrong in their practice. Therefore, it is not uncommon to see patients in Chinese clinics and hospitals diagnosed as suffering from "qigong disease." Because the symptoms of erroneous qigong may include disturbing physical and psycho-emotional sensations, within contemporary Chinese medical psychiatry, there is the disease category of "psychological disturbances due to erroneous qigong." This is also sometimes translated as qigong-induced psychoses. Some of the potentially disturbing subjective physical sensations created by erroneous qigong include numbness of the face and extremities, feelings of fullness and distention and/or soreness and pain, nausea, dizziness and vertigo, and itching and formication. In fact, certain of these sensations may also be the result of even correct qigong. In such cases, it is important for the instructor to identify these as normal, transitory experiences of the movement of qi within the body and thus allay any fears or anxieties the practitioner may have about them.

Qigong-related psychological disturbances are divided into four basic types. The first of these is schizoid psychological disturbances. Mostly this presents as an agitated disease state. Patients may speak deliriously or incoherently, may have auditory hallucinations, may feel afflicted by fear, or may have delusional thoughts. Internally, they feel uncomfortable, and externally, their movements are chaotic and disturbed. The disease course is typically short, and, with cessation of practice and proper remedial treatment, there is usually complete recovery.

The second group of psychological disturbances due to erroneous qigong is hysteria-like syndrome. The symptoms of this condition include laughing and crying without constancy, tetany, spasms and convulsions, taciturnity, decreased movement, weakness of the body and extremities, aphasia, and decreased visual acuity.

The third type of psychological disturbances due to faulty qigong practice is neurotic syndrome. These patients feel the qi moving about inside their body. This feels uncomfortable and the patient develops worries and anxieties, depression, insomnia, profuse dreams, headache, dizziness, etc.

The fourth type of psychological disturbances due to wrong qigong practice is referred to as qigong-induced schizophrenia. In this case, the patient has a history of schizophrenia and the practice of qigong causes the schizophrenia to recur. There are all the same sorts of symptoms as in schizophrenia in general, such as visual and auditory hallucinations, delusional thinking, etc. In this case, the disease course tends to be long.

In addition, erroneous practice of qigong can cause systemic disease, most notably hypertension. Therefore, it is easy to see that, if one is going to practice qigong, A) they should find a form that suits their constitution, B) they should apprentice themselves to a qualified and experienced teacher, C) they should practice according to the instructions they have received from that teacher, and D) they should immediately tell their teacher if there are any worrisome or unusual symptoms. The teacher should then be able to tell the student if such symptoms are normal, transitory experiences or if they are pathological and require professional remedial treatment.

WESTERN PSYCHIATRY'S VIEW OF THIS CONDITION:

Numerous psychological symptoms have been ascribed to "erroneous qigong." The underlying assumption is that symptoms originate when the wrong type of qigong is practiced for a given constitution, age, or identified problem, or when an appropriate kind of qigong is practiced excessively or otherwise unskillfully with physically or psychologically damaging consequences. Chinese medicine distinguishes four basic patterns of psychological disturbances that are consistently observed outcomes of "erroneous qigong." One of these has been formalized into a specific diagnosis in the current editions of the *Chinese Classification of Mental Disorders (CCMD-2)*, and a paral-

lel diagnosis in the *DSM-IV* used in the United States and other Western countries. The contemporary Western classification of this disorder is given as a culture-bound syndrome. In other words, Western psychiatry views psychological disturbances due to erroneous qigong as reported subjective experiences that can take place only within the context of Chinese culture or among individuals who believe in the efficacy of qigong and who then become susceptible to this syndrome following exposure to erroneous qigong. The Western diagnosis of "qigong psychotic reaction" is, therefore, regarded as a distressing belief or culture-specific idiom of distress.

In this context, it is interesting and noteworthy that certain symptom patterns are described as culture-bound syndromes while simultaneously viewed as falling outside of conventional Western psychiatric diagnostic categories. It is not clear how the architects of *DSM-IV* can logically defend labeling a syndrome as aberrant in the context of a diagnostic system while simultaneously placing that syndrome outside of conventional Western nosologic categories that serve as a basis for determining whether a syndrome is or is not aberrant and therefore a disorder. This apparent contradiction will require clarification in future editions of the *Diagnostic and Statistical Manual of Mental Disorders*. This problem points to the broader question of how to identify reasonable criteria for determining whether a symptom pattern is construed as normal or aberrant within a given cultural context. It is well-established that significant cross-cultural differences exist between normal or expected patterns of emotion or behavior and aberrant or pathological patterns. In contemporary Western psychiatry it is argued that less cross-cultural variability exists between disorders that are more biologically driven. To date, this model has not been substantiated by epidemiologic or clinical data. In addition to numerous subtle biological factors, family, social, and cultural variables contribute centrally to the pathogenesis and course of psychiatric illness. By definition, there can be no direct correspondence between a culture-bound syndrome in one culture and psychiatric disorders described in other cultures.

Despite evidence to the contrary, in contemporary Western psychiatry, there is no on-going effort to address the hypothesis that psychiatric symptoms associated with "erroneous qigong" are somehow caused by direct or indirect pathological effects of qi on various aspects of cognitive and emotional functioning. The *Chinese Classification of Mental Disorders* does not include the implicit Western bias that psychological disturbances due to erroneous qigong represent culture-specific idioms of distress. However, the current official Chinese classification system also avoids explicit mention of the possibility that qi directly influences mental or emotional states.

## NOSOLOGY:

There is no direct correspondence between the four patterns of psychological disturbance due to erroneous qigong described below and Western psychiatric disorders. However, aspects of all four patterns bear phenomenological resemblance to several Western psychiatric symptoms or syndromes, including conversion disorders, somatoform disorders, histrionic personality disorder, and, in some cases, schizophrenia or acute exacerbations of other psychotic disorders. Approaches used to differentiate these diagnostic categories are discussed in the following section.

## DIFFERENTIAL DIAGNOSIS:

The initial task in Western medical diagnosis is to rule out possible underlying medical causes of psychiatric symptoms. Epilepsy, disorders of the brain (e.g., tumor, stroke, infection), and substance abuse (including alcohol, stimulants, and heroin) can manifest as auditory hallucinations or other psychotic symptoms, anxiety, depression, emotional lability, bizarre behavioral symptoms, headaches, dizziness, or numerous other symptoms frequently observed as psychological disturbances associated with "erroneous qigong." Careful history-taking will usually point to likely medical etiologies which are then ruled out or confirmed with appropriate tests.

When possible medical causes have been eliminated, the psychiatric differential diagnosis is clarified by a thorough review of history combined with clinical assessment of the patient's mental status. A long-standing pattern of psychotic symptoms with onset before the individual started practicing qigong effectively rules out erroneous qigong as the cause of psychosis but does not necessarily exclude it as an exacerbating factor in the long-term course of a recurring psychotic illness. A history of this sort is consistent with the fourth symptom pattern in which a schizophrenic individual experiences an acute exacerbation of psychotic symptoms (including possibly auditory or visual hallucinations) following the erroneous practice of qigong.

In cases where there is no pre-morbid psychiatric history and psychotic symptoms are experienced following qigong exercises that are subsequently identified as erroneous by someone qualified to make that judgement, at least three diagnostic possibilities must be examined in a Western psychiatric framework. If psychotic symptoms

are transient and resolve with little or no treatment, brief psychotic disorder is the likely diagnosis. However, if the individual experiencing such symptoms operates from a cultural-philosophical framework that assumes the validity of qi and similar energy concepts, the contemporary Western diagnosis is more accurately qigong psychotic reaction. In cases where psychotic symptoms associated with erroneous qigong practice continue for several months or longer and there is no documented history of similar previous symptoms, a contemporary Western view would likely identify qigong as a precipitating stressor of a latent psychotic disorder to which the patient was predisposed. In this case, erroneous qigong would be regarded as the critical stressful factor precipitating a first psychotic episode in someone who is genetically at risk.

Nonpsychotic psychological disturbances due to erroneous qigong are described in the Chinese medical literature as a hysteria-like syndrome and a neurotic syndrome. Both symptom patterns fall outside of the suggested elements of the Western diagnostic category of qigong psychotic reaction as a culture-specific syndrome. Prominent symptoms observed in the hysteria-like syndrome (pattern #2) include inappropriate laughing and crying, tetany, spasms, and convulsions, decreased movement, weakness, aphasia, and decreased visual acuity. This symptom pattern does not correspond to a discreet Western psychiatric syndrome and a time course is not specified to help clarify possibilities in a reasonable Western medical differential diagnosis. Assuming that possible medical causes have been ruled out (including, for instance, seizure disorder and cerebrovascular accident), these symptoms might be described as conversion phenomena in Western psychiatry. When an individual is not consciously aware of psychological distress, such as that which might result from erroneous qigong, Western psychiatry maintains that the distress or conflict is transformed or converted into a symptom that symbolizes the distress or unconscious conflict. For example, an individual who is highly conflicted or ambivalent about going to war might experience sudden unexplained loss of functioning in his or her legs, thus preventing him or her from enlisting. Although no evidence of stroke is found on brain imaging and the patient's neurologic exam is not consistent with any known disorder, the patient believes and acts as though they are paralyzed. In this case, conversion paralysis is a symptom that has resolved the patient's conflict outside of conscious awareness, as paralysis effectively prevents him or her from going to war. Conversion symptoms typically affect motor or sensory functioning, begin suddenly and are associated with equivocal findings on neurological examination or diagnostic studies. Most conversion symptoms resolve within days. However, some persist for weeks or longer, thus making it difficult to discern this psychiatric syndrome from possible but rarely occurring neurologic disorders.

In cases where apparent dramatic physical or psychiatric symptoms follow erroneous qigong and there is no loss of motor or sensory function, histrionic personality disorder is a plausible Western psychiatric diagnosis for the second and third symptom patterns described as sub-types of this Chinese diagnostic category. Histrionic personality disorder is characterized by exaggerated, dramatic emotional displays; a high degree of suggestibility; excessive concern about one's appearance or how others see one, and frequent demands for attention. The histrionic individual who is practicing qigong, for example, might be expected to display exaggerated apparent effects of qigong as a way of seeking attention. He or she might be expected to be highly suggestible to the physical or psychological consequences of erroneous qigong and to exhibit dramatic signs and symptoms even when practicing for a brief period or following a safe or appropriate type of qigong exercise. In general, individuals who have personality disorders may be more susceptible to psychological disturbances due to erroneous qigong and perhaps also to appropriate qigong. According to contemporary Western psychiatric models of personality disorders, these individuals typically experience distress that is disproportionate to an objective appraisal of external stress. There is often a tendency to distort or exaggerate bodily sensations, including unusual somatic sensations that reportedly occur commonly during qigong practice. Because of these maladaptive traits, individuals with personality disorders, including histrionic, borderline, and schizotypal, are probably more susceptible to developing psychiatric disturbances while practicing qigong.

## ETIOLOGY & PATHOPHYSIOLOGY:

The Chinese category of psychological disturbances due to erroneous qigong may correspond partially to several diagnoses in contemporary Western medicine. To date, there is no consensus in Western medicine regarding cause(s) of the psychological disturbances as resulting from erroneous qigong practice. Recent research findings on the putative effects of qigong used to treat neurologic disorders suggest interesting possible biophysical explanations. However, Western medicine regards these explanations as completely speculative and assumes that psychogenic factors constitute a sufficient explanation for consistently observed effects of qigong on human behavior. A second, implicit assumption in the Western explanation is that psychogenic factors, such as suggestibility or intense unconscious conflicts, somehow cause neurobiological changes that manifest as the observed symptom patterns in individuals who are genetically predisposed. This kind of explanatory model is viewed as adequate to explain observations of acute psychotic symptoms in some schizophrenics following qigong exercises.

## WESTERN MEDICAL TREATMENT:

Determination of the most appropriate treatment for symptoms associated with erroneous qigong depends on the kind and severity of symptoms and their identified cause(s). When the symptom pattern is one of psychosis and the severity or duration of symptoms has resulted in significant social or occupational impairment, treatment with an antipsychotic medication is indicated. However, in cases of transient psychosis or mild to moderate impairment, in the absence of a pre-morbid psychotic disorder, symptoms may resolve without pharmacological treatment. There is no specific pharmacological treatment for

---

### DIFFERENTIAL DIAGNOSIS

| 1. MEDICAL DISORDERS | 2. EFFECTS OF SUBSTANCES | 3. PSYCHIATRIC DISORDERS |
|---|---|---|
| A. SEIZURE DISORDERS<br>B. DISORDERS OR INFECTIONS OF THE CNS, INCLUDING TUMORS AND CEREBROVASCULAR ACCIDENT (CVA) | A. ALCOHOL OR ILLICIT SUBSTANCE INTOXICATION OR WITHDRAWAL<br>B. SIDE EFFECTS OF MEDICATIONS (ESPECIALLY THOSE THAT ACT ON CNS DOPAMINE) | A. SCHIZOPHRENIA AND OTHER PSYCHOTIC DISORDERS<br>B. QIGONG PSYCHOTIC REACTION<br>C. CONVERSION DISORDER<br>D. HISTRIONIC PERSONALITY DISORDER (AND SOMETIMES BORDERLINE OR SCHIZOTYPAL PERSONALITY DISORDERS) |

conversion disorders or histrionic personality disorder. In both cases, Western psychiatry uses the approach of aggressively treating the symptom that is associated with the greatest amount of distress or impairment. For example, in the case of an individual who has become symptomatic following erroneous qigong, complaining of intense emotional lability or inappropriate laughing or crying, treatment with a serotonin-selective re-uptake inhibitor (SSRI) such as fluoxetine (Prozac), paroxetine (Paxil), or sertraline (Zoloft) would likely be recommended. Alternatively, if the principal or most impairing complaint is diffuse anxiety, a sedative-hypnotic medication may be a reasonable choice. In cases where the presenting symptom pattern appears to correspond to a conversion disorder, hypnosis is sometimes beneficial in accelerating the course of recovery. If histrionic personality disorder or another personality disorder has been established and linked to the pathogenesis of a symptom pattern (see Differential Diagnosis above) associated with erroneous qigong, pharmacological treatment should be directed toward the most impairing symptoms. Intense individual or group psychotherapy is sometimes helpful in cases of histrionic personality disorder or borderline personality disorder.

## SHORT & LONG-TERM ADVANTAGES & DISADVANTAGES OF WESTERN MEDICAL TREATMENT:

Successful treatment of an identified medical cause will generally result in resolution of associated psychological disturbances that may have been ascribed to erroneous qigong. However, it is important to note that some medical causes are irreversible or minimally responsive to currently available Western medical therapies. When a primary psychiatric disorder is the identified cause (see Differential Diagnosis above), effective pharmacological treatment often results in improved cognitive, social, and occupational functioning. Disadvantages of pharmacological treatment include the risk of side effects, interactions, and toxicities of specific medications. Most antipsychotic medications carry an inherent risk of causing abnormal involuntary movements which may be transient or permanent. The likelihood of developing a permanent movement disorder increases with duration of use and dosage. Newer so-called atypical antipsychotics have a significantly lower associated risk of abnormal involuntary movement disorders.

## PROGNOSIS:

Western psychiatric disorders that appear to be associated with erroneous qigong differ substantially in long-term outcome. Schizophrenia, for example, follows an insidiously declining course that almost always leads to permanent social and occupational impairment. Conversely, a brief psychotic disorder typically resolves in weeks or days without treatment. Conversion disorder generally has a good prognosis and may resolve spontaneously without treatment. Histrionic personality disorder and other personality disorders that may be associated with psychological disturbances due to erroneous qigong persist for the duration of one's life during which symptom severity typically waxes and wanes depending on environmental stresses.

## INDICATIONS FOR REFERRAL TO WESTERN MEDICAL SERVICES:

Urgent medical referral to the nearest available emergency room is indicated when there is evidence of an underlying acute or rapidly progressive medical disorder, including epilepsy, brain tumor, or stroke. Findings of acute psychotic symptoms, active suicidal ideation, or cognitive impairment related to alcohol or other substance abuse are also a basis for urgent medical triage in an emergency room or urgent care facility. Routine psychiatric referral may help to clarify the differential diagnosis when reasonable efforts have been made to exclude acute medical etiologies and the patient continues to complain of persisting symptoms that appear to be related to erroneous qigong following an appropriate course and duration of Chinese medical treatment. In this instance, the goal is to develop an optimized treatment plan combining Chinese and Western modalities.

## CHINESE DISEASE CATEGORIZATION:

Traditionally, what are now referred to in Chinese medicine as psychological disturbances due to erroneous qigong are also referred to as qigong disease (*qi gong bing*), Zen disease (*Chan bing*), and departing fire enters the room (*zou huo ru hui*). *Chan* refers to the silent meditation characteristic of what is commonly called Zen in the West. That this type of meditation can cause disease is not widely known by its Western practitioners. *Zou huo ru hui* is an even more interesting term. *Zuo* means to walk or run. It also means to depart from the usual. *Huo* means fire. As a compound term in everyday Chinese, *zuo huo* means to spark an accidental discharge. However, Chinese is a multivalent language, and this everyday compound term does have a relatively precise technical Chinese medical implication. In this sense, *zuo huo* means the departure of the ministerial fire from its lower source. Ministerial fire is only healthy in the body when it remains level in the lower burner. If it stirs upward, it becomes the enemy of the original qi and becomes a pathological force in the body. *Ru hui* means to enter a room. In this case, the room refers to the heart and/or brain. The character *hui* is written with a house radical on top of the ghost or spirit radical. The full Chinese medical/qigong implication of this phrase is that erroneous qigong can cause the ministerial fire to flame upward to harass the heart spirit.

## CHINESE MEDICAL DISEASE CAUSES & DISEASE MECHANISMS:

In Chinese medicine, the qi, the mind, and the breath are all closely related. In a sense, these are not three separate things but are aspects of a single reality. Numerous Chinese medical classics, such as the *Nei Jing (Inner Classic)* and *Nan Jing (Classic of Difficulties)*, describe how the qi moves through the body in coordination with the breath. It is the lungs' respiration which diffuses and scatters the ancestral or chest qi to spread and extend to the rest of the body. In addition, consciousness in Chinese medicine is referred to as the spirit brilliance, and the spirit is nothing other than the accumulation of qi in the heart. According to many Asian schools of meditation, the thoughts in the mind come and go with the movement of the breath. Therefore, alterations in respiration correspond to alterations in mentation and *vice versa*. Further, it is qi which moves the body in space. Hence, there is likewise a relationship between the movement of the mind, the circulation of qi, and the movement of the body.

Most qigong is a combination of either specific static posture or physical movement coordinated with specific respiration and specific concentration or visualization. Therefore, we can say that qigong affects the flow of qi in the body, and, as we have seen above, specific mental-emotional states are evoked by and correspond to specific directions of qi flow. Thus it is easy to see that erroneous qigong can cause abnormal flows of qi in the body which then causes an uncomfortable, even pathological mental-emotional state. In addition, if one disturbs the free flow of the qi mechanism, for instance, by absorbing more qi than the body can freely diffuse and circulate or by accumulating and concentrating the qi in a certain area of the body, this may easily lead to liver depression qi stagnation. If this qi stagnation endures, depression may transform fire, and fire flaming upward may harass the heart spirit. Depressive heat may also damage and consume yin fluids, thus giving rise to ascendant hyperactivity of yang, vacuity heat, and/or internal stirring of wind.

On another level, if one is too physically active, activity which is yang may also damage and consume yin fluids leading to yang hyperactivity and evil heat. While too much sitting and inactivity, as in Zen meditation, which is yin, may aggravate liver depression and even cause or aggravate both phlegm dampness and blood stasis. This is even more likely if such still, sitting meditation is accompanied by unfulfilled desires, such as wanting to become a Buddha or an Immortal, or if there are excessive worries and anxieties. Especially if one leads the qi in the body upward or concentrates their mind on a point in the upper body, one can lead ministerial fire to counterflow upward. When this disease mechanism causes symptoms of heat harassing upward, it is sometimes referred to as "fire burning the Shaolin monastery."[2]

## TREATMENT BASED ON PATTERN DISCRIMINATION:

### 1. QI STAGNATION & BLOOD STASIS PATTERN

**MAIN SYMPTOMS:** Emotional lability, crying and laughing without constancy, paranoia, tension, visual hallucinations, delusional thoughts, chest and rib-side fullness and oppression, headache, generalized body pain, a dark, stagnant facial complexion, a dark red tongue or possible static spots or macules, engorged, tortuous sublingual veins, and a bowstring, choppy pulse

**ANALYSIS OF SYMPTOMS:** Emotional impetuosity, difficulty staying still, emotional lability, crying and laughing without constancy, etc. are all symptoms indicating that the qi mechanism is disturbed and chaotic and has lost its control. The qi is the commander of the blood, while the blood is the mother of the qi. When the qi moves, the blood moves. Likewise, if the qi becomes chaotic, the blood becomes disquieted. Hence qi and blood lose their regulation and are unable to control themselves (alternate reading: and one is unable to control oneself). Qi and blood depression and stagnation may obstruct and confound the heart orifices, resulting in harassment of the heart spirit. Therefore, one may see emotional lability, crying and laughing without constancy, paranoia, tension, visual hallucinations, and delusional thoughts. Static blood obstructing and stagnating may cause qi stagnation of chest yang. In that case, one may see chest and rib-side fullness and oppression. Qi stagnation and blood stasis result in the channels and network vessels not being free-flowing. Hence there is headache, generalized body pain, a dark, stagnant facial complexion, a dark red tongue with possible static spots or macules, and a bowstring, choppy pulse.

**TREATMENT PRINCIPLES:** Quicken the blood and transform phlegm, rectify the qi and quiet the spirit

**FORMULA & MEDICINALS:** *Dian Kuang Meng Xing Tang* (Withdrawal & Mania Dream-arousing Decoction)

Semen Pruni Persicae (*Tao Ren*), 24g, Radix Bupleuri (*Chai Hu*), 10g, Rhizoma Cyperi Rotundi (*Xiang Fu*), 15g, Radix Auklandiae Lappae (*Mu Xiang*), 10g, Radix Rubrus Paeoniae Lactiflorae (*Chi Shao*), 10g, Rhizoma Pinelliae Ternatae (*Ban Xia*), 10g, Pericarpium Arecae Catechu (*Da Fu Pi*), 15g, Pericarpium Citri Reticulatae Viride (*Qing Pi*), 10g, Pericarpium Citri Reticulatae (*Chen Pi*), 10g, Caulis Akebiae (*Mu Tong*), 15g, Fructus Perillae Frutescentis (*Zi Su Zi*), 10g, mix-fried Radix Glycyrrhizae (*Gan Cao*), 10g

Decoct in water and administer orally in two divided doses, morning and evening, one *ji* per day.

**ANALYSIS OF FORMULA:** Within this formula, a heavy use of Persica combined with Red Peony quickens the blood and transforms stasis. Bupleurum, Cyperus, Green Orange Peel, Orange Peel, and Fructus Perillae are all qi-rectifying ingredients. These promote the normal movement of the qi which then quiets the spirit, Pericarpium Arecae, Pinellia, and Akebia dry dampness and disinhibit water, free the flow and disinhibit the channels and vessels.

**ADDITIONS & SUBTRACTIONS:** If there is simultaneously a bitter taste in the mouth, dry throat, tension, agitation, and easy anger, all showing that qi depression has transformed fire, add Cortex Radicis Moutan (*Dan Pi*), Fructus Gardeniae Jasminoidis (*Zhi Zi*), and Radix Scutellariae Baicalensis (*Huang Qi*) to clear heat and eliminate vexation. If there are visual hallucinations, delusional thoughts, paranoia, tension, headache, and insomnia suggesting heavier static blood obstructing the network vessels, then add Lumbricus (*Di Long*), Bombyx Batryticatus (*Jiang Can*), Buthus Martensis (*Quan Xie*), Scolopendra Subspinipes (*Wu Gong*), and other such worm type medicinals to track and pick out static blood from the vessels and network vessels. If the patient feels like their body is full of so much qi they cannot contain themselves or control themselves, then add Radix Albus Paeoniae Lactiflorae (*Bai Shao*), Sclerotium Poriae Cocos (*Fu Ling*), Flos Inulae Racemosae (*Xuan Fu Hua*), and Radix Angelicae Sinensis (*Dang Gui*) in order to restrain the qi and return it to its source, *i.e.*, the lower burner.

**ACUPUNCTURE:** For predominant qi stagnation, use *Tai Chong* (Liv 3), *He Gu* (LI 4), *Qi Hai* (CV 6), *Qi Men* (Liv 13), *Shen Men* (Ht 7), *Nei Guan* (Per 6).

**ADDITIONS & SUBTRACTIONS:** For blood stasis, add *Xue Hai* (Sp 6) and *Ge Shu* (Bl 17). For depression transforming heat, use *Xing Jian* (Liv 2) instead of *Tai Chong* and *Jian Shi* (Per 5) instead of *Nei Guan*, delete *Qi Men* unless there is marked abdominal distention, and add *Zu Qiao Yin* (GB 44). Use draining technique.

## 2. PHLEGM FIRE HARASSING ABOVE PATTERN

**MAIN SYMPTOMS:** Emotional tension and agitation, impulsive movement, breaking things, mania, lack of wisdom or intelligence, difficulty controlling one's qi, profuse phlegm, chest oppression, a bitter taste in the mouth and bad breath, headache, red eyes, reddish urine, bound stools, a red tongue with thick, slimy, yellow fur, and a bowstring, slippery, rapid pulse

**ANALYSIS OF SYMPTOMS:** If there is habitual bodily yang exuberance or addiction to alcohol and/or tobacco, or excessive eating of fatty, greasy, thick-flavored foods, phlegm dampness may congest and become exuberant. In that case, when one tries to practice qigong, one cannot obtain stillness but the qi mechanism becomes disturbed and chaotic instead. Then phlegm and fire become mixed and internally harass the heart spirit. This then causes emotional tension and agitation, impulsive movement, breaking and damaging things, manic, chaotic behavior, and lack of intelligence or wisdom. If the qi does not gather in the channels, it is difficult for it to control itself. This then leads to spontaneous sensations of qi discharging chaotically around the body and inability to control oneself. Phlegm turbidity internally obstructing with devitalization of chest yang results in profuse phlegm and chest oppression, while phlegm fire ascending to harass the clear orifices results in the bitter taste in the mouth, bad breath, headache, and red eyes. The reddish urine, bound stools, red tongue with thick, slimy, yellow fur, and the bowstring, slippery, rapid pulse are all signs of phlegm fire and congested heat.

**TREATMENT PRINCIPLES:** Transform phlegm and drain fire, clear the heart and quiet the spirit

**FORMULA & MEDICINALS:** *Xiao Xian Xiong Tang* (Minor Sunken Chest Decoction)

Rhizoma Coptidis Chinensis (*Huang Lian*), 6g (added later), Rhizoma Pinelliae Ternatae (*Ban Xia*), 10g, Fructus Trichosanthis Kirlowii (*Gua Lou*), 30g

Decoct in water and administer orally in two divided doses, morning and evening, one *ji* per day.

**ANALYSIS OF FORMULA:** Within this formula, Fructus Trichosanthis is sweet and cold, slippery and disinhibiting. It clears heat and flushes phlegm, broadens the chest and scatters nodulation. It is a main medicinal for promoting the downward movement of phlegm heat. Coptis is bitter and cold and drains fire. It is the adjutant medicinal which helps clear fire evils from the heart. Pinellia is acrid and warm. It downbears the qi and transforms phlegm. When combined with Coptis, Pinellia's acridity opens and Coptis's bitterness downbears. This is a good combination for clearing phlegm fire from the chest and venter. Although the number of medicinals in this formula is small, their effect is great.

**ADDITIONS & SUBTRACTIONS:** If phlegm turbidity is more exuberant, the spirit is not clear, and there is delirious, incoherent speech, add Rhizoma Arisaematis (*Nan Xing*), Bulbus Fritillariae (*Bei Mu*), and Rhizoma Acori Graminei (*Shi Chang Pu*) to dispel phlegm and open the orifices. If the movement is impulsive but the stools are bound, add Radix Et Rhizoma Rhei (*Da Huang*), Mirabilitum (*Mang Xiao*), Cortex Magnoliae Officinalis (*Hou Po*), and Fructus Immaturus Citri Aurantii (*Zhi Shi*) to drain replete heat from the yang ming. If there is a strong, replete form and sudden agitation and stirring with inability to control oneself or manically assaulting other persons, add *Long Hu Wan* (Dragon & Tiger Pills, a Chinese ready-made medicine) to promote vomiting and draining (*i.e.*, diarrhea) to more effectively clear and flush phlegm fire and replete heat.

*Long Hu Wan* consist of: Calculus Bovis (*Niu Huang*), defatted Semen Crotonis Tiglii (*Ba Dou Shuang*), Arsenicum (*Pi Shi*), Cinnabar (*Zhu Sha*).

**ACUPUNCTURE:** *Bai Hui* (GV 20), *Ren Zhong* (GV 26), *Jian Shi* (Per 5), *Feng Long* (St 40), *Nei Ting* (St 44). Use draining technique.

### 3. YIN VACUITY-FIRE EFFULGENCE PATTERN

**MAIN SYMPTOMS:** Emotional depression, difficulty thinking, dull-witted, decreased memory power, mumbling and speaking to oneself, fright palpitations, fear and dread, auditory and visual hallucinations, vexatious heat in the five hearts, a dry mouth and throat, insomnia, night sweats, a red tongue with scanty fur, and a fine, rapid or surging rapid pulse

**ANALYSIS OF SYMPTOMS:** If one is already habitually kidney yin depleted and vacuous, doing too much or erroneous qigong may cause excessive psycho-emotional tension. In addition, compulsively chasing one's thoughts or a desire to emit qi or possess other such supra-normal qigong abilities may cause one to exhaust oneself in one's practice. This exhausts and consumes the essence and blood. If the essence and blood become insufficient, then the sea of marrow will lack nourishment. This then leads to difficulty thinking, dull-wittedness, and decreased memory power. Essence and blood depletion and vacuity leads to heart spirit lack of nourishment. Hence there is emotional depression, mumbling and speaking to oneself, fright palpitations, fear and dread. Yin vacuity leads to vacuity fire flaming upward. Therefore, one sees vexatious heat in the five hearts, a dry mouth and throat, insomnia, and night sweats. The red tongue with scanty fur and the fine, rapid or surging, rapid pulse are signs of yin vacuity with internal heat.

**TREATMENT PRINCIPLES:** Enrich yin and downbear fire, nourish the blood and quiet the spirit

**FORMULA & MEDICINALS:** *Zhi Bai Di Huang Tang Jia Wei* (Anemarrhena & Phellodendron Rehmannia Decoction with Added Flavors)

Rhizoma Anemarrhenae Aspheloidis (*Zhi Mu*), 10g, Cortex Phellodendri (*Huang Bai*), 10g, cooked Radix Rehmanniae (*Shu Di*), 30g, Fructus Corni Officinalis (*Shan Zhu Yu*), 20g, Radix Dioscoreae Oppositae (*Shan Yao*), 18g, Rhizoma Alismatis (*Ze Xie*), 10g, Sclerotium Poriae Cocos (*Fu Ling*), 10g, Cortex Radicis Moutan (*Dan Pi*), 10g, Radix Salviae Miltiorrhizae (*Dan Shen*), 10g, Semen Zizyphi Spinosae (*Suan Zao Ren*), 30g, Succinum (*Hu Po*), 6g (powdered and swallowed with the decocted liquid)

Decoct in water and administer orally in two divided doses, morning and evening, one *ji* per day.

**ANALYSIS OF FORMULA:** Cooked Rehmannia is the ruling medicinal in this formula. It enriches the kidneys and fosters essence. It is assisted by Cornus, which nourishes the liver and kidneys and astringes the essence and blood, and Dioscorea, which supplements and boosts the spleen and kidneys. When these three medicinals are combined together, they very effectively supplement yin. Poria blandly percolates spleen dampness and assists Dioscorea in boosting the spleen. Alisma clears and discharges kidney fire and also prevents cooked Rehmannia's enriching sliminess from causing damage to the spleen or stagnation and stasis. Moutan clears and discharges liver fire. It also controls Cornus's warming. Anemarrhena and Phellodendron are both bitter and cold and enter the kidneys where they control flaming and flaring of vacuity fire. The combination of Salvia, Zizyphus Spinosa, and Succinum quickens the blood, nourishes the blood, and quiets the spirit. When all these medicinals are used together, they enrich yin and downbear fire, nourish the blood and quiet the spirit.

**ADDITIONS & SUBTRACTIONS:** If there is simultaneous phlegm heat, one can add Fructus Trichosanthis Kirlowii (*Gua Lou*), bile-processed Rhizoma Arisaematis (*Dan Nan Xing*), and Concretio Bambusae Siliceae (*Tian Zhu Huang*) to clear phlegm heat. If there is simultaneous heart spirit instability with fear and dread, and restlessness, one can also administer *Ding Zhi Wan* (Stabilize the Mind Pills, a Chinese ready-made medicine) in order to quiet the spirit and stabilize the mind. If there is afternoon tidal heat or bone-steaming and vexation and agitation, one can add Radix Cynanchi Atrati (*Bai Wei*) and Cortex Radicis Lycii Chinensis (*Di Gu Pi*) to clear vacuity heat.

*Ding Zhi Wan* consist of: Radix Panacis Ginseng (*Ren Shen*), Sclerotium Poriae Cocos (*Fu Ling*), Rhizoma Acori Graminei (*Shi Chang Pu*), and Radix Polygalae Tenuifoliae (*Yuan Zhi*).

**ACUPUNCTURE:** *Bai Hui* (GV 20), *Ren Zhong* (GV 26), *He Gu* (LI 4), *Tai Chong* (Liv 3) needled through to *Yong Quan* (Ki 1), *Tai Xi* (Ki 3), *San Yin Jiao* (Sp 6). Use even supplementing-even draining technique.

**CLINICAL TIPS:**

1. In two out of the above three patterns there is qi stagnation (qi stagnation and blood stasis, and phlegm fire). Because yin blood nourishes and moistens the liver, in real life, pattern #3, yin vacuity-fire effulgence, will also typically be complicated by liver depression qi stagnation. Therefore, the overwhelming majority of patients with qigong-induced psychological disturbances have qi stagnation.

2. Also in two out of three patterns there is heat, either phlegm heat, a species of depressive heat, or vacuity heat. Remember, there is no vexation and agitation without evil heat. Body type, age, diet, and type of qigong practiced should be used to help differentiate phlegm heat from vacuity heat.

3. At the very first sign of qigong-induced disease, the patient should stop doing qigong or their practice should be monitored, assessed, and modified by someone competent to do so. Short-term psychotherapy may be useful to clarify the underlying motivations for practicing qigong or a specific type of qigong. Clarifying these motivations may help enable the patient to either stop practicing or modify their practice.

**ENDNOTES**

[1] In an article by B.Y. Ng titled "Qigong-induced Mental Disorders: A Review" appearing in the *Australian-New Zealand Journal of Psychiatry*, Apr. 1999, p. 197-206, the author suggests that qigong-induced psychoses should be more properly called qigong-precipitated psychoses.

[2] The Shaolin monastery is the traditional home of Chan or Zen Buddhism, while *shao lin* literally means "little forest."

# GLOSSARY OF WESTERN PSYCHIATRIC TERMS

**AGORAPHOBIA** An anxiety disorder that occurs alone or in the context of panic disorder and is characterized by persisting anxiety about being in places from which escape might be difficult or impossible in the event of a panic attack. Agoraphobic patients typically minimize or avoid travel, and a pattern of phobic avoidance is not better explained by the existence of a specific phobia or other psychiatric disorder, an underlying medical disorder, medication side effects, or chronic substance abuse.

**ALCOHOL-INDUCED PERSISTING AMNESTIC DISORDER** A disorder of persisting impaired memory characterized by inability to learn new information or to recall previously learned information that is etiologically related to chronic alcohol abuse

**ALCOHOL-RELATED DEMENTIA** A syndrome of dementia that persists following acute intoxication and withdrawal and is etiologically related to the CNS effects of chronic alcohol abuse on memory and cognitive functioning

**ALZHEIMER'S DISEASE (I.E., SENILE DEMENTIA OF THE ALZHEIMER'S TYPE)** A syndrome of global cognitive decline characterized by gradual onset, impaired memory, and one or more disturbances in cognitive functioning, including language disturbance, impaired capacity to perform learned behaviors (apraxia), loss of capacity to recognize familiar objects or people (agnosia), or disturbance

of executive functioning. Alzheimer's disease is diagnosed only when other identifiable causes of dementia have been excluded.

**ANOREXIA NERVOSA** A syndrome characterized by a refusal of the person to maintain a minimally normal body weight, an intense fear of being overweight, and a misperception of the person's own body size and shape

**ANTIPSYCHOTICS** Medications that are used to treat schizophrenia and other psychotic disorders. Most current antipsychotics are dopamine receptor antagonists, but more recently introduced antipsychotics function as combined serotonin and dopamine antagonists.

**ANTISOCIAL PERSONALITY DISORDER** A personality disorder characterized by a persistent pattern of victimizing others through theft or destruction of property, physical assault (including spouse and/or child abuse), or deceit to gain personal profit or pleasure

**ANXIETY** A persisting state of fear that may or may not be associated with a specific object or situation. In generalized anxiety disorder (GAD), for example, the individual experiences nonspecific anxiety symptoms that cause significant social or occupational impairment. In contrast, specific phobias are characterized by intense anxiety responses to specific objects or situations but normal functioning in other contexts.

ASPERGER'S SYNDROME One of the disorders of childhood-onset pervasive developmental delay characterized by grossly impaired social interaction, repetitive stereotyped behaviors, but (in contrast to autism), normal language and normal cognitive development.

ATTENTION DEFICIT-HYPERACTIVITY DISORDER (ADHD) A disorder of childhood-onset persisting inattention and/or hyperactivity that interferes with school performance and social functioning. Symptoms of inattention or hyperactivity are not caused by a medical disorder or the effects of a substance and are not present only during acute episodes of other psychiatric disorders.

AUTISM A disorder of pervasive developmental delay in social interaction, language, and play behavior that begins before age three. The disorder is characterized by profound impairment in verbal and nonverbal behavior, the absence of age-appropriate play behavior, and stereotyped repetitive motor behaviors.

AVOIDANT PERSONALITY DISORDER A personality disorder characterized by extreme social anxiety, low self-esteem, and hypersensitivity to criticism. Individuals with avoidant personality often view themselves as socially inept or inferior and often avoid occupational or social activities because of fear of excessive social contact.

BIPOLAR I DISORDER A serious mood disorder characterized by a persisting pattern of cyclic mood changes alternating between depressive and manic episodes. This disorder results in significant social or occupational impairment and cannot be etiologically related to an underlying medical disorder, the effects of a substance, or another major psychiatric disorder. The diagnosis of bipolar I disorder requires a history of at least one manic episode.

BIPOLAR II DISORDER A mood disorder that is less severe and causes less impairment than bipolar I and is characterized by cyclic mood changes alternating between major depressive and hypomanic episodes. In contrast to mania, psychosis never occurs during a hypomanic episode, and the individual typically continues to work and participate in normal social activities.

BIPOLAR AFFECTIVE DISORDER (BAD) Another term for bipolar disorder (previously manic-depressive disorder)

BODY DYSMORPHIC DISORDER A disorder characterized by preoccupation with a belief that one's appearance is seriously defective. Complaints commonly involve perceived defects in the face or head but can involve any body part. The distress caused by this belief results in significant social or occupational impairment. Symptoms of this disorder cannot be better accounted for by another psychiatric disorder, including anorexia nervosa.

BORDERLINE PERSONALITY DISORDER A personality disorder characterized by a persisting pattern of unstable interpersonal relationships, disturbed self-image, and impulsive self-injurious behaviors. Borderline patients often make suicide attempts or self-mutilate, describe chronic feelings of emptiness, and exhibit inappropriate intense emotions. They may experience transient psychotic or dissociative symptoms when acutely distressed.

BRIEF PSYCHOTIC DISORDER A syndrome characterized by a psychotic disturbance that lasts more than one day but less than one month

BRIQUET'S SYNDROME An obsolete term for hysteria, characterized by anxiety, somatic, depressive, and dissociative symptoms. Current diagnostic categories that include similar phenomenology are conversion disorder and hypochondriasis.

BROCA'S APHASIA Impairment in expressive language that is etiologically related to a lesion in Broca's area in the left frontotemporal cortex (in contrast to Wernecke's aphasia, which is a syndrome of impairment in receptive language that is caused by a lesion in Werneke's area, just posterior to Broca's area)

BULIMIA NERVOSA A syndrome that is characterized by repetitive binge eating and maladaptive approaches to preventing weight gain in response to binge eating, including vomiting, abuse of laxatives, diuretics, or enemas. The disorder lasts at least three months and is not better explained by an underlying medical disorder or another psychiatric disorder.

CIRCADIAN RHYTHM SLEEP DISORDER A persisting sleep disturbance characterized by disrupted night-time sleep and day-time somnolence that is related to a mismatch between an individual's sleep-wake schedule and his or her natural circadian rhythm

COGNITIVE-BEHAVORIAL THERAPY (CBT) A kind of psychotherapy directed at changing behaviors and cognitions that are believed to be causally linked to persisting maladaptive behaviors or distressing symptoms, including generalized anxiety and depressed mood

CO-MORBIDITY The simultaneous existence of two or more disorders in the same person

CONVERSION DISORDER A syndrome characterized by symptoms of apparent dysfunction in sensory or motor functioning in the absence of abnormal findings on neurologic examination or diagnostic testing. The symptom(s) must not be intentionally produced or feigned, must cause considerable social or occupational impairment, and are not etiologically related to other identified medical or psychiatric disorders.

CYCLOTHYMIC DISORDER A syndrome of cyclic mood changes alternating between episodes of hypomania and moderate depression. Symptoms are not severe enough to warrant a diagnosis bipolar disorder.

DELUSIONAL DISORDER A psychotic disorder characterized by persisting non-bizarre delusions in the absence of other psychotic symptoms. The disorder cannot be caused by an identified medical condition or the effects of a substance, and cannot be diagnosed in an individual who has a previous history of schizophrenia or other psychotic disorder.

DEMENTIA A syndrome of persisting decline in global cognitive functioning, including impaired memory, and one or more severe deficits in cognition resulting in severe social and occupational impairment. In dementia, the patient's sensorium remains intact in contrast to delirium, in which the individual is grossly disoriented. Multiple causes have been identified for dementia, including neurologic disorders, numerous medical disorders, toxic exposure, chronic alcohol or illicit substance abuse, and others.

DEPENDENT PERSONALITY DISORDER A personality disorder characterized by an excessive need to be taken care of associated with submissive, clinging behavior, and fear of independence

DEPERSONALIZATION A dissociative symptom characterized by feelings of detachment from one's body or body parts. The individual may report feeling as though he or she is acting or living as though in a dream.

DEPERSONALIZATION DISORDER A kind of dissociative disorder characterized by recurring episodes of depersonalization accompanied by severe emotional distress or impairment. During episodes of depersonalization, the individual retains the capacity to discern reality (i.e., reality testing is intact).

DISSOCIATIVE DISORDERS Syndromes characterized by disruption in the normal "smooth" flow of consciousness resulting in disruptions in memory, identity, or perception. These disorders occur in the absence of identified underlying medical (including neurologic) disorders or other major psychiatric disorders. According to the DSM-IV, dissociative disorders include dissociative amnesia, dissociative fugue, dissociative identity disorder (formerly multiple personality disorder), depersonalization disorder, dissociative trance disorder, and dissociative disorder not otherwise specified

DISSOCIATIVE FUGUE A dissociative disorder characterized by confusion over one's identity and associated impulsive travel from one's home or workplace without memory of having done so.

DISSOCIATIVE IDENTITY DISORDER (DID) A dissociative disorder (not due to a medical condition, the effects of a substance, or another psychiatric disorder) that is characterized by the presence of two or more distinct identities or personality states during normal waking consciousness that recurrently take control of the individual's behavior accompanied. During dissociative states, afflicted individuals are unable to recall important personal information.

DOPAMINE A neurotransmitter whose dysregulation has been implicated in the pathogenesis of schizophrenia

DYSOMNIAS A group of sleep disorders characterized by persisting difficulty initiating or maintaining sleep resulting in excessive daytime sleepiness. These disorders are not due to an underlying medical disorder and do not occur only in the context of a pre-existing psychiatric disorder.

DYSTHYMIC DISORDER A mood disorder characterized by an almost continuous state of moderate depressed mood persisting at least two years in the absence of a major depressive or manic episode

EATING DISORDERS Persisting severe disturbances of eating behavior associated with refusal to maintain normal body weight and maladaptive behaviors performed in order to compensate for distorted cognitions or perceptions about body image. Bulimia nervosa and anorexia nervosa are the two primary eating disorders defined in the DSM-IV.

ELECTROCONVULSIVE THERAPY (ECT) A kind of treatment that is used in contemporary Western psychiatry for severe or refractory mania, psychosis, or depression in which a weak electrical current is passed through the brain when the patient is unconscious under general anesthesia.

GAMMA-AMINO-BUTYRIC ACID (GABA) The principle inhibitory CNS neurotransmitter. Sedative-hypnotic drugs, principally the benzodiazepines, act on the brain by attaching to GABA receptors resulting in a general state of decreased arousal or sedation.

GENDER IDENTITY DISORDER A syndrome characterized by an intense and persistent sense of identity as someone of the opposite gender causing significant emotional distress and social and occupational impairment

GENERALIZED ANXIETY DISORDER (GAD) An anxiety disorder characterized by excessive anxiety, restlessness, inability to concentrate, and worry occurring more days than not for at least six months

GLOBUS HYSTERICUS A kind of conversion disorder that is characterized by the persisting belief that an object is caught in one's throat and is interfering with swallowing. The patient has normal findings on physical and neurologic examination.

GLUTAMATE A principle excitatory CNS neurotransmitter whose dysregulation has recently been implicated in the pathogenesis of schizophrenia

HISTRIONIC PERSONALITY DISORDER A personality disorder characterized by excessive emotionality and attention-seeking behavior

HYPOCHONDRIASIS A syndrome characterized by persisting unfounded fears of having a serious illness based on a misinterpretation of normal bodily functions or minor symptoms. The absence of underlying medical disorders has been verified by physical examination or neurologic evaluation and/or diagnostic testing, and symptoms are not better accounted for by another major psychiatric disorder.

HYPOMANIC EPISODE A period of at least four days in which an individual experiences abnormal and persistently elevated, expansive, or irritable mood concurrently with other symptoms including nondelusional grandiosity, diminished need for sleep, pressured speech, easily being distracted, or increased goal-directed activities. In contrast to a manic episode, a hypomanic episode does not result in social or occupational impairment, and there are no associated psychotic symptoms, including hallucinations or delusions.

HYSTERIA An obsolete diagnostic category commonly used in the latter half of the 19th century characterized by extreme anxiety, somatoform, depressive, and dissociative symptoms, such as paralyses, anesthesias, blindness, seizures, and head and body aches with no medical explanation, as well as dysphoria, hallucinations, and multiple personalities

L-DOPA (I.E., L-DIHYDROXYPHENYLALANINE) The current standard treatment for Parkinson's disease which works by repleting dopamine in neurons of the substantia nigra, the specific brain region whose dysregulation results in Parkinson's disease

LIMBIC SYSTEM Related subcortical evolutionarily primitive brain regions that are centrally involved in the expression and regulation of emotions. Limbic structures include the hypothalamus, amygdala, and various regions in the midbrain.

MAJOR DEPRESSIVE DISORDER A serious mood disorder characterized by a persisting pattern of severe depressive episodes in the absence of a history of manic, mixed, or hypomanic episodes. Depressive episodes are not related to an underlying medical etiology or the effects of substance abuse and are not better explained by another major psychiatric disorder.

MAJOR DEPRESSIVE EPISODE Persisting severe depressed mood of at least two weeks duration in which depression is accompanied by at least four additional symptoms including possibly: changes in appetite, weight loss or gain, sleep disturbance, psychomotor agitation or slowing, fatigue, feelings of worthlessness or guilt, difficulty thinking, and recurrent thoughts of suicide or suicide attempts. The episode is not related to an underlying medical disorder, medication side effects, or the effects of chronic substance abuse and is not better explained by a pre-existing severe psychiatric disorder.

MAJOR DEPRESSIVE EPISODE WITH PSYCHOTIC FEATURES An episode of severe depression that is accompanied by psychotic symptoms, including possibly auditory hallucinations, delusions, or others. Psychotic symptoms occur only during the depressive episode, and are not caused by an underlying medical disorder or the effects of a substance or better explained by another psychiatric disorder.

MANIC EPISODE Persisting euphoric or irritable mood lasting at least one week (or any amount of time when hospitalization is required) accompanied by at least three of the following symptoms: grandiosity, decreased need for sleep, pressured speech, flight of ideas, distractibility, increased goal-directed activity, and excessive involvement in pleasurable activity with a high potential for painful consequences. Psychotic symptoms including hallucinations or delusions sometimes occur during manic episodes.

MONOAMINE OXIDASE INHIBITORS (MAOIs) An older class of antidepressant medications that work through inhibition of the enzyme (monoamine oxidase) that breaks down certain naturally occurring CNS neurotransmitters (the amines), including epinephrine, serotonin, and norepinephrine, thereby resulting in increased availability of these neurotransmitters and associated improvement in depressed mood. MAOIs in current use in Western psychiatry include isocarboxizide (Marplan), phenelzine (Nardil), and tranylcypromine (Parnate).

MOOD DISORDERS Serious disorders that include depressive, manic or mixed mood episodes as primary clinical features. The principal mood disorders described in contemporary Western psychiatry include major depressive disorder (formerly unipolar depression), bipolar disorder (formerly manic-depressive disorder), dysthymic disorder, and cyclothymic disorder.

MOOD EPISODE An enduring pattern of impairing changes in an individual's baseline mood, including depression, mania, hypomania, or mixed depressive-manic states. The type, severity, and pattern of mood symptoms determines typically leads to diagnosis of a specific mood disorder.

NARCISSISTIC PERSONALITY DISORDER A personality disorder characterized by a persisting grandiose sense of self-importance, preoccupation with fantasies of unlimited success or power, arrogant behavior, intense need for admiration, and lack of empathy for others, and sometimes exploitative behavior in efforts to achieve goals

NARCOLEPSY A severe sleep disorder characterized a persisting pattern of sleep attacks accompanied by loss of muscle tone and abnormal EEG activity. The disorder is not caused by an underlying medical disorder, the effects of a substance (including medications) and is not better explained by a pre-existing psychiatric disorder.

NEUROLEPTICS (A SYNONYM FOR ANTIPSYCHOTICS) Medications used to treat schizophrenia and other psychotic disorders. Most currently used neuroleptics work by antagonizing CNS dopamine receptors. More recently introduced neuroleptics have a lower associated risk of side effects, including neurologic syndromes, and work by antagonizing both dopamine and serotonin receptors in the brain.

NEUROSIS (not a currently used term in *DSM-IV* diagnostic descriptions) A kind of mental disorder of moderate severity that is presumed to have its origin in intrapsychic conflicts or other psychodynamic issues

OBSESSIVE-COMPULSIVE DISORDER (OCD) A syndrome characterized by persisting intrusive, seemingly irrational thoughts (obsessions) and associated repetitive ritualized behaviors (compulsions) performed to reduce emotional distress associated with obsessions. The individual may experience predominantly obsessions or compulsions or a combined pattern of obsessions and compulsions. Patients with OCD experience significant, sometimes constant distress and frequent social or occupational impairment because of interfering effects of obsessions and compulsions in their day to day lives.

OBSESSIVE-COMPULSIVE PERSONALITY DISORDER (OCPD) In contrast to OCD, a personality disorder characterized by a long-standing preoccupation with order, perfection, attention to detail, rules, and control. Patients with OCPD have an obsessive personality style but do not experience frank obsessions, and their obsessive-compulsive style typically does not result in significant distress.

OPPOSITIONAL DEFIANT DISORDER A syndrome of disruptive behavior with onset in childhood characterized by defiant, hostile behavior, frequent loss of temper, angry or resentful mood, and deliberate efforts to annoy others. The disorder causes significant impairment in social or academic functioning and is not caused by an underlying medical disorder or major psychiatric disorder.

PAIN DISORDER One of the somatoform disorders characterized by persisting complaints of pain in one or more body areas in the absence of associated medical problems requiring treatment. Complaints of pain cause significant social or occupational impairment and almost continuous subjective distress. Onset or exacerbations of pain are associated with psychological factors or combined psychological-physiological factors. A syndrome characterized by the subjective experience of pain that does not have sufficient medical justification

PANIC ATTACK A transient period of intense anxiety or discomfort associated with several psychological or physiological symptoms, including possibly: palpitations, sweating, trembling, shortness of breath, a choking sensation, chest pain, nausea or abdominal distress, dizziness, depersonalization, derealization, fear of going crazy, fear of dying, tactile sensations (paresthesias), and chills or hot flashes

PANIC DISORDER A severe anxiety disorder characterized by a persisting pattern of recurrent unexpected and un-cued panic attacks that are not etiologically related to an underlying medical disorder, the effects of a substance (including medication side effects), or another major psychiatric disorder

PARANOID PERSONALITY DISORDER A personality disorder characterized by pervasive distrust of other people such that others are virtually always perceived as being threatening or hostile

PARASOMNIAS As opposed to dyssomnias in which the clinical focus is a disturbance in the ability to initiate or maintain sleep, paradomnias are disorders of sleep characterized abnormal physiological or behavioral events that disrupt the normal stages of sleep. Parasomnias include sleep terrors, nightmares, and sleepwalking.

PERIMENOPAUSAL SYNDROME (at present, not a formal diagnosis in the DSM-IV) A disorder that begins close to onset of menopause characterized by vague somatic complaints and depressed mood and lability. Perimenopausal symptoms are believed to result from changes in levels of reproductive hormones but may also be driven by cultural expectations.

PERSONALITY DISORDER An pervasive and enduring pattern of subjective experience and outward behavior that deviates from normal cultural expectations which starts at or before adolescence and is typically associated with significant interpersonal dysfunction and personal distress

PERVASIVE DEVELOPMENTAL DISORDER A broad class of severe developmental disorders with onset during infancy or early childhood characterized by stereotyped behaviors and impairments in numerous developmental areas of functioning, including communication skills and social interactions with peers

POSTPARTUM DEPRESSION (at present, not a formal diagnosis in DSM-IV) Depressed mood with onset soon following the end of a normal term pregnancy. Psychosis is sometimes reported during an episode of post-partum depression. Women who experience depressed mood in the immediate post-partum period are at increased risk of future episodes of major depression.

POST-TRAUMATIC STRESS DISORDER (PSTD) A severe anxiety disorder characterized by a persisting pattern of re-experiencing a potentially life-threatening trauma through flash-backs, recurring dreams or intense fear when exposed to circumstances that remind the patient of the trauma. Patients with PTSD often develop a pattern of avoiding situations that remind them of the traumatic event, and frequently experience feelings of "numbing" and increased arousal, including increased startle response.

PREMENSTRUAL DYSPHORIC DISORDER (PDD) (included in the DSM-IV as a provisional disorder, i.e., a set of research criteria) A mood disorder in women characterized by a persisting pattern of depressed mood starting during the late luteal phase (i.e., pre-menstrually) and typically resolving soon after the beginning of menstruation

PSEUDOSEIZURES Recurring abnormal movements that are similar in appearance to those of seizure disorders but occur in the absence of seizures. Pseudoseizures often occur in individuals who have actual seizure disorders and are sometimes feigned or occur as a kind of conversion disorder.

PSYCHOSURGERY Surgical procedures involving specific brain regions that is performed in efforts to alleviate psychiatric symptoms. This approach is considered as a last resort in cases where the patient is severely impaired by symptoms (e.g., severe OCD) and has been unresponsive to multiple medication trials.

PSYCHOTIC SYMPTOMS A group of symptoms that result from gross impairment in reality testing. Contemporary Western psychiatry classifies psychotic symptoms as positive – ones that manifest as an excess of normal functioning – and negative, in which there is a loss of normal functioning. Positive psychotic symptoms include, for example, auditory hallucinations, delusional beliefs, or grossly disorganized speech or behavior. In contrast, representative negative psychotic symptoms include flattening of affect and diminished spontaneous speech. Psychotic symptoms occur in the context of many medical disorders as a consequence of substance intoxication or medication side effects and in schizophrenia and the other psychotic disorders. The duration, severity, and pattern of psychotic symptoms will determine the most likely psychiatric or medical diagnosis.

PSYCHOTIC DISORDERS A group of severe psychiatric disorders characterized by prominent psychotic symptoms, including loss of reality testing, hallucinations, delusions, disorganized speech or behavior, and others. Schizophrenia, schizoaffective disorder, schizophreniform disorder, and delusional disorder are principal psychotic disorders in the DSM-IV.

REALITY TESTING (LOSS OF) A psychotic symptom commonly seen in schizophrenia characterized by loss of capacity to distinguish between the actual experiences of self in relation to the external physical and social environments and the content of delusional beliefs, auditory hallucinations, or other psychotic symptoms

**SCHIZOAFFECTIVE DISORDER** A psychotic disorder in which prominent depressive or manic symptoms occur together with psychotic symptoms at some times and psychotic symptoms which occur in the absence of mood symptoms at other times during the same two week period

**SCHIZOID PERSONALITY DISORDER** A personality disorder characterized by pervasive detachment from social relationships and restricted range of emotions

**SCHIZOPHRENIA** A psychotic disorder characterized by the presence of two or more prominent psychotic symptoms (including hallucinations, delusions, disorganized speech or behavior, or negative psychotic symptoms) that continue for at least one month, resulting in significant social and occupational impairment. The disorder cannot be related to a history of pervasive developmental disorder, underlying medical causes, or chronic effects of substance abuse, and the total duration of the illness (including residual phase) must last at least six months. Five types of schizophrenia have been defined in contemporary Western psychiatry: paranoid, catatonic, disorganized, undifferentiated, and residual.

**SCHIZOPHRENIFORM DISORDER** A psychotic disorder that is identical to schizophrenia except that total duration of symptoms must be at least one month and less than six months

**SCHIZOTYPAL PERSONALITY DISORDER** A personality disorder characterized by anxiety in social relationships, odd or eccentric behaviors, superstitiousness, a preoccupation with paranormal phenomena, magical thinking, or the use of bizarre or magical rituals in everyday situations

**SEASONAL AFFECTIVE DISORDER (SAD)** A variant of bipolar disorder characterized by cyclic manic, depressive, or mixed mood states that are somehow triggered by external cues related to changing seasons, including principally, increased or decreased day length. Individuals with SAD tend to become depressed during the autumn months and manic during springtime.

**SEDATIVE-HYPNOTICS** A class of drugs that act on the brain by increasing the activity of GABA, thus resulting in general calming or (at higher doses) sedation

**SEIZURE DISORDERS** A group of disorders characterized by intermittent abnormal electrical activity in the CNS associated with abnormal movements, changes in level of consciousness, and numerous psychiatric symptoms both during and after seizure activity

**SEROTONIN** A naturally occurring CNS neurotransmitter whose dysregulation has been implicated in the pathogenesis of major depressive disorder, obsessive-compulsive disorder, and numerous other psychiatric disorders

**SEROTONIN-SELECTIVE RE-UPTAKE INHIBITORS (SSRIs)** A class of antidepressant medications that work by selectively inhibiting the normal reuptake of serotonin from the synaptic region (*i.e.*, between two neurons) into neurons that manufactured serotonin. SSRIs currently used in Western psychiatry include fluoxetine (Prozac), paroxetine (Paxil), sertraline (Zoloft), and citalopram (Celexa).

**SHARED PSYCHOTIC DISORDER** A psychotic disorder characterized by the development of a delusional belief in an individual who is in a close relationship with another person who has a psychotic disorder that includes delusions

**SLEEP DISORDERS** A group of disorders resulting in disruption of normal sleep behavior. The two major kinds of sleep disorders are the dyssomnias – disruptions in the initiation or maintenance of sleep – and the parasomnias – abnormal behaviors that occur during sleep and disrupt it.

**SLEEP TERROR DISORDER** A parasomnia characterized by recurrent episodes of awakening in a state of terror accompanied by autonomic arousal, including elevated heart rate and rapid breathing. Awakening typically occurs in the first hours of sleep, and the individual has no or limited dream recall. The disorder may not be caused by a medical disorder, medication side effects, or substance intoxication or withdrawal.

**SOCIAL PHOBIA** An anxiety disorder characterized by a persisting pattern of intense anxiety and, sometimes, panic attacks in social contexts or performance situations. The phobic individual acknowledges that the level of anxiety experienced is unreasonable. The disorder is not etiologically related to an underlying medical disorder, substance abuse, or another major psychiatric disorder.

**SOMATIZATION** The manifestation of emotional distress as somatic (*i.e.*, bodily) symptoms

**SOMATIZATION DISORDER** A kind of somatoform disorder characterized by chronic and recurrent psychosomatic symptoms, including at least four pain symptoms, two gastrointestinal symptoms, one sexual symptom and one pseudoneurological symptom. There is either no identified underlying medical condition or symptoms are disproportionate to what would be expected in response to an identified disorder.

SOMATOFORM DISORDERS A group of psychiatric disorders characterized by prominent physical complaints in the absence of a medical disorder that can sufficiently explain them. According to the *DSM-IV*, the somatoform disorders include somatization disorder, conversion disorder, pain disorder, hypochondriasis, body dysmorphic disorder, and undifferentiated somatoform disorder.

SPECIFIC PHOBIA An anxiety disorder characterized by persisting fear of a specific circumscribed object or situation, exposure to which almost invariably evokes intense anxiety or panic

SUBSTANCE ABUSE A long-standing maladaptive pattern of substance use resulting in significant social or occupational impairment and persisting distress. Substance abuse is characterized by academic or occupational failure that is related to abuse, associated legal problems, and continuing use of a substance in spite of significant problems that are related to ongoing use.

SUBSTANCE DEPENDENCE In contrast to substance abuse, a maladaptive pattern of substance use associated with tolerance of the effects of a substance from chronic use and the occurrence of physiological signs and symptoms of withdrawal when the substance is discontinued. The alcoholic, for example, experiences a characteristic physiological withdrawal syndrome on discontinuing alcohol after prolonged heavy drinking.

SUBSTANCE-INDUCED MENTAL DISORDERS A group of syndromes, including delirium, dementia, amnestic disorder, psychotic disorder, mood disorder, anxiety disorder, and others that can develop during intoxication or withdrawal or following prolonged abstinence after a period of heavy chronic use

SUBSTANCE WITHDRAWAL A syndrome that occurs following abrupt cessation of certain substances following chronic heavy use characterized by clinically significant distress and impaired social or occupational functioning. Withdrawal is typically manifested as a physiological and psychological symptom pattern that is specific to each substance.

TARDIVE DYSKINESIA A persisting, usually permanent neurologic disorder characterized by abnormal involuntary movements typically affecting muscles of the neck, tongue, and face resulting from CNS effects following chronic use of certain antipsychotic medications

TOURETTE'S DISORDER A kind of tic disorder characterized by persisting combinations of vocal or motor tics that cause significant social or occupational impairment and are not better explained by medication side effects, substance abuse, or an underlying medical disorder

TRANQUILIZERS (A SYNONYM FOR SEDATIVE-HYPNOTICS) A class of medications used to treat symptoms of anxiety or agitation. Most tranquilizers work by increasing GABA, the principal CNS inhibitory neurotransmitter, thus resulting in a general calming effect.

TRICYCLIC ANTIDEPRESSANTS (TCAs) A class of antidepressant medications, including desipramine, imiprimine, and nortriptyline, that share similar pharmacological properties and side effect profiles. Now considered outdated or second tier antidepressants by many Western-trained psychiatrists, these medications are still often used in the treatment of depressive symptoms that are unresponsive or partially responsive to newer antidepressants associated with fewer side effects.

UNDIFFERENTIATED SOMATOFORM DISORDER A somatoform disorder that lasts at least six months and is characterized by a persisting somatic complaint that cannot be adequately explained by identified medical problems, causes significant distress, does not meet full criteria for somatization disorder, and is not the result of malingering

UNIPOLAR DEPRESSION A synonym for major depressive episode. See above.

UP-REGULATION (OF NEUROTRANSMITTER SYSTEMS) An increase in the number of neurotransmitter receptors (or their binding affinities for medications or neurotransmitters) resulting from the prolonged use of certain psychiatric medications, including most antipsychotics and SSRIs

VASCULAR DEMENTIA A kind of dementia characterized by marked impairment in memory and at least one severe cognitive symptom including language disturbance (aphasia), impaired ability to carry out learned tasks (apraxia), loss of capacity to recognize familiar places or faces (agnosia), and diminished executive functioning. There are typically associated neurological signs, and the disorder is etiologically related to identifiable CNS disease.

# COMMON SIDE EFFECTS OF ❖ WESTERN PSYCHIATRIC ❖ MEDICATIONS

SIDE EFFECTS OF COMMONLY PRESCRIBED ANTIDEPRESSANTS

| MEDICATION (COMMON BRAND NAME) | DRY MOUTH, CONSTIPATION, BLURRED VISION | SEDATION | POSTURAL CHANGES IN BLOOD PRESSURE | SEXUAL DYSFUNCYION | GASTROINTESTINAL DISTURBANCES | INSOMNIA |
|---|---|---|---|---|---|---|
| AMITRIPTYLINE (ELAVIL) | HIGH | HIGH | HIGH | HIGH | LOW | NONE |
| CLOMIPRAMINE (ANAFRANIL) | HIGH | HIGH | HIGH | HIGH | LOW | NONE |
| DESIPRAMINE (NORPRAMIN) | SOME | SOME | SOME | HIGH | LOW | SOME |
| DOXEPIN (SINEQUAN) | HIGH | HIGH | HIGH | HIGH | LOW | NONE |
| IMIPRAMINE (TOFRANIL) | HIGH | HIGH | HIGH | HIGH | LOW | NONE |
| NORTRIPTYLINE (PAMELOR) | SOME | SOME | SOME | HIGH | LOW | NONE |
| CITALOPRAM (CELEXA) | NONE | LOW | NONE | HIGH | HIGH | LOW |
| FLUOXETINE (PROZAC) | NONE | NONE | NONE | HIGH | HIGH | HIGH |
| FLUVOXAMINE (LUVOX) | NONE | SOME | NONE | HIGH | HIGH | LOW |

CONTINUED

## SIDE EFFECTS OF COMMONLY PRESCRIBED ANTIDEPRESSANTS, CONTINUED

| MEDICATION (COMMON BRAND NAME) | DRY MOUTH, CONSTIPATION, BLURRED VISION | SEDATION | POSTURAL CHANGES IN BLOOD PRESSURE | SEXUAL DYSFUNCYION | GASTRO-INTESTINAL DISTURBANCES | INSOMNIA |
|---|---|---|---|---|---|---|
| PAROXETINE (PAXIL) | LOW | LOW | NONE | HIGH | HIGH | LOW |
| SERTRALINE (ZOLOFT) | NONE | LOW | NONE | HIGH | HIGH | SOME |
| MAOIS (ISOCARBOXAZID/MARPLAN; PHENELZINE/NARDIL; TRANYLCYPROMINE/PARNATE | SOME | SOME | HIGH | HIGH | LOW | LOW EXCEPT PARNATE (HIGH) |
| BUPROPION (WELLBUTRIN) | NONE | NONE | NONE | NONE | SOME | HIGH |
| MIRTAZAPINE (REMERON) | NONE | NONE | NONE | NONE | LOW | NONE |
| NEFAZODONE (SERZONE) | NONE | HIGH | LOW | NONE | SOME | LOW |
| TRAZADONE (DESYREL) | LOW | HIGH | HIGH | NONE | SOME | NONE |
| VENLAFAXINE (EFFEXOR) | NONE | LOW | LOW | HIGH | HIGH | SOME |

## SIDE EFFECTS OF COMMONLY PRESCRIBED MOOD-STABILIZERS

| MEDICATION (BRAND NAME) | COMMON SIDE EFFECTS |
|---|---|
| LITHIUM CARBONATE (ESKALITH) | NAUSEA, INCREASED URINATION, THIRST, HAND TREMOR, GI DISTRESS (SLURRED SPEECH, CONFUSION WHEN TOXIC) |
| CARBAMAZEPINE (TEGRETOL) | DIZZINESS, SEDATION, NAUSEA, DRY MOUTH CONSTIPATION, HEADACHE |
| VALPROIC ACID (DEPAKOTE) | SEDATION, HAND TREMOR, NAUSEA, DIARRHEA, ABDOMINAL CRAMPS, HAIR LOSS |
| GABA-PENTIN (NEURONTIN) | SEDATION, WEIGHT GAIN, ATAXIA, HEADACHES, NAUSEA |
| LAMOTRAGINE (LAMICTAL) | LIFE-THREATENING SKIN RASHES (RARE) USUALLY IN FIRST WEEKS OF TREATMENT, BENIGN RASH MUCH MORE LIKELY |

## Side effects of commonly prescribed sedative-hypnotics

| Medication (common brand name) | Side effects |
|---|---|
| Flurazepam (Dalmane) | Hangover effect, rebound insomnia after stopping |
| Temazepam (Restoril) | Anterograde amnesia, rebound insomnia after stopping |
| Diphenhydramine (Benadryl) | Dry mouth, constipation,, blurred vision |
| Zolpidem (Ambien) | Hangover effect (less often) |
| Zaleplon (Sonata) | Hangover effect (less often) |
| Chloral hydrate | Gastrointestinal irritation |

## Side effects of commonly prescribed antidepressants

| Medication (common brand name) | Acute or chronic neurologic side effects | Dry mouth, constipation, blurred vision | Sedation | Postural changes in blood pressure |
|---|---|---|---|---|
| Chlorpromazine (Thorazine) | Some | Some | High | High |
| Thioridazine (Mellaril) | Low | High | High | High |
| Perphenazine (Trilafon) | High | Low | Low | Low |
| Haloperidol (Haldol) | High | Low | Low | Low |
| Thiothixene (Navane) | High | Low | Low | Low |
| Clozapine (Clozaril) | Low | High | High | High |
| Quetiapine (Seroquel) | Low | Low | Some | Some |
| Olanzapine (Zyprexa) | Low | Low | Some | Low |
| Risperidone (Risperdal) | Low | Low | Low | Some |

# ❖ BIBLIOGRAPHY ❖

## CHINESE LANGUAGE BIBLIOGRAPHY

"A Clinical Audit of Post Serious Infection Spleen Vacuity Syndrome in Infants" by Lin Guang-yu *et al.*, *Zhong Yi Za Zhi (Journal of Chinese Medicine)*, #1, 1998, p. 38-39

"A Clinical Audit of the Preventive Treatment of Chemotherapy Gastrointestinal Tract Reactions with Chinese Medicinals" by Zhou Xiong-gen, *Shang Hai Zhong Yi Yao Za Zhi (Shanghai Journal of Chinese Medicine & Medicinals)*, #6, 1999, p. 24-25

"A Clinical Audit of the Treatment of 56 Cases of Lily Disease with *Bai He Da Zao Tang* (Lily & Red Date Decoction)" by Yang Wei-hua *et al.*, *Bei Jing Zhong Yi (Beijing Chinese Medicine)*, #3, 1999, p. 35

"A Comparison Between Electro-acupuncture with Chlorpromazine and Chlorpormazine Alone in 60 Schizophrenia Patients" by Zhu-ge D.Y. & Chen J.K., *Zhong Guo Zhong Xi Yi Jie He Za Zhi (Chinese National Journal of Integrated Chinese-Western Medicine)*, #7, 1993, p. 408-409

"A Comparative Clinical Survey of *Duo Dong Ning* (Hyperactivity Calmer) & Ritalin in the Treatment of Pediatric Hyperactivity Syndrome" by Li Xue-rong & Chen Zhi-jian, *Zhong Guo Zhong Xi Yi Jie He Za Zhi (Chinese National Journal of Integrated Chinese-Western Medicine)*, #7, 1999, p. 410-411

"An Analysis of Those with Liver Depression & Serum Levels of [Various] Estrogens" by Wang Xia-ling & Zhou Da-qiao, *Hu Bei Zhong Yi Za Zhi (Hubei Journal of Chinese Medicine)*, #4, 1996, p. 38-39

"An Explanation of the Pattern Discrimination Treatment of 49 Cases of Plum Pit Qi" by Yuan chang-hua, *Si Chuan Zhong Yi (Sichuan Chinese Medicine)*, #11, 1993, p. 33-34

"An Initial Exploration of the Relationship between Spleen-stomach Theory and Neurological-psychiatric Diseases" by Cui Shi-xian, *Shang Hai Zhong Yi Yao Za Zhi (Shanghai Journal of Chinese Medicine & Medicinals)*, #3, 1996, p. 5-6

"A Short Discussion of Experiences Treating Running Piglet" by Zhang Xiao-hui, *Ji Lin Zhong Yi Yao (Jilin Chinese Medicine & Medicinals)*, #1, 1999, p. 42

"A Simple Exploration of the Relationship between 'Resolution' & Depression" by Nan Zhong-bo, *Shang Hai Zhong Yi Yao Za Zhi (Shanghai Journal of Chinese Medicine & Medicinals)*, #2, 1994, p. 14-16

"A Study of the *Nei Jing* & Ancient Chinese Psychiatric Diseases" by Guo Li-wa & Huang Jian, *Bei Jing Zhong Yi (Beijing Chinese Medicine)*, #2, 1996, p. 48-50

"A Survey of the Effects of the Methods of Enriching Yin & Free the Flow of the Orifices on the Psychiatric

Evaluation of Table in Patients with Vascular Dementia" by Wang Can-hui, Liu Tao, Yang Jin *et al.*, *Zhong Guo Zhong Xi Yi Jie He Za Zhi (Chinese National Journal of Integrated Chinese-Western Medicine)*, #7, 1999, p. 405-406

"A Survey of the Treatment of Neurological & Psychiatric Diseases with *Chai Hu Jia Long Gu Mu Li Tang* (Bupleurum Plus Dragon Bone & Oyster Shell Decoction)" by Lin Tian-hua, *Bei Jing Zhong Yi (Beijing Chinese Medicine)*, #3, 1996, p. 47-48
*Bian Zheng Qi Wen (Pattern Discrimination Wondrous News)* by Chen Shi-duo, Chinese Ancient Books Press, Beijing, 1993

*Dian Kuang Xian (Withdrawal, Mania & Epilepsy)* by Zhuang Jia-xu, Chinese National Chinese Medicine & Medicinals Press, Beijing, 1995

*Dian Kuang Xian Juan (A Book on Withdrawal, Mania & Epilepsy)* by Shan Shu-jian & Chen Zi-hua, Chinese National Chinese Medicine & Medicinals Press, Beijing, 1999

*Dao De Jing (The Classic of the Way & Virtue)* by Lao-zi appearing in *The Gate of All Marvelous Things: A Guide to Reading the Tao Te Ching* by Gregory C. Richter, Red Mansions Publishing, SF, 1998

"Epimedium in the Treatment of Climacteric Syndrome" by Hu Wei-yong, *Zhong Yi Za Zhi (Journal of Chinese Medicine)*, #12, 1999, p. 711

"Experiences in the Treatment of Hysterical Disease with Acupuncture" by Huang Xing-yi, *Zhong Guo Zhen Jiu (Chinese Acupuncture & Moxibustion)*, #2, 1995, p. 44

"Experiences Treating Depression with Scalp Acupuncture" by Kong Ze-qi, *Zhong Yi Za Zhi (Journal of Chinese Medicine)*, #8, 1996, p. 472

"Experiential Knowledge of the Treatment of Insomnia with *Xue Fu Zhu Yu Tang* (Blood Mansion Dispel Stasis Decoction)" by Chen Gui-fu, *Hei Long Jiang Zhong Yi Yao Za Zhi (Heilongjiang Journal of Chinese Medicine & Medicinals)*, #5, 1996, p. 35

"Experiential Knowledge of the Treatment of Sleep Anxiety with *Xue Fu Zhu Yu Tang* (Blood Mansion Dispel Stasis Decoction)" by Hu Ji-ming, *Zhen Jiang Zhong Yi Za Zhi (Zhejiang Journal of Chinese Medicine)*, #5, 1993, p. 198

*Fu Ke (Gynecology)* by Yang Yi-ya, Hubei Science & Technology Press, Shijiazhuang, 1996

*Fu Ke Ming Yi Zheng Zhi Jing Hua (An Efflorescence of Famous Gynecologists' Patterns & Treatments)* by Yue Tou-zhen, Shanghai University of Chinese Medicine Press, Shanghai, 1995

*Gu Fang Miao Yong (Ancient Formulas, Wondrous Uses)* by Chen Bao-ming & Zhao Jin-xi, Science & Technology Press, Beijing, 1994

*Han Ying Chang Yong Yi Xue Ci Hui (Chinese-English Glossary of Commonly Used Medical Terms)* by Huang Xiao-kai, People's Health & Hygiene Press, Beijing, 1982

*Huang Di Nei Jing Dao Du (Yellow Emperor's Inner Classic Reference Notes)* by Fu Wei-kang & Wu Hong-zhou, Bashu Book Press, Chengdu, 1988

*Jian Ming Zhong Yi Da Ci Dian (A Plain & Clear Dictionary of Chinese Medicine)* compiled by the Research Institute, Guangzhou College of Chinese Medicine, People's Health & Hygiene Press, Beijing, 1986

*Jin Gui Yao Lue (Essentials from the Golden Cabinet)* by Zhang Zhong-jing, Oriental Healing Arts Institute, Long Beach, CA, 1983

*Jin Yuan Si Da Yi Xue Jia Ming Zhu Ji Cheng (An Anthology of Famous Jin-Yuan Four Great Schools Medical Studies)* edited by Ye Chuan & Jian Yi, Chinese National Chinese Medicine & Medicinal Press, Beijing, 1997

*Jin Yuan Si Da Yi Xue Zhu Si Xiang Zhi Yan Jiu (A Study of Jin-Yuan Four Great Schools of Medicine's Thinking)* edited by Li Cong-fu & Liu Bing-fan, People's Health & Hygiene Press, Beijing, 1983

*Jin Zi Jiu Zhuan Ji (A Collection of Jin Zi-jiu's Teachings)* by Jin Zi-jiu, People's Health & Hygiene Press, Beijing, 1982

*Jing Shen Bing De Zhong Yi Zhi Liao (The Chinese Medical Treatment of Psychiatric Diseases)* by Li Qi-lu, Chinese National Chinese Medicine & Medicinal Press, Beijing, 1994

*Jing Shen Yi Bing Zhong Yi Lin Chuang Zhi Liao (The Clinical Treatment of Psychiatric Disease with Chinese Medicine)* by Huang Yue-dong, Shanghai Science & Technology Press, Shanghai, 1998

"Jottings on the Acupuncture Treatment of Senile Dementia" by He Jun & Li Qiu-yang, *Tian Jin Zhong Yi (Tianjin Chinese Medicine)*, #3, 1993, p. 43

"Knowledge Gained by Experience in the Treatment of

Climacteric Syndrome" by Liu Zong-bao, *Si Chuan Zhong Yi* (*Sichuan Chinese Medicine*), #6, 1999, p. 10

*Lao Nian Chang Xian Bing Zheng Fang Zhi Fa* (*The Prevention & Treatment of Commonly Seen Diseases in the Elderly*) by Wu Jun-xi, Chinese National Chinese Medicine & Medicinal Press, Beijing, 1998

*Lao Nian Qi Chi Dai Zheng De Zhong Yi Zhi Liao* (*The Chinese Medical Treatment of Senile Dementia*) by Hu Long-cai, True China Book Publishers, Taipei, 1997

*Nan Zhi Bing De Liang Fang Miao Fa* (*Fine Formulas & Miraculous Methods for Difficult to Treat Diseases*) by Wu Da-zhou & Ge Xiu-ke, Chinese National Chinese Medicine & Medicinal Press, Beijing, 1992

*Nei Jing Jiang Yi* (*Inner Classic Teaching Materials*) by Cheng Shi-de, Shanghai Science & Technology Press, Shanghai, 1985

"New Uses for *Wan Dai Tang* (Arresting Vaginal Discharge Decoction)" by Qian Sheng, *Zhong Yi Za Zhi* (*Journal of Chinese Medicine*), #9, 1993, p. 550

*Qi Nan Za Zheng Jing Xuan* (*A Carefully Chosen [Collection of] Strange, Difficult Miscellaneous Conditions*) by Huang Yong-yuan, Guangdong Science & Technology Press, Guangzhou, 1996

*Qian Jia Miao Fang* (*Ten Thousand Families' Wondrous Formulas*) compiled by Li Wen-liang & Qi Qiang, People's Liberation Army Press, Beijing, 1985

*Shang Hai Lao Zhong Yi Jing Yan Xuan Bian* (*A Selected Compilation of Shanghai Old Doctors' Experiences*), Shanghai Science & Technology Press, Shanghai, 1984

*Shang Han Lun Lin Chuang Yan Jiu* (*Clinical Studies [Based on] the Treatise on Damage [Due to] Cold*) by Wang Zhan-xi, People's Health & Hygiene Press, Beijing, 1983

*Shen Jing Jing Shen Yi Bing Gu Qin Xiao Fang* (*Ancient & Modern Effective Formulas for Neurological & Psychiatric Diseases*) by Li Xi-ru, Science & Technology Press, Beijing, 1998

*Shen Jing Nei Ke Ji Zheng Shou Ce* (*A Handbook of Neurological, Internal Medicine & Emergency Conditions*) by Zheng Xiang-cai & Lu Guan-yi, Shanxi Science & Technology Press, Xian, 1992

*Shi Yong zhen Jiu Tui Na Zhi Liao Xue* (*A Study of Practical Acupuncture-moxibustion & Tuina Treatments*) by Xia Zhi-ping, Shanghai College of Chinese Medicine Press, Shanghai, 1990

*Shi Yong Zhong Yi Nei Ke Xue* (*A Study of Practical Chinese Medicine Internal Medicine*) by Huang Wen-dong, Shanghai Science & Technology Press, Shanghai, 1985

*Shi Yong Zhong Yi Zhen Duan Xue* (*A Study of Practical Chinese Medicine Diagnosis*) by Liu Tie-tiao, Shanghai Science & Technology Press, Shanghai, 1995

*Shi Yong Zhong Yi Shen Jing Bing Xue* (*A Study of Practical Chinese Medical Neurology*) by Chen Jia-yang, Gansu Science & Technology Press, Lanzhou, 1989

"The Chinese Medical Diagnosis & Treatment of [40 Cases of] Antibiotic-resistant Pediatric Respiratory Tract Infection" by Liu Ying-feng, *Si Chuan Zhong Yi* (*Sichuan Chinese Medicine*), #1, 1996, p. 44-45

"The Chinese Medical Treatment of 20 Cases of Frequently Occurring Somnolence" by Wang Gui-rong & Dan Shu-fu, *Hei Long Jiang Zhong Yi Yao Za Zhi* (*Heilongjiang Journal of Chinese Medicine & Medicinals*), #3, 1995, p. 16

"The Chinese Medicine Treatment of 25 Cases of Amenorrhea as a Result of Neuroleptic Medicines" by He Guo-zhang, *Xin Zhong Yi* (*New Chinese Medicine*), #9, 1995, p. 51-52

"The Clinical Discrimination & Treatment of Manic-depression" by Ding De-zheng, *Shang Hai Zhong Yi Za Zhi* (*Shanghai Journal of Chinese Medicine & Medicinals*), #5, 1995, p. 3-4

"The Outstanding Effectiveness of *Gan Mai Da Zao Tang* (Licorice, Wheat & Red Dates Decoction) in the Treatment of Psychiatric Diseases of the Heart & Liver" by Yuan Can-xing, *Shang Hai Zhong Yi Za Zhi* (*Shanghai Journal of Chinese Medicine & Medicinals*), #7, 1996, p. 4-6

"The Treatment of 10 Cases of Mania with *Gan Sui Gun Tan Tang* (Euphorbia Roll [Away] Phlegm Decoction)" by Lin Tian-zhou, *Zhe Jiang Zhong Yi Za Zhi* (*Zhejiang Journal of Chinese Medicine*), #4, 1993, p. 159

"The Treatment of 12 Cases of Pediatric Convulsions Based on the Liver" by Chen Wei-bin *et al.*, *Shang Hai Zhong Yi Yao Za Zhi* (*Shanghai Journal of Chinese Medicine & Medicinals*), #4, 1999, p. 31

"The Treatment of 17 Cases of Cancer Chemotherapy

Reactions with *Bu Yang Huan Wu Tang* (Supplement Yang & Restore the Five [Viscera] Decoction)" by Gong Hao, *Zhe Jiang Zhong Yi Za Zhi (Zhejiang Journal of Chinese Medicine)*, #2, 1996, p. 67

"The Treatment of 20 Cases of Anti-tubercular Medicine's Gastrointestinal Tract Reactions with Chinese Medicinals" by Wei Chang-chun et al., *Ji Lin Zhong Yi Yao (Jilin Chinese Medicine & Medicinals)*, #4, 1999, p. 17

"The Treatment of 23 Cases of Plum Pit Qi with *Gua Di Dan Fan San* (Melon Pedicle & Chalcanthitum Powder)" by Yang Ding-you, *Zhe Jiang Zhong Yi Za Zhi (Zhejiang Journal of Chinese Medicine)*, #5, 1993, p. 210

"The Treatment of [23 Cases of] Post-breast Cancer Surgery Edema of the Upper Arms by the Methods of Boosting the Qi & Quickening the Blood" by Yang Ji-ping, *Zhe Jiang Zhong Yi Za Zhi (Zhejiang Journal of Chinese Medicine)*, #5, 1995, p. 222

"The Treatment of 30 Cases of Climacteric Syndrome with *Gui Zhi Tang Jia Wei* (Cinnamon Twig Decoction with Added Flavors)" by Ye Feng & Yang Hai-hua, *Zhe Jiang Zhong Yi Za Zhi (Zhejiang Journal of Chinese Medicine)*, #11, 1999, p. 477

"The Treatment of 30 Cases of Post-chemotherapy Gastro-intestinal Tract Reactions with Acupuncture & Massage" by Lin Bei-hong et al., *Si Chuan Zhong Yi (Sichuan Chinese Medicine)*, #9, 1999, p. 52-53

"The Treatment of 31 Cases of Facial Muscle Spasm by Needling the Facial Nerve Trunk & *He Gu* (LI 4)" by Chen Dang-guo, *He Han Zhong Yi (Henan Chinese Medicine)*, #1, 2000, p. 53

"The Treatment of 40 Cases of Plum Pit Qi with *Shun Qi Xiao Shi Hua Tan Tang* (Normalize the Qi, Disperse Food & Transform Phlegm Decoction)" by Jing Ming-mo, *Ji Lin Zhong Yi Yao (Jilin Chinese Medicine & Medicinals)*, #4, 1993, p. 19

"The Treatment of 40 Cases of Post-stroke Depression Mainly by Enriching Yin & Quieting the Spirit" by Xu Chao-gang, *Si Chuan Zhong Yi (Sichuan Chinese Medicine)*, #2, 1999, p. 25

"The Treatment of [40 Cases of] Post-surgical Yin Vacuity Fever with *Sha Shen San Xian Tang* (Glehnia Three Immortals Decoction)" by Zhang Hui-ling, *Zhe Jiang Zhong Yi Za Zhi (Zhejiang Journal of Chinese Medicine)*, #3, 1995, p. 113

"The Treatment of 41 Cases of Female Sexual Disturbance with Chinese Medicine" by Wang Da-yue & Jiang Kun, *Shang Hai Zhong Yi Yao Za Zhi (Shanghai Journal of Chinese Medicine & Medicinals)*, #4, 1999, p. 32-33

"The Treatment of 44 Cases of Withdrawal & Mania with Acupuncture" by Wu Ji-hong, *Zhong Guo Zhen Jiu (Chinese Acupuncture & Moxibustion)*, #5, 1994, p. 8

"The Treatment of 52 Cases of Pediatric Tourette's Syndrome Based on the Lungs" by Xu Zhu-qian, *Zhong Yi Za Zhi (Journal of Chinese Medicine)*, #11, 1993, p. 679

"The Treatment of 58 Cases of Post-liver Cancer Chemotherapy Vomiting with *Zhu Ye Shi Gao Tang* (Bamboo Leaf & Gypsum Decoction)" by Jin Pu-fang, *Zhe Jiang Zhong Yi Za Zhi (Zhejiang Journal of Chinese Medicine)*, #5, 1995, p. 200

"The Treatment of 59 Cases of Cancer Chemotherapy Toxic Reactions with the Methods of Regulating & Rectifying the Spleen & Stomach" by Li Zong-ju, *Si Chuan Zhong Yi (Sichuan Chinese Medicine)*, #10, 1999, p. 24-25

"The Treatment of [62 Cases of] Post-surgical Abdominal Distention with *Zhu Hou Tang* (Post-surgery Decoction)" by Wu Hong-ying, *Shan Dong Zhong Yi Za Zhi (Shandong Journal of Chinese Medicine)*, #1, 1995, p. 34

"The Treatment of 80 Cases of Post-surgical Abortion Excessive Menstruation with *Gu Jing Wan* (Secure the Menses Pills)" by Mi Yang, *Hu Bei Zhong Yi Za Zhi (Hubei Journal of Chinese Medicine)*, #2, 1993, p. 9

"The Treatment of 86 Cases of Elevated Serum Prolactin in Females with *Xian Mai Tang* (Epimedium & Malted Barley Decoction)" by Li Xiao-ping & Zhang Min-jian, *Fu Jian Zhong Yi Yao (Fujian Chinese Medicine & Medicinals)*, #5, 1996, p. 27-28

"The Treatment of 100 Cases of Climacteric Syndrome with *Du Qi Wan Jia Chai Shao Gui* (Capital Qi Pills Plus Bupleurum, Peony & Cinnamon)" by Li Shi-qian, *Si Chuan Zhong Yi (Sichuan Chinese Medicine)*, #8, 1999, p. 49

"The Treatment of Depression with *Suan Gan Ning Xin Tang* (Zizyphus Spinosa & Licorice Calm the Heart Decoction)" by Zhu Bo, *Zhe Jiang Zhong Yi Za Zhi (Zhejiang Journal of Chinese Medicine)*, #12, 1992, p. 544

"The Treatment of Insomnia & Anxiety with *Jia Yi Gui*

*Zang Tang* (Jia & Yi Returning & Treasuring Decoction)" by Ding Ying, *Zhe Jiang Zhong Yi Za Zhi (Zhejiang Journal of Chinese Medicine)*, #10, 1995, p. 446

"The Treatment of Pediatric Hyperactivity Based on the Kidneys" by Wang Shi-biao & Duan Ji-hong, *Shang Hai Zhong Yi Yao Za Zhi (Shanghai Journal of Chinese Medicine & Medicinals)*, #3, 1993, p. 22

"The Treatment of Postpartum Insomnia with *Gui Pi Tang Jia Wei* (Restore the Spleen Decoction with Added Flavors)" by Zhou Yan-yu & Gan Shu-jian, *Ji Lin Zhong Yi Yao (Jilin Chinese Medicine & Medicinals)*, #6, 1999, p. 23

"The Treatment of Running Piglet Disease with *Xuan Fu Dai Zhe Tang* (Inula & Hematite Decoction)" by Qian Tian-lei, *Bei Jing Zhong Yi (Beijing Chinese Medicine)*, #1, 1996, p. 30-31

"The Treatment of Running Piglet with *Yi Guan Jian* (One Link Decoction)" by Qiu Zhi-qiang, *Zhe Jiang Zhong Yi Za Zhi (Zhejiang Journal of Chinese Medicine)*, #10, 1999, p. 431

"The Treatment of 26 Cases of Running Piglet Qi with Acupuncture-moxibustion" by Du Qiu-yao & Wang Lin, *He Nan Zhong Yi (Henan Chinese Medicine)*, #3, 2000, p. 62-63

"The Treatment of Senile Dementia by Needling *Si Shen Cong* (M-HN-1)" by Ye Heng, *Zhe Jiang Zhong Yi Za Zhi (Zhejiang Journal of Chinese Medicine)*, #11, 1993, p. 520

"The Treatment of Three Cases of Insomnia Based on Stasis" by Xu Bin-hua & Xie Qing-lin, *Fu Jian Zhong Yi Yao (Fujian Chinese Medicine & Medicinals)*, #3, 1995, p. 61

"The Treatment of Tourette's Syndrome with Pueraria" by Zhang Wu-sheng, *Zhong Yi Za Zhi (Journal of Chinese Medicine)*, #6, 1999, p. 326

"The Treatment of Withdrawal & Mania with *Mang Xiao Luo Bu Tang* (Mirabilite & Radish Decoction) by Deng Jing-ming, *Zhe Jiang Zhong Yi Za Zhi (Zhejiang Journal of Chinese Medicine)*, #8, 1995, p. 366

"The 'Using Emotions to Overcome Emotions Method' in the Treatment of Psychiatric Diseases" by Liang Guo-yin, *Zhe Jiang Zhong Yi Za Zhi (Zhejiang Journal of Chinese Medicine)*, #9, 1999, p. 399

"The Water Needle Treatment of 26 Cases of Senile Dementia" by Yang Shu-cheng, *Zhe Jiang Zhong Yi Za Zhi (Zhejiang Journal of Chinese Medicine)*, #8, 1995, p. 357

"Wang Ying-yu's Experiences in the Treatment of Withdrawal & Mania" by Cai Sheng-xiang, *Zhe Jiang Zhong Yi Za Zhi (Zhejiang Journal of Chinese Medicine)*, #9, 1996, p. 416

"Wu Shi-yan's Experience in the Treatment of Schizophrenia" by Yao Yuan-shen, *Zhe Jiang Zhong Yi Za Zhi (Zhejiang Journal of Chinese Medicine)*, #4, 1993, p. 177

*Xian Zai Nan Zhi Bing Zhong Yi Zhen Liao Xue (A Study of the Diagnosis & Treatment of Modern, Difficult to Treat Diseases)* by Wu Jun-yu & Bai Yong-ke, Chinese Medicine Ancient Books Press, Beijing, 1993

"Xu Bai-yang's Treatment of Schizophrenia" by Chu Shui-jin, *Shang Hai Zhong Yi Za Zhi (Shanghai Journal of Chinese Medicine & Medicinals)*, #1, 1994, p. 21

*Yan De Xin Zhen Zhi Ning Nan Bing Mi Chi (A Secret Satchel of Yan De-xin's Diagnosis & Treatment of Knotty, Difficult to Treat Diseases)* by Yan De-xin, Literary Press Publishing Co., Shanghai, 1997

*Ye Tian Shi Zhen Zhi Da Quan (A Compendium of Ye Tian-shi's Diagnosis & Treatment)* by Chen Ke-zheng, Chinese National Chinese Medicine & Medicinal Press, Beijing, 1995

*Yi Lin Gai Cuo (Correcting the Errors in the Forest of Medicine)* by Wang Qing-ren, Chinese National Chinese Medicine & Medicinal Press, Beijing, 1995

*Yi Zong Jin Jian (The Golden Mirror of Ancestral Medicine)* by Wu Qian *et al.*, People's Health & Hygiene Press, Beijing, 1985

*Yu Xue Zheng Zhi (Static Blood Patterns & Treatments)* by Zhang Xue-wen, Shanxi Science & Technology Press, Xian, 1986

*Zhen Fa Jiu Fa Xue (A Study of Acupuncture & Moxibustion Methods)* by Xi Yong-hong, Shanghai Science & Technology Press, Shanghai, 1985

*Zhen Jiu Chu Fang Xue (A Study of Acupuncture & Moxibustion Prescriptions)* by Wang Dai, Beijing Publishing Co., Beijing, 1990

*Zhen Jiu Da Cheng (The Great Compendium of Acupuncture & Moxibustion)* by Yang Ji-zhou, People's Health & Hygiene Press, Beijing, 1983

*Zhen Jiu Xue (A Study of Acupuncture & Moxibustion)* by Qiu Mao-liang et al., Shanghai Science & Technology Press, Shanghai, 1985

*Zhen Jiu Yi Xue (An Easy Study of Acupuncture & Moxibustion)* by Li Shou-xian, People's Health & Hygiene Press, Beijing, 1990

*Zhen Jiu Yi Xue You Ji (A Gathering of Case Studies of Acupuncture & Moxibustion)* by Tian Cong-huo, Science & Technology Literature Press, Beijing, 1985

*Zhong Guo Dang Dai Zhen Jiu Ming Jia Yi An (Contemporary Chinese Famous Families Acupuncture-moxibustion Case Histories)* by Wang Xue-tai & Liu Guan-jun, Jilin Science & Technology Press, Changchun, 1991

*Zhong Guo Yi Xue Shi (A History of Chinese Medicine)* by Zhen Zhi-ya, Shanghai Science & Technology Press, Shanghai, 1990

*Zhong Guo Yi Xue Zhen Fa Da Quan (A Grerat Collection of Chinese Medical Diagnostic Methods)* by Ma Zhong-xue, Shandong Science & Technology Press, Jinan, 1991

*Zhong Guo Zhen Jiu Chu Fang Xue (A Study of Chinese Acupuncture & Moxibustion Prescriptions)* by Xiao Shao-qing, Ningxia People's Press, Yingchuan, 1986

*Zhong Guo Zhong Yi Mi Fang Da Quan (A Great Compendium of Chinese National Chinese Medical Secret Formulas)* edited by Hu Zhao-ming, Literary Propagation Publishing Co., Shanghai, 1992

*Zhong Yi Bing Yin Bing Ji Xue (A Study of Chinese Medical Disease Causes & Disease Mechanisms)* by Wu Dun-xu, Shanghai College of Chinese Medicine Press, Shanghai, 1989

*Zhong Yi Ji Chu Li Lun (The Foundation Theories of Chinese Medicine)* by Yin Hui-de, Shanghai Science & Technology Press, Shanghai, 1984

*Zhong Yi Jing Shen Bing Xue (A Study of Chinese Medicine & Psychiatric Disease)* by Li Qing-fu & Liu Du-zhou, Tianjin Science & Technology Press, Tianjin, 1989

*Zhong Yi Lin Chuang Ge Ke (Various Clinical Specialties in Chinese Medicine)* by Zhang En-qin et al., Shanghai College of Chinese Medicine Press, Shanghai, 1990

*Zhong Yi Nei Ke Lin Chuang Shou Ce (Handbook of Chinese Medicine Internal Medicine)* by Xia De-xin, Shanghai Science & Technology Press, Shanghai, 1989

*Zhong Yi Nei Ke Xue (A Study of Chinese Medicine Internal Medicine)* by Zhang Bo-yu, People's Health & Hygiene Press, Beijing, 1988

*Zhong Yi Zhen Duan Xue (A Study of Chinese Medical Diagnosis)* by Deng Tie-tao, People's Health & Hygiene Press, Beijing, 1994

*Zhong Yi Zheng Hou Zhen Duan Zhi Liao Xue (A Study of Chinese Medicine Patterns, Diagnosis & Treatment)* by Cheng Shao-en & Xiao Hong-sheng, Beijing Science & Technology Press, Beijing, 1993

*Zhong Yi Zheng Zhuang Jian Bie Zhen Duan Xue (A Study of Chinese Medicine Symptoms & Differential Diagnosis)* by Zhao Jin-ze, People's Health & Hygiene Press, Beijing, 1984

*Zhong Yi Zhen Jiu Zhi Liao Shen Jing Bing (The Chinese Medical Acupuncture & Moxibustion Treatment of Psychiatric Disease)* by Zhang Hong-du, Zhang Jin-yi & Ding Yu-ling, Shanghai Chinese Medicine Press, Shanghai, 1987

*Zhong Yi Zhi Liao Xue (A Study of Chinese Medical Treatments)* by Sun Guo-jie & Tu Jin-wen, Chinese Medicine & Medicinal Science & Technology Press, Beijing, 1990

*Zhong Yong (The Doctrine of the Mean)* by Kong Zi (Confucius), Sinolingua, Beijing, 1996

## ENGLISH LANGUAGE BIBLIOGRAPHY

*260 Essential Chinese Medicinals* by Bob Flaws, Blue Poppy Press, Boulder, CO, 1999

*Acupuncture and Moxibustion Formulas & Treatments* by Cheng Dan-an, trans. by Wu Ming, Blue Poppy Press, Boulder, CO, 1996

"Acupuncture As Treatment for Borderline Personality Disorder" by Mindy Thompson Fullilove & Michael O. Smith, National Acupuncture Detoxification Assoc. Inc, Vancouver, WA, #3005

*Acupuncture Case Histories from China* edited by Chen Ji-rui & Nissi Wang, Eastland Press, Seattle, 1988

"Acupuncture May Prevent Relapse in Chronic Schizophrenic Patients" by Michael Smith, Tom Atwood & Gloria Turley, National Acupuncture Detoxification Assoc. Inc., Vancouver, WA, #3007

*Aging & Blood Stasis: A New TCM Approach to Geriatrics* by Yan De-xin, Blue Poppy Press, Boulder, CO, 2000

*A Handbook of Menstrual Diseases in Chinese Medicine* by Bob Flaws, Blue Poppy Press, Boulder, CO, 1997

*A History of Medicine* by Ruan Fang-fu, Chinese Culture Books Co., Oakland, CA, 1992

*A Practical Dictionary of Chinese Medicine* by Nigel Wiseman & Feng Ye, Paradigm Publications, Brookline, MA, 1998

"A Theoretical and Practical Approach to Psychodynamics Using Traditional Chinese Medicine" by Daniel A. Weber & Wilhelmina Hoedeman, *Pacific Journal of Oriental Medicine*, #10, p. 27

"Basic Patterns of Psychological Imbalance," National Acupuncture Detoxification Assoc. Inc., Vancouver, WA, #4011

"Body and Mind: The Chinese Perspective" by Hidemi Ishida, *Traditional Acupuncture Society Journal*, #9, 1991, p. 17-27

"Body, Mind and Spirit" by Chris Cook, *Traditional Acupuncture Society Journal*, #6, 1989, p. 14-15

*Chinese-English Manual of Commonly-used Prescriptions in Traditional Chinese Medicine* edited by Ou Ming, Joint Publishing Co. Ltd, Hong Kong, 1989

*Chinese-English Medical Dictionary*, The Commercial Press Ltd. & People's Health & Hygiene Press, Hong Kong, 1988

*Chinese-English Terminology of Traditional Chinese Medicine* by Shuai Xue-zhong *et al.*, Hunan Science & Technology Press, Changsha, 1983

*Chinese Herbal Medicine: Formulas & Strategies* by Dan Bensky & Randall Barolet, Eastland Press, Seattle, 1990

*Chinese Herbal Medicine: Materia Medica* by Dan Bensky & Andrew Gamble, Eastland Press, Seattle, 1993

"Chinese Medicine Preferred," *Journal of Chinese Medicine* (UK), May, 1999, p. 4

"Chinese Psycho-social Medicine: Doctor and Dang-ki, An Inter-cultural Analysis" by Bruce Holbrook, *Bulletin of the Institute of Ethnology*, #37, 1974, p. 85-110

*Clinical Manual of Oriental Medicine* by John Chen, Lotus Herbs, LA, 1998

"Clinical Observation on Needling Extrachannel Points in Treating Mental Depression" by Yang X., Liu X., Luo H. & Jia Y., *Journal of Traditional Chinese Medicine*, #14, p. 14-18

"Commonly Used Chinese Herb Formulas for the Treatment of Mental Disorders" by Heiner Fruehauf, *Journal of Chinese Medicine* (UK), #48, 1995, p. 21-34

*Comprehensive Textbook of Psychiatry*, 7th edition, edited by H. Kaplan & B. Sadock, Williams & Wilkins, Baltimore, 2000

*Concise Chinese-English English-Chinese Dictionary*, Oxford Univ. Press, Oxford, 1999

*Culture & Mental Illness, A Client-centered Approach* by Richard J. Castillo, Brooks-Cole Publishing Co., Pacific Grove, CA, 1997

*Current Therapy in Neurologic Disease*, 5th ed., edited by R.T. Johnson & J.W. Griffin, Mosby, St. Louis, MO, 1997

"Depression and Acupuncture: A Controlled Clinical Trial" by John J.B. Allen, *Psychiatric Times*, Mar., 2000, p. 72-75

*Descartes' Error: Emotion, Reason and the Human Brain* by Antonio R. Damasio, Avon Books, NY, 1994

*Desk Reference to the Diagnostic Criteria from DSM-IV*, American Psychiatric Association Press, Washington, DC, 1994

"Diagnosis Postponed: *Shen Jing Shuai Ruo* and the Transformation of Psychiatry in Post-Mao China" by Lee S., *Culture, Medicine & Psychiatry*, Sept., 1999, p. 381-399

*Diagnostic and Statistical Manual of Mental Disorders*, 4th edition, American Psychiatric Association Press, Washington, DC, 1994

*Dragon Rises, Red Bird Flies* by Leon Hammer, Station Hill Press, Barrytown, NY, 1990

"Driving Out Demons and Snakes: Gu Syndrome and a Forgotten Clinical Approach to Chronic Parasitism" by Heiner Fruehauf, *Journal of Chinese Medicine* (UK), #5, 1998, p. 10-17

*DSM-IV Handbook of Differential Diagnosis* by M. Francis

& A. Pincus, American Psychiatric Association Press, Washington, DC, 1996

"Electroacupuncture: An Alternative to Antidepressants for Treating Affective Diseases?" by Han J.S., *International Journal of Neuroscience*, #1-2, 1986, p. 79-92

"Electro-acupuncture vs. Amitriptyline in the Treatment of Depressive States" by Luo H., Jia Y. & Zhan L., *Journal of Traditional Chinese Medicine*, #5, p. 3-8

"Emotion, Knowing and Culture" by R.I. Levy, *Culture Theory: Essays on Mind, Self & Emotion*, Cambridge Univ. Press, Cambridge, 1984

*English-Chinese Chinese-English Dictionary of Chinese Medicine* by Nigel Wiseman, Hunan Science & Technology Press, Changsha, 1995

*Feeling Good: The New Mood Therapy* by David D. Burns, William Morrow & Co., NY, 1981

"Flowering of the Heart: Perspectives on Counseling Patients in an Acupuncture Setting," www.ormed.edu/users/nkraft/ormed.cc.html

*French's Index of Differential Diagnosis*, 12th ed., edited by F. Dudley Hart, John Wright and Sons, Ltd., NY, 1985

*Fundamentals of Chinese Acupuncture* by Andrew Ellis, Nigel Wiseman & Ken Boss, Paradigm Publications, Brookline, MA, 1988

*Fundamentals of Chinese Medicine* by Nigel Wiseman & Andrew Ellis, Paradigm Publications, Brookline, MA, 1985

*Golden Needle Wang Le-ting: A 20th Century Master's Approach to Acupuncture* by Yu Hui-chan & Han Fu-ru, trans. by Shuai Xue-zhong, Blue Poppy Press, Boulder, CO, 1997

*Grace Unfolding: Psychotherapy in the Spirit of the Tao-te Ching* by Greg Johanson & Ron Kurtz, Belltower, NY, 1991

*Handbook of Medical Psychiatry* by David Moore & James Jefferson, Mosby, St. Louis, MO, 1996

*Harrison's Principles of Internal Medicine*, 14th ed., edited by Braunwald *et al.*, McGraw-Hill Co., NY, 1997

*Health, Stress and Coping* by Aaron Antonovsky, Jossey-Bass & Co., San Francisco, 1979

*Human Change Processes: The Scientific Foundations of Psychotherapy* by Michael J. Mahoney, Basic Books, NY, 1991

"Hysterical Diseases" by Huang Xing-yi, trans. by Tom Dey, *European Journal of Oriental Medicine*, #2, 1996, p. 20-21

"Jin Shubai's Approach to the Treatment of Psychiatric Disorders" trans. by Charles Chace & Zhang Ting-liang, *Traditional Acupuncture Society Journal*, #10, 1991, p. 35-38

*Madness in Late Imperial China: From Illness to Deviance* by Vivien Ng, Univ. of OK Press, Norman, 1990

*Master Hua's Classic of the Central Viscera* by Hua Tuo, trans. by Yang Shou-zhong, Blue Poppy Press, Boulder, CO, 1993

*Medicine in China: A History of Ideas* by Paul U. Unschuld, Univ. of CA Press, Berkeley, CA, 1985

*Mental Dysfunction as Treated by Traditional Chinese Medicine* by C.S. Cheung, Yat Ki Lai & U. Aik Kaw, Traditional Chinese Medical Publisher, San Francisco, 1981

*Merritt's Textbook of Neurology* edited by H. Merritt & L. Rowland, Lippincott, Williams and Wilkins, Baltimore, 1994

"Mind-regulating Acupuncture Treatment of Neurosis Using Points of the Du Channel" by Chengying Y., *International Journal of Clinical Acupuncture*, #2, 1992, p. 193-196

*Nourishing Destiny: The Inner Tradition of Chinese Medicine* by Lonny S. Jarrett, Spirit Path Press, Stockbridge, MA, 1998

*Path of Pregnancy, Vol. 2: A Handbook of Traditional Chinese Postpartum Diseases* by Bob Flaws, Blue Poppy Press, Boulder, CO, 1993

*Practical Therapeutics of Traditional Chinese Medicine* by Yan Wu & Warren Fischer, Paradigm Publications, Brookline, MA, 1997

"Preferences in Help-seeking Among Chinese Students" by Cheung F., *Culture, Medicine and Psychiatry*, #8, 1984, p. 371-380

*Principles of Neurology*, 6th ed., by R. Adams & M. Victor, McGraw-Hill Co., NY, 1997

"Psychiatric Complications of Ma-Huang" by Karl M. Jacobs & Kenneth A. Hirsch, *Psychosomatics*, #1, 2000, p. 58-62

"Psychiatric Functions of Acupuncture," National Acupuncture Detoxification Assoc. Inc., Vancouver, WA, #3003

"Psychiatry in Traditional Chinese Medicine" by Xiehe Liu, *British Journal of Psychiatry*, #138, 1981, p. 429-433

"Psychiatry in Traditional Chinese Medicine" by Jay Chi Cheong & Cheng M.B., *Canadian Psychiatric Association Journal*, Aug., 1970, 399-401

*Psychotherapy East and West* by Alan W. Watts, New American Library, NY, 1963

"Qigong-induced Mental Disorders: A Review" by Ng Beng-yeong, *Australian-New Zealand Journal of Psychiatry*, Apr., 1999, p. 197-206

*Scalp Acupuncture and Clinical Cases* by Jiao Shun-fa, Foreign Languages Press, Beijing, 1997

*Seventy Essential TCM Formulas for Beginners* by Bob Flaws, Blue Poppy Press, Boulder, CO, 1994

"Situational Variations in Help-seeking Behavior Among Chinese Patients" by Cheung F. & Lau B., *Comprehensive Psychiatry*, #23, 1982, p. 253-262

"Somatization: The Interconnectedness in Chinese Society Among culture, Depressive Experiences and the Meaning of Pain" by Arthur Kleinman & Joan Kleinman, *Culture & Depression*, Univ. of CA Press, Berkeley, CA, 1985

"Some Issues in the Diagnosis of Depression in China" by Xu J.M., *Canadian Journal of Psychiatry*, Jun., 1987, p. 368-370

*Soothing the Troubled Mind: Acupuncture and Moxibustion in the Treatment and Prevention of Schizophrenia*, Chinese authors unnamed, trans. by Thomas Dey (a.k.a. Michael Helme), Paradigm Publications, Brookline, MA, 1999

*The American Psychiatric Association Textbook of Psychopharmacology* edited by A.F. Schatzberg & C.B. Nemerov, American Association of Psychiatry Press, Washington, DC, 1995

*The Classic of Difficulties*, trans. by Bob Flaws, Blue Poppy Press, Boulder, CO, 1999

"The Development of Psychiatric Concepts in Traditional Chinese Medicine" by Wen-shing Tseng, *Archives of General Psychiatry*, Oct., 1973, p. 569-575

*The Divine Farmer's Materia Medica* by Tao Hong-jing, trans. by Yang Shou-zhong, Blue Poppy Press, Boulder, CO, 1998

"The Efficacy of Acupuncture in the Treatment of Major Depression in Women" by J.J.B. Allen, Rosa Schnyer & S.K. Hitt, *Psychological Science*, #5, 1998, p. 397-401

*The Essence of Liu Feng-wu's Gynecology* by Liu Feng-wu, trans. by Shuai Xue-zhong & Bob Flaws, Blue Poppy Press, Boulder, CO, 1998

*The Essential Guide to Prescription Drugs* by James W. Long, Harper & Row, NY, 1990

*The Heart & Essence of Dan-xi's Methods of Treatment* by Zhu Dan-xi, trans. by Yang Shou-zhong, Blue Poppy Press, Boulder, CO, 1993

*The Heart Transmission of Medicine* by Liu Yi-ren, trans. by Yang Shou-zhong, Blue Poppy Press, Boulder, CO, 1997

"The Indigenization of Neurasthenia in Hong Kong" by Cheung F.M., *Culture, Medicine & Psychiatry*, Jun., 1989, p. 227-241

*The Merck Manual*, 17th edition, edited by Mark H. Beers & Robert Berkow, Merck Research Laboratories, Rahway, NJ, 1999

*The Pinyin Chinese-English Dictionary* edited by Wu Jing-rong, Beijing Foreign Languages Institute, The Commercial Press, Beijing, 1991

"The Song of the Thirteen Ghost Points" by William (Hung Pui) Yu, *Pacific Journal of Oriental Medicine*, #4, 1995, p. 8-19

"The Supernatural in Far Eastern Concepts of Mental Disease" by Ilza Veith, *Bulletin of the History of Medicine*, #37, p. 139-154

*The Systematic Classic of Acupuncture & Moxibustion* by Huang-fu Mi, trans. by Yang Shou-zhong & Charles Chace, Blue Poppy Press, Boulder, CO, 1994

*The Treatise on the Spleen & Stomach* by Li Dong-yuan, trans. by Yang Shou-zhong, Blue Poppy Press, Boulder, CO 1993

*The Treatment of Disease in TCM, Vol. 1: Diseases of the Head and Face Including Mental-Emotional Disorders* by Philippe Sionneau & Lü Gang, Blue Poppy Press, Boulder, CO, 1996

"The Treatment of Psycho-emotional Disturbances by Acupuncture with Particular Reference to the Du Mai" by Peter Deadman & Mazin Al-Khafaji, *Journal of Chinese Medicine* (UK), #1, 1995, p. 30-34

"The Treatment of Stress Syndromes by Acupuncture" by Qiao Wen-lei, trans. by Fu Zhi-wen, *Journal of Chinese Medicine* (UK), #48, 1995, p. 15-19

"The Way of the Spirit: A Seminar Given by Ted Kaptchuk" by Alan Hext, *Traditional Acupuncture Society Journal*, 37, 1990, p. 30-34

*The Yellow Emperor's Classic of Medicine* trans. by Mao-shing Ni, Shambhala, Boston, 1995

"To Err is Human: Building A Safer Health System," Institute of Medicine Report, edited by L.T. Kohn, J.M. Corrigan & M.S. Donaldson, National Academy Press, Washington, DC, Nov. 29, 1999

*Traditional Medicine in Contemporary China* by Nathan Sivin, University of Michigan, Ann Arbor, 1987

*Understanding Acupuncture* by Stephen J. Birch & Robert L. Felt, Churchill Livingstone, Edinburgh, 1999

"Use of Ear Acupuncture in Treating Persons with Serious Mental Illness and Substance Abuse," National Acupuncture Detoxification Assoc. Inc., Vancouver, WA, #3010

"Use of Herbal Medicine for Treating Psychiatric Disorders in Japan" by S. Kanba, K. Yamada, H. Mizushima & M. Asai, *Psychiatry & Clinical Neuroscience*, Dec. 1998, p. 331-333

## FRENCH LANGUAGE BIBLIOGRAPHY

*Troubles Psychique en Medicine Chinoise* by Philippe Sionneau, Guy Tredaniel Editeur, Paris, 1996

# GENERAL INDEX

# ❖ FORMULA INDEX ❖

# OTHER BOOKS ON CHINESE MEDICINE AVAILABLE FROM:

## BLUE POPPY ENTERPRISES, INC.

Oregon: 4804 SE 69th Avenue, Portland, OR 97206
For ordering 1-800-487-9296  PH. 503-650-6077  FAX 503-650-6076
California: 1815 W. 205th Street, Suite 304, Torrance, CA 90501
For ordering 1-800-293-6697  PH. 424-488-2000  FAX 424-488-2024
Email: info@bluepoppy.com Website: www.bluepoppy.com

ACUPOINT POCKET REFERENCE
by Bob Flaws
ISBN 0-936185-93-7
ISBN 978-0-936185-93-4

ACUPUNCTURE, CHINESE MEDICINE & HEALTHY
WEIGHT LOSS                    Revised Edition
by Juliette Aiyana, L. Ac.
ISBN 1-891845-61-6
ISBN 978-1-891845-61-1

ACUPUNCTURE & IVF
by Lifang Liang
ISBN 0-891845-24-1
ISBN 978-0-891845-24-6

ACUPUNCTURE FOR STROKE REHABILITATION
Three Decades of Information from China
by Hoy Ping Yee Chan, et al.
ISBN 1-891845-35-7
ISBN 978-1-891845-35-2

ACUPUNCTURE PHYSICAL MEDICINE: An Acupuncture
Touchpoint Approach to the Treatment of Chronic Pain,
Fatigue, and Stress Disorders
by Mark Seem
ISBN 1-891845-13-6
ISBN 978-1-891845-13-0

AGING & BLOOD STASIS: A New Approach to TCM Geriatrics
by Yan De-xin
ISBN 0-936185-63-6
ISBN 978-0-936185-63-7

AN ACUPUNCTURISTS GUIDE TO MEDICAL RED FLAGS &
REFERRALS
by Dr. David Anzaldua, MD
ISBN 1-891845-54-3
ISBN 978-1-891845-54-3

BETTER BREAST HEALTH NATURALLY with CHINESE
MEDICINE
by Honora Lee Wolfe & Bob Flaws
ISBN 0-936185-90-2
ISBN 978-0-936185-90-3

BIOMEDICINE: A TEXTBOOK FOR PRACTITIONERS OF
ACUPUNCTURE AND ORIENTAL MEDICINE
by Bruce H. Robinson, MD Second Edition
ISBN 1-891845-62-4
ISBN 978-1-891845-62-8

THE BOOK OF JOOK: Chinese Medicinal Porridges
by Bob Flaws
ISBN 0-936185-60-6
ISBN 978-0-936185-60-0

CHANNEL DIVERGENCES Deeper Pathways of the Web
by Miki Shima and Charles Chase
ISBN 1-891845-15-2
ISBN 978-1-891845-15-4

CHINESE MEDICAL OBSTETRICS
by Bob Flaws
ISBN 1-891845-30-6
ISBN 978-1-891845-30-7

CHINESE MEDICAL PALM IS TRY: Your Health in Your Hand
by Zong Xiao-fan & Gary Liscum
ISBN 0-936185-64-3
ISBN 978-0-936185-64-4

CHINESE MEDICAL PSYCHIATRY: A Textbook and Clinical
Manual
by Bob Flaws and James Lake, MD
ISBN 1-845891-17-9
ISBN 978-1-845891-17-8

CHINESE MEDICINAL TEAS: Simple, Proven, Folk Formulas
for Common Diseases & Promoting Health
by Zong Xiao-fan & Gary Lis cum
ISBN 0-936185-76-7
ISBN 978-0-936185-76-7

CHINESE MEDICINAL WINES & ELIXIRS
by Bob Flaws Revised Edition
ISBN 0-936185-58-9
ISBN 978-0-936185-58-3

CHINESE PEDIATRIC MASSAGE THERAPY: A Parent's &
Practitioner's Guide to the Prevention & Treatment of Childhood
Illness
by Fan Ya-li
ISBN 0-936185-54-6
ISBN 978-0-936185-54-5

CHINESE SCALP ACUPUNCTURE
by Jason Jishun Hao & Linda Lingzhi Hao
ISBN 1-891845-60-8
ISBN 978-1-891845-60-4

CHINESE SELF-MASSAGE THERAPY: The Easy Way to Health
by Fan Ya-li
ISBN 0-936185-74-0
ISBN 978-0-936185-74-3

THE CLASSIC OF DIFFICULTIES: A Translation of the Nan Jing
translation by Bob Flaws
ISBN 1-891845-07-1
ISBN 978-1-891845-07-9

A CLINICIAN'S GUIDE TO USING GRANULE
EXTRACTS
by Eric Brand
ISBN 1-891845-51-9
ISBN 978-1-891845-51-2
A COMPENDIUM OF CHINESE MEDICAL MENSTRUAL
DISEASES
by Bob Flaws
ISBN 1-891845-31-4
ISBN 978-1-891845-31-4

CONCISE CHINESE MATERIA MEDICA
by Eric Brand and Nigel Wiseman
ISBN 0-912111-82-8
ISBN 978-0-912111-82-7

CONTEMPORARY GYNECOLOGY: An Integrated Chinese-
Western Approach
by Lifang Liang
ISBN 1-891845-50-0
ISBN 978-1-891845-50-5

CONTROLLING DIABETES NATURALLY WITH CHINESE
MEDICINE
by Lynn Kuchinski
ISBN 0-936185-06-3
ISBN 978-0-936185-06-2

CURING ARTHRITIS NATURALLY WITH CHINESE
MEDICINE
by Douglas Frank & Bob Flaws
ISBN 0-936185-87-2
ISBN 978-0-936185-87-3

CURING DEPRESSION NATURALLY WITH CHINESE
MEDICINE
by Rosa Schnyer & Bob Flaws
ISBN 0-936185-94-5
ISBN 978-0-936185-94-1

CURING FIBROMYALGIA NATURALLY WITH CHINESE
MEDICINE
by Bob Flaws
ISBN 1-891845-09-8
ISBN 978-1-891845-09-3

CURING HAY FEVER NATURALLY WITH CHINESE
MEDICINE
by Bob Flaws
ISBN 0-936185-91-0
ISBN 978-0-936185-91-0

CURING HEADACHES NATURALLY WITH CHINESE
MEDICINE
by Bob Flaws
ISBN 0-936185-95-3
ISBN 978-0-936185-95-8

CURING IBS NATURALLY WITH CHINESE
MEDICINE
by Jane Bean Oberski
ISBN 1-891845-11-X
ISBN 978-1-891845-11-6

CURING INSOMNIA NATURALLY WITH CHINESE
MEDICINE
by Bob Flaws
ISBN 0-936185-86-4
ISBN 978-0-936185-86-6

CURING PMS NATURALLY WITH CHINESE MEDICINE
by Bob Flaws
ISBN 0-936185-85-6
ISBN 978-0-936185-85-9

DISEASES OF THE KIDNEY & BLADDER
by Hoy Ping Yee Chan, et al.
ISBN 1-891845-37-3
ISBN 978-1-891845-35-6

THE DIVINE FARMER'S MATERIA MEDICA: A Translation of
the Shen Nong Ben Cao
translation by Yang Shouz-zhong
ISBN 0-936185-96-1
ISBN 978-0-936185-96-5

DUI YAO: THE ART OF COMBINING CHINESE HERBAL
MEDICINALS
by Philippe Sionneau
ISBN 0-936185-81-3
ISBN 978-0-936185-81-1

ENDOMETRIOSIS, INFERTILITY AND TRADITIONAL
CHINESE MEDICINE: A Layperson's Guide
by Bob Flaws
ISBN 0-936185-14-7
ISBN 978-0-936185-14-9

THE ESSENCE OF LIU FENG-WU'S GYNECOLOGY
by Liu Feng-wu, translated by Yang Shou-zhong
ISBN 0-936185-88-0
ISBN 978-0-936185-88-0

EXTRA TREATISES BASED ON INVESTIGATION &
INQUIRY: A Translation of Zhu Dan-xi's Ge Zhi Yu Lun
translation by Yang Shou-zhong
ISBN 0-936185-53-8
ISBN 978-0-936185-53-8

FIRE IN THE VALLEY: TCM Diagnosis & Treatment of Vaginal
Diseases
by Bob Flaws
ISBN 0-936185-25-2
ISBN 978-0-936185-25-5

FULFILLING THE ESSENCE:
A Handbook of Traditional & Contemporary Treatments for
Female Infertility
by Bob Flaws
ISBN 0-936185-48-1
ISBN 978-0-936185-48-4

FU QING-ZHU'S GYNECOLOGY
trans. by Yang Shou-zhong and Liu Da-wei
ISBN 0-936185-35-X
ISBN 978-0-936185-35-4

GOLDEN NEEDLE WANG LE-TING: A 20th Century Master's
Approach to Acupuncture
by Yu Hui-chan and Han Fu-ru, trans. by Shuai Xue-zhong
ISBN 0-936185-78-3
ISBN 978-0-936185-78-1

A HANDBOOK OF CHINESE HEMATOLOGY
by Simon Becker
ISBN 1-891845-16-0
ISBN 978-1-891845-16-1

A HANDBOOK OF TCM PATTERNS & THEIR TREATMENTS
Second Edition
by Bob Flaws & Daniel Finney
ISBN 0-936185-70-8
ISBN 978-0-936185-70-5

A HANDBOOK OF TRADITIONAL CHINESE DERMATOLOGY
by Liang Jian-hui, trans. by Zhang Ting-liang
& Bob Flaws
ISBN 0-936185-46-5
ISBN 978-0-936185-46-0

A HANDBOOK OF TRADITIONAL CHINESE GYNECOLOGY
by Zhejiang College of TCM, trans. by Zhang Ting-liang
& Bob Flaws
ISBN 0-936185-06-6 (4th edit.)
ISBN 978-0-936185-06-4

A HANDBOOK of TCM PEDIATRICS
by Bob Flaws
ISBN 0-936185-72-4
ISBN 978-0-936185-72-9

THE HEART & ESSENCE OF DAN-XI'S METHODS OF
TREATMENT
by Xu Dan-xi, trans. by Yang Shou-zhong
ISBN 0-926185-50-3
ISBN 978-0-936185-50-7

HERB TOXICITIES & DRUG INTERACTIONS: A Formula
Approach
by Fred Jennes with Bob Flaws
ISBN 1-891845-26-8
ISBN 978-1-891845-26-0

IMPERIAL SECRETS OF HEALTH & LONGEVITY
by Bob Flaws
ISBN 0-936185-51-1
ISBN 978-0-936185-51-4

INSIGHTS OF A SENIOR ACUPUNCTURIST
by Miriam Lee
ISBN 0-936185-33-3
ISBN 978-0-936185-33-0

INTEGRATED PHARMACOLOGY: Combining Modern
Pharmacology with Chinese Medicine
by Dr. Greg Sperber with Bob Flaws
ISBN 1-891845-41-1
ISBN 978-0-936185-41-3

INTRODUCTION TO THE USE OF PROCESSED CHINESE
MEDICINALS
by Philippe Sionneau
ISBN 0-936185-62-7
ISBN 978-0-936185-62-0

KEEPING YOUR CHILD HEALTHY WITH CHINESE
MEDICINE
by Bob Flaws
ISBN 0-936185-71-6
ISBN 978-0-936185-71-2

THE LAKESIDE MASTER'S STUDY OF THE PULSE
by Li Shi-zhen, trans. by Bob Flaws
ISBN 1-891845-01-2
ISBN 978-1-891845-01-7

MANAGING MENOPAUSE NATURALLY WITH CHINESE
MEDICINE
by Honora Lee Wolfe
ISBN 0-936185-98-8
ISBN 978-0-936185-98-9

MASTER HUA'S CLASSIC OF THE CENTRAL VISCERA
by Hua Tuo, trans. by Yang Shou-zhong
ISBN 0-936185-43-0
ISBN 978-0-936185-43-9

THE MEDICAL I CHING: Oracle of the Healer Within
by Miki Shima
ISBN 0-936185-38-4
ISBN 978-0-936185-38-5

MENOPAIUSE & CHINESE MEDICINE
by Bob Flaws
ISBN 1-891845-40-3
ISBN 978-1-891845-40-6

MOXIBUSTION: A MODERN CLINICAL HANDBOOK
by Lorraine Wilcox
ISBN 1-891845-49-7
ISBN 978-1-891845-49-9

MOXIBUSTION: THE POWER OF MUGWORT FIRE
by Lorraine Wilcox
ISBN 1-891845-46-2
ISBN 978-1-891845-46-8

A NEW AMERICAN ACUPUNTURE By Mark Seem
ISBN 0-936185-44-9
ISBN 978-0-936185-44-6

PLAYING THE GAME: A Step-by-Step Approach to Accepting
Insurance as an Acupuncturist
by Greg Sperber & Tiffany Anderson-Hefner
ISBN 3-131416-11-7
ISBN 978-3-131416-11-7

POCKET ATLAS OF CHINESE MEDICINE
Edited by Marne and Kevin Ergil
ISBN 1-891-845-59-4
ISBN 978-1-891845-59-8

POINTS FOR PROFIT: The Essential Guide to Practice Success
for Acupuncturists                    5th Fully Edited Edition
by Honora Wolfe with Marilyn Allen
ISBN 1-891845-25-X
ISBN 978-1-891845-25-3

PRINCIPLES OF CHINESE MEDICAL ANDROLOGY: An
Integrated Approach to Male Reproductive and Urological
Health by Bob Damone
ISBN 1-891845-45-4
ISBN 978-1-891845-45-1

PRINCE WEN HUI's COOK: Chinese Dietary Therapy
By Bob Flaws & Honora Wolfe
ISBN 0-912111-05-4
ISBN 978-0-912111-05-6

THE PULSE CLASSIC: A Translation of the Mai Jing
by Wang Shu-he, trans. by Yang Shou-zhong
ISBN 0-936185-75-9
ISBN 978-0-936185-75-0

THE SECRET OF CHINESE PULSE DIAGNOSIS
by Bob Flaws
ISBN 0-936185-67-8
ISBN 978-0-936185-67-5

SECRET SHAOLIN FORMULAS FOR THE TREATMENT OF
EXTERNAL INJURY
by De Chan, trans. by Zhang Ting-liang & Bob Flaws
ISBN 0-936185-08-2
ISBN 978-0-936185-08-8

STATEMENTS OF FACT IN TRADITIONAL CHINESE MEDICINE
by Bob Flaws                          Revised & Expanded
ISBN 0-936185-52-X
ISBN 978-0-936185-52-1

STICKING TO THE POINT: A Step-by-Step Approach to TCM
Acupuncture Therapy
by Bob Flaws & Honora Wolfe 2 Condensed Books
ISBN 1-891845-47-0
ISBN 978-1-891845-47-5

A STUDY OF DAOIST ACUPUNCTURE
by Liu Zheng-cai
ISBN 1-891845-08-X
ISBN 978-1-891845-08-6

THE SUCCESSFUL CHINESE HERBALIST
by Bob Flaws and Honora Lee Wolfe
ISBN 1-891845-29-2
ISBN 978-1-891845-29-1

THE SYSTEMATIC CLASSIC OF ACUPUNCTURE &
MOXIBUSTION: A translation of the Jia Yi Jing
by Huang-fu Mi, trans. by Yang Shou-zhong & Charles Chace
ISBN 0-936185-29-5
ISBN 978-0-936185-29-3

THE TAO OF HEALTHY EATING: DIETARY
WISDOM ACCORDING TO CHINESE MEDICINE
by Bob Flaws Second Edition
ISBN 0-936185-92-9
ISBN 978-0-936185-92-7

TEACH YOURSELF TO READ MODERN MEDICAL CHINESE
by Bob Flaws
ISBN 0-936185-99-6
ISBN 978-0-936185-99-6

TEST PREP WORKBOOK FOR BASIC TCM THEORY
by Zhong Bai-song
ISBN 1-891845-43-8
ISBN 978-1-891845-43-7

TEST PREP WORKBOOK FOR THE NCCAOM BIOMEDICINE
MODULE: Exam Preparation & Study Guide
by Zhong Bai-song
ISBN 1-891845-34-9
ISBN 978-1-891845-34-5

TREATING PEDIATRIC BED-WETTING WITH ACUPUNCTURE
& CHINESE MEDICINE
by Robert Helmer
ISBN 1-891845-33-0
ISBN 978-1-891845-33-8

TREATISE on the SPLEEN & STOMACH: A Translation and
annotation of Li Dong-yuan's Pi Wei Lun
by Bob Flaws
ISBN 0-936185-41-4
ISBN 978-0-936185-41-5

THE TREATMENT OF CARDIOVASCULAR DISEASES WITH
CHINESE MEDICINE
by Simon Becker, Bob Flaws & Robert Casañas, MD
ISBN 1-891845-27-6
ISBN 978-1-891845-27-7

THE TREATMENT OF DIABETES MELLITUS WITH CHINESE
MEDICINE
by Bob Flaws, Lynn Kuchinski & Robert Casañas, M.D.
ISBN 1-891845-21-7
ISBN 978-1-891845-21-5

THE TREATMENT OF DISEASE IN TCM, Vol. 1: Diseases of
the Head & Face, Including Mental & Emotional Disorders New
Edition
by Philippe Sion neau & Lü Gang
ISBN 0-936185-69-4
ISBN 978-0-936185-69-9

THE TREATMENT OF DISEASE IN TCM, Vol. II:
Diseases of the Eyes, Ears, Nose, & Throat
by Sionneau & Lü
ISBN 0-936185-73-2
ISBN 978-0-936185-73-6

THE TREATMENT OF DISEASE IN TCM, Vol. III: Diseases of
the Mouth, Lips, Tongue, Teeth & Gums
by Sionneau & Lü
ISBN 0-936185-79-1
ISBN 978-0-936185-79-8

THE TREATMENT OF DISEASE IN TCM, Vol IV: Diseases of
the Neck, Shoulders, Back, & Limbs
by Phi lippe Sion neau & Lü Gang
ISBN 0-936185-89-9
ISBN 978-0-936185-89-7

THE TREATMENT OF DISEASE IN TCM, Vol V: Diseases of
the Chest & Abdomen
by Philippe Sionneau & Lü Gang
ISBN 1-891845-02-0
ISBN 978-1-891845-02-4

THE TREATMENT OF DISEASE IN TCM, Vol VI: Diseases of
the Urogential System & Proctology
by Phi lippe Sion neau & Lü Gang
ISBN 1-891845-05-5
ISBN 978-1-891845-05-5

THE TREATMENT OF DISEASE IN TCM, Vol VII:
General Symptoms
by Phi lippe Sion neau & Lü Gang
ISBN 1-891845-14-4
ISBN 978-1-891845-14-7

THE TREATMENT OF EXTER NAL DIS EASES WITH
ACUPUNCTURE & MOXIBUSTION
by Yan Cui-lan and Zhu Yun-long, trans. by Yang Shou-zhong
ISBN 0-936185-80-5
ISBN 978-0-936185-80-4

THE TREATMENT OF MODERN WESTERN
MEDICAL DISEASES WITH CHINESE MEDICINE
by Bob Flaws & Philippe Sionneau
ISBN 1-891845-20-9
ISBN 978-1-891845-20-8

UNDERSTANDING THE DIFFICULT PATIENT: A Guide for
Practitioners of Oriental Medicine
by Nancy Bilello, RN, L.ac.
ISBN 1-891845-32-2
ISBN 978-1-891845-32-1

WESTERN PHYSICAL EXAM SKILLS FOR PRACTITIONERS
OF ASIAN MEDICINE
by Bruce H. Robinson & Honora Lee Wolfe
ISBN 1-891845-48-9
ISBN 978-1-891845-48-2

YI LIN GAI CUO (Correcting the Errors in the Forest of
Medicine)
by Wang Qing-ren
ISBN 1-891845-39-X
ISBN 978-1-891845-39-0

70 ESSENTIAL CHINESE HERBAL FORMULAS
by Bob Flaws
ISBN 0-936185-59-7
ISBN 978-0-936185-59-0

160 ESSENTIAL CHINESE READY-MADE MEDICINES
by Bob Flaws
ISBN 1-891945-12-8
ISBN 978-1-891945-12-3

630 QUESTIONS & ANSWERS ABOUT CHINESE HERBAL
MEDICINE:
A Work book & Study Guide
by Bob Flaws
ISBN 1-891845-04-7
ISBN 978-1-891845-04-8

260 ESSENTIAL CHINESE MEDICINALS
by Bob Flaws
ISBN 1-891845-03-9
ISBN 978-1-891845-03-1

750 QUESTIONS & ANSWERS ABOUT ACUPUNCTURE
Exam Preparation & Study Guide
by Fred Jennes
ISBN 1-891845-22-5
ISBN 978-1-891845-22-2